DIAMOND
ITALIAN
DICTIONARY

DIAMOND
ITALIAN
DICTIONARY

ITALIAN · ENGLISH   ENGLISH · ITALIAN

Catherine E. Love

This edition published 1994 by
Diamond Books
77–85 Fulham Palace Road
Hammersmith, London W6 8JB

© William Collins Sons & Co. Ltd. 1982

Reprinted 1992

Latest reprint 1994

contributors
Paolo L. Rossi with Davina M. Chaplin,
Fernando Villa, Ennio Bilucaglia

INTRODUCTION

The user whose aim is to read and understand Italian will find in this dictionary a comprehensive and up-to-date wordlist including numerous phrases in current use. He will also find listed alphabetically the main irregular forms with a cross-reference to the basic form where a translation is given, as well as some of the most common abbreviations, acronyms and geographical names.

The user who wishes to communicate and to express himself in Italian will find clear and detailed treatment of all the basic words, with numerous indications pointing to the appropriate translation, and helping him to use it correctly.

INTRODUZIONE

Questo dizionario offre a chi deve leggere e comprendere l'inglese una nomenclatura dettagliata e aggiornata, con vocaboli e locuzioni idiomatiche parlate e scritte della lingua inglese contemporanea. Vi figurano anche, in ordine alfabetico, le principali forme irregolari, con un rimando alla forma di base dove si trova la traduzione, così come i più comuni nomi di luogo, le sigle e le abbreviazioni.

A loro volta, quanti hanno la necessità di esprimersi in inglese trovano in questo dizionario una trattazione chiara ed essenziale di tutti i vocaboli di base, con numerose indicazioni per una esatta traduzione e un uso corretto ed appropriato.

Abbreviations		Abbreviazioni
adjective	**a**	aggettivo
abbreviation	**abbr**	abbreviazione
adverb	**ad**	avverbio
administration	**ADMIN**	amministrazione
flying, air travel	**AER**	aeronautica, viaggi aerei
adjective	**ag**	aggettivo
agriculture	**AGR**	agricoltura
administration	**AMM**	amministrazione
anatomy	**ANAT**	anatomia
architecture	**ARCHIT**	architettura
astronomy, astrology	**ASTR**	astronomia, astrologia
the motor car and motoring	**AUT**	l'automobile
adverb	**av**	avverbio
flying, air travel	**AVIAT**	aeronautica, viaggi aerei
biology	**BIOL**	biologia
botany	**BOT**	botania
British English	**Brit**	inglese di Gran Bretagna
consonant	**C**	consonante
conjunction	**cj**	congiunzione
colloquial usage (! particularly offensive)	**col(!)**	familiare (! da evitare)
commerce, finance, banking	**COMM**	commercio, finanza, banca
conjunction	**cong**	congiunzione
compound element: noun used as adjective and which cannot follow the noun it qualifies	**cpd**	sostantivo usato come aggettivo, non può essere usato né come attributo, né dopo il sostantivo qualificato
cookery	**CULIN, CUC**	cucina
before	**dav**	davanti a
determiner: article, demonstrative etc	**det**	determinativo: articolo, aggettivo dimostrativo o indefinito etc
law	**DIR**	diritto
economics	**ECON**	economia
building	**EDIL**	edilizia
electricity, electronics	**ELEC, ELETTR**	elettricità, elettronica
exclamation	**excl, escl**	esclamazione

feminine	**f**	femminile
colloquial usage (! particularly offensive)	**fam(!)**	familiare (! da evitare)
railways	**FERR**	ferrovia
figurative use	**fig**	figurato
physiology	**FISIOL**	fisiologia
photography	**FOT**	fotografia
(phrasal verb) where the particle cannot be separated from main verb	**fus**	(verbo inglese) la cui particella è inseparabile dal verbo
in most or all senses; generally	**gen**	nella maggior parte dei sensi; generalmente
geography, geology	**GEO**	geografia, geologia
geometry	**GEOM**	geometria
computers	**INFORM**	informatica
schooling, schools and universities	**INS**	insegnamento, sistema scolastico e universitario
invariable	**inv**	invariabile
irregular	**irg**	irregolare
grammar, linguistics	**LING**	grammatica, linguistica
masculine	**m**	maschile
mathematics	**MAT(H)**	matematica
medical term, medicine	**MED**	termine medico, medicina
the weather, meteorology	**METEOR**	il tempo, meteorologia
either masculine or feminine depending on sex	**m/f**	maschile o femminile, secondo il sesso
military matters	**MIL**	esercito, lingua militare
music	**MUS**	musica
noun	**n**	sostantivo
sailing, navigation	**NAUT**	nautica
numeral adjective or noun	**num**	numerale (aggettivo, sostantivo)
oneself	**o.s.**	
derogatory, pejorative	**pej, peg**	peggiorativo
photography	**PHOT**	fotografia
physiology	**PHYSIOL**	fisiologia
plural	**pl**	plurale
politics	**POL**	politica
past participle	**pp**	participio passato
preposition	**prep**	preposizione
psychology, psychiatry	**PSYCH, PSIC**	psicologia, psichiatria

past tense	**pt**	tempo del passato
uncountable noun : not used in the plural	**q**	sostantivo che non si usa al plurale
	qc	qualcosa
	qd	qualcuno
religions, church service	**REL**	religione, liturgia
noun	**s**	sostantivo
somebody	**sb**	
schooling, schools and universities	**SCOL**	insegnamento, sistema scolastico e universitario
singular	**sg**	singolare
(grammatical) subject	**sog**	soggetto (grammaticale)
something	**sth**	
subjunctive	**sub**	congiuntivo
(grammatical) subject	**subj**	soggetto (grammaticale)
technical term, technology	**TECH, TECN**	termine tecnico, tecnologia
telecommunications	**TEL**	telecomunicazioni
typography, printing	**TIP**	tipografia
television	**TV**	televisione
typography, printing	**TYP**	tipografia
American English	**US**	inglese degli Stati Uniti
vowel	**V**	vocale
verb	**vb**	verbo
verb or phrasal verb used intransitively	**vi**	verbo o gruppo verbale con funzione intransitiva
reflexive verb	**vr**	verbo riflessivo
verb or phrasal verb used transitively	**vt**	verbo o gruppo verbale con funzione transitiva
zoology	**ZOOL**	zoologia
registered trademark	**®**	marca depositata
introduces a cultural equivalent	**≈**	introduce un'equivalenza culturale
auxiliary verb 'essere' in compound tenses	**ɜ**	verbo ausiliare 'essere' nei tempi composti

TRASCRIZIONE FONETICA

PHONETIC TRANSCRIPTION

CONSONANTS CONSONANTI

VOWELS VOCALI

NB. The pairing of some vowel sounds only indicates approximate equivalence/La messa in equivalenza di certi suoni indica solo una rassomiglianza approssimativa.

NB. **p, b, t, d, k, g** are not aspirated in Italian/sono seguiti da un'aspirazione in inglese.

			heel bead	iː i	vino idea
			hit pity	ɪ	
				e	stella edera
puppy	p	padre	set tent	ɛ	epoca
baby	b	bambino			eccetto
tent	t	tutto	apple bat	æ a	mamma
daddy	d	dado			amore
cork kiss chord	k	cane che	after car calm	ɑː	
gag guess	g	gola ghiro	fun cousin	ʌ	
so rice kiss	s	sano	over above	ə	
cousin buzz	z	svago esame	urn fern work	əː	
sheep sugar	ʃ	scena	wash pot	ɔ	rosa occhio
pleasure beige	ʒ		born cork	ɔː	ponte
church	tʃ	pece lanciare			ognuno
judge general	dʒ	giro gioco	full soot	u	utile zucca
farm raffle	f	afa faro	boon lewd	uː	
very rev	v	vero bravo			
thin maths	θ				
that other	ð				
little ball	l	letto ala			
	ʎ	gli			
rat brat	r	rete arco			
mummy comb	m	ramo madre			
no ran	n	no fumante			
	ɲ	gnomo			
singing bank	ŋ				
hat reheat	h				
yet	j	buio piacere			
wall bewail	w	uomo guaio			
loch	x				

DIPHTHONGS DITTONGHI

ɪə	beer tier
ɛə	tear fair there
eɪ	date plaice day
aɪ	life buy cry
au	owl foul now
əu	low no
ɔɪ	boil boy oily
uə	poor tour

MISCELLANEOUS

VARIE

* per l'inglese: la 'r' finale viene pronunciata se seguita da una vocale.

' precedes the stressed syllable/precede la sillaba accentata.

ITALIAN PRONUNCIATION

Vowels

Where the vowel **e** or the vowel **o** appears in a stressed syllable it can be either open [ɛ], [ɔ] or closed [e], [o]. As the open or closed pronunciation of these vowels is subject to regional variation, the distinction is of little importance to the user of this dictionary. Phonetic transcription for headwords containing these vowels will therefore only appear where other pronunciation difficulties are present.

Consonants

c before 'e' or 'i' is pronounced *tch*.

ch is pronounced like the 'k' in 'kit'.

g before 'e' or 'i' is pronounced like the 'j' in 'jet'.

gl before 'e' or 'i' is normally pronounced like the 'lli' in 'million', and in a few cases only like the 'gl' in 'glove'.

gn is pronounced like the 'ny' in 'canyon'.

sc before 'e' or 'i' is pronounced *sh*.

z is pronounced like the 'ts' in 'stetson', or like the 'd's' in 'bird's-eye'.

Headwords containing the above consonants and consonantal groups have been given full phonetic transcription in this dictionary.

NB. All double written consonants in Italian are fully sounded: eg. the *tt* in 'tutto' is pronounced as in 'hat *t*rick'.

ITALIANO - INGLESE
ITALIAN - ENGLISH

A

a prep (a + il = **al**, a + lo = **allo**, a + l' = **all'**, a + la = **alla**, a + i = **ai**, a + gli = **agli**, a + le = **alle**) (stato in luogo, tempo) at; in; (moto a luogo, complemento di termine) to; (mezzo) with, by; essere ~ **Roma/alla posta/~ casa** to be in Rome/at the post office/at home; ~ **18 anni** at 18 (years of age); ~ **mezzanotte/Natale** at midnight/ Christmas; **alle 3** at 3 (o'clock); ~ **maggio** in May; ~ **piedi/cavallo** on foot/horseback; **una barca ~ motore** a motorboat; **alla milanese** the Milanese way, in the Milanese fashion; ~ **500 lire il chilo** 500 lire a o per kilo; **viaggiare ~ 100 chilometri l'ora** to travel at 100 kilometres an o per hour; ~ **10 chilometri da Firenze** 10 kilometres from Florence; ~ **domani** see you tomorrow; ~ **uno** ~ **uno** one by one.

a'bate sm abbot.

abbacchi'ato, a [abbak'kjato] ag downhearted, in low spirits.

abbagli'ante [abbaʎ'ʎante] ag dazzling; **~i** smpl (AUT): **accendere gli ~i** to put one's headlights on full beam.

abbagli'are [abbaʎ'ʎare] vt to dazzle; (illudere) to delude; **ab'baglio** sm blunder; **prendere un abbaglio** to blunder, make a blunder.

abbai'are vi to bark.

abba'ino sm dormer window; (soffitta) attic room.

abbando'nare vt to leave, abandon, desert; (trascurare) to neglect; (rinunciare a) to abandon, give up; **~rsi** vr to let o.s. go; **~rsi a** (ricordi, vizio) to give o.s. up to; **abban'dono** sm abandoning; neglecting; (stato) abandonment; neglect; (SPORT) withdrawal; (fig) abandon.

abbas'sare vt to lower; (radio) to turn down; **~rsi** vr (chinarsi) to stoop; (livello, sole) to go down; (fig: umiliarsi) to demean o.s.; ~ **i fari** (AUT) to dip one's lights.

ab'basso escl: ~ **il re!** down with the king!

abbas'tanza [abbas'tantsa] av (a sufficienza) enough; (alquanto) quite, rather, fairly; **un vino ~ dolce** quite a sweet wine, a fairly sweet wine; **averne ~ di qd/qc** to have had enough of sb/sth.

ab'battere vt (muro, casa) to pull down; (ostacolo) to knock down; (albero) to fell; (: sog: vento) to bring down; (bestie da macello) to slaughter; (cane, cavallo) to destroy, put down; (selvaggina, aereo) to shoot down; (fig: sog: malattia) to leave prostrate; **~rsi** vr (avvilirsi) to lose heart.

abba'zia [abbat'tsia] sf abbey.

abbece'dario [abbetʃe'darjo] sm primer.

abbel'lire vt to make beautiful; (ornare) to embellish.

abbeve'rare vt to water; **abbevera'toio** sm drinking trough.

'abbi, 'abbia, abbi'amo, 'abbiano, abbi'ate forme del vb avere.

abbicci [abbit'tʃi] sm inv alphabet; (sillabario) primer; (fig) rudiments pl.

abbi'ente ag well-to-do, well-off.

abbi'etto, a ag = **abietto.**

abbiglia'mento [abbiʎʎa'mento] sm dress q; (indumenti) clothes pl; (industria) clothing industry.

abbigli'are [abbiʎ'ʎare] vt to dress up.

abbi'nare vt to combine, put together.

abbindo'lare vt (fig) to cheat, trick.

abbocca'mento sm talks pl, meeting.

abboc'care vt (tubi, canali) to connect, join up // vi (pesce) to bite; (fig) to swallow the bait; (tubi) to join.

abbona'mento sm subscription; (alle ferrovie etc) season ticket; **fare l'~** to take out a subscription (o season ticket).

abbo'nare vt = **abbuonare**; **~rsi** vr: **~rsi a un giornale** to take out a subscription to a newspaper; **~rsi al teatro/alle ferrovie** to take out a season ticket for the theatre/the train; **abbo'nato, a** sm/f subscriber; season-ticket holder.

abbon'dante ag abundant, plentiful; (giacca) roomy.

abbon'danza [abbon'dantsa] sf abundance.

abbon'dare vi to abound, be plentiful; ~ **in** o **di** to be full of, abound in.

abbor'dabile ag (persona) approachable; (prezzo) reasonable.

abbor'dare vt (nave) to board; (persona) to approach; (argomento) to tackle; ~ **una curva** to take a bend.

abbotto'nare vt to button up, do up.

abboz'zare [abbot'tsare] vt to sketch, outline; (SCULTURA) to rough-hew; ~ **un sorriso** to give a ghost of a smile; **ab'bozzo** sm sketch, outline; (DIR) draft.

abbracci'are [abbrat'tʃare] vt to embrace; (persona) to hug, embrace; (professione) to take up; (contenere) to include; **~rsi** vr to hug o embrace (one another); **~rsi a qd/qc** to cling to sb/sth; **ab'braccio** sm hug, embrace.

abbrevi'are vt to shorten; (parola) to abbreviate, shorten; **abbreviazi'one** sf abbreviation.

abbron'zante [abbron'dzante] *ag* tanning, sun *cpd*.

abbron'zare [abbron'dzare] *vt* (*pelle*) to tan; (*metalli*) to bronze; **~rsi** *vr* to tan, get a tan; **abbronza'tura** *sf* tan, suntan.

abbrusto'lire *vt* (*pane*) to toast; (*caffè*) to roast.

abbui'are *vi* (*annottare*) to grow dark; **~rsi** *vr* to grow dark; (*vista*) to grow dim; (*fig*) to grow sad.

abbuo'nare *vt* (*perdonare*) to forgive.

abbu'ono *sm* (*COMM*) allowance, discount; (*SPORT*) handicap.

abdi'care *vi* to abdicate; **~ a** to give up, renounce; **abdicazi'one** *sf* abdication.

aberrazi'one [aberrat'tsjone] *sf* aberration.

a'bete *sm* fir (tree); **~ rosso** spruce.

abi'etto, a *ag* despicable, abject.

'abile *ag* (*idoneo*) suitable, fit; (*capace*) able; (*astuto*) clever; (*accorto*) skilful; (*MIL*): **~ alla leva** fit for military service; **abilità** *sf inv* ability; cleverness; skill.

abili'tato, a *ag* qualified; **abilitazi'one** *sf* qualification.

a'bisso *sm* abyss, gulf.

abi'tante *sm/f* inhabitant.

abi'tare *vt* to live in, dwell in // *vi*: **~ in campagna/a Roma** to live in the country/in Rome; **abi'tato, a** *ag* inhabited; lived in // *sm* built-up area; **abitazi'one** *sf* residence; house.

'abito *sm* dress *q*; (*da uomo*) suit; (*da donna*) dress; (*abitudine, disposizione, REL*) habit; **~i** *smpl* clothes; **in ~ da sera** in evening dress.

abitu'ale *ag* usual, habitual.

abitu'are *vt*: **~ qd a** to get sb used *o* accustomed to; **~rsi a** to get used to, accustom o.s. to.

abitudi'nario, a *ag* of fixed habits; **~i** *smpl* regular customers.

abi'tudine *sf* habit; **d'~** usually; **per ~** from *o* out of habit.

abiu'rare *vt* to renounce.

abnegazi'one [abnegat'tsjone] *sf* (self-)abnegation, self-denial.

abo'lire *vt* to abolish; (*DIR*) to repeal; **abolizi'one** *sf* abolition; repeal.

abomi'nevole *ag* abominable.

abo'rigeno [abo'ridʒeno] *sm* aborigine.

abor'rire *vt* to abhor, detest.

abor'tire *vi* (*MED: accidentalmente*) to miscarry, have a miscarriage; (*: deliberatamente*) to have an abortion; (*fig*) to miscarry, fail; **a'borto** *sm* miscarriage; abortion; (*fig*) freak.

abrasi'one *sf* abrasion; **abra'sivo, a** *ag*, *sm* abrasive.

abro'gare *vt* to repeal, abrogate.

A'bruzzo *sm*: **l'~**, **gli ~i** the Abruzzi.

'abside *sf* apse.

abu'sare *vi*: **~ di** to abuse, misuse; (*alcool*) to take to excess; (*approfittare, violare*) to take advantage of; **~ dei cibi** to eat to excess; **a'buso** *sm* abuse, misuse; excessive use.

a.C. (*abbr di* **avanti Cristo**) B.C.

'acca *sf* letter H.

acca'demia *sf* (*società*) learned society; (*scuola: d'arte, militare*) academy; **acca'demico, a, ci, che** *ag* academic // *sm* academician.

acca'dere *vb impers* (2) to happen, occur; **acca'duto** *sm* event; **raccontare l'accaduto** to describe what has happened.

accalappi'are *vt* to catch; (*fig*) to trick, dupe.

accal'care *vt* to crowd, throng.

accal'darsi *vr* to grow hot.

accalo'rarsi *vr* (*fig*) to get excited.

accampa'mento *sm* camp.

accam'pare *vt* to encamp; (*fig*) to put forward, advance; **~rsi** *vr* to camp.

accani'mento *sm* fury; (*tenacia*) tenacity, perseverance.

acca'nirsi *vr* (*infierire*) to rage; (*ostinarsi*): **~ in** to persist in; **acca'nito, a** *ag* (*odio, gelosia*) fierce, bitter; (*lavoratore*) assiduous, dogged; (*fumatore*) inveterate.

ac'canto *av* near, nearby; **~ a** *prep* near, beside, close to.

accanto'nare *vt* (*problema*) to shelve; (*somma*) to set aside.

accaparra'mento *sm* (*COMM*) cornering, buying up.

accapar'rare *vt* to corner, buy up; (*versare una caparra*) to pay a deposit on; **~rsi qc** (*fig: simpatia, voti*) to secure sth (for o.s.).

accapigli'arsi [akkapiʎ'ʎarsi] *vr* to come to blows; (*fig*) to quarrel.

accappa'tolo *sm* bathrobe.

accappo'nare *vi*: **mi si accappona la pelle per il freddo** the cold is giving me goosepimples *o* gooseflesh.

accarez'zare [akkaret'tsare] *vt* to caress, stroke, fondle; (*fig*) to toy with.

acca'sarsi *vr* to set up house; to get married.

accasci'arsi [akkaʃ'ʃarsi] *vr* to collapse; (*fig*) to lose heart.

accatto'naggio [akkatto'naddʒo] *sm* begging.

accat'tone, a *sm/f* beggar.

accaval'lare *vt* (*gambe*) to cross; **~rsi** *vr* (*sovrapporsi*) to overlap; (*addensarsi*) to gather.

acce'care [attʃe'kare] *vt* to blind // *vi* (2) to go blind.

ac'cedere [at'tʃedere] *vi* (2): **~ a** to enter; (*richiesta*) to grant, accede to.

accele'rare [attʃele'rare] *vt* to speed up // *vi* (*AUT*) to accelerate; **~ il passo** *o* **vi** to quicken one's pace; **accele'rato, a** *ag* quick, rapid; accelerated // *sm* (*FERR*) slow train; **accelera'tore** *sm* (*AUT*) accelerator; **accelerazi'one** *sf* acceleration.

ac'cendere [at'tʃendere] *vt* (*fuoco, sigaretta*) to light; (*luce, televisione*) to put *o* switch *o* turn on; (*AUT: motore*) to switch on; (*COMM: conto*) to open; (*fig: suscitare*) to inflame, stir up; **~rsi** *vr* (*luce*) to come *o* go on; (*legna*) to catch fire, ignite; **accen-**

'dino sm, accendi'sigaro sm (cigarette) lighter.

accen'nare [attʃen'nare] vt to indicate, point out; (disegno) to sketch; (MUS) to pick out the notes of; to hum // vi: ~ a to beckon to; (col capo) to nod to; (fig: alludere a) to hint at; (: parlare brevemente di) to touch on; (: far vista di) to look as if, (: far atto di) to make as if.

ac'cenno [at'tʃenno] sm (cenno) sign; nod; (allusione) hint.

accensi'one [attʃen'sjone] sf (vedi accendere) lighting; switching on; opening; (AUT) ignition.

accen'tare [attʃen'tare] vt (parlando) to stress; (scrivendo) to accent.

ac'cento [at'tʃento] sm accent; (FONETICA, fig) stress; (inflessione) tone (of voice).

accen'trare [attʃen'trare] vt to centralize.

accentu'are [attʃentu'are] vt to stress, emphasize; ~rsi vr to become more noticeable.

accerchi'are [attʃer'kjare] vt to surround, encircle.

accerta'mento [attʃerta'mento] sm check; assessment.

accer'tare [attʃer'tare] vt to ascertain; (verificare) to check; (reddito) to assess.

ac'ceso, a [at'tʃeso] pp di accendere // ag lit; on; open; (colore) bright.

acces'sibile [attʃes'sibile] ag (luogo) accessible; (persona) approachable; (prezzo) reasonable; (idea): ~ a qd within the reach of sb.

ac'cesso [at'tʃesso] sm access; (MED) attack, fit; (impulso violento) fit, outburst.

acces'sorio, a [attʃes'sɔrjo] ag secondary, of secondary importance; ~i smpl accessories.

ac'cetta [at'tʃetta] sf hatchet.

accet'tabile [attʃet'tabile] ag acceptable.

accet'tare [attʃet'tare] vt to accept; ~ di fare qc to agree to do sth; accettazi'one sf acceptance; (locale di servizio pubblico) reception.

ac'cetto, a [at'tʃetto] ag agreeable; (persona) liked.

accezi'one [attʃet'tsjone] sf meaning.

acchiap'pare [akkjap'pare] vt to catch.

acci'acco, chi [at'tʃakko] sm ailment.

accia'ria [attʃaje'ria] sf steelworks sg.

acci'aio [at'tʃajo] sm steel.

acciden'tale [attʃiden'tale] ag accidental.

acciden'tato, a [attʃiden'tato] ag (terreno etc) uneven.

acci'dente [attʃi'dente] sm (caso imprevisto) accident; (disgrazia) mishap; (MED) stroke; ~i (fam: per rabbia) damn (it)!; (: per meraviglia) good heavens!

ac'cidia [at'tʃidja] sf (REL) sloth.

accigli'ato, a [attʃiʎ'ʎato] ag frowning.

ac'cingersi [at'tʃindʒersi] vr: ~ a fare to be about to do.

acciuf'fare [attʃuf'fare] vt to seize, catch.

acci'uga, ghe [at'tʃuga] sf anchovy.

accla'mare vt (applaudire) to applaud;

(eleggere) to acclaim; acclamazi'one sf applause; acclamation.

acclima'tare vt to acclimatize; ~rsi vr to become acclimatized.

ac'cludere vt to enclose; ac'cluso, a pp di accludere // ag enclosed.

accocco'larsi vr to crouch.

accogli'ente [akkoʎ'ʎente] ag welcoming, friendly; accogli'enza sf reception; welcome.

ac'cogliere [ak'kɔʎʎere] vt (ricevere) to receive; (dare il benvenuto) to welcome; (approvare) to agree to, accept; (contenere) to hold, accommodate.

accol'lato, a ag (vestito) high-necked.

accoltel'lare vt to knife, stab.

ac'colto, a pp di accogliere.

accoman'dita sf (DIR) limited partnership.

accomia'tare vt to dismiss; ~rsi vr: ~rsi (da) to take one's leave (of).

accomoda'mento sm agreement, settlement.

accomo'dante ag accommodating.

accomo'dare vt (aggiustare) to repair, mend; (riordinare) to tidy; (conciliare) to settle; ~rsi vr to make o.s. comfortable o at home; (adattarsi) to make do; ~rsi a sedere/in casa to sit down/come in.

accompagna'mento [akkompaɲɲa'mento] sm (MUS) accompaniment.

accompa'gnare [akkompaɲ'ɲare] vt to accompany, come o go with; (MUS) to accompany; (unire) to couple.

accomu'nare vt to pool, share; (avvicinare) to unite.

acconcia'tura [akkontʃa'tura] sf hairstyle.

ac'concio, a, ci, ce [ak'kontʃo] ag suitable.

accondi'scendere [akkondiʃ'ʃendere] vi: ~ a to agree o consent to; accondi'sceso, a pp di accondiscendere.

acconsen'tire vi: ~ (a) to agree o consent (to).

acconten'tare vt to satisfy; ~rsi di to be satisfied with, content o.s. with.

ac'conto sm part payment; pagare una somma in ~ to pay a sum of money as a deposit.

accoppia'mento sm coupling, pairing off; mating.

accoppi'are vt to couple, pair off; (BIOL) to mate; ~rsi vr to pair off; to mate.

accorci'are [akkor'tʃare] vt to shorten; ~rsi vr to become shorter.

accor'dare vt to reconcile; (colori) to match; (MUS) to tune; (LING): ~ qc con qc to make sth agree with sth; (DIR) to grant; ~rsi vr to agree, come to an agreement; (colori) to match.

ac'cordo sm agreement; (armonia) harmony; (MUS) chord; essere d'~ to agree; andare d'~ to get on well together; d'~! all right!, agreed!

ac'corgersi [ak'kordʒersi] vr: ~ di to notice; (fig) to realize; accorgi'mento sm shrewdness q; (espediente) trick, device.

ac'correre vi (2) to run up.

ac'corto, a pp di **accorgersi** // ag shrewd; **stare ~** to be on one's guard.

accos'tare vt (avvicinare): **~ qc a** to bring sth near to, put sth near to; (avvicinarsi a) to approach; (socchiudere: imposte) to half-close; (: porta) to leave ajar // vi (NAUT) to come alongside; **~rsi a** to draw near, approach; (fig) to support.

accovacci'arsi [akkovat'tʃarsi] vr to crouch.

accoz'zaglia [akkot'tsaʎʎa] sf jumble, hotchpotch; (peg: di persone) mob.

accredi'tare vt (notizia) to confirm the truth of; (COMM) to credit; (diplomato) to accredit; **~rsi** vr (fig) to gain credit.

ac'crescere [ak'kreʃʃere] vt to increase; **~rsi** vr to increase, grow; **accresci'mento** sm increase, growth; **accresci'uto, a** pp di **accrescere**.

accucci'arsi [akkut'tʃarsi] vr (cane) to lie down.

accu'dire vt (anche: vi: **~ a**) to attend to.

accumu'lare vt to accumulate; **accumula'tore** sm (ELETTR) accumulator; **accumulazi'one** sf accumulation.

accura'tezza [akkura'tettsa] sf care; accuracy.

accu'rato, a ag (diligente) careful; (preciso) accurate.

ac'cusa sf accusation; (DIR) charge.

accu'sare vt: **~ qd di qc** to accuse sb of sth; (DIR) to charge sb with sth; **~ ricevuta di** (COMM) to acknowledge receipt of.

accu'sato, a sm/f accused; defendant.

accusa'tore, 'trice sm/f accuser // sm (DIR) prosecutor.

a'cerbo, a [a'tʃerbo] ag bitter; (frutta) sour, unripe.

'acero [atʃero] sm maple.

a'cerrimo, a [a'tʃerrimo] ag very fierce.

a'ceto [a'tʃeto] sm vinegar.

A.C.I. sm (abbr di Automobile Club d'Italia) ≈ A.A.

acidità [atʃidi'ta] sf acidity; sourness.

'acido, a ['atʃido] ag (sapore) acid, sour; (CHIM) acid // sm (CHIM) acid.

'acino ['atʃino] sm berry; **~ d'uva** grape.

'acne sf acne.

'acqua sf water; (pioggia) rain; **~e** sfpl waters; **fare ~** (NAUT) to leak, take in water; **~ corrente** running water; **~ dolce** fresh water; **~ minerale** mineral water; **~ potabile** drinking water; **~ salata** salt water; **~ tonica** tonic water.

acqua'forte, pl acque'forti sf etching.

a'cqualo sm sink.

acqua'ragia [akkwa'radʒa] sf turpentine.

a'cquario sm aquarium; (dello zodiaco): A**~** Aquarius.

acqua'santa sf holy water.

acqua'vite sf brandy.

acquaz'zone [akkwat'tsone] sm cloudburst, heavy shower.

acque'dotto sm aqueduct; waterworks pl, water system.

acque'rello sm watercolour.

acque'rugiola [akkwe'rudʒola] sf drizzle.

acquie'tare vt to appease; (dolore) to ease; **~rsi** vr to calm down.

acqui'rente sm/f purchaser, buyer.

acqui'sire vt to acquire.

acquis'tare vt to purchase, buy; (fig) to gain; **a'cquisto** sm purchase; **fare acquisti** to go shopping.

acqui'trino sm bog, marsh.

acquo'lina sf: **far venire l'~ in bocca a qd** to make sb's mouth water.

a'cquoso, a ag watery.

'acre ag acrid, pungent; (fig) harsh, biting.

a'crobata, i, e sm/f acrobat.

acro'batica sf acrobatics sg.

acroba'zia [akrobat'tsia] sf acrobatic feat.

acu'ire vt to sharpen.

a'culeo sm (ZOOL) sting; (BOT) prickle.

a'cume sm acumen, perspicacity.

a'custica sf (scienza) acoustics sg; (di una sala) acoustics pl.

a'cuto, a ag (appuntito) sharp, pointed; (suono, voce) shrill, piercing; (MAT, LING, MED) acute; (MUS) high-pitched; (fig: dolore, desiderio) intense; (: perspicace) acute, keen.

ad prep (dav V) = **a.**

adagi'are [ada'dʒare] vt to lay o set down carefully; **~rsi** vr to lie down, stretch out.

a'dagio [a'dadʒo] av slowly // sm (MUS) adagio; (proverbio) adage, saying.

adatta'mento sm adaptation.

adat'tare vt to adapt; (applicare) to fit; **~rsi (a)** (ambiente, tempi) to adapt (to).

a'datto, a ag: **~ (a)** suitable (for), right (for).

addebi'tare vt: **~ qc a qd** to debit sb with sth; (fig: incolpare) to blame sb for sth.

adden'sare vt to thicken; **~rsi** vr to thicken; (folla, nuvole) to gather.

adden'tare vt to bite into.

adden'trarsi vr: **~ in** to penetrate, go into.

ad'dentro av inside, within; (fig) deeply; **essere molto ~ in qc** to be well-versed in sth.

addestra'mento sm training.

addes'trare vt, **~rsi** vr to train; **~rsi in qc** to practise sth.

ad'detto, a ag: **~ a** assigned to; (occupato in un lavoro) employed in, attached to // sm employee; (funzionario) attaché; **~ commerciale/stampa** commercial/ press attaché.

addì av (AMM): **~ 3 luglio 1978** on the 3rd of July 1978.

addi'etro av (indietro) behind; (nel passato, prima) before, ago.

ad'dio sm, escl goodbye, farewell.

addirit'tura av (veramente) really, absolutely; (perfino) even; (direttamente) directly, right away.

ad'dirsi vr: **~ a** to suit, be suitable for.

addi'tare vt to point out; (fig) to expose.

addi'tivo *sm* additive.

addizio'nare [additts∫o'nare] *vt* (*MAT*) to add (up); **addizi'one** *sf* addition.

addob'bare *vt* to decorate; **ad'dobbo** *sm* decoration.

addol'cire [addol't∫ire] *vt* (*caffè etc*) to sweeten; (*acqua, fig: carattere*) to soften; ~**rsi** *vr* (*fig*) to mellow, soften.

addolo'rare *vt* to pain, grieve; ~**rsi** (**per**) to be distressed (by).

ad'dome *sm* abdomen.

addomesti'care *vt* to tame.

addormen'tare *vt* to put to sleep; ~**rsi** *vr* to fall asleep.

addos'sare *vt* (*appoggiare*): ~ **qc a qc** to lean sth against sth; (*fig*): ~ **qc a qd** to saddle sb with sth; ~ **la colpa a qd** to lay the blame on sb; ~**rsi qc** (*responsabilità etc*) to shoulder.

ad'dosso *av* (*sulla persona*) on; **mettersi** ~ **il cappotto** to put one's coat on; ~ **a** *prep* (*sopra*) on; (*molto vicino*) right next to.

ad'durre *vt* (*DIR*) to produce; (*citare*) to cite.

adegu'are *vt*: ~ **qc a** to adjust *o* relate sth to; ~**rsi** *vr* to adapt; **adegu'ato, a** *ag* adequate; (*conveniente*) suitable; (*equo*) fair.

a'dempiere, adem'pire *vt* to fulfil, carry out.

ade'rente *ag* adhesive; (*vestito*) close-fitting // *sm/f* follower; **ade'renza** *sf* adhesion; **aderenze** *sfpl* (*fig*) connections, contacts.

ade'rire *vi* (*stare attaccato*) to adhere, stick; ~ **a** to adhere to, stick to; (*fig: società, partito*) to join; (: *opinione*) to support; (*richiesta*) to agree to; **adesi'one** *sf* adhesion; (*fig*) agreement, acceptance; **ade'sivo, a** *ag, sm* adhesive.

a'desso *av* (*ora*) now; (*or ora, poco fa*) just now; (*tra poco*) any moment now.

adia'cente [adja't∫ente] *ag* adjacent.

adi'bire *vt* (*usare*): ~ **qc a** to turn sth into.

adi'rarsi *vr*: ~ (**con** *o* **contro qd per qc**) to get angry (with sb over sth).

a'dire *vt* (*tribunale*) to resort to; ~ **le vie legali** to take legal proceedings.

'adito *sm* entrance; access.

adocchi'are [adok'kjare] *vt* (*scorgere*) to catch sight of; (*occhieggiare*) to eye.

adole'scente [adole∫'∫ente] *ag, sm/f* adolescent; **adole'scenza** *sf* adolescence.

adom'brare *vt* (*fig*) to veil, conceal; ~**rsi** *vr* (*cavallo*) to shy; (*persona*) to grow suspicious; (: *aversene a male*) to be offended.

adope'rare *vt* to use; ~**rsi** *vr* to strive; ~**rsi per qd/qc** to do one's best for sb/sth.

ado'rare *vt* to adore; (*REL*) to adore, worship; **adorazi'one** *sf* adoration; worship.

ador'nare *vt* to adorn.

adot'tare *vt* to adopt; (*decisione, provvedimenti*) to pass; **adot'tivo, a** *ag* (*genitori*) adoptive; (*figlio, patria*) adopted; **adozi'one** *sf* adoption.

adri'atico, a, ci, che *ag* Adriatic // *sm*: **l'A~, il mare A~** the Adriatic, the Adriatic Sea.

adu'lare *vt* to adulate, flatter.

adulte'rare *vt* to adulterate.

adul'terio *sm* adultery; **a'dultero, a** *ag* adulterous // *sm/f* adulterer/adulteress.

a'dulto, a *ag* adult; (*fig*) mature // *sm* adult, grown-up.

adu'nanza [adu'nantsa] *sf* assembly, meeting.

adu'nare *vt*, ~**rsi** *vr* to assemble, gather; **adu'nata** *sf* (*MIL*) parade, muster.

a'dunco, a, chi, che *ag* hooked.

a'ereo, a *ag* air *cpd*; (*radice*) aerial // *sm* aerial; (*abbr di aeroplano*) plane; **aerodi-'namico, a, ci, che** *ag* aerodynamic; (*affusolato*) streamlined // *sf* aerodynamics *sg*; **aero'nautica** *sf* (*scienza*) aeronautics *sg*; **aeronautica militare** air force; **aero'piano** *sm* aeroplane; **aero'porto** *sm* airport; **aero-'sol** *sm inv* aerosol; **aerospazi'ale** *ag* aerospace.

'afa *sf* sultriness.

af'fabile *ag* affable.

affaccen'darsi [affatt∫en'darsi] *vr*: ~ **intorno a qc** to busy o.s. with sth; **affaccen'dato, a** *ag* busy.

affacci'arsi [affat't∫arsi] *vr*: ~ (**a**) to appear (at).

affa'mare *vt* to starve; **affa'mato, a** *ag* starving; (*fig*): **affamato (di)** eager (for).

affan'nare *vt* to leave breathless; (*fig*) to worry; ~**rsi** *vr*: ~**rsi per qd/qc** to worry about sb/sth; **af'fanno** *sm* breathlessness; (*fig*) anxiety, worry; **affan'noso, a** *ag* (*respiro*) difficult; (*fig*) troubled, anxious.

af'fare *sm* (*cosa, faccenda*) matter, affair; (*COMM*) piece of business, (business) deal; (*DIR*) case; (*fam: cosa*) thing; ~**i** *smpl* (*COMM*) business *sg*; **ministro degli A~i esteri** Foreign Secretary; **affa'rista, i** *sm* profiteer, unscrupulous businessman.

affasci'nare [affa∫∫i'nare] *vt* to bewitch; (*fig*) to charm, fascinate.

affati'care *vt* to tire; ~**rsi** *vr* (*durar fatica*) to tire o.s. out.

af'fatto *av* completely; **non ... ~ not ... at all**.

affer'mare *vi* (*dire di sì*) to say yes // *vt* (*dichiarare*) to maintain, affirm; ~**rsi** *vr* to assert o.s., make one's name known; **affermazi'one** *sf* affirmation, assertion; (*successo*) achievement.

affer'rare *vt* to seize, grasp; (*fig: idea*) to grasp; ~**rsi** *vr*: ~**rsi a** to cling to.

affet'tare *vt* (*tagliare a fette*) to slice; (*ostentare*) to affect; **affet'tato, a** *ag* sliced; affected // *sm* sliced cold meat; **affettazi'one** *sf* affectation.

affet'tivo, a *ag* emotional, affective.

af'fetto *sm* affection; **affettu'oso, a** *ag* affectionate.

affezio'narsi [affettsjo'narsi] *vr*: ~ a to grow fond of.

affezi'one [affet'tsjone] *sf* (*affetto*) affection; (*MED*) ailment, disorder.

affian'care *vt* to place side by side; (*MIL*) to flank; (*fig*) to support; ~ qc a qc to place sth next to *o* beside sth; ~rsi a qd to stand beside sb.

affia'tarsi *vr* to get on well together.

affibbi'are *vt* to buckle, do up; (*fig: dare*) to give.

affida'mento *sm* (*fiducia*) confidence, trust; (*garanzia*) assurance; fare ~ su qd to rely on sb.

affi'dare *vt*: ~ qc a qd to entrust sb with sth; ~rsi *vr*: ~rsi a to place one's trust in.

affievo'lirsi *vr* to grow weak.

af'figgere [af'fiddʒere] *vt* to stick up, post up.

affi'lare *vt* to sharpen.

affili'are *vt* to affiliate; ~rsi *vr*: ~rsi a to become affiliated to.

affi'nare *vt* to sharpen.

affinché [affin'ke] *cong* in order that, so that.

af'fine *ag* similar; **affinità** *sf inv* affinity.

affio'rare *vi* to emerge.

affissi'one *sf* bill-posting.

af'fisso, a *pp di* affiggere // *sm* bill, poster; (*LING*) affix.

affit'tare *vt* (*dare in affitto*) to let, rent (out); (*prendere in affitto*) to rent; **af'fitto** *sm* rent; (*contratto*) lease.

af'fliggere [af'fliddʒere] *vt* to torment; ~rsi *vr* to grieve; **af'flitto, a** *pp di* affliggere; **afflizi'one** *sf* distress, torment.

afflosci'arsi [afflof'farsi] *vr* to go limp; (*frutta*) to go soft.

afflu'ente *sm* tributary; **afflu'enza** *sf* flow; (*di persone*) crowd.

afflu'ire *vi* (2) to flow; (*fig: merci, persone*) to pour in; **af'flusso** *sm* influx.

affo'gare *vt, vi* to drown; ~rsi *vr* to drown; (*deliberatamente*) to drown o.s.

affol'lare *vt*, ~rsi *vr* to crowd; **affol-'lato, a** *ag* crowded.

affon'dare *vt* to sink.

affran'care *vt* to free, liberate; (*AMM*) to redeem; (*lettera*) to stamp; (*automaticamente*) to frank; ~rsi *vr* to free o.s.; **affranca'tura** *sf* (*di francobollo*) stamping; franking; (*tassa di spedizione*) postage.

af'franto, a *ag* (*esausto*) worn out; (*abbattuto*) overcome.

af'fresco, schi *sm* fresco.

affret'tare *vt* to quicken, speed up; ~rsi *vr* to hurry; ~rsi a fare qc to hurry *o* hasten to do sth.

affron'tare *vt* (*pericolo etc*) to face; (*assalire: nemico*) to confront; ~rsi *vr* (*reciproco*) to come to blows.

af'fronto *sm* affront, insult.

affumi'care *vt* to fill with smoke; to blacken with smoke; (*alimenti*) to smoke.

affuso'lato, a *ag* tapering.

a'foso, a *ag* sultry, close.

'Africa *sf*: l'~ Africa; **afri'cano, a** *ag*, *sm/f* African.

afrodi'siaco, a, ci, che *ag, sm* aphrodisiac.

a'genda [a'dʒɛnda] *sf* diary.

a'gente [a'dʒɛnte] *sm* agent; ~ di cambio stockbroker; ~ di polizia police officer; ~ di vendita sales agent; **agen-'zia** *sf* agency; (*succursale*) branch; **agenzia immobiliare** estate agent's (office); **agenzia pubblicitaria/viaggi** advertising/travel agency.

agevo'lare [adʒevo'lare] *vt* to facilitate, make easy.

a'gevole [a'dʒevole] *ag* easy; (*strada*) smooth.

agganci'are [aggan'tʃare] *vt* to hook up; (*FERR*) to couple.

ag'geggio [ad'dʒeddʒo] *sm* gadget, contraption.

agget'tivo [addʒet'tivo] *sm* adjective.

agghiacci'are [aggjat'tʃare] *vt* to freeze; (*fig*) to make one's blood run cold; ~rsi *vr* to freeze.

agglor'nare [addʒor'nare] *vt* (*opera, manuale*) to bring up-to-date; (*seduta etc*) to postpone; ~rsi *vr* to bring (*o* keep) o.s. up-to-date.

aggi'rare [addʒi'rare] *vt* to go round; (*fig: ingannare*) to trick; ~rsi *vr* to wander about; il prezzo s'aggira sul milione the price is around the million mark.

aggiudi'care [addʒudi'kare] *vt* to award; (*all'asta*) to knock down; ~rsi qc to win sth.

ag'giungere [ad'dʒundʒere] *vt* to add; **aggi'unto, a** *pp di* aggiungere // *ag* assistant *cpd* // *sm* assistant // *sf* addition; **sindaco aggiunto** deputy mayor.

aggius'tare [addʒus'tare] *vt* (*accomodare*) to mend, repair; (*riassettare*) to adjust; (*fig: lite*) to settle; ~rsi *vr* (*arrangiarsi*) to make do; (*con senso reciproco*) to come to an agreement.

agglome'rato *sm* (*di rocce*) conglomerate; (*di legno*) chipboard; ~ urbano built-up area.

aggrap'parsi *vr*: ~ a to cling to.

aggra'vare *vt* (*aumentare*) to increase; (*appesantire: anche fig*) to weigh down, make heavy; (*fig: pena*) to make worse; ~rsi *vr* (*fig*) to worsen, become worse.

aggrazi'ato, a [aggrat'tsjato] *ag* graceful.

aggre'dire *vt* to attack, assault.

aggre'gare *vt*: ~ qd a qc to admit sb to sth; ~rsi *vr* to join; ~rsi a to join, become a member of; **aggre'gato, a** *ag* associated // *sm* aggregate; **aggregato di case** block of houses.

aggressi'one *sf* aggression; (*atto*) attack, assault.

aggres'sivo, a *ag* aggressive.

aggres'sore *sm* aggressor, attacker.

aggrot'tare *vt*: ~ le sopracciglia to frown.

aggrovigli'are [aggrovi'ʎʎare] *vt* to

tangle; **~rsi** *vr* (*fig*) to become complicated.

aggru'marsi *vr* to clot.

agguan'tare *vt* to catch, seize.

aggu'ato *sm* trap; (*imboscata*) ambush; **tendere un ~ a qd** to set a trap for sb.

agi'ato, a [a'dʒato] *ag* (*vita*) easy; (*persona*) well-off, well-to-do.

'agile ['adʒile] *ag* agile, nimble; **agilità** *sf* agility, nimbleness.

'agio ['adʒo] *sm* ease, comfort; **~i** *smpl* comforts; **mettersi a proprio ~** to make o.s. at home *o* comfortable.

a'gire [a'dʒire] *vi* to act; (*esercitare un'azione*) to take effect; (*TECN*) to work, function; **~ su** (*influire su*) to affect; **~ contro qd** (*DIR*) to take action against sb.

agi'tare [adʒi'tare] *vt* (*bottiglia*) to shake; (*mano, fazzoletto*) to wave; (*fig: turbare*) to disturb; (*: incitare*) to stir (up); (*: dibattere*) to discuss; **~rsi** *vr* (*mare*) to be rough; (*malato, dormitore*) to toss and turn; (*bambino*) to fidget; (*emozionarsi*) to get upset; (*POL*) to agitate; **agi'tato, a** *ag* rough; restless; fidgety; upset, perturbed; **agitazi'one** *sf* agitation; (*POL*) unrest, agitation; **mettere in agitazione qd** to upset *o* distress sb.

'agli ['aʎʎi] *prep* + *det vedi* **a.**

'aglio ['aʎʎo] *sm* garlic.

a'gnello [aɲ'ɲɛllo] *sm* lamb.

'ago, *pl* **aghi** *sm* needle.

ago'nia *sf* agony.

ago'nistico, a, ci, che *ag* athletic; (*fig*) competitive.

agoniz'zare [agonid'dzare] *vi* to be dying.

agopun'tura *sf* acupuncture.

a'gosto *sm* August.

a'grario, a *ag* agrarian, agricultural; (*riforma*) land *cpd* // *sm* landowner // *sf* agriculture.

a'gricolo, a *ag* agricultural, farm *cpd*; **agricol'tore** *sm* farmer; **agricol'tura** *sf* agriculture, farming.

agri'foglio [agri'fɔʎʎo] *sm* holly.

agrimen'sore *sm* land surveyor.

'agro, a *ag* sour, sharp.

a'grume *sm* (*spesso al pl: pianta*) citrus; (*: frutto*) citrus fruit.

aguz'zare [agut'tsare] *vt* to sharpen; **~ gli orecchi** to prick up one's ears.

a'guzzo, a [a'guttso] *ag* sharp.

'ai *prep* + *det vedi* **a.**

'aia *sf* threshing-floor.

'Aia *sf*: **l'~** the Hague.

ai'rone *sm* heron.

aiu'ola *sf* flower bed.

aiu'tante *sm/f* assistant // *sm* (*MIL*) adjutant; (*NAUT*) master-at-arms; **~ di campo** aide-de-camp.

aiu'tare *vt* to help.

ai'uto *sm* help, assistance, aid; (*aiutante*) assistant; **venire in ~ di qd** to come to sb's aid; **~ chirurgo** assistant surgeon.

aiz'zare [ait'tsare] *vt* to incite; **~ i cani contro qd** to set the dogs on sb.

al *prep* + *det vedi* **a.**

'aia, *pl* **'ali** *sf* wing; **fare ~** to fall back, make way; **~ destra/sinistra** (*SPORT*) right/left wing.

ala'bastro *sm* alabaster.

'alacre *ag* quick, brisk.

a'lano *sm* Great Dane.

a'lare *ag* wing *cpd*; **~i** *smpl* firedogs.

'alba *sf* dawn.

Alba'nia *sf*: **l'~** Albania.

'albatro *sm* albatross.

albeggi'are [albed'dʒare] (2) *vi, vb impers* to dawn.

albera'tura *sf* (*NAUT*) masts *pl*.

alberga'tore, 'trice *sm/f* hotelier, hotel-keeper.

alberghi'ero, a [alber'gjɛro] *ag* hotel *cpd*.

al'bergo, ghi *sm* hotel.

'albero *sm* tree; (*NAUT*) mast; (*TECN*) shaft; **~ di Natale** Christmas tree; **~ maestro** mainmast; **~ di trasmissione** transmission shaft.

albi'cocca, che *sf* apricot; **albi'cocco, chi** *sm* apricot tree.

'albo *sm* (*registro*) register, roll; (*AMM*) notice board.

'album *sm* album; **~ da disegno** sketch book.

al'bume *sm* albumen.

albu'mina *sf* albumin.

'alce ['altʃe] *sm* elk.

al'chimia [al'kimia] *sf* alchemy; **alchi-'mista, i** *sm* alchemist.

al'colico, a, ci, che *ag* alcoholic // *sm* alcoholic drink.

alcoliz'zato, a [alkolid'dzato] *sm/f* alcoholic.

'alcool *sm* alcohol; **alco'olico** *etc vedi* **alcolico** *etc.*

al'cova *sf* alcove.

al'cuno, a *det* (*dav sm*: **alcun** +*C*, *V*, **alcuno** + *s impura, gn, pn, ps, x, z*; *dav sf*: **alcuna** +*C*, **alcun'** +*V*) (*nessuno*): **non ... ~** no, not any; **~i(e)** *det pl, pronome pl* some, a few; **non c'è ~a fretta** there's no hurry; there isn't any hurry; **senza alcun riguardo** without any consideration.

a'letta *sf* (*TECN*) fin; tab.

alfa'beto *sm* alphabet.

alfi'ere *sm* standard-bearer; (*MIL*) ensign; (*SCACCHI*) bishop.

al'fine *av* finally, in the end.

'alga, ghe *sf* seaweed *q*, alga.

'algebra ['aldʒebra] *sf* algebra.

Alge'ria [aldʒe'ria] *sf*: **l'~** Algeria.

ali'ante *sm* (*AER*) glider.

'alibi *sm inv* alibi.

alie'nare *vt* (*DIR*) to alienate, transfer; (*rendere ostile*) to alienate; **~rsi qd** to alienate sb; **alie'nato, a** *ag* alienated; transferred; (*fuor di senno*) insane // *sm* lunatic, insane person; **alienazi'one** *sf* alienation; transfer; insanity.

ali'eno, a *ag* (*avverso*): **~ (da)** opposed (to), averse (to).

alimen'tare *vt* to feed; (*TECN*) to feed; to supply; (*fig*) to sustain // *ag* food *cpd*;

alimentazi'one sf feeding; supplying; sustaining; (gli alimenti) diet.

ali'mento sm food; ~i smpl food sg; (DIR) alimony.

a'liquota sf share; (d'imposta) rate.

alis'cafo sm hydrofoil.

'alito sm breath.

all. (abbr di allegato) encl.

'alla prep + det vedi **a**.

allacci'are [allat't∫are] vt (scarpe) to tie, lace (up); (cintura) to do up, fasten; (due località) to link; (luce, gas) to connect; (amicizia) to form.

allaga'mento sm flooding q; flood.

allar'gare vt to widen; (vestito) to let out; (aprire) to open; (fig: dilatare) to extend.

allar'mare vt to alarm.

al'larme sm alarm; ~ aereo air-raid warning.

allat'tare vt to feed.

'alle prep + det vedi **a**.

alle'anza [alle'antsa] sf alliance.

alle'arsi vr to form an alliance; **alle'ato**, **a** ag allied // sm/f ally.

alle'gare vt (accludere) to enclose; (DIR: citare) to cite, adduce; (denti) to set on edge; **alle'gato**, **a** ag enclosed // sm enclosure; **in allegato** enclosed.

allegge'rire [alledd3e'rire] vt to lighten, make lighter; (fig: sofferenza) to alleviate, lessen; (: lavoro, tasse) to reduce; ~rsi vr to put on lighter clothes.

allego'ria sf allegory.

alle'gria sf gaiety, cheerfulness.

al'legro, **a** ag cheerful, merry; (un po' brillo) merry, tipsy; (vivace: colore) bright // sm (MUS) allegro.

allena'mento sm training.

alle'nare vt, ~rsi vr to train; **allena'tore** sm (SPORT) trainer, coach.

allen'tare vt to slacken; (disciplina) to relax; ~rsi vr to become slack; (ingranaggio) to work loose.

aller'gia, **'gie** [aller'd3ia] sf allergy; **al'lergico**, **a**, **ci**, **che** ag allergic.

alles'tire vt (cena) to prepare; (esercito, nave) to equip, fit out; (spettacolo) to stage.

allet'tare vt to lure, entice.

alleva'mento sm breeding, rearing; (luogo) stock farm.

alle'vare vt (animale) to breed, rear; (bambino) to bring up.

allevi'are vt to alleviate.

alli'bire vi (?) to be astounded.

allie'tare vt to cheer up, gladden.

alli'evo sm pupil; (apprendista) apprentice; (MIL) cadet.

alliga'tore sm alligator.

alline'are vt (persone, cose) to line up; (TIP) to align; (fig: economia, salari) to adjust, align; ~rsi vr to line up; (fig: a idee): ~rsi a to come into line with.

'allo prep + det vedi **a**.

al'locco, **a**, **chi**, **che** sm tawny owl // sm/f dolt.

allocuzi'one [allokut'tsjone] sf address, solemn speech.

al'lodola sf (sky)lark.

alloggi'are [allod'd3are] vt to put up, give accommodation to; (MIL) to quarter; to billet // vi to live; (MIL) to be quartered; to be billeted; **al'loggio** sm lodging, accommodation; (appartamento) flat; (MIL) quarters pl; billet.

allontana'mento sm removal; dismissal.

allonta'nare vt to send away, send off; (impiegato) to dismiss; (pericolo) to avert, remove; (estraniare) to alienate; ~rsi vr: ~rsi (da) to go away (from); (estraniarsi) to become estranged (from).

al'lora av (in quel momento) then // cong (in questo caso) well then; (dunque) well then, so; **la gente d'~** people then o in those days; **da ~ in poi** from then on.

al'loro sm laurel.

'alluce ['allut∫e] sm big toe.

allucinazi'one [allut∫inat'tsjone] sf hallucination.

al'ludere vi: ~ a to allude to, hint at.

allu'minio sm aluminium.

allun'gare vt to lengthen; (distendere) to prolong, extend; (diluire) to water down; ~rsi vr to lengthen; (ragazzo) to stretch, grow taller; (sdraiarsi) to lie down, stretch out.

allusi'one sf hint, allusion.

alluvi'one sf flood.

alma'nacco, **chi** sm almanac.

al'meno av at least // cong if only; ~ **piovesse!** if only it would rain!

a'lone sm halo.

'Alpi sfpl: **le** ~ the Alps.

alpi'nismo sm mountaineering, climbing; **alpi'nista**, **i**, **e** sm/f mountaineer, climber.

al'pino, **a** ag Alpine; mountain cpd.

al'quanto av rather, a little; ~, **a** det a certain amount of, some // pronome a certain amount, some; ~i(e) det pl, pronome pl several, quite a few.

alt escl halt!, stop!

alta'lena sf (a funi) swing; (in bilico, anche fig) seesaw.

al'tare sm altar.

alte'rare vt to alter, change; (cibo) to adulterate; (registro) to falsify; (persona) to irritate; ~rsi vr to alter; (cibo) to go bad; (persona) to lose one's temper; **alterazi'one** sf alteration, change; adulteration; falsification; annoyance.

al'terco, **chi** sm altercation, wrangle.

alter'nare vt, ~rsi vr to alternate; **alterna'tivo**, **a** ag alternating // sf (avvicendamento) alternation; (scelta) alternative; **alterna'tore** sm alternator.

al'terno, **a** ag alternate; **a giorni** ~i on alternate days, every other day.

al'tezza [al'tettsa] sf height; width; breadth; depth; pitch; (GEO) latitude; (titolo) highness; (fig: nobiltà) greatness; **essere all'~ di** to be on a level with; (fig) to be up to o equal to; **altez'zoso**, **a** ag haughty.

alti'tudine sf altitude.

'alto, **a** ag high; (persona) tall; (tessuto)

wide, broad; (sonno, acque) deep; (suono) high(-pitched); (GEO) upper; (: settentrionale) northern // sm top (part) // av high; (parlare) aloud, loudly; **il palazzo è ~ 20 metri** the building is 20 metres high; **il tessuto è ~ 70 cm** the material is 70 cm wide; **ad ~a voce** aloud; **a notte ~a** in the dead of night; **in ~** up, upwards; at the top; **dall'~** in o **al basso** up and down; **degli ~i e bassi** (fig) ups and downs; **~a fedeltà** high fidelity, hi-fi; **~a moda** haute couture.

alto'forno sm blast furnace.

altopar'lante sm loudspeaker.

altret'tanto, a ag, pronome as much; (pl) as many // av equally; **tanti auguri! — grazie, ~** all the best! — thank you, the same to you.

'altri pronome inv (qualcuno) somebody; (: in espressioni negative) anybody; (un'altra persona) another (person).

altri'menti av otherwise.

'altro, a det other; **un ~ libro** (supplementare) another book, one more book; (diverso) another book, a different book; **un ~** another (one); **l'~** the other (one); **gli ~i** (la gente) others, other people; **desidera ~?** do you want anything else?; **aiutarsi l'un l'~** to help one another; **l'uno e l'~** both (of them); **l'~ giorno** the other day; **l'~ ieri** the day before yesterday; **domani l'~** the day after tomorrow; **quest'~ mese** next month; **da un giorno all'~** from day to day; (qualsiasi giorno) any day now; **d'~a parte** on the other hand; **tra l'~** among other things; **ci mancherebbe ~!** that's all we need!; **non faccio ~ che studiare** I do nothing but study; **sei contento? — ~ che!/tutt'~!** are you pleased? — and how!/on the contrary!; **noi/voi ~i** us/you (lot).

al'tronde av: **d'~** on the other hand.

al'trove av elsewhere, somewhere else.

al'trui ag inv other people's // sm other people's belongings pl.

altru'ista, i, e ag altruistic.

al'tura sf (rialto) height, high ground; (alto mare) open sea; **pesca d'~** deep-sea fishing.

a'lunno, a sm/f pupil.

alve'are sm hive.

al'zare [al'tsare] vt to raise, lift; (issare) to hoist; (costruire) to build, erect; **~rsi** vr to rise; (dal letto) to get up; (crescere) to grow tall (o taller); **~ le spalle** to shrug one's shoulders; **~ le carte** to cut the cards; **~rsi in piedi** to stand up, get to one's feet; **al'zata** sf lifting, raising; **un'alzata di spalle** a shrug.

a'mabile ag lovable; (vino) sweet.

a'maca, che sf hammock.

amalga'mare vt, **~rsi** vr to amalgamate.

a'mante ag: **~ di** (musica etc) fond of // sm/f lover/mistress.

a'mare vt to love; (amico, musica, sport) to like.

ama'rena sf sour black cherry.

ama'rezza [ama'rettsa] sf bitterness.

a'maro, a ag bitter // sm bitterness; (liquore) bitters pl.

ambasce'ria [ambaʃʃe'ria] sf embassy.

am'bascia, sce [am'baʃʃa] sf (MED) difficulty in breathing; (fig) anguish.

ambasci'ata [ambaʃʃata] sf embassy; (messaggio) message; **ambascia'tore, 'trice** sm/f ambassador/ambassadress.

ambe'due ag inv: **~ i ragazzi** both boys // pronome inv both.

ambien'tare vt to acclimatize; (romanzo, film) to set; **~rsi** vr to get used to one's surroundings.

ambi'ente sm environment; (fig: insieme di persone) milieu; (stanza) room.

ambigui'tà sf inv ambiguity.

am'biguo, a ag ambiguous; (persona) shady.

am'bire vt (anche: vi: **~ a**) to aspire to.

'ambito sm sphere, field.

ambizi'one [ambit'tsjone] sf ambition; **ambizi'oso**, a ag ambitious.

'ambra sf amber; **~ grigia** ambergris.

ambu'lante ag travelling, itinerant.

ambu'lanza [ambu'lantsa] sf ambulance.

ambula'torio sm (studio medico) surgery.

ameni'tà sf inv pleasantness q; (facezia) pleasantry.

a'meno, a ag pleasant; (strano) funny, strange; (spiritoso) amusing.

A'merica sf: **l'~** America; **l'~ latina** Latin America; **ameri'cano**, a ag, sm/f American.

ame'tista sf amethyst.

a'mica sf vedi **amico**.

ami'chevole [ami'kevole] ag friendly.

ami'cizia [ami'tʃittsja] sf friendship; **~e** sfpl (amici) friends.

a'mico, a, ci, che sm/f friend; (amante) boyfriend/girlfriend; **~ del cuore** o **intimo** bosom friend.

'amido sm starch.

ammac'care vt (pentola) to dent; (persona) to bruise; **~rsi** vr to bruise; **ammacca'tura** sf dent; bruise.

ammaes'trare vt (animale) to train; (persona) to teach.

ammai'nare vt to lower, haul down.

amma'larsi vr to fall ill; **amma'lato**, a ag ill, sick // sm/f sick person; (paziente) patient.

ammali'are vt (fig) to enchant, charm; **ammalia'tore, 'trice** sm/f enchanter/enchantress.

am'manco, chi sm (ECON) deficit.

ammanet'tare vt to handcuff.

ammas'sare vt (ammucchiare) to amass; (raccogliere) to gather together; **~rsi** vr to pile up; to gather; **am'masso** sm mass; (mucchio) pile, heap; (ECON) stockpile.

ammat'tire vi (2) to go mad.

ammaz'zare [ammat'tsare] vt to kill; **~rsi** vr (uccidersi) to kill o.s.; (rimanere ucciso) to be killed; **~rsi di lavoro** to work o.s. to death.

am'menda sf amends pl; (DIR, SPORT) fine; fare ~ di qc to make amends for sth.

am'messo, a pp di ammettere // cong: ~ che supposing that.

am'mettere vt to admit; (riconoscere: fatto) to acknowledge, admit; (permettere) to allow, accept; (supporre) to suppose; ammettiamo che ... let us suppose that ... .

ammic'care vi: ~ (a) to wink (at).

amminis'trare vt to run, manage; (REL, DIR) to administer; amministra'tivo, a ag administrative; amministra'tore sm administrator; (direttore di azienda) manager; (consigliere di società) director; amministratore delegato managing director; amministrazi'one sf management; administration.

ammiragli'ato [ammiraʎ'ʎato] sm admiralty.

ammi'raglio [ammi'raʎʎo] sm admiral.

ammi'rare vt to admire; ammira'tore, 'trice sm/f admirer; ammirazi'one sf admiration.

ammis'sibile ag admissible, acceptable.

ammissi'one sf admission; (approvazione) acknowledgment.

ammobili'are vt to furnish.

am'modo, a 'modo av properly // ag inv respectable, nice.

ammol'lare vt (panni etc) to soak.

ammo'niaca sf ammonia.

ammoni'mento sm warning; admonishment.

ammo'nire vt (avvertire) to warn; (rimproverare) to admonish; (DIR) to caution.

ammon'tare vi (2): ~ a to amount to // sm (total) amount.

ammonticchi'are [ammontik'kjare] vt to pile up, heap up.

ammorbi'dire vt to soften.

ammortiz'zare [ammortid'dzare] vt (ECON) to pay off, amortize; (: spese d'impianto) to write off; (AUT, TECN) to absorb, deaden; ammortizza'tore sm (AUT, TECN) shock-absorber.

ammucchi'are [ammuk'kjare] vt, ~rsi vr to pile up, accumulate.

ammuf'fire vi (2) to go mouldy.

ammutina'mento sm mutiny.

ammuti'narsi vr to mutiny.

ammuto'lire vi to be struck dumb.

amne'sia sf amnesia.

amnis'tia sf amnesty.

'amo sm (PESCA) hook; (fig) bait.

a'more sm love; ~i smpl love affairs; il tuo bambino è un ~ your baby's a darling; fare l'~ o all'~ to make love; per ~ o per forza by hook or by crook; amor proprio self-esteem, pride; amo'revole ag loving, affectionate.

a'morfo, a ag amorphous; (fig: persona) lifeless.

amo'roso, a ag (affettuoso) loving, affectionate; (d'amore: sguardo) amorous; (: poesia, relazione) love cpd.

ampi'ezza [am'pjettsa] sf width, breadth; spaciousness; (fig: importanza) scale, size.

'ampio, a ag wide, broad; (spazioso) spacious; (abbondante: vestito) loose; (: gonna) full; (: spiegazione) ample, full.

am'plesso sm (eufemismo) embrace.

ampli'are vt (ingrandire) to enlarge; (allargare) to widen.

amplifi'care vt to amplify; (magnificare) to extol; amplifica'tore sm (TECN, MUS) amplifier.

am'polla sf (vasetto) cruet.

ampol'loso, a ag bombastic, pompous.

ampu'tare vt (MED) to amputate; amputazi'one sf amputation.

anabbagli'ante [anabbaʎ'ʎante] ag (AUT) dipped; ~i smpl dipped headlights.

a'nagrafe sf (registro) register of births, marriages and deaths; (ufficio) registry office.

analfa'beta, i, e ag, sm/f illiterate.

a'nalisi sf inv analysis; (MED: esame) test; ~ grammaticale parsing; ana'lista, i, e sm/f analyst; (PSIC) (psycho)analyst.

analiz'zare [analid'dzare] vt to analyse; (MED) to test.

analo'gia, 'gie [analo'dʒia] sf analogy.

a'nalogo, a, ghi, ghe ag analogous.

'ananas sm inv pineapple.

anar'chia [anar'kia] sf anarchy; a'narchico, a, ci, che ag anarchic(al) // sm/f anarchist.

ana'tema, i sm anathema.

anato'mia sf anatomy; ana'tomico, a, ci, che ag anatomical; (sedile) contoured.

'anatra sf duck.

'anca, che sf (ANAT) hip; (ZOOL) haunch.

'anche ['anke] av also; (perfino) even; vengo anch'io! I'm coming too!; ~ se even if.

an'cora av still; (di nuovo) again; (di più) some more; (: in frasi negative) any more; (persino): più forte even stronger; non ~ not yet; ~ un po' a little more; (di tempo) a little longer.

'ancora sf anchor; gettare/levare l'~ to cast/weigh anchor; anco'raggio sm anchorage; anco'rare vt, ancorarsi vr to anchor.

anda'mento sm progress, movement; course; state.

an'dante ag (corrente) current; (di poco pregio) cheap, second-rate // sm (MUS) andante.

an'dare sm (l'andatura) walk, gait; a lungo ~ in the long run // vi (2) to go; (essere adatto): ~ a to suit; (moneta) to be legal tender; (piacere): il suo comportamento non mi va I don't like the way he behaves; ti va di andare al cinema? do you feel like going to the cinema?; andarsene to go away; questa camicia va lavata this shirt needs a wash o should be washed; ~ a cavallo to ride; ~ in macchina/aereo to go by car/plane; ~ a male to go bad; come va? — bene, grazie! how are you? — fine, thanks!; ne va della nostra vita our lives are at stake; **an'data** *sf* going; (*viaggio*) outward journey; **biglietto di sola andata/di andata e ritorno** single/return ticket; **anda'tura** *sf* (*modo di andare*) walk, gait; (*SPORT*) pace; (*NAUT*) tack.

an'dazzo [an'dattso] *sm* (*peg*) current (bad) practice.

andirivi'eni *sm inv* coming and going.

'andito *sm* corridor, passage.

an'drone *sm* entrance-hall.

a'neddoto *sm* anecdote.

ane'lare *vi*: ~ **a** (*fig*) to long for, yearn for.

a'nelito *sm* (*fig*): ~ **di** longing *o* yearning for.

a'nello *sm* ring; (*di catena*) link.

ane'mia *sf* anaemia; **a'nemico, a, ci, che** *ag* anaemic.

a'nemone *sm* anemone.

aneste'sia *sf* anaesthesia; **anes'tetico, a, ci, che** *ag*, *sm* anaesthetic.

an'fibio, a *ag* amphibious.

anfite'atro *sm* amphitheatre.

an'fratto *sm* ravine.

an'gelico, a, ci, che [an'dʒɛliko] *ag* angelic(al).

'angelo ['andʒelo] *sm* angel; ~ **custode** guardian angel.

anghe'ria [ange'ria] *sf* vexation.

an'gina [an'dʒina] *sf* angina.

angli'cano, a *ag* Anglican.

angli'cismo [angli'tʃizmo] *sm* anglicism.

anglo'sassone *ag* Anglo-Saxon.

ango'lare *ag* angular.

'angolo *sm* corner; (*MAT*) angle.

an'goscia, sce [an'gɔʃʃa] *sf* deep anxiety, anguish *q*; **angosci'oso, a** *ag* (*d'angoscia*) anguished; (*che dà angoscia*) distressing, painful.

angu'illa *sf* eel.

an'guria *sf* watermelon.

an'gustia *sf* (*ansia*) anguish, distress; (*povertà*) poverty, want.

angusti'are *vt* to distress; ~**rsi** *vr*: ~**rsi (per)** to worry (about).

an'gusto, a *ag* (*stretto*) narrow; (*fig*) mean, petty.

'anice ['anitʃe] *sm* (*CUC*) aniseed; (*BOT*) anise.

'anima *sf* soul; (*fig: persona*) person, soul; (: *abitante*) inhabitant.

ani'male *sm*, *ag* animal.

ani'mare *vt* to give life to, liven up; (*incoraggiare*) to encourage; ~**rsi** *vr* to become animated, come to life; **ani'mato, a** *ag* animate; (*vivace*) lively, animated; (: *strada*) busy; **anima'tore, 'trice** *sm/f* guiding spirit; (*CINEMA*) animator; (*di festa*) life and soul; **animazi'one** *sf* liveliness; (*di strada*) bustle; (*CINEMA*) animation.

'animo *sm* (*mente*) mind; (*cuore*) heart; (*coraggio*) courage; (*disposizione*) character, disposition; (*inclinazione*) inclination; (*proposito*) intention; **avere in ~ di fare qc** to intend *o* have a mind to do sth; **fare qc di buon/mal ~** to do sth

willingly/unwillingly; **perdersi d'~** to lose heart; **animosità** *sf* animosity; **ani'moso, a** *ag* hostile; (*coraggioso*) spirited, bold.

'anitra *sf* = **anatra**.

anna'cquare *vt* to water down, dilute.

annaffi'are *vt* to water; **annaffia'toio** *sm* watering can.

an'nali *smpl* annals.

an'nata *sf* year; (*importo annuo*) annual amount.

annebbi'are *vt* (*fig*) to cloud; ~**rsi** *vr* (*tempo*) to become foggy, become misty; (*vista*) to become dim.

annega'mento *sm* drowning.

anne'gare *vt, vi* (*2*) to drown; ~**rsi** *vr* (*accidentalmente*) to drown; (*deliberatamente*) to drown o.s.

anne'rire *vt* to blacken // *vi* (*2*) to become black.

an'nessi *smpl* (*edifici*) outbuildings; ~ **e connessi** appurtenances.

annessi'one *sf* (*POL*) annexation.

an'nesso, a *pp di* **annettere.**

an'nettere *vt* (*POL*) to annex; (*accludere*) to attach.

annichi'lare, annichi'lire [anniki'lare, anniki'lire] *vt* to annihilate.

anni'darsi *vr* to nest.

annienta'mento *sm* annihilation, destruction.

annien'tare *vt* to annihilate, destroy.

anniver'sario, a *ag*: **giorno ~** anniversary // *sm* anniversary.

'anno *sm* year; ~**i fa** years ago.

anno'dare *vt* to knot, tie; (*fig: rapporto*) to form.

annoi'are *vt* to bore; (*seccare*) to annoy; ~**rsi** *vr* to be bored; to be annoyed.

anno'tare *vt* (*registrare*) to note, note down; (*commentare*) to annotate; **annotazi'one** *sf* note; annotation.

annove'rare *vt* to number.

annu'ale *ag* annual.

annu'ario *sm* yearbook.

annu'ire *vi* to nod; (*acconsentire*) to agree.

annulla'mento *sm* annihilation, destruction; cancellation; annulment; quashing.

annul'lare *vt* to annihilate, destroy; (*contratto, francobollo*) to cancel; (*matrimonio*) to annul; (*sentenza*) to quash; (*risultati*) to declare void.

annunci'are [annun'tʃare] *vt* to announce; (*dar segni rivelatori*) to herald; **annuncia'tore, 'trice** *sm/f* (*RADIO, TV*) announcer; **l'Annunciazi'one** *sf* the Annunciation.

an'nuncio [an'nuntʃo] *sm* announcement; (*fig*) sign; ~ **pubblicitario** advertisement; ~**i economici** classified advertisements, small ads.

'annuo, a *ag* annual, yearly.

annu'sare *vt* to sniff, smell; (*fig*) to smell, suspect.

anoma'lia *sf* anomaly.

a'nomalo, a *ag* anomalous.

a'nonimo, a ag anonymous // sm (autore) anonymous writer (o painter etc).

anor'male ag abnormal // sm/f subnormal person; (eufemismo) homosexual; anormalità sf inv abnormality.

'ansa sf (manico) handle; (di fiume) bend, loop.

'ansia, ansietà sf anxiety.

ansi'mare vi to pant.

ansi'oso, a ag anxious.

antago'nismo sm antagonism; antago'nista, i, e sm/f antagonist.

an'tartico, a, ci, che ag Antarctic // sm: l'A~ the Antarctic.

antece'dente [antetʃe'dente] ag preceding, previous.

ante'fatto sm previous events pl; previous history.

antegu'erra sm pre-war period.

ante'nato sm ancestor, forefather.

an'tenna sf (RADIO, TV) aerial; (ZOOL) antenna, feeler; (NAUT) yard.

ante'prima sf preview.

anteri'ore ag (ruota, zampa) front; (fatti) previous, preceding.

antia'ereo, a ag anti-aircraft.

antibi'otico, a, ci, che ag, sm antibiotic.

anti'camera sf anteroom; fare ~ to wait (for an audience).

antichità [antiki'ta] sf inv antiquity; (oggetto) antique.

antici'clone [antitʃi'klone] sm anticyclone.

antici'pare [antitʃi'pare] vt (consegna, visita) to bring forward, anticipate; (somma di denaro) to pay in advance; (notizia) to disclose // vi to be ahead of time; anticipazi'one sf anticipation; (di notizia) advance information; (somma di denaro) advance; an'ticipo sm anticipation; (di denaro) advance; in anticipo early, in advance.

an'tico, a, chi, che ag (quadro, mobili) antique; (dell'antichità) ancient.

anticoncezio'nale [antikontʃettsjo'nale] sm contraceptive.

an'tidoto sm antidote.

An'tille sfpl: le ~ the West Indies.

an'tilope sf antelope.

anti'pasto sm hors d'œuvre.

antipa'tia sf antipathy, dislike; anti'patico, a, ci, che ag unpleasant, disagreeable.

an'tipodi smpl: gli ~ the antipodes.

antiquari'ato sm antique trade.

anti'quario sm antique dealer.

anti'quato, a ag antiquated, old-fashioned.

anti'settico, a, ci, che ag, sm antiseptic.

an'titesi sf antithesis.

anto'logia, 'gie [antolo'dʒia] sf anthology.

'antro sm cavern; (fig) hole.

antro'pofago, gi sm cannibal.

antropo'logia [antropolo'dʒia] sf anthropology.

anu'lare ag ring cpd // sm ring finger.

'anzi ['antsi] av (invece) on the contrary; (o meglio) or rather, or better still; (di più) indeed; ~ che = anziché.

anzianità [antsjani'ta] sf old age; (AMM) seniority.

anzi'ano, a [an'tsjano] ag old; (AMM) senior // sm/f old person; senior member.

anziché [antsi'ke] cong rather than.

anzi'tutto [antsi'tutto] av first of all.

apa'tia sf apathy, indifference; a'patico, a, ci, che ag apathetic, indifferent.

'ape sf bee.

aperi'tivo sm aperitif.

a'perto, a pp di aprire // ag open; all'~ in the open (air).

aper'tura sf opening; (ampiezza) width, spread; (POL) approach; (FOT) aperture; ~ alare wing span; ~ mentale open-mindedness.

'apice ['apitʃe] sm apex; (fig) height.

apicol'tore sm beekeeper.

a'polide ag stateless.

apoples'sia sf (MED) apoplexy.

a'postolo sm apostle.

a'postrofo sm apostrophe.

appa'gare vt to satisfy; ~rsi vr: ~rsi di to be satisfied with.

appai'are vt to couple, pair.

ap'palto sm (COMM) contract; dare/prendere in ~ un lavoro to let out/undertake a job on contract.

appan'nare vt (vetro) to mist; (metallo) to tarnish; (vista) to dim; ~rsi vr to mist over; to tarnish; to grow dim.

appa'rato sm (messinscena) display; (ANAT, TECN) apparatus; ~ scenico (TEATRO) props pl.

apparecchi'are [apparek'kjare] vt to prepare; (tavola) to set // vi to set the table.

appa'recchio [appa'rekkjo] sm piece of apparatus, device; (aeroplano) aircraft inv; ~ televisivo/telefonico television set/telephone.

appa'rente ag apparent; appa'renza sf appearance; in o all'apparenza apparently, to all appearances.

appa'rire vi (2) to appear; (sembrare) to seem, appear; appari'scente ag (colore) garish, gaudy; (bellezza) striking; appari'zione sf apparition.

apparta'mento sm flat, apartment (US).

appar'tarsi vr to withdraw; appar'tato, a ag secluded.

apparte'nere vi: ~ a to belong to.

appassio'nare vt to thrill; (commuovere) to move; ~rsi a qc to take a great interest in sth; to be deeply moved by sth; appassio'nato, a ag passionate; appassionato per la musica passionately fond of music.

appas'sire vi (2) to wither.

appel'lare vt (DIR) to appeal; ~rsi vr (ricorrere): ~rsi a to appeal to; (DIR): ~rsi contro to appeal against; ap'pello sm roll-call; (implorazione, DIR) appeal;

fare appello a to appeal to.

ap'pena av (a stento) hardly, scarcely; (solamente, da poco) just // cong as soon as; ~ furono arrivati ... as soon as they had arrived ...; ~ ... che o quando no sooner ... than.

ap'pendere vt to hang (up).

appen'dice [appen'ditʃe] sf appendix.

appendi'cite [appendi'tʃite] sf appendicitis.

Appen'nini smpl: gli ~ the Apennines.

appesan'tire vt to make heavy; ~rsi vr to grow stout.

ap'peso, a pp di appendere.

appe'tito sm appetite; appeti'toso, a ag appetising; (fig) attractive, desirable.

appia'nare vt to level; (fig) to smooth away, iron out.

appiat'tire vt to flatten; ~rsi vr to become flatter; (farsi piatto) to flatten o.s.; ~rsi al suolo to lie flat on the ground.

appicci'care [appittʃi'kare] vt to stick; (fig): ~ qc a qd to palm sth off on sb; ~rsi vr to stick; (fig: persona) to cling.

appigli'arsi [appiʎ'ʎarsi] vr: ~ a (afferrarsi) to take hold of; (fig) to cling to; ap'piglio sm hold; (fig) pretext.

appiso'larsi vr to doze off.

applau'dire vt, vi to applaud; ap'plauso sm applause.

appli'care vt to apply; (regolamento) to enforce; ~rsi vr to apply o.s.; applica-zi'one sf application; enforcement.

appoggi'are [appod'dʒare] vt (mettere contro): ~ qc a qc to lean o rest sth against sth; (fig: sostenere) to support; ~rsi vr: ~rsi a to lean against; (fig) to rely upon; ap'poggio sm support.

ap'porre vt to affix.

appor'tare vt to bring.

ap'posito, a ag appropriate.

ap'posta av on purpose, deliberately.

appos'tare vt to lie in wait for; ~rsi vr to lie in wait.

appren'dere vt (imparare) to learn; (comprendere) to grasp.

appren'dista, i, e sm/f apprentice.

apprensi'one sf apprehension; appren-'sivo, a ag apprehensive.

ap'presso av (accanto, vicino) close by, near; (dietro) behind; (dopo, più tardi) after, later; ~ a ~rsi a to lean against; (fig) to rely upon; ap'poggio sm support.

appres'tare vt to prepare, get ready; ~rsi vr: ~rsi a fare qc to prepare o get ready to do sth.

apprez'zabile [appret'tsabile] ag noteworthy, significant.

apprezza'mento [apprettsa'mento] sm appreciation; (giudizio) opinion.

apprez'zare [appret'tsare] vt to appreciate.

ap'proccio [ap'prottʃo] sm approach.

appro'dare vi (NAUT) to land; (fig): non ~ a nulla to come to nothing; ap'prodo sm landing; (luogo) landing-place.

approfit'tare vi: ~ di to make the most of, profit by.

approfon'dire vt to deepen; (fig) to study in depth.

appropri'ato, a ag appropriate.

approssi'marsi vr: ~ a to approach.

approssima'tivo, a ag approximate, rough; (impreciso) inexact, imprecise.

appro'vare vt (condotta, azione) to approve of; (candidato) to pass; (progetto di legge) to approve; approvazi'one sf approval.

approvvigiona'mento [approvvidʒona-'mento] sm supplying; stocking up; ~i smpl (MIL) supplies.

approvvigio'nare [approvvidʒo'nare] vt to supply; ~rsi vr to lay in provisions, stock up; ~ qd di qc to supply sb with sth.

appunta'mento sm appointment; (amoroso) date; darsi ~ to arrange to meet (one another).

appun'tare vt (rendere aguzzo) to sharpen; (fissare) to pin, fix; (annotare) to note down.

ap'punto sm note; (rimprovero) reproach // av (proprio) exactly, just; per l'~i, ~! exactly!

appu'rare vt to check, verify.

apribot'tiglie [apribot'tiʎʎe] sm inv bottleopener.

a'prile sm April.

a'prire vt to open; (via, cadavere) to open up; (gas, luce, acqua) to turn on // vi to open; ~rsi vr to open; ~rsi a qd to confide in sb, open one's heart to sb.

apris'catole sm inv tin opener.

a'quario sm = acquario.

'aquila sf (ZOOL) eagle; (fig) genius.

aqui'lone sm (giocattolo) kite; (vento) North wind.

A'rabia 'Saudita sf: l'~ Saudi Arabia.

'arabo, a ag, sm/f Arab // sm Arabic.

a'rachide [a'rakide] sf peanut.

ara'gosta sf crayfish; lobster.

a'raldica sf heraldry.

a'raldo sm herald.

a'rancia, ce [a'rantʃa] sf orange; aran-ci'ata sf orangeade; a'rancio sm (BOT) orange tree; (colore) orange // ag inv (colore) orange.

a'rare vt to plough.

a'ratro sm plough.

a'razzo [a'rattso] sm tapestry.

arbi'traggio [arbi'raddʒo] sm (SPORT) refereeing; umpiring; (DIR) arbitration.

arbi'trare vt (SPORT) to referee; to umpire; (DIR) to arbitrate.

arbi'trario, a ag arbitrary.

ar'bitrio sm will; (abuso, sopruso) arbitrary act.

'arbitro sm arbiter, judge; (DIR) arbitrator; (SPORT) referee; (: TENNIS, CRICKET) umpire.

ar'busto sm shrub.

'arca, che sf (sarcofago) sarcophagus; l'~ di Noè Noah's ark.

ar'caico, a, ci, che ag archaic.
ar'cangelo [ar'kandʒelo] sm archangel.
ar'cano, a ag arcane, mysterious.
ar'cata sf (ARCHIT, ANAT) arch; (ordine di archi) arcade.
archeolo'gia [arkeolo'dʒia] sf archaeology; arche'ologo, a, gi, ghe sm/f archaeologist.
ar'chetto [ar'ketto] sm (MUS) bow.
archi'tetto [arki'tetto] sm architect; architet'tura sf architecture.
ar'chivio [ar'kivjo] sm archives pl.
arci'ere [ar'tʃɛre] sm archer.
ar'cigno, a [ar'tʃiɲɲo] ag grim, severe.
arci'pelago, ghi [artʃi'pelago] sm archipelago.
arci'vescovo [artʃi'veskovo] sm archbishop.
'arco sm (arma, MUS) bow; (ARCHIT) arch; (MAT) arc.
arcoba'leno sm rainbow.
arcu'ato, a ag curved, bent; dalle gambe ~ e bow-legged.
ar'dente ag burning; (fig) burning, ardent.
'ardere vt, vi (2) to burn.
ar'desia sf slate.
ar'dire vi to dare; ar'dito, a ag brave, daring, bold; (sfacciato) bold.
ar'dore sm blazing heat; (fig) ardour, fervour.
'arduo, a ag arduous, difficult.
'area sf area; (EDIL) land, ground.
a'rena sf arena; (sabbia) sand.
are'narsi vr to run aground.
areo'piano sm = aeroplano.
'argano sm winch.
argente'ria [ardʒente'ria] sf silverware, silver.
argenti'ere [ardʒen'tjɛre] sm silversmith.
Argen'tina [ardʒen'tina] sf: l'~ Argentina.
ar'gento [ar'dʒɛnto] sm silver; ~ vivo quicksilver.
ar'gilla [ar'dʒilla] sf clay.
'argine ['ardʒine] sm embankment, bank; (diga) dyke.
argomen'tare vi to argue.
argo'mento sm argument; (motivo) motive; (materia, tema) subject.
argu'ire vt to deduce.
ar'guto, a ag sharp, quick-witted; (spiritoso) witty; ar'guzia sf wit; (battuta) witty remark.
'aria sf air; (espressione, aspetto) air, look; (MUS: melodia) tune; (: di opera) aria; mandare all'~ qc to ruin o upset sth; all'~ aperta in the open (air).
'arido, a ag arid.
arieggi'are [arjed'dʒare] vt (cambiare aria) to air; (imitare) to imitate.
ari'ete sm ram; (MIL) battering ram; (dello zodiaco): A~ Aries.
a'ringa, ghe sf herring inv.
'arista sf (CUC) chine of pork.
aristo'cratico, a, ci, che ag aristocratic.
aristocra'zia [aristokrat'tsia] sf aristocracy.

arit'metica sf arithmetic.
arlec'chino [arlek'kino] sm harlequin.
'arma, i sf weapon, arin; (parte dell'esercito) arm; chiamare alle ~i to call up; sotto le ~i in the army (o forces); alle ~i! to arms!; ~ da fuoco firearm.
ar'madio sm cupboard; (per abiti) wardrobe.
armamen'tario sm equipment, instruments pl.
arma'mento sm (MIL) armament; (: materiale) arms pl, weapons pl; (NAUT) fitting out; manning.
ar'mare vt to arm; (arma da fuoco) to cock; (NAUT: nave) to rig, fit out; to man; (EDIL: volta, galleria) to prop up, shore up; ~rsi vr to arm o.s.; (MIL) to take up arms; ar'mata sf (MIL) army; (NAUT) fleet; arma'tore sm shipowner; arma'tura sf (struttura di sostegno) framework; (impalcatura) scaffolding; (STORIA) armour q, suit of armour.
armis'tizio [armis'tittsjo] sm armistice.
armo'nia sf harmony; ar'monico, a, ci, che ag harmonic; (fig) harmonious; armoni'oso, a ag harmonious.
armoniz'zare [armonid'dzare] vt to harmonize; (colori, abiti) to match // vi to be in harmony; to match.
ar'nese sm tool, implement; (oggetto indeterminato) thing, contraption; male in ~ (malvestito) badly dressed; (di salute malferma) in poor health; (di condizioni economiche) down-at-heel.
'arnia sf hive.
a'roma, i sm aroma; fragrance; ~i smpl herbs and spices; aro'matico, a, ci, che ag aromatic; (cibo) spicy.
'arpa sf (MUS) harp.
ar'peggio [ar'peddʒo] sm (MUS) arpeggio.
ar'pia sf (anche fig) harpy.
arpi'one sm (gancio) hook; (cardine) hinge; (PESCA) harpoon.
arrabat'tarsi vr to do all one can, strive.
arrabbi'are vi (2) (cane) to be affected with rabies; ~rsi vr (essere preso dall'ira) to get angry, fly into a rage; arrabbi'ato, a ag rabid, with rabies; furious, angry.
arrampi'carsi vr to climb (up).
arran'giare [arran'dʒare] vt to arrange; ~rsi vr to manage, do the best one can.
arre'care vt to bring; (causare) to cause.
arreda'mento sm (studio) interior design; (mobili etc) furnishings pl.
arre'dare vt to furnish; ar'redo sm. fittings pl, furnishings pl.
ar'rendersi vr to surrender.
arres'tare vt (fermare) to stop, halt; (catturare) to arrest; ~rsi vr (fermarsi) to stop; ar'resto sm (cessazione) stopping; (fermata) stop; (cattura, MED) arrest; subire un arresto to come to a stop o standstill; mettere agli arresti to place under arrest.
arre'trare vt, vi (2) to withdraw; arre'trato, a ag (lavoro) behind schedule;

(*paese, bambino*) backward; (*numero di giornale*) back cpd.

arric'chire [arrik'kire] *vt* to enrich; **~rsi** *vr* to become rich.

arricci'are [arrit'tʃare] *vt* to curl; **~ il naso** to turn up one's nose.

ar'ringa, ghe *sf* harangue; (*DIR*) address by counsel.

arrischi'are [arris'kjare] *vt* to risk; **~rsi** *vr* to venture, dare; **arrischi'ato, a** *ag* risky; (*temerario*) reckless, rash.

arri'vare *vi* (2) to arrive; (*accadere*) to happen, occur; **~ a** (*livello, grado etc*) to reach; **lui arriva a Roma alle 7** he gets to *o* arrives at Rome at 7; **non ci arrivo** I can't reach it; (*fig: non capisco*) I can't understand it.

arrive'derci [arrive'dertʃi] *escl* goodbye!

arrive'derla *escl* (*forma di cortesia*) goodbye!

arri'vista, i, e *sm/f* go-getter.

ar'rivo *sm* arrival; (*SPORT*) finish, finishing-line.

arro'gante *ag* arrogant.

arro'lare *vb* = **arruolare**.

arros'sire *vi* (*per vergogna, timidità*) to blush, flush; (*per gioia, rabbia*) to flush.

arros'tire *vt* to roast; (*pane*) to toast; (*ai ferri*) to grill.

ar'rosto *sm, ag inv* roast.

arro'tare *vt* to sharpen; (*investire con un veicolo*) to run over.

arroto'lare *vt* to roll up.

arroton'dare *vt* (*forma, oggetto*) to round; (*stipendio*) to add to; (*somma*) to round off.

arruf'fare *vt* to ruffle; (*fili*) to tangle; (*fig: questione*) to confuse.

arruggi'nire [arruddʒi'nire] *vt* to rust; **~rsi** *vr* to rust; (*fig*) to become rusty.

arruola'mento *sm* (*MIL*) enlistment.

arruo'lare (*MIL*) *vt* to enlist; **~rsi** *vr* to enlist, join up.

arse'nale *sm* (*MIL*) arsenal; (*cantiere navale*) dockyard.

ar'senico *sm* arsenic.

'arso, a *pp di* **ardere** // *ag* (*bruciato*) burnt; (*arido*) dry; **ar'sura** *sf* (*calore opprimente*) burning heat; (*siccità*) drought.

'arte *sf* art; (*abilità*) skill.

ar'tefice [ar'tefitʃe] *sm/f* craftsman/woman; (*autore*) author.

ar'teria *sf* artery.

'artico, a, ci, che *ag* Arctic.

artico'lare *ag* (*ANAT*) of the joints, articular // *vt* to articulate; (*suddividere*) to divide, split up.

ar'ticolo *sm* article; **~ di fondo** (*STAMPA*) leader, leading article.

'Artide *sf*: **l'~** the Arctic.

artifici'ale [artifi'tʃale] *ag* artificial.

arti'ficio [arti'fitʃo] *sm* (*espediente*) trick, artifice; (*ricerca di effetto*) artificiality; **artifi'cioso, a** *ag* cunning; (*non spontaneo*) affected.

artigia'nato [artidʒa'nato] *sm* craftsmanship; craftsmen *pl*.

artigi'ano, a [arti'dʒano] *sm/f* craftsman/woman.

artiglie'ria [artiʎʎe'ria] *sf* artillery.

ar'tiglio [ar'tiʎʎo] *sm* claw; (*di rapaci*) talon.

ar'tista, i, e *sm/f* artist; **ar'tistico, a, ci, che** *ag* artistic.

'arto *sm* (*ANAT*) limb.

ar'trite *sf* (*MED*) arthritis.

ar'zillo, a [ar'dzillo] *ag* lively, sprightly.

a'scella [aʃ'ʃella] *sf* (*ANAT*) armpit.

ascen'dente [aʃʃen'dɛnte] *sm* ancestor; (*fig*) ascendancy.

ascensi'one [aʃʃen'sjone] *sf* (*ALPINISMO*) ascent; (*REL*): **l'A~** the Ascension.

ascen'sore [aʃʃen'sore] *sm* lift.

a'scesa [aʃ'ʃesa] *sf* ascent; (*al trono*) accession.

a'sceso [aʃ'ʃesso] *sm* (*MED*) abscess.

a'sceta, i [aʃ'ʃeta] *sm* ascetic.

'ascia, pl 'asce ['aʃʃe] *sf* axe.

asciugacapelli [aʃʃugaka'pelli] *sm* hairdrier.

asciuga'mano [aʃʃuga'mano] *sm* towel.

asciu'gare [aʃʃu'gare] *vt* to dry; **~rsi** *vr* to dry o.s.; (*diventare asciutto*) to dry.

asci'utto, a [aʃ'ʃutto] *ag* dry; (*fig: magro*) lean; (: *burbero*) curt; **restare a bocca ~a** (*fig*) to be disappointed; **restare all'~** (*fig*) to be left penniless.

ascol'tare *vt* to listen to; **ascolta'tore, 'trice** *sm/f* listener; **as'colto** *sm*: **essere** *o* **stare in ascolto** to be listening; **dare** *o* **prestare ascolto (a)** to pay attention (to).

as'falto *sm* asphalt.

asfis'sia *sf* asphyxia, asphyxiation.

'Asia *sf*: **l'A~** Asia; **asi'atico, a, ci, che** *ag, sm/f* Asiatic, Asian.

a'silo *sm* refuge, sanctuary; **~ (d'infanzia)** nursery(-school); **~ politico** political asylum.

'asino *sm* donkey, ass.

'asma *sf* asthma.

'asola *sf* buttonhole.

as'parago, gi *sm* asparagus *q*.

asperità *sf inv* roughness *q*; (*fig*) harshness *q*.

aspet'tare *vt* to wait for; (*anche COMM*) to await; (*aspettarsi*) to expect // *vi* to wait; **~rsi** *vr* to expect; **~ un bambino** to be expecting (a baby); **questo non me l'aspettavo** I wasn't expecting this; **aspetta'tiva** *sf* wait; expectation; **inferiore all'aspettativa** worse than expected.

as'petto *sm* (*apparenza*) aspect, appearance, look; (*punto di vista*) point of view.

aspi'rante *ag* (*attore etc*) aspiring // *sm/f* candidate, applicant.

aspira'polvere *sm inv* vacuum cleaner.

aspi'rare *vt* (*respirare*) to breathe in, inhale; (*sog: apparecchi*) to suck (up) // *vi*: **~ a** to aspire to; **aspira'tore** *sm* extractor fan.

aspi'rina *sf* aspirin.

aspor'tare *vt* (*anche* MED) to remove, take away.

as'prezza [as'prettsa] *sf* sourness, tartness; pungency; harshness; roughness; rugged nature.

'aspro, a *ag* (*sapore*) sour, tart; (*odore*) acrid, pungent; (*voce, clima, fig*) harsh; (*superficie*) rough; (*paesaggio*) rugged.

assaggi'are [assad'dʒare] *vt* to taste; **as-'saggio** *sm* tasting; (*piccola quantità*) taste; (*campione*) sample.

as'sai *av* (*abbastanza*) enough; (*molto*) a lot, much // *ag inv* (*quantità*) a lot of, much; (*numero*) a lot of, many; ~ **contento** very pleased.

assa'lire *vt* to attack, assail.

as'salto *sm* attack, assault.

assassi'nare *vt* to murder; to assassinate; (*fig*) to ruin; **assas'sinio** *sm* murder; assassination; **assas'sino, a** *ag* murderous // *sm/f* murderer; assassin.

'asse *sm* (TECN) axle; (MAT) axis // *sf* board; ~ **f da stiro** ironing board.

assedi'are *vt* to besiege; **as'sedio** *sm* siege.

asse'gnare [assen'nare] *vt* to assign, allot.

as'segno [as'senno] *sm* allowance; (*anche*: ~ **bancario**) cheque; **contro** ~ cash on delivery; ~ **circolare** bank draft; ~ **sbarrato** crossed cheque; ~ **a vuoto** dud cheque; ~**i familiari** family allowance *sg*

assem'blea *sf* assembly.

assen'nato, a *ag* sensible.

as'senso *sm* assent, consent.

as'sente *ag* absent; (*fig*) faraway, vacant; **as'senza** *sf* absence.

asses'sore *sm* (POL) councillor.

assesta'mento *sm* (*sistemazione*) arrangement; (EDIL) settlement.

asses'tare *vt* (*mettere in ordine*) to put in order, arrange; ~**rsi** *vr* to settle in; ~ **un colpo a qd** to deal sb a blow.

asse'tato, a *ag* thirsty, parched.

as'setto *sm* order, arrangement; (NAUT, AER) trim.

assicu'rare *vt* (*accertare*) to ensure; (*infondere certezza*) to assure; (*fermare, legare*) to make fast, secure; (*fare un contratto di assicurazione*) to insure; ~**rsi** *vr* (*accertarsi*): ~**rsi** (**di**) to make sure (of); (*contro il furto etc*): ~**rsi** (**contro**) to insure o.s. (against); **assicurazi'one** *sf* assurance; insurance.

assidera'mento *sm* exposure.

as'siduo, a *ag* (*costante*) assiduous; (*regolare*) regular.

assi'eme *av* (*insieme*) together; ~ **a** *prep* (together) with.

assil'lare *vt* to pester, torment.

as'sillo *sm* (*fig*) worrying thought.

assimi'lare *vt* to assimilate.

as'sise *sfpl* (DIR) assizes; **Corte f d'A~** Court of Assizes.

assis'tente *sm/f* assistant; ~ **sociale** social worker.

assis'tenza [assis'tɛntsa] *sf* assistance,

help; treatment; (*presenza*) presence; ~ **sociale** welfare services *pl*.

as'sistere *vt* (*aiutare*) to assist, help; (*curare*) to treat // *vi*: ~ (**a qc**) (*essere presente*) to be present (at sth), to attend (sth).

'asso *sm* ace; **piantare qd in** ~ to leave sb in the lurch.

associ'are [asso'tʃare] *vt* to associate; (*rendere partecipe*): ~ **qd a** (*affari*) to take sb into partnership in; (*partito*) to make sb a member of; ~**rsi** *vr* to enter into partnership; ~**rsi a** to become a member of, join; (*dolori, gioie*) to share in.

associazi'one [assotʃat'tsjone] *sf* association; (COMM) association, society.

assogget'tare [assoddʒet'tare] *vt* to subject, subjugate.

asso'lato, a *ag* sunny.

assol'dare *vt* to recruit.

as'solto, a *pp di* **assolvere.**

assoluta'mente *av* absolutely.

asso'luto, a *ag* absolute.

assoluzi'one [assolut'tsjone] *sf* (DIR) acquittal; (REL) absolution.

as'solvere *vt* (DIR) to acquit; (REL) to absolve; (*adempiere*) to carry out, perform.

assomigli'are [assomiʎ'ʎare] *vi*: ~ **a** to resemble, look like.

asso'pirsi *vr* to doze off.

assor'bente *ag* absorbent // *sm*: ~ **igienico** sanitary towel.

assor'bire *vt* to absorb; (*fig: far proprio*) to assimilate.

assor'dare *vt* to deafen.

assorti'mento *sm* assortment.

assor'tito, a *ag* assorted; matched, matching.

as'sorto, a *ag* absorbed, engrossed.

assottigli'are [assottiʎ'ʎare] *vt* to make thin, to thin; (*aguzzare: anche fig*) to sharpen; (*ridurre*) to reduce; ~**rsi** *vr* to grow thin; (*fig: ridursi*) to be reduced.

assue'fare *vt* to accustom; ~**rsi a** to get used to, accustom o.s. to.

as'sumere *vt* (*impiegato*) to take on, engage; (*responsabilità*) to assume, take upon o.s.; (*contegno, espressione*) to assume, put on; **as'sunto, a** *pp di* **assumere** // *sm* (*tesi*) proposition.

assurdità *sf inv* absurdity; **dire delle** ~ to talk nonsense.

as'surdo, a *ag* absurd.

'asta *sf* pole; (*modo di vendita*) auction.

as'temio, a *ag* abstemious.

aste'nersi *vr*: ~ (**da**) to abstain (from), refrain (from); (POL) to abstain (from); **astensi'one** *sf* abstention.

aste'risco, schi *sm* asterisk.

asti'nenza [asti'nɛntsa] *sf* abstinence.

'astio *sm* rancour, resentment.

as'tratto, a *ag* abstract.

'astro *sm* star.

'astro... ** *prefisso*: **astrolo'gia [astrolo'dʒia] *sf* astrology; **as'trologo, a, ghi, ghe** *sm/f* astrologer; **astro'nauta, i, e** *sm/f*

astronaut; astro'nave sf space ship; **astrono'mia** sf astronomy; **astro-'nomico, a, ci, che** ag astronomic(al); **as-'tronomo** sm astronomer.

as'tuccio [as'tuttʃo] sm case, box, holder.

as'tuto, a ag astute, cunning, shrewd; **as-'tuzia** sf astuteness, shrewdness; (azione) trick.

ate'ismo sm atheism.

A'tene sf Athens.

'ateo, a ag, sm/f atheist.

at'lante sm atlas.

at'lantico, a, ci, che ag Atlantic // sm: **l'A~, l'Oceano A~** the Atlantic, the Atlantic Ocean.

at'leta, i, e sm/f athlete; **at'letica** sf athletics sg.

atmos'fera sf atmosphere; **atmos'ferico, a, ci, che** ag atmospheric.

a'tomico, a, ci, che ag atomic; (nucleare) atomic, atom cpd, nuclear.

'atomo sm atom.

'atrio sm entrance-hall, lobby.

a'troce [a'trotʃe] ag (che provoca orrore) dreadful; (terribile) atrocious; **atrocità** sf inv atrocity.

attacca'mento sm (fig) attachment, affection.

attacca'panni sm hook, peg; (mobile) hall stand.

attac'care vt (unire) to attach; (far aderire) to stick (on); (appendere) to hang (up); (assalire: anche fig) to attack; (iniziare) to begin, start; (fig: contagiare) to pass on // vi to stick, adhere; **~rsi** vr to stick, adhere; (trasmettersi per contagio) to be contagious; (afferrarsi): **~rsi (a)** to cling (to); (fig: affezionarsi): **~rsi (a)** to become attached (to); **~ discorso** to start a conversation; **at'tacco, chi** sm (punto di unione) junction; (azione offensiva: anche fig) attack; (MED) attack, fit.

atteggia'mento [attedtʒa'mento] sm attitude.

atteggi'arsi [atted'dʒarsi] vr: **~ a** to pose as.

at'tendere vt to wait for, await // vi: **~ a** to attend to.

atte'nersi vr: **~ a** to keep o stick to.

atten'tare vi: **~ a** to make an attempt on; **atten'tato** sm attack; **attentato alla vita di qd** attempt on sb's life.

at'tento, a ag attentive; (accurato) careful, thorough; **stare ~ a qc** to pay attention to sth // escl be careful!

attenu'ante sf (DIR) extenuating circumstance.

attenu'are vt to attenuate; (dolore, rumore) to lessen, deaden; (pena, tasse) to alleviate; **~rsi** vr to ease, abate.

attenzi'one [atten'tsjone] sf attention // escl watch out!, be careful!

atter'raggio [atter'raddʒo] sm landing.

atter'rare vt to bring down // vi to land.

atter'rire vt to terrify; **~rsi** vr to be terrified.

at'teso, a pp di **attendere** // sf waiting; (tempo trascorso aspettando) wait.

attes'tato sm certificate.

'attico, ci sm attic.

at'tiguo, a ag adjacent, adjoining.

attil'lato, a ag (vestito) close-fitting, tight; (persona) dressed up.

'attimo sm moment; **in un ~** in a moment.

atti'nente ag: **~ a** relating to, concerning.

atti'rare vt to attract.

atti'tudine sf (disposizione) aptitude; (atteggiamento) attitude.

atti'vare vt to activate; (far funzionare) to set going, start.

attività sf inv activity; (COMM) assets pl.

at'tivo, a ag active; (COMM) profit-making, credit cpd // sm (COMM) assets pl.

attiz'zare [attit'tsare] vt (fuoco) to poke; (fig) to stir up.

'atto sm act; (azione, gesto) action, act, deed; (DIR: documento) deed, document; **~i** smpl (di congressi etc) proceedings; **mettere in ~** to put into action.

at'tonito, a ag dumbfounded, astonished.

attorcigli'are [attortʃiʎ'ʎare] vt, **~rsi** vr to twist.

at'tore, 'trice sm/f actor/actress.

at'torno av, **~ a** prep round, around, about.

attra'ente ag attractive.

at'trarre vt to attract; **attrat'tiva** sf (fig: fascino) attraction, charm; **at'tratto, a** pp di **attrarre**.

attraver'sare vt to cross; (città, bosco, fig: periodo) to go through; (sog: fiume) to run through.

attra'verso prep through; (da una parte all'altra) across.

attrazi'one [attrat'tsjone] sf attraction.

attrez'zare [attret'tsare] vt to equip; (NAUT) to rig; **attrezza'tura** sf equipment q; rigging; **at'trezzo** sm tool, instrument, (SPORT) piece of equipment.

attribu'ire vt: **~ qc a qd** (assegnare) to give o award sth to sb; (quadro etc) to attribute sth to sb; **attri'buto** sm attribute.

at'trice [at'tritʃe] sf vedi **attore**.

attu'ale ag (presente) present; (di attualità) topical; (che è in atto) actual; **attualità** sf inv topicality; (avvenimento) current event; **essere di attualità** to be topical; to be fashionable.

attu'are vt to carry out; **~rsi** vr to be realized.

attu'tire vt to deaden, reduce; **~rsi** vr to die down.

au'dace [au'datʃe] ag audacious, daring, bold; (provocante) provocative; (sfacciato) impudent, bold; **au'dacia** sf audacity, daring; boldness; provocativeness; impudence.

audiovi'sivo, a ag audiovisual.

audi'torio sm auditorium.

audizi'one [audit'tsjone] sf hearing; (MUS) audition.

augu'rare vt to wish; **~rsi qc** to hope for sth.

au'gurio sm (presagio) omen; (voto di benessere etc) (good) wish; **fare gli ~i a** qd to give sb one's best wishes; **tanti ~i!** all the best!

'aula sf (scolastica) classroom; (universitaria) lecture-theatre; (di edificio pubblico) hall.

aumen'tare vt, vi (2) to increase; **au-'mento** sm increase.

au'reola sf halo.

au'rora sf dawn.

ausili'are ag, sm, sm/f auxiliary.

aus'picio [aus'pitʃo] sm omen; (protezione) patronage; **sotto gli ~i di** under the auspices of.

austerità sf inv austerity.

aus'tero, a ag austere.

Aus'tralia sf: **l'A~** Australia; **austra-li'ano, a** ag, sm/f Australian.

'Austria sf: **l'A~** Austria; **aus'triaco, a, ci, che** ag, sm/f Austrian.

autenti'care vt to authenticate.

au'tentico, a, ci, che ag (quadro, firma) authentic, genuine; (fatto) true, genuine.

au'tista, i sm driver.

'auto sf inv car.

autobiogra'fia sf autobiography.

'autobus sm inv bus.

auto'carro sm lorry.

au'tografo, a ag, sm autograph.

auto'linea sf bus route.

au'toma, i sm automaton.

auto'matico, a, ci, che ag automatic // sm (bottone) snap fastener; (fucile) automatic.

auto'mezzo [auto'mɛddzo] sm motor vehicle.

auto'mobile sf (motor) car.

autono'mia sf autonomy; (di volo) range.

au'tonomo, a ag autonomous.

autop'sia sf post-mortem (examination), autopsy.

auto'radio sf inv (apparecchio) car radio; (autoveicolo) radio car.

au'tore, 'trice sm/f author; **l'~ del furto** the person who committed the robbery.

auto'revole ag authoritative; (persona) influential.

autori'messa sf garage.

autorità sf inv authority.

autoriz'zare [autorid'dzare] vt (permettere) to authorize; (giustificare) to allow, sanction; **autorizzazi'one** sf authorization.

autoscu'ola sf driving school.

autos'top sm hitchhiking; **autostop-'pista, i, e** sm/f hitchhiker.

autos'trada sf motorway.

auto'treno sm articulated lorry.

autove'icolo sm motor vehicle.

au'tunno sm autumn.

avam'braccio, pl(f) cia [avam'brattʃo] sm forearm.

avangu'ardia sf vanguard.

a'vanti av (stato in luogo) in front; (moto: andare, venire) forward; (tempo: prima) before // escl (entrate) come (o go) in!; (MIL) forward!; (suvvia) come on! // ag inv (precedente) before; **il giorno ~** the day before; (che si trova davanti) front cpd // sm inv (SPORT) forward; **~ e indietro** backwards and forwards; **andare ~** to go forward; (precedere) to go ahead; (continuare) to go on; (orologio) to be fast; **essere ~ negli studi** to be well advanced with one's studies.

avanza'mento [avantsa'mento] sm progress; promotion.

avan'zare [avan'tsare] vt (spostare in avanti) to move forward, advance; (domanda) to put forward; (superare) to surpass; (vincere) to beat; (promuovere) to promote; (essere creditore): **~ qc da qd** to be owed sth by sb // vi (2) (andare avanti) to move forward, advance; (fig: progredire) to make progress; (essere d'avanzo) to be left, remain; **~rsi** vr to move forward, advance; **avan'zata** sf (MIL) advance; **a'vanzo** sm (residuo) remains pl, left-overs pl; (MAT) remainder; (COMM) surplus; **averne d'avanzo di qc** to have more than enough of sth.

ava'ria sf (guasto) damage; (: meccanico) breakdown.

ava'rizia [ava'rittsja] sf avarice.

a'varo, a ag avaricious, miserly // sm miser.

a'vena sf oats pl.

a'vere sm (COMM) credit; **~i** smpl (ricchezza) wealth sg, possessions // vt, vb ausiliare to have; vedi **freddo, fame** etc; **~ da mangiare/bere** to have something to eat/drink; **~ da o a fare qc** to have to do sth; **~ (a) che fare o vedere con qd/qc** to have to do with sb/sth; **ho 28 anni** I am 28 (years old); **avercela con qd** to have something against sb.

avia'tore, 'trice sm/f aviator, pilot.

aviazi'one [avjat'tsjone] sf aviation; (MIL) air force.

avidità sf eagerness; greed.

'avido, a ag eager; (peg) greedy.

'avi smpl ancestors, forefathers.

avo'cado sm avocado.

a'vorio sm ivory.

Avv. abbr di **avvocato**.

avvalla'mento sm sinking q; (effetto) depression.

avvalo'rare vt to confirm.

avvantaggi'are [avvantad'dʒare] vt to favour; **~rsi** vr (trarre vantaggio): **~rsi di** to take advantage of; (prevalere): **~rsi negli affari/sui concorrenti** to get ahead in business/of one's competitors.

avvelena'mento sm poisoning.

avvele'nare vt to poison.

avve'nente ag attractive, charming.

avveni'mento sm event.

avve'nire vi, vb impers (2) to happen, occur // sm future.

avven'tarsi vr: **~ su** o **contro qd/qc** to hurl o.s. o rush at sb/sth.

avven'tato, a ag rash, reckless.

av'vento *sm* advent, coming; (*REL*): l'A~ Advent.

avven'tura *sf* adventure; (*amorosa*) affair.

avventu'rarsi *vr* to venture.

avventuri'ere, a *sm/f* adventurer/adventuress.

avventu'roso, a *ag* adventurous.

avve'rarsi *vr* to come true.

av'verbio *sm* adverb.

avver'sare *vt* to oppose.

avver'sario, a *ag* opposing // *sm* opponent, adversary.

avversi'one *sf* aversion.

avversità *sf inv* adversity, misfortune.

av'verso, a *ag* (*contrario*) contrary; (*sfavorevole*) unfavourable.

avver'tenza [avver'tɛntsa] *sf* (*ammonimento*) warning; (*cautela*) care; (*premessa*) foreword; **~e** *sfpl* (*istruzioni per l'uso*) instructions.

avverti'mento *sm* warning.

avver'tire *vt* (*avvisare*) to warn; (*rendere consapevole*) to inform, notify; (*percepire*) to feel.

av'vezzo, a [av'vettso] *ag*: **~ a** used to.

avvia'mento *sm* (*atto*) starting; (*effetto*) start; (*AUT*) starting; (*: dispositivo*) starter; (*COMM*) goodwill.

avvi'are *vt* (*mettere sul cammino*) to direct; (*impresa*) to begin, start; (*motore*) to start; **~rsi** *vr* to set off, set out.

avvicina'mento [avvitʃina'mento] *sm* approach.

avvici'nare [avvitʃi'nare] *vt* to bring near; (*trattare con: persona*) to approach; **~rsi** *vr*: **~rsi (a qd/qc)** to approach (sb/sth), draw near (to sb/sth).

avvili'mento *sm* humiliation; disgrace; discouragement.

avvi'lire *vt* (*umiliare*) to humiliate; (*degradare*) to disgrace; (*scoraggiare*) to dishearten, discourage; **~rsi** *vr* (*abbattersi*) to lose heart.

avvinaz'zato, a [avvinat'tsato] *ag* drunk.

av'vincere [av'vintʃere] *vt* to charm, enthral.

avvinghi'are [avvin'gjare] *vt* to clasp; **~rsi** *vr*: **~rsi a** to cling to.

avvi'sare *vt* (*far sapere*) to inform; (*mettere in guardia*) to warn; **av'viso** *sm* warning; (*annuncio*) announcement; (*: affisso*) notice; (*inserzione pubblicitaria*) advertisement; **a mio avviso** in my opinion.

avvi'tare *vt* to screw down (o in).

avviz'zire [avvit'tsire] *vi* (2) to wither.

avvo'cato, 'essa *sm/f* (*DIR*) barrister; (*fig*) defender, advocate.

av'volgere [av'voldʒere] *vt* to roll up; (*avviluppare*) to wrap up; **~rsi** *vr* (*avvilupparsi*) to wrap o.s. up; **avvol'gibile** *sm* roller blind.

avvol'toio *sm* vulture.

azi'enda [ad'dzjɛnda] *sf* business, firm, concern; **~ agricola** farm.

azi'one [at'tsjone] *sf* action; (*COMM*) share; **azio'nista, i, e** *sm/f* (*COMM*) shareholder.

azzan'nare [attsan'nare] *vt* to sink one's teeth into.

azzar'darsi [addzar'darsi] *vr* to dare; **azzar'dato, a** *ag* (*impresa*) risky; (*risposta*) rash.

az'zardo [ad'dzardo] *sm* risk.

azzuf'farsi [attsuf'farsi] *vr* to come to blows.

az'zurro, a [ad'dzurro] *ag* blue // *sm* (*colore*) blue; **gli ~i** (*SPORT*) the Italian national team.

B

bab'beo *sm* simpleton.

'babbo *sm* (*fam*) dad, daddy; **B~ natale** Father Christmas.

bab'buccia, ce [bab'buttʃa] *sf* slipper; (*per neonati*) bootee.

ba'bordo *sm* (*NAUT*) port side.

ba'cato, a *ag* worm-eaten, rotten.

'bacca, che *sf* berry.

baccalà *sm* dried salted cod.

bac'cano *sm* din, clamour.

bac'cello [bat'tʃɛllo] *sm* pod.

bac'chetta [bak'ketta] *sf* (*verga*) stick, rod; (*di direttore d'orchestra*) baton; (*di tamburo*) drumstick; **~ magica** magic wand.

baci'are [ba'tʃare] *vt* to kiss; **~rsi** *vr* to kiss (one another).

baci'nella [batʃi'nɛlla] *sf* basin.

ba'cino [ba'tʃino] *sm* basin; (*MINERALOGIA*) field, bed; (*ANAT*) pelvis; (*NAUT*) dock.

'bacio ['batʃo] *sm* kiss.

'baco, chi *sm* worm; **~ da seta** silkworm.

ba'dare *vi* (*fare attenzione*) to take care, be careful; (*occuparsi di*): **~ a** to look after, take care of; (*dar ascolto*): **~ a** to pay attention to; **bada ai fatti tuoi!** mind your own business!

ba'dia *sf* abbey.

ba'dile *sm* shovel.

'baffi *smpl* moustache *sg*; (*di animale*) whiskers; **ridere sotto i ~** to laugh up one's sleeve; **leccarsi i ~** to lick one's lips.

bagagli'aio [bagaʎ'ʎajo] *sm* luggage-van; (*AUT*) boot.

ba'gaglio [ba'gaʎʎo] *smpl* luggage *sg*.

bagat'tella *sf* trifle, trifling matter.

bagli'ore [baʎ'ʎore] *sm* flash, dazzling light; **un ~ di speranza** a sudden ray of hope.

ba'gnante [baɲ'ɲante] *sm/f* bather.

ba'gnare [baɲ'ɲare] *vt* to wet; (*inzuppare*) to soak; (*innaffiare*) to water; (*sog: fiume*) to flow through; (*: mare*) to wash, bathe; **~rsi** *vr* (*al mare*) to go swimming *o* bathing; (*in vasca*) to have a bath.

ba'gnino [baɲ'ɲino] *sm* lifeguard.

'bagno ['baɲɲo] *sm* bath; (*locale*) bathroom; **~i** *smpl* (*stabilimento*) baths; **fare il ~** to have a bath; (*nel mare*) to go swimming *o* bathing; **fare il ~ a qd** to give sb a bath.

'**baia** sf bay.

baio'netta sf bayonet.

balaus'trata sf balustrade.

balbet'tare vi to stutter, stammer; (bimbo) to babble // vt to stammer out.

balbuzi'ente [balbut'tsjɛnte] ag stuttering, stammering.

bal'cone sm balcony.

baldac'chino [baldak'kino] sm canopy.

bal'danza [bal'dantsa] sf self-confidence, boldness.

'**baldo**, a ag bold, daring.

bal'doria sf merrymaking q; noisy party.

ba'lena sf whale.

bale'nare (2) vb impers: **balena** there's lightning // vi to flash; **mi balenò un'idea** an idea flashed through my mind; **ba'leno** sm flash of lightning; **in un baleno** in a flash.

ba'lestra sf crossbow.

'**balia** sf wet-nurse.

ba'lìa sf: **in ~ di** at the mercy of; **cadere in ~ di qd** to fall into sb's hands.

'**balla** sf (di merci) bale; (fandonia) (tall) story.

bal'lare vt, vi to dance; **bal'lata** sf ballad.

balle'rina sf dancer; ballet dancer; (scarpa) ballet shoe.

balle'rino sm dancer; ballet dancer.

bal'letto sm ballet.

'**ballo** sm dance; (azione) dancing q; **essere in ~** (fig: persona) to be involved; (: cosa) to be at stake.

ballot'taggio [ballot'taddʒo] sm (POL) second ballot.

balne'are ag seaside cpd; (stagione) bathing.

ba'locco, chi sm toy.

ba'lordo, a ag stupid, senseless; (stordito) stupefied, dopey.

bal'samo sm (aroma) balsam; (lenimento, fig) balm.

'**Baltico** sm: **il (mar) ~** the Baltic (Sea).

balu'ardo sm bulwark.

'**balza** ['baltsa] sf (dirupo) crag; (di stoffa) frill.

bal'zare [bal'tsare] vi to bounce; (lanciarsi) to jump, leap; '**balzo** sm bounce; jump, leap; (del terreno) crag.

bam'bagia [bam'badʒa] sf (ovatta) cotton wool; (cascame) cotton waste.

bam'bina ag, sf vedi **bambino**.

bambi'naia sf nanny, nurse(maid).

bam'bino, a ag child cpd; (non sviluppato) immature // sm/f child.

bam'boccio [bam'bɔttʃo] sm plump child; (pupazzo) rag doll.

'**bambola** sf doll.

bambù sm bamboo.

ba'nale ag banal, commonplace; **banalità** sf inv banality.

ba'nana sf banana; **ba'nano** sm banana tree.

'**banca, che** sf bank.

banca'rella sf stall.

ban'carlo, a ag banking, bank cpd // sm bank clerk.

banca'rotta sf bankruptcy; **fare ~** to go bankrupt.

ban'chetto [ban'ketto] sm banquet.

banchi'ere [ban'kjere] sm banker.

ban'china [ban'kina] sf (di porto) quay; (per pedoni, ciclisti) path; (di stazione) platform; **~ spartitraffico** (AUT) central reservation; **~e non transitabili** (AUT) soft verges.

'**banco, chi** sm bench; (di negozio) counter; (di mercato) stall; (di officina) (work-)bench; (GEO, banca) bank; **~ degli imputati** dock; **~ di prova** (fig) testing ground; **~ dei testimoni** witness box.

banco'nota sf banknote.

'**banda** sf band; (di stoffa) band, stripe; (lato, parte) side.

banderu'ola sf pennant; (METEOR) weathercock, weathervane.

bandi'era sf flag, banner.

ban'dire vt to proclaim; (esiliare) to exile; (fig) to dispense with.

ban'dito sm outlaw, bandit.

bandi'tore sm (di aste) auctioneer.

'**bando** sm proclamation; (esilio) exile, banishment.

bar sm inv bar.

'**bara** sf coffin.

ba'racca, che sf shed, hut; (peg) hovel; **mandare avanti la ~** to keep things going; **far ~** to make merry.

bara'onda sf hubbub, bustle.

ba'rare vi to cheat.

'**baratro** sm abyss.

barat'tare vt: **~ qc con** to barter sth for, swap sth for; **ba'ratto** sm barter.

ba'rattolo sm (di latta) tin; (di vetro) jar; (di coccio) pot.

'**barba** sf beard; **farsi la ~** to shave; **farla in ~ a qd** (fig) to do sth to sb's face; **che ~!** what a bore!

barbabi'etola sf beetroot; **~ da zucchero** sugar beet.

bar'barico, a, ci, che ag barbarian; barbaric.

bar'barie sf barbarity.

'**barbaro**, a ag barbarous; **~i** smpl barbarians.

barbi'ere sm barber.

bar'bone sm (cane) poodle; (vagabondo) tramp.

bar'buto, a ag bearded.

'**barca, che** sf boat; **~ a remi** rowing boat; **barcai'olo** sm boatman; (noleggiatore) boat hirer.

barcol'lare vi to stagger.

bar'cone sm (per ponti di barche) pontoon.

ba'rella sf (lettiga) stretcher.

ba'rile sm barrel, cask.

ba'rista, i, e sm/f barman/maid; bar owner.

ba'ritono sm baritone.

bar'lume sm glimmer, gleam.

ba'rocco, a, chi, che ag, sm baroque.

ba'rometro sm barometer.

ba'rone sm baron; **baro'nessa** sf baroness.

'barra sf bar; (NAUT) helm; (linea grafica) line, stroke.

barri'care vt to barricade; **barri'cata** sf barricade.

barri'era sf barrier; (GEO) reef.

ba'ruffa sf scuffle.

barzel'letta [bardzel'letta] sf joke, funny story.

ba'sare vt to base, found; ~**rsi** vr: ~**rsi su** (sog: fatti, prove) to be based o founded on; (: persona) to base one's arguments on.

'basco, schi sm (copricapo) beret.

'base sf base; (fig: fondamento) basis; (POL) rank and file; **di** ~ basic; **in** ~ **a** on the basis of, according to; **a** ~ **di caffè** coffee-based.

ba'setta sf sideburn.

ba'silica, che sf basilica.

ba'silico sm basil.

'basso, a ag low; (di statura) short; (meridionale) southern // sm bottom, lower part; (MUS) bass; **la** ~**a Italia** southern Italy.

basso'fondo, pl **bassifondi** sm (GEO) shallows pl; **bassifondi** smpl (fig) dregs.

bassorili'evo sm bas-relief.

'basta escl (that's) enough!, that will do!

bas'tardo, a ag (animale, pianta) hybrid, crossbreed; (persona) illegitimate, bastard (peg) // sm/f illegitimate child, bastard (peg).

bas'tare vi, vb impers (2) to be enough, be sufficient; ~ **a qd** to be enough for sb; **basta chiedere a un vigile** you have only to o need only ask a policeman.

basti'mento sm ship, vessel.

basto'nare vt to beat, thrash.

bas'tone sm stick; ~ **da passeggio** walking stick.

bat'taglia [bat'taʎʎa] sf battle; fight.

bat'taglio [bat'taʎʎo] sm (di campana) clapper; (di porta) knocker.

battagli'one [battaʎ'ʎone] sm battalion.

bat'tello sm boat.

bat'tente sm (imposta: di porta) wing, flap; (: di finestra) shutter; (batacchio: di porta) knocker; (: di orologio) hammer.

'battere vt to beat; (grano) to thresh; (percorrere) to scour // vi (bussare) to knock; (urtare): ~ **contro** to hit o strike against; (pioggia, sole) to beat down; (cuore) to beat; (TENNIS) to serve; ~**rsi** vr to fight; ~ **le mani** to clap; ~ **i piedi** to stamp one's feet; ~ **le ore** to strike the hours; ~ **su un argomento** to hammer home an argument; ~ **a macchina** to type; ~ **bandiera italiana** to fly the Italian flag; ~ **in testa** (AUT) to knock; **in un batter d'occhio** in the twinkling of an eye.

bat'teri smpl bacteria.

batte'ria sf battery; (MUS) drums pl.

bat'tesimo sm baptism; christening.

battez'zare [batted'dzare] vt to baptize; to christen.

batticu'ore sm palpitations pl; **avere il** ~ to be frightened to death.

batti'mano sm applause.

batti'panni sm inv carpet-beater.

battis'tero sm baptistry.

battis'trada sm inv (di pneumatico) tread; (di gara) pacemaker.

'battito sm beat, throb; ~ **cardiaco** heartbeat; ~ **della pioggia/ dell'orologio** beating of the rain/ticking of the clock.

bat'tuta sf blow; (di macchina da scrivere) stroke; (MUS) bar; beat; (TEATRO) cue; (di caccia) beating; (POLIZIA) combing, scouring; (TENNIS) service.

ba'ule sm trunk; (AUT) boot.

'bava sf dribble; (di cane etc) slaver, slobber; (di vento) breath.

bava'glino [bavaʎ'ʎino] sm bib.

ba'vaglio [ba'vaʎʎo] sm gag.

'bavero sm collar.

ba'zar [bad'dzar] sm inv bazaar.

baz'zecola [bad'dzekola] sf trifle.

bazzi'care [battsi'kare] vt to frequent // vi: ~ **in/con** to frequent.

beati'tudine sf bliss.

be'ato, a ag blessed; (fig) happy; ~ **te!** lucky you!

bec'caccia, ce [bek'kattʃa] sf woodcock.

bec'care vt to peck; (fig: raffreddore) to pick up, catch; ~**rsi** vr (fig) to squabble.

becheggi'are [bekked'dʒare] vi to pitch.

bec'chino [bek'kino] sm gravedigger.

'becco, chi sm beak, bill; (di caffettiera etc) spout; lip.

Be'fana sf old woman who, according to legend, brings children their presents at the Epiphany; (Epifania) Epiphany; (donna brutta): **b**~ hag, witch.

'beffa sf practical joke; **bef'fardo, a** ag scornful, mocking; **bef'fare** vt (anche: **beffarsi di**) to make a fool of, mock.

'bega, ghe sf quarrel.

'begli ['beʎʎi] **'bei, bel** ag vedi **bello**.

be'lare vi to bleat.

'belga, gi, ghe ag, sm/f Belgian.

'Belgio ['bɛldʒo] sm: **il** ~ Belgium.

bel'lezza [bel'lettsa] sf beauty.

belli'coso, a ag warlike.

bellige'rante [bellidʒe'rante] ag belligerent.

'bello, a ag (dav sm **bel** +C, **bell'** +V, **bello** + s impura, gn, pn, ps, x, z, pl **bei** +C, **begli** + s impura etc o V) beautiful, fine, lovely; (uomo) handsome // sm (bellezza) beauty; (tempo) fine weather // sf (SPORT) decider // av: **fa** ~ the weather is fine, it's fine; **una** ~**a cifra** a considerable sum of money; **un bel niente** absolutely nothing; **è una truffa** ~**a e buona!** it's a real fraud!; **è bell'e finito** it's already finished; **sul più** ~ at the crucial point; **belle arti** fine arts.

'belva sf wild animal.

belve'dere sm inv panoramic viewpoint.

benché [ben'ke] cong although.

'benda sf bandage; (per gli occhi) blindfold; **ben'dare** vt to bandage; to blindfold.

'bene av well; (completamente, affatto): **è**

ben difficile it's very difficult // ag inv: **gente** ~ well-to-do people // sm good; ~**i** smpl (averi) property sg, estate sg; **io sto** ~/**poco** ~ I'm well/not very well; **va** ~ all right; **volere un** ~ **dell'anima a qd** to love sb very much; **un uomo per** ~ a respectable man; **fare** ~ **to do the right thing; fare** ~ **a** (salute) to be good for; **fare del** ~ **a qd** to do sb a good turn; ~**i di consumo** consumer goods.

bene'detto, a pp di **benedire** // ag blessed, holy.

bene'dire vt to bless; to consecrate; **benedizi'one** sf blessing.

benedu'cato, a ag well-mannered.

benefat'tore, 'trice sm/f benefactor/benefactress.

benefi'care vt to help, benefit.

benefi'cenza [benefi'tʃɛntsa] sf charity.

bene'ficio [bene'fitʃo] sm benefit.

be'nefico, a, ci, che ag beneficial; charitable.

bene'merito, a ag meritorious.

be'nessere sm well-being.

benes'tante ag well-to-do.

benes'tare sm consent, approval.

benevo'lenza [benevo'lɛntsa] sf benevolence.

be'nevolo, a ag benevolent.

be'nigno, a [be'niɲɲo] ag kind, kindly; (critica etc) favourable; (MED) benign.

benin'teso av of course.

bensì cong but (rather).

benve'nuto, a ag, sm welcome; **dare il** ~ **a qd** to welcome sb.

ben'zina [ben'dzina] sf petrol; **fare** ~ **to get petrol; benzi'naio** sm petrol pump attendant.

'bere vt to drink; (assorbire) to soak up.

ber'lina sf (AUT) saloon (car).

Ber'lino sf Berlin.

ber'noccolo sm bump; (inclinazione) bent, flair.

ber'retto sm cap.

bersagli'are [bersaʎ'ʎare] vt to shoot at; (colpire ripetutamente, fig) to bombard; **bersagliato dalla sfortuna** dogged by ill fortune.

ber'saglio [ber'saʎʎo] sm target.

bes'temmia sf blasphemy; oath, curse, swearword.

bestemmi'are vi to blaspheme; to curse, swear // vt to blaspheme; to curse, swear at.

'bestia sf animal; ~ **da soma** beast of burden; **besti'ale** ag bestial; brutal; **besti'ame** sm livestock; (bovino) cattle pl.

'bettola sf (peg) dive.

be'tulla sf birch.

be'vanda sf drink, beverage.

bevi'tore, 'trice sm/f drinker.

be'vuto, a pp di **bere** // sf drink.

bi'ada sf fodder.

bianche'ria [bjanke'ria] sf linen; ~ **intima** underwear; ~ **da donna** ladies' underwear, lingerie.

bi'anco, a, chi, che ag white; (non

scritto) blank // sm white; blank, blank space; (intonaco) whitewash // sm/f white, white man/woman; **in** ~ (foglio, assegno) blank; **mangiare in** ~ to follow a bland diet; **pesce in** ~ boiled fish; ~ **dell'uovo** egg-white.

biasi'mare vt to disapprove of, censure; **bi'asimo** sm disapproval, censure.

'bibbia sf bible.

bibe'ron sm inv feeding bottle.

'bibita sf (soft) drink.

biblio'teca, che sf library; (mobile) bookcase; **bibliote'cario, a** sm/f librarian.

bicarbo'nato sm: ~ (**di sodio**) bicarbonate (of soda).

bicchi'ere [bik'kjɛre] sm glass.

bici'cletta [bitʃi'kletta] sf bicycle.

bidé sm inv bidet.

bi'dello, a sm/f (INS) janitor.

bi'done sm drum, can; (anche: ~ **dell'immondizia**) (dust)bin; (fam: truffa) swindle.

bien'nale ag biennial.

bi'etola sf beet.

bifor'carsi vr to fork; **biforcazi'one** sf fork.

biga'mia sf bigamy.

bighello'nare [bigello'nare] vi to loaf (about).

biglotte'ria [bidʒotte'ria] sf costume jewellery; (negozio) jeweller's (selling only costume jewellery).

bigli'ardo [biʎ'ʎardo] sm = **biliardo**.

bigliette'ria [biʎʎette'ria] sf (di stazione) ticket office; booking office; (di teatro) box office.

bigli'etto [biʎ'ʎetto] sm (per viaggi, spettacoli etc) ticket; (cartoncino) card; (anche: ~ **di banca**) (bank)note; ~ **d'auguri/da visita** greetings/visiting card.

bigo'dino sm roller, curler.

bi'gotto, a ag over-pious // sm/f church fiend.

bi'lancia, ce [bi'lantʃa] sf (pesa) scales pl; (: di precisione) balance; (dello zodiaco): **B**~ **Libra**; ~ **commerciale/dei pagamenti** balance of trade/payments; **bilanci'are** vt (pesare) to weigh; (: fig) to weigh up; (pareggiare) to balance.

bi'lancio [bi'lantʃo] sm (COMM) balance(-sheet); (statale) budget; **fare il** ~ **di** (fig) to assess; ~ **consuntivo** (final) balance; ~ **preventivo** budget.

'bile sf bile; (fig) rage, anger.

bili'ardo sm billiards sg; billiard table.

'bilico, chi sm unstable equilibrium; **in** ~ in the balance; **tenere qd in** ~ to keep sb in suspense.

bi'lingue ag bilingual.

bili'one sm (mille milioni) thousand million; (milione di milioni) billion.

'bimbo, a sm/f little boy/girl.

bimen'sile ag fortnightly.

bimes'trale ag two-monthly, bimonthly.

bi'nario sm (railway) track o line;

(*piattaforma*) platform; ~ **morto** dead-end track.

bi'nocolo *sm* binoculars *pl.*

bio... *prefisso*: **bio'chimica** [bio'kimika] *sf* biochemistry; **biodegra'dabile** *ag* biodegradable; **biogra'fia** *sf* biography; **biolo'gia** *sf* biology; **bio'logico, a, ci, che** *ag* biological.

bi'ondo, a *ag* blond, fair.

bir'bante *sm* rogue, rascal.

biri'chino, a [biri'kino] *ag* mischievous // *sm/f* scamp, little rascal.

bi'rillo *sm* skittle; ~**i** *smpl* (*gioco*) skittles *sg*.

'birra *sf* beer; **a tutta** ~ (*fig*) at top speed; **birre'ria** *sf* ≈ bierkeller.

bis *escl, sm inv* encore.

bisbigli'are [bisbi⅄'⅄are] *vt, vi* to whisper; **bis'biglio** *sm* whisper; (*notizia*) rumour; **bisbi'glio** *sm* whispering.

'bisca, sche *sf* gambling-house.

'biscia, sce ['biʃʃa] *sf* snake; ~ **d'acqua** grass snake.

bis'cotto *sm* biscuit.

bises'tile *ag*: **anno** ~ leap year.

bis'lungo, a, ghi, ghe *ag* oblong.

bis'nonno, a *sm/f* great-grandfather/grandmother.

biso'gnare [bizoɲ'ɲare] *vb impers*: **bisogna che tu parta/lo faccia** you'll have to go/do it; **bisogna parlargli** we'll (o I'll) have to talk to him // *vi* (*esser utile*) to be necessary; **mi bisognano quei fogli** I need those sheets of paper.

bi'sogno [bi'zoɲɲo] *sm* need; ~**i** *smpl*: **fare i propri** ~**i** to relieve o.s.; **avere** ~ **di qc/di fare qc** to need sth/to do sth; **al** ~, **in caso di** ~ if need be; **biso'gnoso, a** *ag* needy, poor; **bisognoso di** in need of, needing.

bis'tecca, che *sf* steak, beefsteak.

bisticci'are [bistit'tʃare] *vi*, ~**rsi** *vr* to quarrel, bicker; **bis'ticcio** *sm* quarrel, squabble; (*gioco di parole*) pun.

bis'turi *sm* scalpel.

bi'sunto, a *ag* very greasy.

'bitter *sm inv* bitters *pl.*

bi'vacco, chi *sm* bivouac.

'bivio *sm* fork; (*fig*) dilemma.

'bizza ['biddza] *sf* tantrum; **fare le** ~**e** (*bambino*) to be naughty.

biz'zarro, a [bid'dzarro] *ag* bizarre, strange.

biz'zeffe [bid'dzɛffe]: **a** ~ *av* in plenty, galore.

blan'dire *vt* to soothe; to flatter.

'blando, a *ag* mild, gentle.

bla'sone *sm* coat of arms.

blate'rare *vi* to chatter, blether.

'blatta *sf* cockroach.

blin'dato, a *ag* armoured.

bloc'care *vt* to block; (*isolare*) to isolate, cut off; (*porto*) to blockade; (*prezzi, beni*) to freeze; (*meccanismo*) to jam.

'blocco, chi *sm* block; (*MIL*) blockade; (*dei fitti*) restriction; (*quadernetto*) pad; (*fig: unione*) coalition; (*il bloccare*) blocking;

isolating, cutting-off; blockading; freezing; jamming; **in** ~ (*nell'insieme*) as a whole; (*COMM*) in bulk.

blu *ag inv, sm* dark blue.

'blusa *sf* (*camiciotto*) smock; (*camicetta*) blouse.

'boa *sm inv* (*ZOOL*) boa constrictor; (*sciarpa*) feather boa // *sf* buoy.

bo'ato *sm* rumble, roar.

bo'bina *sf* reel, spool; (*di pellicola*) spool; (*di film*) reel; (*ELETTR*) coil.

'bocca, che *sf* mouth; **in** ~ **al lupo!** good luck!

boc'caccia, ce [bok'kattʃa] *sf* (*smorfia*) grimace.

boc'cale *sm* jug; ~ **da birra** tankard.

boc'cetta [bot'tʃetta] *sf* small bottle.

boccheggi'are [bokked'dʒare] *vi* to gasp.

boc'chino [bok'kino] *sm* (*di sigaretta, sigaro: cannella*) cigarette-holder; cigar-holder; (*di pipa, strumenti musicali*) mouthpiece; ~ **con filtro** filter tip.

'boccia, ce ['bottʃa] *sf* bottle; (*da vino*) decanter, carafe; (*palla*) bowl; **gioco di** ~**ce** bowls *sg*.

bocci'are [bot'tʃare] *vt* (*respingere*) to reject; (*: INS*) to fail; (*nel gioco delle bocce*) to hit; **boccia'tura** *sf* failure.

bocci'olo [bot'tʃolo] *sm* bud.

boc'cone *sm* mouthful, morsel.

boc'coni *av* face downwards.

'boia *sm inv* executioner; hangman.

bol'ata *sf* botch.

boicot'tare *vt* to boycott.

Bo'livia *sf*: **la** ~ Bolivia.

'bolla *sf* bubble; (*MED*) blister; ~ **papale** papal bull.

bol'lare *vt* to stamp; (*fig*) to brand.

bol'lente *ag* boiling; boiling hot.

bol'letta *sf* bill; (*ricevuta*) receipt; **essere in** ~ to be hard up.

bollet'tino *sm* bulletin; (*COMM*) note; ~ **di spedizione** consignment note.

bol'lire *vt, vi* to boil; **bol'lito** *sm* (*CUC*) boiled meat; **bolli'tura** *sf* boiling.

'bollo *sm* stamp.

bol'lore *sm* boiling (point); (*caldo intenso*) torrid heat; ~**i di gioventù** youthful enthusiasm *sg*.

'bomba *sf* bomb; **tornare a** ~ (*fig*) to get back to the point; ~ **atomica** atom bomb.

bombarda'mento *sm* bombardment; bombing.

bombar'dare *vt* to bombard; (*da aereo*) to bomb.

bombardi'ere *sm* bomber.

bom'betta *sf* bowler (hat).

'bombola *sf* cylinder.

bo'naccia, ce [bo'nattʃa] *sf* dead calm.

bo'nario, a *ag* good-natured, kind.

bo'nifica, che *sf* reclamation; reclaimed land.

bo'nifico, ci *sm* (*COMM: abbuono*) discount; (*: versamento*) credit transfer.

bontà *sf* goodness; (*cortesia*) kindness; **aver la** ~ **di fare qc** to be good o kind enough to do sth.

borbot'tare *vi* to mumble; (*stomaco*) to rumble.

'borchia ['borkja] *sf* stud.

borda'tura *sf* (*SARTORIA*) border, trim.

'bordo *sm* (*NAUT*) ship's side; (*orlo*) edge; (*striscia di guarnizione*) border, trim; **prendere a ~** to take on board; **a ~ della macchina** inside the car.

bor'dura *sf* border.

bor'gata *sf* hamlet.

bor'ghese [bor'geze] *ag* (*spesso peg*) middle-class; bourgeois; **abito ~** civilian dress; **borghe'sia** *sf* middle classes *pl*; bourgeoisie.

'borgo, ghi *sm* (*paesino*) village; (*quartiere*) district.

'boria *sf* self-conceit, arrogance; **bori'oso, a** *ag* arrogant.

boro'talco *sm* talcum powder.

bor'raccia, ce [bor'rattʃa] *sf* canteen, water-bottle.

'borsa *sf* bag; (*anche:* **~ da signora**) handbag; (*ECON*): **la B~** (*valori*) the Stock Exchange; **~ nera** black market; **~ della spesa** shopping bag; **~ di studio** grant; **borsai'olo** *sm* pickpocket; **borsel'lino** *sm* purse; **bor'setta** *sf* handbag; **bor'sista, i, e** *sm/f* (*ECON*) speculator; (*INS*) grant-holder.

bos'caglia [bos'kaʎʎa] *sf* woodlands *pl*.

boscai'olo *sm* woodcutter; forester.

'bosco, schi *sm* wood; **bos'coso, a** *ag* wooded.

'bossolo *sm* cartridge-case.

bo'tanico, a, ci, che *ag* botanical // *sm* botanist // *sf* botany.

'botola *sf* trap door.

'botta *sf* blow; (*rumore*) bang.

'botte *sf* barrel, cask.

bot'tega, ghe *sf* shop; (*officina*) workshop; **botte'gaio, a** *sm/f* shopkeeper; **botte-'ghino** *sm* ticket office; (*del lotto*) public lottery office.

bot'tiglia [bot'tiʎʎa] *sf* bottle; **bottiglie-'ria** *sf* wine shop.

bot'tino *sm* (*di guerra*) booty; (*di rapina, furto*) loot.

'botto *sm* bang; crash; **di ~** suddenly.

bot'tone *sm* button; (*BOT*) bud; **botton d'oro** buttercup.

bo'vino, a *ag* bovine; **~i** *smpl* cattle.

boxe [boks] *sf* boxing.

'bozza ['bottsa] *sf* draft; sketch; (*TIP*) proof; **boz'zetto** *sm* sketch.

'bozzolo ['bottsolo] *sm* cocoon.

brac'care *vt* to hunt.

brac'cetto [brat'tʃetto] *sm*: **a ~** arm in arm.

bracci'ale [brat'tʃale] *sm* bracelet; (*distintivo*) armband; **braccia'letto** *sm* bracelet, bangle.

bracci'ante [brat'tʃante] *sm* (*AGR*) day labourer.

bracci'ata [brat'tʃata] *sf* armful; (*nel nuoto*) stroke.

'braccio ['brattʃo] *sm* (*pl(f)* **braccia:** *ANAT*) arm; (*pl(m)* **bracci:** *di gru, fiume*)

arm; (*: di edificio*) wing; **~ di mare** sound; **~ di terra** promontory; **bracci'olo** *sm* (*appoggio*) arm.

'bracco, chi *sm* hound.

bracconi'ere *sm* poacher.

brace ['bratʃe] *sf* embers *pl*; **braci'ere** *sm* brazier.

braci'ola [bra'tʃɔla] *sf* (*CUC*) chop.

'branca, che *sf* branch.

'branchia ['brankja] *sf* (*ZOOL*) gill.

'branco, chi *sm* (*di cani, lupi*) pack; (*di uccelli, pecore*) flock; (*mandria*) herd; (*peg: di persone*) gang, pack.

branco'lare *vi* to grope, feel one's way.

'branda *sf* camp bed.

bran'dello *sm* scrap, shred; **a ~i** in tatters, in rags.

bran'dire *vt* to brandish.

'brano *sm* piece; (*di libro*) passage.

bra'sare *vt* to braise.

Bra'sile *sm*: **il ~** Brazil; **brasili'ano, a** *ag, sm/f* Brazilian.

'bravo, a *ag* (*abile*) clever, capable, skilful; (*buono*) good, honest; (*: bambino*) good; (*coraggioso*) brave; **~!** well done!; (*al teatro*) bravo!

bra'vura *sf* cleverness, skill.

'breccia, ce ['brettʃa] *sf* breach.

bre'tella *sf* (*AUT*) link; **~e** *sfpl* braces.

'breve *ag* brief, short; **in ~** in short.

brevet'tare *vt* to patent.

bre'vetto *sm* patent; **~ di pilotaggio** pilot's licence.

brevità *sf* brevity.

'brezza ['breddza] *sf* breeze.

'bricco, chi *sm* jug, pot; **~ del caffè** coffeepot.

bric'cone, a *sm/f* rogue, rascal.

'briciola ['britʃola] *sf* crumb.

'briciolo ['britʃolo] *sm* bit.

'briga, ghe *sf* (*fastidio*) trouble, bother; **pigliarsi la ~ di fare qc** to take the trouble to do sth.

brigadi'ere *sm* (*dei carabinieri etc*) ≈ sergeant.

bri'gante *sm* bandit.

bri'gare *vi* to scheme.

bri'gata *sf* (*MIL*) brigade; (*gruppo*) group, party.

'briglia ['briʎʎa] *sf* rein; **a ~ sciolta** at full gallop; (*fig*) at full speed.

bril'lante *ag* bright; brilliant; (*che luccica*) shining // *sm* diamond.

bril'lare *vi* to shine; (*mina*) to blow up.

'brillo, a *ag* merry, tipsy.

'brina *sf* hoarfrost.

brin'dare *vi*: **~ a qd/qc** to drink to o toast sb/sth.

'brindisi *sm inv* toast.

'brio *sm* liveliness, go; **bri'oso, a** *ag* lively.

bri'tannico, a, ci, che *ag* British.

'brivido *sm* shiver; (*di ribrezzo*) shudder; (*fig*) thrill.

brizzo'lato, a [brittso'lato] *ag* (*persona*) going grey; (*barba, capelli*) greying.

'brocca, che *sf* jug.

broc'cato *sm* brocade.

'**broccolo** *sm* broccoli *sg*.

'**brodo** *sm* broth; (*per cucinare*) stock; ~ **ristretto** consommé.

'**brogli** ['brɔʎʎi] *smpl* (*DIR*) malpractices.

brogli'accio [broʎ'ʎattʃo] *sm* scribbling pad.

bron'chite [bron'kite] *sf* (*MED*) bronchitis.

'**broncio** ['brontʃo] *sm* sulky expression; **fare il** ~ to sulk.

bronto'lare *vi* to grumble; (*stomaco*) to rumble.

'**bronzo** ['brondzo] *sm* bronze.

bru'care *vt* to browse on, nibble at.

brucia'pelo [brutʃa'pelo]: **a** ~ *av* point-blank.

bruci'are [bru'tʃare] *vt* to burn; (*scottare*) to scald // *vi* (2) to burn; **brucia'tore** *sm* burner; **brucia'tura** *sf* burning *q*; burn; (*scottatura*) scald; **bruci'ore** *sm* burning *o* smarting sensation.

'**bruco**, **chi** *sm* caterpillar; grub.

brughi'era [bru'gjɛra] *sf* heath, moor.

bruli'care *vi* to swarm.

'**brullo**, **a** *ag* bare, bleak.

'**bruma** *sf* mist.

'**bruno**, **a** *ag* brown, dark; (*persona*) dark(-haired).

brusco, **a**, **schi**, **sche** *ag* (*sapore*) sharp; (*modi*, *persona*) brusque, abrupt; (*movimento*) abrupt, sudden.

bru'sio *sm* buzz, buzzing.

bru'tale *ag* brutal; **brutalità** *sf inv* brutality.

'**bruto**, **a** *ag* brute *cpd*; brutal // *sm* brute.

brut'tezza [brut'tettsa] *sf* ugliness.

'**brutto**, **a** *ag* ugly; (*cattivo*) bad; (*malattia*, *strada*, *affare*) nasty, bad; ~ **tempo bad weather; **brut'tura** *sf* (*cosa brutta*) ugly thing; (*sudiciume*) filth; (*azione meschina*) mean action.

Bru'xelles [bry'sɛl] *sf* Brussels.

'**buca**, **che** *sf* hole; (*avvallamento*) hollow; ~ **delle lettere** letterbox.

buca'neve *sm inv* snowdrop.

bu'care *vt* (*forare*) to make a hole (*o* holes) in; (*pungere*) to pierce; (*biglietto*) to punch; ~ **una gomma** to have a puncture.

bu'cato *sm* (*operazione*) washing; (*panni*) wash, washing.

'**buccia**, **ce** ['buttʃa] *sf* skin, peel; (*corteccia*) bark.

bucherel'lare [bukerel'lare] *vt* to riddle with holes.

'**buco**, **chi** *sm* hole.

bu'dello *sm* intestine; (*fig: tubo*) tube; ~ **a** *sfpl* bowels, guts.

bu'dino *sm* pudding.

'**bue** *sm* ox; (*anche:* **carne di** ~) beef.

'**bufalo** *sm* buffalo.

bu'fera *sf* storm; ~ **di vento** gale.

'**buffo**, **a** *ag* funny; (*TEATRO*) comic.

buf'fone *sm* buffoon.

bu'gia, '**gie** [bu'dʒia] *sf* lie; (*candeliere*) candleholder; **bugi'ardo**, **a** *ag* lying, deceitful // *sm/f* liar.

bugi'gattolo [budʒi'gattolo] *sm* poky little room.

'**buio**, **a** *ag* dark // *sm* dark, darkness; **fa** ~ **pesto** it's pitch-dark.

'**bulbo** *sm* (*BOT*) bulb; ~ **oculare** eyeball.

Bulga'ria *sf:* **la** ~ Bulgaria.

bul'lone *sm* bolt.

buongus'taio, **a** *sm/f* gourmet.

buon'gusto *sm* good taste.

bu'ono, **a** *ag* (*dav sm buon + C o V*, **buono** + *s impura*, *gn*, *pn*, *ps*, *x*, *z*; *dav sf* **buon'** + *V*) good; (*benevolo*): ~ (**con**) good (to), kind (to); (*adatto*): ~ **a/da** fit for/to // *sm* good; (*COMM*) voucher, coupon; **alla buona** *ag* simple // *av* in a simple way, without any fuss; **buona fortuna** good luck; **buona notte** good night; **buona sera** good evening; **buon compleanno** happy birthday; **buon divertimento** have a nice time; **buon giorno** good morning (*o* afternoon); **a buon mercato** cheap; **di buon'ora** early; ~ **di cassa** cash voucher; ~ **fruttifero** bond bearing interest; ~ **a nulla** good-for-nothing; ~ **del tesoro** Treasury bill; **buon riposo** sleep well; **buon senso** common sense; **buon viaggio** bon voyage, have a good trip.

buontem'pone, **a** *sm/f* jovial person.

burat'tino *sm* puppet.

'**burbero**, **a** *ag* surly, gruff.

'**burla** *sf* prank, trick; **bur'lare** *vt:* **burlare** *qc/qd*, **burlarsi il** *qc/qd* to make fun of sth/sb.

bu'rocrate *sm* bureaucrat; **buro'cratico**, **a**, **ci**, **che** *ag* bureaucratic; **burocra'zia** *sf* bureaucracy.

bur'rasca, **sche** *sf* storm; **burras'coso**, **a** *ag* stormy.

'**burro** *sm* butter.

bur'rone *sm* ravine.

bus'care *vt* (*anche:* ~**rsi:** *raffreddore*) to get, catch; **buscarle** (*fam*) to get a hiding.

bus'sare *vi* to knock.

'**bussola** *sf* compass; **perdere la** ~ (*fig*) to lose one's bearings.

'**busta** *sf* (*da lettera*) envelope; (*astuccio*) case; **in** ~ **aperta** in an unsealed envelope; ~ **paga** pay packet.

busta'rella *sf* bribe, backhander.

'**busto** *sm* bust; (*indumento*) corset, girdle.

but'tare *vt* to throw; (*anche:* ~ **via**) to throw away; ~ **giù** (*scritto*) to scribble down, dash off; (*cibo*) to gulp down; (*edificio*) to pull down, demolish; (*pasta*, *verdura*) to put into boiling water; ~**rsi dalla finestra** to jump *o* throw o.s. out of the window.

C

ca'bina *sf* (*di nave*) cabin; (*da spiaggia*) beach hut; (*di autocarro*, *treno*) cab; (*di aereo*) cockpit; (*di ascensore*) cage; ~ **telefonica** call box, (tele)phone box *o* booth.

ca'cao *sm* cocoa.

'**caccia** ['kattʃa] *sf* hunting; (*con fucile*)

shooting; (*inseguimento*) chase; (*cacciagione*) game; ~ **grossa** big-game hunting; ~ **all'uomo** manhunt // *sm inv* (*aereo*) fighter; (*nave*) destroyer.

cacciabombardi'ere [kattʃabombar-'djere] *sm* fighter-bomber.

cacciagi'one [kattʃa'dʒone] *sf* game.

cacci'are [kat'tʃare] *vt* to hunt; (*mandar via*) to chase away; (*ficcare*) to shove, stick // *vi* to hunt; ~**rsi** *vr* (*mettersi*): ~**rsi tra la folla** to plunge into the crowd; **dove s'è cacciata la mia borsa?** where has my bag got to?; ~ **fuori qc** to whip *o* pull sth out; ~ **un urlo** to let out a yell; **caccia'tore** *sm* hunter; **cacciatore di frodo** poacher.

caccia'vite [kattʃa'vite] *sm inv* screwdriver.

'cactus *sm inv* cactus.

ca'davere *sm* (dead) body, corpse.

ca'dente *ag* falling; (*casa*) tumbledown; (*persona*) decrepit.

ca'denza [ka'dentsa] *sf* cadence; (*andamento ritmico*) rhythm; (*MUS*) cadenza.

ca'dere *vi* (2) to fall; (*denti, capelli*) to fall out; (*tetto*) to fall in; **questa gonna cade bene** this skirt hangs well; **lasciar cadere** (*anche fig*) to drop; ~ **dal sonno** to be falling asleep on one's feet; ~ **ammalato** to fall ill.

ca'detto *sm* cadet.

ca'duta *sf* fall; ~ **di temperatura** drop in temperature.

caffè *sm inv* coffee; (*locale*) café; ~ **macchiato** coffee with a dash of milk; ~ **macinato** ground coffee.

caffel'latte *sm inv* white coffee.

caffetti'era *sf* coffeepot.

cagio'nare [kadʒo'nare] *vt* to cause, be the cause of.

cagio'nevole [kadʒo'nevole] *ag* delicate, weak.

cagli'are [kaʎ'ʎare] *vi* (2) to curdle.

'cagna ['kaɲɲa] *sf* (*ZOOL, peg*) bitch.

ca'gnesco, a, schi, sche [kaɲ'nesko] *ag* (*fig*): **guardare qd in** ~ to scowl at sb.

cala'brone *sm* hornet.

cala'maio *sm* inkpot; inkwell.

cala'maro *sm* squid.

cala'mita *sf* magnet.

calamità *sf inv* calamity, disaster.

ca'lare *vt* (*far discendere*) to lower; (*MAGLIA*) to decrease // *vi* (2) (*discendere*) to go (*o* come) down; (*tramontare*) to set, go down; ~ **di peso** to lose weight.

'calca *sf* throng, press.

cal'cagno [kal'kaɲɲo] *sm* heel.

cal'care *sm* limestone // *vt* (*premere coi piedi*) to tread, press down; (*premere con forza*) to press down; (*mettere in rilievo*) to stress.

'calce ['kaltʃe] *sm*: **in** ~ at the foot of the page // *sf* lime; ~ **viva** quicklime.

calces'truzzo [kaltʃes'truttso] *sm* concrete.

calci'are [kal'tʃare] *vt, vi* to kick; **calcia- 'tore** *sm* footballer.

cal'cina [kal'tʃina] *sf* (lime) mortar.

'calcio ['kaltʃo] *sm* (*pedata*) kick; (*sport*) football, soccer; (*di pistola, fucile*) butt; (*CHIM*) calcium; ~ **di punizione** (*SPORT*) free kick.

'calco, chi *sm* (*ARTE*) casting, moulding; cast, mould.

calco'lare *vt* to calculate, work out, reckon; (*ponderare*) to weigh (up); **calcola'tore, 'trice** *ag* calculating // *sm* calculator; (*fig*) calculating person // *sf* calculator; **calcolatore elettronico** computer.

'calcolo *sm* (*anche MAT*) calculation; (*infinitesimale etc*) calculus; (*MED*) stone; **fare i propri** ~**i** (*fig*) to weigh the pros and cons; **per** ~ out of self-interest.

cal'daia *sf* boiler.

caldeggi'are [kalded'dʒare] *vt* to support warmly, favour.

'caldo, a *ag* warm; (*molto caldo*) hot; (*fig: appassionato*) keen; hearty // *sm* heat; **ho** ~ I'm warm; I'm hot; **fa** ~ it's warm; it's hot.

calen'dario *sm* calendar.

'calibro *sm* (*di arma*) calibre, bore; (*TECN*) callipers *pl*; (*fig*) calibre; **i grossi** ~**i** (*anche fig*) the big guns.

'calice ['kalitʃe] *sm* goblet; (*REL*) chalice.

ca'ligine [ka'lidʒine] *sf* fog; (*mista con fumo*) smog.

'callo *sm* callus; (*ai piedi*) corn; **fare il** ~ **a qc** to get used to sth.

'calma *sf* calm.

cal'mante *sm* sedative, tranquillizer.

cal'mare *vt* to calm; (*lenire*) to soothe; ~**rsi** *vr* to grow calm, calm down; (*vento*) to abate; (*dolore*) to ease.

calmi'ere *sm* controlled price.

'calmo, a *ag* calm, quiet.

'calo *sm* (*COMM: di prezzi*) fall; (*: di volume*) shrinkage; (*: di peso*) loss.

ca'lore *sm* warmth; heat; **essere in** ~ (*ZOOL*) to be on heat.

calo'ria *sf* calorie.

calo'roso, a *ag* warm.

calpes'tare *vt* to tread on, trample on; **'è vietato** ~ **l'erba'** 'keep off the grass'.

ca'lunnia *sf* slander; (*scritta*) libel.

cal'vario *sm* (*fig*) affliction, cross.

cal'vizie [kal'vittsje] *sf* baldness.

'calvo, a *ag* bald.

'calza ['kaltsa] *sf* (*da donna*) stocking; (*da uomo*) sock.

cal'zare [kal'tsare] *vt* (*scarpe, guanti: mettersi*) to put on; (*: portare*) to wear // *vi* (2) to fit; **calza'tura** *sf* footwear.

calzet'tone [kaltset'tone] *sm* heavy knee-length sock.

cal'zino [kal'tsino] *sm* sock.

calzo'laio [kaltso'lajo] *sm* shoemaker; (*che ripara scarpe*) cobbler; **calzole'ria** *sf* (*negozio*) shoe shop.

calzon'cini [kaltson'tʃini] *smpl* shorts.

cal'zone [kal'tsone] *sm* trouser leg; (*cuc*)

savoury turnover made with pizza dough; ~**i** smpl trousers.

camale'onte sm chameleon.

cambi'ale sf bill (of exchange); (pagherò cambiario) promissory note.

cambia'mento sm change.

cambi'are vt to change; (modificare) to alter, change; (barattare) to exchange // vi (2) to change, alter; ~**rsi** vr (variare abito) to change; ~ **casa** to move (house); ~ **idea** to change one's mind; ~ **aspetto** to change (in appearance); ~ **treno** to change trains.

'cambio sm change; (modifica) alteration, change; (scambio, COMM) exchange; (corso dei cambi) rate (of exchange); (TECN, AUT) gears pl; **in** ~ **di** in exchange for; **dare il** ~ **a qd** to take over from sb.

'camera sf room; (anche: ~ **da letto**) bedroom; (COMM, TECN) chamber; (POL) chamber, house; (FOT) camera; ~ **ardente** mortuary chapel; ~ **d'aria** inner tube; (di pallone) bladder; **C**~ **dei Deputati** Chamber of Deputies, ≈ House of Commons; ~ **a gas** gas chamber; ~ **a un letto/a due letti/matrimoniale** single/twin-bedded/double room; ~ **oscura** (FOT) dark room.

came'rata, i, e sm/f companion, mate // sf dormitory; **camera'tismo** sm comradeship.

cameri'era sf (domestica) maid; (che serve a tavola) waitress; (che fa le camere) chambermaid.

cameri'ere sm (man)servant; (di ristorante) waiter.

came'rino sm (TEATRO) dressing room.

'camice ['kamitʃe] sm (REL) alb; (per medici etc) white coat.

cami'cetta [kami'tʃetta] sf blouse.

ca'micia, cie [ka'mitʃa] sf (da uomo) shirt; (da donna) blouse; ~ **di forza** straitjacket; **camici'otto** sm smock; workman's top.

ca'mino sm chimney; (focolare) fireplace, hearth.

'camion sm inv lorry; **camion'cino** sm van.

cam'mello sm (ZOOL) camel; (tessuto) camel hair.

cam'meo sm cameo.

commi'nare vi to walk; (funzionare) to work, go.

cam'mino sm walk; (sentiero) path; (itinerario, direzione, tragitto) way; **mettersi in** ~ to set o start off; **cammin facendo** on the way.

camo'milla sf camomile; (infuso) camomile tea.

ca'morra sf camorra; racket.

ca'moscio [ka'moʃʃo] sm chamois.

cam'pagna [kam'paɲɲa] sf country, countryside; (POL, COMM, MIL) campaign; **in** ~ in the country; **fare una** ~ to campaign; **campa'gnolo, a** ag country cpd // sf (AUT) land rover.

cam'pale ag field cpd; (fig): **una giornata** ~ a hard day.

cam'pana sf bell; (anche: ~ **di vetro**) bell jar; **campa'nella** sf small bell; (di tenda) curtain ring; (di porta) (ring-shaped) knocker; **campa'nello** sm (all'uscio, da tavola) bell.

campa'nile sm bell tower, belfry; **campani'lismo** sm parochialism.

cam'pare vi (2) to live; (tirare avanti) to get by, manage; ~ **alla giornata** to live from day to day.

cam'pato, a ag: ~ **in aria** unsound, unfounded.

campeggi'are [kamped'dʒare] vi to camp; (risaltare) to stand out; **cam-'peggio** sm camping; (terreno) camp site; **fare (del) campeggio** to go camping.

cam'pestre ag country cpd, rural.

campio'nario, a ag: **fiera** ~**a** trade fair // sm collection of samples.

campio'nato sm championship.

campi'one, 'essa sm/f (SPORT) champion // sm (COMM) sample.

'campo sm field; (MIL) field; (: accampamento) camp; (spazio delimitato: sportivo etc) ground; field; (di quadro) background; ~ **-i** (campagna) the countryside; ~ **da aviazione** airfield; ~ **di concentramento** concentration camp; ~ **di golf** golf course; ~ **da tennis** tennis court; ~ **visivo** field of vision.

campo'santo, pl **campisanti** sm cemetery.

camuf'fare vt to disguise.

'Canada sm: **il** ~ Canada; **cana'dese** ag, sm/f Canadian.

ca'naglia [ka'naʎʎa] sf rabble, mob; (persona) scoundrel, rogue.

ca'nale sm (anche fig) channel; (artificiale) canal.

'canapa sf hemp.

cana'rino sm canary.

cancel'lare [kantʃel'lare] vt (con la gomma) to rub out, erase; (con la penna) to strike out; (annullare) to annul, cancel; (disdire) to cancel.

cancelle'ria [kantʃelle'ria] sf chancery; (quanto necessario per scrivere) stationery.

cancelli'ere [kantʃel'ljɛre] sm chancellor; (di tribunale) clerk of the court.

can'cello [kan'tʃɛllo] sm gate.

can'crena sf gangrene.

'cancro sm (MED) cancer; (dello zodiaco) **C**~ Cancer.

can'dela sf candle; ~ **di accensione** (AUT) sparking plug.

cande'labro sm candelabra.

candeli'ere sm candlestick.

candi'dato, a sm/f candidate; (aspirante a una carica) applicant.

'candido, a ag white as snow; (puro) pure; (sincero) sincere, candid.

can'dito, a ag candied.

can'dore sm brilliant white; purity; sincerity, candour.

'cane sm dog; (di pistola, fucile) cock; **fa un freddo** ~ it's bitterly cold; **non c'era un** ~ there wasn't a soul; **quell'attore è un**

~ he's a rotten actor; ~ **da guardia** guard dog; ~ **lupo** alsatian.

ca'nestro *sm* basket.

cangi'ante [kan'dʒante] *ag* iridescent; **seta** ~ shot silk.

can'guro *sm* kangaroo.

ca'nile *sm* kennel; (*di allevamento*) kennels *pl*; ~ **municipale** dog pound.

ca'nino, a *ag, sm* canine.

'canna *sf* (*pianta*) reed; (: *indica, da zucchero*) cane; (*bastone*) stick, cane; (*di fucile*) barrel; (*di organo*) pipe; ~ **fumaria** chimney flue; ~ **da pesca** (fishing) rod; ~ **da zucchero** sugar cane.

can'nella *sf* (*CUC*) cinnamon.

can'nibale *sm* cannibal.

cannocchi'ale [kannok'kjale] *sm* telescope.

can'none *sm* (*MIL*) gun; (: *STORIA*) cannon; (*tubo*) pipe, tube; (*piega*) box pleat; (*fig*) ace.

can'nuccia, ce [kan'nuttʃa] *sf* (drinking) straw.

ca'noa *sf* canoe.

'canone *sm* canon, criterion; (*mensile, annuo*) rent; fee; **ca'nonico, ci** *sm* (*REL*) canon.

canoniz'zare [kanonid'dzare] *vt* to canonize.

ca'noro, a *ag* (*uccello*) singing, song *cpd*.

canot'taggio [kanot'taddʒo] *sm* rowing.

canotti'era *sf* vest.

ca'notto *sm* small boat, dinghy; canoe.

cano'vaccio [kano'vattʃo] *sm* (*tela*) canvas; (*strofinaccio*) duster; (*trama*) plot.

can'tante *sm/f* singer.

can'tare *vt, vi* to sing; **cantau'tore, 'trice** *sm/f* singer-composer.

canterel'lare *vt* to hum, sing to oneself.

canti'ere *sm* (*EDIL*) (building) site; (*anche:* ~ **navale**) shipyard.

canti'lena *sf* (*filastrocca*) lullaby; (*fig*) sing-song voice.

can'tina *sf* (*locale*) cellar; (*bottega*) wine shop.

'canto *sm* song; (*arte*) singing; (*REL*) chant; chanting; (*poesia*) poem, lyric; (*parte di una poesia*) canto; (*angolo di due muri*) corner; (*parte, lato*) side; **d'altro** ~ on the other hand.

can'tone *sm* (*in Svizzera*) canton.

can'tuccio [kan'tuttʃo] *sm* corner, nook.

ca'nuto, a *ag* white, whitehaired.

canzo'nare [kantso'nare] *vt* to tease.

can'zone [kan'tsone] *sf* song; (*POESIA*) canzone; **canzoni'ere** *sm* (*MUS*) songbook; (*LETTERATURA*) collection of poems.

'caos *sm inv* chaos; **ca'otico, a, ci, che** *ag* chaotic.

C.A.P. *abbr vedi* **codice.**

ca'pace [ka'patʃe] *ag* able, capable; (*ampio, vasto*) large, capacious; **sei ~ di farlo?** can you *o* are you able to do it?; **capacità** *sf inv* ability; (*DIR, di recipiente*) capacity; **capaci'tarsi** *vr*: **capacitarsi di** to make out, understand.

ca'panna *sf* hut.

capan'none *sm* (*AGR*) barn; (*fabbricato industriale*) (factory) shed.

ca'parbio, a *ag* stubborn.

ca'parra *sf* deposit, down payment.

ca'pello *sm* hair; ~**i** *smpl* (*capigliatura*) hair *sg*; **capel'luto, a** *ag* having thick hair.

capez'zale [kapet'tsale] *sm* bolster; (*fig*) bedside.

ca'pezzolo [ka'pettsolo] *sm* nipple.

capi'enza [ka'pjentsa] *sf* capacity.

capigli'atura [kapiʎʎa'tura] *sf* hair.

ca'pire *vt* to understand.

capi'tale *ag* (*mortale*) capital; (*fondamentale*) main, chief // *sf* (*città*) capital // *sm* (*ECON*) capital; **capita'lismo** *sm* capitalism; **capita'lista, i, e** *ag, sm/f* capitalist.

capi'tano *sm* captain.

capi'tare (2) *vi* (*giungere casualmente*) to happen to go, find o.s.; (*accadere*) to happen; (*presentarsi: cosa*) to turn up, present itself // *vb impers* to happen.

capi'tello *sm* (*ARCHIT*) capital.

capito'lare *vi* to capitulate.

ca'pitolo *sm* chapter.

capi'tombolo *sm* headlong fall, tumble.

'capo *sm* head; (*persona*) head, leader; (: *in ufficio*) head, boss; (: *in tribù*) chief; (*di oggetti*) head; top; end; (*GEO*) cape; **andare a ~** to start a new paragraph; **da** ~ over again; ~ **di bestiame** head *inv* of cattle; ~ **di vestiario** item of clothing.

'capo... *prefisso*: **Capo'danno** *sm* New Year; **capo'fitto: a capofitto** *av* headfirst, headlong; **capo'giro** *sm* dizziness *q*; **capola'voro, i** *sm* masterpiece; **capo'linea**, *pl* **capi'linea** *sm* terminus; **capolu'ogo**, *pl* **ghi** *o* **capi-lu'oghi** *sm* chief town, administrative centre; **capo'mastro**, *pl* **i** *o* **capi'mastri** *sm* master builder.

capo'rale *sm* (*MIL*) lance corporal.

'capo... *prefisso*: **capo'saldo**, *pl* **capi'saldi** *sm* stronghold; (*fig: fondamento*) basis, cornerstone; **capostazi'one**, *pl* **capistazi'one** *sm* station master; **capo-'treno**, *pl* **capi'treno** *o* **capo'treni** *sm* guard.

capo'volgere [kapo'voldʒere] *vt* to overturn; (*fig*) to reverse; ~**rsi** *vr* to overturn; (*barca*) to capsize; (*fig*) to be reversed.

capo'volto, a *pp di* **capovolgere.**

'cappa *sf* (*mantello*) cape, cloak; (*del camino*) hood.

cap'pella *sf* (*REL*) chapel; **cappel'lano** *sm* chaplain.

cap'pello *sm* hat.

'cappero *sm* caper.

cap'pone *sm* capon.

cap'potto *sm* (over)coat.

cappuc'cino [kapput'tʃino] *sm* (*frate*) Capuchin monk; (*bevanda*) frothy white coffee.

cap'puccio [kap'puttʃo] *sm* (*copricapo*) hood; (*della biro*) cap.

'**capra** sf (she-)goat; **ca'pretto** sm kid.

ca'**priccio** [ka'prittʃo] sm caprice, whim; (bizza) tantrum; **fare i ~i** to be very naughty; **capricci'oso, a** ag capricious, whimsical; naughty.

Capri'corno sm Capricorn.

capri'ola sf somersault.

capri'olo sm roe deer.

'**capro** sm billy-goat; **~ espiatorio** (fig) scapegoat.

'**capsula** sf capsule; (di proiettile) primer; cap.

cap'tare vt (RADIO, TV) to pick up; (cattivarsi) to gain, win.

carabini'ere sm carabiniere.

ca'raffa sf carafe.

cara'mella sf sweet.

ca'rattere sm character; (caratteristica) characteristic, trait; **avere un buon ~** to be good-natured; **caratte'ristico, a, ci, che** ag characteristic // sf characteristic, trait, peculiarity; **caratteriz'zare** vt to characterize, distinguish.

car'bone sm coal.

carbu'rante sm (motor) fuel.

carbura'tore sm carburettor.

car'cassa sf carcass.

carce'rato, a [kartʃe'rato] sm/f prisoner.

'**carcere** ['kartʃere] sm prison; (pena) imprisonment.

carci'ofo [kar'tʃofo] sm artichoke.

car'diaco, a, ci, che ag cardiac, heart cpd.

cardi'nale ag, sm cardinal.

'**cardine** sm hinge.

'**cardo** sm thistle.

ca'rena sf (NAUT) bottom, hull.

ca'renza [ka'rentsa] sf lack, scarcity; (vitaminica) deficiency.

cares'tia sf famine; (penuria) scarcity, dearth.

ca'rezza [ka'rettsa] sf caress; **carez'zare** vt to caress, stroke, fondle.

'**carica** sf vedi **carico**.

cari'care vt to load; (aggravare: anche fig) to weigh down; (orologio) to wind up; (batteria, MIL) to charge.

carica'tura sf caricature.

'**carico, a, chi, che** ag (che porta un peso): **~ di** loaded o laden with; (fucile) loaded; (orologio) wound up; (batteria) charged; (colore) deep; (caffè, tè) strong // sm (il caricare) loading; (ciò che si carica, ELETTR) load; (fig: peso) burden, weight // sf (mansione ufficiale) office, position; (MIL, TECN, ELETTR) charge; (fig: energia) drive; **persona a ~** dependent; **essere a ~ di qd** (spese etc) to be charged to sb.

'**carie** sf (dentaria) decay.

ca'rino, a ag lovely, pretty, nice; (simpatico) nice.

carità sf charity; **per ~!** (escl di rifiuto) good heavens, no!

carnagi'one [karna'dʒone] sf complexion.

car'nale ag (amore) carnal; (fratello) blood cpd.

'**carne** sf flesh; (bovina, ovina etc) meat; **~ di manzo/maiale/pecora** beef/pork/mutton; **~ tritata** mince, minced meat.

car'nefice [kar'nefitʃe] sm executioner; hangman.

carne'vale sm carnival.

car'nivoro, a ag carnivorous.

car'noso, a ag fleshy.

'**caro, a** ag (amato) dear; (costoso) dear, expensive.

ca'rogna [ka'roɲɲa] sf carrion; (fig: fam) swine.

caro'sello sm merry-go-round.

ca'rota sf carrot.

caro'vana sf caravan.

caro'vita sm high cost of living.

carpenti'ere sm carpenter.

car'pire vt: **~ qc a qd** (segreto etc) to get sth out of sb.

car'poni av on all fours.

car'rabile ag suitable for vehicles.

car'raio, a ag: **passo ~** vehicle entrance.

carreggi'ata [karred'dʒata] sf carriageway.

car'rello sm trolley; (AER) undercarriage; (CINEMA) dolly; (di macchina da scrivere) carriage.

car'retto sm cart.

carri'era sf career; **fare ~** to get on; **a gran ~** at full speed.

carri'ola sf wheelbarrow.

'**carro** sm cart, wagon; **~ armato** tank.

car'rozza [kar'rottsa] sf carriage.

carrozze'ria [karrottse'ria] sf body, coachwork; (officina) coachbuilder's workshop.

carroz'zina [karrot'tsina] sf pram.

'**carta** sf paper; (al ristorante) menu; (GEO) map; plan; (documento, da gioco) card; (costituzione) charter; **~e** sfpl (documenti) papers, documents; **~ assorbente** blotting paper; **~ di credito** credit card; **~ (geografica)** map; **~ d'identità** identity card; **~ igienica** toilet paper; **~ da lettere** writing paper; **~ da parati** wallpaper; **~ verde** (AUT) green card; **~ vetrata** sandpaper.

cartacar'bone, pl **cartecar'bone** sf carbon paper.

car'taccia, ce [kar'tattʃa] sf waste paper.

cartamo'neta sf paper money.

carta'pecora sf parchment.

carta'pesta sf papier-mâché.

car'teggio [kar'teddʒo] sm correspondence.

car'tella sf (scheda) card; (custodia: di cartone) folder; (: di uomo d'affari etc) briefcase; (: di scolaro) schoolbag, satchel.

car'tello sm sign; (pubblicitario) poster; (stradale) sign, signpost; (ECON) cartel; (in dimostrazioni) placard; **cartel'lone** sm (pubblicitario) advertising poster; (della tombola) scoring frame; (TEATRO) playbill; **tenere il cartellone** (spettacolo) to have a long run.

carti'era sf paper mill.

carti'lagine [karti'ladʒine] sf cartilage.

car'toccio [kar'tɔttʃo] sm paper bag.

cartole'ria sf stationer's (shop).

carto'lina sf postcard.

car'tone sm cardboard; (ARTE) cartoon; ~i animati smpl (CINEMA) cartoons.

car'tuccia, ce [kar'tuttʃa] sf cartridge.

'casa sf house; (specialmente la propria casa) home; (COMM) firm, house; **essere a** ~ to be at home; **vado a** ~ **mia/tua** I'm going home/to your house; ~ **di cura** nursing home; ~ **dello studente** student hostel; ~**e popolari** ≈ council houses (o flats).

ca'sacca, che sf military coat; (di fantino) blouse.

casalingo, a, ghi, ghe ag household, domestic; (fatto a casa) home-made; (semplice) homely; (amante della casa) home-loving // sf housewife; ~**ghi** smpl household articles; **cucina** ~**a** plain home cooking.

cas'care vi to fall; **cas'cata** sf fall; (d'acqua) cascade, waterfall.

'casco, schi sm helmet; (del parrucchiere) hair-drier.

ca'sella sf pigeon-hole; ~ **postale** (C.P.) post office box (P.O. box).

ca'sello sm (di autostrada) toll-house.

ca'serma sf barracks pl.

ca'sino sm (confusione) row, racket; (casa di prostituzione) brothel.

casinò sm inv casino.

'caso sm chance; (fatto, vicenda) event, incident; (possibilità) possibility; (MED, LING) case; **a** ~ at random; **per** ~ by chance, by accident; **in ogni** ~, **in tutti i** ~**i** in any case, at any rate; **al** ~ should the opportunity arise; **nel** ~ **che** in case; ~ **mai** if by chance; ~ **limite** borderline case.

'cassa sf case, crate, box; (bara) coffin; (mobile) chest; (involucro: di orologio etc) case; (macchina) cash register; (luogo di pagamento) cash desk; (fondo) fund; (istituto bancario) bank; ~ **mutua** o **malattia** health insurance scheme; ~ **toracica** (ANAT) chest; ~ **di risparmio** savings bank.

cassa'forte, pl casseforti sf safe.

cassa'panca, pl cassapanche o **cassepanche** sf settle.

casseru'ola, casse'rola sf saucepan.

cas'setta sf box; (per registratore) cassette; (CINEMA, TEATRO) box-office takings pl; ~ **di sicurezza** strongbox; ~ **delle lettere** letterbox.

cas'setto sm drawer; **casset'tone** sm chest of drawers.

cassi'ere, a sm/f cashier; (di banca) teller.

'casta sf caste.

cas'tagna [kas'taɲɲa] sf chestnut.

cas'tagno [kas'taɲɲo] sm chestnut (tree).

cas'tello sm castle; (TECN) scaffolding.

casti'gare vt to punish; **cas'tigo, ghi** sm punishment.

castità sf chastity.

'casto, a ag chaste, pure.

cas'toro sm beaver.

cas'trare vt to castrate; to geld; to doctor.

casu'ale ag chance cpd.

cata'comba sf catacomb.

ca'talogo, ghi sm catalogue.

catarifran'gente [catarifran'dʒente] sm (AUT) reflector.

ca'tarro sm catarrh.

ca'tasta sf stack, pile.

ca'tasto sm land register; land registry office.

ca'tastrofe sf catastrophe, disaster.

cate'chismo [kate'kizmo] sm catechism.

catego'ria sf category; **cate'gorico, a, ci, che** ag categorical.

ca'tena sf chain; ~ **di montaggio** assembly line; ~**e da neve** (AUT) snow chains; **cate'naccio** sm bolt.

cate'ratta sf cataract; (chiusa) sluice-gate.

cati'nella sf: **piovere a** ~**e** to pour, rain cats and dogs.

ca'tino sm basin.

ca'trame sm tar.

'cattedra sf teacher's desk; (di università) chair.

catte'drale sf cathedral.

catti'veria sf malice, spite; naughtiness; (atto) spiteful act; (parole) malicious o spiteful remark.

cattività sf captivity.

cat'tivo, a ag bad; (malvagio) bad, wicked; (turbolento: bambino) bad, naughty; (: mare) rough; (odore, sapore) nasty, bad.

cattoli'cesimo [kattoli'tʃezimo] sm Catholicism.

cat'tolico, a, ci, che ag, sm/f (Roman) Catholic.

cat'tura sf capture.

cattu'rare vt to capture.

cauccià [kaut'tʃu] sm rubber.

'causa sf cause; (DIR) lawsuit, case, action; **fare** o **muovere** ~ **a qd** to take legal action against sb.

cau'sare vt to cause.

'caustico, a, ci, che ag caustic.

cau'tela sf caution, prudence.

caute'lare vt to protect.

'cauto, a ag cautious, prudent.

cauzi'one [kaut'tsjone] sf security; (DIR) bail.

cav. abbr di **cavaliere**.

'cava sf quarry; (di carbone) open-cast mine.

caval'care vt (cavallo) to ride; (muro) to sit astride; (sog: ponte) to span; **caval'cata** sf ride; (gruppo di persone) riding party.

cavalca'via sm inv flyover.

cavalcioni [kaval'tʃoni]: **a** ~ **di** prep astride.

cavali'ere sm rider; (feudale, titolo) knight; (soldato) cavalryman; (che accompagna una donna) escort; (: al ballo) partner; **cavalle'resco, a, schi, sche** ag chivalrous; **cavalle'ria** *sf* chivalry; (*milizia a cavallo*) cavalry.

cavalle'rizzo, a [kavalle'rittso] *sm/f* horseman/woman.

caval'letta *sf* grasshopper.

caval'letto *sm* (FOT) tripod; (*da pittore*) easel.

ca'vallo *sm* horse; (SCACCHI) knight; (AUT: anche: ~ **vapore**) horsepower; (*dei pantaloni*) crotch; a ~ on horseback; a ~ **di** astride, straddling; ~ **da corsa** racehorse.

ca'vare *vt* (*togliere*) to draw out, extract, take out; (: *giacca, scarpe*) to take off; (: *fame, sete, voglia*) to satisfy; **cavarsela** to get away with it; to manage, get on all right.

cava'tappi *sm inv* corkscrew.

ca'verna *sf* cave.

ca'vezza [ka'vettsa] *sf* halter.

'cavia *sf* guinea pig.

cavi'ale *sm* caviar.

ca'viglia [ka'viʎʎa] *sf* ankle.

cavil'lare *vi* to quibble.

cavità *sf inv* cavity.

'cavo, a *ag* hollow // *sm* (ANAT) cavity; (*grossa corda*) rope, cable; (ELETTR, TEL) cable.

cavolfi'ore *sm* cauliflower.

'cavolo *sm* cabbage; ~ **di Bruxelles** Brussels sprout.

cazzu'ola [kat'tswola] *sf* trowel.

c/c *abbr di* **conto corrente.**

ce [tʃe] *pron, av vedi* **ci.**

cecità [tʃetʃi'ta] *sf* blindness.

Cecoslo'vacchia [tʃekoslo'vakkja] *sf*: la ~ Czechoslovakia; **cecoslo'vacco, a, chi, che** *ag, sm/f* Czechoslovakian.

'cedere [tʃedere] *vt* (*concedere: posto*) to give up; (DIR) to transfer, make over // *vi* (*cadere*) to give way, subside; ~ (a) to surrender (to), yield (to), give in (to); **ce'devole** *ag* (*terreno*) soft; (*fig*) yielding.

'cedola ['tʃedola] *sf* (COMM) coupon; voucher.

'cedro ['tʃedro] *sm* cedar; (*albero da frutto*) lime tree.

C.E.E. *abbr f vedi* **comunità.**

cef'fone [tʃef'fone] *sm* slap, smack.

ce'larsi [tʃe'larsi] *vr* to hide.

cele'brare [tʃele'brare] *vt* to celebrate; **celebrazi'one** *sf* celebration.

'celebre ['tʃelebre] *ag* famous, celebrated; **celebrità** *sf inv* fame; (*persona*) celebrity.

'celere ['tʃelere] *ag* fast, swift; (*corso*) crash *cpd.*

ce'leste [tʃe'leste] *ag* celestial; heavenly; (*colore*) sky-blue.

celi'bato [tʃeli'bato] *sm* bachelorhood; (REL) celibacy.

'celibe ['tʃelibe] *ag* single, unmarried // *sm* bachelor.

'cella ['tʃella] *sf* cell.

'cellula ['tʃellula] *sf* (BIOL, ELETTR, POL) cell.

cemen'tare [tʃemen'tare] *vt* (*anche fig*) to cement.

ce'mento [tʃe'mento] *sm* cement; ~ **armato** reinforced concrete.

'cena ['tʃena] *sf* dinner; (*leggera*) supper.

ce'nare [tʃe'nare] *vi* to dine, have dinner.

'cencio ['tʃentʃo] *sm* piece of cloth, rag; (*da spolverare*) duster.

'cenere ['tʃenere] *sf* ash.

'cenno ['tʃenno] *sm* (*segno*) sign, signal; (*gesto*) gesture; (*col capo*) nod; (*con la mano*) wave; (*allusione*) hint, mention; (*spiegazione sommaria*) short account; **far** ~ **di sì/no** to nod (one's head)/shake one's head.

censi'mento [tʃensi'mento] *sm* census.

cen'sore [tʃen'sore] *sm* censor.

cen'sura [tʃen'sura] *sf* censorship; censor's office; (*fig*) censure; **censu'rare** *vt* to censor; to censure.

cente'nario, a [tʃente'narjo] *ag* (*che ha cento anni*) hundred-year-old; (*che ricorre ogni cento anni*) centennial, centenary *cpd* // *sm/f* centenarian // *sm* centenary.

cen'tesimo, a [tʃen'tezimo] *ag, sm* hundredth.

cen'tigrado, a [tʃen'tigrado] *ag* centigrade; **20 gradi** ~**i** 20 degrees centigrade.

cen'timetro [tʃen'timetro] *sm* centimetre.

centi'naio, *pl(f)* **aia** [tʃenti'najo] *sm*: **un** ~ (**di**) a hundred; about a hundred.

'cento ['tʃento] *num* a hundred, one hundred.

cen'trale [tʃen'trale] *ag* central // *sf*: ~ **telefonica** (telephone) exchange; ~ **elettrica** electric power station; **centra'lino** *sm* (telephone) exchange; (*di albergo etc*) switchboard; **centrali'nista** *sm/f* operator; **centraliz'zare** *vt* to centralize.

cen'trare [tʃen'trare] *vt* to hit the centre of; (TECN) to centre.

cen'trifuga [tʃen'trifuga] *sf* spin-drier.

'centro ['tʃentro] *sm* centre.

'ceppo ['tʃeppo] *sm* (*di albero*) stump; (*pezzo di legno*) log.

'cera ['tʃera] *sf* wax; (*aspetto*) appearance, look.

ce'ramica, che [tʃe'ramika] *sf* ceramic; (ARTE) ceramics *sg.*

'cerca ['tʃerka] *sf*: **in** *o* **alla** ~ **di in** search of.

cer'care [tʃer'kare] *vt* to look for, search for // *vi*: ~ **di fare qc** to try to do sth.

'cerchia ['tʃerkja] *sf* circle.

'cerchio ['tʃerkjo] *sm* circle; (*giocattolo, di botte*) hoop.

cere'ale [tʃere'ale] *sm* cereal.

cere'brale [tʃere'brale] *ag* cerebral.

ceri'monia [tʃeri'monja] *sf* ceremony; **cerimoni'ale** *sm* etiquette, ceremonial; **cerimoni'oso, a** *ag* formal, ceremonious.

ce'rino [tʃe'rino] *sm* wax match.

'cernia ['tʃernja] *sf* (ZOOL) stone bass.

cerni'era [tʃer'njera] *sf* hinge; ~ **lampo** zip (fastener).

cernita ['tʃernita] *sf* selection.

'cero ['tʃero] *sm* (church) candle.

ce'rotto [tʃe'rotto] *sm* sticking plaster.

cer'tezza [tʃer'tettsa] *sf* certainty.

certifi'care [tʃertifi'kare] *vt* to certify.

certifi'cato *sm* certificate; ~ **medico/di nascita** medical/birth certificate.

'certo, a ['tʃɛrto] *ag* certain; (*sicuro*): ~ **(di/che)** certain *o* sure (of/that) // *det* certain *o* *av* certainly, of course; ~**i** *pronome pl* some; **un** ~ **non so che an** indefinable something; **di una** ~ **a età** past one's prime, not so young; **sì** ~ yes indeed; **no** ~ certainly not; **di** ~ certainly.

cer'tuni [tʃer'tuni] *pronome pl* some (people).

cer'vello, *pl* **i** (*anche: pl(f)* **a** *o* **e**) [tʃer'vɛllo] *sm* brain.

'cervo, a ['tʃɛrvo] *sm/f* stag/hind // *sm* deer; ~ **volante** stag beetle.

cesel'lare [tʃezel'lare] *vt* to chisel; (*fig*) to polish, finish with care.

ce'sello [tʃe'zɛllo] *sm* chisel.

ce'soie [tʃe'zoje] *sfpl* shears.

'cespite ['tʃɛspite] *sm* source of income.

ces'puglio [tʃes'puʎʎo] *sm* bush.

ces'sare [tʃes'sare] *vi* (2), *vt* to stop, cease; ~ **di fare qc** to stop doing sth; **cessate il fuoco** *sm* ceasefire.

'cesso [tʃɛsso] *sm* (*fam*) bog.

'cesta ['tʃesta] *sf* (large) basket.

ces'tino [tʃes'tino] *sm* basket; (*per la carta straccia*) wastepaper basket.

'cesto ['tʃesto] *sm* basket.

'ceto ['tʃɛto] *sm* (social) class.

cetrio'lino [tʃetrio'lino] *sm* gherkin.

cetri'olo [tʃetri'ɔlo] *sm* cucumber.

cfr. (*abbr di* confronta) cf.

che [ke] *pronome* (*relativo: persona: soggetto*) who; (: *oggetto*) whom; (: *cosa*) which, that; **l'uomo** ~ **io vedo** the man (whom) I see; **il libro** ~ **è sul tavolo** the book which *o* that is on the table; **il giorno** ~ ... the day (that) ...; **la sera** ~ **ti ho visto** the evening I saw you; (*interrogativo, esclamativo*) what; ~ **(cosa) fai?** what are you doing?; **a** ~ **(cosa) pensi?** what are you thinking about?; **non sa** ~ **fare** he doesn't know what to do // (*di numero limitato*) which; ~ **vestito ti vuoi mettere?** what (*o* which) dress do you want to put on?; ~ **tipo di film hai visto?** what sort of film did you see?; ~ **bel vestito!** what a lovely dress!; ~ **buono! how delicious!** // *cong* that; **so** ~ **tu c'eri** I know (that) you were there; **voglio** ~ **tu studi** I want you to study; (*affinché*): **vieni qua,** ~ **ti veda** come here, so that I can see you; (*temporale*): **arrival** ~ **eri già partito** you had already left when I arrived; **sono anni** ~ **non lo vedo** I haven't seen him in years; (*in frasi imperative*): ~ **venga pure** let him come by all means; **non** ~ **sia stupido** not that he's stupid; *vedi* **non, più, meno** *etc*.

cheru'bino [keru'bino] *sm* cherub.

cheti'chella [keti'kɛlla]: **alla** ~ *av* stealthily, unobtrusively.

'cheto, a ['keto] *ag* quiet, silent.

chi [ki] *pronome* (*interrogativo: soggetto*) who; (: *oggetto*): **di** ~ **è questo libro?** whose book is this?; **con** ~ **parli?** to whom are you talking?, who are you talking to?; (*relativo: colui/colei che*) he/she who; (: *complemento*): **dillo a** ~ **vuoi** tell it to whoever you like; ~ **dice una cosa** ~ **un'altra** some say one thing some another.

chiacchie'rare [kjakkje'rare] *vi* to chat; (*discorrere futilmente*) to chatter; (*far pettegolezzi*) to gossip; **chi'acchiere** *sfpl* chatter *q*; gossip *q*; **fare due** *o* **quattro chiacchiere** to have a chat; **chiacchie'rone, a** *ag* talkative, chatty; gossipy.

chia'mare [kja'mare] *vt* to call; (*rivolgersi a qd*) to call (in), send for; ~**rsi** *vr* (*aver nome*) to be called; **mi chiamo Paolo** my name is Paolo, I'm called Paolo; ~ **alle armi** to call up; ~ **in giudizio** to summon; **chia'mata** *sf* call; (*MIL*) call-up; **chiamata interurbana** (*TEL*) trunk call.

chia'rezza [kja'rettsa] *sf* clearness, clarity.

chiarifi'care [kjarifi'kare] *vt* (*anche fig*) to clarify.

chia'rire [kja'rire] *vt* to make clear; (*fig: spiegare*) to clear up, explain; ~**rsi** *vr* to become clear.

chi'aro, a ['kjaro] *ag* clear; (*luminoso*) clear, bright; (*colore*) pale, light.

chiaroveg'gente [kjaroved'dʒɛnte] *sm/f* clairvoyant.

chi'asso ['kjasso] *sm* uproar, row; **chias'soso, a** *ag* noisy, rowdy.

chi'ave ['kjave] *sf* key // *ag inv* key *cpd*; ~ **inglese** monkey wrench; **chiavis'tello** *sm* bolt.

chi'azza ['kjattsa] *sf* stain; splash.

chic [ʃik] *ag inv* chic, elegant.

'chicco, chi ['kikko] *sm* (*di cereale, riso*) grain; (*di caffè*) bean; ~ **d'uva** grape.

chi'edere ['kjɛdere] *vt* (*per sapere*) to ask; (*per avere*) to ask for // *vi*: ~ **di qd** to ask after sb; (*chiamare: al telefono*) to ask for *o* want sb; ~ **qc a qd** to ask sb sth; to ask sb for sth.

chi'erico, ci ['kjɛriko] *sm* cleric; altar boy.

chi'esa ['kjɛza] *sf* church.

chi'esto, a *pp di* chiedere.

'chiglia ['kiʎʎa] *sf* keel.

'chilo ['kilo] *sm* (*abbr di* chilogrammo) kilo; **chilo'grammo** *sm* kilogram(me); **chi'lometro** *sm* kilometre.

'chimico, a, ci, che ['kimiko] *ag* chemical // *sm/f* chemist // *sf* chemistry.

'china ['kina] *sf* (*pendio*) slope, descent; (*inchiostro di*) ~ Indian ink.

chi'nare [ki'nare] *vt* to lower, bend; ~**rsi** *vr* to stoop, bend.

chincaglie'ria [kinkaʎʎe'ria] *sf* fancy-goods shop; ~**e** *sfpl* fancy goods, knick-knacks.

chi'nino [ki'nino] *sm* quinine.

chi'occia, ce ['kjɔttʃa] *sf* brooding hen.

chi'occiola ['kjɔttʃola] *sf* snail.

chi'odo ['kjɔdo] *sm* nail; (*fig*) obsession.

chi'oma ['kjɔma] *sf* (*capelli*) head of hair; (*di albero*) foliage.

chi'osco, schi ['kjɔsko] *sm* kiosk.

chi'ostro ['kjɔstro] *sm* cloister.

chirur'gia [kirur'dʒia] *sf* surgery; **chi-'rurgo, ghi** *o* **gi** *sm* surgeon.

chissà [kis'sa] *av* who knows, I wonder.

chi'tarra [ki'tarra] *sf* guitar; **chitar-'rista, i, e** *sm/f* guitarist, guitar player.

chi'udere ['kjudere] *vt* to close, shut; (*luce, acqua*) to put off, turn off; (*definitivamente: fabbrica*) to close down, shut down; (*strada*) to close; (*recingere*) to enclose; (*porre termine*) to end // *vi* to close, shut; to close down, shut down; to end; ~ **rsi** *vr* to shut, close; (*ritirarsi: anche fig*) to shut o.s. away; (*ferita*) to close up.

chi'unque [ki'unkwe] *pronome* (*relativo*) whoever; (*indefinito*) anyone, anybody.

chi'uso, a ['kjuso] *pp* **di chiudere** // *sf* (*di corso d'acqua*) sluice, lock; (*recinto*) enclosure; (*di discorso etc*) conclusion, ending; **chiu'sura** *sf* closing; shutting; closing *o* shutting down; enclosing; putting *o* turning off; ending; (*dispositivo*) catch; fastening; fastener.

ci [tʃi] (*dav* **lo, la, li, le, ne diventa ce**) *pronome* (*personale*) us; (: *complemento di termine*) to us; (: *riflessivo*) ourselves; (: *reciproco*) one another; (*dimostrativo: di ciò, su ciò, in ciò etc*) about (*o on o of*) it; **non so cosa far~** I don't know what to do about it; **che c'entro io?** what have I got to do with it? // *av* (*qui*) here; (*lì*) there; **esser~** *vedi* **essere**.

C.ia (*abbr di* **compagnia**) Co.

cia'batta [tʃa'batta] *sf* mule, slipper.

ci'alda [tʃalda] *sf* (*CUC*) wafer.

ciam'bella [tʃam'bella] *sf* (*CUC*) ring-shaped cake; (*salvagente*) rubber ring.

ci'ao [tʃao] *escl* (*all'arrivo*) hello!; (*alla partenza*) cheerio!, bye!

ciarla'tano [tʃarla'tano] *sm* charlatan.

cias'cuno, a [tʃas'kuno] (*dav sm:* **ciascun** **+C, V, ciascuno +s impura, gn, pn, ps, x, z;** *dav sf:* **ciascuna +C, ciascun' +V**) *det, pronome* each.

'cibo ['tʃibo] *sm* food.

ci'cala [tʃi'kala] *sf* cicada.

cica'trice [tʃika'tritʃe] *sf* scar; **cicatriz-'zarsi** *vr* to form a scar, heal (up).

'cicca ['tʃikka] *sf* cigarette end.

'ciccia ['tʃittʃa] *sf* (*fam: carne*) meat; (: *grasso umano*) fat, flesh.

cice'rone [tʃitʃe'rone] *sm* guide.

cicla'mino [tʃikla'mino] *sm* cyclamen.

ci'clismo [tʃi'klizmo] *sm* cycling; **ci'clista, i, e** *sm/f* cyclist.

'ciclo ['tʃiklo] *sm* cycle; (*di malattia*) course.

ciclomo'tore [tʃiklomo'tore] *sm* moped.

ci'clone [tʃi'klone] *sm* cyclone.

ciclos'tile [tʃiklos'tile] *sm* cyclostyle.

ci'cogna [tʃi'koɲɲa] *sf* stork.

ci'coria [tʃi'kɔria] *sf* chicory.

ci'eco, a, chi, che ['tʃeko] *ag* blind // *sm/f* blind man/woman.

ci'elo ['tʃɛlo] *sm* sky; (*REL*) heaven.

'cifra ['tʃifra] *sf* (*numero*) figure; numeral; (*somma di denaro*) sum, figure; (*monogramma*) monogram, initials *pl*; (*codice*) code, cipher; **ci'frare** *vt* to embroider with a monogram; to code.

'ciglio ['tʃiʎʎo] *sm* (*margine*) edge, verge; (*pl(f)* **ciglia:** *delle palpebre*) eye(lash); eye(lid); (*sopracciglio*) eyebrow.

'cigno ['tʃiɲɲo] *sm* swan.

cigo'lare [tʃigo'lare] *vi* to squeak, creak.

'Cile ['tʃile] *sm:* **il ~** Chile.

cilecca [tʃi'lekka] *sf:* **far ~** to fail.

cili'egia, gie *o* **ge** [tʃi'ljedʒa] *sf* cherry; **cili'egio** *sm* cherry tree.

cilin'drata [tʃilin'drata] *sf* (*AUT*) (cubic) capacity; **una macchina di grossa ~** a big-engined car.

ci'lindro [tʃi'lindro] *sm* cylinder; (*cappello*) top hat.

'cima ['tʃima] *sf* (*sommità*) top; (*di monte*) top, summit; (*estremità*) end; **da ~ a fondo** from top to bottom; (*fig*) from beginning to end.

cimen'tare [tʃimen'tare] *vt* to put to the test.

'cimice ['tʃimitʃe] *sf* (*ZOOL*) bug; (*puntina*) drawing pin.

cimini'era [tʃimi'njɛra] *sf* chimney; (*di nave*) funnel.

cimi'tero [tʃimi'tɛro] *sm* cemetery.

ci'murro [tʃi'murro] *sm* (*di cani*) distemper.

'Cina ['tʃina] *sf:* **la ~** China.

'cinema ['tʃinema] *sm inv* cinema; **cinematogra'fare** *vt* to film; **cine'presa** *sf* cine-camera.

ci'nese [tʃi'nese] *ag, sm/f, sm* Chinese *inv*.

ci'netico, a, ci, che [tʃi'netiko] *ag* kinetic.

'cingere ['tʃindʒere] *vt* (*attorniare*) to surround, encircle; ~ **la vita** con una **cintura** to put a belt round one's waist.

'cinghia ['tʃingja] *sf* strap; (*cintura, TECN*) belt.

cinghi'ale [tʃin'gjale] *sm* wild boar.

cinguet'tare [tʃingwet'tare] *vi* to twitter.

'cinico, a, ci, che ['tʃiniko] *ag* cynical // *sm/f* cynic.

cin'quanta [tʃin'kwanta] *num* fifty; **cinquan'tesimo, a** *num* fiftieth.

cinquan'tina [tʃinkwan'tina] *sf* (*serie*): **una ~** (**di**) about fifty; (*età*): **essere sulla ~** to be about fifty.

'cinque ['tʃinkwe] *num* five; **avere ~ anni** to be five (years old); **il ~ dicembre 1982** the fifth of December 1982; **alle ~** (*ora*) at five (o'clock).

cinque'cento [tʃinkwe'tʃento] *num* five hundred // *sm:* **il C~** the sixteenth century.

'cinto, a ['tʃinto] *pp di* **cingere**.

cin'tura [tʃin'tura] *sf* belt; ~ **di salvataggio** lifebelt; ~ **di sicurezza** (*AUT, AER*) safety belt.

ciò [tʃɔ] *pronome* this; that; ~ **che** what; ~ **nondimeno** in spite of this (*o* that).

ci'occa, che [tʃɔkka] sf (di capelli) lock.

ciocco'iata [tʃokkoˈiata] sf chocolate; (bevanda) (hot) chocolate; **cioccola'tino** sm chocolate; **ciocco'lato** sm chocolate.

cioè [tʃoˈɛ] av that is (to say).

ciondo'lare [tʃondoˈlare] vi to dangle; (fig) to loaf (about); **ci'ondolo** sm pendant.

ci'otola [ˈtʃɔtola] sf bowl.

ci'ottolo [ˈtʃɔttolo] sm pebble; (di strada) cobble(stone).

ci'polla [tʃiˈpolla] sf onion; (di tulipano etc) bulb.

ci'presso [tʃiˈprɛsso] sm cypress (tree).

'cipria [ˈtʃiprja] sf (face) powder.

cipri'ota, i, e [tʃipriˈɔta] ag, sm/f Cypriot.

'Cipro [ˈtʃipro] sm Cyprus.

'circa [ˈtʃirka] av about, roughly // prep about, concerning; **a mezzogiorno ~** about midday.

'circo, chi [ˈtʃirko] sm circus.

circo'lare [tʃirkoˈlare] vi to circulate; (AUT) to drive (along), move (along) // ag circular // sf (AMM) circular; (di autobus) circle (line); **circolazi'one** sf circulation; (AUT): **la circolazione** (the) traffic.

'circolo [ˈtʃirkolo] sm circle.

circon'dare [tʃirkonˈdare] vt to surround.

circonfe'renza [tʃirkonfeˈrɛntsa] sf circumference.

circonvallazi'one [tʃirkonvallatˈtsjone] sf ring road; (per evitare una città) by-pass.

circos'critto, a [tʃirkosˈkritto] pp di **circoscrivere**.

circos'crivere [tʃirkosˈkrivere] vt to circumscribe; (fig) to limit, restrict; **circoscrizi'one** sf (AMM) district, area; **circoscrizione elettorale** constituency.

circos'petto, a [tʃirkosˈpetto] ag circumspect, cautious.

circos'tante [tʃirkosˈtante] ag surrounding, neighbouring.

circos'tanza [tʃirkosˈtantsa] sf circumstance; (occasione) occasion.

cir'cuito [tʃirˈkuito] sm circuit.

'ciste [ˈtʃiste] sf = **cisti**.

cis'terna [tʃisˈtɛrna] sf tank, cistern.

'cisti [ˈtʃisti] sf cyst.

C.I.T. [tʃit] abbr f di Compagnia Italiana Turismo.

ci'tare [tʃiˈtare] vt (DIR) to summon; (autore) to quote; (a esempio, modello) to cite; **citazi'one** sf summons sg; quotation; (di persona) mention.

ci'tofono [tʃiˈtɔfono] sm entry phone; (in uffici) intercom.

città [tʃitˈta] sf inv town; (importante) city; **~ universitaria** university campus.

cittadi'nanza [tʃittadiˈnantsa] sf citizens pl, inhabitants pl of a town (o city); (DIR) citizenship.

citta'dino, a [tʃittaˈdino] ag town cpd; city cpd // sm/f (di uno Stato) citizen; (abitante di città) towndweller.

ci'uco, a, chi, che [ˈtʃuko] sm/f ass, donkey.

ci'uffo [ˈtʃuffo] sm tuft.

ci'vetta [tʃiˈvetta] sf (ZOOL) owl; (fig: donna) coquette, flirt.

'civico, a, ci, che [ˈtʃivico] ag civic; (museo) municipal, town cpd; municipal, city cpd.

ci'vile [tʃiˈvile] ag civil; (non militare) civilian; (nazione) civilized // sm civilian.

civiliz'zare [tʃivilidˈdzare] vt to civilize; **civilizzazi'one** sf civilization.

civiltà [tʃivilˈta] sf civilization; (cortesia) civility.

ci'vismo [tʃiˈvizmo] sm public spirit.

'clacson sm inv (AUT) horn.

cla'more sm (frastuono) din, uproar, clamour; (fig) outcry; **clamo'roso, a** ag noisy; (fig) sensational.

clandes'tino, a ag clandestine; (POL) underground, clandestine // sm/f stowaway.

clari'netto sm clarinet.

'classe sf class; **di ~** (fig) with class; of excellent quality.

classi'cismo [klassiˈtʃizmo] sm classicism.

'classico, a, ci, che ag classical; (tradizionale: moda) classic(al) // sm classic; classical author.

clas'sifica sf classification; (SPORT) placings pl.

classifi'care vt to classify; (candidato, concorrente) to grade; (compito) to mark; **~rsi** vr to be placed; **classificazi'one** sf classification; grading; marking.

'clausola sf (DIR) clause.

'clava sf club.

clavi'cembalo [klaviˈtʃembalo] sm harpsichord.

cla'vicola sf (ANAT) collar bone.

cle'mente ag merciful; (clima) mild; **cle'menza** sf mercy, clemency; mildness.

cleri'cale ag clerical.

'clero sm clergy.

cli'ente sm/f customer, client; **clien'tela** sf customers pl, clientèle.

'clima, i sm climate; **cli'matico, a, ci, che** ag climatic; **climatizzazi'one** sf (TECN) air conditioning.

'clinico, a, ci, che ag clinical // sm (medico) clinician // sf (scienza) clinical medicine; (casa di cura) clinic, nursing home; (ospedale) clinic.

clo'aca, che sf sewer.

cloro'filla sf chlorophyll.

cloro'formio sm chloroform.

club sm inv club.

coabi'tare vi to live together, live under the same roof.

coagu'lare vt to coagulate // vi (2), **~rsi** vr to coagulate; (latte) to curdle.

coalizi'one [koalitˈtsjone] sf coalition.

co'atto, a ag (DIR) compulsory, forced.

'cobra sm inv cobra.

coca'ina sf cocaine.

cocci'nella [kottʃiˈnɛlla] sf ladybird.

'coccio [ˈkɔttʃo] sm earthenware; (vaso) earthenware pot; **~i** smpl fragments (of pottery).

cocci'uto, a [kot'tʃuto] *ag* stubborn, pigheaded.

'**cocco, chi** *sm* (*pianta*) coconut palm; (*frutto*): **noce di ~** coconut // *sm/f* (*fam*) darling.

cocco'drillo *sm* crocodile.

cocco'lare *vt* to cuddle, fondle.

co'cente [ko'tʃente] *ag* (*anche fig*) burning.

co'comero *sm* watermelon.

co'cuzzolo [ko'kuttsolo] *sm* top; (*di capo, cappello*) crown.

'**coda** *sf* tail; (*fila di persone, auto*) queue; (*di abiti*) train; (*dell'occhio*) corner; **mettersi in ~** to queue (up); to join the queue; **~ di cavallo** (*acconciatura*) ponytail.

co'dardo, a *ag* cowardly // *sm/f* coward.

'**codice** ['koditʃe] *sm* code; **~ di avviamento postale (C.A.P.)** postal code; **~ della strada** highway code.

codifi'care *vt* (*DIR*) to codify; (*cifrare*) to code.

coe'rente *ag* coherent; **coe'renza** *sf* coherence.

coesi'one *sf* cohesion.

coe'sistere *vi* (*2*) to coexist.

coe'taneo, a *ag, sm/f* contemporary.

'**cofano** *sm* (*AUT*) bonnet; (*forziere*) chest.

'**cogli** ['koʎʎi] *prep + det vedi* **con**.

'**cogliere** ['kɔʎʎere] *vt* (*fiore, frutto*) to pick, gather; (*sorprendere*) to catch, surprise; (*bersaglio*) to hit; (*fig: momento opportuno etc*) to grasp, seize, take; (: *capire*) to grasp; **~ qd in flagrante** *o* **in fallo** to catch sb red-handed.

co'gnato, a [koɲ'ɲato] *sm/f* brother-/sister-in-law.

cognizi'one [koɲɲit'tsjone] *sf* knowledge.

co'gnome [koɲ'ɲome] *sm* surname.

'**coi** *prep + det vedi* **con**.

coinci'denza [kointʃi'dɛntsa] *sf* coincidence; (*FERR, AER, di autobus*) connection.

coin'volgere [koin'vɔldʒere] *vt*: **~ in** to involve in.

col *prep + det vedi* **con**.

cola'brodo *sm inv* strainer.

cola'pasta *sm inv* colander.

co'lare *vt* (*liquido*) to strain; (*pasta*) to drain; (*oro fuso*) to pour // *vi* (*sudore*) to drip; (*botte*) to leak; (*cera*) to melt; **~ a picco** *vt, vi* (*nave*) to sink.

co'lata *sf* (*di lava*) flow; (*FONDERIA*) casting.

colazi'one [kolat'tsjone] *sf* (*anche*: **prima ~**) breakfast; (*anche*: **seconda ~**) lunch; **fare ~** to have breakfast (*o* lunch).

co'lei *pronome vedi* **colui**.

co'lera *sm* (*MED*) cholera.

'**colica** *sf* (*MED*) colic.

'**colla** *sf* glue; (*di farina*) paste.

collabo'rare *vi* to collaborate; **~ a** to collaborate on; (*giornale*) to contribute to; **collabora'tore, 'trice** *sm/f* collaborator; contributor; **collaborazi'one** *sf* collaboration; contribution.

col'lana *sf* necklace; (*collezione*) collection, series.

col'lant [kɔ'lã] *sm inv* tights *pl*.

col'lare *sm* collar.

col'lasso *sm* (*MED*) collapse.

collau'dare *vt* to test, try out; **col'laudo** *sm* testing *q*; test.

'**colle** *sm* hill.

col'lega, ghi, ghe *sm/f* colleague.

collega'mento *sm* connection; (*MIL*) liaison.

colle'gare *vt* to connect, join, link; **~rsi** *vr* (*RADIO, TV*) to link up; **~rsi con** (*TEL*) to get through to.

col'legio [kol'lɛdʒo] *sm* college; (*convitto*) boarding school; **~ elettorale** (*POL*) constituency.

'**collera** *sf* anger.

col'lerico, a, ci, che *ag* quick-tempered, irascible.

col'letta *sf* collection.

collettività *sf* community.

collet'tivo, a *ag* collective; (*interesse*) general, everybody's; (*biglietto, visita etc*) group *cpd* // *sm* (*POL*) (political) group.

col'letto *sm* collar.

collezio'nare [kollettsjo'nare] *vt* to collect.

collezi'one [kollet'tsjone] *sf* collection.

colli'mare *vi* to correspond, coincide.

col'lina *sf* hill.

col'lirio *sm* eyewash.

collisi'one *sf* collision.

'**collo** *sm* neck; (*di abito*) neck, collar; (*pacco*) parcel; **~ del piede** instep.

colloca'mento *sm* (*impiego*) employment; (*disposizione*) placing, arrangement.

collo'care *vt* (*libri, mobili*) to place; (*persona: trovare un lavoro per*) to find a job for, place; (*COMM: merce*) to find a market for; **~rsi** *vr* to take one's place; to find a job.

col'loquio *sm* conversation, talk; (*ufficiale*) interview, talk; (*INS*) preliminary oral exam.

col'mare *vt*: **~ di** (*anche fig*) to fill with; (*dare in abbondanza*) to load *o* overwhelm with; '**colmo, a** *ag*: **colmo (di)** full (of) // *sm* summit, top; (*fig*) height; **al colmo della disperazione** in the depths of despair; **è il colmo!** it's the last straw!

co'lombo, a *sm/f* dove; pigeon.

co'lonia *sf* colony; (*per bambini*) holiday camp; **acqua di ~** (eau de) cologne; **coloni'ale** *ag* colonial // *sm/f* colonist, settler.

coloniz'zare [kolonid'dzare] *vt* to colonize.

co'lonna *sf* column; **~ vertebrale** spine, spinal column.

colon'nello *sm* colonel.

co'lono *sm* (*coltivatore*) tenant farmer.

colo'rante *sm* colouring.

colo'rare *vt* to colour; (*disegno*) to colour in.

co'lore *sm* colour; **a ~i** in colour, colour

cpd; **farne di tutti i ~i** to get up to all sorts of mischief.

colo'rito, a *ag* coloured; *(viso)* rosy, pink; *(linguaggio)* colourful // *sm (tinta)* colour; *(carnagione)* complexion.

co'loro *pronome pl vedi* **colui.**

colos'sale *ag* colossal, enormous.

co'losso *sm* colossus.

'colpa *sf* fault; *(biasimo)* blame; *(colpevolezza)* guilt; *(azione colpevole)* offence; *(peccato)* sin; **di chi è la ~?** whose fault is it?; **per ~ di** through, owing to; **col'pevole** *ag* guilty.

col'pire *vt* to hit, strike; *(fig)* to strike; **rimanere colpito da qc** to be amazed *o* struck by sth.

'colpo *sm (urto)* knock; (: *affettivo)* blow, shock; (: *aggressivo)* blow; *(di pistola)* shot; *(SPORT)* stroke; shot; blow; *(MED)* stroke; **di ~ suddenly; fare ~** to make a strong impression; **~ di grazia** coup de grâce; **~ di sole** sunstroke; **~ di Stato** coup d'état; **~ di telefono** phone call; **~ di testa** (sudden) impulse *o* whim; **~ di vento** gust (of wind).

coltel'lata *sf* stab.

col'tello *sm* knife; **~ a serramanico** clasp knife.

colti'vare *vt* to cultivate; *(verdura)* to grow, cultivate; *(MINERALOGIA)* to work; **coltiva'tore** *sm* farmer; **coltivazi'one** *sf* cultivation; growing; working.

'colto, a *pp di* **cogliere** // *ag (istruito)* cultured, educated.

'coltre *sf* blanket.

col'tura *sf (di terra)* cultivation; *(di verdura)* growing; cultivation.

co'lui, co'lei, pl co'loro *pronome* the one; **~ che parla** the one *o* the man *o* the person who is speaking; **colei che amo** the one *o* the woman *o* the person (whom) I love.

'coma *sm inv* coma.

comanda'mento *sm (REL)* commandment.

coman'dante *sm (MIL)* commander, commandant; *(di reggimento)* commanding officer; *(NAUT, AER)* captain.

coman'dare *vt* to command; *(imporre)* to order, command; *(meccanismo)* to control; **co'mando** *sm (ingiunzione)* order, command; *(autorità)* command; *(TECN)* control.

combaci'are [kombat'tʃare] *vi* to meet; *(fig: coincidere)* to coincide, correspond.

combat'tente *ag* fighting // *sm* combatant; **ex-~** ex-serviceman.

com'battere *vt* to fight; *(fig)* to combat, fight against // *vi* to fight; **combatti-'mento** *sm* fight; fighting *q;* *(di pugilato)* match.

combi'nare *vt* to combine; *(organizzare)* to arrange; *(fam: fare)* to make, cause; **~rsi** *vr* to combine; *(mettersi d'accordo)* to come to an agreement; **combinazi'one** *sf* combination; *(caso fortuito)* coincidence; *(biancheria)* combinations *pl;* *(tuta: da aviatore)* flying suit; (: *da operaio)* boiler

suit; **per combinazione** by chance.

combus'tibile *ag* combustible // *sm* fuel.

combusti'one *sf* combustion.

com'butta *sf (peg)* gang; **in ~** in league.

'come *av* like; *(in qualità di)* as; *(interrogativo, esclamativo)* how; *(che cosa, prego):* **~?** pardon?, sorry? // *cong* as; *(che, in quale modo)* how; *(appena che, quando)* as soon as; **~ stai?** how are you?; **~ sei cresciuto!** how you've grown!; **~ se** as if, as though; *vedi* **così, tanto.**

co'meta *sf* comet.

'comico, a, ci, che *ag (TEATRO)* comic; *(buffo)* comical // *sm (attore)* comedian, comic actor; *(comicità)* comic spirit, comedy.

co'mignolo [ko'miɲɲolo] *sm* chimney top.

cominci'are [komin'tʃare] *vt, vi* to begin, start; **~ a fare/col fare** to begin to do/by doing.

comi'tato *sm* committee.

comi'tiva *sf* party, group.

co'mizio [ko'mittsjo] *sm (POL)* meeting, assembly.

com'mando *sm inv* commando (squad).

com'media *sf* comedy; *(opera teatrale)* play; (: *che fa ridere)* comedy; *(fig)* playacting *q;* **commedi'ante** *sm/f (peg)* third-rate actor/actress; (: *fig)* sham.

commemo'rare *vt* to commemorate; **commemorazi'one** *sf* commemoration.

commen'tare *vt* to comment on; *(testo)* to annotate; *(RADIO, TV)* to give a commentary on; **commenta'tore, 'trice** *sm/f* commentator; **com'mento** *sm* comment; *(a un testo)* commentary, notes *pl;* *(RADIO, TV)* commentary.

commerci'ale [kommer'tʃale] *ag* commercial, trading; *(peg)* commercial.

commerci'ante [kommer'tʃante] *sm/f* trader, dealer; *(bottegaio)* shopkeeper.

commerci'are [kommer'tʃare] *vi:* **~ in** to deal *o* trade in.

com'mercio [kom'mertʃo] *sm* trade, commerce; **essere in ~** *(prodotto)* to be on the market *o* on sale; **essere nel ~** *(persona)* to be in business; **~ all'ingrosso/al minuto** wholesale/retail trade.

com'messo, a *pp di* **commettere** // *sm/f* shop assistant // *sm (impiegato subalterno)* clerk // *sf (COMM)* order; **~ viaggiatore** commercial traveller.

commes'tibile *ag* edible.

com'mettere *vt* to commit.

commi'nare *vt (DIR)* to threaten; to inflict.

commise'rare *vt* to sympathize with, commiserate with.

commissari'ato *sm (AMM)* commissionership; (: *sede)* commissioner's office; (: *di polizia)* police station.

commis'sario *sm* commissioner; *(di pubblica sicurezza)* ≈ police superintendent; *(SPORT)* steward; *(membro di commissione)* member of a committee *o* board.

commissio'nario sm (COMM) selling agent.

commissi'one sf (incarico) message; errand; (comitato, percentuale) commission; (COMM: ordinazione) order; ~ **i** sfpl (acquisti) shopping sg.

commit'tente sm/f (COMM) purchaser, buyer.

com'mosso, a pp di **commuovere**.

commo'vente ag moving.

commozi'one [kommot'tsjone] sf emotion, deep feeling; ~ **cerebrale** concussion.

commu'overe vt to move, affect; ~**rsi** vr to be moved.

commu'tare vt (pena) to commute; (ELETTR) to change o switch over.

comò sm inv chest of drawers.

como'dino sm bedside table.

comodità sf inv comfort; convenience.

'comodo, a ag comfortable; (facile) easy; (conveniente) convenient; (utile) useful, handy; (persona) easy-going // sm comfort; convenience; **con** ~ at one's convenience o leisure; **fare il proprio** ~ to do as one pleases; **far** ~ to be useful o handy.

compae'sano, a sm/f fellow-countryman; person from the same town.

com'pagine [kom'padʒine] sf (squadra) team.

compa'gnia [kompaɲ'ɲia] sf company; (gruppo) gathering.

com'pagno, a [kom'paɲɲo] sm/f (di classe, gioco) companion; (POL) comrade; (COMM: socio) partner; ~ **di squadra** team mate.

compa'rare vt to compare.

compara'tivo, a ag, sm comparative.

comparazi'one [komparat'tsjone] sf comparison.

compa'rire vi (2) to appear; (spiccare: persona) to stand out; **com'parso, a** pp di **comparire** // sf appearance; (TEATRO) walk-on; (CINEMA) extra.

compartecipazi'one [kompartetʃipat'tsjone] sf sharing; (quota) share; ~ **agli utili** profit-sharing.

comparti'mento sm (suddivisione) division, compartment; (FERR) compartment; (AMM) department.

compassi'one sf compassion, pity; **avere** ~ **di qd** to feel sorry for sb, to pity sb; **compassio'nevole** ag compassionate.

com'passo sm (pair of) compasses pl; callipers pl.

compa'tibile ag (scusabile) excusable; (conciliabile) compatible.

compati'mento sm compassion; indulgence.

compa'tire vt (aver compassione di) to sympathize with, feel sorry for; (scusare) to make allowances for.

compatri'ota, i, e sm/f compatriot.

com'patto, a ag compact; (roccia) solid; (folla) dense; (fig: partito) united, close-knit.

compendi'are vt to summarize.

com'pendio sm summary; (libro) compendium.

compene'trare vt to permeate.

compen'sare vt (equilibrare) to compensate for, make up for; ~ **qd di** (rimunerare) to pay o remunerate sb for; (risarcire) to pay compensation to sb for; (fig: fatiche, dolori) to reward sb for; **com'penso** sm compensation; payment, remuneration; reward; **in compenso** in compensation; (in cambio) in return.

'compera etc = **compra** etc.

compe'tente ag competent; (mancia) apt, suitable; **compe'tenza** sf competence; **competenze** sfpl (onorari) fees.

com'petere vi to compete, vie; (DIR: spettare): ~ **a** to lie within the competence of; **competi'tore, 'trice** sm/f competitor; **competizi'one** sf competition.

compia'cente [kompja'tʃente] ag courteous, obliging; **compia'cenza** sf courtesy.

compia'cere [kompja'tʃere] vi: ~ **a** to gratify, please // vt to humour; ~**rsi** vr (provare soddisfazione): ~**rsi di** o **per qc** to be delighted at sth; (rallegrarsi): ~**rsi con qd** to congratulate sb; (degnarsi): ~**rsi di fare** to be so good as to do; **compiaci'uto, a** pp di **compiacere**.

compi'angere [kom'pjandʒere] vt to sympathize with, feel sorry for; **compi'anto, a** pp di **compiangere**.

'compiere vt (concludere) to finish, end, complete; (adempiere) to carry out, fulfil; ~**rsi** vr (avverarsi) to be fulfilled, come true; ~ **gli anni** to have one's birthday.

compi'lare vt to compile.

com'pire vb = **compiere**.

compi'tare vt to spell out.

'compito sm (incarico) task, duty; (dovere) duty; (INS) exercise; (: a casa) homework.

com'pito, a ag well-mannered, polite.

comple'anno sm birthday.

complemen'tare ag complementary; (INS: materia) subsidiary.

comple'mento sm complement; (MIL) reserve (troops); ~ **oggetto** (LING) direct object.

complessità sf complexity.

comples'sivo, a ag (globale) comprehensive, overall; (totale: cifra) total.

com'plesso, a ag complex // sm (PSIC, EDIL) complex; (MUS: corale) ensemble; (: orchestrina) band; (: di musica pop) group; **in** o **nel** ~ on the whole.

comple'tare vt to complete.

com'pleto, a ag complete; (teatro, autobus) full // sm suit; **al** ~ full; (tutti presenti) all present.

compli'care vt to complicate; ~**rsi** vr to become complicated; **complicazi'one** sf complication.

'complice ['komplitʃe] sm/f accomplice.

complimen'tarsi vr: ~ **con** to congratulate.

compli'mento sm compliment; ~**i** smpl

(cortesia eccessiva) ceremony sg; (ossequi) regards, compliments; ~**i** congratulations!; **senza** ~**il** don't stand on ceremony!; make yourself at home!; help yourself!

complot'tare vi to plot, conspire.

com'plotto sm plot, conspiracy.

compo'nente sm/f member // sm o f component (part).

componi'mento sm (DIR) settlement; (INS) composition; (poetico, teatrale) work.

com'porre vt (musica, testo) to compose; (formare) to make up, form; (motore) to make up, put together; (mettere in ordine) to arrange; (DIR: lite) to settle; (TIP) to set.

comporta'mento sm behaviour.

compor'tare vt (implicare) to involve; (consentire) to permit, allow (of); ~**rsi** vr (condursi) to behave.

composi'tore, 'trice sm/f composer; (TIP) compositor, typesetter.

composizi'one [kompozit'tsjone] sf composition; (DIR) settlement.

com'posta sf vedi **composto**.

compos'tezza [kompos'tettsa] sf composure; decorum.

com'posto, a pp di **comporre** // ag (persona) composed, self-possessed; (: decoroso) dignified; (formato da più elementi) compound cpd // sm compound // sf (CUC) stewed fruit q; (AGR) compost.

'compra sf purchase.

com'prare vt to buy; **compra'tore, 'trice** sm/f buyer, purchaser.

com'prendere vt (contenere) to comprise, consist of; (capire) to understand.

comprensi'one sf understanding.

compren'sivo, a ag (prezzo): ~ **di** inclusive of; (indulgente) understanding.

com'preso, a pp di **comprendere** // ag (incluso) included.

com'pressa sf vedi **compresso**.

compressi'one sf compression; (pressione) pressure.

com'presso, a pp di **comprimere** // ag pressed; compressed; repressed // sf (MED: garza) compress; (: pastiglia) tablet.

com'primere vt (premere) to press; (FISICA) to compress; (fig) to repress.

compro'messo, a pp di **compromettere** // sm compromise.

compro'mettere vt to compromise.

compro'vare vt to confirm.

com'punto, a ag contrite; **compunzi'one** sf compunction.

compu'tare vt to calculate; (addebitare): ~ **qc a qd** to debit sb with sth; **computiste'ria** sf accounting, bookkeeping; **'computo** sm calculation.

comu'nale ag municipal; town cpd, ≈ borough cpd.

comu'nanza [komu'nantsa] sf community.

co'mune ag common; (consueto) common, everyday; (di livello medio) average; (ordinario) ordinary // sm (AMM) commune, ≈ town council; (: sede) town

hall // sf (di persone) commune; **fuori del** ~ out of the ordinary; **mettere in** ~ to share.

comuni'care vt (notizia) to pass on, convey; (malattia) to pass on; (ansia etc) to communicate; (trasmettere: calore etc) to transmit, communicate; (REL) to administer communion to // vi to communicate; ~**rsi** vr (propagarsi): ~**rsi a** to spread to; (REL) to receive communion; **comunica-'tivo, a** ag (sentimento) infectious; (persona) communicative.

comuni'cato sm communiqué.

comunicazi'one [komunikat'tsjone] sf communication; (TEL): ~ **(telefonica)** (telephone) call; **dare la** ~ **a qd** to put sb through; **ottenere la** ~ to get through.

comuni'one sf communion.

comu'nismo sm communism; **comu-'nista, i, e** ag, sm/f communist.

comuni'tà sf inv community; **C**~ **Economica Europea (C.E.E.)** European Economic Community (EEC).

co'munque cong however, no matter how // av (in ogni modo) in any case; (tuttavia) however, nevertheless.

con prep (nei seguenti casi con può fondersi con l'articolo definito: con + il = col, con + gli = cogli, con + i = coi) with; **partire col treno** to leave by train; ~ **mio grande stupore** to my great astonishment; ~ **tutto ciò** for all that.

co'nato sm: ~ **di vomito** retching.

'conca, che sf (GEO) valley.

'concavo, a ag concave.

con'cedere [kon'tʃedere] vt (accordare) to grant; (ammettere) to admit, concede; ~**rsi qc** to treat o.s. to sth, to allow o.s. sth.

concentra'mento [kontʃentra'mento] sm concentration.

concen'trare [kontʃen'trare] vt, ~**rsi** vr to concentrate; **concentrazi'one** sf concentration.

concepi'mento [kontʃepi'mento] sm conception.

conce'pire [kontʃe'pire] vt (bambino) to conceive; (progetto, idea) to conceive (of); (metodo, piano) to devise; (affetto, speranze) to entertain.

con'cernere [kon'tʃernere] vt to concern.

concer'tare [kontʃer'tare] vt (MUS) to harmonize; (ordire) to devise, plan; ~**rsi** vr to agree.

con'certo [kon'tʃerto] sm (MUS) concert; (: componimento) concerto.

concessio'nario [kontʃessjo'narjo] sm (COMM) agent, dealer.

concessi'one [kontʃes'sjone] sf concession.

con'cesso, a [kon'tʃesso] pp di **concedere**.

con'cetto [kon'tʃetto] sm (pensiero, idea) concept; (opinione) opinion.

concezi'one [kontʃet'tsjone] sf conception.

con'chiglia [kon'kiʎʎa] sf shell.

'concia ['kontʃa] sf (di pelle) tanning; (di

tabacco) curing; *(sostanza)* tannin.

conci'are [kon'tʃare] *vt (pelle)* to tan; *(tabacco)* to cure; *(fig: ridurre in cattivo stato)* to beat up; **~rsi** *vr (sporcarsi)* to get in a mess; *(vestirsi male)* to dress badly.

concili'abolo [kontʃi'ljabolo] *sm* clandestine meeting.

concili'are [kontʃi'ljare] *vt* to reconcile; *(contravvenzione)* to pay on the spot; *(favorire: sonno)* to be conducive to, induce; *(procurare: simpatia)* to gain; **~rsi** **qc** to gain *o* win sth (for o.s.); **~rsi qd** to win sb over; **~rsi con** to be reconciled with; **conciliazi'one** *sf* reconciliation; *(DIR)* settlement.

con'cilio [kon'tʃiljo] *sm (REL)* council.

con'cime [kon'tʃime] *sm* manure; *(chimico)* fertilizer.

con'ciso, a [kon'tʃizo] *ag* concise, succinct.

conci'tato, a [kontʃi'tato] *ag* excited, emotional.

concitta'dino, a [kontʃitta'dino] *sm/f* fellow citizen.

con'clave *sm* conclave.

con'cludere *vt* to conclude; *(portare a compimento)* to conclude, finish, bring to an end; *(operare positivamente)* to achieve // *vi (essere convincente)* to be conclusive; **~rsi** *vr* to come to an end, close; **conclusi'one** *sf* conclusion; *(risultato)* result; **conclu'sivo, a** *ag* conclusive; *(finale)* final; **con'cluso, a** *pp di* **concludere**.

concor'danza [konkor'dantsa] *sf (anche LING)* agreement.

concor'dare *vt (tregua)* to agree on; *(LING)* to make agree // *vi* to agree; **concor'dato** *sm* agreement; *(DIR)* composition; *(REL)* concordat.

con'corde *ag (d'accordo)* in agreement; *(simultaneo)* simultaneous.

con'cordia *sf* harmony, concord.

concor'rente *ag* competing; *(MAT)* concurrent // *sm/f* competitor; *(INS)* candidate; **concor'renza** *sf* competition.

con'correre *vi: ~ (in)* *(MAT)* to converge *o* meet (in); *~ (a)* *(competere)* to compete (for); *(: INS: a una cattedra)* to apply (for); *(partecipare: a un'impresa)* to take part (in), contribute (to); **con'corso, a** *pp di* **concorrere** // *sm* competition; *(INS)* competitive examination.

con'creto, a *ag* concrete.

concussi'one *sf (DIR)* extortion.

con'danna *sf* sentence; conviction; condemnation.

condan'nare *vt (DIR): ~ a* to sentence to; *~ per* to convict of; *(disapprovare)* to condemn; **condan'nato, a** *sm/f* convict.

conden'sare *vt*, **~rsi** *vr* to condense; **condensazi'one** *sf* condensation.

condi'mento *sm* seasoning; dressing.

con'dire *vt* to season; *(insalata)* to dress.

condiscen'dente [kondiʃʃen'dente] *ag* compliant; indulgent, easy-going.

condi'scendere [kondiʃ'ʃendere] *vi: ~ a*

to agree to; **condi'sceso, a** *pp di* **condiscendere**.

condi'videre *vt* to share; **condi'viso, a** *pp di* **condividere**.

condizio'nale [kondittsjo'nale] *ag* conditional // *sm (LING)* conditional // *sf (DIR)* suspended sentence.

condizio'nare [kondittsjo'nare] *vt* to condition; *(determinare)* to determine.

condizi'one [kondit'tsjone] *sf* condition; **~i** *sfpl (di pagamento etc)* terms, conditions; **a ~ che** on condition that, provided that.

condogli'anze [kondoʎ'ʎantse] *sfpl* condolences.

condo'minio *sm* joint ownership; *(edificio)* jointly-owned building.

condo'nare *vt (DIR)* to remit; **con'dono** *sm* remission.

con'dotta *sf vedi* **condotto**.

con'dotto, a *pp di* **condurre** // *ag:* **medico ~** local authority doctor *(in country district)* // *sm (canale, tubo)* pipe, conduit; *(ANAT)* duct // *sf (modo di comportarsi)* conduct, behaviour; *(di un affare etc)* handling; *(di acqua)* piping; *(incarico sanitario)* country medical practice controlled by a local authority.

condu'cente [kondu'tʃente] *sm* driver.

con'durre *vt* to conduct; *(azienda)* to manage; *(accompagnare: bambino)* to take; *(automobile)* to drive; *(trasportare: acqua, gas)* to convey, conduct; *(fig)* to lead // *vi* to lead; **condursi** *vr* to behave, conduct o.s.; **~ una vita felice** to lead a happy life.

condut'tore *sm (conducente)* driver; *(FERR)* guard; *(ELETTR, FISICA)* conductor.

con'farsi *vr: ~ a* to suit, agree with.

confederazi'one [konfederat'tsjone] *sf* confederation.

confe'renza [konfe'rentsa] *sf (discorso)* lecture; *(riunione)* conference; **conferenzi'ere, a** *sm/f* lecturer.

confe'rire *vt: ~ qc a qd* to give sth to sb, bestow sth on sb // *vi* to confer.

con'ferma *sf* confirmation.

confer'mare *vt* to confirm.

confes'sare *vt*, **~rsi** *vr* to confess; **confessio'nale** *ag*, *sm* confessional; **confessi'one** *sf* confession; *(setta religiosa)* denomination; **confes'sore** *sm* confessor.

con'fetto *sm* sugared almond; *(MED)* pill.

confezio'nare [konfettsjo'nare] *vt (vestito)* to make (up); *(merci, pacchi)* to package.

confezi'one [konfet'tsjone] *sf* tailoring; dressmaking; packaging; **~i** *sfpl* garments, clothes; **~ regalo** gift pack.

confic'care *vt: ~ qc in* to hammer *o* drive sth into; **~rsi** *vr* to stick.

confi'dare *vi: ~ in* to confide in, rely on // *vt* to confide; **~rsi con qd** to confide in sb; **confi'dente** *sm/f (persona amica)* confidant/confidante; *(spia)* informer; **confi'denza** *sf (familiarità)* intimacy, familiarity; *(fiducia)* trust, confidence; *(rivelazione)* confidence; **confidenzi'ale** *ag* familiar, friendly; (*notizia*) confidential.

configu'rarsi *vr*: ~ a to assume the shape *o* form of; **configurazi'one** *sf* configuration.

confi'nare *vi*: ~ **con** to border on // *vt* (*POL*) to intern; (*fig*) to confine; ~**rsi** *vr* (*isolarsi*): ~**rsi in** to shut o.s. up in; (*fig: limitarsi*): ~**rsi a** to confine o.s. to.

con'fine *sm* boundary; (*di paese*) border, frontier.

con'fino *sm* internment.

confis'care *vt* to confiscate.

conflagrazi'one [konflagrat'tsjone] *sf* conflagration.

con'flitto *sm* conflict.

conflu'enza [konflu'entsa] *sf* (*di fiumi*) confluence; (*di strade*) junction.

conflu'ire *vi* (*fiumi*) to flow into each other, meet; (*strade*) to meet.

con'fondere *vt* to mix up, confuse; (*imbarazzare*) to embarrass; ~**rsi** *vr* (*mescolarsi*) to mingle; (*turbarsi*) to be confused; (*sbagliare*) to get mixed up.

confor'mare *vt* (*adeguare*): ~ a to adapt *o* conform to // *vr*: ~**rsi (a)** to conform (to).

conforme'mente *av* accordingly; ~ a in accordance with.

confor'mista, i, e *sm/f* conformist.

confor'tare *vt* to comfort, console; **confor'tevole** *ag* (*consolante*) comforting; (*comodo*) comfortable; **con'forto** *sm* comfort, consolation; comfort.

confron'tare *vt* to compare.

con'fronto *sm* comparison; **in** *o* **a** ~ **di** in comparison with, compared to; **nei miei** (*o tuoi etc*) ~**i** towards me (*o you etc*).

confusi'one *sf* confusion; (*imbarazzo*) embarrassment.

con'fuso, a *pp di* **confondere** // *ag* (*vedi confondere*) confused; embarrassed.

confu'tare *vt* to refute.

conge'dare [kondʒe'dare] *vt* to dismiss; (*MIL*) to demob; ~**rsi** *vr* to take one's leave; **con'gedo** *sm* (*anche MIL*) leave; **prendere congedo da qd** to take one's leave of sb; **congedo assoluto** (*MIL*) discharge.

conge'gnare [kondʒeɲ'ɲare] *vt* to construct, put together; **con'gegno** *sm* device, mechanism.

conge'lare [kondʒe'lare] *vt* to freeze; **congela'tore** *sm* freezer.

con'genito, a [kon'dʒɛnito] *ag* congenital.

congestio'nare [kondʒestjo'nare] *vt* to congest.

congesti'one [kondʒes'tjone] *sf* congestion.

conget'tura [kondʒet'tura] *sf* conjecture, supposition.

con'giungere [kon'dʒundʒere] *vt* to join (together); (*porre in comunicazione*) to connect, link (up); ~**rsi** *vr* to join (together); to connect, link (up).

congiunti'vite [kondʒunti'vite] *sf* conjunctivitis.

congiun'tivo [kondʒun'tivo] *sm* (*LING*) subjunctive.

congi'unto, a [kon'dʒunto] *pp di* **congiungere** // *ag* (*unito*) joined; (*: da parentela*) related.

congiun'tura [kondʒun'tura] *sf* (*giuntura*) junction, join; (*ANAT*) joint; (*circostanza*) juncture; (*ECON*) economic situation.

congiunzi'one [kondʒun'tsjone] *sf* (*LING*) conjunction.

congi'ura [kon'dʒura] *sf* conspiracy; **congiu'rare** *vi* to conspire.

conglome'rato *sm* (*GEO*) conglomerate; (*fig*) conglomeration; (*EDIL*) concrete.

congratu'larsi *vr*: ~ **con qd per qc** to congratulate sb on sth.

congratulazi'oni [kongratulat'tsjoni] *sfpl* congratulations.

congrega, ghe *sf* band, bunch.

congregazi'one [kongregat'tsjone] *sf* congregation.

con'gresso *sm* congress.

conguagli'are [kongwaʎ'ʎare] *vt* to balance; **congu'aglio** *sm* balancing, adjusting; (*somma di denaro*) balance.

coni'are *vt* to mint, coin; (*fig*) to coin.

'conico, a, ci, che *ag* conical.

co'nifera *sf* conifer.

co'niglio [ko'niʎʎo] *sm* rabbit.

coniu'gare *vt* (*LING*) to conjugate; ~**rsi** *vr* to get married; **coniugazi'one** *sf* (*LING*) conjugation.

'coniuge ['kɔnjudʒe] *sm/f* spouse.

connazio'nale [konnattsjo'nale] *sm/f* fellow-countryman/woman.

connessi'one *sf* connection.

con'nesso, a *pp di* **connettere**.

con'nettere *vt* to connect, join // *vi* (*fig*) to think straight.

conni'vente *ag* conniving.

conno'tati *smpl* distinguishing marks.

'cono *sm* cone; ~ **gelato** ice-cream cone.

cono'scente [konoʃ'ʃente] *sm/f* acquaintance.

cono'scenza [konoʃ'ʃentsa] *sf* (*il sapere*) knowledge *q*; (*persona*) acquaintance; (*facoltà sensoriale*) consciousness *q*; **perdere** ~ to lose consciousness.

co'noscere [ko'noʃʃere] *vt* to know; **ci siamo conosciuti a Firenze** we (first) met in Florence; **conosci'tore, 'trice** *sm/f* connoisseur; **conosci'uto, a** *pp di* **conoscere** // *ag* well-known.

con'quista *sf* conquest.

conquis'tare *vt* to conquer; (*fig*) to gain, win.

consa'crare *vt* (*REL*) to consecrate; (*: sacerdote*) to ordain; (*dedicare*) to dedicate; (*fig: uso etc*) to sanction; ~**rsi a** to dedicate o.s. to.

consangu'ineo, a *sm/f* blood relation.

consa'pevole *ag*: ~ **di** aware *o* conscious of; **consapevo'lezza** *sf* awareness, consciousness.

'conscio, a, sci, sce ['kɔnʃo] *ag*: ~ **di** aware *o* conscious of.

consecu'tivo, a *ag* consecutive;

(*successivo: giorno*) following, next.

con'segna [kon'seɲɲa] *sf* delivery; (*merce consegnata*) consignment; (*custodia*) trust, custody; (MIL: *ordine*) orders *pl*; (: *punizione*) confinement to barracks; (DIR: *di malfattore*) handing over; **alla ~ on delivery; dare qc in ~ a qd** to entrust sth to sb.

conse'gnare [konseɲ'ɲare] *vt* to deliver; (*affidare*) to entrust, hand over; (MIL) to confine to barracks.

consegu'ente *ag* consequent.

consegu'enza [konse'gwɛntsa] *sf* consequence; **per o di ~** consequently.

consegu'ire *vt* to achieve // *vi* (2) to follow, result.

con'senso *sm* consent; (*fra due o più persone*) agreement.

consen'tire *vi*: **~ a** to consent o agree to // *vt* to allow, permit.

con'serva *sf* (CUC) preserve; **~ di frutta** jam; **~ di pomodoro** tomato purée.

conser'vare *vt* (CUC) to preserve; (*custodire*) to keep; (: *dalla distruzione etc*) to preserve, conserve; **~rsi** *vr* to keep; **~rsi sano** to keep healthy.

conserva'tore, 'trice *sm/f* (POL) conservative.

conservazi'one [konservat'tsjone] *sf* preservation.

conside'rare *vt* to consider; (*reputare*) to consider, regard; **~ molto qd** to think highly of sb; **considerazi'one** *sf* consideration; regard, esteem; **conside'revole** *ag* considerable.

consigli'are [konsiʎ'ʎare] *vt* (*persona*) to advise; (*metodo, azione*) to recommend, advise, suggest; **~rsi con qd** to ask sb for advice; **consigli'ere, a** *sm/f* adviser // *sm*: **consigliere d'amministrazione** board member; **consigliere comunale** town councillor; **con'siglio** *sm* (*suggerimento*) advice q, piece of advice; (*assemblea*) council; **consiglio d'amministrazione** board; **il Consiglio dei Ministri** (POL) ≈ the Cabinet.

consis'tente *ag* thick; solid; (*fig*) sound, valid; **consis'tenza** *sf* consistency, thickness; solidity; validity.

consis'tere *vi*: **~ in** to consist of; **consis'tito, a** *pp di* **consistere**.

conso'lare *ag* consular // *vt* (*confortare*) to console, comfort; (*rallegrare*) to cheer up; **~rsi** *vr* to be comforted; to cheer up.

conso'lato *sm* consulate.

consolazi'one [konsolat'tsjone] *sf* consolation q, comfort q.

'console *sm* consul.

consoli'dare *vt* to strengthen, reinforce; (MIL, *terreno*) to consolidate; **~rsi** *vr* to consolidate.

conso'nante *sf* consonant.

conso'nanza [konso'nantsa] *sf* consonance.

con'sorte *sm/f* consort.

con'sorzio [kon'sortsjo] *sm* consortium.

con'stare (2) *vi*: **~ di** to consist of // *vb impers*: **mi consta che** it has come to my knowledge that, it appears that.

consta'tare *vt* to establish, verify; (*notare*) to notice, observe.

consu'eto, a *ag* habitual, usual; **consue'tudine** *sf* habit, custom; (*usanza*) custom.

consul'tare *vt* to consult; **~rsi con qd** to seek the advice of sb; **consultazi'one** *sf* consultation; **consultazioni** *sfpl* (POL) talks.

consu'mare *vt* (*logorare: abiti, scarpe*) to wear out; (*usare*) to consume, use up; (*mangiare, bere*) to consume; (DIR) to consummate; **~rsi** *vr* to wear out; to be used up; (*anche fig*) to be consumed; (*combustibile*) to burn out; **consuma'tore** *sm* consumer; **consumazi'one** *sf* consumption; (*bibita*) drink; (*spuntino*) snack; (DIR) consummation; **con'sumo** *sm* consumption; wear; use.

consun'tivo *sm* (ECON) final balance.

con'sunto, a *ag* worn-out; (*viso*) wasted.

con'tabile *ag* accounts *cpd*, accounting // *sm/f* accountant; **contabilità** *sf* (*attività, tecnica*) accounting, accountancy; (*insieme dei libri etc*) books *pl*, accounts *pl*; (*ufficio*) accounts department.

conta'dino, a *sm/f* countryman/woman; farm worker; (*peg*) peasant.

contagi'are [konta'dʒare] *vt* to infect.

con'tagio [kon'tadʒo] *sm* infection; (*per contatto diretto*) contagion; **contagi'oso, a** *ag* infectious; contagious.

contami'nare *vt* to contaminate; **contaminazi'one** *sf* contamination.

con'tante *sm* cash; **pagare in ~i** to pay cash.

con'tare *vt* to count; (*considerare*) to consider // *vi* to count, be of importance; **~ su qd** to count o rely on sb; **~ di fare qc** to intend to do sth; **conta'tore** *sm* meter.

contat'tare *vt* to contact.

con'tatto *sm* contact.

'conte *sm* count.

conteggi'are [konted'dʒare] *vt* to charge, put on the bill; **con'teggio** *sm* calculation; **conteggio alla rovescia** countdown.

con'tegno [kon'teɲɲo] *sm* (*comportamento*) behaviour; (*atteggiamento*) attitude; **conte'gnoso, a** *ag* reserved, dignified.

contem'plare *vt* to contemplate, gaze at; (DIR) to make provision for.

contempo'raneo, a *ag, sm/f* contemporary.

conten'dente *sm/f* opponent, adversary.

con'tendere *vi* (*competere*) to compete; (*litigare*) to quarrel // *vt* to contest.

conte'nere *vt* to contain; **conteni'tore** *sm* container.

conten'tare *vt* to please, satisfy; **~rsi di** to be satisfied with, content o.s. with.

conten'tezza [konten'tettsa] *sf* contentment.

con'tento, a *ag* pleased, glad; **~ di** pleased with.

conte'nuto *sm* contents *pl*; (*argomento*) content.

con'teso, a *pp di* **contendere** // *sf* dispute, argument.

con'tessa *sf* countess.

contes'tare *vt* (*DIR*) to notify; (*fig*) to dispute.

con'testo *sm* context.

con'tiguo, a *ag*: ~ (a) adjacent (to).

continen'tale *ag, sm/f* continental.

conti'nente *ag* continent // *sm* (*GEO*) continent; (: *terra ferma*) mainland; **conti'nenza** *sf* continence.

contin'gente [kontin'dʒɛnte] *sm* (*COMM*) quota; (*MIL*) contingent; **contin'genza** *sf* circumstance.

continu'are *vt* to continue (with), go on with // *vi* to continue, go on; ~ a fare qc to go on *o* continue doing sth; **continuazi'one** *sf* continuation.

continuità *sf* continuity.

con'tinuo, a *ag* (*numerazione*) continuous; (*pioggia*) continual, constant; (*ELETTR*) corrente ~ a direct current; **di** ~ continually.

'conto *sm* (*calcolo*) calculation; (*COMM, ECON*) account; (*di ristorante, albergo*) bill; (*fig: stima*) consideration, esteem; **fare i** ~ **i con qd** to settle one's account with sb; **fare** ~ **su qd/qc** to count *o* rely on sb; **rendere** ~ **a qd di qc** to be accountable to sb for sth; **tener** ~ **di qd/qc** to take sb/sth into account; **per** ~ **di** on behalf of; **per** ~ **mio** as far as I'm concerned; ~ **corrente** current account; **a** ~ **i fatti, in fin dei** ~ **i** all things considered.

con'torcere [kon'tortʃere] *vt* to twist; (*panni*) to wring (out); ~ **rsi** *vr* to twist, writhe.

contor'nare *vt* to surround.

con'torno *sm* (*linea*) outline, contour; (*ornamento*) border; (*CUC*) vegetables *pl*.

contorsi'one *sf* contortion.

con'torto, a *pp di* **contorcere**.

contrabbandi'ere *a, sm/f* smuggler.

contrab'bando *sm* smuggling, contraband; **merce di** ~ contraband, smuggled goods *pl*.

contraccambi'are *vt* (*favore etc*) to return; **contrac'cambio** *sm* return; **in contraccambio di** in return *o* exchange for.

contrac'colpo *sm* rebound; (*di arma da fuoco*) recoil; (*fig*) repercussion.

contrad'detto, a *pp di* **contraddire**.

contrad'dire *vt* to contradict; **contraddit'torio, a** *ag* contradictory // *sm* debate; **contraddizi'one** *sf* contradiction.

contraf'fare *vt* (*persona*) to mimic; (*alterare: voce*) to disguise; (*firma*) to forge, counterfeit; **contraf'fatto, a** *pp di* **contraffare** // *ag* counterfeit; **contraffazi'one** *sf* mimicking *q*; disguising *q*; forging *q*; (*cosa contraffatta*) forgery.

con'tralto *sm* (*MUS*) contralto.

contrap'peso *sm* counterbalance, counterweight.

contrap'porre *vt* (*opporre*) to oppose, set against; **contrap'posto, a** *pp di* **contrapporre**.

contraria'mente *av*: ~ **a** contrary to.

contrari'are *vt* (*contrastare*) to thwart, oppose; (*irritare*) to annoy, bother; ~ **rsi** *vr* to get annoyed.

contrarietà *sf* adversity; (*fig*) aversion.

con'trario, a *ag* opposite; (*sfavorevole*) unfavourable // *sm* opposite; ~ **a** contrary to; **al** ~ on the contrary.

con'trarre *vt*, **contrarsi** *vr* to contract.

contrasse'gnare [kontrassen'nare] *vt* to mark; **contras'segno** *sm* mark; (*distintivo*) distinguishing mark.

contras'tante *ag* contrasting.

contras'tare *vt* (*avversare*) to oppose; (*impedire*) to bar; (*negare: diritto*) to contest, dispute // *vi*: ~ (**con**) (*essere in disaccordo*) to contrast (with); (*lottare*) to struggle (with); **con'trasto** *sm* contrast; (*conflitto*) conflict; (*litigio*) dispute.

contrat'tacco *sm* counterattack.

contrat'tare *vt*, *vi* to negotiate.

contrat'tempo *sm* hitch.

con'tratto, a *pp di* **contrarre** // *sm* contract; **contrattu'ale** *ag* contractual.

contravve'leno *sm* antidote.

contravve'nire *vi*: ~ **a** (*legge*) to contravene; (*obbligo*) to fail to meet; **contravvenzi'one** *sf* contravention; (*ammenda*) fine.

contrazi'one [kontrat'tsjone] *sf* contraction; (*di prezzi etc*) reduction.

contribu'ente *sm/f* taxpayer; ratepayer.

contribu'ire *vi* to contribute; **contri'buto** *sm* contribution; (*tassa*) tax.

con'trito, a *ag* contrite, penitent.

'contro *prep* against; ~ **di me/lui** against me/him; ~ **pagamento** (*COMM*) on payment // *prefisso*: **contro'battere** *vt* (*fig: a parole*) to answer back; (: *confutare*) to refute; **controfi'gura** *sf* (*CINEMA*) double; **controfir'mare** *vt* to countersign.

control'lare *vt* (*accertare*) to check; (*sorvegliare*) to watch, control; (*tenere nel proprio potere, fig: dominare*) to control; **con'trollo** *sm* check; watch; control; **controllo delle nascite** birth control; **control'lore** *sm* (*FERR, AUTOBUS*) (ticket) inspector.

controprodu'cente [kontroprodu'tʃɛnte] *ag* producing the opposite effect.

contro'senso *sm* (*contraddizione*) contradiction in terms; (*assurdità*) nonsense.

controspio'naggio [kontrospio'naddʒo] *sm* counterespionage.

contro'versia *sf* controversy.

contro'verso, a *ag* controversial.

contro'voglia [kontro'vɔʎʎa] *av* unwillingly.

contu'macia [kontu'matʃa] *sf* (*DIR*) default.

contur'bare *vt* to disturb, upset.

contusi'one *sf* (*MED*) bruise.

convale'scente [konvaleʃˈʃɛnte] *ag, sm/f* convalescent; **convale'scenza** *sf* convalescence.

convali'dare *vt* to confirm.

con'vegno [konˈveɲɲo] *sm* (*incontro*) meeting; (*congresso*) convention, congress; (*luogo*) meeting place.

conve'nevoli *smpl* civilities.

conveni'ente *ag* suitable; (*pratico*) convenient, handy; (*vantaggioso*) profitable, advantageous; (*prezzo*) cheap; **conveni'enza** *sf* suitability; convenience; advantage; **le convenienze** *sfpl* social conventions.

conve'nire *vi* (2: *riunirsi*) to gather, assemble; (*concordare*) to agree; (*essere opportuno, addirsi*) to be suitable; (*tornare utile*) to be worthwhile // *vb impers* (2): **conviene fare questo** it is advisable to do this; **conviene andarsene** we should go; **ne convengo** I agree.

con'vento *sm* (*di frati*) monastery; (*di suore*) convent.

convenzio'nale [konventsjoˈnale] *ag* conventional.

convenzi'one [konvenˈtsjone] *sf* (*DIR*) agreement; (*nella società*) convention; **le ~ i** *sfpl* convention *sg*, social conventions.

conver'gente [konverˈdʒɛnte] *ag* convergent.

con'vergere [konˈvɛrdʒere] *vi* (2) to converge.

conver'sare *vi* to converse.

conversazi'one [konversatˈtsjone] *sf* conversation.

conversi'one *sf* conversion.

con'verso, a *pp di* **convergere**.

conver'tire *vt* (*trasformare*) to change; (*POL, REL*) to convert; **~rsi** *vr*: **~rsi (in)** to change (to); **~rsi (a)** to be converted (to); **conver'tito, a** *sm/f* convert.

con'vesso, a *ag* convex.

con'vincere [konˈvintʃere] *vt* to convince; **~ qd di qc** to convince sb of sth; **~ qd a fare qc** to persuade sb to do sth; **con'vinto, a** *pp di* **convincere**; **convinzi'one** *sf* conviction, firm belief.

convis'suto, a *pp di* **convivere**.

con'vitto *sm* (*INS*) boarding school; **convit'tore, 'trice** *sm/f* boarder.

con'vivere *vi* to live together.

convo'care *vt* to call, convene; (*DIR*) to summon; **convocazi'one** *sf* meeting; summons *sg*.

convogli'are [konvoʎˈʎare] *vt* to convey; (*dirigere*) to direct, send; **con'voglio** *sm* (*di veicoli*) convoy; (*FERR*) train; **convoglio funebre** funeral procession.

convulsi'one *sf* convulsion.

con'vulso, a *ag* (*pianto*) violent, convulsive; (*attività*) feverish.

coope'rare *vi*: **~ (a)** to cooperate (in); **coopera'tiva** *sf* cooperative; **coopera-zi'one** *sf* cooperation.

coordi'nare *vt* to coordinate; **coordi-'nate** *sfpl* (*MAT, GEO*) coordinates; **coordinazi'one** *sf* coordination.

co'perchio [koˈperkjo] *sm* cover; (*di pentola*) lid.

co'perta *sf* cover; (*di lana*) blanket; (*da viaggio*) rug; (*NAUT*) deck.

coper'tina *sf* (*STAMPA*) cover, jacket.

co'perto, a *pp di* **coprire** // *ag* covered; (*cielo*) overcast // *sm* place setting; (*posto a tavola*) place; (*al ristorante*) cover charge; **~ di** covered in *o* with.

coper'tone *sm* (*telo impermeabile*) tarpaulin; (*AUT*) rubber tyre.

coper'tura *sf* (*anche ECON, MIL*) cover; (*di edificio*) roofing.

'copia *sf* copy; (*stesura*) draught, copy; **brutta/bella ~** rough/final draft.

copi'are *vt* to copy; **copia'trice** *sf* copier, copying machine.

copi'one *sm* (*CINEMA, TEATRO*) script.

'coppa *sf* (*bicchiere*) goblet; (*per frutta, gelato*) dish; (*trofeo*) cup, trophy; **~ dell'olio** oil sump.

'coppia *sf* couple.

coprifu'oco, chi *sm* curfew.

copri'letto *sm* bedspread.

co'prire *vt* to cover; (*occupare: carica, posto*) to hold; **~rsi** *vr* (*cielo*) to cloud over; (*vestirsi*) to wrap up, cover up; (*ECON*) to cover o.s.; **~rsi di** (*fiori, muffa*) to become covered in.

co'raggio [koˈraddʒo] *sm* courage, bravery; **coraggi'oso, a** *ag* courageous, brave.

co'rale *ag* choral; (*approvazione*) unanimous.

co'rallo *sm* coral.

co'rano *sm* (*REL*) Koran.

co'razza [koˈrattsa] *sf* armour; (*di animali*) carapace, shell; (*MIL*) armour(-plating); **coraz'zata** *sf* battleship.

corbelle'ria *sf* stupid action; howler; **~e** *sfpl* nonsense *q*.

'corda *sf* cord; (*fune*) rope; (*spago, MUS*) string; **tenere sulla ~ qd** to keep sb on tenterhooks; **tagliare la ~** to slip away, sneak off; **~e vocali** vocal cords.

cordi'ale *ag* cordial, warm // *sm* (*bevanda*) cordial.

cor'doglio [korˈdɔʎʎo] *sm* grief; (*lutto*) mourning.

cor'done *sm* cord, string; (*linea: di polizia*) cordon; **~ ombelicale** umbilical chord.

coreogra'fia *sf* choreography.

core'ografo, a *sm/f* choreographer.

cori'andoli *smpl* confetti *sg*.

cori'care *vt* to put to bed; **~rsi** *vr* to go to bed.

'corna *sfpl vedi* **corno**.

cor'nacchia [korˈnakkja] *sf* crow.

corna'musa *sf* bagpipes *pl*.

'cornea *sf* (*ANAT*) cornea.

cor'netta *sf* (*MUS*) cornet; (*TEL*) receiver.

cor'netto *sm* (*CUC*) croissant; **~ acustico** ear trumpet.

cor'nice [korˈnitʃe] *sf* frame.

'corno *sm* (*ZOOL*: *pl(f)* **~a**, *MUS*) horn; **fare le ~a a qd** to be unfaithful to sb; **cor'nuto, a** *ag* (*con corna*) horned; (*fam!*

marito) cuckolded // *sm* (*fam!*) cuckold; (: *insulto*) bastard (!).

'co'ro *sm* chorus; (*REL*) choir.

co'rona *sf* crown; (*di fiori*) wreath; ~ **del rosario** rosary, rosary beads *pl*; **coro'nare** *vt* to crown.

'corpo *sm* body; (*cadavere*) (dead) body; (*militare, diplomatico*) corps *inv*; (*di opere*) corpus; **prendere** ~ to take shape; **a** ~ **a** ~ hand-to-hand; ~ **di ballo** corps de ballet; ~ **di guardia** guardroom; ~ **insegnante** teaching staff.

corpo'rale *ag* bodily; (*punizione*) corporal.

corpora'tura *sf* build, physique.

corporazi'one [korporat'tsjone] *sf* corporation.

cor'poreo, a *ag* bodily, physical.

corpu'lento, a *ag* stout.

corre'dare *vt*: ~ **di** to provide *o* furnish with; **cor'redo** *sm* equipment; (*di sposa*) trousseau.

cor'reggere [kor'rɛddʒere] *vt* to correct; (*compiti*) to correct, mark.

cor'rente *ag* (*fiume*) flowing; (*acqua del rubinetto*) running; (*moneta, prezzo*) current; (*comune*) everyday // *sm*: **essere al** ~ to be well-informed // *sf* (*movimento di liquido*) current, stream; (*spiffero*) draught; (*ELETTR, METEOR*) current; (*fig*) trend, tendency.

'correre *vi* (2) to run; (*precipitarsi*) to rush; (*partecipare a una gara*) to race, run; (*fig: diffondersi*) to go round // *vt* (*SPORT: gara*) to compete in; (*rischio*) to run; (*pericolo*) to face; ~ **dietro a qd** to run after sb.

cor'retto, a *pp di* correggere // *ag* (*comportamento*) correct, proper.

correzi'one [korret'tsjone] *sf* correction; marking; ~ **di bozze** proofreading.

corri'doio *sm* corridor.

corri'dore *sm* (*SPORT*) runner; (: *su veicolo*) racer.

corri'era *sf* coach, bus.

corri'ere *sm* (*diplomatico, di guerra*) courier; (*posta*) mail, post; (*COMM*) carrier.

corri'gendo, a [korri'dʒendo] *sm/f* (*DIR*) young offender.

corrispon'dente *ag* corresponding // *sm/f* correspondent.

corrispon'denza [korrispon'dentsa] *sf* correspondence.

corris'pondere *vi* to correspond; (*stanze*) to communicate; (*fig: contraccambiare*): ~ **a** to return; **corris'posto, a** *pp di* corrispondere.

corrobo'rare *vt* to strengthen, fortify; (*fig*) to corroborate, bear out.

cor'rodere *vt*, ~**rsi** *vr* to corrode.

cor'rompere *vt* to corrupt; (*comprare*) to bribe.

corrosi'one *sf* corrosion.

corro'sivo, a *ag* corrosive.

cor'roso, a *pp di* corrodere.

cor'rotto, a *pp di* corrompere // *ag* corrupt.

corrucci'arsi [korrut'tʃarsi] *vr* to grow angry *o* vexed.

corru'gare *vt* to wrinkle; ~ **la fronte** to knit one's brows.

corruzi'one [korrut'tsjone] *sf* corruption; bribery.

'corsa *sf* running *q*; (*gara*) race; (*di autobus, taxi*) journey, trip; **fare una** ~ to run, dash; (*SPORT*) to run a race.

cor'sia *sf* (*AUT, SPORT*) lane; (*di ospedale*) ward.

cor'sivo *sm* cursive (writing); (*TIP*) italics *pl*.

'corso, a *pp di* correre // *sm* course; (*strada cittadina*) main street; (*di unità monetaria*) circulation; (*di titoli, valori*) rate, price; **dar libero** ~ **a** to give free expression to; **in** ~ in progress, under way; (*annata*) current; ~ **serale** evening class.

'corte *sf* (court)yard; (*DIR, regale*) court; **fare la** ~ **a qd** to court sb; ~ **marziale** court-martial.

cor'teccia, ce [kor'tettʃa] *sf* bark.

corteggi'are [korted'dʒare] *vt* to court.

cor'teo *sm* procession.

cor'tese *ag* courteous; **corte'sia** *sf* courtesy.

cortigi'ano, a [korti'dʒano] *sm/f* courtier // *sf* courtesan.

cor'tile *sm* (court)yard.

cor'tina *sf* curtain; (*anche fig*) screen.

'corto, a *ag* short; **essere a** ~ **di qc** to be short of sth; ~ **circuito** short-circuit.

'corvo *sm* raven.

'cosa *sf* thing; (*faccenda*) affair, matter, business *q*; (*che*) ~? what?; **a** ~ **pensi?** what are you thinking about?; **a** ~ **e fatte** when it's all over.

'coscia, sce ['kɔʃʃa] *sf* thigh.

cosci'ente [koʃ'ʃɛnte] *ag* conscious; ~ **di** conscious *o* aware of; **cosci'enza** *sf* conscience; (*consapevolezza*) consciousness; **coscienzi'oso, a** *ag* conscientious.

cosci'otto [koʃ'ʃɔtto] *sm* (*CUC*) leg.

cos'critto *sm* (*MIL*) conscript.

coscrizi'one [koskrit'tsjone] *sf* conscription.

così *av* so; (*in questo modo*) like this, like that; ~ **lontano** so far away; **un ragazzo** ~ **intelligente** such an intelligent boy // *ag inv* (*tale*): **non ho mai visto un film** ~ I've never seen such a film // *cong* (*perciò*) so, therefore; ~ ... **come** as ... as; **non è** ~ **bravo come te** he's not as good as you; **come stai?** — ~ ~ how are you? — so-so; **non ho detto** ~ I didn't say that; **e** ~ **via** and so on; **per** ~ **dire** so to speak.

cosìd'detto, a *ag* so-called.

cos'metico, a, ci, che *ag, sm* cosmetic.

'cosmo *sm* cosmos.

cosmo'nauta, i, e *sm/f* cosmonaut.

cosmopo'lita, i, e *ag* cosmopolitan.

cos'pargere [kos'pardʒere] *vt*: ~ **di** to sprinkle with; **cos'parso, a** *pp di* cospargere.

cos'petto *sm*: **al** ~ **di** in front of; in the presence of.

cos'picuo, a *ag* conspicuous, remarkable; (*grande*) considerable, large.

cospi'rare *vi* to conspire; **cospira'tore, 'trice** *sm/f* conspirator; **cospirazi'one** *sf* conspiracy.

'costa *sf* (*tra terra e mare*) coast(line); (*litorale*) shore; (*pendio*) slope; (ANAT) rib.

costà *av* there.

cos'tante *ag* constant; (*persona*) steadfast // *sf* constant.

cos'tare *vi* (2), *vt* to cost; ~ **caro** to be expensive, cost a lot.

costeggi'are [kosted'dʒare] *vt* to be close to; to run alongside.

cos'tei *pronome vedi* **costui.**

costellazi'one [kostellat'tsjone] *sf* constellation.

costernazi'one [kosternat'tsjone] *sf* dismay, consternation.

costi'ero, a *ag* coastal, coast *cpd* // *sf* stretch of coast.

costitu'ire *vt* (*comitato, gruppo*) to set up, form; (*collezione*) to put together, build up; (*sog: elementi, parti: comporre*) to make up, constitute; (*rappresentare*) to constitute; (DIR) to appoint; ~**rsi alla polizia** to give o.s. up to the police.

costituzio'nale [kostituttsjo'nale] *ag* constitutional.

costituzi'one [kostitut'tsjone] *sf* setting up; building up; constitution.

'costo *sm* cost; **a ogni** *o* **qualunque** ~, **a tutti i** ~**i** at all costs.

'costola *sf* (ANAT) rib; (*di libro, pettine*) spine.

costo'letta *sf* (CUC) cutlet.

cos'toro *pronome pl vedi* **costui.**

cos'toso, a *ag* expensive, costly.

cos'tretto, a *pp di* **costringere.**

cos'tringere [kos'trindʒere] *vt*: ~ **qd a fare qc** to force sb to do sth; **costrizi'one** *sf* coercion.

costru'ire *vt* to construct, build; **costruzi'one** *sf* construction, building.

cos'tui, cos'tei, *pl* **cos'toro** *pronome* (*soggetto*) he/she; *pl* they; (*complemento*) him/her; *pl* them.

cos'tume *sm* (*uso*) custom; (*foggia di vestire, indumento*) costume; ~**i** *smpl* morals, morality *sg*; **il buon** ~ public morality; ~ **da bagno** bathing *o* swimming costume, swimsuit; (*da uomo*) bathing *o* swimming trunks *pl*.

co'tenna *sf* hide; (*di maiale*) pigskin; (*del lardo*) rind.

co'togna [ko'toɲɲa] *sf* quince.

co'tone *sm* cotton; ~ **idrofilo** cotton wool.

'cotta *sf* (REL) surplice; (*fam: innamoramento*) crush.

'cottimo *sm* piecework; **lavorare a** ~ to do piecework.

'cotto, a *pp di* **cuocere** // *ag* cooked; (*fam: innamorato*) head-over-heels in love.

cot'tura *sf* cooking; (*in forno*) baking; (*in umido*) stewing.

co'vare *vt* to hatch; (*fig: malattia*) to be

sickening for; (: *odio, rancore*) to nurse // *vi* (*fuoco, fig*) to smoulder.

'covo *sm* den.

co'vone *sm* sheaf.

'cozza ['kottsa] *sf* mussel.

coz'zare [kot'tsare] *vi*: ~ **contro** to bang into, collide with; **'cozzo** *sm* collision.

C.P. *abbr vedi* **casella.**

'crampo *sm* cramp.

'cranio *sm* skull.

cra'tere *sm* crater.

cra'vatta *sf* tie.

cre'anza [kre'antsa] *sf* manners *pl*.

cre'are *vt* to create; **cre'ato** *sm* creation; **crea'tore, 'trice** *ag* creative // *sm* creator; **crea'tura** *sf* creature; (*bimbo*) baby, infant; **creazi'one** *sf* creation; (*fondazione*) foundation, establishment.

cre'dente *sm/f* (REL) believer.

cre'denza [kre'dɛntsa] *sf* belief; (*credito*) credit; (*armadio*) sideboard.

credenzi'ali [kreden'tsjali] *sfpl* credentials.

'credere *vt* to believe // *vi*: ~ **in**, ~ **a** to believe in; ~ **qd onesto** to believe sb (to be) honest; ~ **che** to believe *o* think that; ~**rsi furbo** to think one is clever; **cre'dibile** *ag* credible, believable.

'credito *sm* (*anche* COMM) credit; (*reputazione*) esteem, repute; **comprare a** ~ to buy on credit.

'credo *sm inv* credo.

'credulo, a *ag* credulous.

'crema *sf* cream; (*con uova, zucchero etc*) custard.

cre'mare *vt* to cremate; **cremazi'one** *sf* cremation.

Crem'lino *sm*: **il** ~ the Kremlin.

'crepa *sf* crack.

cre'paccio [kre'pattʃo] *sm* large crack, fissure; (*di ghiacciaio*) crevasse.

crepacu'ore *sm* broken heart.

cre'pare *vi* (2) (*fam!: morire*) to snuff it, kick the bucket; (*spaccarsi*) to crack; ~ **dalle risa** to split one's sides laughing; ~ **dall'invidia** to be green with envy.

crepi'tare *vi* (*fuoco*) to crackle; (*pioggia*) to patter.

cre'puscolo *sm* twilight, dusk.

cre'scendo [kreʃ'ʃendo] *sm* (MUS) crescendo.

'crescere ['kreʃʃere] *vi* (2) to grow; **'crescita** *sf* growth; **cresci'uto, a** *pp di* **crescere.**

'cresima *sf* (REL) confirmation; **cresi'mare** *vt* to confirm.

'crespo, a *ag* (*capelli*) frizzy; (*vestito*) wrinkled // *sm* crêpe.

'cresta *sf* crest; (*di polli, uccelli*) crest, comb.

'creta *sf* chalk; clay.

'Creta *sf* Crete.

cre'tino, a *sm/f* idiot, fool.

cric *sm inv* (TECN) jack.

'cricca, che *sf* clique.

'cricco, chi *sm* = **cric.**

crimi'nale *ag, sm/f* criminal.

'**crimine** sm (DIR) crime.

'**crine** sm horsehair; **crini'era** sf mane.

'**cripta** sf crypt.

crisan'temo sm chrysanthemum.

'**crisi** sf inv crisis; (MED) attack, fit; ~ **di nervi** attack o fit of nerves.

cristalliz'zare [kristalid'dʒare] vi (2), ~**rsi** vr to crystallize; (fig) to become fossilized.

cris'tallo sm crystal.

cristia'nesimo sm Christianity.

cristianità sf Christianity; (i cristiani) Christendom.

cristi'ano, a ag, sm/f Christian.

'**Cristo** sm Christ.

cri'terio sm criterion; (buon senso) (common) sense.

'**critica, che** sf vedi **critico**.

criti'care vt to criticize.

'**critico, a, ci, che** ag critical // sm critic // sf criticism; **la** ~**a** (attività) criticism; (persone) the critics pl.

cri'vello sm riddle.

'**croce** ['krotʃe] sf cross; **in** ~ (di traverso) crosswise; (fig) on tenterhooks; **la C**~ **Rossa** the Red Cross.

croce'figgere [krotʃe'fiddʒere] etc = **crocifiggere** etc.

croce'via [krotʃe'via] sm inv crossroads sg.

croci'ata [kro'tʃata] sf crusade.

cro'cicchio [kro'tʃikkjo] sm crossroads sg.

croci'era [kro'tʃera] sf (viaggio) cruise; (ARCHIT) transept.

croci'figgere [krotʃi'fiddʒere] vt to crucify; **crocifissi'one** sf crucifixion; **croci'fisso, a** pp di **crocifiggere**.

crogi'olo, crogiu'olo [kro'dʒɔlo] sm crucible; (fig) melting pot.

crol'lare vi (2) to collapse; '**crollo** sm collapse; (di prezzi) slump, sudden fall.

cro'mato, a ag chromium-plated.

'**cromo** sm chrome, chromium.

cromo'soma, i sm chromosome.

'**cronaca, che** ['krɔnaka] sf chronicle; (STAMPA) news sg; (: rubrica) column; (TV, RADIO) commentary; **fatto** o **episodio di** ~ news item; ~ **nera** crime news sg; crime column.

'**cronico, a, ci, che** ag chronic.

cro'nista, i sm (STAMPA) reporter, columnist.

cronolo'gia [kronolo'dʒia] sf chronology.

'**crosta** sf crust.

cros'tacei [kros'tatʃei] smpl shellfish.

'**cruccio** ['kruttʃo] sm worry, torment.

cruci'verba sm inv crossword (puzzle).

cru'dele ag cruel; **crudeltà** sf cruelty.

'**crudo, a** ag (non cotto) raw; (aspro) harsh, severe.

cru'miro sm (peg) blackleg, scab.

'**crusca** sf bran.

crus'cotto sm (AUT) dashboard.

'**Cuba** sf Cuba.

'**cubico, a, ci, che** ag cubic.

'**cubo, a** ag cubic // sm cube; **elevare al** ~ (MAT) to cube.

cuc'cagna [kuk'kaɲɲa] sf: **paese della** ~ land of plenty; **albero della** ~ greasy pole (fig).

cuc'cetta [kut'tʃetta] sf (FERR) couchette; (NAUT) berth.

cucchi'ata [kukja'jata] sf spoonful.

cucchia'ino [kukkja'ino] sm teaspoon; coffee spoon.

cucchi'aio [kuk'kjajo] sm spoon.

'**cuccia, ce** ['kuttʃa] sf dog's bed; **a** ~! down!

'**cucciolo** ['kuttʃolo] sm puppy.

cu'cina [ku'tʃina] sf (locale) kitchen; (arte culinaria) cooking, cookery; (le vivande) food, cooking; (apparecchio) cooker; **fare da** ~ to cook; ~ **componibile** fitted kitchen; **cuci'nare** vt to cook.

cu'cire [ku'tʃire] vt to sew, stitch; **cuci-'tura** sf sewing, stitching; (costura) seam.

cucù sm inv, **cu'culo** sm cuckoo.

'**cuffia** sf bonnet, cap; (da bagno) (bathing) cap; (per ascoltare) headphones pl, headset.

cu'gino, a [ku'dʒino] sm/f cousin.

'**cui** pronome (nei complementi indiretti): **la persona a** ~ **accennavo** the person you were referring to o to whom you referred; **il libro di** ~ **parlavo** the book I was talking about o about which I was talking; **il quartiere in** ~ **abito** the district where I live; (inserito tra l'articolo e il sostantivo) whose; **il** ~ **nome** whose name; **la** ~ **madre** whose mother.

culi'naria sf cookery.

'**culla** sf (anche fig) cradle.

cul'lare vt to rock.

culmi'nare vi to culminate.

'**culmine** sm top, summit.

'**culo** sm (fam!) arse (!), bum.

'**culto** sm (religione) religion; (adorazione) worship, adoration; (venerazione: anche fig) cult.

cul'tura sf culture; education, learning; **cultu'rale** ag cultural.

cumu'lare vt to accumulate, amass; **cumula'tivo, a** ag cumulative; (prezzo) inclusive; (biglietto) group cpd.

'**cumulo** sm (mucchio) pile, heap; (METEOR) cumulus.

'**cuneo** sm wedge.

cu'ocere ['kwɔtʃere] vt (alimenti) to cook; (mattoni etc) to fire // vi (2) to cook; **cu'oco, a, chi, che** sm/f cook; **primo cuoco** chef.

cu'oio sm leather; ~ **capelluto** scalp.

cu'ore sm heart; ~**i** smpl (CARTE) hearts; **avere buon** ~ to be kind-hearted; **di (buon)** ~ willingly.

cupi'digia [kupi'didʒa] sf greed, covetousness.

'**cupo, a** ag dark; (fig) gloomy, dismal.

'**cupola** sf dome; cupola.

'**cura** sf care; (MED: trattamento) (course of) treatment; **aver** ~ **di** (occuparsi di) to look after; **a** ~ **di** (libro) edited by.

cu'rare vt (malato, malattia) to treat; (: guarire) to cure; (aver cura di) to take care of; (*testo*) to edit; ~**rsi** *vr* to take care of o.s.; (*MED*) to follow a course of treatment; ~**rsi di** to pay attention to.

cu'rato *sm* parish priest; (*protestante*) vicar.

cura'tore, 'trice *sm/f* (*DIR*) trustee; (*di antologia etc*) editor.

'curia *sf* (*REL*): **la ~ romana** the Roman curia.

curiosità *sf inv* curiosity; (*cosa rara*) curio, curiosity.

curi'oso, a *ag* (*che vuol sapere*) curious, inquiring; (*ficcanaso*) curious, inquisitive; (*bizzarro*) strange, curious.

'curva *sf* curve; (*stradale*) bend, curve.

cur'vare *vt* to bend // *vi* (*veicolo*) to take a bend; (*strada*) to bend, curve; ~**rsi** *vr* to bend; (*legno*) to warp.

'curvo, a *ag* curved; (*piegato*) bent.

cusci'netto [kuʃʃi'netto] *sm* pad; (*TECN*) bearing // *ag inv*: **stato ~** buffer state; **~ a sfere** ball bearing.

cu'scino [kuʃ'ʃino] *sm* cushion; (*guanciale*) pillow.

'cuspide *sf* (*ARCHIT*) spire.

cus'tode *sm/f* keeper, custodian.

cus'todia *sf* care; (*DIR*) custody; (*astuccio*) case, holder.

custo'dire *vt* (*conservare*) to keep; (*assistere*) to look after, take care of; (*fare la guardia*) to guard.

'cute *sf* (*ANAT*) skin.

cu'ticola *sf* cuticle.

C.V. (*abbr di* **cavallo vapore**) h.p.

D

da *prep* (*da + il* = **dal**, *da + lo* = **dallo**, *da + l'* = **dall'**, *da + la* = **dalla**, *da + i* = **dai**, *da + gli* = **dagli**, *da + le* = **dalle**) (*agente*) by; (*provenienza*) from; (*causale*) with; (*moto a luogo: riferito a persone*): **vado ~ Pietro/dal giornalaio** I'm going to Pietro's (house)/to the newsagent's; (*stato in luogo: riferito a persone*): **sono ~ Pietro** I'm at Pietro's (house); (*moto per luogo*) through; (*fuori da*) out of, from; (*tempo*): **vivo qui ~ un anno** I have been living here for a year; **è dalle 3 che ti aspetto** I've been waiting for you since 3 (o'clock); **comportarsi ~ bambino** to behave like a child; **~ bambino piangevo molto** I cried a lot as a *o* when I was a child; **una ragazza dai capelli biondi** a girl with blonde hair; **un vestito ~ 100,000 lire** a 100,000 lire dress; **~ ... a** from ... to; **~ oggi in poi** from today onwards; **l'ho fatto ~ me** I did it myself; **macchina ~ corsa** racing car.

dab'bene *ag* honest, decent.

dac'capo, da 'capo *av* (*di nuovo*) (once) again; (*dal principio*) all over again, from the beginning.

dacché [dak'ke] *cong* since.

'dado *sm* (*da gioco*) dice *o* die (*pl* **dice**); (*CUC*) stock cube; **~i** *smpl* (*game of*) dice.

daf'fare, da 'fare *sm* work, toil.

'dagli ['daʎʎi], **'dai** *prep + det vedi* **da**.

'daino *sm* (*fallow*) deer *inv*; (*pelle*) buckskin.

dal, dall', 'dalla, 'dalle, 'dallo *prep + det vedi* **da**.

'dama *sf* lady; (*nei balli*) partner; (*gioco*) draughts *sg*.

damigi'ana [dami'dʒana] *sf* demijohn.

da'naro *sm* = **denaro**.

da'nese *ag* Danish // *sm/f* Dane // *sm* (*LING*) Danish.

Dani'marca *sf*: **la ~** Denmark.

dan'nare *vt* (*REL*) to damn; **far ~ qd** to drive sb mad; **dannazi'one** *sf* damnation.

danneggi'are [danned'dʒare] *vt* to damage; (*rovinare*) to spoil; (*nuocere*) to harm.

'danno *sm* damage; (*a persona*) harm, injury; **~i** *smpl* (*DIR*) damages; **dan'noso, a** *ag*: **dannoso (a)** harmful (to), bad (for).

Da'nubio *sm*: **il ~** the Danube.

'danza ['dantsa] *sf*: **la ~** dancing; **una ~** a dance.

dan'zare [dan'tsare] *vt, vi* to dance.

dapper'tutto *av* everywhere.

dap'poco *ag inv* inept, worthless.

dap'presso *av* (*vicino*) near, close at hand; (*da vicino*) closely.

dap'prima *av* at first.

'dardo *sm* dart.

'dare *sm* (*COMM*) debit // *vt* to give; (*produrre: frutti, suono*) to produce // *vi* (*guardare*): **~ su** to look (out) onto; **~rsi** *vr*: **~rsi a** to dedicate o.s. to; **~rsi al commercio** to go into business; **~rsi al bere** to take to drink; **~rsi a correre** to start to run; **~ per certo qc** to consider sth certain; **~ per morto qd** to give sb up for dead.

'darsena *sf* dock; dockyard.

'data *sf* date.

da'tare *vt* to date // *vi*: **~ da** to date from.

'dato, a *ag* given // *sm* datum; **~i** *smpl* data *pl*; **~ che** given that.

'dattero *sm* date.

dattilogra'fare *vt* to type; **dattilogra'fia** *sf* typing; **datti'lografo, a** *sm/f* typist.

da'vanti *av* in front; (*dirimpetto*) opposite // *ag inv* front // *sm* front; **~ a** prep in front of; facing, opposite; (*in presenza di*) before, in front of.

davan'zale [davan'tsale] *sm* windowsill.

da'vanzo, d'a'vanzo [da'vantso] *av* more than enough.

dav'vero *av* really, indeed.

'dazio ['dattsjo] *sm* (*somma*) duty; (*luogo*) customs *pl*.

d. C. (*abbr di* **dopo Cristo**) A.D.

'dea *sf* goddess.

'debito, a *ag* due, proper // *sm* debt; (*COMM: dare*) debit; **a tempo ~** at the right time; **debi'tore, 'trice** *sm/f* debtor.

'debole *ag* weak, feeble; (*suono*) faint; (*luce*) dim; **debo'lezza** *sf* weakness.

debut'tare *vi* to make one's début; **de-'butto** *sm* début.

deca'dente *ag* decadent, in decline; **deca-**

'denza sf decline; (DIR) loss, forfeiture.

decaffei'nare vt to decaffeinate.

de'cano sm (REL) dean.

decapi'tare vt to decapitate, behead.

decappot'tabile ag, sf convertible.

dece'duto, a [detʃe'duto] ag deceased.

de'cenne [de'tʃɛnne] ag ten-year-old; (predicativo) ten years old; **de'cennio** sm decade.

de'cente [de'tʃɛnte] ag decent, respectable, proper; (accettabile) satisfactory, decent; **de'cenza** sf decency, propriety.

de'cesso [de'tʃɛsso] sm death; **atto di ~** death certificate.

de'cidere [de'tʃidere] vt: **~ qc** to decide on sth; (questione, lite) to settle sth; **~ di fare/che** to decide to do/that; **~ di qc** (sog: cosa) to determine sth; **~rsi (a fare)** to decide (to do), make up one's mind (to do).

deci'frare [detʃi'frare] vt to decode; (fig) to decipher, make out.

deci'male [detʃi'male] ag decimal.

deci'mare [detʃi'mare] vt to decimate.

'decimo, a ['dɛtʃimo] num tenth.

de'cina [de'tʃina] sf ten; (circa dieci): **una ~ (di)** about ten.

decisi'one [detʃi'zjone] sf decision; **prendere una ~** to make a decision.

de'ciso, a [de'tʃizo] pp di **decidere**.

declas'sare vt to downgrade; to lower in status.

decli'nare vi to go down; (fig: diminuire) to decline; (tramontare) to set, go down // vt to decline; **declinazi'one** sf (LING) declension; **de'clino** sm decline.

de'clivio sm (downward) slope.

decol'lare vi (AER) to take off; **de'collo** sm take-off.

decolo'rare vt to bleach.

decom'porre vt, **decomporsi** vr to decompose; **decomposizi'one** sf decomposition; **decom'posto, a** pp di **decomporre**.

deconge'lare [dekondʒe'lare] vt to defrost.

deco'rare vt to decorate; **decora'tore, 'trice** sm/f (interior) decorator; **decorazi'one** sf decoration.

de'coro sm decorum; **deco'roso, a** ag decorous, dignified.

de'correre vi (2) to pass, elapse; (avere effetto) to run, have effect; **de'corso, a** pp di **decorrere** // sm passing; (evoluzione: anche MED) course.

de'crepito, a ag decrepit.

de'crescere [de'kreʃere] vi (2) (diminuire) to decrease, diminish; (acque) to subside, go down; (prezzi) to go down; **decresci'uto, a** pp di **decrescere**.

de'creto sm decree.

'dedalo sm maze, labyrinth.

'dedica, che sf dedication.

dedi'care vt to dedicate.

'dedito, a ag: **~ a** (studio etc) dedicated o devoted to; (vizio) addicted to.

de'dotto, a pp di **dedurre**.

de'durre vt (concludere) to deduce; (defalcare) to deduct; **deduzi'one** sf deduction.

defal'care vt to deduct.

defe'rente ag respectful, deferential.

defe'rire vt (DIR) to refer.

defezi'one [defet'tsjone] sf defection, desertion.

defici'ente [defi'tʃɛnte] ag (mancante) insufficient; (minorato) mentally deficient; (stupido) idiotic // sm/f mental defective; idiot; **defici'enza** sf shortage; (lacuna) gap; (MED) mental deficiency.

'deficit ['dɛfitʃit] sm inv (ECON) deficit.

defi'nire vt to define; (risolvere) to settle; **defini'tivo, a** ag definitive, final; **definizi'one** sf definition; settlement.

deflazi'one [deflat'tsjone] sf (ECON) deflation.

de'flusso sm (della marea) ebb.

defor'mare vt (alterare) to put out of shape; (corpo) to deform; (pensiero, fatto) to distort; **~rsi** vr to lose its shape.

de'forme ag deformed; disfigured; **deformità** sf inv deformity.

defrau'dare vt: **~ qd di qc** to defraud sb of sth, cheat sb out of sth.

de'funto, a ag late cpd // sm/f deceased.

degene'rare [dedʒene'rare] vi to degenerate; **de'genere** ag degenerate.

de'gente [de'dʒɛnte] ag bedridden.

'degli ['deʎʎi] prep + det vedi **di**.

de'gnarsi [deɲ'ɲarsi] vr: **~ di fare** to deign o condescend to do.

'degno, a [deɲ'ɲo] ag dignified; **~ di** worthy of; **~ di lode** praiseworthy.

degra'dare vt (MIL) to demote; (privare della dignità) to degrade; **~rsi** vr to demean o.s.

degus'tare vt to sample, taste; **degusta-zi'one** sf sampling, tasting.

'dei, del prep + det vedi **di**.

dela'tore, 'trice sm/f police informer.

'delega, ghe sf (procura) proxy.

dele'gare vt to delegate; **dele'gato** sm delegate; **delegazi'one** sf delegation.

del'fino sm dolphin.

delibe'rare vt, vi to deliberate.

delica'tezza [delika'tettsa] sf (anche CUC) delicacy; frailty; thoughtfulness; tactfulness.

deli'cato, a ag delicate; (salute) delicate, frail; (fig: gentile) thoughtful, considerate; (: pieno di tatto) tactful.

delimi'tare vt to circumscribe, define.

deline'are vt to outline; **~rsi** vr to be outlined; (fig) to emerge.

delin'quente sm/f criminal, delinquent; **delin'quenza** sf criminality, delinquency; **delinquenza minorile** juvenile delinquency.

deli'rare vi to be delirious, rave; (fig) to rave.

de'lirio sm delirium; (ragionamento insensato) raving; (fig) frenzy.

de'litto sm crime; **delittu'oso, a** ag criminal.

de'lizia [de'littsja] sf delight; **delizi'oso, a** ag delightful; (cibi) delicious.

dell', 'della, 'delle, 'dello prep + det vedi **di**.

'delta sm inv delta.

delta'piano sm hang-glider; **volo col ~** hang gliding.

de'ludere vt to disappoint; **delusi'one** sf disappointment; **de'luso, a** pp di deludere.

dema'gogo, ghi sm demagogue.

de'manio sm state property.

de'mente ag (MED) demented, mentally deranged; **de'menza** sf dementia; (stupidità) foolishness.

demo'cratico, a, ci, che ag democratic.

democra'zia [demokrat'tsia] sf democracy.

democristi'ano, a ag, sm/f Christian Democrat.

demo'lire vt to demolish; **demolizi'one** sf demolition.

'demone sm demon.

de'monio sm demon, devil; **il D~** the Devil.

demoraliz'zare [demoralid'dzare] vt to demoralize.

de'naro sm money.

deni'grare vt to denigrate, run down.

denomi'nare vt to name; **~rsi** vr to be named o called; **denomina'tore** sm (MAT) denominator; **denominazi'one** sf name; denomination.

deno'tare vt to denote, indicate.

densità sf inv density.

'denso, a ag thick, dense.

den'tale ag dental.

den'tario, a ag dental.

'dente sm tooth; (di forchetta) prong; (GEO: cima) jagged peak; **al ~** (CUC pasta) cooked so as to be firm when eaten; **~i del giudizio** wisdom teeth; **denti'era** sf (set of) false teeth pl.

denti'fricio [denti'fritʃo] sm toothpaste.

den'tista, i, e sm/f dentist.

'dentro av in, inside; (fig: nell'intimo) inwardly, in one's mind // prep in, inside; (entro) within; **~ a, ~ in** in, inside; within; **qui/là ~** in here/there; **~ di sé** (pensare, brontolare) to oneself; **di ~** from inside.

de'nuncia, ce o **cie** [de'nuntʃa], **de-'nunzia** [de'nuntsja] sf denunciation; accusation; declaration; **~ del reddito** (income) tax return.

denunci'are [denun'tʃare], **denunzi'are** [denun'tsjare] vt to denounce; (accusare) to accuse; (dichiarare) to declare.

denutrizi'one [denutrit'tsjone] sf malnutrition.

deodo'rante sm deodorant.

depe'rire vi to waste away.

depila'torio, a ag depilatory.

deplo'rare vt to deplore; to lament; **deplo'revole** ag deplorable.

de'porre vt (depositare) to put down; (rimuovere: da una carica) to remove; (: re) to depose; (DIR) to testify.

depor'tare vt to deport.

deposi'tare vt (GEO, ECON) to deposit; (lasciare) to leave; (merci) to store.

de'posito sm deposit; (luogo) warehouse; depot; (: MIL) depot; **~ bagagli** left-luggage office.

deposizi'one [depozit'tsjone] sf deposition; (da una carica) removal.

de'posto, a pp di deporre.

depra'vare vt to corrupt, deprave.

depre'care vt to deprecate, disapprove of.

depre'dare vt to rob, plunder.

depressi'one sf depression.

de'presso, a pp di deprimere // ag depressed.

deprez'zare [depret'tsare] vt (ECON) to depreciate.

de'primere vt to depress.

depu'rare vt to purify.

depu'tare vt to delegate; **~ qd a** to send sb (as a representative) to; **depu'tato, a** o **'essa** sm/f (POL) deputy, ≈ Member of Parliament; **deputazi'one** sf deputation; (POL) position of deputy, ≈ parliamentary seat.

deraglia'mento [deraʎʎa'mento] sm derailment.

deragli'are [deraʎ'ʎare] vi to be derailed; **far ~** to derail.

dere'litto, a ag derelict.

dere'tano sm bottom, buttocks pl.

de'ridere vt to mock, deride; **derisi'one** sf derision, mockery; **de'riso, a** pp di deridere.

de'riva sf (NAUT, AER) drift; **andare alla ~** (anche fig) to drift.

deri'vare vi (2): **~ da** to derive from // vt to derive; (corso d'acqua) to divert; **derivazi'one** sf derivation; diversion.

dero'gare vi: **~ a** to go against, depart from; (legge) to repeal in part.

der'rate sfpl commodities; **~ alimentari** foodstuffs.

deru'bare vt to rob.

des'critto, a pp di descrivere.

des'crivere vt to describe; **descrizi'one** sf description.

de'serto, a ag deserted // sm (GEO) desert; **isola ~a** desert island.

deside'rare vt to want, wish for; (sessualmente) to desire; **~ fare/che qd faccia** to want o wish to do/sb to do; **desidera fare una passeggiata?** would you like to go for a walk?

desi'derio sm wish; (forte, carnale) desire.

deside'roso, a ag: **~ di** longing o eager for.

desi'gnare [desin'nare] vt to designate, appoint; (data) to fix.

desi'nare vi to dine, have dinner // sm dinner.

de'sistere vi: **~ da** to give up, desist from; **desis'tito, a** pp di desistere.

deso'lare vt (affliggere) to distress, grieve.

deso'lato, a ag (paesaggio) desolate; (persona: spiacente) sorry; **desolazi'one** sf desolation.

'despota, i sm despot.

des'tare vt to wake (up); (fig) to awaken, arouse; **~rsi** vr to wake (up).

desti'nare vt to destine; (assegnare) to appoint, assign; (indirizzare) to address; **~ qc a qd** to intend to give sth to sb, intend sb to have sth.

destinazi'one [destinat'tsjone] sf destination; (uso) purpose.

des'tino sm destiny, fate.

destitu'ire vt to dismiss, remove.

'desto, a ag (wide) awake.

'destra sf vedi **destro**.

destreggi'arsi [destred'dʒarsi] vr to manoeuvre.

des'trezza [des'trettsa] sf skill, dexterity.

'destro, a ag right, right-hand; (abile) skilful, adroit // sf (mano) right hand; (parte) right (side); (POL): **la ~ the** Right; **a ~a** on the right.

dete'nere vt (incarico, primato) to hold; (un bene) to be in possession of; (in prigione) to detain, hold; **dete'nuto, a** sm/f prisoner; **detenzi'one** sf holding; possession; detention.

deter'gente [deter'dʒente] sm detergent.

deterio'rare vt to damage; **~rsi** vr to deteriorate.

determi'nare vt to determine; **~rsi a fare qc** to make up one's mind to do sth; **determinazi'one** sf determination; (decisione) decision.

deter'sivo sm detergent.

detes'tare vt to detest, hate.

deto'nare vi to detonate.

de'trarre vt: **~ (da)** to deduct (from), take away (from); **de'tratto, a** pp di **detrarre**.

detri'mento sm detriment, harm; **a ~ di** to the detriment of.

de'trito sm (GEO) detritus.

dettagli'ante [dettaʎ'ʎante] sm/f (COMM) retailer.

dettagli'are [dettaʎ'ʎare] vt to detail, give full details of.

det'taglio [det'taʎʎo] sm detail; (COMM): **il ~ retail; al ~** (COMM) retail; separately.

det'tare vt to dictate; **det'tato** sm dictation; **detta'tura** sf dictation.

'detto, a pp di **dire** // ag (soprannominato) called, known as; (già nominato) above-mentioned // sm saying; **~ fatto** no sooner said than done.

detur'pare vt to disfigure; (moralmente) to sully.

devas'tare vt to devastate; (fig) to ravage; **devastazi'one** sf devastation; ravages pl.

devi'are vi to swerve, veer off // vt to divert; **deviazi'one** sf (anche AUT) diversion.

devo'luto, a pp di **devolvere**.

devoluzi'one [devolut'tsjone] sf (DIR) devolution, transfer.

de'volvere vt (DIR) to transfer, devolve.

de'voto, a ag (REL) devout, pious; (affezionato) devoted.

devozi'one [devot'tsjone] sf devoutness; (anche REL) devotion.

di prep (di + il = **del**, di + lo = **dello**, di + l' = **dell'**, di + la = **della**, di + i = **dei**, di + gli = **degli**, di + le = **delle**) of; (causa) with; for; of; (mezzo) with; (provenienza) from // det: **del pane** (some) bread; **dei libri** (some) books; **la sorella ~ mio padre** my father's sister; **un sacchetto ~ plastica/orologio d'oro** a plastic bag/gold watch; **tremare ~ paura** to tremble with fear; **un bambino ~ tre anni** a child of three, a three-year-old child; **~ primavera/giugno** in spring/June; **~ mattina/sera** in the morning/evening; **~ notte** by night; at night; in the night; **~ domenica** on Sundays; **~ ... in** from ... to; vedi **più**, **meno** etc.

dia'bete sm diabetes sg.

dia'bolico, a, ci, che ag diabolical.

di'acono sm (REL) deacon.

dia'dema, i sm diadem; (di donna) tiara.

dia'framma, i sm (divisione) screen; (ANAT, FOT) diaphragm.

di'agnosi [di'aɲɲozi] sf diagnosis sg; **diagnosti'care** vt to diagnose.

diago'nale ag, sf diagonal.

dia'gramma, i sm diagram.

dia'letto sm dialect.

di'alogo, ghi sm dialogue.

dia'mante sm diamond.

di'ametro sm diameter.

di'amine escl: **che ~ ... ?** what on earth ... ?

diaposi'tiva sf transparency, slide.

di'ario sm diary.

diar'rea sf diarrhoea.

di'avolo sm devil.

di'battere vt to debate, discuss; **~rsi** vr to struggle; **di'battito** sm debate, discussion.

di'cembre [di'tʃembre] sm December.

dicas'tero sm ministry.

dichia'rare [dikja'rare] vt to declare; **dichiarazi'one** sf declaration.

dician'nove [ditʃan'nɔve] num nineteen.

dicias'sette [ditʃas'sɛtte] num seventeen.

dici'otto [di'tʃɔtto] num eighteen.

dici'tura [ditʃi'tura] sf words pl, wording.

di'dattico, a, ci, che ag didactic.

di'eci ['djɛtʃi] num ten; **die'cina** sf = **decina**.

'diesel ['dizəl] sm inv diesel engine.

di'eta sf diet; **essere a ~** to be on a diet.

di'etro av behind // prep behind; (tempo: dopo) after // sm back, rear; **le zampe di ~** the back legs, the hind legs; **~ richiesta** on demand; (scritta) on application.

di'fendere vt to defend; **difen'sivo, a** ag defensive // sf: **stare sulla difensiva**

(*anche fig*) to be on the defensive; **difen-'sore, a** *sm/f* defender; **avvocato difensore** counsel for the defence; **di'feso, a** *pp di* **difendere** // *sf* defence.

difet'tare *vi* to be defective; ~ **di** to be lacking in, lack; **difet'tivo, a** *ag* defective.

di'fetto *sm* (*mancanza*): ~ **di** lack of; shortage of; (*di fabbricazione*) fault, flaw, defect; (*morale*) fault, failing, defect; (*fisico*) defect; **far** ~ to be lacking; **in** ~ at fault; in the wrong; **difet'toso, a** *ag* defective, faulty.

diffa'mare *vt* to defame, slander; to libel.

diffe'rente *ag* different.

diffe'renza [diffe'rɛntsa] *sf* difference; **a** ~ **di** unlike.

differenzi'ale [differen'tsjale] *ag, sm* differential.

differenzi'are [differen'tsjare] *vt* to differentiate; ~**rsi da** to differentiate o.s. from; to differ from.

diffe'rire *vt* to postpone, defer // *vi* to be different.

dif'ficile [dif'fitʃile] *ag* difficult; (*persona*) hard to please, difficult (to please); (*poco probabile*): **è** ~ **che sia libero** it is unlikely that he'll be free // *sm* difficult part, difficulty; **diffi'coltà** *sf inv* difficulty.

dif'fida *sf* (*DIR*) warning, notice.

diffi'dare *vi*: ~ **di** to be suspicious *o* distrustful of // *vt* (*DIR*) to warn; **diffi-'dente** *ag* suspicious, distrustful; **diffi-'denza** *sf* suspicion, distrust.

dif'fondere *vt* (*calore*) to diffuse; (*notizie*) to spread, circulate; ~**rsi** *vr* to spread; **diffusi'one** *sf* diffusion; spread; (*anche di giornale*) circulation; (*FISICA*) scattering; **dif'fuso, a** *pp di* **diffondere**.

diffi'lato *av* (*direttamente*) straight, directly; (*subito*) straight away.

difte'rite *sf* (*MED*) diphtheria.

'diga, ghe *sf* dam; (*argine litoraneo*) dyke.

dige'rire [didʒe'rire] *vt* to digest; **diges-ti'one** *sf* digestion; **diges'tivo, a** *ag* digestive // *sm* (*after-dinner*) liqueur.

digi'tale [didʒi'tale] *ag* digital; (*delle dita*) finger *cpd*, digital // *sf* (*BOT*) foxglove.

digiu'nare [didʒu'nare] *vi* to starve o.s.; (*REL*) to fast; **digi'uno, a** *ag*: **essere digiuno** not to have eaten // *sm* fast; **a digiuno** on an empty stomach.

dignità [diɲɲi'ta] *sf inv* dignity; **digni-'tario** *sm* dignitary; **digni'toso, a** *ag* dignified.

digressi'one *sf* digression.

digri'gnare [digriɲ'ɲare] *vt*: ~ **i denti** to grind one's teeth.

dila'gare *vi* to flood; (*fig*) to spread.

dilapi'dare *vt* to squander, waste.

dila'tare *vt* to dilate; (*gas*) to cause to expand; (*passaggio, cavità*) to open (up); ~**rsi** *vr* to dilate; (*FISICA*) to expand.

dilazio'nare [dilattsjo'nare] *vt* to delay, defer; **dilazi'one** *sf* delay; (*COMM: di pagamento etc*) extension; (*rinvio*) postponement.

dileggi'are [diled'dʒare] *vt* to mock, deride.

dilegu'are *vi*, ~**rsi** *vr* to vanish, disappear.

di'lemma, i *sm* dilemma.

dilet'tante *sm/f* dilettante; (*anche SPORT*) amateur.

dilet'tare *vt* to give pleasure to, delight; ~**rsi** *vr*: ~**rsi di** to take pleasure in, enjoy.

di'letto, a *ag* dear, beloved // *sm* pleasure, delight.

dili'gente [dili'dʒɛnte] *ag* (*scrupoloso*) diligent; (*accurato*) careful, accurate; **dili-'genza** *sf* diligence; care; (*carrozza*) stagecoach.

dilu'ire *vt* to dilute.

dilun'garsi *vr* (*fig*): ~ **su** to talk at length on *o* about.

dilu'viare *vb impers* to pour (down).

di'luvio *sm* downpour; (*inondazione, fig*) flood.

dima'grire *vi* (*2*) to get thinner, lose weight.

dime'nare *vt* to wave, shake; ~**rsi** *vr* to toss and turn; (*fig*) to struggle; ~ **la coda** (*sog: cane*) to wag its tail.

dimensi'one *sf* dimension; (*grandezza*) size.

dimenti'canza [dimenti'kantsa] *sf* forgetfulness; (*errore*) oversight; slip; **per** ~ inadvertently.

dimenti'care *vt* to forget; ~**rsi di qc** to forget sth.

di'messo, a *pp di* **dimettere** // *ag* (*voce*) subdued; (*uomo, abito*) modest, humble.

dimesti'chezza [dimesti'kettsa] *sf* familiarity.

di'mettere *vt*: ~ **qd da** to dismiss sb from; (*dall'ospedale*) to discharge sb from; ~**rsi (da)** to resign (from).

dimez'zare [dimed'dzare] *vt* to halve.

diminu'ire *vt* to reduce, diminish // *vi* (*2*) to decrease, diminish, go down; **diminu-zi'one** *sf* decreasing, diminishing.

dimissi'oni *sfpl* resignation *sg*; **dare** *o* **presentare le** ~ to resign, hand in one's resignation.

di'mora *sf* residence.

dimo'rare *vi* to reside.

dimos'trare *vt* to demonstrate, show; (*provare*) to prove, demonstrate; ~**rsi** *vr*: ~**rsi molto abile** to show o.s. *o* prove to be very clever; **dimostra'tivo, a** *ag* (*anche LING*) demonstrative; **dimostra-zi'one** *sf* demonstration; proof.

di'namico, a, ci, che *ag* dynamic // *sf* dynamics *sg*.

dina'mismo *sm* dynamism.

dina'mite *sf* dynamite.

'dinamo *sf inv* dynamo.

di'nanzi [di'nantsi]: ~ **a** *prep* in front of.

dinas'tia *sf* dynasty.

dini'ego, ghi *sm* refusal; denial.

din'torno *av* round, (round) about; ~**i** *smpl* outskirts; **nei** ~**i di** in the vicinity *o* neighbourhood of.

'dio, pl 'dei *sm* god; **D**~ God; **gli dei** the gods.

di'ocesi [di'ɔtʃezi] *sf* diocese.

dipa'nare *vt* (*lana*) to wind into a ball; (*fig*) to disentangle, sort out.

diparti'mento *sm* department.

dipen'dente *ag* dependent // *sm/f* employee; **dipen'denza** *sf* dependence; **essere alle dipendenze di qd** to be employed by sb *o* in sb's employ.

di'pendere *vi* (*2*): ~ **da** to depend on; (*finanziariamente*) to be dependent on; (*derivare*) to come from, be due to; **di'peso**, **a** *pp di* **dipendere**.

di'pingere [di'pindʒere] *vt* to paint; ~**rsi** *vr* to make up, put on makeup; **di'pinto**, **a** *pp di* **dipingere** // *sm* painting.

di'ploma, **i** *sm* diploma.

diplo'matico, **a**, **ci**, **che** *ag* diplomatic // *sm* diplomat.

diploma'zia [diplomat'tsia] *sf* diplomacy.

di'porto *sm*: **imbarcazione** *f* **da** ~ pleasure craft.

dira'dare *vt* to thin (out); (*visite*) to reduce, make less frequent; ~**rsi** *vr* to disperse; (*nebbia*) to clear (up).

dira'mare *vt* to issue, send out // *vi*, ~**rsi** *vr* to branch.

'dire *vt* to say; (*segreto, fatto*) to tell; ~ **qc a qd** to tell sb sth; ~ **a qd di fare qc** to tell sb to do sth; ~ **di sì/no** to say yes/no; **si dice che ...** they say that ...; **si direbbe che ...** it looks (*o* sounds) as though ... ; **dica, signora?** (*in un negozio*) yes, Madam, can I help you?

diret'tissimo *sm* (*FERR*) fast (through) train.

di'retto, **a** *pp di* **dirigere** // *ag* direct // *sm* (*FERR*) through train.

diret'tore, **'trice** *sm/f* (*d'impresa*) director; manager/ess; (*di scuola elementare*) headmaster/mistress; ~ **d'orchestra** conductor.

direzi'one [diret'tsjone] *sf* board of directors; management; (*senso di movimento*) direction; **in** ~ **di** in the direction of, towards.

diri'gente [diri'dʒɛnte] *sm/f* executive; (*POL*) leader.

diri'gere [di'ridʒere] *vt* to direct; (*impresa*) to run, manage; (*MUS*) to conduct; ~**rsi** *vr*: ~**rsi verso** *o* **a** to make *o* head for.

diri'gibile [diri'dʒibile] *sm* dirigible.

dirim'petto *av* opposite; ~ **a** *prep* opposite, facing.

di'ritto, **a** *ag* straight; (*onesto*) straight, upright; (*destro*) right // *av* straight, directly; **andare** ~ to go straight on // *sm* right side; (*prerogativa*) right; (*leggi, scienza*): **il** ~ **law**; ~**i** *smpl* (*tasse*) duty *sg*; **stare** ~ to stand upright.

dirit'tura *sf* (*SPORT*) straight; (*fig*) rectitude.

diroc'cato, **a** *ag* tumbledown, in ruins.

dirot'tare *vt* (*nave, aereo*) to change the course of; (*aereo: sotto minaccia*) to hijack; (*traffico*) to divert // *vi* (*nave, aereo*) to change course; **dirotta'tore**, **'trice** *sm/f* hijacker.

di'rotto, **a** *ag* (*pioggia*) torrential; (*pianto*) unrestrained; **piovere a** ~ to pour, rain cats and dogs; **piangere a** ~ to cry one's heart out.

di'rupo *sm* crag, precipice.

disabi'tato, **a** *ag* uninhabited.

disabitu'arsi *vr*: ~ **a** to get out of the habit of.

disac'cordo *sm* disagreement.

disadat'tato, **a** *ag* (*PSIC*) maladjusted.

disa'datto, **a** *ag*: ~ (**a** *o* **per**) unsuited (to).

disa'dorno, **a** *ag* plain, unadorned.

disagi'ato, **a** [diza'dʒato] *ag* poor, needy; (*vita*) hard.

di'sagio [di'zadʒo] *sm* discomfort; (*disturbo*) inconvenience; (*fig: imbarazzo*) embarrassment; ~**i** *smpl* hardship *sg*, poverty *sg*; **essere a** ~ to be ill at ease.

disappro'vare *vt* to disapprove of; **disapprovazi'one** *sf* disapproval.

disap'punto *sm* disappointment.

disar'mare *vt*, *vi* to disarm; **di'sarmo** *sm* (*MIL*) disarmament.

di'sastro *sm* disaster; **disas'troso**, **a** *ag* disastrous.

disat'tento, **a** *ag* inattentive.

disa'vanzo [diza'vantso] *sm* (*ECON*) deficit.

disavve'duto, **a** *ag* careless, thoughtless.

disavven'tura *sf* misadventure, mishap.

dis'brigo, **ghi** *sm* (*prompt*) clearing up *o* settlement.

dis'capito *sm* disadvantage, detriment; **a** ~ **di qd** to sb's cost.

discen'dente [diʃʃen'dɛnte] *ag* descending // *sm/f* descendant.

di'scendere [diʃ'ʃendere] *vt* to go (*o* come) down // *vi* (*2*) to go (*o* come) down; (*strada*) to go down; (*smontare*) to get off; ~ **da** (*famiglia*) to be descended from; ~ **dalla macchina/dal treno** to get out of the car/out of *o* off the train; ~ **da cavallo** to dismount, get off one's horse.

di'scepolo, **a** [diʃ'ʃepolo] *sm/f* disciple.

di'scernere [diʃ'ʃernere] *vt* to discern, make out; **discerni'mento** *sm* judgment, discernment.

di'sceso, **a** [diʃ'ʃeso] *pp di* **discendere** // *sf* descent; (*pendio*) slope; **in** ~**a** (*strada*) downhill.

disci'ogliere [diʃ'ʃɔʎʎere] *vt*, ~**rsi** *vr* to dissolve; (*fondere*) to melt; **disci'olto**, **a** *pp di* **disciogliere**.

disci'plina [diʃʃi'plina] *sf* discipline; **discipli'nare** *ag* disciplinary // *vt* to discipline.

'disco, **schi** *sm* disc; (*SPORT*) discus; (*fonografico*) record, disc; ~ **orario** (*AUT*) parking disc; ~ **volante** flying saucer.

discol'pare *vt* to clear of blame.

disco'noscere [disko'noʃʃere] *vt* to refuse to acknowledge; (*figlio*) to disown; **disconosci'uto**, **a** *pp di* **disconoscere**.

dis'corde *ag* conflicting, clashing; **dis'cordia** *sf* discord; (*dissidio*) disagreement, clash.

dis'correre *vi*: ~ **(di)** to talk (about).

dis'corso, a *pp di* **discorrere** // *sm* speech; (*conversazione*) conversation, talk.

dis'costo, a *ag* faraway, distant // *av* far away; ~ **da** *prep* far from.

disco'teca, che *sf* (*raccolta*) record library; (*luogo di ballo*) discothèque.

discredi'tare *vt* to discredit.

discre'panza [diskre'pantsa] *sf* disagreement.

dis'creto, a *ag* discreet; (*abbastanza buono*) reasonable, fair; **discrezi'one** *sf* discretion; (*giudizio*) judgment, discernment; **a discrezione di** at the discretion of.

discriminazi'one [diskriminat'tsjone] *sf* discrimination.

discussi'one *sf* discussion; (*litigio*) argument.

dis'cusso, a *pp di* **discutere**.

dis'cutere *vt* to discuss, debate; (*contestare*) to question, dispute // *vi* to talk; (*contrastare*) to argue; ~ **di** to discuss.

disde'gnare [disdeɲ'ɲare] *vt* to scorn; **dis'degno** *sm* scorn, disdain.

dis'detto, a *pp di* **disdire** // *sf* retraction; cancellation; (*sfortuna*) bad luck.

dis'dire *vt* (*ritrattare*) to retract, take back; (*annullare*) to cancel.

dise'gnare [diseɲ'ɲare] *vt* to draw; (*progettare*) to design; (*fig*) to outline; **disegna'tore, 'trice** *sm/f* designer.

di'segno [di'seɲɲo] *sm* drawing; design; outline.

diser'tare *vt, vi* to desert; **diser'tore** *sm* (*MIL*) deserter; **diserzi'one** *sf* (*MIL*) desertion.

dis'fare *vt* to undo; (*valigie*) to unpack; (*lavoro, paese*) to destroy; (*neve*) to melt; ~**rsi** *vr* to melt; ~ **il letto** to strip the bed; ~**rsi in lacrime** to dissolve into tears; ~**rsi di qd** (*liberarsi*) to get rid of sb; **dis'fatto, a** *pp di* **disfare** // *sf* (*sconfitta*) rout.

disfunzi'one [disfun'tsjone] *sf* (*MED*) disorder.

disge'lare [dizdʒe'lare] *vt, vi*, ~**rsi** *vr* to thaw; **dis'gelo** *sm* thaw.

dis'grazia [diz'grattsja] *sf* (*sventura*) misfortune; (*incidente*) accident, mishap; **disgrazi'ato, a** *ag* unfortunate // *sm/f* wretch.

disgre'gare *vt*, ~**rsi** *vr* to break up.

disgu'ido *sm*: ~ **postale** error in postal delivery.

disgus'tare *vt* to disgust; ~**rsi** *vr*: ~**rsi di** to be disgusted by.

dis'gusto *sm* disgust; **disgus'toso, a** *ag* disgusting.

disidra'tare *vt* to dehydrate.

disil'ludere *vt* to disillusion, disenchant; **disillusi'one** *sf* disillusion, disenchantment.

disimpa'rare *vt* to forget.

disimpe'gnare [dizimpeɲ'ɲare] *vt* (*oggetto dato in pegno*) to redeem, get out of pawn; (*liberare*) to release, free;

(*sbrigare: ufficio*) to carry out; ~**rsi** *vr* to free o.s.; (*cavarsela*) to manage.

disinfet'tante *ag, sm* disinfectant.

disinfet'tare *vt* to disinfect; **disinfezi'one** *sf* disinfection.

disingan'nare *vt* to disabuse, disillusion.

disinte'grare *vt, vi* (2) to disintegrate.

disinteres'sarsi *vr*: ~ **di** to take no interest in.

disinte'resse *sm* indifference; (*generosità*) unselfishness.

disin'volto, a *ag* casual, free and easy; **disinvol'tura** *sf* casualness, ease.

dislo'care *vt* to station, position.

dismi'sura *sf* excess; **a** ~ to excess, excessively.

disobbe'dire *etc* = **disubbidire** *etc*.

disoccu'pato, a *ag* unemployed // *sm/f* unemployed person; **disoccupazi'one** *sf* unemployment.

disonestà *sf* dishonesty.

diso'nesto, a *ag* dishonest.

disono'rare *vt* to dishonour, bring disgrace upon.

diso'nore *sm* dishonour, disgrace.

di'sopra *av* (*con contatto*) on top; (*senza contatto*) above; (*al piano superiore*) upstairs // *ag inv* (*superiore*) upper; **la gente** ~ the people upstairs; **il piano** ~ the floor above // *sm inv* top, upper part.

disordi'nare *vt* to mess up, disarrange; (*fig*) to upset, confuse; (*MIL*) to throw into disorder // *vi*: ~ **nel bere** *etc* to take drink *etc* to excess; **disordi'nato, a** *ag* untidy; (*privo di misura*) irregular, wild.

di'sordine *sm* (*confusione*) disorder, confusion; (*sregolatezza*) debauchery.

disorien'tare *vt* to disorientate; ~**rsi** *vr* (*fig*) to get confused, lose one's bearings.

di'sotto *av* below, underneath; (*in fondo*) at the bottom; (*al piano inferiore*) downstairs // *ag inv* (*inferiore*) lower; bottom *cpd*; **la gente** ~ the people downstairs; **il piano** ~ the floor below // *sm inv* (*parte inferiore*) lower part; bottom.

dis'paccio [dis'pattʃo] *sm* dispatch.

dispa'rato, a *ag* disparate.

'dispari *ag inv* odd, uneven.

disparità *sf inv* disparity.

dis'parte: **in** ~ *av* (*da lato*) aside, apart; **tenersi** *o* **starsene in** ~ to keep to o.s., hold aloof.

dispendi'oso, a *ag* expensive.

dis'pensa *sf* pantry, larder; (*mobile*) sideboard; (*DIR*) exemption; (*REL*) dispensation; (*fascicolo*) number, issue.

dispen'sare *vt* (*elemosine, favori*) to distribute; (*esonerare*) to exempt.

dispe'rare *vi*: ~ **(di)** to despair (of); ~**rsi** *vr* to despair; **dispe'rato, a** *ag* desperate; **disperazi'one** *sf* desperation.

dis'perdere *vt* (*disseminare*) to disperse; (*MIL*) to scatter, rout; (*fig: consumare*) to waste, squander; ~**rsi** *vr* to disperse; to scatter; **dispersi'one** *sf* dispersion, dispersal; (*FISICA, CHIM*) dispersion; **dis'perso, a** *pp di* **disperdere** // *sm/f* missing person.

dis'petto sm spite q, spitefulness q; **fare un ~ a qd** to play a (nasty) trick on sb; **a ~ di** in spite of; **dispet'toso, a** ag spiteful.

dispia'cere [dispja'tʃere] sm (rammarico) regret, sorrow; (dolore) grief; ~**i** smpl troubles, worries // vi: ~ **a** to displease // vb impers: **mi dispiace (che)** I am sorry (that); **se non le dispiace, me ne vado adesso** if you don't mind, I'll go now; **dispiaci'uto, a** pp di **displacere**.

dispo'nibile ag available.

dis'porre vt (sistemare) to arrange; (preparare) to prepare; (DIR) to order; (persuadere): ~ **qd a** to incline o dispose sb towards // vi (decidere) to decide; (usufruire): ~ **di** to use, have at one's disposal; (essere dotato): ~ **di** to have; **disporsi** vr (ordinarsi) to place o.s., arrange o.s.; **disporsi a fare** to get ready to do; **disposizi'one** sf arrangement, layout; (stato d'animo) mood; (tendenza) bent, inclination; (comando) order; (DIR) provision, regulation; **a disposizione di qd** at sb's disposal; **dis'posto, a** pp di **disporre**.

dis'potico, a, ci, che ag despotic.

disprez'zare [dispret'tsare] vt to despise.

dis'prezzo [dis'prettso] sm contempt.

'disputa sf dispute, quarrel.

dispu'tare (contendere) to dispute, contest; (SPORT: partita) to play; (: gareggiare) to take part in // vi to quarrel; ~ **di** to discuss; ~**rsi qc** to fight for sth.

dissangua'mento sm loss of blood.

disse'care vt to dissect.

dissec'care vt, ~**rsi** vr to dry up.

dissemi'nare vt to scatter; (fig: notizie) to spread.

dis'senso sm dissent; (disapprovazione) disapproval.

dissente'ria sf dysentery.

dissen'tire vi: ~ **(da)** to disagree (with).

dissertazi'one [dissertat'tsjone] sf dissertation.

disser'vizio [disser'vittsjo] sm inefficiency.

disses'tare vt (ECON) to ruin; **dis'sesto** sm (financial) ruin.

disse'tante ag refreshing.

disse'tare vt to quench the thirst of.

dissezi'one [disset'tsjone] sf dissection.

dissi'dente ag, sm/f dissident.

dis'sidio sm disagreement.

dis'simile ag different, dissimilar.

dissimu'lare vt (fingere) to dissemble; (nascondere) to conceal.

dissi'pare vt to dissipate; (scialacquare) to squander, waste; **dissipa'tezza** sf dissipation; **dissipazi'one** sf squandering.

dissoci'are [disso'tʃare] vt to dissociate.

dis'solto, a pp di **dissolvere**.

disso'lubile ag soluble.

disso'luto, a pp di **dissolvere** // ag dissolute, licentious.

dis'solvere vt to dissolve; (neve) to melt;

(fumo) to disperse; ~**rsi** vr to dissolve; to melt; to disperse.

disso'nante ag discordant.

dissu'adere vt: ~ **qd da** to dissuade sb from; **dissu'aso, a** pp di **dissuadere**.

distac'care vt to detach, separate; (SPORT) to leave behind; ~**rsi** vr to be detached; (fig) to stand out; ~**rsi da** (fig: allontanarsi) to grow away from.

dis'tacco, chi sm (separazione) separation; (fig: indifferenza) detachment; (SPORT): **è arrivato con un ~ di 10 minuti dai primi** he came in 10 minutes behind the leaders.

dis'tante av far away // ag distant, far away.

dis'tanza [dis'tantsa] sf distance.

distanzi'are [distan'tsjare] vt to space out, place at intervals; (SPORT) to outdistance; (fig: superare) to outstrip, surpass.

dis'tare vi: **distiamo pochi chilometri da Roma** we are only a few kilometres (away) from Rome.

dis'tendere vt (coperta) to spread out; (gambe) to stretch (out); (mettere a giacere) to lay; (rilassare: muscoli, nervi) to relax; ~**rsi** vr (rilassarsi) to relax; (sdraiarsi) to lie down; **distensi'one** sf stretching; relaxation; (POL) détente.

dis'teso, a pp di **distendere** // sf expanse, stretch.

distil'lare vt to distil.

distille'ria sf distillery.

dis'tinguere vt to distinguish.

dis'tinta sf (nota) note; (elenco) list.

distin'tivo, a ag distinctive; distinguishing // sm badge.

dis'tinto, a pp di **distinguere** // ag (dignitoso ed elegante) distinguished; "~**i saluti**" "Yours faithfully".

distinzi'one [distin'tsjone] sf distinction.

dis'togliere [dis'toʎʎere] vt: ~ **da** to take away from; (fig) to dissuade from; **dis-'tolto, a** pp di **distogliere**.

distorsi'one sf (MED) sprain; (alterazione) distortion.

dis'trarre vt to distract; (divertire) to entertain, amuse; **distrarsi** vr (svagarsi) to amuse o enjoy o.s.; **dis'tratto, a** pp di **distrarre** // ag absent-minded; (disattento) inattentive; **distrazi'one** sf absent-mindedness; inattention; (svago) distraction, entertainment.

dis'tretto sm district.

distribu'ire vt to distribute; (CARTE) to deal (out); (consegnare: posta) to deliver; **distribu'tore** sm (di benzina) petrol pump; (AUT, ELETTR) distributor; (automatico) vending o slot machine; **distribuzi'one** sf distribution; delivery.

distri'care vt to disentangle, unravel.

dis'truggere [dis'truddʒere] vt to destroy; **distrut'tivo, a** ag destructive; **dis'trutto, a** pp di **distruggere**; **distruzi'one** sf destruction.

distur'bare vt to disturb, trouble; (sonno,

lezioni) to disturb, interrupt; ~**rsi** *vr* to put o.s. out.

dis'turbo *sm* trouble, bother, inconvenience; (*indisposizione*) (slight) disorder, ailment; ~**i** *smpl* (RADIO, TV) static *sg*.

disubbidi'ente *ag* disobedient; **disubbidi'enza** *sf* disobedience.

disubbi'dire *vi*: ~ **(a qd)** to disobey (sb).

disugu'ale *ag* unequal; (*diverso*) different; (*irregolare*) uneven.

disu'mano, a *ag* inhuman.

disu'nire *vt* to divide, disunite.

di'suso *sm* disuse; **andare** *o* **cadere in** ~ to fall into disuse.

'dita *fpl di* **dito**.

di'tale *sm* thimble.

'dito, *pl*(*f*) **'dita** *sm* finger; (*misura*) finger, finger's breadth; ~ **(del piede)** toe.

'ditta *sf* firm, business.

ditta'tore *sm* dictator.

ditta'tura *sf* dictatorship.

dit'tongo, ghi *sm* diphthong.

di'urno, a *ag* day *cpd*, daytime *cpd* // *sm* (*anche:* **albergo** ~) *public toilets with washing and shaving facilities etc.*

'diva *sf vedi* **divo**.

diva'gare *vi* to digress; **divagazi'one** *sf* digression.

divam'pare *vi* (*2*) to flare up, blaze up.

di'vano *sm* sofa; divan.

divari'care *vt* to open wide.

di'vario *sm* difference.

dive'nire *vi* (*2*) = **diventare**; **dive'nuto, a** *pp di* **divenire**.

diven'tare *vi* (*2*) to become; ~ **famoso/professore** to become famous/a teacher.

di'verbio *sm* altercation.

diver'gente [diver'dʒɛnte] *ag* divergent.

di'vergere [di'vɛrdʒere] *vi* to diverge.

diversifi'care *vt* to diversify, vary; to differentiate.

diversi'one *sf* diversion.

diversità *sf inv* difference, diversity; (*varietà*) variety.

diver'sivo *sm* diversion, distraction.

di'verso, a *ag* (*differente*): ~ **(da)** different (from); ~**i, e** *det pl* several, various; (COMM) sundry // *pronome pl* several (people), many (people).

diver'tente *ag* amusing.

diverti'mento *sm* amusement, pleasure; (*passatempo*) pastime, recreation.

diver'tire *vt* to amuse, entertain; ~**rsi** *vr* to amuse *o* enjoy o.s.

divi'dendo *sm* dividend.

di'videre *vt* (*anche* MAT) to divide; (*distribuire, ripartire*) to divide (up), split (up).

divi'eto *sm* prohibition; "~ **di sosta**" (AUT) "no parking".

divinco'larsi *vr* to wriggle, writhe.

divinità *sf inv* divinity.

di'vino, a *ag* divine.

di'visa *sf* (MIL *etc*) uniform; (COMM) foreign currency.

divisi'one *sf* division.

di'viso, a *pp di* **dividere**.

'divo, a *sm/f* star.

divo'rare *vt* to devour.

divorzi'are [divor'tsjare] *vi*: ~ **(da qd)** to divorce (sb).

di'vorzio [di'vɔrtsjo] *sm* divorce.

divul'gare *vt* to divulge, disclose; (*rendere comprensibile*) to popularize; ~**rsi** *vr* to spread.

dizio'nario [ditsjo'narjo] *sm* dictionary.

dizi'one [dit'tsjone] *sf* diction; pronunciation.

do *sm* (MUS) C; (: *solfeggiando la scala*) do(h).

'doccia, ce ['dottʃa] *sf* shower; (*condotto*) pipe.

do'cente [do'tʃɛnte] *ag* teaching // *sm/f* teacher; (*di università*) lecturer; **do'cenza** *sf* university teaching *o* lecturing.

'docile ['dɔtʃile] *ag* docile.

documen'tare *vt* to document; ~**rsi** *vr*: ~**rsi (su)** to gather information *o* material (about).

documen'tario, a *ag, sm* documentary.

documentazi'one [dokumentat'tsjone] *sf* documentation.

docu'mento *sm* document; ~**i** *smpl* (*d'identità etc*) papers.

'dodici ['dɔditʃi] *num* twelve.

do'gana *sf* (*ufficio*) customs *pl*; (*tassa*) (customs) duty; **passare la** ~ to go through customs; **doga'nale** *ag* customs *cpd*; **dogani'ere** *sm* customs officer.

'doglie ['dɔʎʎe] *sfpl* (MED) labour *sg*, labour pains.

'dogma, i *sm* dogma.

'dolce ['dolt ʃe] *ag* sweet; (*colore*) soft; (*fig: mite: clima*) mild; (*non ripido: pendio*) gentle // *sm* (*sapore dolce*) sweetness, sweet taste; (CUC: *portata*) sweet, dessert; (: *torta*) cake; **dol'cezza** *sf* sweetness; softness; mildness; gentleness; **dolci'umi** *smpl* sweets.

do'lente *ag* sorrowful, sad.

do'lere *vi* (*2*) to be sore, hurt, ache; ~**rsi** *vr* to complain; (*essere spiacente*): ~**rsi di** to be sorry for; **mi duole la testa** my head aches, I've got a headache.

'dollaro *sm* dollar.

'dolo *sm* (DIR) malice.

Dolo'miti *sfpl*: **le** ~ the Dolomites.

do'lore *sm* (*fisico*) pain; (*morale*) sorrow, grief; **dolo'roso, a** *ag* painful; sorrowful, sad.

do'loso, a *ag* (DIR) malicious.

do'manda *sf* (*interrogazione*) question; (*richiesta*) demand; (: *cortese*) request; (DIR: *richiesta scritta*) application; (ECON): **la** ~ demand; **fare una** ~ **a qd** to ask sb a question.

doman'dare *vt* (*per avere*) to ask for; (*per sapere*) to ask; (*esigere*) to demand; ~**rsi** *vr* to wonder; to ask o.s.; ~ **qc a qd** to ask sb for sth; to ask sb sth.

do'mani *av* tomorrow // *sm*: **il** ~ (*il futuro*) the future; (*il giorno successivo*) the next day; ~ **l'altro** the day after tomorrow.

do'mare vt to tame.

domat'tina av tomorrow morning.

do'menica, che sf Sunday; **di** o **la** ~ **on** Sundays; **domeni'cale** ag Sunday cpd.

do'mestica, che sf vedi **domestico**.

domesti'chezza [domesti'kettsa] sf = **dimestichezza**.

do'mestico, a, ci, che ag domestic // sm/f servant, domestic.

domi'cilio [domi'tʃiljo] sm (DIR) domicile, place of residence.

domi'nare vt to dominate; (fig: sentimenti) to control, master // vi to be in the dominant position; **~rsi** vr (controllarsi) to control o.s.; **~ su** (fig) to surpass, outclass; **dominazi'one** sf domination.

do'minio sm dominion; (fig: campo) field, domain.

do'nare vt to give, present; (per beneficenza etc) to donate // vi (fig): ~ **a** to suit, become; **dona'tore, 'trice** sm/f donor; **donatore di sangue** blood donor; **donazi'one** sf donation.

dondo'lare vt (cullare) to rock; **~rsi** vr to swing, sway; **'dondolo** sm: **sedia/cavallo a dondolo** rocking chair/horse.

'donna sf woman; ~ **di casa** housewife; home-loving woman; ~ **di servizio** maid.

donnai'olo sm ladykiller.

don'nesco, a, schi, sche ag women's, woman's.

'donnola sf weasel.

'dono sm gift.

'dopo av (tempo) afterwards; (luogo) after, next // prep after // cong (temporale): ~ **aver studiato** after having studied; ~ **mangiato va a dormire** after having eaten o after a meal he goes for a sleep // ag inv: **il giorno** ~ the following day; **un anno** ~ a year later; ~ **di me/lui** after me/him.

dopodo'mani av the day after tomorrow.

dopogu'erra sm postwar years pl.

dopo'pranzo [dopo'prandzo] av after lunch (o dinner).

doposci [dopoʃ'ʃi] sm inv après-ski outfit.

doposcu'ola sm inv sort of school club offering extra tuition and recreational facilities.

dopo'tutto av after all.

doppi'aggio [dop'pjaddʒo] sm (CINEMA) dubbing.

doppi'are vt (NAUT) to round; (SPORT) to lap; (CINEMA) to dub.

'doppio, a ag double; (fig: falso) double-dealing, deceitful // sm (quantità): **il** ~ (di) twice as much (o many), double the amount (o number) of; (SPORT) doubles pl // av double.

doppi'one sm duplicate (copy).

doppio'petto sm double-breasted jacket.

do'rare vt to gild; (CUC) to brown; **dora-'tura** sf gilding.

dormicchi'are [dormik'kjare] vi to doze.

dormigli'one, a [dormiʎ'ʎone] sm/f sleepyhead.

dor'mire vt, vi to sleep; **dor'mita** sf (good) sleep.

dormi'torio sm dormitory.

dormi'veglia [dormi'veʎʎa] sm drowsiness.

'dorso sm back; (di montagna) ridge, crest; (di libro) spine; **a** ~ **di cavallo** on horseback.

do'sare vt to measure out; (MED) to dose.

'dose sf quantity, amount; (MED) dose.

'dosso sm (dorso) back; **levarsi di** ~ **i vestiti** to take one's clothes off.

do'tare vt: ~ **di** to provide o supply with; (fig) to endow with; **dotazi'one** sf (insieme di beni) endowment; (di macchine etc) equipment.

'dote sf (di sposa) dowry; (assegnata a un ente) endowment; (fig) gift, talent.

Dott. (abbr di dottore) Dr.

'dotto, a ag (colto) learned // sm (sapiente) scholar; (ANAT) duct.

dotto'rato sm degree; (di ricerca) doctorate, doctor's degree.

dot'tore, essa sm/f doctor.

dot'trina sf doctrine.

Dott.ssa (abbr di dottoressa) Dr.

'dove av where, in which; (in cui) where, in which; (dovunque) wherever; **di** ~ **sei?** where are you from?; **da** ~ **abito vedo tutta la città** I can see the whole city from where I stay; **per** ~ **si passa?** which way should we go?

do'vere sm (obbligo) duty // vt (essere debitore): ~ **qc (a qd)** to owe (sb) sth // vi (seguito dall'infinito: obbligo) to have to; **lui deve farlo** he has to do it, he must do it; **è dovuto partire** he had to leave; **ha dovuto pagare** he had to pay; (: intenzione): **devo partire domani** I'm (due) to leave tomorrow; (: probabilità) **dev'essere tardi** it must be late.

dove'roso, a ag (right and) proper.

do'vunque av (in qualunque luogo) wherever; (dappertutto) everywhere; ~ **io vada** wherever I go.

do'vuto, a ag (causato): ~ **a** due to.

doz'zina [dod'dzina] sf dozen; **una** ~ **di uova** a dozen eggs.

dozzi'nale [doddzi'nale] ag cheap, second-rate.

dra'gare vt to dredge.

'drago, ghi sm dragon.

'dramma, i sm drama; **dram'matico, a, ci, che** ag dramatic; **drammatiz'zare** vt to dramatize; **dramma'turgo, ghi** sm playwright, dramatist.

drappeggi'are [draped'dʒare] vt o drape.

drap'pello sm (MIL) squad; (gruppo) band, group.

dre'naggio [dre'naddʒo] sm drainage.

dre'nare vt to drain.

'dritto, a ag, av = **diritto**.

driz'zare [drit'tsare] vt (far tornare diritto) to straighten; (volgere: sguardo, occhi) to turn, direct; (*innalzare: antenna, muro*) to erect; ~**rsi** *vr* to stand up; ~ **le orecchie** to prick up one's ears.

'**droga, ghe** *sf* (*sostanza aromatica*) spice; (*stupefacente*) drug; **dro'gare** *vt* to season, spice; to drug, dope; **drogarsi** *vr* to take drugs; **dro'gato, a** *sm/f* drug addict.

droghe'ria [droge'ria] *sf* grocer's shop.

drome'dario *sm* dromedary.

'**dubbio, a** *ag* (*incerto*) doubtful, dubious; (*ambiguo*) dubious // *sm* (*incertezza*) doubt; **avere il** ~ **che** to be afraid that, suspect that; **mettere in** ~ **qc** to question sth; **dubbi'oso, a** *ag* doubtful, dubious.

dubi'tare *vi*: ~ **di** to doubt; (*risultato*) to be doubtful of; **dubita'tivo, a** *ag* doubtful, dubious.

'**duca, chi** *sm* duke.

du'chessa [du'kessa] *sf* duchess.

'**due** *num* two.

due'cento [due'tʃɛnto] *num* two hundred // *sm*: **il D**~ the thirteenth century.

du'ello *sm* duel.

'**duna** *sf* dune.

'**dunque** *cong* (*perciò*) so, therefore; (*riprendendo il discorso*) well (then).

du'omo *sm* cathedral.

dupli'cato *sm* duplicate.

'**duplice** ['duplitʃe] *ag* double, twofold; **in** ~ in duplicate.

du'rante *prep* during.

du'rare *vi* to last; (*perseverare*) ~ **in qc/a fare qc** to persist *o* persevere in sth/in doing sth; ~ **fatica a** to have difficulty in; **du'rata** *sf* length (of time); duration; **dura'turo, a** *ag*, **du'revole** *ag* lasting.

du'rezza [du'rettsa] *sf* hardness; stubbornness; harshness; toughness.

'**duro, a** *ag* (*pietra, lavoro, materasso, problema*) hard; (*persona: ostinato*) stubborn, obstinate; (: *severo*) harsh, hard; (*voce*) harsh; (*carne*) tough // *sm* (*persona*) tough guy; ~ **d'orecchi** hard of hearing; ~ **di testa** (*fig: fam*) slow-witted.

du'rone *sm* hard skin.

E

e, *dav V spesso* **ed** *cong* and.

E. (*abbr di est*) E.

è *forma del vb* **essere**.

'**ebano** *sm* ebony.

eb'bene *cong* well (then).

eb'brezza [eb'brettsa] *sf* intoxication.

'**ebbro, a** *ag* drunk; ~ **di** (*gioia etc*) beside o.s. *o* wild with.

'**ebete** *ag* stupid, idiotic.

ebolizi'one [ebollit'tsjone] *sf* boiling; **punto di** ~ boiling point.

e'braico, a, ci, che *ag* Hebrew, Hebraic // *sm* (*LING*) Hebrew.

e'breo, a *ag* Jewish // *sm/f* Jew/Jewess.

ecc *av* (*abbr di eccetera*) etc.

ecce'denza [ettʃe'dɛntsa] *sf* excess, surplus.

ec'cedere [et'tʃedere] *vt* to exceed // *vi* to go too far; ~ **nel bere/mangiare** to indulge in drink/food to excess.

eccel'lente [ettʃel'lɛnte] *ag* excellent; **eccel'lenza** *sf* excellence; (*titolo*) Excellency.

ec'cellere [et'tʃellere] *vi* to excel; ~ **su tutti** to surpass everyone; **ec'celso, a** *pp di* eccellere.

ec'centrico, a, ci, che [et'tʃɛntriko] *ag* eccentric; (*quartiere*) outlying.

ecces'sivo, a [ettʃes'sivo] *ag* excessive.

ec'cesso [et'tʃɛsso] *sm* excess; **all'**~ (*gentile, generoso*) to excess, excessively; **dare in** ~**i** to fly into a rage.

ec'cetera [et'tʃɛtera] *av* et cetera, and so on.

ec'cetto [et'tʃɛtto] *prep* except, with the exception of; ~ **che** *cong* except, other than; ~ **che (non)** unless.

eccettu'are [ettʃettu'are] *vt* to except.

eccezio'nale [ettʃetsjo'nale] *ag* exceptional.

eccezi'one [ettʃet'tsjone] *sf* exception; (*DIR*) objection; **a** ~ **di** with the exception of, except for; **d'**~ exceptional.

ecci'tare [ettʃi'tare] *vt* (*curiosità, interesse*) to excite, arouse; (*folla*) to incite; ~**rsi** *vr* to get excited; **eccita-zi'one** *sf* excitement.

ecclesi'astico, a, ci, che *ag* ecclesiastical, church *cpd*; clerical // *sm* ecclesiastic.

'**ecco** *av* (*per dimostrare*): ~ **il treno!** here's *o* here comes the train!; (*dav pronome*): ~**mi!** here I am!; ~**ne uno!** here's one (of them)!; (*dav pp*): ~ **fatto!** there, that's it done!

echeggi'are [eked'dʒare] *vi* to echo.

e'clissi *sf* eclipse.

'**eco**, *pl(m)* '**echi** *sm o f* echo.

ecolo'gia [ekolo'dʒia] *sf* ecology.

econo'mia *sf* economy; (*scienza*) economics *sg*; (*risparmio: azione*) saving; ~**e** *sfpl* (*denari risparmiati*) savings; **fare** ~**e** to save; **eco'nomico, a, ci, che** *ag* (*ECON*) economic; (*poco costoso*) economical; **econo'mista, i** *sm* economist; **economiz'zare** *vt, vi* to save; **e'conomo, a** *ag* thrifty // *sm/f* (*INS*) bursar.

ed *cong vedi* **e**.

'**edera** *sf* ivy.

e'dicola *sf* newspaper kiosk.

edifi'care *vt* to build; (*fig: teoria, azienda*) to establish; (*indurre al bene*) to edify.

edi'ficio [edi'fitʃo] *sm* building; (*fig*) structure.

e'dile *ag* building *cpd*; **edi'lizio, a** *ag* building *cpd* // *sf* building, building trade.

edi'tore, 'trice *ag* publishing *cpd* // *sm/f* publisher; (*curatore*) editor; **edito'ria** *sf* publishing; **editori'ale** *ag* publishing *cpd* // *sm* editorial, leader.

edizi'one [edit'tsjone] *sf* edition; (*tiratura*) printing; (*di manifestazioni, feste etc*) production.

edu'care *vt* to educate; (*abituare*): ~ (a) to train (for); **edu'cato**, a, ag polite, well-mannered; **educazi'one** *sf* education; (*comportamento*) (good) manners *pl*; **educazione fisica** (*INS*) physical training o education.

effemi'nato, a *ag* effeminate.

efferve'scente [efferveʃ'ʃɛnte] *ag* effervescent.

effet'tivo, a *ag* (*reale*) real, actual; (*operaio, professore*) permanent; (*MIL*) regular // *sm* (*MIL*) strength; (*di patrimonio etc*) sum total.

ef'fetto *sm* effect; (*fig: impressione*) impression; **cercare d'~** to look for attention; **in ~i** in fact, actually; **effettu'are** *vt* to effect, carry out.

effi'cace [effi'katʃe] *ag* effective.

effici'ente [effi'tʃɛnte] *ag* efficient; **efficienza** *sf* efficiency; **in piena efficienza** (*persona*) fit; (*macchina*) in perfect working order.

ef'figie [ef'fidʒe] *sf inv* effigy.

ef'fimero, a *ag* ephemeral.

effusi'one *sf* effusion.

E'geo [e'dʒɛo] *sm*: **l'~, il mare** ~ the Aegean (Sea).

E'gitto [e'dʒitto] *sm*: **l'~** Egypt.

'egli ['eʎʎi] *pronome* he; ~ **stesso** he himself.

ego'ismo *sm* selfishness, egoism; **ego'ista, i, e** *ag* selfish, egoistic // *sm/f* egoist.

egr. *abbr di* **egregio.**

e'gregio, a, gi, gie [e'grɛdʒo] *ag* distinguished; (*nelle lettere*): **E~ Signore** Dear Sir.

eguagli'anza [egwaʎ'ʎantsa] *etc vedi* **uguaglianza** *etc*.

elabo'rare *vt* (*progetto*) to work out, elaborate; (*dati*) to process; (*digerire*) to digest; **elaborazi'one** *sf* elaboration; digestion; **elaborazione dei dati** data processing.

e'lastico, a, ci, che *ag* elastic // *sm* (*gommino*) rubber band; (*per il cucito*) elastic *q*.

ele'fante *sm* elephant.

ele'gante *ag* elegant; **ele'ganza** *sf* elegance.

e'leggere [e'lɛddʒere] *vt* to elect.

elemen'tare *ag* elementary; ~**i** *sfpl* primary school.

ele'mento *sm* element; (*parte componente*) element, component, part; ~**i** *smpl* (*della scienza etc*) elements, rudiments.

ele'mosina *sf* charity, alms *pl*.

elen'care *vt* to list.

e'lenco, chi *sm* list; ~ **telefonico** telephone directory.

e'letto, a *pp di* **eleggere** // *sm/f* (*nominato*) elected member; **eletto'rale** *ag* electoral, election *cpd*; **eletto'rato** *sm*

electorate; **elet'tore, 'trice** *sm/f* voter, elector.

elet'trauto *sm inv* workshop for car electrical repairs; (*tecnico*) car electrician.

elettri'cista, i [elettri'tʃista] *sm* electrician.

elettricità [elettritʃi'ta] *sf* electricity.

e'lettrico, a, ci, che *ag* electric(al).

elettrifi'care *vt* to electrify.

elettriz'zare [elettrid'dzare] *vt* to electrify.

e'lettro... *prefisso*: **elettrocardio-'gramma, i** *sm* electrocardiogram; **e'lettrodo** *sm* electrode; **elettrodo-'mestico, a, ci, che** *ag*: **apparecchi elettrodomestici** domestic (electrical) appliances; **elettroma'gnetico, a, ci, che** *ag* electromagnetic; **elet'trone** *sm* electron; **elet'tronico, a, ci, che** *ag* electronic // *sf* electronics *sg*; **elettro-'treno** *sm* electric train.

ele'vare *vt* to raise; (*edificio*) to erect; (*multa*) to impose; **elevazi'one** *sf* elevation; (*l'elevare*) raising.

elezi'one [elet'tsjone] *sf* election; ~**i** *sfpl* (*POL*) election(s).

'elica, che *sf* propeller.

eli'cottero *sm* helicopter.

elimi'nare *vt* to eliminate; **elimina'toria** *sf* eliminating round.

'elio *sm* helium.

'ella *pronome* she; (*forma di cortesia*) you; ~ **stessa** she herself; you yourself.

el'metto *sm* helmet.

e'logio [e'lɔdʒo] *sm* (*discorso, scritto*) eulogy; (*lode*) praise (*di solito q*).

elo'quente *ag* eloquent; **elo'quenza** *sf* eloquence.

e'ludere *vt* to evade; **elu'sivo, a** *ag* evasive.

ema'nare *vt* to send out, give out; (*fig: leggi, decreti*) to issue // *vi* (*2*): ~ **da** to come from.

emanci'pare [emantʃi'pare] *vt* to emancipate; ~**rsi** *vr* (*fig*) to become liberated o emancipated; **emancipa-zi'one** *sf* emancipation.

em'blema, i *sm* emblem.

embri'one *sm* embryo.

emenda'mento *sm* amendment.

emen'dare *vt* to amend.

emer'genza [emer'dʒɛntsa] *sf* emergency; **in caso di** ~ in an emergency.

e'mergere [e'mɛrdʒere] *vi* to emerge; (*sommergibile*) to surface; (*fig: distinguersi*) to stand out; **e'merso, a** *pp di* **emergere.**

e'messo, a *pp di* **emettere.**

e'mettere *vt* (*suono, luce*) to give out, emit; (*onde radio*) to send out; (*assegno, francobollo*) to issue; (*fig: giudizio*) to express, voice.

emi'crania *sf* migraine.

emi'grante *ag, sm/f* emigrant.

emi'grare *vi* to emigrate; **emigrazi'one** *sf* emigration.

emi'nente *ag* eminent, distinguished; **emi'nenza** *sf* eminence.

emis'fero *sm* hemisphere; ~ **boreale/australe** northern/southern hemisphere.

emissi'one *sf* emission; sending out; issue; (*RADIO*) broadcast.

emit'tente *ag* (*banca*) issuing; (*RADIO*) broadcasting, transmitting // *sf* (*RADIO*) transmitter.

emorra'gia, 'gie [emorra'dʒia] *sf* haemorrhage.

emo'tivo, a *ag* emotional.

emozio'nante [emottsjo'nante] *ag* exciting, thrilling.

emozio'nare [emottsjo'nare] *vt* (*eccitare*) to excite; (*commuovere*) to move; (*turbare*) to upset; **~rsi** *vr* to be excited; to be moved; to be upset.

emozi'one [emot'tsjone] *sf* emotion; (*agitazione*) excitement.

'empio, a *ag* (*sacrilego*) impious; (*spietato*) cruel, pitiless; (*malvagio*) wicked, evil.

em'pire *vt* to fill (up).

em'porio *sm* market, commercial centre; (*grande magazzino*) department store.

emu'lare *vt* to emulate.

emulsi'one *sf* emulsion.

en'ciclica, che [en'tʃiklika] *sf* (*REL*) encyclical.

enciclope'dia [entʃiklope'dia] *sf* encyclopaedia.

endove'noso, a *ag* (*MED*) intravenous.

ener'gia, 'gie [ener'dʒia] *sf* (*FISICA*) energy; (*fig*) energy, strength, vigour; **e'nergico, a, ci, che** *ag* energetic, vigorous; (*efficace*) powerful, strong.

'enfasi *sf* emphasis; (*peg*) bombast, pomposity; **en'fatico, a, ci, che** *ag* pompous.

e'nigma, i *sm* enigma; **enig'matico, a, ci, che** *ag* enigmatic.

E.N.I.T. *abbr di Ente Nazionale Italiano per il Turismo.*

en'nesimo, a *ag* (*MAT, fig*) nth; **per l'~a volta** for the umpteenth time.

e'norme *ag* enormous, huge; **enormità** *sf inv* enormity, huge size; (*assurdità*) absurdity; **non dire ~!** don't talk nonsense!

'ente *sm* (*istituzione*) body, board, corporation; (*FILOSOFIA*) being.

en'trambi, e *pronome pl* both (of them) // *ag pl:* ~ **i ragazzi** both boys, both of the boys.

en'trare *vi* (*2*) to enter, go (*o come*) in; ~ **in** (*luogo*) to enter, go (*o come*) into; (*trovar posto, poter stare*) to fit into; (*essere ammesso a: club etc*) to join, become a member of; ~ **in automobile** to get into the car; **questo non c'entra** (*fig*) that's got nothing to do with it; **en'trata** *sf* entrance, entry; **entrate** *sfpl* (*COMM*) receipts, takings; (*ECON*) income *sg*.

'entro *prep* (*temporale*) within.

entusias'mare *vt* to excite, fill with enthusiasm; **~rsi** (*per qc/qd*) to become enthusiastic (about sth/sb); **entusi'asmo**

sm enthusiasm; **entusi'asta, i, e** *ag* enthusiastic // *sm/f* enthusiast; **entusi'astico, a, ci, che** *ag* enthusiastic.

enume'rare *vt* to enumerate, list.

enunci'are [enun'tʃare] *vt* (*teoria*) to enunciate, set out.

'epico, a, ci, che *ag* epic.

epide'mia *sf* epidemic.

Epifa'nia *sf* Epiphany.

epiles'sia *sf* epilepsy.

e'pilogo, ghi *sm* conclusion.

epi'sodio *sm* episode.

e'pistola *sf* epistle.

e'piteto *sm* epithet.

'epoca, che *sf* (*periodo storico*) age, era; (*tempo*) time; (*GEO*) age.

ep'pure *cong* and yet, nevertheless.

epu'rare *vt* (*POL*) to purge; (: *persona*) to expel, remove.

equa'tore *sm* equator.

equazi'one [ekwat'tsjone] *sf* (*MAT*) equation.

e'questre *ag* equestrian.

equi'latero, a *ag* equilateral.

equili'brare *vt* to balance; **equi'librio** *sm* balance; (*bilancia*) equilibrium.

e'quino, a *ag* horse *cpd*; equine.

equi'nozio [ekwi'nɔttsjo] *sm* equinox.

equipaggi'are [ekwipad'dʒare] *vt* (*di persone*) to man; (*di mezzi*) to equip; **equi'paggio** *sm* crew.

equipa'rare *vt* to make equal.

equità *sf* equity, fairness.

equitazi'one [ekwitat'tsjone] *sf* (horse-)riding.

equiva'lente *ag, sm* equivalent; **equiva'lenza** *sf* equivalence.

equivo'care *vi* to misunderstand; **e'quivoco, a, ci, che** *ag* equivocal, ambiguous; (*sospetto*) dubious // *sm* misunderstanding; **a scanso di equivoci** to avoid any misunderstanding; **giocare sull'equivoco** to equivocate.

'equo, a *ag* fair, just.

'era *sf* era.

'erba *sf* grass; (*aromatica, medicinale*) herb; **in ~** (*fig*) budding; **er'baccia, ce** *sf* weed; **er'boso, a** *ag* grassy.

e'rede *sm/f* heir; **eredità** *sf* (*DIR*) inheritance; (*BIOL*) heredity; **lasciare qc in eredità a qd** to leave *o* bequeath sth to sb; **eredi'tare** *vt* to inherit; **eredi'tario, a** *ag* hereditary.

ere'mita, i *sm* hermit.

ere'sia *sf* heresy; **e'retico, a, ci, che** *ag* heretical // *sm/f* heretic.

e'retto, a *pp di* **erigere** // *ag* erect, upright; **erezi'one** *sf* (*FISIOL*) erection.

er'gastolo *sm* (*DIR: pena*) life imprisonment; (: *luogo di pena*) prison.

'erica *sf* heather.

e'rigere [e'ridʒere] *vt* to erect, raise; (*fig: fondare*) to found.

ermel'lino *sm* ermine.

er'metico, a, ci, che *ag* hermetic.

'ernia *sf* (*MED*) hernia.

e'roe *sm* hero.

ero'gare *vt* (*somme*) to distribute; (: *per beneficenza*) to donate; (*gas, servizi*) to supply.

e'roico, a, ci, che *ag* heroic.

ero'ina *sf* heroine; (*droga*) heroin.

ero'ismo *sm* heroism.

erosi'one *sf* erosion.

e'rotico, a, ci, che *ag* erotic.

'erpice ['erpitʃe] *sm* (*AGR*) harrow.

er'rare *vi* (*vagare*) to wander, roam; (*sbagliare*) to be mistaken; er'roneo, a *ag* erroneous, wrong; er'rore *sm* error, mistake; (*morale*) error; per errore by mistake.

'erta *sf* steep slope; stare all'~ to be on the alert.

eru'dito, a *ag* learned, erudite.

erut'tare *vi* to belch // *vt* (*sog: vulcano*) to throw out.

eruzi'one [erut'tsjone] *sf* eruption.

esacer'bare [ezatʃer'bare] *vt* to exacerbate.

esage'rare [ezadʒe'rare] *vt* to exaggerate // *vi* to exaggerate; (*eccedere*) to go too far; esagerazi'one *sf* exaggeration.

e'sagono *sm* hexagon.

esal'tare *vt* to exalt; (*entusiasmare*) to excite, stir; esal'tato *sm* fanatic.

e'same *sm* examination; (*INS*) exam, examination; dare un ~ to sit an exam; ~ del sangue blood test.

esami'nare *vt* to examine.

e'sanime *ag* lifeless.

esaspe'rare *vt* to exasperate; to exacerbate; ~rsi *vr* to become annoyed *o* exasperated; esasperazi'one *sf* exasperation.

esat'tezza [ezat'tettsa] *sf* exactitude, accuracy, precision.

e'satto, a *pp di* esigere // *ag* (*calcolo, ora*) correct, right, exact; (*preciso*) accurate, precise; (*puntuale*) punctual.

esat'tore *sm* (*di imposte etc*) collector.

esau'dire *vt* to grant, fulfil.

esauri'ente *ag* exhaustive.

esauri'mento *sm* exhaustion; ~ nervoso nervous breakdown.

esau'rire *vt* (*stancare*) to exhaust, wear out; (*provviste, miniera*) to exhaust; ~rsi *vr* to exhaust o.s., wear o.s. out; (*provviste*) to run out; esau'rito, a *ag* exhausted; (*merci*) sold out; (*libri*) out of print; e'sausto, a *ag* exhausted.

'esca, *pl* esche *sf* bait; (*sostanza infiammabile*) tinder.

escande'scenza [eskandeʃ'ʃentsa] *sf*: dare in ~e to lose one's temper, fly into a rage.

'esce, 'esci ['eʃe, 'eʃi] *forme del vb* uscire.

escla'mare *vi* to exclaim, cry out; esclamazi'one *sf* exclamation.

es'cludere *vt* to exclude; esclusi'one *sf* exclusion.

esclu'sivo, a *ag* exclusive // *sf* (*DIR*) exclusive *o* sole rights *pl*.

es'cluso, a *pp di* escludere.

'esco, 'escono *forme del vb* uscire.

'escono *forma del vb* uscire.

escre'menti *smpl* excrement *sg*, faeces.

escursi'one *sf* (*gita*) excursion, trip; (: *a piedi*) hike, walk; (*METEOR*) range.

ese'crare *vt* to loathe, abhor.

esecu'tivo, a *ag, sm* executive.

esecu'tore, 'trice *sm/f* (*MUS*) performer; (*DIR*) executor.

esecuzi'one [ezekut'tsjone] *sf* execution, carrying out; (*MUS*) performance; ~ capitale execution.

esegu'ire *vt* to carry out, execute; (*MUS*) to perform, execute.

e'sempio *sm* example; per ~ for example, for instance; esem'plare *ag* exemplary // *sm* example; (*copia*) copy; esemplifi'care *vt* to exemplify.

esen'tare *vt*: ~ qd/qc da to exempt sb/sth from.

e'sente *ag*: ~ da (*dispensato da*) exempt from; (*privo di*) free from; esenzi'one *sf* exemption.

e'sequie *sfpl* funeral rites; funeral service *sg*.

eser'cente [ezer'tʃente] *sm/f* trader, dealer; shopkeeper.

eserci'tare [ezertʃi'tare] *vt* (*professione*) to practise; (*alienare: corpo, mente*) to exercise, train; (*diritto*) to exercise; (*influenza, pressione*) to exert; ~rsi *vr* to practise; ~rsi alla lotta to practise fighting; esercitazi'one *sf* (*scolastica, militare*) exercise.

e'sercito [e'zertʃito] *sm* army.

eser'cizio [ezer'tʃittsjo] *sm* practise; exercising; (*fisico, di matematica*) exercise; (*ECON*) financial year; (*azienda*) business, concern; in ~ (*medico etc*) practising.

esi'bire *vt* to exhibit, display; (*documenti*) to produce, present; ~rsi *vr* (*attore*) to perform; (*fig*) to show off; esibizi'one *sf* exhibition; (*di documento*) presentation; (*spettacolo*) show, performance.

esi'gente [ezi'dʒente] *ag* demanding; esi-'genza *sf* demand, requirement.

e'sigere [e'zidʒere] *vt* (*pretendere*) to demand; (*richiedere*) to demand, require; (*imposte*) to collect.

e'siguo, a *ag* small, slight.

'esile *ag* slender, slim; (*suono*) faint.

esili'are *vt* to exile; e'silio *sm* exile.

e'simere *vt*: ~ qd/qc da to exempt sb/sth from.

esis'tenza [ezis'tentsa] *sf* existence.

e'sistere *vi* (2) to exist.

esis'tito, a *pp di* esistere.

esi'tare *vi* to hesitate; esitazi'one *sf* hesitation.

'esito *sm* result, outcome.

'esodo *sm* exodus.

esone'rare *vt*: ~ qd da to exempt sb from.

esorbi'tante *ag* exorbitant, excessive.

esorciz'zare [ezortʃid'dʒare] *vt* to exorcize.

e'sordio *sm* début.

esor'tare *vt*: ~ qd a fare to urge sb to do.

e'sotico, a, ci, che *ag* exotic.

es'pandere *vt* to expand; (*confini*) to extend; (*influenza*) to extend, spread; ~**rsi** *vr* to expand; **espansi'one** *sf* expansion; **espan'sivo, a** *ag* expansive, communicative.

espatri'are *vi* (2) to leave one's country.

espedi'ente *sm* expedient.

es'pellere *vt* to expel.

esperi'enza [espe'rjɛntsa] *sf* experience; (*SCIENZA: prova*) experiment; **parlare per** ~ to speak from experience.

esperi'mento *sm* experiment.

es'perto, a *ag, sm* expert.

espi'are *vt* to atone for.

espi'rare *vt, vi* to breathe out.

espli'care *vt* (*attività*) to carry out, perform.

es'plicito, a [es'plitʃito] *ag* explicit.

es'plodere *vi* (*anche fig*) to explode; (*fucile*) to go off // *vt* to fire.

esplo'rare *vt* to explore; **esplora'tore, 'trice** *sm/f* explorer; (*anche:* **giovane esploratore**) (boy) scout/(girl) guide // *sm* (*NAUT*) scout (ship); **esplorazi'one** *sf* exploration.

esplosi'one *sf* explosion; **esplo'sivo, a** *ag, sm* explosive; **es'ploso, a** *pp di* **esplodere.**

espo'nente *sm/f* (*rappresentante*) representative.

es'porre *vt* (*merci*) to display; (*quadro*) to exhibit, show; (*fatti, idee*) to explain, set out; (*porre in pericolo, FOT*) to expose.

espor'tare *vt* to export; **esporta'tore, 'trice** *ag* exporting // *sm* exporter; **esportazi'one** *sf* exportation; export.

esposizi'one [espozit'tsjone] *sf* displaying; exhibiting; setting out; (*anche FOT*) exposure; (*mostra*) exhibition; (*narrazione*) explanation, exposition.

es'posto, a *pp di* **esporre** // *ag*: ~ **a nord** facing north // *sm* (*AMM*) statement, account; (: *petizione*) petition.

espressi'one *sf* expression.

espres'sivo, a *ag* expressive.

es'presso, a *pp di* **esprimere** // *ag* express // *sm* (*lettera*) express letter; (*anche:* **treno** ~) express train; (*anche:* **caffè** ~) espresso.

es'primere *vt* to express; ~**rsi** *vr* to express o.s.

espulsi'one *sf* expulsion; **es'pulso, a** *pp di* **espellere.**

'essa *pronome f*, **'esse** *pronome fpl vedi* **esso.**

es'senza [es'sɛntsa] *sf* essence; **essenzi'ale** *ag* essential; **l'essenziale** the main *o* most important thing.

'essere *sm* being; ~ **umano** human being // *vi, vb con attributo* (2) to be // *vb ausiliare* (2) to have (*o qualche volta* be); è **giovane/professore** he is young/a teacher; è **l'una** it's one o'clock; **sono le otto** it's eight o'clock; **esserci: c'è/ci sono** there is/there are; **che c'è?** what's wrong?; **ci siamo!** here we are!; (*fig*) this

is it!; (: *siamo alle solite*) here we go again!; ~ **di** (*appartenenza*) to belong to; (*origine*) to be from; è **di mio fratello** it belongs to my brother, it's my brother's.

'esso, a *pronome* it; (*fam: riferito a persona: soggetto*) he/she; (: *complemento*) him/her; ~**i, e** *pronome pl* they; (*complemento*) them.

est *sm* east.

'estasi *sf* ecstasy.

es'tate *sf* summer.

es'tatico, a, ci, che *ag* ecstatic.

es'tendere *vt* to extend; ~**rsi** *vr* (*diffondersi*) to spread; (*territorio, confini*) to extend; **estensi'one** *sf* extension; (*di superficie*) expanse; (*MUS*) range.

esteri'ore *ag* outward, external.

es'terno, a *ag* (*porta, muro*) outer, outside; (*scala*) outside; (*alunno, impressione*) external // *sm* outside, exterior // *sm/f* (*allievo*) day pupil; **per uso** ~ for external use only.

'estero, a *ag* foreign // *sm*: **all'**~ abroad.

es'teso, a *pp di* **estendere** // *ag* extensive, large; **scrivere per** ~ to write in full.

es'tetico, a, ci, che *ag* aesthetic // *sf* aesthetics *q*; **este'tista** *sf* beautician.

'estimo *sm* valuation; (*disciplina*) surveying.

es'tinguere *vt* to extinguish, put out; (*debito*) to pay off; ~**rsi** *vr* to go out; (*famiglia, animali*) to become extinct; **es-'tinto, a** *pp di* **estinguere**; **estin'tore** *sm* (fire) extinguisher; **estinzi'one** *sf* putting out; (*di famiglia, animali*) extinction.

es'tivo, a *ag* summer *cpd*.

es'torcere [es'tɔrtʃere] *vt*: ~ **qc (a qd)** to extort sth (from sb); **estorsi'one** *sf* extortion; **es'torto, a** *pp di* **estorcere.**

estradizi'one [estradit'tsjone] *sf* extradition.

es'traneo, a *ag* foreign; (*discorso*) extraneous, unrelated // *sm/f* stranger; **rimanere** ~ **a qc** to take no part in sth.

es'trarre *vt* to extract, pull out; (*minerali*) to mine; (*sorteggiare*) to draw; **es'tratto, a** *pp di* **estrarre** // *sm* extract; (*di documento*) abstract; **estratto conto** statement of account; **estrazi'one** *sf* extraction; mining; drawing *q*; draw.

estre'mista, i, e *sm/f* extremist.

estremità *sf inv* extremity, end // *sfpl* (*ANAT*) extremities.

es'tremo, a *ag, sm* extreme; **l'**~ **Oriente** the Far East.

'estro *sm* (*capriccio*) whim, fancy; (*ispirazione creativa*) inspiration; **es'troso, a** *ag* whimsical, capricious; inspired.

estro'verso, a *ag, sm* extrovert.

estu'ario *sm* estuary.

esube'rante *ag* exuberant.

'esule *sm/f* exile.

età *sf inv* age; **all'**~ **di 8 anni** at the age of 8, at 8 years of age; **raggiungere la maggiore** ~ to come of age; **essere in** ~ **minore** to be under age.

'etere *sm* ether; **e'tereo, a** *ag* ethereal.

eternità *sf* eternity.

e'terno, a *ag* eternal.

etero'geneo, a [etero'dʒɛneo] *ag* heterogeneous.

'etica *sf vedi* etico.

eti'chetta [eti'ketta] *sf* label; (*cerimoniale*) etiquette.

'etico, a, ci, che *ag* ethical // *sf* ethics *sg*.

etimolo'gia, 'gie [etimolo'dʒia] *sf* etymology.

Eti'opia *sf*: l'~ Ethiopia.

'Etna *sm*: l'~ Etna.

'etnico, a, ci, che *ag* ethnic.

e'trusco, a, schi, sche *ag*, *sm/f* Etruscan.

'ettaro *sm* hectare (= 10,000 m²).

'etto *sm abbr di* ettogrammo.

etto'grammo *sm* hectogram(me) (= 100 grams).

Eucaris'tia *sf*: l'~ the Eucharist.

eufe'mismo *sm* euphemism.

Eu'ropa *sf*: l'~ Europe; euro'peo, a *ag*, *sm/f* European.

eutana'sia *sf* euthanasia.

evacu'are *vt* to evacuate; evacuazi'one *sf* evacuation.

e'vadere *vi* (2) (*fuggire*): ~ da to escape from // *vt* (*sbrigare*) to deal with, dispatch; (*tasse*) to evade.

evan'gelico, a, ci, che [evan'dʒɛliko] *ag* evangelical; evange'lista, i *sm* evangelist; evan'gelo *sm* = vangelo.

evapo'rare *vi* to evaporate; evaporazi'one *sf* evaporation.

evasi'one *sf* escape; ~ fiscale tax evasion.

eva'sivo, a *ag* evasive.

e'vaso, a *pp di* evadere // *sm* escapee.

e'vento *sm* event.

eventu'ale *ag* possible.

evi'dente *ag* evident, obvious; evi'denza *sf* obviousness; mettere in evidenza to point out, highlight.

evi'tare *vt* to avoid; ~ di fare to avoid doing; ~ qc a qd to spare sb sth.

'evo *sm* age, epoch.

evo'care *vt* to evoke.

evo'luto, a *pp di* evolvere.

evoluzi'one [evolut'tsjone] *sf* evolution.

e'volversi *vr* to evolve.

ev'viva *escl* hurrah!; ~ il rei long live the king!, hurrah for the king!

ex *prefisso* ex-.

'extra *prep* outside, outwith // *ag inv* first-rate; top-quality // *sm inv* extra; extraconiu'gale *ag* extramarital.

F

fa *forma del vb* fare // *sm inv* (*MUS*) F; (: *solfeggiando la scala*) fa // *av*: 10 anni ~ 10 years ago.

'fabbrica *sf* factory; fabbri'cante *sm* manufacturer, maker; fabbri'care *vt* to build; (*produrre*) to manufacture, make; (*fig*) to fabricate, invent.

'fabbro *sm* (black)smith.

fac'cenda [fat'tʃɛnda] *sf* matter, affair; (*cosa da fare*) task, chore.

fac'chino [fak'kino] *sm* porter.

'faccia, ce ['fattʃa] *sf* face; (*di moneta, disco etc*) side; ~ a ~ face to face.

facci'ata [fat'tʃata] *sf* façade; (*di pagina*) side.

'faccio ['fattʃo] *forma del vb* fare.

fa'ceto, a [fa'tʃeto] *ag* witty, humorous.

'facile ['fatʃile] *ag* easy; (*affabile*) easygoing; (*disposto*): ~ a inclined to, prone to; (*probabile*): è ~ che piova it's likely to rain; facilità *sf* easiness; (*disposizione, dono*) aptitude; facili'tare *vt* to make easier.

facino'roso, a [fatʃino'roso] *ag* violent.

facoltà *sf inv* faculty; (*potere*) power.

facolta'tivo, a *ag* optional; (*fermata d'autobus*) request *cpd*.

'faggio ['faddʒo] *sm* beech.

fagi'ano [fa'dʒano] *sm* pheasant.

fagio'lino [fadʒo'lino] *sm* French bean.

fagi'olo [fa'dʒɔlo] *sm* bean.

fa'gotto *sm* bundle; (*MUS*) bassoon; far ~ (*fig*) to pack up and go.

'fai *forma del vb* fare.

'falce ['faltʃe] *sf* scythe; fal'cetto *sm* sickle; falci'are *vt* to cut; (*fig*) to mow down.

'falco, chi *sm* hawk.

fal'cone *sm* falcon.

'falda *sf* layer, stratum; (*di cappello*) brim; (*di monte*) lower slope; (*di tetto*) pitch; nevica a larghe ~e the snow is falling in large flakes; abito a ~e tails *pl*.

fale'gname [falen'ɲame] *sm* joiner.

fal'lace [fal'latʃe] *ag* misleading; deceptive.

falli'mento *sm* failure; bankruptcy.

fal'lire *vi* (2: *non riuscire*): ~ (in) to fail (in); (*DIR*) to go bankrupt // *vt* (*bersaglio, preda*) to miss; fal'lito, a *ag* unsuccessful; bankrupt // *sm* bankrupt.

'fallo *sm* error, mistake; (*imperfezione*) defect, flaw; (*SPORT*) foul; fault; senza ~ without fail.

falò *sm inv* bonfire.

fal'sare *vt* to distort, misrepresent; fal'sario *sm* forger; counterfeiter; falsifi'care *vt* to forge; (*monete*) to forge, counterfeit.

'falso, a *ag* false; (*errato*) wrong, incorrect; (*falsificato*) forged; fake // *sm* forgery; giurare il ~ to commit perjury.

'fama *sf* fame; (*reputazione*) reputation, name.

'fame *sf* hunger; aver ~ to be hungry; fa'melico, a, ci, che *ag* ravenous.

fa'miglia [fa'miʎʎa] *sf* family.

famili'are *ag* (*della famiglia*) family *cpd*; (*ben noto*) familiar; (*tono*) friendly, informal; (*LING*) informal, colloquial // *sm* relative, relation; familiarità *sf* familiarity; informality.

fa'moso, a *ag* famous, well-known.

fa'nale *sm* (*AUT*) light, lamp; (*NAUT*) beacon; ~ di coda (*AUT*) tail-light.

fa'natico, a, ci, che ag fanatical; (del teatro, calcio etc): ~ **di** o **per** mad o wild about // sm/f fanatic; (tifoso) fan.

fanciul'lezza [fantʃul'lettsa] sf childhood.

fanci'ullo, a [fan'tʃullo] sm/f child.

fan'donia sf tall story; ~**e** sfpl nonsense sg.

fan'fara sf brass band; (musica) fanfare.

'fango, ghi sm mud; **fan'goso, a** ag muddy.

'fanno forma del vb **fare**.

fannul'lone, a sm/f idler, loafer.

fantasci'enza [fantaʃ'ʃentsa] sf science fiction.

fanta'sia sf fantasy, imagination; (capriccio) whim, caprice // ag inv: vestito ~ patterned dress.

fan'tasma, i sm ghost, phantom; (immagine) fantasy.

fantastiche'ria [fantastike'ria] sf daydream.

fan'tastico, a, ci, che ag fantastic; (potenza, ingegno) imaginative.

'fante sm infantryman; (CARTE) jack, knave; **fante'ria** sf infantry.

fan'toccio [fan'tɔttʃo] sm puppet.

far'dello sm bundle; (fig) burden.

'fare vt to make; (operare, agire) to do; (TEATRO) to act; ~ **l'avvocato/il medico** to be a lawyer/doctor; ~ **del tennis** to play tennis; ~ **il morto/l'ignorante** to act dead/the fool; **non fa niente** it doesn't matter; **2 più 2 fa 4** 2 and 2 are o make 4; **non ce la faccio più** I can't go on any longer; **farla** o **qd** to get the better of sb; **farla finita con qc** to have done with sth // vi (essere adatto) to be suitable; (stare per): **fece per parlare quando ...** he was about to speak when ...; ~ **in modo di** to act in such a way that; **faccia pure!** go ahead!; ~ **da** (fare le funzioni di) to act as // vb impers: vedi **bello, freddo** etc; ~ **piangere/ridere qd** to make sb cry/laugh; ~ **venire qd** to have sb come; **fammi vedere** let me see; ~**rsi** vr (diventare) to become; ~**rsi la macchina** to get a car for o.s.; ~**rsi avanti** to come forward; ~**rsi notare** to get o.s. noticed.

far'falla sf butterfly.

fa'rina sf flour.

fa'ringe [fa'rindʒe] sf (ANAT) pharynx.

farma'ceutico, a, ci, che [farma-'tʃeutiko] ag pharmaceutical.

farma'cia, 'cie [farma'tʃia] sf pharmacy; (locale) chemist's (shop), pharmacy; **farma'cista, i, e** sm/f chemist, pharmacist.

'farmaco, ci o **chi** sm drug, medicine.

'faro sm (NAUT) lighthouse; (AER) beacon; (AUT) headlight, headlamp.

'farsa sf farce.

'fascia, sce ['faʃʃa] sf band, strip; (MED) bandage; (di carta) wrapper; (di sindaco, ufficiale) sash; (parte di territorio) strip, belt.

fasci'are [faʃ'ʃare] vt to bandage.

fa'scicolo [faʃ'ʃikolo] sm (di documenti) file, dossier; (di rivista) issue, number; (opuscolo) booklet, pamphlet.

'fascino ['faʃʃino] sm charm, fascination.

'fascio ['faʃʃo] sm bundle, sheaf; (di fiori) bunch.

fa'scismo [faʃ'ʃizmo] sm fascism.

'fase sf phase.

fas'tidio sm (molestia) annoyance, bother, trouble; (scomodo) inconvenience; **dare** ~ **a qd** to bother o annoy sb; **sento** ~ **allo stomaco** my stomach's upset; **fastidi'oso, a** ag annoying, tiresome; (schifiltoso) fastidious.

'fasto sm pomp, splendour.

'fata sf fairy.

fa'tale ag fatal; (inevitabile) inevitable; (fig) irresistible; **fatalità** sf inevitability; (avversità) misfortune; (fato) fate, destiny.

fa'tica, che sf hard work, toil; (sforzo) effort; (di metalli) fatigue; **a** ~ **with** difficulty; **fati'care** vi to toil; **faticare a fare qc** to have difficulty doing sth; **fati'coso, a** ag tiring, exhausting; hard, difficult.

'fato sm fate, destiny.

'fatto, a pp di **fare** // ag: **un uomo** ~ a grown man; ~ **a mano/in casa** hand-/home-made // sm fact; (azione) deed; (di romanzo, film) action, story; (affare, caso) event; **cogliere qd sul** ~ to catch sb red-handed; **il** ~ **sta o è che** the fact remains o is that; **in** ~ **di** as for, as far as ... is concerned.

fat'tore sm (AGR) farm manager; (elemento costitutivo) factor.

fatto'ria sf farm; farmhouse.

fatto'rino sm errand-boy; office-boy.

fat'tura sf (di abito, scarpa) cut, design; (lavorazione) workmanship; (COMM) invoice; (malia) spell.

fattu'rare vt (COMM) to invoice; (vino) to adulterate.

'fatuo, a ag vain, fatuous.

'fauna sf fauna.

fau'tore sm advocate, supporter.

fa'vella sf speech.

fa'villa sf spark.

'favola sf (fiaba) fairy tale; (d'intento morale) fable; (fandonia) yarn; **favo'loso, a** ag fabulous.

fa'vore sm favour; **per** ~ please; **favo-'revole** ag favourable.

favo'rire vt to favour; (il commercio, l'industria, le arti) to promote, encourage; **vuole** ~? won't you help yourself?; **favorisca in salotto** please come into the sitting room; **favo'rito, a** ag, sm/f favourite.

fazi'one [fat'tsjone] sf faction.

fazzo'letto [fattso'letto] sm handkerchief; (per la testa) (head)scarf.

feb'braio sm February.

'febbre sf fever; **aver la** ~ to have a high temperature; ~ **da fieno** hay fever; **feb-'brile** ag (anche fig) feverish.

'feccia, ce ['fettʃa] sf dregs pl.

'fecola sf potato flour.

fecon'dare *vt* to fertilize.

fe'condo, a *ag* fertile.

'fede *sf* (*credenza*) belief, faith; (*REL*) faith; (*fiducia*) faith, trust; (*fedeltà*) loyalty; (*anello*) wedding ring; (*attestato*) certificate; **aver ~ in qd** to have faith in sb; **fe'dele** *ag*: **fedele (a)** faithful (to) // *sm/f* follower; **i fedeli** (*REL*) the faithful; **fedeltà** *sf* faithfulness; (*coniugale*, *RADIO*) fidelity.

'federa *sf* pillowslip, pillowcase.

fede'rale *ag* federal.

federazi'one [federat'tsjone] *sf* federation.

'fegato *sm* liver; (*fig*) guts *pl*, nerve.

'felce ['feltʃe] *sf* fern.

fe'lice [fe'litʃe] *ag* happy; (*fortunato*) lucky; **felicità** *sf* happiness.

felici'tarsi [felitʃi'tarsi] *vr* (*congratularsi*): **~ con qd per qc** to congratulate sb on sth.

fe'lino, a *ag* feline.

'feltro *sm* felt; (*cappello*) felt hat.

'femmina *sf* (*ZOOL*, *TECN*) female; (*figlia*) girl, daughter; (*spesso peg*) woman; **femmi'nile** *ag* feminine; (*sesso*) female; (*lavoro*) woman's // *sm* (*LING*) feminine; **femmi'nismo** *sm* feminism.

'fendere *vt* to split, cleave; (*attraversare*) to force one's way through.

fe'nomeno *sm* phenomenon.

'feretro *sm* coffin.

feri'ale *ag* working *cpd*, work *cpd*, week *cpd*; **giorno ~** weekday.

'ferie *sfpl* holidays.

fe'rire *vt* to injure; (*deliberatamente*: *MIL etc*) to wound; (*colpire*) to hurt; **fe'rita** *sf* injury; wound.

'ferma *sf* (*MIL*) (period of) service; (*CACCIA*): **cane da ~** pointer.

fer'maglio [fer'maʎʎo] *sm* clasp; (*gioiello*) brooch.

fer'mare *vt* to stop, halt; (*POLIZIA*) to detain, hold; (*bottone etc*) to fasten, fix // *vi* to stop; **~rsi** *vr* to stop, halt; **~ l'attenzione su qc** to focus one's attention on sth.

fer'mata *sf* stop; **~ dell'autobus** bus stop.

fer'mento *sm* (*anche fig*) ferment; (*lievito*) yeast.

fer'mezza [fer'mettsa] *sf* (*fig*) firmness, steadfastness.

'fermo, a *ag* still, motionless; (*veicolo*) stationary; (*orologio*) not working; (*saldo*: *anche fig*) firm; (*fissato*: *occhi*) fixed // *escl* stop!; keep still! // *sm* (*chiusura*) catch, lock; (*DIR*) detention.

fe'roce [fe'rotʃe] *ag* (*bestia*) wild, fierce, ferocious; (*persona*) cruel, fierce; (*fame*, *dolore*) raging; **fe'rocia, cie** *sf* ferocity.

ferra'gosto *sm* (*festa*) feast of the Assumption; (*periodo*) August holidays *pl*.

ferra'menta *sfpl* ironmongery *sg*, hardware *sg*; **negozio di ~** ironmonger's, hardware shop.

fer'rare *vt* (*cavallo*) to shoe.

'ferreo, a *ag* iron.

'ferro *sm* iron; **una bistecca ai ~i** a grilled steak; **~ battuto** wrought iron; **~ di cavallo** horseshoe; **~ da stiro** iron.

ferro'via *sf* railway; **le ~e** the railways; **ferrovi'ario, a** *ag* railway *cpd*; **ferrovi'ere** *sm* railwayman.

'fertile *ag* fertile; **fertiliz'zante** *sm* fertilizer.

fer'vente *ag* fervent, ardent.

fer'vore *sm* fervour, ardour; (*punto culminante*) height.

'fesso, a *pp di* **fendere** // *ag* (*fam*: *sciocco*) crazy, cracked.

fes'sura *sf* crack, split; (*per gettone*, *moneta*) slot.

'festa *sf* (*religiosa*) feast; (*pubblica*) holiday; (*compleanno*) birthday; (*onomastico*) name day; (*cerimonia*) celebration, party; **far ~** to have a holiday; to live it up; **far ~ a qd** to give sb a warm welcome.

festeggi'are [fested'dʒare] *vt* to celebrate; (*amici*, *sposi*) to give a warm welcome to.

fes'tino *sm* party; (*con balli*) ball.

fes'tivo, a *ag* Sunday *cpd*; holiday *cpd*; **giorno ~** holiday.

fes'toso, a *ag* merry, joyful.

fe'ticcio [fe'tittʃo] *sm* fetish.

'feto *sm* foetus.

'fetta *sf* slice.

feu'dale *ag* feudal.

FF.SS. *abbr di* *Ferrovie dello Stato*.

fi'aba *sf* fairy tale.

fi'acca *sf* weariness; (*svogliatezza*) listlessness.

fiac'care *vt* to weaken.

fi'acco, a, chi, che *ag* (*stanco*) tired, weary; (*svogliato*) listless; (*debole*) weak; (*mercato*) slack.

fi'accola *sf* torch.

fi'ala *sf* phial.

fi'amma *sf* flame; (*NAUT*) pennant.

fiammeggi'are [fjammed'dʒare] *vi* to blaze.

fiam'mifero *sm* match.

fiam'mingo, a, ghi, ghe *ag* Flemish // *sm/f* Fleming // *sm* (*LING*) Flemish; (*ZOOL*) flamingo; **i F~ghi** the Flemish.

fiancheggi'are [fjanked'dʒare] *vt* to border; (*fig*) to support, back (up); (*MIL*) to flank.

fi'anco, chi *sm* side; (*MIL*) flank; **di ~** sideways, from the side; **a ~ a ~** side by side.

fi'asco, schi *sm* flask; (*fig*) fiasco; **fare ~** to be a fiasco.

fi'ato *sm* breath; (*SPORT*) stamina; **avere il ~ grosso** to be out of breath; **prendere ~** to catch one's breath.

'fibbia *sf* buckle.

'fibra *sf* fibre; (*fig*) constitution.

fic'care *vt* to push, thrust, drive.

'fico, chi *sm* (*pianta*) fig tree; (*frutto*) fig; **~ d'India** prickly pear; **~ secco** dried fig.

fidanza'mento [fidantsa'mento] *sm* engagement.

fidan'zarsi [fidan'tsarsi] *vr* to get engaged; **fidan'zato, a** *sm/f* fiancé/fiancée.

fi'darsi *vr*: ~ **di** to trust; **fi'dato, a** *ag* reliable, trustworthy.

'fido *sm* (*seguace*) loyal follower; (*COMM*) credit.

fi'ducia [fi'dutʃa] *sf* confidence, trust; **incarico di** ~ position of trust, responsible position; **persona di** ~ reliable person.

fi'ele *sm* (*MED*) bile; (*fig*) bitterness.

fie'nile *sm* barn; hayloft.

fi'eno *sm* hay.

fi'era *sf* fair.

fie'rezza [fje'rettsa] *sf* pride.

fi'ero, a *ag* proud; (*crudele*) fierce, cruel; (*audace*) bold.

'fifa *sf* (*fam*): aver ~ to have the jitters.

'figlia ['fiʎʎa] *sf* daughter.

figli'astro, a [fiʎ'ʎastro] *sm/f* stepson/daughter.

'figlio ['fiʎʎo] *sm* son; (*senza distinzione di sesso*) child; ~ **di papà** spoilt, wealthy young man; **figli'occio, a, ci, ce** *sm/f* godchild, godson/daughter.

fi'gura *sf* figure; (*forma, aspetto esterno*) form, shape; (*illustrazione*) picture, illustration; **far** ~ to look smart; **fare una brutta** ~ to make a bad impression.

figu'rare *vt* (*plasmare*) to model; (*simboleggiare*) to symbolize, stand for // *vi* to appear; ~**rsi** *qc* to imagine sth; **figurati!** imagine that!; **ti do noia? - ma figurati!** am I disturbing you? - not at all!

figura'tivo, a *ag* figurative.

'fila *sf* row, line; (*coda*) queue; (*serie*) series, string; **di** ~ in succession; **fare la** ~ to queue; **in** ~ **indiana** in single file.

fila'mento *sm* filament.

filantro'pia *sf* philanthropy.

fi'lare *vt* to spin; (*NAUT*) to pay out // *vi* (*baco, ragno*) to spin; (*liquido*) to trickle out; (*discorso*) to hang together; (*fam: amoreggiare*) to go steady; (*4: muoversi a forte velocità*) to go at full speed; (*: andarsene lestamente*) to make o.s. scarce; ~ **diritto** (*fig*) to toe the line.

filar'monico, a, ci, che *ag* philharmonic.

filas'trocca, che *sf* nursery rhyme.

filate'lia *sf* philately, stamp collecting.

fi'lato, a *ag* spun // *sm* yarn; **3 giorni** ~**i** 3 days running o on end; **fila'tura** *sf* spinning; (*luogo*) spinning mill.

fi'letto *sm* braid, trimming; (*di vite*) thread; (*di carne*) fillet.

fili'ale *ag* filial // *sf* (*di impresa*) branch.

fili'grana *sf* (*in oreficeria*) filigree; (*su carta*) watermark.

film *sm inv* film; **fil'mare** *vt* to film.

'filo *sm* (*anche fig*) thread; (*filato*) yarn; (*metallico*) wire; **per** ~ **e per segno** in detail; ~ **d'erba** blade of grass; ~ **di perle** string of pearls; ~ **spinato** barbed

wire; **con un** ~ **di voce** in a whisper.

'filobus *sm inv* trolley bus.

fi'lone *sm* (*di minerali*) seam, vein; (*pane*) Vienna loaf; (*fig*) trend.

filoso'fia *sf* philosophy; **fi'losofo, a** *sm/f* philosopher.

fil'trare *vt, vi* (2) to filter.

'filtro *sm* filter.

'filza ['filtsa] *sf* (*anche fig*) string.

fin *av, prep* = **fino**.

fi'nale *ag* final // *sm* (*di opera*) end, ending; (*: MUS*) finale // *sf* (*SPORT*) final; **finalità** *sf* (*scopo*) aim, purpose; **final'mente** *av* finally, at last.

fi'nanza [fi'nantsa] *sf* finance; ~**e** *sfpl* (*di individuo, Stato*) finances; **finanzi'ario, a** *ag* financial; **finanzi'ere** *sm* financier; (*guardia di finanza: doganale*) customs officer; (*: tributaria*) inland revenue official.

finché [fin'ke] *cong* (*per tutto il tempo che*) as long as; (*fino al momento in cui*) until; **aspetta** ~ **io (non) sia ritornato** wait until I get back.

'fine *ag* (*lamina, carta*) thin; (*capelli, polvere*) fine; (*vista, udito*) keen, sharp; (*persona: raffinata*) refined, distinguished; (*osservazione*) subtle // *sf* end // *sm* aim, purpose; (*esito*) result, outcome; **secondo** ~ ulterior motive; **in** o **alla** ~ in the end, finally; ~ **settimana** *sm* o *f inv* weekend.

fi'nestra *sf* window; **fines'trino** *sm* (*di treno, auto*) window.

'fingere ['findʒere] *vt* to feign; (*supporre*) to imagine, suppose; ~**rsi** *vr*: ~**rsi ubriaco/pazzo** to pretend to be drunk/mad; ~ **di fare** to pretend to do.

fini'menti *smpl* (*di cavallo etc*) harness *sg*.

fini'mondo *sm* pandemonium.

fi'nire *vt* to finish // *vi* (2) to finish, end; ~ **di fare** (*compiere*) to finish doing; (*smettere*) to stop doing; ~ **ricco** to end up o finish up rich; **fini'tura** *sf* finish.

Fin'landia *sf*: **la** ~ Finland.

'fino, a *ag* (*capelli, seta*) fine; (*oro*) pure; (*fig: acuto*) shrewd // *av* (*spesso troncato in* **fin**: *pure*, anche) even // *prep* (*spesso troncato in* **fin**: *tempo*): **fin quando?** till when?; (*: luogo*): **fin qui** as far as here; ~ **a** (*tempo*) until, till; (*luogo*) as far as, (up) to; **fin da domani** from tomorrow onwards; **fin da ieri** since yesterday; **fin dalla nascita** from o since birth.

fi'nocchio [fi'nɔkkjo] *sm* fennel; (*fam: pederasta*) queer.

fi'nora *av* up till now.

'finto, a *pp di* **fingere** // *sf* pretence, sham; (*SPORT*) feint; **far** ~**a (di fare)** to pretend (to do).

finzi'one [fin'tsjone] *sf* pretence, sham.

fi'occo, chi *sm* (*di nastro*) bow; (*di stoffa, lana*) flock; (*di neve*) flake; (*NAUT*) jib; **coi** ~**chi** (*fig*) first-rate; ~**chi d'avena** oatflakes.

fi'ocina ['fjɔtʃina] *sf* harpoon.

fi'oco, a, chi, che *ag* faint, dim.

fi'onda *sf* catapult.

fio'raio, a *sm/f* florist.

fio'rami *smpl*: **a ~** flowered, with a floral pattern.

fi'ordo *sm* fjord.

fi'ore *sm* flower; **~i** *smpl* (*CARTE*) clubs; **a fior d'acqua/di pelle** on the surface of the water/skin.

fioren'tino, a *ag* Florentine.

fio'retto *sm* (*SCHERMA*) foil.

fio'rire *vi* (2) (*rosa*) to flower; (*albero*) to blossom; (*fig*) to flourish; (*ammuffire*) to become mouldy.

Fi'renze [fi'rɛntse] *sf* Florence.

'firma *sf* signature; (*reputazione*) name.

firma'mento *sm* firmament.

fir'mare *vt* to sign.

fisar'monica *sf* accordion.

fis'cale *ag* fiscal, tax *cpd*.

fischi'are [fis'kjare] *vi* to whistle // *vt* to whistle; (*attore*) to boo, hiss.

'fischio ['fiskjo] *sm* whistle.

'fisco *sm* tax authorities *pl*, ≈ Inland Revenue.

'fisico, a, ci, che *ag* physical // *sm/f* physicist // *sm* physique // *sf* physics *sg*.

fisiolo'gia [fizjolo'dʒia] *sf* physiology.

fisiono'mia *sf* face, physiognomy.

fisiotera'pia *sf* physiotherapy.

fis'sare *vt* to fix, fasten; (*guardare intensamente*) to stare at; (*data, condizioni*) to fix, establish, set; (*prenotare*) to book; **~rsi su** (*sog*: *sguardo, attenzione*) to focus on; (*fig*: *idea*) to become obsessed with; **fissazi'one** *sf* (*PSIC*) fixation.

'fisso, a *ag* fixed; (*stipendio, impiego*) regular; (*occhi*) staring.

'fitta *sf vedi* **fitto**.

fit'tizio, a *ag* fictitious, imaginary.

'fitto, a *ag* thick, dense // *sm* depths *pl*, middle; (*affitto, pigione*) rent // *sf* sharp pain; **a capo ~** head first.

fiu'mana *sf* swollen river; (*fig*) stream, flood.

fi'ume *sm* river.

fiu'tare *vt* to smell, sniff; (*sog*: *animale*) to scent; (*fig*: *inganno*) to get wind of, smell; **fi'uto** *sm* (sense of) smell; (*fig*) nose.

fla'gello [fla'dʒɛllo] *sm* scourge.

fla'grante *ag* flagrant; **cogliere qd in ~** to catch sb red-handed.

fla'nella *sf* flannel.

flash [flaʃ] *sm inv* (*FOT*) flash; (*giornalistico*) newsflash.

'flauto *sm* flute.

'flebile *ag* faint, feeble.

'flemma *sf* (*calma*) coolness, phlegm; (*MED*) phlegm.

fles'sibile *ag* pliable; (*fig*: *che si adatta*) flexible.

'flesso, a *pp di* **flettere**.

flessu'oso, a *ag* supple, lithe.

'flettere *vt* to bend.

F.lli (*abbr di* **fratelli**) Bros.

'flora *sf* flora.

'florido, a *ag* flourishing; (*fig*) glowing with health.

'floscio, a, sci, sce ['floʃʃo] *ag* floppy, soft; (*muscoli*) flabby.

'flotta *sf* fleet.

'fluido, a *ag*, *sm* fluid.

flu'ire *vi* (2) to flow.

fluore'scente [fluoreʃ'ʃɛnte] *ag* fluorescent.

flu'oro *sm* fluorine.

fluo'ruro *sm* fluoride.

'flusso *sm* flow; (*del mare*) flood tide; (*FISICA, MED*) flux; **~ e riflusso** ebb and flow.

fluttu'are *vi* to rise and fall; (*ECON*) to fluctuate; (*fig*) to waver.

fluvi'ale *ag* river *cpd*, fluvial.

'foca, che *sf* (*ZOOL*) seal.

fo'caccia, ce [fo'kattʃa] *sf* kind of pizza; (*dolce*) bun.

'foce ['fotʃe] *sf* (*GEO*) mouth.

foco'laio *sm* (*MED*) centre of infection; (*fig*) hotbed.

foco'lare *sm* hearth, fireside; (*TECN*) furnace.

'fodera *sf* lining; (*di libro, poltrona*) cover; **fode'rare** *vt* to line; to cover.

'fodero *sm* sheath.

'foga *sf* enthusiasm, ardour.

'foggia, ge ['fɔddʒa] *sf* (*maniera*) style; (*aspetto*) form, shape; (*moda*) fashion, style.

'foglia ['fɔʎʎa] *sf* leaf; **~ d'argento/d'oro** silver/gold leaf; **fogli'ame** *sm* foliage, leaves *pl*.

'foglio ['fɔʎʎo] *sm* (*di carta*) sheet (of paper); (*di metallo*) sheet; (*documento*) document; (*banconota*) (bank)note; **~ rosa** (*AUT*) provisional licence; **~ volante** pamphlet.

'fogna ['fɔɲɲa] *sf* drain, sewer; **fogna'tura** *sf* drainage, sewerage.

folgo'rare *vt* (*sog*: *fulmine*) to strike down; (: *alta tensione*) to electrocute.

'folla *sf* crowd, throng.

'folle *ag* mad, insane; (*TECN*) idle; **in ~** (*AUT*) in neutral.

fol'lia *sf* folly, foolishness; foolish act; (*pazzia*) madness, lunacy.

'folto, a *ag* thick.

fomen'tare *vt* to stir up, foment.

fonda'mento *sm* foundation; **~a** *sfpl* (*EDIL*) foundations.

fon'dare *vt* to found; (*edificio*) to lay the foundations for; (*fig*: *dar base*): **~ qc su** to base sth on; **fondazi'one** *sf* founding; (*ente morale*) foundation; **fondazi'oni** *sfpl* (*EDIL*) foundations.

'fondere *vt* (*neve*) to melt; (*metallo*) to fuse, melt; (*fig*: *colori*) to merge, blend // *vi* to melt; **~rsi** *vr* to melt; (*fig*: *partiti, correnti*) to unite, merge; **fonde'ria** *sf* foundry.

'fondo, a *ag* deep // *sm* (*di recipiente, pozzo*) bottom; (*di stanza*) back; (*quantità di liquido che resta, deposito*) dregs *pl*; (*sfondo*) background; (*unità immobiliare*) property, estate; (*somma di denaro*) fund; (*SPORT*) long-distance race; **~i** *smpl* (*denaro*) funds; **in ~ a** at the bottom of; at the back of; **andare a ~** (*nave*) to sink;

conoscere a ~ to know inside out; **in** ~ (fig) after all, all things considered; **andare fino in** ~ **a** (fig) to examine thoroughly; **a** ~ **perduto** (COMM) without security; ~**i di caffè** coffee grounds; ~**i di magazzino** old o unsold stock sg.

fo'netica sf phonetics sg.

fon'tana sf fountain.

'**fonte** sf spring, source; (fig) source.

fo'raggio [fo'raddʒo] sm fodder, forage.

fo'rare vt to pierce, make a hole in; (biglietto) to punch; ~ **una gomma** to burst a tyre.

'**forbici** ['forbitʃi] sfpl scissors.

forbi'cina [forbi'tʃina] sf earwig.

'**forca, che** sf (AGR) fork, pitchfork; (patibolo) gallows sg.

for'cella [for'tʃɛlla] sf fork; (di monte) pass.

for'chetta [for'ketta] sf fork.

for'cina [for'tʃina] sf hairpin.

'**forcipe** ['fortʃipe] sm forceps pl.

fo'resta sf forest.

foresti'ero, a ag foreign // sm/f foreigner.

'**forfora** sf dandruff.

'**forgia, ge** ['fordʒa] sf forge; **forgi'are** vt to forge.

'**forma** sf form; (aspetto esteriore) form, shape; (DIR: procedura) procedure; (per calzature) last; (stampo da cucina) mould; ~**e** sfpl (del corpo) figure, shape; **le** ~**e** (convenzioni) appearances; **essere in** ~ to be in good shape.

formag'gino [formad'dʒino] sm processed cheese.

for'maggio [for'maddʒo] sm cheese.

for'male ag formal; **formalità** sf inv formality.

for'mare vt to form, shape, make; (fig: carattere) to form, mould; ~**rsi** vr to form, take shape; **for'mato** sm format, size; **formazi'one** sf formation; (fig: educazione) training.

for'mica, che sf ant; **formi'caio** sm anthill.

formico'lare vi (2: gamba, braccio) to tingle; (brulicare: anche fig): ~ **di** to be swarming with; **mi formicola la gamba** I've got pins and needles in my leg, my leg's tingling; **formico'lio** sm pins and needles pl; swarming.

formi'dabile ag powerful, formidable; (straordinario) remarkable.

'**formula** sf formula.

formu'lare vt to formulate; to express.

for'nace [for'natʃe] sf (per laterizi etc) kiln; (per metalli) furnace.

for'naio sm baker.

for'nello sm (elettrico, a gas) ring; (di pipa) bowl.

for'nire vt: ~ **qd di qc,** ~ **qc a qd** to provide o supply sb with sth, to supply sth to sb.

'**forno** sm (di cucina) oven; (panetteria) bakery; (TECN: per calce etc) kiln; (: per metalli) furnace.

'**foro** sm (buco) hole; (STORIA) forum; (tribunale) (law) court.

'**forse** av perhaps, maybe; (circa) about; **essere in** ~ to be in doubt.

forsen'nato, a ag mad, insane.

'**forte** ag strong; (suono) loud; (spesa) considerable, great; (passione, dolore) great, deep // av strongly; (velocemente) fast; (a voce alta) loud(ly) // sm (edificio) fort; (specialità) forte, strong point; **essere** ~ **in qc** to be good at sth.

for'tezza [for'tettsa] sf (morale) strength; (luogo fortificato) fortress.

fortifi'care vt to fortify, strengthen.

for'tuito, a ag fortuitous.

for'tuna sf (destino) fortune, luck; (buona sorte) success, fortune; (eredità, averi) fortune; **per** ~ luckily, fortunately; **di** ~ makeshift, improvised; **atterraggio di** ~ emergency landing; **fortu'nato, a** ag lucky, fortunate; (impresa) successful.

forvi'are vt, vi = **fuorviare**.

'**forza** ['fortsa] sf strength; (potere) power; (FISICA) force; ~**e** sfpl (fisiche) strength sg; (MIL) forces // escl come on!; **per** ~ against one's will; (naturalmente) of course; **a viva** ~ by force; **a** ~ **di** by dint of; ~ **maggiore** circumstances beyond one's control; **la** ~ **pubblica** the police pl.

for'zare [for'tsare] vt to force; ~ **qd a fare** to force sb to do; **for'zato, a** ag forced // sm (DIR) prisoner sentenced to hard labour.

fos'chia [fos'kia] sf mist, haze.

'**fosco, a, schi, sche** ag dark, gloomy.

fos'fato sm phosphate.

fosforo sm phosphorous.

'**fossa** sf pit; (di cimitero) grave; ~ **biologica** septic tank.

fos'sato sm ditch; (di fortezza) moat.

fos'setta sf dimple.

'**fossile** ag, sm fossil.

'**fosso** sm ditch; (MIL) trench.

'**foto** sf (abbr di fotografia) photo // pref: **foto'copia** sf photocopy; **fotocopi'are** vt to photocopy; **fotogra'fare** vt to photograph; **fotogra'fia** sf (procedimento) photography; (immagine) photograph; **fo'tografo, a** sm/f photographer; **foto-ro'manzo** sm romantic picture story.

fra prep = **tra**.

fracas'sare vt to shatter, smash; ~**rsi** vr to shatter, smash; (veicolo) to crash; **fra-'casso** sm smash; crash; (baccano) din, racket.

'**fradicio, a, ci, ce** ['fraditʃo] ag (guasto) rotten; (molto bagnato) soaking (wet); **ubriaco** ~ blind drunk.

'**fragile** ['fradʒile] ag fragile; (fig: salute) delicate.

'**fragola** sf strawberry.

frago'roso, a ag crashing, roaring.

fra'grante ag fragrant.

frain'tendere vt to misunderstand; **frain'teso, a** pp di **fraintendere**.

fram'mento sm fragment.

'frana sf landslide; **fra'nare** vi (2) to slip, slide down.

fran'cese [fran'tʃeze] ag French // sm/f Frenchman/woman // sm (LING) French; **i F∼i** the French.

fran'chezza [fran'kettsa] sf frankness, openness.

'Francia ['frantʃa] sf: **la ∼** France.

'franco, a, chi, che ag (COMM) free; (sincero) frank, open, sincere // sm (moneta) franc; **farla ∼a** (fig) to get off scot-free; **∼ di dogana** duty-free; **∼ a domicilio** delivered free of charge; **prezzo ∼ fabbrica** ex-works price; **∼ tiratore** sm sniper.

franco'bollo sm (postage) stamp.

fran'gente [fran'dʒɛnte] sm breaker.

'frangia, ge ['frandʒa] sf fringe; (fig: abbellimento) frill, embellishment.

frantu'mare vt, **∼rsi** vr to break into pieces, shatter; **fran'tumi** smpl pieces, bits; (schegge) splinters.

'frasca, sche sf (leafy) branch.

'frase sf (LING) sentence; (locuzione, espressione, MUS) phrase; **∼ fatta** set phrase.

'frassino sm ash (tree).

frastu'ono sm hubbub, din.

'frate sm friar, monk.

fratel'lanza [fratel'lantsa] sf brotherhood; (associazione) fraternity.

fra'tello sm brother; **∼i** smpl brothers; (nel senso di fratelli e sorelle) brothers and sisters.

fra'terno, a ag fraternal, brotherly.

frat'tanto av in the meantime, meanwhile.

frat'tempo sm: **nel ∼** in the meantime, meanwhile.

frat'tura sf fracture.

fraudo'lento, a ag fraudulent.

frazi'one [frat'tsjone] sf fraction; (borgata): **∼ di comune** hamlet.

'freccia, ce ['frettʃa] sf arrow; **∼ di direzione** (AUT) indicator.

fred'dare vt to shoot dead.

fred'dezza [fred'dettsa] sf coldness.

'freddo, a ag, sm cold; **fa ∼** it's cold; **aver ∼** to be cold; **a ∼** (fig) deliberately; **freddo'loso, a** ag sensitive to the cold.

fred'dura sf pun.

fre'gare vt to rub; (fam: truffare) to take in, cheat; (: rubare) to swipe, pinch; **fregarsene** (fam!): **chi se ne frega?** who gives a damn (about it)?

fre'gata sf rub; (fam) swindle; (NAUT) frigate.

'fregio ['fredʒo] sm (ARCHIT) frieze; (ornamento) decoration.

'fremere vi: **∼ di** to tremble o quiver with; **'fremito** sm tremor, quiver.

fre'nare vt (veicolo) to slow down; (cavallo) to rein in; (lacrime) to restrain, hold back // vi to brake; **∼rsi** vr (fig) to restrain o.s., control o.s.; **fre'nata** sf: **fare una frenata** to brake.

frene'sia sf frenzy; mania; **fre'netico, a, ci, che** ag frenzied.

'freno sm brake; (morso) bit; (fig) check; **∼ a disco** disc brake; **∼ a mano** handbrake.

frequen'tare vt (luoghi) to frequent; (persone) to see (often).

fre'quente ag frequent; **di ∼** frequently; **fre'quenza** sf frequency; (assiduità) attendance.

fres'chezza [fres'kettsa] sf freshness.

'fresco, a, schi, sche ag fresh; (temperatura) cool; (notizia) recent, fresh // sm: **godere il ∼** to enjoy the cool air; **stare ∼** (fig) to be in for it; **mettere al ∼** to put in a cool place.

'fretta sf hurry, haste; **in ∼** in a hurry; **in ∼ e furia** in a mad rush; **aver ∼** to be in a hurry; **fretto'loso, a** ag hurried, rushed.

fri'abile ag (terreno) friable; (pasta) crumbly.

'friggere ['friddʒere] vt to fry // vi (olio etc) to sizzle.

'frigido, a ['fridʒido] ag (MED) frigid.

'frigo sm fridge.

frigo'rifero, a ag refrigerating // sm refrigerator.

fringu'ello sm chaffinch.

frit'tata sf omelette; **fare una ∼** (fig) to make a mess of things.

frit'tella sf (CUC) pancake; (: ripiena) fritter.

'fritto, a pp di **friggere** // ag fried // sm fried food; **∼ misto** mixed fry.

'frivolo, a ag frivolous.

frizi'one [frit'tsjone] sf friction; (di pelle) rub, rub-down; (AUT) clutch.

friz'zante [frid'dzante] ag (acqua) fizzy, sparkling; (vento, fig) biting.

'frizzo ['friddzo] sm witticism.

fro'dare vt to defraud, cheat.

'frode sf fraud; **∼ fiscale** tax evasion.

'frollo, a ag (carne) tender; (: di selvaggina) high; (fig: persona) soft; **pasta ∼a** short(crust) pastry.

'fronda sf (leafy) branch; (di partito politico) internal opposition; **∼e** sfpl foliage sg.

fron'tale ag frontal; (scontro) head-on.

'fronte sf (ANAT) forehead; (di edificio) front, façade // sm (MIL, POL, METEOR) front; **a ∼, di ∼** facing, opposite; **di ∼ a** (posizione) opposite, facing, in front of; (a paragone di) compared with.

fronteggi'are [fronted'dʒare] vt (avversari, difficoltà) to face, stand up to; (sog: edificio) to face.

fronti'era sf border, frontier.

fronzolo ['frondzolo] sm frill.

'frottola sf fib; **∼e** sfpl nonsense sg.

fru'gale ag frugal.

fru'gare vi to rummage // vt to search.

frul'lare vt (CUC) to whisk // vi (uccelli) to flutter; **frulla'tore** sm electric mixer; **frul'lino** sm whisk.

fru'mento sm wheat.

fru'scio [fruʃˈʃo] *sm* rustle; rustling; (*di acque*) murmur.

'frusta *sf* whip; (*CUC*) whisk.

frus'tare *vt* to whip.

frus'tino *sm* riding crop.

frus'trare *vt* to frustrate; **frustrazi'one** *sf* frustration.

'frutta *sf* fruit; (*portata*) dessert; ~ **candita/secca** candied/dried fruit.

frut'teto *sm* orchard.

frutti'vendolo, a *sm/f* greengrocer.

'frutto *sm* fruit; (*fig: risultato*) result(s); (*ECON: interesse*) interest; (: *reddito*) income; ~**i di mare** seafood *sg*.

FS *abbr di Ferrovie dello Stato.*

fu *forma del vb* **essere** // *ag inv:* **il** ~ **Paolo Bianchi** the late Paolo Bianchi.

fuci'lare [futʃiˈlare] *vt* to shoot; **fuci'lata** *sf* rifle shot.

fu'cile [fuˈtʃile] *sm* rifle, gun; (*da caccia*) shotgun, gun.

fu'cina [fuˈtʃina] *sf* forge.

'fuga *sf* flight; (*di gas, liquidi*) leak; (*MUS*) fugue; **prendere la** ~ to take flight, flee.

fu'gace [fuˈgatʃe] *ag* fleeting, transient.

fug'gevole [fudˈdʒevole] *ag* fleeting.

fuggi'asco, a, schi, sche [fudˈdʒasko] *ag, sm/f* fugitive.

fuggi'fuggi [fuddʒiˈfuddʒi] *sm* scramble, stampede.

fug'gire [fudˈdʒire] *vi* (2) to flee, run away; (*fig: passar veloce*) to fly // *vt* to avoid; **fuggi'tivo, a** *sm/f* fugitive, runaway.

'fulcro *sm* fulcrum.

ful'gore *sm* brilliance, splendour.

fu'liggine [fuˈliddʒine] *sf* soot.

fulmi'nare *vt* to strike down; (*sog: alta tensione*) to electrocute.

'fulmine *sm* thunderbolt; lightning *q*.

fumai'olo *sm* (*di nave*) funnel; (*di fabbrica*) chimney-stack.

fu'mare *vi* to smoke; (*emettere vapore*) to steam // *vt* to smoke; **fu'mata** *sf* puff of smoke; (*segnale*) smoke signal; (*di tabacco*) smoke; **fare una fumata** to have a smoke; **fuma'tore, 'trice** *sm/f* smoker.

fu'metto *sm* comic strip; ~**i** *smpl* comics.

'fumo *sm* smoke; (*vapore*) steam; (*il fumare tabacco*) smoking; ~**i** *smpl* fumes; **vendere** ~ to deceive, cheat; **fu'moso, a** *ag* smoky.

fu'nambolo, a *sm/f* tightrope walker.

'fune *sf* rope, cord; (*più grossa*) cable.

'funebre *ag* (*rito*) funeral; (*aspetto*) gloomy, funereal.

fune'rale *sm* funeral.

'fungere [ˈfundʒere] *vi:* ~ **da** to act as.

'fungo, ghi *sm* fungus; (*commestibile*) mushroom; ~ **velenoso** toadstool.

funico'lare *sf* funicular railway.

funi'via *sf* cable railway.

funzio'nare [funtsjoˈnare] *vi* to work, function; (*fungere*): ~ **da** to act as.

funzio'nario [funtsjoˈnarjo] *sm* official.

funzi'one [funˈtsjone] *sf* function; (*carica*) post, position; (*REL*) service; **entrare in** ~ to take up one's post; to take up office.

fu'oco, chi *sm* fire; (*fornello*) ring; (*FOT, FISICA*) focus; **dare** ~ **a qc** to set fire to sth; **far** ~ (*sparare*) to fire; ~ **d'artificio** firework.

fuorché [fworˈke] *cong, prep* except.

fu'ori *av* outside; (*all'aperto*) outdoors, outside; (*fuori di casa, SPORT*) out; (*esclamativo*) get out! // *prep:* ~ (*di*) out of, outside // *sm* outside; **lasciar** ~ **qc/qd** to leave sth/sb out; **far** ~ **qd** (*fam*) to kill sb, do sb in; **essere** ~ **di sé** to be beside o.s.; ~ **luogo** (*inopportuno*) out of place, uncalled for; ~ **mano** out of the way, remote; ~ **pericolo** out of danger; ~ **uso** old-fashioned; obsolete.

fu'ori... *prefisso:* **fuori'bordo** *sm* speedboat (with outboard motor); outboard motor; **fuori'classe** *sm/f inv* (undisputed) champion; **fuorig'ioco** *sm* offside; **fuori'legge** *sm/f inv* outlaw; **fuori'serie** *ag inv* (*auto etc*) custom-built; **fuoru'scito, a, fuoriu'scito, a** *sm/f* exile; **fuorvi'are** *vt* to mislead, put on the wrong track; (*fig*) to lead astray // *vi* to go astray.

'furbo, a *ag* cunning, sly; (*astuto*) shrewd.

fu'rente *ag:* ~ (**contro**) furious (with).

fur'fante *sm* rascal, scoundrel.

fur'gone *sm* van.

'furia *sf* (*ira*) fury, rage; (*fig: impeto*) fury, violence; (*fretta*) rush; **a** ~ **di** by dint of; **montare in** ~ to fly into a rage; **furi'bondo, a** *ag* furious.

furi'oso, a *ag* furious; (*mare, vento*) raging.

fu'rore *sm* fury; (*esaltazione*) frenzy; **far** ~ to be all the rage.

fur'tivo, a *ag* furtive; (*merce*) stolen.

'furto *sm* theft; ~ **con scasso** burglary.

'fusa *sfpl:* **fare le** ~ to purr.

fu'sibile *sm* (*ELETTR*) fuse.

fusi'one *sf* (*di metalli*) fusion, melting; (*colata*) casting; (*COMM*) merger; (*fig*) merging.

'fuso, a *pp di* **fondere** // *sm* (*FILATURA*) spindle; ~ **orario** time zone.

fus'tagno [fusˈtaɲɲo] *sm* corduroy.

'fusto *sm* stem; (*ANAT, di albero*) trunk; (*recipiente: in metallo*) drum, can; (: *in legno*) barrel, cask.

'futile *ag* vain, futile; **futilità** *sf inv* futility.

fu'turo, a *ag, sm* future.

G

gab'bare *vt* to take in, dupe; ~**rsi** *vr:* ~**rsi di qd** to make fun of sb.

'gabbia *sf* cage; (*DIR*) dock; (*da imballaggio*) crate; ~ **dell'ascensore** lift shaft; ~ **toracica** (*ANAT*) rib cage.

gabbi'ano *sm* (sea)gull.

gabi'netto *sm* (*MED etc*) consulting room; (*POL*) cabinet; (*di decenza*) toilet, lavatory; (*INS: di fisica etc*) laboratory.

gagli'ardo, a [gaʎˈʎardo] *ag* strong, vigorous.

gai'ezza [gaˈjettsa] *sf* gaiety, cheerfulness.

'**gaio, a** *ag* gay, cheerful.
'**gala** *sf* (*sfarzo*) pomp; (*festa*) ala.
ga'lante *ag* gallant, courteous; (*avventura, poesia*) amorous; **galante'ria** *sf* gallantry.
galantu'omo, *pl* **galantu'omini** *sm* gentleman.
ga'lassia *sf* galaxy.
gala'teo *sm* (good) manners *pl*.
gale'otto *sm* (*rematore*) galley slave; (*carcerato*) convict.
ga'lera *sf* prison.
'**galla** *sf* (*BOT*) gall; **a ~** afloat.
galleggi'ante [galled'dʒante] *ag* floating // *sm* (*natante*) barge; (*di pescatore, lenza, TECN*) float.
galleggi'are [galled'dʒare] *vi* to float.
galle'ria *sf* (*traforo*) tunnel; (*ARCHIT, d'arte*) gallery; (*TEATRO*) circle; (*strada coperta con negozi*) arcade; **~ del vento** *o* **aerodinamica** (*AER*) wind tunnel.
'**Galles** *sm*: **il ~** Wales.
gal'lina *sf* hen.
'**gallo** *sm* cock.
gal'lone *sm* piece of braid; (*MIL*) stripe; (*misura inglese e americana*) gallon.
galop'pare *vi* to gallop.
ga'loppo *sm* gallop; **al** *o* **di ~** at a gallop.
galvaniz'zare [galvanid'dzare] *vt* to galvanize.
'**gamba** *sf* leg; (*asta: di lettera*) stem; **in ~** (*in buona salute*) well; (*bravo*) bright, smart; **prendere qc sotto ~** (*fig*) to treat sth too lightly.
gambe'retto *sm* prawn; shrimp.
'**gambero** *sm* (*di acqua dolce*) crayfish; (*di mare*) lobster.
'**gambo** *sm* stem; (*di pianta*) stalk, stem; (*TECN*) shank.
'**gamma** *sf* (*MUS*) scale; (*di colori, fig*) range, gamut.
ga'nascia, sce [ga'naʃʃa] *sf* jaw; **~sce del freno** (*AUT*) brake shoes.
'**gancio** ['gantʃo] *sm* hook.
'**ganghero** ['gangero] *sm* (*arpione di ferro*) hinge; (*gancetto*) hook; **uscire dai ~i** (*fig*) to fly into a temper.
'**gara** *sf* competition; (*SPORT*) competition; contest; match; (: *corsa*) race; **fare a ~ to** compete, vie.
garan'tire *vt* to guarantee; (*dare per certo*) to assure.
garan'zia [garan'tsia] *sf* guarantee; (*pegno*) security.
gar'bato, a *ag* courteous, polite.
'**garbo** *sm* (*buone maniere*) politeness, courtesy; (*di vestito etc*) grace, style.
gareggi'are [gared'dʒare] *vi* to compete.
garga'rismo *sm* gargle; **fare i ~i** to gargle.
ga'rofano *sm* carnation; **chiodo di ~** clove.
'**garza** ['gardza] *sf* (*per bende*) gauze.
gar'zone [gar'dzone] *sm* boy; **~ di stalla** stableboy.
gas *sm inv* gas; **a tutto ~** at full speed; **dare ~** (*AUT*) to accelerate; **~ lacrimogeno** tear gas.

ga'solio *sm* diesel oil.
ga's(s)are *vt* to aerate, carbonate; (*asfissiare*) to gas.
gas'soso, a *ag* gaseous; gassy // *sf* lemonade.
'**gastrico, a, ci, che** *ag* gastric.
gastrono'mia *sf* gastronomy.
gat'tino *sm* kitten.
'**gatto, a** *sm/f* cat, tomcat/she-cat; **~ selvatico** wildcat.
gatto'pardo *sm*: **~ africano** serval; **~ americano** ocelot.
gat'tuccio [gat'tuttʃo] *sm* dogfish.
gau'dente *sm/f* pleasure-seeker.
ga'vetta *sf* (*MIL*) mess tin.
'**gazza** ['gaddza] *sf* magpie.
gaz'zella [gad'dzɛlla] *sf* gazelle.
gaz'zetta [gad'dzetta] *sf* news sheet; **G~ Ufficiale** official publication containing details of new laws.
gaz'zoso, a *ag* = **gassoso**.
ge'lare [dʒe'lare] *vt, vi, vb impers* to freeze; **ge'lata** *sf* frost.
gelate'ria [dʒelate'ria] *sf* ice-cream shop.
gela'tina [dʒela'tina] *sf* gelatine; **~ esplosiva** dynamite; **~ di frutta** fruit jelly.
ge'lato, a [dʒe'lato] *ag* frozen // *sm* ice cream.
'**gelido, a** ['dʒɛlido] *ag* icy, ice-cold.
'**gelo** ['dʒɛlo] *sm* (*temperatura*) intense cold; (*brina*) frost; (*fig*) chill; **ge'lone** *sm* chilblain.
gelo'sia [dʒelo'sia] *sf* (*stato d'animo*) jealousy; (*persiana*) shutter.
ge'loso, a [dʒe'loso] *ag* jealous.
'**gelso** ['dʒɛlso] *sm* mulberry (tree).
gelso'mino [dʒelso'mino] *sm* jasmine.
ge'mello, a [dʒe'mɛllo] *ag, sm/f* twin; **~i** *smpl* (*di camicia*) cufflinks; (*dello zodiaco*): **G~i** Gemini *sg*.
'**gemere** ['dʒɛmere] *vi* to moan, groan; (*cigolare*) to creak; (*gocciolare*) to drip, ooze; '**gemito** *sm* moan, groan.
'**gemma** ['dʒɛmma] *sf* (*BOT*) bud; (*pietra preziosa*) gem.
gene'rale [dʒene'rale] *ag, sm* general; **in ~** (*per sommi capi*) in general terms; (*di solito*) usually, in general; **a ~ richiesta** by popular request; **generalità** *sfpl* (*dati d'identità*) particulars; **generaliz'zare** *vt, vi* to generalize.
gene'rare [dʒene'rare] *vt* (*dar vita*) to give birth to; (*produrre*) to produce; (*causare*) to arouse; (*TECN*) to produce, generate; **genera'tore** *sm* (*TECN*) generator; **generazi'one** *sf* generation.
'**genere** ['dʒɛnere] *sm* kind, type, sort; (*BIOL*) genus; (*merce*) article, product; (*LING*) gender; (*ARTE, LETTERATURA*) genre; **in ~** generally, as a rule; **il ~ umano** mankind; **~i alimentari** foodstuffs.
ge'nerico, a, ci, che [dʒe'nɛriko] *ag* generic; (*persona: non specializzata*) general, non-specialized.
'**genero** ['dʒɛnero] *sm* son-in-law.
generosità [dʒenerosi'ta] *sf* generosity.

gene'roso, a [dʒene'roso] *ag* generous.

'genesi ['dʒɛnesi] *sf* genesis.

ge'netico, a, ci, che [dʒe'nɛtiko] *ag* genetic // *sf* genetics *sg*.

gen'giva [dʒen'dʒiva] *sf* (ANAT) gum.

geni'ale [dʒen'jale] *ag* (*persona*) of genius; (*idea*) ingenious, brilliant.

'genio ['dʒɛnjo] *sm* genius; (*attitudine, talento*) talent, flair, genius; **andare a ~ a qd** to be to sb's liking, appeal to sb.

geni'tale [dʒeni'tale] *ag* genital; **~i** *smpl* genitals.

geni'tore [dʒeni'tore] *sm* parent, father *o* mother; **~i** *smpl* parents.

gen'naio [dʒen'najo] *sm* January.

'Genova ['dʒɛnova] *sf* Genoa.

gen'taglia [dʒen'taʎʎa] *sf* (*peg*) rabble.

'gente ['dʒɛnte] *sf* people *pl*.

gen'tile [dʒen'tile] *ag* (*persona, atto*) kind; (: *garbato*) courteous, polite; (*nelle lettere*): **G~ Signore** Dear Sir; (: *sulla busta*): **G~ Signor Fernando Villa** Mr Fernando Villa; **genti'lezza** *sf* kindness; courtesy, politeness; **per gentilezza** (*per favore*) please.

genuflessi'one [dʒenufles'sjone] *sf* genuflection.

genu'ino, a [dʒenu'ino] *ag* genuine.

geogra'fia [dʒeogra'fia] *sf* geography; **geo'grafico, a, ci, che** *ag* geographical.

geolo'gia [dʒeolo'dʒia] *sf* geology; **geo'logico, a, ci, che** *ag* geological.

ge'ometra, i, e [dʒe'ɔmetra] *sm/f* (*professionista*) surveyor.

geome'tria [dʒeome'tria] *sf* geometry; **geo'metrico, a, ci, che** *ag* geometric(al).

ge'ranio [dʒe'ranjo] *sm* geranium.

gerar'chia [dʒerar'kia] *sf* hierarchy.

ge'rente [dʒe'rɛnte] *sm/f* manager/manageress.

'gergo, ghi ['dʒɛrgo] *sm* jargon; slang.

geria'tria [dʒerja'tria] *sf* geriatrics *sg*.

Ger'mania [dʒer'manja] *sf*: **la ~** Germany.

'germe ['dʒɛrme] *sm* germ.

germogli'are [dʒermoʎ'ʎare] *vi* to sprout; to germinate; **ger'moglio** *sm* shoot; bud.

gero'glifico, ci [dʒero'glifiko] *sm* hieroglyphic.

'gesso ['dʒɛsso] *sm* chalk; (SCULTURA, MED, EDIL) plaster; (*minerale*) gypsum.

gestazi'one [dʒestat'tsjone] *sf* gestation.

gestico'lare [dʒestiko'lare] *vi* to gesticulate.

gesti'one [dʒes'tjone] *sf* management.

ges'tire [dʒes'tire] *vt* to run, manage.

'gesto ['dʒɛsto] *sm* gesture.

ges'tore [dʒes'tore] *sm* manager.

Gesù [dʒe'zu] *sm* Jesus.

gesu'ita, i [dʒezu'ita] *sm* Jesuit.

get'tare [dʒet'tare] *vt* to throw; (*anche*: **~ via**) to throw away *o* out; (SCULTURA) to cast; (EDIL) to lay; (*emettere*) to spout, gush; **~rsi in** (*sog: fiume*) to flow into; **~ uno sguardo su** to take a quick look at;

get'tata *sf* (*di cemento, metalli*) cast; (*diga*) jetty.

'getto ['dʒetto] *sm* (*di gas, liquido, AER*) jet; (BOT) shoot; **a ~ continuo** uninterruptedly; **di ~** (*fig*) straight off, in one go.

get'tone [dʒet'tone] *sm* token; (*per giochi*) counter; (: *roulette etc*) chip; **~ telefonico** telephone token.

'ghetto ['getto] *sm* ghetto.

ghiacci'aio [gjat'tʃajo] *sm* glacier.

ghiacci'are [gjat'tʃare] *vt* to freeze; (*fig*): **~ qd** to make sb's blood run cold // *vi* to freeze, ice over.

ghi'accio ['gjattʃo] *sm* ice.

ghiacci'olo [gjat'tʃɔlo] *sm* icicle; (*tipo di gelato*) ice(d) lolly.

ghi'aia ['gjaja] *sf* gravel.

ghi'anda ['gjanda] *sf* (BOT) acorn.

ghi'andola ['gjandola] *sf* gland.

ghigliot'tina [giʎʎot'tina] *sf* guillotine.

ghi'gnare [gin'nare] *vi* to sneer.

ghi'otto, a ['gjotto] *ag* greedy; (*cibo*) delicious, appetizing; **ghiot'tone, a** *sm/f* glutton.

ghiri'bizzo [giri'biddzo] *sm* whim.

ghiri'goro [giri'gɔro] *sm* scribble, squiggle.

ghir'landa [gir'landa] *sf* garland, wreath.

'ghiro ['giro] *sm* dormouse.

'ghisa ['giza] *sf* cast iron.

già [dʒa] *av* already; (*ex, in precedenza*) formerly // *escl* of course!, yes indeed!

gi'acca, che ['dʒakka] *sf* jacket; **~ a vento** windcheater.

giacché [dʒak'ke] *cong* since, as.

giac'chetta [dʒak'ketta] *sf* (light) jacket.

gia'cenza [dʒa'tʃɛntsa] *sf*: **merce in ~** goods in stock; **capitale in ~** uninvested capital; **~e di magazzino** unsold stock.

gia'cere [dʒa'tʃere] *vi* (2) to lie; **giaci'mento** *sm* deposit.

gia'cinto [dʒa'tʃinto] *sm* hyacinth.

gi'ada ['dʒada] *sf* jade.

giaggi'olo [dʒad'dʒɔlo] *sm* iris.

giagu'aro [dʒa'gwaro] *sm* jaguar.

gi'allo ['dʒallo] *ag* yellow; (*carnagione*) sallow // *sm* yellow; (*anche*: **romanzo ~**) detective novel; (*anche*: **film ~**) detective film; **~ dell'uovo** yolk.

giam'mai [dʒam'mai] *av* never.

Giap'pone [dʒap'pone] *sm* Japan; **giappo'nese** *ag, sm/f, sm* Japanese.

gi'ara ['dʒara] *sf* jar.

giardi'naggio [dʒardi'naddʒo] *sm* gardening.

giardini'ere, a [dʒardi'njɛre] *sm/f* gardener // *sf* (*misto di sottaceti*) mixed pickles *pl*; (*automobile*) estate car.

giar'dino [dʒar'dino] *sm* garden; **~ d'infanzia** nursery school; **~ pubblico** public gardens *pl*, (public) park.

giarretti'era [dʒarret'tjɛra] *sf* garter.

giavel'lotto [dʒavel'lɔtto] *sm* javelin.

gi'gante, essa [dʒi'gante] *sm/f* giant // *ag* giant, gigantic; **gigan'tesco, a, schi, sche** *ag* gigantic.

'giglio ['dʒiʎʎo] *sm* lily.

gilè [dʒi'lɛ] *sm inv* waistcoat.

gin [dʒin] *sm* gin.

ginecolo'gia [dʒinekolo'dʒia] *sf* gynaecology.

gi'nepro [dʒi'nepro] *sm* juniper.

gi'nestra [dʒi'nɛstra] *sf* (BOT) broom.

Gi'nevra [dʒi'nevra] *sf* Geneva.

gingil'larsi [dʒindʒil'larsi] *vr* to fritter away one's time.

gin'gillo [dʒin'dʒillo] *sm* plaything.

gin'nasio [dʒin'nazjo] *sm the 4th and 5th year of secondary school in Italy.*

gin'nasta, i, e [dʒin'nasta] *sm/f* gymnast; **gin'nastica** *sf* gymnastics *sg*; keep-fit exercises.

gi'nocchio [dʒi'nɔkkjo], *pl*(m) **gi'nocchi** *o pl*(f) **gi'nocchia** *sm* knee; **stare in ~** to kneel, be on one's knees; **ginocchi'oni** *av* on one's knees.

gio'care [dʒo'kare] *vt* to play; (*scommettere*) to stake, wager, bet; (*ingannare*) to take in // *vi* to play; (*a roulette etc*) to gamble; (*fig*) to play a part, be important; (TECN: *meccanismo*) to be loose; **~ a** (*gioco, sport*) to play; (*cavalli*) to bet on; **gioca'tore, 'trice** *sm/f* player; gambler.

gio'cattolo [dʒo'kattolo] *sm* toy.

gio'chetto [dʒo'ketto] *sm* (*fig*): **è un ~** it's child's play.

gi'oco, chi ['dʒɔko] *sm* game; (*divertimento*, TECN) play; (*al casinò*) gambling; (CARTE) hand; (*insieme di pezzi etc necessari per un gioco*) set; **per ~** for fun; **fare il doppio ~ con qd** to double-cross sb; **~ d'azzardo** game of chance; **~ della palla football; ~ degli scacchi** chess set; **i giochi olimpici** the Olympic games.

gio'coso, a [dʒo'koso] *ag* playful, jesting.

gio'gaia [dʒo'gaja] *sf* (GEO) range of mountains.

gi'ogo, ghi ['dʒɔgo] *sm* yoke.

gi'oia [dʒ'ɔja] *sf* joy, delight; (*pietra preziosa*) jewel, precious stone.

gioiel'leria [dʒojelle'ria] *sf* jeweller's craft; jeweller's (shop).

gioielli'ere, a [dʒojel'ljɛre] *sm/f* jeweller.

gioi'ello [dʒo'jɛllo] *sm* jewel, piece of jewellery; **~i** *smpl* jewellery *sg*.

gioi'oso, a [dʒo'joso] *ag* joyful.

Gior'dania [dʒor'danja] *sf*: **la ~** Jordan.

giorna'laio, a [dʒorna'lajo] *sm/f* newsagent; news-vendor.

gior'nale [dʒor'nale] *sm* (news)paper; (*diario*) diary, journal; (COMM) journal; **~ di bordo** log; **~ radio** radio news *sg*.

giornali'ero, a [dʒorna'ljɛro] *ag* daily; (*che varia: umore*) changeable // *sm/f* day labourer.

giorna'lismo [dʒorna'lizmo] *sm* journalism.

giorna'lista, i, e [dʒorna'lista] *sm/f* journalist.

gior'nata [dʒor'nata] *sf* day; **~ lavorativa** working day.

gi'orno ['dʒorno] *sm* day; (*opposto alla notte*) day, daytime; (*luce del ~*) daylight; **al ~** per day; **di ~** by day; **d'oggi** nowadays.

gi'ostra ['dʒɔstra] *sf* merry-go-round; (*torneo storico*) joust.

gio'vane ['dʒovane] *ag* young; (*giovanile*) youthful // *sm/f* youth/girl, young man/woman; **i ~i** young people; **giova-'nile** *ag* youthful; **giova'notto** *sm* young man.

gio'vare [dʒo'vare] *vi*: **~ a** (*essere utile*) to be useful to; (*far bene*) to be good for // *vb impers* (*essere bene, utile*) to be useful; **~rsi di qc** to take advantage of sth.

giovedì [dʒove'di] *sm* Thursday; **di o il ~** on Thursdays.

gioventù [dʒoven'tu] *sf* youth; (*i giovani*) young people *pl*, youth.

giovi'ale [dʒo'vjale] *ag* jovial, jolly.

giovi'nezza [dʒovi'nettsa] *sf* youth.

gira'dischi [dʒira'diski] *sm inv* record player.

gi'raffa [dʒi'raffa] *sf* giraffe.

giran'dola [dʒiran'dola] *sf* (*fuoco d'artificio*) Catherine wheel; (*giocattolo*) toy windmill; (*banderuola*) weather vane, weather cock.

gi'rare [dʒi'rare] *vt* (*far ruotare*) to turn; (*percorrere, visitare*) to go round; (CINEMA) to shoot; to make; (COMM) to endorse // *vi* to turn; (*più veloce*) to spin; (*andare in giro*) to wander, go around; **~rsi** *vr* to turn; **~ attorno a** to go round; to revolve round; **far ~ la testa a qd** to make sb dizzy; (*fig*) to turn sb's head.

girar'rosto [dʒirar'rɔsto] *sm* (CUC) spit.

gira'sole [dʒira'sole] *sm* sunflower.

gi'rata [dʒi'rata] *sf* (*passeggiata*) stroll; (*con veicolo*) drive; (COMM) endorsement.

gira'volta [dʒira'vɔlta] *sf* twirl, turn; (*curva*) sharp bend; (*fig*) about-turn.

gi'revole [dʒi'revole] *ag* revolving, turning.

gi'rino [dʒi'rino] *sm* tadpole.

'giro ['dʒiro] *sm* (*cerchio*) circle; (*di manovella*) turn; (*viaggio*) tour, excursion; (*passeggiata*) stroll, walk; (*in macchina*) drive; (*in bicicletta*) ride; (SPORT: *della pista*) lap; (*di denaro*) circulation; (CARTE) hand; (TECN) revolution; **prendere in ~ qd** (*fig*) to pull sb's leg; **fare un ~** to go for a walk (*o* a drive *o* a ride); **andare in ~** to go about, walk around; **a stretto ~ di posta** by return of post; **nel ~ di un mese** in a month's time; **~ d'affari** (COMM) turnover; **~ di parole** circumlocution; **~ di prova** (AUT) test drive; **giro'collo** *sm*: **a girocollo** crewneck *cpd*; **gi'rone** *sm* (SPORT) series of games; **girone di andata/ritorno** (CALCIO) first/second half of the season.

gironzo'lare [dʒirondzo'lare] *vi* to stroll about.

girova'gare [dʒirova'gare] *vi* to wander about.

'gita ['dʒita] *sf* excursion, trip.

gi'tano, a [dʒi'tano] *sm/f* gipsy.

giù [dʒu] *av* down; *(dabbasso)* downstairs; **in ~** downwards, down; **~ di lì** *(pressappoco)* thereabouts; **bambini dai 6 anni in ~** children aged 6 and under; **~ per: cadere ~ per le scale** to fall down the stairs; **portare i capelli ~ per le spalle** to have shoulder-length hair; **essere ~** *(fig: di salute)* to be run down; *(: di spirito)* to be depressed.

giub'botto [dʒub'bɔtto] *sm* jerkin.

giubi'lare [dʒubi'lare] *vi* to rejoice // *vt* to pension off.

gi'ubilo ['dʒubilo] *sm* rejoicing.

giudi'care [dʒudi'kare] *vt* to judge; **~ qd/qc bello** to consider sb/sth (to be) beautiful.

gi'udice ['dʒuditʃe] *sm* judge; **~ conciliatore** justice of the peace.

giu'dizio [dʒu'dittsjo] *sm* judgment; *(opinione)* opinion; *(DIR)* judgment, sentence; *(: processo)* trial; *(: verdetto)* verdict; **aver ~** to be wise *o* prudent; **giudizi'oso, a** *ag* prudent, judicious.

gi'ugno ['dʒuɲɲo] *sm* June.

giul'lare [dʒul'lare] *sm* jester.

giu'menta [dʒu'menta] *sf* mare.

gi'unco, chi ['dʒunko] *sm* rush.

gi'ungere ['dʒundʒere] *vi* (2) to arrive // *vt* *(mani etc)* to join; **~ a** to arrive at, reach.

gi'ungla ['dʒungla] *sf* jungle.

gi'unto, a ['dʒunto] *pp di* **giungere** // *sf* addition; *(organo esecutivo, amministrativo)* council, board; **per ~a** into the bargain, in addition; **~a militare** military junta; **giun'tura** *sf* joint.

giuo'care [dʒwo'kare] *vt, vi* = **giocare**; **giu'oco** *sm* = **gioco**.

giura'mento [dʒura'mento] *sm* oath; **~ falso** perjury.

giu'rare [dʒu'rare] *vt* to swear // *vi* to swear, take an oath; **giu'rato, a** *ag*: **nemico giurato** sworn enemy // *sm/f* juror, juryman/woman.

giu'ria [dʒu'ria] *sf* jury.

giu'ridico, a, ci, che [dʒu'ridiko] *ag* legal.

giurisdizi'one [dʒurizdit'tsjone] *sf* jurisdiction.

giurispru'denza [dʒurispru'dɛntsa] *sf* jurisprudence.

giustifi'care [dʒustifi'kare] *vt* to justify; **giustificazi'one** *sf* justification; *(INS)* (note of) excuse.

gius'tizia [dʒus'tittsja] *sf* justice; **giusti'ziare** *vt* to execute, put to death; **giusti'ziere** *sm* executioner.

gi'usto, a ['dʒusto] *ag* *(equo)* fair, just; *(vero)* true, correct; *(adatto)* right, suitable; *(preciso)* exact, correct // *av* *(esattamente)* exactly, precisely; *(per l'appunto, appena)* just; **arrivare ~** to arrive just in time; **ho ~ bisogno di te** you're just the person I need.

glaci'ale [gla'tʃale] *ag* glacial.

'glandola *sf* = **ghiandola**.

gli [ʎi] *det mpl* (dav V, s impura, gn, pn, ps, x, z) the // *pronome* (a lui) to him; (a esso) to

it; (in coppia con lo, la, li, le, ne: a lui, a lei, a loro etc): **glielo do** I'm giving them to him (o her o them).

glice'rina [glitʃe'rina] *sf* glycerine.

gli'ela ['ʎela] *etc vedi* **gli**.

glo'bale *ag* overall.

'globo *sm* globe.

'globulo *sm* globule; *(ANAT)* corpuscle.

'gloria *sf* glory; **glorifi'care** *vt* to exalt, glorify; **glori'oso, a** *ag* glorious.

glos'sario *sm* glossary.

glu'cosio *sm* glucose.

'gnocchi ['ɲɔkki] *smpl* *(CUC)* small dumplings made of semolina pasta or potato.

'gnomo ['ɲɔmo] *sm* gnome.

'gobba *sf* *(ANAT)* hump; *(protuberanza)* bump.

'gobbo, a *ag* hunchbacked; *(ricurvo)* round-shouldered // *sm/f* hunchback.

'goccia, ce ['gottʃa] *sf* drop; **goccio'lare** *vi* (2), *vt* to drip; **goccio'lio** *sm* dripping.

go'dere *vi* *(compiacersi)*: **~ (di)** to be delighted (at), rejoice (at); *(trarre vantaggio)*: **~ di** to enjoy, benefit from // *vt* to enjoy; **~rsi la vita** to enjoy life; **~sela** to have a good time, enjoy o.s.; **godi'mento** *sm* enjoyment.

'goffo, a *ag* clumsy, awkward.

'gola *sf* *(ANAT)* throat; *(golosità)* gluttony, greed; *(di camino)* flue; *(di monte)* gorge; **fare ~** *(anche fig)* to tempt.

golf *sm inv* *(SPORT)* golf; *(maglia)* cardigan.

'golfo *sm* gulf.

go'loso, a *ag* greedy.

'gomito *sm* elbow; *(di strada etc)* sharp bend.

'gomma *sf* rubber; *(colla)* gum; *(per cancellare)* rubber, eraser; *(di veicolo)* tyre; **~ a terra** flat tyre; **gommapi'uma** *sf* ® foam rubber.

'gondola *sf* gondola; **gondoli'ere** *sm* gondolier.

gonfa'lone *sm* banner.

gonfi'are *vt* *(pallone)* to blow up, inflate; *(dilatare, ingrossare)* to swell; *(fig: persona)* to flatter; *(: notizia)* to exaggerate; **~rsi** *vr* to swell; *(fiume)* to rise; **'gonfio, a** *ag* swollen; *(stomaco)* bloated; **gonfi'ore** *sm* swelling.

gongo'lare *vi* to look pleased with o.s.; **~ di gioia** to be overjoyed.

'gonna *sf* skirt.

'gonzo ['gondzo] *sm* simpleton, fool.

gorgheggi'are [gorged'dʒare] *vi* to warble; to trill.

'gorgo, ghi *sm* whirlpool.

gorgogli'are [gorgoʎ'ʎare] *vi* to gurgle.

go'rilla *sm inv* gorilla.

'gotico, a, ci, che *ag, sm* Gothic.

'gotta *sf* gout.

gover'nante *sm/f* ruler // *sf* *(di bambini)* governess; *(donna di servizio)* housekeeper.

gover'nare *vt* *(Stato)* to govern, rule; *(azienda)* to manage, run; *(pilotare, guidare)* to steer; *(bestiame)* to tend, look after; **governa'tivo, a** *ag* government *cpd*, state *cpd*; **governa'tore** *sm* governor.

go'verno *sm* government; management, running; steering; tending; ~ **della casa** housekeeping.

gozzo'viglia [gottso'viʎʎa] *sf* carousing.

gracchi'are [grak'kjare] *vi* to caw.

graci'dare [gratʃi'dare] *vi* to croak.

'gracile ['gratʃile] *ag* frail, delicate.

gra'dasso *sm* boaster.

gradazi'one [gradat'tsjone] *sf* (*sfumatura*) gradation; ~ **alcolica** alcoholic content, strength.

gra'devole *ag* pleasant, agreeable.

gradi'mento *sm* pleasure, satisfaction.

gradi'nata *sf* flight of steps; (*in teatro, stadio*) tiers *pl*.

gra'dino *sm* step; (*ALPINISMO*) foothold.

gra'dire *vt* (*accettare con piacere*) to accept; (*desiderare*) to wish, like; **gra'dito**, **a** *ag* pleasing; welcome.

'grado *sm* (*MAT, FISICA etc*) degree; (*stadio*) degree, level; (*MIL, sociale*) rank; **essere in ~ di fare** to be in a position to do.

gradu'ale *ag* gradual.

gradu'are *vt* to grade; **gradu'ato**, **a** *ag* (*esercizi*) graded; (*scala, termometro*) graduated // *sm* (*MIL*) non-commissioned officer; **graduazi'one** *sf* graduation.

'graffa *sf* (*gancio*) clip; (*segno grafico*) brace.

graffi'are *vt* to scratch.

'graffio *sm* scratch.

gra'fia *sf* spelling; (*scrittura*) handwriting.

'grafico, **a**, **ci**, **che** *ag* graphic // *sm* graph; (*persona*) graphic designer // *sf* graphic arts *pl*.

gra'migna [gra'miɲɲa] *sf* weed; couch grass.

gram'matica, **che** *sf* grammar; **grammati'cale** *ag* grammatical; **grammatico**, **a**, **ci**, **che** *ag* = **grammaticale**.

'grammo *sm* gram(me).

gram'mofono *sm* gramophone.

gran *ag vedi* **grande**.

'grana *sf* (*granello, di minerali, corpi spezzati*) grain; (*fam: seccatura*) trouble; (: *soldi*) cash // *sm inv* Parmesan (cheese).

gra'naio *sm* granary, barn.

gra'nata *sf* (*scopa*) broom; (*frutto*) pomegranate; (*pietra preziosa*) garnet; (*proiettile*) grenade.

Gran Bre'tagna [gran bre'taɲɲa] *sf*: **la ~** Great Britain.

'granchio ['grankjo] *sm* crab; (*fig*) blunder.

grandango'lare *sm* wide-angle lens *sg*.

'grande, *qualche volta* **gran** +*C*, **grand'** +*V ag* (*grosso, largo, vasto*) big, large; (*alto*) tall; (*lungo*) long; (*in sensi astratti*) great // *sm/f* (*persona adulta*) adult, grown-up; (*chi ha ingegno e potenza*) great man/woman; **fare le cose in ~** to do things in style; **una gran bella donna** a very beautiful woman; **non è una gran cosa** *o* **un gran che** it's nothing special; **non ne so gran che** I don't know very much about it.

grandeggi'are [granded'dʒare] *vi* (*emergere per grandezza*): ~ **su** to tower over; (*darsi arie*) to put on airs.

gran'dezza [gran'dettsa] *sf* (*dimensione*) size; magnitude; (*fig*) greatness; **in ~ naturale** lifesize.

grandi'nare *vb impers* to hail.

'grandine *sf* hail.

grandi'oso, **a** *ag* grand, grandiose.

gran'duca, **chi** *sm* grand duke.

gra'nello *sm* (*di cereali, uva*) seed; (*di frutta*) pip; (*di sabbia etc*) grain.

gra'nita *sf* kind of water ice.

gra'nito *sm* granite.

'grano *sm* (*in quasi tutti i sensi*) grain; (*frumento*) wheat; (*di rosario, collana*) bead; ~ **di pepe** peppercorn.

gran'turco *sm* maize.

'granulo *sm* granule; (*MED*) pellet.

'grappa *sf* (*alcool*) rough, strong brandy; (*EDIL*) cramp (iron).

'grappolo *sm* bunch, cluster.

'grasso, **a** *ag* fat; (*cibo*) fatty; (*pelle*) greasy; (*terreno*) rich; (*fig: guadagno, annata*) plentiful; (: *volgare*) coarse, lewd // *sm* (*di persona, animale*) fat; (*sostanza che unge*) grease; **gras'soccio**, **a**, **ci**, **ce** *ag* plump.

'grata *sf* grating.

gra'ticcio [gra'tittʃo] *sm* trellis; (*stuoia*) mat.

gra'ticola *sf* grill.

gra'tifica, **che** *sf* bonus.

'gratis *av* free, for nothing.

grati'tudine *sf* gratitude.

'grato, **a** *ag* grateful; (*gradito*) pleasant, agreeable.

gratta'capo *sm* worry, headache.

grattaci'elo [gratta'tʃɛlo] *sm* skyscraper.

grat'tare *vt* (*pelle*) to scratch; (*raschiare*) to scrape; (*pane, formaggio, carote*) to grate; (*fam: rubare*) to pinch // *vi* (*stridere*) to grate; (*AUT*) to grind; ~**rsi** *vr* to scratch o.s.

grat'tugia, **gie** [grat'tudʒa] *sf* grater; **grattugi'are** *vt* to grate.

gra'tuito, **a** *ag* free; (*fig*) gratuitous.

gra'vame *sm* tax; (*fig*) burden, weight.

gra'vare *vt* to burden // *vi* (2): ~ **su** to weigh on.

'grave *ag* heavy; (*fig: danno, pericolo, peccato etc*) grave, serious; (: *responsabilità*) heavy, grave; (: *contegno*) grave, solemn; (*voce, suono*) deep, low-pitched; (*LING*) **accento** ~ grave accent; **un malato** ~ a person who is seriously ill.

gravi'danza [gravi'dantsa] *sf* pregnancy.

'gravido, **a** *ag* pregnant.

gravità *sf* seriousness; (*anche FISICA*) gravity.

gra'voso, **a** *ag* heavy, onerous.

'grazia ['grattsja] *sf* grace; (*favore*) favour; (*DIR*) pardon; **grazi'are** *vt* (*DIR*) to pardon.

'grazie ['grattsje] *escl* thank you!; ~

mille! *o* **tante!** *o* **infinite!** thank you very much!; ~ a thanks to.

grazi'oso, a [grat'tsjoso] *ag* charming, delightful; (*gentile*) gracious.

'Grecia ['grɛtʃa] *sf*: **la** ~ Greece; **'greco, a, ci, che** *ag, sm/f* Greek.

gre'gario *sm* (*CICLISMO*) supporting rider.

'gregge, pl(f) i ['greddʒe] *sm* flock.

'greggio, a, gi, ge ['greddʒo] *ag* raw, crude, rough; (*fig*) unrefined // *sm* (*anche*: **petrolio** ~) crude (oil).

grembi'ule *sm* apron; (*sopravveste*) overall.

'grembo *sm* lap; (*ventre della madre*) womb.

gre'mire *vt* to pack, cram; ~**rsi** *vr*: ~**rsi (di)** to become packed *o* crowded (with); **gre'mito, a** *ag* packed, crowded.

'gretto, a *ag* mean, stingy; (*fig*) narrow-minded.

'greve *ag* heavy.

'grezzo, a ['greddzo] *ag* = **greggio**.

gri'dare *vi* (*per chiamare*) to shout, cry (out); (*strillare*) to scream, yell // *vt* to shout (out), yell (out).

'grido, pl(m) i *o* **pl(f) a** *sm* shout, cry; scream, yell; (*di animale*) cry; **di** ~ famous.

'grigio, a, gi, gie ['gridʒo] *ag* grey.

'griglia ['griʎʎa] *sf* (*per arrostire*) grill; (*ELETTR*) grid; **alla** ~ (*CUC*) grilled.

gril'letto *sm* trigger.

'grillo *sm* (*ZOOL*) cricket; (*fig*) whim.

grimal'dello *sm* picklock.

'grinta *sf* grim expression; (*SPORT*) fighting spirit.

'grinza [grintsa] *sf* crease, wrinkle; (*ruga*) wrinkle.

grip'pare *vi* (*TECN*) to seize.

gris'sino *sm* bread-stick.

'gronda *sf* eaves *pl*.

gron'daia *sf* gutter.

gron'dare *vi* (2) to pour; (*essere bagnato*): ~ **di** to be soaking *o* dripping with // *vt* to drip with.

'groppa *sf* (*di animale*) back, rump; (*fam*: *dell'uomo*) back, shoulders *pl*.

'groppo *sm* tangle; **avere un** ~ **alla gola** (*fig*) to have a lump in one's throat.

'grossa *sf* (*unità di misura*) gross.

gros'sezza [gros'settsa] *sf* size; thickness.

gros'sista, i, e *sm/f* (*COMM*) wholesaler.

'grosso, a *ag* big, large; (*di spessore*) thick; (*grossolano*: *anche fig*) coarse; (*grave, insopportabile*) serious, great; (*tempo, mare*) rough // *sm*: **il** ~ **di** the bulk of; **farla** ~**a** to do something very stupid; **dirle** ~**e** to tell tall stories; **sbagliarsi di** ~ to be completely wrong.

grosso'lano, a *ag* rough, coarse; (*fig*) coarse, crude.

grosso'modo *av* roughly.

'grotta *sf* cave; grotto.

grot'tesco, a, schi, sche *ag* grotesque.

grovi'era *sm o f* gruyère (cheese).

gro'viglio [gro'viʎʎo] *sm* tangle; (*fig*) muddle.

gru *sf inv* crane.

'gruccia, ce ['gruttʃa] *sf* (*per camminare*) crutch; (*per abiti*) coat-hanger.

gru'gnire [gruɲ'ɲire] *vi* to grunt; **gru'gnito** *sm* grunt.

'grugno, ['gruɲɲo] *sm* snout.

'grullo, a *ag* silly, stupid.

'grumo *sm* (*di sangue*) clot; (*di farina etc*) lump.

'gruppo *sm* group; ~ **sanguigno** blood group.

gruvi'era *sm o f* = **groviera**.

guada'gnare [gwadaɲ'ɲare] *vt* (*ottenere*) to gain; (*soldi, stipendio*) to earn; (*vincere*) to win; (*raggiungere*) to reach.

gua'dagno [gwa'daɲɲo] *sm* earnings *pl*; (*COMM*) profit; (*vantaggio, utile*) advantage, gain; ~ **lordo/netto** gross/net earnings *pl*.

gu'ado *sm* ford; **passare a** ~ to ford.

gu'ai *escl*: ~ **a te** (*o lui etc*)! woe betide you (*o him etc*)!

gua'ina *sf* (*fodero*) sheath; (*indumento per donna*) girdle.

gu'aio *sm* trouble, mishap; (*inconveniente*) trouble, snag.

gua'ire *vi* to whine, yelp.

gu'ancia, ce [gwan'tʃa] *sf* cheek.

guanci'ale [gwan'tʃale] *sm* pillow.

gu'anto *sm* glove.

gu'arda... prefisso: ~**'boschi** *sm inv* forester; ~**'caccia** *sm inv* gamekeeper; ~**'coste** *sm inv* coastguard; (*nave*) coastguard patrol vessel; ~**'linee** *sm inv* (*SPORT*) linesman.

guar'dare *vt* (*con lo sguardo: osservare*) to look at; (*film, televisione*) to watch; (*custodire*) to look after, take care of // *vi* to look; (*badare*): ~ **a** to pay attention to; (*luoghi: esser orientato*): ~ **a** to face; ~**rsi** *vr* to look at o.s.; ~**rsi da** (*astenersi*) to refrain from; (*stare in guardia*) to beware of; ~**rsi da fare** to take care not to do; ~ **a vista qd** to keep a close watch on sb.

guarda'roba *sm inv* wardrobe; (*locale*) cloakroom; **guardarobi'ere, a** *sm/f* cloakroom attendant.

gu'ardia *sf* guard; (*vigilanza, custodia*) watch, guard; **fare la** ~ **a qc/qd** to guard sth/sb; **stare in** ~ (*fig*) to be on one's guard; ~ **di finanza** (*corpo*) customs *pl*; (*persona*) customs officer.

guardi'ano, a *sm/f* (*di carcere*) warder; (*di villa etc*) caretaker; (*di museo*) custodian; ~ **notturno** night watchman.

guar'dingo, a, ghi, ghe *ag* wary, cautious.

guardi'ola *sf* porter's lodge; (*MIL*) look-out tower.

guarigi'one [gwari'dʒone] *sf* recovery.

gua'rire *vt* (*persona, malattia*) to cure; (*ferita*) to heal // *vi* (2) to recover, be cured; to heal (up).

guarnigi'one [gwarni'dʒone] *sf* garrison.

guar'nire *vt* (*ornare*) to decorate, ornament; (: *abiti*) to trim; (*CUC*) to garnish; (*MIL*) to garrison; **guarnizi'one** *sf* decoration; trimming; garnish; (TECN) gasket.

guasta'feste sm/f inv spoilsport.

guas'tare vt to spoil, ruin; (meccanismo) to break; ~**rsi** vr (cibo) to go bad; (meccanismo) to break down; (tempo) to change for the worse; (fig) to be spoiled, be ruined; (: amici) to quarrel, fall out.

gu'asto, a ag (non funzionante) broken; (: telefono) out of order; (andato a male) bad, rotten; (: dente) decayed, bad; (fig: corrotto) depraved // sm breakdown, failure; (danno) damage; (fig) something rotten.

gu'azza ['gwattsa] sf heavy dew.

guazza'buglio [gwattsa'buʎʎo] sm muddle.

gu'azzo ['gwattso] sm puddle, pool; (PITTURA) gouache.

gu'ercio, a, ci, ce ['gwertʃo] ag cross-eyed.

gu'erra sf war; (tecnica: atomica, chimica etc) warfare; **fare la ~ (a)** to wage war (against); **~ mondiale** world war; **guerreggi'are** vi to wage war; **guer'resco, a, schi, sche** ag (di guerra) war cpd; (incline alla guerra) warlike; **guerri'ero, a** ag warlike // sm warrior; **guerrigli'ero** sm guerrilla.

'gufo sm owl.

gu'ida sf guide; (comando, direzione) guidance, direction; (AUT) driving; (: sterzo) steering; (tappeto, di tenda, cassetto) runner; ~ **a destra/sinistra** (AUT) right-/left-hand drive.

gui'dare vt to guide; (condurre a capo) to lead; (auto) to drive; (aereo, nave) to pilot; **sai ~?** can you drive?; **guida'tore** sm (conducente) driver.

guin'zaglio [gwin'tsaʎʎo] sm leash, lead.

gu'isa sf: **a ~ di** like, in the manner of.

guiz'zare [gwit'tsare] vi to dart; to flash; to flicker; to leap.

'guscio ['guʃʃo] sm shell.

gus'tare vt (cibi) to taste; (: assaporare con piacere) to enjoy, savour; (fig) to enjoy, appreciate // vi (piacere) to please; **non mi gusta affatto** I don't like it at all.

'gusto sm taste; (sapore) flavour; (godimento) enjoyment; **al ~ di fragola** strawberry-flavoured; **mangiare di ~** to eat heartily; **prenderci ~: ci ha preso ~** he's acquired a taste for it, he's got to like it; **gus'toso, a** ag tasty; (fig) agreeable.

guttu'rale ag guttural.

H

ha, 'hai [a, ai] forme del vb avere.

'handicap ['handikap] sm inv handicap.

'hanno ['anno] forma del vb avere.

'hascisc ['haʃiʃ] sm hashish.

ho [ɔ] forma del vb avere.

'hobby ['hɔbi] sm inv hobby.

'hockey ['hɔki] sm hockey; ~ **su ghiaccio** ice hockey.

I

i det mpl the.

i'ato sm hiatus.

ibernazi'one [ibernat'tsjone] sf hibernation.

'ibrido, a ag, sm hybrid.

i'cona sf icon.

Id'dio sm God.

i'dea sf idea; (opinione) opinion, view; (ideale) ideal; ~ **fissa** obsession; **neanche o neppure per ~!** not on your life!, certainly not!

ide'ale ag, sm ideal; **idea'lismo** sm idealism; **idea'lista, i, e** sm/f idealist; **idealiz'zare** vt to idealize.

ide'are vt (immaginare) to think up, conceive; (progettare) to plan.

i'dentico, a, ci, che ag identical.

identifi'care vt to identify; **identifica-zi'one** sf identification.

identità sf inv identity.

ideolo'gia, 'gie [ideolo'dʒia] sf ideology.

i'dillico, a, ci, che ag idyllic.

idi'oma, i sm idiom, language; **idio-'matico, a, ci, che** ag idiomatic.

idiosincra'sia sf idiosyncrasy.

idi'ota, i, e ag idiotic // sm/f idiot.

idio'tismo sm idiom, idiomatic phrase.

idola'trare vt to worship; (fig) to idolize.

'idolo sm idol.

idoneità sf suitability.

i'doneo, a ag: ~ **a** suitable for, fit for; (MIL) fit for; (qualificato) qualified for.

i'drante sm hydrant.

i'draulico, a, ci, che ag hydraulic // sm plumber // sf hydraulics sg.

idroe'lettrico, a, ci, che ag hydroelectric.

i'drofilo, a ag: vedi cotone.

idrofo'bia sf rabies sg.

i'drogeno [i'drɔdʒeno] sm hydrogen.

idros'calo sm seaplane base.

idrovo'lante sm seaplane.

i'ena sf hyena.

i'eri av yesterday; ~ **l'altro** the day before yesterday; ~ **sera** yesterday evening.

igi'ene [i'dʒɛne] sf hygiene; ~ **pubblica** public health; **igi'enico, a, ci, che** ag hygienic; (salubre) healthy.

i'gnaro, a [iɲ'ɲaro] ag: ~ **di** unaware of, ignorant of.

i'gnobile [iɲ'ɲɔbile] ag despicable, vile.

igno'minia [iɲɲo'minja] sf ignominy.

igno'rante [iɲɲo'rante] ag ignorant; **igno-'ranza** sf ignorance.

igno'rare [iɲɲo'rare] vt (non sapere, conoscere) to be ignorant o unaware of, not to know; (fingere di non vedere, sentire) to ignore.

i'gnoto, a [iɲ'ɲɔto] ag unknown.

il det m the.

'ilare ag cheerful; **ilarità** sf hilarity, mirth.

illangui'dire vi (2) to grow weak o feeble.

il'lecito, a [il'lɛtʃito] *ag* illicit.

ille'gale *ag* illegal.

illeg'gibile [illed'dʒibile] *ag* illegible.

illegittimità [illedʒittimi'ta] *sf* illegitimacy.

ille'gittimo, a [ille'dʒittimo] *ag* illegitimate.

il'leso, a *ag* unhurt, unharmed.

illette'rato, a *ag* illiterate.

illimi'tato, a *ag* boundless; unlimited.

il'logico, a, ci, che [il'lɔdʒiko] *ag* illogical.

il'ludere *vt* to deceive, delude; ~**rsi** *vr* to deceive o.s., delude o.s.

illumi'nare *vt* to light up; (*con riflettori*) to illuminate, floodlight; (*fig*) to enlighten; ~**rsi** *vr* to light up; **illuminazi'one** *sf* lighting; illumination, floodlighting; (*fig*) flash of inspiration.

illusi'one *sf* illusion; **farsi delle** ~**i** to delude o.s.

illusio'nismo *sm* conjuring.

il'luso, a *pp di* **illudere**.

illus'trare *vt* to illustrate; **illustra'tivo, a** *ag* illustrative; **illustrazi'one** *sf* illustration.

il'lustre *ag* eminent, renowned.

imbacuc'care *vt*, ~**rsi** *vr* to wrap up.

imbal'laggio [imbal'laddʒo] *sm* packing q.

imbal'lare *vt* to pack; (*AUT*) to race; ~**rsi** *vr* (*AUT*) to race.

imbalsa'mare *vt* to embalm.

imbaraz'zare [imbarat'tsare] *vt* (*ostacolare*) to hamper; (*confondere*) to puzzle, perplex; (*mettere in imbarazzo*) to embarrass.

imba'razzo [imba'rattso] *sm* (*ostacolo*) hindrance, obstacle; (*perplessità*) bewilderment, puzzlement; (*disagio*) embarrassment; ~ **di stomaco** indigestion.

imbarca'dero *sm* landing stage.

imbar'care *vt* (*passeggeri*) to embark; (*merci*) to load; ~**rsi** *vr* to board; ~ **acqua** (*NAUT*) to ship water.

imbarcazi'one [imbarkat'tsjone] *sf* (*small*) boat, (*small*) craft *inv*; ~ **di salvataggio** lifeboat.

im'barco, chi *sm* embarkation; loading; boarding; (*banchina*) landing stage.

imbas'tire *vt* (*cucire*) to tack; (*fig: abbozzare*) to sketch, outline.

im'battersi *vr*: ~ **in** (*incontrare*) to bump *o* run into; (*avere la sorte*) to meet with.

imbat'tibile *ag* unbeatable, invincible.

imbavagli'are [imbavaʎ'ʎare] *vt* to gag.

imbec'cata *sf* (*TEATRO*) prompt.

imbe'cille [imbe'tʃille] *ag* idiotic // *sm/f* idiot; (*MED*) imbecile.

imbel'lire *vt* to adorn, embellish.

im'berbe *ag* beardless.

im'bevere *vt* to soak; ~**rsi** *vr*: ~**rsi di** to soak up, absorb.

imbian'care *vt* to whiten; (*muro*) to whitewash // *vi* (2) to become *o* turn white.

imbian'chino [imbjan'kino] *sm* (*house*) painter, painter and decorator.

imboc'care *vt* (*bambino*) to feed; (*fig: imbeccare*): ~ **qd** to prompt sb, put the words into sb's mouth; (*entrare: strada*) to enter, turn into; (*tromba*) to put to one's mouth // *vi*: ~ **in** (*sog: strada*) to lead into; (: *fiume*) to flow into.

imbocca'tura *sf* (*apertura*) opening; mouth; (*ingresso*) entrance; (*MUS*) mouthpiece.

im'bocco, chi *sm* entrance.

imbos'care *vt* to hide; ~**rsi** *vr* (*MIL*) to evade military service.

imbos'cata *sf* ambush.

imbottigli'are [imbottiʎ'ʎare] *vt* to bottle; (*NAUT*) to blockade; (*MIL*) to hem in; ~**rsi** *vr* to be stuck in a traffic jam.

imbot'tire *vt* to stuff; (*giacca*) to pad; **imbot'tita** *sf* quilt; **imbot'titura** *sf* stuffing; padding.

imbrat'tare *vt* to dirty, smear, daub.

imbrigli'are [imbriʎ'ʎare] *vt* to bridle.

imbroc'care *vt* (*fig*) to guess correctly.

imbrogli'are [imbroʎ'ʎare] *vt* to mix up; (*CARTE*) to shuffle; (*fig: raggirare*) to deceive, cheat; (: *confondere*) to confuse, mix up; ~**rsi** *vr* to get tangled; (*fig*) to become confused; **im'broglio** *sm* (*groviglio*) tangle; (*situazione confusa*) mess; (*truffa*) swindle, trick; **imbroglio'ne, a** *sm/f* cheat, swindler.

imbronci'are [imbron'tʃare] *vi* (2) (*anche:* ~**rsi**) to sulk.

imbru'nire *vi*, *vb impers* (2) to grow dark; **sull'**~ at dusk.

imbrut'tire *vt* to make ugly // *vi* (2) to become ugly.

imbu'care *vt* to post.

imbur'rare *vt* to butter.

im'buto *sm* funnel.

imi'tare *vt* to imitate; (*riprodurre*) to copy; (*assomigliare*) to look like; **imitazi'one** *sf* imitation.

immaco'lato, a *ag* spotless; immaculate.

immagazzi'nare [immagaddzi'nare] *vt* to store.

immagi'nare [immadʒi'nare] *vt* to imagine; (*supporre*) to suppose; (*inventare*) to invent; **s'immagini!** don't mention it!, not at all!; **immagi'nario, a** *ag* imaginary; **immaginazi'one** *sf* imagination; (*cosa immaginata*) fancy.

im'magine [im'madʒine] *sf* image; (*rappresentazione grafica, mentale*) picture.

imman'cabile *ag* certain; unfailing.

immangi'abile [imman'dʒabile] *ag* inedible.

immatrico'lare *vt* to register; ~**rsi** *vr* (*INS*) to matriculate, enrol; **immatricolazi'one** *sf* registration; matriculation, enrolment.

imma'turo, a *ag* (*frutto*) unripe; (*persona*) immature; (*prematuro*) premature.

immedesi'marsi *vr*: ~ **in** to identify with.

immedi'ato, a *ag* immediate.

im'memore *ag*: ~ **di** forgetful of.

im'menso, a ag immense.

im'mergere [im'mɛrdʒere] vt to immerse, plunge; ~rsi vr to plunge; (sommergibile) to dive, submerge; (dedicarsi a): ~rsi in to immerse o.s. in.

immeri'tato, a ag undeserved.

immeri'tevole ag undeserving, unworthy.

immersi'one sf immersion; (di sommergibile) submersion, dive; (di palombaro) dive.

im'merso, a pp di immergere.

immi'grante ag, sm/f immigrant.

immi'grare vi (2) to immigrate; immi'grato, a sm/f immigrant; immigrazi'one sf immigration.

immi'nente ag imminent.

immischi'are [immis'kjare] vt: ~ qd in to involve sb in; ~rsi in to interfere o meddle in.

im'mobile ag motionless, still; (beni) ~i smpl real estate sg; immobili'are ag (DIR) property cpd; immobilità sf stillness; immobility; immobiliz'zare vt to immobilize; (ECON) to lock up.

immode'rato, a ag excessive.

immo'desto, a ag immodest.

immo'lare vt to sacrifice, immolate.

immon'dizia [immon'dittsja] sf dirt, filth; (spesso al pl: spazzatura, rifiuti) rubbish q, refuse q.

im'mondo, a ag filthy, foul.

immo'rale ag immoral.

immorta'lare vt to immortalize.

immor'tale ag immortal.

im'mune ag (esente) exempt; (MED, DIR) immune; immunità sf immunity; immunità parlamentare parliamentary privilege; immuniz'zare vt (MED) to immunize.

immu'tabile ag immutable; unchanging.

impacchet'tare [impakket'tare] vt to pack up.

impacci'are [impat'tʃare] vt to hinder, hamper; impacci'ato, a ag awkward, clumsy; (imbarazzato) embarrassed; im'paccio sm obstacle; (imbarazzo) embarrassment; (situazione imbarazzante) awkward situation.

im'pacco, chi sm (MED) compress.

impadro'nirsi vr: ~ di to seize, take possession of; (fig: apprendere a fondo) to master.

impa'gabile ag priceless.

impagli'are [impaʎ'ʎare] vt to stuff (with straw).

impa'lato, a ag (fig) stiff as a poker.

impalca'tura sf scaffolding; (anche fig) framework.

impalli'dire vi (2) to turn pale; (fig) to fade.

impa'nare vt (CUC) to dip in breadcrumbs.

impanta'narsi vr to sink (in the mud); (fig) to get bogged down.

impappi'narsi vr to stammer, falter.

impa'rare vt to learn.

impareggi'abile [impared'dʒabile] ag incomparable.

imparen'tarsi vr: ~ con to marry into.

'impari ag inv (disuguale) unequal; (dispari) odd.

impar'tire vt to bestow, give.

imparzi'ale [impar'tsjale] ag impartial, unbiased.

impas'sibile ag impassive.

impas'tare vt (pasta) to knead; (colori) to mix.

im'pasto sm (anche fig) mixture; (di pane) dough.

im'patto sm impact.

impau'rire vt to scare, frighten // vi (2) (anche: ~rsi) to become scared o frightened.

impazi'ente [impat'tsjɛnte] ag impatient; impazi'enza sf impatience.

impaz'zire [impat'tsire] vi (2) to go mad; ~ per qd/qc to be crazy about sb/sth.

impec'cabile ag impeccable, flawless.

impedi'mento sm obstacle, hindrance.

impe'dire vt (vietare): ~ a qd di fare to prevent sb from doing; (ostruire) to obstruct; (impacciare) to hamper, hinder.

impe'gnare [impeɲ'ɲare] vt (dare in pegno) to pawn; (onore etc) to pledge; (prenotare) to book, reserve; (obbligare) to oblige; (occupare) to keep busy; (MIL: nemico) to engage; ~rsi vr (vincolarsi): ~rsi a fare to undertake to do; (mettersi risolutamente): ~rsi in qc to devote o.s. to sth; impegna'tivo, a ag binding; (lavoro) demanding, exacting; impe'gnato, a ag (occupato) busy; (fig: romanzo, autore) committed, engagé.

im'pegno [im'peɲɲo] sm (obbligo) obligation; (promessa) promise, pledge; (zelo) diligence, zeal; (compito, d'autore) commitment.

impel'lente ag pressing, urgent.

impene'trabile ag impenetrable.

impen'narsi vr (cavallo) to rear up; (AER) to nose up; (fig) to bridle.

impen'sato, a ag unforeseen, unexpected.

impensie'rire vt, ~rsi vr to worry.

impe'rare vi (anche fig) to reign, rule.

impera'tivo, a ag, sm imperative.

impera'tore, 'trice sm/f emperor/empress.

impercet'tibile [impertʃet'tibile] ag imperceptible.

imperdo'nabile ag unforgivable, unpardonable.

imper'fetto, a ag imperfect // sm (LING) imperfect (tense); imperfezi'one sf imperfection.

imperi'ale ag imperial.

imperi'oso, a ag (persona) imperious; (motivo, esigenza) urgent, pressing.

impe'rizia [impe'rittsja] sf lack of experience.

imperma'lirsi vr to take offence.

imperme'abile ag waterproof // sm raincoat.

im'pero sm empire; (forza, autorità) rule, control.

imperscru'tabile ag inscrutable.

imperso'nale ag impersonal.

imperso'nare vt to personify; (TEATRO) to play, act (the part of).

imperter'rito, a ag fearless, undaunted; impassive.

imperti'nente ag impertinent; **imperti-'nenza** sf impertinence.

impertur'babile ag imperturbable.

imperver'sare vi to rage.

'impeto sm (moto, forza) force, impetus; (assalto) onslaught; (fig: impulso) impulse; (: slancio) transport; **con ~** energetically; vehemently.

impet'tito, a ag stiff, erect.

impetu'oso, a ag (vento) strong, raging; (persona) impetuous.

impian'tare vt (motore) to install; (azienda, discussione) to establish, start.

impi'anto sm (installazione) installation; (apparecchiature) plant; (sistema) system; **~ elettrico** wiring; **~ sportivo** sports complex.

impias'trare vt to smear, dirty.

impi'astro sm poultice.

impic'care vt to hang; **~rsi** vr to hang o.s.

impicci'are [impit'tʃare] vt to hinder, hamper; **~rsi** vr to meddle, interfere; **im-'piccio** sm (ostacolo) hindrance; (seccatura) trouble, bother; (affare imbrogliato) mess.

impie'gare vt (usare) to use, employ; (assumere) to employ, take on; (spendere: denaro, tempo) to spend; (investire) to invest; **~rsi** vr to get a job, obtain employment; **impie'gato, a** sm/f employee.

impi'ego, ghi sm (uso) use; (occupazione) employment; (posto) (regular) job, post; (ECON) investment.

impieto'sire vt to move to pity; **~rsi** vr to be moved to pity.

impigli'are [impiʎ'ʎare] vt to catch, entangle; **~rsi** vr to get caught up o entangled.

impi'grire vt to make lazy // vi (2) (anche: **~rsi**) to grow lazy.

impiom'bare vt (pacco) to seal (with lead); (dente) to fill.

impli'care vt to imply; (coinvolgere) to involve; **~rsi** vr to become involved; **implicazi'one** sf implication.

im'plicito, a [im'plitʃito] ag implicit.

implo'rare vt to implore.

impoltro'nire vt to make lazy // vi (2) (anche: **~rsi**) to grow lazy.

impolve'rare vt to cover with dust; **~rsi** vr to get dusty.

impo'nente ag imposing, impressive.

impo'nibile ag taxable // sm taxable income.

impopo'lare ag unpopular; **impopolarità** sf unpopularity.

im'porre vt to impose; (costringere) to force, make; (far valere) to impose, enforce; **imporsi** vr (persona) to assert o.s.; (cosa: rendersi necessario) to become necessary; **~ a qd di fare** to force sb to do, make sb do.

impor'tante ag important; **impor'tanza** sf importance; **dare importanza a qc** to attach importance to sth.

impor'tare vt (introdurre dall'estero) to import // vi (2) to matter, be important // vb impers (2) (essere necessario) to be necessary; (interessare) to matter; **non importa** it doesn't matter!; **non me ne importa** I don't care!; **importazi'one** sf importation; (merci importate) imports pl.

im'porto sm (total) amount.

importu'nare vt to bother.

impor'tuno, a ag irksome, annoying.

imposizi'one [impozit'tsjone] sf imposition; order, command; (onere, imposta) tax.

imposses'sarsi vr: **~ di** to seize, take possession of.

impos'sibile ag impossible; **im-possibilità** sf impossibility; **essere nell'impossibilità di fare qc** to be unable to do sth.

im'posta sf (di finestra) shutter; (tassa) tax; **~ sul reddito** income tax; **~ sul valore aggiunto (I.V.A.)** value added tax (VAT).

impos'tare vt (imbucare) to post; (preparare) to plan, set out; (avviare) to begin, start off; (voce) to pitch.

im'posto, a pp di **imporre**.

impos'tore, a sm/f impostor.

impo'tente ag weak, powerless; (anche MED) impotent; **impo'tenza** sf weakness, powerlessness; impotence.

impove'rire vt to impoverish // vi (2) (anche: **~rsi**) to become poor.

imprati'cabile ag (strada) impassable; (campo da gioco) unplayable.

imprati'chire [imprati'kire] vt to train; **~rsi in qc** to practise sth.

impre'ciso, a [impre'tʃizo] ag imprecise, vague.

impre'gnare [impreɲ'ɲare] vt: **~ (di)** (imbevere) to soak o impregnate (with); (riempire: anche fig) to fill (with).

imprendi'tore sm entrepreneur; (appaltatore) contractor; **piccolo ~** small businessman.

im'presa sf (iniziativa) enterprise; (azione) exploit; (azienda) firm, concern.

impre'sario sm (TEATRO) manager, impresario; **~ di pompe funebri** funeral director.

imprescin'dibile [impreʃʃin'dibile] ag not to be ignored.

impressio'nante ag impressive; upsetting.

impressio'nare vt to impress; (turbare) to upset; (FOT) to expose; **~rsi** vr to be easily upset.

impressi'one sf impression; (fig: sensazione) sensation, feeling; (stampa) printing; **fare ~** to impress; (turbare) to frighten, upset; **fare buona/cattiva ~ a** to make a good/bad impression on.

im'presso, a pp di **imprimere**.

impreve'dibile ag unforeseeable; (persona) unpredictable.

imprevi'dente ag lacking in foresight.

impre'visto, a ag unexpected, unforeseen // sm unforeseen event; **salvo ~i** unless anything unexpected happens.

imprigiona'mento [impridʒona'mento] sm imprisonment.

imprigio'nare [impridʒo'nare] vt to imprison.

im'primere vt (anche fig) to impress, stamp; (stampare) to print; (comunicare: movimento) to transmit, give.

impro'babile ag improbable, unlikely.

im'pronta sf imprint, impression, sign; (di piede, mano) print; (fig) mark, stamp; **~ digitale** fingerprint.

impro'perio sm insult; **~i** smpl abuse sg.

im'proprio, a ag improper.

improvvisa'mente av suddenly; unexpectedly.

improvvi'sare vt to improvise; **~rsi** vr: **~rsi cuoco** to (decide to) act as cook; **improvvi'sata** sf (pleasant) surprise.

improv'viso, a ag (imprevisto) unexpected; (subitaneo) sudden; **all'~** unexpectedly; suddenly.

impru'dente ag unwise, rash.

impu'dente ag impudent; **impu'denza** sf impudence.

impu'dico, a, chi, che ag immodest.

impu'gnare [impuɲ'ɲare] vt to grasp, grip; (DIR) to contest; **impugna'tura** sf grip, grasp; (manico) handle; (: di spada) hilt.

impul'sivo, a ag impulsive.

im'pulso sm impulse.

impu'nito, a ag unpunished.

impun'tarsi vr to stop dead, refuse to budge; (fig) to be obstinate.

impurità sf inv impurity.

im'puro, a ag impure.

impu'tare vt (ascrivere): **~ qc a** to attribute sth to; (DIR: accusare): **~ qd di** to charge sb with, accuse sb of; **impu'tato, a** sm/f (DIR) accused, defendant; **imputa-zi'one** sf (DIR) charge.

imputri'dire vi (2) to rot.

in prep (in + il = **nel**, in + lo = **nello**, in + l' = **nell'**, in + la = **nella**, in + i = **nei**, in + gli = **negli**, in + le = **nelle**) in; (moto a luogo) to; (: dentro) into; (mezzo): **~ autobus/treno** by bus/train; (composizione): **~ marmo** made of marble, marble cpd; **essere ~ casa** to be at home; **andare ~ Austria** to go to Austria; **Maria Bianchi ~ Rossi** Maria Rossi née Bianchi; **siamo ~ quattro** there are four of us.

i'nabile ag: **~ a** incapable of; (fisicamente, MIL) unfit for; **inabilità** sf incapacity.

inabi'tabile ag uninhabitable.

inacces'sibile [inattʃes'sibile] ag inaccessible; (persona) unapproachable.

inaccet'tabile [inattʃet'tabile] ag unacceptable.

ina'datto, a ag: **~ (a)** unsuitable o unfit (for).

inadegu'ato, a ag inadequate.

inadempi'ente sm/f defaulter.

inaffer'rabile ag elusive; (concetto, senso) difficult to grasp.

ina'lare vt to inhale; **inala'tore** sm inhaler.

inalbe'rare vt (NAUT) to hoist, raise; **~rsi** vr (impennarsi) to rear up; (fig) to flare up, fly off the handle.

inalte'rabile ag unchangeable; (colore) fast, permanent; (affetto) constant.

inalte'rato, a ag unchanged.

inami'dare vt to starch; **inamidato, a** ag starched.

inammis'sibile ag inadmissible.

inani'mato, a ag inanimate; (senza vita: corpo) lifeless.

inappa'gabile ag insatiable.

inappel'labile ag (DIR) final, not open to appeal.

inappun'tabile ag irreproachable, flawless.

inar'care vt (schiena) to arch; (sopracciglia) to raise; **~rsi** vr to arch.

inari'dire vt to make arid, dry up // vi (2) (anche: **~rsi**) to dry up, become arid.

inaspet'tato, a ag unexpected.

inas'prire vt to embitter; to exacerbate; **~rsi** vr to grow bitter.

inattac'cabile ag (MIL) unassailable; (fig: fama) unimpeachable; **~ dalle tarme** moth-proof.

inatten'dibile ag unreliable.

inat'teso, a ag unexpected.

inat'tivo, a ag inactive, idle; (CHIM) inactive.

inattu'abile ag impracticable.

inau'dito, a ag unheard of.

inaugu'rale ag inaugural.

inaugu'rare vt to inaugurate, open; (monumento) to unveil; **inaugurazi'one** sf inauguration; unveiling.

inavve'duto, a ag careless, inadvertent.

inavver'tenza [inavver'tɛntsa] sf carelessness, inadvertence.

incagli'are [inkaʎ'ʎare] vi (2) (NAUT: anche: **~rsi**) to run aground // vt (intralciare) to hamper, hinder; **in'caglio** sm (NAUT) running aground; (ostacolo) obstacle, hindrance.

incalco'labile ag incalculable.

incal'lito, a ag calloused; (fig) hardened, inveterate; (: insensibile) hard.

incal'zare [inkal'tsare] vt to follow o pursue closely; (fig) to press // vi (urgere) to be pressing; (essere imminente) to be imminent.

incame'rare vt (DIR) to expropriate.

incammi'nare vt (fig: avviare) to start up; **~rsi** vr to set off.

incande'scente [inkandeʃ'ʃɛnte] ag incandescent, white-hot.

incan'tare vt to enchant, bewitch; **~rsi**

vr (*rimanere intontito*) to be spellbound; to be in a daze; (*meccanismo: bloccarsi*) to jam; **incanta'tore**, **'trice** *ag* enchanting, bewitching // *sm/f* enchanter/enchantress; **incan'tesimo** *sm* spell, charm; **incan'tevole** *ag* charming, enchanting.

in'canto *sm* spell, charm, enchantment; (*asta*) auction; **come per ~** as if by magic; **mettere all'~** to put up for auction.

incanu'tire *vi* (2) to go white.

inca'pace [inka'patʃe] *ag* incapable; **incapacità** *sf* inability; (*DIR*) incapacity.

incapo'nirsi *vr* to be stubborn, be determined.

incap'pare *vi* (2): **~ in** qc/qd (*anche fig*) to run into sth/sb.

incapricci'arsi [inkaprit'tʃarsi] *vr*: **~ di** to take a fancy to *o* for.

incapsu'lare *vt* (*dente*) to crown.

incarce'rare [inkartʃe'rare] *vt* to imprison.

incari'care *vt*: **~ qd di fare** to give sb the responsibility of doing; **~rsi di** to take care *o* charge of; **incari'cato, a** *ag*: **incaricato (di)** in charge (of), responsible (for) // *sm/f* delegate, representative; **incaricato d'affari** (*POL*) chargé d'affaires.

in'carico, chi *sm* task, job.

incar'nare *vt* to embody; **~rsi** *vr* to be embodied; (*REL*) to become incarnate; **incarnazi'one** *sf* incarnation.

incarta'mento *sm* dossier, file.

incar'tare *vt* to wrap (in paper).

incas'sare *vt* (*merce*) to pack (in cases); (*gemma: incastonare*) to set; (*ECON: riscuotere*) to collect; (*PUGILATO: colpi*) to take, stand up to; **in'casso** *sm* cashing, encashment; (*introito*) takings *pl*.

incasto'nare *vt* to set; **incastona'tura** *sf* setting.

incas'trare *vt* to fit in, insert; **~rsi** *vr* to stick; **in'castro** *sm* slot, groove.

incate'nare *vt* to chain up; (*fig*) to tie.

incatra'mare *vt* to tar.

in'cauto, a *ag* imprudent, rash.

inca'vare *vt* to hollow out; **inca'vato, a** *ag* hollow; (*occhi*) sunken; **incava'tura** *sf* hollow; **in'cavo** *sm* hollow; (*solco*) groove.

incendi'are [intʃen'djare] *vt* to set fire to; **~rsi** *vr* to catch fire, burst into flames.

incendi'ario, a [intʃen'djarjo] *ag* incendiary // *sm/f* arsonist.

in'cendio [in'tʃendjo] *sm* fire.

incene'rire [intʃene'rire] *vt* to burn to ashes, incinerate; (*cadavere*) to cremate; **~rsi** *vr* to be burnt to ashes.

in'censo [in'tʃenso] *sm* incense.

incensu'rato, a [intʃensu'rato] *ag* (*DIR*): **essere ~** to have a clean record.

incen'tivo [intʃen'tivo] *sm* incentive.

incep'pare [intʃep'pare] *vt* to obstruct, hamper; **~rsi** *vr* to jam.

ince'rata [intʃe'rata] *sf* (*tela*) tarpaulin; (*impermeabile*) oilskins *pl*.

incer'tezza [intʃer'tettsa] *sf* uncertainty.

in'certo, a [in'tʃerto] *ag* uncertain; (*irresoluto*) undecided, hesitating // *sm* uncertainty.

inces'sante [intʃes'sante] *ag* incessant.

in'cesto [in'tʃesto] *sm* incest.

in'cetta [in'tʃetta] *sf* buying up; **fare ~ di** qc to buy sth up.

inchi'esta [in'kjesta] *sf* investigation, inquiry.

inchi'nare [inki'nare] *vt* to bow; **~rsi** *vr* to bend down; (*per riverenza*) to bow; (: *donna*) to curtsy; **in'chino** *sm* bow; curtsy.

inchio'dare [inkjo'dare] *vt* to nail; (*chiudere con chiodi*) to nail down (*o* up).

inchi'ostro [in'kjostro] *sm* ink; **~ simpatico** invisible ink.

inciam'pare [intʃam'pare] *vi* to trip, stumble.

inci'ampo [in'tʃampo] *sm* obstacle; **essere d'~ a** qd (*fig*) to be in sb's way.

inciden'tale [intʃiden'tale] *ag* incidental.

inci'dente [intʃi'dɛnte] *sm* accident; **~ d'auto** car accident.

inci'denza [intʃi'dɛntsa] *sf* incidence.

in'cidere [in'tʃidere] *vi*: **~ su** to bear upon, affect // *vt* (*tagliare incavando*) to cut into; (*ARTE*) to engrave; to etch; (*canzone*) to record.

in'cinta [in'tʃinta] *ag f* pregnant.

incipi'ente [intʃi'pjɛnte] *ag* incipient.

incipri'are [intʃi'prjare] *vt* to powder.

in'circa [in'tʃirka] *av*: **all'~** more or less, very nearly.

incisi'one [intʃi'zjone] *sf* cut; (*disegno*) engraving; etching; (*registrazione*) recording; (*MED*) incision.

inci'sivo, a [intʃi'zivo] *ag* incisive.

in'ciso [in'tʃizo] *sm*: **per ~** incidentally, by the way.

inci'tare [intʃi'tare] *vt* to incite.

inci'vile [intʃi'vile] *ag* uncivilized; (*villano*) impolite.

incivi'lire [intʃivi'lire] *vt* to civilize.

incl. (*abbr di* **incluso**) encl.

incli'nare *vt* to tilt // *vi* (*fig*): **~ a** qc/a **fare** to incline towards sth/doing; to tend towards sth/to do; **inclinato, a** *ag* (*anche fig*) inclined; **inclinazi'one** *sf* slope; (*fig*) inclination, tendency; **in'cline** *ag*: **incline a** inclined to.

in'cludere *vt* to include; (*accludere*) to enclose; **inclusi'one** *sf* inclusion; **inclu'sivo, a** *ag*: **inclusivo di** inclusive of; **in'cluso, a** *pp di* **includere** // *ag* included; enclosed.

incoe'rente *ag* incoherent; (*contraddittorio*) inconsistent; **incoe'renza** *sf* incoherence; inconsistency.

in'cognito, a [in'kɔɲɲito] *ag* unknown // *sm*: **in ~** incognito // *sf* (*MAT, fig*) unknown quantity.

incol'lare *vt* to glue, gum; (*unire con colla*) to stick together.

incolon'nare *vt* to draw up in columns.

inco'lore *ag* colourless.

incol'pare *vt*: **~ qd di** to charge sb with.

in'colto, a *ag* (*terreno*) uncultivated;

(*trascurato: capelli*) neglected; (*persona*) uneducated.

in'**colume** *ag* safe and sound, unhurt.

in'**combere** *vi* (*sovrastare minacciando*): ~ **su** to threaten, hang over; (*spettare*): ~ **a** to rest *o* be incumbent upon.

incominci'**are** [inkomin'tʃare] *vi* (2), *vt* to begin, start.

in'**comodo, a, ag** uncomfortable; (*inopportuno*) inconvenient // *sm* inconvenience, bother.

incompa'**rabile** *ag* incomparable.

incompa'**tibile** *ag* (*non ammissibile*: *negligenza*) intolerable; (*inconciliabile*) incompatible.

incompe'**tente** *ag* incompetent; incompe'**tenza** *sf* incompetence.

incompi'**uto, a** *ag* unfinished, incomplete.

incom'**pleto, a** *ag* incomplete.

incompren'**sibile** *ag* incomprehensible.

incomprensi'**one** *sf* incomprehension.

incom'**preso, a** *ag* not understood; misunderstood.

inconce'**pibile** [inkontʃe'pibile] *ag* inconceivable.

inconcili'**abile** [inkontʃi'ljabile] *ag* irreconcilable.

inconclu'**dente** *ag* inconclusive; (*persona*) ineffectual.

incondizio'**nato, a** [inkondittsjo'nato] *ag* unconditional.

inconfu'**tabile** *ag* irrefutable.

incongru'**ente, a** *ag* incongruous.

in'**congruo, a** *ag* incongruous.

inconsa'**pevole** *ag*: ~ **di** unaware of, ignorant of.

in'**conscio, a, sci, sce** [in'kɔnʃo] *ag* unconscious // *sm* (*PSIC*): l'~ the unconscious.

inconsis'**tente** *ag* insubstantial; unfounded.

inconso'**labile** *ag* inconsolable.

inconsu'**eto, a** *ag* unusual.

incon'**sulto, a** *ag* rash.

inconti'**nenza** [inkonti'nɛntsa] *sf* incontinence.

incon'**trare** *vt* to meet; (*difficoltà*) to meet with; ~**rsi** *vr* to meet.

incontras'**tabile** *ag* incontrovertible, indisputable.

in'**contro** *av*: ~ **a** (*verso*) towards // *sm* meeting; (*SPORT*) match; meeting; ~ **di calcio** football match.

inconveni'**ente** *sm* drawback, snag.

incoraggia'**mento** [inkoraddʒa'mento] *sm* encouragement.

incoraggi'**are** [inkorad'dʒare] *vt* to encourage.

incornici'**are** [inkorni'tʃare] *vt* to frame.

incoro'**nare** *vt* to crown; incoronazi'**one** *sf* coronation.

incorpo'**rare** *vt* to incorporate; (*fig: annettere*) to annex.

incorreg'**gibile** [inkorred'dʒibile] *ag* incorrigible.

in'**correre** *vi* (2): ~ **in** to meet with, run into.

incorrut'**tibile** *ag* incorruptible.

incosci'**ente** [inkoʃ'ʃɛnte] *ag* (*inconscio*) unconscious; (*irresponsabile*) reckless, thoughtless; incosci'**enza** *sf* unconsciousness; recklessness, thoughtlessness.

incre'**dibile** *ag* incredible, unbelievable.

in'**credulo, a** *ag* incredulous, disbelieving.

incremen'**tare** *vt* to increase; (*dar sviluppo a*) to promote.

incre'**mento** *sm* (*sviluppo*) development; (*aumento numerico*) increase, growth.

incres'**parsi** *vr* (*acqua*) to ripple; (*capelli*) to go frizzy; (*pelle, tessuto*) to wrinkle.

incrimi'**nare** *vt* (*DIR*) to charge.

incri'**nare** *vt*, ~**rsi** *vr* to crack; incrina'**tura** *sf* crack.

incroci'**are** [inkro'tʃare] *vt* to cross; (*incontrare*) to meet // *vi* (*NAUT, AER*) to cruise; ~**rsi** *vr* (*strade*) to cross, intersect; (*persone, veicoli*) to pass each other; ~ **le braccia/le gambe** to fold one's arms/cross one's legs; incrocia'**tore** *sm* cruiser.

in'**crocio** [in'krotʃo] *sm* (*anche FERR*) crossing; (*di strade*) crossroads.

incros'**tare** *vt* to encrust.

incuba'**trice** [inkuba'tritʃe] *sf* incubator.

incubazi'**one** [inkubat'tsjone] *sf* incubation.

'**incubo** *sm* nightmare.

in'**cudine** *sf* anvil.

incul'**care** *vt*: ~ **qc in** to inculcate sth into, instill sth into.

incune'**are** *vt* to wedge.

incu'**rabile** *ag* incurable.

incu'**rante** *ag*: ~ (**di**) heedless (of), careless (of).

incurio'**sire** *vt* to make curious; ~**rsi** *vr* to become curious.

incursi'**one** *sf* raid.

incur'**vare** *vt*, ~**rsi** *vr* to bend, curve.

in'**cusso, a** *pp di* incutere.

incusto'**dito, a** *ag* unguarded, unattended.

in'**cutere** *vt* to arouse; ~ **timore/rispetto a qd** to strike fear into sb/command sb's respect.

'**indaco** *sm* indigo.

indaffa'**rato, a** *ag* busy.

inda'**gare** *vt* to investigate.

in'**dagine** [in'dadʒine] *sf* investigation, inquiry; (*ricerca*) research, study.

indebi'**tare** *vt* to get into debt; ~**rsi** *vr* to run *o* get into debt.

in'**debito, a** *ag* undue; undeserved.

indebo'**lire** *vt*, *vi* (2) (*anche*: ~**rsi**) to weaken.

inde'**cente** [inde'tʃɛnte] *ag* indecent; inde'**cenza** *sf* indecency.

indeci'**frabile** [indetʃi'frabile] *ag* indecipherable.

indecisi'**one** [indetʃi'zjone] *sf* indecisiveness; indecision.

inde'**ciso, a** [inde'tʃizo] *ag* indecisive; (*irresoluto*) undecided.

inde'**fesso, a** *ag* untiring, indefatigable.

indefi'**nibile** *ag* indefinable.

indefi'nito, a ag (anche LING) indefinite; (impreciso, non determinato) undefined.

in'degno, a [in'deɲɲo] ag unworthy.

inde'lebile ag indelible.

indelica'tezza [indelika'tettsa] sf tactlessness.

indemoni'ato, a ag possessed (by the devil).

in'denne ag unhurt, uninjured; **indennità** sf inv (rimborso: di spese) allowance; (: di perdita) compensation, indemnity; **indennità di contingenza** cost-of-living allowance; **indennità di trasferta** travel expenses pl.

indenniz'zare [indennid'dzare] vt to compensate; **inden'nizzo** sm (somma) compensation, indemnity.

indero'gabile ag binding.

indeside'rabile ag undesirable.

indetermi'nato, a ag indefinite, indeterminate.

'India sf: l'∼ India; **indi'ano, a** ag Indian // sm/f (d'India) Indian; (d'America) Red Indian.

indiavo'lato, a ag possessed (by the devil); (vivace, violento) wild.

indi'care vt (mostrare) to show, indicate; (: col dito) to point to, point out; (consigliare) to suggest, recommend; **indica'tivo, a** ag indicative // sm (LING) indicative (mood); **indica'tore** sm (elenco) guide; directory; (TECN) gauge; indicator; **indicazi'one** sf indication; (notizia) information q; **indicazioni per l'uso** instructions for use.

'indice ['inditʃe] sm (ANAT: dito) index finger, forefinger; (lancetta) needle, pointer; (fig: indizio) sign; (TECN, MAT, nei libri) index.

indi'cibile [indi'tʃibile] ag inexpressible.

indietreggi'are [indietred'dʒare] vi to draw back, retreat.

indi'etro av back; (guardare) behind, back; (andare, cadere: anche: all'∼) backwards; **rimanere** ∼ to be left behind; **essere** ∼ (col lavoro) to be behind; (orologio) to be slow; **rimandare** qc ∼ to send sth back.

indiffe'rente ag indifferent; **indiffe'renza** sf indifference.

in'digeno, a [in'didʒeno] ag indigenous, native // sm/f native.

indi'gente [indi'dʒɛnte] ag poverty-stricken, destitute; **indi'genza** sf extreme poverty.

indigesti'one [indidʒes'tjone] sf indigestion.

indi'gesto, a [indi'dʒɛsto] ag indigestible.

indi'gnare [indiɲ'ɲare] vt to fill with indignation; ∼**rsi** vr to be (o get) indignant; **indignazi'one** sf indignation.

indimenti'cabile ag unforgettable.

indipen'dente ag independent; **indipen'denza** sf independence.

indi'retto, a ag indirect.

indiriz'zare [indirit'tsare] vt (dirigere) to direct; (mandare) to send; (lettera) to address; ∼ **la parola a qd** to address sb.

indi'rizzo [indi'rittso] sm address; (direzione) direction; (avvio) trend, course.

indisci'plina [indiʃʃi'plina] sf indiscipline.

indis'creto, a ag indiscreet; **indiscrezi'one** sf indiscretion.

indis'cusso, a ag unquestioned.

indispen'sabile ag indispensable, essential.

indispet'tire vt to irritate, annoy // vi (2) (anche: ∼**rsi**) to get irritated o annoyed.

indis'posto, a pp di **indisporre** // ag indisposed, unwell.

indisso'lubile ag indissoluble.

indis'tinto, a ag indistinct.

indistrut'tibile ag indestructible.

in'divia sf endive.

individu'ale ag individual; **individualità** sf individuality.

individu'are vt (dar forma distinta a) to characterize; (determinare) to locate; (riconoscere) to single out.

indi'viduo sm individual.

indi'viso, a ag undivided.

indizi'are [indit'tsjare] vt: ∼ **qd di qc** to cast suspicion on sb for sth; **indizi'ato, a** ag suspected // sm/f suspect.

in'dizio [in'dittsjo] sm (segno) sign, indication; (POLIZIA) clue; (DIR) piece of evidence.

'indole sf nature, character.

indo'lente ag indolent; **indo'lenza** sf indolence.

indolen'zito, a [indolen'tsito] ag stiff, aching; (intorpidito) numb.

indo'lore ag painless.

indo'mani sm: l'∼ the next day, the following day.

Indo'nesia sf: l'∼ Indonesia.

indos'sare vt (mettere indosso) to put on; (avere indosso) to have on; **indossa'tore, 'trice** sm/f model.

in'dotto, a pp di **indurre.**

indottri'nare vt to indoctrinate.

indovi'nare vt (scoprire) to guess; (immaginare) to imagine, guess; (il futuro) to foretell; **indovi'nato, a** ag successful; (scelta) inspired; **indovi'nello** sm riddle; **indo'vino, a** sm/f fortuneteller.

indubbia'mente av undoubtedly.

in'dubbio, a ag certain, undoubted.

indugi'are [indu'dʒare] vi to take one's time, delay; ∼**rsi** vr (soffermarsi) to linger.

in'dugio [in'dudʒo] sm (ritardo) delay; **senza** ∼ without delay.

indul'gente [indul'dʒɛnte] ag indulgent; (giudice) lenient; **indul'genza** sf indulgence; leniency.

in'dulgere [in'duldʒere] vi: ∼ **a** (accondiscendere) to comply with; (abbandonarsi) to indulge in; **in'dulto, a** pp di **indulgere** // sm (DIR) pardon.

indu'mento sm article of clothing, garment; ∼**i** smpl clothes.

indu'rire vt to harden // vi (2) (anche: ∼**rsi**) to harden, become hard.

in'durre vt to induce, persuade, lead; ~ qd in errore to mislead sb.

in'dustria sf industry; **industri'ale** ag industrial // sm industrialist.

industrializ'zare [industrialid'dzare] vt to industrialize; **industrializzazi'one** sf industrialization.

industri'arsi vr to do one's best, try hard.

industri'oso, a ag industrious, hard-working.

induzi'one [indut'tsjone] sf induction.

inebe'tito, a ag dazed, stunned.

inebri'are vt (anche fig) to intoxicate; ~**rsi** vr to become intoxicated.

inecce'pibile [inettʃe'pibile] ag unexceptionable.

i'nedia sf starvation.

i'nedito, a ag unpublished.

ineffi'cace [ineffi'katʃe] ag ineffective.

ineffici'ente [ineffi'tʃɛnte] ag inefficient.

inegu'ale ag unequal; (irregolare) uneven.

ine'rente ag: ~ a concerning, regarding.

i'nerme ag unarmed; defenceless.

inerpi'carsi vr: ~ (su) to clamber (up).

i'nerte ag inert; (inattivo) indolent, sluggish; **i'nerzia** sf inertia; indolence, sluggishness.

ine'satto, a ag (impreciso) inexact; (erroneo) incorrect; (AMM: non riscosso) uncollected.

inesau'ribile ag inexhaustible.

inesis'tente ag non-existent.

ineso'rabile ag inexorable, relentless.

inesperi'enza [inespe'rjɛntsa] sf inexperience.

ines'perto, a ag inexperienced.

inespli'cabile ag inexplicable.

inesti'mabile ag inestimable.

i'netto, a ag (incapace) inept; (che non ha attitudine): ~ (a) unsuited (to).

inevi'tabile ag inevitable.

i'nezia [i'nɛttsja] sf trifle, thing of no importance.

infagot'tare vt to bundle up, wrap up; ~**rsi** vr to wrap up.

infal'libile ag infallible.

infa'mare vt to defame; **infama'torio, a** ag defamatory.

in'fame ag infamous; (fig: cosa, compito) awful, dreadful; **in'famia** sf infamy.

infan'tile ag child cpd; childlike; (adulto, azione) childish; **letteratura** ~ children's books pl.

in'fanzia [in'fantsja] sf childhood; (bambini) children pl; **prima** ~ babyhood, infancy.

infari'nare vt to cover with (o sprinkle with o dip in) flour; ~ **di zucchero** to sprinkle with sugar; **infarina'tura** sf (fig) smattering.

in'farto sm (MED): ~ (**cardiaco**) coronary.

infasti'dire vt to annoy, irritate; ~**rsi** vr to get annoyed o irritated.

infati'cabile ag tireless, untiring.

in'fatti cong as a matter of fact, in fact, actually.

infatu'arsi vr: ~ **di** o **per** to become infatuated with, fall for; **infatuazi'one** sf infatuation.

in'fausto, a ag unpropitious, unfavourable.

infe'condo, a ag infertile.

infe'dele ag unfaithful; **infedeltà** sf infidelity.

infe'lice [infe'litʃe] ag unhappy; (sfortunato) unlucky, unfortunate; (inopportuno) inopportune, ill-timed; (mal riuscito: lavoro) bad, poor; **infelicità** sf unhappiness.

inferi'ore ag lower; (per intelligenza, qualità) inferior // sm/f inferior; ~ a (numero, quantità) less o smaller than; (meno buono) inferior to; ~ **alla media** below average; **inferiorità** sf inferiority.

inferme'ria sf sick bay.

infermi'ere, a sm/f nurse.

infermità sf inv illness; infirmity.

in'fermo, a ag (ammalato) ill; (debole) infirm; ~ **di mente** mentally ill.

infer'nale ag infernal; (proposito, complotto) diabolical.

in'ferno sm hell.

inferri'ata sf grating.

infervo'rare vt to arouse enthusiasm in; ~**rsi** vr to get excited, get carried away.

infes'tare vt to infest.

infet'tare vt to infect; ~**rsi** vr to become infected; **infet'tivo, a** ag infectious; **in'fetto, a** ag infected; (acque) polluted, contaminated; **infezi'one** sf infection.

inflac'chire [infjak'kire] vt to weaken // vi (2) (anche: ~**rsi**) to grow weak.

inflam'mabile ag inflammable.

inflam'mare vt to set alight; (fig, MED) to inflame; ~**rsi** vr to catch fire; (MED) to become inflamed; (fig): ~**rsi di** to be fired with; **inflammazi'one** sf (MED) inflammation.

inflas'care vt to bottle.

in'fido, a ag unreliable, treacherous.

in'figgere [in'fiddʒere] vt: ~ **qc in** to thrust o drive sth into; ~**rsi in** to penetrate, sink deeply into.

infi'lare vt (ago) to thread; (mettere: chiave) to insert; (: anello, vestito) to slip o put on; ~**rsi** vr: ~**rsi in/per** to slip into/through; ~ **l'uscio** to slip in; to slip out.

infil'trarsi vr to penetrate, seep through; (MIL) to infiltrate; **infiltrazi'one** sf infiltration.

infil'zare [infil'tsare] vt (infilare) to string together; (trafiggere) to pierce.

'infimo, a ag lowest.

in'fine av finally; (insomma) in short.

infinità sf infinity; (in quantità): **un'**~ **di** an infinite number of.

infi'nito, a ag infinite; (LING) infinitive // sm (LING) infinitive; **all'**~ (senza fine) endlessly.

infinocchi'are [infinok'kjare] vt (fam) to hoodwink.

infischi'arsi [infis'kjarsi] *vr*: ~ **di** not to care about.

in'fisso, a *pp di* **infiggere** // *sm* fixture; *(di porta, finestra)* frame.

infit'tire *vt, vi* (2) *(anche:* ~**rsi**) to thicken.

inflazi'one [inflat'tsjone] *sf* inflation.

infles'sibile *ag* inflexible; *(ferreo)* unyielding.

inflessi'one *sf* inflexion.

in'fliggere [in'fliddʒere] *vt* to inflict; **in-'flitto, a** *pp di* **infliggere.**

influ'ente *ag* influential; **influ'enza** *sf* influence; *(MED)* influenza, flu.

influ'ire *vi*: ~ **su** to influence.

in'flusso *sm* influence.

infol'tire *vt, vi* (2) to thicken.

infon'dato, a *ag* unfounded, groundless.

in'fondere *vt*: ~ **qc in qd** to instill sth in sb.

infor'care *vt* to fork (up); *(bicicletta, cavallo)* to get on; *(occhiali)* to put on.

infor'mare *vt* to inform, tell; ~**rsi** *vr*: ~**rsi (di)** to inquire (about); **infor-'matica** *sf* computer science; **informa-'tivo, a** *ag* informative; **informa'tore** *sm* informer; **informazi'one** *sf* piece of information; **informazioni** *sfpl* information *sg*.

in'forme *ag* shapeless.

infor'tunio *sm* accident; ~ **sul lavoro** industrial accident, accident at work.

infos'sarsi *vr* *(avvallarsi)* to sink; *(incavarsi)* to become hollow; **infos'sato, a** *ag* hollow; *(occhi)* deep-set; (: *per malattia)* sunken.

in'frangere [in'frandʒere] *vt* to smash; *(fig: patti)* to break; ~**rsi** *vr* to smash, break; **infran'gibile** *ag* unbreakable; **in-'franto, a** *pp di* **infrangere** // *ag* broken.

infra'rosso, a *ag, sm* infrared.

infrastrut'tura *sf* infrastructure.

infrazi'one [infrat'tsjone] *sf*: ~ **a** breaking of, violation of.

infredda'tura *sf* slight cold.

infreddo'lito, a *ag* cold, chilled.

infre'quente *ag* infrequent, rare.

infruttu'oso, a *ag* fruitless.

infu'ori *av* out; **all'**~ outwards; **all'**~ **di** *(eccetto)* except, with the exception of.

infuri'are *vi* to rage; ~**rsi** *vr* to fly into a rage.

infusi'one *sf* infusion.

in'fuso, a *pp di* **infondere** // *sm* infusion; ~ **di camomilla** camomile tea.

Ing. *abbr di* **ingegnere.**

ingabbi'are *vt* to cage; **ingabbia'tura** *sf* *(EDIL)* supporting frame.

ingaggi'are [ingad'dʒare] *vt* *(assumere con compenso)* to take on, hire; *(SPORT)* to sign on; *(MIL)* to engage; **in'gaggio** *sm* hiring; signing on.

ingan'nare *vt* to deceive; *(coniuge)* to be unfaithful to; *(fisco)* to cheat; *(eludere)* to dodge, elude; *(fig: tempo)* to while away // *vi (apparenza)* to be deceptive; ~**rsi** *vr* to

be mistaken, be wrong; **ingan'nevole** *ag* deceptive.

in'ganno *sm* deceit, deception; *(azione)* trick; *(menzogna, frode)* cheat, swindle; *(illusione)* illusion.

ingarbugli'are [ingarbuʎ'ʎare] *vt* to tangle; *(fig)* to confuse, muddle; ~**rsi** *vr* to become confused *o* muddled.

inge'gnarsi [indʒeɲ'ɲarsi] *vr* to do one's best, try hard; ~ **per vivere** to live by one's wits.

inge'gnere [indʒeɲ'ɲere] *sm* engineer; ~ **civile/navale** civil/naval engineer; **ingegne'ria** *sf* engineering.

in'gegno [in'dʒeɲɲo] *sm* *(intelligenza)* intelligence, brains *pl*; *(capacità creativa)* ingenuity; *(disposizione)* talent; **inge-'gnoso, a** *ag* ingenious, clever.

ingelo'sire [indʒelo'zire] *vt* to make jealous // *vi* (2) *(anche:* ~**rsi**) to become jealous.

in'gente [in'dʒɛnte] *ag* huge, enormous.

ingenuità [indʒenui'ta] *sf* ingenuousness.

in'genuo, a [in'dʒɛnuo] *ag* ingenuous, naïve.

inge'rirsi [indʒe'rirsi] *vr* to interfere, meddle.

inges'sare [indʒes'sare] *vt* *(MED)* to put in plaster; **ingessa'tura** *sf* plaster.

Inghil'terra [ingil'tɛrra] *sf*: **l'**~ England.

inghiot'tire [ingjot'tire] *vt* to swallow.

ingial'lire [indʒal'lire] *vi* (2) to go yellow.

ingigan'tire [indʒigan'tire] *vt* to enlarge, magnify // *vi* (2) to become gigantic *o* enormous.

inginocchi'arsi [indʒinok'kjarsi] *vr* to kneel (down).

ingiù [in'dʒu] *av* down, downwards.

ingi'uria [in'dʒurja] *sf* insult; *(fig: danno)* damage; **ingiuri'are** *vt* to insult, abuse; **ingiuri'oso, a** *ag* insulting, abusive.

ingius'tizia [indʒus'tittsja] *sf* injustice.

ingi'usto, a [in'dʒusto] *ag* unjust, unfair.

in'glese *ag* English // *sm/f* Englishman/woman // *sm* *(LING)* English; **gli I**~**i** the English; **andarsene** *o* **filare all'**~ to take French leave.

ingoi'are *vt* to gulp (down); *(fig)* to swallow (up).

ingol'fare *vt*, ~**rsi** *vr (motore)* to flood.

ingom'brare *vt (strada)* to block; *(stanza)* to clutter up; **in'gombro** *sm* obstacle; *(di macchina)*: **lunghezza/larghezza/al-tezza d'ingombro** maximum length/width/height.

in'gordo, a *ag*: ~ **di** greedy for; *(fig)* greedy *o* eager for.

ingor'garsi *vr* to be blocked up, be choked up.

in'gorgo, ghi *sm* blockage, obstruction; ~ **di traffico** traffic jam.

ingoz'zare [ingot'tsare] *vt (inghiottire)* to gulp down, gobble; *(costringere a mangiare: animali)* to fatten.

ingra'naggio [ingra'naddʒo] *sm* gear; *(fig)* mechanism; ~**i** *smpl* gears, gearing *sg*.

ingra'nare *vi* to mesh, engage // *vt* to

engage; ~ **la marcia** to get into gear.

ingrandi'mento *sm* enlàrgement; extension.

ingran'dire *vt* (*anche* FOT) to enlarge; (*estendere*) to extend; (OTTICA, *fig*) to magnify // *vi* (2) (*anche*: ~**rsi**) to become larger *o* bigger; (*aumentare*) to grow, increase; (*espandersi*) to expand.

ingras'sare *vt* to make fat; (*animali*) to fatten; (AGR: *terreno*) to manure; (*lubrificare*) to oil, lubricate // *vi* (2) (*anche*: ~**rsi**) to get fat, put on weight; **in'grasso** *sm* (*di animali*) fattening; (*di terreno*) manuring *q*; manure.

ingrati'tudine *sf* ingratitude.

in'grato, a *ag* ungrateful; (*lavoro*) thankless, unrewarding.

ingrazi'are [ingrat'tsjare] *vt*: ~**rsi qd** to ingratiate o.s. with sb.

ingredi'ente *sm* ingredient.

in'gresso *sm* (*porta*) entrance; (*atrio*) hall; (*l'entrare*) entrance, entry; (*facoltà di entrare*) admission; **"~ libero"** "admission free".

ingros'sare *vt* to increase; (*folla, livello*) to swell // *vi* (2) (*anche*: ~**rsi**) to increase; to swell.

in'grosso *av*: **all'~** (COMM) wholesale; (*all'incirca*) roughly, about.

ingual'cibile [ingwal'tʃibile] *ag* crease-resistant.

ingua'ribile *ag* incurable.

'inguine *sm* (ANAT) groin.

ini'bire *vt* to forbid, prohibit; (PSIC) to inhibit; **inibizi'one** *sf* prohibition; inhibition.

iniet'tare *vt* to inject; ~**rsi di sangue** (*occhi*) to become bloodshot; **iniezi'one** *sf* injection.

inimi'carsi *vr*: ~ **con qd** to fall out with sb.

inimi'cizia [inimi'tʃittsja] *sf* animosity.

ininter'rotto, a *ag* unbroken; uninterrupted.

iniquità *sf inv* iniquity; (*atto*) wicked action.

i'niquo, a *ag* iniquitous.

inizi'ale [init'tsjale] *ag, sf* initial.

inizi'are [init'tsjare] *vi* (2), *vt* to begin, start; ~ **qd a** to initiate sb into; (*pittura etc*) to introduce sb to.

inizia'tiva [inittsja'tiva] *sf* initiative; ~ **privata** private enterprise.

i'nizio [i'nittsjo] *sm* beginning; **all'~** at the beginning, at the start; **dare ~ a qc** to start sth, get sth going.

innaffi'are *etc* = **annaffiare** *etc*.

innal'zare [innal'tsare] *vt* (*sollevare, alzare*) to raise; (*rizzare*) to erect; ~**rsi** *vr* to rise.

innamo'rare *vt* to enchant, charm; ~**rsi** *vr*: ~**rsi (di qd)** to fall in love (with sb); **innamo'rato, a** *ag* (*che nutre amore*): **innamorato (di)** in love (with); (*appassionato*): **innamorato di** very fond of.

in'nanzi [in'nantsi] *av* (*stato in luogo*) in front, ahead; (*moto a luogo*) forward, on; (*tempo: prima*) before // *prep* (*prima*) before; ~ **a** in front of; **d'ora** ~ from now on.

in'nato, a *ag* innate.

innatu'rale *ag* unnatural.

inne'gabile *ag* undeniable.

innervo'sire *vt*: ~ **qd** to get on sb's nerves; ~**rsi** *vr* to get irritated *o* upset.

innes'care *vt* to prime; **in'nesco, schi** *sm* primer.

innes'tare *vt* (BOT, MED) to graft; (TECN) to engage; (*inserire: presa*) to insert; **in'nesto** *sm* graft; grafting *q*; (TECN) clutch; (ELETTR) connection.

'inno *sm* hymn; ~ **nazionale** national anthem.

inno'cente [inno'tʃɛnte] *ag* innocent; **inno'cenza** *sf* innocence.

in'nocuo, a *ag* innocuous, harmless.

inno'vare *vt* to change, make innovations in; **innovazi'one** *sf* innovation.

innume'revole *ag* innumerable.

inocu'lare *vt* (MED) to inoculate.

ino'doro, a *ag* odourless.

inol'trare *vt* (AMM) to pass on, forward; ~**rsi** *vr* (*addentrarsi*) to advance, go forward.

i'noltre *av* besides, moreover.

inon'dare *vt* to flood; **inondazi'one** *sf* flooding *q*; flood.

inope'roso, a *ag* inactive, idle.

inoppor'tuno, a *ag* untimely, ill-timed; inappropriate; (*momento*) inopportune.

inor'ganico, a, ci, che *ag* inorganic.

inorgo'glire [inorgoʎ'ʎire] *vt* to make proud // *vi* (2) (*anche*: ~**rsi**) to become proud; ~**rsi di qc** to pride o.s. on sth.

inorri'dire *vt* to horrify // *vi* (2) to be horrified.

inospi'tale *ag* inhospitable.

inosser'vato, a *ag* (*non notato*) unobserved; (*non rispettato*) not observed, not kept.

inossi'dabile *ag* stainless.

inqua'drare *vt* (*foto, immagine*) to frame; (*fig*) to situate, set.

inquie'tare *vt* (*turbare*) to disturb, worry; ~**rsi** *vr* to worry, become anxious; (*impazientirsi*) to get upset.

inqui'eto, a *ag* restless; (*preoccupato*) worried, anxious; **inquie'tudine** *sf* anxiety, worry.

inqui'lino, a *sm/f* tenant.

inquina'mento *sm* pollution.

inqui'nare *vt* to pollute.

inqui'sire *vt, vi* to investigate; **inquisi'tore, 'trice** *ag* (*sguardo*) inquiring; (DIR) investigating; **inquisizi'one** *sf* (STORIA) inquisition.

insa'lata *sf* salad; **insalati'era** *sf* salad bowl.

insa'lubre *ag* unhealthy.

insa'nabile *ag* incurable; unhealable.

insangui'nare *vt* to stain with blood.

in'sania *sf* insanity.

insa'puta *sf*: **all'~ di qd** without sb knowing.

insazi'abile [insat'tsjabile] *ag* insatiable.

insce'nare [inʃe'nare] *vt* (*TEATRO*) to stage, put on; (*fig*) to stage.

in'segna [in'seɲɲa] *sf* sign; (*emblema*) sign, emblem; (*bandiera*) flag, banner; ~ e *sfpl* (*decorazioni*) insignia *pl*.

insegna'mento [inseɲɲa'mento] *sm* teaching.

inse'gnante [inseɲ'nante] *ag* teaching // *sm/f* teacher.

inse'gnare [inseɲ'nare] *vt, vi* to teach; ~ a qd qc to teach sb sth; ~ qd a fare qc to teach sb (how) to do sth.

insegui'mento *sm* pursuit, chase.

insegu'ire *vt* to pursue, chase; **insegui'tore, 'trice** *sm/f* pursuer.

inselvati'chire [inselvati'kire] *vi* (2) (*anche*: ~ **rsi**) to grow wild.

insena'tura *sf* inlet, creek.

insen'sato, a *ag* senseless, stupid.

insen'sibile *ag* (*nervo*) insensible; (*movimento*) imperceptible; (*persona*) indifferent.

insepa'rabile *ag* inseparable.

inse'rire *vt* to insert; (*ELETTR*) to connect; ~ rsi *vr* (*fig*): ~ rsi in to become part of; **in'serto** *sm* (*pubblicazione*) insert.

inservi'ente *sm/f* attendant.

inserzi'one [inser'tsjone] *sf* insertion; (*avviso*) advertisement; fare un' ~ (*sul giornale*) to put an advertisement in the paper.

insetti'cida, i [insetti'tʃida] *sm* insecticide.

in'setto *sm* insect.

in'sidia *sf* snare, trap; (*pericolo*) hidden danger; **insidi'are** *vt, vi*: **insidiare a** to lay a trap for; **insidi'oso, a** *ag* insidious.

insi'eme *av* together // *prep*: ~ a o con together with // *sm* whole; (*MAT, servizio, assortimento*) set; (*MODA*) ensemble, outfit; tutti ~ all together; tutto ~ all together; (*in una volta*) at one go; nell' ~ on the whole; d' ~ (*veduta etc*) overall.

insignifi'cante [insiɲɲifi'kante] *ag* insignificant.

insi'gnire [insiɲ'nire] *vt* to decorate.

insin'cero, a [insin'tʃero] *ag* insincere.

insinda'cabile *ag* unquestionable.

insinu'are *vt* (*introdurre*): ~ qc in to slip o slide sth into; (*fig*) to insinuate, imply; ~ rsi *vr*: ~ rsi in to seep into; (*fig*) to creep into; to worm one's way into; **insinuazi'one** *sf* (*fig*) insinuation.

in'sipido, a *ag* insipid.

insis'tente *ag* insistent; persistent; **insis'tenza** *sf* insistence; persistence.

in'sistere *vi*: ~ su qc to insist on sth; ~ in qc/a fare (*perseverare*) to persist in sth/in doing; **insis'tito, a** *pp di* **insistere**.

insoddis'fatto, a *ag* dissatisfied.

insoffe'rente *ag* intolerant.

insolazi'one [insolat'tsjone] *sf* insolation; (*MED*) sunstroke.

inso'lente *ag* insolent; **insolen'tire** *vi* (2) to grow insolent // *vt* to insult, be rude to; **inso'lenza** *sf* insolence.

in'solito, a *ag* unusual, out of the ordinary.

inso'lubile *ag* insoluble.

inso'luto, a *ag* (*non risolto*) unsolved; (*non pagato*) unpaid, outstanding.

insol'vibile *ag* insolvent.

in'somma *av* (*in breve, in conclusione*) in short; (*dunque*) well // *escl* for heaven's sake!

in'sonne *ag* sleepless; **in'sonnia** *sf* insomnia, sleeplessness.

insonno'lito, a *ag* sleepy, drowsy.

insoppor'tabile *ag* unbearable.

in'sorgere [in'sordʒere] *vi* (2) (*ribellarsi*) to rise up, rebel; (*apparire*) to come up, arise.

in'sorto, a *pp di* **insorgere** // *sm/f* rebel, insurgent.

insospet'tire *vt* to make suspicious // *vi* (2) (*anche*: ~ **rsi**) to become suspicious.

inspi'rare *vt* to breathe in, inhale.

in'stabile *ag* (*carico, indole*) unstable; (*tempo*) unsettled; (*equilibrio*) unsteady.

instal'lare *vt* to install; ~ **rsi** *vr* (*sistemarsi*): ~ **rsi in** to settle in; **installazi'one** *sf* installation.

instan'cabile *ag* untiring, indefatigable.

instau'rare *vt* to introduce, institute; ~ **rsi** *vr* to start, begin.

instra'dare *vt* to direct.

insubordinazi'one [insubordinat'tsjone] *sf* insubordination.

insuc'cesso [insut'tʃesso] *sm* failure, flop.

insudici'are [insudi'tʃare] *vt* to dirty; ~ **rsi** *vr* to get dirty.

insuffici'ente [insuffi'tʃente] *ag* insufficient; (*compito, allievo*) inadequate; **insuffici'enza** *sf* insufficiency; inadequacy; (*INS*) fail.

insu'lare *ag* insular.

insu'lina *sf* insulin.

in'sulso, a *ag* (*sciocco*) inane, silly; (*persona*) dull, insipid.

insul'tare *vt* to insult, affront.

in'sulto *sm* insult, affront.

insurrezi'one [insurret'tsjone] *sf* revolt, insurrection.

insussis'tente *ag* non-existent.

intac'care *vt* (*fare tacche*) to cut into; (*corrodere*) to corrode; (*fig: cominciare ad usare: risparmi*) to break into; (: *ledere*) to damage.

intagli'are [intaʎ'ʎare] *vt* to carve; **in'taglio** *sm* carving.

intan'gibile [intan'dʒibile] *ag* untouchable; inviolable.

in'tanto *av* (*nel frattempo*) meanwhile, in the meantime; (*per cominciare*) just to begin with; ~ che *cong* while.

intarsi'are *vt* to inlay; **in'tarsio** *sm* inlaying *q*, marquetry *q*; inlay.

inta'sare *vt* to choke (up), block (up); (*AUT*) to obstruct, block; ~ **rsi** *vr* to become choked o blocked.

intas'care *vt* to pocket.

in'tatto, a *ag* intact; (*puro*) unsullied.

intavo'lare *vt* to start, enter into.

inte'grale ag complete; (MAT): calcolo ~ integral calculus.

inte'grante ag: parte ~ integral part.

inte'grare vt to complete; (MAT) to integrate; ~rsi vr (persona) to integrate; integrazi'one sf integration.

integrità sf integrity.

'integro, a ag (intatto, intero) complete, whole; (retto) upright.

intelaia'tura sf frame; (fig) structure, framework.

intel'letto sm intellect; intellettu'ale ag, sm/f intellectual.

intelli'gente [intelli'dʒɛnte] ag intelligent; intelli'genza sf intelligence; intelli'gibile ag intelligibile.

intem'perie sfpl bad weather sg.

intempes'tivo, a ag untimely.

inten'dente sm principal administrator; inten'denza sf: intendenza di finanza finance office; intendenza generale (MIL) supplies office.

in'tendere vt (avere intenzione): ~ fare qc to intend o mean to do sth; (comprendere) to understand; (udire) to hear; (significare) to mean; ~rsi vr (conoscere): ~rsi di to know a lot about, be a connoisseur of; (accordarsi) to get on (well); intendersela con qd (avere una relazione amorosa) to have an affair with sb; intendi'mento sm (intelligenza) understanding; (proposito) intention; intendi'tore, 'trice sm/f connoisseur, expert.

intene'rire vt (fig) to move (to pity); ~rsi vr (fig) to be moved.

intensifi'care vt, ~rsi vr to intensify.

intensità sf intensity.

inten'sivo, a ag intensive.

in'tenso, a ag intense.

in'tento, a ag (teso, assorto): ~ (a) intent (on), absorbed (in) // sm aim, purpose.

intenzio'nale [intentsjo'nale] ag intentional.

intenzi'one [inten'tsjone] sf intention; (DIR) intent: avere ~ di fare qc to intend to do sth, have the intention of doing sth.

interca'lare sm pet phrase, stock phrase // vt to insert.

inter'cedere [inter'tʃedere] vi to intercede; intercessi'one sf intercession.

intercet'tare [intertʃet'tare] vt to intercept; (telefono) to tap.

inter'correre vi (2) (esserci) to exist; (passare: tempo) to elapse.

inter'detto, a pp di interdire // ag forbidden, prohibited; (sconcertato) dumbfounded // sm (REL) interdict.

inter'dire vt to forbid, prohibit, ban; (REL) to interdict; (DIR) to deprive of civil rights; interdizi'one sf prohibition, ban.

interessa'mento sm interest.

interes'sante ag interesting; essere in stato ~ to be expecting (a baby).

interes'sare vt to interest; (concernere) to concern, be of interest to; (far intervenire): ~ qd a to draw sb's attention

to // vi: ~ a to interest, matter to; ~rsi vr (mostrare interesse): ~rsi a to take an interest in, be interested in; (occuparsi): ~rsi di to take care of.

inte'resse sm (anche COMM) interest.

interfe'renza [interfe'rɛntsa] sf interference.

interfe'rire vi to interfere.

interiezi'one [interjet'tsjone] sf exclamation, interjection.

interi'ora sfpl entrails.

interi'ore ag interior, inner, inside, internal; (fig) inner.

inter'ludio sm (MUS) interlude.

intermedi'ario, a ag, sm/f intermediary.

inter'medio, a ag intermediate.

inter'mezzo [inter'mɛddzo] sm (intervallo) interval; (breve spettacolo) intermezzo.

intermi'nabile ag interminable, endless.

inter'nare vt (arrestare) to intern; (MED) to commit (to a mental institution).

internazio'nale [internattsjo'nale] ag international.

in'terno, a ag (di dentro) internal, interior, inner; (: mare) inland; (nazionale) domestic, home cpd, internal; (allievo) boarding // sm inside, interior; (di paese) interior; (fodera) lining; (di appartamento) flat (number); (TEL) extension // sm/f (INS) boarder; ~i smpl (CINEMA) interior shots; all'~ inside; ministro dell'I'~ Minister of the Interior, ≈ Home Secretary; ~ destro/sinistro (CALCIO) inside right/left.

in'tero, a ag (integro, intatto) whole, entire; (completo, totale) complete; (numero) whole; (non ridotto: biglietto) full.

interpel'lare vt to consult.

inter'porre vt to interpose; interporsi vr to intervene; inter'posto, a pp di interporre.

interpre'tare vt to interpret; interpretazi'one sf interpretation; in'terprete sm interpreter; (TEATRO) actor, performer; (MUS) performer.

interro'gare vt to question; (INS) to test; interroga'tivo, a ag (occhi, sguardo) questioning, inquiring; (LING) interrogative // sm question; (fig) mystery; interroga'torio, a ag interrogatory, questioning // sm (DIR) questioning q; interrogazi'one sf questioning q; (INS) oral test.

inter'rompere vt to interrupt; (studi, trattative) to break off, interrupt; ~rsi vi to break off, stop; inter'rotto, a pp di interrompere.

interrut'tore sm switch.

interruzi'one [interrut'tsjone] sf interruption; break.

interse'care vt, ~rsi vr to intersect.

inter'stizio [inter'stittsjo] sm interstice, crack.

interur'bano, a ag inter-city; (TEL: chiamata) trunk cpd, long-distance; (: telefono) long-distance // sf trunk call, long-distance call.

inter'vallo *sm* interval; (*spazio*) space, gap.

interve'nire *vi* (2) (*partecipare*): ~ **a** to be present at, attend; (*intromettersi: anche* POL) to intervene; (MED: *operare*) to operate; **inter'vento** *sm* presence, attendance; (*inframmettenza*) intervention; (MED) operation.

inter'vista *sf* interview; **intervis'tare** *vt* to interview.

in'teso, a *pp di* **intendere** // *ag* agreed // *sf* (*fra amici, paesi*) understanding; (*accordo*) agreement, understanding, (SPORT) teamwork; **non darsi per ~ di** qc to take no notice of sth.

intes'tare *vt* to head; (*casa*): ~ qc a to put *o* register sth in the name of; ~**rsi** *vr* (*ostinarsi*): ~**rsi a fare** to take it into one's head to do; **intestazi'one** *sf* heading; (*su carta da lettere*) letterhead; (*registrazione*) registration.

intes'tino, a *ag* (*lotte*) internal, civil // *sm* (ANAT) intestine.

inti'mare *vt* to order, command; **intimazi'one** *sf* order, command.

intimidazi'one [intimidat'tsjone] *sf* intimidation.

intimi'dire *vt* to intimidate // *vi* (*anche:* ~**rsi**) to grow shy.

intimità *sf* intimacy; privacy; (*familiarità*) familiarity.

'intimo, a *ag* intimate; (*affetti, vita*) private; (*fig: profondo*) inmost // *sm* (*persona*) intimate *o* close friend; (*dell'animo*) bottom, depths *pl*.

intimo'rire *vt* to frighten; ~**rsi** *vr* to become frightened.

in'tingolo *sm* sauce; (*pietanza*) stew.

intiriz'zire [intirid'dzire] *vt* to numb // *vi* (2) (*anche:* ~**rsi**) to go numb.

intito'lare *vt* to give a title to; (*dedicare*) to dedicate.

intolle'rabile *ag* intolerable.

intolle'rante *ag* intolerant.

intona'care *vt* to plaster.

in'tonaco, ci *o* **chi** *sm* plaster.

into'nare *vt* (*canto*) to start to sing; (*strumenti*) to tune; (*armonizzare*) to match; ~**rsi** *vr* to be in tune; to match; **intonazi'one** *sf* intonation.

inton'tire *vt* to stun, daze // *vi* (2) to be stunned *o* dazed.

in'toppo *sm* stumbling block, obstacle.

in'torno *av* around; ~ **a** *prep* (*attorno a*) around; (*riguardo, circa*) about.

intorpi'dire *vt* to numb; (*fig*) to make sluggish // *vi* (2) (*anche:* ~**rsi**) to grow numb; (*fig*) to become sluggish.

intossi'care *vt* to poison; **intossica-zi'one** *sf* poisoning.

intralci'are [intral'tʃare] *vt* to hamper, hold up.

intransi'gente [intransi'dʒɛnte] *ag* intransigent, uncompromising.

intransi'tivo, a *ag, sm* intransitive.

intrapren'dente *ag* enterprising, go-ahead.

intra'prendere *vt* to undertake.

intrat'tabile *ag* intractable.

intratte'nere *vt* to entertain; to engage in conversation; ~**rsi** *vr* to linger; ~**rsi su** qc to dwell on sth.

intrave'dere *vt* to catch a glimpse of; (*fig*) to foresee.

intrecci'are [intret'tʃare] *vt* (*capelli*) to plait, braid; (*intessere: anche fig*) to weave, interweave, intertwine; ~**rsi** *vr* to intertwine, become interwoven; ~ **le mani** to clasp one's hands; **in'treccio** *sm* (*fig: trama*) plot, story.

in'trepido, a *ag* fearless, dauntless.

intri'gare *vi* to manoeuvre, scheme; ~**rsi** *vr* to interfere, meddle; **in'trigo, ghi** *sm* plot, intrigue.

in'trinseco, a, ci, che *ag* intrinsic; (*amico*) close, intimate.

in'triso, a *ag:* ~ (**di**) soaked (in).

intro'durre *vt* to introduce; (*chiave etc*): ~ **qc in** to insert sth into; (*persone: far entrare*) to show in; **introdursi** *vr* (*moda, tecniche*) to be introduced; **introdursi in** (*persona: penetrare*) to enter; (: *entrare furtivamente*) to steal *o* slip into; **introduzi'one** *sf* introduction.

in'troito *sm* income, revenue.

intro'mettersi *vr* to interfere, meddle; (*interporsi*) to intervene.

intro'verso, a *ag* introverted // *sm* introvert.

in'truglio [in'truʎʎo] *sm* concoction.

intrusi'one *sf* intrusion; interference.

in'truso, a *sm/f* intruder.

intu'ire *vt* to perceive by intuition; (*rendersi conto*) to realise; **in'tuito** *sm* intuition; (*perspicacia*) perspicacity; **intui-zi'one** *sf* intuition.

inu'mano, a *ag* inhuman.

inumi'dire *vt* to dampen, moisten; ~**rsi** *vr* to become damp *o* wet.

i'nutile *ag* useless; (*superfluo*) pointless, unnecessary; **inutilità** *sf* uselessness; pointlessness.

inva'dente *ag* (*fig*) interfering, nosey.

in'vadere *vt* to invade; (*affollare*) to swarm into, overrun; (*sog: acque*) to flood; **invadi'trice** *ag vedi* **invasore**.

invalidità *sf* infirmity; disability; (DIR) invalidity.

in'valido, a *ag* (*infermo*) infirm, invalid; (*al lavoro*) disabled; (DIR) invalid // *sm/f* invalid; disabled person.

in'vano *av* in vain.

invari'abile *ag* invariable.

invasi'one *sf* invasion.

in'vaso, a *pp di* **invadere**.

inva'sore, invadi'trice [invadi'tritʃe] *ag* invading // *sm* invader.

invecchi'are [invek'kjare] *vi* (2) (*persona*) to grow old; (*vino, popolazione*) to age; (*moda*) to become dated // *vt* to age; (*far apparire più vecchio*) to make look older.

in'vece [in'vetʃe] *av* instead; (*al contrario*) on the contrary; ~ **di** *prep* instead of.

inve'ire *vi:* ~ **contro** to rail against.

inven'tare vt to invent; (pericoli, pettegolezzi) to make up, invent.

inven'tario sm inventory; (COMM) stocktaking q.

inven'tivo, a ag inventive // sf inventiveness.

inven'tore sm inventor.

invenzi'one [inven'tsjone] sf invention; (bugia) lie, story.

inver'nale ag winter cpd; (simile all'inverno) wintry.

in'verno sm winter.

invero'simile ag unlikely.

inversi'one sf inversion; reversal; ~ di marcia (AUT) reversing; "divieto d'~" "no U-turns".

in'verso, a ag reverse; opposite; (MAT) inverse // sf contrary, opposite; in senso ~ in the opposite direction; nell'ordine ~ in the reverse order.

inverte'brato, a ag, sm invertebrate.

inver'tire vt to invert, reverse; ~ la marcia to reverse; **inver'tito, a** sm/f homosexual.

investi'gare vt, vi to investigate; **investiga'tore** sm investigator, detective; **investigazi'one** sf investigation, inquiry.

investi'mento sm (ECON) investment; (scontro, urto) crash, collision; (incidente stradale) road accident.

inves'tire vt (denaro) to invest; (sog: veicolo: pedone) to knock down; (: altro veicolo) to crash into; (sog: nave) to collide with; (apostrofare) to assail; (incaricare): ~ qd di to invest sb with; **investi'tura** sf investiture.

invete'rato, a ag inveterate.

invet'tiva sf invective.

invi'are vt to send; **invi'ato, a** sm/f envoy; (STAMPA) correspondent.

in'vidia sf envy; **invidi'are** vt to envy; **invidi'oso, a** ag envious.

invigo'rire vt to strengthen, invigorate // vi (?) (anche: ~rsi) to gain strength.

invin'cibile [invin'tʃibile] ag invincible.

in'vio, 'vii sm sending; (insieme di merci) consignment.

invio'labile ag inviolable.

invipe'rito, a ag furious.

invi'sibile ag invisible.

invi'tare vt to invite; ~ qd a fare to invite sb to do; (sog: cosa) to tempt sb to do; **invi'tato, a** sm/f guest; **in'vito** sm invitation.

invo'care vt (chiedere: aiuto, pace) to cry out for; (appellarsi: la legge, Dio) to appeal to, invoke.

invogli'are [invoʎ'ʎare] vt: ~ qd a fare to tempt sb to do, induce sb to do; ~rsi di to take a fancy to.

involon'tario, a ag (errore) unintentional; (gesto) involuntary.

invol'tino sm (CUC) roulade.

in'volto sm (pacco) parcel; (fagotto) bundle.

in'volucro sm cover, wrapping.

invo'luto, a ag involved, intricate.

invulne'rabile ag invulnerable.

inzacche'rare [intsakke'rare] vt to spatter with mud.

inzup'pare [intsup'pare] vt to soak; ~rsi vr to get soaked.

'io pronome I // sm inv: l'~ the ego, the self; ~ stesso(a) I myself.

l'odio sm iodine.

l'ogurt sm inv = yoghurt.

l'one sm ion.

l'onio sm: lo ~ the Ionian (Sea).

iperme'cato sm hypermarket.

ipertensi'one sf high blood pressure, hypertension.

ip'nosi sf hypnosis; **ip'notico, a, ci, che** ag hypnotic; **ipno'tismo** sm hypnotism; **ipnotiz'zare** vt to hypnotize.

ipocri'sia sf hypocrisy.

i'pocrita, i, e ag hypocritical // sm/f hypocrite.

ipo'teca, che sf mortgage; **ipote'care** vt to mortgage.

i'potesi sf inv hypothesis; **ipo'tetico, a, ci, che** ag hypothetical.

'ippico, a, ci, che ag horse cpd // sf horseracing.

ippocas'tano sm horse chestnut.

ip'podromo sm racecourse.

ippo'potamo sm hippopotamus.

'ira sf anger, wrath.

I'ran sm: l'~ Iran.

I'raq sm: l'~ Iraq.

'iride sf (arcobaleno) rainbow; (ANAT, BOT) iris.

Ir'landa sf: l'~ Ireland; **irlan'dese** ag Irish // sm/f Irishman/woman; **gli Irlandesi** the Irish.

iro'nia sf irony; **i'ronico, a, ci, che** ag ironic(al).

irradi'are vt to radiate; (sog: raggi di luce: illuminare) to shine on, irradiate // vi (?) (diffondersi: anche: ~rsi) to radiate; **irradiazi'one** sf radiation; irradiation.

irragio'nevole [irradʒo'nevole] ag irrational; unreasonable.

irrazio'nale [irrattsjo'nale] ag irrational.

irre'ale ag unreal.

irrecu'sabile ag (offerta) not to be refused; (prova) irrefutable.

irrefu'tabile ag irrefutable.

irrego'lare ag irregular; (terreno) uneven; **irregolarità** sf inv irregularity; unevenness.

irremo'vibile ag (fig) unshakeable, unyielding.

irrepa'rabile ag irreparable; (fig) unavoidable.

irrepe'ribile ag nowhere to be found.

irrequi'eto, a ag restless.

irresis'tibile ag irresistible.

irreso'luto, a ag irresolute.

irrespon'sabile ag irresponsible.

irrevo'cabile ag irrevocable.

irridu'cibile [irridu'tʃibile] ag irreducible; (fig) indomitable.

irri'gare vt (annaffiare) to irrigate; (sog:

fiume etc) to flow through; **irrigazi'one** *sf* irrigation.

irrigi'dire [irridʒi'dire] *vt*, ~**rsi** *vr* to stiffen.

irri'sorio, a *ag* derisory.

irri'tabile *ag* irritable.

irri'tare *vt* (*mettere di malumore*) to irritate, annoy; (*MED*) to irritate; ~**rsi** *vr* (*stizzirsi*) to become irritated *o* annoyed; **irritazi'one** *sf* irritation; annoyance.

ir'rompere *vi*: ~ **in** to burst into.

irro'rare *vt* to sprinkle; (*AGR*) to spray.

irru'ente *ag* (*fig*) impetuous, violent.

irruzi'one [irrut'tsjone] *sf* irruption *q*; **fare** ~ **in** to burst into.

'irto, a *ag* bristly; ~ **di** bristling with.

is'critto, a *pp di* **iscrivere** // *sm/f* member; **per** *o* **in** ~ in writing.

is'crivere *vt* to register, enter; (*persona*) to register, enrol; ~**rsi** *vr*: ~**rsi (a)** (*club, partito*) to join; (*università*) to register *o* enrol (at); (*esame, concorso*) to register *o* enter (for); **iscrizi'one** *sf* (*epigrafe etc*) inscription; (*a scuola, società*) enrolment, registration; (*registrazione*) registration.

Is'landa *sf*: **l'**~ Iceland.

'isola *sf* island; ~ **pedonale** (*AUT*) traffic island.

isola'mento *sm* isolation; (*TECN*) insulation.

iso'lano, a *ag* island *cpd* // *sm/f* islander.

iso'lante *ag* insulating // *sm* insulator.

iso'lare *vt* to isolate; (*TECN*) to insulate; (*: acusticamente*) to soundproof; **iso'lato, a** *ag* isolated; insulated // *sm* (*EDIL*) block.

ispetto'rato *sm* inspectorate.

ispet'tore *sm* inspector.

ispezio'nare [ispettsjo'nare] *vt* to inspect.

ispezi'one [ispet'tsjone] *sf* inspection.

'ispido, a *ag* bristly, shaggy.

ispi'rare *vt* to inspire; ~**rsi** *vr*: ~**rsi a** to draw one's inspiration from; **ispirazi'one** *sf* inspiration.

Isra'ele *sm*: **l'**~ Israel; **israeli'ano, a** *ag, sm/f* Israeli.

is'sare *vt* to hoist.

istan'taneo, a *ag* instantaneous // *sf* (*FOT*) snapshot.

is'tante *sm* instant, moment; **all'**~, **sull'**~ instantly, immediately.

is'tanza [is'tantsa] *sf* petition, request.

is'terico, a, ci, che *ag* hysterical.

iste'rismo *sm* hysteria.

isti'gare *vt* to incite, instigate; **istigazi'one** *sf* instigation.

istin'tivo, a *ag* instinctive.

is'tinto *sm* instinct.

istitu'ire *vt* (*fondare*) to institute, found; (*porre: confronto*) to establish; (*intraprendere: inchiesta*) to set up.

isti'tuto *sm* institute; (*ente, DIR*) institution; ~ **di bellezza** beauty salon.

istituzi'one [istitut'tsjone] *sf* institution.

'istmo *sm* (*GEO*) isthmus.

'istrice ['istritʃe] *sm* porcupine.

istri'one *sm* (*peg*) ham actor.

istru'ire *vt* (*insegnare*) to teach;

(*ammaestrare*) to train; (*informare*) to instruct, inform; (*DIR*) to prepare; **istrut'tivo, a** *ag* instructive; **istrut'tore, 'trice** *sm/f* instructor // *ag*: **giudice istruttore** examining magistrate; **istrut'toria** *sf* (*DIR*) (preliminary) investigation and hearing; **istruzi'one** *sf* education; training; (*direttiva*) instruction; (*DIR*) = **istruttoria**; **istruzioni** *sfpl* (*norme per l'uso*) instructions, directions.

I'talia *sf*: **l'**~ Italy.

itali'ano, a *ag* Italian // *sm/f* Italian // *sm* (*LING*) Italian; **gli I**~**i** the Italians.

itine'rario *sm* itinerary.

itte'rizia [itte'rittsja] *sf* (*MED*) jaundice.

'ittico, a, ci, che *ag* fish *cpd*; fishing *cpd*.

Iugos'lavia *sf* = **Jugoslavia**.

iugos'lavo, a *ag, sm/f* = **jugoslavo, a**.

i'uta *sf* jute.

I.V.A. ['iva] *abbr f vedi* **imposta**.

J

jazz [dʒaz] *sm* jazz.

jeans [dʒinz] *smpl* jeans.

Jugos'lavia [jugoz'lavja] *sf*: **la** ~ Yugoslavia; **jugos'lavo, a** *ag, sm/f* Yugoslav(ian).

'juta ['juta] *sf* = **iuta**.

L

l' *det vedi* **la, lo.**

la *det f* (*dav V* **l'**) the // *pronome* (*dav V* **l'**) (*oggetto: persona*) her; (*: cosa*) it; (*: forma di cortesia*) you // *sm inv* (*MUS*) A; (*: solfeggiando la scala*) la.

là *av* there; **di** ~ (*da quel luogo*) from there; (*in quel luogo*) in there; (*dall'altra parte*) over there; **di** ~ **di** beyond; **per di** ~ that way; **andare in** ~ (*procedere*) to go on, proceed; **più in** ~ further on; (*tempo*) later on; *vedi* **quello.**

'labbro *sm* (*pl(f)*: **labbra**: *solo nel senso ANAT*) lip.

labi'rinto *sm* labyrinth, maze.

labora'torio *sm* (*di ricerca*) laboratory; (*di arti, mestieri*) workshop; ~ **linguistico** language laboratory.

labori'oso, a *ag* (*faticoso*) laborious; (*attivo*) hard-working.

labu'rista, i, e *ag* Labour *cpd* // *sm/f* Labour Party member.

'lacca, che *sf* lacquer.

'laccio ['lattʃo] *sm* noose; (*lazo*) lasso; (*di scarpa*) lace; (*fig*) snare.

lace'rare [latʃe'rare] *vt* to tear to shreds, lacerate; ~**rsi** *vr* to tear; **'lacero, a** *ag* (*logoro*) torn, tattered.

la'conico, a, ci, che *ag* laconic, brief.

'lacrima *sf* tear; (*goccia*) drop; **in** ~**e** in tears; **lacri'mare** *vi* to water; **lacri'mogeno, a** *ag*: *vedi* **gas; lacri'moso, a** *ag* (*commovente*) pitiful, pathetic.

la'cuna *sf* (*fig*) gap.

'ladro *sm* thief; **ladro'cinio** *sm* theft, larceny.

laggiù [lad'dʒu] av down there; (di là) over there.

la'gnarsi [laɲ'narsi] vr: ~ (di) to complain (about).

'lago, ghi sm lake.

'lagrima etc = **lacrima** etc.

la'guna sf lagoon.

'laico, a, ci, che ag (apostolato) lay; (vita) secular; (scuola) non-denominational // sm/f layman/ woman // sm lay brother.

'lama sf blade // sm inv (ZOOL) llama; (REL) lama.

lambic'care vt to distil; ~rsi il cervello to rack one's brains.

lam'bire vt to lick; to lap.

la'mella sf (di metallo etc) thin sheet, thin strip; (di fungo) gill.

lamen'tare vt to lament; ~rsi vr (emettere lamenti) to moan, groan; (rammaricarsi): ~rsi (di) to complain (about); **lamen'tela** sf complaining q; **lamen'tevole** ag (voce) complaining, plaintive; (destino) pitiful; **la'mento** sm moan, groan; wail; **lamen'toso, a** ag plaintive.

la'metta sf razor blade.

lami'era sf sheet metal.

'lamina sf (lastra sottile) thin sheet (o layer o plate); ~ d'oro gold leaf; gold foil; **lami'nare** vt to laminate; **lami'nato, a** ag laminated; (tessuto) lamé // sm laminate; lamé.

'lampada sf lamp; ~ da saldatore blowlamp; ~ da tavolo table lamp.

lampa'dario sm chandelier.

lampa'dina sf light bulb; ~ tascabile pocket torch.

lam'pante ag (fig: evidente) crystal clear, evident.

lampeggi'are [lamped'dʒare] vi (luce, fari) to flash // vb impers: **lampeggia** there's lightning; **lampeggia'tore** sm (AUT) indicator.

lampi'one sm street light o lamp.

'lampo sm (METEOR) flash of lightning; (di luce, fig) flash; ~i smpl lightning q // ag inv: cerniera ~ zip (fastener); guerra ~ blitzkrieg.

lam'pone sm raspberry.

'lana sf wool; ~ d'acciaio steel wool; pura ~ vergine pure new wool; ~ di vetro glass wool.

lan'cetta [lan'tʃetta] sf (indice) pointer, needle; (di orologio) hand.

'lancia ['lantʃa] sf (arma) lance; (: picca) spear; (imbarcazione) launch.

lanciafi'amme [lantʃa'fjamme] sm inv flamethrower.

lanci'are [lan'tʃare] vt to throw, hurl, fling; (SPORT) to throw; (far partire: automobile) to get up to full speed; (bombe) to drop; (razzo, prodotto, moda) to launch; ~rsi vr: ~rsi contro/su to throw o hurl o fling o.s. against/on; ~rsi in (fig) to embark on.

lanci'nante [lantʃi'nante] ag (dolore) shooting, throbbing; (grido) piercing.

'lancio ['lantʃo] sm throwing q; throw; dropping q; drop; launching q; launch; ~ del peso putting the shot.

'landa sf (GEO) moor.

'languido, a ag (fiacco) languid, weak; (tenero, malinconico) languishing.

langu'ire vi to languish; (conversazione) to flag.

langu'ore sm weakness, languor.

lani'ero, a ag wool cpd, woollen.

lani'ficio [lani'fitʃo] sm woollen mill.

la'noso, a ag woolly.

lan'terna sf lantern; (faro) lighthouse.

la'nugine [la'nudʒine] sf down.

lapi'dare vt to stone.

lapi'dario, a ag (fig) terse.

'lapide sf (di sepolcro) tombstone; (commemorativa) plaque.

'lapis sm inv pencil.

'lapsus sm inv slip.

'lardo sm bacon fat, lard.

largheggi'are [larged'dʒare] vi: ~ di o in to be generous o liberal with.

lar'ghezza [lar'gettsa] sf width; breadth; looseness; generosity; ~ di vedute broad-mindedness.

'largo, a, ghi, ghe ag wide; broad; (maniche) wide; (abito: troppo ampio) loose; (fig) generous // sm width; breadth; (mare aperto): il ~ the open sea; ~ due metri two metres wide; ~ di spalle broad-shouldered; ~ di vedute broad-minded; su ~a scala on a large scale; al ~ (NAUT) offshore; farsi ~ tra la folla to push one's way through the crowd.

'larice ['laritʃe] sm (BOT) larch.

la'ringe [la'rindʒe] sf larynx; **larin'gite** sf laryngitis.

'larva sf larva; (fig) shadow.

la'sagne [la'zaɲɲe] sfpl lasagna sg.

lasci'are [laʃ'ʃare] vt to leave; (abbandonare) to leave, abandon, give up; (cessare di tenere) to let go of // vb ausiliare: ~ fare qd to let sb do // vi: ~ di fare (smettere) to stop doing; ~rsi andare/truffare to let o.s. go/be cheated; ~ andare o correre o perdere to let things go their own way; ~ stare qc/qd to leave sth/sb alone.

'lascito ['laʃʃito] sm (DIR) legacy.

la'scivo, a [laʃ'ʃivo] ag lascivious.

'laser ['lazer] ag, sm inv: (raggio) ~ laser (beam).

lassa'tivo, a ag, sm laxative.

'lasso sm: ~ di tempo interval, lapse of time.

lassù av up there.

'lastra sf (di pietra) slab; (di metallo, FOT) plate; (di ghiaccio, vetro) sheet; (radiografica) X-ray (plate).

lastri'care vt to pave; **lastri'cato** sm, **'lastrico, ci** o **chi** sm pavement.

la'tente ag latent.

late'rale ag lateral, side cpd // sm (CALCIO) half-back.

late'rizi [late'rittsi] smpl bricks; tiles.

lati'fondo sm large estate.

la'tino, a *ag, sm* Latin; **~-ameri'cano a** *ag* Latin-American.

lati'tante *sm/f* fugitive (from justice).

lati'tudine *sf* latitude.

'lato, a *ag* (*fig*) wide, broad // *sm* side; (*fig*) aspect, point of view; **in senso ~** broadly speaking.

la'trare *vi* to bark.

la'trina *sf* latrine.

latro'cinio [latro'tʃinjo] *sm* = **ladrocinio.**

'latta *sf* tin (plate); (*recipiente*) tin, can.

lat'taio, a *sm/f* milkman/ dairywoman.

lat'tante *ag* unweaned.

'latte *sm* milk; **~ detergente** cleansing milk *o* lotion; **~ secco** *o* **in polvere** dried *o* powdered milk; **~ scremato** skimmed milk; **'latteo, a** *ag* milky; (*dieta, prodotto*) milk *cpd*; **latte'ria** *sf* dairy; **latti'cini** *smpl* dairy products.

lat'tina *sf* (*di birra etc*) can.

lat'tuga *sf* lettuce.

'laurea *sf* degree; **laure'ando, a** *sm/f* final-year student; **laure'are** *vt* to confer a degree on; **laurearsi** *vr* to graduate; **laure'ato, a** *ag, sm/f* graduate.

'lauro *sm* laurel.

'lava *sf* lava.

la'vabile *ag* washable.

la'vabo *sm* washbasin.

la'vaggio [la'vaddʒo] *sm* washing *q*; **~ del cervello** brainwashing *q*.

la'vagna [la'vaɲɲa] *sf* (GEO) slate; (*di scuola*) blackboard.

la'vanda *sf* (*anche* MED) wash; (BOT) lavender; **lavan'daia** *sf* washerwoman; **lavande'ria** *sf* laundry; **lavanderia automatica** launderette; **lavan'dino** *sm* sink.

lavapi'atti *sm/f* dishwasher.

la'vare *vt* to wash; **~rsi** *vr* to wash, have a wash; **~ a secco** to dry-clean; **~rsi le mani/i denti** to wash one's hands/clean one's teeth.

lava'secco *sm o f inv* drycleaner's.

lavasto'viglie [lavasto'viʎʎe] *sm o f inv* (*macchina*) dishwasher.

lava'toio *sm* (public) washhouse.

lava'trice [lava'tritʃe] *sf* washing machine.

lava'tura *sf* washing *q*; **~ di piatti** dishwater.

lavo'rante *sm* workman.

lavo'rare *vi* to work; (*fig: bar, studio etc*) to do good business // *vt* to work; (*fig: persuadere*) to work on; **~ a** to work on; **~ a maglia** to knit; **~ la terra** to till the land; **lavora'tivo, a** *ag* working; **lavora'tore, 'trice** *sm/f* worker // *ag* working; **lavorazi'one** *sf* manufacture; (*di materie prime*) processing; (*produzione*) production; **lavo'rio** *sm* intense activity.

la'voro *sm* work; (*occupazione*) job, work *q*; (*opera*) piece of work, job; (ECON) labour; **~i forzati** hard labour *sg*; **ministro dei L~i pubblici** Minister of Works.

le *det fpl* the // *pronome* (*oggetto*) them; (: *a lei, a essa*) to her; (: *forma di cortesia*) to you.

le'ale *ag* loyal; (*sincero*) sincere; (*onesto*) fair; **lealtà** *sf* loyalty; sincerity; fairness.

'lebbra *sf* leprosy.

'lecca 'lecca *sm inv* lollipop.

leccapi'edi *sm/f inv* (*peg*) toady, bootlicker.

lec'care *vt* to lick; (*sog: gatto: latte etc*) to lick *o* lap up; (*fig*) to flatter; **~rsi i baffi** *o* **le labbra** to lick one's lips; **lec'cata** *sf* lick.

'leccio ['iettʃo] *sm* holm oak, ilex.

leccor'nia *sf* titbit, delicacy.

'lecito, a ['lɛtʃito] *ag* permitted, allowed.

'ledere *vt* to damage, injure; **~ gli interessi di qd** to be prejudicial to sb's interests.

'lega, ghe *sf* league; (*di metalli*) alloy.

le'gaccio [le'gattʃo] *sm* string, lace.

le'gale *ag* legal // *sm* lawyer; **legalità** *sf* legality, lawfulness; **legaliz'zare** *vt* to authenticate; (*regolarizzare*) to legalize.

le'game (*corda, fig: affettivo*) tie, bond; (*nesso logico*) link, connection.

lega'mento *sm* (ANAT) ligament.

le'gare *vt* (*prigioniero, capelli, cane*) to tie (up); (*libro*) to bind; (CHIM) to alloy; (*fig: collegare*) to bind, join // *vi* (*far lega*) to unite; (*fig*) to get on well.

lega'tario, a *sm/f* (DIR) legatee.

le'gato *sm* (REL) legate; (DIR) legacy, bequest.

lega'tura *sf* tying *q*; binding *q*; (*di libro*) binding; (MUS) ligature.

legazi'one [legat'tsjone] *sf* legation.

'legge ['leddʒe] *sf* law.

leg'genda [led'dʒenda] *sf* (*narrazione*) legend; (*di carta geografica etc*) key, legend; (*di disegno*) caption, legend; **leg-gen'dario, a** *ag* legendary.

'leggere ['lɛddʒere] *vt, vi* to read.

legge'rezza [leddʒe'rettsa] *sf* lightness; thoughtlessness; fickleness.

leg'gero, a [led'dʒɛro] *ag* light; (*agile, snello*) nimble, agile, light; (*tè, caffè*) weak; (*fig: non grave, piccolo*) slight; (: *spensierato*) thoughtless; (: *incostante*) fickle; free and easy; **alla ~a** thoughtlessly.

leggi'adro, a [led'dʒadro] *ag* pretty, lovely; (*movimenti*) graceful.

leg'gibile [led'dʒibile] *ag* legible; (*libro*) readable, worth reading.

leggi'ero, a [led'dʒɛro] *ag* = **leggero.**

leg'gio, 'gii [led'dʒio] *sm* lectern; (MUS) music stand.

legio'nario [ledʒo'narjo] *sm* (*romano*) legionary; (*volontario*) legionnaire.

legi'one [le'dʒone] *sf* legion; **~ straniera** foreign legion.

legisla'tivo, a [ledʒizla'tivo] *ag* legislative.

legisla'tore [ledʒizla'tore] *sm* legislator.

legisla'tura [ledʒizla'tura] *sf* legislature.

legislazi'one [ledʒizlat'tsjone] *sf* legislation.

legittimità [ledʒittimi'ta] *sf* legitimacy.

le'gittimo, a [le'dʒittimo] *ag* legitimate; *(fig: giustificato, lecito)* justified, legitimate; **~a difesa** *(DIR)* self-defence.

'legna ['leɲɲa] *sf* firewood; **le'gname** *sm* wood, timber.

'legno ['leɲɲo] *sm* wood; *(pezzo di —)* piece of wood; **di ~** wooden; **~ compensato** plywood; **le'gnoso, a** *ag* wooden; woody; *(carne)* tough.

le'gumi *smpl* *(BOT)* pulses.

'lei *pronome (soggetto)* she; *(oggetto: per dare rilievo, con preposizione)* her; *(forma di cortesia: anche:* L**~)** you // *sm*: **dare del ~ a qd** to address sb as 'lei'; **~ stessa** she herself, you yourself.

'lembo *sm (di abito, strada)* edge; *(striscia sottile: di terra)* strip.

'lemma, i *sm* headword.

'lemme 'lemme *av* (very) very slowly.

'lena *sf (fig)* energy, stamina.

le'nire *vt* to soothe.

'lente *sf (OTTICA)* lens *sg*; **~ d'ingrandimento** magnifying glass; **~i a contatto** o **corneali** contact lenses.

len'tezza [len'tettsa] *sf* slowness.

len'ticchia [len'tikkja] *sf (BOT)* lentil.

len'tiggine [len'tiddʒine] *sf* freckle.

'lento, a *ag* slow; *(molle: fune)* slack; *(non stretto: vite, abito)* loose.

'lenza ['lɛntsa] *sf* fishing-line.

lenzu'olo [len'tswɔlo] *sm* sheet; **~a** *sfpl* pair of sheets.

le'one *sm* lion; *(dello zodiaco):* L**~** Leo.

leo'pardo *sm* leopard.

'lepido, a *ag* witty.

lepo'rino, a *ag*: **labbro ~** harelip.

'lepre *sf* hare.

'lercio, a, ci, cie ['lertʃo] *ag* filthy.

'lesbica, che *sf* lesbian.

lesi'nare *vt* to be stingy with // *vi*: **~ (su)** to skimp (on), be stingy (with).

lesi'one *sf (MED)* lesion; *(DIR)* injury, damage; *(EDIL)* crack.

le'sivo, a *ag*: **~ (di)** damaging (to), detrimental (to).

'leso, a *pp di* **ledere** // *ag (offeso)* injured.

les'sare *vt (CUC)* to boil.

'lessico, ci *sm* vocabulary; lexicon.

'lesso, a *ag* boiled // *sm* boiled meat.

'lesto, a *ag* quick; *(agile)* nimble; *(cosa: sbrigativa)* hasty, hurried; **~ di mano** *(per rubare)* light-fingered; *(per picchiare)* free with one's fists.

le'tale *ag* lethal; fatal.

leta'maio *sm* dunghill.

le'tame *sm* manure, dung.

le'targo, ghi *sm* lethargy; *(ZOOL)* hibernation.

le'tizia [le'tittsja] *sf* joy, happiness.

'lettera *sf* letter; **~e** *sfpl (letteratura)* literature *sg*; *(studi umanistici)* arts (subjects); **alla ~** literally; **in ~e** in words, in full; **lette'rale** *ag* literal.

lette'rario, o *ag* literary.

lette'rato, a *ag* well-read, scholarly.

lettera'tura *sf* literature.

let'tiga, ghe *sf (portantina)* litter; *(barella)* stretcher.

'letto, a *pp di* **leggere** // *sm* bed; **~ a castello** bunk beds *pl*; **~ a una piazza/a due piazze** o **matrimoniale** single/double bed.

let'tore, 'trice *sm/f* reader; *(INS)* (foreign language) assistant.

let'tura *sf* reading.

leuce'mia [leutʃe'mia] *sf* leukaemia.

'leva *sf* lever; *(MIL)* conscription; **far ~ su qd** to work on sb; **~ del cambio** *(AUT)* gear lever.

le'vante *sm* east; *(vento)* East wind; **il L~** the Levant.

le'vare *vt (occhi, braccio)* to raise; *(sollevare, togliere: tassa, divieto)* to lift; *(indumenti)* to take off, remove; *(rimuovere)* to take away; *(: dal di sopra)* to take off; *(: dal di dentro)* to take out; **~rsi** *vr* to get up; *(sole)* to rise; **le'vata** *sf* rising; *(di posta)* collection.

leva'toio, a *ag*: **ponte ~** drawbridge.

leva'tura *sf* intelligence, mental capacity.

levi'gare *vt* to smooth; *(con carta vetrata)* to sand.

levri'ero *sm* greyhound.

lezi'one [let'tsjone] *sf* lesson; *(all'università, sgridata)* lecture; **fare ~** to teach; to lecture.

lezi'oso, a [let'tsjoso] *ag* affected; simpering.

'lezzo ['leddzo] *sm* stench, stink.

li *pronome pl (oggetto)* them.

lì *av* there; **di** o **da ~** from there; **per di ~** that way; **di ~ a pochi giorni** a few days later; **~ per ~** there and then; at first; **essere** o **(~~)** per fare to be on the point of doing, be about to do; **~ dentro** in there; **~ sotto** under there; **~ sopra** on there; up there; *vedi* **quello**.

Li'bano *sm*: **il ~** the Lebanon.

'libbra *sf (peso)* pound.

li'beccio [li'bettʃo] *sm* south-west wind.

li'bello *sm* libel.

li'bellula *sf* dragonfly.

libe'rale *ag, sm/f* liberal.

liberaliz'zare [liberalid'dzare] *vt* to liberalize.

libe'rare *vt* to free, liberate; *(prigioniero: sog: autorità, TECN)* to release; *(sottrarre a danni)* to rescue; **libera'tore, 'trice** *ag* liberating // *sm/f* liberator; **liberazi'one** *sf* liberation, freeing; release; rescuing.

'libero, a *ag* free; *(strada)* clear; *(non occupato: posto etc)* vacant; not taken; empty; not engaged; **~ di fare qc** free to do sth; **~ da** free from; **~ arbitrio** free will; **~ professionista** professional man; **~ scambio** free trade; **libertà** *sf inv* freedom; *(tempo disponibile)* free time // *sfpl (licenza)* liberties; **in libertà provvisoria/vigilata** on bail/probation; **libertà di riunione** right to hold meetings.

liber'tino, a *ag* libertine.

'Libia *sf*: la ~ Libya; **'libico, a, ci, che** *ag, sm/f* Libyan.

li'bidine *sf* lust; **libidi'noso, a** *ag* lustful, libidinous.

li'bido *sf* libido.

li'braio *sm* bookseller.

li'brarsi *vr* to hover.

li'brario, a *ag* book *cpd.*

libre'ria *sf* (*bottega*) bookshop; (*stanza*) library; (*mobile*) bookcase.

li'bretto *sm* booklet; (*taccuino*) notebook; (*MUS*) libretto; ~ **degli assegni** cheque book; ~ **di risparmio** (*savings*) bankbook, passbook; ~ **universitario** student's report book.

'libro *sm* book; ~ **di cassa** cash book; ~ **paga** payroll.

li'cenza [li'tʃentsa] *sf* (*permesso*) permission, leave; (*di pesca, caccia, circolazione*) permit, licence; (*MIL*) leave; (*INS*) leaving certificate, diploma; (*libertà*) liberty; licence; licentiousness; **andare in** ~ (*MIL*) to go on leave.

licenzia'mento [litʃentsja'mento] *sm* dismissal; **indennità di** ~ redundancy payment.

licenzi'are [litʃen'tsjare] *vt* (*impiegato*) to dismiss; (*INS*) to award a certificate to; ~**rsi** *vr* (*impiegato*) to resign, hand in one's notice; (*INS*) to obtain one's school-leaving certificate.

licenzi'oso, a [litʃen'tsjoso] *ag* licentious.

li'ceo [li'tʃɛo] *sm* (*INS*) secondary school (*for 14- to 19-year-olds*).

li'chene [li'kene] *sm* (*BOT*) lichen.

licitazi'one [litʃitat'tsjone] *sf* (*offerta*) bid.

'lido *sm* beach, shore.

li'eto, a *ag* happy, glad; **"molto** ~**"** (*nelle presentazioni*) "pleased to meet you".

li'eve *ag* light; (*di poco conto*) slight; (*sommesso: voce*) faint, soft.

lievi'tare *vi* (2) (*anche fig*) to rise // *vt* to leaven.

li'evito *sm* yeast; ~ **di birra** brewer's yeast.

'ligio, a, gi, gie ['lidʒo] *ag* faithful, loyal.

'lilla, lillà *sm inv* lilac.

'lima *sf* file.

limacci'oso, a [limat'tʃoso] *ag* slimy; muddy.

li'mare *vt* to file (down); (*fig*) to polish.

'limbo *sm* (*REL*) limbo.

li'metta *sf* nail file.

limi'tare *sm* (*anche fig*) threshold // *vt* to limit, restrict; (*circoscrivere*) to bound, surround; **limita'tivo, a** *ag* limiting, restricting; **limi'tato, a** *ag* limited, restricted; **limitazi'one** *sf* limitation, restriction.

'limite *sm* limit; (*confine*) border, boundary; ~ **di velocità** speed limit.

li'mitrofo, a *ag* neighbouring.

limo'nata *sf* lemonade; lemon squash.

li'mone *sm* (*pianta*) lemon tree; (*frutto*) lemon.

'limpido, a *ag* clear; (*acqua*) limpid, clear.

'lince ['lintʃe] *sf* lynx.

linci'are *vt* to lynch.

'lindo, a *ag* tidy, spick and span; (*biancheria*) clean.

'linea *sf* line; (*di mezzi pubblici di trasporto: itinerario*) route; (: *servizio*) service; **a grandi** ~**e** in outline; **mantenere la** ~ to look after one's figure; **di** ~: **aereo di** ~ airliner; **nave di** ~ liner; ~ **di partenza/d'arrivo** (*SPORT*) starting/finishing line; ~ **di tiro** line of fire.

linea'menti *smpl* features; (*fig*) outlines.

line'are *ag* linear; (*fig*) coherent, logical.

line'etta *sf* (*trattino*) dash; (*d'unione*) hyphen.

lin'gotto *sm* ingot, bar.

'lingua *sf* (*ANAT, CUC*) tongue; (*idioma*) language; **mostrare la** ~ to stick out one's tongue; **di** ~ **italiana** Italian-speaking; ~ **madre** mother tongue; **una** ~ **di terra** a spit of land; **linguacci'uto, a** *ag* gossipy.

lingu'aggio [lin'gwaddʒo] *sm* language.

lingu'etta *sf* (*di strumento*) reed; (*di scarpa, TECN*) tongue; (*di busta*) flap.

lingu'ista, i, e *sm/f* linguist; **lingu'istica, a, ci, che** *ag* linguistic // *sf* linguistics *sg*.

lini'mento *sm* liniment.

'lino *sm* (*pianta*) flax; (*tessuto*) linen.

li'noleum *sm inv* linoleum, lino.

li'corno *sm* unicorn.

lique'fare *vt* (*render liquido*) to liquefy; (*fondere*) to melt; ~**rsi** *vr* to liquefy; to melt.

liqui'dare *vt* (*società, beni; persona: uccidere*) to liquidate; (*persona: sbarazzarsene*) to get rid of; (*conto, problema*) to settle; (*COMM: merce*) to sell off, clear; **liquidazi'one** *sf* liquidation; settlement; clearance sale.

liquidità *sf* liquidity.

'liquido, a *ag, sm* liquid; ~ **per freni** brake fluid.

liqui'rizia [likwi'rittsja] *sf* (*BOT*) liquorice.

li'quore *sm* liqueur.

'lira *sf* (*unità monetaria*) lira; (*MUS*) lyre; ~ **sterlina** pound sterling.

'lirico, a, ci, che *ag* lyric(al); (*MUS*) lyric // *sf* (*poesia*) lyric poetry; (*componimento poetico*) lyric; (*MUS*) opera; **cantante/teatro** ~ opera singer/house.

Lis'bona *sf* Lisbon.

'lisca, sche *sf* (*di pesce*) fishbone.

lisci'are [liʃ'ʃare] *vt* to smooth; (*accarezzare*) to stroke; (*fig*) to flatter.

'liscio, a, sci, sce ['liʃʃo] *ag* smooth; (*capelli*) straight; (*mobile*) plain; (*bevanda alcolica*) neat; (*fig*) straightforward, simple // *av*: **andare** ~ to go smoothly; **passarla** ~**a** to get away with it.

'liso, a *ag* worn out, threadbare.

'lista *sf* (*striscia*) strip; (*elenco*) list; ~ **elettorale** electoral roll; ~ **delle vivande** menu; **lis'tare** *vt* to edge, border.

lis'tino *sm* list; ~ **dei cambi** (*foreign*) exchange rate; ~ **dei prezzi** price list.

lita'nia *sf* l'tany.

'lite *sf* quarrel, argument; (*DIR*) lawsuit.
liti'gare *vi* to quarrel; (*DIR*) to litigate.
li'tigio [li'tidʒo] *sm* quarrel; **litigi'oso, a** *ag* quarrelsome; (*DIR*) litigious.
litogra'fia *sf* (*sistema*) lithography; (*stampa*) lithograph.
lito'rale *ag* coastal, coast *cpd* // *sm* coast.
'litro *sm* litre.
litur'gia, 'gie [litur'dʒia] *sf* liturgy.
li'uto *sm* lute.
li'vella *sf* level; **~ a bolla d'aria** spirit level.
livel'lare *vt* to level, make level; **~rsi** *vr* to become level; (*fig*) to level out, balance out.
li'vello *sm* level; (*fig*) level, standard; **ad alto ~** (*fig*) high-level; **~ del mare** sea level.
'livido, a *ag* livid; (*per percosse*) bruised, black and blue; (*cielo*) leaden // *sm* bruise.
li'vore *sm* malice, spite.
Li'vorno *sf* Livorno, Leghorn.
li'vrea *sf* livery.
'lizza ['littsa] *sf* lists *pl*; **scendere in ~** (*anche fig*) to enter the lists.
lo *det m* (*dav s impura, gn, pn, ps, x, z*; *dav V l'*) the // *pronome* (*dav V l'*) (*oggetto: persona*) him; (: *cosa*) it; **~ sapevo** I knew it; **~ so** I know; **sii buono, anche se lui non ~** be good, even if he isn't.
'lobo *sm* lobe; **~ dell'orecchio** ear lobe.
lo'cale *ag* local // *sm* room; (*luogo pubblico*) premises *pl*; **~ notturno** nightclub; **località** *sf inv* locality; **localiz-'zare** *vt* (*circoscrivere*) to confine, localize; (*accertare*) to locate, place.
lo'canda *sf* inn; **locandi'ere, a** *sm/f* innkeeper.
loca'tario, a *sm/f* tenant.
loca'tore, 'trice *sm/f* landlord/lady.
locazi'one [lokat'tsjone] *sf* (*da parte del locatario*) renting *q*; (*da parte del proprietario*) renting out *q*, letting *q*; (*effetto*) rent(al).
locomo'tiva *sf* locomotive.
locomo'tore *sm* electric locomotive.
locomozi'one [lokomot'tsjone] *sf* locomotion; **mezzi di ~** vehicles, means of transport.
lo'custa *sf* locust.
locuzi'one [lokut'tsjone] *sf* phrase, expression.
lo'dare *vt* to praise.
'lode *sf* praise; (*INS*): **laurearsi con la ~ ≈** to graduate with a first-class honours degree; **lo'devole** *ag* praiseworthy.
loga'ritmo *sm* logarithm.
'loggia, ge ['lɔddʒa] *sf* (*ARCHIT*) loggia; (*circolo massonico*) lodge; **loggi'one** *sm* (*di teatro*): **il loggione** the Gods *sg*.
'logico, a, ci, che ['lɔdʒiko] *ag* logical // *sf* logic.
logo'rare *vt* to wear out; (*sciupare*) to waste; **~rsi** *vr* to wear out; (*fig*) to wear o.s. out.
logo'rio *sm* wear and tear; (*fig*) strain.
'logoro, a *ag* (*stoffa*) worn out,

threadbare; (*persona*) worn out.
lom'baggine [lom'baddʒine] *sf* lumbago.
Lombar'dia *sf*: **la ~** Lombardy.
lom'bata *sf* (*taglio di carne*) loin.
'lombo *sm* (*ANAT*) loin.
lom'brico, chi *sm* earthworm.
'Londra *sf* London.
longevità [londʒevi'ta] *sf* longevity.
lon'gevo, a [lon'dʒevo] *ag* long-lived.
longi'tudine [londʒi'tudine] *sf* longitude.
lonta'nanza [lonta'nantsa] *sf* distance; absence.
lon'tano, a *ag* (*distante*) distant, faraway; (*assente*) absent; (*vago: sospetto*) slight, remote; (*tempo: remoto*) far-off, distant; (*parente*) distant, remote // *av* far; **è ~a la casa?** is it far to the house?, is the house far from here?; **è ~ un chilometro** it's a mile away *o* a mile from here; **più ~** farther; **da *o* di ~** from a distance; **~ da** a long way from; **alla ~a** slightly, vaguely.
'lontra *sf* otter.
lo'quace [lo'kwatʃe] *ag* talkative, loquacious; (*fig: gesto etc*) eloquent.
'lordo, a *ag* dirty, filthy; (*peso, stipendio*) gross; **lor'dura** *sf* filth.
'loro *pronome pl* (*oggetto, con preposizione*) them; (*complemento di termine*) to them; (*soggetto*) they; (*forma di cortesia: anche* **L~**) you; to you; **il(la) ~, i(le) ~** their; (*forma di cortesia: anche* **L~**) your // *pronome* their; (*forma di cortesia: anche* **L~**) yours; **~ stessi(e)** they themselves; you yourselves.
'losco, a, schi, sche *ag* (*fig*) shady, suspicious.
'loto *sm* lotus.
'lotta *sf* struggle, fight; (*SPORT*) wrestling; **lot'tare** *vi* to fight, struggle; to wrestle; **lotta'tore** *sm* wrestler.
lotte'ria *sf* lottery; (*di gara ippica*) sweepstake.
'lotto *sm* (*gioco*) (state) lottery; (*parte*) lot; (*EDIL*) site.
lozi'one [lot'tsjone] *sf* lotion.
'lubrico, a, ci, che *ag* lewd, lascivious.
lubrifi'cante *sm* lubricant.
lubrifi'care *vt* to lubricate.
luc'chetto [luk'ketto] *sm* padlock.
lucci'care [luttʃi'kare] *vi* to sparkle, glitter, twinkle.
'luccio ['luttʃo] *sm* (*ZOOL*) pike.
'lucciola ['luttʃola] *sf* (*ZOOL*) firefly; glowworm.
'luce ['lutʃe] *sf* light; (*finestra*) window; **alla ~ di** by the light of; **fare ~ su qc** (*fig*) to shed *o* throw light on sth; **~ del sole/della luna** sun/moonlight; **lu'cente** *ag* shining.
lu'cerna [lu'tʃerna] *sf* oil-lamp.
lucer'nario [lutʃer'narjo] *sm* skylight.
lu'certola [lu'tʃertola] *sf* lizard.
luci'dare [lutʃi'dare] *vt* to polish; (*ricalcare*) to trace.
lucidità [lutʃidi'ta] *sf* lucidity.
'lucido, a ['lutʃido] *ag* shining, bright;

(*lucidato*) polished; (*fig*) lucid // *sm* shine, lustre; (*per scarpe etc*) polish; (*disegno*) tracing.

lu'cignolo [lu'tʃiɲɲolo] *sm* wick.

lu'crare *vt* to earn, make.

'lucro *sm* profit, gain; **lu'croso, a** *ag* lucrative, profitable.

lu'dibrio *sm* mockery *q*; (*oggetto di scherno*) laughing-stock.

'luglio ['luʎʎo] *sm* July.

'lugubre *ag* gloomy.

'lui *pronome* (*soggetto*) he; (*oggetto: per dare rilievo, con preposizione*) him; ~ **stesso** he himself.

lu'maca, che *sf* slug; (*chiocciola*) snail.

'lume *sm* light; (*lampada*) lamp; (*fig*): **chiedere ~i a qd** to ask sb for advice.

lumi'naria *sf* (*per feste*) illuminations *pl*.

lumi'noso, a *ag* (*che emette luce*) luminous; (*cielo, colore, stanza*) bright; (*sorgente*) of light, light *cpd*; (*fig*) obvious, clear; **idea ~a** bright idea.

'luna *sf* moon; ~ **nuova/piena** new/full moon; ~ **di miele** honeymoon.

'luna park *sm inv* amusement park, funfair.

lu'nare *ag* lunar, moon *cpd*.

lu'nario *sm* almanac.

lu'natico, a, ci, che *ag* whimsical, temperamental.

lunedì *sm inv* Monday; **di o il ~** on Mondays.

lun'gaggine [lun'gaddʒine] *sf* slowness; ~**i della burocrazia** red tape.

lun'ghezza [lun'gettsa] *sf* length; ~ **d'onda** (*FISICA*) wavelength.

'lungo, a, ghi, ghe *ag* long; (*lento: persona*) slow; (*diluito: caffè, brodo*) weak, watery, thin // *sm* length // *prep* along; ~ **3 metri** 3 metres long; **a ~** for a long time; **a ~ andare** in the long run; **di gran ~a** (*molto*) by far; **andare in ~** o **per le lunghe** to drag on; **saperla ~a** to know what's what; **in ~ e in largo** far and wide, all over; ~ **il corso dei secoli** throughout the centuries.

lungo'mare *sm* promenade.

lu'notto *sm* (*AUT*) rear o back window.

lu'ogo, ghi *sm* place; (*posto: di incidente etc*) scene, site; (*punto, passo di libro*) passage; **in ~ di** instead of; **in primo ~** in the first place; **aver ~** to take place; **dar ~ a** to give rise to; ~ **comune** commonplace; ~ **geometrico** locus.

luogote'nente *sm* (*MIL*) lieutenant.

lu'para *sf* sawn-off shotgun.

'lupo, a *sm/f* wolf.

'luppolo *sm* (*BOT*) hop.

'lurido, a *ag* filthy.

lu'singa, ghe *sf* (*spesso al pl*) flattery *q*.

lusin'gare *vt* to flatter; ~**rsi** *vr* (*sperare*) to deceive o.s.; **lusin'ghiero, a** *ag* flattering, gratifying.

lus'sare *vt* to dislocate.

Lussem'burgo *sm*: **il ~** Luxembourg.

'lusso *sm* luxury; **di ~** luxury *cpd*; **lus-su'oso, a** *ag* luxurious.

lussureggi'are [lussured'dʒare] *vi* to be luxuriant.

lus'suria *sf* lust.

lus'trare *vt* to polish, shine.

lustras'carpe *sm/f inv* shoeshine.

lus'trino *sm* sequin.

'lustro, a *ag* shiny; (*pelliccia*) glossy // *sm* shine, gloss; (*fig*) prestige, glory; (*quinquennio*) five-year period.

'lutto *sm* mourning; **essere in/portare il ~** to be in/wear mourning; **luttu'oso, a** *ag* mournful, sad.

M

ma *cong* but; ~ **insomma!** for goodness sake!; ~ **no!** of course not!

'macabro, a *ag* gruesome, macabre.

macché [mak'ke] *escl* not at all!, certainly not!

macche'roni [makke'roni] *smpl* macaroni *sg*.

'macchia ['makkja] *sf* stain, spot; (*chiazza di diverso colore*) spot; splash, patch; (*tipo di boscaglia*) scrub; **macchi'are** *vt* (*sporcare*) to stain, mark; **macchiarsi** *vr* (*persona*) to get o.s. dirty; (*stoffa*) to stain; to get stained o marked.

'macchina ['makkina] *sf* machine; (*elettrica, a vapore*) engine; (*automobile*) car; (*fig: meccanismo*) machinery; **andare in** ~ (*AUT*) to go by car; (*STAMPA*) to go to press; ~ **da cucire** sewing machine; ~ **fotografica** camera; ~ **da scrivere** typewriter; ~ **a vapore** steam engine.

macchi'nare [makki'nare] *vt* to plot.

macchi'nario [makki'narjo] *sm* machinery.

macchi'netta [makki'netta] *sf* (*fam: caffettiera*) percolator; (: *accendino*) lighter.

macchi'nista, i [makki'nista] *sm* (*di treno*) engine-driver; (*di nave*) engineer; (*TEATRO, TV*) stagehand.

macchi'noso, a [makki'noso] *ag* complex, complicated.

mace'donia [matʃe'donja] *sf* fruit salad.

macel'laio [matʃel'lajo] *sm* butcher.

macel'lare [matʃel'lare] *vt* to slaughter, butcher; **macelle'ria** *sf* butcher's (shop); **ma'cello** *sm* (*mattatoio*) slaughterhouse, abattoir; (*fig*) slaughter, massacre; (: *disastro*) shambles *sg*.

mace'rare [matʃe'rare] *vt* to macerate; (*fig*) to mortify; ~**rsi** *vr* to waste away; (*fig*): ~**rsi in** to be consumed with.

ma'cerie [ma'tʃerje] *sfpl* rubble *sg*, debris *sg*.

ma'cigno [ma'tʃiɲɲo] *sm* (*masso*) rock, boulder.

maci'lento, a [matʃi'lento] *ag* emaciated.

'macina ['matʃina] *sf* (*pietra*) millstone; (*macchina*) grinder; **macinacaffè** *sm inv* coffee grinder; **macina'pepe** *sm inv* peppermill.

maci'nare [matʃi'nare] *vt* to grind; **maci'nato** *sm* meal, flour; (*carne*) mince, minced meat.

maci'nino [matʃi'nino] *sm* coffee grinder; peppermill.

'madido, a *ag*: ~ **(di)** wet *o* moist (with).

Ma'donna *sf* (REL) Our Lady. .

mador'nale *ag* enormous, huge.

'madre *sf* mother; (*matrice di bolletta*) counterfoil // *ag inv* mother *cpd*; **ragazza** ~ unmarried mother; **scena** ~ (TEATRO) principal scene.

madre'lingua *sf* mother tongue, native language.

madre'perla *sf* mother-of-pearl.

madri'gale *sm* madrigal.

ma'drina *sf* godmother.

maestà *sf inv* majesty; **maes'toso, a** *ag* majestic.

ma'estra *sf vedi* **maestro.**

maes'trale *sm* north-west wind, mistral.

maes'tranze [maes'trantse] *sfpl* workforce *sg*.

maes'tria *sf* mastery, skill.

ma'estro, a *sm/f* (INS: *anche:* ~ **elementare**) primary teacher; (*persona molto preparata*) expert // *sm* (*artigiano, fig: guida*) master; (MUS) maestro // *ag* (*principale*) main; (*di grande abilità*) masterly, skilful; ~ **di cerimonie** master of ceremonies; ~**a giardiniera** nursery teacher.

'mafia *sf* Mafia; **mafi'oso** *sm* member of the Mafia.

'maga *sf* sorceress.

ma'gagna [ma'gaɲɲa] *sf* defect, flaw, blemish.

ma'gari *escl* (*esprime desiderio*): ~ **fosse vero!** if only it were true!; **ti piacerebbe andare in Scozia?** — ~**!** would you like to go to Scotland? — and how! // *av* (*anche*) even; (*forse*) perhaps.

magaz'zino [magad'dzino] *sm* warehouse; (*grande emporio*) department store.

'maggio ['maddʒo] *sm* May.

maggio'rana [maddʒo'rana] *sf* (BOT) (*sweet*) marjoram.

maggio'ranza [maddʒo'rantsa] *sf* majority.

maggio'rare [maddʒo'rare] *vt* to increase, raise.

maggior'domo [maddʒor'dɔmo] *sm* butler.

maggi'ore [mad'dʒore] *ag* (*comparativo: più grande*) bigger, larger; taller; greater; (: *più vecchio: sorella, fratello*) older, elder; (: *di grado superiore*) senior; (: *più importante*, MIL, MUS) major; (*superlativo*) biggest, largest; tallest; greatest; oldest, eldest // *sm/f* (*di grado*) superior; (*di età*) elder; (MIL) major; (: AER) squadron leader; **la maggior parte** the majority; **maggio'renne** *ag* of age // *sm/f* person who has come of age; **maggio'rente** *sm* notable; **maggior'mente** *av* much more; (*con senso superlativo*) most.

ma'gia [ma'dʒia] *sf* magic; **'magico, a, ci, che** *ag* magic; (*fig*) fascinating, charming, magical.

'magio ['madʒo] *sm* (REL): **i re Magi** the Magi, the Three Wise Men.

magis'tero [madʒis'tero] *sm* (INS) teaching; (*fig: maestria*) skill; **magis'trale** *ag* primary teachers', primary teaching *cpd*; skilful.

magis'trato [madʒis'trato] *sm* magistrate; **magistra'tura** *sf* magistrature; (*magistrati*): **la magistratura** the Bench.

'maglia ['maʎʎa] *sf* stitch; (*lavoro ai ferri*) knitting *q*; (*tessuto, SPORT*) jersey; (*maglione*) jersey, sweater; (*di catena*) link; (*di rete*) mesh; **avviare/diminuire le** ~**e** to cast on/cast off; ~ **diritta/rovescia** plain/purl; **magli'eria** *sf* knitwear; (*negozio*) knitwear shop; **magli'etta** *sf* (*canottiera*) vest; (*tipo camicia*) T-shirt; **magli'ficio** *sm* knitwear factory.

'maglio ['maʎʎo] *sm* mallet; (*macchina*) power hammer.

ma'gnanimo, a [maɲ'ɲanimo] *ag* magnanimous.

ma'gnesia [maɲ'ɲezja] *sf* (CHIM) magnesia.

ma'gnesio [maɲ'ɲezjo] *sm* (CHIM) magnesium.

ma'gnete [maɲ'ɲete] *sm* magnet; **ma'gnetico, a, ci, che** *ag* magnetic; **magne'tismo** *sm* magnetism.

magne'tofono [maɲɲe'tɔfono] *sm* tape recorder.

magnifi'cenza [maɲɲifi'tʃentsa] *sf* magnificence, splendour.

ma'gnifico, a, ci, che [maɲ'ɲifiko] *ag* magnificent, splendid; (*ospite*) generous.

ma'gnolia [maɲ'ɲɔlja] *sf* magnolia.

'mago, ghi *sm* (*stregone*) magician, wizard; (*illusionista*) magician.

ma'grezza [ma'grettsa] *sf* thinness.

'magro, a *ag* (*very*) thin, skinny; (*carne*) lean; (*formaggio*) low-fat; (*fig: scarso, misero*) meagre, poor; (: *meschino: scusa*) poor, lame; **mangiare di** ~ not to eat meat.

'mai *av* (*nessuna volta*) never; (*talvolta*) ever; **non ...** ~ never; ~ **più** never again; **come** ~**?** why (*o* how) on earth?; **chi/dove/quando** ~**?** whoever/wherever/whenever?

mai'ale *sm* (ZOOL) pig; (*carne*) pork.

maio'nese *sf* mayonnaise.

'mais *sm inv* maize.

mai'uscolo, a *ag* (*lettera*) capital; (*fig*) enormous, huge // *sf* capital letter.

mal *av, sm vedi* **male.**

malac'corto, a *ag* rash, careless.

mala'copia *sf* rough copy.

malafede *sf* bad faith.

mala'mente *av* badly; dangerously.

malan'dato, a *ag* (*persona: di salute*) in poor health; (: *di condizioni finanziarie*) badly off; (*trascurato*) shabby.

ma'lanimo *sm* ill will, malevolence; **di** ~ unwillingly.

ma'lanno *sm* (*disgrazia*) misfortune; (*malattia*) ailment.

mala'pena *sf*: **a** ~ hardly, scarcely.

ma'laria *sf* (MED) malaria.

mala'sorte *sf* bad luck.

mala'ticcio, a [mala'tittʃo] *ag* sickly.

ma'lato, a *ag* ill, sick; (*gamba*) bad; (*pianta*) diseased // *sm/f* sick person; (*in ospedale*) patient; **malat'tia** *sf* (*infettiva etc*) illness, disease; (*cattiva salute*) illness, sickness.

malau'gurio *sm* bad o ill omen.

mala'vita *sf* underworld.

mala'voglia [mala'vɔʎʎa] *sf* reluctance, unwillingness; **di ~** unwillingly, reluctantly.

mal'concio, a, ci, ce [mal'kontʃo] *ag* in a sorry state.

malcon'tento *sm* discontent.

malcos'tume *sm* immorality.

mal'destro, a *ag* (*inabile*) inexpert, inexperienced; (*goffo*) awkward.

maldi'cente [maldi'tʃente] *ag* slanderous.

maldis'posto, a *ag:* **~ (verso)** ill-disposed (towards).

'male *av* badly // *sm* (*ciò che è ingiusto, disonesto*) evil; (*danno, svantaggio*) harm; (*sventura*) misfortune; (*dolore fisico, morale*) pain, ache; **di ~ in peggio** from bad to worse; **sentirsi ~** to feel ill; **far ~** (*dolere*) to hurt; **far ~ alla salute** to be bad for one's health; **far del ~ a qd** to hurt o harm sb; **restare o rimanere ~** to be sorry; to be disappointed; to be hurt; **andare a ~** to go bad; **come va? — non c'è ~** how are you? — not bad; **mal di mare** seasickness; **avere mal di gola/testa** to have a sore throat/a headache.

male'detto, a *pp di* **maledire** // *ag* cursed, damned; (*fig: fastidioso*) damned, wretched.

male'dire *vt* to curse; **maledizi'one** *sf* curse; **maledizione!** damn it!

maledu'cato, a *ag* rude, ill-mannered.

male'ficio [male'fitʃo] *sm* witchcraft.

ma'lefico, a, ci, che *ag* (*aria, cibo*) harmful, bad; (*influsso, azione*) evil.

ma'lessere *sm* indisposition, slight illness; (*fig*) uneasiness.

ma'levolo, a *ag* malevolent.

malfa'mato, a *ag* notorious.

mal'fatto, a *ag* (*persona*) deformed; (*cosa*) badly made.

malfat'tore, 'trice *sm/f* wrongdoer.

mal'fermo, a *ag* unsteady, shaky; (*salute*) poor, delicate.

malformazi'one [malformat'tsjone] *sf* malformation.

malgo'verno *sm* maladministration.

mal'grado *prep* in spite of, despite // *cong* although; **mio** (*o tuo etc*) **~** against my (*o your etc*) will.

ma'lia *sf* spell; (*fig: fascino*) charm.

mali'gnare [malin'nare] *vi:* **~ su** to malign, speak ill of.

ma'ligno, a [ma'linno] *ag* (*malvagio*) malicious, malignant; (MED) malignant.

malinco'nia *sf* melancholy, gloom; **malin'conico, a, ci, che** *ag* melancholy.

malincu'ore: a ~ *av* reluctantly, unwillingly.

malintenzio'nato, a [malintentsjo'nato] *ag* ill-intentioned.

malin'teso, a *ag* misunderstood; (*riguardo, senso del dovere*) mistaken, wrong // *sm* misunderstanding.

ma'lizia [ma'littsja] *sf* (*malignità*) malice; (*furbizia*) cunning; (*espediente*) trick; **malizi'oso, a** *ag* malicious; cunning; (*vivace, birichino*) mischievous.

malle'abile *ag* malleable.

malme'nare *vt* to beat up; (*fig*) to ill-treat.

mal'messo, a *ag* (*persona*) shabby, badly-dressed; (*casa*) badly-furnished.

malnu'trito, a *ag* undernourished; **malnutrizi'one** *sf* malnutrition.

ma'locchio [ma'lɔkkjo] *sm* evil eye.

ma'lora *sf* ruin; **andare in ~** to go to the dogs; **va in ~!** go to hell!

ma'lore *sm* feeling of faintness; feeling of discomfort.

mal'sano, a *ag* unhealthy.

malsi'curo, a *ag* unsafe; (*fig*) uncertain; (: *testimonianza*) unreliable.

'malta *sf* (EDIL) mortar.

mal'tempo *sm* bad weather.

'malto *sm* malt.

maltrat'tare *vt* to ill-treat.

malu'more *sm* bad mood; (*irritabilità*) bad temper; (*discordia*) ill feeling; **di ~** in a bad mood.

mal'vagio, a, gi, gie [mal'vadʒo] *ag* wicked, evil.

malversazi'one [malversat'tsjone] *sf* (DIR) embezzlement.

mal'visto, a *ag:* **~ (da)** disliked (by), unpopular (with).

malvi'vente *sm* criminal.

malvolenti'eri *av* unwillingly, reluctantly.

malvo'lere *vt:* **farsi ~ da qd** to make o.s. unpopular with sb // *sm* (*avversione*) ill will; (*scarsa volontà*) unwillingness.

'mamma *sf* mummy, mum; **~ mia!** my goodness!

mam'mario, a *ag* (ANAT) mammary.

mam'mella *sf* (ANAT) breast; (*di vacca, capra etc*) udder.

mam'mifero *sm* mammal.

'mammola *sf* (BOT) violet.

ma'nata *sf* (*colpo*) slap; (*quantità*) handful.

'manca *sf vedi* **manco.**

man'canza [man'kantsa] *sf* lack; (*carenza*) shortage, scarcity; (*fallo*) fault; (*imperfezione*) failing, shortcoming; **per ~ di tempo** through lack of time; **in ~ di meglio** for lack of anything better.

man'care *vi* (2: *essere insufficiente*) to be lacking; (: *venir meno*) to fail; (: *non esserci*) to be missing, not to be there; (: *essere lontano*): **~ (da)** to be away (from) // *vt* to miss; **~ di** to lack; **~ a** (*promessa*) to fail to keep; **tu mi manchi** I miss you; **mancò poco che morisse** he very nearly died; **mancano ancora 10**

sterline we're still £10 short; **manca un quarto alle 6** it's a quarter to 6; **man'cato, a** ag (tentativo) unsuccessful; (artista) failed.

'**mancia, ce** ['mantʃa] sf tip; ~ competente reward.

manci'ata [man'tʃata] sf handful.

man'cino, a [man'tʃino] ag (braccio) left; (persona) left-handed; (fig) underhand.

'**manco, a, chi, che** ag left // sf left hand // av (nemmeno) not even.

man'dare vt to send; (far funzionare: macchina) to drive; (emettere) to send out; (: grido) to give, utter, let out; ~ a chiamare qd to send for sb; ~ giù to send down; (anche fig) to swallow; ~ via to send away; (licenziare) to fire.

manda'rino sm mandarin (orange), tangerine; (cinese) mandarin.

man'data sf (spedizione) sending; (quantità) lot, batch; (di chiave) turn.

manda'tario sm (DIR) representative, agent.

man'dato sm (incarico) commission; (DIR: provvedimento) warrant; (di deputato etc) mandate; (ordine di pagamento) postal o money order; ~ d'arresto warrant for arrest.

man'dibola sf mandible, jaw.

'**mandorla** sf almond; '**mandorlo** sm almond tree.

'**mandria** sf herd.

maneggi'are [maned'dʒare] vt (creta) to mould, work, fashion; (arnesi, utensili) to handle; (: adoperare) to use; (fig: persone) to handle, deal with; **ma'neggio** sm moulding; handling; use; (intrigo) plot, scheme; (per cavalli) riding school.

ma'nesco, a, schi, sche ag free with one's fists.

ma'netta sf hand lever; ~e sfpl handcuffs.

manga'nello sm club.

manga'nese sm manganese.

'**mangano** sm mangle.

mange'reccio, a, ci, ce [mandʒe'rettʃo] ag edible.

mange'ria [mandʒe'ria] sf extortion.

mangia'dischi [mandʒa'diski] sm inv record player.

mangi'are [man'dʒare] vt to eat; (intaccare) to eat into o away; (CARTE, SCACCHI etc) to take // vi to eat // sm eating; (cibo) food; (cucina) cooking; ~rsi le parole to mumble; **mangia'toia** sf feeding-trough.

man'gime [man'dʒime] sm fodder.

'**mango, ghi** sm mango.

ma'nia sf (PSIC) mania; (fig) obsession, craze; **ma'niaco, a, ci, che** ag suffering from a mania; **maniaco (di)** obsessed (by), crazy (about).

'**manica** sf sleeve; (fig: gruppo) gang, bunch; (GEO): **la M**~ the (English) Channel; **essere di** ~ **larga/stretta** to be easy-going/strict; ~ **a vento** (AER) wind sock.

mani'chino [mani'kino] sm (di sarto, vetrina) dummy.

'**manico, ci** sm handle; (MUS) neck.

mani'comio sm mental hospital; (fig) madhouse.

mani'cotto sm muff; (TECN) coupling; sleeve.

mani'cure sf inv manicurist.

mani'era sf way, manner; (stile) style, manner; ~e sfpl manners; in ~ che so that; in ~ da so as to; in tutte le ~e at all costs.

manie'rato, a ag affected.

manifat'tura sf (lavorazione) manufacture; (stabilimento) factory.

manifes'tare vt to show, display; (esprimere) to express; (rivelare) to reveal, disclose // vi to demonstrate; ~rsi vr to show o.s.; ~rsi amico to prove o.s. (to be) a friend; **manifestazi'one** sf show, display; expression; (sintomo) sign, symptom; (dimostrazione pubblica) demonstration; (cerimonia) event.

mani'festo, a ag obvious, evident // sm poster, bill; (scritto ideologico) manifesto.

ma'niglia [ma'niʎʎa] sf handle; (sostegno: negli autobus etc) strap.

manipo'lare vt to manipulate; (alterare: vino) to adulterate; **manipolazi'one** sf manipulation; adulteration.

manis'calco, chi sm farrier.

'**manna** sf (REL) manna.

man'naia sf (del boia) (executioner's) axe; (per carni) cleaver.

man'naro: lupo ~ sm werewolf.

'**mano, i** sf hand; (strato: di vernice etc) coat; **di prima** ~ (notizia) first-hand; **di seconda** ~ second-hand; **man** ~ little by little, gradually; **man** ~ **che** as; **darsi o stringersi la** ~ to shake hands; **mettere le** ~i **avanti** (fig) to safeguard o.s.; **a** ~ by hand; ~i **in alto!** hands up!

mano'dopera sf labour.

ma'nometro sm gauge, manometer.

mano'mettere vt (alterare) to tamper with; (frugare, aprire) to break open illegally; (ledere: diritti) to violate, infringe; **mano'messo, a** pp di **manomettere**.

ma'nopola sf (dell'armatura) gauntlet; (guanto) mitt; (di impugnatura) hand-grip; (pomello) knob.

mano'scritto, a ag handwritten // sm manuscript.

mano'vale sm labourer.

mano'vella sf handle; (TECN) crank; **albero a** ~ crankshaft.

ma'novra sf manoeuvre; (FERR) shunting; **mano'vrare** vt to manoeuvre; (congegno) to operate // vi to manoeuvre.

manro'vescio [manro'veʃʃo] sm slap (with back of hand).

man'sarda sf attic.

mansi'one sf task, duty, job.

mansu'eto, a ag gentle, docile.

man'tello sm cloak; (fig: di neve etc) blanket, mantle; (TECN: involucro) casing, shell; (ZOOL) coat.

mante'nere vt to maintain; (adempiere: promesse) to keep, abide by; (provvedere a) to support, maintain; ~**rsi** vr: ~**rsi calmo/ giovane** to stay calm/young; **manteni'mento** sm maintenance.

'**mantice** ['mantitʃe] sm bellows pl; (di carrozze, automobile) hood.

'**manto** sm cloak; ~ **stradale** road surface.

manu'ale ag manual // sm (testo) manual, handbook.

ma'nubrio sm handle; (di bicicletta etc) handlebars pl; (SPORT) dumbbell.

manu'fatto, a ag manufactured.

manutenzi'one [manuten'tsjone] sf maintenance, upkeep; (d'impianti) maintenance, servicing.

'**manzo** ['mandzo] sm (ZOOL) steer; (carne) beef.

'**mappa** sf (GEO) map; **mappa'mondo** sm map of the world; (globo girevole) globe.

ma'rasma, i sm (fig) decay, decline.

mara'tona sf marathon.

'**marca, che** sf mark; (bollo) stamp; (COMM: di prodotti) brand; (contrassegno, scontrino) ticket, check; ~ **da bollo** official stamp; ~ **di fabbrica** trademark.

mar'care vt (munire di contrassegno) to mark; (a fuoco) to brand; (SPORT: gol) to score; (: avversario) to mark; ~ **visita** (MIL) to report sick.

mar'chese, a [mar'keze] sm/f marquis o marquess/marchioness.

marchi'are [mar'kjare] vt to brand; '**marchio** sm (di bestiame, COMM, fig) brand; **marchio di fabbrica** trademark; **marchio deposotato** registered trademark.

'**marcia, ce** ['martʃa] sf (anche MUS, MIL) march; (funzionamento) running; (il camminare) walking; (AUT) gear; **mettere in** ~ to start; **mettersi in** ~ to get moving; **far** ~ **indietro** (AUT) to reverse; (fig) to back-pedal.

marciapi'ede [martʃa'pjɛde] sm (di strada) pavement; (FERR) platform.

marci'are [mar'tʃare] vi to march; (andare: treno, macchina) to go; (funzionare) to run, work.

'**marcio, a, ci, ce** ['martʃo] ag (frutta, legno) rotten, bad; (MED) festering; (fig) corrupt, rotten.

mar'cire [mar'tʃire] vi (2) (andare a male) to go bad, rot; (suppurare) to fester; (fig) to rot, waste away.

'**marco, chi** sm (unità monetaria) mark.

'**mare** sm sea; **in** ~ at sea; **andare al** ~ (in vacanza etc) to go to the seaside; **il** ~ **del Nord** the North Sea.

ma'rea sf tide; **alta/bassa** ~ high/low tide.

mareggi'ata [mared'dʒata] sf heavy sea.

ma'remma sf (GEO) maremma, swampy coastal area.

mare'moto sm seaquake.

maresci'allo [mareʃ'ʃallo] sm (MIL) marshal; (: sottufficiale) warrant officer.

marga'rina sf margarine.

marghe'rita [marge'rita] sf (ox-eye) daisy, marguerite; **margheri'tina** sf daisy.

margi'nale [mardʒi'nale] ag marginal.

'**margine** ['mardʒine] sm margin; (di bosco, via) edge, border.

ma'rina sf navy; (costa) coast; ~ **militare/mercantile** navy/merchant navy.

mari'naio sm sailor.

mari'nare vt (CUC) to marinate; ~ **la scuola** to play truant; **mari'nata** sf marinade.

ma'rino, a ag sea cpd, marine.

mario'netta sf puppet.

mari'tale ag marital.

mari'tare vt to marry; ~**rsi** vr: ~**rsi a** o **con qd** to marry sb, get married to sb.

ma'rito sm husband.

ma'rittimo, a ag maritime, sea cpd.

mar'maglia [mar'maʎʎa] sf mob, riff-raff.

marmel'lata sf jam; (di agrumi) marmalade.

mar'mitta sf (recipiente) pot; (AUT) silencer.

'**marmo** sm marble.

mar'mocchio [mar'mɔkkjo] sm (fam) tot, kid.

mar'motta sf (ZOOL) marmot.

Ma'rocco sm: **il** ~ Morocco.

'**marra** sf hoe.

mar'rone ag inv brown // sm (BOT) chestnut.

mar'sina sf tails pl, tail coat.

marte'dì sm inv Tuesday; **di** o **il** ~ **on** Tuesdays; ~ **grasso** Shrove Tuesday.

martel'lare vt to hammer // vi to hammer; (pulsare) to throb.

mar'tello sm hammer; (di uscio) knocker.

marti'netto sm (TECN) jack.

'**martire** sm/f martyr; **mar'tirio** sm martyrdom; (fig) agony, torture.

'**martora** sf marten.

martori'are vt to torment, torture.

marza'pane [martsa'pane] sm marzipan.

marzi'ale [mar'tsjale] ag martial.

'**marzo** ['martso] sm March.

mascal'zone [maskal'tsone] sm rascal, scoundrel.

ma'scella [maʃ'ʃella] sf (ANAT) jaw.

'**maschera** ['maskera] sf mask; (travestimento) disguise; (: per un ballo etc) fancy dress; (TEATRO, CINEMA) usher/usherette; (personaggio del teatro) stock character; **maschera'mento** sm disguise; (MIL) camouflage; **masche'rare** vt to mask; (travestire) to disguise; to dress up; (fig: celare) to hide, conceal; (MIL) to camouflage; ~**rsi da** to disguise o.s. as; to dress up as; (fig) to masquerade as.

mas'chile [mas'kile] ag masculine; (sesso, popolazione) male; (abiti) men's; (per ragazzi: scuola) boys'.

'**maschio, a** ['maskjo] ag (BIOL) male; (virile) manly // sm male; (ragazzo) boy; (figlio) son.

masco'lino, a *ag* masculine.

mas'cotte *sf inv* mascot.

'**massa** *sf* mass; (*di errori etc*): **una ~ di** heaps of, masses of; (*di gente*) mass, multitude; (ELETTR) earth; **in ~** (COMM) in bulk; (*tutti insieme*) en masse; **adunata in ~** mass meeting; **la ~ del popolo** the masses *pl*.

massa'crare *vt* to massacre, slaughter; **mas'sacro** *sm* massacre, slaughter; (*fig*) mess, disaster.

massaggi'are [massad'dʒare] *vt* to massage; **mas'saggio** *sm* massage.

mas'saia *sf* housewife.

masse'ria *sf* large farm.

masse'rizie [masse'rittsje] *sfpl* (household) furnishings.

mas'siccio, a, ci, ce [mas'sittʃo] *ag* (*oro, legno*) solid; (*palazzo*) massive; (*corporatura*) stout // *sm* (GEO) massif.

'**massima** *sf vedi* **massimo.**

massi'male *sm* maximum.

'**massimo, a** *ag, sm* maximum // *sf* (*sentenza, regola*) maxim; (METEOR) maximum temperature; **al ~** at (the) most; **in linea di ~a** generally speaking.

'**masso** *sm* rock, boulder.

mas'sone *sm* freemason; **massone'ria** *sf* freemasonry.

masti'care *vt* to chew.

'**mastice** ['mastitʃe] *sm* mastic; (*per vetri*) putty.

mas'tino *sm* mastiff.

masturbazi'one [masturbat'tsjone] *sf* masturbation.

ma'tassa *sf* skein; **trovare il bandolo della ~** (*fig*) to get to the bottom of a complicated matter.

mate'matico, a, ci, che *ag* mathematical // *sm/f* mathematician // *sf* mathematics *sg*.

mate'rasso *sm* mattress; **~ a molle** spring *o* interior-sprung mattress.

ma'teria *sf* (FISICA) matter; (TECN, COMM) material, matter *q*; (*disciplina*) subject; (*argomento*) subject matter, material; **~e prime** raw materials; **materi'ale** *ag* material; '(*fig: grossolano*) rough, rude // *sm* material; (*insieme di strumenti etc*) equipment *q*, materials *pl*; **materia'lista, i, e** *ag* materialistic.

mater'nità *sf* motherhood, maternity; (*clinica*) maternity hospital.

ma'terno, a *ag* (*amore, cura etc*) maternal, motherly; (*nonno*) maternal; (*lingua, terra*) mother *cpd*.

ma'tita *sf* pencil.

ma'trice [ma'tritʃe] *sf* matrix; (COMM) counterfoil.

ma'tricola *sf* (*registro*) register; (*numero*) registration number; (*nell'università*) freshman, fresher.

ma'trigna [ma'triɲɲa] *sf* stepmother.

matrimoni'ale *ag* matrimonial, marriage *cpd*.

matri'monio *sm* marriage, matrimony; (*durata*) marriage, married life; (*cerimonia*) wedding.

ma'trona *sf* (*fig*) matronly woman.

mat'tina *sf* morning; **matti'nata** *sf* morning; (*spettacolo*) matinée, afternoon performance; **mattini'ero, a** *ag*: **essere mattiniero** to be an early riser; **mat'tino** *sm* morning.

'**matto, a** *ag* mad, crazy; (*fig: falso*) false, imitation; (: *opaco*) matt, dull // *sm/f* madman/woman; **avere una voglia ~a di qc** to be dying for sth.

mat'tone *sm* brick.

matto'nella *sf* tile.

matu'rare *vi* (2) (*anche: ~rsi*) (*frutta, grano*) to ripen; (*ascesso*) to come to a head; (*fig: persona, idea,* ECON) to mature // *vt* to ripen; to (make) mature.

maturità *sf* maturity; (*di frutta*) ripeness, maturity; (INS) school-leaving examination, ≈ GCE A-levels.

ma'turo, a *ag* mature; (*frutto*) ripe, mature.

mauso'leo *sm* mausoleum.

'**mazza** ['mattsa] *sf* (*bastone*) club; (*martello*) sledge-hammer; (SPORT: *da golf*) club; (: *da baseball, cricket*) bat.

'**mazzo** ['mattso] *sm* (*di fiori, chiavi etc*) bunch; (*di carte da gioco*) pack.

me *pronome me*; **~ stesso(a)** myself; **sei bravo quanto ~** you are as clever as I (am) *o* as me.

me'andro *sm* meander.

M.E.C. [mɛk] *sm* (*abbr di* **Mercato Comune Europeo**) EEC.

mec'canico, a, ci, che *ag* mechanical // *sm* mechanic // *sf* mechanics *sg*; (*attività tecnologica*) mechanical engineering; (*meccanismo*) mechanism.

mecca'nismo *sm* mechanism.

me'daglia [me'daʎʎa] *sf* medal; **medagli'one** *sm* (ARCHIT) medallion; (*gioiello*) locket.

me'desimo, a *ag* same; (*in persona*): **io ~** I myself.

'**media** *sf vedi* **medio.**

medi'ano, a *ag* median; (*valore*) mean // *sm* (CALCIO) half-back.

medi'ante *prep* by means of.

medi'are *vt* (*fare da mediatore*) to act as mediator in; (MAT) to average.

media'tore, 'trice *sm/f* mediator; (COMM) middle man, agent.

mediazi'one [medjat'tsjone] *sf* mediation.

medica'mento *sm* medicine, drug.

medi'care *vt* to treat; (*ferita*) to dress; **medicazi'one** *sf* treatment, medication; dressing.

medi'cina [medi'tʃina] *sf* medicine; **~ legale** forensic medicine; **medici'nale** *ag* medicinal // *sm* drug, medicine.

'**medico, a, ci, che** *ag* medical // *sm* doctor; **~ generico** general practitioner, G.P.

medie'vale *ag* medieval.

'**medio, a** *ag* average; (*punto, ceto*) middle; (*altezza, statura*) medium // *sm* (*dito*) middle finger // *sf* average; (MAT) mean; (INS: *voto*) end-of-term average.

medi'ocre *ag* mediocre, poor.
medioe'vale *ag* = **medievale**.
medio'evo *sm* Middle Ages *pl*.
medi'tare *vt* to ponder over, meditate on; (*progettare*) to plan, think out // *vi* to meditate; **meditazi'one** *sf* meditation.
mediter'raneo, a *ag* Mediterranean; **il (mare) M~** the Mediterranean (Sea).
me'dusa *sf* (*ZOOL*) jellyfish.
me'gafono *sm* megaphone.
'meglio ['meʎʎo] *av, ag inv* better; (*con senso superlativo*) best // *sm* (*la cosa migliore*) il ~ the best (thing); **alla ~** as best one can; **andar di bene in ~** to get better and better; **fare del proprio ~** to do one's best; **per il ~** for the best; **aver la ~ su qd** to get the better of sb.
'mela *sf* apple; **~ cotogna** quince.
mela'grana *sf* pomegranate.
melan'zana [melan'dzana] *sf* aubergine.
me'lassa *sf* molasses *sg*, treacle.
me'lenso, a *ag* dull, stupid.
mel'lifluo, a *ag* (*peg*) sugary, honeyed.
'melma *sf* mud, mire.
'melo *sm* apple tree.
melo'dia *sf* melody; **me'lodico, a, ci, che** *ag* melodic; **melodi'oso, a** *ag* melodious.
melo'dramma, i *sm* melodrama.
me'lone *sm* (musk)melon.
'membra *sfpl vedi* **membro**.
mem'brana *sf* membrane.
'membro *sm* member; (*pl(f)* ~a: *arto*) limb.
memo'rabile *ag* memorable.
memo'randum *sm inv* memorandum.
me'moria *sf*, **~e** *sfpl* (*opera autobiografica*) memoirs; **a ~** (*imparare, sapere*) by heart; **a ~ d'uomo** within living memory; **memori'ale** *sm* (*raccolta di memorie*) memoirs *pl*; (*DIR*) memorial.
mena'dito: a ~ *av* perfectly, thoroughly; **sapere qc a ~** to have sth at one's fingertips.
me'nare *vt* to lead; (*picchiare*) to hit, beat; (*dare: colpi*) to deal; **~ la coda** (*cane*) to wag its tail.
mendi'cante *sm/f* beggar.
mendi'care *vt* to beg for // *vi* to beg.
'meno *av* less; (*in frasi comparative*): **~ freddo che** not as cold as, less cold than; (*: seguito da nome, pronome*): **~ alto di** not as tall as, less tall than; **~ denaro di** less money than, not as much money as; (*in frasi superlative*): **il(la) ~ bravo(a)** the least clever; (*di temperatura*) below (zero), minus; (*MAT*) minus, less; (*l'ora*): **sono le 8 ~ un quarto** it's a quarter to eight // *ag inv* (*tempo, denaro*) less; (*errori, persone*) fewer // *prep* except (for) // *sm inv* (*la parte minore*): **il ~** the least; (*MAT*) minus; **i ~** (*la minoranza*) the minority; **a ~ che** *cong* unless; **fare a ~ di qc** (*privarsene*) to do without sth; (*rinunciarvi*) to give sth up; **fare a ~ di fumare** to give up smoking; **non potevo fare a ~ di ridere** I couldn't help laughing; **mille lire in ~** a thousand lire less; **~ male** so much the better; thank goodness.

meno'mare *vt* (*danneggiare*) to maim, disable; (*diminuire: meriti*) to diminish, lessen.
meno'pausa *sf* menopause.
'mensa *sf* (*locale*) canteen; (*: MIL*) mess; (*: nelle università*) refectory.
men'sile *ag* monthly // *sm* (*periodico*) monthly (magazine); (*stipendio*) monthly salary.
'mensola *sf* bracket; (*ripiano*) shelf; (*ARCHIT*) corbel.
'menta *sf* mint; (*anche: ~ peperita*) peppermint.
men'tale *ag* mental; **mentalità** *sf inv* mentality.
'mente *sf* mind; **imparare/sapere qc a ~** to learn/know sth by heart; **avere in ~ qc** to have sth in mind; **passare di ~ a qd** to slip sb's mind.
men'tire *vi* to lie.
'mento *sm* chin.
'mentre *cong* (*temporale*) while; (*avversativo*) whereas.
menzio'nare [mentsjo'nare] *vt* to mention.
menzi'one [men'tsjone] *sf* mention; **fare ~ di** to mention.
men'zogna [men'tsɔɲɲa] *sf* lie.
mera'viglia [mera'viʎʎa] *sf* amazement, wonder; (*persona, cosa*) marvel, wonder; **a ~** perfectly, wonderfully; **meravigli'are** *vt* to amaze, astonish; **meravigliarsi (di)** to marvel (at); (*stupirsi*) to be amazed (at), be astonished (at); **meravigli'oso, a** *ag* wonderful, marvellous.
mer'cante *sm* merchant; **~ di cavalli** horse dealer; **mercanteggi'are** *vt* (*onore, voto*) to sell // *vi* to bargain, haggle; **mercan'tile** *ag* commercial, mercantile, merchant *cpd* // *sm* (*nave*) merchantman; **mercan'zia** *sf* merchandise, goods *pl*.
mer'cato *sm* market; **~ dei cambi** exchange market; **M~ Comune (Europeo)** (European) Common Market; **~ nero** black market.
'merce ['mɛrtʃe] *sf* goods *pl*, merchandise; **~ deperibile** perishable goods *pl*.
mercé [mer'tʃe] *sf* mercy.
merce'nario, a [mertʃe'narjo] *ag, sm* mercenary.
merce'ria [mertʃe'ria] *sf* (*bottega, articoli*) haberdashery.
mercoledì *sm inv* Wednesday; **di o il ~** on Wednesdays; **~ delle Ceneri** Ash Wednesday.
mer'curio *sm* mercury.
'merda *sf* (*fam!*) shit (!).
me'renda *sf* afternoon snack.
meridi'ano, a *ag* meridian; midday *cpd*, noonday // *sm* meridian // *sf* (*orologio*) sundial.
meridio'nale *ag* southern // *sm/f* southerner.
meridi'one *sm* south.
me'ringa, ghe *sf* (*CUC*) meringue.
meri'tare *vt* to deserve, merit.
meri'tevole *ag* worthy.

'**merito** sm merit; (valore) worth; **in ~ a** as regards, with regard to; **dare ~ a qd di** to give sb credit for; **meri'torio, a** ag praiseworthy.

mer'letto sm lace.

'**merlo** sm (ZOOL) blackbird; (ARCHIT) battlement.

mer'luzzo [mer'luttso] sm (ZOOL) cod.

mes'chino, a [mes'kino] ag wretched; (scarso) scanty, poor; (persona: gretta) mean; (: limitata) narrow-minded, petty.

'**mescita** ['meʃʃita] sf public house.

mesco'lanza [mesko'lantsa] sf mixture.

mesco'lare vt to mix; (colori) to blend; (mettere in disordine) to mix up, muddle up; (carte) to shuffle; **~rsi** vr to mix; to blend; to get mixed up; (fig): **~rsi in** to get mixed up in, meddle in.

'**mese** sm month.

'**messa** sf (REL) mass; (il mettere): **~ in moto** starting; **~ in piega** set; **~ a punto** (TECN) adjustment; (AUT) tuning; (fig) clarification; **~ in scena** vedi **messinscena**.

messag'gero [messad'dʒero] sm messenger.

mes'saggio [mes'saddʒo] sm message.

mes'sale sm (REL) missal.

'**messe** sf harvest.

Mes'sia sm inv (REL): **il ~** the Messiah.

'**Messico** sm: **il ~** Mexico.

messin'scena [messin'ʃena] sf (TEATRO) production.

'**messo, a** pp di **mettere** // sm messenger.

mesti'ere sm (professione) job; (: manuale) trade; (: artigianale) craft; (fig: abilità nel lavoro) skill, technique; **essere del ~** to know the tricks of the trade.

'**mesto, a** ag sad, melancholy.

'**mestola** sf (CUC) ladle; (EDIL) trowel.

'**mestolo** sm (CUC) ladle.

mestruazi'one [mestruat'tsjone] sf menstruation.

'**meta** sf destination; (fig) aim, goal.

metà sf inv half; (punto di mezzo) middle; **dividere qc a o per ~** to divide sth in half, halve sth; **fare a ~ (di qc con qd)** to go halves (with sb in sth); **a ~ prezzo** at half price; **a ~ strada** halfway.

metabo'lismo sm metabolism.

meta'fisica sf metaphysics sg.

me'tafora sf metaphor.

me'tallico, a, ci, che ag (di metallo) metal cpd; (splendore etc) metallic.

me'tallo sm metal; **metallur'gia** sf metallurgy.

meta'morfosi sf metamorphosis.

me'tano sm methane.

me'teora sf meteor.

meteo'rite sm meteorite.

meteorolo'gia [meteorolo'dʒia] sf meteorology; **meteoro'logico, a, ci, che** ag meteorological, weather cpd.

me'ticcio, a, ci, ce [me'tittʃo] sm/f half-caste, half-breed.

metico'loso, a ag meticulous.

me'todico, a, ci, che ag methodical.

'**metodo** sm method; (manuale) tutor, manual.

'**metrico, a, ci, che** ag metric; (POESIA) metrical // sf metrics sg.

'**metro** sm metre; (nastro) tape measure; (asta) (metre) rule.

me'tropoli sf metropolis.

metropoli'tano, a ag metropolitan // sm (city) policeman // sf underground, subway.

'**mettere** vt to put; (abito) to put on; (: portare) to wear; (installare: telefono) to put in; (fig: provocare): **~ fame/allegria a qd** to make sb hungry/happy; (supporre): **mettiamo che ...** let's suppose o say that ... ; **~rsi** vr (disporsi: faccenda) to turn out; **~rsi a sedere** to sit down; **~rsi a letto** to get into bed; (per malattia) to take to one's bed; **~rsi il cappello** to put on one's hat; **~rsi a** (cominciare) to begin to, start to; **~rsi al lavoro** to set to work; **~rci**: **~rci molta cura/molto tempo** to take a lot of care/a lot of time; **ci ho messo 3 ore per venire** it's taken me 3 hours to get here; **~ a tacere qd/qc** to keep sb/sth quiet; **~ su casa** to set up house; **~ su un negozio** to start a shop; **~ via** to put away.

mez'zadro [med'dzadro] sm (AGR) sharecropper.

mezza'luna [meddza'luna] sf half-moon; (dell'islamismo) crescent; (coltello) (semicircular) chopping knife.

mezza'nino [meddza'nino] sm mezzanine (floor).

mez'zano, a [med'dzano] ag (medio) average, medium // sm/f (intermediario) go-between; (ruffiano) pimp.

mezza'notte [meddza'notte] sf midnight.

'**mezzo, a** ['meddzo] ag half; **un ~ litro/panino** half a litre/roll // av half-; **~ morto** half-dead // sm (metà) half; (parte centrale: di strada etc) middle; (per raggiungere un fine) means sg; (veicolo) vehicle; (nell'indicare l'ora): **le nove e ~** half past nine; **mezzogiorno e ~** half past twelve; **~i smpi** (possibilità economiche) means; **di ~a età** middle-aged; **di ~** middle, in the middle; **andarci di ~** (patir danno) to suffer; **levarsi o togliersi di ~** to get out of the way; **in ~ a** in the middle of; **per o a ~ di** by means of; **~i di comunicazione di massa** mass media pl; **~i pubblici** public transport sg; **~i di trasporto** means of transport.

mezzogi'orno [meddzo'dʒorno] sm midday, noon; (GEO) south; **a ~** at 12 (o'clock) o midday o noon; **il ~ d'Italia** southern Italy.

mez'z'ora, mez'zora [med'dzora] sf half-hour, half an hour.

mi pronome (dav lo, la, li, le, ne diventa me) (oggetto) me; (complemento di termine) to me, (riflessivo) myself // sm (MUS) E; (: solfeggiando la scala) mi.

'**mia** vedi **mio**.

miago'lare vi to miaow, mew.

'mica *sf* (*CHIM*) mica // *av* (*fam*): **non ...** ∼ not ... at all; **non sono** ∼ **stanco** I'm not a bit tired; ∼ **male** not bad.

'miccia, ce ['mittʃa] *sf* fuse.

micidi'ale [mitʃi'djale] *ag* fatal; (*dannosissimo*) deadly.

'microbo *sm* microbe.

mi'crofono *sm* microphone.

micros'copico, a, ci, che *ag* microscopic.

micros'copio *sm* microscope.

mi'dollo, *pl(f)* ∼**a** *sm* (*ANAT*) marrow.

'mie, mi'ei *vedi* **mio.**

mi'ele *sm* honey.

mi'etere *vt* (*AGR*) to reap, harvest; (*fig: vite*) to take, claim.

migli'aio [miʎ'ʎajo], *pl(f)* ∼**a** *sm* thousand; **un** ∼ **(di)** about a thousand; **a** ∼ **a** by the thousand, in thousands.

'miglio ['miʎʎo] *sm* (*BOT*) millet; (*pl(f)* ∼**a:** *unità di misura*) mile; ∼ **marino** *o* **nautico** nautical mile.

miglio'rare [miʎʎo'rare] *vt, vi* to improve.

migli'ore [miʎ'ʎore] *ag* (*comparativo*) better; (*superlativo*) best // *sm*: **il** ∼ **the** best (thing) // *sm/f*: **il(la)** ∼ **the** best (person); **il miglior vino di questa regione** the best wine in this area.

'mignolo ['miɲɲolo] *sm* (*ANAT*) little finger, pinkie; (*: dito del piede*) little toe.

mi'grare *vi* to migrate; **migrazi'one** *sf* migration.

'mila *pl di* **mille.**

Mi'lano *sf* Milan.

milia'rdario, a *sm/f* millionaire.

mili'ardo *sm* milliard, thousand million.

mili'are *ag:* **pietra** ∼ milestone.

mili'one *sm* million; **un** ∼ **di lire** a million lire.

mili'tante *ag, sm/f* militant.

mili'tare *vi* (*MIL*) to be a soldier, serve; (*fig: in un partito*) to be a militant // *ag* military // *sm* serviceman; ∼ **a favore di** (*sog: argomenti etc*) to militate in favour of; **fare il** ∼ to do one's military service.

'milite *sm* soldier.

mi'lizia [mi'littsja] *sf* (*corpo armato*) militia.

millanta'tore, 'trice *sm/f* boaster.

'mille *num* (*pl* **mila**) a *o* one thousand; **dieci mila** ten thousand.

mille'foglie [mille'fɔʎʎe] *sm inv* (*CUC*) cream *o* vanilla slice.

mil'lennio *sm* millennium.

millepi'edi *sm inv* centipede.

mil'lesimo, a *ag, sm* thousandth.

milli'grammo *sm* milligram(me).

mil'limetro *sm* millimetre.

'milza [miltsa] *sf* (*ANAT*) spleen.

mimetiz'zare [mimetid'dzare] *vt* to camouflage; ∼**rsi** *vr* to camouflage o.s.

'mimica *sf* (*arte*) mime.

'mimo *sm* (*attore, componimento*) mime.

mi'mosa *sf* mimosa.

'mina *sf* (*esplosiva*) mine; (*di matita*) lead.

mi'naccia, ce [mi'nattʃa] *sf* threat;

---

minacci'are *vt* to threaten; **minacci'oso, a** *ag* threatening.

mi'nare *vt* (*MIL*) to mine; (*fig*) to undermine.

mina'tore *sm* miner.

mina'torio, a *ag* threatening.

mine'rale *ag, sm* mineral; **mineralo'gia** *sf* mineralogy.

mine'rario, a *ag* (*delle miniere*) mining; (*dei minerali*) ore *cpd*.

mi'nestra *sf* soup; ∼ **in brodo** noodle soup; **mines'trone** *sm* thick vegetable and pasta soup.

mingher'lino, a [minger'lino] *ag* thin, slender.

minia'tura *sf* miniature.

mini'era *sf* mine.

'minimo, a *ag* minimum, least, slightest; (*piccolissimo*) very small, slight; (*il più basso*) lowest, minimum // *sm* minimum; **al** ∼ at least; **girare al** ∼ (*AUT*) to idle.

minis'tero *sm* (*POL, REL*) ministry; (*governo*) government; ∼ **delle Finanze** Ministry of Finance, ≈ Treasury.

mi'nistro *sm* (*POL, REL*) minister; ∼ **delle Finanze** Minister of Finance, ≈ Chancellor of the Exchequer.

mino'ranza [mino'rantsa] *sf* minority.

mino'rato, a *ag* handicapped // *sm/f* physically (*o* mentally) handicapped person.

mi'nore *ag* (*comparativo*) less; (*più piccolo*) smaller; (*numero*) lower; (*inferiore*) lower, inferior; (*meno importante*) minor; (*più giovane*) younger; (*superlativo*) least; smallest; lowest; youngest // *sm/f* (*minorenne*) minor, person under age.

mino'renne *ag* under age // *sm/f* minor, person under age.

mi'nuscolo, a *ag* (*scrittura, carattere*) small; (*piccolissimo*) tiny // *sf* small letter.

mi'nuta *sf* rough copy, draft.

mi'nuto, a *ag* tiny, minute; (*pioggia*) fine; (*corporatura*) delicate, fine; (*lavoro*) detailed // *sm* (*unità di misura*) minute; **al** ∼ (*COMM*) retail.

'mio, 'mia, mi'ei, 'mie *det*: **il** ∼, **la mia** *etc* my // *pronome*: **il** ∼, **la mia** *etc* mine; **i miei** my family; **un** ∼ **amico** a friend of mine.

'miope *ag* short-sighted.

'mira *sf* (*anche fig*) aim; (*bersaglio*) target; (*congegno di mira*) sight; **prendere la** ∼ to take aim; **prendere di** ∼ **qd** (*fig*) to pick on sb.

mi'rabile *ag* admirable, wonderful.

mi'racolo *sm* miracle; **miraco'loso, a** *ag* miraculous.

mi'raggio [mi'raddʒo] *sm* mirage.

mi'rare *vi:* ∼ **a** to aim at.

mi'rino *sm* (*TECN*) sight; (*FOT*) viewer, viewfinder.

mir'tillo *sm* bilberry, whortleberry.

'mirto *sm* myrtle.

mi'santropo, a *sm/f* misanthropist.

mi'scela [miʃ'ʃela] sf mixture; (di caffè) blend.

miscel'lanea [miʃʃel'lanea] sf miscellany.

'mischia ['miskja] sf scuffle.

mischi'are [mis'kjare] vt, ~**rsi** vr to mix, blend.

mis'cuglio [mis'kuʎʎo] sm mixture, hotchpotch, jumble.

mise'rabile ag (infelice) miserable, wretched; (povero) poverty-stricken; (di scarso valore) miserable.

mi'seria sf extreme poverty; (infelicità) misery; ~**e** sfpl (del mondo etc) misfortunes, troubles; **porca** ~! (fam), ~ **ladra!** (fam) blast!, damn!

miseri'cordia sf mercy, pity.

'misero, a ag miserable, wretched; (povero) poverty-stricken; (insufficiente) miserable.

mis'fatto sm misdeed, crime.

mi'sogino [mi'zɔdʒino] sm misogynist.

'missile sm missile.

missio'nario, a ag, sm/f missionary.

missi'one sf mission.

misteri'ose, a ag mysterious.

mis'tero sm mystery.

'mistico, a, ci, che ag mystic(al) // sm mystic.

mistifi'care vt to fool, bamboozle.

'misto, a ag mixed; (scuola) mixed, coeducational // sm mixture.

mis'tura sf mixture.

mi'sura sf measure; (misurazione, dimensione) measurement; (taglia) size; (provvedimento) measure, step; (moderazione) moderation; (MUS) time; (: divisione) bar; (fig: limite) bounds pl, limit; **a** ~ **che** as; **su** ~ made to measure.

misu'rare vt (ambiente, stoffa) to measure; (terreno) to survey; (abito) to try on; (pesare) to weigh; (fig: parole etc) to weigh up; (: spese, cibo) to limit; ~**rsi** vr: ~**rsi con qd** to have a confrontation with sb; to compete with sb; **misu'rato, a** ag (ponderato) measured; (prudente) cautious; (moderato) moderate; **misurazi'one** sf measuring; (di terreni) surveying.

'mite ag mild; (prezzo) moderate, reasonable.

miti'gare vt to mitigate, lessen; (lenire) to soothe, relieve; ~**rsi** vr (odio) to subside; (tempo) to become milder.

'mito sm myth; **mitolo'gia, 'gie** sf mythology.

'mitra sf (REL) mitre // sm inv (arma) sub-machine gun.

mitraglia'trice [mitraʎʎa'tritʃe] sf machine gun.

mit'tente sm/f sender.

'mobile ag mobile; (parte di macchina) moving; (DIR: bene) movable, personal // sm (arredamento) piece of furniture; ~**i** smpl furniture sg.

mo'bilia sf furniture.

mobili'are ag (DIR) personal, movable.

mo'bilio sm = **mobilia**.

mobilità sf motility.

mobili'tare vt to mobilize; **mobilita-zi'one** sf mobilization.

mocas'sino sm moccasin.

'moccolo sm (di candela) candle-end; (fam: bestemmia) oath; (: moccio) snot; **reggere il** ~ to play gooseberry.

'moda sf fashion; **alla** ~, **di** ~ fashionable, in fashion.

modalità sf inv formality.

mo'della sf model.

model'lare vt (creta) to model, shape; ~**rsi** vr: ~**rsi su** to model o.s. on.

mo'dello sm (stampo) mould // ag inv model cpd; ~ **di carta** (SARTORIA) (paper) pattern.

mode'rare vt to moderate; ~**rsi** vr to restrain o.s.; **mode'rato, a** ag moderate.

modera'tore, 'trice sm/f moderator.

moderazi'one [moderat'tsjone] sf moderation.

mo'derno, a ag modern.

mo'destia sf modesty.

mo'desto, a ag modest.

'modico, a, ci, che ag reasonable, moderate.

mo'difica, che sf modification.

modifi'care vt to modify, alter; ~**rsi** vr to alter, change.

'modo sm way, manner; (mezzo) means, way; (occasione) opportunity; (LING) mood; (MUS) mode; ~**i** smpl manners; **a suo** ~, **a** ~ **suo** in his own way; **ad o in ogni** ~ anyway; **di o in** ~ **che** so that; **in** ~ **da** so as to; **in tutti i** ~**i** at all costs; (comunque sia) anyway; (in ogni caso) in any case; **in qualche** ~ somehow or other; ~ **di dire** turn of phrase; **per** ~ **di dire** so to speak.

modu'lare vt to modulate; **modulazi'one** sf modulation; **modulazione di frequenza** frequency modulation.

'modulo sm form; (lunare, di comando) module.

'mogio, a, gi, gie ['mɔdʒo] ag down in the dumps, dejected.

'moglie ['moʎʎe] sf wife.

mo'ine sfpl cajolery sg; (leziosità) affectation sg.

'mola sf millstone; (utensile abrasivo) grindstone.

mo'lare vi to grind // ag (pietra) mill cpd // sm (dente) molar.

'mole sf mass; (dimensioni) size; (edificio grandioso) massive structure.

mo'lecola sf molecule.

moles'tare vt to bother, annoy; **mo'lestia** sf annoyance, bother; **recar molestia a qd** to bother sb; **mo'lesto, a** ag annoying.

'molla sf spring; ~**e** sfpl tongs.

mol'lare vt to release, let go; (NAUT) to ease; (fig: ceffone) to give // vi (cedere) to give in.

'molle ag soft; (peg) flabby, limp; (: fig) weak, feeble; (bagnato) wet.

mol'letta sf (per capelli) hairgrip; (per

panni stesi) clothes peg; ~**e** _stpl_ (_per zucchero_) tongs.

mol'lezza [mol'lettsa] _sf_ softness, flabbiness, limpness; weakness, feebleness; ~**e** _stpl:_ **vivere nelle ~e** to live in the lap of luxury.

'mollica, che _sf_ crumb, soft part; ~**che** _stpl_ (_briciole_) crumbs.

mol'lusco, schi _sm_ mollusc.

'molo _sm_ mole, breakwater; jetty.

mol'teplice [mol'teplitʃe] _ag_ (_formato di più elementi_) complex; (_numeroso_) numerous; (: _interessi, attività_) many, manifold; **molteplicità** _sf_ multiplicity.

moltipli'care _vt_ to multiply; ~**rsi** _vr_ to multiply; to increase in number; **moltiplica'tore** _sm_ multiplier; **moltiplicazi'one** _sf_ multiplication.

molti'tudine _sf_ multitude; **una ~ di** a vast number o a multitude of.

'molto, a _det_ much, a lot of; (_con sostantivi al plurale_): ~**i(e)** many, a lot of; (_lungo: tempo_) long // _av_ a lot; (_in frasi negative_) much; (_intensivo_) very // _pronome_ much, a lot; ~**i(e)** _pronome pl_ many, a lot; ~ **meglio** much o a lot better; ~ **buono** very good; **per ~ (tempo)** for a long time.

momen'taneo, a _ag_ momentary, fleeting.

mo'mento _sm_ moment; **capitare nel ~ buono** to come at the right time; **da un ~ all'altro** at any moment; (_all'improvviso_) suddenly; **al ~ di fare** just as I was (_o you were o he was etc_) doing; **per il ~** for the time being; **dal ~ che** ever since; (_dato che_) since.

'monaca, che _sf_ nun.

'monaco, ci _sm_ monk.

'Monaco _sf_ Monaco; ~ **(di Baviera)** Munich.

mo'narca, chi _sm_ monarch; **monar'chia** _sf_ monarchy.

monas'tero _sm_ (_di monaci_) monastery; (_di monache_) convent; **mo'nastico, a, ci, che** _ag_ monastic.

'monco, a, chi, che _ag_ maimed; (_fig_) incomplete; ~ **d'un braccio** one-armed.

mon'dana _sf_ prostitute.

mon'dano, a _ag_ (_anche fig_) worldly; (_dell'alta società_) society _cpd_; fashionable.

mon'dare _vt_ (_frutta, patate_) to peel; (_piselli_) to shell; (_pulire_) to clean.

mondi'ale _ag_ (_campionato, popolazione_) world _cpd_; (_influenza_) world-wide.

'mondo _sm_ world; (_grande quantità_): **un ~ di** lots of, a host of; **il gran o bel ~** high society.

mo'nello, a _sm/f_ street urchin; (_ragazzo vivace_) scamp, imp.

mo'neta _sf_ coin; (_ECON: valuta_) currency; (_denaro spicciolo_) (small) change; ~ **estera** foreign currency; ~ **legale** legal tender; **mone'tario, a** _ag_ monetary.

mongo'loide _ag, sm/f_ (_MED_) mongol.

'monito _sm_ warning.

'monitor _sm inv_ (_TECN, TV_) monitor.

mo'nocolo _sm_ (_lente_) monocle, eyeglass.

monoco'lore _ag_ (_POL_) one-party.

mono'gramma, i _sm_ monogram.

mo'nologo, ghi _sm_ monologue.

mono'plano _sm_ monoplane.

mono'polio _sm_ monopoly; **monopoliz'zare** _vt_ to monopolize.

mono'sillabo, a _ag_ monosyllabic // _sm_ monosyllable.

monoto'nia _sf_ monotony.

mo'notono, a _ag_ monotonous.

monsi'gnore [monsiɲ'ɲore] _sm_ (_REL: titolo_) Your (o His) Grace.

mon'sone _sm_ monsoon.

monta'carichi [monta'kariki] _sm inv_ hoist, goods lift.

mon'taggio [mon'taddʒo] _sm_ (_TECN_) assembly; (_CINEMA_) editing.

mon'tagna [mon'taɲɲa] _sf_ mountain; (_zona montuosa_): **la ~** the mountains _pl_; ~**e russe** roller coaster _sg_, big dipper _sg_; **monta'gnoso, a** _ag_ mountainous.

monta'naro, a _ag_ mountain _cpd_ // _sm/f_ mountain dweller.

mon'tano, a _ag_ mountain _cpd_; alpine.

mon'tare _vt_ to go (o come) up; (_apparecchiatura_) to set up, assemble; (_CUC_) to whip; (_ZOOL_) to cover; (_incastonare_) to mount, set; (_CINEMA_) to edit // _vi (2)_ to go (o come) up; (_a cavallo_): ~ **bene/male** to ride well/badly; (_aumentare di livello, volume_) to rise; ~**rsi** _vr_ to become big-headed; ~ **qc** to exaggerate sth; ~ **qd o la testa a qd** to turn sb's head; ~ **in bicicletta/treno** to get on a bicycle/train; ~ **a cavallo** to get on o mount a horse.

monta'tura _sf_ assembling _q_; (_di occhiali_) frames _pl_; (_di gioiello_) mounting, setting; (_fig_): ~ **pubblicitaria** publicity stunt.

'monte _sm_ mountain; **a ~** upstream; **mandare a ~ qc** to upset sth, cause sth to fail; **il M~ Bianco** Mont Blanc; ~ **dei pegni** pawnshop.

mon'tone _sm_ (_ZOOL_) ram.

montu'oso, a _ag_ mountainous.

monu'mento _sm_ monument.

'mora _sf_ (_del rovo_) blackberry; (_del gelso_) mulberry; (_DIR_) delay; (: _somma_) arrears _pl_.

mo'rale _ag_ moral // _sf_ (_scienza_) ethics _sg_, moral philosophy; (_complesso di norme_) moral standards _pl_, morality; (_condotta_) morals _pl_; (_insegnamento morale_) moral // _sm_ morale; **moralità** _sf_ morality; (_condotta_) morals _pl_.

'morbido, a _ag_ soft; (_pelle_) soft, smooth.

mor'billo _sm_ (_MED_) measles _sg_.

'morbo _sm_ disease.

mor'boso, a _ag_ (_fig_) morbid.

'morchia ['mɔrkja] _sf_ (_residuo grasso_) dregs _pl_; oily deposit.

mor'dace [mor'datʃe] _ag_ biting, cutting.

mor'dente _sm_ (_fig_) push, drive.

'mordere _vt_ to bite; (_addentare_) to bite into; (_corrodere_) to eat into.

mor'fina _sf_ morphine.

mori'bondo, a _ag_ dying, moribund.

morige'rato, a [moridʒe'rato] ag of good morals.

mo'rire vi (2) to die; (abitudine, civiltà) to die out; ~ **di fame** to die of hunger; (fig) to be starving; ~ **di noia** to be bored to death; **fa un caldo da** ~ it's terribly hot.

mormo'rare vi to murmur; (brontolare) to grumble; **mormo'rìo** sm murmuring; grumbling.

'moro, a ag dark(-haired); dark(-complexioned); i M~i smpl (STORIA) the Moors.

mo'roso, a ag in arrears // sm/f (fam: innamorato) sweetheart.

'morsa sf vice.

morsi'care vt to nibble (at), gnaw (at); (sog: insetto) to bite.

'morso, a pp di **mordere** // sm bite; (di insetto) sting; (parte della briglia) bit; ~i **della fame** pangs of hunger.

mor'taio sm mortar.

mor'tale ag, sm mortal; **mortalità** sf mortality, death rate.

'morte sf death.

mortifi'care vt to mortify.

'morto, a pp di **morire** // ag dead // sm/f dead man/woman; i ~i the dead; **fare il** ~ (nell'acqua) to float on one's back.

mor'torio sm (anche fig) funeral.

mo'saico, ci sm mosaic.

'mosca, sche sf fly; ~ **cieca** blind-man's-buff.

'Mosca sf Moscow.

mos'cato sm muscatel (wine).

mosce'rino [moʃʃe'rino] sm midge, gnat.

mos'chea [mos'kɛa] sf mosque.

mos'chetto [mos'ketto] sm musket.

'moscio, a, sci, sce ['moʃʃo] ag (fig) lifeless.

mos'cone sm (ZOOL) bluebottle; (barca) pedalò; (a remi) kind of pedalo with oars.

'mossa sf movement; (nel gioco) move.

'mosso, a pp di **muovere** // ag (mare) rough; (capelli) wavy; (FOT) blurred; (ritmo, prosa) animated.

mos'tarda sf mustard.

'mostra sf exhibition, show; (ostentazione) show; **in** ~ on show; **far** ~ **di** (fingere) to pretend; **far** ~ **di sé** to show off.

mos'trare vt to show // vi: ~ **di fare** to pretend to do; ~**rsi** vr to appear.

'mostro sm monster; **mostru'oso**, a ag monstrous.

mo'tel sm inv motel.

moti'vare vt (causare) to cause; (giustificare) to justify, account for; **motivazi'one** sf justification; motive; (PSIC) motivation.

mo'tivo sm (causa) reason, cause; (movente) motive; (letterario) (central) theme; (disegno) motif, design, pattern; (MUS) motif; **per quale** ~? why?, for what reason?

'moto sm (anche FISICA) motion; (movimento, gesto) movement; (esercizio fisico) exercise; (sommossa) rising, revolt; (commozione) feeling, impulse // sf inv (motocicletta) motor-bike; **mettere in** ~

to set in motion; (AUT) to start up.

motoci'cletta [mototʃi'kletta] sf motorcycle; **motoci'clismo** sm motorcycling, motorcycle racing; **motoci'clista**, i, e sm/f motorcyclist.

mo'tore, **'trice** ag motor; (TECN) driving // sm engine, motor; a ~ motor cpd, power-driven; ~ **a combustione interna/a reazione** internal combustion/jet engine; **moto'rino** sm moped; **motorino di avviamento** (AUT) starter; **motoriz'zato**, a ag (truppe) motorized; (persona) having a car o transport.

motos'cafo sm motorboat.

mot'teggio [mot'teddʒo] sm banter.

'motto sm (battuta scherzosa) witty remark; (frase emblematica) motto, maxim.

mo'vente sm motive.

movimen'tare vt to liven up.

movi'mento sm movement; (fig) activity, hustle and bustle; (MUS) tempo, movement.

mozi'one [mot'tsjone] sf (POL) motion.

moz'zare [mot'tsare] vt to cut off; (coda) to dock; ~ **il fiato o il respiro a qd** (fig) to take sb's breath away.

mozza'rella [mottsa'rella] sf mozzarella (a moist Neapolitan curd cheese).

mozzi'cone [mottsi'kone] sm stub, butt, end; (anche: ~ **di sigaretta**) cigarette end.

'mozzo sm ['mɔddzo] (MECCANICA) hub; ['mottso] (NAUT) ship's boy; ~ **di stalla** stable boy.

'mucca, che sf cow.

'mucchio ['mukkjo] sm pile, heap; (fig): **un** ~ **di** lots of, heaps of.

'muco, chi sm mucus.

mu'cosa sf mucous membrane.

'muffa sf mould, mildew.

mug'gire [mud'dʒire] vi (vacca) to low, moo; (toro) to bellow; (fig) to roar; **mug'gito** sm low, moo; bellow; roar.

mu'ghetto [mu'getto] sm lily of the valley.

mu'gnaio, a [mun'najo] sm/f miller.

mugo'lare vi (cane) to whimper, whine; (fig: persona) to moan.

muli'nare vi to whirl, spin (round and round).

muli'nello sm (moto vorticoso) eddy, whirl; (per aria) ventilating fan; (di canna da pesca) reel; (NAUT) windlass.

mu'lino sm mill; ~ **a vento** windmill.

'mulo sm mule.

'multa sf fine; **mul'tare** vt to fine.

multico'lore ag multicoloured.

'multiplo, a ag, sm multiple.

'mummia sf mummy.

'mungere ['mundʒere] vt (anche fig) to milk.

munici'pale [munitʃi'pale] ag municipal; town cpd.

muni'cipio [muni'tʃipjo] sm town council, corporation; (edificio) town hall.

mu'nire *vt*: ~ **qc/qd di** to equip sth/sb with.

munizi'oni [munit'tsjoni] *sfpl* (*MIL*) ammunition *sg*.

'munto, a *pp di* **mungere**.

mu'overe *vt* to move; (*ruota, macchina*) to drive; (*sollevare: questione, obiezione*) to raise, bring up, (: *accusa*) to make, bring forward; ~**rsi** *vr* to move; **muoviti!** hurry up!, get a move on!

'mura *sfpl vedi* **muro**.

mu'raglia [mu'raʎʎa] *sf* (high) wall.

mu'rale *ag* wall *cpd*; mural.

mu'rare *vt* (*persona, porta*) to wall up.

mura'tore *sm* mason; bricklayer.

'muro *sm* wall; ~**a** *sfpl* (*cinta cittadina*) walls; a ~ wall *cpd*; (*armadio etc*) built-in; ~ **del suono** sound barrier.

'muschio ['muskjo] *sm* (*ZOOL*) musk; (*BOT*) moss.

musco'lare *ag* muscular, muscle *cpd*.

'muscolo *sm* (*ANAT*) muscle.

mu'seo *sm* museum.

museru'ola *sf* muzzle.

'musica *sf* music; **scrivere una** ~ to write a piece of music; ~ **da ballo/camera** dance/chamber music; **musi'cale** *ag* musical; **musi'cista, i, e** *sm/f* musician.

'muso *sm* muzzle; (*di auto, aereo*) nose; **tenere il** ~ to sulk; **mu'sone, a** *sm/f* sulky person.

'mussola *sf* muslin.

'muta *sf* (*ZOOL*) moulting; (: *di serpenti*) sloughing; (*cambio*) change; (*di sentinella*) relief; (*per immersioni subacquee*) diving suit; (*gruppo di cani*) pack.

muta'mento *sm* change.

mu'tande *sfpl* (*da uomo*) (under)pants; **mutan'dine** *sfpl* (*da donna, bambino*) pants; **mutandine di plastica** plastic pants.

mu'tare *vt, vi* (2) to change, alter; **mutazi'one** *sf* change, alteration; (*BIOL*) mutation; **mu'tevole** *ag* changeable.

muti'lare *vt* to mutilate, maim; (*fig*) to mutilate, deface; **muti'lato, a** *sm/f* disabled person (*through loss of limbs*); **mutilazi'one** *sf* mutilation.

mu'tismo *sm* (*MED*) mutism; (*atteggiamento*) (stubborn) silence.

'muto, a *ag* (*MED*) dumb; (*emozione, dolore, CINEMA*) silent; (*LING*) silent, mute; (*carta geografica*) blank; ~ **per lo stupore** *etc* speechless with amazement *etc*.

'mutua *sf* (*anche*: **cassa** ~) health insurance scheme.

mutu'are *vt* (*fig*) to borrow.

mutu'ato, a *sm/f* member of a health insurance scheme.

'mutuo, a *ag* (*reciproco*) mutual // *sm* (*ECON*) (long-term) loan.

N

N. (*abbr di* **nord**) N.

'nacchere ['nakkere] *sfpl* castanets.

'nafta *sf* naphtha; (*per motori diesel*) diesel oil.

'naia *sf* (*ZOOL*) cobra; (*MIL*) slang term for national service.

'nailon *sm* nylon.

'nanna *sf* (*linguaggio infantile*): **andare a** ~ to go bye-byes.

'nano, a *ag, sm/f* dwarf.

napole'tano, a *ag, sm/f* Neapolitan.

'Napoli *sf* Naples.

'nappa *sf* tassel.

nar'ciso [nar't∫izo] *sm* narcissus.

nar'cosi *sf* narcosis.

nar'cotico, ci *sm* narcotic.

na'rice [na'rit∫e] *sf* nostril.

nar'rare *vt* to tell the story of, recount; **narra'tivo, a** *ag* narrative // *sf* (*branca letteraria*) fiction; **narra'tore, 'trice** *sm/f* narrator; **narrazi'one** *sf* narration; (*racconto*) story, tale.

na'sale *ag* nasal.

'nascere ['na∫∫ere] *vi* (2) (*bambino*) to be born; (*pianta*) to come o spring up; (*fiume*) to rise, have its source; (*sole*) to rise; (*dente*) to come through; (*fig: derivare, conseguire*): ~ **da** to arise from, be born out of; **è nata nel 1952** she was born in 1952; **'nascita** *sf* birth.

nas'condere *vt* to hide, conceal; ~**rsi** *vr* to hide; **nascon'diglio** *sm* hiding place; **nascon'dino** *sm* (*gioco*) hide-and-seek; **nas'costo, a** *pp di* **nascondere** // *ag* hidden; **di nascosto** secretly.

na'sello *sm* (*ZOOL*) hake.

'naso *sm* nose.

'nastro *sm* ribbon; (*magnetico, isolante, SPORT*) tape; ~ **adesivo** adhesive tape; ~ **dattilografico** typewriter ribbon; ~ **trasportatore** conveyor belt.

nas'turzio [nas'turtsjo] *sm* nasturtium.

na'tale *ag* of one's birth // *sm* (*REL*): **N**~ Christmas; (*giorno della nascita*) birthday; **natalità** *sf* birth rate: **nata'lizio, a** *ag* (*del Natale*) Christmas *cpd*; (*di nascita*) of one's birth.

na'tante *ag* floating // *sm* craft *inv*, boat.

'natica, che *sf* (*ANAT*) buttock.

na'tio, a, 'tii, 'tie *ag* native.

Nativita *sf* (*REL*) Nativity.

na'tivo, a *ag, sm/f* native.

'nato, a *pp di* **nascere** // *ag*: **un attore** ~ a born actor; ~**a Pieri** née Pieri.

na'tura *sf* nature; **pagare in** ~ to pay in kind; ~ **morta** still life.

natu'rale *ag* natural; **natura'lezza** *sf* naturalness; **natura'lista, i, e** *sm/f* naturalist.

naturaliz'zare [naturalid'dzare] *vt* to naturalize.

natural'mente *av* naturally; (*certamente, sì*) of course.

naufra'gare *vi* (*nave*) to be wrecked;

(persona) to be shipwrecked; *(fig)* to fall through; **nau'fragio** *sm* shipwreck; *(fig)* ruin, failure; **'naufrago, ghi** *sm* castaway, shipwreck victim.

'nausea *sf* nausea; **nausea'bondo, a** *ag* nauseating, sickening; **nause'are** *vt* to nauseate, make (feel) sick.

'nautico, a, ci, che *ag* nautical // *sf* (art of) navigation.

na'vale *ag* naval.

na'vata *sf* *(anche:* ~ **centrale)** nave; *(anche:* ~ **laterale)** aisle.

'nave *sf* ship, vessel; ~ **cisterna** tanker; ~ **da guerra** warship; ~ **spaziale** spaceship.

na'vetta *sf* shuttle; *(servizio di collegamento)* shuttle (service).

navi'cella [navi'tʃɛlla] *sf (di aerostato)* gondola.

navi'gabile *ag* navigable.

navi'gare *vi* to sail; **navigazi'one** *sf* navigation.

na'viglio [na'viʎʎo] *sm* fleet, ships *pl*; *(canale artificiale)* canal; ~ **da pesca** fishing fleet.

nazio'nale [nattsjo'nale] *ag* national // *sf (SPORT)* national team; **naziona'lismo** *sm* nationalism; **nazionalità** *sf inv* nationality; **nazionaliz'zare** *vt* to nationalize.

nazi'one [nat'tsjone] *sf* nation.

ne *pronome* of him/her/it/them; about him/her/it/them; ~ **riconosco la voce** I recognize his *(o* her) voice; **non parliamone più** let's not talk about him (o her *o* it *o* them) any more; *(con valore partitivo):* **hai dei libri?** — **sì,** ~ **ho** have you any books? — yes, I have (some); **hai del pane?** — **no, non** ~ **ho** have you any bread? — no, I don't have any; **quanti anni hai?** — ~ **ho 17** how old are you? — I'm 17 // *av (moto da luogo)* from there.

né *cong:* ~ ... ~ neither ... nor; ~ **l'uno** ~ **l'altro lo vuole** neither of them wants it; **non parla** ~ **l'italiano** ~ **il tedesco** he speaks neither Italian nor German, he doesn't speak either Italian or German; **non piove** ~ **nevica** it isn't raining or snowing.

ne'anche [ne'anke] *av, cong* not even; **non** ... ~ not even; ~ **se volesse potrebbe venire** he couldn't come even if he wanted to; **non l'ho visto** — ~ **lo** I didn't see him — neither did I o I didn't either; ~ **per idea** *o* **sogno!** not on your life!

'nebbia *sf* fog; *(foschia)* mist; **nebbi'oso, a** *ag* foggy; misty.

necessaria'mente [netʃessarja'mente] *av* necessarily.

neces'sario, a [netʃes'sarjo] *ag* necessary.

necessità [netʃessi'ta] *sf inv* necessity; *(povertà)* need, poverty; **necessi'tare** *vt* to require // *vi (2)* (*aver bisogno)*: **necessitare di** to need // *vb impers* to be necessary.

necro'logio [nekro'lɔdʒo] *sm* obituary notice; *(registro)* register of deaths.

necrosco'pia *sf* postmortem (examination).

ne'fando, a *ag* infamous, wicked.

ne'fasto, a *ag* inauspicious, ill-omened.

ne'gare *vt* to deny; *(rifiutare)* to deny, refuse; ~ **di aver fatto/che** to deny having done/that; **nega'tivo, a** *ag, sf* negative; **negazi'one** *sf* denial; *(contrario)* negation; *(LING)* negative.

neghit'toso, a [negit'toso] *ag* slothful.

ne'gletto, a [ne'ʎʎetto] *ag (trascurato)* neglected.

'negli ['neʎʎi] *prep + det* vedi **in**.

negli'gente [negli'dʒente] *ag* negligent, careless; **negli'genza** *sf* negligence, carelessness.

negozi'ante [negot'tsjante] *sm/f* trader, dealer; *(bottegaio)* shopkeeper.

negozi'are [negot'tsjare] *vt* to negotiate // *vi:* ~ **in** to trade *o* deal in; **negozi'ato** *sm* negotiation.

ne'gozio [ne'gɔttsjo] *sm (locale)* shop; *(affare)* (piece of) business *q*.

'negro, a *ag, sm/f* Negro.

'nei, nei, neil', 'nella, 'nelle, 'nello *prep + det* vedi **in**.

'nembo *sm (METEOR)* nimbus.

ne'mico, a, ci, che *ag* hostile; *(MIL)* enemy *cpd* // *sm/f* enemy; **essere** ~ **di** to be strongly averse *o* opposed to.

nem'meno *av, cong* = **neanche**.

'nenia *sf* dirge; *(motivo monotono)* monotonous tune.

'neo *sm* mole; *(fig)* (slight) flaw.

'neo... *prefisso* neo...; **neo'litico, a, ci, che** *ag* neolithic.

'neon *sm (CHIM)* neon.

neo'nato, a *ag* newborn // *sm/f* newborn baby.

neozelan'dese [neoddzelan'dese] *ag* New Zealand *cpd* // *sm/f* New Zealander.

nep'pure *av, cong* = **neanche**.

'nerbo *sm* lash; *(fig)* strength, backbone; **nerbo'ruto, a** *ag* muscular; robust.

ne'retto *sm (TIP)* bold type.

'nero, a *ag* black; *(scuro)* dark // *sm* black.

nerva'tura *sf (ANAT)* nervous system; *(BOT)* venation; *(ARCHIT, TECN)* rib.

'nervo *sm (ANAT)* nerve; *(BOT)* vein; **avere i** ~**i** to be on edge; **dare sui** ~**i a qd** to get on sb's nerves; **ner'voso, a** *ag* nervous; *(irritabile)* irritable // *sm (fam):* **far venire il nervoso a qd** to get on sb's nerves.

'nespola *sf (BOT)* medlar; *(fig)* blow, punch; **'nespolo** *sm* medlar tree.

'nesso *sm* connection, link.

nes'suno, a *det (dav sm* **nessun** + *C, V,* **nessuno** + *s impura, gn, pn, ps, x, z; dav sf* **nessuna** + *C,* **nessun'** + *V) (non uno)* no, *espressione negativa* + any; *(qualche)* any // *pronome (non uno)* no one, nobody, *espressione negativa* + any(one); *(: cosa)* none, *espressione negativa* + any; *(qualcuno)* anyone, anybody; *(qualcosa)* anything; **non c'è nessun libro** there isn't any book, there is no book; **hai** ~ **a**

obiezione? do you have any objections?; ~ è venuto, non è venuto ~ nobody came; nessun altro no one else, nobody else; nessun'altra cosa nothing else; in nessun luogo nowhere.

net'tare vt to clean // sm ['nɛttare] nectar.

net'tezza [net'tettsa] sf cleanness, cleanliness; ~ urbana cleansing department.

'netto, a ag (pulito) clean; (chiaro) clear, clear-cut; (deciso) definite; (ECON) net.

nettur'bino sm dustman.

neurolo'gia [neurolo'dʒia] sf neurology.

neu'rosi sf = nevrosi.

neu'trale ag neutral; **neutralità** sf neutrality; **neutraliz'zare** vt to neutralize.

'neutro, a ag neutral; (LING) neuter // sm (LING) neuter.

ne'vaio sm snowfield.

'neve sf snow; **nevi'care** vb impers to snow; **nevi'cata** sf snowfall.

ne'vischio [ne'viskjo] sm sleet.

ne'voso, a ag snowy; snow-covered.

nevral'gia [nevral'dʒia] sf neuralgia.

ne'vrosi sf neurosis.

'nibbio sm (ZOOL) kite.

'nicchia ['nikkja] sf niche.

nicchi'are [nik'kjare] vi to shilly-shally, hesitate.

'nichel ['nikel] sm nickel.

nico'tina sf nicotine.

'nido sm nest; a ~ d'ape (tessuto etc) honeycomb cpd.

ni'ente pronome (nessuna cosa) nothing; (qualcosa) anything; non ... ~ nothing, espressione negativa + anything // sm nothing // av (in nessuna misura) non è ~ buono it's not good at all; una cosa da ~ a trivial thing; ~ affatto not at all, not in the least; nient'altro nothing else; nient'altro che nothing but; just, only; ~ di ~ absolutely nothing; per ~ (invano, gratuitamente) for nothing; non ... per ~ not ... at all.

niente'meno, niente'meno av actually, even // escl really!, I say!

'nimbo sm halo.

'ninfa sf nymph.

nin'fea sf water lily.

ninna-'nanna sf lullaby.

'ninnolo sm (balocco) plaything; (gingillo) knick-knack.

ni'pote sm/f (di zii) nephew/niece; (di nonni) grandson/daughter, grandchild.

'nitido, a ag clear; (specchio) bright.

ni'trato sm nitrate.

'nitrico, a, ci, che ag nitric.

ni'trire vi to neigh.

ni'trito sm (di cavallo) neighing q; neigh; (CHIM) nitrite.

nitroglice'rina [nitroglitʃe'rina] sf nitroglycerine.

'niveo, a ag snow-white.

no av (risposta) no; vieni o ~? are you coming or not?; perché ~? why not?

'nobile ag noble // sm/f noble, nobleman/woman; **nobil'iare** ag noble; **nobiltà** sf nobility; (di azione etc) nobleness.

'nocca, che sf (ANAT) knuckle.

nocci'ola [not'tʃola] sf hazelnut.

'nocciolo ['nɔttʃolo] sm (di frutto) stone; (fig) heart, core; [not'tʃolo] (albero) hazel.

'noce ['notʃe] sm (albero) walnut tree // sf (frutto) walnut; ~ moscata nutmeg.

no'civo, a [no'tʃivo] ag harmful, noxious.

'nodo sm (di cravatta, legname, NAUT) knot; (AUT, FERR) junction; (MED, ASTR, BOT) node; (fig: legame) bond, tie; (: punto centrale) heart, crux; avere un ~ alla gola to have a lump in one's throat; no'doso, a ag (tronco) gnarled.

'noi pronome (soggetto) we; (oggetto: per dare rilievo, con preposizione) us; ~ stessi(e) we ourselves; (oggetto) ourselves.

'noia sf boredom; (disturbo, impaccio) bother q, trouble q; avere qd/qc a ~ not to like sb/sth; mi è venuto a ~ I'm tired of it; dare ~ a to annoy; avere delle ~e con qd to have trouble with sb.

noi'altri pronome we.

noi'oso, a ag boring; annoying, troublesome.

noleggi'are [noled'dʒare] vt (prendere a noleggio) to hire; (dare a noleggio) to hire out; (aereo, nave) to charter; **no'leggio** sm hire; charter.

'nolo sm hire; charter; (per trasporto merci) freight; prendere/dare a ~ qc to hire/hire out sth.

'nomade ag nomadic // sm/f nomad.

'nome sm name; (LING) noun; in/a ~ di in the name of; di o per ~ (chiamato) called, named; conoscere qd di ~ to know sb by name; ~ d'arte stage name; ~ depositato trade name; ~ di famiglia surname.

no'mea sf notoriety.

no'mignolo [no'miɲɲolo] sm nickname.

'nomina sf appointment.

nomi'nale ag nominal; (LING) noun cpd.

nomi'nare vt to name; (eleggere) to appoint; (citare) to mention.

nomina'tivo, a ag (LING) nominative; (ECON) registered // sm (LING: anche: caso ~) nominative (case); (AMM) name.

non av not // prefisso non-; vedi affatto, appena etc.

nonché [non'ke] cong (tanto più, tanto meno) let alone; (e inoltre) as well as.

noncu'rante ag: ~ (di) careless (of), indifferent (to); **noncu'ranza** sf carelessness, indifference.

nondi'meno cong (tuttavia) however; (nonostante) nevertheless.

'nonno, a sm/f grandfather/ mother; (in senso più familiare) grandma/grandpa; ~i smpl grandparents.

non'nulla sm inv: un ~ nothing, a trifle.

'nono, a ag, sm ninth.

nonos'tante prep in spite of,

notwithstanding // *cong* although, even though.

nontiscordardimé *sm inv* (BOT) forget-me-not.

nord *sm* North // *ag inv* north; northern; **nor'dest** *sm* North-East; **'nordico, a, ci, che** *ag* nordic, northern European; **nor'dovest** *sm* North-West.

'norma *sf* (*criterio*) norm; (*regola*) regulation, rule; (*avvertenza*) instruction; **a ~ di legge** according to law, as laid down by law.

nor'male *ag* normal; (*che dà una norma: lettera*) standard *cpd*; **normalità** *sf* normality; **normaliz'zare** *vt* to normalize, bring back to normal.

normal'mente *av* normally.

norve'gese [norve'dʒese] *ag, sm/f, sm* Norwegian.

Nor'vegia [nor'vedʒa] *sf*: **la ~** Norway.

nostal'gia [nostal'dʒia] *sf* (*di casa, paese*) homesickness; (*del passato*) nostalgia; **nos'talgico, a, ci, che** *ag* homesick; nostalgic.

nos'trano, a *ag* local; national; home-produced.

'nostro, a *det*: **il(la) ~(a)** *etc* our // *pronome*: **il(la) ~(a)** *etc* ours; **i ~i** (*soldati etc*) our own people.

'nota *sf* (*segno*) mark; (*comunicazione scritta, MUS*) note; (*fattura*) bill; (*elenco*) list; **degno di ~** noteworthy, worthy of note; **~e caratteristiche** distinguishing marks o features.

no'tabile *ag* notable; (*persona*) important // *sm* prominent citizen

no'taio *sm* notary.

no'tare *vt* (*segnare: errori*) to mark; (*registrare*) to note (down), write down; (*rilevare, osservare*) to note, notice; **farsi ~** to get o.s. noticed.

notazi'one [notat'tsjone] *sf* marking; annotation; (MUS) notation.

no'tevole *ag* (*talento*) notable, remarkable; (*peso*) considerable.

no'tifica, che *sf* notification.

notifi'care *vt* (DIR): **~ qc a qd** to notify sb of sth, give sb notice of sth; **notifica-zi'one** *sf* notification.

no'tizia [no'tittsja] *sf* (*piece of*) news *sg*; (*informazione*) piece of information; **~e** *sfpl* news *sg*; information *sg*; **notizi'ario** *sm* (RADIO, TV, STAMPA) news *sg*.

'noto, a *ag* (well-)known.

notorietà *sf* fame; notoriety.

no'torio, a *ag* well-known; (*peg*) notorious.

not'tambulo *sm* night-bird.

not'tata *sf* night; **far ~** to sit up all night.

'notte *sf* night; **di ~** at night; (*durante la notte*) in the night, during the night; **peggio che andar di ~** worse than ever; **~ bianca** sleepless night; **notte'tempo** *av* at night; during the night.

not'turno, a *ag* nocturnal; (*servizio, guardiano*) night *cpd*.

no'vanta *num* ninety; **novan'tesimo, a** *num* ninetieth; **novan'tina** *sf*: **una novantina (di)** about ninety.

'nove *num* nine.

nove'cento [nove'tʃɛnto] *num* nine hundred // *sm*: **il N~** the twentieth century.

no'vella *sf* (LETTERATURA) short story.

novel'lino, a *ag* (*pivello*) green, inexperienced.

no'vello, a *ag* (*piante, patate*) new; (*animale*) young; (*sposo*) newly-married.

no'vembre *sm* November.

novi'lunio *sm* (ASTR) new moon.

novità *sf inv* novelty; (*innovazione*) innovation; (*cosa originale, insolita*) something new; (*notizia*) (piece of) news *sg*; **le ~ della moda** the latest fashions.

novizi'ato [novit'tsjato] *sm* (REL) novitiate; (*tirocinio*) apprenticeship.

no'vizio, a [no'vittsjo] *sm/f* (REL) novice; (*tirocinante*) beginner, apprentice.

nozi'one [not'tsjone] *sf* notion, idea; **~i** *sfpl* basic knowledge *sg*, rudiments.

'nozze ['nɔttse] *sfpl* wedding *sg*, marriage *sg*; **~ d'argento/d'oro** silver/golden wedding *sg*.

ns. *abbr commerciale di* **nostro.**

'nube *sf* cloud; **nubi'fragio** *sm* cloudburst.

'nubile *ag* (*donna*) unmarried, single.

'nuca *sf* nape of the neck.

nucle'are *ag* nuclear.

'nucleo *sm* nucleus; (*gruppo*) team, unit, group; (MIL) squad.

nu'dista, i, e *sm/f* nudist.

nudità *sf inv* nudity, nakedness; (*di paesaggio*) bareness // *sfpl* (*parti nude del corpo*) nakedness *sg*.

'nudo, a *ag* (*persona*) bare, naked, nude; (*membra*) bare, naked; (*montagna*) bare // *sm* (ARTE) nude.

'nulla *pronome, av* = **niente** // *sm*: **il ~** nothing.

nulla'osta *sm inv* authorization.

nullità *sf inv* nullity; (*persona*) nonentity.

'nullo, a *ag* useless, worthless; (DIR) null (and void); (SPORT): **incontro ~** draw.

nume'rale *ag, sm* numeral.

nume'rare *vt* to number; **numerazi'one** *sf* numbering; (*araba, decimale*) notation.

nu'merico, a, ci, che *ag* numerical.

'numero *sm* number; (*romano, arabo*) numeral; (*di spettacolo*) act, turn; **~ civico** house number; **nume'roso, a** *ag* numerous, many; (*con sostantivo sg: adunanza etc*) large.

'nunzio ['nuntsjo] *sm* (REL) nuncio.

nu'ocere ['nwɔtʃere] *vi*: **~ a** to harm, damage; **nuoci'uto, a** *pp di* **nuocere.**

nu'ora *sf* daughter-in-law.

nuo'tare *vi* to swim; (*galleggiare: oggetti*) to float; **nuota'tore, 'trice** *sm/f* swimmer; **nu'oto** *sm* swimming; **nuoto sul dorso** backstroke.

nu'ova *sf vedi* **nuovo.**

nuova'mente *av* again.

nu'ovo, a *ag* new // *sf* (*notizia*) (piece of) news *sg*; **di ~** again; **~ fiammante** *o* **di zecca** brand-new; **la N~a Zelanda** New Zealand.

nutri'ente ag nutritious, nourishing.

nutri'mento sm food, nourishment.

nu'trire vt to feed; (fig: sentimenti) to harbour, nurse; nutri'tivo, a ag nutritional; (alimento) nutritious; nutri-zi'one sf nutrition.

'nuvola sf cloud; 'nuvolo, a ag, nuvo-'loso, a ag cloudy.

nuzi'ale [nut'tsjale] ag nuptial; wedding cpd.

O

o cong (dav V spesso od) or; ~ ... ~ either ... or; ~ l'uno ~ l'altro either (of them).

O. (abbr di ovest) W.

'oasi sf inv oasis.

obbedi'ente etc vedi ubbidiente etc.

obbli'gare vt (costringere): ~ qd a fare to force o oblige sb to do; (DIR) to bind; ~rsi vr: ~rsi a fare to undertake to do; obbli'gato, a ag (costretto, grato) obliged; obbliga'torio, a ag compulsory, obligatory; obbligazi'one sf obligation; (COMM) bond, debenture; 'obbligo, ghi sm obligation; (dovere) duty; avere l'obbligo di fare, essere nell'obbligo di fare to be obliged to do.

ob'brobrio sm disgrace.

obesità sf obesity.

o'beso, a ag obese.

obiet'tare vt to object; ~ su qc to object to sth, raise objections concerning sth.

obiettività sf objectivity.

obiet'tivo, a ag objective; (imparziale) unbiased, impartial // sm (OTTICA, FOT) lens sg, objective; (MIL, fig) objective.

obiet'tore sm objector; ~ di coscienza conscientious objector.

obiezi'one [objet'tsjone] sf objection.

obi'torio sm morgue, mortuary.

o'bliquo, a ag oblique; (inclinato) slanting; (fig) devious, underhand; sguardo ~ sidelong glance.

oblite'rare vt to obliterate.

oblò sm inv porthole.

o'blungo, a, ghi, ghe ag oblong.

'oboe sm (MUS) oboe.

obsolescenza [obsole'ʃentsa] sf (ECON) obsolescence.

'oca, pl 'oche sf goose.

occasi'one sf (caso favorevole) opportunity; (causa, motivo, circostanza) occasion; (COMM) bargain; d'~ (a buon prezzo) bargain cpd; (usato) secondhand.

occhi'aia [ok'kjaja] sf eye socket; ~e sfpl shadows (under the eyes).

occhi'ali [ok'kjali] smpl glasses, spectacles; ~ da sole sunglasses.

occhi'ata [ok'kjata] sf look, glance; dare un'~ a to have a look at.

occhieggi'are [okkjed'dʒare] vt to eye, ogle // vi (apparire qua e là) to peep (out).

occhi'ello [ok'kjɛllo] sm buttonhole; (asola) eyelet.

'occhio ['ɔkkjo] sm eye; ~! careful!, watch out!; a ~ nudo with the naked eye; a quattr'~i privately, tête-à-tête; dare all'~ o nell'~ a qd to catch sb's eye; fare l'~ a qc to get used to sth; tenere d'~ qd to keep an eye on sb; vedere di buon/mal ~ qc to look favourably/unfavourably on sth.

occhio'lino [okkjo'lino] sm: fare l'~ a qd to wink at sb.

occiden'tale [ottʃiden'tale] ag western // sm/f Westerner.

occi'dente [ottʃi'dente] sm west; (POL): l'O~ the West.

oc'cipite [ot'tʃipite] sm back of the head, occiput.

oc'cludere vt to block; occlusi'one sf blockage, obstruction; oc'cluso, a pp di occludere.

occor'rente ag necessary // sm all that is necessary.

occor'renza [okkor'rentsa] sf necessity, need; all'~ in case of need.

oc'correre (?) vi to be needed, be required // vb impers: occorre farlo it must be done; occorre che tu parta you must leave, you'll have to leave; oc'corso, a pp di occorrere.

occul'tare vt to hide, conceal.

oc'culto, a ag hidden, concealed; (scienze, forze) occult.

occu'pare vt to occupy; (manodopera) to employ; (ingombrare) to occupy, take up; ~rsi vr to occupy o.s., keep o.s. busy; (impiegarsi) to get a job; ~rsi di (interessarsi) to take an interest in; (prendersi cura di) to look after, take care of; occu'pato, a ag (MIL, POL) occupied; (persona: affaccendato) busy; (posto, sedia) taken; (toilette, TEL) engaged; occupa'tore, 'trice sm/f occupier, occupa-zi'one sf occupation; (impiego, lavoro) job; (ECON) employment.

o'ceano [o'tʃeano] sm ocean.

'ocra sf ochre.

ocu'lare ag ocular, eye cpd.

ocu'lato, a ag (attento) cautious, prudent; (accorto) shrewd.

ocu'lista, i, e sm/f eye specialist, oculist.

'ode sf ode.

odi'are vt to hate, detest.

odi'erno, a ag today's, of today; (attuale) present.

'odio sm hatred; avere in ~ qc/qd to hate o detest sth/sb; odi'oso, a ag hateful, odious.

odo'rare vt (annusare) to smell; (profumare) to perfume, scent // vi: ~ (di) to smell (of); odo'rato sm sense of smell.

o'dore sm smell; gli ~i smpl (CUC) (aromatic) herbs; odo'roso, a ag sweet-smelling.

of'fendere vt to offend; (violare) to break, violate; (insultare) to insult; (ferire) to injure; ~rsi vr (con senso reciproco) to insult one another; ~rsi (di) to take offence (at), be offended (by); offen'sivo, a ag, sf offensive; offen'sore,

offendi'trice *sm/f* offender; (*MIL*) aggressor.

offe'rente *sm* (*in aste*): **al maggior ~** to the highest bidder.

of'ferto, a *pp di* **offrire** // *sf* offer; (*donazione, anche REL*) offering; (*in gara d'appalto*) tender; (*in aste*) bid; (*ECON*) supply.

of'feso, a *pp di* **offendere** // *ag* offended // *sm/f* offended party // *sf* insult, affront; (*MIL*) attack; (*DIR*) offence.

offi'cina [offi'tʃina] *sf* workshop.

of'frire *vt* to offer; **~rsi** *vr* (*proporsi*) to offer (o.s.), volunteer; (*occasione*) to present itself; (*esporsi*): **~rsi a** to expose o.s. to; **ti offro da bere** I'll buy you a drink.

offus'care *vt* to obscure, darken; (*fig: intelletto*) to dim, cloud; (: *fama*) to obscure, overshadow; **~rsi** *vr* to grow dark; to cloud, grow dim; to be obscured.

of'talmico, a, ci, che *ag* ophthalmic.

oggettività [oddʒettivi'ta] *sf* objectivity.

ogget'tivo, a [oddʒet'tivo] *ag* objective.

og'getto [od'dʒetto] *sm* object; (*materia, argomento*) subject (matter).

'oggi ['ɔddʒi] *av, sm* today; **~ a otto a** week today; **oggigi'orno** *av* nowadays.

o'giva [o'dʒiva] *sf* (*ARCHIT*) diagonal rib; (*MIL*) warhead; **arco a ~** lancet arch.

'ogni ['oɲɲi] *det* every, each; (*tutti*) all; **~ uomo è mortale** all men are mortal; (*con valore distributivo*) every; **viene ~ due giorni** he comes every two days; **~ cosa** everything; **in ~ luogo** everywhere; **~ tanto** every so often; **~ volta che** every time that.

Ognis'santi [oɲɲis'santi] *sm* All Saints' Day.

o'gnuno [oɲ'ɲuno] *pronome* everyone, everybody.

'ohi *escl* oh!; (*esprimente dolore*) ow!

ohimè *escl* oh dear!

O'landa *sf*: **l'~** Holland; **olan'dese** *ag* Dutch // *sm* (*LING*) Dutch // *sm/f* Dutchman/woman; **gli Olandesi** the Dutch.

oleo'dotto *sm* oil pipeline.

ole'oso, a *ag* oily; (*che contiene olio*) oil-yielding.

ol'fatto *sm* sense of smell.

oli'are *vt* to oil; **olia'tore** *sm* oil-can, oiler.

oli'era *sf* oil cruet.

olim'piadi *sfpl* Olympic games; **o'limpico, a, ci, che** *ag* Olympic.

'olio *sm* oil; **sott'~** (*CUC*) in oil; **~ d'oliva** olive oil; **~ di fegato di merluzzo** cod liver oil.

o'liva *sf* olive; **oli'vastro, a** *ag* olive(-coloured); (*carnagione*) sallow; **oli'veto** *sm* olive grove; **o'livo** *sm* olive tree.

'olmo *sm* elm.

oltraggi'are [oltrad'dʒare] *vt* to outrage; to offend gravely.

ol'traggio [ol'traddʒo] *sm* outrage; offence, insult; **~ alla magistratura** contempt of court; **oltraggi'oso, a** *ag* offensive.

ol'tralpe *av* beyond the Alps.

ol'tranza [ol'trantsa] *sf*: **a ~** to the last, to the bitter end.

'oltre *av* (*più in là*) further; (*di più: aspettare*) longer, more // *prep* (*di là da*) beyond, over, on the other side of; (*più di*) more than, over; (*in aggiunta a*) besides; (*eccetto*): **~ a** except, apart from; **oltre'mare** *av* overseas; **oltrepas'sare** *vt* to go beyond, exceed.

o'maggio [o'maddʒo] *sm* (*dono*) gift; (*segno di rispetto*) homage, tribute; **~i** *smpl* (*complimenti*) respects; **rendere ~ a** to pay homage o tribute to; **copia in ~** (*STAMPA*) complimentary copy.

ombeli'cale *ag* umbilical.

ombe'lico, chi *sm* navel.

'ombra *sf* (*zona non assolata, fantasma*) shade; (*sagoma scura*) shadow; **sedere all'~** to sit in the shade.

ombreggi'are [ombred'dʒare] *vt* to shade.

om'brello *sm* umbrella; **ombrel'lone** *sm* beach umbrella.

om'bretto *sm* eyeshadow.

om'broso, a *ag* shady, shaded; (*cavallo*) nervous, skittish; (*persona*) touchy, easily offended.

ome'lia *sf* (*REL*) homily, sermon.

omeopa'tia *sf* homoeopathy.

omertà *sf* conspiracy of silence.

o'messo, a *pp di* **omettere**.

o'mettere *vt* to omit, leave out; **~ di fare** to omit o fail to do.

omi'cida, i, e [omi'tʃida] *ag* homicidal, murderous // *sm/f* murderer/eress.

omi'cidio [omi'tʃidjo] *sm* murder; **~ colposo** culpable homicide.

omissi'one *sf* omission.

omogeneiz'zato [omodʒeneid'dzato] *sm* baby food.

omo'geneo, a [omo'dʒɛneo] *ag* homogeneous.

omolo'gare *vt* to approve, recognize; to ratify.

o'monimo, a *sm/f* namesake // *sm* (*LING*) homonym.

omosessu'ale *ag, sm/f* homosexual.

'oncia, ce ['ontʃa] *sf* ounce.

'onda *sf* wave; **mettere o mandare in ~** (*RADIO, TV*) to broadcast; **~e corte/medie/lunghe** short/medium/long wave; **on'data** *sf* wave, billow; (*fig*) wave, surge; **a ondate** in waves; **ondata di caldo** heatwave.

'onde *cong* (*affinché: con il congiuntivo*) so that, in order that; (: *con l'infinito*) so as to, in order to.

ondeggi'are [onded'dʒare] *vi* (*acqua*) to ripple; (*muoversi sulle onde: barca*) to rock, roll; (*fig: muoversi come le onde, barcollare*) to sway; (: *essere incerto*) to waver.

ondula'torio, a *ag* undulating; (*FISICA*) undulatory, wave *cpd*.

ondulazi'one [ondulat'tsjone] *sf* undulation; (*acconciatura*) wave; **~ permanente** permanent wave, perm.

'**onere** *sm* burden; ~**i fiscali** taxes; one-'**roso, a** *ag* (*fig*) heavy, onerous.

onestà *sf* honesty.

o'**nesto, a** *ag* (*probo, retto*) honest; (*giusto*) fair; (*casto*) chaste, virtuous.

'**onice** ['onitʃe] *sf* onyx.

onnipo'tente *ag* omnipotent.

onnisci'ente [onniʃ'ʃɛnte] *ag* omniscient.

onniveg'gente [onnived'dʒɛnte] *ag* all-seeing.

ono'**mastico, ci** *sm* name-day.

ono'**ranze** [ono'rantse] *sfpl* honours.

ono'**rare** *vt* to honour; (*far onore a*) to do credit to; ~**rsi** *vr*: ~**rsi di** to feel honoured at, be proud of.

ono'**rario, a** *ag* honorary // *sm* fee.

o'**nore** *sm* honour; **in ~ di** in honour of; **fare gli ~i di casa** to play host (*o* hostess); **fare ~ a** to honour; (*pranzo*) to do justice to; (*famiglia*) to be a credit to; **farsi ~** to distinguish o.s.; **ono'revole** *ag* honourable // *sm/f* (*POL*) Member of Parliament; **onorifi'cenza** *sf* honour; decoration; **ono'rifico, a, ci, che** *ag* honorary.

'**onta** *sf* shame, disgrace.

'**O.N.U.** ['ɔnu] *sf* (*abbr di Organizzazione delle Nazioni Unite*) UN, UNO.

o'**paco, a, chi, che** *ag* (*vetro*) opaque; (*metallo*) dull, matt.

o'**pale** *sm o f* opal.

'**opera** *sf* work; (*azione rilevante*) action, deed, work; (*MUS*) work; opus; (: *melodramma*) opera; (: *teatro*) opera house; (*ente*) institution, organization; ~ **d'arte** work of art; ~**e pubbliche** public works.

ope'**raio, a** *ag* working-class; workers' // *sm/f* worker; **classe** ~**a** working class.

ope'**rare** *vt* to carry out, make; (*MED*) to operate on // *vi* to operate, work; (*rimedio*) to act, work; (*MED*) to operate; ~**rsi** *vr* to occur, take place; **opera'tivo, a** *ag* operative, operating; **opera'tore, 'trice** *sm/f* operator; (*MED*) surgeon; (*TV, CINEMA*) cameraman; **operatore economico** agent, broker; **opera'torio, a** *ag* (*MED*) operating; **operazi'one** *sf* operation.

ope'**retta** *sf* (*MUS*) operetta, light opera.

ope'**roso, a** *ag* busy, active, hard-working.

opi'**ficio** [opi'fitʃo] *sm* factory, works *pl*.

opini'**one** *sf* opinion.

'**oppio** *sm* opium.

oppo'**nente** *ag* opposing // *sm/f* opponent.

op'**porre** *vt* to oppose; **opporsi** *vr*: **opporsi (a qc)** to oppose (sth); to object (to sth); ~ **resistenza/un rifiuto** to offer resistance/refuse.

opportu'**nista, i, e** *sm/f* opportunist.

opportu'**nità** *sf inv* opportunity; (*convenienza*) opportuneness, timeliness.

oppor'**tuno, a** *ag* timely, opportune.

opposi'**tore** *sm* opposer, opponent.

opposizi'**one** [oppozit'tsjone] *sf* opposition; (*DIR*) objection.

op'**posto, a** *pp di* **opporre** // *ag* opposite; (*opinioni*) conflicting // *sm* opposite, contrary; **all'**~ on the contrary.

oppressi'**one** *sf* oppression.

oppres'**sivo, a** *ag* oppressive.

op'**presso, a** *pp di* **opprimere**.

oppres'**sore** *sm* oppressor.

op'**primere** *vt* (*premere, gravare*) to weigh down; (*estenuare: sog: caldo*) to suffocate, oppress; (*tiranneggiare: popolo*) to oppress.

oppu'**gnare** [oppuɲ'ɲare] *vt* (*fig*) to refute.

op'**pure** *cong* or (else).

op'**tare** *vi*: ~ **per** to opt for.

opu'**lento, a** *ag* (*ricco*) rich, wealthy; (: *arredamento etc*) opulent.

o'**puscolo** *sm* booklet, pamphlet.

opzi'**one** [op'tsjone] *sf* option.

'**ora** *sf* (*60 minuti*) hour; (*momento*) time; **che ~ è?, che ~e sono?** what time is it?; **non veder l'~ di** fare to long to do, look forward to doing; **alla buon'**~**!** at last!; ~ **legale (estiva)** summer time; ~ **locale** local time; ~ **di punta** (*AUT*) rush hour // *av* (*adesso*) now; (*poco fa*): **è uscito proprio** ~ he's just gone out; (*tra poco*) presently, in a minute; (*correlativo*): ~ ... ~ **now ... now; d'**~ **in avanti** from now on; **or** ~ just now, a moment ago.

o'**racolo** *sm* oracle.

'**orafo** *sm* goldsmith.

o'**rale** *ag, sm* oral.

ora'**mai** *av* = **ormai**.

o'**rario, a** *ag* hourly; (*velocità*) per hour // *sm* timetable, schedule; (*di ufficio, visite etc*) hours *pl*, time(s *pl*).

ora'**tore, 'trice** *sm/f* speaker; orator.

ora'**torio, a** *ag* oratorical // *sm* (*REL*) oratory; (*MUS*) oratorio // *sf* (*arte*) oratory.

or'**bene** *cong* so, well (then).

'**orbita** *sf* (*ASTR, FISICA*) orbit; (*ANAT*) (eye-)socket.

or'**chestra** [or'kɛstra] *sf* orchestra; **orches'trale** *ag* orchestral // *sm/f* orchestra player; **orches'trare** *vt* to orchestrate; (*fig*) to mount, stage-manage.

orchi'**dea** [orki'dɛa] *sf* orchid.

'**orcio** ['ortʃo] *sm* jar.

'**orco, chi** *sm* ogre.

'**orda** *sf* horde.

or'**digno** [or'diɲɲo] *sm* (*esplosivo*) explosive device.

ordi'**nale** *ag, sm* ordinal.

ordina'**mento** *sm* order, arrangement; (*regolamento*) regulations *pl*, rules *pl*; ~ **scolastico/giuridico** education/legal system.

ordi'**nanza** [ordi'nantsa] *sf* (*DIR, MIL*) order; (*persona: MIL*) orderly, batman; **d'**~ (*MIL*) regulation *cpd*.

ordi'**nare** *vt* (*mettere in ordine*) to arrange, organize; (*COMM*) to order; (*prescrivere: medicina*) to prescribe; (*comandare*): ~ **a qd di fare qc** to order *o* command sb to do sth; (*REL*) to ordain.

ordi'**nario, a** *ag* (*comune*) ordinary;

everyday; standard; (*grossolano*) **coarse,** **common** // *sm* ordinary; (*INS: di università*) full professor.

ordina'tivo, a *ag* regulating, regulative.

ordi'nato, a *ag* tidy, orderly.

ordinazi'one [ordinat'tsjone] *sf* (*COMM*) order; (*REL*) ordination.

'ordine *sm* order; (*carattere*): **d'~** **pratico** of a practical nature; **all'~** (*COMM: assegno*) to order; **di prim'~** first-class; **fino a nuovo ~** until further notice; **mettere in ~** to put in order, tidy (up); **~ del giorno** (*di seduta*) agenda; (*MIL*) order of the day; **l'~ pubblico** law and order; **~i** (**sacri**) (*REL*) Holy orders.

or'dire *vt* (*fig*) to plot, scheme; **or'dito** *sm* (*fig*) plot.

orec'chino [orek'kino] *sm* earring.

o'recchio [o'rekkjo], *pl*(*f*) **o'recchie** *sm* (*ANAT*) ear.

orecchi'oni [orek'kjoni] *smpl* (*MED*) mumps *sg*.

o'refice [o'rɛfitʃe] *sm* goldsmith; jeweller; **orefice'ria** *sf* (*arte*) goldsmith's art; (*negozio*) jeweller's (shop).

'orfano, a *ag* orphan(ed) // *sm/f* orphan; **~ di padre/madre** fatherless/motherless; **orfano'trofio** *sm* orphanage.

orga'netto *sm* barrel organ; (*armonica a bocca*) mouth organ; (*fisarmonica*) accordion.

or'ganico, a, ci, che *ag* organic // *sm* personnel, staff.

organi'gramma, i *sm* organization chart.

orga'nismo *sm* (*BIOL*) organism; (*corpo umano*) body; (*AMM*) body, organism.

orga'nista, i, e *sm/f* organist.

organiz'zare [organid'dzare] *vt* to organize; **~rsi** *vr* to get organized; **organizza'tore, 'trice** *ag* organizing // *sm/f* organizer; **organizzazi'one** *sf* organization.

'organo *sm* organ; (*di congegno*) part; (*portavoce*) spokesman, mouthpiece.

or'gasmo *sm* (*FISIOL*) orgasm; (*fig*) agitation, anxiety.

'orgia, ge [ˈɔrdʒa] *sf* orgy.

or'goglio [orˈɡoʎʎo] *sm* pride; **orgogli'oso, a** *ag* proud.

orien'tale *ag* oriental; eastern; east.

orienta'mento *sm* positioning; orientation; direction; **senso di ~** sense of direction; **~ professionale** careers guidance.

orien'tare *vt* (*situare*) to position; (*fig*) to direct, orientate; **~rsi** *vr* to find one's bearings; (*fig: tendere*) to tend, lean; (: *indirizzarsi*): **~rsi verso** to take up, go in for.

ori'ente *sm* east; **l'O~** the East, the Orient.

o'rigano *sm* oregano.

origi'nale [oridʒi'nale] *ag* original; (*bizzarro*) eccentric // *sm* original; **originalità** *sf* originality; eccentricity.

origi'nare [oridʒi'nare] *vt* to bring about,

produce // *vi* (2): **~ da** to arise *o* spring from.

origi'nario, a [oridʒi'narjo] *ag* original; **essere ~ di** to be a native of; (*provenire da*) to originate from; to be native to.

o'rigine [o'ridʒine] *sf* origin; **all'~** originally; **d'~ inglese** of English origin; **dare ~ a** to give rise to.

origli'are [oriʎ'ʎare] *vi*: **~ (a)** to eavesdrop (on).

o'rina *sf* urine; **ori'nale** *sm* chamberpot.

ori'nare *vi* to urinate // *vt* to pass; **orina'toio** *sm* (*public*) urinal.

ori'undo, a *ag*: **~ (di)** native (of).

orizzon'tale [oriddzon'tale] *ag* horizontal.

oriz'zonte [orid'dzonte] *sm* horizon.

or'lare *vt* to hem; **orla'tura** *sf* hemming *q*; hem.

'orlo *sm* edge, border; (*di recipiente*) rim, brim; (*di vestito etc*) hem.

'orma *sf* (*di persona*) footprint; (*di animale*) track; (*impronta, traccia*) mark, trace.

or'mai *av* by now, by this time; (*adesso*) now; (*quasi*) almost, nearly.

ormeggi'are [ormed'dʒare] *vt* (*NAUT*) to moor; **or'meggio** *sm* (*atto*) mooring *q*; (*luogo*) moorings *pl*.

or'mone *sm* hormone.

ornamen'tale *ag* ornamental, decorative.

orna'mento *sm* ornament, decoration.

or'nare *vt* to adorn, decorate; **or'nato, a** *ag* ornate.

ornitolo'gia [ornitolo'dʒia] *sf* ornithology.

'oro *sm* gold; **d'~, in ~** gold *cpd*; **d'~** (*fig*) golden.

orologe'ria [orolodʒe'ria] *sf* watchmaking *q*; watchmaker's (shop); clockmaker's (shop); **bomba a ~** time bomb.

orologi'aio [orolo'dʒajo] *sm* watchmaker; clockmaker.

oro'logio [oro'lɔdʒo] *sm* clock; (*da tasca, da polso*) watch; **~ da polso** wristwatch; **~ a sveglia** alarm clock.

o'roscopo *sm* horoscope.

or'rendo, a *ag* (*spaventoso*) horrible, awful; (*bruttissimo*) hideous.

or'ribile *ag* horrible.

'orrido, a *ag* fearful, horrid.

orripi'lante *ag* hair-raising, horrifying.

or'rore *sm* horror; **avere in ~ qd/qc** to loathe *o* detest sb/sth.

orsacchi'otto [orsak'kjɔtto] *sm* teddy bear.

'orso *sm* bear; **~ bruno/bianco** brown/polar bear.

or'taggio [or'taddʒo] *sm* vegetable.

or'tica, che *sf* (*stinging*) nettle.

orti'caria *sf* nettle rash.

orticol'tura *sf* horticulture.

'orto *sm* vegetable garden, kitchen garden; **~ industriale** market garden.

orto'dosso, a *ag* orthodox.

ortogra'fia *sf* spelling.

orto'lano, a *sm/f* (*venditore*) greengrocer.

ortope'dia *sf* orthopaedics *sg*; **orto-**

'pedico, a, ci, che ag orthopaedic // sm orthopaedic specialist.

orzai'olo [ordza'jɔlo] sm (MED) stye.

or'zata [or'dzata] sf barley water.

'orzo ['ɔrdzo] sm barley.

o'sare vt, vi to dare; ~ fare to dare (to) do.

oscenità [oʃeni'ta] sf inv obscenity.

o'sceno, a [oʃɛno] ag obscene; (ripugnante) ghastly.

oscil'lare [oʃil'lare] vi (pendolo) to swing; (dondolare: al vento etc) to rock; (variare) to fluctuate; (TECN) to oscillate; (fig): ~ fra to waver o hesitate between; oscilla-zi'one sf oscillation; (di prezzi, temperatura) fluctuation.

oscura'mento sm darkening; obscuring; (in tempo di guerra) blackout.

oscu'rare vt to darken, obscure; (fig) to obscure; ~rsi vr to grow dark.

os'curo, a ag dark; (fig) obscure; humble, lowly // sm: all'~ in the dark; tenere qd all'~ di qc to keep sb in the dark about sth.

ospe'dale sm hospital.

ospi'tale ag hospitable; ospitalità sf hospitality.

ospi'tare vt to give hospitality to; (sog: albergo) to accommodate.

'ospite sm/f (persona che ospita) host/hostess; (persona ospitata) guest.

os'pizio [os'pittsjo] sm (per vecchi etc) home.

'ossa sfpl vedi osso.

ossa'tura sf (ANAT) skeletal structure, frame; (TECN, fig) framework.

'osseo, a ag bony; (tessuto etc) bone cpd.

osse'quente ag respectful, deferential; ~ alla legge law-abiding.

os'sequio sm deference, respect; ~i smpl (saluto) respects, regards; ossequi'oso, a ag obsequious.

osser'vanza [osser'vantsa] sf observance.

osser'vare vt to observe, watch; (esaminare) to examine; (notare, rilevare) to notice, observe; (DIR: la legge) to observe, respect; (mantenere: silenzio) to keep, observe; far ~ qc a qd to point sth out to sb; osserva'tore, 'trice ag observant, perceptive // sm/f observer; osserva'torio sm (ASTR) observatory; (MIL) observation post; osservazi'one sf observation; (di legge etc) observance; (considerazione critica) observation, remark; (rimprovero) reproof; in osservazione under observation.

ossessio'nare vt to obsess, haunt; (tormentare) to torment, harass.

ossessi'one sf obsession.

os'sesso, a ag (spiritato) possessed.

os'sia cong that is, to be precise.

ossi'dare vt, ~rsi vr to oxidize.

'ossido sm oxide; ~ di carbonio carbon monoxide.

ossige'nare [ossidʒe'nare] vt to oxygenate; (decolorare) to bleach.

os'sigeno sm oxygen.

'osso sm (pl(f) ossa nel senso ANAT) bone; d'~ (bottone etc) of bone, bone cpd.

osso'buco, pl ossi'buchi sm (CUC) marrowbone; (: piatto) stew made with knuckle of veal in tomato sauce.

os'suto, a ag bony.

ostaco'lare vt to block, obstruct.

os'tacolo sm obstacle; (EQUITAZIONE) hurdle, jump.

os'taggio [os'taddʒo] sm hostage.

'oste, os'tessa sm/f innkeeper.

osteggi'are [osted'dʒare] vt to oppose, be opposed to.

os'tello sm: ~ della gioventù youth hostel.

osten'sorio sm (REL) monstrance.

osten'tare vt to make a show of, flaunt; ostentazi'one sf ostentation, show.

oste'ria sf inn.

os'tessa sf vedi oste.

os'tetrico, a, ci, che ag obstetric // sm obstetrician // sf midwife.

'ostia sf (REL) host; (per medicinali) wafer.

'ostico, a, ci, che ag (fig) harsh, hard, difficult; unpleasant.

os'tile ag hostile; ostilità sf inv hostility // sfpl (MIL) hostilities.

osti'narsi vr to insist, dig one's heels in; ~ a fare to persist (obstinately) in doing; osti'nato, a ag (caparbio) obstinate; (tenace) persistent, determined; ostina-zi'one sf obstinacy; persistence.

ostra'cismo [ostra'tʃizmo] sm ostracism.

'ostrica, che sf oyster.

ostru'ire vt to obstruct, block; ostru-zi'one sf obstruction, blockage.

'otre sm (recipiente) goatskin.

ottago'nale ag octagonal.

ot'tagono sm octagon.

ot'tanta num eighty; ottan'tesimo, a num eightieth; ottan'tina sf: una ottantina (di) about eighty.

ot'tavo, a num eighth // sf octave.

ottempe'rare vi: ~ a to comply with, obey.

ottene'brare vt to darken; (fig) to cloud.

otte'nere vt to obtain, get; (risultato) to achieve, obtain.

'ottico, a, ci, che ag (della vista: nervo) optic; (dell'ottica) optical // sm optician // sf (scienza) optics sg; (FOT: lenti, prismi etc) optics pl.

ottima'mente av excellently, very well.

otti'mismo sm optimism; otti'mista, i, a sm/f optimist.

'ottimo, a ag excellent, very good.

'otto num eight.

ot'tobre sm October.

otto'cento [otto'tʃɛnto] num eight hundred // sm: l'O~ the nineteenth century.

ot'tone sm brass; gli ~i (MUS) the brass.

ottuage'nario, a [ottuadʒe'narjo] ag, sm/f octogenarian.

ot'tundere vt (fig) to dull.

ottu'rare vt to close (up); (dente) to fill; ottura'tore sm (FOT) shutter; (nelle armi) breechblock; **otturazi'one** *sf* closing (up); *(dentaria)* filling.

ot'tuso, a *pp di* **ottundere** // *ag (smussato)* blunt, dull; *(MAT, fig)* obtuse; *(suono)* dull.

o'vaia *sf,* **o'vaio** *sm (ANAT)* ovary.

o'vale *ag, sm* oval.

o'vatta *sf* cotton wool; *(per imbottire)* padding, wadding.

ovazi'one [ovat'tsjone] *sf* ovation.

'ovest *sm* west.

o'vile *sm* pen, enclosure.

o'vino, a *ag* sheep *cpd,* ovine.

ovulazi'one [ovulat'tsjone] *sf* ovulation.

'ovulo *sm (FISIOL)* ovum.

ov'vero *cong (ossia)* that is, to be precise; *(oppure)* or (else).

ovvi'are *vi:* ~ **a** to obviate.

'ovvio, a *ag* obvious.

ozi'are [ot'tsjare] *vi* to laze, idle.

'ozio ['ɔttsjo] *sm* idleness; *(tempo libero)* leisure; **ore d'** ~ leisure time; **stare in** ~ to be idle; **ozi'oso, a** *ag* idle.

o'zono [o'dzɔno] *sm* ozone.

P

pa'cato, a *ag* quiet, calm.

pac'chetto [pak'ketto] *sm* packet.

'pacco, chi *sm* parcel; *(involto)* bundle.

'pace ['patʃe] *sf* peace; **darsi** ~ to resign o.s.

pacifi'care [patʃifi'kare] *vt (riconciliare)* to reconcile, make peace between; *(mettere in pace)* to pacify.

pa'cifico, a, ci, che [pa'tʃifiko] *ag (persona)* peaceable; *(vita)* peaceful; *(fig: indiscusso)* indisputable; *(: ovvio)* obvious, clear // *sm:* **il P~, l'Oceano P~** the Pacific (Ocean).

paci'fista, i, e [patʃi'fista] *sm/f* pacifist.

pa'della *sf* frying pan; *(per infermi)* bedpan.

padigli'one [padiʎ'ʎone] *sm* pavilion; *(AUT)* roof.

'Padova *sf* Padua.

'padre *sm* father; ~**i** *smpl (antenati)* forefathers; **pa'drino** *sm* godfather.

padro'nanza [padro'nantsa] *sf* command, mastery.

pa'drone, a *sm/f* master/mistress; *(proprietario)* owner; *(datore di lavoro)* employer; **essere** ~ **di sé** to be in control of o.s.; ~ **di casa** master/mistress of the house; *(per gli inquilini)* landlord/lady; **padroneggi'are** *vt* to rule, command; *(fig: sentimenti)* to master, control; *(: materia)* to master, know thoroughly.

pae'saggio [pae'zaddʒo] *sm* landscape.

pae'sano, a *ag* country *cpd* // *sm/f* villager; countryman.

pa'ese *sm* country; land; region; village; **i P~i Bassi** the Netherlands.

paf'futo, a *ag* chubby, plump.

'paga, ghe *sf* pay, wages *pl.*

paga'mento *sm* payment.

pa'gano, a *ag, sm/f* pagan.

pa'gare *vt* to pay; *(acquisto, fig: colpa)* to pay for; *(contraccambiare)* to repay, pay back // *vi* to pay; **quanto l'hai pagato?** how much did you pay for it?; ~ **un assegno a qd** *(sog: banca)* to cash sb a cheque.

pa'gella [pa'dʒɛlla] *sf (INS)* report card.

'paggio ['paddʒo] *sm* page(boy).

paghe'rò [page'rɔ] *sm* , *inv* acknowledgement of a debt, IOU.

'pagina ['padʒina] *sf* page.

'paglia ['paʎʎa] *sf* straw.

pagliac'cetto [paʎʎat'tʃetto] *sm (per bambini)* rompers *pl.*

pagli'accio [paʎ'ʎattʃo] *sm* clown.

pagli'etta [paʎ'ʎetta] *sf (cappello per uomo)* (straw) boater; *(per tegami etc)* steel wool.

pagli'uzza [paʎ'ʎuttsa] *sf* (blade of) straw; *(d'oro etc)* tiny particle, speck.

pa'gnotta [paɲ'ɲɔtta] *sf* round loaf.

pa'goda *sf* pagoda.

'paio, *pl(f)* **'paia** *sm* pair; **un** ~ **di** *(alcuni)* a couple of.

pai'olo, paiu'olo *sm* (copper) pot.

'pala *sf* shovel; *(di remo, ventilatore, elica)* blade; *(di ruota)* paddle.

pa'lato *sm* palate.

pa'lazzo [pa'lattso] *sm (reggia)* palace; *(edificio)* building; ~ **di giustizia** courthouse; ~ **dello sport** sports stadium.

pal'chetto [pal'ketto] *sm* shelf.

'palco, chi *sm (TEATRO)* box; *(tavolato)* platform, stand; *(ripiano)* layer.

palco'scenico, ci [palkoʃ'ʃeniko] *sm (TEATRO)* stage.

pale'sare *vt* to reveal, disclose; ~**rsi** *vr* to reveal *o* show o.s.

pa'lese *ag* clear, evident.

Pales'tina *sf:* **la** ~ Palestine.

pa'lestra *sf* gymnasium; *(esercizio atletico)* exercise, training; *(fig)* training ground, school.

pa'letta *sf* spade; *(per il focolare)* shovel; *(del capostazione)* signalling disc.

pa'letto *sm* stake, peg; *(spranga)* bolt.

'palio *sm (gara):* **il P**~ horserace run at Siena; **mettere qc in** ~ to offer sth as a prize.

paliz'zata [palit'tsata] *sf* palisade.

'palla *sf* ball; *(pallottola)* bullet; ~ **canestro** *sm* basketball; ~ **nuoto** *sm* water polo; ~ **volo** *sm* volleyball.

pallia'tivo *sm* palliative; *(fig)* stopgap measure.

'pallido, a *ag* pale.

pal'lina *sf (bilia)* marble.

pallon'cino [pallon'tʃino] *sm* balloon; *(lampioncino)* chinese lantern.

pal'lone *sm (palla)* ball; *(CALCIO)* football; *(aerostato)* balloon; **gioco del** ~ football.

pal'lore *sm* pallor, paleness.

pal'lottola *sf* pellet; (*proiettile*) bullet.
'palma *sf* (ANAT) = palmo; (BOT, *simbolo*) palm; ~ da datteri date palm.
'palmo *sm* (ANAT) palm; restare con un ~ di naso to be badly disappointed.
'palo *sm* (*legno appuntito*) stake; (*sostegno*) pole; fare da o li ~ (*fig*) to act as look-out.
palom'baro *sm* diver.
pa'lombo *sm* (*pesce*) dogfish.
pal'pare *vt* to feel, finger.
'palpebra *sf* eyelid.
palpi'tare *vi* (*cuore, polso*) to beat; (: *più forte*) to pound, throb; (*fremere*) to quiver; palpitazi'one *sf* palpitation; 'palpito *sm* (*del cuore*) beat; (*fig: d'amore etc*) throb.
paltò *sm inv* overcoat.
pa'lude *sf* marsh, swamp; palu'doso, a *ag* marshy, swampy.
pa'lustre *ag* marsh *cpd*, swamp *cpd*.
'pampino *sm* vine leaf.
pana'cea [pana'tʃɛa] *sf* panacea.
'panca, che *sf* bench.
pan'cetta [pan'tʃetta] *sf* (CUC) bacon.
pan'chetto [pan'ketto] *sm* stool; footstool.
pan'china [pan'kina] *sf* garden seat; (*di giardino pubblico*) (park) bench.
'pancia, ce ['pantʃa] *sf* belly, stomach; mettere o fare ~ to be getting a paunch; avere mal di ~ to have stomach ache o a sore stomach.
panci'otto [pan'tʃɔtto] *sm* waistcoat.
pan'cone *sm* workbench.
'pancreas *sm* pancreas.
'panda *sm inv* panda.
pande'monio *sm* pandemonium.
'pane *sm* bread; (*pagnotta*) loaf (of bread); (*forma*): un ~ di burro/cera *etc* a pat of butter/bar of wax *etc*; ~ integrale wholemeal bread; ~ tostato toast.
panette'ria *sf* (*forno*) bakery; (*negozio*) baker's (shop), bakery.
panetti'ere, a *sm/f* baker.
panet'tone *sm* a kind of spiced brioche with sultanas, eaten at Christmas.
pangrat'tato *sm* breadcrumbs *pl*.
'panico, a, ci, che *ag, sm* panic.
pani'ere *sm* basket.
pani'ficio [pani'fitʃo] *sm* (*forno*) bakery; (*negozio*) baker's (shop), bakery.
pa'nino *sm* roll; ~ imbottito filled roll; sandwich.
'panna *sf* (CUC) cream; (TECN) breakdown; essere in ~ to have broken down; ~ montata whipped cream.
pan'nello *sm* panel.
'panno *sm* cloth; ~i *smpl* (*abiti*) clothes.
pan'nocchia [pan'nɔkkja] *sf* (*di mais etc*) ear.
panno'lino *sm* (*per bambini*) nappy.
pano'rama, i *sm* panorama; pano-'ramico, a, ci, che *ag* panoramic.
panta'loni *smpl* trousers *pl*, pair of trousers.
pan'tano *sm* bog.
pan'tera *sf* panther.
pan'tofola *sf* slipper.

panto'mima *sf* pantomime.
pan'zana [pan'tsana] *sf* fib, tall story.
pao'nazzo, a [pao'nattso] *ag* purple.
'papa, i *sm* pope.
papà *sm inv* dad(dy).
pa'pale *ag* papal.
pa'pato *sm* papacy.
pa'pavero *sm* poppy.
'papero, a *sm/f* (ZOOL) gosling // *sf* (*fig*) slip of the tongue, blunder.
'papiro *sm* papyrus.
'pappa *sf* baby's cereal.
pappa'gallo *sm* parrot; (*fig: uomo*) Romeo, wolf.
pappa'gorgia, ge [pappa'gɔrdʒa] *sf* double chin.
'para *sf*: suole di ~ crepe soles.
pa'rabola *sf* (MAT) parabola; (REL) parable.
para'brezza [para'breddza] *sm inv* (AUT) windscreen.
paraca'dute *sm inv* parachute; paracadu'tista, i, e *sm/f* parachutist.
para'carro *sm* kerbstone.
para'diso *sm* paradise.
parados'sale *ag* paradoxical.
para'dosso *sm* paradox.
para'fango, ghi *sm* mudguard.
paraf'fina *sf* paraffin, paraffin wax.
parafra'sare *vt* to paraphrase.
para'fulmine *sm* lightning conductor.
pa'raggi [pa'raddʒi] *smpl*: nel ~ in the vicinity, in the neighbourhood.
parago'nare *vt*: ~ con/a to compare with/to.
para'gone *sm* comparison; (*esempio analogo*) analogy, parallel; reggere al ~ to stand comparison.
pa'ragrafo *sm* paragraph.
pa'ralisi *sf* paralysis; para'litico, a, ci, che *ag, sm/f* paralytic.
paraliz'zare [paralid'dzare] *vt* to paralyze.
paral'lelo, a *ag* parallel // *sm* (GEO) parallel; (*comparazione*): fare un ~ tra to draw a parallel between // *sf* parallel (line); ~e *sfpl* (*attrezzo ginnico*) parallel bars.
para'lume *sm* lampshade.
pa'rametro *sm* parameter.
para'noia *sf* paranoia; para'noico, a, ci, che *ag, sm/f* paranoiac.
para'occhi [para'ɔkki] *smpl* blinkers.
para'petto *sm* parapet.
para'piglia [para'piʎʎa] *sm* commotion, uproar.
pa'rare *vt* (*addobbare*) to adorn, deck; (*proteggere*) to shield, protect; (*scansare: colpo*) to parry; (CALCIO) to save // *vi*: dove vuole andare a ~? what are you driving at?; ~rsi *vr* (*presentarsi*) to appear, present o.s.
para'sole *sm inv* parasol, sunshade.
paras'sita, i *sm* parasite.
pa'rata *sf* (SPORT) save; (MIL) review, parade.
para'tia *sf* (*di nave*) bulkhead.

para'urti *sm inv* (*AUT*) bumper.

para'vento *sm* folding screen.

par'cella [par'tʃɛlla] *sf* account, fee (*of lawyer etc*).

parcheggi'are [parked'dʒare] *vt* to park; **par'cheggio** *sm* parking *q*; (*luogo*) car park.

par'chimetro [par'kimetro] *sm* parking meter.

'parco, chi *sm* park; (*spazio per deposito*) depot; (*complesso di veicoli*) fleet.

'parco, a, chi, che *ag*: ~ **(in)** (*sobrio*) moderate (in); (*avaro*) sparing (with).

pa'recchio, a [pa'rekkjo] *det* quite a lot of; (*tempo*) quite a lot of, a long; ~**i(e)** *det pl* quite a lot of, several // *pronome* quite a lot, quite a bit; (*tempo*) quite a while, a long time; ~**i(e)** *pronome pl* quite a lot, several // *av* (*con ag*) quite, rather; (*con vb*) quite a lot, quite a bit.

pareggi'are [pared'dʒare] *vt* to make equal; (*terreno*) to level, make level; (*bilancio, conti*) to balance // *vi* (*SPORT*) to draw; **par'reggio** *sm* (*ECON*) balance; (*SPORT*) draw.

paren'tado *sm* relatives *pl*, relations *pl*.

pa'rente *sm/f* relative, relation.

paren'tela *sf* (*vincolo di sangue*, *fig*) relationship; (*insieme dei parenti*) relations *pl*, relatives *pl*.

pa'rentesi *sf* (*segno grafico*) bracket, parenthesis; (*frase incisa*) parenthesis; (*digressione*) parenthesis, digression.

pa'rere *sm* (*opinione*) opinion; (*consiglio*) advice, opinion; **a mio** ~ in my opinion // (2) *vi* to seem, appear // *vb impers*: **pare che** it seems *o* appears that; they say that; **mi pare che** it seems to me that; **fai come ti pare** do as you like; **che ti pare del mio libro?** what do you think of my book?

pa'rete *sf* wall.

'pari *ag inv* (*uguale*) equal, same; (*in giochi*) equal; drawn, tied; (*fig: adeguato*): ~ **a** equal to; (*MAT*) even // *sm* (*POL: di Gran Bretagna*) peer // *sm/f* peer, equal; **alla** ~ on the same level; **ragazza alla** ~ **au pair** girl; **mettersi alla** ~ **con** to place o.s. on the same level as; **mettersi in** ~ **con** to catch up with; **andare di** ~ **passo con qd** to keep pace with sb.

Pa'rigi [pa'ridʒi] *sf* Paris.

pa'riglia [pa'riʎʎa] *sf* pair; **rendere la** ~ to give tit for tat.

parità *sf* parity, equality; (*SPORT*) draw, tie.

parlamen'tare *ag* parliamentary // *sm/f* member of parliament // *vi* to negotiate, parley.

parla'mento *sm* parliament.

parlan'tina *sf* (*fam*) talkativeness; **avere una buona** ~ to have the gift of the gab.

par'lare *vi* to speak, talk; (*confidare cose segrete*) to talk // *vt* to speak; ~ **(a qd) di** to speak *o* talk (to sb) about; **parla'tore, 'trice** *sm/f* speaker; **parla'torio** *sm* (*di carcere etc*) visiting room; (*REL*) parlour.

parmigi'ano [parmi'dʒano] *sm* (*grana*) Parmesan (cheese).

paro'dia *sf* parody.

pa'rola *sf* word; (*facoltà*) speech; ~**e** *sfpl* (*chiacchiere*) talk *sg*; **chiedere la** ~ to ask permission to speak; ~ **d'onore** word of honour; ~ **d'ordine** (*MIL*) password; ~**e incrociate** crossword (puzzle) *sg*; **paro'laccia, ce** *sf* bad word, swearword.

par'rocchia [par'rɔkkja] *sf* parish; parish church.

'parroco, ci *sm* parish priest.

par'rucca, che *sf* wig.

parrucchi'ere, a [parruk'kjɛre] *sm/f* hairdresser // *sm* barber.

parsi'monia *sf* frugality, thrift.

'parso, a *pp di* **parere**.

'parte *sf* part; (*lato*) side; (*quota spettante a ciascuno*) share; (*direzione*) direction; (*POL*) party; faction; (*DIR*) party; **a** ~ *ag* separate // *av* separately; **scherzi a** ~ joking aside; **a** ~ **ciò** apart from that; **da** ~ (*in disparte*) to one side, aside; **d'altra** ~ on the other hand; **da** ~ **di** (*per conto di*) on behalf of; **da** ~ **mia** as far as I'm concerned, as for me; **da** ~ **a** ~ right through; **da ogni** ~ on all sides, everywhere; (*moto da luogo*) from all sides; **prendere** ~ **a qc** to take part in sth; **mettere qd a** ~ **di qc** to inform sb of sth.

parteci'pare [partetʃi'pare] *vi*: ~ **a** to take part in, participate in; (*utili etc*) to share in; (*spese etc*) to contribute to; (*dolore, successo di qd*) to share (in); **partecipazi'one** *sf* participation; sharing; (*ECON*) interest; **partecipazione agli utili** profit-sharing; **par'tecipe** *ag* participating; **essere partecipe di** to take part in, participate in; to share (in); (*consapevole*) to be aware of.

parteggi'are [parted'dʒare] *vi*: ~ **per** to side with, be on the side of.

par'tenza [par'tɛntsa] *sf* departure; (*SPORT*) start; **essere in** ~ to be about to leave, be leaving.

parti'cella [parti'tʃɛlla] *sf* particle.

parti'cipio [parti'tʃipjo] *sm* participle.

partico'lare *ag* (*specifico*) particular; (*proprio*) personal, private; (*speciale*) special, particular; (*caratteristico*) distinctive, characteristic; (*fuori dal comune*) peculiar // *sm* detail, particular; **in** ~ in particular, particularly; **particolareggi'are** *vt* to give full details of, detail; **particolarità** *sf inv* particularity; detail; characteristic, feature.

partigi'ano, a [parti'dʒano] *ag* partisan // *sm* (*fautore*) supporter, champion; (*MIL*) partisan.

par'tire *vi* (2) to go, leave; (*allontanarsi*) to go (*o* drive *etc*) away *o* off; (*petardo, colpo*) to go off; (*fig: avere inizio, SPORT*) to start; **sono partita da Roma alle 7** I left Rome at 7; **il volo parte da Ciampino** the flight leaves from Ciampino; **a** ~ **da** from.

par'tita *sf* (*COMM*) lot, consignment; (*ECON: registrazione*) entry, item; (*CARTE, SPORT:*

gioco) game; (: *competizione*) match, game; ~ **di caccia** hunting party.

par'tito *sm* (POL) party; (*decisione*) decision, resolution; (*persona da maritare*) match.

'parto *sm* (MED) delivery, (child)birth; labour; **parto'rire** *vt* to give birth to; (*fig*) to produce.

parzi'ale [par'tsjale] *ag* (*limitato*) partial; (*non obiettivo*) biased, partial.

'pascere ['paʃʃere] *vi* to graze // *vt* (*brucare*) to graze on; (*far pascolare*) to graze, pasture; (*nutrire: persone, animali*) to feed, nourish; **pasci'uto, a** *pp di* **pascere**.

pasco'lare *vt, vi* to graze.

'pascolo *sm* pasture.

'Pasqua *sf* Easter; **pas'quale** *ag* Easter *cpd*.

pas'sabile *ag* fairly good, passable.

pas'saggio [pas'saddʒo] *sm* passing *q*, passage; (*traversata*) crossing *q*, passage; (*luogo, prezzo della traversata, brano di libro etc*) passage; (*su veicolo altrui*) lift; (SPORT) pass; **di** ~ (*persona*) passing through; ~ **pedonale/a livello** pedestrian/level crossing.

pas'sante *sm/f* passer-by // *sm* loop.

passa'porto *sm* passport.

pas'sare *vi* (2) (*andare*) to go; (*veicolo, pedone*) to pass (by), go by; (*fare una breve sosta: postino etc*) to come, call; (: *amico: per fare una visita*) to call *o* drop in; (*sole, aria, luce*) to get through; (*trascorrere: giorni, tempo*) to pass, go by; (*fig: proposta di legge*) to be passed; (: *dolore*) to pass, go away; (: *essere trasferito*): ~ **di ... in** to pass from ... to; (CARTE) to pass // *vt* (*attraversare*) to cross; (*trasmettere: messaggio*): ~ **qc a qd** to pass sth on to sb; (*dare*): ~ **qc a qd** to pass sth *o* sb, give sb sth; (*trascorrere: tempo*) to spend; (*superare: esame*) to pass; (*triturare: verdura*) to strain; (*approvare*) to pass, approve; (*oltrepassare, sorpassare: anche fig*) to go beyond, pass; (*fig: subire*) to go through; ~ **per** (*anche fig*) to go through; ~ **per stupido/un genio** to be taken for a fool/a genius; ~ **sopra** (*anche fig*) to pass over; ~ **attraverso** (*anche fig*) to go through; ~ **alla storia** to pass into history; ~ **a un esame** to go up (to the next class) after an exam; ~ **inosservato** to go unnoticed; ~ **di moda** to go out of fashion; **le passo il Signor X** (*al telefono*) here is Mr X; **I'm putting you through to Mr X; lasciar** ~ **qd/qc** to let sb/sth through; **passarsela: come te la passi?** how are you getting on *o* along?

pas'sata *sf*: **dare una** ~ **di vernice a qc** to give sth a coat of paint; **dare una** ~ **al giornale** to have a look at the paper, skim through the paper.

passa'tempo *sm* pastime, hobby.

pas'sato, a *ag* past; (*sfiorito*) faded // *sm* past; (LING) past (tense); ~ **prossimo** (LING) present perfect; ~ **remoto** (LING)

past historic; ~ **di verdura** (CUC) vegetable purée.

passaver'dura *sm inv* vegetable mill.

passeg'gero, a [passed'dʒero] *ag* passing // *sm/f* passenger.

passeggi'are [passed'dʒare] *vi* to go for a walk; (*in veicolo*) to go for a drive; **passeggi'ata** *sf* walk; drive; (*luogo*) promenade; **fare una passeggiata** to go for a walk (*o* drive); **passeg'gino** *sm* pushchair; **pas'seggio** *sm* walk, stroll; (*luogo*) promenade.

passe'rella *sf* footbridge; (*di nave, aereo*) gangway; (*pedana*) catwalk.

'passero *sm* sparrow.

pas'sibile *ag*: ~ **di** liable to.

passi'one *sf* passion.

pas'sivo, a *ag* passive // *sm* (LING) passive; (ECON) debit; (: *complesso dei debiti*) liabilities *pl*.

'passo *sm* step; (*andatura*) pace; (*rumore*) (foot)step; (*orma*) footprint; (*passaggio, fig: brano*) passage; (*valico*) pass; **a** ~ **d'uomo** at walking pace; ~ **(a)** ~ **step by step; fare due** *o* **quattro** ~**i** to go for a walk *o* a stroll; **'**~ **carraio'** 'vehicle entrance — keep clear'.

'pasta *sf* (CUC) dough; (: *impasto per dolce*) pastry; (: *anche*: ~ **alimentare**) pasta; (*massa molle di materia*) paste; (*fig: indole*) nature; ~**e** *sfpl* (*pasticcini*) pastries; ~ **di legno** wood pulp.

pastasci'utta [pastaʃ'ʃutta] *sf* pasta.

pas'tella *sf* batter.

pas'tello *sm* pastel.

pas'tetta *sf* (CUC) = **pastella**.

pas'ticca, che *sf* = **pastiglia**.

pasticce'ria [pastittʃe'ria] *sf* (*pasticcini*) pastries *pl*, cakes *pl*; (*negozio*) cake shop; (*arte*) confectionery.

pasticci'are [pastit'tʃare] *vt* to mess up, make a mess of // *vi* to make a mess.

pasticci'ere, a [pastit'tʃere] *sm/f* pastrycook; confectioner.

pas'ticcio [pas'tittʃo] *sm* (CUC) pie; (*lavoro disordinato, imbroglio*) mess; **trovarsi nei** ~**i** to get into trouble.

pasti'ficio [pasti'fitʃo] *sm* pasta factory.

pas'tiglia [pas'tiʎʎa] *sf* pastille, lozenge.

pas'tina *sf* small pasta shapes used in soup.

pasti'naca, che *sf* parsnip.

'pasto *sm* meal.

pasto'rale *ag* pastoral.

pas'tore *sm* shepherd; (REL) pastor, minister; (*anche*: **cane** ~) sheepdog.

pastoriz'zare [pastorid'dzare] *vt* to pasteurize.

pas'toso, a *ag* doughy; pasty; (*fig: voce, colore*) mellow, soft.

pas'trano *sm* greatcoat.

pas'tura *sf* pasture.

pa'tata *sf* potato; ~**e fritte** chips, French fried potatoes; **pata'tine** *sfpl* (*potato*) crisps.

pata'trac *sm* (*crollo: anche fig*) crash.

pa'tella *sf* (ZOOL) limpet.

pa'tema, i *sm* anxiety, worry.

pa'tente sf licence; (anche: ~ **di guida**) driving licence.

paternità sf paternity, fatherhood.

pa'terno, a ag (affetto, consigli) fatherly; (casa, autorità) paternal.

pa'tetico, a, ci, che ag pathetic; (commovente) moving, touching.

'pathos ['patos] sm pathos.

pa'tibolo sm gallows sg, scaffold.

'patina sf (su rame etc) patina; (sulla lingua) fur, coating.

pa'tire vt, vi to suffer.

pa'tito, a sm/f enthusiast, fan, lover.

patolo'gia [patolo'dʒia] sf pathology; **pato'logico, a, ci, che** ag pathological.

'patria sf homeland.

patri'arca, chi sm patriarch.

pa'trigno [pa'trippo] sm stepfather.

patri'monio sm estate, property; (fig) heritage.

patri'ota, i, e sm/f patriot; **patri'ottico, a, ci, che** ag patriotic; **patriot'tismo** sm patriotism.

patroci'nare [patrotʃi'nare] vt (DIR: difendere) to defend; (sostenere) to sponsor, support; **patro'cinio** sm defence; support, sponsorship.

patro'nato sm patronage; (istituzione benefica) charitable institution o society.

pa'trono sm (REL) patron saint; (socio di patronato) patron; (DIR) counsel.

'patta sf (di pantaloni) fly.

patteggi'are [patted'dʒare] vt, vi to negotiate.

patti'naggio [patti'naddʒo] sm skating.

patti'nare vi to skate; **pattina'tore, 'trice** sm/f skater; **'pattino** sm skate; (di slitta) runner; (AER) skid; (TECN) sliding block; **pattini (da ghiaccio)** (ice) skates; **pattini a rotelle** roller skates; [pat'tino] (barca) kind of pedalo with oars.

'patto sm (accordo) pact, agreement; (condizione) term, condition; **a ~ che** on condition that.

pat'tuglia [pat'tuʎʎa] sf (MIL) patrol.

pattu'ire vt to reach an agreement on.

pattumi'era sf (dust)bin.

pa'ura sf fear; **aver ~ di/di fare/che** to be frightened o afraid of/of doing/that; **far ~ a** to frighten; **per ~ di/che** for fear of/that; **pau'roso, a** ag (che fa paura) frightening; (che ha paura) fearful, timorous.

'pausa sf (sosta) break; (nel parlare, MUS) pause.

pavi'mento sm floor.

pa'vone sm peacock; **pavoneggi'arsi** vr to strut about, show off.

pazien'tare [pattsjen'tare] vi to be patient.

pazi'ente [pat'tsjɛnte] ag, sm/f patient; **pazi'enza** sf patience.

paz'zesco, a, schi, sche [pat'tsesko] ag mad, crazy.

paz'zia [pat'tsia] sf (MED) madness, insanity; (azione) folly; (di azione, decisione) madness, folly.

'pazzo, a ['pattso] ag (MED) mad, insane; (strano) wild, mad // sm/f madman/woman; ~ **di** (gioia etc) mad o crazy with; ~ **per qc/qd** mad o crazy about sth/sb.

'pecca, che sf defect, flaw, fault.

peccami'noso, a ag sinful.

pec'care vi to sin; (fig) to err.

pec'cato sm sin; **è un ~ che** it's a pity that; **che ~!** what a shame o pity!

pecca'tore, 'trice sm/f sinner.

'pece ['petʃe] sf pitch.

'pecora sf sheep; **peco'raio** sm shepherd; **peco'rino** sm sheep's milk cheese.

peculi'are ag: ~ **di** peculiar to.

pecuni'ario, a ag financial, money cpd.

pe'daggio [pe'daddʒo] sm toll.

pedago'gia [pedago'dʒia] sf pedagogy, educational methods pl.

peda'lare vi to pedal; (andare in bicicletta) to cycle.

pe'dale sm pedal.

pe'dana sf (SPORT: nel salto) springboard; (: nella scherma) piste; (tappetino) rug.

pe'dante ag pedantic // sm/f pedant.

pe'data sf (impronta) footprint; (colpo) kick.

pede'rasta, i sm pederast; homosexual.

pe'destre ag prosaic, pedestrian.

pedi'atra, i, e sm/f paediatrician; **pedia-'tria** sf paediatrics sg.

pedi'cure sm/f inv chiropodist.

pe'dina sf (della dama) draughtsman; (fig) pawn.

pedi'nare vt to shadow, tail.

pedo'nale ag pedestrian.

pe'done, a sm/f pedestrian // sm (SCACCHI) pawn.

'peggio ['peddʒo] av, ag inv worse // sm o f: **il o la ~** the worst; **alla ~** at worst, if the worst comes to the worst; **peggiora-'mento** sm worsening; **peggio'rare** vt to make worse, worsen // vi to grow worse, worsen; **peggiora'tivo, a** ag pejorative; **peggi'ore** ag (comparativo) worse; (superlativo) worst // sm/f: **il(la) peggiore** the worst (person).

'pegno ['peɲɲo] sm (DIR) security, pledge; (nei giochi di società) forfeit; (fig) pledge, token; **dare in ~ qc** to pawn sth.

pe'lame sm (di animale) coat, fur.

pe'lare vt (spennare) to pluck; (spellare) to skin; (sbucciare) to peel; (fig) to make pay through the nose; ~**rsi** vr to go bald.

pel'lame sin skins pl, hides pl.

'pelle sf skin; (di animale) skin, hide; (cuoio) leather; **avere la ~ d'oca** to have goose pimples o goose flesh.

pellegri'naggio [pellegri'naddʒo] sm pilgrimage.

pelle'grino, a sm/f pilgrim.

pelle'rossa, pelli'rossa, pl pelli'rosse sm/f Red Indian.

pellette'ria sf leather goods pl; leather goods shop.

pelli'cano sm pelican.

pellicce'ria [pellittʃe'ria] sf (negozio)

furrier's (shop); (*quantità di pellicce*) furs pl.

pel'liccia, ce [pel'littʃa] *sf* (*mantello di animale*) coat, fur; (*indumento*) fur coat.

pel'licola *sf* (*membrana sottile*) film, layer; (*FOT, CINEMA*) film.

'pelo *sm* hair; (*pelame*) coat, hair; (*pelliccia*) fur; (*di tappeto*) pile; (*di liquido*) surface; **per un ~: per un ~ non ho perduto il treno** I very nearly missed the train; **c'è mancato un ~ che affogasse** he escaped drowning by the skin of his teeth; **pe'loso, a** *ag* hairy.

'peltro *sm* pewter.

pe'luria *sf* down.

'pena *sf* (*DIR*) sentence; (*punizione*) punishment; (*sofferenza*) sadness *q*, sorrow; (*fatica*) trouble *q*, effort; (*difficoltà*) difficulty; **far ~** to be pitiful; **mi fai ~** I feel sorry for you; **prendersi o darsi la ~ di fare** to go to the trouble of doing; **~ di morte** death sentence; **~ pecuniaria** fine; **pe'nale** *ag* penal; **penalità** *sf inv* penalty; **penaliz'zare** *vt* (*SPORT*) to penalize.

pe'nare *vi* (*patire*) to suffer; (*faticare*) to struggle.

pen'dente *ag* hanging; leaning // *sm* (*ciondolo*) pendant; (*orecchino*) drop earring; **pen'denza** *sf* slope, slant; (*grado d'inclinazione*) gradient; (*ECON*) outstanding account.

'pendere *vi* (*essere appeso*): **~ da** to hang from; (*essere inclinato*) to lean; (*fig: incombere*): **~ su** to hang over.

pen'dio, 'dii *sm* slope, slant; (*luogo in pendenza*) slope.

'pendola *sf* pendulum clock.

pendo'lare *ag* pendulum *cpd*, pendular // *sm/f* commuter.

'pendolo *sm* (*peso*) pendulum; (*anche*: **orologio a ~**) pendulum clock.

'pene *sm* penis.

pene'trante *ag* piercing, penetrating.

pene'trare *vi* to come *o* get in // *vt* to penetrate; **~ in** to enter; (*sog: proiettile*) to penetrate; (: *acqua, aria*) to go *o* come into.

penicil'lina [penitʃil'lina] *sf* penicillin.

pe'nisola *sf* peninsula.

peni'tente *ag, sm/f* penitent; **peni'tenza** *sf* penitence; (*punizione*) penance.

penitenzi'ario [peniten'tsjarjo] *sm* prison.

'penna *sf* (*di uccello*) feather; (*per scrivere*) pen; **~ a feltro/ stilografica/a sfera** felt-tip/ fountain/ballpoint pen.

pennel'lare *vi* to paint.

pen'nello *sm* brush; (*per dipingere*) (paint)brush; **a ~** (*perfettamente*) to perfection, perfectly; **~ per la barba** shaving brush.

pen'nino *sm* nib.

pen'none *sm* (*NAUT*) yard; (*stendardo*) banner, standard.

pe'nombra *sf* half-light, dim light.

pe'noso, a *ag* painful, distressing; (*faticoso*) tiring, laborious.

pen'sare *vi* to think // *vt* to think; (*inventare, escogitare*) to think out; **~ a** to think of; (*amico, vacanze*) to think of *o* about; (*problema*) to think about; **~ di fare qc** to think of doing sth.

pensi'ero *sm* thought; (*modo di pensare, dottrina*) thinking *q*; (*preoccupazione*) worry, care, trouble; **stare in ~ per qd** to be worried about sb; **pensie'roso, a** *ag* thoughtful.

'pensile *ag* hanging.

pensio'nante *sm/f* (*presso una famiglia*) lodger; (*di albergo*) guest.

pensio'nato, a *sm/f* pensioner.

pensi'one *sf* (*al prestatore di lavoro*) pension; (*vitto e alloggio*) board and lodging; (*albergo*) boarding house; **andare in ~** to retire.

pen'soso, a *ag* thoughtful, pensive, lost in thought.

pen'tagono *sm* pentagon.

Pente'coste *sf* Pentecost, Whit Sunday.

penti'mento *sm* repentance, contrition.

pen'tirsi *vr*: **~ di** to repent of; (*rammaricarsi*) to regret, be sorry for.

'pentola *sf* pot; **~ a pressione** pressure cooker.

pe'nultimo, a *ag* last but one, penultimate.

pe'nuria *sf* shortage.

penzo'lare [pendzo'lare] *vi* to dangle, hang loosely; **penzo'loni** *av* dangling, hanging down; **stare penzoloni** to dangle, hang down.

'pepe *sm* pepper; **~ macinato/in grani** ground/whole pepper.

pepe'rone *sm* pepper, capsicum; (*piccante*) chili.

pe'pita *sf* nugget.

per *prep* for; (*moto attraverso luogo*) through; (*mezzo, modo*) by; (*causa*) because of, owing to // *cong*: **~ fare** (so as) to do, in order to do; **~ aver fatto** for having done; **partire ~ l'Inghilterra** to leave for England; **sedere ~ terra** to sit on the ground; **~ lettera/ferrovia** by letter/rail; **assentarsi ~ malattia** to be off because of *o* through *o* owing to illness; **uno ~ uno** one by one; **~ persona** per person; **moltiplicare/dividere 9 ~ 3** to multiply/divide 9 by 3; **~ cento** per cent; **~ poco che sia** however little it may be, little though it may be.

'pera *sf* pear.

pe'raltro *av* moreover, what's more.

per'bene *ag inv* respectable, decent // *av* (*con cura*) properly, well.

percentu'ale [pertʃentu'ale] *sf* percentage.

perce'pire [pertʃe'pire] *vt* (*sentire*) to perceive; (*ricevere*) to receive; **percet'tibile** *ag* perceptible; **percezi'one** *sf* perception.

perché [per'ke] *av* why // *cong* (*causale*) because; (*finale*) in order that, so that; (*consecutivo*): **è troppo forte ~ si possa batterlo** he's too strong to be beaten.

perciò [per'tʃɔ] *cong* so, for this (*o* that) reason.

per'correre *vt* (*luogo*) to go all over; (: *paese*) to travel up and down, go all over; (*distanza*) to cover.

per'corso, a *pp di* **percorrere** // *sm* (*tragitto*) journey; (*tratto*) route.

per'cosso, a *pp di* **percuotere** // *sf* blow.

percu'otere *vt* to hit, strike.

percussi'one *sf* percussion; **strumenti a ~** (*MUS*) percussion instruments.

'perdere *vt* to lose; (*lasciarsi sfuggire*) to miss; (*sprecare: tempo, denaro*) to waste; (*mandare in rovina: persona*) to ruin // *vi* to lose; (*serbatoio etc*) to leak; **~rsi** *vr* (*smarrirsi*) to get lost; (*svanire*) to disappear, vanish; **saper ~** to be a good loser; **lascia ~!** forget it!, never mind!

perdigi'orno [perdi'dʒorno] *sm/f inv* idler, waster.

'perdita *sf* loss; (*spreco*) waste; (*fuoriuscita*) leak; **in ~** (*COMM*) at a loss; **a ~ d'occhio** as far as the eye can see.

perdi'tempo *sm* waste of time // *sm/f inv* waster, idler.

perdo'nare *vt* to pardon, forgive; (*scusare*) to excuse, pardon.

per'dono *sm* forgiveness; (*DIR*) pardon.

perdu'rare *vi* to go on, last; (*perseverare*) to persist.

perduta'mente *av* desperately, passionately.

per'duto, a *pp di* **perdere**.

peregri'nare *vi* to wander, roam.

pe'renne *ag* eternal, perpetual, perennial; (*BOT*) perennial.

peren'torio, a *ag* peremptory; (*decisivo*) final.

per'fetto, a *ag* perfect // *sm* (*LING*) perfect (tense).

perfezio'nare [perfettsjo'nare] *vt* to improve, perfect; **~rsi** *vr* to improve; (*INS*) to specialize.

perfezi'one [perfet'tsjone] *sf* perfection.

'perfido, a *ag* perfidious, treacherous.

per'fino *av* even.

perfo'rare *vt* to perforate; to punch a hole (*o* holes) in; (*banda, schede*) to punch; (*trivellare*) to drill; **perfora'tore, 'trice** *sm/f* punch-card operator // *sm* (*utensile*) punch; **perforatore di schede** card punch // *sf* (*TECN*) boring *o* drilling machine; (*INFORM*) card punch; **perforazi'one** *sf* perforation; punching; drilling; (*INFORM*) punch; (*MED*) perforation.

perga'mena *sf* parchment.

'pergamo *sm* pulpit.

perico'lante *ag* precarious.

pe'ricolo *sm* danger; **mettere in ~** to endanger, put in danger; **perico'loso, a** *ag* dangerous.

perife'ria *sf* periphery; (*di città*) outskirts *pl*.

pe'rifrasi *sf* circumlocution.

pe'rimetro *sm* perimeter.

peri'odico, a, ci, che *ag* periodic(al); (*MAT*) recurring // *sm* periodical.

pe'riodo *sm* period.

peripe'zie [peripet'tsie] *sfpl* ups and downs, vicissitudes.

pe'rire *vi* (2) to perish, die.

peris'copio *sm* periscope.

pe'rito, a *ag* expert, skilled // *sm/f* expert; (*agronomo, navale*) surveyor; **un ~ chimico** a qualified chemist.

pe'rizia [pe'rittsja] *sf* (*abilità*) ability; (*consulenza*) expert opinion; expert's report; (*valutazione*) survey, appraisal.

'perla *sf* pearl; **per'lina** *sf* bead.

perlus'trare *vt* to patrol.

perma'loso, a *ag* touchy.

perma'nente *ag* permanent // *sf* permanent wave, perm; **perma'nenza** *sf* permanence; (*soggiorno*) stay.

perma'nere *vi* (2) to remain.

perme'are *vt* to permeate.

per'messo, a *pp di* **permettere** // *sm* (*autorizzazione*) permission, leave; (*dato a militare, impiegato*) leave; (*licenza*) licence, permit; (*MIL: foglio*) pass; **~?, è ~?** (*posso entrare?*) may I come in?; (*posso passare?*) excuse me; **~ di lavoro/pesca** work/fishing permit.

per'mettere *vt* to allow, permit; **~ a qd di fare/qc** to allow sb to do/sth.

permutazi'one [permutat'tsjone] *sf* (*baratto*) exchange, barter; (*MAT*) permutation.

per'nice [per'nitʃe] *sf* partridge.

pernici'oso, a [perni'tʃoso] *ag* pernicious.

'perno *sm* pivot.

pernot'tare *vi* to spend the night, stay overnight.

'pero *sm* pear tree.

però *cong* (*ma*) but; (*tuttavia*) however, nevertheless.

pero'rare *vt* to defend, support.

perpendico'lare *ag, sf* perpendicular.

perpen'dicolo *sm* plumbline; **a ~** perpendicularly.

perpe'trare *vt* to perpetrate.

perpetu'are *vt* to perpetuate.

per'petuo, a *ag* perpetual.

per'plesso, a *ag* perplexed; uncertain, undecided.

perqui'sire *vt* to search; **perquisizi'one** *sf* (*police*) search.

persecu'tore *sm* persecutor.

persecuzi'one [persekut'tsjone] *sf* persecution.

persegu'ire *vt* to pursue.

persegui'tare *vt* to persecute.

perseve'rante *ag* persevering; **perseve-'ranza** *sf* perseverance.

perseve'rare *vi* to persevere.

'Persia *sf*: **la ~** Persia.

persi'ano, a *ag, sm/f* Persian // *sf* shutter; **~ a avvolgibile** Venetian blind.

'persico, a, ci, che *ag* (*GEO*) Persian; **il golfo P~** the Persian Gulf.

per'sino *av* = **perfino**.

persis'tente *ag* persistent.

per'sistere *vi* to persist; **~ a fare** to

persist in doing; **persis'tito, a** *pp di* **persistere.**

'perso, a *pp di* **perdere.**

per'sona *sf* person; (*qualcuno*): **una ~** someone, somebody, *espressione interrogativa* + anyone *o* anybody; **~e** *stpl* people; **non c'è ~ che ...** there's nobody who ..., there isn't anybody who ... .

perso'naggio [perso'naddʒo] *sm* (*persona ragguardevole*) personality, figure; (*tipo*) character, individual; (*LETTERATURA*) character.

perso'nale *ag* personal // *sm* staff; personnel.

personalità *sf inv* personality.

personifi'care *vt* to personify; to embody.

perspi'cace [perspi'katʃe] *ag* shrewd, discerning.

persu'adere *vt* to persuade; **~ qd di qc/a fare** to persuade sb of sth/to do; **persuasi'one** *sf* persuasion; **persua'sivo, a** *ag* persuasive; **persu'aso, a** *pp di* **persuadere.**

per'tanto *cong* (*quindi*) so, therefore.

'pertica, che *sf* pole.

perti'nace [perti'natʃe] *ag* determined; persistent.

perti'nente *ag*: **~ (a)** relevant (to), pertinent (to).

per'tosse *sf* whooping cough.

per'tugio [per'tudʒo] *sm* hole, opening.

pertur'bare *vt* to disrupt; (*persona*) to disturb, perturb; **perturbazi'one** *sf* disruption; perturbation; **perturbazione atmosferica** atmospheric disturbance.

per'vadere *vt* to pervade; **per'vaso, a** *pp di* **pervadere.**

perve'nire *vi* (2): **~ a** to reach, arrive at, come to; (*venire in possesso*): **gli pervenne una fortuna** he inherited a fortune; **far ~ qc a** to have sth sent to; **perve'nuto, a** *pp di* **pervenire.**

perversi'one *sf* perversion.

per'verso, a *ag* depraved; perverse.

perver'tire *vt* to pervert.

p. es. (*abbr di per esempio*) e.g.

'pesa *sf* weighing *q*; weighbridge.

pe'sante *ag* heavy; (*fig: noioso*) dull, boring.

pe'sare *vt* to weigh // *vi* (*avere un peso*) to weigh; (*essere pesante*) to be heavy; (*fig*) to carry weight; **~ su** (*fig*) to lie heavy on; to influence; to hang over; **mi pesa sgridarlo** I find it hard to scold him.

'pesca *sf* (*pl:* **pesche:** *frutto*) peach; (*il pescare*) fishing; **andare a ~** to go fishing; **~ con la lenza** angling.

pes'care *vt* to fish for; (*annegato*) to fish out; (*fig: trovare*) to get hold of, find.

pesca'tore *sm* fisherman; angler.

'pesce ['peʃʃe] *sm* fish *gen inv;* **P~i** (*dello zodiaco*) Pisces; **~ d'aprile!** April Fool!; **~ spada** swordfish; **pesce'cane** *sm* shark.

pesche'reccio [peske'rettʃo] *sm* fishing boat.

pesche'ria [peske'ria] *sf* fishmonger's (shop).

peschi'era [pes'kjɛra] *sf* fishpond.

pesci'vendolo, a [peʃʃi'vɛndolo] *sm/f* fishmonger.

'pesco, schi *sm* peach tree.

pes'coso, a *ag* abounding in fish.

'peso *sm* weight; (*SPORT*) shot; **rubare sul ~** to give short weight; **~ lordo/netto** gross/net weight; **~ piuma/mosca/gallo/medio/massimo** (*PUGILATO*) feather/fly/bantam/middle/heavyweight.

pessi'mismo *sm* pessimism; **pessi'mista, i, e** *ag* pessimistic // *sm/f* pessimist.

'pessimo, a *ag* very bad, awful.

pes'tare *vt* to tread on, trample on; (*sale, pepe*) to grind; (*uva, aglio*) to crush; **~ il muso a qd** to smash sb's face in.

'peste *sf* plague; (*persona*) nuisance, pest.

pes'tello *sm* pestle.

pesti'lenza [pesti'lɛntsa] *sf* pestilence; (*fetore*) stench.

'pesto, a *ag* (*alimentari*) ground; crushed // *sm* (*CUC*) sauce made with basil, garlic, cheese and oil; **c'è buio ~** it's pitch-dark; **occhio ~** black eye.

'petalo *sm* (*BOT*) petal.

pe'tardo *sm* banger, firecracker.

petizi'one [petit'tsjone] *sf* petition.

'peto *sm* (*fam!*) fart (!).

petro'chimica [petro'kimika] *sf* petrochemical industry.

petroli'era *sf* (*nave*) oil tanker.

petro'lifero, a *ag* oil-bearing; oil *cpd.*

pe'trolio *sm* oil, petroleum; (*per lampada, fornello*) paraffin.

pettego'lare *vi* to gossip.

pettego'lezzo [pettego'leddzo] *sm* gossip *q;* **fare ~i** to gossip.

pet'tegolo, a *ag* gossipy // *sm/f* gossip.

petti'nare *vt* to comb (the hair of); **~rsi** *vr* to comb one's hair; **pettina'tura** *sf* combing *q;* (*acconciatura*) hairstyle.

'pettine *sm* comb; (*ZOOL*) scallop.

petti'rosso *sm* robin.

'petto *sm* chest; (*seno*) breast, bust; (*CUC: di carne bovina*) brisket; (: *di pollo etc*) breast; **a doppio ~** (*abito*) double-breasted; **petto'ruto, a** *ag* broad-chested; full-breasted; (*fig*) haughty, puffed up with pride.

petu'lante *ag* insolent.

'pezza ['pɛttsa] *sf* piece of cloth; (*toppa*) patch; (*cencio*) rag, cloth.

pez'zato, a [pet'tsato] *ag* piebald.

pez'zente [pet'tsɛnte] *sm/f* beggar.

'pezzo ['pɛttso] *sm* (*gen*) piece; (*brandello, frammento*) piece, bit; (*di macchina, arnese etc*) part; (*STAMPA*) article; (*di tempo*): **aspettare un ~** to wait quite a while *o* some time; **in o da ~i** in pieces; **andare in ~i** to break into pieces; **un bel ~ d'uomo** a fine figure of a man; **abito a due ~i** two-piece suit; **~ di cronaca** (*STAMPA*) report; **~ grosso** (*fig*) bigwig; **~ di ricambio** spare part.

pia'cente [pja'tʃɛnte] ag attractive, pleasant.

pia'cere [pja'tʃere] vi (2) to please; **una ragazza che piace** a likeable girl; an attractive girl; **~ a: mi piace** I like it; **quei ragazzi non mi piacciono** I don't like those boys; **gli piacerebbe andare al cinema** he would like to go to the cinema // sm pleasure; (favore) favour; '**~r** (nelle presentazioni) 'pleased to meet you!'; **con ~** certainly, with pleasure; **per ~!** please; **fare un ~ a qd** to do sb a favour; **piacevole** ag pleasant, agreeable; **piaci'uto, a** pp di piacere.

pi'aga, ghe sf (lesione) sore; (ferita: anche fig) wound; (fig: flagello) scourge, curse; (: persona) pest, nuisance.

piagnis'teo [pjaɲɲis'tɛo] sm whining, whimpering.

piagnuco'lare [pjaɲɲuko'lare] vi to whimper.

pi'alla sf (arnese) plane; **pial'lare** vt to plane.

pi'ana sf stretch of level ground; (più esteso) plain.

pianeggi'ante [pjaned'dʒante] ag flat, level.

piane'rottolo sm landing.

pia'neta sm (ASTR) planet.

pi'angere ['pjandʒere] vi to cry, weep; (occhi) to water // vt to cry, weep; (lamentare) to bewail, lament; (: morto) to mourn (for).

pianifi'care vt to plan; **pianificazi'one** sf planning.

pia'nista, i, e sm/f pianist.

pi'ano, a ag (piatto) flat, level; (MAT) plane; (facile) straightforward, simple; (chiaro) clear, plain // av (adagio) slowly; (a bassa voce) softly; (con cautela) slowly, carefully // sm (MAT) plane; (GEO) plain; (livello) level, plane; (di edificio) floor; (programma) plan; (MUS) piano; **plan ~** very slowly; (poco a poco) little by little; **in primo/secondo ~** in the foreground/background; **di primo ~** (fig) prominent, high-ranking; **~ stradale** roadway.

piano'forte sm piano, pianoforte.

pi'anta sf (BOT) plant; (ANAT: anche: **~ del piede**) sole (of the foot); (grafico) plan; (topografica) map; **in ~ stabile** on the permanent staff; **piantagi'one** sf plantation; **pian'tare** vt to plant; (conficcare) to drive o hammer in; (tenda) to put up, pitch; (fig: lasciare) to leave, desert; **~rsi davanti a qd** to plant o.s. in front of sb; **piantala!** (fam) cut it out!

pianter'reno sm ground floor.

pi'anto, a pp di piangere // sm tears pl, crying.

pian'tone sm (vigilante) sentry, guard; (soldato) orderly; (AUT) steering column.

pia'nura sf plain.

pi'astra sf plate; (di pietra) slab.

pias'trella sf tile.

pias'trina sf (MIL) identity disc.

piatta'forma sf (anche fig) platform.

pi'atto, a ag flat; (fig: scialbo) dull // sm (recipiente, vivanda) dish; (portata) course; (parte piana) flat (part); **~i** smpl (MUS) cymbals; **~ fondo** soup dish; **~ forte** main course; **~ dei giradischi** turntable.

pi'azza ['pjattsa] sf square; (COMM) market; **far ~ pulita** to make a clean sweep; **piazza'forte, pl piazze'forti** sf (MIL) stronghold; **piaz'zale** sm (large) square.

piaz'zare [pjat'tsare] vt to place; (COMM) to market, sell; **~rsi** vr (SPORT) to be placed.

piaz'zista, i [pjat'tsista] sm (COMM) commercial traveller.

piaz'zola [pjat'tsɔla] sf (AUT) lay-by.

'**picca, che** sf pike; **~che** sfpl (CARTE) spades.

pic'cante ag hot, pungent; (fig) racy; biting.

pic'carsi vr: **~ di fare** to pride o.s. on one's ability to do; **~ per qc** to take offence at sth.

pic'chetto [pik'ketto] sm (MIL, di scioperanti) picket.

picchi'are [pik'kjare] vt (percuotere) to thrash, beat; (colpire) to strike, hit // vi (bussare) to knock; (: con forza) to bang; (colpire) to hit, strike; **picchi'ata** sf knock; bang; blow; (percosse) beating, thrashing; (AER) dive.

picchiet'tare [pikkjet'tare] vt (punteggiare) to spot, dot; (colpire) to tap.

'**picchio** ['pikkjo] sm woodpecker.

pic'cino, a [pit'tʃino] ag tiny, very small.

piccio'naia [pittʃo'naja] sf pigeon-loft; (TEATRO): **la ~** the Gods sg.

picci'one [pit'tʃone] sm pigeon.

'**picco, chi** sm peak; **a ~** vertically.

'**piccolo, a** ag small; (oggetto, mano, di età: bambino) small, little (dav sostantivo); (di breve durata: viaggio) short; (fig) mean, petty // sm/f child, little one; **~i** smpl (di animale) young pl; **in ~** in miniature.

pic'cone sm pick-(axe).

pic'cozza [pik'kɔttsa] sf ice-axe.

pic'nic sm inv picnic.

pi'docchio [pi'dɔkkjo] sm louse.

pi'ede sm foot; (di mobile) leg; **in ~i** standing; **a ~ in** on foot; **a ~i nudi** barefoot; **su due ~i** (fig) at once; **prendere ~** (fig) to gain ground, catch on; **sul ~ di guerra** (MIL) ready for action; **~ di porco** crowbar.

piedis'tallo, piedes'tallo sm pedestal.

pi'ega, ghe sf (piegatura, GEO) fold; (di gonna) pleat; (di pantaloni) crease; (grinza) wrinkle, crease; (fig: andamento) turn.

pie'gare vt to fold; (braccia, gambe, testa) to bend // vi to bend; **~rsi** vr to bend; (fig): **~rsi (a)** to yield (to), submit (to); **piega'tura** sf folding q; bending q; fold; bend; **pieghet'tare** vt to pleat; **pie'ghevole** ag pliable, flexible; (porta) folding; (fig) yielding, docile.

Pie'monte sm: **il ~** Piedmont.

pi'ena sf vedi pieno.

pi'eno, a ag full; (muro, mattone) solid //

sm (*colmo*) height, peak; (*carico*) full load // sf (*di fiume*) flood, spate; (*gran folla*) crowd, throng; ~ **di** full of; **in** ~**a notte** in the middle of the night; **fare il** ~ **(di benzina)** to fill up (with petrol).

pietà sf pity; (*REL*) piety; **senza** ~ pitiless, merciless; **avere** ~ **di** (*compassione*) to pity, feel sorry for; (*misericordia*) to have pity o mercy on.

pie'tanza [pje'tantsa] sf dish; (*main*) course.

pie'toso, a ag (*compassionevole*) pitying, compassionate; (*che desta pietà*) pitiful.

pi'etra sf stone; ~ **preziosa** precious stone, gem; **pie'traia** sf (*terreno*) stony ground; **pie'trame** sm stones pl; **pietrifi-'care** vt to petrify; (*fig*) to transfix, paralyze.

'piffero sm (*MUS*) pipe.

pigi'ama [pi'dʒama] sm pyjamas pl.

'pigia 'pigia ['pidʒa'pidʒa] sm crowd, press.

pigi'are [pi'dʒare] vt to press; **pigia'trice** sf (*macchina*) wine press.

pigi'one [pi'dʒone] sf rent; **dare/prendere a** ~ to let o rent out/rent.

pigli'are [piʎ'ʎare] vt to take, grab; (*afferrare*) to catch.

'piglio ['piʎʎo] sm look, expression.

pig'mento sm pigment.

pig'meo, a sm/f pygmy.

'pigna ['piɲɲa] sf pine cone.

pi'gnolo, a [piɲ'ɲɔlo] ag pernickety.

pigo'lare vi to cheep, chirp.

pi'grizia [pi'grittsja] sf laziness.

'pigro, a ag lazy; (*fig: ottuso*) slow, dull.

'pila sf (*catasta, di ponte*) pile; (*ELETTR*) battery; (*vasca*) basin.

pi'lastro sm pillar.

'pillola sf pill; **prendere la** ~ to be on the pill.

pi'lone sm (*di ponte*) pier; (*di linea elettrica*) pylon.

pi'lota, i, e sm/f pilot; (*AUT*) driver // ag inv pilot cpd; ~ **automatico** automatic pilot; **pilo'tare** vt to pilot; to drive.

piluc'care vt (*acini d'uva*) to pick off, pluck (one at a time); (*biscotto*) to nibble at.

pi'mento sm pimento, allspice.

pinaco'teca, che sf art gallery.

pi'neta sf pinewood.

ping-'pong [piŋ'pɔŋ] sm table tennis.

'pingue ag fat, corpulent; **pingu'edine** sf corpulence.

pingu'ino sm (*ZOOL*) penguin.

'pinna sf fin; (*di pinguino, spatola di gomma*) flipper.

pin'nacolo sm pinnacle.

'pino sm pine (tree); **pi'nolo** sm pine kernel.

'pinza ['pintsa] sf pliers pl; (*MED*) forceps pl; (*ZOOL*) pincer.

pinzette [pin'tsette] sfpl tweezers pl.

'pio, a, 'pii, 'pie ag pious; (*opere, istituzione*) charitable, charity cpd.

---

pi'oggia, ge ['pjɔddʒa] sf rain.

pi'olo sm peg; (*di scala*) rung.

piom'bare vi to fall heavily; (*gettarsi con impeto*): ~ **su** to fall upon, assail // vt (*dente*) to fill; **quel vestito piomba bene** that dress hangs well; **piomba'tura** sf (*di dente*) filling.

piom'bino sm (*sigillo*) (lead) seal; (*del filo a piombo*) plummet; (*PESCA*) sinker.

pi'ombo sm (*CHIM*) lead; (*sigillo*) (lead) seal; (*proiettile*) (lead) shot; **a** ~ (*cadere*) straight down.

pioni'ere, a sm/f pioneer.

pi'oppo sm poplar.

pi'overe (2) vb impers to rain // vi (*fig: scendere dall'alto*) to rain down; (: *affluire in gran numero*): ~ **in** to pour into; **pioviggi'nare** vb impers to drizzle; **pio-'voso, a** ag rainy.

pi'ovra sf octopus.

'pipa sf pipe.

pipì sf (*fam*): **fare** ~ to have a wee (wee).

pipis'trello sm (*ZOOL*) bat.

pi'ramide sf pyramid.

pi'rata, i sm pirate; ~ **della strada** hit-and-run driver.

Pire'nei smpl: **i** ~ the Pyrenees.

'pirico, a, ci, che ag: **polvere** ~**a** gunpowder.

pi'rite sf pyrite.

piro'etta sf pirouette.

piro'filo, a ag heat-resistant.

pi'roga, ghe sf dug-out canoe.

pi'romane sm/f pyromaniac; arsonist.

pi'roscafo sm steamer, steamship.

pisci'are [piʃ'ʃare] vi (*fam!*) to piss (!), pee (!).

pi'scina [piʃ'ʃina] sf (*swimming*) pool; (*stabilimento*) (swimming) baths pl.

pi'sello sm pea.

piso'lino sm nap.

'pista sf (*traccia*) track, trail; (*di stadio*) track; (*di pattinaggio*) rink; (*da sci*) run; (*AER*) runway; (*di circo*) ring; ~ **da ballo** dance floor.

pis'tacchio [pis'takkjo] sm pistachio (tree); pistachio (nut).

pis'tillo sm (*BOT*) pistil.

pis'tola sf pistol, gun; ~ **a spruzzo** spray gun.

pis'tone sm piston.

pi'tocco, chi sm skinflint, miser.

pi'tone sm python.

pit'tore, 'trice sm/f painter; **pitto'resco, a, schi, sche** ag picturesque; **pit'torico, a, ci, che** ag of painting, pictorial.

pit'tura sf painting; **pittu'rare** vt to paint.

più av more; (*in frasi comparative*) more, aggettivo corto + ...er; (*in frasi superlative*) most, aggettivo corto + ...est; (*negativo*): **non** ... ~ no more, *espressione negativa* + any more; no longer; (*di temperatura*) above zero; (*MAT*) plus // prep plus, besides // ag inv more; (*parecchi*) several // sm inv (*la parte maggiore*): **il** ~ the most; (*MAT*) plus (sign); **i** ~ the majority; ~ **che/di** more than; ~ **grande che**

bigger than; ~ **di 10 persone/te** more than 10 people/you; **il ~ intelligente/grande** the most intelligent/biggest; **di ~** more; (*inoltre*) what's more, moreover; **3 ore/litri di ~ che** 3 hours/litres more than; **3 chili in ~** 3 kilos more, 3 extra kilos; **a ~ non posso** as much as possible; **al ~ presto** as soon as possible; **al ~ tardi** at the latest; **o meno** more or less; **né ~ né meno** no more, no less.

piucchepper'fetto [pjukkepper'fetto] *sm* (LING) pluperfect, past perfect.

pi'uma *sf* feather; **~e** *sfpl* down *sg*; (*piumaggio*) plumage *sg*, feathers; **piu'maggio** *sm* plumage, feathers *pl*; **piu'mino** *sm* (eider)down; (*coperta*) eiderdown; (*per cipria*) powder puff; (*per spolverare*) feather duster.

piut'tosto *av* rather; **~ che** (*anziché*) rather than.

pi'vello, a *sm/f* greenhorn.

'pizza ['pittsa] *sf* pizza; **pizze'ria** *sf* place *where pizzas are made, sold or eaten.*

pizzi'cagnolo, a [pittsi'kaɲɲolo] *sm/f* specialist grocer.

pizzi'care [pittsi'kare] *vt* (*stringere*) to nip, pinch; (*pungere*) to sting; (MUS) to pluck // *vi* (*prudere*) to itch, be itchy; (*sentir bruciare*) to sting, tingle; (*cibo*) to be hot *o* spicy.

pizziche'ria [pittsike'ria] *sf* delicatessen (shop).

'pizzico, chi ['pittsiko] *sm* (*pizzicotto*) pinch, nip; (*piccola quantità*) pinch, dash; (*d'insetto*) sting, bite.

pizzi'cotto [pittsi'kɔtto] *sm* pinch, nip.

'pizzo ['pittso] *sm* (*merletto*) lace; (*barbetta*) goatee beard.

pla'care *vt* to placate, soothe; **~rsi** *vr* to calm down.

'placca, che *sf* plate; (*con iscrizione*) plaque; (*d'eczema etc*) patch; **plac'care** *vt* to plate; **placcato in oro/argento** gold-/silver-plated.

pla'centa [pla'tʃɛnta] *sf* placenta.

'placido, a ['platʃido] *ag* placid, calm.

plagi'are [pla'dʒare] *vt* (*copiare*) to plagiarize; **'plagio** *sm* plagiarism.

pla'nare *vi* (AER) to glide.

'plancia, ce ['plantʃa] *sf* (NAUT) bridge.

'plancton *sm* plankton.

plane'tario, a *ag* planetary // *sm* (*locale*) planetarium.

'plasma *sm* plasma.

plas'mare *vt* to mould, shape.

'plastico, a, ci, che *ag* plastic // *sm* (*rappresentazione*) relief model; (*esplosivo*): **bomba al ~** plastic bomb // *sf* (*arte*) plastic arts *pl*; (MED) plastic surgery; (*sostanza*) plastic.

plasti'lina *sf* (*ᴿ*) plasticine (*ᴿ*).

'platano *sm* plane tree.

pla'tea *sf* (TEATRO) stalls *pl*.

'platino *sm* platinum.

pla'tonico, a, ci, che *ag* platonic.

plau'sibile *ag* plausible.

'plauso *sm* (*fig*) approval.

ple'baglia [ple'baʎʎa] *sf* (*peg*) rabble, mob.

'plebe *sf* common people; **ple'beo, a** *ag* plebeian; (*volgare*) coarse, common; **plebi'scito** *sm* plebiscite.

ple'nario, a *ag* plenary.

pleni'lunio *sm* full moon.

'plettro *sm* plectrum.

pleu'rite *sf* pleurisy.

'plico, chi *sm* bundle; (*pacco*) parcel; **in ~ a parte** (COMM) under separate cover.

plo'tone *sm* (MIL) platoon; **~ d'esecuzione** firing squad.

'plumbeo, a *ag* leaden.

plu'rale *ag, sm* plural; **pluralità** *sf* plurality; (*di voti etc*) majority.

plusva'lore *sm* (ECON) surplus.

pluvi'ale *ag* rain *cpd*, pluvial.

pneu'matico, a, ci, che *ag* inflatable; pneumatic // *sm* (AUT) tyre.

po' *av, sm vedi* **poco.**

'poco, a, chi, che *ag* (*quantità*) little, negazione + (very) much; (*numero*) few, negazione + (very) many // *av* little, espressione negativa + much; (*con ag*) espressione negativa + very // *pronome* (very) little; **~chi(che)** *pronome pl* few // *sm*: **il ~ che guadagna ...** what little he earns ...; **un po'** a little, a bit; **sono un po' stanco** I'm a bit tired; **un po' di soldi/pane** a little money/bread; **~ prima/dopo** shortly before/afterwards; **~ fa** a short time ago; **a ~ a ~** little by little; **fra ~ o un po'** in a little while.

po'dere *sm* (AGR) farm.

pode'roso, a *ag* powerful.

podestà *sm inv* (*nel fascismo*) podestà, mayor.

'podio *sm* dais, platform; (MUS) podium.

po'dismo *sm* (SPORT) track events *pl*.

po'ema, i *sm* poem.

poe'sia *sf* (*arte*) poetry; (*componimento*) poem.

po'eta, 'essa *sm/f* poet/poetess; **poe'tare** *vi* to write poetry; **po'etico, a, ci, che** *ag* poetic(al).

poggi'are [pod'dʒare] *vt* to lean, rest; (*posare*) to lay, place; **poggia'testa** *sm inv* (AUT) headrest.

'poggio ['pɔddʒo] *sm* hillock, knoll.

'poi *av* then; (*avversario*) but; (*alla fine*) finally, at last; **e ~** and (then).

poiché [poi'ke] *cong* since, as.

'poker *sm* poker.

po'lacco, a, chi, che *ag* Polish // *sm/f* Pole.

po'lare *ag* polar.

'polca, che *sf* polka.

po'lemico, a, ci, che *ag* polemic(al), controversial // *sf* controversy.

po'lenta *sf* (CUC) sort of thick porridge made *with maize flour.*

'poli... *prefisso*: **poli'clinico, ci** *sm* polyclinic; **poliga'mia** *sf* polygamy; **po'ligono** *sm* polygon.

'polio(mie'lite) *sf* polio(myelitis).

'polipo *sm* polyp.

polisti'rolo sm polystyrene.
poli'tecnico, ci sm postgraduate technical college.
politiciz'zare [politit∫id'dzare] vt to politicize.
po'litico, a, ci, che ag political // sm/f politician // sf politics sg; (linea di condotta) policy.
poli'zia [polit'tsia] sf police; ~ giudiziaria ≈ Criminal Investigation Department, ≈ C.I.D.; ~ stradale traffic police; **polizi'esco, a schi, sche** ag police cpd; (film, romanzo) detective cpd; **poli-zi'otto** sm policeman; **cane poliziotto** police dog; **donna poliziotto** policewoman.
'polizza ['polittsa] sf (COMM) bill; ~ di assicurazione insurance policy; ~ di carico bill of lading.
pol'laio sm henhouse.
pollai'olo, a sm/f poulterer.
pol'lame sm poultry.
pol'lastro (ZOOL) cockerel.
'pollice ['pollit∫e] sm thumb.
'polline sm pollen.
'pollo sm chicken.
pol'mone sm lung; **polmo'nite** sf pneumonia.
'polo sm (GEO, FISICA) pole; (gioco) polo.
Po'lonia sf: la ~ Poland.
'polpa sf flesh, pulp; (carne) lean meat.
pol'paccio [pol'patt∫o] sm (ANAT) calf.
pol'petta sf (CUC) meatball; **polpet'tone** sm (CUC) meatloaf.
'polpo sm octopus.
pol'poso, a ag fleshy.
pol'sino sm cuff.
'polso sm (ANAT) wrist; (pulsazione) pulse; (fig: forza) drive, vigour.
pol'tiglia [pol'tiλλa] sf (composto) mash, mush; (fango) mire.
pol'trire vi to laze about.
pol'trona sf armchair; (TEATRO: posto) seat in the front stalls.
pol'trone ag lazy, slothful.
'polvere sf dust; (anche: ~ da sparo) (gun)powder; (sostanza ridotta minutissima) powder, dust; **latte in ~** dried o powdered milk; **caffè in ~** instant coffee; **sapone in ~** soap powder; ~ di carbone coal dust; **polveri'era** sf powder magazine; **polveriz'zare** vt to pulverize; (nebulizzare) to atomize; (fig) to crush, pulverize; to smash; **polve'rone** sm thick cloud of dust; **polve'roso, a** ag dusty.
po'mata sf ointment, cream.
po'mello sm knob.
pomeridi'ano, a ag afternoon cpd; **nelle ore ~e** in the afternoon.
pome'riggio [pome'ridd3o] sm afternoon.
'pomice ['pomit∫e] sf pumice.
'pomo sm (mela) apple; (ornamentale) knob; (di sella) pommel; ~ d'Adamo (ANAT) Adam's apple.
pomo'doro sm tomato.
'pompa sf pump; (sfarzo) pomp (and ceremony); ~e funebri funeral parlour

sg, undertaker's sg; **pom'pare** vt to pump; (trarre) to pump out; (gonfiare d'aria) to pump up.
pom'pelmo sm grapefruit.
pompi'ere sm fireman.
pom'poso, a ag pompous.
ponde'rare vt to ponder over, consider carefully.
ponde'roso, a ag (anche fig) weighty.
po'nente sm west.
'ponte sm bridge; (di nave) deck; (: anche: ~ di comando) bridge; (impalcatura) scaffold; **fare il ~** (fig) to take the extra day off (between 2 public holidays); **governo/soluzione ~** interim government/solution; ~ aereo airlift; ~ sospeso suspension bridge; ~ di volo flight deck.
pon'tefice [pon'tefit∫e] sm (REL) pontiff.
pontifi'care vi (anche fig) to pontificate; **pontifi'cato** sm pontificate; **ponti'ficio, a, ci, cie** ag papal.
popo'lano, a ag popular, of the people.
popo'lare ag popular; (quartiere, clientela) working-class // vt (rendere abitato) to populate; (abitare) to inhabit; **~rsi** vr to fill with people; **popolarità** sf popularity; **popolazi'one** sf population.
'popolo sm people; **popo'loso, a** ag densely populated.
po'pone sm melon.
'poppa sf (di nave) stern; (mammella) breast.
pop'pare vt to suck.
poppa'toio sm (feeding) bottle.
porcel'lana [port∫el'lana] sf porcelain, china; piece of china.
porcel'lino, a [port∫el'lino] sm/f piglet.
porche'ria [porke'ria] sf filth, muck; (fig) obscenity; (: azione disonesta) dirty trick; (cosa mal fatta) rubbish.
por'cile [por't∫ile] sm pigsty.
por'cino, a [por't∫ino] ag of pigs, pork cpd // sm (fungo) type of edible mushroom.
'porco, ci sm pig; (carne) pork.
porcos'pino sm porcupine.
'porgere ['pord3ere] vt to hand, give; (tendere) to hold out.
pornogra'fia sf pornography; **porno-'grafico, a, ci, che** ag pornographic.
'poro sm pore; **po'roso, a** ag porous.
'porpora sf purple; **di ~** purple.
'porre vt (mettere) to put; (collocare) to place; (posare) to lay (down), put (down); (fig: supporre): **poniamo che ...** let's suppose that ...; **porsi** vr (mettersi): **porsi a sedere/in cammino** to sit down/set off; ~ una domanda a qd to ask sb a question, put a question to sb; ~ mente a qc to turn one's mind to sth.
'porro sm (BOT) leek; (MED) wart.
'porta sf door; (SPORT) goal; ~e sfpl (di città) gates; ~ principale main door; front door; a ~e chiuse (DIR) in camera.
'porta... prefisso: **portaba'gagli** sm inv (facchino) porter; (AUT, FERR) luggage

rack; **portabandi'era** sm inv standard bearer; **porta'cenere** sm inv ashtray; **portachi'avi** sm inv keyring; **porta-'cipria** sm inv powder compact; **por-ta'erei** sf inv (nave) aircraft carrier // sm inv (aereo) aircraft transporter; **porta-fi'nestra**, pl **portefi'nestre** sf French window; **porta'foglio** sm (busta) wallet; (borsa) briefcase; (POL, BORSA) portfolio; **portafor'tuna** sm inv lucky charm; mascot; **portagl'oie** sm inv, **porta-gioi'elli** sm inv jewellery box.

por'tale sm portal.

porta'lettere sm/f inv postman/woman.

porta'mento sm carriage, bearing; (fig) behaviour, conduct.

portamo'nete sm inv purse.

por'tante ag (muro etc) supporting, load-bearing.

portan'tina sf sedan chair; (per ammalati) stretcher.

por'tare vt (sostenere, sorreggere: peso, bambino, pacco) to carry; (indossare: abito, occhiali) to wear; (: capelli lunghi) to have; (avere: nome, titolo) to have, bear; (recare): ~ qc a qd to take (o bring) sth to sb; (fig: sentimenti) to bear; ~rsi vr (trasferirsi) to go; (agire) to behave, act; ~ i bambini a spasso to take the children for a walk; ~ fortuna to bring good luck.

portasiga'rette sm inv cigarette case.

portas'pilli sm inv pincushion.

por'tata sf (vivanda) course; (AUT) carrying (o loading) capacity; (di arma) range; (volume d'acqua) (rate of) flow; (fig: limite) scope, capability; (: importanza) impact, import; **alla ~ di qd** at sb's level, within sb's capabilities; **a/fuori ~ (di)** within/out of reach (of); **a ~ di mano** within (arm's) reach.

por'tatile ag portable.

por'tato, a ag (incline): ~ **a fare** inclined o apt to do.

porta'tore, 'trice sm/f (anche COMM) bearer; (MED) carrier.

portau'ovo sm inv eggcup.

porta'voce [porta'votʃe] sm/f inv spokesman/woman // sm inv loudhailer.

por'tento sm wonder, marvel.

'portico, a sm portico.

porti'era sf door.

porti'ere sm (portinaio) doorman, commissionaire; (nel calcio) goalkeeper.

porti'naio, a sm/f porter, doorkeeper.

portine'ria sf porter's lodge.

'porto, a pp di **porgere** // sm (NAUT) harbour, port; (spesa di trasporto) carriage // sm inv port (wine); ~ **abusivo d'armi** unlawful carrying of arms.

Porto'gallo sm: **il ~** Portugal; **porto-'ghese** ag, sm/f, sm Portuguese.

por'tone sm main entrance, main door.

portu'ale ag harbour cpd, port cpd // sm dock worker.

porzi'one [por'tsjone] sf portion, share; (di cibo) portion, helping.

'posa sf laying q; settling q; (riposo) rest,

peace; (FOT) exposure; (atteggiamento, di modello) pose.

po'sare vt to put (down), lay (down) // vi (fig: fondarsi): ~ **su** to be based on; (: atteggiarsi) to pose; (liquidi) to settle; ~**rsi** vr (ape, aereo) to land.

po'sata sf piece of cutlery; ~**e** sfpl cutlery sg.

po'sato, a ag serious.

pos'critto sm postscript.

posi'tivo, a ag positive; (persona: pratica) down-to-earth, practical; **di ~** (certo) for sure.

posizi'one [pozit'tsjone] sf position; **prendere ~** (fig) to take a stand; **luci di ~** (AUT) sidelights.

posolo'gia, 'gie [pozolo'dʒia] sf dosage, directions pl for use.

pos'porre vt to place after; (differire) to postpone, defer; **pos'posto, a** pp di **posporre**.

posse'dere vt to own, possess; (qualità, virtù) to have, possess; (conoscere a fondo: lingua etc) to have a thorough knowledge of; (sog: ira etc) to possess; **possedi-'mento** sm possession.

posses'sivo, a ag possessive.

pos'sesso sm ownership q; possession.

posses'sore sm owner.

pos'sibile ag possible // sm: **fare tutto il ~** to do everything possible; **nei limiti del ~** as far as possible; **al più tardi ~** as late as possible; **possibilità** sf inv possibility // sfpl (mezzi) means; **aver la possibilità di fare** to be in a position to do; to have the opportunity to do.

possi'dente sm/f landowner.

'posta sf (servizio) post, postal service; (corrispondenza) post, mail; (ufficio postale) post office; (nei giochi d'azzardo) stake; ~**e** sfpl (amministrazione) post office; ~ **aerea** airmail; **ministro delle P~e e Telecomunicazioni** Postmaster General; **posta'giro** sm postal giro; **pos'tale** ag postal, post office cpd.

post'bellico, a, ci, che ag postwar.

posteggi'are [posted'dʒare] vt, vi to park; **pos'teggio** sm car park; **posteggio per auto pubbliche** taxi rank.

postelegra'fonico, a, ci, che ag postal, telegraphic and telephonic.

posteri'ore ag (dietro) back; (dopo) later // sm (fam) behind.

posterità sf posterity.

pos'ticcio, a, ci, ce [pos'tittʃo] ag false // sm hairpiece.

postici'pare [postitʃi'pare] vt to defer, postpone.

pos'tilla sf marginal note.

pos'tino sm postman.

'posto, a pp di **porre** // sm (sito, posizione) place; (impiego) job; (spazio libero) room, space; (di parcheggio) space; (sedile: al teatro, in treno etc) seat; (MIL) post; **a ~** (in ordine) in place, tidy; (fig) settled; (: persona) reliable; **mettere a ~ qd** (dargli un lavoro) to fix sb up with a job; **al ~ di**

in place of; **sul ~** on the spot; **~ di blocco** roadblock.

pos'tribolo *sm* brothel.

'postumo, a *ag* posthumous; (*tardivo*) belated; **~i** *smpl* (*conseguenze*) after-effects, consequences.

po'tabile *ag* drinkable; **acqua ~** drinking water.

po'tare *vt* to prune.

po'tassio *sm* potassium.

po'tente *ag* (*nazione*) strong, powerful; (*veleno*) potent, strong; **po'tenza** *sf* power; (*forza*) strength.

potenzi'ale [poten'tsjale] *ag, sm* potential.

po'tere *vb + infinito* can; (*sog: persona*) can, to be able to; (*autorizzazione*) can, may; (*possibilità, ipotesi*) may // *vb impers*: **può darsi** perhaps; **può darsi che** perhaps, it may be that // *sm* power; **avresti potuto dirmelo!** you could o might have told me!; **non ne posso più** I'm exhausted; I can't take any more; **~ d'acquisto** purchasing power.

potestà *sf* (*potere*) power; (*DIR*) authority.

'povero, a *ag* poor; (*disadorno*) plain, bare // **i~i** *smpl* poor man/woman; **i ~i** the poor; **~ di** lacking in, having little; **povertà** *sf* poverty.

pozi'one [pot'tsjone] *sf* potion.

'pozza ['pottsa] *sf* pool.

poz'zanghera [pot'tsangera] *sf* puddle.

'pozzo ['pottso] *sm* well; (*cava: di carbone*) pit; (*di miniera*) shaft; **~ petrolifero** oil well.

pran'zare [pran'dzare] *vi* to dine, have dinner; to lunch, have lunch.

'pranzo ['prandzo] *sm* dinner; (*a mezzogiorno*) lunch.

'prassi *sf* usual procedure.

'pratica, che *sf* practice; (*esperienza*) experience; (*conoscenza*) knowledge, familiarity; (*tirocinio*) training, practice; (*AMM: affare*) matter, case; (: *incartamento*) file, dossier; **~che** *sfpl* dealings, negotiations; **in ~** (*praticamente*) in practice; **mettere in ~** to put into practice.

prati'cabile *ag* (*progetto*) practicable, feasible; (*luogo*) passable, practicable.

prati'cante *sm/f* apprentice, trainee; (*REL*) (regular) churchgoer.

prati'care *vt* to practise; (*attuare*) to put into practice; (*frequentare: persona*) to associate o mix with; (: *luogo*) to frequent; (*eseguire*) to carry out, perform; (: *apertura, buco*) to make.

'pratico, a, ci, che *ag* practical; **~ di** (*esperto*) experienced o skilled in; (*familiare*) familiar with.

'prato *sm* meadow; (*di giardino*) lawn.

preavvi'sare *vt* to forewarn; to inform in advance; **preav'viso** *sm* notice; **telefonata con preavviso** telefonico personal o person to person call.

pre'cario, a *ag* precarious.

precauzi'one [prekaut'tsjone] *sf* caution, care; (*misura*) precaution.

prece'dente [pretʃe'dɛnte] *ag* previous //

sm precedent; **il discorso/film ~** the previous o preceding speech/film; **prece'denza** *sf* priority, precedence; (*AUT*) right of way.

pre'cedere [pre'tʃedere] *vt* to precede; (*camminare, guidare innanzi*) to be ahead of.

pre'cetto [pre'tʃetto] *sm* precept; (*MIL*) call-up notice.

precet'tore [pretʃet'tore] *sm* (private) tutor.

precipi'tare [pretʃipi'tare] *vi* (2) (*cadere: anche fig*) to fall headlong, plunge (down) // *vt* (*gettare dall'alto in basso*) to hurl, fling; (*fig: affrettare*) to rush; **~rsi** *vr* (*gettarsi*) to hurl o fling o.s.; (*affrettarsi*) to rush; **precipitazi'one** *sf* (*METEOR*) precipitation; (*fig*) haste; **precipi'toso, a** *ag* (*caduta, fuga*) headlong; (*fig: avventato*) rash, reckless; (: *affrettato*) hasty, rushed.

preci'pizio [pretʃi'pittsjo] *sm* precipice; **a ~** (*fig: correre*) headlong.

pre'cipuo, a [pre'tʃipuo] *ag* principal, main.

preci'sare [pretʃi'zare] *vt* to state, specify; (*spiegare*) to explain (in detail).

precisi'one [pretʃiz'jone] *sf* precision, accuracy.

pre'ciso, a [pre'tʃizo] *ag* (*esatto*) precise; (*accurato*) accurate, precise; (*uguale*): **2 vestiti ~i** 2 dresses exactly the same; **sono le 9 ~e** it's exactly 9 o'clock.

pre'cludere *vt* to block, obstruct; **pre'cluso, a** *pp di* **precludere**.

pre'coce [pre'kɔtʃe] *ag* early; (*bambino*) precocious; (*vecchiaia*) premature.

precon'cetto, a [prekon'tʃetto] *ag* preconceived.

precur'sore *sm* forerunner, precursor.

'preda *sf* (*bottino*) booty; (*animale, fig*) prey; **essere ~ di** to fall prey to; **essere in ~ a** to be prey to; **preda'tore** *sm* predator.

predeces'sore, a [predetʃes'sore] *sm/f* predecessor.

pre'della *sf* platform, dais; altar-step.

predesti'nare *vt* to predestine.

pre'detto, a *pp di* **predire**.

'predica, che *sf* sermon; (*fig*) lecture, talking-to.

predi'care *vt, vi* to preach.

predi'cato *sm* (*LING*) predicate.

predi'letto, a *pp di* **prediligere** // *ag, sm/f* favourite.

predilezi'one [predilet'tsjone] *sf* fondness, partiality; **avere una ~ per qc/qd** to be partial to sth/fond of sb.

predi'ligere [predi'lidʒere] *vt* to prefer, have a preference for.

pre'dire *vt* to foretell, predict.

predis'porre *vt* to get ready, prepare; **~ qd a qc** to predispose sb to sth; **predis'posto, a** *pp di* **predisporre**.

predizi'one [predit'tsjone] *sf* prediction.

predomi'nare *vi* to predominate; (*prevalere*) to prevail; **predo'minio** *sm* predominance; supremacy.

prefabbri'cato, a ag (*EDIL*) prefabricated.

prefazi'one [prefat'tsjone] *sf* preface, foreword.

prefe'renza [prefe'rɛntsa] *sf* preference; **preferenzi'ale** *ag* preferential.

prefe'rire *vt* to prefer, like better; ~ **il caffè al tè** to prefer coffee to tea, like coffee better than tea.

pre'fetto *sm* prefect; **prefet'tura** *sf* prefecture.

pre'figgere [pre'fiddʒere] *vt* to fix *o* arrange in advance; ~**rsi uno scopo** to set o.s. a goal.

pre'fisso, a *pp di* **prefiggere** // *sm* (*LING*) prefix; (*TEL*) dialling code.

pre'gare *vi* to pray // *vt* (*REL*) to pray to; (*implorare*) to beg; (*chiedere*): ~ **qd di fare** to ask sb to do; **farsi** ~ to need coaxing *o* persuading.

pre'gevole [pre'dʒevole] *ag* valuable.

preghi'era [pre'gjera] *sf* (*REL*) prayer; (*domanda*) request.

pregi'arsi [pre'dʒarsi] *vr*: **mi pregio di farle sapere che ...** I am pleased *o* honoured to inform you that ... .

'pregio ['prɛdʒo] *sm* (*stima*) esteem, regard; (*qualità*) (good) quality, merit; (*valore*) value, worth.

pregiudi'care [predʒudi'kare] *vt* to prejudice, harm, be detrimental to; **pregiudi'cato, a** *sm/f* (*DIR*) previous offender.

pregiu'dizio [predʒu'dittsjo] *sm* (*idea errata*) prejudice; (*danno*) harm *q*.

'pregno, a ['preɲɲo] *ag* (*gravido*) pregnant; (*saturo*): ~ **di** full of, saturated with.

'prego *escl* (*a chi ringrazia*) don't mention it!; (*invitando qd ad accomodarsi*) please sit down!; (*invitando qd ad andare prima*) after you!

pregus'tare *vt* to look forward to.

preis'torico, a, ci, che *ag* prehistoric.

pre'lato *sm* prelate.

prele'vare *vt* (*denaro*) to withdraw; (*campione*) to take; (*sog: polizia*) to take, capture.

preli'evo *sm* (*MED*): **fare un** ~ **(di)** to take a sample (of).

prelimi'nare *ag* preliminary; ~**i** *smpl* preliminary talks; preliminaries.

pre'ludio *sm* prelude.

pre-ma'man [prema'mã] *sm inv* maternity dress.

prema'turo, a *ag* premature.

premeditazi'one [premeditat'tsjone] *sf* (*DIR*) premeditation; **con** ~ *ag* premeditated // *av* with intent.

'premere *vt* to press // *vi*: ~ **su** to press down on; (*fig*) to put pressure on; ~ **a** (*fig: importare*) to matter to.

pre'messo, a *pp di* **premettere** // *sf* introductory statement, introduction.

pre'mettere *vt* to put before; (*dire prima*) to start by saying, state first.

premi'are *vt* to give a prize to; to reward.

premi'nente *ag* pre-eminent.

'premio *sm* prize, award; (*ricompensa*) reward; (*COMM*) premium; (*AMM: indennità*) bonus.

premu'nirsi *vr*: ~ **di** to provide o.s. with; ~ **contro** to protect o.s. from, guard o.s. against.

pre'mura *sf* (*fretta*) haste, hurry; (*riguardo*) attention, care; **premu'roso, a** *ag* thoughtful, considerate.

prena'tale *ag* antenatal.

'prendere *vt* to take; (*andare a prendere*) to get, fetch; (*ottenere*) to get; (*guadagnare*) to get, earn; (*catturare: ladro, pesce*) to catch; (*collaboratore, dipendente*) to take on; (*passeggero*) to pick up; (*chiedere: somma, prezzo*) to charge, ask; (*trattare: persona*) to handle // *vi* (*colla, cemento*) to set; (*pianta*) to take; (*fuoco: nel camino*) to catch; (: *incendio*) to start; (*voltare*): ~ **a destra** to turn (to the) right; ~**rsi** *vr* (*azzuffarsi*): ~**rsi a pugni** to come to blows; ~ **a fare qc** to start doing sth; ~ **qd/qc per** (*scambiare*) to take sb/sth for; ~ **le armi** to take up arms; ~ **fuoco** to catch fire; ~ **parte a** to take part in; ~**rsi cura di qd/qc** to look after sb/sth; **prendersela** (*adirarsi*) to get annoyed; (*preoccuparsi*) to get upset, worry.

preno'tare *vt* to book, reserve; **prenotazi'one** *sf* booking, reservation.

preoccu'pare *vt* to worry; to preoccupy; ~**rsi** *vr*: ~**rsi di qd/qc** to worry about sb/sth; ~**rsi per qd** to be anxious for sb; **preoccupazi'one** *sf* worry, anxiety.

prepa'rare *vt* to prepare; (*esame, concorso*) to prepare for; ~**rsi** *vr*: ~**rsi (a qc/a fare)** to get ready *o* prepare (o.s.) (for sth/to do); **prepara'tivi** *smpl* preparations; **prepa'rato** *sm* (*prodotto*) preparation; **prepara'torio, a** *ag* preparatory; **preparazi'one** *sf* preparation.

pre'porre *vt* to place before; (*fig*) to prefer.

preposizi'one [prepozit'tsjone] *sf* (*LING*) preposition.

pre'posto, a *pp di* **preporre**.

prepo'tente *ag* domineering, arrogant; (*bisogno, desiderio*) overwhelming, pressing // *sm/f* bully; **prepo'tenza** *sf* arrogance; arrogant behaviour.

pre'puzio [pre'puttsjo] *sm* (*ANAT*) foreskin.

preroga'tiva *sf* prerogative.

'presa *sf* taking *q*; catching *q*; (*di città*) capture; (*indurimento: di cemento*) setting; (*appiglio, SPORT*) hold; (*ELETTR*): ~ **(di corrente)** socket; (: *al muro*) point; (*piccola quantità: di sale etc*) pinch; (*CARTE*) trick; **far** ~ to catch, hold; (*cemento*) to set; (*pianta*) to take root; ~ **d'acqua** water supply point; tap; ~ **d'aria** air inlet; ~ **di terra** (*ELETTR*) earth; **essere alle** ~**e con qc** (*fig*) to be struggling with sth.

pre'sagio [pre'zadʒo] *sm* omen.

presa'gire [preza'dʒire] vt to foresee.
'presbite ag long-sighted.
presbiteri'ano, a ag, sm/f Presbyterian.
presbi'terio sm presbytery.
pre'scindere [preʃ'ʃindere] vi: ~ **da** to leave out of consideration; **a** ~ **da** apart from.
pres'critto, a pp di **prescrivere**.
pres'crivere vt to prescribe; **prescrizi'one** sf (MED, DIR) prescription; (norma) rule, regulation.
presen'tare vt to present; (far conoscere): ~ **qd (a)** to introduce sb (to); (AMM: inoltrare) to submit; ~**rsi** vr (in comune etc) to report, come; (in giudizio) to appear; (farsi conoscere) to introduce o.s.; (occasione) to arise; ~**rsi candidato** (POL) to stand as a candidate; ~**rsi bene/male** to look good/bad; **presentazi'one** sf presentation; introduction.
pre'sente ag present; (questo) this // sm present; **i** ~ **i** those present; **aver** ~ **qc/qd** to remember sth/sb.
presenti'mento sm premonition.
pre'senza [pre'zɛntsa] sf presence; (aspetto esteriore) appearance; ~ **di spirito** presence of mind.
pre'sepio, pre'sepe sm crib.
preser'vare vt to protect; to save; **preserva'tivo** sm sheath, condom.
'preside sm/f (INS) headmaster/mistress; (di facoltà universitaria) dean.
presi'dente sm (POL) president; (di assemblea, COMM) chairman; **presiden'tessa** sf president; president's wife; chairwoman; **presi'denza** sf presidency; office of president; chairmanship; **presidenzi'ale** ag presidential.
presidi'are vt to garrison; **pre'sidio** sm garrison.
presi'edere vt to preside over // vi: ~ **a** to direct, be in charge of.
'preso, a pp di **prendere**.
'pressa sf crowd, throng; (TECN) press.
pressap'poco av about, roughly.
pres'sare vt to press.
pressi'one sf pressure; **far** ~ **su qd** to put pressure on sb; ~ **sanguigna** blood pressure.
'presso av (vicino) nearby, close at hand // prep (vicino a) near; (accanto a) beside, next to; (in casa di): ~ **qd** at sb's home; (nelle lettere) care of (abbr c/o); **lavora** ~ **di noi** he works for o with us.
pressuriz'zare [pressurid'dzare] vt to pressurize.
presta'nome sm/f inv (peg) figurehead.
pres'tante ag good-looking.
pres'tare vt to lend; ~**rsi** vr (adoperarsi): ~**rsi per qd/a fare** to help sb/to do; (essere adatto): ~**rsi a** to lend itself to, be suitable for; ~ **aiuto** to lend a hand; ~ **orecchio** to listen; **prestazi'oni** stpl (di macchina, atleta) performance sg; (di persona: servizi) services.
prestigia'tore, 'trice [prestidʒa'tore] sm/f conjurer.

pres'tigio [pres'tidʒo] sm (potere) prestige; (illusione): **gioco di** ~ conjuring trick.
'prestito sm lending q; loan; **dar in** o **a** ~ to lend; **prendere in** ~ to borrow.
'presto av (tra poco) soon; (in fretta) quickly; (di buon'ora) early; **a** ~ see you soon; **fare** ~ **a fare** qc to hurry up and do sth; (non costare fatica) to have no trouble doing sth; **si fa** ~ **a criticare** it's easy to criticize.
pre'sumere vt to presume, assume // vi: ~ **di** to overrate; **pre'sunto, a** pp di **presumere**.
presuntu'oso, a ag presumptuous.
presunzi'one [prezun'tsjone] sf presumption.
presup'porre vt to suppose; to presuppose.
'prete sm priest.
preten'dente sm/f pretender // sm (corteggiatore) suitor.
pre'tendere vt (esigere) to demand, require; (sostenere): ~ **che** to claim that // vi (presumere) to think, presume; **pretende di avere sempre ragione** he thinks he's always right; ~ **a** to lay claim to; **pretensi'one** sf claim; pretentiousness; **pretenzi'oso, a** ag pretentious.
pre'teso, a pp di **pretendere** // sf (esigenza) claim, demand; (presunzione, sfarzo) pretentiousness; **senza** ~**e** unpretentious.
pre'testo sm pretext, excuse.
pre'tore sm magistrate.
preva'lente ag prevailing; **preva'lenza** sf predominance.
preva'lere vi to prevail; **pre'valso, a** pp di **prevalere**.
preve'dere vt (indovinare) to foresee; (presagire) to foretell; (considerare) to make provision for.
preve'nire vt (anticipare) to forestall; to anticipate; (evitare) to avoid, prevent; (avvertire): ~ **qd (di)** to warn sb (of); to inform sb (of).
preventi'vare vt (COMM) to estimate.
preven'tivo, a ag preventive // sm (COMM) estimate.
prevenzi'one [preven'tsjone] sf prevention; (preconcetto) prejudice.
previ'dente ag showing foresight; prudent; **previ'denza** sf foresight; **istituto di previdenza** provident institution; **previdenza sociale** social security.
previsi'one sf forecast, prediction; ~**i meteorologiche** o **del tempo** weather forecast sg.
pre'visto, a pp di **prevedere** // ag foreseen, expected; **più/meno del** ~ more/less than expected.
prezi'oso, a [pret'tsjoso] ag precious; invaluable // sm jewel; valuable.
prez'zemolo [pret'tsemolo] sm parsley.
'prezzo ['prettso] sm price; ~

d'acquisto/di vendita buying/ selling price.

prigi'one [pri'dʒone] *sf* prison; **prigio'nia** *sf* imprisonment; **prigioni'ero, a** *ag* captive // *sm/f* prisoner.

'prima *sf vedi* **primo** // *av* before; (*in anticipo*) in advance, beforehand; (*per l'addietro*) at one time, formerly; (*più presto*) sooner, earlier; (*in primo luogo*) first // *cong:* **~ di fare/che parta** before doing/he leaves; **~ di** *prep* before; **~ o poi** sooner or later.

pri'mario, a *ag* primary; (*principale*) chief, leading, primary.

pri'mate *sm* (*REL*) primate.

pri'mato *sm* supremacy; (*SPORT*) record.

prima'vera *sf* spring; **primave'rile** *ag* spring *cpd*.

primeggi'are [primed'dʒare] *vi* to excel, be one of the best.

primi'tivo, a *ag* primitive; original.

pri'mizie [pri'mittsje] *sfpl* early produce *sg*.

'primo, a *ag* first; (*fig*) initial; basic; prime // *sf* (*TEATRO*) first night; (*CINEMA*) première; (*AUT*) first (gear); **le ~e ore del mattino** the early hours of the morning; **al ~ di maggio** at the beginning of May; **viaggiare in ~a** to travel first-class; **in ~ luogo** first of all, in the first place; **di prim'ordine** *o* **~a qualità** first-class, first-rate; **in un ~ tempo** at first; **~a donna** leading lady; (*di opera lirica*) prima donna.

primo'genito, a [primo'dʒenito] *ag, sm/f* firstborn.

primordi'ale *ag* primordial.

'primula *sf* primrose.

princi'pale [printʃi'pale] *ag* main, principal // *sm* manager, boss.

princi'pato [printʃi'pato] *sm* principality.

'principe ['printʃipe] *sm* prince; **~ ereditario** crown prince; **princi'pessa** *sf* princess.

principi'ante [printʃi'pjante] *sm/f* beginner.

principi'are [printʃi'pjare] *vt, vi* to start, begin.

prin'cipio [prin'tʃipjo] *sm* (*inizio*) beginning, start; (*origine*) origin, cause; (*concetto, norma*) principle; **al** *o* **in ~** at first; **per ~** on principle.

pri'ore *sm* (*REL*) prior.

priorità *sf* priority.

'prisma, i *sm* prism.

pri'vare *vt:* **~ qd di** to deprive sb of; **~rsi di** to go *o* do without.

priva'tiva *sf* (*ECON*) monopoly.

pri'vato, a *ag* private // *sm/f* private citizen; **in ~** in private.

privazi'one [privat'tsjone] *sf* privation, hardship.

privilegi'are [privile'dʒare] *vt* to grant a privilege to.

privi'legio [privi'lɛdʒo] *sm* privilege.

'privo, a *ag:* **~ di** without, lacking.

pro *prep* for, on behalf of // *sm inv* (*utilità*) advantage, benefit; **a che ~?** what's the

use?; **il ~ e il contro** the pros and cons.

pro'babile *ag* probable, likely; **probabilità** *sf inv* probability.

pro'bante *ag* convincing.

probità *sf* integrity, probity.

pro'blema, i *sm* problem.

pro'boscide [pro'bɔʃʃide] *sf* (*di elefante*) trunk.

procacci'are [prokat'tʃare] *vt* to get, obtain.

pro'cedere [pro'tʃedere] *vi* to proceed; (*comportarsi*) to behave; (*iniziare*): **~ a** to start; **~ contro** (*DIR*) to start legal proceedings against; **procedi'mento** *sm* (*modo di condurre*) procedure; (*di avvenimenti*) course; (*comportamento*) behaviour; (*TECN*) process; **proce'dura** *sf* (*DIR*) procedure.

proces'sare [protʃes'sare] *vt* (*DIR*) to try.

processi'one [protʃes'sjone] *sf* procession.

pro'cesso [pro'tʃesso] *sm* (*DIR*) trial; **proceedings** *pl*; (*metodo*) process.

pro'cinto [pro'tʃinto] *sm:* **in ~ di fare** about to do, on the point of doing.

pro'clama, i *sm* proclamation.

procla'mare *vt* to proclaim; **proclamazi'one** *sf* proclamation, declaration.

procrastinazi'one [prokrastinat'tsjone] *sf* procrastination.

procre'are *vt* to procreate.

pro'cura *sf* (*DIR*) proxy; power of attorney; (*ufficio*) attorney's office.

procu'rare *vt:* **~ qc a qd** (*provvedere*) to get *o* obtain sth for sb; (*causare: noie etc*) to bring *o* give sb sth.

procura'tore, 'trice *sm/f* (*DIR*) ≈ solicitor; (: *chi ha la procura*) attorney, proxy; **~ generale** (*in corte d'appello*) public prosecutor; (*in corte di cassazione*) Attorney General; **~ della Repubblica** (*in corte d'assise, tribunale*) public prosecutor.

prodi'gare *vt* to be lavish with; **~rsi per qd** to do all one can for sb.

pro'digio [pro'didʒo] *sm* marvel, wonder; (*persona*) prodigy; **prodigi'oso, a** *ag* prodigious; phenomenal.

'prodigo, a, ghi, ghe *ag* lavish, extravagant.

pro'dotto, a *pp di* **produrre** // *sm* product; **~i agricoli** farm produce *sg*.

pro'durre *vt* to produce; **prodursi** *vr* (*attore*) to perform, appear; **produttività** *sf* productivity; **produt'tivo, a** *ag* productive; **produt'tore, 'trice** *sm/f* producer; **produzi'one** *sf* production; (*rendimento*) output.

pro'emio *sm* introduction, preface.

Prof. (*abbr di* **professore**) Prof.

profa'nare *vt* to desecrate.

pro'fano, a *ag* (*mondano*) secular; profane; (*sacrilego*) profane.

profe'rire *vt* to utter.

profes'sare *vt* to profess; (*medicina etc*) to practise.

professio'nale *ag* professional.

professi'one *sf* profession; **professio-'nista, i, e** *sm/f* professional.

profes'sore, 'essa *sm/f* (*INS*) teacher; (: *di università*) lecturer; (: *titolare di cattedra*) professor.

pro'feta, i *sm* prophet; **profetiz'zare** *vt* to prophesy; **profe'zia** *sf* prophecy.

pro'ficuo, a *ag* useful, profitable.

profi'lare *vt* to outline; (*ornare: vestito*) to edge; (*aereo*) to streamline; **~rsi** *vr* to stand out, be silhouetted; to loom up.

pro'filo *sm* profile; (*contorno*) contour, line; (*breve descrizione*) sketch, outline; **di ~** in profile.

profit'tare *vi*: **~ in** to make progress in; **~ di** (*trarre profitto*) to profit by; (*approfittare*) to take advantage of.

pro'fitto *sm* advantage, profit, benefit; (*fig: progresso*) progress; (*COMM*) profit.

pro'fondere *vt* (*lodi*) to lavish; (*denaro*) to squander; **~rsi in** to be profuse in.

profondità *sf inv* depth.

pro'fondo, a *ag* deep; (*rancore, meditazione*) profound // *sm* depth(s *pl*), bottom; **~ 8 metri** 8 metres deep.

'profugo, a, ghi, ghe *sm/f* refugee.

profu'mare *vt* to perfume // *vi* (2) to be fragrant; **~rsi** *vr* to put on perfume *o* scent.

profume'ria *sf* perfumery; (*negozio*) perfume shop; **~e** *sfpl* perfumes.

pro'fumo *sm* (*prodotto*) perfume, scent; (*fragranza*) scent, fragrance.

profusi'one *sf* profusion; **a ~ in** plenty.

pro'fuso, a *pp di* **profondere**.

proget'tare [prod3et'tare] *vt* to plan; (*TECN: edificio*) to plan, design; **pro'getto** *sm* plan; (*idea*) plan, project; **progetto di legge** bill.

pro'gramma, i *sm* programme; (*TV, RADIO*) programmes *pl*; (*INS*) syllabus, curriculum; (*INFORM*) program; **program-'mare** *vt* (*TV, RADIO*) to put on; (*INFORM*) to program; (*ECON*) to plan; **programma-'tore, 'trice** *sm/f* (*INFORM*) computer programmer; (*ECON*) planner; **program-mazi'one** *sf* programming; planning.

progre'dire *vi* to progress, make progress.

progressi'one *sf* progression.

progres'sivo, a *ag* progressive.

pro'gresso *sm* progress *q*; **fare ~i** to make progress.

proi'bire *vt* to forbid, prohibit; **proibi-'tivo, a** *ag* prohibitive; **proibizi'one** *sf* prohibition.

proiet'tare *vt* (*gettare*) to throw out (*o* off *o* up); (*CINEMA*) to project; (: *presentare*) to show, screen; (*luce, ombra*) to throw, cast, project; **proi'ettile** *sm* projectile, bullet (*o* shell *etc*); **proiet'tore** *sm* (*CINEMA*) projector; (*AUT*) headlamp; (*MIL*) searchlight; **proiezi'one** *sf* (*CINEMA*) projection; showing.

'prole *sf* children *pl*, offspring.

proletari'ato *sm* proletariat.

prole'tario, a *ag, sm* proletarian.

prolife'rare *vi* (*fig*) to proliferate.

pro'lifico, a, ci, che *ag* prolific.

pro'lisso, a *ag* verbose.

'prologo, ghi *sm* prologue.

pro'lunga, ghe *sf* (*di cavo elettrico etc*) extension.

prolun'gare *vt* (*discorso, attesa*) to prolong; (*linea, termine*) to extend.

prome'moria *sm inv* memorandum.

pro'messa *sf* promise.

pro'messo, a *pp di* **promettere**.

pro'mettere *vt* to promise // *vi* to be *o* look promising; **~ a qd di fare** to promise sb that one will do.

promi'nente *ag* prominent; **promi-'nenza** *sf* prominence.

promiscuità *sf* promiscuousness.

promon'torio *sm* promontory, headland.

pro'mosso, a *pp di* **promuovere**.

promo'tore *sm* promoter, organizer.

promozi'one [promot'tsjone] *sf* promotion.

promul'gare *vt* to promulgate.

promu'overe *vt* to promote.

proni'pote *sm/f* (*di nonni*) great-grandchild, great-grandson/grand-daughter; (*di zii*) great-nephew/ niece.

pro'nome *sm* (*LING*) pronoun.

pronosti'care *vt* to foretell, predict; to presage.

pron'tezza [pron'tettsa] *sf* readiness; quickness, promptness.

'pronto, a *ag* ready; (*rapido*) fast, quick, prompt; **~! (*TEL*) hello!; **~ all'ira** quick-tempered; **~ soccorso** first aid.

prontu'ario *sm* manual, handbook.

pro'nuncia [pro'nuntʃa] *etc* = **pronunzia** *etc*.

pro'nunzia [pro'nuntsja] *sf* pronunciation; **pronunzi'are** *vt* (*parola, sentenza*) to pronounce; (*dire*) to utter; (*discorso*) to deliver; **pronunziarsi** *vr* to declare one's opinion; **pronunzi'ato, a** *ag* (*spiccato*) pronounced, marked; (*sporgente*) prominent.

propa'ganda *sf* propaganda.

propa'gare *vt* (*fig*) to spread; (*BIOL*) to propagate; **~rsi** *vr* to spread; to propagate; (*FISICA*) to be propagated.

pro'pendere *vi*: **~ per** to favour, lean towards; **propensi'one** *sf* inclination, propensity; **pro'penso, a** *pp di* **propendere**.

propi'nare *vt* to administer.

pro'pizio, a [pro'pittsjo] *ag* favourable.

pro'porre *vt* (*suggerire*): **~ qc (a qd)/di fare** to suggest sth (to sb)/doing, propose to do; (*candidato*) to put forward; (*legge, brindisi*) to propose; **proporsi di fare** to propose *o* intend to do; **proporsi una meta** to set o.s. a goal.

proporzio'nale [proportsjo'nale] *ag* proportional.

proporzio'nare [proportsjo'nare] *vt*: **~ qc a** to proportion *o* adjust sth to.

proporzi'one [propor'tsjone] *sf* proportion; **in ~ a** in proportion to.

pro'posito *sm* (*intenzione*) intention, aim;

(*argomento*) subject, matter; **a ~ di** regarding, with regard to; **di ~** (*apposta*) deliberately, on purpose; **a ~** by the way; **capitare a ~** (*cosa, persona*) to turn up at the right time.

proposizi'one [propozit'tsjone] *sf* (*LING*) clause; (: *periodo*) sentence.

pro'posto, a *pp di* **proporre** // *sf* suggestion; proposal.

proprietà *sf inv* (*diritto*) ownership; (*ciò che si possiede*) property *gen* q, estate; (*caratteristica*) property; (*correttezza*) correctness; **proprie'tario, a** *sm/f* owner; (*di albergo etc*) proprietor, owner; (*per l'inquilino*) landlord/lady.

'proprio, a *ag* (*possessivo*) own; (: *impersonale*) one's; (*esatto*) exact, correct, proper; (*senso, significato*) literal; (*LING*: *nome*) proper; (*particolare*): **~ di** characteristic of, peculiar to // *av* (*precisamente*) just, exactly, precisely; (*davvero*) really; (*affatto*): **non ... ~** not ... at all.

propulsi'one *sf* propulsion.

'prora *sf* (*NAUT*) bow(s *pl*), prow.

'proroga, ghe *sf* extension; postponement; **proro'gare** *vt* to extend; (*differire*) to postpone, defer.

pro'rompere *vi* to burst out; **pro'rotto, a** *pp di* **prorompere**.

'prosa *sf* prose; **pro'saico, a, ci, che** *ag* (*fig*) prosaic, mundane.

pro'sciogliere [proʃ'ʃɔʎʎere] *vt* to release; (*DIR*) to acquit; **prosci'olto, a** *pp di* **prosciogliere**.

prosciu'gare [proʃʃu'gare] *vt* (*terreni*) to drain, reclaim; **~rsi** *vr* to dry up.

prosci'utto [proʃ'ʃutto] *sm* ham.

pros'critto, a *pp di* **proscrivere** // *sm* exile.

pros'crivere *vt* to exile, banish.

prosecuzi'one [prosekut'tsjone] *sf* continuation.

prosegui'mento *sm* continuation; **buon ~!** all the best!; (*a chi viaggia*) enjoy the rest of your journey!

prosegu'ire *vt* to carry on with, continue // *vi* to carry on, go on.

prospe'rare *vi* to thrive; **prosperità** *sf* prosperity; **'prospero, a** *ag* (*fiorente*) flourishing, thriving, prosperous; (*favorevole*) favourable; **prospe'roso, a** *ag* (*robusto*) hale and hearty; (: *ragazza*) buxom.

prospet'tare *vt* (*esporre*) to point out, show; **~rsi** *vr* to look, appear.

prospet'tiva *sf* (*ARTE*) perspective; (*veduta*) view; (*fig*: *previsione*) prospect.

pros'petto *sm* (*veduta*) view, prospect; (*facciata*) façade, front; (*tabella*) table.

prospici'ente [prospi'tʃente] *ag*: **~ qc** facing *o* overlooking sth.

prossimità *sf* nearness, proximity; **in ~ di** near (to), close to.

'prossimo, a *ag* (*vicino*): **~ a** near (to), close to; (*che viene subito dopo*) next; (*parente*) close // *sm* neighbour, fellow man.

prosti'tuta *sf* prostitute; **prostituzi'one** *sf* prostitution.

pros'trare *vt* (*fig*) to exhaust, wear out; **~rsi** *vr* (*fig*) to humble o.s.

protago'nista, i, e *sm/f* protagonist.

pro'teggere [pro'tɛddʒere] *vt* to protect.

prote'ina *sf* protein.

pro'tendere *vt* to stretch out; **pro'teso, a** *pp di* **protendere**.

pro'testa *sf* protest; (*dichiarazione*) protestation, profession.

protes'tante *ag, sm/f* Protestant.

protes'tare *vt, vi* to protest; **~rsi** *vr*: **~rsi innocente** *etc* to protest one's innocence *o* that one is innocent *etc*.

protet'tivo, a *ag* protective.

pro'tetto, a *pp di* **proteggere**.

protetto'rato *sm* protectorate.

protet'tore, 'trice *sm/f* protector; (*sostenitore*) patron.

protezi'one [protet'tsjone] *sf* protection; (*patrocinio*) patronage.

protocol'lare *vt* to register // *ag* formal; of protocol.

proto'collo *sm* protocol; (*registro*) register of documents.

proto'tipo *sm* prototype.

pro'trarre *vt* (*prolungare*) to prolong; (*differire*) to put off; **pro'tratto, a** *pp di* **protrarre**.

protube'ranza [protube'rantsa] *sf* protuberance, bulge.

'prova *sf* (*esperimento, cimento*) test, trial; (*tentativo*) attempt, try; (*MAT, testimonianza, documento etc*) proof; (*DIR*) evidence q, proof; (*INS*) exam, test; (*TEATRO*) rehearsal; (*di abito*) fitting; **a ~ di** (*in testimonianza di*) as proof of; **a ~ di fuoco** fireproof; **mettere in ~** (*vestito*) to try on; **mettere alla ~** to put to the test; **viaggio** *o* **corsa di ~** test *o* trial run; **~ generale** (*TEATRO*) dress rehearsal.

pro'vare *vt* (*sperimentare*) to test; (*tentare*) to try, attempt; (*assaggiare*) to try, taste; (*sperimentare in sé*) to experience; (*sentire*) to feel; (*cimentare*) to put to the test; (*dimostrare*) to prove; (*abito*) to try on // *vi* to try; **~rsi** *vr*: **~rsi (a fare)** to try *o* attempt (to do); **~ a fare** to try *o* attempt to do.

proveni'enza [prove'njɛntsa] *sf* origin, source.

prove'nire *vi* (*2*): **~ da** to come from.

pro'venti *smpl* revenue *sg*.

prove'nuto, a *pp di* **provenire**.

pro'verbio *sm* proverb.

pro'vetta *sf* test tube.

pro'vetto, a *ag* skilled, experienced.

pro'vincia, ce *o* **cie** [pro'vintʃa] *sf* province; **provinci'ale** *ag* provincial.

pro'vino *sm* (*CINEMA*) screen test; (*campione*) specimen.

provo'cante *ag* (*attraente*) provocative.

provo'care *vt* (*causare*) to cause, bring about; (*eccitare*: *riso, pietà*) to arouse; (*irritare, sfidare*) to provoke; **provoca-**

'torio, a ag provocative; **provocazi'one** sf provocation.

provve'dere vi (disporre): ~ **(a)** to provide (for); (prendere un provvedimento) to take steps, act // vt to provide, supply; ~**rsi** vr: ~**rsi di** to provide o.s. with; **provvedi'mento** sm measure; (di previdenza) precaution.

provvi'denza [provvi'dcntsa] sf: la ~ providence; **provvidenzi'ale** ag providential.

provvigi'one [provvi'dʒone] sf (COMM) commission.

provvi'sorio, a ag temporary; (DIR) provisional.

prov'vista sf provision, supply.

'prua sf (NAUT) = **prora**.

pru'dente ag cautious, careful, prudent; (assennato) sensible, wise; **pru'denza** sf prudence; (cautela) caution, care.

'prudere vi to itch, be itchy.

'prugna ['pruɲɲa] sf plum; ~ **secca** prune; **'prugno** sm plum tree.

prurigi'noso, a [pruridʒi'noso] ag itchy.

pru'rito sm itchiness q; itch.

P.S. (abbr di postscriptum) P.S.; abbr di **Pubblica Sicurezza**.

pseu'donimo sm pseudonym.

psica'nalisi sf psychoanalysis; **psicana-'lista, i, e** sm/f psychoanalyst; **psicana-liz'zare** vt to psychoanalyse.

'psiche ['psike] sf (PSIC) psyche.

psichi'atra, i, e [psi'kjatra] sm/f psychiatrist; **psichia'tria** sf psychiatry.

psicolo'gia [psikolo'dʒia] sf psychology; **psico'logico, a, ci, che** ag psychological; **psi'cologo, a, gi, ghe** sm/f psychologist.

psico'patico, a, ci, che ag psychopathic // sm/f psychopath.

P.T. (abbr di Posta e Telegrafi) P.O.

pubbli'care vt to publish.

pubblicazi'one [pubblikat'tsjone] sf publication; ~**i (matrimoniali)** sfpl (marriage) banns.

pubbli'cista, i, e [pubbli'tʃista] sm/f (STAMPA) occasional contributor.

pubblicità [pubblitʃi'ta] sf (diffusione) publicity; (attività) advertising; (annunci nei giornali) advertisements pl; **pubblici-'tario, a** ag advertising cpd; (trovata, film) publicity cpd.

'pubblico, a, ci, che ag public; (statale: scuola etc) state cpd // sm public; (spettatori) audience; **in ~** in public; ~ **funzionario** civil servant; **P~ Ministero** Public Prosecutor's Office; **la P~a Sicurezza** the Police.

'pube sm (ANAT) pubis.

pubertà sf puberty.

'pudico, a, ci, che ag modest.

pu'dore sm modesty.

puericul'tura sf paediatric nursing; infant care.

pue'rile ag childish.

pugi'lato [pudʒi'lato] sm boxing.

'pugile ['pudʒile] sm boxer.

pugna'lare [puɲɲa'lare] vt to stab.

pu'gnale [puɲ'ɲale] sm dagger.

'pugno ['puɲɲo] sm fist; (colpo) punch; (quantità) fistful.

'pulce ['pultʃe] sf flea.

pul'cino [pul'tʃino] sm chick.

pu'ledro, a sm/f colt/filly.

pu'leggia, ge [pu'leddʒa] sf pulley.

pu'lire vt to clean; (lucidare) to polish; **pu-'lito, a** ag (anche fig) clean; (ordinato) neat, tidy // sf quick clean; **puli'tura** sf cleaning; **pu'lizia** sf cleaning; cleanness; **fare le pulizie** to do the cleaning, do the housework.

'pullman sm inv coach.

pul'lover sm inv pullover, jumper.

pullu'lare vi to swarm, teem.

pul'mino sm minibus.

'pulpito sm pulpit.

pul'sante sm (push-)button.

pul'sare vi to pulsate, beat; **pulsazi'one** sf beat.

pul'viscolo sm fine dust.

'puma sm inv puma.

pun'gente [pun'dʒente] ag prickly; stinging; (anche fig) biting.

'pungere ['pundʒere] vt to prick; (sog: insetto, ortica) to sting; (: freddo) to bite; (fig) to wound, offend.

pungigli'one [pundʒiʎ'ʎone] sm sting.

pungo'lare vt to goad.

pu'nire vt to punish; **puni'tivo, a** ag punitive; **punizi'one** sf punishment.

'punta sf point; (parte terminale) tip, end; (di monte) peak; (di costa) promontory; (minima parte) touch, trace; **in ~ di piedi** on tip-toe; **ore di ~** peak hours; **uomo di ~** front-rank o leading man.

pun'tare vt (piedi a terra, gomiti sul tavolo) to plant; (scommettere: pistola) to point; (scommettere) to bet // vi (mirare): ~ **a** to aim at; (avviarsi): ~ **su** to head o make for; (fig: contare): ~ **su** to count o rely on.

pun'tata sf (gita) short trip; (scommessa) bet; (parte di opera) instalment; **romanzo a ~e** serial.

punteggi'are [punted'dʒare] vt to dot; (forare) to make holes in; (LING) to punctuate; **puntaggia'tura** sf (LING) punctuation.

pun'teggio [pun'teddʒo] sm score.

puntel'lare vt to support.

pun'tello sm prop, support.

pun'tiglio [pun'tiʎʎo] sm obstinacy, stubbornness.

pun'tina sf: ~ **da disegno** drawing pin.

pun'tino sm dot; **fare qc a ~** to do sth properly.

'punto, a pp di **pungere** // sm (segno, macchiolina) dot; (LING) full stop; (MAT, momento, di punteggio, fig: argomento) point; (posto) spot; (a scuola) mark; (nel cucire, nella maglia, MED) stitch // av: **non ... ~** not ... at all; **due ~i** sm (LING) colon; **sul ~ di fare** (just) about to do; **fare il ~** (NAUT) to take a bearing; (fig): **fare il ~ su qc** to define sth; **alle 6 in ~** at 6 o'clock sharp o on the dot; **essere a buon**

~ to have reached a satisfactory stage; **mettere a** ~ to adjust; (*motore*) to tune; (*cannocchiale*) to focus; (*fig*) to settle; **di** ~ **in bianco** point-blank; ~ **cardinale** point of the compass, cardinal point; ~ **debole** weak point; ~ **esclamativo/ interrogativo** exclamation/question mark; ~ **di riferimento** landmark; (*fig*) point of reference; ~ **di vendita** retail outlet; ~ **e virgola** semicolon; ~ **di vista** (*fig*) point of view; ~**i di sospensione** suspension points.

puntu'ale *ag* punctual; precise, exact; **puntualità** *sf* punctuality; precision, exactness.

pun'tura *sf* (*di ago*) prick; (*di insetto*) sting, bite; (*MED*) puncture; (: *iniezione*) injection; (*dolore*) sharp pain.

punzecchi'are [puntsek'kjare] *vt* to prick; (*fig*) to tease.

pun'zone [pun'tsone] *sm* (*per metalli*) stamp, die.

'pupa *sf* doll.

pu'pazzo [pu'pattso] *sm* puppet.

pu'pillo, a *sm/f* (*DIR*) ward; (*prediletto*) favourite, pet // *sf* (*ANAT*) pupil.

purché [pur'ke] *cong* provided that, on condition that.

'pure *cong* (*tuttavia*) and yet, nevertheless; (*anche se*) even if // *av* (*anche*) too, also; **pur di** (*al fine di*) just to; **faccia** ~**!** go ahead!, please do!

purè *sm*, **pu'rea** *sf* (*CUC*) purée; (*di patate*) mashed potatoes.

pu'rezza [pu'rettsa] *sf* purity.

'purga, ghe *sf* (*MED*) purging *q*; purge; (*POL*) purge.

pur'gante *sm* (*MED*) purgative, purge.

pur'gare *vt* (*MED, POL*) to purge; (*pulire*) to clean.

purga'torio *sm* purgatory.

purifi'care *vt* to purify; (*metallo*) to refine.

puri'tano, a *ag, sm/f* Puritan.

'puro, a *ag* pure; (*acqua*) clear, limpid; (*vino*) undiluted; **puro'sangue** *sm/f inv* thoroughbred.

pur'troppo *av* unfortunately.

pus *sm* pus.

pusil'lanime *ag* fainthearted.

'pustola *sf* pimple.

puti'ferio *sm* rumpus, row.

putre'fare *vi* (2) to putrefy, rot; **putre-'fatto, a** *pp di* **putrefare**.

'putrido, a *ag* putrid, rotten.

put'tana *sf* (*fam!*) whore (!).

'puzza ['puttsa] *sf* = **puzzo**.

puz'zare [put'tsare] *vi* to stink.

'puzzo ['puttso] *sm* stink, foul smell.

'puzzola ['puttsola] *sf* polecat.

puzzo'lente [puttso'lɛnte] *ag* stinking.

Q

qua *av* here; **in** ~ (*verso questa parte*) this way; **da un anno in** ~ for a year now; **per di** ~ (*passare*) this way; **al di** ~ **di**

(*fiume, strada*) on this side of; *vedi* **questo**.

qua'derno *sm* notebook; (*per scuola*) exercise book.

qua'drangolo *sm* quadrangle.

qua'drante *sm* quadrant; (*di orologio*) face.

qua'drare *vi* (*bilancio*) to balance, tally; (*descrizione*) to correspond; (*fig*): ~ **a** to please, be to one's liking // *vt* (*MAT*) to square; **non mi quadra** I don't like it; **qua'drato, a** *ag* square; (*fig: equilibrato*) level-headed, sensible // *sm* (*MAT*) square; (*PUGILATO*) ring; **5 al quadrato** 5 squared.

qua'dretto *sm*: **a** ~**i** (*tessuto*) checked.

quadri'foglio [kwadri'fɔʎʎo] *sm* four-leaf clover.

'quadro *sm* (*pittura*) painting, picture; (*quadrato*) square; (*tabella*) table, chart; (*TECN*) board, panel; (*TEATRO*) scene; (*fig: scena, spettacolo*) sight; (: *descrizione*) outline, description; ~**i** *smpl* (*POL*) party organizers; (*MIL*) cadres; (*CARTE*) diamonds.

qua'drupede *sm* quadruped.

quadrupli'care *vt* to quadruple.

qua'druplo, a *ag, sm* quadruple.

quaggiù [kwad'dʒu] *av* down here.

'quaglia ['kwaʎʎa] *sf* quail.

'qualche ['kwalke] *det* some; (*alcuni*) a few; (*in espressioni interrogative*) any; (*uno*): **c'è** ~ **medico?** is there a doctor?; **ho comprato** ~ **libro** I've bought some *o* a few books; **hai** ~ **sigaretta?** have you any cigarettes?; **una persona di** ~ **rilievo** a person of some importance; ~ **cosa** = **qualcosa**; **in** ~ **modo** somehow; ~ **volta** sometimes; **qualche'duno** *pronome* = **qualcuno**.

qual'cosa *pronome* something; (*in espressioni interrogative*) anything; **qual-cos'altro** something else; anything else; ~ **di nuovo** something new; anything new.

qual'cuno *pronome* (*persona*) someone, somebody; (: *in espressioni interrogative*) anyone, (*alcuni*) some; ~ **è favorevole a noi** some are on our side; **qualcun altro** someone *o* somebody else; anyone *o* anybody else.

'quale (*spesso troncato in* **qual**) *det* what; (*discriminativo*) which; (*come*) as // *pronome* (*interrogativo*) what; which; (*relativo*) which // ~ (*persona: soggetto*) who; (: *oggetto, con preposizione*) whom; (*cosa*) which; (*possessivo*): **la signora della** ~ **ammiriamo la bellezza** the lady whose beauty we admire // *av* (*in qualità di*) as; ~ **disgrazia!** what a misfortune!

qua'lifica, che *sf* qualification; (*titolo*) title.

qualifi'care *vt* to qualify; (*definire*): ~ **qd/qc come** to describe sb/sth as; ~**rsi** *vr* (*anche SPORT*) to qualify; **qualifica-'tivo, a** *ag* qualifying; **qualificazi'one** *sf* qualification.

qualità *sf inv* quality; **in** ~ **di** in one's capacity as.

qua'lora *cong* in case, if.

qual'siasi, qua'lunque *det inv* any; *(quale che sia)* whatever; *(discriminativo)* whichever; *(posposto: mediocre)* poor, indifferent; ordinary; ~ **cosa accada** whatever happens; **a ~ costo** at any cost, whatever the cost; **l'uomo ~** the man in the street; ~ **persona** anyone, anybody.

'quando *cong, av* when; ~ **sarò ricco** when I'm rich; **da ~** *(dacché)* since; *(interrogativo)*: **da ~ sei qui?** how long have you been here?; **quand'anche** even if.

quantità *sf inv* quantity; *(gran numero)*: **una ~ di** a great deal of; a lot of; **in grande ~** in large quantities.

'quanto, a *det (interrogativo: quantità)* how much; (: *numero)* how many; *(esclamativo)* what a lot of, how much *(o* many); *(relativo)* as much ... as; as many ... as; **ho ~ denaro mi occorre** I have as much money as I need // *pronome (interrogativo)* how much; how many; (: *tempo)* how long; *(relativo)* as much as; as many as; ~ **i(e)** *pronome pl (persone)* all those who // *av (interrogativo: con ag, av)* how; (: *con vb)* how much; *(esclamativo: con ag, av)* how; (: *con vb)* how much, what a lot; *(con valore relativo)* as much as; **studierò ~ posso** I'll study as much as *o* all I can; **~i ne abbiamo oggi?** what is the date today?; **~i anni hai?** how old are you?; ~ **costa?, quant'è?** how much does it cost?, how much is it?; **in ~** *av (in qualità di)* as; *(poiché)* since; **per ~ sia brava, fa degli errori** however good she may be, she makes mistakes; **per ~ io sappia** as far as I know; ~ **a** as regards, as for; ~ **prima** as soon as possible; ~ **tempo?** how long?, how much time?; ~ **più ... tanto meno** the more ... the less; ~ **più ... tanto più** the more ... the more.

quan'tunque *cong* although, though.

qua'ranta *num* forty.

quaran'tena *sf* quarantine.

quaran'tesimo, a *num* fortieth.

quaran'tina *sf*: **una ~ (di)** about forty.

qua'resima *sf*: **la ~** Lent.

'quarta *sf vedi* **quarto.**

quar'tetto *sm* quartet(te).

quarti'ere *sm* district, area; *(MIL)* quarters *pl*; ~ **generale** headquarters *pl*, HQ.

'quarto, a *ag* fourth // *sm* fourth; *(quarta parte)* quarter // *sf (AUT)* fourth (gear); ~ **d'ora** quarter of an hour; **le 6 e un ~** a quarter past six.

'quarzo ['kwartso] *sm* quartz.

'quasi *av* almost, nearly // *cong (anche:* ~ **che)** as if; **(non) ... ~ mai** hardly ever; ~ **~ me ne andrei** I've half a mind to leave.

quassù *av up* here.

'quatto, a *ag* crouched, squatting; *(silenzioso)* silent; ~ **~** very quietly; stealthily.

quat'tordici [kwat'torditʃi] *num* fourteen.

quat'trini *smpl* money *sg*, cash *sg*.

'quattro *num* four; **in ~ e quatt'rotto** in less than no time; **quattro'cento** *num* four hundred // *sm*: **il Quattrocento** the fifteenth century; **quattro'mila** *num* four thousand.

'quello, a *det (dav sm* **quel** + *C,* **quell'** + *V,* **quello** + *s impura, gn, pn, ps, x, z; pl* **quei** + *C,* **quegli** + *V o s impura, gn, pn, ps, x, z; dav sf* **quella** + *C,* **quell'** + *V; pl* **quelle)** that; those *pl //* *pronome* that (one); those (ones) *pl*; *(ciò)* that; **~(a) che** the one who; **~i(e) che** those who; **ho fatto ~ che potevo** I did what I could; **~(a) ... lì** *o* **là** *det* that; **quell'uomo lì** that man; **~(a) lì** *o* **là** *pronome* that one.

'quercia, ce ['kwertʃa] *sf* oak (tree); *(legno)* oak.

que'rela *sf (DIR)* (legal) action; **quere'lare** *vt* to bring an action against.

que'sito *sm* question, query; problem.

questio'nare *vi*: ~ **di/su qc** to argue about/over sth.

questio'nario *sm* questionnaire.

questi'one *sf* problem, question; *(affare)* matter; issue; *(litigio)* quarrel; **in ~** in question; **fuor di ~** out of the question; **è ~ di tempo** it's a matter *o* question of time.

'questo, a *det* this; these *pl //* *pronome* this (one); those (ones) *pl*; *(ciò)* this; **~(a) ... qui** *o* **qua** *det* this; ~ **ragazzo qui** this boy; **~(a) qui** *o* **qua** *pronome* this one; **io prendo ~ cappotto, tu prendi quello** I'll take this coat, you take that one; **preferisce ~i o quelli?** do you prefer these (ones) or those (ones)?; **vengono Paolo e Folco:** ~ **da Roma, quello da Palermo** Paolo and Folco are coming: the latter from Rome, the former from Palermo; **quest'oggi** today.

ques'tore *sm ≈* chief constable.

'questua *sf* collection (of alms).

ques'tura *sf* police headquarters *pl*.

qui *av* here; **da** *o* **di ~** from here; **di ~ in avanti** from now on; **di ~ a poco/una settimana** in a little while/a week's time; ~ **dentro/sopra/vicino** in/up/near here; *vedi* **questo.**

quie'tanza [kwje'tantsa] *sf* receipt.

quie'tare *vt* to calm, soothe.

qui'ete *sf* quiet, quietness; calmness; stillness; peace.

qui'eto, a *ag* quiet; *(calmo)* calm, still; *(tranquillo)* quiet, calm; *(pacifico)* peaceful; *(pacato)* peaceable.

'quindi *av* then // *cong* therefore, so.

'quindici ['kwinditʃi] *num* fifteen.

quindi'cina [kwindi'tʃina] *sf (serie)*: **una ~ (di)** about fifteen; **fra una ~ di giorni** in a fortnight.

quin'quennio *sm* period of five years.

quin'tale *sm* quintal *(100 kg)*.

'quinte *sfpl (TEATRO)* wings.

quin'tetto *sm* quintet(te).

'quinto, a *num* fifth.

'quorum *sm* quorum.

'quota *sf (ripartizione)* quota, share; *(rata)* instalment; *(AER)* height, altitude; *(IPPICA)* odds *pl*; **prendere/perdere** ~ (AER) to gain/lose height *o* altitude.

quo'tare *vt* (BORSA) to quote; **quotazi'one** *sf* quotation.

quotidi'ano, a *ag* daily; (*banale*) everyday // *sm* (*giornale*) daily (paper).

quozi'ente [kwot'tsjente] *sm* (MAT) quotient; ~ **d'intelligenza** intelligence quotient, IQ.

R

ra'barbaro *sm* rhubarb.

'rabbia *sf* (*ira*) anger, rage; (*accanimento, furia*) fury; (MED: *idrofobia*) rabies *sg*.

rab'bino *sm* rabbi.

rabbi'oso, a *ag* angry, furious; (*facile all'ira*) quick-tempered; (*forze, acqua etc*) furious, raging; (MED) rabid, mad.

rabbo'nire *vt*, ~**rsi** *vr* to calm down.

rabbrivi'dire *vi* (2) to shudder, shiver.

rabbui'arsi *vr* to grow dark.

raccapez'zare [rakkapet'tsare] *vt* (*denaro*) to scrape together; (*senso*) to make out, understand; ~**rsi** *vr*: **non** ~**rsi** to be at a loss.

raccapricci'ante [rakkaprit'tʃante] *ag* horrifying.

raccatta'palle *sm inv* (SPORT) ballboy.

raccat'tare *vt* to pick up.

rac'chetta [rak'ketta] *sf* (*per tennis*) racket; (*per ping-pong*) bat; ~ **da neve** snowshoe; ~ **da sci** ski stick.

racchi'udere [rak'kjudere] *vt* to contain; **racchi'uso, a** *pp di* **racchiudere**.

rac'cogliere [rak'kɔʎʎere] *vt* to collect; (*raccattare*) to pick up; (*frutti, fiori*) to pick, pluck; (AGR) to harvest; (*approvazione, voti*) to win; (*profughi*) to take in; ~**rsi** *vr* to gather; (*fig*) to gather one's thoughts; to meditate; **raccogli'mento** *sm* meditation; **raccogli'tore, 'trice** *sm/f* collector // *sm* (*cartella*) folder, binder; **raccoglitore a fogli mobili** loose-leaf binder.

rac'colto, a *pp di* **raccogliere** // *ag* (*rannicchiato*) curled up; (*pensoso*) thoughtful; (*assorto*) absorbed, engrossed // *sm* (AGR) crop, harvest // *sf* collecting *q*; collection; (AGR) harvesting *q*, gathering *q*; harvest, crop; (*adunata*) gathering.

raccoman'dare *vt* to recommend; (*affidare*) to entrust; (*lettera*) to register; ~**rsi a qd** to commend o.s. to sb; **mi raccomando!** don't forget!; **raccoman'data** *sf* (*anche:* **lettera raccomandata**) registered letter; **raccomandazi'one** *sf* recommendation.

raccomo'dare *vt* (*rassettare*) to put in order; (*riparare*) to repair, mend.

raccon'tare *vt*: ~ **(a qd)** (*dire*) to tell (sb); (*narrare*) to relate to (sb), tell (sb) about; **rac'conto** *sm* telling *q*, relating *q*; (*fatto raccontato*) story, tale.

raccorci'are [rakkor'tʃare] *vt* to shorten.

raccor'dare *vt* to link up, join; **rac'cordo** *sm* (TECN: *giunzione*) connection, joint;

(AUT: *di autostrada*) slip road; **raccordo anulare** (AUT) ring road.

ra'chitico, a, ci, che [ra'kitiko] *ag* suffering from rickets; (*fig*) scraggy, scrawny.

rachi'tismo [raki'tizmo] *sm* (MED) rickets *sg*.

racimo'lare [ratʃimo'lare] *vt* (*fig*) to scrape together, glean.

'rada *sf* (*natural*) harbour.

'radar *sm* radar.

raddol'cire [raddol'tʃire] *vt* to sweeten; (*fig*: *lenire*) to ease, soothe; (: *voce, colori*) to soften; ~**rsi** *vr* (*tempo*) to grow milder.

raddoppi'are *vt* to double; (*accrescere*: *anche fig*) to redouble, increase // *vi* to double.

raddriz'zare [raddrit'tsare] *vt* to straighten; (*fig*: *correggere*) to put straight, correct.

'radere *vt* (*barba*) to shave off; (*mento*) to shave; (*fig*: *rasentare*) to graze; to skim; ~**rsi** *vr* to shave (o.s.); ~ **al suolo** to raze to the ground.

radi'ale *ag* radial.

radi'are *vt* to strike off.

radia'tore *sm* radiator.

radiazi'one [radjat'tsjone] *sf* (FISICA) radiation; (*cancellazione*) striking off.

radi'cale *ag* radical // *sm* (LING) root.

ra'dicchio [ra'dikkjo] *sm* chicory.

ra'dice [ra'ditʃe] *sf* root.

'radio *sf inv* radio // *sm* (CHIM) radium; **radioattività** *sf* radioactivity; **radioat-'tivo, a** *ag* radioactive; **radiodiffusi'one** *sf* (*radio*) broadcasting; **radiogra'fia** *sf* radiography; (*foto*) X-ray photograph; **radiogra'fare** *vt* to X-ray; **radi'ologo, a, gi, ghe** *sm/f* radiologist.

radi'oso, a *ag* radiant.

radiostazi'one [radjostat'tsjone] *sf* radio station.

'rado, a *ag* (*capelli*) sparse, thin; (*visite*) infrequent; **di** ~ rarely.

radu'nare *vt*, ~**rsi** *vr* to gather, assemble.

ra'dura *sf* clearing.

'rafano *sm* radish.

raffazzo'nare [raffattso'nare] *vt* to patch up.

raf'fermo, a *ag* stale.

'raffica, che *sf* (METEOR) gust (of wind); (*di colpi*: *scarica*) burst of gunfire.

raffigu'rare *vt* to represent.

raffi'nare *vt* to refine; **raffina'tezza** *sf* refinement; **raffi'nato, a** *ag* refined; **raffine'ria** *sf* refinery.

raffor'zare [raffor'tsare] *vt* to reinforce.

raffredda'mento *sm* cooling.

raffred'dare *vt* to cool; (*fig*) to dampen, have a cooling effect on; ~**rsi** *vr* to grow cool *o* cold; (*prendere raffreddore*) to catch a cold; (*fig*) to cool (off).

raffred'dore *sm* (MED) cold.

raf'fronto *sm* comparison.

'rafia *sf* (*fibra*) raffia.

ra'gazzo, a [ra'gattso] *sm/f* boy/girl; (*fam*:

fidanzato) boyfriend/girlfriend.

raggi'ante [rad'dʒante] *ag* radiant, shining.

'raggio ['raddʒo] *sm (di sole etc)* ray; *(MAT, distanza)* radius; *(di ruota etc)* spoke; ~ **d'azione** range; ~**i X** X-rays.

raggi'rare [raddʒi'rare] *vt* to take in, trick; **rag'giro** *sm* trick.

raggi'ungere [rad'dʒundʒere] *vt* to reach; *(persona: riprendere)* to catch up (with); *(bersaglio)* to hit; *(fig: meta)* to achieve; **raggi'unto, a** *pp di* **raggiungere**.

raggomito'larsi *vr* to curl up.

raggrane'llare *vt* to scrape together.

raggrin'zare [raggrin'tsare] *vt, vi (2) (anche: ~rsi)* to wrinkle.

raggrup'pare *vt* to group (together).

ragguagli'are [raggwaʎ'ʎare] *vt (paragonare)* to compare; *(informare)* to inform; **raggu'aglio** *sm* comparison; piece of information.

ragguar'devole *ag (degno di riguardo)* distinguished, notable; *(notevole: somma)* considerable.

'ragia ['radʒa] *sf* resin; **acqua** ~ turpentine.

ragiona'mento [radʒona'mento] *sm* reasoning *q*; arguing *q*; argument.

ragio'nare [radʒo'nare] *vi (usare la ragione)* to reason; *(discorrere)*: ~ **(di)** to argue (about).

ragi'one [ra'dʒone] *sf* reason; *(dimostrazione, prova)* argument, reason; *(diritto)* right; **aver** ~ to be right; **aver** ~ **di qd** to get the better of sb; **in** ~ **di** at the rate of; to the amount of; according to; **a** *o* **con** ~ rightly, justly; **perdere la** ~ to become insane; *(fig)* to take leave of one's senses; **a ragion veduta** after due consideration.

ragione'ria [radʒone'ria] *sf* accountancy; accounts department.

ragio'nevole [radʒo'nevole] *ag* reasonable.

ragioni'ere, a [radʒo'njɛre] *sm/f* accountant.

ragli'are [raʎ'ʎare] *vi* to bray.

ragna'tela [raɲɲa'tela] *sf* cobweb, spider's web.

'ragno ['raɲɲo] *sm* spider.

ragù *sm inv (CUC)* meat sauce; stew.

RAI-TV [raiti'vu] *abbr f di Radio televisione italiana.*

rallegra'menti *smpl* congratulations.

ralle'grare *vt* to cheer up; ~**rsi** *vr* to cheer up; *(provare allegrezza)* to rejoice; ~**rsi con qd** to congratulate sb.

rallenta'mento *sm* slowing down; lessening, slackening.

rallen'tare *vt* to slow down; *(fig)* to lessen, slacken // *vi* to slow down; ~**rsi** *vr (fig)* to lessen, slacken (off).

raman'zina [raman'dzina] *sf* lecture, telling-off.

'rame *sm (CHIM)* copper.

ramificazi'one [ramifikat'tsjone] *sf* ramification.

rammari'carsi *vr:* ~ **(di)** *(rincrescersi)* to be sorry (about), regret; *(lamentarsi)* to complain (about); **ram'marico, chi** *sm* regret.

rammen'dare *vt* to mend; *(calza)* to darn; **ram'mendo** *sm* mending *q*; darning *q*; mend; darn.

rammen'tare *vt* to remember, recall; *(richiamare alla memoria)*: ~ **qc a qd** to remind sb of sth; ~**rsi** *vr:* ~**rsi (di qc)** to remember (sth).

rammol'lire *vt* to soften // *vi (2) (anche:* ~**rsi)** to go soft.

'ramo *sm* branch.

ramo'scello [ramoʃ'ʃello] *sm* twig.

'rampa *sf* flight (of stairs); ~ **di lancio** launching pad.

rampi'cante *ag (BOT)* climbing.

ram'pino *sm (gancio)* hook; *(NAUT)* grapnel; *(fig)* pretext, excuse.

ram'pone *sm* harpoon; *(ALPINISMO)* crampon.

'rana *sf* frog.

'rancido, a ['rantʃido] *ag* rancid.

ran'core *sm* rancour, resentment.

ran'dagio, a, gi, gie *o* **ge** [ran'dadʒo] *ag (gatto, cane)* stray.

ran'dello *sm* club, cudgel.

'rango, ghi *sm (condizione sociale, MIL: riga)* rank.

rannicchi'arsi [rannik'kjarsi] *vr* to crouch, huddle.

rannuvo'larsi *vr* to cloud over, become overcast.

ra'nocchio [ra'nɔkkjo] *sm (edible)* frog.

'rantolo *sm* wheeze; *(di agonizzanti)* death rattle.

'rapa *sf (BOT)* turnip.

ra'pace [ra'patʃe] *ag (animale)* predatory; *(fig)* rapacious, grasping // *sm* bird of prey.

ra'pare *vt (capelli)* to crop, cut very short.

'rapida *sf vedi* **rapido.**

rapidità *sf* speed.

'rapido, a *ag* fast; *(esame, occhiata)* quick, rapid // *sm (FERR)* express (train) // *sf (di fiume)* rapid.

rapi'mento *sm* kidnapping; *(fig)* rapture.

ra'pina *sf* robbery; *(bottino)* loot; ~ **a mano armata** armed robbery; **rapi'nare** *vt* to rob; **rapina'tore, 'trice** *sm/f* robber.

ra'pire *vt (cose)* to steal; *(persone)* to kidnap; *(fig)* to enrapture, delight; **rapi-'tore, 'trice** *sm/f* kidnapper.

rappez'zare [rappet'tsare] *vt* to patch.

rappor'tare *vt (riferire)* to report; *(confrontare)* to compare; *(riprodurre)* to reproduce.

rap'porto *sm (resoconto)* report; *(legame)* relationship; *(MAT, TECN)* ratio; ~**i** *smpl (fra persone, paesi)* relations; ~**i sessuali** sexual intercourse *sg*.

rap'prendersi *vr* to coagulate, clot; *(latte)* to curdle.

rappre'saglia [rappre'saʎʎa] *sf* reprisal, retaliation.

rappresen'tante *sm/f* representative;

rappresen'tanza *sf* delegation, deputation; (*COMM: ufficio, sede*) agency.

rappresen'tare *vt* to represent; (*TEATRO*) to perform; **rappresenta'tivo, a** *ag* representative; **rappresentazi'one** *sf* representation; performing *q*; (*spettacolo*) performance.

rap'preso, a *pp di* **rapprendere.**

rapso'dia *sf* rhapsody.

rare'fare *vt*, **~rsi** *vr* to rarefy; **rare'fatto, a** *pp di* **rarefare.**

rarità *sf inv* rarity.

'raro, a *ag* rare.

ra'sare *vt* (*barba etc*) to shave off; (*siepi, erba*) to trim, cut; **~rsi** *vr* to shave (o.s.).

raschi'are [ras'kjare] *vt* to scrape; (*macchia, fango*) to scrape off // *vi* to clear one's throat.

rasen'tare *vt* (*andar rasente*) to keep close to; (*sfiorare*) to skim along (*o* over); (*fig*) to border on.

ra'sente *prep*: **~ (a)** close to, very near.

'raso, a *pp di* **radere** // *ag* (*barba*) shaved; (*capelli*) cropped; (*con misure di capacità*) level; (*pieno: bicchiere*) full to the brim // *sm* (*tessuto*) satin; **~ terra** close to the ground; **un cucchiaio ~** a level spoonful.

ra'soio *sm* razor; **~ elettrico** electric shaver *o* razor.

ras'segna [ras'seɲɲa] *sf* (*MIL*) inspection, review; (*esame*) inspection; (*resoconto*) review, survey; (*pubblicazione letteraria etc*) review; (*mostra*) exhibition, show; **passare in ~** (*MIL*) to inspect, review.

rasse'gnare [rasseɲ'nare] *vt* to resign, relinquish; **~rsi** *vr* (*accettare*) to resign o.s.; **rassegnazi'one** *sf* resignation.

rassere'narsi *vr* (*tempo*) to clear up.

rasset'tare *vt* to tidy, put in order; (*aggiustare*) to repair, mend.

rassicu'rare *vt* to reassure.

rasso'dare *vt* to harden, stiffen; (*fig*) to strengthen, consolidate.

rassomigli'anza [rassomiʎ'ʎantsa] *sf* resemblance.

rassomigli'are [rassomiʎ'ʎare] *vi*: **~ a** to resemble, look like.

rastrel'lare *vt* to rake; (*fig: perlustrare*) to comb.

rastrelli'era *sf* rack; (*per piatti*) dishrack.

ras'trello *sm* rake.

'rata *sf* (*quota*) instalment; **pagare a ~e** to pay by instalments *o* on hire purchase; **rate'are, rateiz'zare** *vt* to divide into instalments.

ratifi'care *vt* (*DIR*) to ratify.

'ratto *sm* (*DIR*) abduction; (*ZOOL*) rat.

rattop'pare *vt* to patch; **rat'toppo** *sm* patching *q*; patch.

rattrap'pire *vt* to make stiff; **~rsi** *vr* to be stiff.

rattris'tare *vt* to sadden; **~rsi** *vr* to become sad.

'rauco, a, chi, che *ag* hoarse.

rava'nello *sm* radish.

ravi'oli *smpl* ravioli *sg*.

ravve'dersi *vr* to mend one's ways.

ravvici'nare [ravvitʃi'nare] *vt* (*avvicinare*): **~ qc a** to bring sth nearer to; (*: due tubi*) to bring closer together; (*riconciliare*) to reconcile, bring together.

ravvi'sare *vt* to recognize.

ravvi'vare *vt* to revive; (*fig*) to brighten up, enliven; **~rsi** *vr* to revive; to brighten up.

razio'cinio [ratsjo'tʃinjo] *sm* reasoning *q*; reason; (*buon senso*) common sense.

razio'nale [rattsjo'nale] *ag* rational.

razio'nare [rattsjo'nare] *vt* to ration.

razi'one [rat'tsjone] *sf* ration; (*porzione*) portion, share.

'razza ['rattsa] *sf* race; (*ZOOL*) breed; (*discendenza, stirpe*) stock, race; (*sorta*) sort, kind.

raz'zia [rat'tsia] *sf* raid, foray.

razzi'ale [rat'tsjale] *ag* racial.

raz'zismo [rat'tsizmo] *sm* racism, racialism.

raz'zista, i, e [rat'tsista] *ag, sm/f* racist, racialist.

'razzo ['raddzo] *sm* rocket.

razzo'lare [rattso'lare] *vi* (*galline*) to scratch about.

re *sm inv* (*sovrano*) king; (*MUS*) D; (*: solfeggiando la scala*) re.

rea'gire [rea'dʒire] *vi* to react.

re'ale *ag* real; (*di, da re*) royal // *sm*: **il ~** reality; **rea'lismo** *sm* realism; **rea'lista, i, e** *sm/f* realist; (*POL*) royalist.

realiz'zare [realid'dzare] *vt* (*progetto etc*) to realize, carry out; (*sogno, desiderio*) to realize, fulfil; (*scopo*) to achieve; (*COMM: titoli etc*) to realize; (*CALCIO etc*) to score; **~rsi** *vr* to be realized; **realizzazi'one** *sf* realization; fulfilment; achievement; **realizzazione scenica** stage production.

real'mente *av* really, actually.

realtà *sf inv* reality.

re'ato *sm* offence.

reat'tore *sm* (*FISICA*) reactor; (*AER: aereo*) jet; (*: motore*) jet engine.

reazio'nario, a [reattsjo'narjo] *ag* (*POL*) reactionary.

reazi'one [reat'tsjone] *sf* reaction.

'rebbio *sm* prong.

recapi'tare *vt* to deliver.

re'capito *sm* (*indirizzo*) address; (*consegna*) delivery.

re'care *vt* (*portare*) to bring; (*avere su di sé*) to carry, bear; (*cagionare*) to cause, bring; **~rsi** *vr* to go.

re'cedere [re'tʃedere] *vi* to withdraw.

recensi'one [retʃen'sjone] *sf* review; **recen'sire** *vt* to review; **recen'sore, a** *sm/f* reviewer.

re'cente [re'tʃente] *ag* recent; **di ~** recently.

recessi'one [retʃes'sjone] *sf* (*ECON*) recession.

re'cidere [re'tʃidere] *vt* to cut off, chop off.

reci'divo, a [retʃi'divo] *sm/f* (*DIR*) second (*o* habitual) offender, recidivist.

re'cinto [re'tʃinto] *sm* enclosure; (*ciò che*

recinge) fence; surrounding wall.

recipi'ente [retʃi'pjɛnte] *sm* container.

re'ciproco, a, ci, che [re'tʃiproko] *ag* reciprocal.

re'ciso, a [re'tʃizo] *pp di* **recidere**.

'recita ['rɛtʃita] *sf* performance.

'recital ['rɛtʃital] *sm inv* recital.

reci'tare [retʃi'tare] *vt (poesia, lezione)* to recite; *(dramma)* to perform; *(ruolo)* to play *o* act (the part of); **recitazi'one** *sf* recitation; *(di attore)* acting.

recla'mare *vi* to complain // *vt (richiedere)* to demand, claim; *(necessitare)* to need, require.

ré'clame [re'klam] *sf inv* advertising *q*; advert(isement).

re'clamo *sm* complaint.

reclusi'one *sf (DIR)* imprisonment.

re'cluso, a *sm/f* prisoner.

'recluta *sf* recruit; **recluta'mento** *sm* recruitment; **reclu'tare** *vt* to recruit.

re'condito, a *ag* secluded; *(fig)* secret, hidden.

recriminazi'one [rekriminat'tsjone] *sf* recrimination.

recrude'scenza [rekrudeʃ'ʃɛntsa] *sf* fresh outbreak.

redar'guire *vt* to rebuke.

re'datto, a *pp di* **redigere; redat'tore, 'trice** *sm/f (giornalista)* writer; sub-editor; *(di casa editrice)* editor; **redazi'one** *sf* writing; editing; *(sede)* editorial office(s); *(personale)* editorial staff; *(versione)* version.

reddi'tizio, a [reddi'tittsjo] *ag* profitable.

'reddito *sm* income; *(dello Stato)* revenue; *(di un capitale)* yield.

re'dento, a *pp di* **redimere**.

redenzi'one [reden'tsjone] *sf* redemption.

re'digere [re'didʒere] *vt* to write; *(contratto)* to draw up.

re'dimere *vt* to deliver; *(REL)* to redeem.

'redini *sfpl* reins.

redi'vivo, a *ag* returned to life, reborn.

'reduce ['rɛdutʃe] *ag:* ~ **da** returning from, back from // *sm/f* survivor.

'refe *sm* thread.

refe'rendum *sm inv* referendum.

refe'renza [refe'rɛntsa] *sf* reference.

re'ferto *sm* medical report.

refet'torio *sm* refectory.

refrat'tario, a *ag* refractory; *(fig):* **essere** ~ **alla matematica** to have no aptitude for mathematics.

refrige'rare [refridʒe'rare] *vt* to refrigerate; *(rinfrescare)* to cool, refresh; **refrigerazi'one** *sf* refrigeration.

rega'lare *vt* to give (as a present), make a present of.

re'gale *ag* regal.

re'galo *sm* gift, present.

re'gata *sf* regatta.

reg'gente [red'dʒɛnte] *sm/f* regent; **reg'genza** *sf* regency.

'reggere ['rɛddʒere] *vt (tenere)* to hold; *(sostenere)* to support, bear, hold up; *(portare)* to carry, bear; *(resistere)* to

withstand; *(dirigere: impresa)* to manage, run; *(governare)* to rule, govern; *(LING)* to take, be followed by // *vi (resistere):* ~ **a** to stand up to, hold out against; *(sopportare):* ~ **a** to stand; *(durare)* to last; ~**rsi** *vr (stare ritto)* to stand; *(fig: dominarsi)* to control o.s.; ~**rsi sulle gambe** *o* **in piedi** to stand up.

'reggia, ge ['rɛddʒa] *sf* royal palace.

reggi'calze [reddʒi'kaltse] *sm inv* suspender belt.

reggi'mento [reddʒi'mento] *sm (MIL)* regiment.

reggi'petto [reddʒi'pɛtto] *sm*, **reggi'seno** [reddʒi'seno] *sm* bra.

re'gia, 'gie [re'dʒia] *sf (TV, CINEMA etc)* direction.

re'gime [re'dʒime] *sm (POL)* regime; *(DIR: aureo, patrimoniale etc)* system; *(MED)* diet; *(TECN)* (engine) speed; **essere a** ~ to be on a diet.

re'gina [re'dʒina] *sf* queen.

'regio, a, gi, gie ['rɛdʒo] *ag* royal.

regio'nale [redʒo'nale] *ag* regional.

regi'one [re'dʒone] *sf* region; *(territorio)* region, district, area.

re'gista, i, e [re'dʒista] *sm/f (TV, CINEMA etc)* director.

regis'trare [redʒis'trare] *vt (AMM)* to register; *(COMM)* to enter; *(notare)* to note, take note of; *(canzone, conversazione, sog: strumento di misura)* to record; *(mettere a punto)* to adjust, regulate; **registra'tore** *sm (strumento di misura)* recorder, register; *(magnetofono)* tape recorder; *(classificatore)* folder; **registratore di cassa** cash register; **registrazi'one** *sf* recording; *(AMM)* registration; *(COMM)* entry.

re'gistro [re'dʒistro] *sm (libro)* register; ledger; logbook; *(DIR)* registry; *(MUS, TECN)* register.

re'gnare [ren'pare] *vi* to reign, rule; *(fig)* to reign.

'regno ['renpo] *sm* kingdom; *(periodo)* reign; *(fig)* realm; **il** ~ **animale/vegetale** the animal/vegetable kingdom; **il R~ Unito** the United Kingdom.

'regola *sf* rule; **a** ~ **d'arte** duly; perfectly; **in** ~ in order.

regola'mento *sm (complesso di norme)* regulations *pl*; *(di debito)* settlement; ~ **di conti** *(fig)* settling of scores.

rego'lare *ag* regular; *(in regola: domanda)* in order, lawful // *vt* to regulate, control; *(apparecchio)* to adjust, regulate; *(questione, conto, debito)* to settle; ~**rsi** *vr (moderarsi):* ~**rsi nel bere/nello spendere** to control one's drinking/spending; *(comportarsi)* to behave, act; **regolarità** *sf inv* regularity.

'regolo *sm* ruler; ~ **calcolatore** slide rule.

reinte'grare *vt* to restore; *(in una carica)* to reinstate.

relatività *sf* relativity.

rela'tivo, a *ag* relative.

relazi'one [relat'tsjone] *sf* (*fra cose, persone*) relation(ship); (*resoconto*) report, account; ~**i** *sfpl* (*conoscenze*) connections.

rele'gare *vt* to banish; (*fig*) to relegate.

religi'one [reli'dʒone] *sf* religion; (*rispetto*) veneration, reverence; **reli-gi'oso, a** *ag* religious // *sm/f* monk/nun.

re'liqua *sf* relic.

re'litto *sm* wreck; (*fig*) down-and-out.

re'mare *vi* to row.

remini'scenze [reminiʃ'ʃentse] *sfpl* reminiscences.

remissi'one *sf* remission; (*deferenza*) submissiveness, compliance.

remis'sivo, a *ag* submissive, compliant.

'remo *sm* oar.

re'moto, a *ag* remote.

'rendere *vt* (*ridare*) to return, give back; (: *saluto etc*) to return; (*produrre*) to yield, bring in; (*esprimere, tradurre*) to render; (*far diventare*): ~ **qc possibile** to make sth possible; ~ **la vista a qd** to restore sb's sight; ~ **grazie a qd** to thank sb; ~**rsi utile** to make o.s. useful; ~**rsi conto di qc** to realize sth.

rendi'conto *sm* (*rapporto*) report, account; (*COMM*) statement of account.

rendi'mento *sm* (*reddito*) yield; (*di manodopera, TECN*) efficiency; (*capacità di produrre*) output; (*di studenti*) performance.

'rendita *sf* (*di individuo*) private *o* unearned income; (*COMM*) revenue; ~ **annua** annuity.

'rene *sm* kidney.

'reni *sfpl* back *sg*.

reni'tente *ag* reluctant, unwilling; ~ **ai consigli di qd** unwilling to follow sb's advice; **essere** ~ **alla leva** (*MIL*) to fail to report for military service.

'renna *sf* reindeer *inv*.

'Reno *sm*: **il** ~ **the** Rhine.

'reo, a *sm/f* (*DIR*) offender.

re'parto *sm* department, section; (*MIL*) detachment.

repel'lente *ag* repulsive.

repen'taglio [repen'taʎʎo] *sm*: **mettere a** ~ to jeopardize, risk.

repen'tino, a *ag* sudden, unexpected.

repe'ribile *ag* to be found, available.

re'perto *sm* (*ARCHEOLOGIA*) find; (*MED*) report.

reper'torio *sm* (*TEATRO*) repertory; (*elenco*) index, (alphabetical) list.

'replica, che *sf* repetition; reply, answer; (*obiezione*) objection; (*TEATRO, CINEMA*) repeat performance; (*copia*) replica.

repli'care *vt* (*ripetere*) to repeat; (*rispondere*) to answer, reply.

repressi'one *sf* repression.

re'presso, a *pp di* **reprimere**.

re'primere *vt* to suppress, repress.

re'pubblica, che *sf* republic; **repub-bli'cano, a** *ag, sm/f* republican.

repu'tare *vt* to consider, judge.

reputazi'one [reputat'tsjone] *sf* reputation.

'requie *sf* rest.

requi'sire *vt* to requisition.

requi'sito *sm* requirement.

requisizi'one [rekwizit'tsjone] *sf* requisition.

'resa *sf* (*l'arrendersi*) surrender; (*restituzione, rendimento*) return; ~ **dei conti** rendering of accounts; (*fig*) day of reckoning.

resi'dente *ag* resident; **resi'denza** *sf* residence; **residenzi'ale** *ag* residential.

re'siduo, a *ag* residual, remaining // *sm* remainder; (*CHIM*) residue.

'resina *sf* resin.

resis'tente *ag* (*che resiste*): ~ **a** resistant to; (*forte*) strong; (*duraturo*) long-lasting, durable; ~ **al caldo** heat-resistant; **resis-'tenza** *sf* resistance; (*di persona*) endurance, resistance.

re'sistere *vi* to resist; ~ **a** (*assalto, tentazioni*) to resist; (*dolore, sog: pianta*) to withstand; (*non patir danno*) to be resistant to; **resis'tito, a** *pp di* **resistere**.

'reso, a *pp di* **rendere**.

reso'conto *sm* report, account.

respin'gente [respin'dʒente] *sm* (*FERR*) buffer.

res'pingere [res'pindʒere] *vt* to drive back, repel; (*rifiutare*) to reject; (*INS: bocciare*) to fail; **res'pinto, a** *pp di* **respingere**.

respi'rare *vi* to breathe; (*fig*) to get one's breath; to breathe again // *vt* to breathe (in), inhale; **respira'tore** *sm* respirator; **respira'torio, a** *ag* respiratory; **respirazi'one** *sf* breathing; **respirazione artificiale** artificial respiration; **res'piro** *sm* breathing *q*; (*singolo atto*) breath; (*fig*) respite, rest; **mandare un respiro di sollievo** to give a sigh of relief.

respon'sabile *ag* responsible // *sm/f* person responsible; (*capo*) person in charge; ~ **di** responsible for; (*DIR*) liable for; **responsabilità** *sf inv* responsibility; (*legale*) liability.

res'ponso *sm* answer.

'ressa *sf* crowd, throng.

res'tare *vi* (2) (*rimanere*) to remain, stay; (*diventare*): ~ **orfano/cieco** to become *o* be left an orphan/become blind; (*trovarsi*): ~ **sorpreso** to be surprised; (*avanzare*) to be left, remain; ~ **d'accordo** to agree; **non resta più niente** there's nothing left; **restano pochi giorni** there are only a few days left.

restau'rare *vt* to restore; **restaura-zi'one** *sf* (*POL*) restoration; **res'tauro** *sm* (*di edifici etc*) restoration.

res'tio, a, 'tii, 'tie *ag* restive; (*persona*): ~ **a** reluctant to.

restitu'ire *vt* to return, give back; (*energie, forze*) to restore.

'resto *sm* remainder, rest; (*denaro*) change; (*MAT*) remainder; ~**i** *smpl* leftovers; (*di città, mortali*) remains; **del** ~ moreover, besides.

res'tringere [res'trindʒere] *vt* to reduce; (*vestito*) to take in; (*stoffa*) to shrink; (*fig*) to restrict, limit; **~rsi** vr (strada) to narrow; (stoffa) to shrink; (persone) to draw closer together; **restrizi'one** sf restriction.

'rete sf net; (fig) trap, snare; (di recinzione) wire netting; (AUT, FERR, di spionaggio etc) network; **segnare una ~** (CALCIO) to score a goal.

reti'cente [reti'tʃɛnte] ag reticent.

retico'lato sm grid; (rete metallica) wire netting.

'retina sf (ANAT) retina.

re'torico, a, ci, che ag rhetorical // sf rhetoric.

retribu'ire vt to pay; (premiare) to reward; **retribuzi'one** sf payment; reward.

re'trivo, a ag (fig) reactionary.

'retro sm inv back // av (dietro): **vedi ~** see over(leaf).

retro'cedere [retro'tʃɛdere] vi (2) to withdraw // vt (CALCIO) to relegate; (MIL) to degrade.

retroda'tare vt (AMM) to backdate.

re'trogrado, a ag (fig) reactionary, backward-looking.

retrogu'ardia sf (MIL) rearguard.

retro'marcia [retro'martʃa] sf (AUT) reverse; (: dispositivo) reverse gear.

retrospet'tivo, a ag retrospective.

retrovi'sore sm (AUT) driving mirror.

'retta sf (MAT) straight line; (di convitto) charge for bed and board; (fig: ascolto): **dar ~ a** to listen to, pay attention to.

rettango'lare ag rectangular.

ret'tangolo, a ag right-angled // sm rectangle.

ret'tifica, che sf rectification, correction.

rettifi'care vt (curva) to straighten; (fig) to rectify, correct.

'rettile sm reptile.

retti'lineo, a ag rectilinear; (fig: condotta) upright, honest.

retti'tudine sf rectitude, uprightness.

'retto, a pp di **reggere** // ag straight; (MAT): **angolo ~** right angle; (onesto) honest, upright; (giusto, esatto) correct, proper, right.

ret'tore sm (REL) rector; (di università) ≈ chancellor.

reuma'tismo sm rheumatism.

reve'rendo, a ag: **il ~ padre Belli** the Reverend Father Belli.

rever'sibile ag reversible.

revisio'nare vt (componimento) to revise; (conti) to audit; (TECN) to overhaul, service; (DIR: processo) to review.

revisi'one sf revision; auditing q; audit; servicing q; overhaul; review.

revi'sore sm: **~ di conti/bozze** auditor/proofreader.

'revoca sf revocation.

revo'care vt to revoke.

re'volver sm inv revolver.

riabili'tare vt to rehabilitate; (fig) to restore to favour; **riabilitazi'one** sf rehabilitation.

rial'zare [rial'tsare] vt to raise, lift; (alzare di più) to heighten, raise; (aumentare: prezzi) to increase, raise // vi (2) (prezzi) to rise, increase; **ri'alzo** sm (di prezzi) increase, rise; (sporgenza) rise.

ria'prire vt, **~rsi** vr to reopen, open again.

ri'armo sm (MIL) rearmament.

rias'setto sm (di stanza etc) rearrangement; (ordinamento) reorganization.

rias'sumere vt (riprendere) to resume; (impiegare di nuovo) to re-employ; (sintetizzare) to summarize; **rias'sunto, a** pp di **riassumere** // sm summary.

ria'vere vt to have again; (avere indietro) to get back; (riacquistare) to recover; **~rsi** vr to recover.

riba'dire vt (fig) to confirm.

ri'balta sf flap; (TEATRO: proscenio) front of the stage; (: apparecchio d'illuminazione) footlights pl; (fig) limelight.

ribal'tabile ag (sedile) tip-up.

ribal'tare vt, vi (2) (anche: **~rsi**) to turn over, tip over.

ribas'sare vt to lower, bring down // vi (2) to come down, fall; **ri'basso** sm reduction, fall.

ri'battere vt to return, hit back; (confutare) to refute // vi to retort; **~ su qc** (fig) to harp on about sth.

ribel'larsi vr: **~ (a)** to rebel (against); **ri'belle** ag (soldati) rebel; (ragazzo) rebellious // sm/f rebel; **ribelli'one** sf rebellion.

'ribes sm inv currant; redcurrant; **~ nero** blackcurrant.

ribol'lire vi (fermentare) to ferment; (fare bolle) to bubble, boil; (fig) to seethe.

ri'brezzo [ri'breddzo] sm disgust, loathing; **far ~ a** to disgust.

ribut'tante ag disgusting, revolting.

rica'dere vi (2) to fall again; (scendere a terra, fig: nel peccato etc) to fall back; (vestiti, capelli etc) to hang (down); (riversarsi: fatiche, colpe): **~ su** to fall on; **rica'duta** sf (MED) relapse.

rical'care vt (disegni) to trace; (fig) to follow faithfully.

rica'mare vt to embroider.

ricambi'are vt to change again; (contraccambiare) to repay, return; **ri'cambio** sm exchange, return; (FISIOL) metabolism; **ricambi** smpl, **pezzi di ricambio** spare parts.

ri'camo sm embroidery.

ricapito'lare vt to recapitulate, sum up.

ricat'tare vt to blackmail; **ricatta'tore, 'trice** sm/f blackmailer; **ri'catto** sm blackmail.

rica'vare vt (estrarre) to draw out, extract; (ottenere) to obtain, gain; **ri'cavo** sm proceeds pl.

ric'chezza [rik'kettsa] sf wealth; (fig) richness; **~e** sfpl (beni) wealth sg, riches.

'riccio, a ['rittʃo] ag curly // sm (ZOOL) hedgehog; (: anche: **~ di mare**) sea urchin; **'ricciolo** sm curl; **ricci'uto, a** ag curly.

'ricco, a, chi, che ag rich; (persona, paese) rich, wealthy // sm/f rich man/woman; **i ~chi** the rich; **~ di** full of; rich in.

ri'cerca, che [ri'tʃerka] sf search; (indagine) investigation, inquiry; (studio): **la ~** research; **una ~** piece of research.

ricer'care [ritʃer'kare] vt (cercare con cura) to look for, search for; (indagare) to investigate; (tentare di scoprire: verità etc) to try to find; **ricer'cato, a** ag (apprezzato) much sought-after; (affettato) studied, affected // sm (POLIZIA) wanted man.

ri'cetta [ri'tʃetta] sf (MED) prescription; (CUC) recipe.

ricettazi'one [ritʃettat'tsjone] sf (DIR) receiving (stolen goods).

ri'cevere [ri'tʃevere] vt to receive; (stipendio, lettera) to get, receive; (accogliere: ospite) to welcome; (vedere: cliente, rappresentante etc) to see // vi to receive visitors; to see clients etc; **ricevi-'mento** sm receiving q; (accoglienza) welcome, reception; (trattenimento) reception; **ricevi'tore** sm (TECN) receiver; **ricevitore delle imposte** tax collector; **rice'vuta** sf receipt; **ricezi'one** sf (RADIO, TV) reception.

richia'mare [rikja'mare] vt (chiamare indietro, ritelefonare) to call back; (ambasciatore, truppe) to recall; (rimproverare) to reprimand; (attirare) to attract, draw; (riportare) to cite; **~rsi a** (riferirsi a) to refer to; **~ qc alla mente** to recall sth; **richi'amo** sm call; (MIL, di ambasciatore) recall; (attrazione) attraction, call, appeal.

richi'edere [ri'kjedere] vt to ask again for; (chiedere indietro): **~ qc** to ask for sth back; (chiedere: per sapere) to ask; (: per avere) to ask for; (AMM: documenti) to apply for; (esigere) to need, require; **richi'esto, a** pp di **richiedere** // sf (domanda) request; (AMM) application, request; (esigenza) demand, request; **a richiesta** on request.

'ricino ['ritʃino] sm: **olio di ~** castor oil.

ricognizi'one [rikoɲɲit'tsjone] sf (MIL) reconnaissance; (DIR) recognition, acknowledgement.

ricominci'are [rikomin'tʃare] vt, vi to start again, begin again.

ricom'pensa sf reward.

ricompen'sare vt to reward.

riconcili'are [rikontʃi'ljare] vt to reconcile; **~rsi** vr to be reconciled; **riconciliazi'one** sf reconciliation.

ricono'scente [rikonoʃ'ʃɛnte] ag grateful; **ricono'scenza** sf gratitude.

rico'noscere [riko'noʃʃere] vt to recognize; (DIR: figlio, debito) to acknowledge; (ammettere: errore) to admit, acknowledge; (MIL) to reconnoitre; **riconosci'mento** sm recognition; acknowledgement; (identificazione)

identification; **riconosci'uto, a** pp di **riconoscere**.

rico'prire vt to re-cover; (coprire) to cover; (occupare: carica) to hold.

ricor'dare vt to remember, recall; (richiamare alla memoria): **~ qc a qd** to remind sb of sth; **~rsi** vr: **~rsi (di)** to remember; **~rsi di qc/di aver fatto** to remember sth/having done.

ri'cordo sm memory; (regalo) keepsake, souvenir; (di viaggio) souvenir; **~i** smpl (memorie) memoirs.

ricor'rente ag recurrent, recurring; **ricor'renza** sf recurrence; (festività) anniversary.

ri'correre vi (2) (ripetersi) to recur; **~ a** (rivolgersi) to turn to; (: DIR) to appeal to; (servirsi di) to have recourse to; **ri'corso, a** pp di **ricorrere** // sm recurrence; (DIR) appeal; **far ricorso a = ricorrere a**.

ricostitu'ire vt to re-establish, reconstitute; (MED) to restore.

ricostru'ire vt (casa) to rebuild; (fatti) to reconstruct; **ricostruzi'one** sf rebuilding q; reconstruction.

ri'cotta sf soft white unsalted cheese made from sheep's milk.

ricove'rare vt to give shelter to; **~ qd in ospedale** to admit sb to hospital.

ri'covero sm shelter, refuge; admission (to hospital); (per vecchi, indigenti) home.

ricre'are vt to recreate; (rinvigorire) to restore; (fig: distrarre) to amuse.

ricreazi'one [rikreat'tsjone] sf recreation, entertainment; (INS) break.

ri'credersi vr to change one's mind.

ricupe'rare vt (rientrare in possesso di) to recover, get back; (tempo perduto) to make up for; (NAUT) to salvage; (: naufraghi) to rescue; (delinquente) to rehabilitate.

ricu'sare vt to refuse.

ridacchi'are [ridak'kjare] vi to snigger.

ri'dare vt to return, give back.

'ridere vi to laugh; (deridere, beffare): **~ di** to laugh at, make fun of.

ri'detto, a pp di **ridire**.

ri'dicolo, a ag ridiculous, absurd.

ridimensio'nare vt to reorganize; (fig) to see in the right perspective.

ri'dire vt to repeat; (criticare) to find fault with; to object to; **trova sempre qualcosa da ~** he always manages to find fault.

ridon'dante ag redundant.

ri'dotto, a pp di **ridurre**.

ri'durre vt (anche CHIM, MAT) to reduce; (prezzo, spese) to cut, reduce; (accorciare: vestito) to shorten; (: opera letteraria) to abridge; (: RADIO, TV) to adapt; **ridursi** vr (diminuirsi) to be reduced, shrink; **ridursi a** to be reduced to; **ridursi pelle e ossa** to be reduced to skin and bone; **ridu-zi'one** sf reduction; abridgement; adaptation.

riempi'mento sm filling.

riem'pire vt to fill (up); (modulo) to fill in o out; **~rsi** vr to fill (up); (mangiare

troppo) to stuff o.s.; ~ qc di to fill sth (up) with; **riempi'tivo, a** *ag* filling // *sm* (*anche fig*) filler.

rien'tranza [rien'trantsa] *sf* recess; indentation.

rien'trare *vi* (2) (*entrare di nuovo*) to go (*o* come) back in; (*tornare*) to return; (*fare una rientranza*) to go in, curve inwards; to be indented; (*riguardare*): ~ **in** to be included among, form part of; **ri'entro** *sm* (*ritorno*) return; (*anche ASTR*) re-entry.

riepilo'gare *vt* to summarize // *vi* to recapitulate.

ri'fare *vt* to do again; (*riparare*) to repair; (*imitare*) to imitate, copy; **~rsi** *vr* (*ristabilirsi: malato*) to recover; (: *tempo*) to clear up; (*ricominciare*) to start again; (*vendicarsi*) to get even; (*risarcirsi*): **~rsi di** to make up for; **~rsi il letto** to make the bed; **~rsi una vita** to make a new life for o.s.; **ri'fatto, a** *pp di* rifare.

riferi'mento *sm* reference; **in** *o* **con** ~ **a** with reference to.

rife'rire *vt* (*riportare*) to report; (*ascrivere*): ~ **qc a** to attribute sth to // *vi* to make a report; **~rsi** *vr*: **~rsi a** to refer to.

rifi'nire *vt* to finish off, put the finishing touches to; **rifini'tura** *sf* finish; finishing touches *pl.*

rifiu'tare *vt* to refuse; ~ **di fare** to refuse to do; **rifi'uto** *sm* refusal; **rifiuti** *smpl* (*spazzatura*) rubbish *sg*, refuse *sg.*

riflessi'one *sf* (*FISICA, meditazione*) reflection; (*il pensare*) thought, reflection; (*osservazione*) remark.

rifles'sivo, a *ag* (*persona*) thoughtful, reflective; (*LING*) reflexive.

ri'flesso, a *pp di* riflettere // *sm* (*di luce, rispecchiamento*) reflection; (*FISIOL*) reflex; **di** *o* **per** ~ indirectly.

ri'flettere *vt* to reflect // *vi* to think; **~rsi** *vr* to be reflected; ~ **su** to think about.

riflet'tore *sm* reflector; (*proiettore*) floodlight; searchlight.

ri'flusso *sm* flowing back; (*della marea*) ebb.

ri'fondere *vt* (*rimborsare*) to refund, repay.

ri'forma *sf* reform; (*MIL*) declaration of unfitness for service; discharge (*on health grounds*); **la R**~ (*REL*) the Reformation.

rifor'mare *vt* to re-form; (*cambiare, innovare*) to reform; (*MIL: recluta*) to declare unfit for service; (: *soldato*) to invalid out, discharge; **riforma'torio** *sm* (*DIR*) approved school.

riforni'mento *sm* supplying, providing; restocking; **~i** *smpl* supplies, provisions.

rifor'nire *vt* (*provvedere*): ~ **di** to supply *o* provide with; (*fornire di nuovo: casa etc*) to restock.

ri'frangere [ri'frandʒere] *vt* to refract; **ri'fratto, a** *pp di* rifrangere; **rifrazi'one** *sf* refraction.

rifug'gire [rifud'dʒire] *vi* (2) to escape again; (*fig*): ~ **da** to shun.

rifugi'arsi [rifu'dʒarsi] *vr* to take refuge; **rifugi'ato, a** *sm/f* refugee.

ri'fugio [ri'fudʒo] *sm* refuge, shelter; ~ **antiaereo** air-raid shelter.

'riga, ghe *sf* line; (*striscia*) stripe; (*di persone, cose*) line, row; (*regolo*) ruler; (*scriminatura*) parting; **mettersi in** ~ to line up; **a ~ghe** (*foglio*) lined; (*vestito*) striped.

ri'gagnolo [ri'gaɲɲolo] *sm* rivulet.

ri'gare *vt* (*foglio*) to rule // *vi*: ~ **diritto** (*fig*) to toe the line.

rigat'tiere *sm* junk dealer.

riget'tare [ridʒet'tare] *vt* (*gettare indietro*) to throw back; (*fig: respingere*) to reject; (*vomitare*) to bring *o* throw up; **ri'getto** *sm* (*anche MED*) rejection.

rigidità [ridʒidi'ta] *sf* rigidity; stiffness; severity, rigours *pl*; strictness; ~ **cadaverica** rigor mortis.

'rigido, a [ˈridʒido] *ag* rigid, stiff; (*membro etc: indurito*) stiff; (*METEOR*) harsh, severe; (*fig*) strict.

rigi'rare [ridʒi'rare] *vt* to turn; (*ripercorrere*) to go round; (*fig: persona*) to get round; **~rsi** *vr* to turn round; (*nel letto*) to turn over; ~ **il discorso** to change the subject; **ri'giri** *smpl* (*fig*) tricks.

'rigo, ghi *sm* line; (*MUS*) staff, stave.

rigogli'oso, a [rigoʎˈʎoso] *ag* (*anche fig*) exuberant.

ri'gonfio, a *ag* swollen.

ri'gore *sm* (*METEOR*) harshness, rigours *pl*; (*fig*) severity, strictness; (*anche:* **calcio di** ~) penalty; **di** ~ compulsory; **a rigor di termini** strictly speaking; **rigo'roso, a** *ag* (*severo: persona*) strict, stern; (: *disciplina*) rigorous, strict; (*preciso*) rigorous.

rigover'nare *vt* to wash (up).

riguar'dare *vt* to look at again; (*considerare*) to regard, consider; (*concernere*) to regard, concern; **~rsi** *vr* (*aver cura di sé*) to look after o.s.; **~rsi da** to beware of, keep away from.

rigu'ardo *sm* (*attenzione*) care; (*considerazione*) regard, respect; ~ **a** concerning, with regard to; **non aver ~i nell'agire/nel parlare** to act/speak freely.

rilasci'are [rilaʃˈʃare] *vt* (*rimettere in libertà*) to release; (*AMM: documenti*) to issue; **ri'lascio** *sm* release; issue.

rilas'sare *vt* to relax; **~rsi** *vr* to relax; (*moralità*) to become slack.

rile'gare *vt* (*libro*) to bind; **rilega'tura** *sf* binding.

ri'leggere [ri'leddʒere] *vt* to reread, read again; (*rivedere*) to read over.

ri'lento: a ~ *av* slowly.

rileva'mento *sm* (*topografico, statistico*) survey; (*NAUT*) bearing.

rile'vante *ag* considerable; important.

rile'vare *vt* (*ricavare*) to find; (*notare*) to notice; (*mettere in evidenza*) to point out; (*venire a conoscere: notizia*) to learn; (*raccogliere: dati*) to gather, collect; (*TOPO-*

GRAFIA) to survey; (*MIL*) to relieve; (*COMM*) to take over.

rili'evo *sm* (*ARTE*, *GEO*) relief; (*fig*: *rilevanza*) importance; (*osservazione*) point, remark; (*TOPOGRAFIA*) survey; **dar ~ a o mettere in ~ qc** (*fig*) to bring sth out, highlight sth.

rilut'tante *ag* reluctant; **rilut'tanza** *sf* reluctance.

'rima *sf* rhyme.

riman'dare *vt* to send again; (*restituire*, *rinviare*) to send back, return; (*differire*): **~ qc** (*a*) to postpone sth *o* put sth off (till); (*fare riferimento*): **~ qd a** to refer sb to; **essere rimandato** (*INS*) to have to repeat one's exams; **ri'mando** *sm* (*rinvio*) return; (*dilazione*) postponement; (*riferimento*) cross-reference.

rima'nente *ag* remaining // *sm* rest, remainder; **I ~i** (*persone*) the rest of them, the others; **rima'nenza** *sf* rest, remainder; **rimanenze** *sfpl* (*COMM*) unsold stock *sg*.

rima'nere *vi* (2) (*restare*) to remain, stay; (*avanzare*) to be left, remain; (*restare stupito*) to be amazed; (*restare, mancare*): **rimangono poche settimane a Pasqua** there are only a few weeks left till Easter; **rimane da vedere se** it remains to be seen whether; (*diventare*): **~ vedovo** to be left a widower; (*trovarsi*): **~ confuso/sorpreso** to be confused/surprised.

rimar'chevole [rimar'kevole] *ag* remarkable.

ri'mare *vt*, *vi* to rhyme.

rimargi'nare [rimardʒi'nare] *vt*, *vi* (*anche:* **~rsi**) to heal.

ri'masto, a *pp di* **rimanere**.

rima'sugli [rima'suʎʎi] *smpl* leftovers.

rimbal'zare [rimbal'tsare] *vi* to bounce back, rebound; (*proiettile*) to ricochet; **rim'balzo** *sm* rebound; ricochet.

rimbam'bire *vi* (2) to be in one's dotage; (*rincretinire*) to grow foolish.

rimboc'care *vt* (*orlo*) to turn up; (*coperta*) to tuck in; (*maniche, pantaloni*) to turn *o* roll up.

rimbom'bare *vi* to resound.

rimbor'sare *vt* to pay back, repay; **rim'borso** *sm* repayment.

rimedi'are *vi* (2): **~ a** to remedy // *vt* (*fam: procurarsi*) to get *o* scrape together.

ri'medio *sm* (*medicina*) medicine; (*cura*, *fig*) remedy, cure.

rimesco'lare *vt* to mix well, stir well; (*carte*) to shuffle; **sentirsi ~ il sangue** (*per paura*) to feel one's blood run cold; (*per rabbia*) to feel one's blood boil.

ri'messa *sf* (*locale: per veicoli*) garage; (: *per aerei*) hangar; (*COMM: di merce*) consignment; (: *di denaro*) remittance; (*CALCIO*): anche: **~ in gioco** throw-in; **vendere a ~** (*COMM*) to sell at a loss.

ri'messo, a *pp di* **rimettere**.

ri'mettere *vt* (*mettere di nuovo*) to put back; (*indossare di nuovo*): **~ qc** to put sth back on, put sth on again; (*restituire*) to

return, give back; (*affidare*) to entrust; (: *decisione*) to refer; (*condonare*) to remit; (*COMM: merci*) to deliver; (: *denaro*) to remit; (*vomitare*) to bring up; (*rimandare*): **~ qc (a)** to postpone sth *o* put sth off (until); **~rsi al bello** (*tempo*) to clear up; **~rsi in salute** to get better, recover one's health.

'rimmel *sm inv* ® mascara.

rimoder'nare *vt* to modernize.

rimon'tare *vt* (*meccanismo*) to reassemble; (*scale*) to go up again; (*SPORT*) to overtake // *vi* (2) to go back up; **~ a** (*risalire a*) to date *o* go back to; **~ a cavallo** to remount.

rimorchi'are [rimor'kjare] *vt* to tow; **rimorchia'tore** *sm* (*NAUT*) tug(boat).

ri'morchio [ri'mɔrkjo] *sm* tow; (*traino*) trailer.

ri'morso *sm* remorse.

rimozi'one [rimot'tsjone] *sf* removal; (*da un impiego*) dismissal; (*PSIC*) repression.

rim'pasto *sm* (*POL*) reshuffle.

rimpatri'are *vi* (2) to return home // *vt* to repatriate; **rim'patrio** *sm* repatriation.

rimpi'angere [rim'pjandʒere] *vt* to regret; (*persona*) to miss; **rimpi'anto, a** *pp di* **rimpiangere** // *sm* regret.

rimpiat'tino *sm* hide-and-seek.

rimpiaz'zare [rimpjat'tsare] *vt* to replace.

rimpicco'lire *vt* to make smaller // *vi* (2) (*anche:* **~rsi**) to become smaller.

rimpin'zare [rimpin'tsare] *vt*: **~ di** to cram *o* stuff with.

rimprove'rare *vt* to rebuke, reprimand; **rim'provero** *sm* rebuke, reprimand.

rimugi'nare [rimudʒi'nare] *vt* (*fig*) to turn over in one's mind.

rimunerazi'one [rimunerat'tsjone] *sf* remuneration; (*premio*) reward.

rimu'overe *vt* to remove; (*destituire*) to dismiss; (*fig: distogliere*) to dissuade.

Rinasci'mento [rinaʃʃi'mento] *sm*: **il ~** the Renaissance.

ri'nascita [ri'naʃʃita] *sf* rebirth, revival.

rincal'zare [rinkal'tsare] *vt* (*sostenere*) to support, prop up; (*lenzuola*) to tuck in; **rin'calzo** *sm* support, prop; (*rinforzo*) reinforcement; (*SPORT*) reserve (player); **rincalzi** *smpl* (*MIL*) reserves.

rinca'rare *vt* to increase the price of // *vi* (2) to go up, become more expensive.

rinca'sare *vi* (2) to go home.

rinchi'udere [rin'kjudere] *vt* to shut (*o* lock) up; **~rsi** *vr*: **~rsi in** to shut o.s. up in; **~rsi in se stesso** to withdraw into o.s.; **rinchi'uso, a** *pp di* **rinchiudere**.

rin'correre *vt* to chase, run after; **rin'corso, a** *pp di* **rincorrere** // *sf* short run.

rin'crescere [rin'kreʃʃere] *vb impers* (2): **mi rincresce che/di non poter fare** I'm sorry that/I can't do, I regret that/being unable to do; **rincresci'mento** *sm* regret; **rincresci'uto, a** *pp di* **rincrescere**.

rincu'lare *vi* (2) to draw back; (*arma*) to recoil.

rinfacci'are [rinfat'tʃare] vt (fig): ~ qc a qd to throw sth in sb's face.

rinfor'zare [rinfor'tsare] vt to reinforce, strengthen // vi (2) (anche: ~rsi) to grow stronger; **rin'forzo** sm reinforcement; (appoggio: anche fig) support; **rinforzi** smpl (MIL) reinforcements.

rinfran'care vt to encourage, reassure.

rinfres'care vt (atmosfera, temperatura) to cool (down); (abito, pareti) to freshen up // vi (2) (tempo) to grow cooler; ~rsi vr (ristorarsi) to refresh o.s.; (lavarsi) to freshen up; **rin'fresco, schi** sm (festa) party; **rinfreschi** smpl refreshments.

rin'fusa sf: alla ~ in confusion, higgledy-piggledy.

ringhi'are [rin'gjare] vi to growl, snarl.

ringhi'era [rin'gjɛra] sf railing; (delle scale) banister(s pl).

ringiova'nire [rindʒova'nire] vt (sog: vestito, acconciatura etc): ~ qd to make sb look younger; (: vacanze etc) to rejuvenate // vi (2) (anche: ~rsi) to become (o look) younger.

ringrazia'menti [ringrattsja'menti] smpl thanks.

ringrazi'are [ringrat'tsjare] vt to thank; ~ qd di qc to thank sb for sth.

rinne'gare vt (fede) to renounce; (figlio) to disown, repudiate; **rinne'gato, a** sm/f renegade.

rinnova'mento sm renewal.

rinno'vare vt to renew; (ripetere) to repeat, renew; ~rsi vr (fenomeno) to be repeated, recur; **rin'novo** sm renewal; recurrence.

rinoce'ronte [rinotʃe'ronte] sm rhinoceros.

rino'mato, a ag renowned, celebrated.

rinsal'dare vt to strengthen.

rinsa'vire vi (2) to come to one's senses.

rintoc'care vi (campana) to toll; (orologio) to strike.

rintracci'are [rintrat'tʃare] vt to track down.

rintro'nare vi to boom, roar // vt (assordare) to deafen; (stordire) to stun.

rintuz'zare [rintut'tsare] vt (fig: sentimento) to check, repress; (: accusa) to refute.

ri'nuncia [ri'nuntʃa] etc = **rinunzia** etc.

ri'nunzia [ri'nuntsja] sf renunciation.

rinunzi'are [rinun'tsjare] vi: ~ a to give up, renounce.

rinve'nire vt to find, recover; (scoprire) to discover, find out // vi (2) (riprendere i sensi) to come round; (riprendere l'aspetto naturale) to revive.

rinvi'are vt (rimandare indietro) to send back, return; (differire): ~ qc (a) to postpone sth o put sth off (till); to adjourn sth (till); (fare un rimando): ~ qd a to refer sb to.

rinvigo'rire vt to strengthen.

rin'vio, 'vii sm (rimando) return; (differimento) postponement; (: di seduta) adjournment; (in un testo) cross-reference.

ri'one sm district, quarter.

riordi'nare vt (rimettere in ordine) to tidy; (riorganizzare) to reorganize.

riorganiz'zare [riorganid'dzare] vt to reorganize.

ripa'gare vt to repay.

ripa'rare vt (proteggere) to protect, defend; (correggere: male, torto) to make up for; (: errore) to put right; (aggiustare) to repair // vi (mettere rimedio): ~ a to make up for; ~rsi vr (rifugiarsi) to take refuge o shelter; **riparazi'one** sf (di un torto) reparation; (di guasto, scarpe) repairing q; repair; (risarcimento) compensation.

ri'paro sm (protezione) shelter, protection; (rimedio) remedy.

ripar'tire vt (dividere) to divide up; (distribuire) to share out // vi (2) to set off again; to leave again.

ripas'sare vi (2) to come (o go) back // vt (scritto, lezione) to go over (again).

ripen'sare vi to think; (cambiare pensiero) to change one's mind; (tornare col pensiero): ~ a to recall.

ripercu'otere vt (luce) to reflect, throw back; (suono) to throw back; ~rsi vr (luce) to be reflected; (suoni) to reverberate; (fig): ~rsi su to have repercussions on.

ripercussi'one sf reflection; reverberation; ~i sfpl (fig) repercussions.

ri'petere vt to repeat; (ripassare) to go over; **ripetizi'one** sf repetition; (di lezione) revision; **ripetizioni** sfpl (INS) private tutoring o coaching sg.

ripi'ano sm (GEO) terrace; (di mobile) shelf.

'ripido, a ag steep.

ripie'gare vt to refold; (piegare più volte) to fold (up) // vi (MIL) to retreat, fall back; ~rsi vr to bend; **ripi'ego, ghi** sm expedient; **vivere di ripieghi** to live by one's wits.

ripi'eno, a ag full; (CUC) stuffed; (: panino) filled // sm (CUC) stuffing.

ri'porre vt (porre al suo posto) to put back, replace; (mettere via) to put away; (fiducia, speranza): ~ qc in qd to place o put sth in sb.

ripor'tare vt (portare indietro) to bring (o take) back; (riferire) to report; (citare) to quote; (ricevere) to receive, get; (MAT) to carry; (COMM) to carry forward; ~rsi a (anche fig) to go back to; (riferirsi a) to refer to; ~ danni to suffer damage.

ripo'sare vt (bicchiere, valigia) to put down; (dare sollievo) to rest // vi to rest; ~rsi vr to rest; **ri'poso** sm rest; (MIL): **riposo!** at ease!; **a riposo** (in pensione) retired; **giorno di riposo** day off.

ripos'tiglio [ripos'tiʎʎo] sm lumber-room; hiding-place.

ri'posto, a pp di **riporre**.

ri'prendere vt (prigioniero, fortezza) to recapture; (prendere indietro) to take back; (ricominciare: lavoro) to resume; (andare a prendere) to fetch, come back for; (assumere di nuovo: impiegati) to take on again, re-employ; (*rimproverare*) to tell off; (*restringere: abito*) to take in; (*CINEMA*) to shoot // *vi* to revive; ~**rsi** *vr* to recover; (*correggersi*) to correct o.s.; **ri'preso, a** *pp di* **riprendere** // *sf* recapture; resumption; (*economica, da malattia, emozione*) recovery; (*AUT*) acceleration *q*; (*TEATRO, CINEMA*) rerun; (*CINEMA: presa*) shooting *q*; shot; (*SPORT*) second half; (: *PUGILATO*) round; **a più riprese** on several occasions, several times.

ripristi'nare *vt* to restore.

ripro'durre *vt* to reproduce; **riprodursi** *vr* (*BIOL*) to reproduce; (*riformarsi*) to form again; **riprodut'tivo, a** *ag* reproductive; **riproduzi'one** *sf* reproduction; **riproduzione vietata** all rights reserved.

ripudi'are *vt* to repudiate, disown.

ripu'gnante [ripun'nante] *ag* disgusting, repulsive.

ripu'gnare [ripun'nare] *vi*: ~ **a qd** to repel *o* disgust sb.

ripu'lire *vt* to clean up; (*sog: ladri*) to clean out; (*perfezionare*) to polish, refine.

ri'quadro *sm* square; (*ARCHIT*) panel.

ri'saia *sf* paddy field.

risa'lire *vi* (2) (*ritornare in su*) to go back up; ~ **a** (*ritornare con la mente*) to go back to; (*datare da*) to date back to, go back to.

risal'tare *vi* (*fig: distinguersi*) to stand out; (*ARCHIT*) to project, jut out; **ri'salto** *sm* prominence; (*sporgenza*) projection; **mettere** *o* **porre in risalto qc** to make sth stand out.

risa'nare *vt* (*guarire*) to heal, cure; (*rendere salubre, bonificare*) to reclaim; (*fig: emendare*) to improve.

risa'pere *vt*: ~ **qc** to come to know of sth.

risarci'mento [risartʃi'mento] *sm* compensation.

risar'cire [risar'tʃire] *vt* (*cose*) to pay compensation for; (*persona*): ~ **qd di qc** to compensate sb for sth.

ri'sata *sf* laugh.

riscalda'mento *sm* heating; ~ **centrale** central heating.

riscal'dare *vt* (*scaldare*) to heat; (: *mani, persona*) to warm; (*minestra*) to reheat; ~**rsi** *vr* to warm up.

riscat'tare *vt* (*prigioniero*) to ransom, pay a ransom for; (*DIR*) to redeem; ~**rsi** *vr* (*da disonore*) to redeem o.s.; **ris'catto** *sm* ransom; redemption.

rischia'rare [riskja'rare] *vt* (*illuminare*) to light up; (*colore*) to make lighter; ~**rsi** *vr* (*tempo*) to clear up; (*cielo*) to clear; (*fig: volto*) to brighten up; ~**rsi la voce** to clear one's throat.

rischi'are [ris'kjare] *vt* to risk // *vi*: ~ **di fare qc** to risk *o* run the risk of doing sth.

'rischio ['riskjo] *sm* risk; **rischi'oso, a** *ag* risky, dangerous.

riscia'cquare [riʃʃa'kware] *vt* to rinse.

riscon'trare *vt* (*confrontare: due cose*) to compare; (*esaminare*) to check, verify; (*rilevare*) to find; **ris'contro** *sm* comparison; check, verification; (*AMM:*

lettera di risposta) reply; **mettere a riscontro** to compare.

ris'cosso, a *pp di* **riscuotere** // *sf* (*riconquista*) recovery, reconquest.

riscossi'one *sf* collection.

ris'cuotere *vt* (*anche fig*) to shake, rouse, stir; (*ritirare una somma dovuta*) to collect; (: *stipendio*) to draw, collect; (*fig: successo etc*) to win, earn; ~**rsi** *vr*: ~**rsi (da)** to shake o.s. (out of), rouse o.s. (from).

risenti'mento *sm* resentment.

risen'tire *vt* to hear again; (*provare*) to feel // *vi*: ~ **di** to feel (*o* show) the effects of; ~**rsi** *vr*: ~**rsi per** to take offence at, resent; **risen'tito, a** *ag* resentful.

ri'serbo *sm* reserve.

ri'serva *sf* reserve; (*di caccia, pesca*) preserve; (*restrizione, di indigeni*) reservation; **di** ~ (*provviste etc*) in reserve.

riser'vare *vt* (*tenere in serbo*) to keep, put aside; (*prenotare*) to book, reserve; **riser-'vato, a** *ag* (*prenotato, fig: persona*) reserved; (*confidenziale*) confidential; **riserva'tezza** *sf* reserve.

risi'edere *vi*: ~ **a/in** to reside in.

'risma *sf* (*di carta*) ream; (*fig*) kind, sort.

'riso, a *pp di* **ridere** // *sm* (*pl*(*f*) ~**a**: *di ridere*): **un** ~ **a** laugh; **il** ~. laughter; (*pianta*) rice.

riso'lino *sm* snigger.

ri'solto, a *pp di* **risolvere**.

risolu'tezza [risolu'tettsa] *sf* determination.

riso'luto, a *ag* determined, resolute.

risoluzi'one [risolut'tsjone] *sf* solving *q*; (*MAT*) solution; (*decisione*) resolution.

ri'solvere *vt* (*difficoltà, controversia*) to resolve; (*problema*) to solve; (*decidere*): ~ **di fare** to resolve to do; ~**rsi** *vr* (*decidersi*): ~**rsi a fare** to make up one's mind to do; (*andare a finire*): ~**rsi in** to end up, turn out; ~**rsi in nulla** to come to nothing.

riso'nanza [riso'nantsa] *sf* resonance; **aver vasta** ~ (*fig: fatto etc*) to be known far and wide.

riso'nare *vt, vi* = **risuonare**.

ri'sorgere [ri'sordʒere] *vi* (2) to rise again; **risorgi'mento** *sm* revival; **il Risorgimento** (*STORIA*) the Risorgimento.

ri'sorsa *sf* expedient, resort; ~**e** *sfpl* (*naturali, finanziarie etc*) resources; **persona piena di** ~**e** resourceful person.

ri'sorto, a *pp di* **risorgere**.

ri'sotto *sm* (*CUC*) risotto.

risparmi'are *vt* to save; (*evitare di consumare, non uccidere*) to spare // *vi* to save; ~ **qc a qd** to spare sb sth.

ris'parmio *sm* saving *q*; (*denaro*) savings *pl*.

rispet'tabile *ag* respectable.

rispet'tare *vt* to respect; **farsi** ~ to command respect.

rispet'tivo, a *ag* respective.

ris'petto *sm* respect; ~**i** *smpl* (*saluti*) respects, regards; ~ **a** (*in paragone a*) compared to; (*in relazione a*) as regards, as for; **rispet'toso, a** *ag* respectful.

ris'plendere *vi* to shine.

rispon'dente *ag*: ~ **a** in keeping *o* conformity with; **rispon'denza** *sf* correspondence; harmony; agreement.

ris'pondere *vi* to answer, reply; (*freni*) to respond; ~ **a** (*domanda*) to answer, reply to; (*persona*) to answer; (*invito*) to reply to; (*provocazione, sog: veicolo, apparecchio*) to respond to; (*corrispondere a*) to correspond to; (: *speranze, bisogno*) to answer; ~ **di** to answer for; **ris'posto, a** *pp di* **rispondere** // *sf* answer, reply; **in** *o* **per risposta a** in reply to.

'rissa *sf* brawl.

ristabi'lire *vt* to re-establish, restore; (*persona: sog: riposo etc*) to restore to health; ~**rsi** *vr* to recover.

rista'gnare [ristaɲ'ɲare] *vi* (*acqua*) to become stagnant; (*sangue*) to cease flowing; (*fig: industria*) to stagnate; **ris-'tagno** *sm* stagnation.

ris'tampa *sf* reprinting *q*; reprint.

ristam'pare *vt* to reprint.

risto'rante *sm* restaurant.

risto'rarsi *vr* to have something to eat and drink; (*riposarsi*) to rest, have a rest; **ris'toro** *sm* (*bevanda, cibo*) refreshment; (*sollievo*) relief.

ristret'tezza [ristret'tettsa] *sf* (*strettezza*) narrowness; (*fig: scarsezza*) scarcity, lack; (: *meschinità*) meanness; ~**e** *sfpl* (*povertà*) financial straits.

ris'tretto, a *pp di* **restringere** // *ag* (*racchiuso*) enclosed, hemmed in; (*angusto*) narrow; (*limitato*): ~ **(a)** restricted *o* limited (to); (*riassunto, condensato*) condensed; ~ **di mente** narrow-minded.

risucchi'are [risuk'kjare] *vt* to suck in.

risul'tare *vi* (2) (*conseguire*) to result, ensue; (*dimostrarsi*) to prove (to be), turn out (to be); (*riuscire*) to be, come out; ~ **da** (*provenire*) to result from, be the result of; **risul'tato** *sm* result.

risuo'nare *vi* (*rimbombare*) to resound, reverberate; (: *stanza*) to be resonant.

risurrezi'one [risurret'tsjone] *sf* (*REL*) resurrection.

risusci'tare [risuʃʃi'tare] *vt* to resuscitate, restore to life; (*fig*) to revive, bring back // *vi* (2) to rise (from the dead).

ris'veglio [riz've ʎʎo] *sm* waking up; (*fig*) revival.

ris'volto *sm* (*di giacca*) lapel; (*di pantaloni*) turn-up; (*di manica*) cuff; (*di tasca*) flap; (*di libro*) inside flap; (*fig*) implication.

ritagli'are [rita ʎ'ʎare] *vt* (*tagliar via*) to cut out; **ri'taglio** *sm* (*di giornale*) cutting, clipping; (*di stoffa etc*) scrap.

ritar'dare *vi* (*persona, treno*) to be late; (*orologio*) to be slow // *vt* (*rallentare*) to slow down; (*impedire*) to delay, hold up; (*differire*) to postpone, delay; **ritarda-'tario, a** *sm/f* latecomer.

ri'tardo *sm* delay; (*di persona aspettata*)

lateness *q*; (*fig: mentale*) backwardness; **in** ~ late.

ri'tegno [ri'teɲɲo] *sm* restraint.

rite'nere *vt* (*trattenere*) to hold back; (: *somma*) to deduct; (*giudicare*) to consider, believe; ~ **qc a memoria** to know sth by heart; **rite'nuta** *sf* (*sul salario*) deduction.

riti'rare *vt* to withdraw; (*POL: richiamare*) to recall; (*andare a prendere: pacco etc*) to collect, pick up; ~**rsi** *vr* to withdraw; (*da un'attività*) to retire; (*stoffa*) to shrink; (*marea*) to recede; **riti'rata** *sf* (*MIL*) retreat; (*latrina*) lavatory; **ri'tiro** *sm* withdrawal; recall; collection; retirement; shrinking; (*luogo appartato*) retreat.

'ritmico, a, ci, che *ag* rhythmic(al).

'ritmo *sm* rhythm; (*fig*) rate; (: *della vita*) pace, tempo.

'rito *sm* rite; **di** ~ usual, customary.

ritoc'care *vt* (*disegno, fotografia*) to touch up; (*testo*) to alter; **ri'tocco, chi** *sm* touching up *q*; alteration.

ritor'nare *vi* (2) to return, go (*o* come) back; (*ripresentarsi*) to recur; (*ridiventare*): ~ **ricco** to become rich again // *vt* (*restituire*) to return, give back.

ritor'nello *sm* refrain.

ri'torno *sm* return; **essere di** ~ to be back; **far** ~ **di fiamma** (*AUT*) to backfire.

ri'trarre *vt* (*trarre indietro, via*) to withdraw; (*distogliere: sguardo*) to turn away; (*rappresentare*) to portray, depict; (*ricavare*) to get, obtain.

ritrat'tare *vt* (*disdire*) to retract, take back.

ri'tratto, a *pp di* **ritrarre** // *sm* portrait.

ri'troso, a *ag* (*restio*): ~ **(a)** reluctant (to); (*schivo*) shy; **andare a** ~ to go backwards.

ritro'vare *vt* to find; (*salute*) to regain; (*persona*) to find; to meet again; ~**rsi** *vr* (*essere, capitare*) to find o.s.; (*raccapezzarsi*) to find one's way; (*con senso reciproco*) to meet (again); **ri'trovo** *sm* meeting place; **ritrovo notturno** night club.

'ritto, a *ag* (*in piedi*) standing, on one's feet; (*levato in alto*) erect, raised; (: *capelli*) standing on end; (*posto verticalmente*) upright.

ritu'ale *ag, sm* ritual.

riuni'one *sf* (*adunanza*) meeting; (*riconciliazione*) reunion.

riu'nire *vt* (*ricongiungere*) to join (together); (*riconciliare*) to reunite, bring together (again); ~**rsi** *vr* (*adunarsi*) to meet; (*tornare a stare insieme*) to be reunited.

riu'scire [riuʃʃire] *vi* (2) (*uscire di nuovo*) to go out again, go back out; (*aver esito: fatti, azioni*) to go, turn out; (*aver successo*) to succeed, be successful; (*essere, apparire*) to be, prove; (*raggiungere il fine*) to manage, succeed; ~ **a fare qc** to manage to do *o* succeed in doing *o* be able to do sth; **questo mi riesce nuovo** this is new to me; **riu'scita** *sf* (*esito*) result, outcome; (*buon esito*) success; **cattiva riuscita** failure.

'riva *sf* (*di fiume*) bank; (*di lago, mare*) shore.

ri'vale *sm/f* rival; **rivalità** *sf* rivalry.

ri'valsa *sf* (*rivincita*) revenge; (*risarcimento*) compensation.

rivalu'tare *vt* (ECON) to revalue.

rive'dere *vt* to see again; (*ripassare*) to revise; (*verificare*) to check.

rive'lare *vt* to reveal; (*divulgare*) to reveal, disclose; (*dare indizio*) to reveal, show; ~**rsi** *vr* (*manifestarsi*) to be revealed; ~**rsi onesto** *etc* to prove to be honest *etc*; **rivela'tore, 'trice** *ag* revealing // *sm* (TECN) detector; (FOT) developer; **rivelazi'one** *sf* revelation.

rivendi'care *vt* to claim, demand.

ri'vendita *sf* (*bottega*) retailer's (shop).

rivendi'tore, 'trice *sm/f* retailer.

riverbe'rare *vt* to reflect; **ri'verbero** *sm* (*di luce, calore*) reflection; (*di suono*) reverberation.

rive'renza [rive'rɛntsa] *sf* reverence; (*inchino*) bow; curtsey.

rive'rire *vt* (*rispettare*) to revere; (*salutare*) to pay one's respects to.

river'sare *vt* (*anche fig*) to pour; ~**rsi** *vr* (*fig: persone*) to pour out.

rivesti'mento *sm* (*materiale*) covering; coating.

rives'tire *vt* (*provvedere di abiti*) to dress; (*indossare*) to put on; (*fig: carica*) to hold; (*ricoprire*) to cover; to coat; ~**rsi** *vr* to get dressed again; to change (one's clothes); ~ **con isolante termico** to lag, insulate.

rivi'era *sf* coast; **la ~ italiana** the Italian Riviera.

ri'vincita [ri'vintʃita] *sf* (SPORT) return match; (*fig*) revenge.

rivis'suto, a *pp di* **rivivere**.

ri'vista *sf* review; (*periodico*) magazine, review; (TEATRO) revue; variety show.

ri'vivere *vi* (2) (*riacquistare forza*) to come alive again; (*tornare in uso*) to be revived // *vt* to relive.

'rivo *sm* stream.

ri'volgere [ri'vɔldʒere] *vt* (*attenzione, sguardo*) to turn, direct; (*parole*) to address; (*distogliere*): ~ **da** to turn away from; ~**rsi** *vr* to turn round; (*fig: dirigersi per informazioni*): ~**rsi a** to go and see, go and speak to; (: *ufficio*) to enquire at; **rivolgi'mento** *sm* upheaval.

ri'volta *sf* revolt, rebellion.

rivol'tare *vt* to turn over; (*con l'interno all'esterno*) to turn inside out; (*provocare disgusto: stomaco*) to upset, turn; (: *fig*) to revolt; to outrage; ~**rsi** *vr* (*ribellarsi*): ~**rsi (a)** to rebel (against).

rivol'tella *sf* revolver.

ri'volto, a *pp di* **rivolgere**.

rivoluzio'nare [rivoluttsjo'nare] *vt* to revolutionize.

rivoluzio'nario, a [rivoluttsjo'narjo] *ag, sm/f* revolutionary.

rivoluzi'one [rivolut'tsjone] *sf* revolution.

riz'zare [rit'tsare] *vt* to raise, erect; ~**rsi**

vr to stand up; (*capelli*) to stand on end.

'roba *sf* stuff, things *pl*; (*possessi, beni*) belongings *pl*, things *pl*, possessions *pl*; ~ **da mangiare** things *pl* to eat, food; ~ **da matti** sheer madness *o* lunacy.

'robot *sm inv* robot.

ro'busto, a *ag* robust, sturdy; (*solido: catena*) strong.

'rocca, che *sf* fortress.

rocca'forte *sf* stronghold.

roc'chetto [rok'ketto] *sm* reel, spool.

'roccia, ce ['rɔttʃa] *sf* rock.

ro'daggio [ro'daddʒo] *sm* running in; **in ~** running in.

ro'dare *vt* (AUT, TECN) to run in.

'rodere *vt* to gnaw (at); (*distruggere poco a poco*) to eat into.

'Rodi *sf* Rhodes.

rodi'tore *sm* (ZOOL) rodent.

rodo'dendro *sm* rhododendron.

'rogna ['rɔɲɲa] *sf* (MED) scabies *sg*; (*fig*) bother, nuisance.

ro'gnone [roɲ'ɲone] *sm* (CUC) kidney.

'rogo, ghi *sm* (*per cadaveri*) (*funeral*) pyre; (*supplizio*): **il ~** the stake.

rol'lio *sm* roll(ing).

'Roma *sf* Rome.

Roma'nia *sf*: **la ~** Romania.

ro'manico, a, ci, che *ag* Romanesque.

ro'mano, a *ag, sm/f* Roman.

romanti'cismo [romanti'tʃizmo] *sm* romanticism.

ro'mantico, a, ci, che *ag* romantic.

ro'manza [ro'mandza] *sf* (MUS, LETTERATURA) romance.

roman'zesco, a, schi, sche [roman'dzesko] *ag* (*cavalleresco*) romance *cpd*; (*del romanzo*) of the novel; (*fig*) storybook *cpd*.

romanzi'ere [roman'dzjere] *sm* novelist.

ro'manzo, a [ro'mandzo] *ag* (LING) romance *cpd* // *sm* (*medievale*) romance; (*moderno*) novel; ~ **d'appendice** serial (story).

rom'bare *vi* to rumble, thunder, roar.

'rombo *sm* rumble, thunder, roar; (MAT) rhombus; (ZOOL) turbot; brill.

ro'meno, a *ag, sm/f, sm* = **rumeno, a**.

'rompere *vt* to break; (*conversazione, fidanzamento*) to break off // *vi* to break; ~**rsi** *vr* to break; ~ **in pianto** to burst into tears; ~**rsi un braccio** to break an arm; **rompi'capo** *sm* worry, headache; (*indovinello*) puzzle; (*in enigmistica*) brainteaser; **rompi'collo** *sm* daredevil; **a rompicollo** *av* at breakneck speed; **rompighi'accio** *sm* (NAUT) icebreaker; **rompis'catole** *sm/f inv* (*fam*) pest, pain in the neck.

'ronda *sf* (MIL) rounds *pl*, patrol.

ron'della *sf* (TECN) washer.

'rondine *sf* (ZOOL) swallow.

ron'done *sm* (ZOOL) swift.

ron'zare [ron'dzare] *vi* to buzz, hum.

ron'zino [ron'dzino] *sm* (*peg: cavallo*) nag.

'rosa *sf* rose // *ag inv, sm* pink; **ro'saio** *sm* (*pianta*) rosebush, rose tree; (*giardino*)

rose garden; **ro'sario** sm (REL) rosary;
ro'sato, a ag pink, rosy // sm (vino) rosé
(wine); **ro'seo, a** ag (anche fig) rosy; **ro-
'setta** sf (diamante) rose diamond;
(rondella) washer.
rosicchi'are [rosik'kjare] vt to gnaw (at);
(mangiucchiare) to nibble (at).
rosma'rino sm rosemary.
'roso, a pp di **rodere**.
roso'lare vt (CUC) to brown.
roso'lia sf (MED) German measles sg,
rubella.
ro'sone sm rosette; (vetrata) rose window.
'rospo sm (ZOOL) toad.
ros'setto sm (per labbra) lipstick; (per
guance) rouge.
'rosso, a ag, sm, sm/f red; **il mar R~** the
Red Sea; **~ d'uovo** egg yolk; **ros'sore** sm
flush, blush; (fig) shame.
rosticce'ria [rostittʃe'ria] sf shop selling
roast meat and other cooked food.
'rostro sm rostrum; (becco) beak.
ro'tabile ag (percorribile): **strada ~**
carriageway; (FERR): **materiale** m **~**
rolling stock.
ro'taia sf rut, track; (FERR) rail; **le ~e**
(FERR) the rails, the track sg.
ru'tare vt, vi to rotate; **rotazi'one** sf
rotation.
rote'are vt, vi to whirl; **~ gli occhi** to roll
one's eyes.
ro'tella sf small wheel; (di mobile) castor.
roto'lare vt, vi (2) to roll; **~rsi** vr to roll
(about).
'rotolo sm roll; **andare a ~i** (fig) to go to
rack and ruin.
ro'tondo, a ag round // sf rotunda.
ro'tore sm rotor.
'rotta sf (AER, NAUT) course, route; (MIL)
rout; **a ~ di collo** at breakneck speed;
essere in ~ con qd to be on bad terms
with sb.
rot'tame sm fragment, scrap, broken bit;
(relitto: anche fig) wreck; **~i di ferro**
scrap iron.
'rotto, a pp di **rompere** // ag broken;
(calzoni) torn, split; (persona: pratico, resistente): **~ a** accustomed o inured to; **per
il ~ della cuffia** by the skin of one's
teeth.
rot'tura sf breaking q; break; breaking
off; (MED) fracture, break.
ro'vente ag red-hot.
'rovere sm oak.
rovesci'are [rovef'ʃare] vt (versare in giù)
to pour; (: accidentalmente) to spill; (capovolgere) to turn upside down; (gettare a
terra) to knock down; (: fig: governo) to
overthrow; (piegare all'indietro: testa) to
throw back; **~rsi** vr to pour down; to spill;
(fig: persone) to pour (out).
ro'vescio, sci [ro'veʃʃo] sm other side,
wrong side; (della mano) back; (di moneta)
reverse; (pioggia) sudden downpour; (fig)
setback; (MAGLIA: anche: **punto ~**) purl
(stitch); (TENNIS) backhand (stroke); **a ~**
upside-down; inside-out; **capire qc a ~** to
misunderstand sth.

ro'vina sf ruin; **~e** sfpl ruins; **andare in
~** (andare a pezzi) to collapse; (fig) to go
to rack and ruin.
rovi'nare vi (2) to collapse, fall down //
vt (far cadere giù: casa) to demolish;
(danneggiare, fig) to ruin; **rovi'noso, a** ag
disastrous; damaging; violent.
rovis'tare vt (casa) to ransack; (tasche) to
rummage in (o through).
'rovo sm (BOT) blackberry bush, bramble
bush.
'rozzo, a ['roddzo] ag rough, coarse.
'ruba sf: **andare a ~** to sell like hot
cakes.
ru'bare vt to steal; **~ qc a qd** to steal sth
from sb.
rubi'netto sm tap.
ru'bino sm ruby.
ru'brica, che sf (STAMPA) column;
(quadernetto) index book; address book.
'rude ag tough, rough.
'ruderi smpl ruins.
rudimen'tale ag rudimentary, basic.
rudi'menti smpl rudiments; basic
principles; basic knowledge sg.
ruffi'ano sm pimp.
'ruga, ghe sf wrinkle.
'ruggine ['ruddʒine] sf rust.
rug'gire [rud'dʒire] vi to roar.
rugi'ada [ru'dʒada] sf dew.
ru'goso, a ag wrinkled.
rul'lare vi (tamburo, nave) to roll; (aereo)
to taxi.
'rullo sm (di tamburi) roll; (arnese
cilindrico, TIP) roller; **~ compressore**
steam roller; **~ di pellicola** roll of film.
rum sm rum.
ru'meno, a ag, sm/f, sm Romanian.
rumi'nare vt (ZOOL) to ruminate; (fig) to
ruminate o over, chew over.
ru'more sm: **un ~** a noise, a sound; (fig)
a rumour; **il ~** noise; **rumoreggi'are** vi
to make a noise; **rumo'roso, a** ag noisy.
ru'olo sm (elenco) roll, register, list;
(TEATRO, fig) role, part; **di ~** permanent,
on the permanent staff.
ru'ota sf wheel; **a ~** (forma) circular; **~
anteriore/posteriore** front/back wheel;
~ di scorta spare wheel.
'rupe sf cliff.
ru'rale ag rural, country cpd.
ru'scello [ruf'ʃello] sm stream.
'ruspa sf excavator.
rus'sare vi to snore.
'Russia sf: **la ~** Russia; **'russo, a** ag,
sm/f, sm Russian.
'rustico, a, ci, che ag rustic; (fig) rough,
unrefined.
rut'tare vi to belch; **'rutto** sm belch.
'ruvido, a ag rough, coarse.
ruzzo'lare [ruttso'lare] vi (2) to tumble
down; **ruzzo'loni** av: **cadere ruzzoloni**
to tumble down; **fare le scale ruzzoloni**
to tumble down the stairs.

S

S. (*abbr di* sud) S.

sa *forma del vb* sapere.

'sabato *sm* Saturday; **di** *o* **il** ~ **on** Saturdays.

'sabbia *sf* sand; ~**e mobili** quicksand(s); **sabbi'oso, a** *ag* sandy.

sabo'taggio [sabo'taddʒo] *sm* sabotage.

sabo'tare *vt* to sabotage.

'sacca, che *sf* bag; (*bisaccia*) haversack; (*insenatura*) inlet; ~ **da viaggio** travelling bag.

sacca'rina *sf* saccharin(e).

sac'cente [sat'tʃɛnte] *sm/f* know-all.

saccheggi'are [sakked'dʒare] *vt* to sack, plunder; **sac'cheggio** *sm* sack(ing).

sac'chetto [sak'ketto] *sm* (small) bag; (small) sack.

'sacco, chi *sm* bag; (*per carbone etc*) sack; (ANAT, BIOL) sac; (*tela*) sacking; (*saccheggio*) sack(ing); (*fig: grande quantità*): **un** ~ **di** lots of, heaps of; ~ **a pelo** sleeping bag.

sacer'dote [satʃer'dote] *sm* priest; **sacer-'dozio** *sm* priesthood.

sacra'mento *sm* sacrament.

sacrifi'care *vt* to sacrifice; ~**rsi** *vr* to sacrifice o.s.; (*privarsi di qc*) to make sacrifices.

sacri'ficio [sakri'fitʃo] *sm* sacrifice.

sacri'legio [sakri'ledʒo] *sm* sacrilege.

'sacro, a *ag* sacred.

sacro'santo, a *ag* sacrosanct.

'sadico, a, ci, che *ag* sadistic // *sm/f* sadist.

sa'dismo *sm* sadism.

sa'etta *sf* arrow; (*fulmine: anche fig*) thunderbolt; flash of lightning.

sa'fari *sm inv* safari.

sa'gace [sa'gatʃe] *ag* shrewd, sagacious.

sag'gezza [sad'dʒettsa] *sf* wisdom.

saggi'are [sad'dʒare] *vt* (*metalli*) to assay; (*fig*) to test.

'saggio, a, gi, ge ['saddʒo] *ag* wise // *sm* (*persona*) sage; (*operazione sperimentale*) test; (: *dell'oro*) assay; (*fig: prova*) proof; (*campione indicativo*) sample; (*ricerca, esame critico*) essay.

Sagit'tario [sadʒit'tarjo] *sm* Sagittarius.

'sagoma *sf* (*profilo*) outline, profile; (*forma*) form, shape; (TECN) template.

'sagra *sf* festival.

sagres'tano *sm* sacristan; sexton.

sagres'tia *sf* sacristy; (*culto protestante*) vestry.

'sai *forma del vb* sapere.

'sala *sf* hall; (*stanza*) room; ~ **d'aspetto** waiting room; ~ **da ballo** ballroom; ~ **operatoria** operating theatre; ~ **da pranzo** dining room; ~ **per concerti** concert hall.

sala'mandra *sf* salamander.

ʒa'lame *sm* salami *q*, salami sausage.

sala'moia *sf* (CUC) brine.

sa'lare *vt* to salt.

salari'ato, a *sm/f* wage-earner.

sa'lario *sm* pay, wages *pl*.

sa'lato, a *ag* (*sapore*) salty; (CUC) salted, salt *cpd*; (*fig: discorso etc*) biting, sharp; (: *prezzi*) steep, stiff.

sal'dare *vt* (*congiungere*) to join, bind; (*parti metalliche*) to solder; (: *con saldatura autogena*) to weld; (*conto*) to settle, pay; **salda'tura** *sf* soldering; welding; (*punto saldato*) soldered joint; weld.

sal'dezza [sal'dettsa] *sf* firmness; strength.

'saldo, a *ag* (*resistente, forte*) strong, firm; (*ferma*) firm, steady, stable; (*fig*) firm, steadfast // *sm* (*svendita*) sale; (*di conto*) settlement; (ECON) balance.

'sale *sm* salt; (*fig*) wit.

'salice ['salitʃe] *sm* willow; ~ **piangente** weeping willow.

sali'ente *ag* (*fig*) salient, main.

sali'era *sf* salt cellar.

sa'lino, a *ag* saline // *sf* saltworks *sg*.

sa'lire *vi* (2) to go (*o* come) up; (*aereo etc*) to climb, go up; (*passeggero*) to get on; (*sentiero, prezzi, livello*) to go up, rise // *vt* (*scale, gradini*) to go (*o* come) up; ~ **su** to climb up onto; ~ **sul treno/sull'autobus** to board the train/the bus; ~ **in macchina** to get into the car; **sa'lita** *sf* climb, ascent; (*erta*) hill, slope; **in salita** *ag, av* uphill.

sa'liva *sf* saliva.

'salma *sf* corpse.

'salmo *sm* psalm.

sal'mone *sm* salmon.

sa'lotto *sm* lounge, sitting room; (*mobilio*) lounge suite.

sal'pare *vi* (2) (NAUT) to set sail; (*anche*: ~ **l'ancora**) to weigh anchor.

'salsa *sf* (CUC) sauce; ~ **di pomodoro** tomato sauce.

sal'siccia, ce [sal'sittʃa] *sf* pork sausage.

sal'tare *vi* to jump, leap; (*esplodere*) to blow up, explode; (: *valvola*) to blow; (*rompersi*) to snap, burst; (*venir via*) to pop off // *vt* to jump (over), leap (over); (*fig: pranzo, capitolo*) to skip, miss (out); (CUC) to sauté; **far** ~ to blow up; to burst open.

saitel'lare *vi* to skip; to hop.

saltim'banco *sm* acrobat.

'salto *sm* jump; (SPORT) jumping; **fare un** ~ to jump, leap; **fare un** ~ **da qd** to pop over to sb's (place); ~ **in alto/lungo** high/long jump; ~ **con l'asta** pole vaulting; ~ **mortale** somersault.

saltu'ario, a *ag* occasional, irregular.

sa'lubre *ag* healthy, salubrious.

salume'ria *sf* delicatessen.

sa'lumi *smpl* salted pork meats.

salu'tare *ag* healthy; (*fig*) salutary, beneficial // *vt* (*per dire buon giorno, fig*) to greet; (*per dire addio*) to say goodbye to; (MIL) to salute.

sa'lute *sf* health; ~**!** (*a chi starnutisce*) bless you!; (*nei brindisi*) cheers!; **bere alla** ~ **di qd** to drink (to) sb's health.

sa'luto *sm* (*gesto*) wave; (*parola*) greeting;

(MIL) salute; ~i smpl greetings; **cari ~i** best regards; **vogliate gradire i nostri più distinti ~i** Yours faithfully.

'salva sf salvo.

salvacon'dotto sm (MIL) safe-conduct.

salva'gente [salva'dʒɛnte] sm (NAUT) lifebuoy; (stradale) traffic island; ~ **a ciambella**; ~ **a giubbotto** lifejacket.

salvaguar'dare vt to safeguard.

sal'vare vt to save; (trarre da un pericolo) to rescue; (proteggere) to protect; ~**rsi** vr to save o.s.; to escape; **salva'taggio** sm rescue; **salva'tore, 'trice** sm/f saviour; **salvazi'one** sf (REL) salvation.

'salve escl (fam) hi!

sal'vezza [sal'vettsa] sf salvation; (sicurezza) safety.

'salvia sf (BOT) sage.

'salvo, a ag safe, unhurt, unharmed; (fuori pericolo) safe, out of danger // prep (eccetto) except; ~ **che** cong (a meno che) unless; (eccetto che) except (that); ~ **imprevisti** barring accidents.

sam'buco sm elder (tree).

sa'nare vt to heal, cure; (fig) to put right.

sana'torio sm sanatorium.

san'cire [san'tʃire] vt to sanction.

'sandalo sm (BOT) sandalwood; (calzatura) sandal.

'sangue sm blood; **farsi cattivo ~** to fret, get in a state; ~ **freddo** (fig) sang-froid, calm; **a ~ freddo** in cold blood; **sangu'igno, a** ag blood cpd; (colore) blood-red; **sangui'nare** vi to bleed; **sangui'noso, a** ag bloody; (cruento) bitter, mortal; **sangui'suga** sf leech.

sanità sf health; (salubrità) healthiness; **Ministro della S~** Minister of Health; ~ **mentale** sanity.

sani'tario, a ag health cpd; (condizioni) sanitary // sm (AMM) doctor.

'sanno forma del vb **sapere**.

'sano, a ag healthy; (denti, costituzione) healthy, sound; (integro) whole, unbroken; (fig: politica, consigli) sound; ~ **di mente** sane; **di ~a pianta** completely, entirely; ~ **e salvo** safe and sound.

santifi'care vt to sanctify; (canonizzare) to canonize; (venerare) to honour.

santità sf sanctity; holiness; **Sua/Vostra** ~ (titolo di Papa) His/Your Holiness.

'santo, a ag holy; (fig) saintly; (seguito da nome proprio: dav sm **san** + C, **sant'** + V, **santo** + s impura, gn, pn, ps, x, z; dav sf **santa** + C, **sant'** + V) saint // sm/f saint; **la S~a Sede** the Holy See; **il S~ Spirito** the Holy Spirit o Ghost.

santu'ario sm sanctuary.

sanzio'nare [santsjo'nare] vt to sanction.

sanzi'one [san'tsjone] sf sanction; (penale, civile) sanction, penalty.

sa'pere vt to know; (essere capace di): **so nuotare** I know how to swim, I can swim // vi: ~ **di** (aver sapore) to taste of; (aver odore) to smell of; **sa di muffa** it smells of mould, it smells mouldy // sm knowledge; **far ~ qc a qd** to inform sb about sth, let sb know sth.

sapi'enza [sa'pjɛntsa] sf wisdom.

sa'pone sm soap; ~ **da bucato** washing soap; **sapo'netta** sf cake o bar o tablet of soap.

sa'pore sm taste, flavour; **sapo'rito, a** ag tasty; (fig: arguto) witty; (: piccante) racy.

sappi'amo forma del vb **sapere**.

saraci'nesca [sarat∫i'neska] sf (serranda) rolling shutter.

sar'casmo sm sarcasm q; sarcastic remark; **sar'castico, a, ci, che** ag sarcastic.

Sar'degna [sar'deɲɲa] sf: **la ~** Sardinia.

sar'dina sf sardine.

'sardo, a ag, sm/f Sardinian.

sar'donico, a, ci, che ag sardonic.

'sarto, a sm/f tailor/dressmaker; **sarto'ria** sf tailor's (shop); dressmaker's (shop); (più grande) fashion house; (arte) couture.

'sasso sm stone; (ciottolo) pebble; (masso) rock.

sas'sofono sm saxophone.

sas'soso, a ag stony; pebbly.

'Satana sm Satan; **sa'tanico, a, ci, che** ag satanic, fiendish.

sa'tellite sm, ag satellite.

'satira sf satire; **sa'tirico, a, ci, che** ag satiric(al).

satu'rare vt to saturate; **saturazi'one** sf saturation; **'saturo, a** ag saturated; (fig): **saturo di** full of.

'sauna sf sauna.

Sa'voia sf: **la ~** Savoy.

savoi'ardo, a ag of Savoy, Savoyard // sm (biscotto) sponge finger.

sazi'are [sat'tsjare] vt to satisfy, satiate; ~**rsi** vr (riempirsi di cibo): ~**rsi (di)** to eat one's fill (of); (fig): ~**rsi di** to grow tired o weary of.

'sazio, a ['sattsjo] ag: ~ **(di)** sated (with), full (of); (fig: stufo) fed up (with), sick (of).

sba'dato, a ag careless, inattentive.

sbadigli'are [zbadiʎ'ʎare] vi to yawn; **sba'diglio** sm yawn.

sbagli'are [zbaʎ'ʎare] vt to make a mistake, get wrong // vi to make a mistake, be mistaken, be wrong; (operare in modo non giusto) to err; ~**rsi** vr to make a mistake, be mistaken, be wrong; ~ **la mira/strada** to miss one's aim/take the wrong road; ~ **qd con qd altro** to mistake sb for sb else; **'sbaglio** sm mistake, error; (morale) error.

sbal'lare vt (merce) to unpack.

sballot'tare vt to toss (about).

sbalor'dire vt to stun, amaze // vi to be stunned, be amazed; **sbalordi'tivo, a** ag amazing; (prezzo) incredible, absurd.

sbal'zare [zbal'tsare] vt to throw, hurl; (fig: da una carica) to remove, dismiss // vi (2) (balzare) to bounce; (saltare) to leap, bound; **'sbalzo** sm bounce; leap; (spostamento improvviso) jolt, jerk; **a sbalzi** jerkily; (fig) in fits and starts.

sban'dare vi (NAUT) to list; (AER) to bank; (AUT) to skid; ~**rsi** vr (folla) to disperse;

(*truppe*) to disband; (*fig: famiglia*) to break up.

sbandie'rare vt (*bandiera*) to wave; (*fig*) to parade, show off.

sbaragli'are [zbaraʎ'ʎare] vt (*MIL*) to rout; (*in gare sportive etc*) to beat, defeat.

sba'raglio [zba'raʎʎo] sm rout; defeat; **gettarsi allo ~** to risk everything.

sbaraz'zarsi [zbarat'tsarsi] vr: **~ di** to get rid of, rid o.s. of.

sbar'care vt (*passeggeri*) to disembark; (*merci*) to unload // vi (2) to disembark; **~ il lunario** (*fig*) to make ends meet; **'sbarco** sm disembarkation; unloading; (*MIL*) landing.

'sbarra sf bar; (*di passaggio a livello*) barrier; (*DIR*): **presentarsi alla ~** to appear before the court.

sbarra'mento sm (*stradale*) roadblock, barricade; (*diga*) dam, barrage; (*MIL*) barrage.

sbar'rare vt (*strada etc*) to block, bar; (*assegno*) to cross; **~ il passo** to bar the way; **~ gli occhi** to open one's eyes wide.

'sbattere vt (*porta*) to slam, bang; (*tappeti, ali, CUC*) to beat; (*urtare*) to knock, hit // vi (*porta*) to slam, bang; (*agitarsi: ali, vele etc*) to flap; **sbat'tuto, a** ag (*viso, aria*) dejected, worn out; (*uovo*) beaten.

sba'vare vi to dribble; (*colore*) to smear, smudge.

sbia'dire vi (2) (*anche: ~rsi*), vt to fade; **sbia'dito, a** ag faded; (*fig*) colourless, dull.

sbian'care vt to whiten; (*tessuto*) to bleach // vi (2) (*impallidire*) to grow pale o white.

sbi'eco, a, chi, che ag (*storto*) squint, askew; **di ~: guardare qd di ~** (*fig*) to look askance at sb; **tagliare una stoffa di ~** to cut a material on the bias.

sbigot'tire vt to dismay, stun // vi (2) (*anche: ~rsi*) to be dismayed.

sbilanci'are [zbilan'tʃare] vt to throw off balance // vi (*perdere l'equilibrio*) to overbalance; (*pendere da una parte*) to be unbalanced; **~rsi** vr (*fig*): **non si sbilancia mai** (*nel parlare*) he always weighs his words; (*nello spendere*) he never spends beyond his means.

sbirci'are [zbir'tʃare] vt to cast sidelong glances at, eye.

'sbirro sm (*peg*) cop.

sbizzar'rirsi [zbiddzar'rirsi] vr to indulge one's whims.

sbloc'care vt to unblock, free; (*freno*) to release; (*prezzi, affitti*) to decontrol.

sboc'care vi (2): **~ in** (*fiume*) to flow into; (*strada*) to lead into; (*persona*) to come (out) into; (*fig: concludersi*) to end (up) in.

sboc'cato, a ag (*persona*) foul-mouthed; (*linguaggio*) foul.

sbocci'are [zbot'tʃare] vi (2) (*fiore*) to bloom, open (out).

'sbocco, chi sm (*apertura*) opening; (*uscita*) way out; (*di fiume*) mouth; (*COMM*) outlet; (: *mercato*) market.

sbol'lire vi (2) (*fig*) to cool down, calm down.

'sbornia sf (*fam*): **prendere una ~** to get plastered.

sbor'sare vt (*denaro*) to pay out.

sbot'tare vi (2) to burst out; **~ a ridere/per la collera** to burst out laughing/explode with anger.

sbotto'nare vt to unbutton, undo.

sbracci'ato, a [zbrat'tʃato] ag (*camicia*) sleeveless; (*persona*) bare-armed.

sbrai'tare vi to yell, bawl.

sbra'nare vt to tear to pieces.

sbricio'lare [zbritʃo'lare] vt, **~rsi** vr to crumble.

sbri'gare vt to deal with, get through; (*cliente*) to attend to, deal with; **~rsi** vr to hurry (up); **sbriga'tivo, a** ag (*persona, modo*) quick, expeditious; (*giudizio*) hasty.

sbrindel'lato, a ag tattered, in tatters.

sbrodo'lare vt to stain, dirty.

'sbronzo, a ['zbrontso] ag (*fam*) tight // sf: **prendere una ~a** to get tight o plastered.

sbu'care vi (2) to come out, emerge; (*apparire improvvisamente*) to pop out (o up).

sbucci'are [zbut'tʃare] vt (*arancia, patata*) to peel; (*piselli*) to shell; (*braccio*) to graze.

sbudel'larsi vr: **~ dalle risa** to split one's sides laughing.

sbuf'fare vi (*persona, cavallo*) to snort; (: *ansimare*) to puff, pant; (*treno*) to puff; **'sbuffo** sm snort; puff, pant; (*di aria, fumo, vapore*) puff.

'scabbia sf (*MED*) scabies sg.

'scabro, a ag rough, harsh.

sca'broso, a ag (*fig: delicato*) delicate, awkward; (: *difficile*) difficult.

scacchi'era [skak'kjɛra] sf chessboard.

scacci'are [skat'tʃare] vt to chase away o out, drive away o out.

'scacco, chi sm (*pezzo del gioco*) chessman; (*quadretto di scacchiera*) square; (*fig*) setback, reverse; **~chi** smpl (*gioco*) chess sg; **a ~chi** (*tessuto*) check(ed); **scacco'matto** sm checkmate.

sca'dente ag shoddy, of poor quality.

sca'denza [ska'dentsa] sf (*di cambiale, contratto*) maturity; (*di passaporto*) expiry date; **a breve/lunga ~** short-/long-term; **lo farò a breve ~** I'll do it in the near future.

sca'dere vi (2) (*contratto etc*) to expire; (*debito*) to fall due; (*valore, forze, peso*) to decline, go down.

sca'fandro sm (*di palombaro*) diving suit; (*di astronauta*) space-suit.

scaf'fale sm shelf; (*mobile*) set of shelves.

'scafo sm (*NAUT, AER*) hull.

scagio'nare [skadʒo'nare] vt to exonerate, free from blame.

'scaglia ['skaʎʎa] sf (*ZOOL*) scale; (*scheggia*) chip, flake.

scagli'are [skaʎ'ʎare] vt (*lanciare: anche fig*) to hurl, fling; **~rsi** vr: **~rsi su o contro** to hurl o fling o.s. at; (*fig*) to rail at.

scaglio'nare [ska⋏⋏o'nare] *vt* (*pagamenti*) to space out, spread out; (*MIL*) to echelon; **scagli'one** *sm* echelon; (*GEO*) terrace.

'scala *sf* (*a gradini etc*) staircase, stairs *pl*; (*a pioli, di corda*) ladder; (*MUS, GEO, di colori, valori, fig*) scale; **~e** *sfpl* (*scalinata*) stairs; **su vasta ~/~ ridotta** on a large/small scale; **~ a libretto** stepladder; **~ mobile** escalator; (*ECON*) sliding scale; **~ mobile dei salari** index-linked pay scale.

sca'lare *vt* (*ALPINISMO, muro*) to climb, scale; (*debito*) to scale down, reduce; **sca'lata** *sf* scaling *q*, climbing *q*; climb; **scala'tore, 'trice** *sm/f* climber.

scalda'bagno [skalda'baɲɲo] *sm* water-heater.

scal'dare *vt* to heat; **~rsi** *vr* to warm up, heat up; (*al sole*) to warm o.s.; (*fig*) to get excited.

scal'fire *vt* to scratch.

scalf'nata *sf* staircase.

sca'lino *sm* (*anche fig*) step; (*di scala a pioli*) rung.

'scalo *sm* (*NAUT*) slipway; (: *porto d'approdo*) port of call; (*AER*) stopover; **fare ~ (a)** (*NAUT*) to call (at), put in (at); (*AER*) to land (at), make a stop (at); **~ merci** (*FERR*) goods yard.

scalop'pina *sf* (*CUC*) escalope.

scal'pello *sm* chisel.

scal'pore *sm* noise, row; **far ~** to make a noise; (*fig*) to cause a sensation *o* a stir.

'scaltro, a *ag* cunning, shrewd.

scal'zare [skal'tsare] *vt* (*albero*) to bare the roots of; (*muro, fig: autorità*) to undermine; (: *escludere: collega*) to oust; **~ i piedi** to take off one's socks and shoes.

'scalzo, a ['skaltso] *ag* barefoot.

scambi'are *vt* to exchange; (*confondere*): **~ qd/qc per** to take *o* mistake sb/sth for; **mi hanno scambiato il cappello** they've given me the wrong hat.

scambi'evole *ag* mutual, reciprocal.

'scambio *sm* exchange; (*FERR*) points *pl*; **~ di persona** case of mistaken identity.

scampa'gnata [skampaɲ'ɲata] *sf* trip to the country.

scampa'nare *vi* to peal.

scam'pare *vt* (*salvare*) to rescue, save; (*evitare: morte, prigione*) to escape // *vi* (*2*): **~ (a qc)** to survive (sth), escape (sth); **scamparla bella** to have a narrow escape; **'scampo** *sm* escape; **cercare scampo nella fuga** to seek safety in flight.

'scampolo *sm* scrap; (*di tessuto*) remnant.

scanala'tura *sf* (*incavo*) channel, groove.

scandagli'are [skanda⋏'⋏are] *vt* (*NAUT*) to sound; (*fig*) to sound out; to probe.

scandaliz'zare [skandalid'dzare] *vt* to shock, scandalize; **~rsi** *vr* to be shocked.

'scandalo *sm* scandal; **scanda'loso, a** *ag* scandalous, shocking.

Scandi'navia *sf*: **la ~** Scandinavia; **scandi'navo, a** *ag, sm/f* Scandinavian.

scan'dire *vt* (*versi*) to scan; (*parole*) to

articulate, pronounce distinctly; **~ il tempo** (*MUS*) to beat time.

scan'nare *vt* (*animale*) to butcher, slaughter; (*persona*) to cut *o* slit the throat of.

'scanno *sm* seat, bench.

scansafa'tiche [skansafa'tike] *sm/f inv* idler, loafer.

scan'sare *vt* (*rimuovere*) to move (aside), shift; (*schivare: schiaffo*) to dodge; (*sfuggire*) to avoid; **~rsi** *vr* to move aside.

scan'sia *sf* shelves *pl*; (*per libri*) bookcase.

'scanso *sm*: **a ~ di** in order to avoid, as a precaution against.

scanti'nato *sm* basement.

scanto'nare *vi* to turn the corner; (*svignarsela*) to sneak off.

scapes'trato, a *ag* dissolute.

'scapito *sm* (*perdita*) loss; (*danno*) damage, detriment; **a ~ di** to the detriment of.

'scapola *sf* shoulder blade.

'scapolo *sm* bachelor.

scappa'mento *sm* (*AUT*) exhaust.

scap'pare *vi* (*2*) (*fuggire*) to escape; (*andare via in fretta*) to rush off; **lasciarsi ~ un'occasione** to let an opportunity go by; **~ di prigione** to escape from prison; **~ di mano** (*oggetto*) to slip out of one's hands; **~ di mente a qd** to slip sb's mind; **mi scappò detto** I let it slip; **scap'pata** *sf* quick visit *o* call; (*scappatella*) escapade; **scappa'tella** *sf* escapade; **scappa'toia** *sf* way out.

scara'beo *sm* beetle.

scarabocchi'are [skarabok'kjare] *vt* to scribble, scrawl; **scara'bocchio** *sm* scribble, scrawl.

scara'faggio [skara'faddʒo] *sm* cockroach.

scaraven'tare *vt* to fling, hurl; (*fig: impiegato*) to shift.

scarce'rare [skartʃe'rare] *vt* to release (from prison).

'scarica, che *sf* (*di arma da fuoco, ELETTR, FISIOL*) discharge; (*di piàrmi*) volley of shots; (*di sassi, pugni*) hail, shower.

scari'care *vt* (*merci, camion etc*) to unload; (*passeggeri*) to set down, put off; (*arma*) to unload; (: *sparare, ELETTR*) to discharge; (*sog: corso d'acqua*) to empty, pour; (*fig: liberare da un peso*) to unburden, relieve; **~rsi** *vr* (*orologio*) to run *o* wind down; (*accumulatore*) to go flat *o* dead; (*fig: rilassarsi*) to unwind; **scarica'tore** *sm* loader; (*di porto*) docker.

'scarico, a, chi, che *ag* unloaded; (*orologio*) run down; (*accumulatore*) dead, flat; (*fig: libero*): **~ di** free from // *sm* (*di merci, materiali*) unloading; (*di immondizie*) dumping, tipping; (: *luogo*) rubbish dump; (*TECN: deflusso*) draining; (: *dispositivo*) drain; (*AUT*) exhaust.

scarlat'tina *sf* scarlet fever.

scar'latto, a *ag* scarlet.

'scarno, a *ag* thin, bony.

'scarpa *sf* shoe; **~e da tennis** tennis shoes.

scar'pata sf escarpment.

scarseggi'are [skarsed'dʒare] vi to be scarce; ~ **di** to be short of, lack.

scar'sezza [skar'settsa] sf scarcity, lack.

'scarso, a ag (insufficiente) insufficient, meagre; (povero: annata) poor, lean; (INS: nota) poor; ~ **di** lacking in; **3 chili ~i** just under 3 kilos, barely 3 kilos.

scarta'mento sm (FERR) gauge; ~ **normale/ridotto** standard/ narrow gauge.

scar'tare vt (pacco) to unwrap; (idea) to reject; (MIL) to declare unfit for military service; (carte da gioco) to discard; (CALCIO) to dodge (past) // vi to swerve.

'scarto sm (cosa scartata, anche COMM) reject; (di veicolo) swerve; (differenza) gap, difference.

scassi'nare vt to break, force.

'scasso sm vedi **furto.**

scate'nare vt (fig) to incite, stir up; ~**rsi** vr (fig) to break out; to rage.

'scatola sf box; (di latta) tin, can; **cibi in** ~ tinned o canned foods; ~ **cranica** cranium.

scat'tare vt (fotografia) to take // vi (2) (congegno, molla etc) to be released; (balzare) to spring up; (SPORT) to put on a spurt; (fig: per l'ira) to fly into a rage; ~ **in piedi** to spring to one's feet.

'scatto sm (dispositivo) release; (: di arma da fuoco) trigger mechanism; (rumore) click; (balzo) jump, start; (SPORT) spurt; (fig: di ira etc) fit; (: di stipendio) increment; **di** ~ suddenly.

scatu'rire vi (2) to gush, spring.

scaval'care vt (ostacolo) to pass (o climb) over; (fig) to get ahead of, overtake.

sca'vare vt (terreno) to dig; (legno) to hollow out; (tesoro) to dig up; (città) to excavate.

'scavo sm excavating q; excavation.

'scegliere ['ʃeʎʎere] vt to choose, select.

sce'icco, chi [ʃe'ikko] sm sheik.

scelle'rato, a [ʃelle'rato] ag wicked, evil.

scel'lino [ʃel'lino] sm shilling.

'scelto, a ['ʃelto] pp di **scegliere** // ag (di prima scelta) carefully chosen; select; (di ottima qualità: merce) choice, top quality; (MIL: specializzato) crack cpd, highly skilled // sf choice; selection; **frutta o formaggi a** ~**a** a choice of fruit or cheese.

sce'mare [ʃe'mare] vt to diminish, reduce.

'scemo, a ['ʃemo] ag stupid, silly.

'scempio ['ʃempjo] sm slaughter, massacre; (fig) ruin; **far** ~ **di** (fig) to play havoc with, ruin.

'scena ['ʃɛna] sf (gen) scene; (palcoscenico) stage; **le** ~**e** (fig: teatro) the stage; **fare una** ~ to make a scene; **andare in** ~ to be staged o put on o performed; **mettere in** ~ to stage.

sce'nario [ʃe'narjo] sm scenery; (di film) scenario.

sce'nata [ʃe'nata] sf row, scene.

'scendere ['ʃɛndere] vi (2) to go (o come) down; (strada, sole) to go down; (passeggero: fermarsi) to get out, alight;

(fig: temperatura, prezzi) to go o come down, fall, drop // vt (scale, pendio) to go (o come) down; ~ **dal treno** to get off o out of the train; ~ **da cavallo** to dismount, get off one's horse.

'scenico, a, ci, che ['ʃɛniko] ag stage cpd, scenic.

scervel'lato, a [ʃervel'lato] ag feather-brained, scatterbrained.

'sceso, a ['ʃeso] pp di **scendere.**

scetti'cismo [ʃetti'tʃizmo] sm scepticism; **'scettico, a, ci, che** ag sceptical.

'scettro ['ʃɛttro] sm sceptre.

'scheda ['skɛda] sf (index) card; ~ **elettorale** ballot paper; ~ **perforata** punch card; **sche'dare** vt (dati) to file; (libri) to catalogue; (registrare: anche POLIZIA) to put on one's files; **sche'dario** sm file; (mobile) filing cabinet.

'scheggia, ge ['skeddʒa] sf splinter, sliver.

'scheletro ['skɛletro] sm skeleton.

'schema, i ['skɛma] sm (diagramma) diagram, sketch; (progetto, abbozzo) outline, plan.

'scherma ['skerma] sf fencing.

scher'maglia [sker'maʎʎa] sf (fig) skirmish.

'schermo ['skermo] sm shield, screen; (CINEMA, TV) screen.

scher'nire [sker'nire] vt to mock, sneer at; **'scherno** sm mockery, derision.

scher'zare [sker'tsare] vi to joke.

'scherzo ['skertso] sm joke; (tiro) trick; (MUS) scherzo; **è uno** ~**!** (una cosa facile) it's child's play!, it's easy!; **per** ~ in jest; for a joke o a laugh; **fare un brutto** ~ **a** qd to play a nasty trick on sb; **scher'zoso, a** ag joking, jesting; (cagnolino etc) playful.

schiaccia'noci [skjattʃa'notʃi] sm inv nutcracker.

schiacci'are [skjat'tʃare] vt (dito) to crush; (noci) to crack; ~ **un pisolino** to have a nap.

schiaffeggi'are [skjaffed'dʒare] vt to slap.

schi'affo ['skjaffo] sm slap.

schiamaz'zare [skjamat'tsare] vi to squawk, cackle.

schian'tare [skjan'tare] vt to break, tear apart; ~**rsi** vr to break (up), shatter; **schi'anto** sm (rumore) crash; tearing sound; (fig: tormento) provare uno **schianto al cuore** to feel a wrench at one's heart; **è uno schianto!** (fam) it's (o he's o she's) terrific!

schia'rire [skja'rire] vt to lighten, make lighter // vi (2) (anche: ~**rsi**) to grow lighter; (tornar sereno) to clear, brighten up; ~**rsi la voce** to clear one's throat.

schiavitù [skjavi'tu] sf slavery.

schi'avo, a ['skjavo] sm/f slave.

schi'ena ['skjɛna] sf (ANAT) back; **schie-'nale** sm (di sedia) back.

schi'era ['skjɛra] sf (MIL) rank; (gruppo) group, band.

schiera'mento [skjera'mento] sm lining up, drawing up; (SPORT) formation; line-up.

schie'rare [skje'rare] *vt* (*esercito*) to line up, draw up, marshal; **~rsi** *vr* to line up; (*fig*) to take sides.

schi'etto, a ['skjɛtto] *ag* (*puro*) pure; (*fig*) frank, straightforward; sincere.

'schifo ['skifo] *sm* disgust; **fare ~** (*essere fatto male, dare pessimi risultati*) to be awful; **mi fa ~** it makes me sick, it's disgusting; **quel libro è uno ~** that book's rotten; **schi'foso, a** *ag* disgusting, revolting; (*molto scadente*) rotten, lousy.

schioc'care [skjok'kare] *vt* (*frusta*) to crack; (*dita*) to snap; (*lingua*) to click; **~ le labbra** to smack one's lips.

schi'udere ['skjudere] *vt*, **~rsi** *vr* to open.

schi'uma ['skjuma] *sf* foam; (*di sapone*) lather; (*fig: feccia*) scum; **schiu'mare** *vt* to skim // *vi* to foam.

schi'uso, a ['skjuso] *pp di* **schiudere**.

schi'vare [ski'vare] *vt* to dodge, avoid.

'schivo, a ['skivo] *ag* (*ritroso*) stand-offish, reserved; (*timido*) shy; **~ a fare** loath to do, reluctant to do.

schizo'frenico, a, ci, che [skidzo'frɛniko] *ag* schizophrenic.

schiz'zare [skit'tsare] *vt* (*spruzzare*) to spurt, squirt; (*sporcare*) to splash, spatter; (*fig: abbozzare*) to sketch // *vi* to spurt, squirt; (*saltar fuori*) to dart up (*o off etc*).

schizzi'noso, a [skittsi'noso] *ag* fussy, finicky.

'schizzo ['skittso] *sm* (*di liquido*) spurt; splash, spatter; (*abbozzo*) sketch.

sci [ʃi] *sm* (*attrezzo*) ski; (*attività*) skiing; **~ nautico** water-skiing.

'scia, *pl* **'scie** [ʃia] *sf* (*di imbarcazione*) wake; (*di profumo*) trail.

scià [ʃa] *sm inv* shah.

sci'abola ['ʃabola] *sf* sabre.

scia'callo [ʃa'kallo] *sm* jackal.

sciac'quare [ʃak'kware] *vt* to rinse.

scia'gura [ʃa'gura] *sf* disaster, calamity; misfortune; **sciagu'rato, a** *ag* unfortunate; (*malvagio*) wicked.

scialac'quare [ʃalak'kware] *vt* to squander.

scia'lare [ʃa'lare] *vi* to lead a life of luxury.

sci'albo, a ['ʃalbo] *ag* pale, dull; (*fig*) dull, colourless.

sci'alle ['ʃalle] *sm* shawl.

scia'luppa [ʃa'luppa] *sf* (*anche*: **~ di salvataggio**) lifeboat.

sci'ame ['ʃame] *sm* swarm.

scian'cato, a [ʃan'kato] *ag* lame; (*mobile*) rickety.

sci'are [ʃi'are] *vi* to ski.

sci'arpa ['ʃarpa] *sf* scarf; (*fascia*) sash.

scia'tore, 'trice [ʃia'tore] *sm/f* skier.

sci'atto, a ['ʃatto] *ag* (*persona, aspetto*) slovenly, unkempt; (*lavoro*) sloppy, careless.

scien'tifico, a, ci, che [ʃen'tifiko] *ag* scientific.

sci'enza ['ʃɛntsa] *sf* science; (*sapere*) knowledge; **~e** *sfpl* (*INS*) science *sg*; **~e**

naturali natural sciences; **scienzi'ato, a** *sm/f* scientist.

'scimmia ['ʃimmja] *sf* monkey; **scimmiot'tare** *vt* to ape, mimic.

scimpanzé [ʃimpan'tse] *sm inv* chimpanzee.

scimu'nito, a [ʃimu'nito] *ag* silly, idiotic.

'scindere ['ʃindere] *vt*, **~rsi** *vr* to split (up).

scin'tilla [ʃin'tilla] *sf* spark; **scintil'lare** *vi* to spark; (*acqua, occhi*) to sparkle.

scioc'chezza [ʃok'kettsa] *sf* stupidity *q*; stupid *o* foolish thing; **dire ~e** to talk nonsense.

sci'occo, a, chi, che ['ʃɔkko] *ag* stupid, foolish.

sci'ogliere ['ʃɔʎʎere] *vt* (*nodo*) to untie; (*animale*) to untie, release; (*fig: persona*): **~ da** to release from; (*neve*) to melt; (*nell'acqua: zucchero etc*) to dissolve; (*fig: problema*) to resolve; (: *muscoli*) to loosen up; (*fig: porre fine a: contratto*) to cancel; (: *società, matrimonio*) to dissolve; (*adempiere: voto etc*) to fulfil; **~rsi** *vr* to loosen, come untied; to melt; to dissolve.

sciol'tezza [ʃol'tettsa] *sf* agility; suppleness; ease.

sci'olto, a ['ʃɔlto] *pp di* **sciogliere** // *ag* loose; (*agile*) agile, nimble; supple; (*disinvolto*) free and easy; **versi ~i** (*POESIA*) blank verse.

sciope'rante [ʃope'rante] *sm/f* striker.

sciope'rare [ʃope'rare] *vi* to strike, go on strike.

sci'opero ['ʃopero] *sm* strike; **fare ~** to strike; **~ bianco** work-to-rule; **~ selvaggio** wildcat strike; **~ a singhiozzo** on-off strike.

sci'rocco [ʃi'rɔkko] *sm* sirocco.

sci'roppo [ʃi'rɔppo] *sm* syrup.

'scisma ['ʃizma] *sm* (*REL*) schism.

scissi'one [ʃis'sjone] *sf* (*anche fig*) split, division; (*FISICA*) fission.

'scisso, a ['ʃisso] *pp di* **scindere**.

sciu'pare [ʃu'pare] *vt* (*abito, libro, appetito*) to spoil, ruin; (*tempo, denaro*) to waste; **~rsi** *vr* to get spoilt *o* ruined; (*rovinarsi la salute*) to ruin one's health.

scivo'lare [ʃivo'lare] *vi* (*2*) to slide *o* glide along; (*involontariamente*) to slip, slide; **'scivolo** *sm* slide; (*TECN*) chute.

scle'rosi *sf* sclerosis.

scoc'care *vt* (*freccia*) to shoot // *vi* (*2*) (*guizzare*) to shoot up; (*battere: ora*) to strike.

scocci'are [skot'tʃare] (*fam*) *vt* to bother, annoy; **~rsi** *vr* to be bothered *o* annoyed.

sco'della *sf* bowl.

scodinzo'lare [skodintso'lare] *vi* to wag its tail.

scogli'era [skoʎ'ʎera] *sf* reef; cliff.

'scoglio ['skoʎʎo] *sm* (*al mare*) rock.

scol'attolo *sm* squirrel.

sco'lare *ag*: **età ~** school age // *vt* to drain // *vi* (*2*) to drip.

scola'resca *sf* schoolchildren *pl*, pupils *pl*.

sco'laro, a *sm/f* pupil, schoolboy/girl.

sco'lastico, a, ci, che *ag* school *cpd*; scholastic.

scol'lare *vt* (*staccare*) to unstick; **~rsi** *vr* to come unstuck; **scolla'tura** *sf* neckline.

'scolo *sm* drainage.

scolo'rire *vt* to fade; to discolour // *vi* (*2*) (*anche:* **~rsi**) to fade; to become discoloured; (*impallidire*) to turn pale.

scol'pire *vt* to carve, sculpt.

scombi'nare *vt* to mess up, upset.

scombusso'lare *vt* to upset.

scom'messo, a *pp di* **scommettere** // *sf* bet, wager.

scom'mettere *vt, vi* to bet.

scomo'dare *vt* to trouble, bother; to disturb; **~rsi** *vr* to put o.s. out; **~rsi a fare** to go to the bother *o* trouble of doing.

'scomodo, a *ag* uncomfortable; (*sistemazione, posto*) awkward, inconvenient.

scompagi'nare [skompadʒi'nare] *vt* to upset, disarrange; (*TIP*) to break up.

scompa'rire *vi* (*2*) to disappear, vanish; (*fig*) to be insignificant; **scom'parso, a** *pp di* **scomparire** // *sf* disappearance.

scomparti'mento *sm* (*FERR*) compartment.

scom'parto *sm* compartment, division.

scompigli'are [skompiʎ'ʎare] *vt* (*cassetto, capelli*) to mess up, disarrange; (*fig: piani*) to upset; **scom'piglio** *sm* mess, confusion.

scom'porre *vt* (*disfare*) to break up, take to pieces; (*scompigliare*) to disarrange, mess up; **scomporsi** *vr* (*fig*) to get upset, lose one's composure; **scom'posto, a** *pp di* **scomporre** // *ag* (*gesto*) unseemly; (*capelli*) ruffled, dishevelled.

sco'munica *sf* excommunication.

scomuni'care *vt* to excommunicate.

sconcer'tare [skontʃer'tare] *vt* to disconcert, bewilder.

'sconcio, a, ci, ce ['skontʃo] *ag* (*osceno*) indecent, obscene // *sm* (*cosa riprovevole, mal fatta*) disgrace.

sconfes'sare *vt* to renounce, disavow; to repudiate.

scon'figgere [skon'fiddʒere] *vt* to defeat, overcome.

sconfi'nare *vi* to cross the border; (*in proprietà privata*) to trespass; (*fig*) **~ da** to stray *o* digress from; **sconfi'nato, a** *ag* boundless, unlimited.

scon'fitto, a *pp di* **sconfiggere** // *sf* defeat.

scon'forto *sm* despondency.

scongiu'rare [skondʒu'rare] *vt* (*implorare*) to entreat, beseech, implore; (*eludere: pericolo*) to ward off, avert; **scongi'uro** *sm* entreaty; (*esorcismo*) exorcism; **fare gli scongiuri** to touch wood.

scon'nesso, a *pp di* **sconnettere** // *ag* (*fig: discorso*) incoherent, rambling.

sconosci'uto, a [skonoʃ'ʃuto] *ag* unknown; new, strange // *sm/f* stranger; unknown person.

sconquas'sare *vt* to shatter, smash; (*scombussolare*) to upset.

sconside'rato, a *ag* thoughtless, rash.

sconsigli'are [skonsiʎ'ʎare] *vt:* **~ qc a qd** to advise sb against sth; **~ qd da fare qc** to advise sb not to do *o* against doing sth.

sconso'lato, a *ag* inconsolable; desolate.

scon'tare *vt* (*detrarre*) to deduct; (*debito*) to pay off; (*COMM*) to discount; (*pena*) to serve; (*colpa, errori*) to pay for, suffer for.

scon'tato, a *ag* (*previsto*) foreseen, taken for granted; **dare per ~ che** to take it for granted that.

scon'tento, a *ag:* **~ (di)** discontented *o* dissatisfied (with) // *sm* discontent, dissatisfaction.

'sconto *sm* discount.

scon'trarsi *vr* (*treni etc*) to crash, collide; (*venire a combattimento, fig*) to clash; **~ con** to crash into, collide with.

scon'trino *sm* ticket.

'scontro *sm* clash, encounter; crash, collision.

scon'troso, a *ag* sullen, surly; (*permaloso*) touchy.

sconveni'ente *ag* unseemly, improper.

scon'volgere [skon'voldʒere] *vt* to throw into confusion, upset; (*turbare*) to shake, disturb, upset; **scon'volto, a** *pp di* **sconvolgere**.

'scopa *sf* broom; (*CARTE*) Italian card game; **sco'pare** *vt* to sweep.

sco'perto, a *pp di* **scoprire** // *ag* uncovered; (*capo*) uncovered, bare; (*luogo*) open, exposed; (*MIL*) exposed, without cover; (*conto*) overdrawn // *sf* discovery.

'scopo *sm* aim, purpose; **a che ~?** what for?

scoppi'are *vi* (*2*) (*spaccarsi*) to burst; (*esplodere*) to explode; (*fig*) to break out; **~ in pianto** *o* **a piangere** to burst out crying; **~ dalle risa** *o* **dal ridere** to split one's sides laughing; **'scoppio** *sm* explosion; (*di tuono, arma etc*) crash, bang; (*fig: di risa, ira*) fit, outburst; (: *di guerra*) outbreak; **a scoppio ritardato** delayed-action.

scoppiet'tare *vi* to crackle.

sco'prire *vt* to discover; (*liberare da ciò che copre*) to uncover; (: *monumento*) to unveil; **~rsi** *vr* to put on lighter clothes; (*fig*) to give o.s. away.

scoraggi'are [skorad'dʒare] *vt* to discourage; **~rsi** *vr* to become discouraged, lose heart.

scorcia'toia [skortʃa'toja] *sf* short cut.

'scorcio ['skortʃo] *sm* (*ARTE*) foreshortening; (*di secolo, periodo*) end, close.

scor'dare *vt* to forget; **~rsi** *vr:* **~rsi di qc/di fare** to forget sth/to do.

'scorgere ['skordʒere] *vt* to make out, distinguish, see.

'scorno *sm* ignominy, disgrace.

scorpacci'ata [skorpat'tʃata] *sf:* **fare**

una ~ (di) to stuff o.s. (with), eat one's fill (of).

scorpi'one sm scorpion; (dello zodiaco): S~ Scorpio.

scorraz'zare [skorrat'tsare] vi to run about.

'scorrere vt (giornale, lettera) to run o skim through // vi (2) (scivolare) to glide, slide; (colare, fluire) to run, flow; (trascorrere) to pass (by).

scor'retto, a ag incorrect; (sgarbato) impolite; (sconveniente) improper.

scor'revole ag (porta) sliding; (fig: stile) fluent, flowing.

scorri'banda sf (MIL) raid; (escursione) trip, excursion.

'scorso, a pp di scorrere // ag last // sf quick look, glance.

scor'soio a ag: nodo ~ noose.

'scorta sf (di personalità, convoglio) escort; (provvista) supply, stock; **scor'tare** vt to escort.

scor'tese ag discourteous, rude; **scorte-'sia** sf lack of courtesy, rudeness.

scorti'care vt to skin.

'scorto, a pp di scorgere.

'scorza ['skɔrdza] sf (di albero) bark; (di agrumi) peel, skin; (di pesce, serpente) skin.

sco'sceso, a [skoʃ'feso] ag steep.

'scosso, a pp di scuotere // ag (turbato) shaken, upset // sf jerk, jolt, shake; (ELETTR, fig) shock.

scos'tante ag (fig) off-putting, unpleasant.

scos'tare vt to move (away), shift; ~rsi vr to move away.

scostu'mato, a ag immoral, dissolute.

scot'tare vt (ustionare) to burn; (: con liquido bollente) to scald; (sog: offesa) to hurt, offend // vi to burn; (caffè) to be too hot; **scotta'tura** sf burn; scald.

'scotto, a ag overcooked // sm (fig): pagare lo ~ (di) to pay the penalty (for).

sco'vare vt to drive out, flush out; (fig) to discover.

'Scozia ['skɔttsia] sf: la ~ Scotland; scoz-'zese ag Scottish // sm/f Scot.

scredi'tare vt to discredit.

screpo'lare vt, ~rsi vr to crack; **screpola'tura** sf cracking q; crack.

screzi'ato, a [skret'tsjato] ag streaked, speckled.

'screzio ['skrettsjo] sm disagreement.

scricchio'lare [skrikkjo'lare] vi to creak, squeak.

'scricciolo ['skrittʃolo] sm wren.

'scrigno ['skrinno] sm casket.

scrimina'tura sf parting.

'scritto, a pp di scrivere // ag written // sm writing; (lettera) letter, note // sf inscription; ~i smpl (letterari etc) writing sg; per o in ~ in writing.

scrit'toio sm writing desk.

scrit'tore, 'trice sm/f writer.

scrit'tura sf writing; (COMM) entry; (contratto) contract; (REL): la Sacra S~ the Scriptures pl; ~e sfpl (COMM) accounts, books.

scrittu'rare vt (TEATRO, CINEMA) to sign up, engage; (COMM) to enter.

scriva'nia sf desk.

scri'vente sm/f writer.

'scrivere vt to write; **come lo si scrive?** how is it spelt?, how do you write it?

scroc'cone, a sm/f scrounger.

'scrofa sf (ZOOL) sow.

scrol'lare vt to shake; ~rsi vr (anche fig) to give o.s. a shake; ~ le spalle/il capo to shrug one's shoulders/shake one's head.

scrosci'are [skroʃ'fare] vi (2) (pioggia) to pour down, pelt down; (torrente, fig: applausi) to thunder, roar; **'scroscio** sm pelting; thunder, roar; (di applausi) burst.

scros'tare vt (intonaco) to scrape off, strip; ~rsi vr to peel off, flake off.

'scrupolo sm scruple; (meticolosità) care, conscientiousness; **scrupo'loso, a** ag scrupulous; conscientious, thorough.

scru'tare vt to search, scrutinize; (intenzioni, causa) to examine, scrutinize.

scruti'nare vt (voti) to count; **scru'tinio** sm (votazione) ballot; (insieme delle operazioni) poll; (INS) (meeting for) assignment of marks at end of a term or year.

scu'cire [sku'tʃire] vt (orlo etc) to unpick, undo.

scude'ria sf stable.

scu'detto sm (SPORT) (championship) shield; (distintivo) badge.

'scudo sm shield.

scul'tore, 'trice sm/f sculptor.

scul'tura sf sculpture.

scu'ola sf school; ~ elemen- tare/materna/media primary/nur- sery/secondary school; ~ guida driving school.

scu'otere vt to shake; ~rsi vr to jump, be startled; (fig: muoversi) to rouse o.s., stir o.s.; (: commuoversi) to be shaken.

'scure sf axe.

'scuro, a ag dark; (fig: espressione) grim // sm darkness; dark colour; (imposta) (window) shutter; verde/rosso etc ~ dark green/red etc.

scur'rile ag scurrilous.

'scusa sf excuse; ~e sfpl apology sg, apologies; **chiedere ~ a qd (per)** to apologize to sb (for); **chiedo ~** I'm sorry; (disturbando etc) excuse me.

scu'sare vt to excuse; ~rsi vr: ~rsi (di) to apologize (for); **(mi) scusi** I'm sorry; (per richiamare l'attenzione) excuse me.

sde'gnare [zden'nare] vt to scorn, despise; ~rsi vr (adirarsi) to get angry.

'sdegno ['zdenno] sm scorn, disdain; **sde-'gnoso, a** ag scornful, disdainful.

sdolci'nato, a [zdoltʃi'nato] ag mawkish, oversentimental.

sdoppi'are vt (dividere) to divide o split in two.

sdrai'arsi vr to stretch out, lie down.

'sdraio sm: sedia a ~ deck chair.

sdruccio'lare [zdruttʃo'lare] vi (2) to slip, slide.

se pronome vedi si // cong if; (in frasi

interrogative indirette) if, whether; **non so** ~ **scrivere o telefonare** I don't know whether *o* if I should write or phone; ~ **mai** if, if ever; (*caso mai*) in case; ~ **solo** *o* **solamente** if only.

sé *pronome* (*gen*) oneself; (*esso, essa, lui, lei, loro*) itself; himself; herself; themselves; ~ **stesso(a)** *pronome* oneself; itself; himself; herself; ~ **stessi(e)** *pronome pl* themselves.

seb'bene *cong* although, though.

sec. (*abbr di* **secolo**) c.

'secca *sf vedi* **secco**.

sec'care *vt* to dry; (*prosciugare*) to dry up; (*fig: importunare*) to annoy, bother; (: *annoiare*) to bore // *vi* (2) to dry; to dry up; ~**rsi** *vr* to dry; to dry up; (*fig*) to grow annoyed; to grow bored; **secca'tura** *sf* (*fig*) bother *q*, trouble *q*.

'secchia ['sekkja] *sf* bucket, pail.

'secco, a, chi, che *ag* dry; (*fichi, pesce*) dried; (*foglie, ramo*) withered; (*magro: persona*) thin, skinny; (*fig: risposta, modo di fare*) curt, abrupt; (: *colpo*) clean, sharp // *sm* (*siccità*) drought // *sf* (*del mare*) shallows *pl*; **restarci** ~ (*fig: morire sul colpo*) to drop dead; **mettere in** ~ (*barca*) to beach; **rimanere in** *o* **a** ~ (*NAUT*) to run aground; (*fig*) to be left in the lurch.

seco'lare *ag* age-old, centuries-old; (*laico, mondano*) secular.

'secolo *sm* century; (*epoca*) age.

se'conda *sf vedi* **secondo**.

secon'dario, a *ag* secondary.

se'condo, a *ag* second // *sm* second; (*di pranzo*) main course // *sf* (*AUT*) second (gear) // *prep* according to; (*nel modo prescritto*) in accordance with; ~ **me** in my opinion, to my mind; **di** ~**a classe** second-class; **di** ~**a mano** second-hand; **viaggiare in** ~**a** to travel second-class; **a** ~**a di** *prep* according to; in accordance with.

secrezi'one [sekret'tsjone] *sf* secretion.

'sedano *sm* celery.

seda'tivo, a *ag, sm* sedative.

'sede *sf* seat; (*di ditta*) head office; (*di organizzazione*) headquarters *pl*; **in** ~ **di** (*in occasione di*) during; ~ **sociale** registered office.

seden'tario, a *ag* sedentary.

se'dere *vi* (2) to sit, be seated; ~**rsi** *vr* to sit down // *sm* (*deretano*) behind, bottom.

'sedia *sf* chair.

sedi'cente [sedi'tʃɛnte] *ag* self-styled.

'sedici ['seditʃi] *num* sixteen.

se'dile *sm* seat; (*nei giardini*) bench.

sedi'mento *sm* sediment.

sedizi'one [sedit'tsjone] *sf* revolt, rebellion; **sedizi'oso, a** *ag* seditious; rebellious.

se'dotto, a *pp di* **sedurre**.

sedu'cente [sedu'tʃɛnte] *ag* seductive; (*proposta*) very attractive.

se'durre *vt* to seduce.

se'duta *sf* session, sitting; (*riunione*)

meeting; (*di modello*) sitting; ~ **stante** (*fig*) immediately.

seduzi'one [sedut'tsjone] *sf* seduction; (*fascino*) charm, appeal.

'sega, ghe *sf* saw.

'segale *sf* rye.

se'gare *vt* to saw; (*recidere*) to saw off; **sega'tura** *sf* (*residuo*) sawdust.

'seggio ['sɛddʒo] *sm* seat; ~ **elettorale** polling station.

'seggiola ['sɛddʒola] *sf* chair; **seggio'lone** *sm* (*per bambini*) highchair.

seggio'via [sɛddʒo'via] *sf* chairlift.

seghe'ria [sege'ria] *sf* sawmill.

seg'mento *sm* segment.

segna'lare [seɲɲa'lare] *vt* (*manovra etc*) to signal; to indicate; (*annunciare*) to announce; to report; (*fig: far conoscere*) to point out; (: *persona*) to single out; ~**rsi** *vr* (*distinguersi*) to distinguish o.s.

se'gnale [seɲ'ɲale] *sm* signal; (*cartello*) sign; ~ **d'allarme** alarm signal; (*FERR*) communication chord; ~ **orario** time signal; **segna'letica** *sf* signalling, signposting; **segnaletica stradale** roadsigns *pl*.

se'gnare [seɲ'ɲare] *vt* to mark; (*prendere nota*) to note; (*indicare*) to indicate, mark; (*SPORT: goal*) to score; ~**rsi** *vr* (*REL*) to make the sign of the cross, cross o.s.

'segno ['seɲɲo] *sm* sign; (*impronta, contrassegno*) mark; (*limite*) limit, bounds *pl*; (*bersaglio*) target; **fare** ~ **di sì/no** to nod (one's head)/shake one's head; **fare** ~ **a qd di fermarsi** to motion (to) sb to stop; **cogliere** *o* **colpire nel** ~ (*fig*) to hit the mark.

segre'gare *vt* to segregate, isolate; **segregazi'one** *sf* segregation.

segre'tario, a *sm/f* secretary; ~ **comunale** town clerk; ~ **di Stato** Secretary of State.

segrete'ria *sf* (*di ditta, scuola*) (secretary's) office; (*d'organizzazione internazionale*) secretariat; (*POL etc: carica*) office of Secretary.

segre'tezza [segre'tettsa] *sf* secrecy.

se'greto, a *ag* secret // *sm* secret; secrecy *q*; **in** ~ in secret, secretly.

segu'ace [se'gwatʃe] *sm/f* follower, disciple.

segu'ente *ag* following, next.

segu'ire *vt* to follow; (*frequentare: corso*) to attend // *vi* (2) to follow; (*continuare: testo*) to continue.

segui'tare *vt* to continue, carry on with // *vi* to continue, carry on.

'seguito *sm* (*scorta*) suite, retinue; (*discepoli*) followers *pl*; (*favore*) following; (*serie*) sequence, series *sg*; (*continuazione*) continuation; (*conseguenza*) result; **di** ~ at a stretch, on end; **in** ~ later on; **in** ~ **a, a** ~ **di** following; (*a causa di*) as a result of, owing to.

'sei *forma del vb* **essere** // *num* six.

sei'cento [sei'tʃɛnto] *num* six hundred // *sm*: **il S**~ the seventeenth century.

selci'ato [sel'tʃato] *sm* pavement.

selezio'nare [selettsjo'nare] *vt* to select.
selezi'one [selet'tsjone] *sf* selection.
'sella *sf* saddle; **sel'lare** *vt* to saddle.
selvag'gina [selvad'dʒina] *sf* (*animali*)
game.
sel'vaggio, a, gi, ge [sel'vaddʒo] *ag* wild;
(*tribù*) savage, uncivilized; (*fig*) savage,
fierce; unsociable // *sm/f* savage.
sel'vatico, a, ci, che *ag* wild.
se'maforo *sm* (*AUT*) traffic lights *pl*.
sem'brare (2) *vi* to seem // *vb impers*:
sembra che it seems that; **mi sembra
che** it seems to me that; I think (that); ~
di essere to seem to be.
'seme *sm* seed; (*sperma*) semen; (*CARTE*)
suit.
se'mestre *sm* half-year; (*INS*) semester.
'semi... *prefisso* semi...; **semi'cerchio** *sm*
semicircle; **semifi'nale** *sf* semifinal;
semi'freddo, a *ag* (*CUC*) chilled // *sm* ice-
cream cake.
'semina *sf* (*AGR*) sowing.
semi'nare *vt* to sow.
semi'nario *sm* seminar; (*REL*) seminary.
se'mitico, a, ci, che *ag* semitic.
sem'mai = se mai; *vedi* **se**.
'semola *sf* bran.
semo'lino *sm* semolina.
'semplice ['semplitʃe] *ag* simple; (*di un
solo elemento*) single; **semplice'mente** *av*
simply; **semplicità** *sf* simplicity;
semplifi'care *vt* to simplify.
'sempre *av* always; (*ancora*) still; **posso**
~ **tentare** I can always try, anyway, I
can try; **per** ~ forever; **una volta per** ~
once and for all; ~ **che** *cong* provided
(that); ~ **più** more and more; ~ **meno**
less and less.
sempre'verde *ag, sm* o *f* (*BOT*) evergreen.
'senape *sf* (*CUC*) mustard.
se'nato *sm* senate; **sena'tore, 'trice** *sm/f*
senator.
se'nile *ag* senile.
'senno *sm* judgment, (common) sense.
'seno *sm* (*petto*) breast; (*ventre materno,
fig*) womb; (*GEO*) inlet, creek; (*ANAT*) sinus;
(*MAT*) sine.
sen'sato, a *ag* sensible.
sensazio'nale [sensattsjo'nale] *ag*
sensational.
sensazi'one [sensat'tsjone] *sf* sensation;
fare ~ to cause a sensation, create a stir.
sen'sibile *ag* sensitive; (*ai sensi*)
perceptible; (*rilevante, notevole*)
appreciable, noticeable; ~ **a** sensitive to;
sensibilità *sf* sensitivity.
'senso *sm* (*FISIOL, istinto*) sense;
(*impressione, sensazione*) feeling,
sensation; (*significato*) meaning, sense;
(*direzione*) direction; ~ **a** (*coscienza*)
consciousness *sg*; (*sensualità*) senses; **ciò
non ha** ~ that doesn't make sense; **fare**
~ **a** (*ripugnare*) to disgust, repel; ~
comune common sense; **in** ~
orario/antiorario clockwise/anticlock-
wise; ~ **unico**, ~ **vietato** (*AUT*) one-way
street.

sensu'ale *ag* sensual; **sensuous;
sensualità** *sf* sensuality; sensuousness.
sen'tenza [sen'tɛntsa] *sf* (*DIR*) sentence;
(*massima*) maxim; **sentenzi'are** *vi* (*DIR*)
to pass judgment.
senti'ero *sm* path.
sentimen'tale *ag* sentimental; (*vita,
avventura*) love *cpd*.
senti'mento *sm* feeling.
senti'nella *sf* sentry.
sen'tire *vt* (*percepire al tatto, fig*) to feel;
(*udire*) to hear; (*ascoltare*) to listen to;
(*odore*) to smell; (*avvertire con il gusto,
assaggiare*) to taste // *vi*: ~ **di** (*avere
sapore*) to taste of; (*avere odore*) to smell
of; ~ **rsi bene/male** to feel well/unwell o
ill; ~ **rsi di fare qc** (*essere disposto*) to
feel like doing sth.
sen'tito, a *ag* (*sincero*) sincere, warm;
per ~ **dire** by hearsay.
'senza ['sɛntsa] *prep, cong* without; ~ **dir
nulla** without saying a word; **fare** ~ **qc**
to do without sth; ~ **di me** without me; ~
che io lo sapessi without me o my
knowing; **senz'altro** of course, certainly;
~ **dubbio** no doubt; ~ **scrupoli**
unscrupulous; ~ **amici** friendless.
sepa'rare *vt* to separate; (*dividere*) to
divide; (*tenere distinto*) to distinguish;
~ **rsi** *vr* (*coniugi*) to separate, part;
(*amici*) to part, leave each other; ~ **rsi da**
(*coniuge*) to separate o part from; (*amico,
socio*) to part company with; (*oggetto*) to
part with; **separazi'one** *sf* separation.
se'polcro *sm* sepulchre.
se'polto, a *pp di* **seppellire**.
seppel'lire *vt* to bury.
'seppia *sf* cuttlefish // *ag inv* sepia.
se'quenza [se'kwɛntsa] *sf* sequence.
seques'trare *vt* (*DIR*) to impound;
(*rapire*) to kidnap; (*costringere in un luogo*)
to keep, confine; **se'questro** *sm* (*DIR*)
impoundment; **sequestro di persona**
kidnapping; illegal confinement.
'sera *sf* evening; **di** ~ in the evening;
domani ~ tomorrow evening, tomorrow
night; **se'rale** *ag* evening *cpd*; **se'rata** *sf*
evening; (*ricevimento*) party.
ser'bare *vt* to keep; (*mettere da parte*) to
put aside; ~ **rancore/odio verso qd** to
bear sb a grudge/hate sb.
serba'toio *sm* tank; (*di apparecchio
igienico*) cistern; (*TECN*) reservoir.
'serbo *sm*: **mettere** (o **tenere** o **avere**) **in**
~ **qc** to put (o keep) sth aside.
sere'nata *sf* (*MUS*) serenade.
serenità *sf* serenity.
se'reno, a *ag* (*tempo, cielo*) clear; (*fig*)
serene, calm.
ser'gente [ser'dʒente] *sm* (*MIL*) sergeant.
'serie *sf inv* (*successione*) series *inv*;
(*gruppo, collezione: di chiavi etc*) set;
(*SPORT*) division; league; (*COMM*): **modello
di** ~ **/fuori** ~ standard/custom-built
model; **in** ~ in quick succession; (*COMM*)
mass *cpd*.
serietà *sf* seriousness; reliability.
'serio, a *ag* serious; (*impiegato*)

responsible, reliable; *(ditta, cliente)* reliable, dependable; **sul ~** *(davvero)* really, truly; *(seriamente)* seriously, in earnest.

ser'mone *sm* sermon.

serpeggi'are [serped'dʒare] *vi* to wind; *(fig)* to spread.

ser'pente *sm* snake; **~ a sonagli** rattlesnake.

'serra *sf* greenhouse; hothouse.

ser'randa *sf* roller shutter.

ser'rare *vt* to close, shut; *(a chiave)* to lock; *(stringere)* to tighten; *(premere: nemico)* to close in on; **~ i pugni/i denti** to clench one's fists/teeth; **~ le file** to close ranks.

serra'tura *sf* lock.

'serva *sf vedi* **servo.**

ser'vire *vt* to serve; *(clienti: al ristorante)* to wait on; *(: al negozio)* to serve, attend to; *(fig: giovare)* to aid, help // *vi* (TENNIS) to serve; *(essere utile)*: **~ a qd** to be of use to sb; **~ a qc/a fare** *(utensile etc)* to be used for sth/for doing; **~ (a qd) di** to serve as (for sb); **~rsi** *vr (usare)*: **~rsi di** to use; *(prendere: cibo)*: **~rsi (di)** to help o.s. (to); *(essere cliente abituale)*: **~rsi da** to be a regular customer at, go to.

servitù *sf* servitude; slavery; captivity; *(personale di servizio)* servants *pl*, domestic staff.

servizi'evole [servit'tsjevole] *ag* obliging, willing to help.

ser'vizio [ser'vittsjo] *sm* service; *(compenso: al ristorante)* service (charge); (STAMPA, TV, RADIO) report; *(da tè, caffè etc)* set, service; **~i** *smpl (di casa)* kitchen and bathroom; (ECON) services; **essere di ~** to be on duty; **fare ~** to operate; *(essere aperto)* to be open; *(essere di turno)* to be on duty; **~ militare** military service; **~i segreti** secret service sg.

'servo, a *sm/f* servant.

ses'santa *num* sixty.

sessan'tina *sf*: **una ~ (di)** about sixty.

sessi'one *sf* session.

'sesso *sm* sex; **sessu'ale** *ag* sexual, sex *cpd.*

ses'tante *sm* sextant.

'sesto, a *ag, sm* sixth.

'seta *sf* silk.

'sete *sf* thirst; **avere ~** to be thirsty.

'setola *sf* bristle.

'setta *sf* sect.

set'tanta *num* seventy.

settan'tina *sf*: **una ~ (di)** about seventy.

'sette *num* seven.

sette'cento [sette'tʃento] *num* seven hundred // *sm*: **il S~** the eighteenth century.

set'tembre *sm* September.

settentrio'nale *ag* northern.

settentri'one *sm* north.

'settico, a, ci, che *ag* (MED) septic.

setti'mana *sf* week; **settima'nale** *ag, sm* weekly.

'settimo, a *ag, sm* seventh.

set'tore *sm* sector.

severità *sf* severity.

se'vero, a *ag* severe.

se'vizie [se'vittsje] *sfpl* torture *sg*; **sevizi'are** *vt* to torture.

sezio'nare [settsjo'nare] *vt* to divide into sections; (MED) to dissect.

sezi'one [set'tsjone] *sf* section; (MED) dissection.

sfaccen'dato, a [sfattʃen'dato] *ag* idle.

sfacci'ato, a [sfat'tʃato] *ag (maleducato)* cheeky, impudent; *(vistoso)* gaudy.

sfa'celo [sfa'tʃɛlo] *sm (fig)* ruin, collapse.

sfal'darsi *vr* to flake (off).

'sfarzo ['sfartso] *sm* pomp, splendour.

sfasci'are [sfaʃ'ʃare] *vt (ferita)* to unbandage; *(distruggere: porta)* to smash, shatter; **~rsi** *vr (rompersi)* to smash, shatter; *(fig)* to collapse.

sfa'tare *vt (leggenda)* to explode.

sfavil'lare *vi* to spark, send out sparks; *(risplendere)* to sparkle.

sfavo'revole *ag* unfavourable.

'sfera *sf* sphere; **'sferico, a, ci, che** *ag* spherical.

sfer'rare *vt (fig: colpo)* to land, deal; *(: attacco)* to launch.

sfer'zare [sfer'tsare] *vt* to whip; *(fig)* to lash out at.

sfiata'toio *sm* blowhole.

sfi'brare *vt (indebolire)* to exhaust, enervate.

'sfida *sf* challenge; **sfi'dare** *vt* to challenge; *(fig)* to defy, brave.

sfi'ducia [sfi'dutʃa] *sf* distrust, mistrust.

sfigu'rare *vt (persona)* to disfigure; *(quadro, statua)* to deface // *vi (far cattiva figura)* to make a bad impression.

sfi'lare *vt* to unthread; *(abito, scarpe)* to slip off // *vi (truppe)* to march past; *(atleti)* to parade; **~rsi** *vr (perle etc)* to come unstrung; *(calza)* to run, ladder; **sfi'lata** *sf* march past; parade; **sfilata di moda** fashion show.

'sfinge ['sfindʒe] *sf* sphinx.

sfi'nito, a *ag* exhausted.

sfio'rare *vt* to brush (against); *(argomento)* to touch upon.

sfio'rire *vi* (2) to wither, fade.

sfo'cato, a *ag* (FOT) out of focus.

sfoci'are [sfo'tʃare] *vi* (2): **~ in** to flow into.

sfo'gare *vt* to vent, pour out; **~rsi** *vr (sfogare la propria rabbia)* to give vent to one's anger; *(confidarsi)*: **~rsi (con)** to pour out one's feelings (to); **non sfogarti su di me!** don't take your bad temper out on me!

sfoggi'are [sfod'dʒare] *vt, vi* to show off.

'sfoglia ['sfɔʎʎa] *sf* sheet of pasta dough; **pasta ~** (CUC) puff pastry.

sfogli'are [sfoʎ'ʎare] *vt (libro)* to leaf through.

'sfogo, ghi *sm* outlet; *(eruzione cutanea)* rash; *(fig)* outburst; **dare ~ a** *(fig)* to give vent to.

sfolgo'rare *vi* to blaze.

sfol'lare *vt* to empty, clear // *vi* (2) to disperse; (*in tempo di guerra*): ~ **(da)** to evacuate.

sfon'dare *vt* (*porta*) to break down; (*scarpe*) to wear a hole in; (*cesto, scatola*) to burst, knock the bottom out of; (*MIL*) to break through // *vi* (*riuscire*) to make a name for o.s.

'sfondo *sm* background.

sfor'mato *sm* (*CUC*) type of soufflé.

sfor'nire *vt*: ~ **di** to deprive of.

sfor'tuna *sf* misfortune, ill luck *q*; **sfor-tu'nato, a** *ag* unlucky; (*impresa, film*) unsuccessful.

sfor'zare [sfor'tsare] *vt* to force; ~**rsi** *vr*: ~**rsi di** *o* **a** *o* **per fare** to try hard to do.

'sforzo ['sfortso] *sm* effort; (*tensione eccessiva, TECN*) strain.

sfrat'tare *vt* to evict; **'sfratto** *sm* eviction.

sfrecci'are [sfret'tʃare] *vi* (2) to shoot *o* flash past.

sfregi'are [sfre'dʒare] *vt* to slash, gash; (*persona*) to disfigure; (*quadro*) to deface; **'sfregio** *sm* gash; scar; (*fig*) insult.

sfre'nato, a *ag* (*fig*) unrestrained, unbridled.

sfron'tato, a *ag* shameless.

sfrutta'mento *sm* exploitation.

sfrut'tare *vt* (*terreno*) to overwork, exhaust; (*miniera*) to exploit, work; (*fig*: *operai, occasione, potere*) to exploit.

sfug'gire [sfud'dʒire] *vi* (2) to escape; ~ **a** (*custode*) to escape (from); (*morte*) to escape; ~ **a qd** (*dettaglio, nome*) to escape sb; ~ **di mano a qd** to slip out of sb's hand (*o* hands); **sfug'gita: di sfuggita** *ad* (*rapidamente, in fretta*) in passing.

sfu'mare *vt* (*colori, contorni*) to soften, shade off // *vi* (2) to shade (off), fade; (*svanire*) to vanish, disappear; (*fig*: *speranze*) to come to nothing; **sfuma'tura** *sf* shading off *q*; (*tonalità*) shade, tone; (*fig*) touch, hint.

sfuri'ata *sf* (*scatto di collera*) fit of anger; (*rimprovero*) sharp rebuke.

sga'bello *sm* stool.

sgabuz'zino [sgabud'dzino] *sm* lumber room.

sgambet'tare *vi* to kick one's legs about; to scurry along.

sgam'betto *sm*: **far lo** ~ **a qd** to trip sb up.

sganasci'arsi [zganaʃ'farsi] *vr*: ~ **dalle risa** to roar with laughter.

sganci'are [zgan'tʃare] *vt* to unhook; (*FERR*) to uncouple; (*bombe*: *da aereo*) to release, drop; (*fig*: *fam*: *soldi*) to fork out.

sganghe'rato, a [zgange'rato] *ag* (*porta*) off its hinges; (*auto*) ramshackle; (*riso*) wild, boisterous.

sgar'bato, a *ag* rude, impolite.

'sgarbo *sm*: **fare uno** ~ **a qd** to be rude to sb.

sgattaio'lare *vi* to sneak away *o* off.

sge'lare [zdʒe'lare] *vi* (2), *vt* to thaw.

'sghembo, a ['zgembo] *ag* (*obliquo*) slanting; (*storto*) crooked.

sghignaz'zare [zɡiɲɲat'tsare] *vi* to laugh scornfully.

sgob'bare *vi* (*fam*: *scolaro*) to swot; (: *operaio*) to slog.

sgoccio'lare [zgottʃo'lare] *vt* (*vuotare*) to drain (to the last drop) // *vi* (*acqua*) to drip; (*recipiente*) to drain.

sgo'larsi *vr* to talk (*o* shout *o* sing) o.s. hoarse.

sgomb(e)'rare *vt* to clear; (*andarsene da*: *stanza*) to vacate; (*evacuare*) to evacuate.

'sgombro, a *ag*: ~ **(di)** clear (of), free (from) // *sm* (*trasloco*) removal; (*ZOOL*) mackerel.

sgomen'tare *vt* to dismay; ~**rsi** *vr* to be dismayed; **sgo'mento, a** *ag* dismayed // *sm* dismay, consternation.

sgonfi'are *vt* to let down, deflate; ~**rsi** *vr* to go down.

'sgorbio *sm* blot; scribble.

sgor'gare *vi* (2) to gush (out).

sgoz'zare [zgot'tsare] *vt* to cut the throat of.

sgra'devole *ag* unpleasant, disagreeable.

sgra'dito, a *ag* unpleasant, unwelcome.

sgra'nare *vt* (*piselli*) to shell; ~ **gli occhi** to open one's eyes wide.

sgran'chirsi [zgran'kirsi] *vr* to stretch; ~ **le gambe** to stretch one's legs.

sgranocchi'are [zgranok'kjare] *vt* to munch.

'sgravio *sm*: ~ **fiscale** tax relief.

sgrazi'ato, a [zgrat'tsjato] *ag* clumsy, ungainly.

sgreto'lare *vt* to cause to crumble; ~**rsi** *vr* to crumble.

sgri'dare *vt* to scold; **sgri'data** *sf* scolding.

sgual'cire [zgwal'tʃire] *vt* to crumple (up), crease.

sgual'drina *sf* (*peg*) slut.

sgu'ardo *sm* (*occhiata*) look, glance; (*espressione*) look (in one's eye).

sguaz'zare [zgwat'tsare] *vi* (*nell'acqua*) to splash about; (*nella melma*) to wallow; ~ **nella ricchezza** to be rolling in money.

sguinzagli'are [zgwintsaʎ'ʎare] *vt* to let off the leash.

sgusci'are [zguʃ'ʃare] *vt* to shell // *vi* (*uccelli*) to hatch; (*sfuggire di mano*) to slip; (*fig*) to slip *o* slink away.

'shampoo ['ʃampo] *sm inv* shampoo.

shock [ʃɔk] *sm inv* shock.

si *pronome* (*dav lo, la, li, le, ne diventa se*) (*riflessivo*) oneself, *m* himself, *f* herself, *soggetto non umano* itself; *pl* themselves; (*reciproco*) one another, each other; (*passivante*): **lo** ~ **ripara facilmente** it is easily repaired; (*possessivo*): **lavarsi le mani** to wash one's hands; (*impersonale*): ~ **vede che è felice** one *o* you can see that he's happy; (*noi*): **tra poco** ~ **parte** we're leaving soon; (*la gente*): ~ **dice che**

they *o* people say that // *sm* (*MUS*) B; (: *solfeggiando la scala*) ti.

sì *av* yes.

'sia *cong*: ~ ... ~ (*o ... o*): ~ **che lavori,** ~ **che non lavori** whether he works or not; (*tanto ... quanto*): **verranno ~ Luigi** ~ **suo fratello** both Luigi and his brother will be coming.

sia'mese *ag* siamese.

si'amo *forma del vb* essere.

Si'beria *sf*: **la** ~ Siberia.

sibi'lare *vi* to hiss; (*fischiare*) to whistle; **'sibilo** *sm* hiss; whistle.

si'cario *sm* hired killer.

sicché [sik'ke] *cong* (*perciò*) so (that), therefore; (*e quindi*) (and) so.

siccità [sittʃi'ta] *sf* drought.

sic'come *cong* since, as.

Si'cilia [si'tʃilja] *sf*: **la** ~ Sicily; **sicili'ano, a** *ag, sm/f* Sicilian.

sico'moro *sm* sycamore.

sicu'rezza [siku'rettsa] *sf* safety; security; (*fiducia*) confidence; (*certezza*) certainty; **di** ~ safety *cpd*; **la** ~ **stradale** road safety.

si'curo, a *ag* safe; (*ben difeso*) secure; (*fiducioso*) confident; (*certo*) sure, certain; (*notizia, amico*) reliable; (*esperto*) skilled // *av* (*anche*): **di** ~) certainly; **essere/mettere al** ~ to be safe/put in a safe place; **sentirsi** ~ to feel safe *o* secure.

siderur'gia [siderur'dʒia] *sf* iron and steel industry.

'sidro *sm* cider.

si'epe *sf* hedge.

si'ero *sm* (*MED*) serum.

si'esta *sf* siesta, (afternoon) nap.

si'ete *forma del vb* essere.

si'filide *sf* syphilis.

si'fone *sm* siphon.

Sig. (*abbr di signore*) Mr.

siga'retta *sf* cigarette.

'sigaro *sm* cigar.

Sigg. (*abbr di signori*) Messrs.

sigil'lare [sidʒil'lare] *vt* to seal.

si'gillo [si'dʒillo] *sm* seal.

'sigla *sf* initials *pl*; acronym, abbreviation; ~ **musicale** signature tune.

si'glare *vt* to initial.

Sig.na *abbr di* signorina.

signifi'care [siɲɲifi'kare] *vt* to mean; **significa'tivo, a** *ag* significant; **signifi-'cato** *sm* meaning.

si'gnora [siɲ'ɲora] *sf* lady; **la** ~ X Mrs ['mɪsɪz] X; **buon giorno S**~/**Signore/Signorina** good morning; (*deferente*) good morning Madam/ Sir/Madam; (*quando si conosce il nome*) good morning Mrs/Mr/Miss X; **Gentile S**~/**Signore/Signorina** (*in una lettera*) Dear Madam/Sir/Madam; **il signor Rossi e** ~ Mr Rossi and his wife; ~ **e e signori** ladies and gentlemen.

si'gnore [siɲ'ɲore] *sm* gentleman; (*padrone*) lord, master; (*REL*): **il S**~ the Lord; **il signor X** Mr ['mɪstə*] X; **i** ~ **i**

Bianchi (*coniugi*) Mr and Mrs Bianchi; *vedi anche* **signora.**

signo'rile [siɲɲo'rile] *ag* refined.

signo'rina [siɲɲo'rina] *sf* young lady; **la** ~ X Miss X; *vedi anche* **signora.**

Sig.ra (*abbr di* signora) Mrs.

silenzia'tore [silentsja'tore] *sm* silencer.

si'lenzio [si'lentsjo] *sm* silence; **silen-zi'oso, a** *ag* silent, quiet.

'sillaba *sf* syllable.

silu'rare *vt* to torpedo; (*fig: privare del comando*) to oust.

si'luro *sm* torpedo.

simboleggi'are [simboled'dʒare] *vt* to symbolize.

sim'bolico, a, ci, che *ag* symbolic(al).

simbo'lismo *sm* symbolism.

'simbolo *sm* symbol.

'simile *ag* (*analogo*) similar; (*di questo tipo*): **un uomo** ~ such a man, a man like this; **libri** ~ **i** such books; ~ **a** similar to; **i suoi** ~ **i** one's fellow men; one's peers.

simme'tria *sf* symmetry; **sim'metrico, a, ci, che** *ag* symmetrical.

simpa'tia *sf* (*inclinazione*) liking; (*partecipazione ai sentimenti di qd*) sympathy; **avere** ~ **per qd** to like sb, have a liking for sb; **sim'patico, a, ci, che** *ag* nice, friendly; pleasant; likeable.

simpatiz'zare [simpatid'dzare] *vi*: ~ **con** to take a liking to.

sim'posio *sm* symposium.

simu'lare *vt* to sham, simulate; (*TECN*) to simulate; **simulazi'one** *sf* shamming; simulation.

simul'taneo, a *ag* simultaneous.

sina'goga, ghe *sf* synagogue.

sincerità [sintʃeri'ta] *sf* sincerity.

sin'cero, a [sin'tʃero] *ag* sincere; genuine; heartfelt.

'sincope *sf* syncopation; (*MED*) blackout.

sincroniz'zare [sinkronid'dzare] *vt* to synchronize.

sinda'cale *ag* (trade-)union *cpd*; **sindaca-'lista, i, e** *sm/f* trade unionist.

sinda'cato *sm* (*di lavoratori*) (trade) union; (*AMM, ECON, DIR*) syndicate, trust, pool; ~ **dei datori di lavoro** employers' association, employers' federation.

'sindaco, ci *sm* mayor.

'sindrome *sf* (*MED*) syndrome.

sinfo'nia *sf* (*MUS*) symphony.

singhioz'zare [singjot'tsare] *vi* to sob; to hiccup.

singhi'ozzo [sin'gjottso] *sm* sob; (*MED*) hiccup; **avere il** ~ to have the hiccups; **a** ~ (*fig*) by fits and starts.

singo'lare *ag* (*insolito*) remarkable, singular; (*LING*) singular // *sm* (*LING*) singular; (*TENNIS*): ~ **mas-chile/femminile** men's/women's singles.

'singolo, a *ag* single, individual // *sm* (*persona*) individual; (*TENNIS*) = singolare.

si'nistro, a *ag* left, left-hand; (*fig*) sinister // *sm* (*incidente*) accident // *sf* (*POL*) left (wing); a ~ a on the left; (*direzione*) to the left.

'**sino** *prep* = **fino**.

si'**nonimo, a** *ag* synonymous // *sm* synonym; ~ **di** synonymous with.

sin'**tassi** *sf* syntax.

'**sintesi** *sf* synthesis; (*riassunto*) summary, résumé.

sin'**tetico, a, ci, che** *ag* synthetic.

sintetiz'**zare** [sintetid'dzare] *vt* to synthesize; (*riassumere*) to summarize.

sinto'**matico, a, ci, che** *ag* symptomatic.

'**sintomo** *sm* symptom.

sinu'**oso, a** *ag* (*strada*) winding.

si'**parlo** *sm* (TEATRO) curtain.

si'**rena** *sf* (*apparecchio*) siren; (*nella mitologia, fig*) siren, mermaid.

'**Siria** *sf*: **la ~ Syria; siri'ano, a** *ag, sm/f* Syrian.

si'**ringa, ghe** *sf* syringe.

'**sismico, a, ci, che** *ag* seismic.

sis'**mografo** *sm* seismograph.

sis'**tema, i** *sm* system; method, way; **cambiare** ~ to change one's way of life.

siste'**mare** *vt* (*mettere a posto*) to tidy, put in order; (*risolvere: questione*) to sort out, settle; (*procurare un lavoro a*) to find a job for; (*dare un alloggio a*) to settle, find accommodation for; ~**rsi** *vr* to settle down; (*trovarsi un lavoro*) to get fixed up with a job; **ti sistemo io!** I'll soon sort you out!

siste'**matico, a, ci, che** *ag* systematic.

sistemazi'**one** [sistemat'tsjone] *sf* arrangement; order; settlement; employment; accommodation.

situ'**are** *vt* to site, situate; **situ'ato, a** *ag*: **situato a/su** situated at/on.

situazi'**one** [situat'tsjone] *sf* situation.

slacci'**are** [zlat'tʃare] *vt* to undo, unfasten.

slanci'**arsi** [zlan'tʃarsi] *vr* to dash, fling o.s.; **slanci'ato, a** *ag* slender; '**slancio** *sm* dash, leap; (*fig*) surge.

sla'**vato, a** *ag* faded, washed out; (*fig: viso, occhi*) pale, colourless.

'**slavo, a** *ag* Slav(onic), Slavic.

sle'**ale** *ag* disloyal; (*concorrenza etc*) unfair.

sle'**gare** *vt* to untie.

'**slitta** *sf* sledge; (*trainata*) sleigh.

slit'**tare** *vi* (2) to slide; (AUT) to skid.

slo'**gare** *vt* (MED) to dislocate.

sloggi'**are** [zlod'dʒare] *vt* (*inquilino*) to turn out; (*nemico*) to drive out, dislodge // *vi* to move out.

smacchi'**are** [zmak'kjare] *vt* to remove stains from.

'**smacco, chi** *sm* humiliating defeat.

smagli'**ante** [zmaʎ'ʎante] *ag* brilliant, dazzling.

smagli'**are** [zmaʎ'ʎare] *vt*, ~**rsi** *vr* (*calza*) to ladder.

smalizi'**ato, a** [smalit'tsjato] *ag* shrewd, cunning.

smal'**tare** *vt* to enamel; (*a vetro*) to glaze; (*unghie*) to varnish.

smal'**tire** *vt* (*merce*) to sell; (: *svendere*) to sell off; (*rifiuti*) to dispose of; (*cibo*) to digest; ~ **la sbornia** to sober up.

'**smalto** *sm* (*anche: di denti*) enamel; (*per ceramica*) glaze; ~ **per unghie** nail varnish.

'**smania** *sf* agitation, restlessness; (*fig*) longing, desire; **avere la ~ addosso** to have the fidgets; **smani'are** *vi* (*agitarsi*) to be restless *o* agitated; (*fig*): **smaniare di fare** to long *o* yearn to do.

smantel'**lare** *vt* to dismantle.

smarri'**mento** *sm* loss; (*fig*) bewilderment; dismay.

smar'**rire** *vt* to lose; (*non riuscire a trovare*) to mislay; ~**rsi** *vr* (*perdersi*) to lose one's way, get lost; (: *oggetto*) to go astray; (*fig: turbarsi*) to be bewildered; (*essere sbigottito*) to be dismayed.

smasche'**rare** [zmaske'rare] *vt* to unmask.

smemo'**rato, a** *ag* forgetful.

smen'**tire** *vt* (*negare*) to deny; (*sbugiardare*) to give the lie to; (*sconfessare*) to retract, take back; ~**rsi** *vr* to be inconsistent (in one's behaviour); **smen'tita** *sf* denial; retraction.

sme'**raldo** *sm* emerald.

smerci'**are** [zmer'tʃare] *vt* (COMM) to sell; (: *svendere*) to sell off.

sme'**riglio** [zme'riʎʎo] *sm* emery.

'**smesso, a** *pp di* **smettere**.

'**smettere** *vt* to stop; (*vestiti*) to stop wearing // *vi* to stop, cease; ~ **di fare** to stop doing.

'**smilzo, a** ['zmiltso] *ag* thin, lean.

sminu'**ire** *vt* to diminish, lessen; (*fig*) to belittle.

sminuz'**zare** [zminut'tsare] *vt* to break into small pieces; to crumble.

smis'**tare** *vt* (*pacchi etc*) to sort; (FERR) to shunt.

smisu'**rato, a** *ag* boundless, immeasurable; (*grandissimo*) immense, enormous.

smobili'**tare** *vt* to demobilize, demob (*col*).

smo'**dato, a** *ag* immoderate.

'**smoking** ['zmɔukiŋ] *sm inv* dinner jacket.

smon'**tare** *vt* (*mobile, macchina etc*) to take to pieces, dismantle; (*far scendere: da veicolo*) to let off, drop (off); (*fig: scoraggiare*) to dishearten // *vi* (2) (*scendere: da cavallo*) to dismount; (: *da treno*) to get off; (*terminare il lavoro*) to stop (work); ~**rsi** *vr* to lose heart; to lose one's enthusiasm.

'**smorfia** *sf* grimace; (*atteggiamento lezioso*) simpering; **fare** ~**e** to make faces; to simper; **smorfi'oso, a** *ag* simpering.

'**smorto, a** *ag* (*viso*) pale, wan; (*colore*) dull.

smor'**zare** [zmor'tsare] *vt* (*suoni*) to deaden; (*colori*) to tone down; (*luce*) to dim; (*sete*) to quench; (*entusiasmo*) to dampen; ~**rsi** *vr* (*attutirsi*) to fade away.

'**smosso, a** *pp di* **smuovere**.

smotta'mento *sm* landslide.

'smunto, a *ag* haggard, pinched.

smu'overe *vt* to move, shift; (*fig: commuovere*) to move; (: *dall'inerzia*) to rouse, stir; ‹ ~**rsi** *vr* to move, shift.

smus'sare *vt* (*angolo*) to round off, smooth; (*lama etc*) to blunt; ~**rsi** *vr* to become blunt.

snatu'rato, a *ag* inhuman, heartless.

'snello, a *ag* (*agile*) agile; (*svelto*) slender, slim.

sner'vare *vt* to enervate, wear out; ~**rsi** *vr* to become enervated.

sni'dare *vt* to drive out, flush out.

snob'bare *vt* to snub.

sno'bismo *sm* snobbery.

snoccio'lare [znotːfoˈlare] *vt* (*frutta*) to stone; (*fig: orazioni*) to rattle off; (: *verità*) to blab; (: *fam: soldi*) to shell out.

sno'dare *vt* to untie, undo; (*rendere agile, mobile*) to loosen; ~**rsi** *vr* to come loose; (*articolarsi*) to bend; (*strada, fiume*) to wind.

so *forma del vb* **sapere.**

so'ave *ag* sweet, gentle, soft.

sobbal'zare [sobbalˈtsare] *vi* to jolt, jerk; (*trasalire*) to jump, start; **sob'balzo** *sm* jerk, jolt; jump, start.

sobbar'carsi *vr*: ~ **a** to take on, undertake.

sob'borgo, ghi *sm* suburb.

sobil'lare *vt* to stir up, incite.

'sobrio, a *ag* temperate; sober.

socchi'udere [sokˈkjudere] *vt* (*porta*) to leave ajar; (*occhi*) to half-close; **socchi'uso, a** *pp di* **socchiudere.**

soc'correre *vt* to help, assist; **soc'corso, a** *pp di* **soccorrere** // *sm* help, aid, assistance; **soccorsi** *smpl* (*MIL*) reinforcements.

socialdemo'cratico, a, ci, che [sotʃaldemoˈkratiko] *sm/f* Social Democrat.

soci'ale [soˈtʃale] *ag* social; (*di associazione*) club *cpd*, association *cpd*.

socia'lismo [sotʃaˈlizmo] *sm* socialism; **socia'lista, i, e** *ag, sm/f* socialist.

società [sotʃeˈta] *sf inv* society; (*sportiva*) club; (*COMM*) company; ~ **per azioni** (S.p.A.) limited company.

soci'evole [soˈtʃevole] *ag* sociable.

'socio [ˈsotʃo] *sm* (*DIR, COMM*) partner; (*membro di associazione*) member.

'soda *sf* (*CHIM*) soda; (*acqua gassata*) soda (water).

soda'lizio [sodaˈlittsjo] *sm* association, society.

soddis'fare *vt, vi*: ~ **a** to satisfy; (*impegno*) to fulfil; (*debito*) to pay off; (*richiesta*) to meet, comply with; (*offesa*) to make amends for; **soddis'fatto, a** *pp di* **soddisfare** // *ag* satisfied; satisfied or happy *o* satisfied with; pleased with; **soddisfazi'one** *sf* satisfaction.

'sodo, a *ag* firm, hard; (*fig*) sound // *av* (*picchiare, lavorare*) hard; **dormire** ~ to sleep soundly.

sofà *sm inv* sofa.

soffe'renza [soffeˈrɛntsa] *sf* suffering.

sof'ferto, a *pp di* **soffrire.**

soffi'are *vt* to blow; (*notizia, segreto*) to whisper // *vi* to blow; ~**rsi il naso** to blow one's nose; ~ **qc/qd a qd** (*fig*) to pinch *o* steal sth/sb from sb; ~ **via qc** to blow sth away.

'soffice [ˈsoffitʃe] *ag* soft.

'soffio *sm* (*di vento*) breath; (*di fumo*) puff; (*MED*) murmur.

sof'fitta *sf* attic.

sof'fitto *sm* ceiling.

soffo'care *vi* (*anche*: ~**rsi**) to suffocate, choke // *vt* to suffocate, choke; (*fig*) to stifle, suppress; **soffocazi'one** *sf* suffocation.

sof'friggere [sofˈfriddʒere] *vt* to fry lightly.

sof'frire *vt* to suffer, endure; (*sopportare*) to bear, stand // *vi* to suffer; to be in pain; ~ (**di**) **qc** (*MED*) to suffer from sth.

sof'fritto, a *pp di* **soffriggere.**

sofisti'care *vt* (*vino, cibo*) to adulterate // *vi* to split hairs, quibble; **sofisti'cato, a** *ag* sophisticated.

sogget'tivo, a [soddʒetˈtivo] *ag* subjective.

sog'getto, a [sodˈdʒɛtto] *ag*: ~ **a** (*sottomesso*) subject to; (*esposto: a variazioni, danni etc*) subject *o* liable to // *sm* subject.

soggezi'one [soddʒetˈtsjone] *sf* subjection; (*timidezza*) awe; **avere** ~ **di qd** to stand in awe of sb; to be ill at ease in sb's presence.

sogghi'gnare [soggiɲˈpare] *vi* to sneer.

soggior'nare [soddʒorˈnare] *vi* to stay; **soggi'orno** *sm* (*invernale, marino*) stay; (*stanza*) living room.

'soglia [ˈsɔʎʎa] *sf* doorstep; (*anche fig*) threshold.

sogli'ola [ˈsɔʎʎola] *sf* (*ZOOL*) sole.

so'gnare [soɲˈpare] *vt, vi* to dream; ~ **a occhi aperti** to daydream; **sogna'tore, 'trice** *sm/f* dreamer.

'sogno [ˈsoɲpo] *sm* dream.

'soia *sf* (*BOT*) soya.

sol *sm* (*MUS*) G; (: *solfeggiando la scala*) so(h).

so'laio *sm* (*soffitta*) attic.

sola'mente *av* only, just.

so'lare *ag* solar, sun *cpd*.

'solco, chi *sm* (*scavo, fig: ruga*) furrow; (*incavo*) rut, track; (*di disco*) groove; (*scia*) wake.

sol'dato *sm* soldier; ~ **semplice** private.

'soldo *sm* (*fig*): **non avere un** ~ to be penniless; **non vale un** ~ it's not worth a penny; ~**i** *smpl* (*denaro*) money *sg*.

'sole *sm* sun; (*luce*) sun(light); (*tempo assolato*) sun(shine); **prendere il** ~ to sunbathe.

so'lenne *ag* solemn; **solennità** *sf* solemnity; grand occasion.

sol'fato *sm* (*CHIM*) sulphate.

sol'furo *sm* (*CHIM*) sulphur.

soli'dale *ag* (*DIR*) joint and several.
solidarietà *sf* solidarity.
solidifi'care *vt, vi* (2) (*anche:* ~rsi) to solidify.
solidità *sf* solidity.
'solido, a *ag* solid; (*forte, robusto*) sturdy, solid; (*fig: ditta*) sound, solid // *sm* (*MAT*) solid.
soli'loquio *sm* soliloquy.
so'lista, i, e *ag* solo // *sm/f* soloist.
solita'mente *av* usually, as a rule.
soli'tario, a *ag* (*senza compagnia*) solitary, lonely; (*solo, isolato*) solitary, lone; (*deserto*) lonely // *sm* (*gioiello, gioco*) solitaire.
'solito, a *ag* usual; **essere** ~ **fare** to be in the habit of doing; **di** ~ usually; **più tardi del** ~ later than usual; **come al** ~ as usual.
soli'tudine *sf* solitude.
solleci'tare [sollet∫i'tare] *vt* (*lavoro*) to speed up; (*persona*) to urge on; (*chiedere con insistenza*) to press for, request urgently; (*stimolare*): ~ **qd a fare** to urge sb to do; (*TECN*) to stress; **sollecitazi'one** *sf* entreaty, request; (*fig*) incentive; (*TECN*) stress.
sol'lecito, a [sol'let∫ito] *ag* prompt, quick // *sm* (*lettera*) reminder; **solleci'tudine** *sf* promptness, speed.
solleti'care *vt* to tickle.
solle'vare *vt* to lift, raise; (*fig: persona: alleggerire*): ~ (**da**) to relieve (of); (: *dar conforto*) to comfort, relieve; (: *questione*) to raise; (: *far insorgere*) to stir (to revolt); ~rsi *vr* to rise; (*fig: riprendersi*) to recover; (: *ribellarsi*) to rise up.
solli'evo *sm* relief; (*conforto*) comfort.
'solo, a *ag* alone; (*in senso spirituale: isolato*) lonely; (*unico*): **un** ~ **libro** only one book, a single book; (*con ag numerale*): **veniamo noi tre** ~ **i** just *o* only the three of us are coming // *av* (*soltanto*) only, just; **non** ~ **... ma anche** not only ... but also; **fare qc da** ~ to do sth (all) by oneself; **da me** ~ single-handed, on my own.
sol'stizio [sol'stittsjo] *sm* solstice.
sol'tanto *av* only.
so'lubile *ag* (*sostanza*) soluble.
soluzi'one [solut'tsjone] *sf* solution.
sol'vente *ag, sm* solvent.
'soma *sf* load, burden; **bestia da** ~ beast of burden.
so'maro *sm ass, donkey.
somigli'anza   [somiʎ'ʎantsa]   *sf* resemblance.
somigli'are [somiʎ'ʎare] *vi* (2): ~ **a** to be like, resemble; (*nell'aspetto fisico*) to look like; ~rsi *vr* to be (*o* look) alike.
'somma *sf* (*MAT*) sum; (*di denaro*) sum (of money); (*complesso di varie cose*) whole amount, sum total.
som'mare *vt* to add up; (*aggiungere*) to add; **tutto sommato** all things considered.
som'mario, a *ag* (*racconto, indagine*) brief; (*giustizia*) summary // *sm* summary.

som'mergere [som'merdʒere] *vt* to submerge.
sommer'gibile [sommer'dʒibile] *sm* submarine.
som'merso, a *pp di* **sommergere**.
som'messo, a *ag* (*voce*) soft, subdued.
somminis'trare *vt* to give, administer.
sommità *sf inv* top; (*di monte*) summit, top; (*fig*) height.
'sommo, a *ag* highest, topmost; (*fig*) supreme; (the) greatest // *sm* (*fig*) height; **per** ~**i capi** briefly, covering the main points.
som'mossa *sf* uprising.
so'naglio [so'naʎʎo] *sm* bell.
so'nare *etc* = **suonare** *etc*.
son'daggio [son'daddʒo] *sm* sounding; probe; boring, drilling; (*indagine*) survey; ~ (**d'opinioni**) (opinion) poll.
son'dare *vt* (*NAUT*) to sound; (*atmosfera, piaga*) to probe; (*MINERALOGIA*) to bore, drill; (*fig*) to sound out; to probe.
so'netto *sm* sonnet.
son'nambulo, a *sm/f* sleepwalker.
sonnecchi'are [sonnek'kjare] *vi* to doze, nod.
son'nifero *sm* sleeping drug (*o* pill).
'sonno *sm* sleep; **prendere** ~ to fall asleep; **aver** ~ to be sleepy.
'sono *forma del vb* **essere**.
so'noro, a *ag* (*ambiente*) resonant; (*voce*) sonorous, ringing; (*onde, film*) sound *cpd*.
sontu'oso, a *ag* sumptuous; lavish.
sopo'rifero, a *ag* soporific.
soppe'sare *vt* to weigh in one's hand(s), feel the weight of; (*fig*) to weigh up.
soppi'atto: di ~ *av* secretly; furtively.
soppor'tare *vt* (*reggere*) to support; (*subire: perdita, spese*) to bear, sustain; (*soffrire: dolore*) to bear, endure; (*sog: cosa: freddo*) to withstand; (*sog: persona: freddo, vino*) to take; (*tollerare*) to put up with, tolerate.
soppressi'one *sf* suppression; deletion.
sop'presso, a *pp di* **sopprimere**.
sop'primere *vt* (*carica, privilegi, testimone*) to do away with; (*pubblicazione*) to suppress; (*parola, frase*) to delete.
'sopra *prep* (*gen*) on; (*al di sopra di, più in alto di*) above; over; (*riguardo a*) on, about // *av* on top; (*attaccato, scritto*) on it; (*al di sopra*) above; (*al piano superiore*) upstairs; **donne** ~ **i 30 anni** women over 30 (years of age); **dormirci** ~ (*fig*) to sleep on it.
so'prabito *sm* overcoat.
soprac'ciglio   [soprat't∫iʎʎo],   *pl(f)* **soprac'ciglia** *sm* eyebrow.
sopracco'perta *sf* (*di letto*) bedspread; (*di libro*) jacket.
soprad'detto, a *ag* aforesaid.
sopraf'fare *vt* to overcome, overwhelm; **sopraf'fatto, a** *pp di* **sopraffare**.
sopraf'fino, a *ag* excellent; (*fig*) consummate, supreme.
sopraggi'ungere [soprad'dʒundʒere] *vi* (2) (*giungere all'improvviso*) to arrive (un-

expectedly); (accadere) to occur (unexpectedly).

soprannatu'rale ag supernatural.

sopran'nome sm nickname.

so'prano, a sm/f (persona) soprano // sm (voce) soprano.

soprappensi'ero av lost in thought.

sopras'salto sm: di ~ with a start; suddenly.

soprasse'dere vi: ~ a to delay, put off.

soprat'tutto av (anzitutto) above all; (specialmente) especially.

sopravve'nire vi (2) to arrive, appear; (fatto) to occur.

sopravvis'suto, a pp di sopravvivere.

soprav'vivere vi (2) to survive; (continuare a vivere): ~ (in) to live on (in); ~ a (incidente etc) to survive; (persona) to outlive.

soprinten'dente sm/f supervisor; (statale: di belle arti etc) keeper; soprinten'denza sf (ente): soprintendenza alle Antichità e ai Monumenti ≈ National Trust.

so'pruso sm abuse of power; fare un ~ a qd to treat sb unjustly.

soq'quadro sm: mettere a ~ to turn upside-down.

sor'betto sm sorbet, water ice.

sor'bire vt to sip; (fig) to put up with.

'sordido, a ag sordid; (fig: gretto) stingy.

sor'dina sf: in ~ softly; (fig) on the sly.

sordità sf deafness.

'sordo, a ag deaf; (rumore) muffled; (dolore) dull; (lotta) silent, hidden // sm/f deaf person; sordo'muto, a ag deaf-and-dumb // sm/f deaf-mute.

so'rella sf sister; sorel'lastra sf stepsister.

sor'gente [sor'dʒente] sf (acqua che sgorga) spring; (di fiume, FISICA, fig) source.

'sorgere ['sordʒere] vi (2) to rise; (scaturire) to spring, rise; (fig: difficoltà) to arise.

sormon'tare vt (fig) to overcome, surmount.

sorni'one, a ag sly.

sorpas'sare vt (AUT) to overtake; (fig) to surpass; (: eccedere) to exceed, go beyond; ~ in altezza to be higher than; (persona) to be taller than.

sor'prendere vt (cogliere: in flagrante etc) to catch; (stupire, prendere a un tratto) to surprise; ~rsi vr: ~rsi (di) to be surprised (at); sor'preso, a pp di sorprendere // sf surprise.

sor'reggere [sor'reddʒere] vt to support, hold up; (fig) to sustain; sor'retto, a pp di sorreggere.

sor'ridere vi to smile; sor'riso, a pp di sorridere // sm smile.

'sorso sm sip.

'sorta sf sort, kind; di ~ whatever, of any kind, at all.

'sorte sf (fato) fate, destiny; (evento fortuito) chance; tirare a ~ to draw lots.

sor'teggio [sor'teddʒo] sm draw.

sorti'legio [sorti'ledʒo] sm witchcraft q; (incantesimo) spell; fare un ~ a qd to cast a spell on sb.

sor'tire vi (2) (uscire a sorte) to come out, be drawn.

sor'tita sf (MIL) sortie.

'sorto, a pp di sorgere.

sorvegli'anza [sorveʎ'ʎantsa] sf watch; supervision; (POLIZIA, MIL) surveillance.

sorvegli'are [sorveʎ'ʎare] vt (bambino, bagagli, prigioniero) to watch, keep an eye on; (malato) to watch over; (territorio, casa) to watch o keep watch over; (lavori) to supervise.

sorvo'lare vt (territorio) to fly over // vi: ~ su (fig) to skim over.

'sosia sm inv double.

sos'pendere vt (appendere) to hang (up); (interrompere, privare di una carica) to suspend; (rimandare) to defer; ~ un quadro al muro/un lampadario al soffitto to hang a picture on the wall/a chandelier from the ceiling; sospensi'one sf (anche CHIM, AUT) suspension; deferment; sos'peso, a pp di sospendere // ag (appeso): sospeso a hanging on (o from); (fig) anxious; in sospeso in abeyance; (conto) outstanding; tenere in sospeso (fig) to keep in suspense.

sospet'tare vt to suspect // vi: ~ di to suspect; (diffidare) to be suspicious of.

sos'petto, a ag suspicious // sm suspicion; sospet'toso, a ag suspicious.

sos'pingere [sos'pindʒere] vt to drive, push; sos'pinto, a pp di sospingere.

sospi'rare vi to sigh // vt to long for, yearn for; sos'piro sm sigh.

'sosta sf (fermata) stop, halt; (pausa) pause, break; senza ~ non-stop, without a break.

sostan'tivo sm noun, substantive.

sos'tanza [sos'tantsa] sf substance; ~e sfpl (ricchezze) wealth sg, possessions; in ~ in short, to sum up; sostanzi'oso, a ag (cibo) nourishing, substantial.

sos'tare vi (fermarsi) to stop (for a while), stay; (fare una pausa) to take a break.

sos'tegno [sos'teɲɲo] sm support.

soste'nere vt to support; (prendere su di sé) to take on, bear; (resistere) to withstand, stand up to; (affermare): ~ che to maintain that; ~rsi vr to hold o.s. up, support o.s.; (fig) to keep up one's strength; ~ gli esami to sit exams; sosteni'tore, 'trice sm/f supporter.

sosta'mento sm maintenance.

soste'nuto, a ag (riservato) reserved, aloof; (stile) elevated; (prezzo) continuing high.

sostitu'ire vt (mettere al posto di): ~ qd/qc a to substitute sb/sth for; (prendere il posto di: persona) to substitute for; (: cosa) to take the place of.

sosti'tuto, a sm/f substitute.

sostituzi'one [sostitut'tsjone] sf substitution; in ~ di as a substitute for, in place of.

sotta'ceti [sotta'tʃeti] smpl pickles.

sot'tana *sf* (*sottoveste*) underskirt; (*gonna*) skirt; (*REL*) soutane, cassock.

sotter'fugio [sotter'fudʒo] *sm* subterfuge.

sotter'raneo, a *ag* underground // *sm* cellar // *sf* (*FERR*) underground.

sotter'rare *vt* to bury.

sottigli'ezza [sottiʎ'ʎettsa] *sf* thinness; slimness; (*fig*: *acutezza*) subtlety; shrewdness; ~e *sfpl* (*pedanteria*) quibbles.

sot'tile *ag* thin; (*figura, caviglia*) thin, slim, slender; (*fine*: *polvere, capelli*) fine; (*fig*: *leggero*) light; (*: vista*) sharp, keen; (*: olfatto*) fine, discriminating; (*: mente*) subtle; shrewd.

sottin'tendere *vt* (*intendere qc non espresso*) to understand; (*implicare*) to imply; **sottin'teso, a** *pp di* **sottintendere** // *sm* allusion; **parlare senza sottintesi** to speak plainly.

'sotto *prep* under; (*più in basso di*) below // *av* underneath, beneath; below; (*al piano inferiore*) downstairs; ~ **il monte** at the foot of the mountain; ~ **la pioggia/il sole** in the rain/sun(shine); ~ **terra** underground; ~ **voce** in a low voice; **chiuso** ~ **vuoto** vacuum packed.

sottoline'are *vt* to underline; (*fig*) to emphasize, stress.

sottoma'rino, a *ag* (*flora*) submarine; (*cavo, navigazione*) underwater // *sm* (*NAUT*) submarine.

sotto'messo, a *pp di* **sottomettere**.

sotto'mettere *vt* to subdue, subjugate; ~**rsi** *vr* to submit.

sottopas'saggio [sottopas'saddʒo] *sm* (*AUT*) underpass; (*pedonale*) subway, underpass.

sotto'porre *vt* (*costringere*) to subject; (*fig*: *presentare*) to submit; **sottoporsi** *vr* to submit; **sottoporsi a** (*subire*) to undergo; **sotto'posto, a** *pp di* **sottoporre**.

sottos'critto, a *pp di* **sottoscrivere**.

sottos'crivere *vt* // *vi*: ~ **a** to subscribe to; **sottoscrizi'one** *sf* signing; subscription.

sottosegre'tario *sm*: ~ **di Stato** Under-Secretary of State.

sotto'sopra *av* upside-down.

sotto'terra *av* underground.

sotto'titolo *sm* subtitle.

sotto'veste *sf* underskirt.

sotto'voce [sotto'votʃe] *av* in a low voice.

sot'trarre *vt* (*MAT*) to subtract, take away; ~ **qd/qc a** (*togliere*) to remove sb/sth from; (*salvare*) to save *o* rescue sb/sth from; ~ **qc a qd** (*rubare*) to steal sth from sb; **sottrarsi** *vr*: **sottrarsi a** (*sfuggire*) to escape; (*evitare*) to avoid; **sot'tratto, a** *pp di* **sottrarre**; **sottrazi'one** *sf* subtraction; removal.

sovi'etico, a, ci, che *ag* Soviet // *sm/f* Soviet citizen.

sovraccari'care *vt* to overload.

sovrac'carico, a, chi, che *ag*: ~ (**di**) overloaded (with) // *sm* excess load; ~ **di lavoro** extra work.

sovrannatu'rale *ag* = **soprannaturale**.

so'vrano, a *ag* sovereign; (*fig*: *sommo*) supreme // *sm/f* sovereign, monarch.

sovras'tare *vi* (*2*): ~ **a**, *vt* (*vallata, fiume*) to overhang; (*fig*) to hang over, threaten.

sovrinten'dente *sm/f* = **soprintendente**; **sovrinten'denza** *sf* = **soprintendenza**.

sovru'mano, a *ag* superhuman.

sovvenzi'one [sovven'tsjone] *sf* subsidy, grant.

sovver'sivo, a *ag* subversive.

'sozzo, a ['sottso] *ag* filthy, dirty.

S.p.A. *abbr vedi* **società**.

spac'care *vt* to split, break; (*legna*) to chop; ~**rsi** *vr* to split, break; **spacca'tura** *sf* split.

spacci'are [spat'tʃare] *vt* (*vendere*) to sell (off); (*mettere in circolazione*) to circulate; ~**rsi** *vr*: ~**rsi per** (*farsi credere*) to pass o.s. off as, pretend to be; **spaccia'tore, 'trice** *sm/f* (*di droga*) pusher; (*di denaro falso*) dealer; **'spaccio** *sm* sale; (*bottega*) shop.

'spacco, chi *sm* (*fenditura*) split, crack; (*strappo*) tear; (*di gonna*) slit.

spac'cone *sm/f* boaster, braggart.

'spada *sf* sword.

spae'sato, a *ag* disorientated, lost.

spa'ghetti [spa'getti] *smpl* (*CUC*) spaghetti *sg*.

'Spagna ['spaɲɲa] *sf*: **la** ~ Spain; **spa'gnolo, a** *ag* Spanish // *sm/f* Spaniard // *sm* (*LING*) Spanish; **gli Spagnoli** the Spanish.

'spago, ghi *sm* string, twine.

spai'ato, a *ag* (*calza, guanto*) odd.

spalan'care *vt*, ~**rsi** *vr* to open wide.

spa'lare *vt* to shovel.

'spalla *sf* shoulder; (*fig*: *TEATRO*) stooge; ~**e** *sfpl* (*dorso*) back; **spalleggi'are** *vt* to back up, support.

spal'letta *sf* (*parapetto*) parapet.

spalli'era *sf* (*di sedia etc*) back; (*di letto*: *da capo*) head(board); (*: da piedi*) foot(board); (*GINNASTICA*) wall bars *pl*.

spal'mare *vt* to spread.

'spandere *vt* to spread; (*versare*) to pour (out); ~**rsi** *vr* to spread; ~ **lacrime** to shed tears; **'spanto, a** *pp di* **spandere**.

spa'rare *vt* to fire // *vi* (*far fuoco*) to fire; (*tirare*) to shoot; **spara'tore** *sm* gunman; **spara'toria** *sf* exchange of shots.

sparecchi'are [sparek'kjare] *vt*: ~ (**la tavola**) to clear the table.

spa'reggio [spa'reddʒo] *sm* (*SPORT*) play-off.

'spargere ['spardʒere] *vt* (*gettare all'intorno*) to scatter, strew; (*versare*: *vino*) to spill; (*: lacrime, sangue*) to shed; (*diffondere*) to spread; (*emanare*) to give off (*o* out); ~**rsi** *vr* to spread; **spargi'mento** *sm* scattering, strewing; spilling; shedding; **spargimento di sangue** bloodshed.

spa'rire *vi* (*2*) to disappear, vanish.

spar'lare *vi*: ~ **di** to run down, speak ill of.

'sparo sm shot.

sparpagli'are [sparpaʎʎ'are] vt, **~rsi** vr to scatter.

'sparso, a pp di **spargere** // ag scattered; (sciolto) loose.

spar'tire vt (eredità, bottino) to share out; (avversari) to separate.

sparti'traffico sm inv (AUT) central reservation.

spa'ruto, a ag (viso etc) haggard.

sparvi'ero sm (ZOOL) sparrowhawk.

spasi'mare vi to be in agony; **~ di fare** (fig) to yearn to do; **~ per qd** to be madly in love with sb.

'spasimo sm pang; **'spasmo** sm (MED) spasm; **spas'modico, a, ci, che** ag (angoscioso) agonizing; (MED) spasmodic.

spassio'nato, a ag dispassionate, impartial.

'spasso sm (divertimento) amusement, enjoyment; **andare a ~** to go out for a walk; **essere a ~** (fig) to be out of work; **mandare qd a ~** to send sb packing.

'spatola sf spatula.

spau'racchio [spau'rakkjo] sm scarecrow.

spau'rire vt to frighten, terrify.

spa'valdo, a ag arrogant, bold.

spaventa'passeri sm inv scarecrow.

spaven'tare vt to frighten, scare; **~rsi** vr to be frightened, be scared; to get a fright; **spa'vento** sm fear, fright; **far spavento a** qd to give sb a fright; **spaven'toso, a** ag frightening, terrible; (fig: fam) tremendous, fantastic.

spazien'tire [spattsjen'tire] vi (2) (anche: **~rsi**) to lose one's patience.

'spazio ['spattsjo] sm space; **spazi'oso, a** ag spacious.

spazzaca'mino [spattsaka'mino] sm chimney sweep.

spaz'zare [spat'tsare] vt to sweep; (foglie etc) to sweep up; (cacciare) to sweep away; **spazza'tura** sf sweepings pl; (immondizia) rubbish; **spaz'zino** sm street sweeper.

'spazzola ['spattsola] sf brush; **~ per abiti** clothesbrush; **~ da capelli** hairbrush; **spazzo'lare** vt to brush; **spazzo'lino** sm (small) brush; **spazzolino da denti** toothbrush.

specchi'arsi [spek'kjarsi] vr to look at o.s. in a mirror; (riflettersi) to be mirrored, be reflected; (fig): **~ in qd** to model o.s. on sb.

'specchio ['spekkjo] sm mirror.

speci'ale [spe'tʃale] ag special; **specia'lista, i, e** sm/f specialist; **specialità** sf inv speciality; (branca di studio) special field, speciality; **specializ'zarsi** vr: **specializzarsi (in)** to specialize (in); **special'mente** av especially, particularly.

'specie ['spetʃe] sf inv (BIOL, BOT, ZOOL) species inv; (tipo) kind, sort // av especially, particularly; **fare ~ a qd** to surprise sb; **la ~ umana** mankind.

specifi'care [spetʃifi'kare] vt to specify, state.

spe'cifico, a, ci, che [spe'tʃifiko] ag specific.

specu'lare vi to speculate; **~ su** (COMM) to speculate in; (meditare) to speculate on; (sfruttare) to exploit; **speculazi'one** sf speculation.

spe'dire vt to send; **spedizi'one** sf sending; (collo) parcel, consignment; (scientifica etc) expedition.

'spegnere ['speɲɲere] vt (fuoco, sigaretta) to put out, extinguish; (apparecchio elettrico) to turn o switch off; (fig: suoni, passioni) to stifle; (debito) to extinguish; **~rsi** vr to go out; to go off; (morire) to pass away.

spel'lare vt (scuoiare) to skin; (scorticare) to graze; **~rsi** vr to peel.

'spendere vt to spend.

spen'nare vt to pluck.

spensie'rato, a ag carefree.

'spento, a pp di **spegnere** // ag (suono) muffled; (colore) dull; (civiltà, vulcano) extinct.

spe'ranza [spe'rantsa] sf hope.

spe'rare vt to hope for // vi: **~ in** to trust in; **~ che/di fare** to hope that/to do; **lo spero, spero di sì** I hope so.

sper'duto, a ag (isolato) out-of-the-way; (persona: smarrita, a disagio) lost.

spergi'uro, a [sper'dʒuro] sm/f perjurer // sm perjury.

sperimen'tale ag experimental.

sperimen'tare vt to experiment with, test; (fig) to test, put to the test.

'sperma, i sm (BIOL) sperm.

spe'rone sm spur.

sperpe'rare vt to squander.

'spesa sf (somma di denaro) expense; (costo) cost; (acquisto) purchase; (fam: acquisto del cibo quotidiano) shopping; **~e** sfpl expenses; (COMM) costs; charges; **fare la ~** to do the shopping; **a ~e di** (a carico di) at the expense of; **~e generali** overheads; **~e postali** postage sg; **~e di viaggio** travelling expenses.

'speso, a pp di **spendere**.

'spesso, a ag (fitto) thick; (frequente) frequent // av often; **~e volte** frequently, often.

spes'sore sm thickness.

spet'tabile ag (abbr: Spett.: in lettere): **~ ditta X** Messrs X and Co.

spet'tacolo sm (rappresentazione) performance, show; (vista, scena) sight; **dare ~ di sé** to make an exhibition o a spectacle of o.s.; **spettaco'loso, a** ag spectacular.

spet'tanza [spet'tantsa] sf (competenza) concern; **non è di mia ~** it's no concern of mine.

spet'tare vi (2): **~ a** (decisione) to be up to; (stipendio) to be due to; **spetta a te decidere** it's up to you to decide.

spetta'tore, 'trice sm/f (CINEMA, TEATRO) member of the audience; (di avvenimento) onlooker, witness.

spetti'nare vt: ~ **qd** to ruffle sb's hair; ~**rsi** vr to get one's hair in a mess.

'spettro sm (fantasma) spectre; (FISICA) spectrum.

'spezie ['spɛttsje] sfpl (CUC) spices.

spez'zare [spet'tsare] vt (rompere) to break; (fig: interrompere) to break up; ~**rsi** vr to break.

spezza'tino [spettsa'tino] sm (CUC) stew.

spezzet'tare [spettset'tare] vt to break up (o chop) into small pieces.

'spia sf spy; (confidente della polizia) informer; (ELETTR) indicating light; warning light; (fessura) spy hole, peephole; (fig: sintomo) sign, indication.

spia'cente [spja'tʃɛnte] ag sorry; **essere ~ di qc/di fare qc** to be sorry about sth/for doing sth.

spia'cevole [spja'tʃevole] ag unpleasant, disagreeable.

spi'aggia, ge ['spjaddʒa] sf beach.

spia'nare vt (terreno) to level, make level; (edificio) to raze to the ground; (pasta) to roll out; (rendere liscio) to smooth (out).

spi'ano sm: **a tutto ~** (lavorare) non-stop, without a break; (spendere) lavishly.

spian'tato, a ag penniless, ruined.

spi'are vt to spy on; (occasione etc) to watch o wait for.

spi'azzo ['spjattso] sm open space; (radura) clearing.

spic'care vt (staccare) to detach, cut off; (foglia, fiore) to pick, pluck; (parole) to pronounce distinctly; (assegno, mandato di cattura) to issue // vi (risaltare) to stand out; ~ **il volo** to fly up; (fig) to take flight; ~ **un balzo** to take a leap; **spic'cato, a** ag (marcato) marked, strong; (notevole) remarkable.

'spicchio ['spikkjo] sm (di agrumi) segment; (di aglio) clove; (parte) piece, slice.

spicci'arsi [spit'tʃarsi] vr to hurry up.

'spicciolo, a [spittʃolo] ag: **moneta ~a, ~i** smpl (small) change.

'spicco, chi sm prominence; **fare ~** to stand out.

spi'edo sm (CUC) spit.

spie'gare vt (far capire) to explain; (tovaglia) to unfold; (vele) to unfurl; ~**rsi** vr to explain o.s., make o.s. clear; **il problema si spiega** one can understand the problem; **spiegazi'one** sf explanation; **avere una spiegazione con qd** to have it out with sb.

spiegaz'zare [spjegat'tsare] vt to crease, crumple.

spie'tato, a ag ruthless, pitiless.

spiffe'rare vt (fam) to blurt out, blab // vi to whistle.

'spiga, ghe sf (BOT) ear.

spigli'ato, a [spiʎ'ʎato] ag self-possessed, self-confident.

spigo'lare vt (anche fig) to glean.

'spigolo sm corner; (MAT) edge.

'spilla sf brooch; (da cravatta, cappello) pin.

spil'lare vt (vino, fig) to tap; ~ **denaro/notizie a qd** to tap sb for money/information.

'spillo sm pin; (spilla) brooch; ~ **di sicurezza** o **da balia** safety pin; ~ **di sicurezza** (MIL) (safety) pin.

spi'lorcio, a, ci, ce [spi'lortʃo] ag mean, stingy.

'spina sf (BOT) thorn; (ZOOL) spine, prickle; (di pesce) bone; (ELETTR) plug; (di botte) bunghole; **birra alla ~** draught beer; ~ **dorsale** (ANAT) backbone.

spi'nacio [spi'natʃo] sm spinach q.

spi'nale ag (ANAT) spinal.

'spingere ['spindʒere] vt to push; (condurre: anche fig) to drive; (stimolare): ~ **qd a fare** to urge o press sb to do; ~**rsi** vr (inoltrarsi) to push on, carry on; ~**rsi troppo lontano** (anche fig) to go too far; **fin dove spinge lo sguardo** as far as the eye can see.

spi'noso, a ag thorny, prickly.

'spinto, a pp di **spingere** // sf (urto) push; (FISICA) thrust; (fig: stimolo) incentive, spur; (: appoggio) string-pulling q; **dare una ~a a qd** (fig) to pull strings for sb.

spio'naggio [spio'naddʒo] sm espionage, spying.

spi'overe vi (2) (scorrere) to flow down; (ricadere) to hang down, fall.

'spira sf coil.

spi'raglio [spi'raʎʎo] sm (fessura) chink, narrow opening; (raggio di luce, fig) glimmer, gleam; **uno ~ d'aria** a breath of air.

spi'rale sf spiral; (contraccettivo) coil; **a ~** spiral(-shaped).

spi'rare vi (vento) to blow; (2: morire) to expire, pass away.

spiri'tato, a ag possessed; (fig: persona, espressione) wild.

spiri'tismo sm spiritualism.

'spirito sm (REL, CHIM, disposizione d'animo, di legge etc, fantasma) spirit; (pensieri, intelletto) mind; (arguzia) wit; (umorismo) humour, wit; **lo S~ Santo** the Holy Spirit o Ghost.

spirito'saggine [spirito'saddʒine] sf witticism; (peg) wisecrack.

spiri'toso, a ag witty.

spiritu'ale ag spiritual.

'splendere vi to shine.

'splendido, a ag splendid; (splendente) shining; (sfarzoso) magnificent, splendid.

splen'dore sm splendour; (luce intensa) brilliance, brightness.

spodes'tare vt to deprive of power; (sovrano) to depose.

'spoglia ['spoʎʎa] sf vedi **spoglio**.

spogli'are [spoʎ'ʎare] vt (svestire) to undress; (privare, fig: depredare): ~ **qd di qc** to deprive sb of sth; (togliere ornamenti: anche fig): ~ **qd/qc di** to strip sb/sth of; (fare lo spoglio di) to go through, peruse; ~**rsi** vr to undress, strip; ~**rsi di** (ricchezze etc) to deprive o.s. of, give up; (pregiudizi) to rid o.s. of; **spoglia'toio** sm dressing room; (di scuola etc) cloakroom;

(SPORT) changing room; **'spoglio, a** ag (*pianta, terreno*) bare; (*privo*): ~ **di** stripped of; lacking in, without // sm going through, perusal // sf (ZOOL) skin, hide; (: *di rettile*) slough; **spoglie** sfpl (*preda*) spoils, booty sg.

'spola sf shuttle; (*bobina di filo*) cop; **fare la** ~ **(fra)** to go to and fro o shuttle (between).

spol'pare vt to strip the flesh off.

spolve'rare vt (anche CUC) to dust; (con spazzola) to brush; (con battipanni) to beat; (fig) to polish off // vi to dust.

'sponda sf (di fiume) bank; (di mare, lago) shore; (bordo) edge.

spon'taneo, a ag spontaneous; (persona) unaffected, natural.

spopo'lare vt to depopulate // vi (attirare folla) to draw the crowds; ~**rsi** vr to become depopulated.

spo'radico, a, ci, che ag sporadic.

spor'care vt to dirty, make dirty; (fig) to sully, soil; ~**rsi** vr to get dirty.

spor'cizia [spor'tfittsja] sf (stato) dirtiness; (sudiciume) dirt, filth; (cosa sporca) dirt q, something dirty; (fig: cosa oscena) obscenity.

'sporco, a, chi, che ag dirty, filthy.

spor'genza [spor'dʒɛntsa] sf projection.

'sporgere ['spordʒere] vt to put out, stretch out // vi (2) (venire in fuori) to stick out; (protendersi) to jut out; ~**rsi** vr to lean out; ~ **querela contro qd** (DIR) to take legal action against sb.

sport sm inv sport.

'sporta sf shopping bag.

spor'tello sm (di treno, auto etc) door; (di banca, ufficio) window, counter.

spor'tivo, a ag (gara, giornale) sports cpd; (persona) sporty; (abito) casual; (spirito, atteggiamento) sporting.

'sporto, a pp di **sporgere**.

'sposa sf bride; (moglie) wife.

sposa'lizio [spoza'littsjo] sm wedding.

spo'sare vt to marry; (fig: idea, fede) to espouse; ~**rsi** vr to get married, marry; ~**rsi con qd** to marry sb, get married to sb.

'sposo sm (bride)groom; (marito) husband; **gli** ~**i** smpl the newlyweds.

spos'sato, a ag exhausted, weary.

spos'tare vt to move, shift; (cambiare: orario) to change; ~**rsi** vr to move.

'spranga, ghe sf (sbarra) bar; (catenaccio) bolt.

'sprazzo ['sprattso] sm (di sole etc) flash; (fig: di gioia etc) burst.

spre'care vt to waste; ~**rsi** vr (persona) to waste one's energy; **'spreco** sm waste.

spre'gevole [spre'dʒevole] ag contemptible, despicable.

spregiudi'cato, a [spredʒudi'kato] ag unprejudiced, unbiased; (peg) unscrupulous.

'spremere vt to squeeze.

spre'muta sf fresh juice; ~ **d'arancia** fresh orange juice.

sprez'zante [spret'tsante] ag scornful, contemptuous.

sprigio'nare [spridʒo'nare] vt to give off, emit; ~**rsi** vr to emanate; (uscire con impeto) to burst out.

spriz'zare [sprit'tsare] vt, vi (2) to spurt; ~ **gioia/salute** to be bursting with joy/health.

sprofon'dare vi (2) to sink; (casa) to collapse; (suolo) to give way, subside; ~**rsi** vr: ~**rsi in** (poltrona) to sink into; (fig) to become immersed o absorbed in.

spro'nare vt to spur (on).

'sprone sm (sperone, fig) spur.

sproporzio'nato, a [sproportsjo'nato] ag disproportionate, out of all proportion.

sproporzi'one [spropor'tsjone] sf disproportion.

sproposi'tato, a ag (lettera, discorso) full of mistakes; (fig: costo) excessive, enormous.

spro'posito sm blunder; **a** ~ at the wrong time; (rispondere, parlare) irrelevantly.

sprovve'duto, a ag (privo): ~ **di** lacking in, without; (impreparato) unprepared.

sprov'visto, a ag (mancante): ~ **di** lacking in, without; **alla** ~**a** unawares.

spruz'zare [sprut'tsare] vt (a nebulizzazione) to spray; (aspergere) to sprinkle; (inzaccherare) to splash; **'spruzzo** sm spray; splash.

'spugna ['spuɲɲa] sf (ZOOL) sponge; (tessuto) towelling; **spu'gnoso, a** ag spongy.

'spuma sf (schiuma) foam; (bibita) mineral water.

spu'mante sm sparkling wine.

spu'mare vi to foam.

spumeggi'ante [spumed'dʒante] ag (vino, fig) sparkling.

spu'mone sm (CUC) mousse.

spun'tare vt (coltello) to break the point of; (capelli) to trim // vi (2) (uscire: germogli) to sprout; (: capelli) to begin to grow; (: denti) to come through; (apparire) to appear (suddenly); ~**rsi** vr to become blunt, lose its point; **spuntaria** (fig) to make it, win through.

spun'tino sm snack.

'spunto sm (TEATRO, MUS) cue; (fig) starting point; (di vino) sour taste; **dare lo** ~ **a** (fig) to give rise to.

spur'gare vt (fogna) to clean, clear; ~**rsi** vr (MED) to expectorate.

spu'tare vt to spit out; (fig) to belch (out) // vi to spit; **'sputo** sm spittle q, spit q.

'squadra sf (strumento) (set) square; (gruppo) team, squad; (di operai) gang, squad; (MIL) squad; (: AER, NAUT) squadron; (SPORT) team; **a** o **in** ~ straight; ~ **doppia** o **a T** T-square.

squa'drare vt to square, make square; (osservare) to look at closely.

squa'driglia [skwa'driʎʎa] sf (AER) flight; (NAUT) squadron.

squa'drone sm squadron.

squagli'arsi [skwaʎ'ʎarsi] vr to melt; (fig) to sneak off.

squa'lifica *sf* disqualification.

squalifi'care *vt* to disqualify.

'squallido, a *ag* wretched, bleak.

squal'lore *sm* wretchedness, bleakness.

'squalo *sm* shark.

'squama *sf* scale; **squa'mare** *vt* to scale; **squamarsi** *vr* to flake *o* peel (off).

squarcia'gola [skwartʃa'gola]: **a ~** *av* at the top of one's voice.

squar'tare *vt* to quarter, cut up.

squattri'nato, a *ag* penniless.

squili'brare *vt* to unbalance; **squili-'brato, a** *ag* (*PSIC*) unbalanced; **squi'li-brio** *sm* (*differenza, sbilancio*) imbalance; (*PSIC*) unbalance.

squil'lante *ag* shrill, sharp.

squil'lare *vi* (*campanello, telefono*) to ring (out); (*tromba*) to blare; **'squillo** *sm* ring, ringing *q*; blare; **ragazza f squillo** *inv* call girl.

squi'sito, a *ag* exquisite; (*cibo*) delicious.

squit'tire *vi* (*uccello*) to squawk; (*topo*) to squeak.

sradi'care *vt* to uproot; (*fig*) to eradicate.

sragio'nare [zradʒo'nare] *vi* to talk nonsense, rave.

srego'lato, a *ag* (*senza ordine: vita*) disorderly; (*smodato*) immoderate; (*dissoluto*) dissolute.

'stabile *ag* stable, steady; (*tempo: non variabile*) settled; (*TEATRO: compagnia*) resident // *sm* (*edificio*) building.

stabili'mento *sm* establishing *q*; (*edificio*) establishment; (*fabbrica*) plant, factory; **~ carcerario** prison.

stabi'lire *vt* to establish; (*fissare: prezzi, data*) to fix; (*decidere*) to decide; **~rsi** *vr* (*prendere dimora*) to settle.

stabilità *sf* stability.

stabiliz'zare [stabilid'dzare] *vt* to stabilize; **stabilizza'tore** *sm* stabilizer.

stac'care *vt* (*levare*) to detach, remove; (*separare: anche fig*) to separate, divide; (*strappare*) to tear off (*o* out); (*scandire: parole*) to pronounce clearly; (*SPORT*) to leave behind; **~rsi** *vr* (*bottone etc*) to come off; (*scostarsi*): **~rsi (da)** to move away (from); (*fig: separarsi*): **~rsi da** to leave; **non ~ gli occhi da qd** not to take one's eyes off sb.

'stadio *sm* (*SPORT*) stadium; (*periodo, fase*) phase, stage.

'staffa *sf* (*di sella*) stirrup.

staf'fetta *sf* (*messo*) dispatch rider; (*SPORT*) relay race.

stagio'nale [stadʒo'nale] *ag* seasonal.

stagio'nare [stadʒo'nare] *vt* (*legno*) to season; (*formaggi, vino*) to mature.

stagi'one [sta'dʒone] *sf* season; **alta/bassa ~** high/low season.

stagli'arsi [staʎ'ʎarsi] *vr* to stand out, be silhouetted.

sta'gnante [staɲ'ɲante] *ag* stagnant.

sta'gnare [staɲ'ɲare] *vt* (*vaso, tegame*) to tin-plate; (*barca, botte*) to make watertight; (*sangue*) to stop // *vi* to stagnate.

'stagno, a ['staɲɲo] *ag* watertight; (*a tenuta d'aria*) airtight // *sm* (*acquitrino*) pond; (*CHIM*) tin.

sta'gnola [staɲ'ɲola] *sf* tinfoil.

stalag'mite *sf* stalagmite.

stalat'tite *sf* stalactite.

'stalla *sf* (*per bovini*) cowshed; (*per cavalli*) stable.

stal'lone *sm* stallion.

sta'mani, stamat'tina *av* this morning.

'stampa *sf* (*TIP, FOT*: tecnica) printing; (*impressione, copia fotografica*) print; (*insieme di quotidiani, giornalisti etc*) press; **~e** *sfpl* printed matter.

stam'pare *vt* to print; (*pubblicare*) to publish; (*coniare*) to strike, coin; (*imprimere: anche fig*) to impress.

stampa'tello *sm* block letters *pl*.

stam'pella *sf* crutch.

'stampo *sm* mould; (*fig: indole*) type, kind, sort.

sta'nare *vt* to drive out.

stan'care *vt* to tire, make tired; (*annoiare*) to bore; (*infastidire*) to annoy; **~rsi** *vr* to get tired, tire o.s. out; **~rsi (di)** to grow weary (of), grow tired (of).

stan'chezza [staŋ'kettsa] *sf* tiredness, fatigue.

'stanco, a, chi, che *ag* tired; **~ di** tired of, fed up with.

standardiz'zare [standardid'dzare] *vt* to standardize.

'stanga, ghe *sm* bar; (*di carro*) shaft.

stan'gata *sf* (*colpo: anche fig*) blow; (*INS*) poor result; (*CALCIO*) shot.

sta'notte *av* tonight; (*notte passata*) last night.

'stante *prep* owing to, because of; **a sé ~** (*appartamento, casa*) independent, separate.

stan'tio, a, 'tii, 'tie *ag* stale; (*burro*) rancid; (*fig*) old.

stan'tuffo *sm* piston.

'stanza ['stantsa] *sf* room; (*POESIA*) stanza; **~ da letto** bedroom.

stanzi'are [stan'tsjare] *vt* to allocate.

stap'pare *vt* to uncork; to uncap.

'stare *vi* (2) (*restare in un luogo*) to stay, remain; (*abitare*) to stay, live; (*essere situato*) to be, be situated; (*anche: ~ in piedi*) to be, stand; (*essere, trovarsi*) to be; (*dipendere*): **se stesse in me** if it were up to me, if it depended on me; (*seguito da gerundio*): **sta studiando** he's studying; **starci** (*esserci spazio*): **nel baule non ci sta più niente** there's no more room in the boot; (*accettare*) to accept; **ci stai?** is that okay with you?; **~ a** (*attenersi a*) to follow, stick to; (*seguito dall'infinito*): **stiamo a discutere** we're talking; (*toccare a*): **sta a te giocare** it's your turn to play; **~ per fare qc** to be about to do sth; **come sta?** how are you?; **io sto bene/male** I'm very well/not very well; **~ a qd** (*abiti etc*) to fit sb; **queste scarpe mi stanno strette** these shoes are tight for me; **il rosso ti sta bene** red suits you.

starnu'tire *vi* to sneeze; **star'nuto** *sm* sneeze.

sta'sera *av* this evening, tonight.

sta'tale *ag* state *cpd*; government *cpd* // *sm/f* state employee, local authority employee; (*nell'amministrazione*) ≈ civil servant.

sta'tista, i *sm* statesman.

sta'tistico, a, ci, che *ag* statistical // statistics *sg*.

'stato, a *pp di* **essere, stare** // *sm* (*condizione*) state, condition; (*POL*) state; (*DIR*) status; **essere in ~ d'accusa** (*DIR*) to be committed for trial; **~ d'assedio/d'emergenza** state of siege/emergency; **~ maggiore** (*MIL*) staff; **gli S—i Uniti (d'America)** the United States (of America).

'statua *sf* statue.

statuni'tense *ag* United States *cpd*, of the United States.

sta'tura *sf* (*ANAT*) height, stature; (*fig*) stature.

sta'tuto *sm* (*DIR*) statute; constitution.

sta'volta *av* this time.

stazio'nario, a [stattsjo'narjo] *ag* stationary; (*fig*) unchanged.

stazi'one [stat'tsjone] *sf* station; (*balneare, termale*) resort; **~ degli autobus** bus station; **~ balneare** seaside resort; **~ invernale** winter sports resort; **~ di polizia** police station (*in small town*); **~ di servizio** service *o* petrol *o* filling station; **~ trasmittente** (*RADIO, TV*) transmitting station.

'stecca, che *sf* stick; (*di ombrello*) rib; (*di sigarette*) carton; (*MED*) splint; (*stonatura*): **fare una ~** to sing (*o* play) a wrong note.

stec'cato *sm* fence.

stec'chito, a [stek'kito] *ag* dried up; (*persona*) skinny; **lasciar ~ qd** (*fig*) to leave sb flabbergasted.

'stella *sf* star; **~ alpina** (*BOT*) edelweiss; **~ di mare** (*ZOOL*) starfish.

'stelo *sm* stem; (*asta*) rod; **lampada a ~** standard lamp.

'stemma, i *sm* coat of arms.

stempe'rare *vt* to dilute; to dissolve, melt; (*colori*) to mix.

sten'dardo *sm* standard.

'stendere *vt* (*braccia, gambe*) to stretch (out); (*tovaglia*) to spread (out); (*bucato*) to hang out; (*mettere a giacere*) to lay (down); (*spalmare: colore*) to spread; (*mettere per iscritto*) to draw up; **~rsi** *vr* (*coricarsi*) to stretch out, lie down; (*estendersi*) to extend, stretch.

stenodatti'lografo, a *sm/f* shorthand typist.

stenogra'fare *vt* to take down in shorthand; **stenogra'fia** *sf* shorthand.

sten'tare *vi*: **~ a fare** to find it hard to do, have difficulty doing.

'stento *sm* (*fatica*) difficulty; **~i** *smpl* (*privazioni*) hardship *sg*, privation *sg*; **a ~** *av* with difficulty, barely.

'sterco *sm* dung.

'stereo('fonico, a, ci, che) *ag* stereo(phonic).

stereoti'pato, a *ag* stereotyped.

'sterile *ag* sterile; (*terra*) barren; (*fig*) futile, fruitless; **sterilità** *sf* sterility.

steriliz'zare [sterilid'dzare] *vt* to sterilize; **sterilizzazi'one** *sf* sterilization.

ster'lina *sf* pound (sterling).

stermi'nare *vt* to exterminate, wipe out.

stermi'nato, a *ag* immense; endless.

ster'minio *sm* extermination, destruction.

'sterno *sm* (*ANAT*) breastbone.

ster'zare [ster'tsare] *vt, vi* (*AUT*) to steer; **'sterzo** *sm* steering; (*volante*) steering wheel.

'steso, a *pp di* **stendere**.

'stesso, a *ag* same; (*rafforzativo: in persona, proprio*): **il re ~** the king himself *o* in person // *pronome*: **lo(la) ~(a)** the same (one); **i suoi ~i avversari lo ammirano** even his enemies admire him; **fa lo ~** it doesn't matter; **per me è lo ~** it's all the same to me, it doesn't matter to me; *vedi* **io, tu** *etc*.

ste'sura *sf* drafting *q*, drawing up *q*; draft.

stetos'copio *sm* stethoscope.

'stigma, i *sm* stigma.

'stigmate *sfpl* (*REL*) stigmata.

stil'lare *vt* to draw up, draft.

'stile *sm* style; **sti'lista, i** *sm* stylist; designer; **stiliz'zato, a** *ag* stylized.

stil'lare *vi* (2) (*trasudare*) to ooze; (*gocciolare*) to drip; **~rsi il cervello** (*fig*) to rack one's brains; **stilli'cidio** *sm* drip, dripping.

stilo'grafica, che *sf* (*anche:* **penna ~**) fountain pen.

'stima *sf* esteem; valuation; assessment, estimate.

sti'mare *vt* (*persona*) to esteem, hold in high regard; (*terreno, casa etc*) to value; (*stabilire in misura approssimativa*) to estimate, assess; (*ritenere*): **~ che** to consider that; **~rsi fortunato** to consider o.s. (to be) lucky.

stimo'lante *ag* stimulating // *sm* (*MED*) stimulant.

stimo'lare *vt* to stimulate; (*incitare*): **~ qd (a fare)** to spur sb on (to do).

'stimolo *sm* (*sollecitazione*) stimulus, spur; (*FISIOL, PSIC*) stimulus; **lo ~ della fame/del rimorso** the pangs of hunger/remorse.

'stinco, chi *sm* shin; shinbone.

'stingere ['stindʒere] *vt, vi* (2) (*anche:* **~rsi**) to fade; **'stinto, a** *pp di* **stingere**.

sti'pare *vt* to cram, pack; **~rsi** *vr* (*accalcarsi*) to crowd, throng.

sti'pendio *sm* salary.

'stipite *sm* (*di porta, finestra*) jamb.

stipu'lare *vt* (*redigere*) to draw up.

sti'rare *vt* (*abito*) to iron; (*distendere*) to stretch; **~rsi** *vr* (*fam*) to stretch (o.s.); **stira'tura** *sf* ironing.

'stirpe *sf* birth, stock; descendants *pl*.

stiti'chezza [stiti'kettsa] *sf* constipation.

'stitico, a, ci, che *ag* constipated.

'stiva *sf* (*di nave*) hold.
sti'vale *sm* boot.
'stizza ['stittsa] *sf* anger, vexation; stiz-
  'zirsi *vr* to lose one's temper; stiz'zoso, a
  ag (*persona*) quick-tempered, irascible;
  (*risposta*) angry.
stocca'fisso *sm* stockfish, dried cod.
stoc'cata *sf* (*colpo*) stab, thrust; (*fig*) gibe,
  cutting remark.
'stoffa *sf* material, fabric; (*fig*): aver la ~
  di to have the makings of.
'stoico, a, ci, che *ag* stoic(al).
'stola *sf* stole.
'stolto, a *ag* stupid, foolish.
'stomaco, chi *sm* stomach; dare di ~ to
  vomit, be sick.
sto'nare *vt* to sing (*o* play) out of tune //
  vi to be out of tune, sing (*o* play) out of
  tune; (*fig*) to be out of place, jar; (: *colori*)
  to clash; stona'tura *sf* (*suono*) false note.
stop *sm inv* (TEL) stop; (AUT: *cartello*) stop
  sign; (: *fanalino d'arresto*) brake-light.
'stoppa *sf* tow.
'stoppia *sf* (AGR) stubble.
stop'pino *sm* wick; (*miccia*) fuse.
'storcere ['stɔrtʃere] *vt* to twist; ~rsi *vr*
  to writhe, twist; ~ il naso (*fig*) to turn up
  one's nose; ~rsi la caviglia to twist
  one's ankle.
stor'dire *vt* (*intontire*) to stun, daze; ~rsi
  vr: ~rsi col bere to drown one's
  sorrows; stor'dito, a *ag* stunned; (*sbadato*)
  scatterbrained, heedless.
'storia *sf* (*scienza, avvenimenti*) history;
  (*racconto, bugia*) story; (*faccenda,
  questione*) business *q*; (*pretesto*) excuse,
  pretext; ~e *sfpl* (*smancerie*) fuss *sg*;
  'storico, a, ci, che *ag* historic(al) // *sm*
  historian.
stori'one *sm* (ZOOL) sturgeon.
stor'mire *vi* to rustle.
'stormo *sm* (*di uccelli*) flock.
stor'nare *vt* (COMM) to transfer.
'storno *sm* starling.
storpi'are *vt* to cripple, maim; (*fig:
  parole*) to mangle.
'storpio, a *ag* crippled, maimed.
'storto, a *pp di* storcere // *ag* (*chiodo*)
  twisted, bent; (*gamba, quadro*) crooked;
  (*fig: ragionamento*) false, wrong // *sf*
  (*distorsione*) sprain, twist; (*recipiente*)
  retort.
sto'viglie [sto'viʎʎe] *sfpl* dishes *pl*,
  crockery.
'strabico, a, ci, che *ag* squint-eyed;
  (*occhi*) squint.
stra'bismo *sm* squinting.
stra'carico, a, chi, che *ag* overloaded.
stracci'are [strat'tʃare] *vt* to tear.
'straccio, a, ci, ce ['strattʃo] *ag* torn //
  sm rag; (*per pulire*) cloth, duster; carta
  ~a waste paper; stracci'vendolo *sm*
  ragman.
stra'cotto, a *ag* overcooked // *sm* (CUC)
  beef stew.
'strada *sf* road; (*di città*) street; (*cammino,
  via, fig*) way; farsi ~ (*fig*) to do well for

o.s.; essere fuori ~ (*fig*) to be on the
  wrong track; ~ facendo on the way; ~
  senza uscita dead end; stra'dale *ag* road
  cpd.
strafalci'one [strafal'tʃone] *sm* blunder,
  howler.
stra'fare *vi* to overdo it; stra'fatto, a *pp
  di* strafare.
strafot'tente *ag*: è ~ he doesn't give a
  damn, he couldn't care less.
'strage ['stradʒe] *sf* massacre, slaughter.
stralu'nare *vt*: ~ gli occhi to roll one's
  eyes; stralu'nato, a *ag* (*occhi*) rolling;
  (*persona*) beside o.s., very upset.
stramaz'zare [stramat'tsare] *vi* (2) to
  fall heavily.
'strambo, a *ag* strange, queer.
strampa'lato, a *ag* odd, eccentric.
stra'nezza [stra'nettsa] *sf* strangeness.
strango'lare *vt* to strangle; ~rsi *vr* to
  choke.
strani'ero, a *ag* foreign // *sm/f* foreigner.
'strano, a *ag* strange, odd.
straordi'nario, a *ag* extraordinary;
  (*treno etc*) special // *sm* (*lavoro*)
  overtime.
strapaz'zare [strapat'tsare] *vt* to ill-treat;
  ~rsi *vr* to tire o.s. out, overdo things;
  stra'pazzo *sm* strain, fatigue; da
  strapazzo (*fig*) third-rate.
strapi'ombo *sm* overhanging rock; a ~
  overhanging.
strapo'tere *sm* excessive power.
strap'pare *vt* to pull out; (*pagina etc*) to
  tear off, tear out; (*fazzoletto, lenzuolo,
  foglio*) to tear, rip; (*sradicare*) to pull up;
  ~ qc a qd to snatch sth from sb; (*fig*) to
  wrest sth from sb; ~rsi *vr* (*lacerarsi*) to
  rip, tear; (*rompersi*) to break; 'strappo *sm*
  pull, tug; tear, rip; fare uno strappo alla
  regola to make an exception to the rule;
  strappo muscolare torn muscle.
strapun'tino *sm* jump *o* foldaway seat.
strari'pare *vi* to overflow.
strasci'care [straʃʃi'kare] *vt* to trail;
  (*piedi*) to drag; (*parole*) to drawl.
'strascico, chi ['straʃʃiko] *sm* (*di abito*)
  train; (*conseguenza*) after-effect.
strata'gemma, i [strata'dʒemma] *sm*
  stratagem.
strate'gia, 'gie [strate'dʒia] *sf* strategy;
  stra'tegico, a, ci, che *ag* strategic.
'strato *sm* layer; (*rivestimento*) coat,
  coating; (GEO, *fig*) stratum; (METEOR)
  stratus.
stratos'fera *sf* stratosphere.
strava'gante *ag* odd, eccentric; strava-
  'ganza *sf* eccentricity.
stra'vecchio, a [stra'vɛkkjo] *ag* very old.
stra'vizio [stra'vittsjo] *sm* excess.
stra'volgere [stra'vɔldʒere] *vt* (*volto*) to
  contort; (*fig: animo*) to trouble deeply; (:
  verità) to twist, distort; stra'volto, a *pp di*
  stravolgere.
strazi'are [strat'tsare] *vt* to torture,
  torment; 'strazio *sm* torture; (*fam:
  persona, libro*) bore.

'strega, ghe sf witch.

stre'gare vt to bewitch.

stre'gone sm (mago) wizard; (di tribù) witch doctor.

'stregua sf: **alla ~ di** by the same standard as.

stre'mare vt to exhaust.

'stremo sm very end; **essere allo ~** to be at the end of one's tether.

'strenna sf Christmas present.

'strenuo, a ag brave, courageous.

strepi'toso, a ag clamorous, deafening; (fig: successo) resounding.

'stretta sf vedi stretto.

stretta'mente av tightly; (rigorosamente) strictly.

stret'tezza [stret'tettsa] sf narrowness; **~e** sfpl poverty sg, straitened circumstances.

'stretto, a pp di stringere // ag (non largo) narrow; (: gonna, serrato: nodo) tight; (intimo: parente, amico) close; (rigoroso: osservanza) strict; (preciso: significato) precise, exact // sm (braccio di mare) strait // sf (di mano) grasp; (finanziaria) squeeze; (fig: dolore, turbamento) pang; **a denti ~i** with clenched teeth; **lo ~ necessario** the bare minimum; **essere alle ~e** to have one's back to the wall; **stret'toia** sf bottleneck; (fig) tricky situation.

stri'ato, a ag streaked.

stri'dente ag strident.

'stridere vi (porta) to squeak; (animale) to screech, shriek; (colori) to clash; **'strido,** pl(f) **strida** sm screech, shriek; **stri'dore** sm screeching, shrieking; **'stridulo, a** ag shrill.

stril'lare vt, vi to scream, shriek; **'strillo** sm scream, shriek.

stril'lone sm newspaper seller.

strimin'zito, a [strimin'tsito] ag (misero) shabby; (molto magro) skinny.

strimpel'lare vt (MUS) to strum.

'stringa, ghe sf lace.

strin'gato, a ag (fig) concise.

'stringere ['strindʒere] vt (avvicinare due cose) to press (together), squeeze (together); (tenere stretto) to hold tight, clasp, clutch; (avvitare) to tighten; (abito) to take in; (sog: scarpe) to pinch, be tight for; (fig: concludere: patto) to make; (: accelerare: passo, tempo) to quicken // vi (incalzare) to be pressing; **~rsi** vr (accostarsi): **~rsi (a)** to draw close (to), press o.s. (to); (restringersi) to squeeze up; **~ la mano a qd** to shake sb's hand; **~ le labbra/gli occhi** to tighten one's lips/screw up one's eyes.

'striscia, sce ['striʃʃa] sf (di carta, tessuto etc) strip; (riga) stripe; **~sce (pedonali)** zebra crossing sg.

strisci'are [striʃ'ʃare] vt (piedi) to drag; (muro, macchina) to graze // vi to crawl, creep; **~rsi** vr: **~rsi a** (sfregarsi) to rub against; (fig) to grovel before o in front of.

'striscio ['striʃʃo] sm graze; (MED) smear; **colpire di ~** to graze.

strito'lare vt to grind.

striz'zare [strit'tsare] vt (arancia) to squeeze; (panni) to wring (out); **~ l'occhio** to wink.

'strofe sf inv, **'strofa** sf strophe.

strofi'naccio [strofi'nattʃo] sm duster, cloth.

strofi'nare vt to rub.

stron'care vt to break off; (fig: ribellione) to suppress, put down; (: film, libro) to tear to pieces.

stropicci'are [stropit'tʃare] vt to rub.

stroz'zare [strot'tsare] vt (soffocare) to choke, strangle; **~rsi** vr to choke; **strozza'tura** sf (restringimento) narrowing; (di strada etc) bottleneck.

'struggere ['struddʒere] vt (sciogliere) to melt; (fig) to consume; **~rsi** vr to melt; (fig): **~rsi di** to be consumed with.

strumen'tale ag (MUS) instrumental.

strumentaliz'zare [strumentalid'dzare] vt to exploit, use to one's own ends.

stru'mento sm (arnese, fig) instrument, tool; (MUS) instrument; **~ a corda/fiato** stringed/wind instrument.

'strutto sm lard.

strut'tura sf structure; **struttu'rare** vt to structure.

'struzzo ['struttso] sm ostrich.

stuc'care vt (muro) to plaster; (vetro) to putty; (decorare con stucchi) to stucco.

stuc'chevole [stuk'kevole] ag nauseating; (fig) tedious, boring.

'stucco, chi sm plaster; (da vetri) putty; (ornamentale) stucco; **rimanere di ~** (fig) to be dumbfounded.

stu'dente, 'essa sm/f student; (scolaro) pupil, schoolboy/girl; **studen'tesco, a, schi, sche** ag student cpd; school cpd.

studi'are vt to study; **~rsi** vr (sforzarsi): **~rsi di fare** to try o endeavour to do.

'studio sm studying; (ricerca, saggio, stanza) study; (di professionista) office; (di artista, CINEMA, TV, RADIO) studio; **~i** smpl (INS) studies.

studi'oso, a ag studious, hardworking // sm/f scholar.

'stufa sf stove; **~ elettrica** electric fire o heater.

stu'fare vt (CUC) to stew; (fig: fam) to bore; **stu'fato** sm (CUC) stew; **'stufo, a** ag (fam): **essere stufo di** to be fed up with, be sick and tired of.

stu'oia sf mat.

stupefa'cente [stupefa'tʃente] ag stunning, astounding // sm drug, narcotic.

stu'pendo, a ag marvellous, wonderful.

stupi'daggine [stupi'daddʒine] sf stupid thing (to do o say).

stupidità sf stupidity.

'stupido, a ag stupid.

stu'pire vt to amaze, stun // vi (2) (anche: **~rsi**) to be amazed, be stunned.

stu'pore sm amazement, astonishment.

'stupro sm rape.

'stura sf: **dare la ~ a** (bottiglia) to uncork; (sentimenti) to give vent to.

stu'rare vt (lavandino) to clear.

stuzzica'denti [stuttsika'denti] sm toothpick.

stuzzi'care [stuttsi'kare] vt (ferita etc) to poke (at), prod (at); (fig) to tease; ~ i denti to pick one's teeth.

su prep (su + il = **sul**, su + lo = **sullo**, su + l' = **sull'**, su + la = **sulla**, su + i = **sui**, su + gli = **sugli**, su + le = **sulle**) on; (moto a luogo) on, on to; (intorno a, riguardo a) about, on; (approssimazione: circa) about, around // av up; (sopra) (up) above // escl come on! in ~ av up(wards); prezzi dalle mille lire in ~ prices from 1000 lire (upwards); una ragazza sui 17 anni a girl of about 17 (years of age); in 3 casi ~ 10 in 3 cases out of 10.

'sua vedi suo.

su'bacqueo, a ag underwater // sm skindiver.

sub'buglio [sub'buʎʎo] sm confusion, turmoil.

subcosci'ente [subkoʃ'ʃɛnte] ag, sm subconscious.

'subdolo, a ag underhand, sneaky.

suben'trare vi (2): ~ a qd in qc to take over sth from sb.

su'bire vt to suffer, endure.

subis'sare vt (fig): ~ di to overwhelm with, load with.

subi'taneo, a ag sudden.

'subito av immediately, at once, straight away.

su'blime ag sublime.

subodo'rare vt (insidia etc) to smell, suspect.

subordi'nato, a ag subordinate; (dipendente): ~ a dependent on, subject to // sm/f subordinate.

subur'bano, a ag suburban.

succe'daneo [suttʃe'daneo] sm substitute.

suc'cedere [sut'tʃɛdere] vi (2) (prendere il posto di qd): ~ a to succeed; (venire dopo): ~ a to follow; (accadere) to happen; ~rsi vr to follow each other; ~ al trono to succeed to the throne; **successi'one** sf succession; **succes'sivo, a** ag successive; **suc'cesso, a** pp di succedere // sm (esito) outcome; (buona riuscita) success; **succes'sore** sm successor.

succhi'are [suk'kjare] vt to suck (up).

suc'cinto, a [sut'tʃinto] ag (discorso) succinct; (abito) brief.

'succo, chi sm juice; (fig) essence, gist; **suc'coso, a** ag juicy; (fig) pithy; **succu'lento, a** ag succulent.

succur'sale sf branch (office).

sud sm south // ag inv south; (lato) south, southern.

su'dare vi to perspire, sweat; ~ freddo to come out in a cold sweat; **su'data** sf sweat; ho fatto una bella sudata per finirlo in tempo it was a real sweat to get it finished in time.

sud'detto, a ag above-mentioned.

sud'dito, a sm/f subject.

suddi'videre vt to subdivide; **suddivisi'one** sf subdivision.

su'dest sm south-east.

'sudicio, a, ci, ce ['suditʃo] ag dirty, filthy; **sudici'ume** sm dirt, filth.

su'dore sm perspiration, sweat.

su'dovest sm south-west.

'sue vedi suo.

suffici'ente [suffi'tʃɛnte] ag enough, sufficient; (borioso) self-important; (INS) satisfactory; **suffici'enza** sf self-importance; pass mark; aver **sufficienza di qc** to have enough of sth; a **sufficienza** av enough.

suf'fisso sm (LING) suffix.

suf'fragio [suf'fradʒo] sm (voto) vote; ~ universale universal suffrage.

suggel'lare [suddʒel'lare] vt (fig) to seal.

suggeri'mento [suddʒeri'mento] sm suggestion; (consiglio) piece of advice, advice q.

sugge'rire [suddʒe'rire] vt (risposta) to tell; (consigliare) to advise; (proporre) to suggest; (TEATRO) to prompt; **suggeri'tore, 'trice** sm/f (TEATRO) prompter.

suggestio'nare [suddʒestjo'nare] vt to influence.

suggesti'one [suddʒes'tjone] sf (PSIC) suggestion; (istigazione) instigation.

sugges'tivo, a [suddʒes'tivo] ag (paesaggio) evocative; (teoria) interesting, attractive.

'sughero ['sugero] sm cork.

'sugli ['suʎʎi] prep + det vedi su.

'sugna ['suɲɲa] sf suet.

'sugo, ghi sm (succo) juice; (di carne) gravy; (condimento) sauce; (fig) gist, essence.

'sui prep + det vedi su.

sui'cida, i, e [sui'tʃida] ag suicidal // sm/f suicide.

suici'darsi [suitʃi'darsi] vr to commit suicide.

sui'cidio [sui'tʃidjo] sm suicide.

su'ino, a ag: carne ~a pork // sm pig; ~ i smpl swine pl.

sul, sull', 'sulla, 'sulle, 'sullo prep + det vedi su.

sul'tanina ag f: (uva) ~ sultana.

sul'tano, a sm/f sultan/sultana.

'sunto sm summary.

'suo, 'sua, 'sue, su'oi det: il ~, la sua etc (di lui) his; (di lei) her; (di esso) its; (con valore indefinito) one's, his/her; (forma di cortesia: anche: S~) your // pronome: il ~, la sua etc his; hers; yours; i suoi (parenti) one's family.

su'ocero, a ['swɔtʃero] sm/f father/mother-in-law; i ~i smpl father-and mother-in-law.

su'oi vedi suo.

su'ola sf (di scarpa) sole.

su'olo sm (terreno) ground; (terra) soil.

suo'nare vt (MUS) to play; (campana) to ring; (ore) to strike; (clacson, allarme) to sound // vi to play; (telefono, campana) to ring; (ore) to strike; (clacson, fig: parole) to sound.

su'ono sm sound.

su'ora *sf* (REL) sister.

supe'rare *vt* (*oltrepassare: limite*) to exceed, surpass; (*percorrere*) to cover; (*attraversare: fiume*) to cross; (*sorpassare: veicolo*) to overtake; (*fig: essere più bravo di*) to surpass, outdo; (: *difficoltà*) to overcome; (: *esame*) to get through; ~ **qd in altezza/peso** to be taller/heavier than sb; **ha superato la cinquantina** he's over fifty.

su'perbia *sf* pride.

su'perbo, a *ag* proud; (*fig*) magnificent, superb.

superfici'ale [superfi'tʃale] *ag* superficial.

super'ficie, ci [super'fitʃe] *sf* surface.

su'perfluo, a *ag* superfluous.

superi'ore *ag* (*piano, arto, classi*) upper; (*più elevato: temperatura, livello*): ~ **(a)** higher (than); (*migliore*): ~ **(a)** superior (to); ~, **a** *sm/f* (*anche* REL) superior; **superiorità** *sf* superiority.

superla'tivo, a *ag, sm* superlative.

supermer'cato *sm* supermarket.

su'perstite *ag* surviving // *sm/f* survivor.

superstizi'one [superstit'tsjone] *sf* superstition; **superstizi'oso, a** *ag* superstitious.

su'pino, a *ag* supine.

suppel'lettile *sf* furnishings *pl*.

suppergiù [supper'dʒu] *av* more or less, roughly.

supple'mento *sm* supplement.

sup'plente *ag* temporary; (*insegnante*) supply *cpd* // *sm/f* temporary member of staff; supply teacher.

'supplica, che *sf* (*preghiera*) plea; (*domanda scritta*) petition, request.

suppli'care *vt* to implore, beseech.

sup'plire *vi*: ~ **a** to make up for, compensate for.

sup'plizio [sup'plittsjo] *sm* torture.

sup'porre *vt* to suppose.

sup'porto *sm* (*sostegno*) support.

supposizi'one [suppozit'tsjone] *sf* supposition.

sup'posta *sf* (MED) suppository.

sup'posto, a *pp di* **supporre**.

suppu'rare *vi* to suppurate.

suprema'zia [supremat'tsia] *sf* supremacy.

su'premo, a *ag* supreme.

surge'lare [surdʒe'lare] *vt* to (deep-)freeze.

sur'plus *sm inv* (ECON) surplus.

surriscal'dare *vt* to overheat.

surro'gato *sm* substitute.

suscet'tibile [suʃʃet'tibile] *ag* (*sensibile*) touchy, sensitive; (*soggetto*): ~ **di miglioramento** that can be improved, open to improvement.

susci'tare [suʃʃi'tare] *vt* to provoke, arouse.

su'sina *sf* plum; **su'sino** *sm* plum (tree).

sussegu'ire *vt* to follow; ~**rsi** *vr* to follow one another.

sussidi'ario, a *ag* subsidiary; auxiliary.

sus'sidio *sm* subsidy.

sussis'tenza [sussis'tɛntsa] *sf* subsistence.

sus'sistere *vi* (2) to exist; to be valid *o* sound.

sussul'tare *vi* to shudder.

sussur'rare *vt, vi* to whisper, murmur; **sus'surro** *sm* whisper, murmur.

su'tura *sf* (MED) suture; **sutu'rare** *vt* to stitch up, suture.

sva'gare *vt* (*distrarre*) to distract; (*divertire*) to amuse; ~**rsi** *vr* to amuse o.s.; to enjoy o.s.

'svago, ghi *sm* (*riposo*) relaxation; (*ricreazione*) amusement; (*passatempo*) pastime.

svaligi'are [zvali'dʒare] *vt* to rob, burgle.

svalu'tare *vt* (ECON) to devalue; (*fig*) to belittle; **svalutazi'one** *sf* devaluation.

sva'nire *vi* (2) to disappear, vanish.

svan'taggio [zvan'taddʒo] *sm* disadvantage; (*inconveniente*) drawback, disadvantage.

svapo'rare *vi* (2) to evaporate.

svari'ato, a *ag* varied; various.

'svastica *sf* swastika.

sve'dese *ag* Swedish // *sm/f* Swede // *sm* (LING) Swedish.

'sveglia ['zveʎʎa] *sf* waking up; (*orologio*) alarm (clock); **suonare la** ~ (MIL) to sound the reveille.

svegli'are [zveʎ'ʎare] *vt* to wake up; (*fig*) to awaken, arouse; ~**rsi** *vr* to wake up; (*fig*) to be revived, reawaken.

'sveglio, a ['zveʎʎo] *ag* awake; (*fig*) alert, quick-witted.

sve'lare *vt* to reveal.

'svelto, a *ag* (*passo*) quick; (*mente*) quick, alert; (*linea*) slim, slender; **alla** ~**a** *av* quickly.

'svendita *sf* (COMM) (clearance) sale.

sveni'mento *sm* fainting fit, faint.

sve'nire *vi* (2) to faint.

sven'tare *vt* to foil, thwart.

sven'tato, a *ag* (*distratto*) scatterbrained; (*imprudente*) rash.

svento'lare *vt, vi* to wave, flutter.

sven'trare *vt* to disembowel.

sven'tura *sf* misfortune; **sventu'rato, a** *ag* unlucky, unfortunate.

sve'nuto, a *pp di* **svenire**.

svergo'gnato, a [zvergoɲ'ɲato] *ag* shameless.

sver'nare *vi* to spend the winter.

sves'tire *vt* to undress; ~**rsi** *vr* to get undressed.

'Svezia ['zvɛttsja] *sf*: **la** ~ Sweden.

svez'zare [zvet'tsare] *vt* to wean.

svi'are *vt* to divert; (*fig*) to lead astray; ~**rsi** *vr* to go astray.

svi'gnarsela [zviɲ'ɲarsela] *vr* to slip away, sneak off.

svilup'pare *vt*, ~**rsi** *vr* to develop.

svi'luppo *sm* development.

svinco'lare *vt* to free, release; (*merce*) to clear; **'svincolo** *sm* clearance; (*stradale*) link road.

svi'sare *vt* to distort.

svisce'rare [zviʃʃe'rare] *vt* (*fig:
argomento*) to examine in depth; **svisce-
'rato, a** *ag* (*amore*) passionate; (*lodi*)
obsequious.

'svista *sf* oversight.

svi'tare *vt* to unscrew.

'Svizzera ['zvittsera] *sf:* **la** ~ Switzerland.

'svizzero, a ['zvittsero] *ag, sm/f* Swiss.

svogli'ato, a [zvoʎ'ʎato] *ag* listless;
(*pigro*) lazy.

svolaz'zare [zvolat'tsare] *vi* to flutter.

'svolgere ['zvɔldʒere] *vt* to unwind;
(*srotolare*) to unroll; (*fig: argomento*) to
develop; (: *piano, programma*) to carry out;
~**rsi** *vr* to unwind; to unroll; (*fig: aver
luogo*) to take place; (: *procedere*) to go on;
svolgi'mento *sm* development;
(*andamento*) course.

'svolta *sf* (*atto*) turning *q*; (*curva*) turn,
bend; (*fig*) turning-point.

svol'tare *vi* to turn.

'svolto, a *pp di* **svolgere**.

svuo'tare *vt* to empty (out).

T

tabac'caio, a *sm/f* tobacconist.

tabacche'ria [tabakke'ria] *sf*
tobacconist's (shop).

ta'bacco, chi *sm* tobacco.

ta'bella *sf* (*tavola*) table; (*elenco*) list.

taber'nacolo *sm* tabernacle.

tabù *ag, sm inv* taboo.

tabula'tore *sm* tabulator.

'tacca, che *sf* notch, nick; **di mezza** ~
(*fig*) mediocre.

tac'cagno, a [tak'kaɲɲo] *ag* mean, stingy.

tac'cheggio [tak'keddʒo] *sm* shoplifting.

tac'chino [tak'kino] *sm* turkey.

'taccia, ce ['tattʃa] *sf* bad reputation.

'tacco, chi *sm* heel.

taccu'ino *sm* notebook.

ta'cere [ta'tʃere] *vi* to be silent *o* quiet;
(*smettere di parlare*) to fall silent // *vt* to
keep to oneself, say nothing about; **far** ~
qd to make sb be quiet; (*fig*) to silence sb.

ta'chimetro [ta'kimetro] *sm*
speedometer.

'tacito, a ['tatʃito] *ag* silent; (*sottinteso*)
tacit, unspoken.

taci'turno, a [tatʃi'turno] *ag* taciturn.

ta'fano *sm* horsefly.

taffe'ruglio [taffe'ruʎʎo] *sm* brawl,
scuffle.

taffettà *sm* taffeta.

'taglia ['taʎʎa] *sf* (*statura*) height; (*misura*)
size; (*riscatto*) ransom; (*ricompensa*)
reward.

taglia'carte [taʎʎa'karte] *sm inv*
paperknife.

tagli'ando [taʎ'ʎando] *sm* coupon.

tagli'are [taʎ'ʎare] *vt* to cut; (*recidere,
interrompere*) to cut off; (*intersecare*) to
cut across, intersect; (*carne*) to carve;
(*vini*) to blend // *vi* to cut; (*prendere una
scorciatoia*) to take a short-cut; ~ **corto**
(*fig*) to cut short.

taglia'telle [taʎʎa'tɛlle] *sfpl* tagliatelle *pl.*

tagli'ente [taʎ'ʎɛnte] *ag* sharp.

'taglio ['taʎʎo] *sm* cutting *q*; cut; (*parte
tagliente*) cutting edge; (*di abito*) cut, style;
(*di stoffa: lunghezza*) length; (*di vini*)
blending; **di** ~ on edge, edgeways;
banconote di piccolo/grosso ~ notes
of small/large denomination.

tagli'ola [taʎ'ʎola] *sf* trap, snare.

tagliuz'zare [taʎʎut'tsare] *vt* to cut into
small pieces.

'talco *sm* talcum powder.

'tale *det* such; (*intensivo*): **un** ~/~**i**
such (a)/such ... // *pronome* (*questa, quella
persona già menzionata*) the one, the
person; (*indefinito*): **un(una)** ~ someone;
il ~ **giorno alla** ~ **ora** on such and such
a day at such and such a time; ~ **quale:
il tuo vestito è** ~ **quale il mio** your
dress is just *o* exactly like mine;
quel/quella ~ that person, that
man/woman.

ta'lento *sm* talent.

talis'mano *sm* talisman.

tallon'cino [tallon'tʃino] *sm* counterfoil.

tal'lone *sm* heel.

tal'mente *av* so.

ta'lora *av* = **talvolta**.

'talpa *sf* (*ZOOL*) mole.

tal'volta *av* sometimes, at times.

tambu'rello *sm* tambourine.

tambu'rino *sm* drummer.

tam'buro *sm* drum.

Ta'migi [ta'midʒi] *sm:* **il** ~ the Thames.

tampo'nare *vt* (*otturare*) to plug; (*urtare:
macchina*) to crash *o* ram into.

tam'pone *sm* (MED) wad, pad; (*per timbri*)
ink-pad; (*respingente*) buffer; ~
assorbente tampon.

'tana *sf* lair, den.

'tanfo *sm* stench; musty smell.

tan'gente [tan'dʒɛnte] *ag* (MAT): ~ **a**
tangential to // *sf* tangent; (*quota*) share.

tan'gibile [tan'dʒibile] *ag* tangible.

'tango, ghi *sm* tango.

tan'nino *sm* tannin.

tan'tino: un ~ *av* a little, a bit.

'tanto, a *det* (*pane, acqua, soldi*) so much;
(*persone, libri*) so many // *pronome* so
much (*o* many) // *av* (*con ag, av*) so; (*con
vb*) so much, such a lot; (: *così a lungo*) so
long; **due volte** ~ twice as much; ~ ...
quanto: ho ~**i libri quanti (ne hanno)
loro** I have as many books as they have *o*
as them; **conosco** ~ **Carlo quanto suo
padre** I know both Carlo and his father; **è**
~ **bella quanto buona** she is as beautiful
as she is good; ~ **più** ... **e** ~ **più** the more
... the more; **un** ~: **costa un** ~ **al metro**
it costs so much per metre; **guardare con**
~ **d'occhi** to gaze wide-eyed at; ~ **per
cambiare** just for a change; **una volta** ~
just once; ~ **è inutile** in any case it's
useless; **di** ~ **in** ~, **ogni** ~ every so
often.

tapi'oca *sf* tapioca.

'tappa *sf* (*luogo di sosta, fermata*) stop, halt;

(*parte di un percorso*) stage, leg; (*SPORT*) lap; **a** ~**e** in stages.

tap'pare *vt* to plug, stop up; (*bottiglia*) to cork.

tap'peto *sm* carpet; (*anche:* **tappetino**) rug; (*di tavolo*) cloth; (*SPORT*): **andare al** ~ to go down for the count; **mettere sul** ~ (*fig*) to bring up for discussion.

tappez'zare [tappet'tsare] *vt* (*con carta*) to paper; (*rivestire*): ~ **qc (di)** to cover sth (with); **tappezze'ria** *sf* (*tessuto*) tapestry; (*carta da parato*) wallpaper; (*arte*) upholstery; **far da tappezzeria** (*fig*) to be a wallflower; **tappezzi'ere** *sm* upholsterer.

'tappo *sm* stopper; (*in sughero*) cork.

ta'rantola *sf* tarantula.

tarchi'ato, a [tar'kjato] *ag* stocky, thickset.

tar'dare *vi* to be late // *vt* to delay; ~ **a fare** to delay doing.

'tardi *av* late; **più** ~ later (on); **al più** ~ at the latest; **far** ~ to be late; (*restare alzato*) to stay up late.

tar'divo, a *ag* (*primavera*) late; (*rimedio*) belated, tardy; (*fig: bambino*) retarded.

'tardo, a *ag* (*lento, fig: ottuso*) slow; (*tempo: avanzato*) late.

'targa, ghe *sf* plate; (*AUT*) number plate.

ta'riffa *sf* rates *pl*; fares *pl*; tariff; (*prezzo*) rate; fare; (*elenco*) price list; tariff.

'tarlo *sm* woodworm.

'tarma *sf* moth.

ta'rocco, chi *sm* tarot card; ~**chi** *smpl* (*gioco*) tarot *sg*.

tartagli'are [tarta'ʎʎare] *vi* to stutter, stammer.

'tartaro, a *ag, sm* (*in tutti i sensi*) tartar.

tarta'ruga, ghe *sf* tortoise; (*di mare*) turtle; (*materiale*) tortoiseshell.

tar'tina *sf* canapé.

tar'tufo *sm* (*BOT*) truffle.

'tasca, sche *sf* pocket; **tas'cabile** *ag* (*libro*) pocket *cpd*; **tasca'pane** *sm* haversack; **tas'chino** *sm* breast pocket.

'tassa, e *sf* (*imposta*) tax; (*doganale*) duty; (*per iscrizione: a scuola etc*) fee; ~ **di circolazione/di soggiorno** road/tourist tax.

tas'sametro *sm* taximeter.

tas'sare *vt* to tax; to levy a duty on.

tassa'tivo, a *ag* peremptory.

tassazi'one [tassat'tsjone] *sf* taxation.

tas'sello *sm* plug; wedge.

tassì *sm inv* = **taxi; tas'sista, i, e** *sm/f* taxi driver.

'tasso *sm* (*di natalità, d'interesse etc*) rate; (*BOT*) yew; (*ZOOL*) badger; ~ **di cambio/d'interesse** rate of exchange/interest.

tas'tare *vt* to feel; ~ **il terreno** (*fig*) to see how the land lies.

tasti'era *sf* keyboard.

'tasto *sm* key; (*tatto*) touch, feel.

tas'toni *av*: **procedere (a)** ~ to grope one's way forward.

'tattico, a, ci, che *ag* tactical // *sf* tactics *pl*.

'tatto *sm* (*senso*) touch; (*fig*) tact; **duro al** ~ hard to the touch; **aver** ~ to be tactful, have tact.

tatu'aggio [tatu'addʒo] *sm* tattooing; (*disegno*) tattoo.

tatu'are *vt* to tattoo.

'tavola *sf* table; (*asse*) plank, board; (*lastra*) tablet; (*quadro*) panel (painting); (*illustrazione*) plate; ~ **calda** snack bar.

tavo'lato *sm* boarding; (*pavimento*) wooden floor.

tavo'letta *sf* tablet, bar.

'tavolo *sm* table.

tavo'lozza [tavo'lɔttsa] *sf* (*ARTE*) palette.

'taxi *sm inv* taxi.

'tazza ['tattsa] *sf* cup; ~ **da caffè/tè** coffee/tea cup.

te *pronome* (*soggetto: in forme comparative, oggetto*) you.

tè *sm inv* tea; (*trattenimento*) tea party.

tea'trale *ag* theatrical.

te'atro *sm* theatre.

'tecnico, a, ci, che *ag* technical // *sm/f* technician // *sf* technique; (*tecnologia*) technology.

tecnolo'gia [teknolo'dʒia] *sf* technology.

te'desco, a, schi, sche *ag, sm/f, sm* German.

'tedio *sm* tedium, boredom.

te'game *sm* (*CUC*) pan.

'tegola *sf* tile.

tei'era *sf* teapot.

'tela *sf* (*tessuto*) cloth; (*per vele, quadri*) canvas; (*dipinto*) canvas, painting; (*TEATRO*) curtain; ~ **cerata** oilcloth; (*copertone*) tarpaulin.

te'laio *sm* (*apparecchio*) loom; (*struttura*) frame.

tele'camera *sf* television camera.

telecomunicazi'oni [telekomunikat'tsjoni] *sfpl* telecommunications.

tele'cronaca *sf* television report.

tele'ferica, che *sf* cableway.

telefo'nare *vi* to telephone, ring; to make a phone call // *vt* to telephone; ~ **a** to phone up, ring up, call up.

telefo'nata *sf* (telephone) call; ~ **a carico del destinatario** reverse charge call.

tele'fonico, a, ci, che *ag* (tele)phone *cpd*.

telefo'nista, i, e *sm/f* telephonist; (*d'impresa*) switchboard operator.

te'lefono *sm* telephone; ~ **a gettoni** ≈ pay phone.

telegior'nale [teledʒor'nale] *sm* television news (programme).

telegra'fare *vt, vi* to telegraph, cable.

telegra'fia *sf* telegraphy; **tele'grafico, a, ci, che** *ag* telegraph *cpd*, telegraphic; **te'legrafo** *sm* telegraph; (*ufficio*) telegraph office.

tele'gramma, i *sm* telegram.

telepa'tia *sf* telepathy.

teles'copio *sm* telescope.

teleselezi'one [teleselet'tsjone] *sf* ≈ subscriber trunk dialling.

telespetta'tore, 'trice *sm/f* (television) viewer.

televisi'one *sf* television.

televi'sore *sm* television set.

'telex *sm inv* telex.

'tema, i *sm* theme; (*INS*) essay, composition.

teme'rario, a *ag* rash, reckless.

te'mere *vt* to fear, be afraid of; (*essere sensibile a: freddo, calore*) to suffer from; (*sog: cose*) to be easily damaged by // *vi* to fear; (*essere preoccupato*): ~ **per** to worry about, fear for; ~ **di/che** to be afraid of/that.

temperama'tite *sm inv* pencil sharpener.

tempera'mento *sm* temperament.

tempe'rare *vt* (*aguzzare*) to sharpen; (*fig*) to moderate, control, temper.

tempe'rato, a *ag* moderate, temperate; (*clima*) temperate.

tempera'tura *sf* temperature.

tempe'rino *sm* penknife.

tem'pesta *sf* storm; ~ **di sabbia/neve** sand/snowstorm.

tempes'tivo, a *ag* timely.

tempes'toso, a *ag* stormy.

'templa *sf* (*ANAT*) temple.

'tempio *sm* (*edificio*) temple.

'tempo *sm* (*METEOR*) weather; (*cronologico*) time; (*epoca*) time, times *pl*; (*di film, gioco: parte*) part; (*MUS*) time; (: *battuta*) beat; (*LING*) tense; **un** ~ once; ~ **fa** some time ago; **al** ~ **stesso** *o* **a un** ~ at the same time; **per** ~ early; **aver fatto il suo** ~ to have had its (*o his etc*) day; **primo/secondo** ~ (*TEATRO*) first/second part; (*SPORT*) first/second half; **in** ~ **utile** in due time *o* course.

tempo'rale *ag* temporal // *sm* (*METEOR*) (thunder)storm.

tempo'raneo, a *ag* temporary.

temporeggi'are [tempored'dʒare] *vi* to play for time, temporize.

tem'prare *vt* to temper.

te'nace [te'natʃe] *ag* strong, tough; (*fig*) tenacious; **te'nacia** *sf* tenacity.

te'naglie [te'naʎʎe] *sfpl* pincers *pl.*

'tenda *sf* (*riparo*) awning; (*di finestra*) curtain; (*per campeggio etc*) tent.

ten'denza [ten'dɛntsa] *sf* tendency; (*orientamento*) trend; **avere** ~ **a qc** to have a bent for sth.

'tendere *vt* (*allungare al massimo*) to stretch, draw tight; (*porgere: mano*) to hold out; (*fig: trappola*) to lay, set // *vi*: ~ **a qc/a fare** to tend towards sth/to do; ~ **l'orecchio** to prick up one's ears; **il tempo tende al caldo** the weather is getting hot.

ten'dina *sf* curtain.

'tendine *sm* tendon, sinew.

ten'done *sm* (*da circo*) tent.

'tenebre *sfpl* darkness *sg*; **tene'broso, a** *ag* dark, gloomy.

te'nente *sm* lieutenant.

te'nere *vt* to hold; (*conservare, mantenere*) to keep; (*ritenere, considerare*) to consider;

(*spazio: occupare*) to take up, occupy; (*seguire: strada*) to keep to // *vi* to hold; (*colori*) to be fast; (*dare importanza*): ~ **a** to care about; ~ **a fare** to want to do, be keen to do; ~**rsi** *vr* (*stare in una determinata posizione*) to stand; (*stimarsi*) to consider o.s.; (*aggrapparsi*): ~**rsi a** to hold on to; (*attenersi*): ~**rsi a** to stick to; ~ **una conferenza** to give a lecture; ~ **conto di qc** to take sth into consideration; ~ **presente qc** to bear sth in mind.

tene'rezza [tene'rettsa] *sf* tenderness.

'tenero, a *ag* tender; (*pietra, cera, colore*) soft; (*fig*) tender, loving.

'tenia *sf* tapeworm.

'tennis *sm* tennis.

te'nore *sm* tenor, way; (*contenuto*) content; (*MUS*) tenor; ~ **di vita** way of life; (*livello*) standard of living.

tensi'one *sf* tension.

ten'tacolo *sm* (*ZOOL*) tentacle.

ten'tare *vt* (*indurre*) to tempt; (*provare*): ~ **qc/di fare** to attempt *o* try sth/to do; **tenta'tivo** *sm* attempt; **tentazi'one** *sf* temptation.

tenten'nare *vi* to shake, be unsteady; (*fig*) to hesitate, waver // *vt*: ~ **il capo** to shake one's head.

ten'toni *av*: **andare (a)** ~ to grope one's way.

'tenue *ag* (*sottile*) fine; (*colore*) soft; (*fig*) slender, slight.

te'nuta *sf* (*capacità*) capacity; (*divisa*) uniform; (*abito*) dress; (*AGR*) estate; **a** ~ **d'aria** airtight; ~ **di strada** roadholding power.

teolo'gia [teolo'dʒia] *sf* theology; **teo-'logico, a, ci, che** *ag* theological; **te'ologo, gi** *sm* theologian.

teo'rema, i *sm* theorem.

teo'ria *sf* theory; **te'orico, a, ci, che** *ag* theoretic(al).

'tepido, a *ag* = **tiepido.**

te'pore *sm* warmth.

'teppa *sf* mob, hooligans *pl*; **tep'pismo** *sm* hooliganism; **tep'pista, i** *sm* hooligan.

tera'pia *sf* therapy.

tergicris'tallo [terdʒikris'tallo] *sm* windscreen wiper.

tergiver'sare [terdʒiver'sare] *vi* to shilly-shally.

'tergo *sm*: **a** ~ behind; **vedi a** ~ please turn over.

ter'male *ag* thermal; **stazione** *f* ~ spa.

'terme *sfpl* thermal baths.

'termico, a, ci, che *ag* thermic; (*unità*) thermal.

termi'nale *ag, sm* terminal.

termi'nare *vt* to end; (*lavoro*) to finish // *vi* to end.

'termine *sm* term; (*fine, estremità*) end; (*di territorio*) boundary, limit; **contratto a** ~ (*COMM*) forward contract; **a breve/lungo** ~ short-/long-term; **parlare senza mezzi** ~**i** to talk frankly, not to mince one's words.

terminolo'gia [terminolo'dʒia] *sf* terminology.

'**termite** sf termite.
ter'**mometro** sm thermometer.
'**termos** sm inv = **thermos.**
termosi'**fone** sm radiator; (**riscaldamento** a) ~ central heating.
ter'**mostato** sm thermostat.
'**terra** sf (gen, ELETTR) earth; (sostanza) soil, earth; (opposto al mare) land q; (regione, paese) land; (argilla) clay; ~e sfpl (possedimento) lands, land sg; **a** o **per** ~ (stato) on the ground (o floor); (moto) to the ground, down; **mettere a** ~ (ELETTR) to earth.
terra'**cotta** sf terracotta; **vasellame** m **di** ~ earthenware.
terra'**ferma** sf dry land, terra firma; (continente) mainland.
terrapi'**eno** sm embankment, bank.
ter'**razza** [ter'rattsa] sf, ter'**razzo** [ter-'rattso] sm terrace.
terre'**moto** sm earthquake.
ter'**reno, a** ag (vita, beni) earthly // sm (suolo, fig) ground; (COMM) land q, plot (of land); site; (SPORT, MIL) field.
ter'**restre** ag (superficie) of the earth, earth's; (di terra: battaglia, animale) land cpd; (REL) earthly, worldly.
ter'**ribile** ag terrible, dreadful.
terrifi'**cante** ag terrifying.
territori'**ale** ag territorial.
terri'**torio** sm territory.
ter'**rore** sm terror; **terro'rismo** sm terrorism; **terro'rista, i, e** sm/f terrorist; **terroriz'zare** vt to terrorize.
'**terso, a** ag clear.
'**terzo, a** ['tɛrtso] ag third // sm (frazione) third; (DIR) third party; ~**i** smpl (altri) others, other people.
'**tesa** sf brim.
'**teschio** ['tɛskjo] sm skull.
'**tesi** sf thesis.
'**teso, a** pp di **tendere** // ag (tirato) taut, tight; (fig) tense.
tesore'**ria** sf treasury.
tesori'**ere** sm treasurer.
te'**soro** sm treasure; **il Ministero del T**~ the Treasury.
'**tessera** sf (documento) card.
'**tessere** vt to weave; '**tessile** ag, sm textile; **tessili** smpl (operai) textile workers; **tessi'tore, 'trice** sm/f weaver; **tessi'tura** sf weaving.
tes'**suto** sm fabric, material; (BIOL) tissue; (fig) web.
'**testa** sf head; (di cose: estremità, parte anteriore) head, front; **di** ~ ag (vettura etc) front; **fare** ~ **a** qd (nemico etc) to face sb; **fare di** ~ **propria** to go one's own way; **in** ~ (SPORT) in the lead; ~ **o croce?** heads or tails?; **avere la** ~ **dura** to be stubborn; ~ **di serie** (TENNIS) seed, seeded player.
testa'**mento** sm (atto) will; (REL): **T**~ Testament.
tes'**tardo, a** ag stubborn, pig-headed.
tes'**tata** sf (parte anteriore) head; (intestazione) heading.

'**teste** sm/f witness.
tes'**ticolo** sm testicle.
testi'**mone** sm/f (DIR) witness.
testimoni'**anza** [testimo'njantsa] sf testimony.
testimoni'**are** vt to testify; (fig) to bear witness to, testify to // vi to give evidence, testify.
'**testo** sm text; **fare** ~ (fig: persona) to be an authority; (: opera) to be the standard work; **testu'ale** ag textual; literal, word for word.
tes'**tuggine** [tes'tuddʒine] sf tortoise; (di mare) turtle.
'**tetano** sm (MED) tetanus.
'**tetro, a** ag gloomy.
'**tetto** sm roof; **tet'toia** sf shed; (di piattaforma etc) roofing.
'**Tevere** sm: **il** ~ the Tiber.
'**thermos** ⓡ ['tɛrmos] sm inv vacuum o Thermos ⓡ flask.
ti pronome (dav lo, la, li, le, ne diventa te) (oggetto) you; (complemento di termine) (to) you; (riflessivo) yourself.
ti'**ara** sf (REL) tiara.
'**tibia** sf tibia, shinbone.
tic sm inv tic, (nervous) twitch; (fig) mannerism.
ticchet'**tio** [tikket'tio] sm clicking; (di orologio) ticking; (della pioggia) patter.
'**ticchio** ['tikkjo] sm (ghiribizzo) whim; (tic) tic, (nervous) twitch.
ti'**epido, a** ag lukewarm, tepid.
ti'**fare** vi: ~ **per** to be a fan of; (parteggiare) to side with.
'**tifo** sm (MED) typhus; (fig): **fare il** ~ **per** to be a fan of.
tifoi'**dea** sf typhoid.
ti'**fone** sm typhoon.
ti'**foso, a** sm/f (SPORT etc) fan.
'**tiglio** ['tiʎʎo] sm lime (tree), linden (tree).
'**tigre** sf tiger.
tim'**ballo** sm (strumento) kettle drum; (CUC) timbale.
'**timbro** sm stamp; (MUS) timbre, tone.
'**timido, a** ag shy; timid.
'**timo** sm thyme.
ti'**mone** sm (NAUT) rudder; **timoni'ere** sm helmsman.
ti'**more** sm (paura) fear; (rispetto) awe; **timo'roso, a** ag timid, timorous.
'**timpano** sm (ANAT) eardrum; (MUS): ~**i** smpl kettledrums, timpani.
'**tingere** ['tindʒere] vt to dye.
'**tino** sm vat.
ti'**nozza** [ti'nɔttsa] sf tub.
'**tinta** sf (materia colorante) dye; (colore) colour, shade; **tinta'rella** sf (fam) (sun)tan.
tintin'**nare** vi to tinkle.
'**tinto, a** pp di **tingere.**
tinto'**ria** sf (officina) dyeworks sg; (lavasecco) dry cleaner's (shop).
tin'**tura** sf (operazione) dyeing; (colorante) dye; ~ **di iodio** tincture of iodine.
'**tipico, a, ci, che** ag typical.

'tipo *sm* type; (*genere*) kind, type; (*fam*) chap, fellow.

tipogra'fia *sf* typography; (*procedimento*) letterpress (printing); (*officina*) printing house; **tipo'grafico, a, ci, che** *ag* typographic(al); letterpress *cpd*; **ti'pografo** *sm* typographer.

ti'raggio [ti'radd3o] *sm* (*di camino etc*) draught.

tiranneggi'are [tiranned'd3are] *vt* to tyrannize.

tiran'nia *sf* tyranny.

ti'ranno, a *ag* tyrannical // *sm* tyrant.

ti'rare *vt* (*gen*) to pull; (*estrarre*): ~ qc da to take *o* pull sth out of; to get sth out of; to extract sth from; (*chiudere: tenda etc*) to draw, pull; (*tracciare, disegnare*) to draw, trace; (*lanciare: sasso, palla*) to throw; (*stampare*) to print; (*pistola, freccia*) to fire // *vi* (*pipa, camino*) to draw; (*vento*) to blow; (*abito*) to be tight; (*fare fuoco*) to fire; (*fare del tiro*, CALCIO) to shoot; ~ avanti *vi* to struggle on // *vt* to keep going; ~ fuori *vt* (*estrarre*) to take out, pull out; ~ giù *vt* (*abbassare*) to bring down; ~ su *vt* to pull up; (*capelli*) to put up; (*fig: bambino*) to bring up; ~rsi indietro to move back.

tira'tore *sm* gunman; **un buon** ~ a good shot; ~ **scelto** marksman.

tira'tura *sf* (*azione*) printing; (*di libro*) (print) run; (*di giornale*) circulation.

'tirchio, a ['tirkjo] *ag* mean, stingy.

'tiro *sm* shooting *q*, firing *q*; (*colpo, sparo*) shot; (*di palla: lancio*) throwing *q*; throw; (*fig*) trick; **cavallo da** ~ draught horse; ~ **a segno** target shooting; (*luogo*) shooting range.

tiro'cinio [tiro't∫injo] *sm* apprenticeship; (*professionale*) training.

ti'roide *sf* thyroid (gland).

Tir'reno *sm*: **il** (*mar*) ~ the Tyrrhenian Sea.

ti'sana *sf* herb tea.

tito'lare *ag* appointed; (*sovrano*) titular // *sm/f* incumbent; (*proprietario*) owner; (*CALCIO*) regular player.

'titolo *sm* title; (*di giornale*) headline; (*diploma*) qualification; (*COMM*) security; (*: azione*) share; **a che** ~? for what reason?; **a** ~ **di amicizia** out of friendship; **a** ~ **di premio** as a prize; **a** ~ **di credito** share; ~ **di proprietà** title deed.

titu'bante *ag* hesitant, irresolute.

'tizio, a ['tittsjo] *sm/f* fellow, chap.

tiz'zone [tit'tsone] *sm* brand.

toc'cante *ag* touching.

toc'care *vt* to touch; (*tastare*) to feel; (*fig: riguardare*) to concern; (*: commuovere*) to touch, move; (*: pungere*) to hurt, wound; (*: far cenno a: argomento*) to touch on, mention // *vi* (*2*): ~ **a** (*accadere*) to happen to; (*spettare*) to be up to; **tocca a te difenderci** it's up to you to defend us; **a chi tocca?** whose turn is it?; **mi toccò pagare** I had to pay.

'tocco, chi *sm* touch; (*ARTE*) stroke, touch; **il** ~ (*l'una*) one o'clock, one p.m.

'toga, ghe *sf* toga; (*di magistrato, professore*) gown.

'togliere ['tɔʎʎere] *vt* (*rimuovere*) to take away (*o* off), remove; (*riprendere, non concedere più*) to take away, remove; (*MAT*) to take away, subtract; (*liberare*) to free; ~ qc a qd to take sth (away) from sb; **ciò non toglie che** nevertheless, be that as it may; ~rsi **il cappello** to take off one's hat.

to'letta *sf* toilet; (*mobile*) dressing table.

tolle'ranza [tolle'rantsa] *sf* tolerance.

tolle'rare *vt* to tolerate.

'tolto, a *pp di* **togliere.**

to'maia *sf* (*di scarpa*) upper.

'tomba *sf* tomb.

tom'bino *sm* manhole cover.

'tombola *sf* (*gioco*) tombola; (*ruzzolone*) tumble.

tombo'lare *vi* (*2*) to tumble.

'tomo *sm* volume.

'tonaca, che *sf* (*REL*) habit.

to'nare *vi* = **tuonare.**

'tondo, a *ag* round.

'tonfo *sm* splash; (*rumore sordo*) thud.

'tonico, a, ci, che *ag, sm* tonic.

tonifi'care *vt* (*muscoli, pelle*) to tone up; (*irrobustire*) to invigorate, brace.

tonnel'laggio [tonnel'ladd3o] *sm* (*NAUT*) tonnage.

tonnel'lata *sf* ton.

'tonno *sm* tuna (fish).

'tono *sm* (*gen*) tone; (*MUS: di pezzo*) key; (*di colore*) shade, tone.

ton'silla *sf* tonsil; **tonsil'lite** *sf* tonsillitis.

ton'sura *sf* tonsure.

'tonto, a *ag* dull, stupid.

to'pazio [to'pattsjo] *sm* topaz.

'topo *sm* mouse.

topogra'fia *sf* topography.

'toppa *sf* (*serratura*) keyhole; (*pezza*) patch.

to'race [to'rat∫e] *sm* chest.

'torba *sf* peat.

'torbido, a *ag* (*liquido*) cloudy; (*: fiume*) muddy; (*fig*) dark; troubled; **pescare nel** ~ (*fig*) to fish in troubled water.

'torcere ['tɔrt∫ere] *vt* to twist; (*biancheria*) to wring (out); ~rsi *vr* to twist, writhe.

torchi'are [tor'kjare] *vt* to press; **'torchio** *sm* press; **torchio tipografico/per uva** printing/wine press.

'torcia, ce ['tɔrt∫a] *sf* torch.

torci'collo [tort∫i'kɔllo] *sm* stiff neck.

'tordo *sm* thrush.

To'rino *sf* Turin.

tor'menta *sf* snowstorm.

tormen'tare *vt* to torment; ~rsi *vr* to fret, worry o.s.; **tor'mento** *sm* torment.

torna'conto *sm* advantage, benefit.

tor'nado *sm* tornado.

tor'nante *sm* hairpin bend.

tor'nare *vi* (*2*) to return, go (*o* come) back; (*ridiventare: anche fig*) to become (again); (*riuscire giusto, esatto: conto*) to work out; (*risultare*) to turn out (to be), prove (to be); ~ **utile** to prove o turn out (to be) useful.

torna'sole *sm inv* litmus.

tor'neo *sm* tournament.

tornio *sm* lathe.

'toro *sm* bull; (*dello zodiaco*): T~ Taurus.

tor'pedine *sf* torpedo; **torpedini'era** *sf* torpedo boat.

tor'pore *sm* torpor, drowsiness; (*pigrizia*) torpor, sluggishness.

'torre *sf* tower; (*SCACCHI*) rook, castle.

torrefazi'one [torrefat'tsjone] *sf* roasting.

tor'rente *sm* torrent; **torrenzi'ale** *ag* torrential.

tor'retta *sf* turret.

'torrido, a *ag* torrid.

torri'one *sm* keep.

tor'rone *sm* nougat.

torsi'one *sf* twisting; torsion.

'torso *sm* torso, trunk; (*ARTE*) torso.

'torsolo *sm* (*di cavolo etc*) stump; (*di frutta*) core.

'torta *sf* cake.

torti'era *sf* cake tin.

'torto, a *pp di* **torcere** // *ag* (*ritorto*) twisted; (*storto*) twisted, crooked // *sm* (*ingiustizia*) wrong; (*colpa*) fault; **a ~** wrongly; **aver ~** to be wrong.

'tortora *sf* turtle dove.

tortu'oso, a *ag* (*strada*) twisting; (*fig*) tortuous.

tor'tura *sf* torture; **tortu'rare** *vt* to torture.

'torvo, a *ag* menacing, grim.

tosa'erba *sm o f inv* (lawn)mower.

to'sare *vt* (*pecora*) to shear; (*siepe*) to clip, trim.

Tos'cana *sf*: **la ~** Tuscany.

'tosse *sf* cough; **~ convulsa** o **canina** whooping cough.

'tossico, a, ci, che *ag* toxic.

tossi'comane *sm/f* drug addict.

tos'sire *vi* to cough.

tosta'pane *sm inv* toaster.

tos'tare *vt* to toast; (*caffè*) to roast.

'tosto, a *ag*: **faccia ~a** cheek.

to'tale *ag, sm* total; **totalità** *sf*: **la totalità di** all of, the total amount (o number) of; **the whole + sg**; **totali'tario, a** *ag* totalitarian; **totaliz'zare** *vt* to total; (*SPORT: punti*) to score.

toto'calcio [toto'kaltʃo] *sm* football pools *pl*.

to'vaglia [to'vaʎʎa] *sf* tablecloth; **tova-gli'olo** *sm* napkin.

'tozzo, a ['tɔttso] *ag* squat // *sm*: **~ di pane** crust of bread.

tra *prep* (*di due persone, cose*) between; (*di più persone, cose*) among(st); (*tempo: entro*) within, in; **~ 5 giorni** in 5 days' time; **litigano ~ (di) loro** they're fighting amongst themselves; **~ breve** soon; **~ sé e sé** (*parlare etc*) to oneself.

traba'llare *vi* to stagger, totter.

trabuc'care *vi* (*2*) to overflow.

traboc'chetto [trabok'ketto] *sm* (*fig*) trap.

tracan'nare *vt* to gulp down.

'traccia, ce ['trattʃa] *sf* (*segno, striscia*) trail, track; (*orma*) tracks *pl*; (*residuo, testimonianza*) trace, sign; (*abbozzo*) outline.

tracci'are [trat'tʃare] *vt* to trace, mark (out); (*disegnare*) to draw; (*fig: abbozzare*) to outline; **tracci'ato** *sm* (*grafico*) layout, plan.

tra'chea [tra'kɛa] *sf* windpipe, trachea.

tra'colla *sf* shoulder strap; **borsa a ~** shoulder bag.

tra'collo *sm* (*fig*) collapse, crash.

traco'tante *ag* overbearing, arrogant.

tradi'mento *sm* betrayal; (*DIR, MIL*) treason.

tra'dire *vt* to betray; (*coniuge*) to be unfaithful to; (*doveri: mancare*) to fail in; (*rivelare*) to give away, reveal; **tradi'tore, 'trice** *sm/f* traitor.

tradizio'nale [tradittsjo'nale] *ag* traditional.

tradizi'one [tradit'tsjone] *sf* tradition.

tra'dotto, a *pp di* **tradurre**.

tra'durre *vt* to translate; (*spiegare*) to render, convey; **tradut'tore, 'trice** *sm/f* translator; **traduzi'one** *sf* translation.

tra'ente *sm/f* (*ECON*) drawer.

trafe'lato, a *ag* out of breath.

traffi'cante *sm/f* dealer; (*peg*) trafficker.

traffi'care *vi* (*commerciare*): **~ (in)** to trade (in), deal (in); (*affaccendarsi*) to busy o.s. // *vt* (*peg*) to traffic in.

'traffico, ci *sm* traffic; (*commercio*) trade, traffic.

tra'figgere [tra'fiddʒere] *vt* to run through, stab; (*fig*) to pierce; **tra'fitto, a** *pp di* **trafiggere**.

trafo'rare *vt* to bore, drill; **tra'foro** *sm* (*azione*) boring, drilling; (*galleria*) tunnel.

tra'gedia [tra'dʒedja] *sf* tragedy.

tra'ghetto [tra'getto] *sm* crossing; (*barca*) ferry(boat).

'tragico, a, ci, che ['tradʒiko] *ag* tragic // *sm* (*autore*) tragedian.

tra'gitto [tra'dʒitto] *sm* (*passaggio*) crossing; (*viaggio*) journey.

tragu'ardo *sm* (*SPORT*) finishing line; (*fig*) goal, aim.

traiet'toria *sf* trajectory.

trai'nare *vt* to drag, haul; (*rimorchiare*) to tow; **'traino** *sm* (*carro*) wagon; (*slitta*) sledge; (*carico*) load.

tralasci'are [tralaʃ'ʃare] *vt* (*studi*) to interrupt; (*dettagli*) to leave out, omit.

'tralcio ['traltʃo] *sm* (*BOT*) shoot.

tra'liccio [tra'littʃo] *sm* (*tela*) ticking; (*struttura*) trellis; (*ELETTR*) pylon.

tram *sm inv* tram.

'trama *sf* (*filo*) weft, woof; (*fig: argomento, maneggio*) plot.

traman'dare *vt* to pass on, hand down.

tra'mare *vt* (*fig*) to scheme, plot.

tram'busto *sm* turmoil.

trames'tio *sm* bustle.

tramez'zino [tramed'dzino] *sm* sandwich.

tra'mezzo [tra'mɛddzo] *sm* (*EDIL*) partition.

'tramite *prep* through.

tramon'tare *vi* (2) to set, go down; **tra-'monto** *sm* setting; (*del sole*) sunset.

tramor'tire *vi* (2) *vt* to stun.

trampo'lino *sm* (*per tuffi*) springboard, diving board; (*per lo sci*) ski-jump.

'trampolo *sm* stilt.

tramu'tare *vt* (*trasferire*) to transfer; (*mutare*) to change, transform.

'trancia, ce ['trantʃa] *sf* slice; (*cesoia*) shearing machine.

tra'nello *sm* trap.

trangugi'are [trangu'dʒare] *vt* to gulp down.

'tranne *prep* except (for), but (for).

tranquil'lante *sm* (*MED*) tranquillizer.

tranquillità *sf* calm, stillness; quietness; peace of mind.

tranquilliz'zare [trankwillid'dzare] *vt* to reassure.

tran'quillo, a *ag* calm, quiet; (*bambino, scolaro*) quiet; (*sereno*) with one's mind at rest; **sta' ~** don't worry.

transat'lantico, a, ci, che *ag* transatlantic // *sm* transatlantic liner.

tran'satto, a *pp di* **transigere**.

transazi'one [transat'tsjone] *sf* compromise; (*DIR*) settlement; (*COMM*) transaction, deal.

tran'senna *sf* barrier.

tran'setto *sm* transept.

tran'sigere [tran'sidʒere] *vi* (*DIR*) to reach a settlement; (*venire a patti*) to compromise, come to an agreement.

tran'sistor *sm*, **transis'tore** *sm* transistor.

transi'tabile *ag* passable.

transi'tare *vi* (2) to pass.

transi'tivo, a *ag* transitive.

'transito *sm* transit; **di ~** (*merci*) in transit; (*stazione*) transit *cpd*; **divieto di ~** no thoroughfare.

transi'torio, a *ag* transitory, transient; (*provvisorio*) provisional.

transizi'one [transit'tsjone] *sf* transition.

tran'via *sf* tramway.

'trapano *sm* (*utensile*) drill; (: *MED*) trepan.

trapas'sare *vt* to pierce.

tra'passo *sm* passage.

trape'lare *vi* (2) to leak, drip; (*fig*) to leak out.

tra'pezio [tra'pɛttsjo] *sm* (*MAT*) trapezium; (*attrezzo ginnico*) trapeze.

trapian'tare *vt* to transplant; **trapi'anto** *sm* transplanting; (*MED*) transplant.

'trappola *sf* trap.

tra'punta *sf* quilt.

'trarre *vt* to draw, pull; (*portare*) to take; (*prendere, tirare fuori*) to take (out), draw; (*derivare*) to obtain; **~ origine da qc** to have its origins *o* originate in sth.

trasa'lire *vi* to start, jump.

trasan'dato, a *ag* shabby.

trasbor'dare *vt* to transfer; (*NAUT*) to tran(s)ship // *vi* to change.

trascenden'tale [traʃʃenden'tale] *ag* transcendental.

trasci'nare [traʃʃi'nare] *vt* to drag; **~rsi** *vr* to drag o.s. along; (*fig*) to drag on.

tras'correre *vt* (*tempo*) to spend, pass; (*libro*) to skim (through) // *vi* (2) to pass; **tras'corso, a** *pp di* **trascorrere**.

tras'critto, a *pp di* **trascrivere**.

tras'crivere *vt* to transcribe; **trascri-zi'one** *sf* transcription.

trascu'rare *vt* to neglect; (*non considerare*) to disregard; **trascura'tezza** *sf* carelessness, negligence; **trascu'rato, a** *ag* (*casa*) neglected; (*persona*) careless, negligent.

traseco'lato, a *ag* astounded, amazed.

trasferi'mento *sm* transfer; (*trasloco*) removal, move.

trasfe'rire *vt* to transfer; **~rsi** *vr* to move; **tras'ferta** *sf* transfer; (*indennità*) travelling expenses *pl*; (*SPORT*) away game.

trasfigu'rare *vt* to transfigure.

trasfor'mare *vt* to transform, change; **trasforma'tore** *sm* transformer; **trasformazi'one** *sf* transformation.

trasfusi'one *sf* (*MED*) transfusion.

trasgre'dire *vt* to disobey, contravene.

tras'lato, a *ag* metaphorical, figurative.

traslo'care *vt* to move, transfer; **~rsi** *vr* to move; **tras'loco, chi** *sm* removal.

tras'messo, a *pp di* **trasmettere**.

tras'mettere *vt* (*passare*): **~ qc a qd** to pass sth on to sb; (*mandare*) to send; (*TECN, TEL, MED*) to transmit; (*TV, RADIO*) to broadcast; **trasmetti'tore** *sm* transmitter; **trasmissi'one** *sf* (*gen, FISICA, TECN*) transmission; (*passaggio*) transmission, passing on; (*TV, RADIO*) broadcast; **trasmit'tente** *sf* transmitting *o* broadcasting station.

traso'gnato, a [trasoɲ'nato] *ag* dreamy.

traspa'rente *ag* transparent; **traspa-'renza** *sf* transparency.

traspa'rire *vi* (2) to show (through).

traspi'rare *vi* (2) to perspire; (*fig*) to come to light, leak out; **traspirazi'one** *sf* perspiration.

traspor'tare *vt* to carry, move; (*merce*) to transport, convey; **lasciarsi ~ (da qc)** to let o.s. be carried away (by sth); **tras-'porto** *sm* transport.

trastul'lare *vt* to amuse; **~rsi** *vr* to amuse o.s.

trasu'dare *vi* (2) (*filtrare*) to ooze; (*sudare*) to sweat // *vi* to ooze with.

trasver'sale *ag* transverse, cross(-); running at right angles.

trasvo'lare *vt* to fly over // *vi* (*fig*): **~ su** to barely touch on.

'tratta *sf* (*ECON*) draft; (*di persone*): **la ~ delle bianche** the white slave trade.

tratta'mento *sm* treatment; (*servizio*) service.

trat'tare *vt* (*gen*) to treat; (*commerciare*) to deal in; (*svolgere: argomento*) to discuss, deal with; (*negoziare*) to negotiate // *vi*: ~ **di** to deal with; ~ **con** (*persona*) to deal with; **si tratta di ...** it's about ...; **tratta-'tive** *sfpl* negotiations; **trat'tato** *sm* (*testo*) treatise; (*accordo*) treaty; **trattazi'one** *sf* treatment.

tratteggi'are [tratted'dʒare] *vt* (*disegnare: a tratti*) to sketch, outline; (*: col tratteggio*) to hatch.

tratte'nere *vt* (*far rimanere: persona*) to detain; (*intrattenere: ospiti*) to entertain; (*tenere, frenare, reprimere*) to hold back, keep back; (*trattenere dal consegnare*) to hold, keep; (*detrarre: somma*) to deduct; ~**rsi** *vr* (*astenersi*) to restrain o.s., stop o.s.; (*soffermarsi*) to stay, remain.

tratteni'mento *sm* entertainment; (*festa*) party.

tratte'nuta *sf* deduction.

trat'tino *sm* dash; (*in parole composte*) hyphen.

'tratto, a *pp* di **trarre** // *sm* (*di penna, matita*) stroke; (*parte*) part, piece; (*di strada*) stretch; (*di mare, cielo*) expanse; (*di tempo*) period (of time); (*modo di comportarsi*) ways *pl*, manners *pl*; ~**i** *smpl* (*lineamenti, caratteristiche*) features; **a un** ~, **d'un** ~ suddenly.

trat'tore *sm* tractor.

tratto'ria *sf* restaurant.

'trauma, i *sm* trauma; **trau'matico, a, ci, che** *ag* traumatic.

tra'vaglio [tra'vaʎʎo] *sm* (*angoscia*) pain, suffering; (*MED*) pains *pl*; ~ **di parto** labour pains.

trava'sare *vt* to decant.

trava'tura *sf* beams *pl*.

tra'versa *sf* (*trave*) crosspiece; (*via*) sidestreet; (*FERR*) sleeper; (*CALCIO*) crossbar.

traver'sare *vt* to cross; **traver'sata** *sf* crossing; (*AER*) flight, trip.

traver'sie *sfpl* mishaps, misfortunes.

traver'sina *sf* (*FERR*) sleeper.

tra'verso, a *ag* oblique; **di** ~ *ag* askew // *av* sideways; **andare di** ~ (*cibo*) to go down the wrong way; **guardare di** ~ to look askance at.

travesti'mento *sm* disguise.

traves'tire *vt* to disguise; ~**rsi** *vr* to disguise o.s.; **traves'tito, a** *ag* disguised, in disguise // *sm* (*PSIC*) transvestite.

travi'are *vt* (*fig*) to lead astray.

travi'sare *vt* (*fig*) to distort, misrepresent.

tra'volgere [tra'vɔldʒere] *vt* to sweep away, carry away; (*fig*) to overwhelm; **tra'volto, a** *pp* di **travolgere**.

trazi'one [trat'tsjone] *sf* traction.

tre *num* three.

trebbi'are *vt* to thresh; **trebbia'trice** *sf* threshing machine.

'treccia, ce ['trettʃa] *sf* plait, braid.

tre'cento [tre'tʃɛnto] *num* three hundred // *sm*: **il T**~ the fourteenth century.

'tredici ['treditʃi] *num* thirteen.

'tregua *sf* truce; (*fig*) respite.

tre'mare *vi* to tremble, shake; ~ **di** (*freddo etc*) to shiver o tremble with; (*paura*) to shake o tremble with.

tre'mendo, a *ag* terrible, awful.

tremen'tina *sf* turpentine.

tre'mila *num* three thousand.

'tremito *sm* trembling *q*; shaking *q*; shivering *q*.

tremo'lare *vi* to tremble; (*luce*) to flicker; (*foglie*) to quiver.

tre'more *sm* tremor.

'treno *sm* train; ~ **di gomme** set of tyres; ~ **merci** goods train; ~ **viaggiatori** passenger train.

'trenta *num* thirty; **tren'tesimo, a** *ag* thirtieth; **tren'tina** *sf*: **una trentina (di)** thirty or so, about thirty.

'trepido, a *ag* anxious.

treppi'ede *sm* tripod; (*CUC*) trivet.

'tresca, sche *sf* (*fig*) intrigue; (*: relazione amorosa*) affair.

'trespolo *sm* trestle.

tri'angolo *sm* triangle.

tribolazi'one [tribolat'tsjone] *sf* suffering, tribulation.

tribù *sf inv* tribe.

tri'buna *sf* (*podio*) platform; (*in aule etc*) gallery; (*di stadio*) stand.

tribu'nale *sm* court.

tribu'tare *vt* to bestow.

tribu'tario, a *ag* (*imposta*) fiscal, tax *cpd*; (*GEO*): **essere** ~ **di** to be a tributary of.

tri'buto *sm* tax; (*fig*) tribute.

tri'checo, chi [tri'kɛko] *sm* (*ZOOL*) walrus.

tri'ciclo [tri'tʃiklo] *sm* tricycle.

trico'lore *ag* three-coloured // *sm* tricolour; (*bandiera italiana*) Italian flag.

tri'dente *sm* trident.

tri'foglio [tri'fɔʎʎo] *sm* clover.

'triglia ['triʎʎa] *sf* red mullet.

trigonome'tria *sf* trigonometry.

tril'lare *vi* (*MUS*) to trill.

tri'mestre *sm* period of three months; (*INS*) term; (*COMM*) quarter.

'trina *sf* lace.

trin'cea [trin'tʃea] *sf* trench; **trince'rare** *vt* to entrench.

trinci'are [trin'tʃare] *vt* to cut up.

Trinità *sf* (*REL*) Trinity.

'trio, pl 'trii *sm* trio.

trion'fale *ag* triumphal, triumphant.

trion'fante *ag* triumphant.

trion'fare *vi* to triumph, win; ~ **su** to triumph over, overcome; **tri'onfo** *sm* triumph.

tripli'care *vt* to triple.

'triplice ['triplitʃe] *ag* triple; **in** ~ **copia** in triplicate.

'triplo, a *ag* triple; treble // *sm*: **il** ~ (**di**) three times as much (as); **una somma** ~**a** a sum three times as great, three times as much money.

'tripode *sm* tripod.

'trippa *sf* (*CUC*) tripe.

'triste *ag* sad; (*luogo*) dreary, gloomy; **tris'tezza** *sf* sadness; gloominess.

'tristo, a *ag* (*cattivo*) wicked, evil;

(*meschino*) sorry, poor; **fare una** ~**a figura** to cut a poor figure.

trita'carne *sm inv* mincer.

tri'tare *vt* to mince.

'trito, a *ag* (*tritato*) minced.

'trittico, ci *sm* (*ARTE*) triptych.

tri'vella *sf* drill; **trivel'lare** *vt* to drill.

trivi'ale *ag* vulgar, low.

tro'feo *sm* trophy.

'trogolo *sm* (*per maiali*) trough.

'tromba *sf* (*MUS*) trumpet; (*AUT*) horn; ~ **d'aria** whirlwind; ~ **delle scale** stairwell.

trom'bone *sm* trombone.

trom'bosi *sf* thrombosis.

tron'care *vt* to cut off; (*spezzare*) to break off.

'tronco, a, chi, che *ag* cut off; broken off; (*LING*) truncated; (*fig*) cut short // *sm* (*BOT, ANAT*) trunk; (*fig: tratto*) section; (: *pezzo: di lancia*) stump.

troneggi'are [troned'dʒare] *vi:* ~ (**su**) to tower (over).

'tronfio, a *ag* conceited.

'trono *sm* throne.

tropi'cale *ag* tropical.

'tropico, ci *sm* tropic; ~**ci** *smpl* tropics.

'troppo, a *det, pronome* (*quantità*) too much; (*numero*) too many // *av* (*con vb*) too much; (*con ag, av*) too; **di** ~: **qualche tazza di** ~ a few cups too many, a few extra cups; **3000 lire di** ~ 3000 lire too much.

'trota *sf* trout.

trot'tare *vi* to trot; **trotterel'lare** *vi* to trot along; (*bambino*) to toddle; **'trotto** *sm* trot.

'trottola *sf* spinning top.

tro'vare *vt* to find; (*giudicare*): **trovo che** I find o think that; ~**rsi** *vr* (*incontrarsi*) to meet; (*essere, stare*) to be; (*arrivare, capitare*) to find o.s.; **andare a** ~ **qd** to go and see sb; ~ **qd colpevole** to find sb guilty; ~**rsi bene** to feel well; **tro'vata** *sf* good idea.

truc'care *vt* (*falsare*) to fake; (*attore etc*) to make up; (*travestire*) to disguise; (*SPORT*) to fix; (*AUT*) to soup up; ~**rsi** *vr* to make up (one's face); **trucca'tore, 'trice** *sm/f* (*CINEMA, TEATRO*) make-up artist.

'trucco, chi *sm* trick; (*cosmesi*) make-up.

'truce ['trutʃe] *ag* fierce.

truci'dare [trutʃi'dare] *vt* to slaughter.

truci'olo ['trutʃolo] *sm* shaving.

'truffa *sf* fraud, swindle; **truf'fare** *vt* to swindle, cheat.

'truppa *sf* troop.

tu *pronome* you; **dare del** ~ **a qd** to address sb as 'tu'.

'tua *vedi* **tuo**.

'tuba *sf* (*MUS*) tuba; (*cappello*) top hat.

tu'bare *vi* to coo.

tuba'tura *sf*, **tubazi'one** [tubat'tsjone] *sf* piping q, pipes *pl*.

tuberco'losi *sf* tuberculosis.

tu'betto *sm* tube.

'tubo *sm* tube; pipe; ~ **digerente** (*ANAT*)

alimentary canal, digestive tract; ~ **di scappamento** (*AUT*) exhaust pipe.

'tue *vedi* **tuo**.

tuf'fare *vt* to plunge, dip; ~**rsi** *vr* to plunge, dive; **'tuffo** *sm* dive; (*breve bagno*) dip.

tu'gurio *sm* hovel.

tuli'pano *sm* tulip.

tumefazi'one [tumefat'tsjone] *sf* (*MED*) swelling.

'tumido, a *ag* swollen.

tu'more *sm* (*MED*) tumour.

tu'multo *sm* uproar, commotion; (*sommossa*) riot; (*fig*) turmoil; **tumul-tu'oso, a** *ag* rowdy, unruly; (*fig*) turbulent, stormy.

'tunica, che *sf* tunic.

Tuni'sia *sf:* **la** ~ Tunisia.

'tuo, 'tua, tu'oi, 'tue *det:* **il** ~, **la tua** *etc* your // *pronome:* **il** ~, **la tua** *etc* yours.

tuo'nare *vi* to thunder; **tuona** it is thundering, there's some thunder.

tu'ono *sm* thunder.

tu'orlo *sm* yoik.

tu'racciolo [tu'rattʃolo] *sm* cap, top; (*di sughero*) cork.

tu'rare *vt* to stop, plug; (*con sughero*) to cork; ~**rsi il naso** to hold one's nose.

turba'mento *sm* disturbance; (*di animo*) anxiety, agitation.

tur'bante *sm* turban.

tur'bare *vt* to disturb, trouble.

tur'bina *sf* turbine.

turbi'nare *vi* to whirl.

'turbine *sm* whirlwind; ~ **di polvere/sabbia** dust/sandstorm.

turbo'lento, a *ag* turbulent; (*ragazzo*) boisterous, unruly.

turbo'lenza [turbo'lentsa] *sf* turbulence.

turboreat'tore *sm* turbojet engine.

tur'chese [tur'kese] *sf* turquoise.

Tur'chia [tur'kia] *sf:* **la** ~ Turkey.

tur'chino, a [tur'kino] *ag* deep blue.

'turco, a, chi, che *ag* Turkish // *sm/f* Turk/Turkish woman // *sm* (*LING*) Turkish.

tu'rismo *sm* tourism; tourist industry; **tu-'rista, i, e** *sm/f* tourist; **tu'ristico, a, ci, che** *ag* tourist *cpd*.

'turno *sm* turn; (*di lavoro*) shift; **di** ~ (*soldato, medico, custode*) on duty; **a** ~ (*rispondere*) in turn; (*lavorare*) in shifts; **fare a** ~ **a fare qc** to take turns to do sth; **è il suo** ~ it's your (o his *etc*) turn.

'turpe *ag* filthy, vile; **turpi'loquio** *sm* obscene language.

'tuta *sf* overalls *pl*; (*SPORT*) tracksuit.

tu'tela *sf* (*DIR: di minore*) guardianship; (: *protezione*) protection; (*difesa*) defence; **tute'lare** *vt* to protect, defend.

tu'tore, 'trice *sm/f* (*DIR*) guardian.

tutta'via *cong* nevertheless, yet.

'tutto, a *det* all; ~ **il latte** all the milk, the whole of the milk; ~**a la sera** all evening, the whole evening; ~**a una bottiglia** a whole bottle; ~**i i ragazzi** all the boys; ~**e le sere** every evening //

pronome everything, all; ~**i(e)** *pronome pl* all (of them); (*ognuno*) everyone // *av* (*completamente*) completely, quite // *sm* whole; (*l'intero*): **il ~** all of it, the whole lot; ~**i e due** both *o* each of us (*o* them); ~**i e cinque** all five of us (*o* them); **a ~a velocità** at full *o* top speed; **del ~** completely; **in ~** in all; **tutt'altro** on the contrary; (*affatto*) not at all; **tutt'altro che felice** anything but happy; ~ **considerato** all things considered; **a tutt'oggi** so far, up till now; **tutt'al più** at (the) most; (*al più tardi*) at the latest; ~**e le volte che** every time (that).

tutto'fare *ag inv*: **domestica ~** general maid; **ragazzo ~** office boy // *sm inv* handyman.

tut'tora *av* still.

U

ubbidi'ente *ag* obedient; **ubbidi'enza** *sf* obedience.

ubbi'dire *vi* to obey; ~ **a** to obey; (*sog: veicolo, macchina*) to respond to.

ubiquità *sf:* **non ho il dono dell'~** I can't be everywhere at once.

ubria'care *vt:* ~ **qd** to get sb drunk; (*sog: alcool*) to make sb drunk; (*fig*) to make sb's head spin *o* reel; ~**rsi** *vr* to get drunk; ~**rsi di** (*fig*) to become intoxicated with.

ubria'chezza [ubria'kettsa] *sf* drunkenness.

ubri'aco, a, chi, che *ag, sm/f* drunk.

uccelli'era [uttʃel'ljɛra] *sf* aviary.

uc'cello [ut'tʃello] *sm* bird.

uc'cidere [ut'tʃidere] *vt* to kill; ~**rsi** *vr* (*suicidarsi*) to kill o.s.; (*perdere la vita*) to be killed; **uccisi'one** *sf* killing; **uc'ciso, a** *pp di* **uccidere**; **ucci'sore, uccidi'trice** *sm/f* killer.

u'dibile *ag* audible.

udi'enza [u'djentsa] *sf* audience; (*DIR*) hearing, sitting.

u'dire *vt* to hear; **udi'tivo, a** *ag* auditory; **u'dito** *sm* (sense of) hearing; **udi'tore, 'trice** *sm/f* listener; (*INS*) unregistered student (*attending lectures*); **udi'torio** *sm* (*persone*) audience.

uffici'ale [uffi'tʃale] *ag* official // *sm* (*AMM*) official, officer; (*MIL*) officer; ~ **di stato civile** registrar.

uf'ficio [uf'fitʃo] *sm* (*gen*) office; (*dovere*) duty; (*mansione*) task, function, job; (*agenzia*) agency, bureau; (*REL*) service; **d'~** *ag* office *cpd*; official // *av* officially; ~ **di collocamento** employment office; ~ **postale** post office.

uffici'oso, a [uffi'tʃoso] *ag* unofficial.

'ufo: a ~ *av* free, for nothing.

uggi'oso, a [ud'dʒoso] *ag* tiresome; (*tempo*) dull.

uguagli'anza [ugwaʎ'ʎantsa] *sf* equality.

uguagli'are [ugwaʎ'ʎare] *vt* to make equal; (*essere uguale*) to equal, be equal to; (*livellare*) to level; ~**rsi a** *o* **con qd** (*paragonarsi*) to compare o.s. to sb.

ugu'ale *ag* equal; (*identico*) identical, the

same; (*uniforme*) level, even; **ugual'mente** *av* equally; (*lo stesso*) all the same.

'ulcera ['ultʃera] *sf* ulcer.

u'liva *etc* = **oliva** *etc*.

ulteri'ore *ag* further.

ulti'mare *vt* to finish, complete.

ulti'matum *sm inv* ultimatum.

'ultimo, a *ag* (*finale*) last; (*estremo*) farthest, utmost; (*recente: notizia, moda*) latest; (*fig: sommo, fondamentale*) ultimate // *sm/f* last (one); **fino all'~** to the last, until the end; **da ~, in ~** in the end; **abitare all'~ piano** to live on the top floor.

ultravio'letto, a *ag* ultraviolet.

ulu'lare *vi* to howl; **ulu'lato** *sm* howling *q*; howl.

umanità *sf* humanity; **umani'tario, a** *ag* humanitarian.

u'mano, a *ag* human; (*comprensivo*) humane.

umbi'lico *sm* = **ombelico**.

umet'tare *vt* to dampen, moisten.

umidità *sf* dampness; humidity.

'umido, a *ag* damp; (*mano, occhi*) moist; (*clima*) humid // *sm* dampness; **carne in ~** stew.

'umile *ag* humble.

umili'are *vt* to humiliate; ~**rsi** *vr* to humble o.s.; **umiliazi'one** *sf* humiliation.

umiltà *sf* humility, humbleness.

u'more *sm* (*disposizione d'animo*) mood; (*carattere*) temper; **di buon/cattivo ~** in a good/bad mood.

umo'rismo *sm* humour; **avere il senso dell'~** to have a sense of humour; **umo'rista, i, e** *sm/f* humorist; **umo'ristico, a, ci, che** *ag* humorous, funny.

un, un', una *vedi* **uno**.

u'nanime *ag* unanimous; **unanimità** *sf* unanimity; **all'unanimità** unanimously.

unci'netto [untʃi'netto] *sm* crochet hook.

un'cino [un'tʃino] *sm* hook.

'undici ['unditʃi] *num* eleven.

'ungere ['undʒere] *vt* to grease, oil; (*REL*) to anoint; (*fig*) to flatter, butter up; ~**rsi** *vr* (*sporcarsi*) to get covered in grease; ~**rsi con la crema** to put on cream.

unghe'rese [unge'rese] *ag, sm/f, sm* Hungarian.

Unghe'ria [unge'ria] *sf:* **l'~** Hungary.

'unghia ['ungja] *sf* (*ANAT*) nail; (*di animale*) claw; (*di rapace*) talon; (*di cavallo*) hoof; **unghi'ata** *sf* (*graffio*) scratch.

ungu'ento *sm* ointment.

'unico, a, ci, che *ag* (*solo*) only; (*ineguagliabile*) unique; (*singolo: binario*) single.

uni'corno *sm* unicorn.

unifi'care *vt* to unite, unify; (*sistemi*) to standardize; **unificazi'one** *sf* uniting; unification; standardization.

uni'forme *ag* uniform; (*superficie*) even // *sf* (*divisa*) uniform; **uniformità** *sf* uniformity; evenness.

unilate'rale *ag* one-sided; (*DIR*) unilateral.

uni'one *sf* union; (*fig: concordia*) unity, harmony; **l'U~ Sovietica** the Soviet Union.

u'nire *vt* to unite; (*congiungere*) to join, connect; (*: ingredienti, colori*) to combine; (*in matrimonio*) to unite, join together; **~rsi** *vr* to unite; (*in matrimonio*) to be joined together; **~ qc a** to unite sth with; to join *o* connect sth with; to combine sth with; **~rsi a** (*gruppo, società*) to join.

u'nisono *sm:* **all'~** in unison.

unità *sf inv* (*unione, concordia*) unity; (*MAT, MIL, COMM, di misura*) unit; **uni'tario, a** *ag* unitary; **prezzo unitario** price per unit.

u'nito, a *ag* (*paese*) united; (*famiglia*) close; (*tinta*) solid.

univer'sale *ag* universal; general.

università *sf inv* university; **universi'tario, a** *ag* university *cpd* // *sm/f* (*studente*) university student; (*insegnante*) academic, university lecturer.

uni'verso *sm* universe.

'uno, a *det, num* (*dav sm un + C, V, uno + s impura, gn, pn, ps, x, z; dav sf un' + V, una + C*) *det* a, an + *vocale* // *num* one // *pronome* (*un tale*) someone, somebody; (*con valore impersonale*) one, you // *sf:* **è l'~a** it's one o'clock.

'unto, a *pp di* **ungere** // *ag* greasy, oily // *sm* grease; **untu'oso, a** *ag* greasy, oily.

u'omo, *pl* **u'omini** *sm* man; **da ~** (*abito, scarpe*) men's, for men; **~ d'affari** businessman; **~ di paglia** stooge; **~ rana** frogman.

u'opo *sm:* **all'~** if necessary.

u'ovo, *pl(f)* **u'ova** *sm* egg; **~ affogato** poached egg; **~ bazzotto/sodo** soft-/hard-boiled egg; **~ alla coque** boiled egg; **~ di Pasqua** Easter egg; **uova strapazzate** scrambled eggs.

ura'gano *sm* hurricane.

u'ranio *sm* (*CHIM*) uranium.

urba'nesimo *sm* urbanization.

urba'nistica *sf* town planning.

ur'bano, a *ag* urban, city *cpd*, town *cpd*; (*fig*) urbane.

ur'gente [ur'dʒente] *ag* urgent; **ur'genza** *sf* urgency; **in caso d'urgenza** in (case of) an emergency; **d'urgenza** *ag* emergency // *av* urgently, as a matter of urgency.

'urgere [urdʒere] *vi* to be urgent; to be needed urgently.

u'rina *sf* = **orina**.

ur'lare *vi* (*persona*) to scream, yell; (*animale, vento*) to howl // *vt* to scream, yell.

'urlo, *pl(m)* **'urli,** *pl(f)* **'urla** *sm* scream, yell; howl.

'urna *sf* urn; (*elettorale*) ballot-box; **andare alle ~e** to go to the polls.

urrà *escl* hurrah!

U.R.S.S. *abbr f:* **l'~** the USSR.

ur'tare *vt* to bump into, knock against; (*fig: irritare*) to annoy // *vi:* **~ contro** *o* **in** to bump into, knock against, crash into; (*fig: imbattersi*) to come up against; **~rsi**

vr (*reciproco: scontrarsi*) to collide; (*: fig*) to clash; (*irritarsi*) to get annoyed; **'urto** *sm* (*colpo*) knock, bump; (*scontro*) crash, collision; (*fig*) clash.

U.S.A. ['uza] *abbr mpl:* **gli ~** the U.S.A.

u'sanza [u'zantsa] *sf* custom; (*moda*) fashion.

u'sare *vt* to use, employ // *vi* (*servirsi*): **~ di** to use; (*: diritto*) to exercise; (*essere di moda*) to be fashionable; (*essere solito*): **~ fare** to be in the habit of doing, be accustomed to doing; **u'sato, a** *ag* used; (*consumato*) worn; (*di seconda mano*) used, second-hand; **secondo l'usato** as usual; **fuori dell'usato** unusual.

usci'ere [uʃʃere] *sm* usher.

'uscio ['uʃʃo] *sm* door.

u'scire [uʃʃire] *vi* (2) (*gen*) to come out; (*partire, andare a passeggio, a uno spettacolo etc*) to go out; (*essere sorteggiato: numero*) to come up; **~ da** (*gen*) to leave; (*posto*) to go (*o* come) out of, leave; (*solco, vasca etc*) to come out of; (*muro*) to stick out of; (*competenza etc*) to be outside; (*infanzia, adolescenza*) to leave behind; (*famiglia nobile etc*) to come from; **~ da** *o* **di casa** to go out; (*fig*) to leave home; **~ in automobile** to go out in the car, go for a drive; **~ di strada** (*AUT*) to go off *o* leave the road.

u'scita [uʃʃita] *sf* (*passaggio, varco*) exit, way out; (*per divertimento*) outing; (*ECON: somma*) expenditure; (*TEATRO*) entrance; (*fig: battuta*) witty remark; **~ di sicurezza** emergency exit.

usi'gnolo [uziɲ'ɲɔlo] *sm* nightingale.

'uso *sm* (*utilizzazione*) use; (*esercizio*) practice; (*abitudine*) custom; **a ~ di** for (the use of); **d'~** (*corrente*) in use; **fuori ~** out of use.

usti'one *sf* burn.

usu'ale *ag* common, everyday.

u'sura *sf* usury; (*logoramento*) wear (and tear); **usu'raio** *sm* usurer.

usur'pare *vt* to usurp.

uten'sile *sm* tool, implement; **~i da cucina** kitchen utensils.

u'tente *sm/f* user.

'utero *sm* uterus.

'utile *ag* useful // *sm* . (*vantaggio*) advantage, benefit; (*ECON: profitto*) profit; **utilità** *sf* usefulness *q*; use; (*vantaggio*) benefit; **utili'tario, a** *ag* utilitarian // *sf* (*AUT*) economy car.

utiliz'zare [utilid'dzare] *vt* to use, make use of, utilize; **utilizzazi'one** *sf* utilization, use.

'uva *sf* grapes *pl;* **~ passa** raisins *pl;* **~ spina** gooseberry.

V

v. (*abbr di vedi*) v.

va'cante *ag* vacant.

va'canza [va'kantsa] *sf* (*l'essere vacante*) vacancy; (*riposo, ferie*) holiday(s *pl*); (*giorno di permesso*) day off, holiday; **~e** *sfpl* (*periodo di ferie*) holidays, vacation *sg;*

essere/andare in ~ to be/go on holiday; ~ e estive summer holiday(s).

'vacca, che sf cow.

vacci'nare [vatt∫i'nare] vt to vaccinate; vaccinazi'one sf vaccination.

vac'cino [vat't∫ino] sm (MED) vaccine.

vacil'lare [vat∫il'lare] vi to sway, wobble; (luce) to flicker; (fig: memoria, coraggio) to be failing, falter.

'vacuo, a ag (fig) empty, vacuous // sm vacuum.

vaga'bondo, a sm/f tramp, vagrant; (fannullone) idler, loafer.

va'gare vi to wander.

vagheggi'are [vaged'dʒare] vt to long for, dream of.

va'gina [va'dʒina] sf vagina.

va'gire [va'dʒire] vi to whimper.

'vaglia ['vaʎʎa] sm inv money order; ~ postale postal order.

vagli'are [vaʎ'ʎare] vt to sift; (fig) to weigh up; 'vaglio sm sieve.

'vago, a, ghi, ghe ag vague.

va'gone sm (FERR: per passeggeri) coach; (: per merci) truck, wagon; ~ letto sleeper, sleeping car; ~ ristorante dining o restaurant car.

vai'olo sm smallpox.

va'langa, ghe sf avalanche.

va'lente ag able, talented.

va'lere vi (2) (avere forza, potenza) to have influence; (essere valido) to be valid; (avere vigore, autorità) to hold, apply; (essere capace: poeta, studente) to be good, be able // vt (prezzo, sforzo) to be worth; (corrispondere) to correspond to; (procurare): ~ qc a qd to earn sb sth; ~ rsi di to make use of, take advantage of; far ~ (autorità etc) to assert; vale a dire that is to say; ~ la pena to be worth the effort o worth it.

va'levole ag valid.

vali'care vt to cross.

'valico, chi sm (passo) pass.

validità sf validity.

'valido, a ag valid; (in buona salute) fit; (efficace) effective; (forte) strong.

valige'ria [validʒe'ria] sf leather goods pl; leather goods factory; leather goods shop.

va'ligia, gie o ge [va'lidʒa] sf (suit)case; fare le ~ gie to pack (up); ~ diplomatica diplomatic bag.

val'lata sf valley.

'valle sf valley; a ~ (di fiume) downstream; scendere a ~ to go downhill.

vàl'letto sm valet.

va'lore sm (gen) value; (merito) merit, worth; (coraggio) valour, courage; (COMM: titolo) security; ~ i smpl (oggetti preziosi) valuables; mettere in ~ (bene) to exploit; (fig) to highlight, show off to advantage.

valoriz'zare [valorid'dzare] vt (terreno) to develop; (fig) to make the most of.

valo'roso, a ag valorous.

'valso, a pp di valere.

va'luta sf currency, money; (BANCA): ~ 15 gennaio interest to run from January 15th.

valu'tare vt (casa, gioiello, fig) to value; (stabilire: peso, entrate, fig) to estimate; valutazi'one sf valuation; estimate.

'valva sf (ZOOL, BOT) valve.

'valvola sf (TECN, ANAT) valve; (ELETTR) fuse.

'valzer ['valtser] sm inv waltz.

vam'pata sf (di fiamma) blaze; (di calore) blast; (: al viso) flush.

vam'piro sm vampire.

vanda'lismo sm vandalism.

'vandalo sm vandal.

vaneggi'are [vaned'dʒare] vi to rave.

'vanga, ghe sf spade; van'gare vt to dig.

van'gelo [van'dʒɛlo] sm gospel.

va'niglia [va'niʎʎa] sf vanilla.

vanità sf vanity; vani'toso, a ag vain, conceited.

'vano, a ag vain // sm (spazio) space; (apertura) opening; (stanza) room.

van'taggio [van'taddʒo] sm advantage; portarsi in ~ (SPORT) to take the lead; vantaggi'oso, a ag advantageous; favourable.

van'tare vt to praise, speak highly of; ~ rsi vr to boast; vante'ria sf boasting; 'vanto sm boasting; (merito) virtue, merit; (gloria) pride.

'vanvera sf: a ~ haphazardly; parlare a ~ to talk nonsense.

va'pore sm vapour; (anche: ~ acqueo) steam; (nave) steamer; a ~ (turbina etc) steam cpd; al ~ (CUC) steamed; vapo'retto sm steamer; vapori'era sf (FERR) steam engine; vaporiz'zare vt to vaporize.

va'rare vt (NAUT, fig) to launch; (DIR) to pass.

var'care vt to cross.

'varco, chi sm passage; aprirsi un ~ tra la folla to push one's way through the crowd.

vari'abile ag variable; (tempo, umore) changeable, variable // sf (MAT) variable.

vari'ante sf variant.

vari'are vt to vary // vi to vary; (subire variazioni) to vary, change; ~ di camera/opinione to change rooms/one's mind; variazi'one sf variation; change.

va'rice [va'rit∫e] sf varicose vein.

vari'cella [vari't∫ɛlla] sf chickenpox.

vari'coso, a ag varicose.

varie'gato, a ag variegated.

varietà sf inv variety // sm inv variety show.

'vario, a ag varied; (parecchi: col sostantivo al pl) various; (mutevole: umore) changeable; vario'pinto, a ag multicoloured.

'varo sm (NAUT, fig) launch; (di leggi) passing.

va'saio sm potter.

'vasca, **sche** *sf* basin; (*anche:* ~ **da bagno**) bathtub, bath.

va'scello [va'ʃɛllo] *sm* (NAUT) vessel, ship.

vase'lina *sf* vaseline.

vasel'lame *sm* china; ~ d'oro/d'argento gold/silver plate.

'vaso *sm* (*recipiente*) pot; (: *barattolo*) jar; (: *decorativo*) vase; (ANAT) vessel; ~ da fiori vase; (*per piante*) flowerpot.

vas'soio *sm* tray.

'vasto, a *ag* vast, immense.

Vati'cano *sm*: il ~ the Vatican.

ve *pronome, av vedi* **vi**.

vecchi'aia [vek'kjaja] *sf* old age.

'vecchio, a ['vɛkkjo] *ag* old // *sm/f* old man/woman; i ~i the old.

'vece ['vetʃe] *sf*: in ~ di in the place of, for; fare le ~i di qd to take sb's place.

ve'dere *vt, vi* to see; ~rsi *vr* to meet, see one another; avere a che ~ con to have sth to do with; far ~ qc a qd to show sb sth; farsi ~ to show o.s.; (*farsi vivo*) to show one's face.

ve'detta *sf* (*sentinella, posto*) look-out; (NAUT) patrol boat.

'vedovo, a *sm/f* widower/widow.

ve'duta *sf* view.

vee'mente *ag* vehement; violent.

vege'tale [vedʒe'tale] *ag, sm* vegetable.

vege'tare [vedʒe'tare] *vi* to vegetate; vegetari'ano, a *ag, sm/f* vegetarian; vegetazi'one *sf* vegetation.

'vegeto, a ['vɛdʒeto] *ag* (*pianta*) thriving; (*persona*) strong, vigorous.

'veglia ['veʎʎa] *sf* wakefulness; (*sorveglianza*) watch; (*trattenimento*) evening gathering; stare a ~ to keep watch; fare la ~ a un malato to watch over a sick person.

vegli'are [veʎ'ʎare] *vi* to be awake; to stay o sit up; (*stare vigile*) to watch; to keep watch // *vt* (*malato, morto*) to watch over, sit up with.

ve'icolo *sm* vehicle.

'vela *sf* (NAUT: *tela*) sail; (*sport*) sailing.

ve'lare *vt* to veil; ~rsi *vr* (*occhi, luna*) to mist over; (*voce*) to become husky; ~rsi il viso to cover one's face (with a veil); ve'lato, a *ag* veiled.

veleggi'are [veled'dʒare] *vi* to sail; (AER) to glide.

ve'leno *sm* poison; vele'noso, a *ag* poisonous.

veli'ero *sm* sailing ship.

ve'lina *sf* (*anche*: carta ~: *per imballare*) tissue paper; (: *per copie*) flimsy paper; (*copia*) carbon copy.

ve'livolo *sm* aircraft.

velleità *sf inv* vain ambition, vain desire.

'vello *sm* fleece.

vel'luto *sm* velvet; ~ a coste cord.

'velo *sm* veil; (*tessuto*) voile.

ve'loce [ve'lotʃe] *ag* fast, quick // *av* fast, quickly; velo'cista, i, e *sm/f* (*sport*) sprinter; velocità *sf* speed; (AUT: *marcia*) gear; velocità di crociera cruising speed; velocità del suono speed of sound.

ve'lodromo *sm* velodrome.

'vena *sf* (*gen*) vein; (*filone*) vein, seam; (*fig: ispirazione*) inspiration; (: *umore*) mood; essere in ~ di qc to be in the mood for sth.

ve'nale *ag* (*prezzo, valore*) market *cpd*; (*fig*) venal; mercenary.

ven'demmia *sf* (*raccolta*) grape harvest; (*quantità d'uva*) grape crop, grapes *pl*; (*vino ottenuto*) vintage; vendemmi'are *vt* to harvest // *vi* to harvest the grapes.

'vendere *vt* to sell; 'vendesi 'for sale'.

ven'detta *sf* revenge.

vendi'care *vt* to avenge; ~rsi *vr*: ~rsi (di) to avenge o.s. (for); (*per rancore*) to take one's revenge (for); vendica'tivo, a *ag* vindictive.

'vendita *sf* sale; la ~ (*attività*) selling; (*smercio*) sales *pl*; in ~ on sale; ~ all'asta sale by auction; vendi'tore *sm* seller, vendor; (*gestore di negozio*) trader, dealer.

ve'nefico, a, ci, che *ag* poisonous.

vene'rabile *ag*, vene'rando, a *ag* venerable.

vene'rare *vt* to venerate.

venerdì *sm inv* Friday; di o il ~ on Fridays; V~ Santo Good Friday.

ve'nereo, a *ag* venereal.

Ve'nezia [ve'nɛttsja] *sf* Venice; venezi'ano, a *ag, sm/f* Venetian.

veni'ale *ag* venial.

ve'nire *vi* (2) to come; (*riuscire: dolce, fotografia*) to turn out; (*come ausiliare: essere*): viene ammirato da tutti he is admired by everyone; ~ da to come from; quanto viene? how much does it cost?; far ~ (*mandare a chiamare*) to send for; ~ giù to come down; ~ meno (*svenire*) to faint; ~ meno a qc to fail in sth; ~ su to come up; ~ via to come away.

ven'taglio [ven'taʎʎo] *sm* fan.

ven'tata *sf* gust (of wind).

ven'tenne *ag*: una ragazza ~ a twenty-year-old girl, a girl of twenty.

ven'tesimo, a *ag, sm* twentieth.

'venti *num* twenty.

venti'lare *vt* to ventilate; (*fig: esaminare*) to discuss; ventila'tore *sm* ventilator, fan; ventilazi'one *sf* ventilation.

ven'tina *sf*: una ~ (di) around twenty, twenty or so.

'vento *sm* wind.

ven'tosa *sf* (ZOOL) sucker; (*di gomma*) suction pad.

ven'toso, a *ag* windy.

'ventre *sm* stomach.

ven'triloquo *sm* ventriloquist.

ven'tura *sf* (*good*) fortune.

ven'turo, a *ag* next, coming.

ve'nuto, a *pp di* venire // *sf* coming, arrival.

vera'mente *av* really.

ve'randa *sf* veranda(h).

ver'bale ag verbal // sm (di riunione) minutes pl.

'verbo sm (LING) verb; (parola) word; (REL): il V~ the Word.

ver'boso, a ag verbose, wordy.

'verde ag, sm green; **essere al ~** to be broke; **~ bottiglia/oliva** ag inv bottle/olive green.

verde'rame sm verdigris.

ver'detto sm verdict.

ver'dura sf vegetables pl.

vere'condo, a ag modest.

'verga, ghe sf rod.

ver'gato a ag (foglio) ruled.

vergi'nale [verdʒi'nale] ag virginal.

'vergine ['verdʒine] sf virgin; (dello zodiaco): V~ Virgo // ag virgin; (ragazza): **essere ~** to be a virgin; **verginità** sf virginity.

ver'gogna [ver'goɲɲa] sf shame; (timidezza) shyness, embarrassment; **vergo'gnarsi** vr: **vergognarsi (di)** to be o feel ashamed (of); to be shy (about), be embarrassed (about); **vergo'gnoso, a** ag ashamed; (timido) shy, embarrassed; (causa di vergogna: azione) shameful.

ve'ridico, a, ci, che ag truthful.

ve'rifica, che sf checking q, check.

verifi'care vt (controllare) to check; (confermare) to confirm, bear out.

verità sf inv truth.

veriti'ero, a ag (che dice la verità) truthful; (conforme a verità) true.

'verme sm worm.

vermi'celli [vermi'tʃelli] smpl vermicelli sg.

ver'miglio [ver'miʎʎo] sm vermilion, scarlet.

'vermut sm inv vermouth.

ver'nacolo sm vernacular.

ver'nice [ver'nitʃe] sf (colorazione) paint; (trasparente) varnish; (pelle) patent leather; (fig) veneer; **vernici'are** vt to paint; to varnish; **vernicia'tura** sf painting; varnishing.

'vero, a ag (veridico: fatti, testimonianza) true; (autentico) real // sm (verità) truth; (realtà) (real) life; **un ~ e proprio delinquente** a real criminal, an out and out criminal.

vero'simile ag likely, probable.

ver'ruca, che sf wart.

versa'mento sm (pagamento) payment; (deposito di denaro) deposit.

ver'sante sm slopes pl, side.

ver'sare vt (fare uscire: vino, farina) to pour (out); (spargere: lacrime, sangue) to shed; (rovesciare) to spill; (ECON) to pay; (: depositare) to deposit, pay in; **~rsi** vr (rovesciarsi) to spill; (fiume, folla): **~rsi (in)** to pour (into).

versa'tile ag versatile.

ver'sato, a ag: **~ in** to be (well-) versed in.

ver'setto sm (REL) verse.

versi'one sf version; (traduzione) translation.

'verso sm (di poesia) verse, line; (di animale, uccello, venditore ambulante) cry; (direzione) direction; (modo) way; (di foglio di carta) verso; (di moneta) reverse; **~i** smpl (poesia) verse sg; **non c'è ~ di persuaderlo** there's no way of persuading him, he can't be persuaded // prep (in direzione di) toward(s); (nei pressi di) near, around (about); (in senso temporale) about, around; **~ di me** towards me; **~ pagamento** (COMM) upon payment.

'vertebra sf vertebra.

verti'cale ag, sf vertical.

'vertice ['vertitʃe] sm summit, top; (MAT) vertex; **conferenza al ~** (POL) summit conference.

ver'tigine [ver'tidʒine] sf dizziness q; dizzy spell; (MED) vertigo; **avere le ~i** to feel dizzy; **vertigi'noso, a** ag (altezza) dizzy; (fig) breathtakingly high (o deep etc).

ve'scica, che [veʃ'ʃika] sf (ANAT) bladder; (MED) blister.

'vescovo sm bishop.

'vespa sf wasp.

'vespro sm (REL) vespers pl.

ves'sillo sm standard; (bandiera) flag.

ves'taglia [ves'taʎʎa] sf dressing gown.

'veste sf garment; (rivestimento) covering; (qualità, facoltà) capacity; **~i** sfpl clothes, clothing sg; **in ~ ufficiale** (fig) in an official capacity; **in ~ di** in the guise of, as; **vesti'ario** sm wardrobe, clothes pl.

ves'tibolo sm (entrance) hall.

ves'tigio, pl(m) gi o pl(f) gia [ves'tidʒo] sm trace.

ves'tire vt (bambino, malato) to dress; (avere indosso) to have on, wear; **~rsi** vr to dress, get dressed; **ves'tito, a** ag dressed // sm garment; (da donna) dress; (da uomo) suit; **vestiti** smpl clothes; **vestito di bianco** dressed in white.

Ve'suvio sm: **il ~** Vesuvius.

vete'rano, a ag, sm/f veteran.

veteri'nario, a ag veterinary // sm veterinary surgeon, vet // sf veterinary medicine.

'veto sm inv veto.

ve'traio sm glassmaker; glazier.

ve'trato, a ag (porta, finestra) glazed; (che contiene vetro) glass cpd // sf glass door (o window); (di chiesa) stained glass window.

vetre'ria sf (stabilimento) glassworks sg; (oggetti di vetro) glassware.

ve'trina sf (di negozio) (shop) window; (armadio) display cabinet; **vetri'nista, i, e** sm/f window dresser.

vetri'olo sm vitriol.

'vetro sm glass; (per finestra, porta) pane (of glass); **ve'troso, a** ag vitreous.

'vetta sf peak, summit, top.

vet'tore sm (MAT, FISICA) vector; (DIR) carrier.

vetto'vaglie [vetto'vaʎʎe] sfpl supplies.

vet'tura sf (carrozza, FERR) carriage; (autovettura) (motor) car.

vezzeggi'are [vettsed'dʒare] vt to fondle,

caress; **vezzeggia'tivo** *sm* (*LING*) term of endearment.

'vezzo ['vettso] *sm* habit; **~i** *smpl* (*smancerie*) affected ways; (*leggiadria*) charms; **vez'zoso, a** *ag* (*grazioso*) charming, pretty; (*lezioso*) affected.

vi, *dav lo, la, li, le, ne diventa* **ve** *pronome* (*oggetto*) you; (*complemento di termine*) (to) you; (*riflessivo*) yourselves; (*reciproco*) each other // *av* (*lì*) there; (*qui*) here; **~ è/sono** there is/are.

'via *sf* (*gen*) way; (*strada*) street; (*sentiero, pista*) path, track; (*AMM: procedimento*) channels *pl* // *prep* (*passando per*) via, by way of // *av* away // *escl* go away!; (*suvvia*) come on!; (*SPORT*) go! // *sm* (*SPORT*) starting signal; **per ~ di** (*a causa di*) because of, on account of; **per ~ d'esempio** by way of example; **in o per ~ che** the way; **per ~ aerea** by air; (*lettere*) by airmail; **~ ~ che** (*a mano a mano*) as; **dare il ~** (*SPORT*) to give the starting signal; **dare il ~ a** (*fig*) to start; **V~ lattea** (*ASTR*) Milky Way; **~ di mezzo** middle course; **in ~ provvisoria** provisionally.

viabilità *sf* (*di strada*) practicability; (*rete stradale*) roads *pl*, road network.

via'dotto *sm* viaduct.

viaggi'are [viad'dʒare] *vi* to travel; **viaggia'tore, 'trice** *ag* travelling // *sm* traveller; (*passeggero*) passenger.

vi'aggio ['vjaddʒo] *sm* travel(ling); (*tragitto*) journey, trip; **~ di nozze** honeymoon.

vi'ale *sm* avenue.

via'vai *sm* coming and going, bustle.

vi'brare *vi* to vibrate; (*agitarsi*): **~ (di)** to quiver (with); **vibrazi'one** *sf* vibration.

vi'cario *sm* (*apostolico etc*) vicar.

'vice ['vitʃe] *sm/f* deputy // *prefisso*: **~'console** *sm* vice-consul; **~diret'tore** *sm* assistant manager.

vi'cenda [vi'tʃenda] *sf* event; **a ~** in turn; **vicen'devole** *ag* mutual, reciprocal.

vice'versa [vitʃe'versa] *av* vice versa; **da Roma a Pisa e ~** from Rome to Pisa and back.

vici'nanza [vitʃi'nantsa] *sf* nearness, closeness; **~e** *sfpl* neighbourhood, vicinity.

vici'nato [vitʃi'nato] *sm* neighbourhood; (*vicini*) neighbours *pl*.

vi'cino, a [vi'tʃino] *ag* (*gen*) near; (*nello spazio*) near, nearby; (*accanto*) next; (*nel tempo*) near, close at hand // *sm/f* neighbour // *av* near, close; **da ~** (*guardare*) close up; (*esaminare, seguire*) closely; (*conoscere*) well, intimately; **~ a** *prep* near (to), close to; (*accanto a*) beside; **~ di casa** neighbour.

vicissi'tudini [vitʃissi'tudini] *sfpl* trials and tribulations.

'vicolo *sm* alley; **~ cieco** blind alley.

vie'tare *vt* to forbid; (*AMM*) to prohibit; **~ a qd di fare** to forbid sb to do; to prohibit sb from doing; **'vietato**

fumare/l'ingresso' 'no smoking/admittance'.

vi'gente [vi'dʒɛnte] *ag* in force.

vigi'lante [vidʒi'lante] *ag* vigilant, watchful; **vigi'lanza** *sf* vigilance.

vigi'lare [vidʒi'lare] *vt* to watch over, keep an eye on // *vi*: **~ a** to attend to, see to; **~ che** to make sure that, see to it that.

'vigile ['vidʒile] *ag* watchful // *sm* (*anche*: **~ urbano**) policeman (*in towns*); **~ del fuoco** fireman.

vi'gilia [vi'dʒilja] *sf* (*giorno antecedente*) eve; **la ~ di Natale** Christmas Eve.

vigli'acco, a, chi, che [viʎ'ʎakko] *ag* cowardly // *sm/f* coward.

'vigna ['viɲɲa] *sf*, **vi'gneto** [viɲ'ɲeto] *sm* vineyard.

vi'gnetta [viɲ'ɲetta] *sf* cartoon.

vi'gore *sm* vigour; (*DIR*): **essere/entrare in ~** to be in/come into force; **vigo'roso, a** *ag* vigorous.

'vile *ag* (*spregevole*) low, mean, base; (*codardo*) cowardly.

vili'pendio *sm* contempt, scorn; public insult.

'villa *sf* villa.

vil'laggio [vil'laddʒo] *sm* village.

villa'nia *sf* rudeness, lack of manners; **fare/dire una ~ a qd** to be rude to sb.

vil'lano, a *ag* rude, ill-mannered // *sm* boor.

villeggi'are [villed'dʒare] *vi* to holiday, spend one's holidays; **villeggia'tura** *sf* holiday(s *pl*).

vil'lino *sm* small house (with a garden), cottage.

vil'loso, a *ag* hairy.

viltà *sf* cowardice *q*; cowardly act.

'vimine *sm* wicker; **mobili di ~i** wicker furniture *sg*.

'vincere ['vintʃere] *vt* (*in guerra, al gioco, una gara*) to defeat, beat; (*premio, guerra, partita*) to win; (*fig*) to overcome, conquer // *vi* to win; **~ qd in bellezza** to be better-looking than sb; **'vincita** *sf* win; (*denaro vinto*) winnings *pl*; **vinci'tore** *sm* winner; (*MIL*) victor.

vinco'lare *vt* to bind; (*COMM: denaro*) to tie up; **'vincolo** *sm* (*fig*) bond, tie; (*DIR: servitù*) obligation.

vi'nicolo, a *ag* wine *cpd*.

'vino *sm* wine; **~ bianco/rosso** white/red wine.

'vinto, a *pp di* **vincere**.

vi'ola *sf* (*BOT*) violet; (*MUS*) viola // *ag, sm inv* (*colore*) purple.

vio'lare *vt* (*chiesa*) to desecrate, violate; (*giuramento, legge*) to violate; **violazi'one** *sf* desecration; violation.

violen'tare *vt* to use violence on; (*donna*) to rape.

vio'lento, a *ag* violent; **vio'lenza** *sf* violence; **violenza carnale** rape.

vio'letto, a *ag, sm* (*colore*) violet // *sf* violet.

violi'nista, i, e *sm/f* violinist.

vio'lino *sm* violin.

violon'cello [violon'tʃello] sm cello.
vi'ottolo sm path, track.
'vipera sf viper, adder.
vi'raggio [vi'raddʒo] sm (NAUT, AER) turn; (FOT) toning.
vi'rare vt (NAUT) to haul (in), heave (in) // vi (NAUT, AER) to turn; (FOT) to tone; ~ di bordo (NAUT) to tack.
virginità [virdʒini'ta] sf = **verginità**.
'virgola sf (LING) comma; (MAT) point; **virgo'lette** sfpl inverted commas, quotation marks.
vi'rile ag (proprio dell'uomo) masculine; (non puerile, da uomo) manly, virile; **virilità** sf masculinity; manliness; (sessuale) virility.
virtù sf inv virtue; **in** o **per** ~ **di** by virtue of, by.
virtu'ale ag virtual.
virtu'oso, a ag virtuous // sm/f (MUS etc) virtuoso.
viru'lento, a ag virulent.
'virus sm inv virus.
'viscere ['viʃʃere] sm (ANAT) internal organ // sfpl (di animale) entrails pl; (fig) bowels pl.
'vischio ['viskjo] sm (BOT) mistletoe; (pania) birdlime; **vischi'oso, a** ag sticky.
'viscido, a ['viʃʃido] ag slimy.
vis'conte, 'essa sm/f viscount/ viscountess.
vis'coso, a ag viscous.
vi'sibile ag visible.
visi'bilio sm profusion; **andare in** ~ **to** go into raptures.
visibilità sf visibility.
visi'era sf (di elmo) visor; (di berretto) peak.
visi'one sf vision; **prendere** ~ **di qc** to examine sth, look sth over; **prima/seconda** ~ (CINEMA) first/second showing.
'visita sf visit; (MED) visit, call; (: esame) examination; **visi'tare** vt to visit; (MED) to visit, call on; (: esaminare) to examine; **visita'tore, 'trice** sm/f visitor.
vi'sivo, a ag visual.
'viso sm face.
vi'sone sm mink.
'vispo, a ag quick, lively.
vis'suto, a pp di **vivere**.
'vista sf (facoltà) (eye)sight; (fatto di vedere): **la** ~ **di** the sight of; (veduta) view; **sparare a** ~ to shoot on sight; **in** ~ sight; **perdere qd di** ~ to lose sight of sb; (fig) to lose touch with sb; **a** ~ **d'occhio** as far as the eye can see; (fig) before one's very eyes; **far** ~ **di fare** to pretend to do.
'visto, a pp di **vedere** // sm visa.
vis'toso, a ag gaudy, garish; (ingente) considerable.
visu'ale ag visual.
'vita sf life; (ANAT) waist; **a** ~ for life.
vi'tale ag vital; **vitalità** sf vitality; **vita-'lizio, a** ag life cpd // sm life annuity.
vita'mina sf vitamin.

'vite sf (BOT) vine; (TECN) screw.
vi'tello sm (ZOOL) calf; (carne) veal; (pelle) calfskin.
vi'ticcio [vi'tittʃo] sm (BOT) tendril.
viticol'tore sm wine grower; **viticol'tura** sf wine growing.
'vitreo, a ag vitreous; (occhio, sguardo) glassy.
'vittima sf victim.
'vitto sm food; (in un albergo etc) board; ~ **e alloggio** board and lodging.
vit'toria sf victory; **vittori'oso, a** ag victorious.
vitupe'rare vt to rail at o against.
'viva escl: ~ **il re!** long live the king!
vi'vace [vi'vatʃe] ag (vivo, animato) lively; (: mente) lively, sharp; (colore) bright; **vivacità** sf vivacity; liveliness; brightness.
vi'vaio sm (di pesci) hatchery; (AGR) nursery.
vi'vanda sf food; (piatto) dish.
vi'vente ag living, alive; **i** ~**i** the living.
'vivere vi (2) to live // vt to live; (passare: brutto momento) to live through, go through; (sentire: gioie, pene di qd) to share // sm life; (anche: **modo di** ~) way of life; ~**i** smpl food sg, provisions; ~ **di** to live on.
'vivido, a ag (colore) vivid, bright.
vivifi'care vt to enliven, give life to; (piante etc) to revive.
vivisezi'one [viviset'tsjone] sf vivisection.
'vivo, a ag (vivente) alive, living; (: animale) live; (fig) lively; (: colore) bright, brilliant; **i** ~**i** the living; ~ **e vegeto** hale and hearty; **farsi** ~ to show one's face; to be heard from; **ritrarre al** ~ to paint from life; **pungere qd nel** ~ (fig) to cut sb to the quick.
vizi'are [vit'tsjare] vt (bambino) to spoil; (corrompere moralmente) to corrupt; **vi-zi'ato, a** ag spoilt; (aria, acqua) polluted.
'vizio ['vittsjo] sm vice; (cattiva abitudine) bad habit; (imperfezione) flaw, defect; (errore) fault, mistake; **vizi'oso, a** ag depraved; defective; (inesatto) incorrect, wrong.
vocabo'lario sm (dizionario) dictionary; (lessico) vocabulary.
vo'cabolo sm word.
vo'cale ag vocal // sf vowel.
vocazi'one [vokat'tsjone] sf vocation; (fig) natural bent.
'voce ['votʃe] sf voice; (diceria) rumour; (di un elenco, in bilancio) item; **aver** ~ **in capitolo** (fig) to have a say in the matter.
voci'are [vo'tʃare] vi to shout, yell.
'voga sf (NAUT) rowing; (usanza): **essere in** ~ to be in fashion o in vogue.
vo'gare vi to row.
'voglia ['vɔʎʎa] sf desire, wish; (macchia) birthmark; **aver** ~ **di qc/di fare** to feel like sth/like doing; (più forte) to want sth/to do.
'voi pronome you; **vo'altri** pronome you (lot).

vo'lano *sm* (SPORT) shuttlecock; (TECN) flywheel.

vo'lante *ag* flying // *sm* (steering) wheel.

volan'tino *sm* leaflet.

vo'lare *vi* (*uccello, aereo, fig*) to fly; (*cappello*) to blow away *o* off, to fly away *o* off; ~ **via** to fly away *o* off.

vo'lata *sf* flight; (*d'uccelli*) flock, flight; (*corsa*) rush; (SPORT) final sprint.

vo'latile *ag* (CHIM) volatile // *sm* (ZOOL) bird.

volenti'eri *av* willingly; '~' 'with pleasure', 'I'd be glad to'.

vo'lere *sm* will; ~**i** *smpl* wishes // *vt* to want; (*esigere, richiedere*) to demand, require; **vuole un po' di formaggio?** would you like some cheese?; ~ **che qd faccia** to want sb to do; **vorrei questo** I would like this; ~**rci** (*essere necessario*): **quanto ci vuole per andare da Roma a Firenze?** how long does it take to go from Rome to Florence?; **ci vogliono 4 metri di stoffa** 4 metres of material are required, you will need 4 metres of material; ~ **bene a qd** to love sb; ~ **male a qd** to dislike sb; **volerne a qd** to bear sb a grudge; ~ **dire (che)** to mean (that); **senza** ~ without meaning to, unintentionally.

vol'gare *ag* vulgar; **l'opinione** ~ common opinion; **volgarità** *sf* vulgarity; **volgariz'zare** *vt* to popularize.

'volgere ['vɔldʒere] *vt* to turn // *vi* to turn; (*tendere*): ~ **a**: **il tempo volge al brutto** the weather is breaking; **un rosso che volge al viola** a red verging on purple; ~**rsi** *vr* to turn; ~ **al peggio** to take a turn for the worse.

'volgo *sm* common people.

voli'era *sf* aviary.

voli'tivo, a *ag* strong-willed.

'volo *sm* flight; **al** ~: **colpire qc al** ~ to hit sth as it flies past; **capire al** ~ to understand straight away.

volontà *sf* will; **a** ~ (*mangiare, bere*) as much as one likes; **buona/cattiva** ~ goodwill/lack of goodwill.

volon'tario, a *ag* voluntary // *sm* (MIL) volunteer.

volonte'roso, a *ag* willing.

'volpe *sf* fox.

'volta *sf* (*momento, circostanza*) time; (*turno, giro*) turn; (*curva*) turn, bend; (ARCHIT) vault; **a mia** (*o* **tua** *etc*) ~ in turn; **una** ~ once; **due** ~**e** twice; **una cosa per** ~ one thing at a time; **una** ~ **per tutte** once and for all; **a** ~**e** at times, sometimes; **una** ~ **che** (*temporale*) once; (*causale*) since; **3** ~ **e 4** 3 times 4.

volta'faccia [volta'fattʃa] *sm inv* (fig) volte-face.

vol'taggio [vol'taddʒo] *sm* (ELETTR) voltage.

vol'tare *vt* to turn; (*girare: moneta*) to turn over; (*rigirare*) to turn round // *vi* to turn; ~**rsi** *vr* to turn; to turn over; to turn round.

volteggi'are [volted'dʒare] *vi* (*volare*) to

circle; (*in equitazione*) to do trick riding; (*in ginnastica*) to vault; to perform acrobatics.

'volto, a *pp di* **volgere** // *sm* face.

vo'lubile *ag* changeable, fickle.

vo'lume *sm* volume; **volumi'noso, a** *ag* voluminous, bulky.

voluttà *sf* sensual pleasure *o* delight; **voluttu'oso, a** *ag* voluptuous.

vomi'tare *vt, vi* to vomit; **'vomito** *sm* vomiting *q*; vomit.

'vongola *sf* clam.

vo'race [vo'ratʃe] *ag* voracious, greedy.

vo'ragine [vo'radʒine] *sf* abyss, chasm.

'vortice ['vɔrtitʃe] *sm* whirlwind; whirlpool; (fig) whirl.

'vostro, a *det*: **il(la)** ~**(a)** *etc* your // *pronome*: **il(la)** ~**(a)** *etc* yours.

vo'tante *sm/f* voter.

vo'tare *vi* to vote // *vt* (*sottoporre a votazione*) to take a vote on; (*approvare*) to vote for; (REL): ~ **qc a** to dedicate sth to; **votazi'one** *sf* vote, voting; **votazioni** *sfpl* (POL) votes; (INS) marks.

vo'tivo, a *ag* (REL) votive.

'voto *sm* (POL) vote; (INS) mark; (REL) vow; (: *offerta*) votive offering.

vs. *abbr commerciale di* **vostro**.

vul'canico, a, ci, che *ag* volcanic.

vul'cano *sm* volcano.

vulne'rabile *ag* vulnerable.

vuo'tare *vt*, ~**rsi** *vr* to empty.

vu'oto, a *ag* empty; (fig: *privo*): ~ **di** (*senso etc*) devoid of // *sm* empty space, gap; (*spazio in bianco*) blank; (FISICA) vacuum; (fig: *mancanza*) gap, void; **a mani** ~**e** empty-handed; ~ **d'aria** air pocket; ~ **a rendere** returnable bottle.

W X Y

watt [vat] *sm inv* watt.

'whisky ['wiski] *sm inv* whisky.

'xeres ['kscres] *sm inv* sherry.

xero'copia [ksero'kɔpja] *sf* xerox, photocopy.

xi'lofono [ksi'lɔfono] *sm* xylophone.

yacht [jɔt] *sm inv* yacht.

'yoghurt ['jɔgurt] *sm inv* yoghourt.

Z

zabai'one [dzaba'jone] *sm* dessert made of egg yolks, sugar and marsala.

'zacchera ['tsakkera] *sf* splash of mud.

zaf'fata [tsaf'fata] *sf* (*tanfo*) stench.

zaffe'rano [dzaffe'rano] *sm* saffron.

zaf'firo [dzaf'firo] *sm* sapphire.

'zagara ['dzagara] *sf* orange blossom.

'zaino ['dzaino] *sm* rucksack.

'zampa ['tsampa] *sf* (*di animale: gamba*) leg; (: *piede*) paw: **a quattro** ~**e** on all fours.

zampil'lare [tsampil'lare] *vi* to gush, spurt; **zam'pillo** *sm* gush, spurt.

zam'pogna [tsam'poɲɲa] *sf* instrument similar to bagpipes.

'zanna ['tsanna] *sf* (*di elefante*) tusk; (*di carnivori*) fang.

zan'zara [dzan'dzara] *sf* mosquito; **zanzari'era** *sf* mosquito net.

'zappa ['tsappa] *sf* hoe; **zap'pare** *vt* to hoe.

zar, za'rina [tsar, tsa'rina] *sm/f* tsar/tsarina.

'zattera ['dzattera] *sf* raft.

za'vorra [dza'vɔrra] *sf* ballast.

'zazzera ['tsattsera] *sf* shock of hair.

'zebra ['dzɛbra] *sf* zebra; **~e** *sfpl* (AUT) zebra crossing *sg*.

'zecca, che ['tsekka] *sf* (ZOOL) tick; (*officina di monete*) mint.

ze'lante [dze'lante] *ag* zealous.

'zelo ['dzɛlo] *sm* zeal.

'zenit ['dzɛnit] *sm* zenith.

'zenzero ['dzendzero] *sm* ginger.

'zeppa ['tseppa] *sf* wedge.

'zeppo, a ['tseppo] *ag*: **~ di** crammed *o* packed with.

zer'bino [dzer'bino] *sm* doormat.

'zero ['dzɛro] *sm* zero, nought; **vincere per tre a ~** (SPORT) to win three-nil.

'zeta ['dzɛta] *sm o f* zed, (the letter) z.

'zia ['tsia] *sf* aunt.

zibel'lino [dzibel'lino] *sm* sable.

'zigomo ['dzigomo] *sm* cheekbone.

zig'zag [dzig'dzag] *sm inv* zigzag; **andare a ~** to zigzag.

zim'bello [dzim'bɛllo] *sm* (*oggetto di burle*) laughing-stock.

'zinco ['dzinko] *sm* zinc.

'zingaro, a ['dzingaro] *sm/f* gipsy.

'zio ['tsio], *pl* **'zii** *sm* uncle; **zii** *smpl* (*zio e zia*) uncle and aunt.

zi'tella [dzi'tɛlla] *sf* spinster; (*peg*) old maid.

'zitto, a ['tsitto] *ag* quiet, silent; **sta' ~!** be quiet!

'zoccolo ['tsɔkkolo] *sm* (*calzatura*) clog; (*di cavallo etc*) hoof; (*basamento*) base; plinth.

zo'diaco [dzo'diako] *sm* zodiac.

'zolfo ['tsolfo] *sm* sulphur.

'zolla ['dzɔlla] *sf* clod (of earth).

zol'letta [dzol'letta] *sf* sugar lump.

'zona ['dzɔna] *sf* zone, area; **~ di depressione** (METEOR) trough of low pressure; **~ verde** (*di abitato*) green area.

'zonzo ['dzondzo]: **a ~** *av*: **andare a ~** to wander about, stroll about.

zoo ['dzɔo] *sm inv* zoo.

zoolo'gia [dzoolo'dʒia] *sf* zoology; **zoo-'logico, a, ci, che** *ag* zoological; **zo'ologo, a, gi, ghe** *sm/f* zoologist.

zoppi'care [tsoppi'kare] *vi* to limp; to be shaky, rickety.

'zoppo, a ['tsɔppo] *ag* lame; (*fig: mobile*) shaky, rickety.

zoti'cone [dzoti'kone] *sm* lout.

'zucca, che ['tsukka] *sf* marrow; pumpkin.

zucche'rare [tsukke'rare] *vt* to put sugar in.

zuccheri'era [tsukke'rjɛra] *sf* sugar bowl.

zuccheri'ficio [tsukkeri'fitʃo] *sm* sugar refinery.

zucche'rino, a [tsukke'rino] *ag* sugary, sweet.

'zucchero ['tsukkero] *sm* sugar; **zucche-'roso, a** *ag* sugary.

zuc'chino [tsuk'kino] *sm* courgette, zucchini.

'zuffa ['tsuffa] *sf* brawl.

zufo'lare [tsufo'lare] *vt, vi* to whistle.

'zuppa ['tsuppa] *sf* soup; (*fig*) mixture, muddle; **~ inglese** (CUC) ≈ trifle; **zup-pi'era** *sf* soup tureen.

'zuppo, a ['tsuppo] *ag*: **~ (di)** drenched (with), soaked (with).

ENGLISH · ITALIAN
INGLESE · ITALIANO

A

a, an [eɪ, ə, æn, ən, n] *det* un (uno + *s impure, gn, pn, ps, x, z),* f una (un' + *vowel);* **3 a day/week** 3 al giorno/la *or* alla settimana; **10 km an hour** 10 km all'ora.

A [eɪ] *n* (*MUS*) la *m*.

A.A. *n* (*abbr of Automobile Association*) ≈ A.C.I.; *abbr of Alcoholics Anonymous.*

aback [ə'bæk] *ad:* **to be taken ∼** essere sbalordito(a).

abandon [ə'bændən] *vt* abbandonare // *n* abbandono.

abashed [ə'bæʃt] *a* imbarazzato(a).

abate [ə'beɪt] *vi* calmarsi.

abattoir ['æbətwɑ:*] *n* mattatoio.

abbey ['æbɪ] *n* abbazia, badia.

abbot ['æbət] *n* abate *m*.

abbreviate [ə'bri:vɪeɪt] *vt* abbreviare; **abbreviation** [-'eɪʃən] *n* abbreviazione *f*.

abdicate ['æbdɪkeɪt] *vt* abdicare a // *vi* abdicare; **abdication** [-'keɪʃən] *n* abdicazione *f*.

abdomen ['æbdəmɛn] *n* addome *m*.

abduct [æb'dʌkt] *vt* rapire; **abduction** [-ʃən] *n* rapimento.

abet [ə'bɛt] *vt see* **aid.**

abeyance [ə'beɪəns] *n*: **in ∼** in sospeso.

abhor [əb'hɔ:*] *vt* aborrire; **∼rent** *a* odioso(a).

abide [ə'baɪd] *vt* sopportare; **to ∼ by** *vt fus* conformarsi a.

ability [ə'bɪlɪtɪ] *n* abilità *f inv*.

ablaze [ə'bleɪz] *a* in fiamme; **∼ with light** risplendente di luce.

able ['eɪbl] *a* capace; **to be ∼ to do sth** essere capace di fare qc, poter fare qc; **∼-bodied** *a* robusto(a); **ably** *ad* abilmente.

abnormal [æb'nɔ:ml] *a* anormale.

aboard [ə'bɔ:d] *ad* a bordo // *prep* a bordo di.

abolish [ə'bɔlɪʃ] *vt* abolire.

abolition [æbəu'lɪʃən] *n* abolizione *f*.

abominable [ə'bɔmɪnəbl] *a* abominevole.

aborigine [æbə'rɪdʒɪnɪ] *n* aborigeno/a.

abort [ə'bɔ:t] *vt* abortire; **∼ion** [ə'bɔ:ʃən] *n* aborto; **∼ive** *a* abortivo(a).

abound [ə'baund] *vi* abbondare; **to ∼ in** abbondare di.

about [ə'baut] *prep* intorno a, riguardo a // *ad* circa; (*here and there*) qua e là; **it takes ∼ 10 hours** ci vogliono circa 10 ore; **at ∼ 2 o'clock** verso le due; **it's ∼ here** è qui dintorno; **to walk ∼ the town** camminare per la città; **to be ∼ to:** **he was ∼ to cry** lui stava per piangere; **what** *or* **how ∼ doing this?** che ne pensa di fare questo?; **∼ turn** *n* dietro front *m inv*.

above [ə'bʌv] *ad, prep* sopra; **mentioned ∼** suddetto; **costing ∼ £10** che costa più di 10 sterline; **∼ all** soprattutto; **∼board** *a* aperto(a); onesto(a).

abrasive [ə'breɪzɪv] *a* abrasivo(a).

abreast [ə'brɛst] *ad* di fianco; **3 ∼** per 3 di fronte; **to keep ∼ of** tenersi aggiornato su.

abridge [ə'brɪdʒ] *vt* ridurre.

abroad [ə'brɔ:d] *ad* all'estero.

abrupt [ə'brʌpt] *a* (*steep*) erto(a); (*sudden*) improvviso(a); (*gruff, blunt*) brusco(a).

abscess ['æbsɪs] *n* ascesso.

abscond [əb'skɔnd] *vi* scappare.

absence ['æbsəns] *n* assenza.

absent ['æbsənt] *a* assente; **∼ee** [-'ti:] *n* assente *m/f*; **∼eeism** [-'ti:ɪzəm] *n* assenteismo; **∼-minded** *a* distratto(a).

absolute ['æbsəlu:t] *a* assoluto(a); **∼ly** [-'lu:tlɪ] *ad* assolutamente.

absolve [əb'zɔlv] *vt*: **to ∼ sb (from)** assolvere qd (da).

absorb [əb'zɔ:b] *vt* assorbire; **to be ∼ed in a book** essere immerso in un libro; **∼ent** *a* assorbente; **∼ent cotton** *n* (*US*) cotone *m* idrofilo.

abstain [əb'steɪn] *vi*: **to ∼ (from)** astenersi (da).

abstemious [əb'sti:mɪəs] *a* astemio(a).

abstention [əb'stɛnʃən] *n* astensione *f*.

abstinence ['æbstɪnəns] *n* astinenza.

abstract ['æbstrækt] *a* astratto(a) // *n* (*summary*) riassunto.

absurd [əb'sə:d] *a* assurdo(a); **∼ity** *n* assurdità *f inv*.

abundance [ə'bʌndəns] *n* abbondanza; **abundant** *a* abbondante.

abuse *n* [ə'bju:s] abuso; (*insults*) ingiurie *fpl* // *vt* [ə'bju:z] abusare di; **abusive** *a* ingiurioso(a).

abysmal [ə'bɪzməl] *a* spaventoso(a).

abyss [ə'bɪs] *n* abisso.

academic [ækə'dɛmɪk] *a* accademico(a); (*pej: issue*) puramente formale // *n* universitario/a.

academy [ə'kædəmɪ] *n* (*learned body*) accademia; (*school*) scuola privata; **military/naval ∼** scuola militare/navale; **∼ of music** conservatorio.

accede [æk'si:d] *vi*: **to ∼ to** (*request*) accedere a; (*throne*) ascendere a.

accelerate [æk'sɛləreɪt] *vt,vi* accelerare; **acceleration** [-'reɪʃən] *n* accelerazione *f*; **accelerator** *n* acceleratore *m*.

accent ['æksɛnt] *n* accento.

accept [ək'sɛpt] *vt* accettare; **∼able** *a* accettabile; **∼ance** *n* accettazione *f*.

access ['æksɛs] *n* accesso; **to have ∼ to**

(*information, library, person*) avere accesso a; ~**ible** [æk'sɛsəbl] a accessibile; ~**ion** [æk'sɛʃən] n ascesa.
accessory [æk'sɛsərɪ] n accessorio; **toilet accessories** npl articoli mpl da toilette.
accident ['æksɪdənt] n incidente m; (*chance*) caso; **by** ~ per caso; ~**al** [-'dɛntl] a accidentale; ~**ally** [-'dɛntəlɪ] ad per caso; ~**prone** a: **he's very** ~**-prone** è un vero passaguai.
acclaim [ə'kleɪm] vt acclamare // n acclamazione f.
acclimatize [ə'klaɪmətaɪz] vt: **to become** ~**d** acclimatarsi.
accommodate [ə'kɔmədeɪt] vt alloggiare; (*oblige, help*) favorire.
accommodating [ə'kɔmədeɪtɪŋ] a compiacente.
accommodation [əkɔmə'deɪʃən] n alloggio.
accompaniment [ə'kʌmpənɪmənt] n accompagnamento.
accompany [ə'kʌmpənɪ] vt accompagnare.
accomplice [ə'kʌmplɪs] n complice m/f.
accomplish [ə'kʌmplɪʃ] vt compiere; ~**ed** a (*person*) esperto(a); ~**ment** n compimento; realizzazione f; ~**ments** npl doti fpl.
accord [ə'kɔːd] n accordo // vt accordare; **of his own** ~ di propria iniziativa; ~**ance** n: **in** ~**ance with** in conformità con; ~**ing to** prep secondo; ~**ingly** ad in conformità.
accordion [ə'kɔːdɪən] n fisarmonica.
accost [ə'kɔst] vt avvicinare.
account [ə'kaunt] n (*COMM*) conto; (*report*) descrizione f; **by all** ~**s** a quanto si dice; **of little** ~ di poca importanza; **on** ~ in acconto; **on no** ~ per nessun motivo; **on** ~ **of** a causa di; **to take into** ~, **take** ~ **of** tener conto di; **to** ~ **for** spiegare; giustificare; ~**able** a responsabile.
accountancy [ə'kauntənsɪ] n ragioneria.
accountant [ə'kauntənt] n ragioniere/a.
accumulate [ə'kjuːmjuleɪt] vt accumulare // vi accumularsi; **accumulation** [-'leɪʃən] n accumulazione f.
accuracy ['ækjurəsɪ] n precisione f.
accurate ['ækjurɪt] a preciso(a); ~**ly** ad precisamente.
accusation [ækju'zeɪʃən] n accusa.
accuse [ə'kjuːz] vt accusare; ~**d** n accusato/a.
accustom [ə'kʌstəm] vt abituare; ~**ed** a (*usual*) abituale; ~**ed to** abituato(a) a.
ace [eɪs] n asso; **within an** ~ **of** a un pelo da.
ache [eɪk] n male m, dolore m // vi (*be sore*) far male, dolere; **my head** ~**s** mi fa male la testa; **I'm aching all over** mi duole dappertutto.
achieve [ə'tʃiːv] vt (*aim*) raggiungere; (*victory, success*) ottenere; (*task*) compiere; ~**ment** n compimento; successo.
acid ['æsɪd] a acido(a) // n acido; ~**ity** [ə'sɪdɪtɪ] n acidità.

acknowledge [ək'nɔlɪdʒ] vt (*letter*) confermare la ricevuta di; (*fact*) riconoscere; ~**ment** n conferma; riconoscimento.
acne ['æknɪ] n acne f.
acorn ['eɪkɔːn] n ghianda.
acoustic [ə'kuːstɪk] a acustico(a); ~**s** n,npl acustica.
acquaint [ə'kweɪnt] vt: **to** ~ **sb with sth** far sapere qc a qd; **to be** ~**ed with** (*person*) conoscere; ~**ance** n conoscenza; (*person*) conoscente m/f.
acquire [ə'kwaɪə*] vt acquistare.
acquisition [ækwɪ'zɪʃən] n acquisto.
acquisitive [ə'kwɪzɪtɪv] a a cui piace accumulare le cose.
acquit [ə'kwɪt] vt assolvere; **to** ~ **o.s. well** comportarsi bene; ~**tal** n assoluzione f.
acre ['eɪkə*] n acro (= 4047 m²).
acrimonious [ækrɪ'məunɪəs] a astioso(a).
acrobat ['ækrəbæt] n acrobata m/f.
acrobatics [ækrəu'bætɪks] n acrobatica // npl acrobazie fpl.
across [ə'krɔs] prep (*on the other side*) dall'altra parte di; (*crosswise*) attraverso // ad dall'altra parte; in larghezza; **to walk** ~ (**the road**) attraversare (la strada); ~ **from** di fronte a.
act [ækt] n atto; (*in music-hall etc*) numero; (*LAW*) decreto // vi agire; (*THEATRE*) recitare; (*pretend*) fingere // vt (*part*) recitare; **to** ~ **Hamlet** recitare la parte di Amleto; **to** ~ **the fool** fare lo stupido; **to** ~ **as** agire da; ~**ing** a che fa le funzioni di // n (*of actor*) recitazione f; (*activity*): **to do some** ~**ing** fare del teatro (or del cinema).
action ['ækʃən] n azione f; (*MIL*) combattimento; (*LAW*) processo; **out of** ~ fuori combattimento; fuori servizio; **to take** ~ agire.
activate ['æktɪveɪt] vt (*mechanism*) fare funzionare; (*CHEM, PHYSICS*) rendere attivo(a).
active ['æktɪv] a attivo(a).
activity [æk'tɪvɪtɪ] n attività f inv.
actor ['æktə*] n attore m.
actress ['æktrɪs] n attrice f.
actual ['æktjuəl] a reale, vero(a); ~**ly** ad realmente; infatti.
acumen ['ækjumən] n acume m.
acupuncture ['ækjupʌŋkt(ə*] n agopuntura.
acute [ə'kjuːt] a acuto(a).
ad [æd] n abbr of **advertisement**.
A.D. ad (*abbr of Anno Domini*) d.C.
Adam ['ædəm] n Adamo; ~**'s apple** n pomo di Adamo.
adamant ['ædəmənt] a adamantino(a).
adapt [ə'dæpt] vt adattare // vi: **to** ~ (**to**) adattarsi (a); ~**able** a (*device*) adattabile; (*person*) che sa adattarsi; ~**ation** [ædæp-'teɪʃən] n adattamento; ~**er** n (*ELEC*) adattatore m.
add [æd] vt aggiungere; (*figures: also:* **to** ~

up) addizionare // vi: **to ~ to** (increase) aumentare.

adder ['ædə*] n vipera.

addict ['ædıkt] n tossicomane m/f; (fig) fanatico/a; **~ed** [ə'dıktıd] a: **to be ~ed to** (drink etc) essere dedito a; (fig: football etc) essere tifoso di; **~ion** [ə'dıkʃən] n (MED) tossicomania.

addition [ə'dıʃən] n addizione f; **in ~** inoltre; **in ~ to** oltre; **~al** a supplementare.

additive ['ædıtıv] n additivo.

address [ə'drɛs] n indirizzo; (talk) discorso // vt indirizzare; (speak to) fare un discorso a.

adenoids ['ædınɔıdz] npl adenoidi fpl.

adept ['ædɛpt] a: **~ at** esperto(a) in.

adequate ['ædıkwıt] a adeguato(a); sufficiente.

adhere [əd'hıə*] vi: **to ~ to** aderire a; (fig: rule, decision) seguire.

adhesion [əd'hi:ʒən] n adesione f.

adhesive [əd'hi:zıv] a adesivo(a) // n adesivo.

adjacent [ə'dʒeısənt] a adiacente; **~ to** accanto a.

adjective ['ædʒɛktıv] n aggettivo.

adjoining [ə'dʒɔınıŋ] a accanto inv, adiacente // prep accanto a.

adjourn [ə'dʒɜːn] vt rimandare // vi aggiornare; (go) spostarsi.

adjust [ə'dʒʌst] vt aggiustare; (COMM) rettificare // vi: **to ~ (to)** adattarsi (a); **~able** a regolabile; **~ment** n adattamento; (of prices, wages) aggiustamento.

adjutant ['ædʒətənt] n aiutante m.

ad-lib [æd'lıb] vt,vi improvvisare // n improvvisazione f.

administer [əd'mınıstə*] vt amministrare; (justice) somministrare.

administration [ədmınıs'treıʃən] n amministrazione f.

administrative [əd'mınıstrətıv] a amministrativo(a).

administrator [əd'mınıstreıtə*] n amministratore/trice.

admiral ['ædmərəl] n ammiraglio; **A~ty** n Ammiragliato; Ministero della Marina.

admiration [ædmə'reıʃən] n ammirazione f.

admire [əd'maıə*] vt ammirare; **~r** n ammiratore/trice.

admission [əd'mıʃən] n ammissione f; (to exhibition, night club etc) ingresso; (confession) confessione f.

admit [əd'mıt] vt ammettere; far entrare; (agree) riconoscere; **to ~ of** lasciare adito a; **to ~ to** riconoscere; **~tance** n ingresso; **~tedly** ad bisogna pur riconoscere (che).

admonish [əd'mɒnıʃ] vt ammonire.

ado [ə'du:] n: **without (any) more ~** senza più indugi.

adolescence [ædəu'lɛsns] n adolescenza.

adolescent [ædəu'lɛsnt] a,n adolescente (m/f).

adopt [ə'dɒpt] vt adottare; **~ed** a adottivo(a); **~ion** [ə'dɒpʃən] n adozione f.

adore [ə'dɔː*] vt adorare.

adorn [ə'dɔːn] vt adornare.

adrenalin [ə'drɛnəlın] n adrenalina.

Adriatic (Sea) [eıdrı'ætık(si:)] n Adriatico.

adrift [ə'drıft] ad alla deriva.

adroit [ə'drɔıt] a abile, destro(a).

adult ['ædʌlt] n adulto/a.

adulterate [ə'dʌltəreıt] vt adulterare.

adultery [ə'dʌltərı] n adulterio.

advance [əd'vɑːns] n avanzamento; (money) anticipo // vt avanzare; (date, money) anticipare // vi avanzare; **in ~** in anticipo; **~d** a avanzato(a); (SCOL: studies) superiore; **~ment** n avanzamento.

advantage [əd'vɑːntıdʒ] n (also TENNIS) vantaggio; **to take ~ of** approfittarsi di; **~ous** [ædvən'teıdʒəs] a vantaggioso(a).

advent ['ædvənt] n avvento; **A ~** Avvento.

adventure [əd'vɛntʃə*] n avventura; **adventurous** a avventuroso(a).

adverb ['ædvɜːb] n avverbio.

adversary ['ædvəsərı] n avversario/a.

adverse ['ædvɜːs] a avverso(a); **in ~ circumstances** nelle avversità; **~ to** contrario(a) a.

adversity [əd'vɜːsıtı] n avversità.

advert ['ædvɜːt] n abbr of **advertisement**.

advertise ['ædvətaız] vi(vt) fare pubblicità or réclame (a); fare un'inserzione (per vendere).

advertisement [əd'vɜːtısmənt] n (COMM) réclame f inv, pubblicità f inv; (in classified ads) inserzione f.

advertising ['ædvətaızıŋ] n pubblicità.

advice [əd'vaıs] n consigli mpl; (notification) avviso; **piece of ~** consiglio.

advisable [əd'vaızəbl] a consigliabile.

advise [əd'vaız] vt consigliare; **to ~ sb of sth** informare qd di qc; **~r** n consigliere/a; **advisory** [-ərı] a consultivo(a).

advocate ['ædvəkeıt] vt propugnare.

aegis ['i:dʒıs] n: **under the ~ of** sotto gli auspici di.

aerial ['ɛərıəl] n antenna // a aereo(a).

aeroplane ['ɛərəpleın] n aeroplano.

aerosol ['ɛərəsɔl] n aerosol m inv.

aesthetic [ıs'θɛtık] n estetico(a).

affable ['æfəbl] a affabile.

affair [ə'fɛə*] n affare m; (also: love ~) relazione f amorosa.

affect [ə'fɛkt] vt toccare; (feign) fingere; **~ation** [æfɛk'teıʃən] n affettazione f; **~ed** a affettato(a).

affection [ə'fɛkʃən] n affezione f; **~ate** a affettuoso(a).

affiliated [ə'fılıeıtıd] a affiliato(a).

affinity [ə'fınıtı] n affinità f inv.

affirmation [æfə'meıʃən] n affermazione f.

affirmative [ə'fɜːmətıv] a affermativo(a) // n: **in the ~** affermativamente.

affix [ə'fıks] vt apporre; attaccare.

afflict [ə'flɪkt] vt affliggere; ~ion [ə'flɪkʃən] n afflizione f.

affluence ['æfluəns] n abbondanza; opulenza.

affluent ['æfluənt] a abbondante; opulente; (person) ricco(a).

afford [ə'fɔːd] vt permettersi; (provide) fornire; I can't ~ the time non ho veramente il tempo.

affront [ə'frʌnt] n affronto; ~ed a insultato(a).

afield [ə'fiːld] ad: far ~ lontano.

afloat [ə'fləut] a, ad a galla.

afoot [ə'fut] ad: there is something ~ si sta preparando qualcosa.

aforesaid [ə'fɔːsɛd] a suddetto(a), predetto(a).

afraid [ə'freɪd] a impaurito(a); to be ~ of aver paura di; to be ~ of doing or to do aver paura di fare; I am ~ that I'll be late mi dispiace, ma farò tardi.

afresh [ə'frɛʃ] ad di nuovo.

Africa ['æfrɪkə] n Africa; ~n a, n africano(a).

aft [ɑːft] ad a poppa, verso poppa.

after ['ɑːftə°] prep,ad dopo; what/who are you ~? che/chi cerca?; ~ all dopo tutto; ~-effects npl conseguenze fpl; (of illness) postumi mpl; ~life n vita dell'al di là; ~math n conseguenze fpl; in the ~math of nel periodo dopo; ~noon n pomeriggio; ~-shave (lotion) n dopobarba m inv; ~thought n: as an ~thought come aggiunta; ~wards ad dopo.

again [ə'gɛn] ad di nuovo; to begin/see ~ ricominciare/rivedere; not ... ~ non ... più; ~ and ~ ripetutamente.

against [ə'gɛnst] prep contro; ~ a blue background su uno sfondo azzurro.

age [eɪdʒ] n età f inv // vt,vi invecchiare; it's been ~s since secoli che; to come of ~ diventare maggiorenne; ~d a (elderly): [ˈeɪdʒɪd] anziano(a); ~d 10 di 10 anni; the ~d ['eɪdʒɪd] gli anziani; ~ group n generazione f; ~less a senza età; ~ limit n limite m d'età.

agency ['eɪdʒənsɪ] n agenzia; through or by the ~ of grazie a.

agenda [ə'dʒɛndə] n ordine m del giorno.

agent ['eɪdʒənt] n agente m.

aggravate ['ægrəveɪt] vt aggravare; (annoy) esasperare.

aggregate ['ægrɪgeɪt] n aggregato; on ~ (SPORT) con punteggio complessivo.

aggression [ə'grɛʃən] n aggressione f.

aggressive [ə'grɛsɪv] a aggressivo(a); ~ness n aggressività.

aggrieved [ə'griːvd] a addolorato(a).

aghast [ə'gɑːst] a sbigottito(a).

agile ['ædʒaɪl] a agile.

agitate ['ædʒɪteɪt] vt turbare; agitare // vi: to ~ for agitarsi per; **agitator** n agitatore/trice.

ago [ə'gəu] ad: 2 days ~ 2 giorni fa; not long ~ poco tempo fa.

agonizing ['ægənaɪzɪŋ] a straziante.

agony ['ægənɪ] n agonia.

agree [ə'griː] vi: to ~ (with) essere d'accordo (con); (LING) concordare (con); to ~ to sth/to do sth accettare qc/di fare qc; to ~ that (admit) ammettere che; to ~ on sth accordarsi su qc; garlic doesn't ~ with me l'aglio non mi va; ~able a gradevole; (willing) disposto(a); are you ~able to this? sei d'accordo con questo?; ~d a (time, place) stabilito(a); to be ~d essere d'accordo; ~ment n accordo; in ~ment d'accordo.

agricultural [ægrɪ'kʌltʃərəl] a agricolo(a).

agriculture ['ægrɪkʌltʃə°] n agricoltura.

aground [ə'graund] ad: to run ~ arenarsi.

ahead [ə'hɛd] ad avanti; davanti; ~ of davanti a; (fig: schedule etc) in anticipo su; ~ of time in anticipo; go ~! avanti!; go right or straight ~ tiri diritto; they were (right) ~ of us erano (proprio) davanti a noi.

aid [eɪd] n aiuto // vt aiutare; to ~ and abet (LAW) essere complice di.

aide [eɪd] n (person) aiutante m.

ailment ['eɪlmənt] n indisposizione f.

aim [eɪm] vt: to ~ sth at (such as gun) mirare qc a, puntare qc a; (camera, remark) rivolgere qc a; (missile) lanciare qc contro; (blow etc) tirare qc a // vi (also: to take ~) prendere la mira // n mira; to ~ at mirare; to ~ to do aver l'intenzione di fare; ~less a, ~lessly ad senza scopo.

air [ɛə°] n aria // vt aerare; (grievances, ideas) esprimere pubblicamente // cpd (currents) d'aria; (attack) aereo(a); ~bed n materassino gonfiabile; ~borne a in volo; aerotrasportato(a); ~ conditioning n condizionamento d'aria; ~-cooled a raffreddato(a) ad aria; ~craft n, pl inv apparecchio; ~craft carrier n portaerei f inv; A~ Force n aviazione f militare; ~gun n fucile m ad aria compressa; ~ hostess n hostess f inv; ~ily ad con disinvoltura; ~ letter n aerogramma m; ~line n linea aerea; ~liner n aereo di linea; ~lock n cassa d'aria; by ~mail per via aerea; ~plane n (US) aeroplano; ~port n aeroporto; ~ raid n incursione f aerea; ~sick a che ha il mal d'aereo; ~strip n pista d'atterraggio; ~tight a ermetico(a); ~y a arioso(a); (manners) non curante.

aisle [aɪl] n (of church) navata laterale; navata centrale.

ajar [ə'dʒɑː°] a a socchiuso(a).

alarm [ə'lɑːm] n allarme m // vt allarmare; ~ clock n sveglia; ~ist n allarmista m.

Albania [æl'beɪnɪə] n Albania.

album ['ælbəm] n album m inv; (L.P.) 33 giri m inv, L.P. m inv.

alchemy ['ælkɪmɪ] n alchimia.

alcohol ['ælkəhɔl] n alcool m; ~ic [-'hɔlɪk] a alcolico(a) // n alcolizzato(a); ~ism n alcolismo.

alcove ['ælkəuv] n alcova.

alderman ['ɔːldəmən] n consigliere m comunale.

ale [eɪl] n birra.

alert [ə'lɜːt] a vivo(a); (watchful) vigile // n allarme m; **on the ~** all'erta.

algebra ['ældʒɪbrə] n algebra.

Algeria [æl'dʒɪərɪə] n Algeria; **~n** a, n algerino(a).

alias ['eɪlɪæs] ad alias // n pseudonimo, falso nome m.

alibi ['ælɪbaɪ] n alibi m inv.

alien ['eɪlɪən] n straniero/a // a: **~ (to)** estraneo(a) a; **~ate** vt alienare; **~ation** [-'neɪʃən] n alienazione f.

alight [ə'laɪt] a acceso(a) // vi scendere; (bird) posarsi.

align [ə'laɪn] vt allineare; **~ment** n allineamento.

alike [ə'laɪk] a simile // ad sia ... sia; **to look ~** assomigliarsi.

alimony ['ælɪmənɪ] n (payment) alimenti mpl.

alive [ə'laɪv] a vivo(a); (active) attivo(a); **~ with** pieno(a) di; **~ to** conscio(a) di.

alkali ['ælkəlaɪ] n alcali m inv.

all [ɔːl] a tutto(a), tutti(e) pl // pronoun tutto m; (pl) tutti(e) // ad tutto; **~ wrong/alone** tutto sbagliato/solo; **~ the time/his life** tutto il tempo/tutta la sua vita; **~ five** tutti e cinque; **~ of them** tutti(e); **~ of it** tutto; **~ of us went** ci siamo andati tutti; **it's not as hard** etc **as ~ that** non è mica così duro etc; **~ in ~** tutto sommato.

allay [ə'leɪ] vt (fears) dissipare.

allegation [ælɪ'geɪʃən] n asserzione f.

allege [ə'ledʒ] vt asserire; **~dly** [ə'ledʒɪdlɪ] ad secondo quanto si asserisce.

allegiance [ə'liːdʒəns] n fedeltà.

allegory ['ælɪgərɪ] n allegoria.

allergic [ə'lɜːdʒɪk] a: **~ to** allergico(a) a.

allergy ['ælədʒɪ] n allergia.

alleviate [ə'liːvɪeɪt] vt sollevare.

alley ['ælɪ] n vicolo; (in garden) vialetto.

alliance [ə'laɪəns] n alleanza.

allied ['ælaɪd] a alleato(a).

alligator ['ælɪgeɪtə*] n alligatore m.

all-important ['ɔːlɪm'pɔːtənt] a importantissimo(a).

all-in ['ɔːlɪn] a (also ad: charge) tutto compreso; **~ wrestling** n lotta americana.

all-night ['ɔːl'naɪt] a aperto(a) (or che dura) tutta la notte.

allocate ['æləkeɪt] vt (share out) distribuire; (duties, sum, time): **to ~ sth to** assegnare qc a; **to ~ sth for** stanziare qc per.

allocation [æləu'keɪʃən] n: **~ (of money)** stanziamento.

allot [ə'lɔt] vt (share out) spartire; (time): **to ~ sth to** dare qc a; (duties): **to ~ sth to** assegnare qc a; **~ment** n (share) spartizione f; (garden) lotto di terra.

all-out ['ɔːlaut] a (effort etc) totale // ad: **to go all out for** mettercela tutta per.

allow [ə'lau] vt (practice, behaviour) permettere; (sum to spend etc) accordare; (sum, time estimated) dare; (concede): **to ~ that** ammettere che; **to ~ sb to do** permettere a qd di fare; **to ~ for** vt fus tener conto di; **~ance** n (money received) assegno; indennità f inv; (TAX) detrazione f di imposta; **to make ~ances for** tener conto di.

alloy ['ælɔɪ] n lega.

all right ['ɔːl'raɪt] ad (feel, work) bene; (as answer) va bene.

all-round ['ɔːl'raund] a completo(a).

all-time ['ɔːl'taɪm] a (record) assoluto(a).

allude [ə'luːd] vi: **to ~ to** alludere a.

alluring [ə'ljuərɪŋ] a seducente.

allusion [ə'luːʒən] n allusione f.

ally ['ælaɪ] n alleato.

almighty [ɔːl'maɪtɪ] a onnipotente.

almond ['ɑːmənd] n mandorla.

almost ['ɔːlməust] ad quasi.

alms [ɑːmz] n elemosina.

alone [ə'ləun] a solo(a); **to leave sb ~** lasciare qd in pace; **to leave sth ~** lasciare stare qc.

along [ə'lɔŋ] prep lungo // ad: **is he coming ~?** viene con noi?; **he was hopping/limping ~** lui veniva saltellando/zoppicando; **~ with** insieme con; **~side** prep accanto a; lungo // ad accanto.

aloof [ə'luːf] a distaccato(a) // ad a distanza, a disparte.

aloud [ə'laud] ad ad alta voce.

alphabet ['ælfəbet] n alfabeto.

alpine ['ælpaɪn] a alpino(a).

Alps [ælps] npl: **the ~** le Alpi.

already [ɔːl'redɪ] ad già.

alright ['ɔːl'raɪt] ad = **all right**.

also ['ɔːlsəu] ad anche.

altar ['ɔltə*] n altare m.

alter ['ɔltə*] vt,vi alterare; **~ation** [ɔltə'reɪʃən] n modificazione f, alterazione f.

alternate a [ɔl'tɜːnɪt] alterno(a) // vi ['ɔltəneɪt] alternare; **on ~ days** ogni due giorni; **alternating** a (current) alternato(a).

alternative [ɔl'tɜːnətɪv] a (solutions) alternativo(a); (solution) altro(a) // n (choice) alternativa; (other possibility) altra possibilità; **~ly** ad alternativamente.

alternator ['ɔltəneɪtə*] n (AUT) alternatore m.

although [ɔːl'ðəu] cj benché + sub, sebbene + sub.

altitude ['æltɪtjuːd] n altitudine f.

alto ['æltəu] n contralto.

altogether [ɔːltə'geðə*] ad del tutto, completamente; (on the whole) tutto considerato; (in all) in tutto.

altruistic [æltru'ɪstɪk] a altruistico(a).

aluminium [ælju'mɪnɪəm] n alluminio.

always ['ɔːlweɪz] ad sempre.

am [æm] vb see **be**.

a.m. *ad* (*abbr of ante meridiem*) della mattina.

amalgamate [ə'mælgəmeɪt] *vt* amalgamare // *vi* amalgamarsi; **amalgamation** [-'meɪʃən] *n* amalgamazione *f*; (*COMM*) fusione *f*.

amass [ə'mæs] *vt* ammassare.

amateur ['æmətə*] *n* dilettante *m/f* // *a* (*SPORT*) dilettante; **~ish** *a* (*pej*) da dilettante.

amaze [ə'meɪz] *vt* stupire; **~ment** *n* stupore *m*.

ambassador [æm'bæsədə*] *n* ambasciatore/trice.

amber ['æmbə*] *n* ambra; **at ~** (*AUT*) giallo.

ambiguity [æmbɪ'gjuɪtɪ] *n* ambiguità *f inv*.

ambiguous [æm'bɪgjuəs] *a* ambiguo(a).

ambition [æm'bɪʃən] *n* ambizione *f*.

ambitious [æm'bɪʃəs] *a* ambizioso(a).

ambivalent [æm'bɪvələnt] *a* (*attitude*) ambivalente.

amble ['æmbl] *vi* (*gen*: **to ~ along**) camminare tranquillamente.

ambulance ['æmbjuləns] *n* ambulanza.

ambush ['æmbuʃ] *n* imboscata // *vt* fare un'imboscata a.

amenable [ə'miːnəbl] *a*: **~ to** (*advice etc*) ben disposto(a) a.

amend [ə'mend] *vt* (*law*) emendare; (*text*) correggere // *vi* emendarsi; **to make ~s** fare ammenda; **~ment** *n* emendamento; correzione *f*.

amenity [ə'miːnɪtɪ] *n* amenità *f inv*.

America [ə'merɪkə] *n* America; **~n** *a, n* americano(a).

amethyst ['æmɪθɪst] *n* ametista.

amiable ['eɪmɪəbl] *a* amabile, gentile.

amicable ['æmɪkəbl] *a* amichevole.

amid(st) [ə'mɪd(st)] *prep* fra, tra, in mezzo a.

amiss [ə'mɪs] *a,ad*: **there's something ~** c'è qualcosa che non va bene; **to take sth ~** aversene a male.

ammunition [æmju'nɪʃən] *n* munizioni *fpl*.

amnesia [æm'niːzɪə] *n* amnesia.

amnesty ['æmnɪstɪ] *n* amnistia.

amok [ə'mɔk] *ad*: **to run ~** diventare pazzo(a) furioso(a).

among(st) [ə'mʌŋ(st)] *prep* fra, tra, in mezzo a.

amoral [æ'mɔrəl] *a* amorale.

amorous ['æmərəs] *a* amoroso(a).

amorphous [ə'mɔːfəs] *a* amorfo(a).

amount [ə'maunt] *n* somma; ammontare *m*; quantità *f inv* // *vi*: **to ~ to** (*total*) ammontare a; (*be same as*) essere come.

amp(ère) ['æmp(ɛə*)] *n* ampère *m inv*.

amphibious [æm'fɪbɪəs] *a* anfibio(a).

amphitheatre ['æmfɪθɪətə*] *n* anfiteatro.

ample ['æmpl] *a* ampio(a); spazioso(a); (*enough*): **this is ~** questo è più che sufficiente; **to have ~ time/room** avere assai tempo/posto.

amplifier ['æmplɪfaɪə*] *n* amplificatore *m*.

amplify ['æmplɪfaɪ] *vt* amplificare.

amply ['æmplɪ] *ad* ampiamente.

amputate ['æmpjuteɪt] *vt* amputare.

amuck [ə'mʌk] *ad* = **amok**.

amuse [ə'mjuːz] *vt* divertire; **~ment** *n* divertimento.

an [æn, ən, n] *det see* **a**.

anaemia [ə'niːmɪə] *n* anemia.

anaemic [ə'niːmɪk] *a* anemico(a).

anaesthetic [ænɪs'θetɪk] *a* anestetico(a) // *n* anestetico.

anaesthetist [æ'niːsθɪtɪst] *n* anestesista *m/f*.

analogy [ə'nælədʒɪ] *n* analogia.

analyse ['ænəlaɪz] *vt* analizzare.

analysis, *pl* **analyses** [ə'næləsɪs, -siːz] *n* analisi *f inv*.

analyst ['ænəlɪst] *n* analista *m/f*.

analytic(al) [ænə'lɪtɪk(əl)] *a* analitico(a).

anarchist ['ænəkɪst] *a* anarchico(a) // *n* anarchista *m/f*.

anarchy ['ænəkɪ] *n* anarchia.

anathema [ə'næθɪmə] *n* anatema *m*.

anatomical [ænə'tɔmɪkəl] *a* anatomico(a).

anatomy [ə'nætəmɪ] *n* anatomia.

ancestor ['ænsɪstə*] *n* antenato/a.

ancestral [æn'sɛstrəl] *a* avito(a).

ancestry ['ænsɪstrɪ] *n* antenati *mpl*; ascendenza.

anchor ['æŋkə*] *n* ancora // *vi* (*also*: **to drop ~**) gettar l'ancora // *vt* ancorare; **~age** *n* ancoraggio.

anchovy ['æntʃəvɪ] *n* acciuga.

ancient ['eɪnʃənt] *a* antico(a); (*fig*) anziano(a).

and [ænd] *cj* e (*often ed before vowel*); **~ so on** e così via; **come ~ sit here** vieni a sedere qui; **better ~ better** sempre meglio.

Andes ['ændiːz] *npl*: **the ~** le Ande.

anecdote ['ænɪkdəut] *n* aneddoto.

anemia [ə'niːmɪə] *etc* = **anaemia** *etc*.

anesthetic [ænɪs'θetɪk] *etc* = **anaesthetic** *etc*.

anew [ə'njuː] *ad* di nuovo.

angel ['eɪndʒəl] *n* angelo.

anger ['æŋgə*] *n* rabbia // *vt* arrabbiare.

angina [æn'dʒaɪnə] *n* angina pectoris.

angle ['æŋgl] *n* angolo; **from their ~** dal loro punto di vista // *vi*: **to ~ for** (*fig*) cercare di farsi fare; **~r** *n* pescatore *m* con la lenza.

Anglican ['æŋglɪkən] *a,n* anglicano(a).

anglicize ['æŋglɪsaɪz] *vt* anglicizzare.

angling ['æŋglɪŋ] *n* pesca con la lenza.

Anglo- ['æŋgləu] *prefix* anglo...; **~Saxon** *a,n* anglosassone (*m/f*).

angrily ['æŋgrɪlɪ] *ad* con rabbia.

angry ['æŋgrɪ] *a* arrabbiato(a), furioso(a); **to be ~ with sb/at sth** essere in collera con qd/per qc; **to get ~** arrabbiarsi; **to make sb ~** fare arrabbiare qd.

anguish ['æŋgwɪʃ] *n* angoscia.

angular ['æŋgjulə*] *a* angolare.

animal ['ænɪməl] *a, n* animale (*m*).

animate *vt* ['ænɪmeɪt] animare // *a* ['ænɪmɪt] animato(a); **~d** *a* animato(a).

animosity [ænɪ'mɔsɪtɪ] *n* animosità.

aniseed ['ænisiːd] n semi mpl di anice.

ankle ['æŋkl] n caviglia.

annex n ['ænɛks] (also: **annexe**) edificio annesso // vt [ə'nɛks] annettere; **~ation** [-'eɪʃən] n annessione f.

annihilate [ə'naɪəleɪt] vt annientare.

anniversary [ænɪ'vɜːsərɪ] n anniversario.

annotate ['ænəuteɪt] vt annotare.

announce [ə'nauns] vt annunciare; **~ment** n annuncio; (letter, card) partecipazione f; **~r** n (RADIO, TV: between programmes) annunciatore/trice; (in a programme) presentatore/trice.

annoy [ə'nɔɪ] vt dare fastidio a; **don't get ~ed!** non irritarti!; **~ance** n noia; **~ing** a noioso(a).

annual ['ænjuəl] a annuale // n (BOT) pianta annua; (book) annuario; **~ly** ad annualmente.

annuity [ə'njuːɪtɪ] n annualità f inv; **life ~** vitalizio.

annul [ə'nʌl] vt annullare; (law) rescindere; **~ment** n annullamento; rescissione f.

annum ['ænəm] n see **per**.

anoint [ə'nɔɪnt] vt ungere.

anomaly [ə'nɒməlɪ] n anomalia.

anonymous [ə'nɒnɪməs] a anonimo(a).

anorak ['ænəræk] n giacca a vento.

another [ə'nʌðə*] a: **~ book** (one more) un altro libro, ancora un libro; (a different one) un altro libro // pronoun un altro(un'altra), ancora uno(a); see also **one**.

answer ['ɑːnsə*] n risposta; soluzione f // vi rispondere // vt (reply to) rispondere a; (problem) risolvere; (prayer) esaudire; **to ~ the phone** rispondere (al telefono); **in ~ to your letter** in risposta alla sua lettera; **to ~ the bell** rispondere al campanello; **to ~ the door** aprire la porta; **to ~ back** vi ribattere; **to ~ for** vt fus essere responsabile di; **to ~ to** vt fus (description) corrispondere a; **~able** a: **~able (to sb/for sth)** responsabile (verso qd/di qc).

ant [ænt] n formica.

antagonism [æn'tægənɪzəm] n antagonismo.

antagonist [æn'tægənɪst] n antagonista m/f; **~ic** [æntægə'nɪstɪk] a antagonistico(a).

antagonize [æn'tægənaɪz] vt provocare l'ostilità di.

Antarctic [ænt'ɑːktɪk] n Antartide f // a antartico(a).

antelope ['æntɪləup] n antilope f.

antenatal ['æntɪ'neɪtl] a prenatale; **~ clinic** n assistenza medica preparto.

antenna, pl **~e** [æn'tɛnə, -niː] n antenna.

anthem ['ænθəm] n antifona; **national ~** inno nazionale.

ant-hill ['ænthɪl] n formicaio.

anthology [æn'θɒlədʒɪ] n antologia.

anthropology [ænθrə'pɒlədʒɪ] n antropologia.

anti- ['æntɪ] prefix anti-... .

anti-aircraft ['æntɪ'ɛəkrɑːft] a antiaereo(a).

antibiotic ['æntɪbaɪ'ɒtɪk] a antibiotico(a) // n antibiotico.

anticipate [æn'tɪsɪpeɪt] vt prevedere; pregustare; (wishes, request) prevenire.

anticipation [æntɪsɪ'peɪʃən] n anticipazione f; (expectation) aspettative fpl; **thanking you in ~** vi ringrazio in anticipo.

anticlimax ['æntɪ'klaɪmæks] n: **it was an ~** fu una completa delusione.

anticlockwise ['æntɪ'klɒkwaɪz] a in senso antiorario.

antics ['æntɪks] npl buffonerie fpl.

anticyclone ['æntɪ'saɪkləun] n anticiclone m.

antidote ['æntɪdəut] n antidoto.

antifreeze ['æntɪ'friːz] n anticongelante m.

antipathy [æn'tɪpəθɪ] n antipatia.

antiquated ['æntɪkweɪtɪd] a antiquato(a).

antique [æn'tiːk] n antichità f inv // a antico(a); **~ dealer** n antiquario/a; **~ shop** n negozio d'antichità.

antiquity [æn'tɪkwɪtɪ] n antichità f inv.

antiseptic [æntɪ'sɛptɪk] a antisettico(a) // n antisettico.

antisocial ['æntɪ'səuʃəl] a antisociale.

antlers ['æntləz] npl palchi mpl.

anus ['eɪnəs] n ano.

anvil ['ænvɪl] n incudine f.

anxiety [æŋ'zaɪətɪ] n ansia; (keenness): **~ to do** smania di fare.

anxious ['æŋkʃəs] a ansioso(a), inquieto(a); (keen): **~ to do/that** impaziente di fare/che + sub.

any ['ɛnɪ] det (in negative and interrogative sentences = some) del, dell', dello, dei, degli, della, delle; alcuno(a); qualche; nessuno(a); (no matter which) non importa che; (each and every) tutto(a), ogni; **I haven't ~ bread/books** non ho pane/libri; **come (at) ~ time** vieni a qualsiasi ora; **at ~ moment** da un momento all'altro; **in ~ case** in ogni caso; **at ~ rate** ad ogni modo // pronoun uno(a) qualsiasi; (anybody) chiunque; (in negative and interrogative sentences): **I haven't ~** non ne ho; **have you got ~?** ne hai?; **can ~ of you sing?** c'è qualcuno che sa cantare? // ad (in negative sentences) per niente; (in interrogative and conditional constructions) **I can't hear him ~ more** non lo sento più; **are you feeling ~ better?** ti senti un po' meglio?; **do you want ~ more soup?** vuoi ancora della minestra?; **~body** pronoun qualsiasi persona; (in interrogative sentences) qualcuno; (in negative sentences): **I don't see ~body** non vedo nessuno; **~how** ad in qualsiasi modo; **~one = ~body**; **~thing** pronoun (see anybody) qualsiasi cosa; qualcosa; non ... niente, non ... nulla; **~time** ad in qualunque momento; quando vuole; **~way** ad in qualsiasi modo; in or ad ogni modo; **~where** ad (see anybody) da qualsiasi parte; da qualche parte; **I don't see him ~where** non lo vedo da nessuna parte.

apart [ə'pɑːt] ad (to one side) a parte; (separately) separatamente; **10 miles/a long way ~** a 10 miglia di distanza/molto lontani l'uno dall'altro; **they are living ~** sono separati; **~ from** prep a parte, eccetto.

apartheid [ə'pɑːteɪt] n apartheid f.

apartment [ə'pɑːtmənt] n (US) appartamento; **~s** npl appartamento ammobiliato.

apathetic [æpə'θetɪk] a apatico(a).

apathy ['æpəθɪ] n apatia.

ape [eɪp] n scimmia // vt scimmiottare.

aperitif [ə'perɪtɪv] n aperitivo.

aperture ['æpətʃuə*] n apertura.

apex ['eɪpeks] n apice m.

aphrodisiac [æfrəu'dɪzɪæk] a afrodisiaco(a) // n afrodisiaco.

apiece [ə'piːs] ad ciascuno(a).

aplomb [ə'plɒm] n disinvoltura.

apologetic [əpɔlə'dʒetɪk] a (tone, letter) di scusa; **to be very ~ about** scusarsi moltissimo di.

apologize [ə'pɒlədʒaɪz] vi: **to ~ (for sth to sb)** scusarsi (di qc a qd), chiedere scusa (a qd per qc).

apology [ə'pɒlədʒɪ] n scuse fpl.

apoplexy ['æpəpleksɪ] n apoplessia.

apostle [ə'pɒsl] n apostolo.

apostrophe [ə'pɒstrəfɪ] n (segno) apostrofo.

appal [ə'pɔːl] vt atterrire; sgomentare; **~ling** a spaventoso(a).

apparatus [æpə'reɪtəs] n apparato.

apparent [ə'pærənt] a evidente; **~ly** ad evidentemente.

apparition [æpə'rɪʃən] n apparizione f.

appeal [ə'piːl] vi (LAW) appellarsi alla legge // n (LAW) appello; (request) richiesta; (charm) attrattiva; **to ~ for** chiedere (con insistenza); **to ~ to** (subj: person) appellarsi a; (subj: thing) piacere a; **to ~ to sb for mercy** chiedere pietà a qd; **it doesn't ~ to me** mi dice poco.

appear [ə'pɪə*] vi apparire; (LAW) comparire; (publication) essere pubblicato(a); (seem) sembrare; **it would ~ that** sembra che; **to ~ in Hamlet** recitare nell'Amleto; **to ~ on TV** presentarsi in televisione; **~ance** n apparizione f; apparenza; (look, aspect) aspetto; **to put in or make an ~ance** fare atto di presenza.

appease [ə'piːz] vt calmare, appagare.

appendage [ə'pendɪdʒ] n aggiunta.

appendicitis [əpendɪ'saɪtɪs] n appendicite f.

appendix, pl **appendices** [ə'pendɪks, -sɪːz] n appendice f.

appetite ['æpɪtaɪt] n appetito.

appetizing ['æpɪtaɪzɪŋ] a appetitoso(a).

applaud [ə'plɔːd] vt,vi applaudire.

applause [ə'plɔːz] n applauso.

apple ['æpl] n mela; **~ tree** n melo.

appliance [ə'plaɪəns] n apparecchio.

applicable [ə'plɪkəbl] a applicabile.

applicant ['æplɪkənt] n candidato.

application [æplɪ'keɪʃən] n applicazione f; (for a job, a grant etc) domanda.

applied [ə'plaɪd] a applicato(a).

apply [ə'plaɪ] vt (paint, ointment): **to ~ (to)** dare (a); (theory, technique): **to ~ (to)** applicare (a) // vi: **to ~ to** (ask) rivolgersi a; (be suitable for, relevant to) riguardare, riferirsi a; **to ~ (for)** (permit, grant, job) fare domanda (per); **to ~ the brakes** frenare; **to ~ o.s. to** dedicarsi a.

appoint [ə'pɔɪnt] vt nominare; **~ment** n nomina; (arrangement to meet) appuntamento.

appraisal [ə'preɪzl] n valutazione f.

appreciable [ə'priːʃəbl] a apprezzabile.

appreciate [ə'priːʃɪeɪt] vt (like) apprezzare; (be grateful for) essere riconoscente di; (be aware of) rendersi conto di // vi (COMM) aumentare.

appreciation [əpriːʃɪ'eɪʃən] n apprezzamento; (COMM) aumento del valore.

appreciative [ə'priːʃɪətɪv] a (person) sensibile; (comment) elogiativo(a).

apprehend [æprɪ'hend] vt arrestare; (understand) comprendere.

apprehension [æprɪ'henʃən] n inquietudine f.

apprehensive [æprɪ'hensɪv] a apprensivo(a).

apprentice [ə'prentɪs] n apprendista m/f; **~ship** n apprendistato.

approach [ə'prəutʃ] vi avvicinarsi // vt (come near) avvicinarsi a; (ask, apply to) rivolgersi a; (subject, passer-by) avvicinare // n approccio; accesso; (to problem) modo di affrontare; **~able** a accessibile.

appropriate vt [ə'prəuprɪeɪt] (take) appropriarsi // a [ə'prəuprɪɪt] appropriato(a); adatto(a); **~ly** ad in modo appropriato.

approval [ə'pruːvəl] n approvazione f; **on ~** (COMM) in prova, in esame.

approve [ə'pruːv] vt, vi approvare; **to ~ of** vt fus approvare; **~d school** n riformatorio; **approvingly** ad in approvazione.

approximate [ə'prɒksɪmɪt] a approssimativo(a); **~ly** ad circa; **approximation** [-'meɪʃən] n approssimazione f.

apricot ['eɪprɪkɒt] n albicocca.

April ['eɪprəl] n aprile m; **~ fool!** pesce d'aprile!

apron ['eɪprən] n grembiule m.

apt [æpt] a (suitable) adatto(a); (able) capace; (likely): **to be ~ to do** avere tendenza a fare.

aptitude ['æptɪtjuːd] n abilità f inv.

aqualung ['ækwəlʌŋ] n autorespiratore m.

aquarium [ə'kwɛərɪəm] n acquario.

Aquarius [ə'kwɛərɪəs] n Acquario.

aquatic [ə'kwætɪk] a acquatico(a).

aqueduct ['ækwɪdʌkt] n acquedotto.

Arab ['ærəb] n arabo/a.
Arabia [ə'reɪbɪə] n Arabia; ~n a arabo(a).
Arabic ['ærəbɪk] a arabico(a) // n arabo.
arable ['ærəbl] a arabile.
arbitrary ['ɑːbɪtrərɪ] a arbitrario(a).
arbitrate ['ɑːbɪtreɪt] vi arbitrare;
  arbitration [-'treɪʃən] n (LAW) arbitrato;
  (INDUSTRY) arbitraggio.
arbitrator ['ɑːbɪtreɪtə*] n arbitro.
arc [ɑːk] n arco.
arcade [ɑː'keɪd] n portico; (passage with
  shops) galleria.
arch [ɑːtʃ] n arco; (of foot) arco plantare //
  vt inarcare // a malizioso(a).
archaeologist [ɑːkɪ'ɔlədʒɪst] n
  archeologo/a.
archaeology [ɑːkɪ'ɔlədʒɪ] n archeologia.
archaic [ɑː'keɪɪk] a arcaico(a).
archbishop [ɑːtʃ'bɪʃəp] n arcivescovo.
arch-enemy ['ɑːtʃ'enɪmɪ] n arcinemico/a.
archer ['ɑːtʃə*] n arciere m; ~y n tiro
  all'arco.
archetype ['ɑːkɪtaɪp] n archetipo.
archipelago [ɑːkɪ'pelɪgəu] n arcipelago.
architect ['ɑːkɪtekt] n architetto; ~ural
  [ɑːkɪ'tektʃərəl] a architettonico(a); ~ure
  ['ɑːkɪtektʃə*] n architettura.
archives ['ɑːkaɪvz] npl archivi mpl.
archway ['ɑːtʃweɪ] n arco.
Arctic ['ɑːktɪk] a artico(a) // n: the ~
  l'Artico.
ardent ['ɑːdənt] a ardente.
arduous ['ɑːdjuəs] a arduo(a).
are [ɑː*] vb see be.
area ['ɛərɪə] n (GEOM) area; (zone) zona; (:
  smaller) settore m; **dining ~** n zona
  pranzo.
arena [ə'riːnə] n arena.
aren't [ɑːnt] = are not.
Argentina [ɑːdʒən'tiːnə] n Argentina;
  Argentinian [-'tɪnɪən] a, n argentino(a).
arguable ['ɑːgjuəbl] a discutibile.
argue ['ɑːgjuː] vi (quarrel) litigare;
  (reason) ragionare; **to ~ that** sostenere
  che.
argument ['ɑːgjumənt] n (reasons)
  argomento; (quarrel) lite f, (debate)
  discussione f; ~ative [ɑːgju'mentətɪv] a
  litigioso(a).
arid ['ærɪd] a arido(a).
Aries ['ɛərɪz] n Ariete m.
arise [ə'raɪz], pt **arose**, pp **arisen** [ə'raɪz, -'rəuz,
  -'rɪzn] vi alzarsi; (opportunity, problem)
  presentarsi; **to ~ from** risultare da.
aristocracy [ærɪs'tɔkrəsɪ] n aristocrazia.
aristocrat ['ærɪstəkræt] n aristocratico/a;
  ~ic [-'krætɪk] a aristocratico(a).
arithmetic [ə'rɪθmətɪk] n aritmetica.
ark [ɑːk] n: **Noah's A~** l'arca di Noè.
arm [ɑːm] n braccio; (MIL: branch) arma //
  vt armare; ~s npl (weapons) armi fpl; ~
  in ~ a braccetto; ~**band** n bracciale m;
  ~**chair** n poltrona; ~**ed** a armato(a);
  ~**ed robbery** n rapina a mano armata;
  ~**ful** n bracciata.
armistice ['ɑːmɪstɪs] n armistizio.
armour ['ɑːmə*] n armatura; (also:

~**-plating**) corazza, blindatura; (MIL:
  tanks) mezzi mpl blindati; ~**ed car** n
  autoblinda f inv; ~**y** n arsenale m.
armpit ['ɑːmpɪt] n ascella.
army ['ɑːmɪ] n esercito.
aroma [ə'rəumə] n aroma; ~**tic**
  [ærə'mætɪk] a aromatico(a).
arose [ə'rəuz] pt of **arise**.
around [ə'raund] ad attorno, intorno //
  prep intorno a; (fig: about): ~ **£5/3
  o'clock** circa 5 sterline/le 3; **is he ~?** è
  in giro?
arouse [ə'rauz] vt (sleeper) svegliare;
  (curiosity, passions) suscitare.
arrange [ə'reɪndʒ] vt sistemare;
  (programme) preparare; ~**ment** n
  sistemazione f; (plans etc): ~**ments**
  progetti mpl, piani mpl.
array [ə'reɪ] n: ~ **of** fila di.
arrears [ə'rɪəz] npl arretrati mpl; **to be in
  ~ with one's rent** essere in arretrato
  con l'affitto.
arrest [ə'rest] vt arrestare; (sb's attention)
  attirare // n arresto; **under ~** in arresto.
arrival [ə'raɪvəl] n arrivo; (person)
  arrivato/a.
arrive [ə'raɪv] vi arrivare; **to ~ at** vt fus
  (fig) raggiungere.
arrogance ['ærəgəns] n arroganza.
arrogant ['ærəgənt] a arrogante.
arrow ['ærəu] n freccia.
arsenal ['ɑːsɪnl] n arsenale m.
arsenic ['ɑːsnɪk] n arsenico.
arson ['ɑːsn] n incendio doloso.
art [ɑːt] n arte f, (craft) mestiere m; **A~s**
  npl (SCOL) Lettere fpl; ~ **gallery** n
  galleria d'arte.
artefact ['ɑːtɪfækt] n manufatto.
artery ['ɑːtərɪ] n arteria.
artful ['ɑːtful] a furbo(a).
arthritis [ɑː'θraɪtɪs] n artrite f.
artichoke ['ɑːtɪtʃəuk] n carciofo.
article ['ɑːtɪkl] n articolo.
articulate a [ɑː'tɪkjulɪt] (person) che si
  esprime forbitamente; (speech)
  articolato(a) // vi [ɑː'tɪkjuleɪt] articolare;
  ~**d lorry** n autotreno.
artificial [ɑːtɪ'fɪʃəl] a artificiale; ~
  respiration n respirazione f artificiale.
artillery [ɑː'tɪlərɪ] n artiglieria.
artisan ['ɑːtɪzæn] n artigiano/a.
artist ['ɑːtɪst] n artista m/f; ~**ic** [ɑː'tɪstɪk]
  a artistico(a); ~**ry** n arte f.
artless ['ɑːtlɪs] a semplice, ingenuo(a).
as [æz, əz] cj (cause) siccome, poiché; (time:
  moment) come, quando; (: duration)
  mentre; (manner) come; (in the capacity
  of) da; ~ **big** ~ tanto grande quanto;
  twice ~ **big** ~ due volte più grande che;
  big ~ it is grande com'è; ~ **she said**
  come lei ha detto; ~ **if** or **though** come
  se + sub; ~ **for** or **to** quanto a; ~ **or so
  long** ~ cj finché; purché; ~ **much** (~)
  tanto(a) (... quanto(a)); ~ **many** (~)
  tanti(e) (... quanti(e)); ~ **soon** ~ cj
  appena; ~ **such** ad come tale; ~ **well** ad

anche; ~ **well** ~ *cj* come pure; *see also* **so, such**.

asbestos [æz'bɛstəs] *n* asbesto, amianto.

ascend [ə'sɛnd] *vt* salire; ~**ancy** *n* ascendente *m*.

ascent [ə'sɛnt] *n* salita.

ascertain [æsə'teɪn] *vt* accertare.

ascetic [ə'sɛtɪk] *a* ascetico(a).

ascribe [ə'skraɪb] *vt*: **to ~ sth to** attribuire qc a.

ash [æʃ] *n* (*dust*) cenere *f*; ~ (**tree**) frassino.

ashamed [ə'feɪmd] *a* vergognoso(a); **to be ~ of** vergognarsi di; **to be ~ (of o.s.) for having done** vergognarsi di aver fatto.

ashen ['æʃn] *a* (*pale*) livido(a).

ashore [ə'ʃɔː] *ad* a terra; **to go ~** sbarcare.

ashtray ['æʃtreɪ] *n* portacenere *m*.

Asia ['eɪʃə] *n* Asia; ~ **Minor** *n* Asia minore; ~**n** *a, n* asiatico(a); ~**tic** [eɪsɪ'ætɪk] *a* asiatico(a).

aside [ə'saɪd] *ad* da parte // *n* a parte *m*; **to take sb ~** prendere qd a parte.

ask [ɑːsk] *vt* (*request*) chiedere; (*question*) domandare; (*invite*) invitare; **to ~ sb sth/sb to do sth** chiedere qc a qd/a qd di fare qc; **to ~ sb about sth** chiedere a qd di qc; **to ~ (sb) a question** fare una domanda (a qd); **to ~ sb out to dinner** invitare qd a mangiare fuori; **to ~ after** *vt fus* chiedere di; **to ~ for** *vt fus* chiedere.

askance [ə'skɑːns] *ad*: **to look ~ at sb** guardare qd di traverso.

askew [ə'skjuː] *ad* di traverso, storto.

asleep [ə'sliːp] *a* addormentato(a); **to be ~** dormire; **to fall ~** addormentarsi.

asparagus [əs'pærəgəs] *n* asparagi *mpl*.

aspect ['æspɛkt] *n* aspetto.

aspersions [əs'pəːʃənz] *npl*: **to cast ~ on** diffamare.

asphalt ['æsfælt] *n* asfalto.

asphyxiate [æs'fɪksɪeɪt] *vt* asfissiare; **asphyxiation** [-'eɪʃən] *n* asfissia.

aspiration [æspə'reɪʃən] *n* aspirazione *f*.

aspire [əs'paɪə] *vi*: **to ~ to** aspirare a.

aspirin ['æsprɪn] *n* aspirina.

ass [æs] *n* asino.

assail [ə'seɪl] *vt* assalire; ~**ant** *n* assalitore *m*.

assassin [ə'sæsɪn] *n* assassino; ~**ate** *vt* assassinare; ~**ation** [əsæsɪ'neɪʃən] *n* assassinio.

assault [ə'sɔːlt] *n* (MIL) assalto; (*gen: attack*) aggressione *f*; (LAW): ~ (**and battery**) minacce *fpl* e vie di fatto *fpl* // *vt* assaltare; aggredire; (*sexually*) violentare.

assemble [ə'sɛmbl] *vt* riunire; (TECH) montare // *vi* riunirsi.

assembly [ə'sɛmblɪ] *n* (*meeting*) assemblea; (*construction*) montaggio; ~ **line** *n* catena di montaggio.

assent [ə'sɛnt] *n* assenso, consenso // *vi* assentire.

assert [ə'səːt] *vt* asserire; (*insist on*) far valere; ~**ion** [ə'səːʃən] *n* asserzione *f*; ~**ive** *a* assertivo(a).

assess [ə'sɛs] *vt* valutare; ~**ment** *n* valutazione *f*.

asset ['æsɛt] *n* vantaggio; ~**s** *npl* beni *mpl*; disponibilità *fpl*; attivo.

assign [ə'saɪn] *vt* (*date*) fissare; (*task*): **to ~ sth to** assegnare qc a; (*resources*): **to ~ sth to** riservare qc a; (*cause, meaning*): **to ~ sth to** attribuire qc a; ~**ment** *n* compito.

assimilate [ə'sɪmɪleɪt] *vt* assimilare; **assimilation** [-'leɪʃən] *n* assimilazione *f*.

assist [ə'sɪst] *vt* assistere, aiutare; ~**ance** *n* assistenza, aiuto; ~**ant** *n* assistente *m/f*; (*also*: **shop ~ant**) commesso/a.

assizes [ə'saɪzɪz] *npl* assise *fpl*.

associate *a* [ə'səuʃɪt] associato(a); (*member*) aggiunto(a) // *n* collega *m/f*; (*in business*) socio/a // *vb* [ə'səuʃɪeɪt] *vt* associare // *vi*: **to ~ with sb** frequentare qd.

association [əsəusɪ'eɪʃən] *n* associazione *f*; ~ **football** *n* (gioco del) calcio.

assorted [ə'sɔːtɪd] *a* assortito(a).

assortment [ə'sɔːtmənt] *n* assortimento.

assume [ə'sjuːm] *vt* supporre; (*responsibilities etc*) assumere; (*attitude, name*) prendere; ~**d name** *n* nome *m* falso.

assumption [ə'sʌmpʃən] *n* supposizione *f*, ipotesi *f inv*.

assurance [ə'ʃuərəns] *n* assicurazione *f*; (*self-confidence*) fiducia in se stesso.

assure [ə'ʃuə] *vt* assicurare.

asterisk ['æstərɪsk] *n* asterisco.

astern [ə'stəːn] *ad* a poppa.

asthma ['æsmə] *n* asma; ~**tic** [æs'mætɪk] *a,n* asmatico(a).

astir [ə'stəː] *ad* in piedi; (*excited*) in fermento.

astonish [ə'stɔnɪʃ] *vt* stupire; ~**ment** *n* stupore *m*.

astound [ə'staund] *vt* sbalordire.

astray [ə'streɪ] *ad*: **to go ~** smarrirsi; (*fig*) traviarsi.

astride [ə'straɪd] *prep* a cavalcioni di.

astrologer [əs'trɔlədʒə] *n* astrologo/a.

astrology [əs'trɔlədʒɪ] *n* astrologia.

astronaut ['æstrənɔːt] *n* astronauta *m/f*.

astronomer [əs'trɔnəmə] *n* astronomo/a.

astronomical [æstrə'nɔmɪkəl] *a* astronomico(a).

astronomy [əs'trɔnəmɪ] *n* astronomia.

astute [əs'tjuːt] *a* astuto(a).

asylum [ə'saɪləm] *n* asilo; (*building*) manicomio.

at [æt] *prep* a; (*because of: following surprised, annoyed etc*) di; con; ~ **Paolo's** da Paolo; ~ **the baker's** dal panettiere; ~ **times** talvolta.

ate [eɪt] *pt of* **eat**.

atheism ['eɪθɪɪzəm] *n* ateismo.

atheist ['eɪθɪɪst] *n* ateo/a.

Athens ['æθɪnz] *n* Atene *f*.

athlete ['æθliːt] *n* atleta *m/f*.

athletic [æθ'lɛtɪk] *a* atletico(a); ~**s** *n* atletica.

Atlantic [ət'læntɪk] *a* atlantico(a) // *n*: **the**

~ (Ocean) l'Atlantico, l'Oceano Atlantico.

atlas ['ætləs] *n* atlante *m*.

atmosphere ['ætməsfɪə*] *n* atmosfera.

atmospheric [ætməs'ferɪk] *a* atmosferico(a); ~s *n* (RADIO) scariche *fpl*.

atom ['ætəm] *n* atomo; ~ic [ə'tɒmɪk] *a* atomico(a); ~(ic) bomb *n* bomba atomica; ~izer ['ætəmaɪzə*] *n* atomizzatore *m*.

atone [ə'təun] *vi*: to ~ for espiare.

atrocious [ə'trəuʃəs] *a* (very bad) pessimo(a).

atrocity [ə'trɒsɪtɪ] *n* atrocità *f inv*.

attach [ə'tætʃ] *vt* attaccare; (document, letter) allegare; (MIL: troops) assegnare; to be ~ed to sb/sth (to like) essere affezionato(a) a qd/qc; ~é [ə'tæʃeɪ] *n* addetto; ~é case *n* valigetta per documenti; ~ment *n* (tool) accessorio; (love): ~ment (to) affetto (per).

attack [ə'tæk] *vt* attaccare; (task etc) iniziare; (problem) affrontare // *n* attacco; (also: heart ~) infarto.

attain [ə'teɪn] *vt* (also: to ~ to) arrivare a, raggiungere; ~ments *npl* cognizioni *fpl*.

attempt [ə'tempt] *n* tentativo // *vt* tentare; ~ed murder (LAW) tentato omicidio; to make an ~ on sb's life attentare alla vita di qd.

attend [ə'tend] *vt* frequentare; (meeting, talk) andare a; (patient) assistere; to ~ to *vt fus* (needs, affairs etc) prendersi cura di; (customer) occuparsi di; ~ance *n* (being present) presenza; (people present) gente *f* presente; ~ant *n* custode *m/f*; persona di servizio // *a* concomitante.

attention [ə'tenʃən] *n* attenzione *f*; ~s premure *fpl*, attenzioni *fpl*; ~! (MIL) attenti!; at ~ (MIL) sull'attenti; for the ~ of (ADMIN) per l'attenzione di.

attentive [ə'tentɪv] *a* attento(a); (kind) premuroso(a); ~ly *ad* attentamente.

attest [ə'test] *vi*: to ~ to attestare.

attic ['ætɪk] *n* soffitta.

attire [ə'taɪə*] *n* abbigliamento.

attitude ['ætɪtjuːd] *n* atteggiamento; posa.

attorney [ə'tɜːnɪ] *n* (lawyer) avvocato; (having proxy) mandatario; A~ General *n* (Brit) Procuratore *m* Generale; (US) Ministro della Giustizia; power of ~ *n* procura.

attract [ə'trækt] *vt* attirare; ~ion [ə'trækʃən] *n* (gen pl: pleasant things) attrattiva; (PHYSICS, fig: towards sth) attrazione *f*; ~ive *a* attraente.

attribute *n* ['ætrɪbjuːt] attributo // *vt* [ə'trɪbjuːt]: to ~ sth to attribuire qc a.

attrition [ə'trɪʃən] *n*: war of ~ guerra di logoramento.

aubergine ['əubəʒiːn] *n* melanzana.

auburn ['ɔːbən] *a* tizianesco(a).

auction ['ɔːkʃən] *n* (also: sale by ~) asta // *vt* (also: to sell by ~) vendere all'asta; (also: to put up for ~) mettere all'asta; ~eer [-'nɪə*] *n* banditore *m*.

audacity [ɔː'dæsɪtɪ] *n* audacia.

audible ['ɔːdɪbl] *a* udibile.

audience ['ɔːdɪəns] *n* (people) pubblico; spettatori *mpl*; ascoltatori *mpl*; (interview) udienza.

audio-visual [ɔːdɪəu'vɪzjuəl] *a* audiovisivo(a).

audit ['ɔːdɪt] *n* revisione *f*, verifica // *vt* rivedere, verificare.

audition [ɔː'dɪʃən] *n* audizione *f*.

auditor ['ɔːdɪtə*] *n* revisore *m*.

auditorium [ɔːdɪ'tɔːrɪəm] *n* sala, auditorio.

augment [ɔːg'ment] *vt,vi* aumentare.

augur ['ɔːgə*] *vt* (be a sign of) predire // *vi*: it ~s well promette bene.

August ['ɔːgəst] *n* agosto.

august [ɔː'gʌst] *a* augusto(a).

aunt [ɑːnt] *n* zia; ~ie, ~y *n* zietta.

au pair ['əu'pɛə*] *n* (also: ~ girl) (ragazza *f*) alla pari *inv*.

aura ['ɔːrə] *n* aura.

auspices ['ɔːspɪsɪz] *npl*: under the ~ of sotto gli auspici di.

auspicious [ɔːs'pɪʃəs] *a* propizio(a).

austere [ɔs'tɪə*] *a* austero(a).

Australia [ɔs'treɪlɪə] *n* Australia; ~n *a, n* australiano(a).

Austria ['ɔstrɪə] *n* Austria; ~n *a, n* austriaco(a).

authentic [ɔː'θentɪk] *a* autentico(a).

author ['ɔːθə*] *n* autore/trice.

authoritarian [ɔːθɒrɪ'tɛərɪən] *a* autoritario(a).

authoritative [ɔː'θɒrɪtətɪv] *a* (account etc) autorevole; (manner) autoritario(a).

authority [ɔː'θɒrɪtɪ] *n* autorità *f inv*; (permission) autorizzazione *f*; the authorities *npl* le autorità.

authorize ['ɔːθəraɪz] *vt* autorizzare.

auto ['ɔːtəu] *n* (US) auto *f inv*.

autobiography [ɔːtəbaɪ'ɒgrəfɪ] *n* autobiografia.

autocratic [ɔːtə'krætɪk] *a* autocratico(a).

autograph ['ɔːtəgrɑːf] *n* autografo // *vt* firmare.

automatic [ɔːtə'mætɪk] *a* automatico(a) // *n* (gun) arma automatica; (car) automobile *f* con cambio automatico; ~ally *ad* automaticamente.

automation [ɔːtə'meɪʃən] *n* automazione *f*.

automaton, *pl* **automata** [ɔː'tɔmətən, -tə] *n* automa *m*.

automobile ['ɔːtəməbiːl] *n* (US) automobile *f*.

autonomy [ɔː'tɔnəmɪ] *n* autonomia.

autopsy ['ɔːtɔpsɪ] *n* autopsia.

autumn ['ɔːtəm] *n* autunno.

auxiliary [ɔːg'zɪlɪərɪ] *a* ausiliario(a) // *n* ausiliare *m/f*.

avail [ə'veɪl] *vt*: to ~ o.s. of servirsi di; approfittarsi di // *n*: to no ~ inutilmente.

availability [əveɪlə'bɪlɪtɪ] *n* disponibilità.

available [ə'veɪləbl] *a* disponibile; every ~ means tutti i mezzi disponibili.

avalanche ['ævəlɑːnʃ] *n* valanga.

avant-garde ['ævɑ̃'gɑːd] *a* d'avanguardia.

avarice ['ævərɪs] *n* avarizia.

Ave. abbr of **avenue**.

avenge [ə'vɛndʒ] vt vendicare.

avenue ['ævənjuː] n viale m.

average ['ævərɪdʒ] n media // a medio(a) // vt (a certain figure) fare di or in media; **on** ~ in media; **above/below (the)** ~ sopra/sotto la media.

averse [ə'vɜːs] a: **to be** ~ **to sth/doing** essere avverso(a) a qc/a fare.

aversion [ə'vɜːʃən] n avversione f.

avert [ə'vɜːt] vt evitare, prevenire; (one's eyes) distogliere.

aviation [eɪvɪ'eɪʃən] n aviazione f.

avid ['ævɪd] a avido(a).

avocado [ævə'kɑːdəʊ] n (also: ~ **pear**) avocado m inv.

avoid [ə'vɔɪd] vt evitare; ~**able** a evitabile; ~**ance** n l'evitare m.

await [ə'weɪt] vt aspettare; ~**ing attention** (COMM: letter) in attesa di risposta; (: order) in attesa di essere evaso.

awake [ə'weɪk] a sveglio(a) // vb (pt **awoke** [ə'wəʊk], pp **awoken** [ə'wəʊkən] or **awaked**) vt svegliare // vi svegliarsi; ~ **to** consapevole di; ~**ning** [ə'weɪknɪŋ] n risveglio.

award [ə'wɔːd] n premio; (LAW) decreto // vt assegnare; (LAW: damages) decretare.

aware [ə'wɛə*] a: ~ **of** (conscious) conscio(a) di; (informed) informato(a) di; **to become** ~ **of** accorgersi di; **politically/socially** ~ politicamente/socialmente preparato; ~**ness** n consapevolezza.

awash [ə'wɒʃ] a: ~ **(with)** inondato(a) (da).

away [ə'weɪ] a,ad via; lontano(a); **two kilometres** ~ a due chilometri di distanza; **two hours** ~ **by car** a due ore di distanza in macchina; **the holiday was two weeks** ~ ci mancavano due settimane alle vacanze; ~ **from** lontano da; **he's** ~ **for a week** è andato via per una settimana; **he was working/pedalling** etc ~ la particella indica la continuità e l'energia dell'azione: lui lavorava/pedalava etc più che poteva; **to fade/wither** etc ~ la particella rinforza l'idea della diminuzione; ~ **match** n (SPORT) partita fuori casa.

awe [ɔː] n timore m; ~**-inspiring**, ~**some** a imponente.

awful ['ɔːfəl] a terribile; ~**ly** ad (very) terribilmente.

awhile [ə'waɪl] ad (per) un po'.

awkward ['ɔːkwəd] a (clumsy) goffo(a); (inconvenient) scomodo(a); (embarrassing) imbarazzante.

awning ['ɔːnɪŋ] n (of tent) veranda; (of shop, hotel etc) tenda.

awoke, awoken [ə'wəʊk, -kən] pt,pp of **awake**.

awry [ə'raɪ] ad di traverso // a storto(a); **to go** ~ andare a monte.

axe [æks] n scure f // vt (project etc) abolire; (jobs) sopprimere.

axiom ['æksɪəm] n assioma m.

axis, pl **axes** ['æksɪs, -siːz] n asse m.

axle ['æksl] n (also: ~-**tree**) asse m.

ay(e) [aɪ] excl (yes) sì.

B

B [biː] n (MUS) si m.

B.A. abbr see **bachelor**.

babble ['bæbl] vi cianciare; mormorare // n ciance fpl; mormorio.

baby ['beɪbɪ] n bambino/a; ~ **carriage** n (US) carrozzina; ~**hood** n prima infanzia; ~**ish** a infantile; ~**-sit** vi fare il (or la) babysitter.

bachelor ['bætʃələ*] n scapolo; **B**~ **of Arts/Science (B.A./B.Sc.)** ≈ laureato/a in lettere/scienze; ~**hood** n celibato.

back [bæk] n (of person, horse) dorso, schiena; (of hand) dorso; (of house, car) didietro; (of train) coda; (of chair) schienale m; (of page) rovescio; (FOOTBALL) difensore m // vt (candidate: also: ~ **up**) appoggiare; (horse: at races) puntare su; (car) guidare a marcia indietro // vi indietreggiare; (car etc) fare marcia indietro // a (in compounds) posteriore, di dietro; arretrato(a); ~ **seats/wheels** (AUT) sedili mpl/ruote fpl posteriori; ~ **payments/rent** arretrati mpl // ad (not forward) indietro; (returned): **he's** ~ lui è tornato; **he ran** ~ tornò indietro di corsa; (restitution): **throw the ball** ~ ritira la palla; **can I have it** ~? posso riaverlo?; (again): **he called** ~ ha richiamato; **to** ~ **down** vi fare marcia indietro; **to** ~ **out** vi (of promise) tirarsi indietro; ~**ache** n mal m di schiena; ~**bencher** n membro del Parlamento senza potere amministrativo; ~**biting** n maldicenza; ~**bone** n spina dorsale; ~-**cloth** n scena di sfondo; ~**date** vt (letter) retrodatare; ~**dated pay rise** aumento retroattivo; ~**er** n sostenitore/trice; (comm) fautore m; ~**fire** vi (AUT) dar ritorni di fiamma; (plans) fallire; ~**gammon** n tavola reale; ~**ground** n sfondo; (of events) background m inv; (basic knowledge) base f; (experience) esperienza; **family** ~**ground** ambiente m familiare; ~**ground noise** n rumore m di fondo; ~**hand** n (TENNIS: also: ~**hand stroke**) rovescio; ~**handed** a (fig) ambiguo(a); ~**hander** n (bribe) bustarella; ~**ing** n (fig) appoggio; ~**lash** n contraccolpo, ripercussione f; ~**log** n: ~**log of work** lavoro arretrato; ~ **number** n (of magazine etc) numero arretrato; ~ **pay** n arretrato di paga; ~**side** n (col) sedere m; ~**stroke** n nuoto sul dorso; ~**ward** a (movement) indietro inv; (person) tardivo(a); (country) arretrato(a); ~**ward and forward movement** movimento avanti e indietro; ~**wards** ad indietro; (fall, walk) all'indietro; ~**water** n (fig) posto morto; ~**yard** n cortile m dietro la casa.

bacon ['beɪkən] n pancetta.

bacteria [bæk'tɪərɪə] npl batteri mpl.

bad [bæd] a cattivo(a); (child) cattivello(a); (meat, food) andato(a) a male; **his ~ leg** la sua gamba malata.

bade [bæd] pt of **bid**.

badge [bædʒ] n insegna; (of policemen) stemma m.

badger ['bædʒə*] n tasso // vt tormentare.

badly ['bædlɪ] ad (work, dress etc) male; **~ wounded** gravemente ferito; **he needs it ~** ne ha gran bisogno; **~ off** a povero(a).

badminton ['bædmɪntən] n badminton m.

bad-tempered ['bæd'tempəd] a irritabile; di malumore.

baffle ['bæfl] vt (puzzle) confondere.

bag [bæg] n sacco; (handbag etc) borsa; (of hunter) carniere m; bottino // vt (col: take) mettersi in tasca; prendersi; **~s under the eyes** borse sotto gli occhi.

baggage ['bægɪdʒ] n bagagli mpl.

baggy ['bægɪ] a largo(a) largo(a).

bagpipes ['bægpaɪps] npl cornamusa.

Bahamas [bə'hɑːməz] npl: **the ~** le isole Bahama.

bail [beɪl] n cauzione f // vt (prisoner: gen: **to grant ~ to**) concedere la libertà provvisoria su cauzione a; (boat: also: ~ **out**) aggottare; see **bale**; **to ~ out** vt (prisoner) ottenere la libertà provvisoria su cauzione di.

bailiff ['beɪlɪf] n usciere m; fattore m.

bait [beɪt] n esca.

bake [beɪk] vt cuocere al forno // vi cuocersi al forno; **~d beans** npl fagioli mpl all'uccelletto; **~r** n fornaio/a; panetteria/e; **~ry** n panetteria; **baking powder** n lievito in polvere.

balaclava ['bælə'klɑːvə] n (also: ~ **helmet**) passamontagna m inv.

balance ['bæləns] n equilibrio; (COMM: sum) bilancio; (scales) bilancia // vt tenere in equilibrio; (pros and cons) soppesare; (budget) far quadrare; (account) pareggiare; (compensate) contrappesare; **~ of trade/payments** bilancia commerciale/dei pagamenti; **~d** a (personality, diet) equilibrato(a); **~ sheet** n bilancio.

balcony ['bælkənɪ] n balcone m.

bald [bɔːld] a calvo(a); **~ness** n calvizie f.

bale [beɪl] n balla; **to ~ out** vi (of a plane) gettarsi col paracadute.

baleful ['beɪlful] a funesto(a).

balk [bɔːk] vi: **to ~ (at)** tirarsi indietro (davanti a); (horse) recalcitrare (davanti a).

ball [bɔːl] n palla; (football) pallone m; (for golf) pallina; (dance) ballo.

ballad ['bæləd] n ballata.

ballast ['bæləst] n zavorra.

ballerina ['bælə'riːnə] n ballerina.

ballet ['bæleɪ] n balletto.

ballistics [bə'lɪstɪks] n balistica.

balloon [bə'luːn] n pallone m.

ballot ['bælət] n scrutinio; **~ box** n urna (per le schede); **~ paper** n scheda.

ball-point pen ['bɔːlpɔɪnt'pen] n penna a sfera.

ballroom ['bɔːlrum] n sala da ballo.

balsam ['bɔːlsəm] n balsamo.

Baltic [bɔːltɪk] a,n: **the ~ (Sea)** il (mare) Baltico.

bamboo [bæm'buː] n bambù m.

bamboozle [bæm'buːzl] vt (col) corbellare.

ban [bæn] n interdizione f // vt interdire.

banal [bə'nɑːl] a banale.

banana [bə'nɑːnə] n banana.

band [bænd] n banda; (at a dance) orchestra; (MIL) fanfara; **to ~ together** vi collegarsi.

bandage ['bændɪdʒ] n benda.

bandit ['bændɪt] n bandito.

bandwagon ['bændwægən] n: **to jump on the ~** (fig) seguire la corrente.

bandy ['bændɪ] vt (jokes, insults) scambiare; **to ~ about** vt far circolare.

bandy-legged ['bændɪ'legɪd] a dalle gambe storte.

bang [bæŋ] n botta; (of door) lo sbattere; (blow) colpo // vt battere (violentemente); (door) sbattere // vi scoppiare; sbattere; **to ~ at the door** picchiare alla porta.

bangle ['bæŋgl] n braccialetto.

banish ['bænɪʃ] vt bandire.

banister(s) ['bænɪstə(z)] n(pl) ringhiera.

banjo, **~es** or **~s** ['bændʒəu] n banjo m inv.

bank [bæŋk] n (for money) banca, banco; (of river, lake) riva, sponda; (of earth) banco // vi (AVIAT) inclinarsi in virata; (COMM): **they ~ with Pitt's** sono clienti di Pitt's; **to ~ on** vt fus contare su; **~ account** n conto di banca; **~er** n banchiere m; **B~ holiday** n giorno di festa (in cui le banche sono chiuse); **~ing** n attività bancaria; professione f di banchiere; **~ing hours** npl orario di sportello; **~note** n banconota; **~ rate** n tasso bancario.

bankrupt ['bæŋkrʌpt] a, n fallito(a); **to go ~** fallire; **~cy** n fallimento.

banner ['bænə*] n bandiera.

bannister(s) ['bænɪstə(z)] n(pl) = **banister(s)**.

banns [bænz] npl pubblicazioni fpl di matrimonio.

banquet ['bæŋkwɪt] n banchetto.

banter ['bæntə*] n scherzi mpl bonari.

baptism ['bæptɪzəm] n battesimo.

baptize [bæp'taɪz] vt battezzare.

bar [bɑː*] n barra; (of window etc) sbarra; (of chocolate) tavoletta; (fig) ostacolo; restrizione f; (pub) bar m inv; (counter: in pub) banco; (MUS) battuta // vt (road, window) sbarrare; (person) escludere; (activity) interdire; **~ of soap** saponetta; **the B~** (LAW) l'Ordine m degli avvocati; **~ none** senza eccezione.

barbaric [bɑː'bærɪk] a barbarico(a).

barbecue ['bɑːbɪkjuː] n barbecue m inv.

barbed wire ['bɑːbd'waɪə*] n filo spinato.

barber ['bɑːbə*] n barbiere m.

barbiturate [bɑː'bɪtjurɪt] n barbiturico.

bare [bɛə*] a nudo(a) // vt scoprire,

denudare; (*teeth*) mostrare; **the ~ essentials** lo stretto necessario; **~back** ad senza sella; **~faced** a sfacciato(a); **~foot** a,ad scalzo(a); **~headed** a,ad a capo scoperto; **~ly** ad appena.

bargain ['bɑːgɪn] n (*transaction*) contratto; (*good buy*) affare m // vi trattare; **into the ~** per giunta.

barge [bɑːdʒ] n chiatta; **to ~ in** vi (*walk in*) piombare dentro; (*interrupt talk*) intromettersi a sproposito; **to ~ into** vt fus urtare contro.

baritone ['bærɪtəʊn] n baritono.

bark [bɑːk] n (*of tree*) corteccia; (*of dog*) abbaio // vi abbaiare.

barley ['bɑːlɪ] n orzo.

barmaid ['bɑːmeɪd] n cameriera al banco.

barman ['bɑːmən] n barista m.

barmy ['bɑːmɪ] a (*col*) tocco(a).

barn [bɑːn] n granaio.

barnacle ['bɑːnəkl] n cirripede m.

barometer [bəˈrɒmɪtə*] n barometro.

baron ['bærən] n barone m; **~ess** n baronessa.

barracks ['bærəks] npl caserma.

barrage ['bærɑːʒ] n (MIL) sbarramento.

barrel ['bærəl] n barile m; (*of gun*) canna; **~ organ** n organetto a cilindro.

barren ['bærən] a sterile; (*hills*) arido(a).

barricade [bærɪˈkeɪd] n barricata // vt barricare.

barrier ['bærɪə*] n barriera.

barring ['bɑːrɪŋ] prep salvo.

barrister ['bærɪstə*] n avvocato/essa (*con diritto di parlare davanti a tutte le corti*).

barrow ['bærəʊ] n (*cart*) carriola.

bartender ['bɑːtendə*] n (US) barista m.

barter ['bɑːtə*] n baratto // vt: **to ~ sth for** barattare qc con.

base [beɪs] n base f // vt: **to ~ sth on** basare qc su // a vile; **coffee-~d** a base di caffè; **a Paris-~d firm** una ditta con sede centrale a Parigi; **~ball** n baseball m; **~ment** n seminterrato; (*of shop*) interrato.

bases ['beɪsiːz] npl of **basis**; ['beɪsɪz] npl of **base**.

bash [bæʃ] vt (*col*) picchiare; **~ed in** a sfondato(a).

bashful ['bæʃful] a timido(a).

basic ['beɪsɪk] a rudimentale; essenziale; **~ally** [-lɪ] ad fondamentalmente; sostanzialmente.

basil ['bæzl] n basilico.

basin ['beɪsn] n (*vessel, also* GEO) bacino; (*also*: **wash~**) lavabo.

basis, pl **bases** ['beɪsɪs, -siːz] n base f.

bask [bɑːsk] vi: **to ~ in the sun** crogiolarsi al sole.

basket ['bɑːskɪt] n cesta; (*smaller*) cestino; (*with handle*) paniere m; **~ball** n pallacanestro f.

bass [beɪs] n (MUS) basso; **~ clef** n chiave f di basso.

bassoon [bəˈsuːn] n fagotto.

bastard ['bɑːstəd] n bastardo/a; (*col!*) stronzo (!).

baste [beɪst] vt (CULIN) ungere con grasso; (SEWING) imbastire.

bat [bæt] n pipistrello; (*for baseball etc*) mazza; (*for table tennis*) racchetta; **off one's own ~** di propria iniziativa; **he didn't ~ an eyelid** non battè ciglio.

batch [bætʃ] n (*of bread*) infornata; (*of papers*) cumulo.

bated ['beɪtɪd] a: **with ~ breath** col fiato sospeso.

bath [bɑːθ, pl bɑːðz] n (*see also* **baths**) bagno; (*bathtub*) vasca da bagno // vt far fare il bagno a; **to have a ~** fare un bagno; **~chair** n poltrona a rotelle.

bathe [beɪð] vi fare il bagno // vt bagnare; **~r** n bagnante m/f.

bathing ['beɪðɪŋ] n bagni mpl; **~ cap** n cuffia da bagno; **~ costume** n costume m da bagno.

bath: **~room** n stanza da bagno; **~s** npl bagni mpl pubblici; **~ towel** n asciugamano da bagno.

batman ['bætmən] n (MIL) attendente m.

baton ['bætən] n bastone m; (MUS) bacchetta.

battalion [bəˈtælɪən] n battaglione m.

batter ['bætə*] vt battere // n pastetta; **~ed** a (*hat*) sformato(a); (*pan*) ammaccato(a); **~ed wife/baby** consorte f/bambino(a) maltrattato(a); **~ing ram** n ariete m.

battery ['bætərɪ] n batteria; (*of torch*) pila.

battle ['bætl] n battaglia // vi battagliare, lottare; **~field** n campo di battaglia; **~ments** npl bastioni mpl; **~ship** n nave f da guerra.

baulk [bɔːlk] vi = **balk**.

bawdy ['bɔːdɪ] a piccante.

bawl [bɔːl] vi urlare.

bay [beɪ] n (*of sea*) baia; **to hold sb at ~** tenere qd a bada.

bayonet ['beɪənɪt] n baionetta.

bay window ['beɪ'wɪndəʊ] n bovindo.

bazaar [bəˈzɑː*] n bazar m inv; vendita di beneficenza.

b. & b., B. & B. abbr see **bed**.

BBC n abbr of British Broadcasting Corporation.

B.C. ad (abbr of before Christ) a.C.

be, pt **was, were**, pp **been** [biː, wɒz, wɜː*, biːn] vi essere; **how are you?** come sta?; **I am warm** ho caldo; **it is cold** fa freddo; **how much is it?** quanto costa?; **he is four (years old)** ha quattro anni; **2 and 2 are 4** 2 più 2 fa 4; **where have you been?** dov'è stato?; dov'è andato?

beach [biːtʃ] n spiaggia // vt tirare in secco; **~wear** n articoli mpl da spiaggia.

beacon ['biːkən] n (*lighthouse*) faro; (*marker*) segnale m.

bead [biːd] n perlina.

beak [biːk] n becco.

beaker ['biːkə*] n coppa.

beam [biːm] n trave f; (*of light*) raggio // vi brillare; **~ing** a (*sun, smile*) raggiante.

bean [biːn] n fagiolo; (*of coffee*) chicco.

bear [bɛə*] n orso // vb (pt **bore**, pp **borne**

[bɔ:°, bɔ:n]) *vt* portare; (*endure*) sopportare // *vi*: **to ~ right/left** piegare a destra/sinistra; **to ~ the responsibility of** assumersi la responsabilità di; **~able** a sopportabile.

beard [bɪəd] *n* barba; **~ed** a barbuto(a).

bearer ['bɛərə°] *n* portatore *m*.

bearing ['bɛərɪŋ] *n* portamento; (*behaviour*) condotta; (*connection*) rapporto; (**ball**) **~s** *npl* cuscinetti *mpl* a sfere; **to take a ~** fare un rilevamento; **to find one's ~s** orientarsi.

beast [bi:st] *n* bestia; **~ly** a meschino(a); (*weather*) da cani.

beat [bi:t] *n* battimento; (*MUS*) tempo; battuta; (*of policeman*) giro // *vt* (*pt* **beat**, *pp* **beaten**) battere; **off the ~en track** fuori mano; **to ~ about the bush** menare il cane per l'aia; **to ~ time** battere il tempo; **to ~ off** *vt* respingere; **to ~ up** *vt* (*col: person*) picchiare; (*eggs*) sbattere; **~er** *n* (*for eggs, cream*) frullino; **~ing** *n* bastonata.

beautician [bju:'tɪʃən] *n* estetista *m/f*.

beautiful ['bju:tɪful] a bello(a); **~ly** *ad* splendidamente.

beauty ['bju:tɪ] *n* bellezza; **~ salon** *n* istituto di bellezza; **~ spot** *n* neo; (*TOURISM*) luogo pittoresco.

beaver ['bi:və°] *n* castoro.

becalmed [bɪ'kɑ:md] a in bonaccia.

became [bɪ'keɪm] *pt of* **become**.

because [bɪ'kɔz] *cj* perché; **~ of** *prep* a causa di.

beckon ['bɛkən] *vt* (*also*: **~ to**) chiamare con un cenno.

become [bɪ'kʌm] *vt* (*irg: like* **come**) diventare; **to ~ fat/thin** ingrassarsi/dimagrire; **what has ~ of him?** che gli è successo?

becoming [bɪ'kʌmɪŋ] a (*behaviour*) che si conviene; (*clothes*) grazioso(a).

bed [bɛd] *n* letto; (*of flowers*) aiuola; (*of coal, clay*) strato; **~ and breakfast** (**b. & b.**) *n* (*terms*) camera con colazione; **~clothes** *npl* biancheria e coperte *fpl* da letto.

bedlam ['bɛdləm] *n* manicomio (*fig*).

bedraggled [bɪ'dræɡld] a fradicio(a).

bed: ~ridden a costretto(a) a letto; **~room** *n* camera da letto; **~side** *n*: at sb's **~side** al capezzale di qd; **~sit(ter)** *n* monolocale *m*; **~spread** *n* copriletto.

bee [bi:] *n* ape *f*.

beech [bi:tʃ] *n* faggio.

beef [bi:f] *n* manzo.

beehive ['bi:haɪv] *n* alveare *m*.

beeline ['bi:laɪn] *n*: **to make a ~ for** buttarsi a capo fitto verso.

been [bi:n] *pp of* **be**.

beer [bɪə°] *n* birra.

beetle ['bi:tl] *n* scarafaggio; coleottero.

beetroot ['bi:tru:t] *n* barbabietola.

befall [bɪ'fɔ:l] *vi(vt)* (*irg: like* **fall**) accadere (a).

before [bɪ'fɔ:°] *prep* (*in time*) prima di; (*in space*) davanti a // *cj* prima che + *sub*; prima di // *ad* prima; **the week ~** la

settimana prima; **I've seen it ~** l'ho già visto; **I've never seen it ~** è la prima volta che lo vedo; **~hand** *ad* in anticipo.

befriend [bɪ'frɛnd] *vt* assistere; mostrarsi amico a.

beg [bɛɡ] *vi* chiedere l'elemosina // *vt* chiedere in elemosina; (*favour*) chiedere; (*entreat*) pregare.

began [bɪ'ɡæn] *pt of* **begin**.

beggar ['bɛɡə°] *n* (*also*: **~man**, **~woman**) mendicante *m/f*.

begin, *pt* **began**, *pp* **begun** [bɪ'ɡɪn, -'ɡæn, -'ɡʌn] *vt*, *vi* cominciare; **~ner** *n* principiante *m/f*; **~ning** *n* inizio, principio.

begrudge [bɪ'ɡrʌdʒ] *vt*: **to ~ sb sth** dare qc a qd a malincuore; invidiare qd per qc.

begun [bɪ'ɡʌn] *pp of* **begin**.

behalf [bɪ'hɑ:f] *n*: **on ~ of** per conto di; a nome di.

behave [bɪ'heɪv] *vi* comportarsi; (*well*: *also*: **~ o.s.**) comportarsi bene.

behaviour [bɪ'heɪvjə°] *n* comportamento, condotta.

beheld [bɪ'hɛld] *pt,pp of* **behold**.

behind [bɪ'haɪnd] *prep* dietro; (*followed by pronoun*) dietro di; (*time*) in ritardo con // *ad* dietro; in ritardo // *n* didietro.

behold [bɪ'həuld] *vt* (*irg: like* **hold**) vedere, scorgere.

beige [beɪʒ] a beige *inv*.

being ['bi:ɪŋ] *n* essere *m*; **to come into ~** cominciare ad esistere.

belated [bɪ'leɪtɪd] a tardo(a).

belch [bɛltʃ] *vi* ruttare // *vt* (*gen*: **~ out**: *smoke etc*) eruttare.

belfry ['bɛlfrɪ] *n* campanile *m*.

Belgian ['bɛldʒən] a, *n* belga (*m/f*).

Belgium ['bɛldʒəm] *n* Belgio.

belie [bɪ'laɪ] *vt* smentire.

belief [bɪ'li:f] *n* (*opinion*) opinione *f*, convinzione *f*; (*trust, faith*) fede *f*; (*acceptance as true*) credenza.

believe [bɪ'li:v] *vt,vi* credere; **~r** *n* credente *m/f*.

belittle [bɪ'lɪtl] *vt* sminuire.

bell [bɛl] *n* campana; (*small, on door, electric*) campanello.

belligerent [bɪ'lɪdʒərənt] a (*at war*) belligerante; (*fig*) bellicoso(a).

bellow ['bɛləu] *vi* muggire.

bellows ['bɛləuz] *npl* soffietto.

belly ['bɛlɪ] *n* pancia.

belong [bɪ'lɔŋ] *vi*: **to ~ to** appartenere a; (*club etc*) essere socio di; **this book ~s here** questo libro va qui; **~ings** *npl* cose *fpl*, roba.

beloved [bɪ'lʌvɪd] a adorato(a).

below [bɪ'ləu] *prep* sotto, al di sotto di // *ad* sotto, di sotto; giù; **see ~** vedi sotto o oltre.

belt [bɛlt] *n* cintura; (*TECH*) cinghia // *vt* (*thrash*) picchiare // *vi* (*col*) filarsela.

bench [bɛntʃ] *n* panca; (*in workshop*) banco; **the B~** (*LAW*) la Corte.

bend [bɛnd] *vb* (*pt,pp* **bent** [bɛnt]) *vt* curvare; (*leg, arm*) piegare // *vi* curvarsi;

piegarsi // *n* (*in road*) curva; (*in pipe, river*) gomito; **to ~ down** *vi* chinarsi; **to ~ over** *vi* piegarsi.

beneath [bɪ'niːθ] *prep* sotto, al di sotto di; (*unworthy of*) indegno(a) di // *ad* sotto, di sotto.

benefactor ['bɛnɪfæktə*] *n* benefattore *m*.

beneficial [bɛnɪ'fɪʃəl] *a* che fa bene; vantaggioso(a).

benefit ['bɛnɪfɪt] *n* beneficio, vantaggio; (*allowance of money*) indennità *f inv* // *vt* far bene a // *vi*: **he'll ~ from it** ne trarrà beneficio *or* profitto.

Benelux ['bɛnɪlʌks] *n* Benelux *m*.

benevolent [bɪ'nɛvələnt] *a* benevolo(a).

bent [bɛnt] *pt,pp of* **bend** // *n* inclinazione *f* // *a* (*col: dishonest*) losco(a); **to be ~ on** essere deciso(a) a.

bequeath [bɪ'kwiːð] *vt* lasciare in eredità.

bequest [bɪ'kwɛst] *n* lascito.

bereavement [bɪ'riːvmənt] *n* lutto.

beret ['bɛreɪ] *n* berretto.

Bermuda [bəː'mjuːdə] *n* le Bermude.

berry ['bɛrɪ] *n* bacca.

berserk [bə'səːk] *a*: **to go ~** montare su tutte le furie.

berth [bəːθ] *n* (*bed*) cuccetta; (*for ship*) ormeggio // *vi* (*in harbour*) entrare in porto; (*at anchor*) gettare l'ancora.

beseech, *pt,pp* **besought** [bɪ'siːtʃ, -'sɔːt] *vt* implorare.

beset, *pt,pp* **beset** [bɪ'sɛt] *vt* assalire.

beside [bɪ'saɪd] *prep* accanto a; **to be ~ o.s. (with anger)** essere fuori di sé.

besides [bɪ'saɪdz] *ad* inoltre, per di più // *prep* oltre a; a parte.

besiege [bɪ'siːdʒ] *vt* (*town*) assediare; (*fig*) tempestare.

besought [bɪ'sɔːt] *pt,pp of* **beseech**.

best [bɛst] *a* migliore // *ad* meglio; **the ~ part of** (*quantity*) la maggior parte di; **at ~** tutt'al più; **to make the ~ of sth** cavare il meglio possibile da qc; **to the ~ of my ability** al massimo delle mie capacità; **~ man** *n* testimone *m* dello sposo.

bestow [bɪ'stəu] *vt* accordare; (*title*) conferire.

bestseller ['bɛst'sɛlə*] *n* bestseller *m inv*.

bet [bɛt] *n* scommessa // *vt,vi* (*pt,pp* **bet** *or* **betted**) scommettere.

betray [bɪ'treɪ] *vt* tradire; **~al** *n* tradimento.

better ['bɛtə*] *a* migliore // *ad* meglio // *vt* migliorare // *n*: **to get the ~ of** avere la meglio su; **you had ~ do it** è meglio che lo faccia; **he thought ~ of it** cambiò idea; **to get ~** migliorare; (*fig*): **you'd be ~ off this way** starebbe meglio così.

betting ['bɛtɪŋ] *n* scommesse *fpl*; **~ shop** *n* ufficio dell'allibratore.

between [bɪ'twiːn] *prep* tra // *ad* in mezzo, nel mezzo.

beverage ['bɛvərɪdʒ] *n* bevanda.

beware [bɪ'wɛə*] *vt,vi*: **to ~ (of)** stare attento(a) (a).

bewildered [bɪ'wɪldəd] *a* sconcertato(a), confuso(a).

bewitching [bɪ'wɪtʃɪŋ] *a* affascinante.

beyond [bɪ'jɔnd] *prep* (*in space*) oltre; (*exceeding*) al di sopra di // *ad* di là; **~ doubt** senza dubbio; **~ repair** irreparabile.

bias ['baɪəs] *n* (*prejudice*) pregiudizio; (*preference*) preferenza; **~(s)ed** *a* parziale.

bib [bɪb] *n* bavaglino.

Bible ['baɪbl] *n* Bibbia.

bicker ['bɪkə*] *vi* bisticciare.

bicycle ['baɪsɪkl] *n* bicicletta.

bid [bɪd] *n* offerta; (*attempt*) tentativo // *vb* (*pt* **bade** [bæd] *or* **bid**, *pp* **bidden** ['bɪdn] *or* **bid**) *vi* fare un'offerta // *vt* fare un'offerta di; **to ~ sb good day** dire buon giorno a qd; **~der** *n*: **the highest ~der** il maggior offerente; **~ding** *n* offerte *fpl*.

bide [baɪd] *vt*: **to ~ one's time** aspettare il momento giusto.

bier [bɪə*] *n* bara.

big [bɪg] *a* grande; grosso(a).

bigamy ['bɪgəmɪ] *n* bigamia.

bigheaded ['bɪg'hɛdɪd] *a* presuntuoso(a).

bigot ['bɪgət] *n* persona gretta; **~ed** *a* gretto(a); **~ry** *n* grettezza.

bigwig ['bɪgwɪg] *n* (*col*) pezzo grosso.

bike [baɪk] *n* bici *f inv*.

bikini [bɪ'kiːnɪ] *n* bikini *m inv*.

bile [baɪl] *n* bile *f*.

bilingual [baɪ'lɪŋgwəl] *a* bilingue.

bilious ['bɪlɪəs] *a* biliare; (*fig*) bilioso(a).

bill [bɪl] *n* conto; (*POL*) atto; (*US: banknote*) banconota; (*of bird*) becco; **to fit** *or* **fill the ~** (*fig*) fare al caso.

billet ['bɪlɪt] *n* alloggio.

billfold ['bɪlfəuld] *n* (*US*) portafoglio.

billiards ['bɪlɪədz] *n* biliardo.

billion ['bɪlɪən] *n* (*Brit*) bilione *m*; (*US*) miliardo.

bin [bɪn] *n* bidone *m*; **bread~** *n* cassetta *f* portapane *inv*.

bind, *pt,pp* **bound** [baɪnd, baund] *vt* legare; (*oblige*) obbligare; **~ing** *n* (*of book*) legatura // *a* (*contract*) vincolante.

bingo ['bɪŋgəu] *n* gioco simile alla tombola.

binoculars [bɪ'nɔkjuləz] *npl* binocolo.

bio... [baɪə'...] *prefix*: **~chemistry** *n* biochimica; **~graphy** [baɪ'ɔgrəfɪ] *n* biografia; **~logical** *a* biologico(a); **~logist** [baɪ'ɔlədʒɪst] *n* biologo/a; **~logy** [baɪ'ɔlədʒɪ] *n* biologia.

birch [bəːtʃ] *n* betulla.

bird [bəːd] *n* uccello; (*col: girl*) bambola; **~ watcher** *n* ornitologo/a dilettante.

birth [bəːθ] *n* nascita; **~ certificate** *n* certificato di nascita; **~ control** *n* controllo delle nascite; contraccezione *f*; **~day** *n* compleanno; **~place** *n* luogo di nascita; **~ rate** *n* indice *m* di natalità.

biscuit ['bɪskɪt] *n* biscotto.

bishop ['bɪʃəp] *n* vescovo.

bit [bɪt] *pt of* **bite** // *n* pezzo; (*of tool*) punta;

(*of horse*) morso; **a ~ of** un po' di; **a ~ mad/dangerous** un po' matto/pericoloso.

bitch [bitʃ] n (*dog*) cagna; (*col!*) vacca.

bite [bait] vt,vi (*pt bit* [bit], *pp bitten* ['bitn]) mordere // n morso; (*insect* ~) puntura; (*mouthful*) boccone m; **let's have a ~** (**to eat**) mangiamo un boccone; **to ~ one's nails** mangiarsi le unghie.

biting ['baitiŋ] a pungente.

bitten ['bitn] pp of **bite**.

bitter ['bitə*] a amaro(a); (*wind, criticism*) pungente // n (*beer*) birra amara; **to the ~ end** a oltranza; **~ness** n amarezza; gusto amaro; **~sweet** a agrodolce.

bivouac ['bivuæk] n bivacco.

bizarre [bi'zɑ:*] a bizzarro(a).

blab [blæb] vi parlare troppo.

black [blæk] a nero(a) // n nero // vt (*INDUSTRY*) boicottare; **to give sb a ~ eye** dare un occhio nero a qd; **~ and blue** a tutto(a) pesto(a); **~berry** n mora; **~bird** n merlo; **~board** n lavagna; **~currant** n ribes m inv; **~en** vt annerire; **~leg** n crumiro; **~list** n lista nera; **~mail** n ricatto // vt ricattare; **~mailer** n ricattatore/trice; **~ market** n mercato nero; **~out** n oscuramento; (*fainting*) svenimento; **the B~ Sea** il Mar Nero; **~ sheep** n pecora nera; **~smith** n fabbro ferraio.

bladder ['blædə*] n vescica.

blade [bleid] n lama; (*of oar*) pala; **~ of grass** filo d'erba.

blame [bleim] n colpa // vt: **to ~ sb/sth for sth** dare la colpa di qc a qd/qc; **who's to ~?** chi è colpevole?; **~less** a irreprensibile.

bland [blænd] a mite; (*taste*) blando(a).

blank [blæŋk] a bianco(a); (*look*) distratto(a) // n spazio vuoto; (*cartridge*) cartuccia a salve.

blanket ['blæŋkit] n coperta.

blare [blɛə*] vi strombettare.

blasé ['blɑ:zei] a blasé inv.

blasphemy ['blæsfimi] n bestemmia.

blast [blɑ:st] n raffica di vento; esplosione f // vt far saltare; **~-off** n (*SPACE*) lancio.

blatant ['bleitənt] a flagrante.

blaze [bleiz] n (*fire*) incendio; (*fig*) vampata // vi (*fire*) ardere, fiammeggiare; (*fig*) infiammarsi // vt: **to ~ a trail** (*fig*) tracciare una via nuova.

blazer ['bleizə*] n blazer m inv.

bleach [bli:tʃ] n (*also*: **household ~**) varechina // vt (*linen*) sbiancare; **~ed** a (*hair*) decolorato(a).

bleak [bli:k] a tetro(a).

bleary-eyed ['bliəri'aid] a dagli occhi offuscati.

bleat [bli:t] vi belare.

bleed, *pt,pp* **bled** [bli:d, bled] vt dissanguare // vi sanguinare; **my nose is ~ing** mi viene fuori sangue dal naso.

blemish ['blemiʃ] n macchia.

blend [blend] n miscela // vt mescolare // vi (*colours etc*) armonizzare.

bless, *pt,pp* **blessed** or **blest** [bles, blest]

vt benedire; **~ you!** (*sneezing*) salute!; **to be ~ed with** godere di; **~ing** n benedizione f; fortuna.

blew [blu:] pt of **blow**.

blight [blait] n (*of plants*) golpe f // vt (*hopes etc*) deludere.

blimey ['blaimi] excl (*col*) accidenti!

blind [blaind] a cieco(a) // n (*for window*) cortina // vt accecare; **to turn a ~ eye** (**on** or **to**) chiudere un occhio (su); **~ alley** n vicolo cieco; **~ corner** n svolta cieca; **~fold** n benda // a,ad bendato(a) // vt bendare gli occhi a; **~ness** n cecità; **~ spot** n (*AUT etc*) punto cieco; (*fig*) punto debole.

blink [bliŋk] vi battere gli occhi; (*light*) lampeggiare; **~ers** npl paraocchi mpl.

bliss [blis] n estasi f.

blister ['blistə*] n (*on skin*) vescica; (*on paintwork*) bolla // vi (*paint*) coprirsi di bolle.

blithe [blaið] a gioioso(a), allegro(a).

blitz [blits] n blitz m.

blizzard ['blizəd] n bufera di neve.

bloated ['bləutid] a gonfio(a).

blob [blɔb] n (*drop*) goccia; (*stain, spot*) macchia.

block [blɔk] n blocco; (*in pipes*) ingombro; (*toy*) cubo; (*of buildings*) isolato // vt bloccare; **~ade** [-'keid] n blocco // vt assediare; **~age** n ostacolo; **~head** n testa di legno; **~ of flats** n caseggiato; **in ~ letters** a stampatello.

bloke [bləuk] n (*col*) tizio.

blonde [blɔnd] a,n biondo(a).

blood [blʌd] n sangue m; **~ donor** n donatore/trice di sangue; **~ group** n gruppo sanguigno; **~less** a (*coup*) senza sangue; **~ poisoning** n setticemia; **~ pressure** n pressione f sanguigna; **~shed** n spargimento di sangue; **~shot** a: **~shot eyes** occhi iniettati di sangue; **~stained** a macchiato(a) di sangue; **~stream** n flusso del sangue; **~thirsty** a assetato(a) di sangue; **~ transfusion** n trasfusione f di sangue; **~y** a sanguinoso(a); (*col!*): **this ~y ...** questo maledetto ...; **~y awful/good** (*col!*) veramente terribile/forte; **~y-minded** a perverso(a), ostinato(a).

bloom [blu:m] n fiore m // vi essere in fiore; **~ing** a (*col*): **this ~ing ...** questo dannato ... .

blossom ['blɔsəm] n fiore m; (*with pl sense*) fiori mpl // vi essere in fiore.

blot [blɔt] n macchia // vt macchiare; **to ~ out** vt (*memories*) cancellare; (*view*) nascondere; (*nation, city*) annientare.

blotchy ['blɔtʃi] a (*complexion*) coperto(a) di macchie.

blotting paper ['blɔtiŋpeipə*] n carta assorbente.

blouse [blauz] n (*feminine garment*) camicetta.

blow [bləu] n colpo // vb (*pt blew*, *pp blown* [blu:, bləun]) vi soffiare // vt (*col*) far saltare; **to ~ one's nose** soffiarsi il naso; **to ~ a whistle** fischiare; **to ~**

away *vt* portare via; **to ~ down** *vt* abbattere; **to ~ off** *vt* far volare via; **to ~ off course** far uscire di rotta; **to ~ out** *vi* scoppiare; **to ~ over** *vi* calmarsi; **to ~ up** *vi* saltare in aria // *vt* far saltare in aria; *(tyre)* gonfiare; *(PHOT)* ingrandire; **~lamp** *n* lampada a benzina per saldare; **~out** *n (of tyre)* scoppio.

blubber ['blʌbə*] *n* grasso di balena // *vi (pej)* piangere forte.

bludgeon ['blʌdʒən] *vt* prendere a randellate.

blue [blu:] *a* azzurro(a); **~ film/joke** film/barzelletta pornografico(a); **to have the ~s** essere depresso(a); **~bell** *n* giacinto di bosco; **~bottle** *n* moscone *m*; **~ jeans** *npl* blue-jeans *mpl*; **~print** *n (fig)* progetto.

bluff [blʌf] *vi* bluffare // *n* bluff *m inv* // *a (person)* brusco(a); **to call sb's ~** mettere alla prova il bluff di qd.

blunder ['blʌndə*] *n* abbaglio // *vi* prendere un abbaglio.

blunt [blʌnt] *a* smussato(a); spuntato(a); *(person)* brusco(a) // *vt* smussare; spuntare; **~ly** *ad* chiaro; bruscamente.

blur [blə:*] *n* cosa offuscata // *vt* offuscare.

blurt [blə:t]: **to ~ out** *vt* lasciarsi sfuggire.

blush [blʌʃ] *vi* arrossire // *n* rossore *m*.

blustery ['blʌstəri] *a (weather)* burrascoso(a).

B.O. *n (abbr of body odour)* odori *mpl* del corpo.

boar [bɔ:*] *n* cinghiale *m*.

board [bɔ:d] *n* tavola; *(on wall)* tabellone *m*; *(committee)* consiglio, comitato; *(in firm)* consiglio d'amministrazione // *vt (ship)* salire a bordo di; *(train)* salire su; **~ and lodging** *n* vitto e alloggio; **full ~** pensione *f* completa; **with ~ and lodging** *(job)* inclusivo di vitto e alloggio; **to go by the ~** *(fig)*: **which goes by the ~** che viene abbandonato; **to ~ up** *vt (door)* chiudere con assi; **~er** *n* pensionante *m/f*; *(SCOL)* convittore/trice; **~ing house** *n* pensione *f*; **~ing school** *n* collegio; **~ room** *n* sala del consiglio.

boast [bəust] *vi* vantare // *vt* vantarsi di // *n* vanteria; vanto; **~ful** *a* vanaglorioso(a).

boat [bəut] *n* nave *f*; *(small)* barca; **~er** *n (hat)* paglietta; **~ing** *n* canottaggio.

bob [bɔb] *vi (boat, cork on water: also: ~ up and down)* andare su e giù // *n (col)* = **shilling; to ~ up** *vi* saltare fuori.

bobbin ['bɔbin] *n* bobina; *(of sewing machine)* rocchetto.

bobby ['bɔbi] *n (col)* ≈ poliziotto.

bobsleigh ['bɔbslei] *n* bob *m inv*.

bodice ['bɔdis] *n* corsetto.

bodily ['bɔdili] *a* fisico(a), corporale // *ad* corporalmente; interamente; in persona.

body ['bɔdi] *n (also: of car)* carrozzeria; *(of plane)* fusoliera; *(fig: quantity)* quantità *f inv*; **a wine with ~** un vino corposo; **~guard** *n* guardia del corpo; **~work** *n* carrozzeria.

bog [bɔg] *n* palude *f* // *vt*: **to get ~ged down** *(fig)* impantanarsi.

boggle ['bɔgl] *vi*: **the mind ~s** è incredibile.

bogus ['bəugəs] *a* falso(a); finto(a).

boil [bɔil] *vt*, *vi* bollire // *n (MED)* foruncolo; **to ~ down** *vi (fig)*: **to ~ down to** ridursi a; **~er** *n* caldaia; **~er suit** *n* tuta; **~ing hot** *a* bollente.

boisterous ['bɔistərəs] *a* chiassoso(a).

bold [bəuld] *a* audace; *(child)* impudente; *(outline)* chiaro(a); *(colour)* deciso(a); **~ness** *n* audacia; impudenza.

Bolivia [bə'liviə] *n* Bolivia.

bollard ['bɔləd] *n (NAUT)* bitta; *(AUT)* colonnina luminosa.

bolster ['bəulstə*] *n* capezzale *m*; **to ~ up** *vt* sostenere.

bolt [bəult] *n* chiavistello; *(with nut)* bullone *m* // *vt* serrare; *(food)* mangiare in fretta // *vi* scappare via; **a ~ from the blue** *(fig)* un fulmine a ciel sereno.

bomb [bɔm] *n* bomba // *vt* bombardare; **~ard** [bɔm'ba:d] *vt* bombardare.

bombastic [bɔm'bæstik] *a* ampolloso(a).

bomb disposal ['bɔmdispəuzl] *n*: **~ unit** corpo degli artificieri.

bomber ['bɔmə*] *n* bombardiere *m*.

bombshell ['bɔmʃel] *n (fig)* notizia bomba.

bona fide ['bəunə'faidi] *a* sincero(a); *(offer)* onesto(a).

bond [bɔnd] *n* legame *m*; *(binding promise, FINANCE)* obbligazione *f*.

bone [bəun] *n* osso; *(of fish)* spina, lisca // *vt* disossare; togliere le spine a; **~-dry** *a* asciuttissimo(a).

bonfire ['bɔnfaiə*] *n* falò *m inv*.

bonnet ['bɔnit] *n* cuffia; *(Brit: of car)* cofano.

bonus ['bəunəs] *n* premio.

bony ['bəuni] *a (arm, face, MED: tissue)* osseo(a); *(meat)* pieno di ossi; *(fish)* pieno(a) di spine.

boo [bu:] *excl* ba! // *vt* fischiare // *n* fischio.

booby trap ['bu:bitræp] *n* trappola.

book [buk] *n* libro; *(of stamps etc)* blocchetto; *(COMM)*: **~s** conti *mpl* // *vt (ticket, seat, room)* prenotare; *(driver)* multare; *(football player)* ammonire; **~able** *a*: **seats are ~able** si possono prenotare i posti; **~case** *n* scaffale *m*; **~ing office** *n* biglietteria; **~-keeping** *n* contabilità; **~let** *n* libricino; **~maker** *n* allibratore *m*; **~seller** *n* libraio; **~shop** *n* libreria; **~stall** *n* bancarella di libri; **~store** *n* = **~shop**.

boom [bu:m] *n (noise)* rimbombo; *(busy period)* boom *m inv* // *vi* rimbombare; andare a gonfie vele.

boomerang ['bu:məræŋ] *n* boomerang *m inv*.

boon [bu:n] *n* vantaggio.

boorish ['buəriʃ] *a* maleducato(a).

boost [bu:st] *n* spinta // *vt* spingere.

boot [bu:t] *n* stivale *m*; *(for hiking)* scarpone *m* da montagna; *(for football etc)* scarpa; *(Brit: of car)* portabagagli *m inv*; **to ~** *(in addition)* per giunta, in più.

booth [bu:ð] *n (at fair)* baraccone *m*; *(of*

cinema, telephone etc) cabina.
booty ['bu:tɪ] *n* bottino.
booze [bu:z] (*col*) *n* alcool *m* // *vi* trincare.
border ['bɔ:də°] *n* orlo; margine *m*; (*of a country*) frontiera; **to ~ on** *vt fus* confinare con; **~line** *n* (*fig*) linea di demarcazione; **~line case** *n* caso limite.
bore [bɔ:°] *pt of* **bear** // *vt* (*hole*) perforare; (*person*) annoiare // *n* (*person*) seccatore/trice; (*of gun*) calibro; **~dom** *n* noia.
boring ['bɔ:rɪŋ] *a* noioso(a).
born [bɔ:n] *a*: **to be ~** nascere; **I was ~ in 1960** sono nato nel 1960; **~ blind** nato(a) cieco(a); **a ~ comedian** un comico nato.
borne [bɔ:n] *pp of* **bear**.
borough ['bʌrə] *n* municipio.
borrow ['bɔrəu] *vt*: **to ~ sth (from sb)** prendere in prestito qc (da qd).
borstal ['bɔ:stl] *n* riformatorio.
bosom ['buzəm] *n* petto; (*fig*) seno; **~ friend** *n* amico/a del cuore.
boss [bɔs] *n* capo // *vt* comandare; **~y** *a* prepotente.
bosun ['bəusn] *n* nostromo.
botanical [bə'tænɪkl] *a* botanico(a).
botanist ['bɔtənɪst] *n* botanico/a.
botany ['bɔtənɪ] *n* botanica.
botch [bɔtʃ] *vt* (*also*: **~ up**) fare un pasticcio di.
both [bəuθ] *a* entrambi, tutte due // *pronoun*: **~ (of them)** entrambi; **~ of us went, we ~ went** ci siamo andati tutt'e due // *ad*: **they sell ~ meat and poultry** vendono insieme la carne ed il pollame.
bother ['bɔðə°] *vt* (*worry*) preoccupare; (*annoy*) infastidire // *vi* (*gen*: **~ o.s.**) preoccuparsi; **can you be ~ed doing it?** ti va di farlo? // *n*: **it is a ~ to have to do** è una seccatura dover fare; **it was no ~ finding** non c'era problema nel trovare.
bottle ['bɔtl] *n* bottiglia; (*baby's*) biberon *m inv* // *vt* imbottigliare; **to ~ up** *vt* contenere; **~neck** *n* ingorgo; **~-opener** *n* apribottiglie *m inv*.
bottom ['bɔtəm] *n* fondo; (*buttocks*) sedere *m* // *a* più basso(a); ultimo(a); **at the ~ of** in fondo a; **~less** *a* senza fondo.
bough [bau] *n* ramo.
bought [bɔ:t] *pt,pp of* **buy**.
boulder ['bəuldə°] *n* masso (tondeggiante).
bounce [bauns] *vi* (*ball*) rimbalzare; (*cheque*) essere restituito(a) // *vt* far rimbalzare // *n* (*rebound*) rimbalzo; **~r** *n* buttafuori *m inv*.
bound [baund] *pt,pp of* **bind** // *n* (*gen pl*) limite *m*; (*leap*) salto // *vi* (*leap*) saltare; (*limit*) delimitare // *a*: **to be ~ to do sth** (*obliged*) essere costretto a fare qc; **out of ~s** il cui accesso è vietato; **he's ~ to fail** (*likely*) è certo di fallire; **~ for** diretto(a) a.
boundary ['baundrɪ] *n* confine *m*.
boundless ['baundlɪs] *a* illimitato(a).

bout [baut] *n* periodo; (*of malaria etc*) attacco; (*BOXING etc*) incontro.
bow *n* [bəu] nodo; (*weapon*) arco; (*MUS*) archetto; [bau] inchino // *vi* [bau] inchinarsi; (*yield*): **to ~ to** *or* **before** sottomettersi a.
bowels [bauəlz] *npl* intestini *mpl*; (*fig*) viscere *fpl*.
bowl [bəul] *n* (*for eating*) scodella; (*for washing*) bacino; (*ball*) boccia; (*of pipe*) fornello // *vi* (*CRICKET*) servire (la palla); **~s** *n* gioco delle bocce; **to ~ over** *vt* (*fig*) sconcertare.
bow-legged ['bəulɛgɪd] *a* dalle gambe storte.
bowler ['bəulə°] *n* giocatore *m* di bocce; (*CRICKET*) giocatore che serve la palla; (*also*: **~ hat**) bombetta.
bowling ['bəulɪŋ] *n* (*game*) gioco delle bocce; **~ alley** *n* pista da bowling; **~ green** *n* campo di bocce.
bow tie ['bəu'taɪ] *n* cravatta a farfalla.
box [bɔks] *n* scatola; (*THEATRE*) palco // *vi* fare del pugilato; **~er** *n* (*person*) pugile *m*; (*dog*) boxer *m inv*; **~ing** *n* (*SPORT*) pugilato; **B~ing Day** *n* Santo Stefano; **~ing gloves** *npl* guantoni *mpl* da pugile; **~ office** *n* biglietteria; **~ room** *n* ripostiglio.
boy [bɔɪ] *n* ragazzo; (*servant*) servo.
boycott ['bɔɪkɔt] *n* boicottaggio // *vt* boicottare.
boyfriend ['bɔɪfrɛnd] *n* ragazzo.
boyish ['bɔɪʃ] *a* di *or* da ragazzo.
B.R. *abbr of* British Rail.
bra [brɑ:] *n* reggipetto, reggiseno.
brace [breɪs] *n* sostegno; (*on teeth*) apparecchio correttore; (*tool*) trapano // *vt* rinforzare, sostenere; **~s** *npl* bretelle *fpl*; **to ~ o.s.** (*fig*) farsi coraggio.
bracelet ['breɪslɪt] *n* braccialetto.
bracing ['breɪsɪŋ] *a* invigorante.
bracken ['brækən] *n* felce *f*.
bracket ['brækɪt] *n* (*TECH*) mensola; (*group*) gruppo; (*TYP*) parentesi *f inv* // *vt* mettere fra parentesi.
brag [bræg] *vi* vantarsi.
braid [breɪd] *n* (*trimming*) passamano; (*of hair*) treccia.
brain [breɪn] *n* cervello; **~s** *npl* cervella *fpl*; **he's got ~s** è intelligente; **~wash** *vt* fare un lavaggio di cervello a; **~wave** *n* lampo di genio; **~y** *a* intelligente.
braise [breɪz] *vt* brasare.
brake [breɪk] *n* (*on vehicle*) freno // *vt, vi* frenare.
bramble ['bræmbl] *n* rovo.
bran [bræn] *n* crusca.
branch [brɑ:ntʃ] *n* ramo; (*COMM*) succursale *f* // *vi* diramarsi.
brand [brænd] *n* marca // *vt* (*cattle*) marcare (a ferro rovente); (*fig: pej*): **to ~ sb a communist** *etc* definire qd come comunista *etc*.
brandish ['brændɪʃ] *vt* brandire.
brand-new ['brænd'nju:] *a* nuovo(a) di zecca.

brandy ['brændɪ] n brandy m inv.

brash [bræʃ] a sfacciato(a).

brass [brɑːs] n ottone m; the ~ (MUS) gli ottoni; ~ **band** n fanfara.

brassière ['bræsɪəˀ] n reggipetto, reggiseno.

brat [bræt] n (pej) marmocchio, monello/a.

bravado [brəˈvɑːdəu] n spavalderia.

brave [breɪv] a coraggioso(a) // n guerriero m pelle rossa inv // vt affrontare; ~ry n coraggio.

brawl [brɔːl] n rissa.

brawn [brɔːn] n muscolo; (meat) carne f di testa di maiale; ~y a muscoloso(a).

bray [breɪ] vi ragliare.

brazen ['breɪzn] a svergognato(a) // vt: to ~ **it out** fare lo sfacciato.

brazier ['breɪzɪəˀ] n braciere m.

Brazil [brəˈzɪl] n Brasile m; ~**ian** a, n brasiliano(a); ~ **nut** n noce f del Brasile.

breach [briːtʃ] vt aprire una breccia in // n (gap) breccia, varco; (breaking): ~ **of contract** rottura di contratto; ~ **of the peace** violazione f dell'ordine pubblico.

bread [brɛd] n pane m; ~ **and butter** n pane e burro; (fig) mezzi mpl di sussistenza; ~**bin** n cassetta f portapane inv; ~**crumbs** npl briciole fpl; (CULIN) pangrattato; ~ **line** n: to be on the ~ line avere appena denaro per vivere.

breadth [brɛtθ] n larghezza.

breadwinner ['brɛdwɪnəˀ] n chi guadagna il pane per tutta la famiglia.

break [breɪk] vb (pt broke [brəuk], pp broken ['brəukən]) vt rompere; (law) violare // vi rompersi; (weather) cambiare // n (gap) breccia; (fracture) rottura; (rest, also SCOL) intervallo; (: short) pausa; (chance) possibilità f inv; to ~ **one's leg** etc rompersi la gamba etc; to ~ **a record** battere un primato; to ~ **the news to sb** comunicare per primo la notizia a qd; to ~ **down** vt (figures, data) analizzare // vi crollare; (MED) avere un esaurimento (nervoso); (AUT) guastarsi; to ~ **even** vi coprire le spese; to ~ **free** or **loose** vi spezzare i legami; to ~ **in** vt (horse etc) domare // vi (burglar) fare irruzione; to ~ **into** vt fus (house) fare irruzione in; to ~ **off** vi (speaker) interrompersi; (branch) troncarsi; to ~ **open** vt (door etc) sfondare; to ~ **out** vi evadere; to ~ **out in spots** coprirsi di macchie; to ~ **up** vi (partnership) sciogliersi; (friends) separarsi // vt fare in pezzi, spaccare; (fight etc) interrompere, far cessare; ~**able** a fragile; ~**age** n rottura; ~**down** n (AUT) guasto, panna; (in communications) interruzione f, (MED) esaurimento nervoso; ~**down service** n servizio riparazioni; ~**er** n frangente m.

breakfast ['brɛkfəst] n colazione f.

breakthrough ['breɪkθruː] n (MIL) breccia; (fig) passo avanti.

breakwater ['breɪkwɔːtəˀ] n frangiflutti m inv.

breast [brɛst] n (of woman) seno; (chest) petto; ~-**stroke** n nuoto a rana.

breath [brɛθ] n fiato; **out of** ~ senza fiato; ~**alyser** n test di verifica per la sobrietà.

breathe [briːð] vt, vi respirare; ~**r** n attimo di respiro.

breathless ['brɛθlɪs] a senza fiato.

breath-taking ['brɛθteɪkɪŋ] a sbalorditivo(a).

breed [briːd] vb (pt, pp bred [brɛd]) vt allevare // vi riprodursi // n razza, varietà f inv; ~**ing** n riproduzione f; allevamento.

breeze [briːz] n brezza.

breezy ['briːzɪ] a arioso(a); allegro(a).

brevity ['brɛvɪtɪ] n brevità f.

brew [bruː] vt (tea) fare un infuso di; (beer) fare; (plot) tramare // vi (tea) essere in infusione; (beer) essere in fermentazione; (fig) bollire in pentola; ~**er** n birraio; ~**ery** n fabbrica di birra.

bribe [braɪb] n bustarella // vt comprare; ~**ry** n corruzione f.

brick [brɪk] n mattone m; ~**layer** n muratore m.

bridal ['braɪdl] a nuziale.

bride [braɪd] n sposa; ~**groom** n sposo; ~**smaid** n damigella d'onore.

bridge [brɪdʒ] n ponte m; (NAUT) ponte di comando; (of nose) dorso; (CARDS, DENTISTRY) bridge m inv // vt (river) fare un ponte sopra; (gap) colmare.

bridle ['braɪdl] n briglia // vt tenere a freno; (horse) mettere la briglia a; ~ **path** n pista per traffico animale.

brief [briːf] a breve // n (LAW) comparsa // vt dare istruzioni a; ~**s** npl mutande fpl; ~**case** n cartella; ~**ing** n istruzioni fpl.

brigade [brɪˈgeɪd] n (MIL) brigata.

brigadier [brɪgəˈdɪəˀ] n generale m di brigata.

bright [braɪt] a luminoso(a); (person) sveglio(a); (colour) vivace; ~**en** vt (room) rendere luminoso(a); ornare // vi schiarirsi; (person: gen: ~**en up**) rallegrarsi.

brilliance ['brɪljəns] n splendore m.

brilliant ['brɪljənt] a splendente.

brim [brɪm] n orlo; ~**ful** a pieno(a) or colmo(a) fino all'orlo; (fig) pieno(a).

brine [braɪn] n acqua salmastra; (CULIN) salamoia.

bring, pt, pp brought [brɪŋ, brɔːt] vt portare; to ~ **about** vt causare; to ~ **back** vt riportare; to ~ **down** vt portare giù; abbattere; to ~ **forward** vt portare avanti; (in time) anticipare; to ~ **off** vt (task, plan) portare a compimento; to ~ **out** vt (meaning) mettere in evidenza; to ~ **round** or to ~ vt (unconscious person) far rinvenire; to ~ **up** vt allevare; (question) introdurre.

brink [brɪŋk] n orlo.

brisk [brɪsk] a vivace.

bristle ['brɪsl] n setola // vi rizzarsi; **bristling with** irto(a) di.

Britain ['brɪtən] n Gran Bretagna.

British ['brɪtɪʃ] a britannico(a); the ~ npl i Britannici; the ~ **Isles** npl le Isole Britanniche.

Briton ['brɪtən] n britannico/a.
brittle ['brɪtl] a fragile.
broach [brəʊtʃ] vt (subject) affrontare.
broad [brɔːd] a largo(a); (distinction) generale; (accent) spiccato(a); **in ~ daylight** in pieno giorno; **~ hint** n allusione f esplicita; **~cast** n trasmissione f // vb (pt,pp **broadcast**) vt trasmettere per radio (or per televisione) // vi fare una trasmissione; **~casting** n radio f inv; televisione f; **~en** vt allargare // vi allargarsi; **~ly** ad (fig) in generale; **~-minded** a di mente aperta.
brochure ['brəʊʃjʊə*] n dépliant m inv.
broil [brɔɪl] vt cuocere a fuoco vivo.
broke [brəʊk] pt of **break** // a (col) squattrinato(a); **~n** pp of **break** // a: **~n leg** etc gamba etc rotta; **in ~n French/English** in un francese/inglese stentato; **~n-hearted** a: **to be ~n-hearted** avere il cuore spezzato.
broker ['brəʊkə*] n agente m.
bronchitis [brɔŋ'kaɪtɪs] n bronchite f.
bronze [brɔnz] n bronzo; **~d** a abbronzato(a).
brooch [brəʊtʃ] n spilla.
brood [bruːd] n covata // vi (hen) covare; (person) rimuginare.
brook [brʊk] n ruscello.
broom [brum] n scopa; **~stick** n manico di scopa.
Bros. abbr of **Brothers**.
broth [brɔθ] n brodo.
brothel ['brɔθl] n bordello.
brother ['brʌðə*] n fratello; **~hood** n fratellanza; confraternità f inv; **~-in-law** n cognato; **~ly** a fraterno(a).
brought [brɔːt] pt,pp of **bring**.
brow [braʊ] n fronte f; (rare, gen: eye~) sopracciglio; (of hill) cima; **~beat** vt intimidire.
brown [braʊn] a bruno(a), marrone // n (colour) color m bruno or marrone // vt (CULIN) rosolare; **~ie** n giovane esploratrice f.
browse [braʊz] vi (among books) curiosare fra i libri.
bruise [bruːz] n ammaccatura // vt ammaccare // vi (fruit) ammaccarsi.
brunette [bruː'nɛt] n bruna.
brunt [brʌnt] n: **the ~ of** (attack, criticism etc) il peso maggiore di.
brush [brʌʃ] n spazzola; (quarrel) schermaglia // vt spazzolare; (gen: **~ past**, **~ against**) sfiorare; (to **~ aside** vt scostare; **to ~ up** vt (knowledge) rinfrescare; **~-off** n: **to give sb the ~-off** dare il ben servito a qd; **~wood** n macchia.
Brussels ['brʌslz] n Bruxelles; **~ sprout** n cavolo di Bruxelles.
brutal ['bruːtl] a brutale; **~ity** [bruː'tælɪtɪ] n brutalità.
brute [bruːt] n bestia.
B.Sc. abbr see **bachelor**.
bubble ['bʌbl] n bolla // vi ribollire; (sparkle, fig) essere effervescente.

buck [bʌk] n maschio (di camoscio, caprone, coniglio etc); (US: col) dollaro // vi sgroppare; **to pass the ~ (to sb)** scaricare (su di qd) la propria responsabilità; **to ~ up** vi (cheer up) rianimarsi.
bucket ['bʌkɪt] n secchio.
buckle ['bʌkl] n fibbia // vt affibbiare; (warp) deformare.
bud [bʌd] n gemma; (of flower) boccio // vi germogliare; (flower) sbocciare.
Buddha ['bʊdə] n Budda m.
budding ['bʌdɪŋ] a (flower) in boccio; (poet etc) in erba.
buddy ['bʌdɪ] n (US) compagno.
budge [bʌdʒ] vt scostare // vi spostarsi.
budgerigar ['bʌdʒərɪgɑː*] n pappagallino.
budget ['bʌdʒɪt] n bilancio preventivo // vi: **to ~ for sth** fare il bilancio per qc.
budgie ['bʌdʒɪ] n = **budgerigar**.
buff [bʌf] a color camoscio // n (enthusiast) appassionato/a.
buffalo, pl **~** or **~es** ['bʌfələʊ] n bufalo; (US) bisonte m.
buffer ['bʌfə*] n respingente m; **~ state** n stato cuscinetto.
buffet n ['bʊfeɪ] (bar, food) buffet m inv // vt ['bʌfɪt] schiaffeggiare; scuotere; urtare.
buffoon [bə'fuːn] n buffone m.
bug [bʌg] n (insect) cimice f; (: gen) insetto; (fig: germ) virus m inv; (spy device) microfono spia // vt mettere sotto controllo; **~bear** n spauracchio.
bugle ['bjuːgl] n tromba.
build [bɪld] n (of person) corporatura // vt (pt,pp **built** [bɪlt]) costruire; **~er** n costruttore m; **~ing** n costruzione f; edificio; (also: **~ing trade**) edilizia; **~ing society** n società di credito edilizio; **to ~ up** vt accumulare; aumentare; **~-up** n (of gas etc) accumulo.
built [bɪlt] pt,pp of **build**; **well-~** a (person) robusto(a); **~-in** a (cupboard) a muro; (device) incorporato(a); **~-up area** n abitato.
bulb [bʌlb] n (BOT) bulbo; (ELEC) lampadina; **~ous** a bulboso(a).
Bulgaria [bʌl'gɛərɪə] n Bulgaria.
bulge [bʌldʒ] n rigonfiamento // vi essere protuberante or rigonfio(a); **to be bulging with** essere pieno(a) or zeppo(a) di.
bulk [bʌlk] n massa, volume m; **in ~** a pacchi (or cassette etc); (COMM) all'ingrosso; **the ~ of** il grosso di; **~head** n paratia; **~y** a grosso(a); voluminoso(a).
bull [bʊl] n toro; **~dog** n buldog m inv.
bulldozer ['bʊldəʊzə*] n bulldozer m inv.
bullet ['bʊlɪt] n pallottola.
bulletin ['bʊlɪtɪn] n bollettino.
bullfight ['bʊlfaɪt] n corrida; **~er** n torero; **~ing** n tauromachia.
bullion ['bʊljən] n oro or argento in lingotti.
bullock ['bʊlək] n giovenco.
bull's-eye ['bʊlzaɪ] n centro del bersaglio.
bully ['bʊlɪ] n prepotente m // vt

angariare; (*frighten*) intimidire; ~ing *n* prepotenze *fpl*.

bum [bʌm] *n* (*col: backside*) culo; (*tramp*) vagabondo/a; to ~ **around** *vi* fare il vagabondo.

bumblebee ['bʌmblbi:] *n* (*ZOOL*) bombo.

bump [bʌmp] *n* (*blow*) colpo; (*jolt*) scossa; (*on road etc*) protuberanza; (*on head*) bernoccolo // *vt* battere; to ~ **along** *vi* procedere sobbalzando; to ~ **into** *vt fus* scontrarsi con; ~er *n* (*Brit*) paraurti *m inv* // *a*: ~er **harvest** raccolto eccezionale.

bumptious ['bʌmpʃəs] *a* presuntuoso(a).

bumpy ['bʌmpɪ] *a* dissestato(a).

bun [bʌn] *n* focaccia; (*of hair*) crocchia.

bunch [bʌntʃ] *n* (*of flowers, keys*) mazzo; (*of bananas*) ciuffo; (*of people*) gruppo; ~ **of grapes** grappolo d'uva.

bundle ['bʌndl] *n* fascio // *vt* (*also: ~ up*) legare in un fascio; (*put*): to ~ **sth/sb into** spingere qc/qd in; to ~ **off** *vt* (*person*) mandare via in gran fretta.

bung [bʌŋ] *n* tappo // *vt* (*throw*) buttare.

bungalow ['bʌŋgələu] *n* bungalow *m inv*.

bungle ['bʌŋgl] *vt* abborracciare.

bunion ['bʌnjən] *n* callo (al piede).

bunk [bʌŋk] *n* cuccetta; ~ **beds** *npl* letti *mpl* a castello.

bunker ['bʌŋkə°] *n* (*coal store*) ripostiglio per il carbone; (*MIL, GOLF*) bunker *m inv*.

bunny ['bʌnɪ] *n* (*also*: ~ **rabbit**) coniglietto; ~ **girl** *n* coniglietta.

bunting ['bʌntɪŋ] *n* pavesi *mpl*, bandierine *fpl*.

buoy [bɔɪ] *n* boa; to ~ **up** *vt* tenere a galla; (*fig*) sostenere; ~**ancy** *n* (*of ship*) galleggiabilità; ~**ant** *a* galleggiante; (*fig*) vivace.

burden ['bə:dn] *n* carico, fardello // *vt* caricare; (*oppress*) opprimere.

bureau, *pl* ~**x** [bjuə'rəu, -z] *n* (*furniture*) scrivania; (*office*) ufficio, agenzia.

bureaucracy [bjuə'rɔkrəsɪ] *n* burocrazia.

bureaucrat ['bjuərəkræt] *n* burocrate *m/f*; ~**ic** [-'krætɪk] *a* burocratico(a).

burglar ['bə:glə°] *n* scassinatore *m*; ~ **alarm** *n* campanello antifurto; ~**ize** *vt* (*US*) svaligiare; ~**y** *n* furto con scasso.

burgle ['bə:gl] *vt* svaligiare.

burial ['bɛrɪəl] *n* sepoltura; ~ **ground** *n* cimitero.

burly ['bə:lɪ] *a* robusto(a).

Burma ['bə:mə] *n* Birmania.

burn [bə:n] *vt,vi* (*pt,pp* **burned** *or* **burnt** [bə:nt]) bruciare // *n* bruciatura, scottatura; to ~ **down** *vt* distruggere col fuoco; ~**ing question** *n* questione *f* scottante.

burnish ['bə:nɪʃ] *vt* brunire.

burnt [bə:nt] *pt,pp* of **burn**.

burp [bə:p] (*col*) *n* rutto // *vi* ruttare.

burrow ['bʌrəu] *n* tana // *vt* scavare.

bursar ['bə:sə°] *n* economo/a; ~**y** *n* borsa di studio.

burst [bə:st] *vb* (*pt,pp* **burst**) *vt* far scoppiare (*or* esplodere) // *vi* esplodere;

(*tyre*) scoppiare // *n* scoppio; (*also*: ~ **pipe**) rottura nel tubo, perdita; ~ **of energy** scoppio d'energia; ~ **of laughter** scoppio di risa; ~ **blood vessel** rottura di un vaso sanguigno; to ~ **into flames/tears** scoppiare in fiamme/lacrime; to be ~**ing with** essere pronto a scoppiare di; to ~ **into** *vt fus* (*room etc*) irrompere in; to ~ **open** *vi* aprirsi improvvisamente; (*door*) spalancarsi; to ~ **out laughing** scoppiare a ridere; to ~ **out of** *vt fus* precipitarsi fuori da.

bury ['bɛrɪ] *vt* seppellire; to ~ **one's face in one's hands** nascondere la faccia tra le mani.

bus, ~**es** [bʌs, 'bʌsɪz] *n* autobus *m inv*.

bush [buʃ] *n* cespuglio; (*scrub land*) macchia.

bushel ['buʃl] *n* staio.

bushy ['buʃɪ] *a* cespuglioso(a).

business ['bɪznɪs] *n* (*matter*) affare *m*; (*trading*) affari *mpl*; (*firm*) azienda; (*job, duty*) lavoro; to be away on ~ essere andato via per affari; it's none of my ~ questo non mi riguarda; he means ~ non scherza; ~**like** *a* serio(a); efficiente; ~**man** *n* uomo d'affari.

bus-stop ['bʌsstɔp] *n* fermata d'autobus.

bust [bʌst] *n* busto; (*ANAT*) seno // *a* (*broken*) rotto(a); to go ~ fallire.

bustle ['bʌsl] *n* movimento, attività // *vi* darsi da fare; ~**ling** *a* (*person*) indaffarato(a); (*town*) animato(a).

busy ['bɪzɪ] *a* occupato(a); (*shop, street*) molto frequentato(a) // *vt*: to ~ **o.s.** darsi da fare; ~**body** *n* ficcanaso.

but [bʌt] *cj* ma // *prep* eccetto, tranne; **nothing** ~ null'altro che; ~ **for** senza, se non fosse per; **all** ~ **finished** quasi finito; **anything** ~ **finished** tutt'altro che finito.

butane ['bju:teɪn] *n* butano.

butcher ['butʃə°] *n* macellaio // *vt* macellare.

butler ['bʌtlə°] *n* maggiordomo.

butt [bʌt] *n* (*cask*) grossa botte *f*; (*thick end*) estremità *f* più grossa; (*of gun*) calcio; (*of cigarette*) mozzicone *m*; (*fig: target*) oggetto // *vt* cozzare.

butter ['bʌtə°] *n* burro // *vt* imburrare.

butterfly ['bʌtəflaɪ] *n* farfalla.

buttocks ['bʌtəks] *npl* natiche *fpl*.

button ['bʌtn] *n* bottone *m* // *vt* abbottonare; ~**hole** *n* asola, occhiello // *vt* attaccare un bottone a.

buttress ['bʌtrɪs] *n* contrafforte *f*.

buxom ['bʌksəm] *a* formoso(a).

buy [baɪ] *vt* (*pt,pp* **bought** [bɔːt]) comprare; to ~ **sb sth/sth from sb** comprare qc per qd/qc da qd; to ~ a **drink** offrire da bere a qd; to ~ **up** *vt* accaparrare; ~**er** *n* compratore/trice.

buzz [bʌz] *n* ronzio; (*col: phone call*) colpo di telefono // *vi* ronzare.

buzzard ['bʌzəd] *n* poiana.

buzzer ['bʌzə°] *n* cicalino.

by [baɪ] *prep* da; (*beside*) accanto a; vicino

a, presso; (*before*): ~ **4 o'clock** entro le 4 // *ad see* **pass, go** *etc*; ~ **bus/car** in autobus/macchina; **paid** ~ **the hour** pagato(a) a ore; **to increase** *etc* ~ **the hour** aumentare di ora in ora; **(all)** ~ **oneself** tutto(a) solo(a); ~ **the way** a proposito; ~ **and large** nell'insieme; ~ **and** ~ di qui a poco *or* presto.

bye(-bye) ['baɪ('baɪ)] *excl* ciao!, arrivederci!

by(e)-law ['baɪlɔː] *n* legge *f* locale.

by-election ['baɪɪlekʃən] *n* elezione *f* straordinaria.

bygone ['baɪgɒn] *a* passato(a) // *n*: **let** ~**s be** ~**s** mettiamoci una pietra sopra.

bypass ['baɪpɑːs] *n* circonvallazione *f* // *vt* fare una deviazione intorno a.

by-product ['baɪprɒdʌkt] *n* sottoprodotto; (*fig*) conseguenza secondaria.

bystander ['baɪstændə*] *n* spettatore/trice.

byword ['baɪwɔːd] *n*: **to be a** ~ **for** essere sinonimo di.

C

C [siː] *n* (*MUS*) do.

C. *abbr of* **centigrade**.

cab [kæb] *n* taxi *m inv*; (*of train, truck*) cabina; (*horse-drawn*) carrozza.

cabaret ['kæbəreɪ] *n* cabaret *m inv*.

cabbage ['kæbɪdʒ] *n* cavolo.

cabin ['kæbɪn] *n* capanna; (*on ship*) cabina; ~ **cruiser** *n* cabinato.

cabinet ['kæbɪnɪt] *n* (*POL*) gabinetto; (*furniture*) armadietto; (*also*: **display** ~) vetrinetta; **cocktail** ~ *n* mobile *m* bar *inv*; ~-**maker** *n* stipettaio.

cable ['keɪbl] *n* cavo; fune *f*; (*TEL*) cablogramma *m* // *vt* telegrafare; ~-**car** *n* funivia; ~-**gram** *n* cablogramma *m*; ~ **railway** *n* funicolare *f*.

cache [kæʃ] *n* nascondiglio; **a** ~ **of food** *etc* un deposito segreto di viveri *etc*.

cackle ['kækl] *vi* schiamazzare.

cactus, *pl* **cacti** ['kæktəs, -taɪ] *n* cacto.

caddie ['kædɪ] *n* caddie *m inv*.

cadet [kə'dɛt] *n* (*MIL*) cadetto.

cadge [kædʒ] *vt* accattare; **to** ~ **a meal (off sb)** scroccare un pranzo (a qd).

Caesarean [siː'zɛərɪən] *a*: ~ **(section)** operazione *f* cesarea.

café ['kæfeɪ] *n* caffè *m inv*; **cafeteria** [kæfɪ'tɪərɪə] *n* self-service *m inv*.

caffein(e) ['kæfiːn] *n* caffeina.

cage [keɪdʒ] *n* gabbia.

cagey ['keɪdʒɪ] *a* (*col*) chiuso(a); guardingo(a).

cajole [kə'dʒəʊl] *vt* allettare.

cake [keɪk] *n* torta; ~ **of soap** saponetta; ~**d** *a*: ~**d with** incrostato(a) di.

calamity [kə'læmɪtɪ] *n* calamità *f inv*.

calcium ['kælsɪəm] *n* calcio.

calculate ['kælkjuleɪt] *vt* calcolare; **calculating** *a* calcolatore(trice); **calculation** [-'leɪʃən] *n* calcolo; **calculator** *n* calcolatrice *f*.

calculus ['kælkjuləs] *n* calcolo.

calendar ['kæləndə*] *n* calendario; ~ **month** *n* mese *m* (secondo il calendario); ~ **year** *n* anno civile.

calf, calves [kɑːf, kɑːvz] *n* (*of cow*) vitello; (*of other animals*) piccolo; (*also*: ~**skin**) (pelle *f* di) vitello; (*ANAT*) polpaccio.

calibre ['kælɪbə*] *n* calibro.

call [kɔːl] *vt* (*gen, also TEL*) chiamare // *vi* chiamare; (*visit*: *also*: ~ **in**, ~ **round**): **to** ~ **(for)** passare (a prendere) // *n* (*shout*) grido, urlata; visita; **(telephone)** ~ telefonata; **to be on** ~ essere disponibile; **to** ~ **for** *vt fus* richiedere; **to** ~ **off** *vt* disdire; **to** ~ **on** *vt fus* (*visit*) passare da; (*request*): **to** ~ **on sb to do** chiedere a qd di fare; **to** ~ **up** *vt* (*MIL*) richiamare; ~**box** *n* cabina telefonica; ~**er** *n* persona che chiama; visitatore/trice; ~ **girl** *n* ragazza *f* squillo *inv*; ~**ing** *n* vocazione *f*; ~**ing card** *n* (*US*) biglietto da visita.

callous ['kæləs] *a* indurito(a), insensibile.

calm [kɑːm] *n* calma // *a* calmo(a); ~**ly** *ad* con calma; ~**ness** *n* calma; **to** ~ **down** *vi* calmarsi // *vt* calmare.

calorie ['kælərɪ] *n* caloria.

calve [kɑːv] *vi* figliare.

calves [kɑːvz] *npl of* **calf**.

camber ['kæmbə*] *n* (*of road*) bombatura.

Cambodia [kæm'bəʊdjə] *n* Cambogia.

came [keɪm] *pt of* **come**.

camel ['kæml] *n* cammello.

cameo ['kæmɪəʊ] *n* cammeo.

camera ['kæmərə] *n* macchina fotografica; (*also*: **cine-**~, **movie** ~) cinepresa; **in** ~ **a porte chiuse**; ~**man** *n* cameraman *m inv*.

camouflage ['kæməflɑːʒ] *n* camuffamento; (*MIL*) mimetizzazione *f* // *vt* camuffare; mimetizzare.

camp [kæmp] *n* campeggio; (*MIL*) campo // *vi* campeggiare; accamparsi.

campaign [kæm'peɪn] *n* (*MIL, POL etc*) campagna // *vi* (*also fig*) fare una campagna.

campbed ['kæmp'bɛd] *n* brandina.

camper ['kæmpə*] *n* campeggiatore/trice.

camping ['kæmpɪŋ] *n* campeggio.

campsite ['kæmpsaɪt] *n* campeggio.

campus ['kæmpəs] *n* campus *m inv*.

can [kæn] *auxiliary vb* potere; (*know how to*) sapere; **I** ~ **swim** *etc* so nuotare *etc*; **I** ~ **speak French** so parlare francese // *n* (*of milk*) scatola; (*of oil*) bidone *m*; (*of water*) tanica; (*tin*) scatola // *vt* mettere in scatola.

Canada ['kænədə] *n* Canada *m*.

Canadian [kə'neɪdɪən] *a, n* canadese (*m/f*).

canal [kə'næl] *n* canale *m*.

canary [kə'nɛərɪ] *n* canarino.

cancel ['kænsəl] *vt* annullare; (*train*) sopprimere; (*cross out*) cancellare; ~**lation** [-'leɪʃən] *n* annullamento; soppressione *f*; cancellazione *f*; (*TOURISM*) prenotazione *f* annullata.

cancer ['kænsə*] n cancro; C~ (sign)
Cancro.

candid ['kændɪd] a onesto(a).

candidate ['kændɪdeɪt] n candidato.

candle ['kændl] n candela; by ~light a
lume di candela; ~stick n (also: ~
holder) bugia; (bigger, ornate) candeliere
m.

candour ['kændə*] n sincerità.

candy ['kændɪ] n zucchero candito; (US)
caramella; ~-floss n zucchero filato.

cane [keɪn] n canna; (SCOL) verga // vt
punire a colpi di verga.

canine ['kænaɪn] a canino(a).

canister ['kænɪstə*] n scatola metallica.

cannabis ['kænəbɪs] n (drug) hascisc m.

canned ['kænd] a (food) in scatola.

cannibal ['kænɪbəl] n cannibale m/f;
~ism n cannibalismo.

cannon, pl ~ or ~s ['kænən] n (gun)
cannone m; ~-ball n palla di cannone.

cannot ['kænɔt] = can not.

canny ['kænɪ] a furbo(a).

canoe [kə'nu:] n canoa; (SPORT) canotto;
~ing n (SPORT) canottaggio; ~ist n
canottiere m.

canon ['kænən] n (clergyman) canonico;
(standard) canone m.

canonize ['kænənaɪz] vt canonizzare.

can opener ['kænəupnə*] n apriscatole m
inv.

canopy ['kænəpɪ] n baldacchino.

cant [kænt] n gergo.

can't [kænt] = can not.

cantankerous [kæn'tæŋkərəs] a
stizzoso(a).

canteen [kæn'ti:n] n mensa; (of cutlery)
portaposate m inv.

canter ['kæntə*] n piccolo galoppo.

cantilever ['kæntɪli:və*] n trave f a sbalzo.

canvas ['kænvəs] n tela; under ~
(camping) sotto la tenda; (NAUT) sotto la
vela.

canvass ['kænvəs] vt: ~ing sollecitazione
f.

canyon ['kænjən] n canyon m inv.

cap [kæp] n (also FOOTBALL) berretto; (of
pen) coperchio; (of bottle) tappo // vt
tappare; (outdo) superare; ~ped with
ricoperto(a) di.

capability [keɪpə'bɪlɪtɪ] n capacità f inv,
abilità f inv.

capable ['keɪpəbl] a capace; ~ of capace
di; suscettibile di.

capacity [kə'pæsɪtɪ] n capacità f inv; (of lift
etc) capienza; in his ~ as nella sua
qualità di; to work at full ~ lavorare al
massimo delle proprie capacità.

cape [keɪp] n (garment) cappa; (GEO) capo.

capital ['kæpɪtl] n (also: ~ city) capitale
f; (money) capitale m; (also: ~ letter)
(lettera) maiuscola; ~ gains npl utili mpl
di capitale; ~ism n capitalismo; ~ist a
capitalista; ~ punishment n pena
capitale.

capitulate [kə'pɪtjuleɪt] vi capitolare.

capricious [kə'prɪʃəs] a capriccioso(a).

Capricorn ['kæprɪkɔ:n] n Capricorno.

capsize [kæp'saɪz] vt capovolgere // vi
capovolgersi.

capstan ['kæpstən] n argano.

capsule ['kæpsju:l] n capsula.

captain ['kæptɪn] n capitano // vt
capitanare.

caption ['kæpʃən] n leggenda.

captivate ['kæptɪveɪt] vt avvincere.

captive ['kæptɪv] a, n prigioniero(a).

captivity [kæp'tɪvɪtɪ] n prigionia; in ~
(animal) in servitù.

capture ['kæptʃə*] vt catturare, prendere;
(attention) attirare // n cattura.

car [ka:*] n macchina, automobile f.

carafe [kə'ræf] n caraffa.

caramel ['kærəməl] n caramello.

carat ['kærət] n carato.

caravan ['kærəvæn] n roulotte f inv.

caraway ['kærəweɪ] n: ~ seed seme m di
cumino.

carbohydrates [ka:bəu'haɪdreɪts] npl
(foods) carboidrati mpl.

carbon ['ka:bən] n carbonio; ~ copy n
copia f carbone inv; ~ paper n carta
carbone.

carburettor [ka:bju'retə*] n carburatore
m.

carcass ['ka:kəs] n carcassa.

card [ka:d] n carta; (visiting ~ etc)
biglietto; (Christmas ~ etc) cartolina;
~board n cartone m; ~ game n gioco di
carte.

cardiac ['ka:dɪæk] a cardiaco(a).

cardigan ['ka:dɪgən] n cardigan m inv.

cardinal ['ka:dɪnl] a, n cardinale (m).

card index ['ka:dɪndɛks] n schedario.

care [kɛə*] n cura, attenzione f; (worry)
preoccupazione f // vi: to ~ about
interessarsi di; would you ~ to/for ...? ti
piacerebbe ...?; I wouldn't ~ to do it non
lo vorrei fare; in sb's ~ alle cure di qd;
to take ~ fare attenzione; to take ~ of
vt curarsi di; to ~ for vt fus aver cura di;
(like) volere bene a; I don't ~ non me ne
importa; I couldn't ~ less non me ne
importa un bel niente.

career [kə'rɪə*] n carriera // vi (also: ~
along) andare di (gran) carriera.

carefree ['kɛəfri:] a sgombro(a) di
preoccupazioni.

careful ['kɛəful] a attento(a); (cautious)
cauto(a); (be) ~! attenzione!; ~ly ad con
cura; cautamente.

careless ['kɛəlɪs] a negligente; (heedless)
spensierato(a); ~ly ad trascuratamente,
senza cura; ~ness n negligenza; spen-
sieratezza.

caress [kə'rɛs] n carezza // vt
accarezzare.

caretaker ['kɛəteɪkə*] n custode m.

car-ferry ['ka:fɛrɪ] n traghetto.

cargo, ~es ['ka:gəu] n carico.

Caribbean [kærɪ'bi:ən] a: the ~ (Sea) il
Mar dei Caraibi.

caricature ['kærɪkətjuə*] n caricatura.

carnal ['ka:nl] a carnale.

carnation [kɑːˈneɪʃən] n garofano.

carnival [ˈkɑːnɪvəl] n (public celebration) carnevale m.

carol [ˈkærəl] n: (Christmas) ~ canto di Natale.

carp [kɑːp] n (fish) carpa; **to** ~ **at** vt fus trovare a ridire su.

car park [ˈkɑːpɑːk] n parcheggio.

carpenter [ˈkɑːpɪntə*] n carpentiere m.

carpentry [ˈkɑːpɪntrɪ] n carpenteria.

carpet [ˈkɑːpɪt] n tappeto // vt coprire con tappeto.

carriage [ˈkærɪdʒ] n vettura; trasporto; (of typewriter) carrello; (bearing) portamento; ~ **way** n (part of road) strada rotabile.

carrier [ˈkærɪə*] n (of disease) portatore/trice; (COMM) impresa di trasporti; (NAUT) portaerei m inv; (on car, bicycle) portabagagli m inv; ~ **bag** n sacchetto.

carrot [ˈkærət] n carota.

carry [ˈkærɪ] vt (subj: person) portare; (: vehicle) trasportare; (a motion, bill) far passare; (involve: responsibilities etc) comportare // vi (sound) farsi sentire; **to be carried away** (fig) farsi trascinare; **to** ~ **on** vi: **to** ~ **on with** s/h/doing continuare qc/a fare // vt mandare avanti; **to** ~ **out** vt (orders) eseguire; (investigation) svolgere; ~**cot** n culla portabile.

cart [kɑːt] n carro // vt trasportare con carro.

cartilage [ˈkɑːtɪlɪdʒ] n cartilagine f.

carton [ˈkɑːtən] n (box) scatola di cartone; (of yogurt) cartone m; (of cigarettes) stecca.

cartoon [kɑːˈtuːn] n (PRESS) disegno umoristico; (satirical) caricatura; (comic strip) fumetto; (CINEMA) disegno animato; ~**ist** n disegnatore/trice; caricaturista m/f; fumettista m/f.

cartridge [ˈkɑːtrɪdʒ] n (for gun, pen) cartuccia; (for camera) caricatore m; (music tape) cassetta; (of record player) testina.

carve [kɑːv] vt (meat) trinciare; (wood, stone) intagliare; **carving** n (in wood etc) scultura; **carving knife** n trinciante m.

car wash [ˈkɑːwɒʃ] n lavaggio auto.

cascade [kæsˈkeɪd] n cascata // vi scendere a cascata.

case [keɪs] n caso; (LAW) causa, processo; (box) scatola; (also: suit~) valigia; **he hasn't put forward his** ~ **very well** non ha dimostrato bene il suo caso; **in** ~ **of** in caso di; **in** ~ **he** caso mai lui; **just in** ~ in caso di bisogno.

cash [kæʃ] n denaro; (COMM) denaro liquido; (COMM: in payment) pagamento in contanti // vt incassare; **to pay (in)** ~ pagare in contanti; ~ **with order/on delivery** (COMM) pagamento all'ordinazione/contro assegno; ~**book** n giornale m di cassa; ~**desk** n cassa.

cashew [kæˈʃuː] n (also: ~ **nut**) anacardio.

cashier [kæˈʃɪə*] n cassiere(a).

cashmere [kæʃˈmɪə*] n cachemire m.

cash register [ˈkæʃredʒɪstə*] n registratore m di cassa.

casing [ˈkeɪsɪŋ] n rivestimento.

casino [kəˈsiːnəu] n casinò m inv.

cask [kɑːsk] n botte f.

casket [ˈkɑːskɪt] n cofanetto; (US: coffin) bara.

casserole [ˈkæsərəul] n casseruola; (food) stufato (nella casseruola).

cast [kɑːst] vt (pt, pp cast) (throw) gettare; (shed) perdere; spogliarsi di; (metal) gettare, fondere // n (THEATRE) complesso di attori; (mould) forma; (also: plaster ~) ingessatura; (THEATRE): **to** ~ **sb as Hamlet** scegliere qd per la parte di Amleto; **to** ~ **one's vote** votare, dare il voto; **to** ~ **off** vi (NAUT) salpare.

castanets [kæstəˈnɛts] npl castagnette fpl.

castaway [ˈkɑːstəwəɪ] n naufrago/a.

caste [kɑːst] n casta.

casting [ˈkɑːstɪŋ] a: ~ **vote** voto decisivo.

cast iron [ˈkɑːstˈaɪən] n ferro battuto.

castle [ˈkɑːsl] n castello; (fortified) rocca.

castor [ˈkɑːstə*] n (wheel) rotella; ~ **oil** n olio di ricino; ~ **sugar** n zucchero semolato.

castrate [kæsˈtreɪt] vt castrare.

casual [ˈkæʒjul] a (by chance) casuale, fortuito(a); (irregular: work etc) avventizio(a); (unconcerned) noncurante, indifferente; ~ **wear** n casual m; ~ **labour** n manodopera avventizia; ~**ly** ad con disinvoltura; casualmente.

casualty [ˈkæʒjultɪ] n ferito/a; (dead) morto/a, vittima; **heavy casualties** npl grosse perdite fpl.

cat [kæt] n gatto.

catalogue [ˈkætəlɒg] n catalogo.

catalyst [ˈkætəlɪst] n catalizzatore m.

catapult [ˈkætəpʌlt] n catapulta, fionda.

cataract [ˈkætərækt] n (also MED) cateratta.

catarrh [kəˈtɑː*] n catarro.

catastrophe [kəˈtæstrəfɪ] n catastrofe f; **catastrophic** [kætəˈstrɒfɪk] a catastrofico(a).

catch [kætʃ] vb (pt, pp caught [kɔːt]) vt (train, thief, cold) acchiappare; (ball) chiappare; (person: by surprise) sorprendere; (understand) sorprendere; (get entangled) impigliare // vi (fire) prendere // n (fish etc caught) retata, presa; (trick) inganno; (TECH) gancio; **to** ~ **sb's attention** or **eye** attirare l'attenzione di qd; **to** ~ **fire** prendere fuoco; **to** ~ **sight of** scorgere; **to** ~ **up** vi mettersi in pari // vt (also: ~ **up with**) raggiungere.

catching [ˈkætʃɪŋ] a (MED) contagioso(a).

catchment area [ˈkætʃmənt'eərɪə] n (SCOL) circoscrizione f scolare; (GEO) bacino pluviale.

catch phrase [ˈkætʃfreɪz] n slogan m inv; frase f fatta.

catchy [ˈkætʃɪ] a orecchiabile.

catechism ['kætɪkɪzəm] n (REL) catechismo.

categoric(al) [kætɪ'gɔrɪk(əl)] a categorico(a).

categorize ['kætɪgəraɪz] vt categorizzare.

category ['kætɪgərɪ] n categoria.

cater ['keɪtə*] vi (gen: ~ **for**) provvedere da mangiare (per); **to ~ for** vt fus (needs) provvedere a; (readers, consumers) incontrare i gusti di; ~**er** n fornitore m; ~**ing** n approvvigionamento; ~**ing trade** n settore m ristoranti.

caterpillar ['kætəpɪlə*] n bruco; ~ **track/vehicle** n catena/trattore m a cingoli.

cathedral [kə'θi:drəl] n cattedrale f, duomo.

catholic ['kæθəlɪk] a universale; aperto(a); eclettico(a); **C ~** a,n (REL) cattolico(a).

cattle ['kætl] npl bestiame m, bestie fpl.

caught [kɔ:t] pt,pp of **catch**.

cauliflower ['kɒlɪflauə*] n cavolfiore m.

cause [kɔ:z] n causa // vt causare; **there is no ~ for concern** non c'è ragione di preoccuparsi.

causeway ['kɔ:zweɪ] n strada rialzata.

caustic ['kɔ:stɪk] a caustico(a).

caution ['kɔ:ʃən] n prudenza; (warning) avvertimento // vt avvertire; ammonire.

cautious ['kɔ:ʃəs] a cauto(a); ~**ly** ad prudentemente; ~**ness** n cautela.

cavalry ['kævəlrɪ] n cavalleria.

cave [keɪv] n caverna, grotta; **to ~ in** vi (roof etc) crollare; ~**man** n uomo delle caverne.

cavern ['kævən] n caverna.

caviar(e) ['kævɪɑ:*] n caviale m.

cavity ['kævɪtɪ] n cavità f inv.

cavort [kə'vɔ:t] vi far capriole.

CBI n (abbr of Confederation of British Industries) ≈ Confindustria.

cc abbr of cubic centimetres; carbon copy.

cease [si:s] vt,vi cessare; ~**-fire** n cessate il fuoco m inv; ~**less** a incessante, continuo(a).

cedar ['si:də*] n cedro.

cede [si:d] vt cedere.

ceiling ['si:lɪŋ] n soffitto.

celebrate ['sɛlɪbreɪt] vt,vi celebrare; ~**d** a celebre; **celebration** [-'breɪʃən] n celebrazione f.

celebrity [sɪ'lɛbrɪtɪ] n celebrità f inv.

celery ['sɛlərɪ] n sedano.

celestial [sɪ'lɛstɪəl] a celeste.

celibacy ['sɛlɪbəsɪ] n celibato.

cell [sɛl] n cella; (ELEC) elemento (di batteria).

cellar ['sɛlə*] n sottosuolo, cantina.

'cello ['tʃɛləu] n violoncello.

cellophane ['sɛləfeɪn] n cellophane m.

cellulose ['sɛljuləus] n cellulosa.

Celtic ['kɛltɪk, 'sɛltɪk] a celtico(a).

cement [sə'mɛnt] n cemento // vt cementare.

cemetery ['sɛmɪtrɪ] n cimitero.

cenotaph ['sɛnətɑ:f] n cenotafio.

censor ['sɛnsə*] n censore m; ~**ship** n censura.

censure ['sɛnʃə*] vt riprovare, censurare.

census ['sɛnsəs] n censimento.

cent [sɛnt] n (US: coin) centesimo, = 1:100 di un dollaro; see also **per**.

centenary [sɛn'ti:nərɪ] n centenario.

centi... prefix: ~**grade** a centigrado(a); ~**metre** n centimetro.

centipede ['sɛntɪpi:d] n centopiedi m inv.

central ['sɛntrəl] a centrale; ~ **heating** n riscaldamento centrale; ~**ize** vt accentrare.

centre ['sɛntə*] n centro; ~**-forward** n (SPORT) centroavanti m inv; ~**-half** n (SPORT) centromediano.

centrifugal [sɛn'trɪfjugəl] a centrifugo(a).

century ['sɛntjurɪ] n secolo.

ceramic [sɪ'ræmɪk] a ceramico(a).

cereal ['si:rɪəl] n cereale m.

ceremony ['sɛrɪmənɪ] n cerimonia; **to stand on ~** fare complimenti.

certain ['sə:tən] a certo(a); **to make ~ of** assicurarsi di; **for ~** per certo, di sicuro; ~**ly** ad certamente, certo; ~**ty** n certezza.

certificate [sə'tɪfɪkɪt] n certificato; diploma m.

certify ['sə:tɪfaɪ] vt certificare // vi: **to ~ to** attestare a.

cervix ['sə:vɪks] n cervice f.

cessation [sə'seɪʃən] n cessazione f, arresto.

cesspool ['sɛspu:l] n pozzo nero.

cf. (abbr = compare) cfr., confronta.

chafe [tʃeɪf] vt fregare, irritare.

chaffinch ['tʃæfɪntʃ] n fringuello.

chain [tʃeɪn] n catena // vt (also: ~ **up**) incatenare; ~ **reaction** n reazione f a catena; **to ~ smoke** vi fumare una sigaretta dopo l'altra; ~ **store** n negozio a catena.

chair [tʃɛə*] n sedia; (armchair) poltrona; (of university) cattedra // vt (meeting) presiedere; ~**lift** n seggiovia; ~**man** n presidente m.

chalet ['ʃæleɪ] n chalet m inv.

chalice ['tʃælɪs] n calice m.

chalk [tʃɔ:k] n gesso.

challenge ['tʃælɪndʒ] n sfida // vt sfidare; (statement, right) mettere in dubbio; **to ~ sb to a fight/game** sfidare qd a battersi/ad una partita; **to ~ sb to do** sfidare qd a fare; ~**r** n (SPORT) sfidante m/f; **challenging** a sfidante; provocatorio(a).

chamber ['tʃeɪmbə*] n camera; ~ **of commerce** camera di commercio; ~**maid** n cameriera; ~ **music** n musica da camera.

chamois ['ʃæmwɑ:] n camoscio; ~ **leather** ['ʃæmɪlɛðə*] n pelle f di camoscio.

champagne [ʃæm'peɪn] n champagne m inv.

champion ['tʃæmpɪən] n campione/essa; ~**ship** n campionato.

chance [tʃɑ:ns] n caso; (opportunity)

occasione f; (*likelihood*) possibilità f inv // vt: to ~ it rischiarlo // a fortuito(a); there is little ~ of his coming è molto improbabile che venga; to take a ~ arrischiarlo; by ~ per caso.

chancel ['tʃɑːnsəl] n coro.

chancellor ['tʃɑːnsələ*] n cancelliere m; C~ of the Exchequer n Cancelliere dello Scacchiere.

chandelier [ʃændə'lɪə*] n lampadario.

change [tʃeɪndʒ] vt cambiare; (*transform*): to ~ sb into trasformare qd in // vi cambiarsi; (*be transformed*): to ~ into trasformarsi in // n cambiamento; (*money*) resto; to ~ one's mind cambiare idea; a ~ of clothes una cambiata; for a ~ tanto per cambiare; small ~ spiccioli mpl, moneta; ~able a (*weather*) variabile; ~over n cambiamento, passaggio.

changing ['tʃeɪndʒɪŋ] a che cambia; (*colours*) cangiante; ~ room n (*in shop*) camerino; (*SPORT*) spogliatoio.

channel ['tʃænl] n canale m; (*of river, sea*) alveo // vt canalizzare; through the usual ~s per le solite vie; the (English) C~ la Manica; the C~ Islands le Isole Normanne.

chant [tʃɑːnt] n canto; salmodia // vt cantare; salmodiare.

chaos ['keɪɒs] n caos m.

chaotic [keɪ'ɒtɪk] a caotico(a).

chap [tʃæp] n (*col: man*) tipo // vt (*skin*) screpolare.

chapel ['tʃæpəl] n cappella.

chaperon ['ʃæpərəun] n accompagnatrice f // vt accompagnare.

chaplain ['tʃæplɪn] n cappellano.

chapter ['tʃæptə*] n capitolo.

char [tʃɑː*] vt (*burn*) carbonizzare // vi (*cleaner*) lavorare come domestica (a ore) // n = charlady.

character ['kærɪktə*] n carattere m; (*in novel, film*) personaggio; (*eccentric*) originale m; ~istic [-'rɪstɪk] a caratteristico(a) // n caratteristica; ~ize vt caratterizzare.

charade [ʃə'rɑːd] n sciarada.

charcoal ['tʃɑːkəul] n carbone m di legna.

charge [tʃɑːdʒ] n accusa; (*cost*) prezzo; (*of gun, battery, MIL: attack*) carica // vt (*LAW*): to ~ sb (with) accusare qd (di); (*gun, battery, MIL: enemy*) caricare; (*customer*) fare pagare a; (*sum*) fare pagare // vi (*gen with: up, along etc*) lanciarsi; ~s npl: bank ~s commissioni fpl bancarie; labour ~s costi mpl del lavoro; to ~ in/out precipitarsi dentro/fuori; is there a ~? c'è da pagare?; there's no ~ non c'è niente da pagare; to take ~ of incaricarsi di; to be in ~ of essere responsabile per; to have ~ of sb aver cura di qd; to ~ an expense (up) to sb addebitare una spesa a qd.

chariot ['tʃærɪət] n carro.

charitable ['tʃærɪtəbl] a caritatevole.

charity ['tʃærɪtɪ] n carità; opera pia.

charlady ['tʃɑːleɪdɪ] n domestica a ore.

charm [tʃɑːm] n fascino; amuleto // vt affascinare, incantare; ~ing a affascinante.

chart [tʃɑːt] n tabella; grafico; (*map*) carta nautica // vt fare una carta nautica di.

charter ['tʃɑːtə*] vt (*plane*) noleggiare // n (*document*) carta; ~ed accountant n ragioniere/a professionista; ~ flight n volo m charter inv.

chase [tʃeɪs] vt inseguire; (*away*) cacciare // n caccia.

chasm ['kæzəm] n abisso.

chassis ['ʃæsɪ] n telaio.

chastity ['tʃæstɪtɪ] n castità.

chat [tʃæt] vi (*also*: have a ~) chiacchierare // n chiacchierata.

chatter ['tʃætə*] vi (*person*) ciarlare // n ciarle fpl; ~box n chiacchierone/a.

chatty ['tʃætɪ] a (*style*) familiare; (*person*) chiacchierino(a).

chauffeur ['ʃəufə*] n autista m.

cheap [tʃiːp] a a buon mercato; (*joke*) grossolano(a); (*poor quality*) di cattiva qualità // ad a buon mercato; ~en vt ribassare; (*fig*) avvilire.

cheat [tʃiːt] vi imbrogliare; (*at school*) copiare // vt ingannare; (*rob*) defraudare // n imbroglione m; copione m; (*trick*) inganno.

check [tʃek] vt verificare; (*passport, ticket*) controllare; (*halt*) fermare; (*restrain*) contenere // n verifica; controllo; (*curb*) freno; (*bill*) conto; (*pattern: gen pl*) quadretti mpl; (*US*) = cheque; to ~ in vi (*in hotel*) registrare; (*at airport*) presentarsi all'accettazione // vt (*luggage*) depositare; to ~ off vt segnare; to ~ out vi (*in hotel*) saldare il conto // vt (*luggage*) ritirare; to ~ up vi: to ~ up (on sth) investigare (qc); to ~ up on sb informarsi sul conto di qd; ~ers n (*US*) dama; ~mate n scaccomatto; ~up n (*MED*) controllo medico.

cheek [tʃiːk] n guancia; (*impudence*) faccia tosta; ~bone n zigomo; ~y a sfacciato(a).

cheer [tʃɪə*] vt applaudire; (*gladden*) rallegrare // vi applaudire // n (*gen pl*) applausi mpl; evviva mpl; ~s! salute!; to ~ up vi rallegrarsi, farsi animo // vt rallegrare; ~ful a allegro(a); ~io excl ciao!

cheese [tʃiːz] n formaggio; ~board n piatto da formaggio.

chef [ʃef] n capocuoco.

chemical ['kemɪkəl] a chimico(a) // n prodotto chimico.

chemist ['kemɪst] n farmacista m/f; (*scientist*) chimico/a; ~ry n chimica; ~'s (shop) n farmacia.

cheque [tʃek] n assegno; ~book n libretto degli assegni.

chequered ['tʃekəd] a (*fig*) eclettico(a).

cherish ['tʃerɪʃ] vt aver caro; (*hope etc*) nutrire.

cherry ['tʃerɪ] n ciliegia.

chess [tʃes] n scacchi mpl; ~board n scacchiera; ~man n pezzo degli scacchi.

chest [tʃɛst] n petto; (box) cassa; ~ of drawers n cassettone m.

chestnut ['tʃɛsnʌt] n castagna; ~ (tree) n castagno.

chew [tʃuː] vt masticare; ~ing gum n chewing gum m.

chic [ʃiːk] a elegante.

chick [tʃɪk] n pulcino.

chicken ['tʃɪkɪn] n pollo; ~ feed n (fig) miseria; ~ pox n varicella.

chicory ['tʃɪkərɪ] n cicoria.

chief [tʃiːf] n capo // a principale; ~ly ad per lo più, soprattutto.

chiffon ['ʃɪfɔn] n chiffon m inv.

chilblain ['tʃɪlbleɪn] n gelone m.

child, pl ~ren [tʃaɪld, 'tʃɪldrən] n bambino/a; ~birth n parto; ~hood n infanzia; ~ish a puerile; ~like a fanciullesco(a); ~ minder n bambinaia.

Chile ['tʃɪlɪ] n Cile m; ~an a, n cileno(a).

chill [tʃɪl] n freddo; (MED) infreddatura // vt raffreddare; ~y a freddo(a), gelido(a); (sensitive to cold) freddoloso(a); to feel ~y sentirsi infreddolito(a).

chime [tʃaɪm] n carillon m inv // vi suonare, scampanare.

chimney ['tʃɪmnɪ] n camino.

chimpanzee [tʃɪmpæn'ziː] n scimpanzé m inv.

chin [tʃɪn] n mento.

china ['tʃaɪnə] n porcellana.

China ['tʃaɪnə] n Cina.

Chinese [tʃaɪ'niːz] a cinese // n cinese m/f; (LING) cinese m.

chink [tʃɪŋk] n (opening) fessura; (noise) tintinnio.

chip [tʃɪp] n (gen pl: CULIN) patatina fritta; (of wood, glass, stone) scheggia // vt (cup, plate) scheggiare; ~pings npl: loose ~pings brecciame m.

chiropodist [kɪ'rɔpədɪst] n pedicure m/f inv.

chirp [tʃəːp] n cinguettio // vi cinguettare.

chisel ['tʃɪzl] n cesello.

chit [tʃɪt] n biglietto.

chivalrous ['ʃɪvəlrəs] a cavalleresco(a).

chivalry ['ʃɪvəlrɪ] n cavalleria; cortesia.

chives [tʃaɪvz] npl erba cipollina.

chloride ['klɔːraɪd] n cloruro.

chlorine ['klɔːriːn] n cloro.

chock [tʃɔk] n zeppa; ~-a-block, ~-full a pieno(a) zeppo(a).

chocolate ['tʃɔklɪt] n (substance) cioccolato, cioccolata; (drink) cioccolata; (a sweet) cioccolatino.

choice [tʃɔɪs] n scelta // a scelto(a).

choir ['kwaɪə*] n coro; ~boy n corista m fanciullo.

choke [tʃəuk] vi soffocare // vt soffocare; (block) ingombrare // n (AUT) valvola dell'aria.

cholera ['kɔlərə] n colera m.

choose, pt **chose**, pp **chosen** [tʃuːz, tʃəuz, 'tʃəuzn] vt scegliere; to ~ to do decidere di fare; preferire fare.

chop [tʃɔp] vt (wood) spaccare; (CULIN: also:

~ up) tritare // n colpo netto; (CULIN) braciola; to ~ down vt (tree) abbattere; ~py a (sea) mosso(a); ~sticks npl bastoncini mpl cinesi.

choral ['kɔːrəl] a corale.

chord [kɔːd] n (MUS) accordo.

chore [tʃɔː*] n faccenda; household ~s faccende fpl domestiche.

choreographer [kɔrɪ'ɔgrəfə*] n coreografo/a.

chorister ['kɔrɪstə*] n corista m/f.

chortle ['tʃɔːtl] vi ridacchiare.

chorus ['kɔːrəs] n coro; (repeated part of song, also fig) ritornello.

chose [tʃəuz] pt of **choose**.

chosen ['tʃəuzn] pp of **choose**.

Christ [kraɪst] n Cristo.

christen ['krɪsn] vt battezzare; ~ing n battesimo.

Christian ['krɪstɪən] a, n cristiano(a); ~ity [-'ænɪtɪ] n cristianesimo; cristianità; ~ name n prenome m.

Christmas ['krɪsməs] n Natale m; ~ card n cartolina di Natale; ~ Eve n la vigilia di Natale; ~ tree n albero di Natale.

chrome [krəum] n = **chromium plating**.

chromium ['krəumɪəm] n cromo; ~ plating n cromatura.

chromosome ['krəuməsəum] n cromosoma m.

chronic ['krɔnɪk] a cronico(a).

chronicle ['krɔnɪkl] n cronaca.

chronological [krɔnə'lɔdʒɪkəl] a cronologico(a).

chrysanthemum [krɪ'sænθəməm] n crisantemo.

chubby ['tʃʌbɪ] a paffuto(a).

chuck [tʃʌk] vt buttare, gettare; to ~ out vt buttar fuori; to ~ (up) vt piantare.

chuckle ['tʃʌkl] vi ridere sommessamente.

chum [tʃʌm] n compagno/a.

chunk [tʃʌŋk] n pezzo; (of bread) tocco.

church [tʃəːtʃ] n chiesa; ~yard n sagrato.

churn [tʃəːn] n (for butter) zangola; (also: milk ~) bidone m.

chute [ʃuːt] n cascata; (also: rubbish ~) canale m di scarico; (children's slide) scivolo.

CID n (abbr of Criminal Investigation Department) ≈ polizia giudiziaria.

cider ['saɪdə*] n sidro.

cigar [sɪ'gɑː*] n sigaro.

cigarette [sɪgə'rɛt] n sigaretta; ~ case n portasigarette m inv; ~ end n mozzicone m; ~ holder n bocchino.

cinch [sɪntʃ] n (col): it's a ~ è presto fatto.

cinder ['sɪndə*] n cenere f.

cine ['sɪnɪ]: ~-camera n cinepresa; ~-film n pellicola.

cinema ['sɪnəmə] n cinema m inv.

cine-projector [sɪnɪprə'dʒɛktə*] n proiettore m.

cinnamon ['sɪnəmən] n cannella.

cipher ['saɪfə*] n cifra; (fig: faceless

employee etc) persona di nessun conto.
circle ['sɔːkl] *n* cerchio; (*of friends etc*) circolo; (*in cinema*) galleria // *vi* girare in circolo // *vt* (*surround*) circondare; (*move round*) girare intorno a.
circuit ['sɔːkɪt] *n* circuito; ~**ous** [sɔːˈkjuɪtəs] *a* indiretto(a).
circular ['sɔːkjuləʳ] *a, n* circolare (*f*).
circulate ['sɔːkjuleɪt] *vi* circolare // *vt* far circolare; **circulation** [-ˈleɪʃən] *n* circolazione *f*; (*of newspaper*) tiratura.
circumcise ['sɔːkəmsaɪz] *vt* circoncidere.
circumference [səˈkʌmfərəns] *n* circonferenza.
circumstances ['sɔːkəmstənsɪz] *npl* circostanze *fpl*; (*financial condition*) condizioni *fpl* finanziarie.
circus ['sɔːkəs] *n* circo.
cistern ['sɪstən] *n* cisterna; (*in toilet*) serbatoio d'acqua.
cite [saɪt] *vt* citare.
citizen ['sɪtɪzn] *n* (*POL.*) cittadino/a; (*resident*): **the ~s of this town** gli abitanti di questa città; ~**ship** *n* cittadinanza.
citrus fruit ['sɪtrəsˈfruːt] *n* agrume *m*.
city ['sɪtɪ] *n* città *f inv*; **the C~** la Città di Londra (*centro commerciale*).
civic ['sɪvɪk] *a* civico(a).
civil ['sɪvɪl] *a* civile; ~ **engineer** *n* ingegnere *m* civile; ~**ian** [sɪˈvɪlɪən] *a, n* borghese (*m/f*).
civilization [sɪvɪlaɪˈzeɪʃən] *n* civiltà *f inv*.
civilized ['sɪvɪlaɪzd] *a* civilizzato(a); (*fig*) cortese.
civil: ~ **law** *n* codice *m* civile; (*study*) diritto civile; ~ **servant** *n* impiegato/a statale; **C~ Service** *n* amministrazione *f* statale; ~ **war** *n* guerra civile.
claim [kleɪm] *vt* rivendicare; sostenere, pretendere; (*damages*) richiedere // *vi* (*for insurance*) richiedere // *n* rivendicazione *f*; pretesa; (*right*) diritto; (*insurance*) ~ richiesta; ~**ant** *n* (*ADMIN, LAW*) rivendicatore/trice.
clam [klæm] *n* vongola.
clamber ['klæmbəʳ] *vi* arrampicarsi.
clammy ['klæmɪ] *a* (*weather*) caldo(a) umido(a); (*hands*) viscido(a).
clamp [klæmp] *n* grappa; pinza; morsa // *vt* ammorsare.
clan [klæn] *n* clan *m inv*.
clang [klæŋ] *n* fragore *m*, suono metallico.
clap [klæp] *vi* applaudire; ~**ping** *n* applausi *mpl*.
claret ['klærət] *n* vino di Bordeaux.
clarification [klærɪfɪˈkeɪʃən] *n* (*fig*) chiarificazione *f*, schiarimento.
clarify ['klærɪfaɪ] *vt* chiarificare, schiarire.
clarinet [klærɪˈnɛt] *n* clarinetto.
clarity ['klærɪtɪ] *n* chiarità.
clash [klæʃ] *n* frastuono; (*fig*) scontro // *vi* scontrarsi; cozzare.
clasp [klɑːsp] *n* fermaglio, fibbia // *vt* stringere.
class [klɑːs] *n* classe *f* // *vt* classificare.

classic ['klæsɪk] *a* classico(a) // *n* classico; ~**al** *a* classico(a).
classification [klæsɪfɪˈkeɪʃən] *n* classificazione *f*.
classify ['klæsɪfaɪ] *vt* classificare.
classmate ['klɑːsmeɪt] *n* compagno/a di classe.
classroom ['klɑːsrum] *n* aula.
clatter ['klætəʳ] *n* acciottolio; scalpitìo // *vi* acciottolare; scalpitare.
clause [klɔːz] *n* clausola; (*LING*) proposizione *f*.
claustrophobia [klɔːstrəˈfəubɪə] *n* claustrofobia.
claw [klɔː] *n* tenaglia; (*of bird of prey*) artiglio; (*of lobster*) pinza // *vt* graffiare; afferrare.
clay [kleɪ] *n* argilla.
clean [kliːn] *a* pulito(a); (*clear, smooth*) liscio(a) // *vt* pulire; **to ~ out** *vt* far piazza pulita di; **to ~ up** *vi* far pulizia // *vt* (*also fig*) ripulire; ~**er** *n* (*person*) donna delle pulizie; (*also*: **dry ~er**) tintore/a; (*product*) smacchiatore *m*; ~**ing** *n* pulizia; ~**liness** ['klɛnlɪnɪs] *n* pulizia.
cleanse [klɛnz] *vt* pulire; purificare; ~**r** *n* detergente *m*.
clean-shaven ['kliːnˈʃeɪvn] *a* sbarbato(a).
clean-up ['kliːnˈʌp] *n* pulizia.
clear [klɪəʳ] *a* chiaro(a); (*road, way*) libero(a) // *vt* sgombrare; liberare; (*table*) sparecchiare; (*COMM: goods*) liquidare; (*LAW: suspect*) discolpare; (*obstacle*) superare // *vi* (*weather*) rasserenarsi; (*fog*) andarsene // *ad*: ~ **of** distante da; **to ~ up** *vi* schiarirsi // *vt* mettere in ordine; (*mystery*) risolvere; ~**ance** *n* (*removal*) sgombro; (*free space*) spazio; (*permission*) autorizzazione *f*, permesso; ~**ance sale** *n* vendita di liquidazione; ~**-cut** *a* ben delineato(a), distinto(a); ~**ing** *n* radura; (*BANKING*) clearing *m*; ~**ly** *ad* chiaramente; ~**way** *n* (*Brit*) strada con divieto di sosta.
clef [klɛf] *n* (*MUS*) chiave *f*.
clench [klɛntʃ] *vt* stringere.
clergy ['klɔːdʒɪ] *n* clero; ~**man** *n* ecclesiastico.
clerical ['klɛrɪkəl] *a* d'impiegato; (*REL*) clericale.
clerk [klɑːk, (*US*) klɔːrk] *n* impiegato/a; (*US: salesman/ woman*) commesso/a.
clever ['klɛvəʳ] *a* (*mentally*) intelligente; (*deft, skilful*) abile; (*device, arrangement*) ingegnoso(a).
cliché ['kliːʃeɪ] *n* cliché *m inv*.
click [klɪk] *vi* scattare.
client ['klaɪənt] *n* cliente *m/f*; ~**ele** [kliːːɑːnˈtɛl] *n* clientela.
cliff [klɪf] *n* scogliera scoscesa, rupe *f*.
climate ['klaɪmɪt] *n* clima *m*.
climax ['klaɪmæks] *n* culmine *m*.
climb [klaɪm] *vi* salire; (*clamber*) arrampicarsi // *vi* salire; (*CLIMBING*) scalare // *n* salita; arrampicata; scalata; **to ~ down** *vi* scendere; ~**er** *n* (*also*: **rock ~er**) rocciatore/trice; alpinista

m/f; ~ing n (also: rock ~ing)
alpinismo.

clinch [klɪntʃ] vt (deal) concludere.

cling, pt, pp **clung** [klɪŋ, klʌŋ] vi: to ~
(to) tenersi stretto (a); (of clothes) aderire
strettamente (a).

clinic ['klɪnɪk] n clinica; ~al a clinico(a).

clink [klɪŋk] vi tintinnare.

clip [klɪp] n (for hair) forcina; (also: paper
~) graffetta; (holding hose etc) anello
d'attacco // vt (also: ~ **together**: papers)
attaccare insieme; (hair, nails) tagliare;
(hedge) tosare; ~**pers** npl macchinetta
per capelli; (also: **nail** ~**pers**) forbicine
fpl per le unghie.

clique [kli:k] n cricca.

cloak [kləuk] n mantello; ~**room** n (for
coats etc) guardaroba m inv; (W.C.)
gabinetti mpl.

clock [klɔk] n orologio; ~**wise** ad in senso
orario; ~**work** n movimento or
meccanismo a orologeria.

clog [klɔg] n zoccolo // vt intasare.

cloister ['klɔɪstə*] n chiostro.

close a, ad and derivatives [kləus] a
vicino(a); (writing, texture) fitto(a);
(watch) stretto(a); (examination)
attento(a); (weather) afoso(a) // ad vicino,
dappresso; a ~ **friend** un amico intimo;
to have a ~ **shave** (fig) scamparla bella
// vb and derivatives [kləuz] vt chiudere //
vi (shop etc) chiudere; (lid, door etc)
chiudersi; (end) finire // n (end) fine f; to
~ **down** vt chiudere (definitivamente) //
vi cessare (definitivamente); ~**d** a
chiuso(a); ~**d shop** n azienda o fabbrica
che impiega solo aderenti ai sindacati; ~**ly**
ad (examine, watch) da vicino.

closet ['klɔzɪt] n (cupboard) armadio.

close-up ['kləusʌp] n primo piano.

closure ['kləuʒə*] n chiusura.

clot [klɔt] n (also: **blood** ~) coagulo; (col:
idiot) scemo/a // vi coagularsi; ~**ted
cream** n panna rappresa.

cloth [klɔθ] n (material) tessuto, stoffa;
(also: **tea**~) strofinaccio.

clothe [kləuð] vt vestire; ~**s** npl abiti mpl,
vestiti mpl; ~**s line** n corda (per stendere
il bucato); ~**s peg** n molletta.

clothing ['kləuðɪŋ] n = **clothes.**

cloud [klaud] n nuvola; ~**burst** n
acquazzone m; ~**y** a nuvoloso(a); (liquid)
torbido(a).

clout [klaut] n (blow) colpo // vt dare un
colpo a.

clove [kləuv] n chiodo di garofano; ~ **of**
garlic spicchio d'aglio.

clover ['kləuvə*] n trifoglio.

clown [klaun] n pagliaccio // vi (also: ~
about, ~ **around**) fare il pagliaccio.

club [klʌb] n (society) club m inv, circolo;
(weapon, GOLF) mazza // vt bastonare //
vi: to ~ **together** associarsi; ~**s** npl
(CARDS) fiori mpl; ~**house** n sede f del
circolo.

cluck [klʌk] vi chiocciare.

clue [klu:] n indizio; (in crosswords)

definizione f; **I haven't a** ~ non ho la
minima idea.

clump [klʌmp] n: ~ **of trees** folto
d'alberi.

clumsy ['klʌmzɪ] a (person) goffo(a),
maldestro(a); (object) malfatto(a), mal
costruito(a).

clung [klʌŋ] pt, pp of **cling.**

cluster ['klʌstə*] n gruppo // vi
raggrupparsi.

clutch [klʌtʃ] n (grip, grasp) presa, stretta;
(AUT) frizione f // vt afferrare, stringere
forte; to ~ **at** aggrapparsi a.

clutter ['klʌtə*] vt ingombrare.

Co. abbr of **county**; **company.**

c/o abbr of care of) presso.

coach [kəutʃ] n (bus) pullman m inv; (horse-
drawn, of train) carrozza; (SPORT)
allenatore/trice // vt allenare.

coagulate [kəu'ægjuleɪt] vi coagularsi.

coal [kəul] n carbone m; ~ **face** n fronte f;
~ **field** n bacino carbonifero.

coalition [kəuə'lɪʃən] n coalizione f.

coalman, coal merchant ['kəulmən,
'kəulmətʃənt] n negoziante m di carbone.

coalmine ['kəulmaɪn] n miniera di
carbone.

coarse [kɔ:s] a (salt, sand etc) grosso(a);
(cloth, person) rozzo(a).

coast [kəust] n costa // vi (with cycle etc)
scendere a ruota libera; ~**al** a
costiero(a); ~**guard** n guardia costiera;
~**line** n linea costiera.

coat [kəut] n cappotto; (of animal) pelo; (of
paint) mano f // vt coprire; ~ **of arms** n
stemma m; ~ **hanger** n attaccapanni m
inv; ~**ing** n rivestimento.

coax [kəuks] vt indurre (con moine).

cobbles, cobblestones ['kɔblz,
'kɔblstəunz] npl ciottoli mpl.

cobra ['kəubrə] n cobra.

cobweb ['kɔbweb] n ragnatela.

cocaine [kə'keɪn] n cocaina.

cock [kɔk] n (rooster) gallo; (male bird)
maschio // vt (gun) armare; to ~ **one's
ears** (fig) drizzare le orecchie; ~**erel** n
galletto; ~**-eyed** a (fig) storto(a);
strampalato(a).

cockle ['kɔkl] n cardio.

cockney ['kɔknɪ] n cockney m/f inv
(abitante dei quartieri popolari dell'East End
di Londra).

cockpit ['kɔkpɪt] n (in aircraft) abitacolo.

cockroach ['kɔkrəutʃ] n blatta.

cocktail ['kɔkteɪl] n cocktail m inv; ~
shaker n shaker m inv.

cocoa ['kəukəu] n cacao.

coconut ['kəukənʌt] n noce f di cocco.

cocoon [kə'ku:n] n bozzolo.

cod [kɔd] n merluzzo.

code [kəud] n codice m.

codify ['kəudɪfaɪ] vt codificare

coeducational ['kəuedju'keɪʃənl] a
misto(a).

coerce [kəu'ɔ:s] vt costringere; **coercion**
[·'ɔ:ʃən] n coercizione f.

coexistence ['kəuɪg'zɪstəns] n coesistenza.

coffee ['kɔfɪ] n caffè m inv; ~ **grounds** npl fondi mpl di caffè; ~**pot** n caffettiera; ~ **table** n tavolino da tè.

coffin ['kɔfɪn] n bara.

cog [kɔg] n dente m; ~**wheel** n ruota dentata.

cogent ['kəudʒənt] a convincente.

coherent [kəu'hɪərənt] a coerente.

coil [kɔɪl] n rotolo; (one loop) anello; (contraceptive) spirale f // vt avvolgere.

coin [kɔɪn] n moneta // vt (word) coniare; ~**age** n sistema m monetario.

coincide [kəuɪn'saɪd] vi coincidere; ~**nce** [kəu'ɪnsɪdəns] n combinazione f.

coke [kəuk] n coke m.

colander ['kɔləndə*] n colino.

cold [kəuld] a freddo(a) // n freddo; (MED) raffreddore m; **it's** ~ fa freddo; **to be** ~ aver freddo; **to have** ~ **feet** avere i piedi freddi; (fig) aver la fifa; **to give sb the** ~ **shoulder** ignorare qd; ~**ly** ad freddamente; ~ **sore** n erpete m.

coleslaw ['kəulslɔ:] n insalata di cavolo e di salsa maionese.

collaborate [kə'læbəreɪt] vi collaborare; **collaboration** [-'reɪʃən] n collaborazione f; **collaborator** n collaboratore/trice.

collage [kɔ'lɑ:ʒ] n collage m inv.

collapse [kə'læps] vi crollare // n crollo; (MED) collasso.

collapsible [kə'læpsəbl] a pieghevole.

collar ['kɔlə*] n (of coat, shirt) colletto; ~**bone** n clavicola.

colleague ['kɔli:g] n collega m/f.

collect [kə'lɛkt] vt adunare; raccogliere; (as a hobby) fare collezione di; (call and pick up) prendere; (mail) raccogliere; (money owed, pension) riscuotere; (donations, subscriptions) fare una colletta di // vi adunarsi, riunirsi; ammucchiarsi; ~**ed** a: ~**ed works** opere fpl raccolte; ~**ion** [kə'lɛkʃən] n collezione f; raccolta; (for money) colletta.

collector [kə'lɛktə*] n collezionista m/f; (of taxes) esattore m.

college ['kɔlɪdʒ] n collegio.

collide [kə'laɪd] vi: **to** ~ (**with**) scontrarsi (con).

colliery ['kɔlɪərɪ] n miniera di carbone.

collision [kə'lɪʒən] n collisione f, scontro.

colloquial [kə'ləukwɪəl] a familiare.

colon ['kəulən] n (sign) due punti mpl; (MED) colon m inv.

colonel ['kə:nl] n colonnello.

colonial [kə'ləunɪəl] a coloniale.

colonize ['kɔlənaɪz] vt colonizzare.

colony ['kɔlənɪ] n colonia.

colossal [kə'lɔsl] a colossale.

colour ['kʌlə*] n colore m // vt colorare; dipingere; (news) svisare; ~**s** npl (of party, club) emblemi mpl; ~ **bar** n discriminazione f razziale (in locali etc); ~**-blind** a daltonico(a); ~**ed** a colorato(a); (photo) a colori // n: ~**eds** gente f di colore; ~ **film** n (for camera)

pellicola a colori; ~**ful** a pieno(a) di colore, a vivaci colori; (personality) colorato(a); ~ **television** n televisione f a colori.

colt [kəult] n puledro.

column ['kɔləm] n colonna; ~**ist** ['kɔləmnɪst] n articolista m/f.

coma ['kəumə] n coma m inv.

comb [kəum] n pettine m // vt (hair) pettinare; (area) battere a tappeto.

combat ['kɔmbæt] n combattimento // vt combattere, lottare contro.

combination [kɔmbɪ'neɪʃən] n combinazione f.

combine vb [kəm'baɪn] vt combinare; (one quality with another) unire (a) // vi unirsi; (CHEM) combinarsi // n ['kɔmbaɪn] lega; (ECON) associazione f; ~ (**harvester**) n mietitrebbia.

combustible [kəm'bʌstɪbl] a combustibile.

combustion [kəm'bʌstʃən] n combustione f.

come, pt **came**, pp **come** [kʌm, keɪm] vi venire; arrivare; **to** ~ **to** (decision etc) raggiungere; **to** ~ **about** vi succedere; **to** ~ **across** vt fus trovare per caso; **to** ~ **along** vi = **to come on**; **to** ~ **apart** vi andare in pezzi; staccarsi; **to** ~ **away** vi venire via; staccarsi; **to** ~ **back** vi ritornare; **to** ~ **by** vt fus (acquire) ottenere; procurarsi; **to** ~ **down** vi discendere; (prices) calare; (buildings) essere demolito(a); **to** ~ **forward** vi farsi avanti; presentarsi; **to** ~ **from** vt venire da; provenire da; **to** ~ **in** vi entrare; **to** ~ **in for** vt fus (criticism etc) ricevere; **to** ~ **into** vt fus (money) ereditare; **to** ~ **off** vi (button) staccarsi; (stain) andar via; (attempt) riuscire; **to** ~ **on** vi (pupil, undertaking) fare progressi; ~ **on!** avanti!, andiamo!, forza!; **to** ~ **out** vi uscire; (strike) entrare in sciopero; **to** ~ **to** vi rinvenire; **to** ~ **up** vi venire su; **to** ~ **up against** vt fus (resistance, difficulties) urtare contro; **to** ~ **up with** vt fus: he came up with an idea venne fuori con un'idea; **to** ~ **upon** vt fus trovare per caso; ~**back** n (THEATRE etc) ritorno.

comedian [kə'mi:dɪən] n comico.

comedown ['kʌmdaun] n rovescio.

comedy ['kɔmɪdɪ] n commedia.

comet ['kɔmɪt] n cometa.

comfort ['kʌmfət] n comodità f inv, benessere m; (solace) consolazione f, conforto // vt consolare, confortare; ~**s** npl comodi mpl; ~**able** a comodo(a); ~ **station** n (US) gabinetti mpl.

comic ['kɔmɪk] a (also: ~**al**) comico(a) // n comico; (magazine) giornaletto; ~ **strip** n fumetto.

coming ['kʌmɪŋ] n arrivo; ~(**s**) **and going(s)** n(pl) andirivieni m inv.

comma ['kɔmə] n virgola.

command [kə'mɑ:nd] n ordine m, comando; (MIL: authority) comando; (mastery) padronanza // vt comandare; **to** ~ **sb to do** ordinare a qd di fare; ~**eer**

[kəmən'dɪə*] *vt* requisire; ~**er** *n* capo; (*MIL*) comandante *m*; ~**ing officer** *n* comandante *m*.

commando [kə'mɑːndəʊ] *n* commando *m inv*; membro di un commando.

commemorate [kə'mɛməreɪt] *vt* commemorare; **commemoration** [-'reɪʃən] *n* commemorazione *f*.

commence [kə'mɛns] *vt*, *vi* cominciare.

commend [kə'mɛnd] *vt* lodare; raccomandare; ~**able** *a* lodevole; ~**ation** [kɔmən'deɪʃən] *n* lode *f*; raccomandazione *f*.

commensurate [kə'mɛnʃərɪt] *a*: ~ **with** proporzionato(a) a.

comment ['kɔment] *n* commento // *vi* fare commenti; ~**ary** ['kɔməntəri] *n* commentario; (*SPORT*) radiocronaca; telecronaca; ~**ator** ['kɔmənteɪtə*] *n* commentatore/trice; radiocronista *m/f*; telecronista *m/f*.

commerce ['kɔməs] *n* commercio.

commercial [kə'mɔːʃəl] *a* commerciale // *n* (*TV*: *also*: ~ **break**) pubblicità *f inv*; ~**ize** *vt* commercializzare; ~ **television** *n* televisione *f* commerciale; ~ **traveller** *n* commesso viaggiatore; ~ **vehicle** *n* veicolo commerciale.

commiserate [kə'mɪzəreɪt] *vi*: **to** ~ **with** condolersi con.

commission [kə'mɪʃən] *n* commissione *f* // *vt* (*MIL*) nominare (al comando); (*work of art*) commissionare; **out of** ~ (*NAUT*) in disarmo; ~**aire** [kəmɪʃə'neə*] *n* (*at shop, cinema etc*) portiere *m* in livrea; ~**er** *n* commissario; (*POLICE*) questore *m*.

commit [kə'mɪt] *vt* (*act*) commettere; (*to sb's care*) affidare; **to** ~ **o.s.** (**to do**) impegnarsi (a fare); **to** ~ **suicide** suicidarsi; ~**ment** *n* impegno; promessa.

committee [kə'mɪtɪ] *n* comitato.

commodity [kə'mɔdɪtɪ] *n* prodotto, articolo; (*food*) derrata.

common ['kɔmən] *a* comune; (*pej*) volgare; (*usual*) normale // *n* terreno comune; **the C**~**s** *npl* la Camera dei Comuni; **in** ~ in comune; **it's** ~ **knowledge that** è di dominio pubblico che; ~**er** *n* cittadino/a (non nobile); ~ **ground** *n* (*fig*) terreno comune; ~ **law** *n* diritto consuetudinario; ~**ly** *ad* comunemente, usualmente; **C**~ **Market** *n* Mercato Comune; ~**place** *a* banale, ordinario(a); ~**room** *n* sala di riunione; (*SCOL*) sala dei professori; ~ **sense** *n* buon senso; **the C**~**wealth** *n* il Commonwealth.

commotion [kə'məʊʃən] *n* confusione *f*, tumulto.

communal ['kɔmjuːnl] *a* (*life*) comunale; (*for common use*) pubblico(a).

commune *n* ['kɔmjuːn] (*group*) comune *m* // *vi* [kə'mjuːn]: **to** ~ **with** mettersi in comunione con.

communicate [kə'mjuːnɪkeɪt] *vt* comunicare, trasmettere // *vi*: **to** ~ (**with**) comunicare (con).

communication [kəmjuːnɪ'keɪʃən] *n*

comunicazione *f*; ~ **cord** *n* segnale *m* d'allarme.

communion [kə'mjuːnɪən] *n* comunione *f*.

communiqué [kə'mjuːnɪkeɪ] *n* comunicato.

communism ['kɔmjunɪzəm] *n* comunismo; **communist** *a*,*n* comunista (*m/f*).

community [kə'mjuːnɪtɪ] *n* comunità *f inv*; ~ **centre** *n* circolo ricreativo; ~ **chest** *n* (*US*) fondo di beneficenza.

commutation ticket [kɔmjuː'teɪʃɔntɪkɪt] *n* (*US*) biglietto di abbonamento.

commute [kə'mjuːt] *vi* fare il pendolare // *vt* (*LAW*) commutare; ~**r** *n* pendolare *m/f*.

compact *a* [kəm'pækt] compatto(a) // *n* ['kɔmpækt] (*also*: **powder** ~) portacipria.

companion [kəm'pænɪən] *n* compagno/a; ~**ship** *n* compagnia.

company ['kʌmpənɪ] *n* (*also COMM, MIL, THEATRE*) compagnia; **he's good** ~ è di buona compagnia; **we have** ~ abbiamo ospiti; **to keep sb** ~ tenere compagnia a qd; **to part** ~ **with** separarsi da.

comparable ['kɔmpərəbl] *a* comparabile.

comparative [kəm'pærətɪv] *a* comparativo(a); (*LING*) comparato(a); ~**ly** *ad* relativamente.

compare [kəm'pɛə*] *vt*: **to** ~ **sth/sb with/to** confrontare qc/qd con/a // *vi*: **to** ~ (**with**) reggere il confronto (con); **comparison** [-'pærɪsn] *n* confronto; **in comparison** (**with**) a confronto di).

compartment [kəm'pɑːtmənt] *n* compartimento; (*RAIL*) scompartimento.

compass ['kʌmpəs] *n* bussola; ~**es** *npl* compassi *mpl*.

compassion [kəm'pæʃən] *n* compassione *f*; ~**ate** *a* compassionevole.

compatible [kəm'pætɪbl] *a* compatibile.

compel [kəm'pɛl] *vt* costringere, obbligare; ~**ling** *a* (*fig*: *argument*) irresistibile.

compendium [kəm'pɛndɪəm] *n* compendio.

compensate ['kɔmpənseɪt] *vt* risarcire // *vi*: **to** ~ **for** compensare; **compensation** [-'seɪʃən] *n* compensazione *f*; (*money*) risarcimento.

compère ['kɔmpɛə*] *n* presentatore/trice.

compete [kəm'piːt] *vi* (*take part*) concorrere; (*vie*): **to** ~ (**with**) fare concorrenza (a).

competence ['kɔmpɪtəns] *n* competenza.

competent ['kɔmpɪtənt] *a* competente.

competition [kɔmpɪ'tɪʃən] *n* gara; concorso; (*ECON*) concorrenza.

competitive [kəm'pɛtɪtɪv] *a* di concorso; di concorrenza.

competitor [kəm'pɛtɪtə*] *n* concorrente *m/f*.

compile [kəm'paɪl] *vt* compilare.

complacency [kəm'pleɪsnsɪ] *n* compiacenza di sé.

complacent [kəm'pleɪsənt] *a* compiaciuto(a) di sé.

complain [kəm'pleɪn] *vi*: **to** ~ (**about**) lagnarsi (di); (*in shop etc*) reclamare (per); **to ~ of** vt fus (MED) accusare; **~t** n lamento; reclamo; (MED) malattia.

complement ['kɔmplɪmənt] n complemento; (especially of ship's crew etc) effettivo; **~ary** [kɔmplɪ'mɛntərɪ] a complementare.

complete [kəm'pliːt] a completo(a) // vt completare, compire; (a form) riempire; **~ly** ad completamente; **completion** n completamento.

complex ['kɔmplɛks] a complesso(a) // n (PSYCH, buildings etc) complesso.

complexion [kəm'plɛkʃən] n (of face) carnagione f; (of event etc) aspetto.

complexity [kəm'plɛksɪtɪ] n complessità f inv.

compliance [kəm'plaɪəns] n acquiescenza; **in ~ with** (orders, wishes etc) in conformità con.

compliant [kəm'plaɪənt] a acquiescente, arrendevole.

complicate ['kɔmplɪkeɪt] vt complicare; **~d** a complicato(a); **complication** [-'keɪʃən] n complicazione f.

compliment n ['kɔmplɪmənt] complimento // vt ['kɔmplɪmɛnt] fare un complimento a; **~s** npl complimenti mpl; rispetti mpl; **~ary** [-'mɛntərɪ] a complimentoso(a), elogiativo(a); (free) in omaggio; **~ary ticket** n biglietto d'omaggio.

comply [kəm'plaɪ] vi: **to ~ with** assentire a; conformarsi a.

component [kəm'pəunənt] n componente m.

compose [kəm'pəuz] vt comporre; **to ~ o.s.** ricomporsi; **~d** a calmo(a); **~d of** composto(a) di; **~r** n (MUS) compositore/trice.

composition [kɔmpə'zɪʃən] n composizione f.

compost ['kɔmpɔst] n composta, concime m.

composure [kəm'pəuʒə*] n calma.

compound ['kɔmpaund] n (CHEM, LING) composto; (enclosure) recinto // a composto(a); **~ fracture** n frattura composta; **~ interest** n interesse m composto.

comprehend [kɔmprɪ'hɛnd] vt comprendere, capire; **comprehension** [-'hɛnʃən] n comprensione f.

comprehensive [kɔmprɪ'hɛnsɪv] a comprensivo(a); **~ policy** n (INSURANCE) polizza che copre tutti i rischi; **~ (school)** n scuola secondaria aperta a tutti.

compress vt [kəm'prɛs] comprimere // n ['kɔmprɛs] (MED) compressa; **~ion** [-'prɛʃən] n compressione f.

comprise [kəm'praɪz] vt (also: **be ~d of**) comprendere.

compromise ['kɔmprəmaɪz] n compromesso // vt compromettere // vi venire a un compromesso.

compulsion [kəm'pʌlʃən] n costrizione f.

compulsive [kəm'pʌlsɪv] a (reason, demand) stringente; (PSYCH) inguaribile.

compulsory [kəm'pʌlsərɪ] a obbligatorio(a).

computer [kəm'pjuːtə*] n computer m inv; **~ize** vt computerizzare; **~ programming** n programmazione f di computer.

comrade ['kɔmrɪd] n compagno/a; **~ship** n cameratismo.

con [kɔn] vt (col) truffare.

concave ['kɔn'keɪv] a concavo(a).

conceal [kən'siːl] vt nascondere.

concede [kən'siːd] vt concedere // vi fare una concessione.

conceit [kən'siːt] n presunzione f, vanità; **~ed** a presuntuoso(a), vanitoso(a).

conceivable [kən'siːvəbl] a concepibile.

conceive [kən'siːv] vt concepire // vi concepire un bambino.

concentrate ['kɔnsəntreɪt] vi concentrarsi // vt concentrare.

concentration [kɔnsən'treɪʃən] n concentrazione f; **~ camp** n campo di concentramento.

concept ['kɔnsɛpt] n concetto.

conception [kən'sɛpʃən] n concezione f.

concern [kən'səːn] n affare m; (COMM) azienda, ditta; (anxiety) preoccupazione f // vt riguardare; **to be ~ed (about)** preoccuparsi (di); **~ing** prep riguardo a, circa.

concert ['kɔnsət] n concerto; **in ~** di concerto; **~ed** [kən'səːtɪd] a concertato(a); **~ hall** n sala da concerti.

concertina [kɔnsə'tiːnə] n piccola fisarmonica // vi ridursi come una fisarmonica.

concerto [kən'tʃəːtəu] n concerto.

concession [kən'sɛʃən] n concessione f.

conciliation [kənsɪlɪ'eɪʃən] n conciliazione f.

conciliatory [kən'sɪlɪətrɪ] a conciliativo(a).

concise [kən'saɪs] a conciso(a).

conclave ['kɔnkleɪv] n riunione f segreta; (REL) conclave m.

conclude [kən'kluːd] vt concludere; **conclusion** [-'kluːʒən] n conclusione f; **conclusive** [-'kluːsɪv] a conclusivo(a).

concoct [kən'kɔkt] vt inventare.

concourse ['kɔŋkɔːs] n (hall) atrio.

concrete ['kɔŋkriːt] n conglomerato (di cemento) // a concreto(a); di cemento.

concur [kən'kəː*] vi concordare.

concurrently [kən'kʌrntlɪ] ad simultaneamente.

concussion [kən'kʌʃən] n commozione f cerebrale.

condemn [kən'dɛm] vt condannare; **~ation** [kɔndɛm'neɪʃən] n condanna.

condensation [kɔndɛn'seɪʃən] n condensazione f.

condense [kən'dɛns] vi condensarsi // vt condensare; **~d milk** n latte m condensato.

condescend [kɔndɪ'sɛnd] vi condiscendere; **~ing** a condiscendente.

condition [kən'dɪʃən] n condizione f // vt condizionare, regolare; **on ~ that** a condizione che + *sub*, a condizione di; ~al a condizionale.

condolences [kən'dəulənsız] *npl* condoglianze *fpl*.

condone [kən'dəun] *vt* condonare.

conducive [kən'dju:sıv] *a*: ~ to favorevole a.

conduct *n* ['kɒndʌkt] condotta // *vt* [kən'dʌkt] condurre; (*manage*) dirigere; amministrare; (*MUS*) dirigere; **to ~ o.s.** comportarsi; ~**ed tour** *n* gita accompagnata; ~**or** *n* (*of orchestra*) direttore *m* d'orchestra; (*on bus*) bigliettaio; (*ELEC*) conduttore *m*; ~**ress** *n* (*on bus*) bigliettaia.

conduit ['kɒndıt] *n* condotto; tubo.

cone [kəun] *n* cono; (*BOT*) pigna.

confectionery [kən'fekʃənərı] *n* dolciumi *mpl*.

confederation [kənfedə'reıʃən] *n* confederazione *f*.

confer [kən'fɔ:*] *vt*: **to ~ sth on** conferire qc a // *vi* conferire.

conference ['kɒnfərns] *n* congresso.

confess [kən'fes] *vt* confessare, ammettere // *vi* confessarsi; ~**ion** [-'feʃən] *n* confessione *f*; ~**ional** [-'feʃənl] *n* confessionale *m*; ~**or** *n* confessore *m*.

confetti [kən'fetı] *n* coriandoli *mpl*.

confide [kən'faıd] *vi*: **to ~ in** confidarsi con.

confidence ['kɒnfıdns] *n* confidenza; (*trust*) fiducia; (*also*: **self-~**) sicurezza di sé; ~ **trick** *n* truffa; **confident** *a* confidente, sicuro(a) di sé; **confidential** [kɒnfı'denʃəl] *a* riservato(a).

confine [kən'faın] *vt* limitare; (*shut up*) rinchiudere; ~**s** ['kɒnfaınz] *npl* confini *mpl*; ~**d** *a* (*space*) ristretto(a); ~**ment** *n* prigionia; (*MIL*) consegna; (*MED*) parto.

confirm [kən'fɔ:m] *vt* confermare; (*REL*) cresimare; ~**ation** [kɒnfə'meıʃən] *n* conferma; cresima; ~**ed** *a* inveterato(a).

confiscate ['kɒnfıskeıt] *vt* confiscare; **confiscation** [-'keıʃən] *n* confisca.

conflict *n* ['kɒnflıkt] conflitto // *vi* [kən-'flıkt] essere in conflitto; ~**ing** *a* contrastante.

conform [kən'fɔ:m] *vi*: **to ~ (to)** conformarsi (a); ~**ist** *n* conformista *m/f*.

confound [kən'faund] *vt* confondere; ~**ed** *a* maledetto(a).

confront [kən'frʌnt] *vt* confrontare; (*enemy*, *danger*) affrontare; ~**ation** [kɒnfrən'teıʃən] *n* confronto.

confuse [kən'fju:z] *vt* imbrogliare; (*one thing with another*) confondere; **confusing** *a* che fa confondere; **confusion** [-'fju:ʒən] *n* confusione *f*.

congeal [kən'dʒi:l] *vi* (*blood*) congelarsi.

congenial [kən'dʒi:nıəl] *a* (*person*) simpatico(a); (*thing*) congeniale.

congenital [kən'dʒenıtl] *a* congenito(a).

conger eel ['kɒngərı:l] *n* grongo.

congested [kən'dʒestıd] *a* congestionato(a).

congestion [kən'dʒestʃən] *n* congestione *f*.

conglomeration [kənglɒmə'reıʃən] *n* conglomerazione *f*.

congratulate [kən'grætjuleıt] *vt*: **to ~ sb (on)** congratularsi con qd (per *or* di); **congratulations** [-'leıʃənz] *npl* auguri *mpl*; (*on success*) complimenti *mpl*.

congregate [kɒngrıgeıt] *vi* congregarsi, riunirsi.

congregation [kɒngrı'geıʃən] *n* congregazione *f*.

congress ['kɒngres] *n* congresso; ~**man** *n* (*US*) membro del Congresso.

conical ['kɒnıkl] *a* conico(a).

conifer ['kɒnıfə*] *n* conifero.

conjecture [kən'dʒektʃə*] *n* congettura // *vt*, *vi* congetturare.

conjugal ['kɒndʒugl] *a* coniugale.

conjunction [kən'dʒʌŋkʃən] *n* congiunzione *f*.

conjunctivitis [kəndʒʌŋktı'vaıtıs] *n* congiuntivite *f*.

conjure ['kʌndʒə*] *vt* prestigiare; **to ~ up** *vt* (*ghost*, *spirit*) evocare; (*memories*) rievocare; ~**r** *n* prestidigitatore/trice; **conjuring trick** *n* gioco di prestigio.

conk [kɒŋk]: **to ~ out** *vi* (*col*) andare in panne.

conman ['kɒnmæn] *n* truffatore *m*.

connect [kə'nekt] *vt* connettere, collegare; (*ELEC*) collegare; (*fig*) associare // *vi* (*train*): **to ~ with** essere in coincidenza con; **to be ~ed with** aver rapporti con; essere imparentato con; ~**ion** [-ʃən] *n* relazione *f*, rapporto; (*ELEC*) connessione *f*; (*TEL*) collegamento; **in ~ion with** con riferimento a.

connexion [kə'nekʃən] *n* = **connection**.

conning tower ['kɒnıŋtauə*] *n* torretta di comando.

connive [kə'naıv] *vi*: **to ~ at** essere connivente in.

connoisseur [kɒnı'sə*] *n* conoscitore/trice.

connotation [kɒnə'teıʃən] *n* connotazione *f*.

conquer ['kɒŋkə*] *vt* conquistare; (*feelings*) vincere; ~**or** *n* conquistatore *m*.

conquest ['kɒŋkwest] *n* conquista.

cons [kɒnz] *npl* see **pro**, **convenience**.

conscience ['kɒnʃəns] *n* coscienza.

conscientious [kɒnʃı'enʃəs] *a* coscienzioso(a); ~ **objector** *n* obiettore *m* di coscienza.

conscious ['kɒnʃəs] *a* consapevole; (*MED*) conscio(a); ~**ness** *n* consapevolezza; coscienza; **to lose/regain** ~**ness** perdere/ riprendere coscienza.

conscript ['kɒnskrıpt] *n* coscritto; ~**ion** [kən'skrıpʃən] *n* coscrizione *f*.

consecrate ['kɒnsıkreıt] *vt* consacrare.

consecutive [kən'sekjutıv] *a* consecutivo(a).

consensus [kən'sensəs] *n* consenso.

consent [kən'sent] *n* consenso // *vi*: **to ~ (to)** acconsentire (a).

consequence ['kɒnsıkwəns] *n* conseguenza, risultato; importanza.

consequently ['kɒnsɪkwəntlɪ] *ad* di conseguenza, dunque.

conservation [kɒnsəː'veɪʃən] *n* conservazione *f.*

conservative [kən'səːvətɪv] *a* conservativo(a); (*cautious*) cauto(a); **C~** *a, n* conservatore(trice).

conservatory [kən'səːvətrɪ] *n* (*greenhouse*) serra.

conserve [kən'səːv] *vt* conservare.

consider [kən'sɪdə*] *vt* considerare; (*take into account*) tener conto di.

considerable [kən'sɪdərəbl] *a* considerevole, notevole.

considerate [kən'sɪdərɪt] *a* premuroso(a).

consideration [kənsɪdə'reɪʃən] *n* considerazione *f;* (*reward*) rimunerazione *f;* **out of ~ for** per riguardo a; **under ~** in esame.

considering [kən'sɪdərɪŋ] *prep* in considerazione di.

consign [kən'saɪn] *vt* consegnare; (*send: goods*) spedire; **~ment** *n* consegna; spedizione *f.*

consist [kən'sɪst] *vi:* **to ~ of** constare di, essere composto(a) di.

consistency [kən'sɪstənsɪ] *n* consistenza; (*fig*) concordanza; coerenza.

consistent [kən'sɪstənt] *a* coerente; (*constant*) costante; **~ with** compatibile con.

consolation [kɒnsə'leɪʃən] *n* consolazione *f.*

console *vt* [kən'səul] consolare // *n* ['kɒnsəul] mensola.

consolidate [kən'sɒlɪdeɪt] *vt* consolidare.

consonant ['kɒnsənənt] *n* consonante *f.*

consortium [kən'sɔːtɪəm] *n* consorzio.

conspicuous [kən'spɪkjuəs] *a* cospicuo(a).

conspiracy [kən'spɪrəsɪ] *n* congiura, cospirazione *f.*

conspire [kən'spaɪə*] *vi* congiurare, cospirare.

constable ['kʌnstəbl] *n* ≈ poliziotto, agente *m* di polizia; **chief ~** *n* capo della polizia.

constant ['kɒnstənt] *a* costante; continuo(a); **~ly** *ad* costantemente, continuamente.

constellation [kɒnstə'leɪʃən] *n* costellazione *f.*

consternation [kɒnstə'neɪʃən] *n* costernazione *f.*

constipated ['kɒnstɪpeɪtəd] *a* stitico(a).

constipation [kɒnstɪ'peɪʃən] *n* stitichezza.

constituency [kən'stɪtjuənsɪ] *n* collegio elettorale.

constituent [kən'stɪtjuənt] *n* elettore/trice; (*part*) elemento componente.

constitute ['kɒnstɪtjuːt] *vt* costituire.

constitution [kɒnstɪ'tjuːʃən] *n* costituzione *f;* **~al** *a* costituzionale.

constrain [kən'streɪn] *vt* costringere; **~ed** *a* costretto(a); **~t** *n* costrizione *f.*

constrict [kən'strɪkt] *vt* comprimere; opprimere.

construct [kən'strʌkt] *vt* costruire; **~ion** [-ʃən] *n* costruzione *f;* **~ive** *a* costruttivo(a).

construe [kən'struː] *vt* interpretare.

consul ['kɒnsl] *n* console *m;* **~ate** ['kɒnsjulɪt] *n* consolato.

consult [kən'sʌlt] *vt* consultare; **~ancy** *n:* **~ancy fee** spese *fpl* di consultazione; **~ant** *n* (*MED*) consulente *m* medico; (*other specialist*) consulente; **~ation** [kɒnsəl'teɪʃən] *n* consultazione *f;* (*MED, LAW*) consulto; **~ing room** *n* ambulatorio.

consume [kən'sjuːm] *vt* consumare; **~r** *n* consumatore/trice; **~r society** *n* società dei consumi.

consummate ['kɒnsʌmeɪt] *vt* consumare.

consumption [kən'sʌmpʃən] *n* consumo; (*MED*) consunzione *f.*

contact ['kɒntækt] *n* contatto; (*person*) conoscenza // *vt* mettersi in contatto con; **~ lenses** *npl* lenti *fpl* a contatto.

contagious [kən'teɪdʒəs] *a* contagioso(a).

contain [kən'teɪn] *vt* contenere; **to ~ o.s.** contenersi; **~er** *n* recipiente *m;* (*for shipping etc*) container *m.*

contaminate [kən'tæmɪneɪt] *vt* contaminare; **contamination** [-'neɪʃən] *n* contaminazione *f.*

cont'd *abbr of* continued.

contemplate ['kɒntəmpleɪt] *vt* contemplare; (*consider*) pensare a (*or* di); **contemplation** [-'pleɪʃən] *n* contemplazione *f.*

contemporary [kən'tɛmpərərɪ] *a* contemporaneo(a); (*design*) moderno(a) // *n* contemporaneo/a.

contempt [kən'tɛmpt] *n* disprezzo; **~ible** *a* spregevole; **~uous** *a* sdegnoso(a).

contend [kən'tɛnd] *vt:* **to ~ that** sostenere che // *vi:* **to ~ with** lottare contro; **~er** *n* contendente *m/f;* concorrente *m/f.*

content [kən'tɛnt] *a* contento(a), soddisfatto(a) // *vt* contentare, soddisfare // *n* ['kɒntɛnt] contenuto; **~s** *npl* contenuto; (*of barrel etc: capacity*) capacità *f inv;* (**table of**) **~s** indice *m;* **to be ~ with** essere contento di; **~ed** *a* contento(a), soddisfatto(a).

contention [kən'tɛnʃən] *n* contesa; (*argument*) affermazione *f.*

contentment [kən'tɛntmənt] *n* contentezza.

contest *n* ['kɒntɛst] lotta; (*competition*) gara, concorso // *vt* [kən'tɛst] contestare; impugnare; (*compete for*) contendere; **~ant** [kən'tɛstənt] *n* concorrente *m/f;* (*in fight*) avversario/a.

context ['kɒntɛkst] *n* contesto.

continent ['kɒntɪnənt] *n* continente *m;* **the C~** l'Europa continentale; **~al** [-'nɛntl] *a* continentale // *n* abitante *m/f* dell'Europa continentale.

contingency [kən'tɪndʒənsɪ] *n* eventualità *f inv;* **~ plan** *n* misura d'emergenza.

contingent [kən'tɪndʒənt] *n* contingenza; **to be ~ upon** dipendere da.

continual [kənˈtɪnjuəl] a continuo(a); ~ly ad di continuo.

continuation [kəntɪnjuˈeɪʃən] n continuazione f; (after interruption) ripresa; (of story) seguito.

continue [kənˈtɪnjuː] vi continuare // vt continuare; (start again) riprendere.

continuity [kɒntɪˈnjuɪtɪ] n continuità.

continuous [kənˈtɪnjuəs] a continuo(a), ininterrotto(a).

contort [kənˈtɔːt] vt contorcere; ~ion [-ˈtɔːʃən] n contorcimento; (of acrobat) contorsione f; ~ionist [-ˈtɔːʃənɪst] n contorsionista m/f.

contour [ˈkɒntuə*] n contorno, profilo; (also: ~ line) curva di livello.

contraband [ˈkɒntrəbænd] n contrabbando.

contraception [kɒntrəˈsɛpʃən] n contraccezione f.

contraceptive [kɒntrəˈsɛptɪv] a contraccettivo(a) // n contraccettivo.

contract n [ˈkɒntrækt] contratto // vb [kənˈtrækt] vi (COMM): to ~ to do sth fare un contratto per fare qc; (become smaller) contrarre; ~ion [-ʃən] n contrazione f; ~or n imprenditore m.

contradict [kɒntrəˈdɪkt] vt contraddire; ~ion [-ʃən] n contraddizione f.

contralto [kənˈtræltəu] n contralto.

contraption [kənˈtræpʃən] n (pej) aggeggio.

contrary [ˈkɒntrərɪ] a contrario(a); (unfavourable) avverso(a), contrario(a); [kənˈtrɛərɪ] (perverse) bisbetico(a) // n contrario; on the ~ al contrario; unless you hear to the ~ a meno che non si disdica.

contrast n [ˈkɒntrɑːst] contrasto // vt [kənˈtrɑːst] mettere in contrasto; ~ing a contrastante, di contrasto.

contravene [kɒntrəˈviːn] vt contravvenire.

contribute [kənˈtrɪbjuːt] vi contribuire // vt: to ~ £10/an article to dare 10 sterline/un articolo a; to ~ to contribuire a; (newspaper) scrivere per; **contribution** [kɒntrɪˈbjuːʃən] n contribuzione f; **contributor** n (to newspaper) collaboratore/trice.

contrite [ˈkɒntraɪt] a contrito(a).

contrivance [kənˈtraɪvəns] n congegno; espediente m.

contrive [kənˈtraɪv] vt inventare; escogitare // vi: to ~ to do fare in modo di fare.

control [kənˈtrəul] vt dominare; (firm, operation etc) dirigere; (check) controllare // n autorità; controllo; ~s npl comandi mpl; to be in ~ of aver autorità su; essere responsabile di; controllare; **circumstances beyond** ~ circostanze fpl che non dipendono da noi; ~ **point** n punto di controllo; ~ **tower** n (AVIAT) torre f di controllo.

controversial [kɒntrəˈvəːʃl] a controverso(a), polemico(a).

controversy [ˈkɒntrəvəːsɪ] n controversia, polemica.

convalesce [kɒnvəˈlɛs] vi rimettersi in salute.

convalescence [kɒnvəˈlɛsns] n convalescenza.

convalescent [kɒnvəˈlɛsnt] a, n convalescente (m/f).

convector [kənˈvɛktə*] n convettore m.

convene [kənˈviːn] vt convocare // vi convenire, adunarsi.

convenience [kənˈviːnɪəns] n convenienza; at your ~ a suo comodo; **all modern** ~s, all mod cons tutte le comodità moderne.

convenient [kənˈviːnɪənt] a conveniente, comodo(a).

convent [ˈkɒnvənt] n convento.

convention [kənˈvɛnʃən] n convenzione f; (meeting) convegno; ~al a convenzionale.

converge [kənˈvəːdʒ] vi convergere.

conversant [kənˈvəːsnt] a: to be ~ with essere al corrente di; essere pratico(a) di.

conversation [kɒnvəˈseɪʃən] n conversazione f; ~al a non formale; ~al Italian l'italiano parlato.

converse [ˈkɒnvəːs] n contrario, opposto; ~ly [-ˈvəːslɪ] ad al contrario, per contro.

conversion [kənˈvəːʃən] n conversione f; ~ table n tavola di equivalenze.

convert vt [kənˈvəːt] (REL, COMM) convertire; (alter) trasformare // n [ˈkɒnvəːt] convertito/a; ~ible n macchina decappottabile.

convex [ˈkɒnˈvɛks] a convesso(a).

convey [kənˈveɪ] vt trasportare; (thanks) comunicare; (idea) dare; ~or belt n nastro trasportatore.

convict vt [kənˈvɪkt] dichiarare colpevole // n [ˈkɒnvɪkt] condannato; ~ion [-ʃən] n condanna; (belief) convinzione f.

convince [kənˈvɪns] vt convincere, persuadere; **convincing** a convincente.

convivial [kənˈvɪvɪəl] a allegro(a).

convoy [ˈkɒnvɔɪ] n convoglio.

convulse [kənˈvʌls] vt sconvolgere; to be ~d with laughter contorcersi dalle risa.

convulsion [kənˈvʌlʃən] n convulsione f.

coo [kuː] vi tubare.

cook [kuk] vt cucinare, cuocere // vi cuocere; (person) cucinare // n cuoco/a; ~book n = ~ery book; ~er n fornello, cucina; ~ery n cucina; ~ery book n libro di cucina; ~ie n (US) biscotto; ~ing n cucina.

cool [kuːl] a fresco(a); (not afraid) calmo(a); (unfriendly) freddo(a); (impertinent) sfacciato(a) // vt raffreddare, rinfrescare // vi raffreddarsi, rinfrescarsi; ~ing tower n torre f di raffreddamento; ~ness n freschezza; sangue m freddo, calma.

coop [kuːp] n stia // vt: to ~ up (fig) stipare.

cooperate [kəuˈɒpəreɪt] vi cooperare, collaborare; **cooperation** [-ˈreɪʃən] n cooperazione f, collaborazione f.

cooperative [kəuˈɒpərətɪv] a

cooperativo(a) // n cooperativa.
coordinate [kəu'ɔːdɪneɪt] vt coordinare; **coordination** [-'neɪʃən] n coordinazione f.
coot [kuːt] n folaga.
cop [kɔp] n (col) sbirro.
cope [kəup] vi farcela; **to ~ with** (problems) far fronte a.
co-pilot ['kəu'paɪlət] n secondo pilota m.
copious ['kəupiəs] a copioso(a), abbondante.
copper ['kɔpə*] n rame m; (col: policeman) sbirro; **~s** npl spiccioli mpl.
copse [kɔps] n bosco ceduo.
copulate ['kɔpjuleɪt] vi accoppiarsi.
copy ['kɔpɪ] n copia; (book etc) esemplare m // vt copiare; **~cat** n (pej) copione m; **~right** n diritto d'autore; **~writer** n redattore m pubblicitario.
coral ['kɔrəl] n corallo; **~ reef** n barriera corallina.
cord [kɔːd] n corda; (fabric) velluto a coste.
cordial ['kɔːdɪəl] a, n cordiale (m).
cordon ['kɔːdn] n cordone m; **to ~ off** vt fare cordone a.
corduroy ['kɔːdərɔɪ] n fustagno.
core [kɔː*] n (of fruit) torsolo; (TECH) centro // vt estrarre il torsolo da.
cork [kɔːk] n sughero; (of bottle) tappo; **~age** n somma da pagare se il cliente porta il proprio vino; **~screw** n cavatappi m inv.
cormorant ['kɔːmərnt] n cormorano.
corn [kɔːn] n grano; (US: maize) granturco; (on foot) callo; **~ on the cob** (CULIN) pannocchia cotta.
cornea ['kɔːnɪə] n cornea.
corned beef ['kɔːnd'biːf] n carne f di manzo in scatola.
corner ['kɔːnə*] n angolo; (AUT) curva // vt mettere in un angolo; mettere con le spalle al muro; (COMM: market) accaparrare // vi prendere una curva; **~ flag** n (FOOTBALL) bandierina d'angolo; **~ kick** n calcio d'angolo; **~stone** n pietra angolare.
cornet ['kɔːnɪt] n (MUS) cornetta; (of ice-cream) cono.
cornflour ['kɔːnflauə*] n farina finissima di granturco.
cornice ['kɔːnɪs] n cornicione m; cornice f.
Cornwall ['kɔːnwəl] n Cornovaglia.
corny ['kɔːnɪ] a (col) trito(a).
corollary [kə'rɔlərɪ] n corollario.
coronary ['kɔrənərɪ] n trombosi f coronaria.
coronation [kɔrə'neɪʃən] n incoronazione f.
coroner ['kɔrənə*] n magistrato incaricato di indagare la causa di morte in circostanze sospettose.
coronet ['kɔrənɪt] n diadema m.
corporal ['kɔːpərl] n caporalmaggiore m // a: **~ punishment** pena corporale.
corporate ['kɔːpərɪt] a costituito(a) (in corporazione); comune.
corporation [kɔːpə'reɪʃən] n (of town) consiglio comunale; (COMM) ente m; **~ tax** n imposta societaria.

corps [kɔː*], pl **corps** [kɔːz] n corpo.
corpse [kɔːps] n cadavere m.
corpuscle ['kɔːpʌsl] n corpuscolo.
corral [kə'rɑːl] n recinto.
correct [kə'rɛkt] a (accurate) corretto(a), esatto(a); (proper) corretto(a) // vt correggere; **~ion** [-ʃən] n correzione f.
correlate ['kɔrɪleɪt] vt mettere in correlazione.
correspond [kɔrɪs'pɔnd] vi corrispondere; **~ence** n corrispondenza; **~ence course** n corso per corrispondenza; **~ent** n corrispondente m/f.
corridor ['kɔrɪdɔː*] n corridoio.
corroborate [kə'rɔbəreɪt] vt corroborare, confermare.
corrode [kə'rəud] vt corrodere // vi corrodersi; **corrosion** [-'rəuʒən] n corrosione f.
corrugated ['kɔrəgeɪtɪd] a increspato(a); ondulato(a); **~ iron** n lamiera di ferro ondulata.
corrupt [kə'rʌpt] a corrotto(a) // vt corrompere; **~ion** [-ʃən] n corruzione f.
corset ['kɔːsɪt] n busto.
Corsica ['kɔːsɪkə] n Corsica.
cortège [kɔː'teːʒ] n corteo.
cosh [kɔʃ] n randello (corto).
cosmetic [kɔz'mɛtɪk] n cosmetico.
cosmonaut ['kɔzmənɔːt] n cosmonauta m/f.
cosmopolitan [kɔzmə'pɔlɪtn] a cosmopolita.
cosmos ['kɔzmɔs] n cosmo.
cosset ['kɔsɪt] vt vezzeggiare.
cost [kɔst] n costo // vb (pt, pp cost) vi costare // vt stabilire il prezzo di; **it ~s £5/too much** costa 5 sterline/troppo; **it ~ him his life/the job** gli costò la vita/il suo lavoro; **at all ~s** a ogni costo.
co-star ['kəustɑː*] n attore/trice della stessa importanza del protagonista.
costly ['kɔstlɪ] a costoso(a), caro(a).
cost price ['kɔst'praɪs] n prezzo all'ingrosso.
costume ['kɔstjuːm] n costume m; (lady's suit) tailleur m inv; (also: **swimming ~**) costume da bagno; **~ jewellery** n bigiotteria.
cosy ['kəuzɪ] a intimo(a).
cot [kɔt] n (child's) lettino.
cottage ['kɔtɪdʒ] n cottage m inv; **~ cheese** n fiocchi mpl di latte magro.
cotton ['kɔtn] n cotone m; **~ dress** etc vestito etc di cotone; **~ wool** n cotone idrofilo.
couch [kautʃ] n sofà m inv // vt esprimere.
cough [kɔf] vi tossire // n tosse f; **~ drop** n pasticca per la tosse.
could [kud] pt of **can**.
council ['kaunsl] n concilio; **city or town ~** n concilio comunale; **~ estate** n quartiere m di case popolari; **~ house** n casa popolare; **~lor** n consigliere/a.
counsel ['kaunsl] n avvocato; consultazione f; **~lor** n consigliere/a.
count [kaunt] vt, vi contare // n conto;

(*nobleman*) conte *m*; to ~ on *vt* fus contare su; to ~ up *vt* addizionare; ~down *n* conto alla rovescia.

countenance ['kauntinəns] *n* volto, aspetto // *vt* approvare.

counter ['kauntə*] *n* banco // *vt* opporsi a; (*blow*) parare // *ad*: ~ to contro; in opposizione a; ~act *vt* agire in opposizione a; (*poison etc*) annullare gli effetti di; ~attack *n* contrattacco // *vt* contrattaccare; ~balance *vt* contrappesare; ~-espionage *n* controspionaggio.

counterfeit ['kauntəfit] *n* contraffazione *f*, falso // *vt* contraffare, falsificare // *a* falso(a).

counterfoil ['kauntəfɔil] *n* matrice *f*.

counterpart ['kauntəpa:t] *n* (*of document etc*) copia; (*of person*) corrispondente *m/f*.

countess ['kauntis] *n* contessa.

countless ['kauntlis] *a* innumerevole.

country ['kʌntri] *n* paese *m*; (*native land*) patria; (*as opposed to town*) campagna; (*region*) regione *f*; ~ dancing *n* danza popolare; ~ house *n* villa in campagna; ~man *n* (*national*) compatriota *m*; (*rural*) contadino; ~side *n* campagna.

county ['kaunti] *n* contea.

coup, ~s [ku:, -z] *n* colpo; (*also*: ~ d'état) colpo di Stato.

coupé [ku:'pei] *n* coupé *m inv*.

couple ['kʌpl] *n* coppia // *vt* (*carriages*) agganciare; (*TECH*) accoppiare; (*ideas, names*) associare; a ~ of un paio di.

couplet ['kʌplit] *n* distico.

coupling ['kʌpliŋ] *n* (*RAIL*) agganciamento.

coupon ['ku:pɔn] *n* buono; (*COMM*) coupon *m inv*.

courage ['kʌridʒ] *n* coraggio; ~ous [kə'reidʒəs] a coraggioso(a).

courier ['kuriə*] *n* corriere *m*; (*for tourists*) guida.

course [kɔ:s] *n* corso; (*of ship*) rotta; (*for golf*) campo; (*part of meal*) piatto; first ~ primo piatto; of ~ ad senz'altro, naturalmente; ~ of action modo d'agire; ~ of lectures corso di lezioni.

court [kɔ:t] *n* corte *f*; (*TENNIS*) campo // *vt* (*woman*) fare la corte a; out of ~ (*LAW*: settle) in via amichevole; to take to ~ sottoporre alla magistratura.

courteous ['kə:tiəs] a cortese.

courtesan [kɔ:ti'zæn] *n* cortigiana.

courtesy ['kə:təsi] *n* cortesia.

court-house ['kɔ:thaus] *n* (*US*) palazzo di giustizia.

courtier ['kɔ:tiə*] *n* cortigiano/a.

court-martial, *pl* **courts-martial** ['kɔ:t-'ma:ʃəl] *n* corte *f* marziale.

courtroom ['kɔ:trum] *n* tribunale *m*.

courtyard ['kɔ:tja:d] *n* cortile *m*.

cousin ['kʌzn] *n* cugino/a.

cove [kəuv] *n* piccola baia.

covenant ['kʌvənənt] *n* accordo.

cover ['kʌvə*] *vt* coprire // *n* (*of pan*) coperchio; (*over furniture*) fodera; (*of book*) copertina; (*shelter*) riparo; (*COMM*) copertura; under ~ al riparo; ~age *n* reportage *m*; (*INSURANCE*) copertura; ~charge *n* coperto; ~ing *n* copertura; ~ing letter *n* lettera d'accompagnamento.

covet ['kʌvit] *vt* bramare.

cow [kau] *n* vacca.

coward ['kauəd] *n* vigliacco/a; ~ice [-is] *n* vigliaccheria; ~ly a vigliacco(a).

cowboy ['kaubɔi] *n* cow-boy *m inv*.

cower ['kauə*] *vi* acquattarsi.

cowshed ['kauʃed] *n* stalla.

coxswain ['kɔksn] *n* (*abbr*: cox) timoniere *m*; (*of ship*) nocchiere *m*.

coy [kɔi] a falsamente timido(a).

crab [kræb] *n* granchio; ~ apple *n* mela selvatica.

crack [kræk] *n* fessura, crepa; incrinatura; (*noise*) schiocco; (: *of gun*) scoppio // *vt* spaccare; incrinare; (*whip*) schioccare; (*nut*) schiacciare // a (*troops*) fuori classe; to ~ up *vi* crollare; ~ed a (*col*) matto(a); ~er *n* cracker *m inv*; petardo.

crackle ['krækl] *vi* crepitare; **crackling** *n* crepitio; (*of pork*) cotenna croccante (del maiale).

cradle ['kreidl] *n* culla.

craft [kra:ft] *n* mestiere *m*; (*cunning*) astuzia; (*boat*) naviglio; ~sman *n* artigiano; ~smanship *n* abilità; ~y a furbo(a), astuto(a).

crag [kræg] *n* roccia.

cram [kræm] *vt* (*fill*): to ~ sth with riempire qc di; (*put*): to ~ sth into stipare qc in; ~ming *n* (*fig*: *pej*) sgobbare *m*.

cramp [kræmp] *n* crampo; ~ed a ristretto(a).

crampon [kræmpən] *n* (*CLIMBING*) rampone *m*.

cranberry ['krænbəri] *n* mirtillo.

crane [krein] *n* gru *f inv*.

cranium, *pl* **crania** ['kreiniəm, 'kreiniə] *n* cranio.

crank [kræŋk] *n* manovella; (*person*) persona stramba; ~shaft *n* albero a manovelle.

cranny ['kræni] *n see* **nook**.

crash [kræʃ] *n* fragore *m*; (*of car*) incidente *m*; (*of plane*) caduta // *vt* (*car*) fracassare // *vi* (*plane*) fracassarsi; (*two cars*) scontrarsi; (*fig*) fallire, andare in rovina; to ~ into scontrarsi con; ~ course *n* corso intensivo; ~ helmet *n* casco; ~ landing *n* atterraggio di fortuna.

crate [kreit] *n* gabbia.

crater ['kreitə*] *n* cratere *m*.

cravat(e) [krə'væt] *n* fazzoletto da collo.

crave [kreiv] *vi*: to ~ for desiderare ardentemente.

crawl [krɔ:l] *vi* strisciare carponi; (*vehicle*) avanzare lentamente // *n* (*SWIMMING*) crawl *m*.

crayfish ['kreifiʃ] *n*, *pl inv* gambero (d'acqua dolce).

crayon ['kreiən] *n* matita colorata.

craze [kreɪz] n mania.

crazy ['kreɪzɪ] a matto(a); ~ **paving** n lastricato m a mosaico irregolare.

creak [kriːk] vi cigolare, scricchiolare.

cream [kriːm] n crema; (fresh) panna // a (colour) color crema inv; ~ **cake** n torta alla crema; ~ **cheese** n mascarpone m; ~y a cremoso(a).

crease [kriːs] n grinza; (deliberate) piega // vt sgualcire.

create [kriː'eɪt] vt creare; **creation** [-ʃən] n creazione f; **creative** a creativo(a); **creator** n creatore/trice.

creature ['kriːtʃə*] n creatura.

crèche, creche [krɛʃ] n asilo infantile.

credence n credenza, fede f.

credentials [krɪ'dɛnʃlz] npl (papers) credenziali fpl.

credibility [krɛdɪ'bɪlɪtɪ] n credibilità.

credible ['krɛdɪbl] a credibile.

credit ['krɛdɪt] n credito; onore m // vt (COMM) accreditare; (believe: also: **give** ~ **to**) credere, prestar fede a; ~**s** npl (CINEMA) titoli mpl; **to** ~ **sb with** (fig) attribuire a qd; **to one's** ~ a proprio onore; **to take the** ~ **for** farsi il merito di; ~**able** a che fa onore, degno(a) di lode; ~ **card** n carta di credito; ~**or** n creditore/trice.

credulity [krɪ'djuːlɪtɪ] n credulità.

creed [kriːd] n credo; dottrina.

creek [kriːk] n insenatura; (US) piccolo fiume m.

creep, pt, pp **crept** [kriːp, krɛpt] vi avanzare furtivamente (or pian piano); (plant) arrampicarsi; ~**er** n pianta rampicante; ~y a (frightening) che fa accapponare la pelle.

cremate [krɪ'meɪt] vt cremare; **cremation** [-ʃən] n cremazione f.

crematorium, pl **crematoria** [krɛmə'tɔːrɪəm, -'tɔːrɪə] n forno crematorio.

creosote ['krɪəsəut] n creosoto.

crêpe [kreɪp] n crespo; ~ **bandage** n fascia elastica.

crept [krɛpt] pt, pp of **creep**.

crescendo [krɪ'ʃɛndəu] n crescendo.

crescent ['krɛsnt] n forma di luna crescente; strada semicircolare.

cress [krɛs] n crescione m.

crest [krɛst] n cresta; (of helmet) pennacchiera; (of coat of arms) cimiero; ~**fallen** a mortificato(a).

Crete [kriːt] n Creta.

crevasse [krɪ'væs] n crepaccio.

crevice ['krɛvɪs] n fessura, crepa.

crew [kruː] n equipaggio; **to have a** ~-**cut** avere i capelli a spazzola; ~-**neck** n girocollo.

crib [krɪb] n culla; (REL) presepio // vt (col) copiare.

crick [krɪk] n crampo.

cricket ['krɪkɪt] n (insect) grillo; (game) cricket m; ~**er** n giocatore m di cricket.

crime [kraɪm] n crimine m; **criminal** ['krɪmɪnl] a, n criminale (m/f).

crimson ['krɪmzn] a color cremisi inv.

cringe [krɪndʒ] vi acquattarsi; (fig) essere servile.

crinkle ['krɪŋkl] vt arricciare, increspare.

cripple ['krɪpl] n zoppo/a // vt azzoppare.

crisis, pl **crises** ['kraɪsɪs, -siːz] n crisi f inv.

crisp [krɪsp] a croccante; (fig) frizzante; vivace; deciso(a); ~**s** npl patatine fpl fritte.

criss-cross ['krɪskrɔs] a incrociato(a).

criterion, pl **criteria** [kraɪ'tɪərɪən, -'tɪərɪə] n criterio.

critic ['krɪtɪk] n critico; ~**al** a critico(a); ~**ally** ad criticamente; ~**ally ill** gravemente malato; ~**ism** ['krɪtɪsɪzm] n critica; ~**ize** ['krɪtɪsaɪz] vt criticare.

croak [krəuk] vi gracchiare.

crochet ['krəuʃeɪ] n lavoro all'uncinetto.

crockery ['krɔkərɪ] n vasellame m.

crocodile ['krɔkədaɪl] n coccodrillo.

crocus ['krəukəs] n croco.

croft [krɔft] n piccolo podere m; ~**er** n affittuario di un piccolo podere.

crony ['krəunɪ] n (col) amicone/a.

crook [kruk] n truffatore m; (of shepherd) bastone m; ~**ed** ['krukɪd] a curvo(a), storto(a); (action) disonesto(a).

crop [krɔp] n raccolto; **to** ~ **up** vi presentarsi.

cropper ['krɔpə*] n: **to come a** ~ (col) fare fiasco.

croquet ['krəukeɪ] n croquet m.

croquette [krə'kɛt] n crocchetta.

cross [krɔs] n croce f; (BIOL) incrocio // vt (street etc) attraversare; (arms, legs, BIOL) incrociare; (cheque) sbarrare // a di cattivo umore; **to** ~ **out** vt cancellare; **to** ~ **over** vi attraversare; ~**bar** n traversa; ~**breed** n incrocio; ~**country** (**race**) n cross-country m inv; ~-**examination** n interrogatorio in contraddittorio; ~-**examine** vt (LAW) interrogare in contraddittorio; ~-**eyed** a strabico(a); ~**ing** n incrocio; (sea-passage) traversata; (also: **pedestrian** ~**ing**) passaggio pedonale; ~**roads** n incrocio; ~ **section** n (BIOL) sezione f trasversale; (in population) settore m rappresentativo; ~**wind** n vento di traverso; ~**word** n cruciverba m inv.

crotch [krɔtʃ] n (of garment) pattina.

crotchet ['krɔtʃɪt] n (MUS) semiminima.

crotchety ['krɔtʃɪtɪ] a (person) burbero(a).

crouch [krautʃ] vi acquattarsi; rannicchiarsi.

crouton ['kruːtɔn] n crostino.

crow [krəu] n (bird) cornacchia; (of cock) canto del gallo // vi (cock) cantare; (fig) vantarsi; cantar vittoria.

crowbar ['krəubɑː*] n piede m di porco.

crowd [kraud] n folla // vt affollare, stipare // vi affollarsi; ~**ed** a affollato(a); ~**ed with** stipato(a) di.

crown [kraun] n corona; (of head) calotta cranica; (of hat) cocuzzolo; (of hill) cima // vt incoronare; ~ **jewels** npl gioielli mpl della Corona; ~ **prince** *n* principe *m* ereditario.

crow's-nest ['krəuznɛst] *n* (*on sailing-ship*) coffa.

crucial ['kru:ʃl] *a* cruciale, decisivo(a).

crucifix ['kru:sifiks] *n* crocifisso; ~**ion** [-'fikʃən] *n* crocifissione *f*.

crucify ['kru:sifai] *vt* crocifiggere, mettere in croce.

crude [kru:d] *a* (*materials*) greggio(a); non raffinato(a); (*fig*: *basic*) crudo(a), primitivo(a); (: *vulgar*) rozzo(a), grossolano(a); ~ **(oil)** *n* (petrolio) greggio.

cruel ['kruəl] *a* crudele; ~**ty** *n* crudeltà *f inv*.

cruet ['kru:it] *n* ampolla.

cruise [kru:z] *n* crociera // *vi* andare a velocità di crociera; (*taxi*) circolare; ~**r** *n* incrociatore *m*; **cruising speed** *n* velocità *f inv* di crociera.

crumb [krʌm] *n* briciola.

crumble ['krʌmbl] *vt* sbriciolare // *vi* sbriciolarsi; (*plaster etc*) sgretolarsi; (*land, earth*) franare; (*building, fig*) crollare; **crumbly** *a* friabile.

crumpet ['krʌmpit] *n* crostino da tè.

crumple ['krʌmpl] *vt* raggrinzare, spiegazzare.

crunch [krʌntʃ] *vt* sgranocchiare; (*underfoot*) scricchiolare // *n* (*fig*) punto *or* momento cruciale; ~**y** *a* croccante.

crusade [kru:'seid] *n* crociata; ~**r** *n* crociato.

crush [krʌʃ] *n* folla // *vt* schiacciare; (*crumple*) sgualcire; ~**ing** *a* schiacciante.

crust [krʌst] *n* crosta.

crutch [krʌtʃ] *n* gruccia.

crux [krʌks] *n* nodo.

cry [krai] *vi* piangere; (*shout*) urlare // *n* urlo, grido; **to ~ off** *vi* ritirarsi; ~**ing** *a* (*fig*) palese; urgente.

crypt [kript] *n* cripta.

cryptic ['kriptik] *a* ermetico(a).

crystal ['kristl] *n* cristallo; ~**-clear** *a* cristallino(a); **crystallize** *vi* cristallizzarsi.

cu. *abbr*: ~ **ft.** = *cubic feet*; ~ **in.** = *cubic inches*.

cub [kʌb] *n* cucciolo.

Cuba ['kju:bə] *n* Cuba; ~**n** *a*, *n* cubano(a).

cubbyhole ['kʌbihəul] *n* angolino.

cube [kju:b] *n* cubo // *vt* (*MATH*) elevare al cubo; ~ **root** *n* radice *f* cubica; **cubic** *a* cubico(a).

cubicle ['kju:bikl] *n* scompartimento separato; cabina.

cuckoo ['kuku:] *n* cucù *m inv*; ~ **clock** *n* orologio a cucù.

cucumber ['kju:kʌmbə*] *n* cetriolo.

cud [kʌd] *n*: **to chew the** ~ ruminare.

cuddle ['kʌdl] *vt* abbracciare, coccolare // *vi* abbracciarsi; **cuddly** *a* da coccolare.

cudgel ['kʌdʒl] *n* randello.

cue [kju:] *n* stecca; (*THEATRE etc*) segnale *m*.

cuff [kʌf] *n* (*of shirt, coat etc*) polsino; (*US*)

= **turn-up**; **off the** ~ *ad* a braccio; ~**link** *n* gemello.

cuisine [kwi'zi:n] *n* cucina.

cul-de-sac ['kʌldəsæk] *n* vicolo cieco.

culinary ['kʌlinəri] *a* culinario(a).

culminate ['kʌlmineit] *vi* culminare; **culmination** [-'neiʃən] *n* culmine *m*.

culpable ['kʌlpəbl] *a* colpevole.

culprit ['kʌlprit] *n* colpevole *m/f*.

cult [kʌlt] *n* culto.

cultivate ['kʌltiveit] *vt* (*also fig*) coltivare; **cultivation** [-'veiʃən] *n* coltivazione *f*.

cultural ['kʌltʃərəl] *a* culturale.

culture ['kʌltʃə*] *n* (*also fig*) cultura; ~**d** *a* colto(a).

cumbersome ['kʌmbəsəm] *a* ingombrante.

cumulative ['kju:mjulətiv] *a* cumulativo(a).

cunning ['kʌniŋ] *n* astuzia, furberia // *a* astuto(a), furbo(a).

cup [kʌp] *n* tazza; (*prize*) coppa.

cupboard ['kʌbəd] *n* armadio.

cupola ['kju:pələ] *n* cupola.

cup-tie ['kʌptai] *n* partita di coppa.

curable ['kjuərəbl] *a* curabile.

curate ['kjuərit] *n* cappellano.

curator [kju'reitə*] *n* direttore *m* (*di museo etc*).

curb [kə:b] *vt* tenere a freno // *n* freno; (*US*) = **kerb**.

curdle ['kə:dl] *vi* cagliare.

curds [kə:ds] *npl* latte *m* cagliato.

cure [kjuə*] *vt* guarire; (*CULIN*) trattare; affumicare; essiccare // *n* rimedio.

curfew ['kə:fju:] *n* coprifuoco.

curio ['kjuəriəu] *n* curiosità *f inv*.

curiosity [kjuəri'ɔsiti] *n* curiosità.

curious ['kjuəriəs] *a* curioso(a).

curl [kə:l] *n* riccio // *vt* ondulare; (*tightly*) arricciare // *vi* arricciarsi; **to ~ up** *vi* avvolgersi a spirale; rannicchiarsi; ~**er** *n* bigodino.

curling ['kə:liŋ] *n* (*SPORT*) curling *m*.

curly ['kə:li] *a* ricciuto(a).

currant ['kʌrnt] *n* sultanina.

currency ['kʌrnsi] *n* moneta; **foreign** ~ divisa estera; **to gain** ~ (*fig*) acquistare larga diffusione.

current ['kʌrnt] *a*, *n* corrente (*f*); ~ **account** *n* conto corrente; ~ **affairs** *npl* attualità *fpl*; ~**ly** *ad* attualmente.

curriculum [kə'rikjuləm], *pl* ~**s** *or* **curricula** [-lə] *n* curriculum *m inv*; ~ **vitae** *n* curriculum vitae *m inv*.

curry ['kʌri] *n* curry *m inv* // *vt*: **to ~ favour with** cercare di attirarsi i favori di; **chicken** ~ pollo al curry.

curse [kə:s] *vt* maledire // *vi* bestemmiare // *n* maledizione *f*; bestemmia.

cursory ['kə:səri] *a* superficiale.

curt [kə:t] *a* secco(a).

curtail [kə:'teil] *vt* (*visit etc*) accorciare; (*expenses etc*) ridurre, decurtare.

curtain ['kə:tn] *n* tenda.

curts(e)y ['kə:tsi] *n* inchino, riverenza // *vi* fare un inchino *or* una riverenza.

curve [kə:v] n curva // vi curvarsi.

cushion ['kuʃən] n cuscino // vt (shock) fare da cuscinetto a.

custard ['kʌstəd] n (for pouring) crema.

custodian [kʌs'təudiən] n custode m/f.

custody ['kʌstədi] n (of child) tutela; (for offenders) arresto.

custom ['kʌstəm] n costume m, usanza; (LAW) consuetudine f; (COMM) clientela; ~ary a consueto(a).

customer ['kʌstəmə*] n cliente m/f.

custom-made ['kʌstəm'meid] a (clothes) fatto(a) su misura; (other goods) fatto(a) su ordinazione.

customs ['kʌstəmz] npl dogana; ~ duty n dazio doganale; ~ officer n doganiere m.

cut [kʌt] vb (pt, pp cut) vt tagliare; (shape, make) intagliare; (reduce) ridurre // vi tagliare; (intersect) tagliarsi // n taglio; (in salary etc) riduzione f; **power** ~ mancanza di corrente elettrica; to ~ a tooth mettere un dente; to ~ down (on) vt fus ridurre; to ~ off vt tagliare; (fig) isolare; to ~ out vt tagliare fuori; eliminare; ritagliare; ~back n riduzione f.

cute [kju:t] a grazioso(a); (clever) astuto(a).

cut glass [kʌt'glɑ:s] n cristallo.

cuticle ['kju:tikl] n (on nail) cuticola.

cutlery ['kʌtləri] n posate fpl.

cutlet ['kʌtlit] n costoletta.

cut: ~out n interruttore m; ~-price a a prezzo ridotto; ~throat n assassino.

cutting ['kʌtiŋ] a tagliente; (fig) pungente // n (PRESS) ritaglio (di giornale); (RAIL) trincea.

cuttlefish ['kʌtlfiʃ] n seppia.

cut-up ['kʌtʌp] a stravolto(a).

cwt abbr of **hundredweight(s)**.

cyanide ['saiənaid] n cianuro.

cyclamen ['sikləmən] n ciclamino.

cycle ['saikl] n ciclo; bicicletta // vi andare in bicicletta.

cycling ['saikliŋ] n ciclismo.

cyclist ['saiklist] n ciclista m/f.

cyclone ['saikləun] n ciclone m.

cygnet ['signit] n cigno giovane.

cylinder ['silində*] n cilindro; ~ capacity n cilindrata; ~-head gasket n guarnizione f della testata del cilindro.

cymbals ['simblz] npl cembali mpl.

cynic ['sinik] n cinico/a; ~al a cinico(a); ~ism ['sinisizəm] n cinismo.

cypress ['saipris] n cipresso.

Cypriot ['sipriət] a, n cipriota (m/f).

Cyprus ['saiprəs] n Cipro.

cyst [sist] n cisti f inv.

czar [zɑ:*] n zar m inv.

Czech [tʃɛk] a ceco(a) // n ceco/a; (LING) ceco.

Czechoslovakia [tʃɛkəslə'vækiə] n Cecoslovacchia; ~n a, n cecoslovacco(a).

D

D [di:] n (MUS) re m; ~-day n giorno dello sbarco degli alleati in Normandia.

dab [dæb] vt (eyes, wound) tamponare; (paint, cream) applicare (con leggeri colpetti); **a ~ of paint** un colpetto di vernice.

dabble ['dæbl] vi: to ~ in occuparsi (da dilettante) di.

dad, daddy [dæd, 'dædi] n babbo, papà m inv; **daddy-long-legs** n tipula.

daffodil ['dæfədil] n giunchiglia.

daft [dɑ:ft] a sciocco(a).

dagger ['dægə*] n pugnale m.

daily ['deili] a quotidiano(a), giornaliero(a) // n quotidiano // ad tutti i giorni.

dainty ['deinti] a delicato(a), grazioso(a).

dairy ['dɛəri] n (shop) latteria; (on farm) caseificio // a caseario(a).

daisy ['deizi] n margherita.

dale [deil] n valle f.

dally ['dæli] vi trastullarsi.

dam [dæm] n diga // vt sbarrare; costruire dighe su.

damage ['dæmidʒ] n danno; danni mpl; (fig) danno // vt danneggiare; (fig) recar danno a; ~s npl (LAW) danni.

damn [dæm] vt condannare; (curse) maledire // n (col): **I don't give a ~** non me ne importa un fico // a (col): **this ~ ... questo maledetto ...**; ~ (it)! accidenti!; ~ing a (evidence) schiacciante.

damp [dæmp] a umido(a) // n umidità, umido // vt (also: ~en) (cloth, rag) inumidire, bagnare; (enthusiasm etc) spegnere; ~ness n umidità, umido.

damson ['dæmzən] n susina damaschina.

dance [dɑ:ns] n danza, ballo; (ball) ballo // vi ballare; ~ **hall** n dancing m inv, sala da ballo; ~r n danzatore/trice; (professional) ballerino/a.

dancing ['dɑ:nsiŋ] n danza, ballo.

dandelion ['dændilaiən] n dente m di leone.

dandruff ['dændrəf] n forfora.

Dane [dein] n danese m/f.

danger ['deindʒə*] n pericolo; **there is a ~ of fire** c'è pericolo di incendio; **in ~** in pericolo; **he was in ~ of falling** rischiava di cadere; ~ous a pericoloso(a).

dangle ['dæŋgl] vt dondolare; (fig) far balenare // vi pendolare.

Danish ['deiniʃ] a danese // n (LING) danese m.

dapper ['dæpə*] a lindo(a).

dare [dɛə*] vt: to ~ sb to do sfidare qd a fare // vi: to ~ (to) do sth osare fare qc; ~devil n scavezzacollo m/f; **daring** a audace, ardito(a).

dark [dɑ:k] a (night, room) buio(a), scuro(a); (colour, complexion) scuro(a); (fig) cupo(a), tetro(a), nero(a) // n: **in the ~** al buio; **in the ~ about** (fig)

all'oscuro di; **after** ~ a notte fatta; **~en**
vt (room) oscurare; (photo, painting) far
scuro(a) // vi oscurarsi; imbrunirsi; ~
glasses npl occhiali mpl scuri; **~ness** n
oscurità, buio; ~ **room** n camera oscura.
darling ['dɑ:lɪŋ] a caro(a) // n tesoro.
darn [dɑ:n] vt rammendare.
dart [dɑ:t] n freccetta // vi: **to ~ towards**
precipitarsi verso; **to ~ away** guizzare
via; **~s** n tiro al bersaglio (con freccette);
~board n bersaglio (per freccette).
dash [dæʃ] n (sign) lineetta // vt (missile)
gettare; (hopes) infrangere // vi: **to ~**
towards precipitarsi verso; **to ~ away** vi
scappare via; **~board** n cruscotto; **~ing**
a ardito(a).
data ['deɪtə] npl dati mpl; ~ **processing** n
elaborazione f (elettronica) dei dati.
date [deɪt] n data; appuntamento; (fruit)
dattero // vt datare; **to ~ a** fino a oggi;
out of ~ scaduto(a); (old-fashioned)
passato(a) di moda; **~d the 13th** datato il
13; **~d a** passato(a) di moda; **~line** n
linea del cambiamento di data.
daub [dɔ:b] vt imbrattare.
daughter ['dɔ:tə°] n figlia; **~-in-law** n
nuora.
daunt [dɔ:nt] vt intimidire; **~less** a
intrepido(a).
dawdle ['dɔ:dl] vi bighellonare.
dawn [dɔ:n] n alba // vi (day) spuntare;
(fig) venire in mente.
day [deɪ] n giorno; (as duration) giornata;
(period of time, age) tempo, epoca; **the ~**
before il giorno avanti or prima; **by ~** di
giorno; **~break** n spuntar m del giorno;
~dream n sogno a occhi aperti // vi
sognare a occhi aperti; **~light** n luce f del
giorno; **~time** n giorno.
daze [deɪz] vt (subject: drug) inebetire; (:
blow) stordire // n: **in a ~** inebetito(a);
stordito(a).
dazzle ['dæzl] vt abbagliare.
dead [dɛd] a morto(a); (numb)
intirizzito(a) // ad assolutamente,
perfettamente; **he was shot ~** fu colpito
a morte; ~ **on time** in perfetto orario; ~
tired stanco(a) morto(a); **to stop ~**
fermarsi in tronco; **the ~** i morti; **~en** vi
(blow, sound) ammortire; (make numb)
intirizzire; ~ **end** n vicolo cieco; **~ heat**
n (SPORT) **to finish in a ~ heat** finire
alla pari; **~line** n scadenza; **~lock** n
punto morto; **~ly** a mortale; (weapon,
poison) micidiale; **~pan** a a faccia
impassibile.
deaf [dɛf] a sordo(a); **~-aid** n apparecchio
per la sordità; **~en** vt assordare; **~ening**
a fragoroso(a), assordante; **~ness** n
sordità; **~-mute** n sordomuto/a.
deal [di:l] n accordo; affare m // vt (pt, pp
dealt [dɛlt]) (blow, cards) dare; **a great ~**
(of) molto(a); **to ~ with** vt fus (COMM)
fare affari con, trattare con; (handle)
occuparsi di; (be about: book etc) trattare
di; **~er** n commerciante m/f; **~ings** npl
(COMM) relazioni fpl; (relations) rapporti
mpl.

dean [di:n] n (SCOL) preside m di facoltà (or
di collegio).
dear [dɪə°] a caro(a) // n: **my ~** caro
mio/cara mia; ~ **me!** Dio mio!; **D~**
Sir/Madam (in letter) Egregio(a)
Signore(a); **D~ Mr/Mrs X** Gentile
Signor/Signora X; **~ly** ad (love)
moltissimo; (pay) a caro prezzo.
dearth [də:θ] n scarsità, carestia.
death [dɛθ] n morte f; (ADMIN) decesso;
~bed n letto di morte; ~ **certificate** n
atto di decesso; ~ **duties** npl (Brit)
imposta or tassa di successione; **~ly** a di
morte; ~ **penalty** n pena di morte; ~
rate n indice m di mortalità.
debar [dɪ'bɑ:°] vt: **to ~ sb from doing**
impedire a qd di fare.
debase [dɪ'beɪs] vt (currency) adulterare;
(person) degradare.
debatable [dɪ'beɪtəbl] a discutibile.
debate [dɪ'beɪt] n dibattito // vt dibattere;
discutere // vi (consider): **to ~ whether**
riflettere se.
debauchery [dɪ'bɔ:tʃərɪ] n dissolutezza.
debit ['dɛbɪt] n debito // vt: **to ~ a sum**
to sb addebitare una somma a qd.
debris ['dɛbri:] n detriti mpl.
debt [dɛt] n debito; **to be in ~** essere
indebitato(a); **~or** n debitore/trice.
début ['deɪbju:] n debutto.
decade ['dɛkeɪd] n decennio.
decadence ['dɛkədəns] n decadenza.
decanter [dɪ'kæntə°] n caraffa.
decay [dɪ'keɪ] n decadimento;
imputridimento; (fig) rovina; (also: **tooth**
~) carie f // vi (rot) imputridire; (fig)
andare in rovina.
decease [dɪ'si:s] n decesso; **~d** n
defunto/a.
deceit [dɪ'si:t] n inganno; **~ful** a
ingannevole, perfido(a).
deceive [dɪ'si:v] vt ingannare.
decelerate [di:'sɛləreɪt] vt, vi rallentare.
December [dɪ'sɛmbə°] n dicembre m.
decency ['di:sənsɪ] n decenza.
decent ['di:sənt] a decente; **they were**
very ~ about it si sono comportati da
signori riguardo a ciò.
decentralize [di:'sɛntrəlaɪz] vt
decentrare.
deception [dɪ'sɛpʃən] n inganno.
deceptive [dɪ'sɛptɪv] a ingannevole.
decibel ['dɛsɪbɛl] n decibel m inv.
decide [dɪ'saɪd] vt (person) far prendere
una decisione a; (question, argument)
risolvere, decidere // vi decidere,
decidersi; **to ~ to do/that** decidere di
fare/che; **to ~ on** decidere per; **~d a**
(resolute) deciso(a); (clear, definite)
netto(a), chiaro(a); **~dly** [-dɪdlɪ] ad
indubbiamente; decisamente.
deciduous [dɪ'sɪdjuəs] a deciduo(a).
decimal ['dɛsɪməl] a, n decimale (m); ~
point n ≈ virgola.
decimate ['dɛsɪmeɪt] vt decimare.
decipher [dɪ'saɪfə°] vt decifrare.
decision [dɪ'sɪʒən] n decisione f.

decisive [dɪ'saɪsɪv] a decisivo(a).

deck [dɛk] n (NAUT) ponte m; (of bus): top ~ imperiale m; (of cards) mazzo; ~**chair** n sedia a sdraio; ~ **hand** n marinaio.

declaration [dɛklə'reɪʃən] n dichiarazione f.

declare [dɪ'klɛə*] vt dichiarare.

decline [dɪ'klaɪn] n (decay) declino; (lessening) ribasso // vt declinare; rifiutare // vi declinare; diminuire.

decode [di:'kəud] vt decifrare.

decompose [di:kəm'pəuz] vi decomporre; **decomposition** [di:kɔmpə'zɪʃən] n decomposizione f.

decontaminate [di:kən'tæmɪneɪt] vt decontaminare.

décor ['deɪkɔ:*] n decorazione f.

decorate ['dɛkəreɪt] vt (adorn, give a medal to) decorare; (paint and paper) tinteggiare e tappezzare; **decoration** [-'reɪʃən] n (medal etc, adornment) decorazione f; **decorative** ['dɛkərətɪv] a decorativo(a); **decorator** n decoratore m.

decoy ['di:kɔɪ] n zimbello.

decrease n ['di:kri:s] diminuzione f // vt, vi [di:'kri:s] diminuire.

decree [dɪ'kri:] n decreto; ~ **nisi** n sentenza provvisoria di divorzio.

decrepit [dɪ'krɛpɪt] a decrepito(a).

dedicate ['dɛdɪkeɪt] vt consacrare; (book etc) dedicare.

dedication [dɛdɪ'keɪʃən] n (devotion) dedizione f.

deduce [dɪ'dju:s] vt dedurre.

deduct [dɪ'dʌkt] vt: to ~ sth (from) dedurre qc (da); (from wage etc) trattenere qc (da); ~**ion** [dɪ'dʌkʃən] n (deducting) deduzione f; (from wage etc) trattenuta; (deducing) deduzione f, conclusione f.

deed [di:d] n azione f, atto; (LAW) atto.

deep [di:p] a profondo(a); **4 metres** ~ profondo(a) 4 metri // ad: ~ **in snow** affondato(a) nella neve; ~ **in water** in acqua fino alle ginocchia; ~**en** vt (hole) approfondire // vi approfondirsi; (darkness) farsi più buio; ~**-freeze** n congelatore m // vt congelare; ~**-sea** a: ~**-sea diving** n immersione f in alto mare; ~**-sea fishing** n pesca d'alto mare; ~**-seated** a (beliefs) radicato(a); ~**-set** a (eyes) infossato(a).

deer [dɪə*] n, pl inv: **the** ~ i cervidi; **(red)** ~ cervo; **(fallow)** ~ daino; **(roe)** ~ capriolo; ~**skin** n pelle f di daino.

deface [dɪ'feɪs] vt imbrattare.

defamation [dɛfə'meɪʃən] n diffamazione f.

default [dɪ'fɔ:lt] vi (LAW) essere contumace; (gen) essere inadempiente // n: **by** ~ (LAW) in contumacia; (SPORT) per abbandono; ~**er** n (in debt) inadempiente m/f.

defeat [dɪ'fi:t] n sconfitta // vt (team, opponents) sconfiggere; (fig: plans, efforts) frustrare; ~**ist** a,n disfattista (m/f).

defect n ['di:fɛkt] difetto // vi [dɪ'fɛkt]: to

~ **to the enemy/the West** passare al nemico/all'Ovest; ~**ive** [dɪ'fɛktɪv] a difettoso(a).

defence [dɪ'fɛns] n difesa; **in** ~ **of** in difesa di; ~**less** a senza difesa.

defend [dɪ'fɛnd] vt difendere; ~**ant** n imputato/a; ~**er** n difensore/a.

defensive [dɪ'fɛnsɪv] a difensivo(a).

defer [dɪ'fə:*] vt (postpone) differire, rinviare.

deference ['dɛfərəns] n deferenza; riguardo.

defiance [dɪ'faɪəns] n sfida; **in** ~ **of** a dispetto di.

defiant [dɪ'faɪənt] a di sfida.

deficiency [dɪ'fɪʃənsɪ] n deficienza; carenza.

deficient [dɪ'fɪʃənt] a deficiente; insufficiente; **to be** ~ **in** mancare di.

deficit ['dɛfɪsɪt] n disavanzo.

defile vb [dɪ'faɪl] vt contaminare // vi sfilare // n ['di:faɪl] gola, stretta.

define [dɪ'faɪn] vt definire.

definite ['dɛfɪnɪt] a (fixed) definito(a), preciso(a); (clear, obvious) ben definito(a), esatto(a); (LING) determinativo(a); **he was** ~ **about it** ne era sicuro; ~**ly** ad indubbiamente.

definition [dɛfɪ'nɪʃən] n definizione f.

definitive [dɪ'fɪnɪtɪv] a definitivo(a).

deflate [di:'fleɪt] vt sgonfiare.

deflation [di:'fleɪʃən] n (ECON) deflazione f.

deflect [dɪ'flɛkt] vt deflettere, deviare.

deform [dɪ'fɔ:m] vt deformare; ~**ed** a deforme; ~**ity** n deformità f inv.

defraud [dɪ'frɔ:d] vt defraudare.

defray [dɪ'freɪ] vt: to ~ **sb's expenses** sostenere le spese di qd.

defrost [di:'frɔst] vt (fridge) disgelare.

deft [dɛft] a svelto(a), destro(a).

defunct [dɪ'fʌŋkt] a defunto(a).

defuse [di:'fju:z] vt disarmare.

defy [dɪ'faɪ] vt sfidare; (efforts etc) resistere a.

degenerate vi [dɪ'dʒɛnəreɪt] degenerare // a [dɪ'dʒɛnərɪt] degenere.

degradation [dɛgrə'deɪʃən] n degradazione f.

degrading [dɪ'greɪdɪŋ] a degradante.

degree [dɪ'gri:] n grado; laurea (universitaria); **a (first)** ~ **in maths** una laurea in matematica.

dehydrated [di:haɪ'dreɪtɪd] a disidratato(a); (milk, eggs) in polvere.

de-ice [di:'aɪs] vt (windscreen) disgelare.

deign [deɪn] vi: to ~ **to do** degnarsi di fare.

deity ['di:ɪtɪ] n deità f inv; dio/dea.

dejected [dɪ'dʒɛktɪd] a abbattuto(a), avvilito(a).

dejection [dɪ'dʒɛkʃən] n abbattimento, avvilimento.

delay [dɪ'leɪ] vt (journey, operation) ritardare, rinviare; (travellers, trains) ritardare // n ritardo; **without** ~ senza ritardo; ~**ed-action** a a azione ritardata.

delegate n ['dɛlɪgɪt] delegato/a // vt ['dɛlɪgeɪt] delegare.
delegation [dɛlɪ'geɪʃən] n delegazione f.
delete [dɪ'li:t] vt cancellare.
deliberate a [dɪ'lɪbərɪt] (intentional) intenzionale; (slow) misurato(a) // vi [dɪ'lɪbəreɪt] deliberare, riflettere; ~ly ad (on purpose) deliberatamente.
delicacy ['dɛlɪkəsɪ] n delicatezza.
delicate ['dɛlɪkɪt] a delicato(a).
delicatessen [dɛlɪkə'tɛsn] n salumeria.
delicious [dɪ'lɪʃəs] a delizioso(a), squisito(a).
delight [dɪ'laɪt] n delizia, gran piacere m // vt dilettare; **to take ~ in** divertirsi a; ~ful a delizioso(a); incantevole.
delinquency [dɪ'lɪŋkwənsɪ] n delinquenza.
delinquent [dɪ'lɪŋkwənt] a,n delinquente (m/f).
delirium [dɪ'lɪrɪəm] n delirio.
deliver [dɪ'lɪvə*] vt (mail) distribuire; (goods) consegnare; (speech) pronunciare; (free) liberare; (MED) far partorire; **to ~ a message** fare un'ambasciata; **to ~ the goods** (fig) partorire; ~y n consegna; distribuzione f; (of speaker) modo di proporre; (MED) parto; **to take ~y of** prendere in consegna.
delta ['dɛltə] n delta m.
delude [dɪ'lu:d] vt deludere, illudere.
deluge ['dɛljuːdʒ] n diluvio.
delusion [dɪ'luːʒən] n illusione f.
delve [dɛlv] vi: **to ~ into** frugare in; (subject) fare ricerche in.
demagogue ['dɛməgɔg] n demagogo.
demand [dɪ'mɑːnd] vt richiedere // n domanda; (ECON, claim) richiesta; **in ~** ricercato(a), richiesto(a); **on ~** a richiesta; ~ing a (boss) esigente; (work) impegnativo(a).
demarcation [diːmɑː'keɪʃən] n demarcazione f.
demean [dɪ'miːn] vt: **to ~ o.s.** umiliarsi.
demeanour [dɪ'miːnə*] n comportamento; contegno.
demented [dɪ'mɛntɪd] a demente, impazzito(a).
demise [dɪ'maɪz] n decesso.
demobilize [diː'məʊbɪlaɪz] vt smobilitare.
democracy [dɪ'mɔkrəsɪ] n democrazia.
democrat ['dɛməkræt] n democratico/a; ~ic [dɛmə'krætɪk] a democratico(a).
demolish [dɪ'mɔlɪʃ] vt demolire.
demolition [dɛmə'lɪʃən] n demolizione f.
demonstrate ['dɛmənstreɪt] vt dimostrare, provare.
demonstration [dɛmən'streɪʃən] n dimostrazione f; (POL) manifestazione f, dimostrazione.
demonstrative [dɪ'mɔnstrətɪv] a dimostrativo(a).
demonstrator ['dɛmənstreɪtə*] n (POL) dimostrante m/f.
demoralize [dɪ'mɔrəlaɪz] vt demoralizzare.
demote [dɪ'məʊt] vt far retrocedere.
demure [dɪ'mjʊə*] a contegnoso(a).

den [dɛn] n tana, covo.
denial [dɪ'naɪəl] n diniego; rifiuto.
denigrate ['dɛnɪgreɪt] vt denigrare.
denim ['dɛnɪm] n tessuto di cotone ritorto; ~s npl blue jeans mpl.
Denmark ['dɛnmɑːk] n Danimarca.
denomination [dɪnɔmɪ'neɪʃən] n (money) valore m; (REL) confessione f.
denominator [dɪ'nɔmɪneɪtə*] n denominatore m.
denote [dɪ'nəʊt] vt denotare.
denounce [dɪ'naʊns] vt denunciare.
dense [dɛns] a fitto(a); (stupid) ottuso(a), duro(a); ~ly ad: ~ly wooded fittamente boscoso; ~ly populated densamente popolato(a).
density ['dɛnsɪtɪ] n densità f inv.
dent [dɛnt] n ammaccatura // vt (also: **make a ~ in**) ammaccare.
dental ['dɛntl] a dentale; ~ **surgeon** n medico/a dentista.
dentifrice ['dɛntɪfrɪs] n dentifricio.
dentist ['dɛntɪst] n dentista m/f; ~ry n odontoiatria.
denture ['dɛntʃə*] n dentiera.
deny [dɪ'naɪ] vt negare; (refuse) rifiutare.
deodorant [diː'əʊdərənt] n deodorante m.
depart [dɪ'pɑːt] vi partire; **to ~ from** (leave) allontanarsi da, partire da.
department [dɪ'pɑːtmənt] n (COMM) reparto; (SCOL) sezione f, dipartimento; (POL) ministero; ~ **store** n grande magazzino.
departure [dɪ'pɑːtʃə*] n partenza; (fig): ~ **from** allontanamento da.
depend [dɪ'pɛnd] vi: **to ~ on** dipendere da; (rely on) contare su; **it ~s** dipende; ~**able** a fidato(a); (car etc) affidabile; ~**ence** n dipendenza; ~**ant**, ~**ent** n persona a carico.
depict [dɪ'pɪkt] vt (in picture) dipingere; (in words) descrivere.
depleted [dɪ'pliːtɪd] a diminuito(a).
deplorable [dɪ'plɔːrəbl] a deplorabile, lamentevole.
deplore [dɪ'plɔː*] vt deplorare.
deploy [dɪ'plɔɪ] vt dispiegare.
depopulation ['diːpɔpjʊ'leɪʃən] n spopolamento.
deport [dɪ'pɔːt] vt deportare; espellere; ~**ation** [diːpɔː'teɪʃən] n deportazione f, ~**ment** n portamento.
depose [dɪ'pəʊz] vt deporre.
deposit [dɪ'pɔzɪt] n (COMM, GEO) deposito; (of ore, oil) giacimento; (CHEM) sedimento; (part payment) acconto; (for hired goods etc) cauzione f // vt depositare; dare in acconto; mettere or lasciare in deposito; ~ **account** n conto vincolato; ~**or** n depositante m/f.
depot ['dɛpəʊ] n deposito.
deprave [dɪ'preɪv] vt depravare, corrompere, pervertire.
depravity [dɪ'prævɪtɪ] n depravazione f.
depreciate [dɪ'priːʃɪeɪt] vi svalutare // vi svalutarsi; **depreciation** [-'eɪʃən] n svalutazione f.

depress [dɪ'prɛs] vt deprimere; (*press down*) premere; ~**ed** a (*person*) depresso(a), abbattuto(a); (*area*) depresso(a); ~**ing** a deprimente; ~**ion** [dɪ'prɛʃən] n depressione f.
deprivation [dɛprɪ'veɪʃən] n privazione f; (*loss*) perdita.
deprive [dɪ'praɪv] vt: to ~ **sb of** privare qd di; ~**d** a disgraziato(a).
depth [dɛpθ] n profondità f inv; **in the ~s of** nel profondo di; nel cuore di; **in the ~s of winter** in pieno inverno; ~ **charge** n carica di profondità.
deputation [dɛpju'teɪʃən] n deputazione f, delegazione f.
deputize ['dɛpjutaɪz] vi: to ~ **for** svolgere le funzioni di.
deputy ['dɛpjutɪ] a: ~ **head** vice-presidente m/f; (*SCOL*) vicepreside m/f // n (*replacement*) supplente m/f; (*second in command*) vice m/f.
derail [dɪ'reɪl] vt far deragliare; to be ~**ed** essere deragliato; ~**ment** n deragliamento.
deranged [dɪ'reɪndʒd] a: to be ~ (*mentally*) ~ essere pazzo(a).
derelict ['dɛrɪlɪkt] a abbandonato(a).
deride [dɪ'raɪd] vt deridere.
derision [dɪ'rɪʒən] n derisione f.
derisive [dɪ'raɪsɪv] a di derisione.
derisory [dɪ'raɪsərɪ] a (*sum*) irrisorio(a).
derivation [dɛrɪ'veɪʃən] n derivazione f.
derivative [dɪ'rɪvətɪv] n derivato // a derivato(a).
derive [dɪ'raɪv] vt: to ~ **sth from** derivare qc da; trarre qc da // vi: to ~ **from** derivare da.
derogatory [dɪ'rɔgətərɪ] a denigratorio(a).
derrick ['dɛrɪk] n gru f inv; (*for oil*) derrick m inv.
descend [dɪ'sɛnd] vt, vi discendere, scendere; to ~ **from** discendere da; ~**ant** n discendente m/f.
descent [dɪ'sɛnt] n discesa; (*origin*) discendenza, famiglia.
describe [dɪs'kraɪb] vt descrivere; **description** [-'krɪpʃən] n descrizione f; (*sort*) genere m, specie f; **descriptive** [-'krɪptɪv] a descrittivo(a).
desecrate ['dɛsɪkreɪt] vt profanare.
desert n ['dɛzət] deserto // vb [dɪ'zɜːt] vt lasciare, abbandonare // vi (*MIL*) disertare; ~**er** n disertore m; ~**ion** [dɪ'zɜːʃən] n diserzione f.
deserve [dɪ'zɜːv] vt meritare; **deserving** a (*person*) meritevole, degno(a); (*cause*) meritorio(a).
design [dɪ'zaɪn] n (*sketch*) disegno; (*layout, shape*) linea; (*pattern*) fantasia; (*COMM*) disegno tecnico; (*intention*) intenzione f // vt disegnare; progettare; to have ~**s on** aver mire su.
designate vt ['dɛzɪgneɪt] designare // a ['dɛzɪgnɪt] designato(a); **designation** [-'neɪʃən] n designazione f.
designer [dɪ'zaɪnə*] n (*ART, TECH*)

disegnatore/trice; (*of fashion*) modellista m/f.
desirability [dɪzaɪərə'bɪlɪtɪ] n desiderabilità; vantaggio.
desirable [dɪ'zaɪərəbl] a desiderabile.
desire [dɪ'zaɪə*] n desiderio, voglia // vt desiderare, volere.
desk [dɛsk] n (*in office*) scrivania; (*for pupil*) banco; (*in shop, restaurant*) cassa; (*in hotel*) ricevimento; (*at airport*) accettazione f.
desolate ['dɛsəlɪt] a desolato(a).
desolation [dɛsə'leɪʃən] n desolazione f.
despair [dɪs'pɛə*] n disperazione f // vi: to ~ **of** disperare di.
despatch [dɪs'pætʃ] n,vt = **dispatch**.
desperate ['dɛspərɪt] a disperato(a); (*fugitive*) capace di tutto; ~**ly** ad disperatamente; (*very*) terribilmente, estremamente.
desperation [dɛspə'reɪʃən] n disperazione f.
despicable [dɪs'pɪkəbl] a disprezzabile.
despise [dɪs'paɪz] vt disprezzare, sdegnare.
despite [dɪs'paɪt] prep malgrado, a dispetto di, nonostante.
despondent [dɪs'pɔndənt] a abbattuto(a), scoraggiato(a).
dessert [dɪ'zɜːt] n dolce m; frutta; ~ **spoon** n cucchiaio da dolci.
destination [dɛstɪ'neɪʃən] n destinazione f.
destine ['dɛstɪn] vt destinare.
destiny ['dɛstɪnɪ] n destino.
destitute ['dɛstɪtjuːt] a indigente, bisognoso(a).
destroy [dɪs'trɔɪ] vt distruggere; ~**er** n (*NAUT*) cacciatorpediniere m inv.
destruction [dɪs'trʌkʃən] n distruzione f.
destructive [dɪs'trʌktɪv] a distruttivo(a).
detach [dɪ'tætʃ] vt staccare, distaccare; ~**able** a staccabile; ~**ed** a (*attitude*) distante; ~**ed house** n villa; ~**ment** n (*MIL*) distaccamento; (*fig*) distacco.
detail ['diːteɪl] n particolare m, dettaglio // vt dettagliare, particolareggiare; **in** ~ nei particolari; ~**ed** a particolareggiato(a).
detain [dɪ'teɪn] vt trattenere; (*in captivity*) detenere.
detect [dɪ'tɛkt] vt scoprire, scorgere; (*MED, POLICE, RADAR etc*) individuare; ~**ion** [dɪ'tɛkʃən] n scoperta; individuazione f; ~**ive** n agente m investigativo; **private** ~**ive** investigatore m privato; ~**ive story** n giallo; ~**or** n rivelatore m.
detention [dɪ'tɛnʃən] n detenzione f; (*SCOL*) permanenza forzata per punizione.
deter [dɪ'tɜː*] vt distogliere.
detergent [dɪ'tɜːdʒənt] n detersivo.
deteriorate [dɪ'tɪərɪəreɪt] vi deteriorarsi; **deterioration** [-'reɪʃən] n deterioramento.
determination [dɪtɜːmɪ'neɪʃən] n determinazione f.
determine [dɪ'tɜːmɪn] vt determinare; ~**d** a (*person*) risoluto(a), deciso(a).
deterrent [dɪ'tɛrənt] n deterrente m.

detest [dɪˈtɛst] vt detestare; ~**able** a detestabile, abominevole.

detonate [ˈdɛtəneɪt] vi detonare; esplodere // vt far detonare or esplodere; **detonator** n detonatore m.

detour [ˈdiːtuə°] n deviazione f.

detract [dɪˈtrækt] vi: to ~ **from** detrarre da.

detriment [ˈdɛtrɪmənt] n: to the ~ **of** a detrimento di; ~**al** [dɛtrɪˈmɛntl] a: ~**al to** dannoso(a) a, nocivo(a) a.

devaluation [dɪvæljuˈeɪʃən] n svalutazione f.

devalue [ˈdiːˈvæljuː] vt svalutare.

devastate [ˈdɛvəsteɪt] vt devastare.

devastating [ˈdɛvəsteɪtɪŋ] a devastatore(trice).

develop [dɪˈvɛləp] vt sviluppare; (habit) prendere (gradualmente) // vi svilupparsi; (facts, symptoms: appear) manifestarsi, rivelarsi; ~**er** n (PHOT) sviluppatore m; (of land) imprenditore/trice; ~**ing country** paese m in via di sviluppo; ~**ment** n sviluppo.

deviate [ˈdiːvɪeɪt] vi deviare.

deviation [diːvɪˈeɪʃən] n deviazione f.

device [dɪˈvaɪs] n (apparatus) congegno.

devil [ˈdɛvl] n diavolo; demonio; ~**ish** a diabolico(a).

devious [ˈdiːvɪəs] a (means) indiretto(a), tortuoso(a); (person) subdolo(a).

devise [dɪˈvaɪz] vt escogitare, concepire.

devoid [dɪˈvɔɪd] a: ~ **of** privo(a) di.

devote [dɪˈvəut] vt: to ~ **sth to** dedicare qc a; ~**d** a devoto(a); **to be** ~**d to** essere affezionato(a) a; ~**e** [dɛvəuˈtiː] n (MUS, SPORT) appassionato/a.

devotion [dɪˈvəuʃən] n devozione f, attaccamento; (REL) atto di devozione, preghiera.

devour [dɪˈvauə°] vt divorare.

devout [dɪˈvaut] a pio(a), devoto(a).

dew [djuː] n rugiada.

dexterity [dɛksˈtɛrɪtɪ] n destrezza.

diabetes [daɪəˈbiːtiːz] n diabete m; **diabetic** [-ˈbɛtɪk] a diabetico(a) // n diabetico.

diagnose [daɪəgˈnəuz] vt diagnosticare.

diagnosis, pl diagnoses [daɪəgˈnəusɪs, -siːz] n diagnosi f inv.

diagonal [daɪˈægənl] a, n diagonale (f).

diagram [ˈdaɪəgræm] n diagramma m.

dial [ˈdaɪəl] n quadrante m; (on telephone) disco combinatore // vt (number) fare; ~**ling tone** n segnale m di linea libera.

dialect [ˈdaɪəlɛkt] n dialetto.

dialogue [ˈdaɪəlɔg] n dialogo.

diameter [daɪˈæmɪtə°] n diametro.

diamond [ˈdaɪəmənd] n diamante m; (shape) rombo; ~**s** npl (CARDS) quadri mpl.

diaper [ˈdaɪəpə°] n (US) pannolino.

diaphragm [ˈdaɪəfræm] n diaframma m.

diarrhoea [daɪəˈriːə] n diarrea.

diary [ˈdaɪərɪ] n (daily account) diario; (book) agenda.

dice [daɪs] n, pl inv dado // vt (CULIN) tagliare a dadini.

dictate vt [dɪkˈteɪt] dettare // n [ˈdɪkteɪt] dettame m.

dictation [dɪkˈteɪʃən] n dettato.

dictator [dɪkˈteɪtə°] n dittatore m; ~**ship** n dittatura.

diction [ˈdɪkʃən] n dizione f.

dictionary [ˈdɪkʃənrɪ] n dizionario.

did [dɪd] pt of **do**.

die [daɪ] n (pl: **dies**) conio; matrice f; stampo // vi morire; to ~ **away** vi spegnersi a poco a poco; to ~ **down** vi abbassarsi; to ~ **out** vi estinguersi.

Diesel [ˈdiːzəl]: ~ **engine** n motore m diesel inv.

diet [ˈdaɪət] n alimentazione f; (restricted food) dieta // vi (also: be on a ~) stare a dieta.

differ [ˈdɪfə°] vi: to ~ **from sth** differire da qc; essere diverso(a) da qc; to ~ **from sb over sth** essere in disaccordo con qd su qc; ~**ence** n differenza; (quarrel) screzio; ~**ent** a diverso(a); ~**ential** [-ˈrɛnʃəl] n (AUT, wages) differenziale m; ~**entiate** [-ˈrɛnʃɪeɪt] vi differenziarsi; to ~**entiate between** discriminare or fare differenza fra; ~**ently** ad diversamente.

difficult [ˈdɪfɪkəlt] a difficile; ~**y** n difficoltà f inv.

diffident [ˈdɪfɪdənt] a sfiduciato(a).

diffuse a [dɪˈfjuːs] diffuso(a) // vt [dɪˈfjuːz] diffondere, emanare.

dig [dɪg] vt (pt, pp **dug** [dʌg]) (hole) scavare; (garden) vangare // n (prod) gomitata; (fig) frecciata; to ~ **into** (snow, soil) scavare; to ~ **up** vt scavare; (tree etc) sradicare.

digest vt [daɪˈdʒɛst] digerire; ~**ible** [dɪˈdʒɛstəbl] a digeribile; ~**ion** [dɪˈdʒɛstʃən] n digestione f.

digit [ˈdɪdʒɪt] n cifra; (finger) dito; ~**al** a digitale.

dignified [ˈdɪgnɪfaɪd] a dignitoso(a).

dignitary [ˈdɪgnɪtərɪ] n dignitario.

dignity [ˈdɪgnɪtɪ] n dignità.

digress [daɪˈgrɛs] vi: to ~ **from** divagare da; ~**ion** [daɪˈgrɛʃən] n digressione f.

digs [dɪgz] npl (Brit: col) camera ammobiliata.

dilapidated [dɪˈlæpɪdeɪtɪd] a cadente.

dilate [daɪˈleɪt] vt dilatare // vi dilatarsi.

dilatory [ˈdɪlətərɪ] a dilatorio(a).

dilemma [daɪˈlɛmə] n dilemma m.

diligent [ˈdɪlɪdʒənt] a diligente.

dilute [daɪˈluːt] vt diluire; (with water) annacquare.

dim [dɪm] a (light, eyesight) debole; (memory, outline) vago(a); (stupid) lento(a) d'ingegno // vt (light) abbassare.

dime [daɪm] n (US) = 10 cents.

dimension [dɪˈmɛnʃən] n dimensione f.

diminish [dɪˈmɪnɪʃ] vt, vi diminuire.

diminutive [dɪˈmɪnjutɪv] a minuscolo(a) // n (LING) diminutivo.

dimly [ˈdɪmlɪ] ad debolmente; indistintamente.

dimple [ˈdɪmpl] n fossetta.

din [dɪn] n chiasso, fracasso.

dine [dain] vi pranzare.

dinghy ['dɪŋgi] n battello pneumatico; (also: **sailing** ~) dinghy m inv.

dingy ['dɪndʒi] a grigio(a).

dining ['daɪnɪŋ] cpd: ~ **car** n vagone m ristorante; ~ **room** n sala da pranzo.

dinner ['dɪnə*] n pranzo; (public) banchetto; ~ **jacket** n smoking m inv; ~ **party** n cena.

diocese ['daɪəsɪs] n diocesi f inv.

dip [dɪp] n discesa; (in sea) bagno // vt immergere; bagnare; (AUT: lights) abbassare // vi abbassarsi.

diphtheria [dɪf'θɪərɪə] n difterite f.

diphthong ['dɪfθɒŋ] n dittongo.

diploma [dɪ'pləumə] n diploma m.

diplomacy [dɪ'pləuməsɪ] n diplomazia.

diplomat ['dɪpləmæt] n diplomatico; ~**ic** [dɪplə'mætɪk] a diplomatico(a); ~**ic corps** n corpo diplomatico.

dipstick ['dɪpstɪk] n (AUT) indicatore m di livello dell'olio.

dire [daɪə*] a terribile; estremo(a).

direct [daɪ'rɛkt] a diretto(a) // vt dirigere; **can you ~ me to ...?** mi può indicare la strada per ...?; ~ **current** n corrente f continua.

direction [dɪ'rɛkʃən] n direzione f; ~**s** npl (advice) chiarimenti mpl; ~**s for use** istruzioni fpl.

directly [dɪ'rɛktlɪ] ad (in straight line) direttamente; (at once) subito.

director [dɪ'rɛktə*] n direttore/trice; amministratore/trice; (THEATRE, CINEMA) regista m/f.

directory [dɪ'rɛktərɪ] n elenco.

dirt [dɜːt] n sporcizia; immondizia; ~-**cheap** a da due soldi; ~**y** a sporco(a) // vt sporcare; ~**y trick** n brutto scherzo.

disability [dɪsə'bɪlɪtɪ] n invalidità f inv; (LAW) incapacità f inv.

disabled [dɪs'eɪbld] a invalido(a); (maimed) mutilato(a); (through illness, old age) inabile.

disadvantage [dɪsəd'vɑːntɪdʒ] n svantaggio; ~**ous** [dɪsædvɑːn'teɪdʒəs] a svantaggioso(a).

disagree [dɪsə'griː] vi (differ) discordare; (be against, think otherwise): **to ~ (with)** essere in disaccordo (con), dissentire (da); **garlic ~s with me** l'aglio non mi va; ~**able** a sgradevole; (person) antipatico(a); ~**ment** n disaccordo.

disallow ['dɪsə'lau] vt respingere.

disappear [dɪsə'pɪə*] vi scomparire; ~**ance** n scomparsa.

disappoint [dɪsə'pɔɪnt] vt deludere; ~**ment** n delusione f.

disapproval [dɪsə'pruːvəl] n disapprovazione f.

disapprove [dɪsə'pruːv] vi: **to ~ of** disapprovare.

disarm [dɪs'ɑːm] vt disarmare; ~**ament** n disarmo.

disaster [dɪ'zɑːstə*] n disastro; **disastrous** a disastroso(a).

disband [dɪs'bænd] vt sbandare; (MIL) congedare.

disbelief ['dɪsbə'liːf] n incredulità.

disc [dɪsk] n disco.

discard [dɪs'kɑːd] vt (old things) scartare; (fig) abbandonare.

disc brake ['dɪskbreɪk] n freno a disco.

discern [dɪ'sɜːn] vt discernere, distinguere; ~**ing** a perspicace.

discharge vt [dɪs'tʃɑːdʒ] (duties) compiere; (ELEC, waste etc) scaricare; (MED) emettere; (patient) dimettere; (employee) licenziare; (soldier) congedare; (defendant) liberare // n ['dɪstʃɑːdʒ] (ELEC) scarica; (MED) emissione f; (dismissal) licenziamento; congedo; liberazione f.

disciple [dɪ'saɪpl] n discepolo.

disciplinary ['dɪsɪplɪnərɪ] a disciplinare.

discipline ['dɪsɪplɪn] n disciplina // vt disciplinare; (punish) punire.

disc jockey ['dɪskdʒɔkɪ] n disc jockey m inv.

disclaim [dɪs'kleɪm] vt ripudiare.

disclose [dɪs'kləuz] vt rivelare, svelare; **disclosure** [-'kləuʒə*] n rivelazione f.

disco ['dɪskəu] n abbr of **discothèque**.

discoloured [dɪs'kʌləd] a scolorito(a); ingiallito(a).

discomfort [dɪs'kʌmfət] n disagio; (lack of comfort) scomodità f inv.

disconcert [dɪskən'sɜːt] vt sconcertare.

disconnect [dɪskə'nɛkt] vt sconnettere, staccare; (ELEC, RADIO) staccare; (gas, water) chiudere; ~**ed** a (speech, thought) sconnesso(a).

disconsolate [dɪs'kɔnsəlɪt] a sconsolato(a).

discontent [dɪskən'tɛnt] n scontentezza; ~**ed** a scontento(a).

discontinue [dɪskən'tɪnjuː] vt smettere, cessare; '~**d**' (COMM) 'sospeso'.

discord ['dɪskɔːd] n disaccordo; (MUS) dissonanza; ~**ant** [dɪs'kɔːdənt] a discordante; dissonante.

discothèque ['dɪskəutɛk] n discoteca.

discount n ['dɪskaunt] sconto // vt [dɪs'kaunt] scontare.

discourage [dɪs'kʌrɪdʒ] vt scoraggiare; **discouraging** a scoraggiante.

discourteous [dɪs'kɜːtɪəs] a scortese.

discover [dɪs'kʌvə*] vt scoprire; ~**y** n scoperta.

discredit [dɪs'krɛdɪt] vt screditare; mettere in dubbio.

discreet [dɪs'kriːt] a discreto(a).

discrepancy [dɪs'krɛpənsɪ] n discrepanza.

discretion [dɪs'krɛʃən] n discrezione f.

discriminate [dɪs'krɪmɪneɪt] vi: **to ~ between** distinguere tra; **to ~ against** discriminare contro; **discriminating** a fine, giudizioso(a); **discrimination** [-'neɪʃən] n discriminazione f; (judgment) discernimento.

discus ['dɪskəs] n disco.

discuss [dɪ'skʌs] vt discutere; (debate) dibattere; ~**ion** [dɪ'skʌʃən] n discussione f.

disdain [dɪs'deɪn] n disdegno.

disease [dɪ'ziːz] n malattia.
disembark [dɪsɪm'baːk] vt,vi sbarcare.
disembodied [dɪsɪm'bɔdɪd] a disincarnato(a).
disembowel [dɪsɪm'bauəl] vt sbudellare, sventrare.
disenchanted [dɪsɪn'tʃɑːntɪd] a disincantato(a), disilluso(a).
disengage [dɪsɪn'geɪdʒ] vt disimpegnare; (TECH) distaccare; (AUT) disinnestare.
disentangle [dɪsɪn'tæŋgl] vt sbrogliare.
disfavour [dɪs'feɪvə*] n sfavore m; disgrazia.
disfigure [dɪs'fɪgə*] vt sfigurare.
disgrace [dɪs'greɪs] n vergogna; (disfavour) disgrazia // vt disonorare, far cadere in disgrazia; ~ful a scandaloso(a), vergognoso(a).
disgruntled [dɪs'grʌntld] a scontento(a), di cattivo umore.
disguise [dɪs'gaɪz] n travestimento // vt travestire; in ~ travestito(a).
disgust [dɪs'gʌst] n disgusto, nausea // vt disgustare, far schifo a; ~ing a disgustoso(a); ripugnante.
dish [dɪʃ] n piatto; to do or wash the ~es fare i piatti; to ~ up vt servire; (facts, statistics) presentare; ~cloth n (for drying) asciugatoio; (for washing) strofinaccio.
dishearten [dɪs'hɑːtn] vt scoraggiare.
dishevelled [dɪ'ʃevəld] a arruffato(a); scapigliato(a).
dishonest [dɪs'ɔnɪst] a disonesto(a); ~y n disonestà.
dishonour [dɪs'ɔnə*] n disonore m; ~able a disonorevole.
dishwasher ['dɪʃwɔʃə*] n lavastoviglie f inv; (person) sguattero/a.
disillusion [dɪsɪ'luːʒən] vt disilludere, disingannare // n disillusione f.
disinfect [dɪsɪn'fɛkt] vt disinfettare; ~ant n disinfettante m.
disintegrate [dɪs'ɪntɪgreɪt] vi disintegrarsi.
disinterested [dɪs'ɪntrəstɪd] a disinteressato(a).
disjointed [dɪs'dʒɔɪntɪd] a sconnesso(a).
disk [dɪsk] n = disc.
dislike [dɪs'laɪk] n antipatia, avversione f // vt: he ~s it non gli piace.
dislocate ['dɪsləkeɪt] vt slogare; disorganizzare.
dislodge [dɪs'lɔdʒ] vt rimuovere, staccare; (enemy) sloggiare.
disloyal [dɪs'lɔɪəl] a sleale.
dismal ['dɪzml] a triste, cupo(a).
dismantle [dɪs'mæntl] vt smantellare, smontare; (fort, warship) disarmare.
dismay [dɪs'meɪ] n costernazione f // vt sgomentare.
dismiss [dɪs'mɪs] vt congedare; (employee) licenziare; (idea) scacciare; (LAW) respingere; ~al n congedo; licenziamento.
dismount [dɪs'maunt] vi scendere.

disobedience [dɪsə'biːdɪəns] n disubbidienza.
disobedient [dɪsə'biːdɪənt] a disubbidiente.
disobey [dɪsə'beɪ] vt disubbidire.
disorder [dɪs'ɔːdə*] n disordine m; (rioting) tumulto; (MED) disturbo; ~ly a disordinato(a); tumultuoso(a).
disorganize [dɪs'ɔːgənaɪz] vt disorganizzare.
disown [dɪs'əun] vt ripudiare.
disparaging [dɪs'pærɪdʒɪŋ] a spregiativo(a), sprezzante.
disparity [dɪs'pærɪtɪ] n disparità f inv.
dispassionate [dɪs'pæʃənət] a calmo(a), freddo(a); imparziale.
dispatch [dɪs'pætʃ] vt spedire, inviare // n spedizione f, invio; (MIL, PRESS) dispaccio.
dispel [dɪs'pɛl] vt dissipare, scacciare.
dispensary [dɪs'pɛnsərɪ] n farmacia; (in chemist's) dispensario.
dispense [dɪs'pɛns] vt distribuire, amministrare; to ~ with vt fus fare a meno di; ~r n (container) distributore m; **dispensing chemist** n farmacista m/f.
dispersal [dɪs'pɔːsl] n dispersione f.
disperse [dɪs'pɔːs] vt disperdere; (knowledge) disseminare // vi disperdersi.
dispirited [dɪs'pɪrɪtɪd] a scoraggiato(a), abbattuto(a).
displace [dɪs'pleɪs] vt spostare; ~d person n (POL) profugo/a.
display [dɪs'pleɪ] n mostra; esposizione f; (of feeling etc) manifestazione f; (screen) schermo; (pej) ostentazione f // vt mostrare; (goods) esporre; (results) affiggere; (departure times) indicare.
displease [dɪs'pliːz] vt dispiacere a, scontentare; **displeasure** [-'plɛʒə*] n dispiacere m.
disposable [dɪs'pəuzəbl] a (pack etc) a perdere; (income) disponibile.
disposal [dɪs'pəuzl] n (of rubbish) evacuazione f; distruzione f; at one's ~ alla sua disposizione.
dispose [dɪs'pəuz] vi disporre; to ~ of vt (time, money) disporre di; (unwanted goods) sbarazzarsi di; (problem) sbrigarsi; ~d a: ~d to do disposto(a) a fare; **disposition** [-'zɪʃən] n disposizione f; (temperament) carattere m.
disproportionate [dɪsprə'pɔːʃənət] a sproporzionato(a).
disprove [dɪs'pruːv] vt confutare.
dispute [dɪs'pjuːt] n disputa; (also: **industrial ~**) controversia (sindacale) // vt contestare; (matter) discutere; (victory) disputare.
disqualification [dɪskwɔlɪfɪ'keɪʃən] n squalifica; ~ (**from driving**) ritiro della patente.
disqualify [dɪs'kwɔlɪfaɪ] vt (SPORT) squalificare; to ~ sb from sth/from doing rendere qd incapace a qc/a fare; squalificare qd da qc/da fare.
disquiet [dɪs'kwaɪət] n inquietudine f.
disregard [dɪsrɪ'gɑːd] vt non far caso a, non badare a.

disrepair [dɪsrɪ'pɛə*] n cattivo stato.

disreputable [dɪs'rɛpjutəbl] a (person) di cattiva fama.

disrespectful [dɪsrɪ'spɛktful] a che manca di rispetto.

disrupt [dɪs'rʌpt] vt mettere in disordine; ~ion [-'rʌpʃən] n disordine m; interruzione f.

dissatisfaction [dɪssætɪs'fækʃən] n scontentezza, insoddisfazione f.

dissatisfied [dɪs'sætɪsfaɪd] a: ~ (with) scontento(a) or insoddisfatto(a) (di).

dissect [dɪ'sɛkt] vt sezionare.

disseminate [dɪ'sɛmɪneɪt] vt disseminare.

dissent [dɪ'sɛnt] n dissenso.

disservice [dɪs'sɜːvɪs] n: to do sb a ~ fare un cattivo servizio a qd.

dissident ['dɪsɪdnt] a dissidente.

dissimilar [dɪ'sɪmɪlə*] a: ~ (to) dissimile or diverso(a) (da).

dissipate ['dɪsɪpeɪt] vt dissipare; ~d a dissipato(a).

dissociate [dɪ'səʊʃɪeɪt] vt dissociare.

dissolute ['dɪsəluːt] a dissoluto(a), licenzioso(a).

dissolve [dɪ'zɒlv] vt dissolvere, sciogliere // vi dissolversi, sciogliersi; (fig) svanire.

dissuade [dɪ'sweɪd] vt: to ~ sb (from) dissuadere qd (da).

distance ['dɪstns] n distanza; in the ~ in lontananza.

distant ['dɪstnt] a lontano(a), distante; (manner) riservato(a), freddo(a).

distaste [dɪs'teɪst] n ripugnanza; ~ful a ripugnante, sgradevole.

distemper [dɪs'tɛmpə*] n (paint) tempera.

distend [dɪs'tɛnd] vt dilatare // vi dilatarsi.

distil [dɪs'tɪl] vt distillare; ~lery n distilleria.

distinct [dɪs'tɪŋkt] a distinto(a); (preference, progress) definito(a); ~ion [dɪs'tɪŋkʃən] n distinzione f; (in exam) lode f; ~ive a distintivo(a); ~ly ad chiaramente; manifestamente.

distinguish [dɪs'tɪŋgwɪʃ] vt distinguere; discernere; ~ed a (eminent) eminente; ~ing a (feature) distinto(a), caratteristico(a).

distort [dɪs'tɔːt] vt distorcere; (TECH) deformare; ~ion [dɪs'tɔːʃən] n distorsione f; deformazione f.

distract [dɪs'trækt] vt distrarre; ~ed a distratto(a); ~ion [dɪs'trækʃən] n distrazione f; to drive sb to ~ion spingere qd alla pazzia.

distraught [dɪs'trɔːt] a stravolto(a).

distress [dɪs'trɛs] n angoscia; (pain) dolore m // vt affliggere; ~ing a doloroso(a); ~ signal n segnale m di pericolo.

distribute [dɪs'trɪbjuːt] vt distribuire; **distribution** [-'bjuːʃən] n distribuzione f; **distributor** n distributore m.

district ['dɪstrɪkt] n (of country) regione f; (of town) quartiere m; (ADMIN) distretto; ~ attorney n (US) ≈ sostituto procuratore m della Repubblica; ~ nurse n (Brit) infermiera di quartiere.

distrust [dɪs'trʌst] n diffidenza, sfiducia // vt non aver fiducia in.

disturb [dɪs'tɜːb] vt disturbare; (inconvenience) scomodare; ~ance n disturbo; (political etc) tumulto; (by drunks etc) disordini mpl; ~ing a sconvolgente.

disuse [dɪs'juːs] n: to fall into ~ cadere in disuso.

disused [dɪs'juːzd] a abbandonato(a).

ditch [dɪtʃ] n fossa // vt (col) piantare in asso.

dither ['dɪðə*] vi vacillare.

ditto ['dɪtəʊ] ad idem.

divan [dɪ'væn] n divano.

dive [daɪv] n tuffo; (of submarine) immersione f; (AVIAT) picchiata; (pej) buco // vi tuffarsi; ~r n tuffatore/trice; palombaro.

diverge [daɪ'vɜːdʒ] vi divergere.

diverse [daɪ'vɜːs] a vario(a).

diversify [daɪ'vɜːsɪfaɪ] vt diversificare.

diversion [daɪ'vɜːʃən] n (AUT) deviazione f; (distraction) divertimento; (MIL) diversione f.

diversity [daɪ'vɜːsɪtɪ] n diversità f inv, varietà f inv.

divert [daɪ'vɜːt] vt deviare; (amuse) divertire.

divide [dɪ'vaɪd] vt dividere; (separate) separare // vi dividersi.

dividend ['dɪvɪdɛnd] n dividendo.

divine [dɪ'vaɪn] a divino(a).

diving ['daɪvɪŋ] n tuffo; ~ board n trampolino.

divinity [dɪ'vɪnɪtɪ] n divinità f inv; teologia.

division [dɪ'vɪʒən] n divisione f; separazione f.

divorce [dɪ'vɔːs] n divorzio // vt divorziare da; ~d a divorziato(a); ~e [-'siː] n divorziato/a.

divulge [daɪ'vʌldʒ] vt divulgare, rivelare.

D.I.Y. a,n abbr of **do-it-yourself.**

dizziness ['dɪzɪnɪs] n vertigini fpl.

dizzy ['dɪzɪ] a (height) vertiginoso(a); to feel ~ avere il capogiro.

DJ n abbr of **disc jockey.**

do, pt **did**, pp **done** [duː, dɪd, dʌn] vt, vi fare; **he didn't laugh, did he** no riso; ~ **you want any?** ne vuole?; **he laughed, didn't he?** lui ha riso, vero?; ~ **they?** ah sì?, vero?; **who broke it? - I did** chi l'ha rotto? - sono stato io; ~ **you agree? - I** ~ è d'accordo? - sì; **to** ~ **one's nails** farsi le unghie; **to** ~ **one's teeth** pulirsi i denti; **will it** ~? andrà bene?; **to** ~ **without** sth fare a meno di qc; **to** ~ **away with** vt fus abolire; **to** ~ **up** vt abbottonare; allacciare; (house etc) rimettere a nuovo.

docile ['dəʊsaɪl] a docile.

dock [dɒk] n bacino; (LAW) banco degli imputati // vi entrare in bacino; ~er n scaricatore m.

dockyard ['dɒkjɑːd] n cantiere m navale.

doctor ['dɒktə*] n medico/a; (Ph.D. etc) dottore/essa.

doctrine ['dɔktrɪn] n dottrina.

document ['dɔkjumənt] n documento; **~ary** [-'mɛntərɪ] a documentario(a) // n documentario; **~ation** [-'teɪʃən] n documentazione f.

doddering ['dɔdərɪŋ] a traballante.

dodge [dɔdʒ] n trucco; schivata // vt schivare, eludere.

dodgems ['dɔdʒəmz] npl autoscontro.

dog [dɔg] n cane m; **~ collar** n collare m di cane; (fig) collarino; **~-eared** a (book) con orecchie.

dogged ['dɔgɪd] a ostinato(a), tenace.

dogma ['dɔgmə] n dogma m; **~tic** [-'mætɪk] a dogmatico(a).

doings ['duːɪŋz] npl attività fpl.

do-it-yourself [duːɪtjɔː'sɛlf] n il far da sé.

doldrums ['dɔldrəmz] npl: **to be in the ~** essere giù.

dole [dəul] n (Brit) sussidio di disoccupazione; **to be on the ~** vivere del sussidio; **to ~ out** vt distribuire.

doleful ['dəulful] a triste, doloroso(a).

doll [dɔl] n bambola; **to ~ o.s. up** farsi bello(a).

dollar ['dɔlə*] n dollaro.

dolphin ['dɔlfɪn] n delfino.

domain [də'meɪn] n dominio.

dome [dəum] n cupola.

domestic [də'mɛstɪk] a (duty, happiness, animal) domestico(a); (policy, affairs, flights) nazionale; **~ated** a addomesticato(a).

domicile ['dɔmɪsaɪl] n domicilio.

dominant ['dɔmɪnənt] a dominante.

dominate ['dɔmɪneɪt] vt dominare; **domination** [-'neɪʃən] n dominazione f; **domineering** [-'nɪərɪŋ] a despotico(a), autoritario(a).

dominion [də'mɪnɪən] n dominio; sovranità; dominion m inv.

domino ['dɔmɪnəu] n domino; **~es** n (game) gioco del domino.

don [dɔn] n docente m/f universitario(a) // vt indossare.

donate [də'neɪt] vt donare; **donation** [də'neɪʃən] n donazione f.

done [dʌn] pp of **do**.

donkey ['dɔŋkɪ] n asino.

donor ['dəunə*] n donatore/trice.

don't [dəunt] vb = **do not**.

doom [duːm] n destino; rovina // vt: **to be ~ed (to failure)** essere predestinato(a) a fallire; **~sday** n il giorno del Giudizio.

door [dɔː*] n porta; **~bell** n campanello; **~ handle** n maniglia; **~man** n (in hotel) portiere m in livrea; (in block of flats) portinaio; **~mat** n stuoia della porta; **~step** n gradino della porta.

dope [dəup] n (col: drugs) roba // vt (horse etc) drogare.

dopey ['dəupɪ] a (col) inebetito(a).

dormant ['dɔːmənt] a inattivo(a); (fig) latente.

dormitory ['dɔːmɪtrɪ] n dormitorio.

dormouse, pl **dormice** ['dɔːmaus, -maɪs] n ghiro.

dose [dəus] n dose f; (bout) attacco.

doss house ['dɔshaus] n asilo notturno.

dot [dɔt] n punto; macchiolina; **on the ~** in punto.

dote [dəut]: **to ~ on** vt fus essere infatuato(a) di.

dotted line [dɔtɪd'laɪn] n linea puntata.

double ['dʌbl] a doppio(a) // ad (fold) in due, doppio; (twice): **to cost ~ (sth)** costare il doppio (di qc) // n sosia m inv; (CINEMA) controfigura // vt raddoppiare; (fold) piegare doppio or in due // vi raddoppiarsi; **at the ~** a passo di corsa; **~s** n (TENNIS) doppio; **~ bass** n contrabbasso; **~ bed** n letto matrimoniale; **~ bend** n doppia curva; **~-breasted** a a doppio petto; **~cross** vt fare il doppio gioco con; **~decker** n autobus m inv a due piani; **~ parking** n parcheggio in doppia fila; **~ room** n camera per due; **doubly** ad doppiamente.

doubt [daut] n dubbio // vt dubitare di; **to ~ that** dubitare che + sub; **~ful** a dubbioso(a), incerto(a); (person) equivoco(a); **~less** ad indubbiamente.

dough [dəu] n pasta, impasto; **~nut** n bombolone m.

dove [dʌv] n colombo/a.

dovetail ['dʌvteɪl] n: **~ joint** n incastro a coda di rondine // vi (fig) combaciare.

dowdy ['daudɪ] a trasandato(a); malvestito(a).

down [daun] n (fluff) piumino // ad giù, di sotto // prep giù per // vt (col: drink) scolarsi; **~ with X!** abbasso X!; **~-at-heel** a scalcagnato(a); (fig) trasandato(a); **~cast** a abbattuto(a); **~fall** n caduta; rovina; **~hearted** a scoraggiato(a); **~hill** ad: **to go ~hill** andare in discesa; **~ payment** n acconto; **~pour** n scroscio di pioggia; **~right** a onesto(a), franco(a); (refusal) assoluto(a); **~stairs** ad giù di sotto; al piano inferiore; **~stream** ad a valle; **~-to-earth** a pratico(a); **~town** ad in città // a (US): **~town Chicago** il centro di Chicago; **~ward** ['daunwəd] a,ad, **~wards** ['daunwədz] ad in giù, in discesa.

dowry ['daurɪ] n dote f.

doz. abbr of **dozen**.

doze [dəuz] vi sonnecchiare; **to ~ off** vi appisolarsi.

dozen ['dʌzn] n dozzina; **a ~ books** una dozzina di libri.

Dr. abbr of **doctor**; **drive** (n).

drab [dræb] a tetro(a), grigio(a).

draft [drɑːft] n abbozzo; (COMM) tratta; (US: MIL) contingente m; (: call-up) leva // vt abbozzare; see also **draught**.

drag [dræg] vt trascinare; (river) dragare // vi trascinarsi // n (col) noioso/a; noia, fatica; **to ~ on** vi tirar avanti lentamente.

dragonfly ['drægənflaɪ] n libellula.

drain [dreɪn] n canale m di scolo; (for sewage) fogna; (on resources) salasso // vt (land, marshes) prosciugare; (vegetables) scolare; (reservoir etc) vuotare // vi (water) defluire (via); **~age** n prosciugamento; fognatura; **~ing board, ~board**

(*US*) *n* asciugapiatti *m inv*; ~**pipe** *n* tubo di scarico.

drama ['drɑːmə] *n* (*art*) dramma *m*, teatro; (*play*) commedia; (*event*) dramma; ~**tic** [drə'mætɪk] *a* drammatico(a); ~**tist** ['dræmətɪst] *n* drammaturgo/a.

drank [dræŋk] *pt of* **drink**.

drape [dreɪp] *vt* drappeggiare; ~**s** *npl* (*US*) tende *fpl*; ~**r** *n* negoziante *m/f* di stoffe.

drastic ['dræstɪk] *a* drastico(a).

draught [drɑːft] *n* corrente *f* d'aria; (*NAUT*) pescaggio; ~**s** *n* (gioco della) dama; **on** ~ (*beer*) alla spina; ~**board** *n* scacchiera.

draughtsman ['drɑːftsmən] *n* disegnatore *m*.

draw [drɔː] *vb* (*pt* **drew**, *pp* **drawn** [druː, drɔːn]) *vt* tirare; (*attract*) attirare; (*picture*) disegnare; (*line, circle*) tracciare; (*money*) ritirare // *vi* (*SPORT*) pareggiare // *n* pareggio; estrazione *f*; attrazione *f*; **to** ~ **to a close** avvicinarsi alla conclusione; **to** ~ **near** *vi* avvicinarsi; **to** ~ **out** *vi* (*lengthen*) allungarsi // *vt* (*money*) ritirare; **to** ~ **up** *vi* (*stop*) arrestarsi, fermarsi // *vt* (*document*) compilare; ~**back** *n* svantaggio, inconveniente *m*; ~**bridge** *n* ponte *m* levatoio.

drawer [drɔː*] *n* cassetto.

drawing ['drɔːɪŋ] *n* disegno; ~ **board** *n* tavola da disegno; ~ **pin** *n* puntina da disegno; ~ **room** *n* salotto.

drawl [drɔːl] *n* pronuncia strascicata.

drawn [drɔːn] *pp of* **draw**.

dread [drɛd] *n* terrore *m* // *vt* tremare all'idea di; ~**ful** *a* terribile.

dream [driːm] *n* sogno // *vt, vi* (*pt, pp* **dreamed** *or* **dreamt** [drɛmt]) sognare; ~**er** *n* sognatore/trice; ~**y** *a* sognante.

dreary ['drɪərɪ] *a* tetro(a); monotono(a).

dredge [drɛdʒ] *vt* dragare; ~**r** *n* draga; (*also.* **sugar** ~**r**) spargizucchero *m inv*.

dregs [drɛgz] *npl* feccia.

drench [drɛntʃ] *vt* inzuppare.

dress [drɛs] *n* vestito; (*clothing*) abbigliamento // *vt* vestire; (*wound*) fasciare; (*food*) condire; preparare // *vi* vestirsi; **to** ~ **up** *vi* vestirsi a festa; (*in fancy dress*) vestirsi in costume; ~ **circle** *n* prima galleria; ~**er** *n* (*THEATRE*) assistente *m/f* del camerino; (*furniture*) credenza; ~**ing** *n* (*MED*) benda; (*CULIN*) condimento; ~**ing gown** *n* vestaglia; ~**ing room** *n* (*THEATRE*) camerino; (*SPORT*) spogliatoio; ~**ing table** *n* toilette *f inv*; ~**maker** *n* sarta; ~**making** *n* sartoria; confezioni *fpl* per donna; ~ **rehearsal** *n* prova generale; ~ **shirt** *n* camicia da sera.

drew [druː] *pt of* **draw**.

dribble ['drɪbl] *vi* gocciolare; (*baby*) sbavare.

dried [draɪd] *a* (*fruit, beans*) secco(a); (*eggs, milk*) in polvere.

drift [drɪft] *n* (*of current etc*) direzione *f*, forza; (*of sand etc*) turbine *m*; (*of snow*) cumulo; turbine; (*general meaning*) senso

// *vi* (*boat*) essere trasportato(a) dalla corrente; (*sand, snow*) ammucchiarsi; ~**wood** *n* resti *mpl* della mareggiata.

drill [drɪl] *n* trapano; (*MIL*) esercitazione *f* // *vt* trapanare // *vi* (*for oil*) fare perforazioni.

drink [drɪŋk] *n* bevanda, bibita // *vt, vi* (*pt* **drank**, *pp* **drunk** [dræŋk, drʌŋk]) bere; **to have a** ~ bere qualcosa; ~**er** *n* bevitore/trice; ~**ing water** *n* acqua potabile.

drip [drɪp] *n* goccia; gocciolamento; (*MED*) apparecchio per fleboclisi // *vi* gocciolare; (*washing*) sgocciolare; (*wall*) trasudare; ~**-dry** *a* (*shirt*) che non si stira; ~**ping** *n* grasso d'arrosto; ~**ping wet** *a* fradicio(a).

drive [draɪv] *n* passeggiata *or* giro in macchina; (*also*: ~**way**) viale *m* d'accesso; (*energy*) energia; (*PSYCH*) impulso; bisogno; (*push*) sforzo eccezionale; campagna; (*SPORT*) drive *m inv*; (*TECH*) trasmissione *f*; propulsione *f*; presa // *vb* (*pt* **drove**, *pp* **driven** ['drəuv, 'drɪvn]) *vt* guidare; (*nail*) piantare; (*push*) cacciare, spingere; (*TECH: motor*) azionare; far funzionare // *vi* (*AUT: at controls*) guidare; (: *travel*) andare in macchina; **left-/right-hand** ~ guida a sinistra/destra.

driver ['draɪvə*] *n* conducente *m/f*; (*of taxi*) tassista *m*; (*of bus*) autista *m*.

driving ['draɪvɪŋ] *a*: ~ **rain** *n* pioggia sferzante // *n* guida; ~ **instructor** *n* istruttore/trice di scuola guida; ~ **lesson** *n* lezione *f* di guida; ~ **licence** *n* (*Brit*) patente *f* di guida; ~ **school** *n* scuola *f* guida *inv*; ~ **test** *n* esame *m* di guida.

drizzle ['drɪzl] *n* pioggerella // *vi* piovigginare.

droll [drəul] *a* buffo(a).

dromedary ['drɒmədərɪ] *n* dromedario.

drone [drəun] *n* ronzio; (*male bee*) fuco.

drool [druːl] *vi* sbavare.

droop [druːp] *vi* abbassarsi; languire.

drop [drɒp] *n* goccia; (*fall*) caduta; (*also*: **parachute** ~) lancio; (*of cliff*) discesa // *vt* lasciare cadere; (*voice, eyes, price*) abbassare; (*set down from car*) far scendere // *vi* cascare; **to** ~ **off** *vi* (*sleep*) addormentarsi; **to** ~ **out** *vi* (*withdraw*) ritirarsi; (*student etc*) smettere di studiare; ~**pings** *npl* sterco.

dross [drɒs] *n* scoria; scarto.

drought [draut] *n* siccità *f inv*.

drove [drəuv] *pt of* **drive** // *n*: ~**s of people** una moltitudine di persone.

drown [draun] *vt* affogare // *vi* affogarsi.

drowsy ['drauzɪ] *a* sonnolento(a), assonnato(a).

drudge [drʌdʒ] *n* bestia da fatica; ~**ry** ['drʌdʒərɪ] *n* lavoro faticoso.

drug [drʌg] *n* farmaco; (*narcotic*) droga // *vt* drogare; ~ **addict** *n* tossicomane *m/f*; ~**gist** *n* (*US*) persona che gestisce un drugstore; ~**store** *n* (*US*) drugstore *m inv*.

drum [drʌm] *n* tamburo; (*for oil, petrol*) fusto; ~**mer** *n* batterista *m/f*.

drunk [drʌŋk] *pp of* **drink** // a ubriaco(a); ebbro(a) // *n* ubriacone/a; **~ard** ['drʌŋkəd] *n* ubriacone/a; **~en** a ubriaco(a); da ubriaco; **~enness** *n* ubriachezza; ebbrezza.

dry [draɪ] a secco(a); (*day, clothes*) asciutto(a) // *vt* seccare; (*clothes*) asciugare // *vi* asciugarsi; **to ~ up** *vi* seccarsi; **~-cleaner's** *n* lavasecco *m inv*; **~er** *n* essiccatore *m*; **~ rot** *n* fungo del legno.

dual ['djuəl] a doppio(a); **~ carriageway** *n* strada a doppia carreggiata; **~ nationality** *n* doppia nazionalità; **~-purpose** a doppio uso.

dubbed [dʌbd] a (*CINEMA*) doppiato(a); (*nicknamed*) soprannominato(a).

dubious ['djuːbɪəs] a dubbio(a).

duchess ['dʌtʃɪs] *n* duchessa.

duck [dʌk] *n* anatra // *vi* abbassare la testa; **~ling** *n* anatroccolo.

duct [dʌkt] *n* condotto; (*ANAT*) canale *m*.

dud [dʌd] *n* (*shell*) proiettile *m* che fa cilecca; (*object, tool*): **it's a ~** è inutile, non funziona // a (*cheque*) a vuoto; (*note, coin*) falso(a).

due [djuː] a dovuto(a); (*expected*) atteso(a); (*fitting*) giusto(a) // *n* dovuto // ad: **~ north** diritto verso nord; **~s** *npl* (*for club, union*) quota; (*in harbour*) diritti *mpl* di porto; **in ~ course** a tempo debito; finalmente; **~ to** dovuto a; a causa di.

duel ['djuəl] *n* duello.

duet [djuː'ɛt] *n* duetto.

dug [dʌg] *pt, pp of* **dig.**

duke [djuːk] *n* duca *m*.

dull [dʌl] a noioso(a); ottuso(a); (*sound, pain*) sordo(a); (*weather, day*) fosco(a), scuro(a); (*blade*) smussato(a) // *vt* (*pain, grief*) attutire; (*mind, senses*) intorpidire.

duly ['djuːlɪ] ad (*on time*) a tempo debito; (*as expected*) debitamente.

dumb [dʌm] a muto(a); (*stupid*) stupido(a); **dumbfounded** [dʌm'faundɪd] a stupito(a), stordito(a).

dummy ['dʌmɪ] *n* (*tailor's model*) manichino; (*SPORT*) finto; (*for baby*) tettarella // a falso(a), finto(a).

dump [dʌmp] *n* mucchio di rifiuti; (*place*) luogo di scarico; (*MIL*) deposito // *vt* (*put down*) scaricare; mettere giù; (*get rid of*) buttar via; (*ECON*) dumping *m*; (*of rubbish*): **'no ~ing'** 'vietato lo scarico'.

dumpling ['dʌmplɪŋ] *n* specie di gnocco.

dunce [dʌns] *n* asino.

dune [djuːn] *n* duna.

dung [dʌŋ] *n* concime *m*.

dungarees [dʌŋgə'riːz] *npl* tuta.

dungeon ['dʌndʒən] *n* prigione *f* sotterranea.

dupe [djuːp] *vt* gabbare, ingannare.

duplicate *n* ['djuːplɪkət] doppio // *vt* ['djuːplɪkeɪt] raddoppiare; (*on machine*) ciclostilare; **in ~** in duplice copia.

durable ['djuərəbl] a durevole; (*clothes, metal*) resistente.

duration [djuə'reɪʃən] *n* durata.

duress [djuə'rɛs] *n*: **under ~** sotto costrizione.

during ['djuərɪŋ] *prep* durante, nel corso di.

dusk [dʌsk] *n* crepuscolo; **~y** a scuro(a).

dust [dʌst] *n* polvere *f* // *vt* (*furniture*) spolverare; (*cake etc*): **to ~ with** cospargere con; **~bin** *n* (*Brit*) pattumiera; **~er** *n* straccio per la polvere; **~ jacket** *n* sopraccoperta; **~man** *n* (*Brit*) netturbino; **~y** a polveroso(a).

Dutch [dʌtʃ] a olandese // *n* (*LING*) olandese *m*; **the ~** gli Olandesi; **~man/woman** *n* olandese *m/f*.

duty ['djuːtɪ] *n* dovere *m*; (*tax*) dazio, tassa; **duties** *npl* mansioni *fpl*; **on ~** di servizio; **off ~** libero(a), fuori servizio; **~-free** a esente da dazio.

dwarf [dwɔːf] *n* nano/a // *vt* far apparire piccolo.

dwell, *pt, pp* **dwelt** [dwɛl, dwɛlt] *vi* dimorare; **to ~ on** *vt fus* indugiare su; **~ing** *n* dimora.

dwindle ['dwɪndl] *vi* diminuire, decrescere.

dye [daɪ] *n* tinta // *vt* tingere.

dying ['daɪɪŋ] a morente, moribondo(a).

dyke [daɪk] *n* diga.

dynamic [daɪ'næmɪk] a dinamico(a); **~s** *n or npl* dinamica.

dynamite ['daɪnəmaɪt] *n* dinamite *f*.

dynamo ['daɪnəməu] *n* dinamo *f inv*.

dynasty ['dɪnəstɪ] *n* dinastia.

dysentery ['dɪsntrɪ] *n* dissenteria.

E

E [iː] *n* (*MUS*) mi *m*.

each [iːtʃ] *det* ogni, ciascuno(a) // *pronoun* ciascuno(a), ognuno(a); **~ one** ognuno(a), ognuno(a); **~ other** si (*or* ci *etc*); **they hate ~ other** si odiano (l'un l'altro); **you are jealous of ~ other** siete gelosi l'uno dell'altro.

eager ['iːgə*] a impaziente; desideroso(a); ardente; **to be ~ to do sth** non veder l'ora di fare qc; essere desideroso di fare qc; **to be ~ for** essere desideroso di, aver gran voglia di.

eagle ['iːgl] *n* aquila.

ear [ɪə*] *n* orecchio; (*of corn*) pannocchia; **~ache** *n* mal *m* d'orecchi; **~drum** *n* timpano.

earl [əːl] *n* conte *m*.

early ['əːlɪ] ad presto, di buon'ora; (*ahead of time*) in anticipo // a precoce; anticipato(a); che si fa vedere di buon'ora; **have an ~ night/start** vada a letto/parta presto; **in the ~ or ~ in the spring/19th century** all'inizio della primavera/dell'Ottocento; **~ retirement** *n* ritiro anticipato.

earmark ['ɪəmɑːk] *vt*: **to ~ sth for** destinare qc a.

earn [əːn] *vt* guadagnare; (*rest, reward*) meritare; **this ~ed him much praise, he ~ed much praise for this** si è attirato grandi lodi per questo.

earnest ['ə:nɪst] *a* serio(a); **in ~** *ad* sul serio.

earnings ['ə:nɪŋz] *npl* guadagni *mpl*; (*salary*) stipendio.

earphones ['ɪəfəunz] *npl* cuffia.

earring ['ɪərɪŋ] *n* orecchino.

earshot ['ɪəʃɔt] *n*: **out of/within ~** fuori portata/a portata di orecchio.

earth [ə:θ] *n* (*gen, also* ELEC) terra; (*of fox etc*) tana // *vt* (ELEC) mettere a terra; **~enware** *n* terracotta; stoviglie *fpl* di terracotta // *a* di terracotta; **~quake** *n* terremoto; **~ tremor** *n* scossa sismica; **~y** *a* (*fig*) grossolano(a).

earwig ['ɪəwɪg] *n* forbicina.

ease [i:z] *n* agio, comodo // *vt* (*soothe*) calmare; (*loosen*) allentare; **to ~ sth out/in** tirare fuori/infilare qc con delicatezza; facilitare l'uscita/l'entrata di qc; **life of ~** vita comoda; **at ~** all'agio; (MIL) a riposo; **to ~ off** *or* **up** *vi* diminuire; (*slow down*) rallentarsi; (*fig*) rilassarsi.

easel ['i:zl] *n* cavalletto.

easily ['i:zɪlɪ] *ad* facilmente.

east [i:st] *n* est *m* // *a* dell'est // *ad* a oriente; **the E~** l'Oriente *m*.

Easter ['i:stə*] *n* Pasqua.

easterly ['i:stəlɪ] *a* dall'est, d'oriente.

eastern ['i:stən] *a* orientale, d'oriente.

East Germany [i:st'dʒə:mənɪ] *n* Germania dell'Est.

eastward(s) ['i:stwəd(z)] *ad* verso est, verso levante.

easy ['i:zɪ] *a* facile; (*manner*) disinvolto(a) // *ad*: **to take it** *or* **things ~** prendersela con calma; **~ chair** *n* poltrona; **~ going** *a* accomodante.

eat, *pt* **ate**, *pp* **eaten** [i:t, eɪt, 'i:tn] *vt* mangiare; **to ~ into** *vt fus* rodere; **~able** *a* mangiabile; (*safe to eat*) commestibile.

eaves [i:vz] *npl* gronda.

eavesdrop ['i:vzdrɔp] *vi*: **to ~ (on a conversation)** origliare (una conversazione).

ebb [ɛb] *n* riflusso // *vi* rifluire; (*fig: also*: **~ away**) declinare.

ebony ['ɛbənɪ] *n* ebano.

ebullient [ɪ'bʌlɪənt] *a* esuberante.

eccentric [ɪk'sɛntrɪk] *a,n* eccentrico(a).

ecclesiastic [ɪkli:zɪ'æstɪk] *n* ecclesiastico; **~al** *a* ecclesiastico(a).

echo, **~es** ['ɛkəu] *n* eco *m or f* // *vt* ripetere; fare eco a // *vi* echeggiare; dare un eco.

eclipse [ɪ'klɪps] *n* eclissi *f inv* // *vt* eclissare.

ecology [ɪ'kɔlədʒɪ] *n* ecologia.

economic [i:kə'nɔmɪk] *a* economico(a); **~al** *a* economico(a); (*person*) economo(a); **~s** *n* economia.

economist [ɪ'kɔnəmɪst] *n* economo/a.

economize [ɪ'kɔnəmaɪz] *vi* risparmiare, fare economia.

economy [ɪ'kɔnəmɪ] *n* economia.

ecstasy ['ɛkstəsɪ] *n* estasi *f inv*; **to go into**

ecstasies over andare in estasi davanti a; **ecstatic** [-'tætɪk] *a* estatico(a), in estasi.

ecumenical [i:kju'mɛnɪkl] *a* ecumenico(a).

eczema ['ɛksɪmə] *n* eczema *m*.

eddy ['ɛdɪ] *n* mulinello.

edge [ɛdʒ] *n* margine *m*; (*of table, plate, cup*) orlo; (*of knife etc*) taglio // *vt* bordare; **on ~** (*fig*) = **edgy**; **to have the ~ on** essere in vantaggio su; **to ~ away from** sgattaiolare da; **~ways** *ad* di fianco; **he couldn't get a word in ~ways** non riuscì a dire una parola.

edgy ['ɛdʒɪ] *a* nervoso(a).

edible ['ɛdɪbl] *a* commestibile; (*meal*) mangiabile.

edict ['i:dɪkt] *n* editto.

edifice ['ɛdɪfɪs] *n* edificio.

edit ['ɛdɪt] *vt* curare; **~ion** [ɪ'dɪʃən] *n* edizione *f*; **~or** *n* (*in newspaper*) redattore/trice; redattore/trice capo; (*of sb's work*) curatore/trice; **~orial** [-'tɔ:rɪəl] *a* redazionale, editoriale // *n* editoriale *m*.

educate ['ɛdjukeɪt] *vt* istruire; educare.

education [ɛdju'keɪʃən] *n* educazione *f*; (*schooling*) istruzione *f*; **~al** *a* pedagogico(a); scolastico(a); istruttivo(a).

EEC *n* (*abbr of European Economic Community*) C.E.E. *f* (*Comunità Economica Europea*).

eel [i:l] *n* anguilla.

eerie ['ɪərɪ] *a* che fa accapponare la pelle.

effect [ɪ'fɛkt] *n* effetto // *vt* effettuare; **~s** *npl* (THEATRE) effetti *mpl* scenici; **to take ~** (*law*) entrare in vigore; (*drug*) fare effetto; **in ~** effettivamente; **~ive** *a* efficace; **~iveness** *n* efficacia.

effeminate [ɪ'fɛmɪnɪt] *a* effeminato(a).

effervescent [ɛfə'vɛsnt] *a* effervescente.

efficacy ['ɛfɪkəsɪ] *n* efficacia.

efficiency [ɪ'fɪʃənsɪ] *n* efficienza; rendimento effettivo.

efficient [ɪ'fɪʃənt] *a* efficiente.

effigy ['ɛfɪdʒɪ] *n* effigie *f*.

effort ['ɛfət] *n* sforzo; **~less** *a* senza sforzo, facile.

effrontery [ɪ'frʌntərɪ] *n* sfrontatezza.

e.g. *ad* (*abbr of exempli gratia*) per esempio, p.es.

egalitarian [ɪgælɪ'tɛərɪən] *a* egualitario(a).

egg [ɛg] *n* uovo; **to ~ on** *vt* incitare; **~cup** *n* portauovo *m inv*; **~plant** *n* melanzana; **~shell** *n* guscio d'uovo.

ego ['i:gəu] *n* ego *m inv*.

egotist ['ɛgəutɪst] *n* egotista *m/f*.

Egypt ['i:dʒɪpt] *n* Egitto; **~ian** [ɪ'dʒɪpʃən] *a, n* egiziano(a).

eiderdown ['aɪdədaun] *n* piumino.

eight [eɪt] *num* otto; **~een** *num* diciotto; **eighth** [eɪtθ] *num* ottavo(a); **~y** *num* ottanta.

Eire ['ɛərə] *n* Repubblica d'Irlanda.

either ['aɪðə*] *det* l'uno(a) o l'altro(a); (*both, each*) ciascuno(a); **on ~ side** su ciascun lato // *pronoun*: **~ (of them)** (o) l'uno(a) o l'altro(a); **I don't like ~** non mi piace né l'uno né l'altro // ad neanche; **no, I don't** ~ no, neanch'io // cj: ~ **good or bad** o buono o cattivo.

ejaculation [ɪdʒækju'leɪʃən] n (PHYSIOL) eiaculazione f.

eject [ɪ'dʒɛkt] vt espellere; lanciare; ~ **or seat** n sedile m eiettabile.

eke [iːk]: **to** ~ **out** vt far durare; aumentare.

elaborate a [ɪ'læbərɪt] elaborato(a), minuzioso(a) // vb [ɪ'læbəreɪt] vt elaborare // vi fornire i particolari.

elapse [ɪ'læps] vi trascorrere, passare.

elastic [ɪ'læstɪk] a elastico(a) // n elastico; ~ **band** n elastico.

elated [ɪ'leɪtɪd] a pieno(a) di gioia.

elation [ɪ'leɪʃən] n gioia.

elbow ['ɛlbəu] n gomito.

elder ['ɛldə*] a maggiore, più vecchio(a) // n (tree) sambuco; **one's** ~s i più anziani; ~**ly** a anziano(a).

eldest ['ɛldɪst] a,n: **the** ~ **(child)** il(la) maggiore (dei bambini).

elect [ɪ'lɛkt] vt eleggere; **to** ~ **to do** decidere di fare // a: **the president** ~ il presidente designato; ~**ion** [ɪ'lɛkʃən] n elezione f; ~**ioneering** [ɪlɛkʃə'nɪərɪŋ] n propaganda elettorale; ~**or** n elettore/trice; ~**oral** a elettorale; ~**orate** n elettorato.

electric [ɪ'lɛktrɪk] a elettrico; ~**al** a elettrico(a); ~ **blanket** n coperta elettrica; ~ **chair** n sedia elettrica; ~ **cooker** n cucina elettrica; ~ **current** n corrente f elettrica; ~ **fire** n stufa elettrica.

electrician [ɪlɛk'trɪʃən] n elettricista m.

electricity [ɪlɛk'trɪsɪtɪ] n elettricità.

electrify [ɪ'lɛktrɪfaɪ] vt (RAIL) elettrificare; (audience) elettrizzare.

electro... [ɪ'lɛktrəu] prefix: **electrocute** [-kjuːt] vt fulminare; **electrode** [ɪ'lɛktrəud] n elettrodo.

electron [ɪ'lɛktrɔn] n elettrone m.

electronic [ɪlɛk'trɔnɪk] a elettronico(a); ~s n elettronica.

elegance ['ɛlɪgəns] n eleganza.

elegant ['ɛlɪgənt] a elegante.

element ['ɛlɪmənt] n elemento; (of heater, kettle etc) resistenza; ~**ary** [-'mɛntərɪ] a elementare.

elephant ['ɛlɪfənt] n elefante/essa.

elevate ['ɛlɪveɪt] vt elevare.

elevation [ɛlɪ'veɪʃən] n elevazione f; (height) altitudine f.

elevator ['ɛlɪveɪtə*] n elevatore m; (US: lift) ascensore m.

eleven [ɪ'lɛvn] num undici; ~**ses** npl caffè m a metà mattina; ~**th** a undicesimo(a).

elf, elves [ɛlf, ɛlvz] n elfo.

elicit [ɪ'lɪsɪt] vt: **to** ~ **(from)** trarre (da), cavare fuori (da).

eligible ['ɛlɪdʒəbl] a eleggibile; (for membership) che ha i requisiti.

eliminate [ɪ'lɪmɪneɪt] vt eliminare; **elimination** n eliminazione f.

élite [eɪ'liːt] n élite f inv.

ellipse [ɪ'lɪps] n ellisse f.

elm [ɛlm] n olmo.

elocution [ɛlə'kjuːʃən] n elocuzione f.

elongated ['iːlɔŋgeɪtɪd] a allungato(a).

elope [ɪ'ləup] vi (lovers) scappare; ~**ment** n fuga romantica.

eloquence ['ɛlɔkwəns] n eloquenza.

eloquent ['ɛlɔkwənt] a eloquente.

else [ɛls] ad altro; **something** ~ qualcos'altro; **somewhere** ~ altrove; **everywhere** ~ in qualsiasi altro luogo; **where** ~? in quale altro luogo?; **little** ~ poco altro; ~**where** ad altrove.

elucidate [ɪ'luːsɪdeɪt] vt delucidare.

elude [ɪ'luːd] vt eludere.

elusive [ɪ'luːsɪv] a elusivo(a); (answer) evasivo(a).

elves [ɛlvz] npl of elf.

emaciated [ɪ'meɪsɪeɪtɪd] a emaciato(a).

emanate ['ɛməneɪt] vi: **to** ~ **from** emanare da.

emancipate [ɪ'mænsɪpeɪt] vt emancipare; **emancipation** [-'peɪʃən] n emancipazione f.

embalm [ɪm'bɑːm] vt imbalsamare.

embankment [ɪm'bæŋkmənt] n (of road, railway) terrapieno; (riverside) argine m; (dyke) diga.

embargo [ɪm'bɑːgəu], ~**es** [ɪm'bɑːgəu] n embargo.

embark [ɪm'bɑːk] vi: **to** ~ **(on)** imbarcarsi (su) // vt imbarcare; **to** ~ **on** (fig) imbarcarsi in; ~**ation** [ɛmbɑː'keɪʃən] n imbarco.

embarrass [ɪm'bærəs] vt imbarazzare; ~**ing** a imbarazzante; ~**ment** n imbarazzo.

embassy ['ɛmbəsɪ] n ambasciata.

embed [ɪm'bɛd] vt conficcare, incastrare.

embellish [ɪm'bɛlɪʃ] vt abbellire.

embers ['ɛmbəz] npl braci fpl.

embezzle [ɪm'bɛzl] vt appropriarsi indebitamente di; ~**ment** n appropriazione f indebita, malversazione f.

embitter [ɪm'bɪtə*] vt amareggiare; inasprire.

emblem ['ɛmbləm] n emblema m.

embodiment [ɪm'bɔdɪmənt] n personificazione f, incarnazione f.

embody [ɪm'bɔdɪ] vt (features) racchiudere, comprendere; (ideas) dar forma concreta a, esprimere.

embossed [ɪm'bɔst] a in rilievo; goffrato(a).

embrace [ɪm'breɪs] vt abbracciare // n abbraccio.

embroider [ɪm'brɔɪdə*] vt ricamare; (fig: story) abbellire; ~**y** n ricamo.

embryo ['ɛmbrɪəu] n (also fig) embrione m.

emerald ['ɛmərəld] n smeraldo.

emerge [ɪ'məːdʒ] vi apparire, sorgere.

emergence [ɪ'məːdʒəns] n apparizione f.

emergency [ɪ'məːdʒənsɪ] n emergenza; **in an** ~ in caso di emergenza; ~ **exit** n uscita di sicurezza.

emergent [ɪ'məːdʒənt] a: ~ **nation** paese :.. in via di sviluppo.

emery ['ɛmərɪ] n: ~ **board** n limetta di carta smerigliata; ~ **paper** n carta smerigliata.

emetic [ɪ'mɛtɪk] n emetico.

emigrant ['ɛmɪgrənt] n emigrante m/f.

emigrate ['ɛmɪgreɪt] vi emigrare; **emigration** [-'greɪʃən] n emigrazione f.

eminence ['ɛmɪnəns] n eminenza.

eminent ['ɛmɪnənt] a eminente.

emission [ɪ'mɪʃən] n emissione f.

emit [ɪ'mɪt] vt emettere.

emotion [ɪ'məʊʃən] n emozione f; ~**al** a (person) emotivo(a); (scene) commovente; (tone, speech) carico(a) d'emozione; ~**ally** ad: ~**ally disturbed** con turbe emotive.

emotive [ɪ'məʊtɪv] a emotivo(a).

emperor ['ɛmpərə*] n imperatore m.

emphasis, pl **ases** ['ɛmfəsɪs, -siːz] n enfasi f inv; importanza.

emphasize ['ɛmfəsaɪz] vt (word, point) sottolineare; (feature) mettere in evidenza.

emphatic [ɛm'fætɪk] a (strong) vigoroso(a); (unambiguous, clear) netto(a); ~**ally** ad vigorosamente; nettamente.

empire ['ɛmpaɪə*] n impero.

empirical [ɛm'pɪrɪkl] a empirico(a).

employ [ɪm'plɔɪ] vt impiegare; ~**ee** [-'iː] n impiegato/a; ~**er** n principale m/f, datore m di lavoro; ~**ment** n impiego; ~**ment agency** n agenzia di collocamento.

empower [ɪm'paʊə*] vt: to ~ **sb to do** concedere autorità a qd di fare.

empress ['ɛmprɪs] n imperatrice f.

emptiness ['ɛmptɪnɪs] n vuoto.

empty ['ɛmptɪ] a vuoto(a); (threat, promise) vano(a) // vt vuotare // vi vuotarsi; (liquid) scaricarsi; **on an** ~ **stomach** a stomaco vuoto; ~-**handed** a a mani vuote.

emulate ['ɛmjuleɪt] vt emulare.

emulsion [ɪ'mʌlʃən] n emulsione f; ~ (paint) n colore m a tempera.

enable [ɪ'neɪbl] vt: to ~ **sb to do** permettere a qd di fare.

enamel [ɪ'næməl] n smalto.

enamoured [ɪ'næməd] a: ~ **of** innamorato(a) di.

enchant [ɪn'tʃɑːnt] vt incantare; (subj: magic spell) catturare; ~**ing** a incantevole, affascinante.

encircle [ɪn'sɜːkl] vt accerchiare.

encl. (abbr of enclosed) all.

enclose [ɪn'kləʊz] vt (land) circondare, recingere; (letter etc): to ~ (**with**) allegare (con); **please find** ~**d** trovi qui accluso.

enclosure [ɪn'kləʊʒə*] n recinto; (COMM) allegato.

encore [ɔŋ'kɔː*] excl, n bis (m inv).

encounter [ɪn'kaʊntə*] n incontro // vt incontrare.

encourage [ɪn'kʌrɪdʒ] vt incoraggiare; ~**ment** n incoraggiamento.

encroach [ɪn'krəʊtʃ] vi: to ~ (**up**)**on**

(rights) usurpare; (time) abusare di; (land) oltrepassare i limiti di.

encyclop(a)edia [ɛnsaɪkləʊ'piːdɪə] n enciclopedia.

end [ɛnd] n fine f; (aim) fine m; (of table) bordo estremo // vt finire; (also: **bring to an** ~, **put an** ~ **to**) mettere fine a // vi finire; **to come to an** ~ arrivare alla fine, finire; **in the** ~ alla fine; **at the** ~ **of the street** in fondo alla strada; **on** ~ (object) ritto(a); **for 5 hours on** ~ per 5 ore di fila; **to** ~ **up** vi: **to** ~ **up in** finire in.

endanger [ɪn'deɪndʒə*] vt mettere in pericolo.

endearing [ɪn'dɪərɪŋ] a accattivante.

endeavour [ɪn'dɛvə*] n sforzo, tentativo // vi: **to** ~ **to do** cercare or sforzarsi di fare.

ending ['ɛndɪŋ] n fine f, conclusione f; (LING) desinenza.

endless ['ɛndlɪs] a senza fine; (patience, resources) infinito(a).

endorse [ɪn'dɔːs] vt (cheque) girare; (approve) approvare, appoggiare; ~**ment** n (on driving licence) contravvenzione registrata sulla patente.

endow [ɪn'daʊ] vt (provide with money) devolvere denaro a; (equip): **to** ~ **with** fornire di, dotare di.

end product ['ɛndprɔdəkt] n prodotto finito; (fig) risultato.

endurance [ɪn'djuərəns] n resistenza; pazienza.

endure [ɪn'djuə*] vt sopportare, resistere a // vi durare.

enemy ['ɛnəmɪ] a,n nemico(a).

energetic [ɛnə'dʒɛtɪk] a energico(a); attivo(a).

energy ['ɛnədʒɪ] n energia.

enervating ['ɛnəveɪtɪŋ] a debilitante.

enforce [ɪn'fɔːs] vt (LAW) applicare, far osservare; ~**d** a forzato(a).

engage [ɪn'geɪdʒ] vt assumere; (subj: activity, MIL) impegnare; (attention) occupare // vi (TECH) ingranare; **to** ~ **in** impegnarsi in; ~**d** a (busy, in use) occupato(a); (betrothed) fidanzato(a); **to get** ~**d** fidanzarsi; ~**ment** n impegno, obbligo; appuntamento; (to marry) fidanzamento; (MIL) combattimento; ~**ment ring** n anello di fidanzamento.

engaging [ɪn'geɪdʒɪŋ] a attraente.

engender [ɪn'dʒɛndə*] vt produrre, causare.

engine ['ɛndʒɪn] n (AUT) motore m; (RAIL) locomotiva; ~ **failure** n guasto al motore; ~ **trouble** n panne f.

engineer [ɛndʒɪ'nɪə*] n ingegnere m; (US: RAIL) macchinista m; ~**ing** n ingegneria; (of bridges, ships, machine) tecnica di costruzione.

England ['ɪŋglənd] n Inghilterra.

English ['ɪŋglɪʃ] a inglese // n (LING) inglese m; **the** ~ gli Inglesi; ~**man/woman** n inglese m/f.

engrave [ɪn'greɪv] vt incidere.

engraving [ɪn'greɪvɪŋ] n incisione f.

engrossed [ɪn'grəʊst] *a*: ~ **in** assorbito(a) da, preso(a) da.

engulf [ɪn'gʌlf] *vt* inghiottire.

enhance [ɪn'hɑːns] *vt* accrescere.

enigma [ɪ'nɪgmə] *n* enigma *m*; ~**tic** [enɪg'mætɪk] *a* enigmatico(a).

enjoy [ɪn'dʒɔɪ] *vt* godere; (*have: success, fortune*) avere; **I ~ dancing** mi piace ballare; **to ~ oneself** godersela, divertirsi; ~**able** *a* piacevole; ~**ment** *n* piacere *m*, godimento.

enlarge [ɪn'lɑːdʒ] *vt* ingrandire // *vi*: **to ~ on** (*subject*) dilungarsi su; ~**ment** *n* (*PHOT*) ingrandimento.

enlighten [ɪn'laɪtn] *vt* illuminare; dare schiarimenti a; ~**ed** *a* illuminato(a); ~**ment** *n* progresso culturale; schiarimenti *mpl*; (*HISTORY*): **the E~ment** l'Illuminismo.

enlist [ɪn'lɪst] *vt* arruolare; (*support*) procurare // *vi* arruolarsi.

enmity ['enmɪtɪ] *n* inimicizia.

enormity [ɪ'nɔːmɪtɪ] *n* enormità *f inv*.

enormous [ɪ'nɔːməs] *a* enorme.

enough [ɪ'nʌf] *a, n*: ~ **time/books** assai tempo/libri; **have you got** ~? ne ha abbastanza *or* a sufficienza? // *ad*: **big** ~ abbastanza grande; **he has not worked** ~ non ha lavorato abbastanza; ~! basta!; **it's hot** ~ (**as it is**)! fa caldo assai così!; **... which, funnily** ~ ... che, strano a dirsi.

enquire [ɪn'kwaɪə*] *vt,vi* = **inquire**.

enrich [ɪn'rɪtʃ] *vt* arricchire.

enrol [ɪn'rəʊl] *vt* iscrivere // *vi* iscriversi; ~**ment** *n* iscrizione *f*.

ensign *n* (*NAUT*) ['ensən] bandiera; (*MIL*) ['ensaɪn] portabandiera *m inv*.

enslave [ɪn'sleɪv] *vt* fare schiavo.

ensue [ɪn'sjuː] *vi* seguire, risultare.

ensure [ɪn'ʃuə*] *vt* assicurare; garantire; **to ~ that** assicurarsi che.

entail [ɪn'teɪl] *vt* comportare.

enter ['entə*] *vt* (*room*) entrare in; (*club*) associarsi a; (*army*) arruolarsi in; (*competition*) partecipare a; (*sb for a competition*) iscrivere; (*write down*) registrare; **to ~ into** *vt fus* (*explanation*) cominciare a dare; (*debate*) partecipare a; (*agreement*) concludere; **to ~ (up)on** *vt fus* cominciare.

enterprise ['entəpraɪz] *n* (*undertaking, company*) impresa; (*spirit*) iniziativa.

enterprising ['entəpraɪzɪŋ] *a* intraprendente.

entertain [entə'teɪn] *vt* divertire; (*invite*) ricevere; (*idea, plan*) nutrire; ~**er** *n* comico/a; ~**ing** *a* divertente; ~**ment** *n* (*amusement*) divertimento; (*show*) spettacolo.

enthralled [ɪn'θrɔːld] *a* affascinato(a).

enthusiasm [ɪn'θuːzɪæzəm] *n* entusiasmo.

enthusiast [ɪn'θuːzɪæst] *n* entusiasta *m/f*; ~**ic** [-'æstɪk] *a* entusiasta, entusiastico(a).

entice [ɪn'taɪs] *vt* allettare, sedurre.

entire [ɪn'taɪə*] *a* intero(a); ~**ly** *ad* completamente, interamente; ~**ty** [ɪn'taɪərətɪ] *n*: **in its** ~**ty** nel suo complesso.

entitle [ɪn'taɪtl] *vt* (*allow*): **to ~ sb to do** dare il diritto a qd di fare; ~**d** *a* (*book*) che si intitola; **to be** ~**d to do** avere il diritto di fare.

entrance *n* ['entrns] entrata, ingresso; (*of person*) entrata // *vt* [ɪn'trɑːns] incantare, rapire; ~ **fee** *n* tassa d'iscrizione; (*to museum etc*) prezzo d'ingresso.

entrant ['entrnt] *n* partecipante *m/f*; concorrente *m/f*.

entreat [en'triːt] *vt* supplicare; ~**y** *n* supplica, preghiera.

entrenched [en'trentʃd] *a* radicato(a).

entrust [ɪn'trʌst] *vt*: **to ~ sth to** affidare qc a.

entry ['entrɪ] *n* entrata; (*way in*) entrata, ingresso; (*item: on list*) iscrizione *f*; (*in dictionary*) voce *f*; **'no ~'** 'vietato l'ingresso'; (*AUT*) 'divieto di accesso'; ~ **form** *n* modulo d'iscrizione.

entwine [ɪn'twaɪn] *vt* intrecciare.

enumerate [ɪ'njuːməreɪt] *vt* enumerare.

enunciate [ɪ'nʌnsɪeɪt] *vt* enunciare; pronunciare.

envelop [ɪn'veləp] *vt* avvolgere, avviluppare.

envelope ['envələʊp] *n* busta.

envious ['envɪəs] *a* invidioso(a).

environment [ɪn'vaɪərnmənt] *n* ambiente *m*; ~**al** [-'mentl] *a* ecologico(a); ambientale.

envisage [ɪn'vɪzɪdʒ] *vt* immaginare; prevedere.

envoy ['envɔɪ] *n* inviato/a.

envy ['envɪ] *n* invidia // *vt* invidiare.

enzyme ['enzaɪm] *n* enzima *m*.

ephemeral [ɪ'femərl] *a* effimero(a).

epic ['epɪk] *n* poema *m* epico // *a* epico(a).

epidemic [epɪ'demɪk] *n* epidemia.

epilepsy ['epɪlepsɪ] *n* epilessia; **epileptic** [-'leptɪk] *a,n* epilettico(a).

epilogue ['epɪlɒg] *n* epilogo.

Epiphany [ɪ'pɪfənɪ] *n* Epifania.

episode ['epɪsəʊd] *n* episodio.

epistle [ɪ'pɪsl] *n* epistola.

epitaph ['epɪtɑːf] *n* epitaffio.

epitome [ɪ'pɪtəmɪ] *n* epitome *f*; quintessenza; **epitomize** *vt* compendiare; essere l'emblema di.

epoch ['iːpɒk] *n* epoca.

equable ['ekwəbl] *a* uniforme; equanime.

equal ['iːkwl] *a, n* uguale (*m/f*) // *vt* uguagliare; ~ **to** (*task*) all'altezza di; ~**ity** [iː'kwɒlɪtɪ] *n* uguaglianza; ~**ize** *vt,vi* pareggiare; ~**izer** *n* pareggio; ~**ly** *ad* ugualmente; ~**(s) sign** *n* segno d'uguaglianza.

equanimity [ekwə'nɪmɪtɪ] *n* equanimità.

equate [ɪ'kweɪt] *vt*: **to ~ sth with** considerare qc uguale a; (*compare*) paragonare qc con; **equation** [ɪ'kweɪʃən] *n* (*MATH*) equazione *f*.

equator [ɪ'kweɪtə*] *n* equatore *m*.

equilibrium [iːkwɪ'lɪbrɪəm] *n* equilibrio.

equinox ['iːkwɪnɒks] *n* equinozio.

equip [ɪ'kwɪp] *vt* equipaggiare, attrezzare; **to ~ sb/sth with** fornire qd/qc di;

~ment n attrezzatura; (electrical etc) apparecchiatura.

equitable ['ɛkwɪtəbl] a equo(a), giusto(a).

equity ['ɛkwɪti] n equità; **equities** npl (COMM) azioni fpl ordinarie.

equivalent [ɪ'kwɪvəlnt] a, n equivalente (m).

equivocal [ɪ'kwɪvəkl] a equivoco(a); (open to suspicion) dubbio(a).

era ['ɪərə] n era, età f inv.

eradicate [ɪ'rædɪkeɪt] vt sradicare.

erase [ɪ'reɪz] vt cancellare; **~r** n gomma.

erect [ɪ'rɛkt] a eretto(a) // vt costruire; (monument, tent) alzare.

erection [ɪ'rɛkʃən] n erezione f.

ermine ['ɜːmɪn] n ermellino.

erode [ɪ'rəʊd] vt erodere; (metal) corrodere; **erosion** [ɪ'rəʊʒən] n erosione f.

erotic [ɪ'rɒtɪk] a erotico(a); **~ism** [ɪ'rɒtɪsɪzm] n erotismo.

err [ɜː°] vi errare; (REL) peccare.

errand ['ɛrnd] n commissione f.

erratic [ɪ'rætɪk] a imprevedibile; (person, mood) incostante.

erroneous [ɪ'rəʊnɪəs] a erroneo(a).

error ['ɛrə°] n errore m.

erudite ['ɛrʊdaɪt] a erudito(a).

erupt [ɪ'rʌpt] vi erompere; (volcano) mettersi (or essere) in eruzione; **~ion** [ɪ'rʌpʃən] n eruzione f.

escalate ['ɛskəleɪt] vi intensificarsi; **escalation** [-'leɪʃən] n escalation f; (of prices) aumento.

escalator ['ɛskəleɪtə°] n scala mobile.

escapade [ɛskə'peɪd] n scappatella; avventura.

escape [ɪ'skeɪp] n evasione f; fuga; (of gas etc) fuga, fuoriuscita // vi fuggire; (from jail) evadere, scappare; (fig) sfuggire; (leak) uscire // vt sfuggire a; to **~ from** sb sfuggire a qd; **escapism** n evasione f (dalla realtà).

escort n ['ɛskɔːt] scorta; (male companion) cavaliere m // vt [ɪ'skɔːt] scortare; accompagnare.

Eskimo ['ɛskɪməʊ] n esquimese m/f.

especially [ɪ'spɛʃlɪ] ad specialmente, soprattutto; espressamente.

espionage ['ɛspɪɒnɑːʒ] n spionaggio.

Esquire [ɪ'skwaɪə°] n (abbr Esq.): J. Brown, ~ Signor J. Brown.

essay ['ɛseɪ] n (SCOL) composizione f; (LITERATURE) saggio.

essence ['ɛsns] n essenza.

essential [ɪ'sɛnʃl] a essenziale; (basic) fondamentale; **~ly** ad essenzialmente.

establish [ɪ'stæblɪʃ] vt stabilire; (business) mettere su; (one's power etc) confermare; **~ment** n stabilimento; the E**~ment** le autorità; l'Establishment m.

estate [ɪ'steɪt] n proprietà f inv; beni mpl, patrimonio; **~ agent** n agente m immobiliare; **~ car** n (Brit) giardiniera.

esteem [ɪ'stiːm] n stima.

esthetic [ɪs'θɛtɪk] a (US) = **aesthetic**.

estimate n ['ɛstɪmət] stima; (COMM) preventivo // vt ['ɛstɪmeɪt] stimare,

valutare; **estimation** [-'meɪʃən] n stima; opinione f.

estuary ['ɛstjuərɪ] n estuario.

etching ['ɛtʃɪŋ] n acquaforte f.

eternal [ɪ'tɜːnl] a eterno(a).

eternity [ɪ'tɜːnɪtɪ] n eternità f.

ether ['iːθə°] n etere m.

ethical ['ɛθɪkl] a etico(a), morale.

ethics ['ɛθɪks] n etica // npl morale f.

ethnic ['ɛθnɪk] a etnico(a).

etiquette ['ɛtɪkɛt] n etichetta.

eulogy ['juːlədʒɪ] n elogio.

euphemism ['juːfəmɪzm] n eufemismo.

euphoria [juː'fɔːrɪə] n euforia.

Europe ['juərəp] n Europa; **~an** [-'piːən] a, n europeo(a).

euthanasia [juːθə'neɪzɪə] n eutanasia.

evacuate [ɪ'vækjueɪt] vt evacuare; **evacuation** [-'eɪʃən] n evacuazione f.

evade [ɪ'veɪd] vt eludere; (question, duties etc) evadere.

evaluate [ɪ'væljueɪt] vt valutare.

evangelist [ɪ'vændʒəlɪst] n evangelista m.

evaporate [ɪ'væpəreɪt] vi evaporare // vt far evaporare; **~d milk** n latte m evaporato; **evaporation** [-'reɪʃən] n evaporazione f.

evasion [ɪ'veɪʒən] n evasione f; scappatoia.

evasive [ɪ'veɪsɪv] a evasivo(a).

eve [iːv] n: on the ~ of alla vigilia di.

even ['iːvn] a regolare; (number) pari inv // ad anche, perfino; ~ **more** anche più; he loves her ~ **more** la ama anche di più; ~ **so** ciò nonostante; to ~ **out** vi pareggiare; to **get** ~ **with** sb dare la pari a qd.

evening ['iːvnɪŋ] n sera; (as duration, event) serata; in the ~ la sera; ~ **class** n corso serale; ~ **dress** n (man's) frac m, smoking m; (woman's) vestito da sera.

event [ɪ'vɛnt] n avvenimento; (SPORT) gara; in the ~ of in caso di; **~ful** a denso(a) di eventi.

eventual [ɪ'vɛntʃuəl] a finale; **~ity** [-'ælɪtɪ] n possibilità f inv; eventualità f inv; **~ly** ad finalmente.

ever ['ɛvə°] ad mai; (at all times) sempre; the **best** ~ il migliore che ci sia mai stato; **have you** ~ **seen it?** l'ha mai visto?; **hardly** ~ non ... quasi mai; ~ **since** ad da allora // cj sin da quando; ~ **so pretty** così bello(a); **~green** n sempreverde m; **~lasting** a eterno(a).

every ['ɛvrɪ] det ogni; ~ **day** tutti i giorni, ogni giorno; **other/third day** ogni due/tre giorni; ~ **other car** una macchina su due; ~ **now and then** ogni tanto, di quando in quando; **~body** pronoun ognuno, tutti pl; **~day** a quotidiano(a); di ogni giorno; **~one** = **~body**; **~thing** pronoun tutto, ogni cosa; **~where** ad in ogni luogo, dappertutto.

evict [ɪ'vɪkt] vt sfrattare; **~ion** [ɪ'vɪkʃən] n sfratto.

evidence ['ɛvɪdns] n (proof) prova; (of witness) testimonianza; (sign): to **show** ~ of dare segni di; to **give** ~ deporre; in ~

(obvious) in evidenza; in vista.

evident ['ɛvɪdnt] *a* evidente; ~ly *ad* evidentemente.

evil ['iːvl] *a* cattivo(a), maligno(a) // *n* male *m*.

evocative [ɪ'vɔkətɪv] *a* evocativo(a).

evoke [ɪ'vəuk] *vt* evocare.

evolution [iːvə'luːʃən] *n* evoluzione *f*.

evolve [ɪ'vɔlv] *vt* elaborare // *vi* svilupparsi, evolversi.

ewe [juː] *n* pecora.

ex- [ɛks] *prefix* ex.

exact [ɪg'zækt] *a* esatto(a) // *vt*: to ~ sth (from) estorcere qc (da); esigere qc (da); ~ing *a* esigente; *(work)* faticoso(a); ~itude *n* esattezza, precisione *f*; ~ly *ad* esattamente.

exaggerate [ɪg'zædʒəreɪt] *vt,vi* esagerare; **exaggeration** [-'reɪʃən] *n* esagerazione *f*.

exalt [ɪg'zɔːlt] *vt* esaltare; elevare.

exam [ɪg'zæm] *n* (SCOL) *abbr of* **examination**.

examination [ɪgzæmɪ'neɪʃən] *n* (SCOL) esame *m*; (MED) controllo.

examine [ɪg'zæmɪn] *vt* esaminare; (LAW: *person*) interrogare; ~r *n* esaminatore/trice.

example [ɪg'zɑːmpl] *n* esempio; **for** ~ ad or per esempio.

exasperate [ɪg'zɑːspəreɪt] *vt* esasperare.

excavate ['ɛkskəveɪt] *vt* scavare; **excavation** [-'veɪʃən] *n* escavazione *f*; **excavator** *n* scavatore *m*, scavatrice *f*.

exceed [ɪk'siːd] *vt* superare; *(one's powers, time limit)* oltrepassare; ~ingly *ad* eccessivamente.

excel [ɪk'sɛl] *vi* eccellere // *vt* sorpassare.

excellence ['ɛksələns] *n* eccellenza.

Excellency ['ɛksələnsɪ] *n*: **His** ~ Sua Eccellenza.

excellent ['ɛksələnt] *a* eccellente.

except [ɪk'sɛpt] *prep* (*also*: ~ **for**, ~**ing**) salvo, all'infuori di, eccetto // *vt* escludere; ~ **if/when** salvo se/quando; ~ **that** salvo che; ~**ion** [ɪk'sɛpʃən] *n* eccezione *f*; **to take** ~**ion to** trovare a ridire su; ~**ional** [ɪk'sɛpʃənl] *a* eccezionale.

excerpt ['ɛksəpt] *n* estratto.

excess [ɪk'sɛs] *n* eccesso; ~ **fare** *n* supplemento; ~ **baggage** *n* bagaglio in eccedenza; ~**ive** *a* eccessivo(a).

exchange [ɪks'tʃeɪndʒ] *n* scambio; (*also*: **telephone** ~) centralino // *vt* scambiare; ~ **market** *n* mercato dei cambi.

exchequer [ɪks'tʃɛkə*] *n* Scacchiere *m*, ≈ ministero delle Finanze.

excisable [ɪk'saɪzəbl] *a* soggetto(a) a dazio.

excise *n* ['ɛksaɪz] imposta, dazio // *vt* [ɛk'saɪz] recidere; ~ **duties** *npl* dazi *mpl*.

excite [ɪk'saɪt] *vt* eccitare; **to get** ~**d** eccitarsi; ~**ment** *n* eccitazione *f*; agitazione *f*; ~**citing** *a* avventuroso(a); *(film, book)* appassionante.

exclaim [ɪk'skleɪm] *vi* esclamare; **exclamation** [ɛksklə'meɪʃən] *n*

esclamazione *f*; **exclamation mark** *n* punto esclamativo.

exclude [ɪk'skluːd] *vt* escludere; **exclusion** [ɪk'skluːʒən] *n* esclusione *f*.

exclusive [ɪk'skluːsɪv] *a* esclusivo(a); *(club)* selettivo(a); *(district)* snob *inv* // *ad* (COMM) non compreso; ~ **of VAT** I.V.A. esclusa; ~**ly** *ad* esclusivamente; ~ **rights** *npl* (COMM) diritti *mpl* esclusivi.

excommunicate [ɛkskə'mjuːnɪkeɪt] *vt* scomunicare.

excrement ['ɛkskrəmənt] *n* escremento.

excruciating [ɪk'skruːʃɪeɪtɪŋ] *a* straziante, atroce.

excursion [ɪk'skəːʃən] *n* escursione *f*, gita.

excuse *n* [ɪk'skjuːs] scusa // *vt* [ɪk'skjuːz] scusare; **to** ~ **sb from** *(activity)* dispensare qd da; ~ **me!** mi scusi!

execute ['ɛksɪkjuːt] *vt* (*prisoner*) giustiziare; *(plan etc)* eseguire.

execution [ɛksɪ'kjuːʃən] *n* esecuzione *f*; ~**er** *n* boia *m inv*.

executive [ɪg'zɛkjutɪv] *n* (COMM) dirigente *m*; (POL) esecutivo // *a* esecutivo(a).

executor [ɪg'zɛkjutə*] *n* esecutore(trice) testamentario(a).

exemplary [ɪg'zɛmplərɪ] *a* esemplare.

exemplify [ɪg'zɛmplɪfaɪ] *vt* esemplificare.

exempt [ɪg'zɛmpt] *a* esentato(a) // *vt*: ~ **sb from** esentare qd da; ~**ion** [ɪg-'zɛmpʃən] *n* esenzione *f*.

exercise ['ɛksəsaɪz] *n* esercizio // *vt* esercitare; *(dog)* portar fuori; **to take** ~ fare del movimento; ~ **book** *n* quaderno.

exert [ɪg'zəːt] *vt* esercitare; **to** ~ **o.s.** sforzarsi.

exhaust [ɪg'zɔːst] *n* (*also*: ~ **fumes**) scappamento; *(also*: ~ **pipe**) tubo di scappamento // *vt* esaurire; ~**ed** *a* esaurito(a); ~**ion** [ɪg'zɔːstʃən] *n* esaurimento; ~**ive** *a* esauriente.

exhibit [ɪg'zɪbɪt] *n* (ART) oggetto esposto; (LAW) documento or oggetto esibito // *vt* esporre; *(courage, skill)* dimostrare; ~**ion** [ɛksɪ'bɪʃən] *n* mostra, esposizione *f*; ~**ionist** [ɛksɪ'bɪʃənɪst] *n* esibizionista *m/f*; ~**or** *n* espositore/trice.

exhilarating [ɪg'zɪləreɪtɪŋ] *a* esilarante; stimolante.

exhort [ɪg'zɔːt] *vt* esortare.

exile ['ɛksaɪl] *n* esilio; esiliato/a // *vt* esiliare; **in** ~ in esilio.

exist [ɪg'zɪst] *vi* esistere; ~**ence** *n* esistenza; **to be in** ~**ence** esistere.

exit ['ɛksɪt] *n* uscita.

exonerate [ɪg'zɔnəreɪt] *vt*: **to** ~ **from** discolpare da.

exorcize ['ɛksɔːsaɪz] *vt* esorcizzare.

exotic [ɪg'zɔtɪk] *a* esotico(a).

expand [ɪk'spænd] *vt* espandere; estendere; allargare // *vi* (*trade etc*) svilupparsi, ampliarsi; espandersi; *(gas)* espandersi; *(metal)* dilatarsi.

expanse [ɪk'spæns] *n* distesa, estensione *f*.

expansion [ɪk'spænʃən] *n* sviluppo; espansione *f*; dilatazione *f*.

expatriate *n* [ɛks'pætrɪət] espatriato/a // *vt* [ɛks'pætrɪeɪt] espatriare.

expect [ɪk'spɛkt] vt (anticipate) prevedere, aspettarsi, prevedere or aspettarsi che + sub; (count on) contare su; (hope for) sperare; (require) richiedere, esigere; (suppose) supporre; (await, also baby) aspettare // vi: to be ~ing essere in stato interessante; to ~ sb to do aspettarsi che qd faccia; ~ant a pieno(a) di aspettative; ~ant mother n gestante f; ~ation [ɛkspɛk'teɪʃən] n aspettativa; speranza.

expedience, expediency [ɛk'spi:dɪəns, ɛk'spi:dɪənsɪ] n convenienza.

expedient [ɪk'spi:dɪənt] a conveniente; vantaggioso(a) // n espediente m.

expedite ['ɛkspədaɪt] vt sbrigare; facilitare.

expedition [ɛkspə'dɪʃən] n spedizione f.

expel [ɪk'spɛl] vt espellere.

expend [ɪk'spɛnd] vt spendere; (use up) consumare; ~able a sacrificabile; ~iture [ɪk'spɛndɪtʃə*] n spesa; spese fpl.

expense [ɪk'spɛns] n spesa; spese fpl; (high cost) costo; ~s npl (COMM) spese fpl, indennità fpl; at the ~ of a spese di; ~ account n nota f spese inv.

expensive [ɪk'spɛnsɪv] a caro(a), costoso(a).

experience [ɪk'spɪərɪəns] n esperienza // vt (pleasure) provare; (hardship) soffrire; ~d a esperto(a).

experiment [ɪk'spɛrɪmənt] n esperimento, esperienza // vi fare esperimenti; ~al [-'mɛntl] a sperimentale.

expert ['ɛkspə:t] a, n esperto(a); ~ise [-'ti:z] n competenza.

expire [ɪk'spaɪə*] vi (period of time, licence) scadere; **expiry** n scadenza.

explain [ɪk'spleɪn] vt spiegare; **explanation** [ɛksplə'neɪʃən] n spiegazione f; **explanatory** [ɪk'splænətrɪ] a esplicativo(a).

explicit [ɪk'splɪsɪt] a esplicito(a); (definite) netto(a).

explode [ɪk'spləud] vi esplodere.

exploit n ['ɛksplɔɪt] impresa // vt [ɪk'splɔɪt] sfruttare; ~ation [-'teɪʃən] n sfruttamento.

exploration [ɛksplə'reɪʃən] n esplorazione f.

exploratory [ɪk'splɔrətrɪ] a (fig: talks) esplorativo(a).

explore [ɪk'splɔ:*] vt esplorare; (possibilities) esaminare; ~r n esploratore/trice.

explosion [ɪk'spləuʒən] n esplosione f.

explosive [ɪk'spləusɪv] a esplosivo(a) // n esplosivo.

exponent [ɪk'spəunənt] n esponente m/f.

export vt [ɪk'spɔ:t] esportare // n ['ɛkspɔ:t] esportazione f; articolo di esportazione // cpd d'esportazione; ~ation [-'teɪʃən] n esportazione f; ~er n esportatore m.

expose [ɪk'spəuz] vt esporre; (unmask) smascherare; to ~ o.s. (LAW) oltraggiare il pudore.

exposure [ɪk'spəuʒə*] n esposizione f; (PHOT) posa; (MED) assideramento; ~meter n esposimetro.

expound [ɪk'spaund] vt esporre.

express [ɪk'sprɛs] a (definite) chiaro(a), espresso(a); (letter etc) espresso inv // n (train) espresso // ad (send) espresso // vt esprimere; ~ion [ɪk'sprɛʃən] n espressione f; ~ive a espressivo(a); ~ly ad espressamente.

expulsion [ɪk'spʌlʃən] n espulsione f.

exquisite [ɛk'skwɪzɪt] a squisito(a).

extend [ɪk'stɛnd] vt (visit) protrarre; (street) prolungare; (building) ampliare; (offer) offrire, porgere // vi (land) estendersi.

extension [ɪk'stɛnʃən] n prolungamento; estensione f; (building) annesso; (to wire, table) prolunga; (telephone) interno; (: in private house) apparecchio addizionale.

extensive [ɪk'stɛnsɪv] a esteso(a), ampio(a); (damage) su larga scala; (alterations) notevole; (inquiries) esauriente; (use) grande; **he's travelled** ~ly ha viaggiato molto.

extent [ɪk'stɛnt] n estensione f; to some ~ fino a un certo punto; to what ~? fino a che punto?

exterior [ɛk'stɪərɪə*] a esteriore, esterno(a) // n esteriore m, esterno; aspetto (esteriore).

exterminate [ɪk'stə:mɪneɪt] vt sterminare; **extermination** [-'neɪʃən] n sterminio.

external [ɛk'stə:nl] a esterno(a), esteriore.

extinct [ɪk'stɪŋkt] a estinto(a); ~ion [ɪk'stɪŋkʃən] n estinzione f.

extinguish [ɪk'stɪŋgwɪʃ] vt estinguere; ~er n estintore m.

extort [ɪk'stɔ:t] vt: to ~ sth (from) estorcere qc (da); ~ion [ɪk'stɔ:ʃən] n estorsione f; ~ionate [ɪk'stɔ:ʃnət] a esorbitante.

extra ['ɛkstrə] a extra inv, supplementare // ad (in addition) di più // n supplemento; (THEATRE) comparso.

extra... ['ɛkstrə] prefix extra... .

extract vt [ɪk'strækt] estrarre; (money, promise) strappare // n ['ɛkstrækt] estratto; (passage) brano; ~ion [ɪk'strækʃən] n estrazione f; (descent) origine f.

extradite ['ɛkstrədaɪt] vt estradare; **extradition** [-'dɪʃən] n estradizione f.

extramarital [ɛkstrə'mærɪtl] a extraconiugale.

extramural [ɛkstrə'mjuərl] a fuori dell'università.

extraneous [ɛk'streɪnɪəs] a: ~ to estraneo(a) a.

extraordinary [ɪk'strɔ:dnrɪ] a straordinario(a).

extra time [ɛkstrə'taɪm] n (FOOTBALL) tempo supplementare.

extravagant [ɪk'strævəgənt] a stravagante; (in spending) dispendioso(a).

extreme [ɪk'stri:m] a estremo(a) // n estremo; ~ly ad estremamente;

extremist *a,n* estremista (*m/f*).
extremity [ɪk'strɛmɪtɪ] *n* estremità *f inv*.
extricate ['ɛkstrɪkeɪt] *vt*: **to ~ sth (from)** districare qc (da).
extrovert ['ɛkstrəvɜːt] *n* estroverso/a.
exuberant [ɪg'zjuːbərnt] *a* esuberante.
exude [ɪg'zjuːd] *vt* trasudare; (*fig*) emanare.
exult [ɪg'zʌlt] *vi* esultare, gioire.
eye [aɪ] *n* occhio; (*of needle*) cruna // *vt* osservare; **to keep an ~ on** tenere d'occhio; **in the public ~** esposto(a) al pubblico; **~ball** *n* globo dell'occhio; **~brow** *n* sopracciglio; **~catching** *a* che colpisce l'occhio; **~drops** *npl* gocce *fpl* oculari, collirio; **~lash** *n* ciglio; **~lid** *n* palpebra; **~opener** *n* rivelazione *f*; **~shadow** *n* ombretto; **~sight** *n* vista; **~sore** *n* pugno nell'occhio; **~ witness** *n* testimone *m/f* oculare.
eyrie ['ɪərɪ] *n* nido (d'aquila).

F

F [ɛf] *n* (*MUS*) fa *m*.
F. *abbr of* Fahrenheit.
fable ['feɪbl] *n* favola.
fabric ['fæbrɪk] *n* stoffa, tessuto.
fabrication [fæbrɪ'keɪʃən] *n* fabbricazione *f*; falsificazione *f*.
fabulous ['fæbjuləs] *a* favoloso(a); (*col: super*) favoloso(a), fantastico(a).
façade [fə'sɑːd] *n* facciata.
face [feɪs] *n* faccia, viso, volto; (*expression*) faccia; (*grimace*) smorfia; (*of clock*) quadrante *m*; (*of building*) facciata; (*side, surface*) faccia // *vt* fronteggiare; (*fig*) affrontare; **to lose ~** perdere la faccia; **in the ~ of** (*difficulties etc*) di fronte a; **on the ~ of it** a prima vista; **to ~ up to** *vt fus* affrontare, far fronte a; **~ cloth** *n* guanto di spugna; **~ cream** *n* crema per il viso; **~ lift** *n* lifting *m inv*; (*of façade etc*) ripulita.
facet ['fæsɪt] *n* faccetta, sfaccettatura; (*fig*) sfaccettatura.
facetious [fə'siːʃəs] *a* faceto(a).
face-to-face ['feɪstə'feɪs] *ad* a faccia a faccia.
face value ['feɪs'væljuː] *n* (*of coin*) valore *m* facciale *or* nominale; **to take sth at ~** (*fig*) giudicare qc dalle apparenze.
facial ['feɪʃəl] *a* facciale.
facile ['fæsaɪl] *a* facile.
facilitate [fə'sɪlɪteɪt] *vt* facilitare.
facility [fə'sɪlɪtɪ] *n* facilità; **facilities** *npl* attrezzature *fpl*.
facsimile [fæk'sɪmɪlɪ] *n* facsimile *m inv*.
fact [fækt] *n* fatto; **in ~** infatti.
faction ['fækʃən] *n* fazione *f*.
factor ['fæktə*] *n* fattore *m*.
factory ['fæktərɪ] *n* fabbrica, stabilimento.
factual ['fæktjuəl] *a* che si attiene ai fatti.
faculty ['fækəltɪ] *n* facoltà *f inv*.
fad [fæd] *n* mania; capriccio.
fade [feɪd] *vi* sbiadire, sbiadirsi; (*light,

sound, hope) attenuarsi, affievolirsi; (*flower*) appassire.
fag [fæg] *n* (*col: cigarette*) cicca; **~ end** *n* mozzicone *m*; **~ged out** *a* (*col*) stanco(a) morto(a).
fail [feɪl] *vt* (*exam*) non superare; (*candidate*) bocciare; (*subj: courage, memory*) mancare a // *vi* fallire; (*student*) essere respinto(a); (*supplies*) mancare; (*eyesight, health, light*) venire a mancare; **to ~ to do sth** (*neglect*) mancare di fare qc; (*be unable*) non riuscire a fare qc; **without ~** senza fallo; certamente; **~ing** *n* difetto // *prep* in mancanza di; **~ure** ['feɪljə*] *n* fallimento; (*person*) fallito/a; (*mechanical etc*) guasto.
faint [feɪnt] *a* debole; (*recollection*) vago(a); (*mark*) indistinto(a) // *vi* svenire; **to feel ~** sentirsi svenire; **~hearted** *a* pusillanime; **~ly** *ad* debolmente; vagamente; **~ness** *n* debolezza.
fair [fɛə*] *a* (*person, decision*) giusto(a), equo(a); (*hair etc*) biondo(a); (*skin, complexion*) bianco(a); (*weather*) bello(a), clemente; (*good enough*) assai buono(a); (*sizeable*) bello(a) // *ad* (*play*) lealmente // *n* fiera; **~ copy** *n* bella copia; **~ly** *ad* equamente; (*quite*) abbastanza; **~ness** *n* equità, giustizia.
fairy ['fɛərɪ] *n* fata; **~ tale** *n* fiaba.
faith [feɪθ] *n* fede *f*; (*trust*) fiducia; (*sect*) religione *f*, fede *f*; **~ful** *a* fedele; **~fully** *ad* fedelmente.
fake [feɪk] *n* (*painting etc*) contraffazione *f*; (*photo*) trucco; (*person*) impostore/a // *a* falso(a); // *vt* simulare, falsare; (*painting*) contraffare; (*photo*) truccare; (*story*) falsificare.
falcon ['fɔːlkən] *n* falco, falcone *m*.
fall [fɔːl] *n* caduta; (*in temperature*) abbassamento; (*in price*) ribasso; (*US: autumn*) autunno // *vi* (*pt* fell, *pp* fallen [fɛl, 'fɔːlən]) cadere; (*temperature, price*) abbassare; **~s** *npl* (*waterfall*) cascate *fpl*; **to ~ flat** *vi* (*on one's face*) cadere bocconi; (*joke*) fare cilecca; (*plan*) fallire; **to ~ behind** *vi* rimanere indietro; **to ~ down** *vi* (*person*) cadere; (*building, hopes*) crollare; **to ~ for** *vt fus* (*trick*) cascarci dentro; (*person*) prendere una cotta per; **to ~ in** *vi* crollare; (*MIL*) mettersi in riga; **to ~ off** *vi* cadere; (*diminish*) diminuire, abbassarsi; **to ~ out** *vi* (*friends etc*) litigare; **to ~ through** *vi* (*plan, project*) fallire.
fallacy ['fæləsɪ] *n* errore *m*; falso ragionamento.
fallen ['fɔːlən] *pp of* fall.
fallible ['fæləbl] *a* fallibile.
fallout ['fɔːlaut] *n* fall-out *m*.
fallow ['fæləu] *a* incolto(a); a maggese.
false [fɔːls] *a* falso(a); **~ alarm** *n* falso allarme *m*; **~ hood** *n* menzogna; **~ly** *ad* (*accuse*) a torto; **~ teeth** *npl* denti *mpl* finti.
falter ['fɔːltə*] *vi* esitare, vacillare.
fame [feɪm] *n* fama, celebrità.
familiar [fə'mɪlɪə*] *a* familiare; (*common*)

comune; (*close*) intimo(a); **to be ~ with**
(*subject*) conoscere; **~ity** [fəmɪlɪˈærɪtɪ] *n*
familiarità; intimità; **~ize** [fəˈmɪlɪəraɪz]
vt: **to ~ize sb with sth** far conoscere qc
a qd.

family [ˈfæmɪlɪ] *n* famiglia; **~ allowance**
n assegni *mpl* familiari; **~ doctor** *n*
medico di famiglia; **~ life** *n* vita
familiare.

famine [ˈfæmɪn] *n* carestia.

famished [ˈfæmɪʃt] *a* affamato(a).

famous [ˈfeɪməs] *a* famoso(a); **~ly** *ad* (*get*
on) a meraviglia.

fan [fæn] *n* (*folding*) ventaglio; (*ELEC*)
ventilatore *m*; (*person*) ammiratore/trice;
tifoso/a // *vt* far vento a; (*fire, quarrel*)
alimentare; **to ~ out** *vi* spargersi (a
ventaglio).

fanatic [fəˈnætɪk] *n* fanatico/a; **~al** *a*
fanatico(a).

fan belt [ˈfænbɛlt] *n* cinghia del
ventilatore.

fancied [ˈfænsɪd] *a* immaginario(a).

fanciful [ˈfænsɪful] *a* fantasioso(a);
(*object*) di fantasia.

fancy [ˈfænsɪ] *n* desiderio; immaginazione
f, fantasia; (*whim*) capriccio // *cpd* (di)
fantasia *inv* // *vt* (*feel like, want*) aver
voglia di; **to take a ~ to** incapricciarsi
di; **~ dress** *n* costume *m* (per maschera);
~-dress ball *n* ballo in maschera.

fang [fæŋ] *n* zanna; (*of snake*) dente *m*.

fanlight [ˈfænlaɪt] *n* lunetta.

fantastic [fænˈtæstɪk] *a* fantastico(a).

fantasy [ˈfæntəzɪ] *n* fantasia,
immaginazione *f*; fantasticheria; chimera.

far [fɑː*] *a*: **the ~ side/end** l'altra
parte/l'altro capo // *ad* lontano; **~ away,
~ off** lontano, distante; **~ better** assai
migliore; **~ from** lontano da; **by ~** di
gran lunga; **go as ~ as the farm** vada
fino alla fattoria; **as ~ as I know** per
quel che so; **~away** *a* lontano(a).

farce [fɑːs] *n* farsa.

farcical [ˈfɑːsɪkəl] *a* farsesco(a).

fare [fɛə*] *n* (*on trains, buses*) tariffa; (*in*
taxi) prezzo della corsa; (*food*) vitto, cibo
// *vi* passarsela.

Far East [fɑːˈriːst] *n*: **the ~** l'Estremo
Oriente *m*.

farewell [fɛəˈwɛl] *excl, n* addio; **~ party** *n*
festa d'addio.

far-fetched [ˈfɑːˈfɛtʃt] *a* gonfiato(a).

farm [fɑːm] *n* fattoria, podere *m* // *vt*
coltivare; **~er** *n* coltivatore/trice;
agricoltore/trice; **~hand** *n* bracciante *m*
agricolo; **~house** *n* fattoria; **~ing** *n*
agricoltura; **~land** *n* terreno da coltivare;
~yard *n* aia.

far-reaching [ˈfɑːˈriːtʃɪŋ] *a* di vasta
portata.

far-sighted [ˈfɑːˈsaɪtɪd] *a* presbite; (*fig*)
lungimirante.

fart [fɑːt] (*col!*) *n* scoreggia(!) // *vi*
scoreggiare (!).

farther [ˈfɑːðə*] *ad* più lontano.

farthest [ˈfɑːðɪst] *superlative of* **far**.

fascia [ˈfeɪʃə] *n* (*AUT*) cruscotto.

fascinate [ˈfæsɪneɪt] *vt* affascinare;
fascination [-ˈneɪʃən] *n* fascino.

fascism [ˈfæʃɪzəm] *n* fascismo.

fascist [ˈfæʃɪst] *a,n* fascista (*m/f*).

fashion [ˈfæʃən] *n* moda; (*manner*)
maniera, modo // *vt* foggiare, formare; **in
~** alla moda; **out of ~** passato(a) di
moda; **~able** *a* alla moda, di moda; **~
show** *n* sfilata di modelli.

fast [fɑːst] *a* rapido(a), svelto(a), veloce;
(*clock*): **to be ~** andare avanti; (*dye,
colour*) solido(a) // *ad* rapidamente;
(*stuck, held*) saldamente // *a* digiuno // *vi*
digiunare; **~ asleep** profondamente
addormentato.

fasten [ˈfɑːsn] *vt* chiudere, fissare; (*coat*)
abbottonare, allacciare // *vi* chiudersi,
fissarsi; **~er, ~ing** *n* fermaglio,
chiusura.

fastidious [fæsˈtɪdɪəs] *a* esigente, difficile.

fat [fæt] *a* grasso(a) // *n* grasso.

fatal [ˈfeɪtl] *a* fatale; mortale;
disastroso(a); **~ism** *n* fatalismo; **~ity**
[fəˈtælɪtɪ] *n* (*road death etc*) morto/a,
vittima; **~ly** *ad* a morte.

fate [feɪt] *n* destino; (*of person*) sorte *f*;
~ful *a* fatidico(a).

father [ˈfɑːðə*] *n* padre *m*; **~-in-law** *n*
suocero; **~ly** *a* paterno(a).

fathom [ˈfæðəm] *n* braccio (= 1828 *mm*) //
vt (*mystery*) penetrare, sondare.

fatigue [fəˈtiːg] *n* stanchezza; (*MIL*) corvé *f*.

fatten [ˈfætn] *vt, vi* ingrassare.

fatty [ˈfætɪ] *a* (*food*) grasso(a).

fatuous [ˈfætjuəs] *a* fatuo(a).

faucet [ˈfɔːsɪt] *n* (*US*) rubinetto.

fault [fɔːlt] *n* colpa; (*TENNIS*) fallo; (*defect*)
difetto; (*GEO*) faglia // *vt* criticare; **it's my
~** è colpa mia; **to find ~ with** trovare
da ridire su; **at ~** in fallo; **to a ~**
eccessivamente; **~less** *a* perfetto(a);
senza difetto; impeccabile; **~y** *a*
difettoso(a).

fauna [ˈfɔːnə] *n* fauna.

favour [ˈfeɪvə*] *n* favore *m*, cortesia,
piacere *m* // *vt* (*proposition*) favorire,
essere favorevole a; (*pupil etc*) favorire;
(*team, horse*) dare per vincente; **to do sb
a ~** fare un favore *or* una cortesia a qd;
in ~ of in favore di; **~able** *a* favorevole;
(*price*) di favore; **~ably** *ad*
favorevolmente; **~ite** [-rɪt] *a,n*
favorito(a); **~itism** *n* favoritismo.

fawn [fɔːn] *n* daino // *a* marrone chiaro *inv*
// *vi*: **to ~ (up)on** adulare servilmente.

fear [fɪə*] *n* paura, timore *m* // *vt* aver
paura di, temere; **for ~ of** per paura di;
~ful *a* pauroso(a); (*sight, noise*) terribile,
spaventoso(a); **~less** *a* intrepido(a),
senza paura.

feasibility [fiːzəˈbɪlɪtɪ] *n* praticabilità.

feasible [ˈfiːzəbl] *a* possibile, realizzabile.

feast [fiːst] *n* festa, banchetto; (*REL*: *also*:
~ day) festa // *vi* banchettare; **to ~ on**
godersi, gustare.

feat [fiːt] *n* impresa, fatto insigne.

feather [ˈfɛðə*] *n* penna.

feature [ˈfiːtʃə*] *n* caratteristica; (*article*)

articolo // vt (subj: film) avere come protagonista // vi figurare; **~s** npl (of face) fisionomia; ~ **film** n film m inv principale; **~less** a anonimo(a), senza caratteri distinti.

February ['fɛbruərɪ] n febbraio.

fed [fɛd] pt,pp of **feed; to be ~ up** essere stufo(a).

federal ['fɛdərəl] a federale.

federation [fɛdə'reɪʃən] n federazione f.

fee [fiː] n pagamento; (of doctor, lawyer) onorario; (of school, college etc) tasse fpl scolastiche; (for examination) tassa d'esame.

feeble ['fiːbl] a debole; **~-minded** a deficiente.

feed [fiːd] n (of baby) pappa // vt (pt, pp **fed** [fɛd]) nutrire; (horse etc) dare da mangiare a; (fuel) alimentare; **to ~ material into sth** imboccare qc con materiali; **to ~ data/information into sth** nutrire qc di data/informazioni; **to ~ on** vt fus nutrirsi di; **~back** n feed-back m; **~ing bottle** n biberon m inv.

feel [fiːl] n sensazione f; (of substance) tatto // vt (pt, pp **felt** [fɛlt]) toccare; palpare; tastare; (cold, pain, anger) sentire; (grief) provare; (think, believe): **to ~ (that)** pensare che; **to ~ hungry/cold** aver fame/freddo; **to ~ lonely/better** sentirsi solo/meglio; **it ~s soft** è morbido al tatto; **to ~ like** (want) aver voglia di; **to ~ about** or **around for** cercare a tastoni; **to ~ about** or **around in one's pocket for** frugarsi in tasca per cercare; **~er** n (of insect) antenna; **to put out a ~er** fare un sondaggio; **~ing** n sensazione f; sentimento; **my ~ing is that...** ho l'impressione che...

feet [fiːt] npl of **foot**.

feign [feɪn] vt fingere, simulare.

fell [fɛl] pt of **fall** // vt (tree) abbattere; (person) atterrare.

fellow ['fɛləu] n individuo, tipo; compagno; (of learned society) membro; **their ~ prisoners/students** i loro compagni di prigione/studio; **~ citizen** n concittadino/a; **~ countryman** n compatriota m; **~ men** npl simili mpl; **~ship** n associazione f; compagnia; specie di borsa di studio universitaria.

felony ['fɛlənɪ] n reato, crimine m.

felt [fɛlt] pt, pp of **feel** // n feltro; **~-tip pen** n pennarello.

female ['fiːmeɪl] n femmina // a femminile; (BIOL, ELEC) femmina inv; **male and ~ students** studenti e studentesse; **~ impersonator** n travestito.

feminine ['fɛmɪnɪn] a, n femminile (m).

feminist ['fɛmɪnɪst] n femminista m/f.

fence [fɛns] n recinto; (col: person) ricettatore/trice // vt (also: **~ in**) recingere // vi schermire; **fencing** n (SPORT) scherma.

fend [fɛnd] vi: **to ~ for o.s.** arrangiarsi.

fender ['fɛndə*] n parafuoco; (US) parafango; paraurti m inv.

ferment vi [fə'mɛnt] fermentare // n ['fɜːmɛnt] agitazione f, eccitazione f; **~ation** [-'teɪʃən] n fermentazione f.

fern [fɜːn] n felce f.

ferocious [fə'rəuʃəs] a feroce.

ferocity [fə'rɔsɪtɪ] n ferocità.

ferry ['fɛrɪ] n (small) traghetto; (large: also: **~boat**) nave f traghetto inv // vt traghettare.

fertile ['fɜːtaɪl] a fertile; (BIOL) fecondo(a); **fertility** [fə'tɪlɪtɪ] n fertilità; fecondità; **fertilize** ['fɜːtɪlaɪz] vt fertilizzare; fecondare; **fertilizer** n fertilizzante m.

fervent ['fɜːvənt] a ardente, fervente.

fester ['fɛstə*] vi suppurare.

festival ['fɛstɪvəl] n (REL) festa; (ART, MUS) festival m inv.

festive ['fɛstɪv] a di festa; **the ~ season** la stagione delle feste.

festivities [fɛs'tɪvɪtɪz] npl festeggiamenti mpl.

fetch [fɛtʃ] vt andare a prendere; (sell for) essere venduto(a) per.

fetching ['fɛtʃɪŋ] a attraente.

fête [feɪt] n festa.

fetish ['fɛtɪʃ] n feticcio.

fetters ['fɛtəz] npl catene fpl.

fetus ['fiːtəs] n (US) = **foetus**.

feud [fjuːd] n contesa, lotta // vi essere in lotta.

feudal ['fjuːdl] a feudale; **~ism** n feudalesimo.

fever ['fiːvə*] n febbre f; **~ish** a febbrile.

few [fjuː] a (pochi(e); **they were ~** erano pochi; **a ~** a qualche inv // pronoun alcuni(e); **~er** a meno inv; meno numerosi(e); **~est** a il minor numero di.

fiancé [fɪ'ɑ̃:ŋseɪ] n fidanzato; **~e** n fidanzata.

fiasco [fɪ'æskəu] n fiasco.

fib [fɪb] n piccola bugia.

fibre ['faɪbə*] n fibra; **~-glass** n fibra di vetro.

fickle ['fɪkl] a incostante, capriccioso(a).

fiction ['fɪkʃən] n narrativa, romanzi mpl; finzione f; **~al** a immaginario(a).

fictitious [fɪk'tɪʃəs] a fittizio(a).

fiddle ['fɪdl] n (MUS) violino; (cheating) imbroglio; truffa // vt (accounts) falsificare, falsare; **to ~ with** vt fus gingillarsi con; **~r** n violinista m/f.

fidelity [fɪ'dɛlɪtɪ] n fedeltà; (accuracy) esattezza.

fidget ['fɪdʒɪt] vi agitarsi; **~y** a agitato(a).

field [fiːld] n campo; **~ glasses** npl binocolo (da campagna); **~ marshal** n feldmaresciallo; **~work** n ricerche fpl esterne.

fiend [fiːnd] n demonio; **~ish** a demoniaco(a).

fierce [fɪəs] a (look, fighting) fiero(a); (wind) furioso(a); (attack) feroce; (enemy) acerrimo(a).

fiery ['faɪərɪ] a ardente; infocato(a).

fifteen [fɪf'tiːn] num quindici.

fifth [fɪfθ] num quinto(a).

fiftieth ['fɪftɪɪθ] num cinquantesimo(a).

fifty ['fɪftɪ] *num* cinquanta.

fig [fɪg] *n* fico.

fight [faɪt] *n* zuffa, rissa; (MIL) battaglia, combattimento; (against cancer etc) lotta // *vb* (*pt, pp* **fought** [fɔːt]) *vt* picchiare; combattere; (cancer, alcoholism) lottare contro, combattere // *vi* battersi, combattere; **~er** *n* combattente *m*; (*plane*) aeroplano da caccia; **~ing** *n* combattimento.

figment ['fɪgmənt] *n*: **a ~ of the imagination** un parto della fantasia.

figurative ['fɪgjʊrətɪv] *a* figurato(a).

figure ['fɪgə*] *n* (DRAWING, GEOM) figura; (number, cipher) cifra; (body, outline) forma // *vi* (appear) figurare; (US: make sense) spiegarsi; **to ~ out** *vt* riuscire a capire; calcolare; **~head** *n* (NAUT) polena; (pej) prestanome *m/f inv.*

filament ['fɪləmənt] *n* filamento.

file [faɪl] *n* (tool) lima; (dossier) incartamento; (folder) cartellina; (for loose leaf) raccoglitore *m*; (row) fila // *vt* (nails, wood) limare; (papers) archiviare; (LAW: claim) presentare; passare agli atti; **to ~ in/out** *vi* entrare/uscire in fila; **to ~ past** *vt fus* marciare in fila davanti a.

filing ['faɪlɪŋ] *n* archiviare *m*; **~s** *npl* limatura; **~ cabinet** *n* casellario.

fill [fɪl] *vt* riempire; (tooth) otturare; (job) coprire // *n*: **to eat one's ~** mangiare a sazietà; **to ~ in** (hole) riempire; (form) compilare; **to ~ up** *vt* riempire // *vi* (AUT) fare il pieno; **~ it up, please** (AUT) mi faccia il pieno, per piacere.

fillet ['fɪlɪt] *n* filetto.

filling ['fɪlɪŋ] *n* (CULIN) impasto, ripieno; (for tooth) otturazione *f*; **~ station** *n* stazione *f* di rifornimento.

fillip ['fɪlɪp] *n* incentivo, stimolo.

film [fɪlm] *n* (CINEMA) film *m inv*; (PHOT) pellicola; (thin layer) velo // *vt* (scene) filmare; **~ star** *n* divo/a dello schermo.

filter ['fɪltə*] *vt* (pt, pp filtrare; **~ lane** *n* (AUT) corsia di svincolo; **~ tip** *n* filtro.

filth [fɪlθ] *n* sporcizia; (fig) oscenità; **~y** *a* lordo(a), sozzo(a); (language) osceno(a).

fin [fɪn] *n* (of fish) pinna.

final ['faɪnl] *a* finale, ultimo(a); definitivo(a) // *n* (SPORT) finale *f*; **~s** *npl* (SCOL) esami *mpl* finali; **~e** [fɪ'nɑːlɪ] *n* finale *m*; **~ist** *n* (SPORT) finalista *m/f*; **~ize** *vt* mettere a punto; **~ly** *ad* (lastly) alla fine; (eventually) finalmente.

finance [faɪ'næns] *n* finanza; **~s** *npl* finanze *fpl* // *vt* finanziare.

financial [faɪ'nænʃəl] *a* finanziario(a).

financier [faɪ'nænsɪə*] *n* finanziatore *m*.

find [faɪnd] *vt* (pt, pp **found** [faʊnd]) trovare; (lost object) ritrovare // *n* trovata, scoperta; **to ~ sb guilty** (LAW) giudicare qd colpevole; **to ~ out** *vt* informarsi di; (truth, secret) scoprire; (person) cogliere in fallo; **~ings** *npl* (LAW) sentenza, conclusioni *fpl*; (of report) conclusioni.

fine [faɪn] *a* bello(a); ottimo(a); fine // *ad* (well) molto bene; (small) finemente // *n* (LAW) contravvenzione *f*, ammenda; multa

// *vt* (LAW) fare una contravvenzione a; multare; **~ arts** *npl* belle arti *fpl*.

finery ['faɪnərɪ] *n* abiti *mpl* eleganti.

finesse [fɪ'nɛs] *n* finezza.

finger ['fɪŋgə*] *n* dito // *vt* toccare, tastare; **~nail** *n* unghia; **~print** *n* impronta digitale; **~tip** *n* punta del dito.

finicky ['fɪnɪkɪ] *a* esigente, pignolo(a); minuzioso(a).

finish ['fɪnɪʃ] *n* fine *f*; (polish etc) finitura // *vt* finire; (use up) esaurire // *vi* finire; (session) terminare; **to ~ off** *vt* compiere; (kill) uccidere; **to ~ up** *vi, vt* finire; **~ing line** *n* linea d'arrivo; **~ing school** *n* scuola privata di perfezionamento (per signorine).

finite ['faɪnaɪt] *a* limitato(a); (verb) finito(a).

Finland ['fɪnlənd] *n* Finlandia.

Finn [fɪn] *n* finlandese *m/f*; **~ish** *a* finlandese // *n* (LING) finlandese *m*.

fiord [fjɔːd] *n* fiordo.

fir [fəː*] *n* abete *m*.

fire [faɪə*] *n* fuoco; incendio // *vt* (discharge): **to ~ a gun** scaricare un fucile; (fig) infiammare; (dismiss) licenziare // *vi* sparare, far fuoco; **on ~** in fiamme; **~ alarm** *n* allarme *m* d'incendio; **~arm** *n* arma da fuoco; **~ brigade** *n* (corpo dei) pompieri *mpl*; **~ engine** *n* autopompa; **~ escape** *n* scala di sicurezza; **~ extinguisher** *n* estintore *m*; **~man** *n* pompiere *m*; **~place** *n* focolare *m*; **~side** *n* angolo del focolare; **~ station** *n* caserma dei pompieri; **~wood** *n* legna; **~work** *n* fuoco d'artificio.

firing ['faɪərɪŋ] *n* (MIL) spari *mpl*, tiro; **~ squad** *n* plotone *m* d'esecuzione.

firm [fəːm] *a* fermo(a) // *n* ditta, azienda.

first [fəːst] *a* primo(a) // *ad* (before others) il primo, la prima; (before other things) per primo; (when listing reasons etc) per prima cosa // *n* (person: in race) primo/a; (SCOL) laurea con lode; (AUT) prima; **at ~** dapprima, all'inizio; **~ of all** prima di tutto; **~-aid kit** *n* cassetta pronto soccorso; **~-class** *a* di prima classe; **~-hand** *a* di prima mano; **~ lady** *n* (US) moglie *f* del presidente; **~ly** *ad* in primo luogo; **~ name** *n* prenome *m*; **~ night** *n* (THEATRE) prima; **~-rate** *a* di prima qualità, ottimo(a).

fiscal ['fɪskəl] *a* fiscale.

fish [fɪʃ] *n, pl inv* pesce *m* // *vi* pescare; **to go ~ing** andare a pesca; **~erman** *n* pescatore *m*; **~ery** *n* zona da pesca; **~ fingers** *npl* bastoncini *mpl* di pesce (surgelati); **~ing boat** *n* barca da pesca; **~ing line** *n* lenza; **~ing rod** *n* canna da pesca; **~monger** *n* pescivendolo; **~y** *a* (fig) sospetto(a).

fission ['fɪʃən] *n* fissione *f*.

fissure ['fɪʃə*] *n* fessura.

fist [fɪst] *n* pugno.

fit [fɪt] *a* (MED, SPORT) in forma; (proper) adatto(a), appropriato(a); conveniente // *vt* (subj: clothes) stare bene a; (adjust) aggiustare; (*put in*, *attach*) mettere; installare; (*equip*) fornire, equipaggiare // *vi* (*clothes*) stare bene; (*parts*) andare bene, adattarsi; (*in space, gap*) entrare // *n* (*MED*) accesso, attacco; ~ **to** in grado di; ~ **for** adatto(a) a; degno(a) di; **this dress is a tight/good** ~ questo vestito è stretto/sta bene; **by** ~**s and starts** a sbalzi; **to** ~ **in** vi accordarsi; adattarsi; **to** ~ **out** (*also*: ~ **up**) *vt* equipaggiare; ~**ful** saltuario(a); ~**ment** n componibile *m*; ~**ness** *n* (*MED*) forma fisica; (*of remark*) appropriatezza; ~**ter** *n* aggiustatore *m* or montatore *m* meccanico; (*DRESSMAKING*) sarto/a; ~**ting** *a* appropriato(a) // *n* (*of dress*) prova; (*of piece of equipment*) montaggio, aggiustaggio; ~**tings** *npl* impianti *mpl*.

five [faɪv] *num* cinque; ~**r** *n* (*Brit*: *col*) biglietto da cinque sterline.

fix [fɪks] *vt* fissare; mettere in ordine; (*mend*) riparare // *n*: **to be in a** ~ essere nei guai; ~**ed** [fɪkst] *a* (*prices etc*) fisso(a); ~**ture** ['fɪkstʃə*] *n* impianto (fisso), (*SPORT*) incontro (del calendario sportivo).

fizz [fɪz] *vi* frizzare.

fizzle ['fɪzl] *vi* frizzare; **to** ~ **out** *vi* finire in nulla.

fizzy ['fɪzɪ] *a* frizzante; gassato(a).

fjord [fjɔːd] *n* = **fiord**.

flabbergasted ['flæbəgɑːstɪd] *a* sbalordito(a).

flabby ['flæbɪ] *a* flaccido(a).

flag [flæg] *n* bandiera; (*also*: ~**stone**) pietra da lastricare // *vi* avvizzire; affievolirsi; **to** ~ **down** *vt* fare segno (di fermarsi) a.

flagon ['flægən] *n* bottiglione *m*.

flagpole ['flægpəul] *n* albero.

flagrant ['fleɪgrənt] *a* flagrante.

flair [flɛə*] *n* (*for business etc*) fiuto; (*for languages etc*) facilità.

flake [fleɪk] *n* (*of rust, paint*) scaglia; (*of snow, soap powder*) fiocco // *vi* (*also*: ~ **off**) sfaldarsi.

flamboyant [flæm'bɔɪənt] *a* sgargiante.

flame [fleɪm] *n* fiamma.

flamingo [flə'mɪŋgəu] *n* fenicottero, fiammingo.

flammable ['flæməbl] *a* infiammabile.

flan [flæn] *n* flan *m inv*.

flange [flændʒ] *n* flangia; (*on wheel*) suola.

flank [flæŋk] *n* fianco.

flannel ['flænl] *n* (*also*: **face** ~) guanto di spugna; (*fabric*) flanella; ~**s** *npl* pantaloni *mpl* di flanella.

flap [flæp] *n* (*of pocket*) patta; (*of envelope*) lembo // *vt* (*wings*) battere // *vi* (*sail, flag*) sbattere; (*col: also*: **be in a** ~) essere in agitazione.

flare [flɛə*] *n* razzo; (*in skirt etc*) svasatura; **to** ~ **up** *vi* andare in fiamme; (*fig: person*) infiammarsi di rabbia; (*: revolt*) scoppiare; ~**d** *a* (*trousers*) svasato(a).

flash [flæʃ] *n* vampata; (*also*: **news** ~) notizia *f* lampo *inv*; (*PHOT*) flash *m inv* // *vt* accendere e spegnere; (*send*: *message*) trasmettere // *vi* brillare; (*light on*

ambulance, eyes etc) lampeggiare; **in a** ~ in un lampo; **to** ~ **one's headlights** lampeggiare; **he** ~**ed by** or **past** ci passò davanti come un lampo; ~**back** *n* flashback *m inv*; ~**bulb** *n* cubo *m* flash *inv*; ~**er** *n* (*AUT*) lampeggiatore *m*.

flashy ['flæʃɪ] *a* (*pej*) vistoso(a).

flask [flɑːsk] *n* fiasco; (*CHEM*) beuta; (*also*: **vacuum** ~) thermos *m inv* ®.

flat [flæt] *a* piatto(a); (*tyre*) sgonfio(a), a terra; (*denial*) netto(a); (*MUS*) bemolle *inv*; (*: voice*) stonato(a) // *n* (*Brit: rooms*) appartamento, (*MUS*) bemolle *m*; (*AUT*) pneumatico sgonfio; ~**ly** *ad* recisamente; ~**ten** *vt* (*also*: ~ **ten out**) appiattare.

flatter ['flætə*] *vt* lusingare; ~**er** *n* adulatore/trice; ~**ing** *a* lusinghiero(a); ~**y** *n* adulazione *f*.

flaunt [flɔːnt] *vt* fare mostra di.

flavour ['fleɪvə*] *n* gusto, sapore *m* // *vt* insaporire, aggiungere sapore a; **vanilla-**~**ed** al gusto di vaniglia; ~**ing** *n* essenza (artificiale).

flaw [flɔː] *n* difetto; ~**less** *a* senza difetti.

flax [flæks] *n* lino; ~**en** *a* biondo(a).

flea [fliː] *n* pulce *f*.

fledg(e)ling ['fledʒlɪŋ] *n* uccellino.

flee, *pt*, *pp* **fled** [fliː, fled] *vt* fuggire da // *vi* fuggire, scappare.

fleece [fliːs] *n* vello // *vt* (*col*) pelare.

fleet [fliːt] *n* flotta; (*of lorries etc*) convoglio, parco.

fleeting ['fliːtɪŋ] *a* fugace, fuggitivo(a); (*visit*) volante.

Flemish ['flemɪʃ] *a* fiammingo(a) // *n* (*LING*) fiammingo.

flesh [fleʃ] *n* carne *f*.

flew [fluː] *pt of* **fly**.

flex [fleks] *n* filo (flessibile) // *vt* flettere; (*muscles*) contrarre; ~**ibility** [-'bɪlɪtɪ] *n* flessibilità; ~**ible** *a* flessibile.

flick [flɪk] *n* colpetto; scarto; **to** ~ **through** *vt fus* sfogliare.

flicker ['flɪkə*] *vi* tremolare // *n* tremolio.

flier ['flaɪə*] *n* aviatore *m*.

flight [flaɪt] *n* volo; (*escape*) fuga; (*also*: ~ **of steps**) scalinata; **to take** ~ darsi alla fuga; **to put to** ~ mettere in fuga; ~ **deck** *n* (*AVIAT*) cabina di controllo; (*NAUT*) ponte *m* di comando.

flimsy ['flɪmzɪ] *a* (*fabric*) inconsistente; (*excuse*) meschino(a).

flinch [flɪntʃ] *vi* ritirarsi; **to** ~ **from** tirarsi indietro di fronte a.

fling, *pt*, *pp* **flung** [flɪŋ, flʌŋ] *vt* lanciare, gettare.

flint [flɪnt] *n* selce *f*; (*in lighter*) pietrina.

flip [flɪp] *n* colpetto.

flippant ['flɪpənt] *a* senza rispetto, irriverente.

flirt [flɜːt] *vi* flirtare // *n* civetta; ~**ation** [-'teɪʃən] *n* flirt *m inv*.

flit [flɪt] *vi* svolazzare.

float [fləut] *n* galleggiante *m*; (*in procession*) carro // *vi* galleggiare // *vt* far galleggiare; (*loan, business*) lanciare; ~**ing** *a* a galla.

flock [flɔk] n gregge m; (of people) folla.

flog [flɔg] vt flagellare.

flood [flʌd] n alluvione m; (of words, tears etc) diluvio // vt allagare; **in ~** in pieno; **~ing** n alluvionamento; **~light** n riflettore m // vt illuminare a giorno.

floor [flɔ:*] n pavimento; (storey) piano; (fig: at meeting): **the ~** il pubblico // vt pavimentare; (knock down) atterrare; **first ~** (Brit), **second ~** (US) primo piano; **~board** n tavellone m di legno; **~ show** n spettacolo di varietà.

flop [flɔp] n fiasco // vi (fail) far fiasco.

floppy ['flɔpɪ] a floscio(a), molle.

flora ['flɔ:rə] n flora.

floral ['flɔ:rl] a floreale.

Florence ['flɔrəns] n Firenze f; **Florentine** ['flɔrəntaɪn] a fiorentino(a).

florid ['flɔrɪd] a (complexion) florido(a); (style) fiorito(a).

florist ['flɔrɪst] n fioraio/a.

flounce [flauns] n balzo; **to ~ out** vi uscire stizzito(a).

flounder ['flaundə*] vi annaspare // n (ZOOL) passera di mare.

flour ['flauə*] n farina.

flourish ['flʌrɪʃ] vi fiorire // vt brandire // n abbellimento; svolazzo; (of trumpets) fanfara; **~ing** a prosperoso(a), fiorente.

flout [flaut] vt disprezzare.

flow [fləu] n flusso; circolazione f // vi fluire; (traffic, blood in veins) circolare; (hair) scendere; **~ chart** n schema m di flusso.

flower ['flauə*] n fiore m // vi fiorire; **~ bed** n aiuola; **~pot** n vaso da fiori; **~y** a fiorito(a).

flown [fləun] pp of **fly**.

flu [flu:] n influenza.

fluctuate ['flʌktjueɪt] vi fluttuare, oscillare; **fluctuation** [-'eɪʃən] n fluttuazione f, oscillazione f.

fluency ['flu:ənsɪ] n facilità, scioltezza; (in foreign language) buona conoscenza della lingua parlata.

fluent ['flu:ənt] a (speech) facile, sciolto(a); corrente; **he speaks ~ Italian** parla l'italiano correntemente; **~ly** ad con facilità; correntemente.

fluff [flʌf] n lanugine f; **~y** a lanuginoso(a); (toy) di peluche.

fluid ['flu:ɪd] a fluido(a) // n fluido; **~ ounce** n = 0.028 l; 0.05 pints.

fluke [flu:k] n (col) colpo di fortuna.

flung [flʌŋ] pt,pp of **fling**.

fluorescent [fluə'resnt] a fluorescente.

fluoride ['fluəraɪd] n fluoruro.

flurry ['flʌrɪ] n (of snow) tempesta; **a ~ of activity/excitement** una febbre di attività/improvvisa agitazione.

flush [flʌʃ] n rossore m; (fig) ebbrezza // vt ripulire con un getto d'acqua // vi arrossire // a: **~ with** a livello di, pari a; **~ against** aderente a; **to ~ the toilet** tirare la catena, tirare lo scarico; **~ed** a tutto(a) rosso(a).

fluster ['flʌstə*] n agitazione f; **~ed** a sconvolto(a).

flute [flu:t] n flauto.

flutter ['flʌtə*] n agitazione f; (of wings) frullio // vi (bird) battere le ali.

flux [flʌks] n: **in a state of ~** in continuo mutamento.

fly [flaɪ] n (insect) mosca; (on trousers: also: **flies**) bracchetta // vb (pt **flew**, pp **flown** [flu:, fləun]) vt pilotare; (passengers, cargo) trasportare (in aereo); (distances) percorrere // vi volare; (passengers) andare in aereo; (escape) fuggire; (flag) sventolare; **to ~ open** vi spalancarsi all'improvviso; **~ing** n (activity) aviazione f; (action) volo // a: **~ing visit** visita volante; **with ~ing colours** con risultati brillanti; **~ing saucer** n disco volante; **~ing start** n: **to get off to a ~ing start** partire come un razzo; **~over** n (Brit: bridge) cavalcavia m inv; **~past** n parata aerea; **~sheet** n (for tent) sopratetto; **~wheel** n volano.

foal [fəul] n puledro.

foam [fəum] n schiuma // vi schiumare; **~ rubber** n gommapiuma ®.

fob [fɔb] vt: **to ~ sb off with** appioppare qd con; sbarazzarsi di qd con.

focal ['fəukəl] a focale.

focus ['fəukəs] n (pl: **~es**) fuoco; (of interest) centro // vt (field glasses etc) mettere a fuoco; **in ~** a fuoco; **out of ~** sfocato(a).

fodder ['fɔdə*] n foraggio.

foe [fəu] n nemico.

foetus ['fi:təs] n feto.

fog [fɔg] n nebbia; **~gy** a nebbioso(a); **it's ~gy** c'è nebbia.

foible ['fɔɪbl] n debolezza, punto debole.

foil [fɔɪl] vt confondere, frustrare // n lamina di metallo; (also: **kitchen ~**) foglio di alluminio; (FENCING) fioretto.

fold [fəuld] n (bend, crease) piega; (AGR) ovile m; (fig) gregge m // vt piegare; **to ~ up** vi (map etc) piegarsi; (business) crollare // vt (map etc) piegare, ripiegare; **~er** n (for papers) cartella; cartellina; (brochure) dépliant m inv; **~ing** a (chair, bed) pieghevole.

foliage ['fəulɪdʒ] n fogliame m.

folk [fəuk] npl gente f // a popolare; **~s** npl famiglia; **~lore** ['fəuklɔ:*] n folclore m; **~song** n canto popolare.

follow ['fɔləu] vt seguire // vi seguire; (result) conseguire, risultare; **he ~ed suit** lui ha fatto lo stesso; **to ~ up** vt (victory) sfruttare; (letter, offer) fare seguito a; (case) seguire; **~er** n seguace m/f, discepolo/a; **~ing** a seguente, successivo(a) // n seguito, discepoli mpl.

folly ['fɔlɪ] n pazzia, follia.

fond [fɔnd] a (memory, look) tenero(a), affettuoso(a); **to be ~ of** volere bene a.

fondle ['fɔndl] vt accarezzare.

fondness ['fɔndnɪs] n affetto.

font [fɔnt] n fonte m (battesimale).

food [fu:d] n cibo; **~ poisoning** n

intossicazione f; **~stuffs** npl generi fpl alimentari.

fool [fu:l] n sciocco/a; (HISTORY: of king) buffone m; (CULIN.) frullato // vt ingannare // vi (gen: **~ around**) fare lo sciocco; **~hardy** a avventato(a); **~ish** a scemo(a), stupido(a); imprudente; **~proof** a (plan etc) sicurissimo(a).

foot [fut] n (pl: **feet** [fi:t]) piede m; (measure) piede (= 304 mm; 12 inches); (of animal) zampa // vt (bill) pagare; **on ~** a piedi; **~ and mouth (disease)** n afta epizootica; **~ball** n pallone m; (sport) calcio; **~baller** n calciatore m; **~brake** n freno a pedale; **~bridge** n passerella; **~hills** npl contrafforti fpl; **~hold** n punto d'appoggio; **~ing** n (fig) posizione f; **to lose one's ~ing** mettere un piede in fallo; **on an equal ~ing** in condizioni di parità; **~lights** npl luci fpl della ribalta; **~man** n lacchè m inv; **~note** n nota (a piè di pagina); **~path** n sentiero; (in street) marciapiede m; **~sore** a coi piedi doloranti o dolenti; **~step** n passo; **~wear** n calzatura.

for [fɔ:*] prep per // cj poiché; **~ all his money/he says ...** nonostante or malgrado tutto il suo denaro/quel che dice ...; **I haven't seen him ~ a week** è una settimana che non lo vedo, non lo vedo da una settimana; **he went down ~ the paper** è sceso a prendere il giornale; **~ sale** da vendere.

forage ['fɔrɪdʒ] vi foraggiare.

foray ['fɔreɪ] n incursione f.

forbad(e) [fə'bæd] pt of **forbid**.

forbearing [fɔ:'bɛərɪŋ] a paziente, tollerante.

forbid, pt **forbad(e)**, pp **forbidden** [fə'bɪd, -'bæd, -'bɪdn] vt vietare, interdire; **~den** a vietato(a); **~ding** a arcigno(a), d'aspetto minaccioso.

force [fɔ:s] n forza // vt forzare; **the F~s** npl le forze armate; **in ~** (in large numbers) in gran numero; (law) in vigore; **to come into ~** entrare in vigore; **~d** [fɔ:st] a forzato(a); **~ful** a forte, vigoroso(a).

forceps ['fɔ:seps] npl forcipe m.

forcibly ['fɔ:səblɪ] ad con la forza; (vigorously) vigorosamente.

ford [fɔ:d] n guado // vt guadare.

fore [fɔ:*] n: **to the ~** in prima linea; **to come to the ~** mettersi in evidenza.

forearm ['fɔ:rɑ:m] n avambraccio.

foreboding [fɔ:'bəudɪŋ] n presagio di male.

forecast ['fɔ:kɑ:st] n previsione f // vt (irg: like **cast**) prevedere.

forecourt ['fɔ:kɔ:t] n (of garage) corte f esterna.

forefathers ['fɔ:fɑ:ðəz] npl antenati mpl, avi mpl.

forefinger ['fɔ:fɪŋɡə*] n (dito) indice m.

forego [fɔ:'ɡəu] vt = **forgo**.

foregone ['fɔ:ɡɔn] a: **it's a ~ conclusion** è una conclusione scontata.

foreground ['fɔ:ɡraund] n primo piano.

forehead ['fɔrɪd] n fronte f.

foreign ['fɔrɪn] a straniero(a); (trade) estero(a); **~ body** n corpo estraneo; **~er** n straniero/a; **~ exchange market** n mercato delle valute; **~ exchange rate** n cambio; **~ minister** n ministro degli Affari esteri.

foreman ['fɔ:mən] n caposquadra m.

foremost ['fɔ:məust] a principale; più in vista.

forensic [fə'rɛnsɪk] a: **~ medicine** medicina legale.

forerunner ['fɔ:rʌnə*] n precursore m.

foresee, pt **foresaw**, pp **foreseen** [fɔ:'si:, -'sɔ:, -'si:n] vt prevedere; **~able** a prevedibile.

foresight ['fɔ:saɪt] n previdenza.

forest ['fɔrɪst] n foresta.

forestall [fɔ:'stɔ:l] vt prevenire.

forestry ['fɔrɪstrɪ] n silvicoltura.

foretaste ['fɔ:teɪst] n pregustazione f.

foretell, pt,pp **foretold** [fɔ:'tɛl, -'təuld] vt predire.

forever [fə'rɛvə*] ad per sempre; (fig) sempre, di continuo.

forewent [fɔ:'wɛnt] pt of **forego**.

foreword ['fɔ:wəd] n prefazione f.

forfeit ['fɔ:fɪt] n ammenda, pena // vt perdere; (one's happiness, health) giocarsi.

forgave [fə'ɡeɪv] pt of **forgive**.

forge [fɔ:dʒ] n fucina // vt (signature, money) contraffare, falsificare; (wrought iron) fucinare, foggiare; **to ~ ahead** vi tirare avanti; **~r** n contraffattore m; **~ry** n falso; (activity) contraffazione f.

forget, pt **forgot**, pp **forgotten** [fə'ɡɛt, -'ɡɔt, -'ɡɔtn] vt,vi dimenticare; **~ful** a di corta memoria; **~ful of** dimentico(a) di.

forgive, pt **forgave**, pp **forgiven** [fə'ɡɪv, -'ɡeɪv, -'ɡɪvn] vt perdonare; **~ness** n perdono.

forgo, pt **forwent**, pp **forgone** [fɔ:'ɡəu, -'wɛnt, -'ɡɔn] vt rinunciare a.

forgot [fə'ɡɔt] pt of **forget**.

forgotten [fə'ɡɔtn] pp of **forget**.

fork [fɔ:k] n (for eating) forchetta; (for gardening) forca; (of roads) bivio; (of railways) inforcazione f // vi (road) biforcarsi; **to ~ out** (col: pay) vt sborsare // vi pagare; **~ed** [fɔ:kt] a (lightning) a zigzag; **~-lift truck** n carrello elevatore.

form [fɔ:m] n forma; (scol) classe f; (questionnaire) scheda // vt formare; **in top ~** in gran forma.

formal ['fɔ:məl] a (offer, receipt) vero(a) e proprio(a); (person) cerimonioso(a); (occasion, dinner) formale, ufficiale; (ART, PHILOSOPHY) formale; **~ly** ad ufficialmente; formalmente; cerimoniosamente.

format ['fɔ:mæt] n formato.

formation [fɔ:'meɪʃən] n formazione f.

formative ['fɔ:mətɪv] a: **~ years** anni mpl formativi.

former ['fɔ:mə*] a vecchio(a) (before n), ex inv (before n); **the ~ ... the latter** quello ... questo; **~ly** ad in passato.

formidable ['fɔ:mɪdəbl] a formidabile.

formula ['fɔːmjulə] n formula.
formulate ['fɔːmjuleɪt] vt formulare.
forsake, pt **forsook,** pp **forsaken**
[fə'seɪk, -'suk, -'seɪkən] vt abbandonare.
fort [fɔːt] n forte m.
forte ['fɔːtɪ] n forte m.
forth [fɔːθ] ad in avanti; **to go back and ~**
andare avanti e indietro; **and so ~** e così
via; **~coming** a prossimo(a); (character)
aperto(a), comunicativo(a); **~right** a
franco(a), schietto(a).
fortieth ['fɔːtɪɪθ] num quarantesimo(a).
fortification [fɔːtɪfɪ'keɪʃən] n
fortificazione f.
fortify ['fɔːtɪfaɪ] vt fortificare.
fortitude ['fɔːtɪtjuːd] n forza d'animo.
fortnight ['fɔːtnaɪt] n quindici giorni mpl,
due settimane fpl; **~ly** a bimensile // ad
ogni quindici giorni.
fortress ['fɔːtrɪs] n fortezza, rocca.
fortuitous [fɔː'tjuːɪtəs] a fortuito(a).
fortunate ['fɔːtʃənɪt] a fortunato(a); **it is**
~ that è una fortuna che; **~ly** ad
fortunatamente.
fortune ['fɔːtʃən] n fortuna; **~teller** n
indovino/a.
forty ['fɔːtɪ] num quaranta.
forum ['fɔːrəm] n foro.
forward ['fɔːwəd] a (ahead of schedule) in
anticipo; (movement, position) in avanti;
(not shy) aperto(a); diretto(a);
sfacciato(a) // ad avanti // n (SPORT)
avanti m inv // vt (letter) inoltrare;
(parcel, goods) spedire; (fig) promuovere,
appoggiare; **to move ~** avanzare; **~(s)**
ad avanti.
forwent [fɔː'wɛnt] pt of **forgo**.
fossil ['fɔsl] a,n fossile (m).
foster ['fɔstə*] vt incoraggiare, nutrire;
(child) adottare; **~ brother** n fratello
adottivo; fratello di latte; **~ child** n
bambino(a) adottato(a); **~ mother** n
madre f adottiva; nutrice f.
fought [fɔːt] pt, pp of **fight**.
foul [faul] a (smell, food) cattivo(a);
(weather) sporco(a); (language) osceno(a);
(deed) infame // n (FOOTBALL) fallo // vt
sporcare; (football player) commettere un
fallo su.
found [faund] pt, pp of **find** // vt (establish)
fondare; **~ation** [-'deɪʃən] n (act)
fondazione f; (base) base f; (also: **~ation**
cream) fondo tinta; **~ations** npl (of
building) fondamenta fpl.
founder ['faundə*] n fondatore/ trice // vi
affondare.
foundry ['faundrɪ] n fonderia.
fount [faunt] n fonte f; **~ain** ['fauntɪn] n
fontana; **~ain pen** n penna stilografica.
four [fɔː*] num quattro; **on all ~s** a
carponi; **~some** ['fɔːsəm] n partita a
quattro; uscita in quattro; **~teen** num
quattordici; **~th** num quarto(a).
fowl [faul] n pollame m; volatile m.
fox [fɔks] n volpe f // vt confondere.
foyer ['fɔɪeɪ] n atrio; (THEATRE) ridotto.
fraction ['frækʃən] n frazione f.

fracture ['fræktʃə*] n frattura // vt
fratturare.
fragile ['frædʒaɪl] a fragile.
fragment ['frægmənt] n frammento;
~ary a frammentario(a).
fragrance ['freɪgrəns] n fragranza,
profumo.
fragrant ['freɪgrənt] a fragrante,
profumato(a).
frail [freɪl] a debole, delicato(a).
frame [freɪm] n (of building) armatura; (of
human, animal) ossatura, corpo; (of picture)
cornice f; (of door, window) telaio; (of
spectacles: also: **~s**) montatura; **~ of**
mind n stato d'animo; **~work** n struttura.
France [frɑːns] n Francia.
franchise ['fræntʃaɪz] n (POL) diritto di
voto.
frank [fræŋk] a franco(a), aperto(a) // vt
(letter) affrancare; **~ly** ad francamente,
sinceramente; **~ness** n franchezza.
frantic ['fræntɪk] a frenetico(a).
fraternal [frə'tɜːnl] a fraterno(a).
fraternity [frə'tɜːnɪtɪ] n (club)
associazione f; (spirit) fratellanza.
fraternize ['frætənaɪz] vi fraternizzare.
fraud [frɔːd] n frode f, inganno, truffa;
impostore/a.
fraudulent ['frɔːdjulənt] a fraudolento(a).
fraught [frɔːt] a: **~ with** pieno(a) di,
intriso(a) da.
fray [freɪ] n baruffa // vt logorare // vi
logorarsi; **her nerves were ~ed** aveva i
nervi a pezzi.
freak [friːk] n fenomeno, mostro // cpd
fenomenale.
freckle ['frɛkl] n lentiggine f.
free [friː] a libero(a); (gratis) gratuito(a);
(liberal) generoso(a) // vt (prisoner,
jammed person) liberare; (jammed object)
districare; **~ (of charge)** ad
gratuitamente; **~dom** ['friːdəm] n libertà;
~-for-all n parapiglia m generale; **~**
kick n calcio libero; **~lance** a
indipendente; **~ly** ad liberamente;
(liberally) liberalmente; **~mason** n
massone m; **~ trade** n libero scambio;
~way n (US) superstrada; **~wheel** vi
andare a ruota libera; **~ will** n libero
arbitrio; **of one's own ~ will** di
spontanea volontà.
freeze [friːz] vb (pt **froze,** pp **frozen** [frəuz,
'frəuzn]) vi gelare // vt gelare; (food)
congelare; (prices, salaries) bloccare // n
gelo; blocco; **~r** n congelatore m.
freezing ['friːzɪŋ] a: **~ cold** a gelido(a);
~ point n punto di congelamento; **3**
degrees below ~ 3 gradi sotto zero.
freight [freɪt] n (goods) merce f, merci fpl;
(money charged) spese fpl di trasporto; **~**
car n (US) carro m merci inv; **~er** n
(NAUT) nave f da carico.
French [frɛntʃ] a francese // n (LING)
francese m; **the ~** i Francesi; **~ fried**
potatoes npl patate fpl fritte; **~man** n
francese m; **~ window** n portafinestra;
~woman n francese f.
frenzy ['frɛnzɪ] n frenesia.

frequency ['fri:kwənsɪ] n frequenza.
frequent a ['fri:kwənt] frequente // vt [frɪ'kwent] frequentare; **~ly** ad frequentemente, spesso.
fresco ['freskəu] n affresco.
fresh [freʃ] a fresco(a); (new) nuovo(a); (cheeky) sfacciato(a); **~en** vi (wind, air) rinfrescare; **to ~en up** vi rinfrescarsi; **~ly** ad di recente, di fresco; **~ness** n freschezza; **~water** a (fish) d'acqua dolce.
fret [fret] vi agitarsi, affliggersi.
friar ['fraɪə*] n frate m.
friction ['frɪkʃən] n frizione f, attrito.
Friday ['fraɪdɪ] n venerdì m inv.
fridge [frɪdʒ] n frigo, frigorifero.
fried [fraɪd] pt, pp of **fry** // a fritto(a).
friend [frend] n amico/a; **~liness** n amichevolezza; **~ly** a amichevole; **~ship** n amicizia.
frieze [fri:z] n fregio.
frigate ['frɪgɪt] n (NAUT: modern) fregata.
fright [fraɪt] n paura, spavento; **~en** vt spaventare, far paura a; **~ening** a spaventoso(a), pauroso(a); **~ful** a orribile; **~fully** ad terribilmente.
frigid ['frɪdʒɪd] a (woman) frigido(a).
frill [frɪl] n balza.
fringe [frɪndʒ] n frangia; (edge: of forest etc) margine m; (fig): **on the ~** al margine.
frisk [frɪsk] vt perquisire.
frisky ['frɪskɪ] a vivace, vispo(a).
fritter ['frɪtə*] n frittella; **to ~ away** vt sprecare.
frivolity [frɪ'vɔlɪtɪ] n frivolezza.
frivolous ['frɪvələs] a frivolo(a).
frizzy ['frɪzɪ] a crespo(a).
fro [frəu] see **to**.
frock [frɔk] n vestito.
frog [frɔg] n rana; **~man** n uomo m rana inv.
frolic ['frɔlɪk] vi sgambettare.
from [frɔm] prep da; **~ a pound/January** da una sterlina in poi/da gennaio in poi; **~ what he says** a quanto dice.
front [frʌnt] n (of house, dress) davanti m inv; (of train) testa; (of book) copertina; (promenade: also: **sea ~**) lungomare m; (MIL, POL, METEOR) fronte m; (fig: appearances) fronte f // a primo(a); anteriore, davanti inv; **~al** a frontale; **~ door** n porta d'entrata; (of car) sportello anteriore; **~ier** ['frʌntɪə*] n frontiera; **~ page** n prima pagina; **~ room** n (Brit) salotto; **~-wheel drive** n trasmissione f anteriore.
frost [frɔst] n gelo; (also: **hoar ~**) brina; **~bite** n congelamento; **~ed** a (glass) smerigliato(a); **~y** a (window) coperto(a) di ghiaccio; (welcome) gelido(a).
froth ['frɔθ] n spuma; schiuma.
frown [fraun] n cipiglio // vi accigliarsi.
froze [frəuz] pt of **freeze**; **~n** pp of **freeze** // a (food) congelato(a).
frugal ['fru:gəl] a frugale.
fruit [fru:t] n, pl inv frutto; (collectively)

frutta; **~ful** a fruttuoso(a); (plant) fruttifero(a); (soil) fertile; **~ion** [fru:'ɪʃən] n: **to come to ~ion** realizzarsi; **~ machine** n macchina f mangiasoldi inv; **~ salad** n macedonia.
frustrate [frʌs'treɪt] vt frustrare; **~d** a frustrato(a); **frustration** [-'treɪʃən] n frustrazione f.
fry [fraɪ], pt, pp **fried** [fraɪ, -d] vt friggere; **the small ~** i pesci piccoli; **~ing pan** n padella.
ft. abbr of **foot, feet.**
fuchsia ['fju:ʃə] n fucsia.
fudge [fʌdʒ] n (CULIN) specie di caramella a base di latte, burro e zucchero.
fuel [fjuəl] n (for heating) combustibile m; (for propelling) carburante m; **~ oil** n nafta; **~ tank** n deposito m nafta inv; (on vehicle) serbatoio (della benzina).
fugitive ['fju:dʒɪtɪv] n fugitivo/a, profugo/a.
fulfil [ful'fɪl] vt (function) compiere; (order) eseguire; (wish, desire) soddisfare, appagare; **~ment** n (of wishes) soddisfazione f, appagamento.
full [ful] a pieno(a); (details, skirt) ampio(a) // ad: **to know ~ well that** sapere benissimo che; **~ employment** piena occupazione; **~ fare** tariffa completa; a **~ two hours** due ore intere; **at ~ speed** a tutta velocità; **in ~** per intero; **~back** n (RUGBY, FOOTBALL) terzino; **~-length** a (portrait) in piedi; **~ moon** n luna piena; **~-sized** a (portrait etc) a grandezza naturale; **~ stop** n punto; **~-time** a (work) a tempo pieno // n (SPORT) fine f partita; **~y** ad interamente, pienamente, completamente.
fumble ['fʌmbl] vi brancolare, andare a tentoni // vt (ball) lasciarsi sfuggire; **to ~ with** vt fus trafficare.
fume [fju:m] vi essere furioso(a); **~s** npl esalazioni fpl, vapori mpl.
fumigate ['fju:mɪgeɪt] vt suffumicare.
fun [fʌn] n divertimento, spasso; **to have ~** divertirsi; **for ~** per scherzo; **it's not much ~** non è molto divertente; **to make ~ of** vt fus prendersi gioco di.
function ['fʌŋkʃən] n funzione f; cerimonia; ricevimento // vi funzionare; **~al** a funzionale.
fund [fʌnd] n fondo, cassa; (source) fondo; (store) riserva; **~s** npl fondi mpl.
fundamental [fʌndə'mentl] a fondamentale; **~s** npl basi fpl; **~ly** ad essenzialmente, fondamentalmente.
funeral ['fju:nərəl] n funerale m; **~ service** n ufficio funebre.
fun fair ['fʌnfeə*] n luna park m inv.
fungus, pl **fungi** ['fʌŋgəs, -gaɪ] n fungo; (mould) muffa.
funnel ['fʌnl] n imbuto; (of ship) ciminiera.
funny ['fʌnɪ] a divertente, buffo(a); (strange) strano(a), bizzarro(a).
fur [fə:*] n pelo; pelliccia; (in kettle etc) deposito calcare; **~ coat** n pelliccia.
furious ['fjuərɪəs] a furioso(a); (effort)

accanito(a); ~ly ad furiosamente; accanitamente.

furlong ['fɔ:lɒŋ] n = 201.17 m (termine ippico).

furlough ['fɔ:ləu] n (US) congedo, permesso.

furnace ['fɔ:nɪs] n fornace f.

furnish ['fɔ:nɪʃ] vt ammobiliare; (supply) fornire; ~ings npl mobili mpl, mobilia.

furniture ['fɔ:nɪtʃə*] n mobili mpl; piece of ~ mobile m.

furrow ['fʌrəu] a solco.

furry ['fɔ:rɪ] a (animal) peloso(a).

further ['fɔ:ðə*] a supplementare, altro(a); nuovo(a); più lontano(a) // ad più lontano; (more) di più; (moreover) inoltre // vt favorire, promuovere; **until ~ notice** fino a nuovo avviso; **college of ~ education** n istituto statale con corsi specializzati (di formazione professionale, aggiornamento professionale etc); ~**more** [fɔ:ðə'mɔ:*] ad inoltre, per di più.

furthest ['fɔ:ðɪst] superlative of **far**.

furtive ['fɔ:tɪv] a furtivo(a).

fury ['fjuərɪ] n furore m.

fuse [fju:z] n fusibile m; (for bomb etc) miccia, spoletta // vt fondere; (ELEC): to ~ **the lights** far saltare i fusibili // vi fondersi; ~ **box** n cassetta dei fusibili.

fuselage ['fju:zəlɑ:ʒ] n fusoliera.

fusion ['fju:ʒən] n fusione f.

fuss [fʌs] n chiasso, trambusto, confusione f; (complaining) storie fpl; **to make a ~** fare delle storie; ~**y** a (person) puntiglioso(a), esigente; che fa le storie; (dress) carico(a) di fronzoli; (style) elaborato(a).

futile ['fju:taɪl] a futile.

futility [fju:'tɪlɪtɪ] n futilità.

future ['fju:tʃə*] a futuro(a) // n futuro, avvenire m; (LING) futuro; **in ~** in futuro; **futuristic** [-'rɪstɪk] a futuristico(a).

fuzzy ['fʌzɪ] a (PHOT) indistinto(a), sfocato(a); (hair) crespo(a).

G

g. abbr of **gram(s)**.

G [dʒi:] n (MUS) sol m.

gabble ['gæbl] vi borbottare; farfugliare.

gable ['geɪbl] n timpano.

gadget ['gædʒɪt] n aggeggio.

gag [gæg] n bavaglio; (joke) facezia, scherzo // vt imbavagliare.

gaiety ['geɪtɪ] n gaiezza.

gaily ['geɪlɪ] ad allegramente.

gain [geɪn] n guadagno, profitto // vt guadagnare // vi (watch) andare avanti; **to ~ in/by** aumentare di/con; **to ~ 3lbs (in weight)** crescere di 3 libbre; ~**ful** a profittevole, lucrativo(a).

gainsay [geɪn'seɪ] vt irg (like say) contraddire; negare.

gait [geɪt] n andatura.

gal. abbr of **gallon**.

gala ['gɑ:lə] n gala.

galaxy ['gæləksɪ] n galassia.

gale [geɪl] n vento forte; burrasca.

gallant ['gælənt] a valoroso(a); (towards ladies) galante, cortese.

gall-bladder ['gɔ:lblædə*] n cistifellea.

gallery ['gælərɪ] n galleria.

galley ['gælɪ] n (ship's kitchen) cambusa; (ship) galea.

gallon ['gæln] n gallone m (= 4.543 l; 8 pints).

gallop ['gæləp] n galoppo // vi galoppare.

gallows ['gæləuz] n forca.

gallstone ['gɔ:lstəun] n calcolo biliare.

gambit ['gæmbɪt] n (fig): (opening) ~ prima mossa.

gamble ['gæmbl] n azzardo, rischio calcolato // vt, vi giocare; **to ~ on** (fig) giocare su; ~**r** n giocatore/trice d'azzardo; **gambling** n gioco d'azzardo.

game [geɪm] n gioco; (event) partita; (HUNTING) selvaggina // a coraggioso(a); (ready): **to be ~ (for sth/to do)** essere pronto(a) (a qc/a fare); **big ~** n selvaggina grossa; ~**keeper** n guardacaccia m inv.

gammon ['gæmən] n (bacon) prosciutto praga; (ham) prosciutto affumicato.

gang [gæŋ] n banda, squadra // vi: **to ~ up on sb** far combutta contro qd.

gangrene ['gæŋgri:n] n cancrena.

gangster ['gæŋstə*] n gangster m inv.

gangway ['gæŋweɪ] n passerella; (of bus) passaggio.

gaol [dʒeɪl] n, vt = **jail**.

gap [gæp] n buco; (in time) intervallo; (fig) lacuna; vuoto.

gape [geɪp] vi restare a bocca aperta; **gaping** a (hole) squarciato(a).

garage ['gærɑ:ʒ] n garage m inv.

garbage ['gɑ:bɪdʒ] n immondizie fpl, rifiuti mpl; ~ **can** n (US) bidone m della spazzatura.

garbled ['gɑ:bld] a deformato(a); ingarbugliato(a).

garden ['gɑ:dn] n giardino // vi lavorare nel giardino; ~**er** n giardiniere/a; ~**ing** n giardinaggio.

gargle ['gɑ:gl] vi fare gargarismi // n gargarismo.

gargoyle ['gɑ:gɔɪl] n gargouille f inv.

garish ['gɛərɪʃ] a vistoso(a).

garland ['gɑ:lənd] n ghirlanda; corona.

garlic ['gɑ:lɪk] n aglio.

garment ['gɑ:mənt] n indumento.

garnish ['gɑ:nɪʃ] vt guarnire.

garret ['gærɪt] n soffitta.

garrison ['gærɪsn] n guarnigione f // vt guarnire.

garrulous ['gærjuləs] a ciarliero(a), loquace.

garter ['gɑ:tə*] n giarrettiera.

gas [gæs] n gas m inv; (US: gasoline) benzina // vt asfissiare con il gas; (MIL) gasare; ~ **cooker** n cucina a gas; ~ **fire** n radiatore m a gas.

gash [gæʃ] n sfregio // vt sfregiare.

gasket ['gæskɪt] n (AUT) guarnizione f.

gasmask ['gæsmɑːsk] n maschera f antigas inv.

gas meter ['gæsmiːtə*] n contatore m del gas.

gasoline ['gæsəliːn] n (US) benzina.

gasp [gɑːsp] vi ansare, boccheggiare; (fig) tirare il fiato.

gas ring ['gæsrɪŋ] n fornello a gas.

gas stove ['gæsstəuv] n cucina a gas.

gassy ['gæsɪ] a gassoso(a).

gastric ['gæstrɪk] a gastrico(a).

gastronomy [gæs'trɒnəmɪ] n gastronomia.

gate [geɪt] n cancello; ~**crash** vt partecipare senza invito a; ~**way** n porta.

gather ['gæðə*] vt (flowers, fruit) cogliere; (pick up) raccogliere; (assemble) radunare; raccogliere; (understand) capire // vi (assemble) radunarsi; to ~ **speed** acquistare velocità; ~**ing** n adunanza.

gauche [gəuʃ] a goffo(a), maldestro(a).

gaudy ['gɔːdɪ] a vistoso(a).

gauge [geɪdʒ] n (standard measure) calibro; (RAIL) scartamento; (instrument) indicatore m // vt misurare.

gaunt [gɔːnt] a scarno(a); (grim, desolate) desolato(a).

gauntlet ['gɔːntlɪt] n (fig): to run the ~ through an angry crowd passare sotto il fuoco di una folla ostile.

gauze [gɔːz] n garza.

gave [geɪv] pt of **give**.

gawp [gɔːp] vi: to ~ **at** guardare a bocca aperta.

gay [geɪ] a (person) gaio(a), allegro(a); (colour) vivace, vivo(a); (col) omosessuale.

gaze [geɪz] n sguardo fisso; to ~ **at** vt fus guardare fisso.

gazelle [gə'zɛl] n gazzella.

gazumping [gə'zʌmpɪŋ] n il fatto di non mantenere una promessa di vendita per accettare un prezzo più alto.

G.R. abbr see **great**.

G.C.E. n (abbr of General Certificate of Education) ≈ maturità.

gear [gɪə*] n attrezzi mpl, equipaggiamento; roba; (TECH) ingranaggio; (AUT) marcia; in **top/low/bottom** ~ in quarta (or quinta)/seconda/prima; in ~ in marcia; out of ~ in folle; ~ **box** n scatola del cambio; ~ **lever**, ~ **shift** (US) n leva del cambio.

geese [giːs] npl of **goose**.

gelatin(e) ['dʒɛlətiːn] n gelatina.

gelignite ['dʒɛlɪgnaɪt] n nitroglicerina.

gem [dʒɛm] n gemma.

Gemini ['dʒɛmɪnaɪ] n Gemelli mpl.

gender ['dʒɛndə*] n genere m.

general ['dʒɛnərl] n generale m // a generale; in ~ in genere; ~ **election** n elezioni fpl generali; ~**ization** [-'zeɪʃən] n generalizzazione f; ~**ize** vi generalizzare; ~**ly** ad generalmente; ~ **practitioner** (G.P.) n medico generico.

generate ['dʒɛnəreɪt] vt generare.

generation [dʒɛnə'reɪʃən] n generazione f.

generator ['dʒɛnəreɪtə*] n generatore m.

generosity [dʒɛnə'rɒsɪtɪ] n generosità.

generous ['dʒɛnərəs] a generoso(a); (copious) abbondante.

genetics [dʒɪ'nɛtɪks] n genetica.

Geneva [dʒɪ'niːvə] n Ginevra.

genial ['dʒiːnɪəl] a geniale, cordiale.

genitals ['dʒɛnɪtlz] npl genitali mpl.

genitive ['dʒɛnɪtɪv] n genitivo.

genius ['dʒiːnɪəs] n genio.

gent [dʒɛnt] n abbr of **gentleman**.

genteel [dʒɛn'tiːl] a raffinato(a), distinto(a).

gentle ['dʒɛntl] a delicato(a); (person) dolce.

gentleman ['dʒɛntlmən] n signore m; (well-bred man) gentiluomo.

gentleness ['dʒɛntlnɪs] n delicatezza; dolcezza.

gently ['dʒɛntlɪ] ad delicatamente.

gentry ['dʒɛntrɪ] n nobiltà minore.

gents [dʒɛnts] n W.C. m (per signori).

genuine ['dʒɛnjuɪn] a autentico(a); sincero(a).

geographic(al) [dʒɪə'græfɪk(l)] a geografico(a).

geography [dʒɪ'ɒgrəfɪ] n geografia.

geological [dʒɪə'lɒdʒɪkl] a geologico(a).

geologist [dʒɪ'ɒlədʒɪst] n geologo/a.

geology [dʒɪ'ɒlədʒɪ] n geologia.

geometric(al) [dʒɪə'mɛtrɪk(l)] a geometrico(a).

geometry [dʒɪ'ɒmɪtrɪ] n geometria.

geranium [dʒɪ'reɪnjəm] n geranio.

germ [dʒəːm] n (MED) microbo; (BIOL, fig) germe m.

German ['dʒəːmən] a tedesco(a) // n tedesco/a; (LING) tedesco; ~ **measles** n rosolia.

Germany ['dʒəːmənɪ] n Germania.

germination [dʒəːmɪ'neɪʃən] n germinazione f.

gestation [dʒɛs'teɪʃən] n gestazione f.

gesticulate [dʒɛs'tɪkjuleɪt] vi gesticolare.

gesture ['dʒɛstjə*] n gesto.

get [gɛt], pt, pp got, pp gotten (US) [gɛt, gɔt, 'gɔtn] vt (obtain) avere, ottenere; (receive) ricevere; (find) trovare; (buy) comprare; (catch) acchiappare; (fetch) andare a prendere; (understand) comprendere, capire; (have): to have got avere; (become): to ~ **rich/old** arricchirsi/invecchiare // vi: to ~ to (place) andare a; arrivare a; pervenire a; **he got across the bridge/under the fence** lui ha attraversato il ponte/è passato sotto il recinto; to ~ **ready/washed/shaved** etc prepararsi/lavarsi/farsi la barba etc; to ~ **sb to do sth** far fare qc a qd; to ~ **sth through/out of** far passare qc per/uscire qc da; to ~ **about** vi muoversi; (news) diffondersi; to ~ **along** vi (agree) andare d'accordo; (depart) andarsene; (manage) = **to get by**; to ~ **at** vt fus (attack) prendersela con; (reach) raggiungere, arrivare a; to ~ **away** vi partire, andarsene; (*escape*) scappare; to ~ **away with** *vt fus* cavarsela; farla franca; to ~ **back** *vi* (*return*) ritornare, tornare // *vt* riottenere, riavere; to ~ **by** *vi* (*pass*) passare; (*manage*) farcela; to ~ **down** *vi*, *vt fus* scendere // *vt* far scendere; (*depress*) buttare giù; to ~ **down to** *vt fus* (*work*) mettersi a (fare); to ~ **in** *vi* entrare; (*train*) arrivare; (*arrive home*) ritornare, tornare; to ~ **into** *vt fus* entrare in; to ~ **into a rage** incavolarsi; to ~ **off** *vi* (*from train etc*) scendere; (*depart: person, car*) andare via; (*escape*) cavarsela // *vt* (*remove: clothes, stain*) levare // *vt fus* (*train, bus*) scendere da; to ~ **on** *vi* (*at exam etc*) andare; (*agree*): to ~ **on (with)** andare d'accordo (con) // *vt fus* montare in; (*horse*) montare su; to ~ **out** *vi* uscire; (*of vehicle*) scendere // *vt* tirar fuori, far uscire; to ~ **out of** *vt fus* uscire da; (*duty etc*) evitare; to ~ **over** *vt fus* (*illness*) riaversi da; to ~ **round** *vt fus* aggirare; (*fig: person*) rigirare; to ~ **through** *vi* (TEL) avere la linea; to ~ **through to** *vt fus* (TEL) avere la linea; to ~ **together** *vi* riunirsi // *vt* raccogliere; (*people*) adunare; to ~ **up** *vi* (*rise*) alzarsi // *vt fus* far alzare; to ~ **up to** *vt fus* (*reach*) raggiungere; (*prank etc*) fare; ~**away** *n* fuga.

geyser ['giːzə*] *n* scaldabagno; (GEO) geyser *m inv*.

Ghana ['gɑːnə] *n* Ghana *m*; ~**ian** [-'neɪən] *a, n* ganaense (*m/f*).

ghastly ['gɑːstlɪ] *a* orribile, orrendo(a).

gherkin ['gəːkɪn] *n* cetriolino.

ghetto ['gɛtəu] *n* ghetto.

ghost [gəust] *n* fantasma *m*, spettro; ~**ly** *a* spettrale.

giant ['dʒaɪənt] *n* gigante/essa // *a* gigante, enorme.

gibberish ['dʒɪbərɪʃ] *n* farfugliare *m*.

gibe [dʒaɪb] *n* frecciata.

giblets ['dʒɪblɪts] *npl* frattaglie *fpl*.

giddiness ['gɪdɪnɪs] *n* vertigine *f*.

giddy ['gɪdɪ] *a* (*dizzy*): to be ~ aver le vertigini; (*height*) vertiginoso(a).

gift [gɪft] *n* regalo; (*donation, ability*) dono; ~**ed** *a* dotato(a).

gigantic [dʒaɪ'gæntɪk] *a* gigantesco(a).

giggle ['gɪgl] *vi* ridere scioccamente.

gild [gɪld] *vt* dorare.

gill [dʒɪl] *n* (*measure*) = 0.14 l; 0.25 pints; ~**s** [gɪlz] *npl* (*of fish*) branchie *fpl*.

gilt [gɪlt] *n* doratura // *a* dorato(a).

gimlet ['gɪmlɪt] *n* succhiello.

gimmick ['gɪmɪk] *n* ... ucco.

gin [dʒɪn] *n* (*liquor*) gin *m*.

ginger ['dʒɪndʒə*] *n* zenzero; ~ **ale**, ~ **beer** *n* bibita gassosa allo zenzero; ~**bread** *n* pan *m* di zenzero; ~**-haired** *a* rossiccio(a).

gingerly ['dʒɪndʒəlɪ] *ad* cautamente.

gingham ['gɪŋəm] *n* percalle *m* a righe *or* quadretti.

gipsy ['dʒɪpsɪ] *n* zingaro/a.

giraffe [dʒɪ'rɑːf] *n* giraffa.

girder ['gəːdə*] *n* trave *f*.

girdle ['gəːdl] *n* (*corset*) guaina.

girl [gəːl] *n* ragazza; (*young unmarried woman*) signorina; (*daughter*) figlia, figliola; ~**friend** *n* (*of girl*) amica; (*of boy*) ragazza; ~**ish** *a* da ragazza.

girth [gəːθ] *n* circonferenza; (*of horse*) cinghia.

gist [dʒɪst] *n* succo.

give [gɪv] *n* (*of fabric*) elasticità // *vb* (*pt* **gave**, *pp* **given** [geɪv, 'gɪvn]) *vt* dare // *vi* cedere; to ~ **sb sth**, ~ **sth to sb** dare qc a qd; to ~ **a cry/sigh** emettere un grido/sospiro; to ~ **away** *vt* dare via; (*give free*) fare dono di; (*betray*) tradire; (*disclose*) rivelare; (*bride*) condurre all'altare; to ~ **back** *vt* rendere; to ~ **in** *vi* cedere // *vt* consegnare; to ~ **off** *vt* emettere; to ~ **out** *vt* distribuire; annunciare; to ~ **up** *vi* rinunciare // *vt* rinunciare a; to ~ **up smoking** smettere di fumare; to ~ **o.s. up** arrendersi; to ~ **way** *vi* cedere; (AUT) dare la precedenza.

glacier ['glæsɪə*] *n* ghiacciaio.

glad [glæd] *a* lieto(a), contento(a); ~**den** *vt* rallegrare, allietare.

gladly ['glædlɪ] *ad* volentieri.

glamorous ['glæmərəs] *a* attraente, seducente.

glamour ['glæmə*] *n* attrattiva.

glance [glɑːns] *n* occhiata, sguardo // *vi*: to ~ **at** dare un'occhiata a; to ~ **off** (*bullet*) rimbalzare su; **glancing** *a* (*blow*) che colpisce di striscio.

gland [glænd] *n* ghiandola.

glare [glɛə*] *n* riverbero, luce *f* abbagliante; (*look*) sguardo furioso // *vi* abbagliare; to ~ **at** guardare male; **glaring** *a* (*mistake*) madornale.

glass [glɑːs] *n* (*substance*) vetro; (*tumbler*) bicchiere *m*; (*also*: **looking** ~) specchio; ~**es** *npl* occhiali *mpl*; ~**house** *n* serra; ~**ware** *n* vetrame *m*; ~**y** *a* (*eyes*) vitreo(a).

glaze [gleɪz] *vt* (*door*) fornire di vetri; (*pottery*) smaltare // *n* vetrina; ~**d** *a* (*eye*) vitreo(a); (*tiles, pottery*) smaltato(a).

glazier ['gleɪzɪə*] *n* vetraio.

gleam [gliːm] *n* barlume *m*; raggio // *vi* luccicare; ~**ing** *a* lucente.

glee [gliː] *n* allegrezza, gioia; ~**ful** *a* allegro(a), gioioso(a).

glen [glɛn] *n* valletta.

glib [glɪb] *a* dalla parola facile; facile.

glide [glaɪd] *vi* scivolare; (AVIAT, *birds*) planare // *n* scivolata; planata; ~**r** *n* (AVIAT) aliante *m*; **gliding** *n* (AVIAT) volo a vela.

glimmer ['glɪmə*] *vi* luccicare // *n* barlume *m*.

glimpse [glɪmps] *n* impressione *f* fugace // *vt* vedere al volo.

glint [glɪnt] *n* luccichio // *vi* luccicare.

glisten ['glɪsn] *vi* luccicare.

glitter ['glɪtə*] *vi* scintillare // *n* scintillio.

gloat [gləut] *vi*: to ~ **(over)** gongolare di piacere (per).

global ['gləubl] *a* globale.

globe [gləub] *n* globo, sfera.

gloom [glu:m] *n* oscurità, buio; (*sadness*) tristezza, malinconia; ~**y** *a* fosco(a), triste.

glorify ['glɔ:rɪfaɪ] *vt* glorificare.

glorious ['glɔ:rɪəs] *a* glorioso(a); magnifico(a).

glory ['glɔ:rɪ] *n* gloria; splendore *m* // *vi*: **to ~ in** gloriarsi di *or* in.

gloss [glɔs] *n* (*shine*) lucentezza; **to ~ over** *vt fus* scivolare su.

glossary ['glɔsərɪ] *n* glossario.

glossy ['glɔsɪ] *a* lucente; ~ (**magazine**) *n* rivista di lusso.

glove [glʌv] *n* guanto.

glow [gləʊ] *vi* ardere; (*face*) essere luminoso(a) // *n* bagliore *m*; (*of face*) rossore *m*.

glower ['glaʊə*] *vi*: **to ~ (at sb)** guardare (qd) in cagnesco.

glucose ['glu:kəʊs] *n* glucosio.

glue [glu:] *n* colla // *vt* incollare.

glum [glʌm] *a* abbattuto(a).

glut [glʌt] *n* eccesso // *vt* saziare; (*market*) saturare.

glutton ['glʌtn] *n* ghiottone/a; **a ~ for work** un(a) patito(a) del lavoro; ~**ous** *a* ghiotto(a), goloso(a); ~**y** *a* ghiottoneria; (*sin*) gola.

glycerin(e) ['glɪsəri:n] *n* glicerina.

gm, gms *abbr of* gram(s).

gnarled [nɑ:ld] *a* nodoso(a).

gnat [næt] *n* moscerino.

gnaw [nɔ:] *vt* rodere.

gnome [nəʊm] *n* gnomo.

go [gəʊ] *vb* (*pt* **went**, *pp* **gone** [wɛnt, gɔn]) *vi* andare; (*depart*) partire, andarsene; (*work*) funzionare; (*be sold*): **to ~ for £10** essere venduto per 10 sterline; (*fit, suit*): **to ~ with** andare bene con; (*become*): **to ~ pale** diventare pallido(a); **to ~ mouldy** ammuffire; (*break etc*) cedere // *n* (*pl*: ~**es**): **to have a ~ (at)** provare; **to be on the ~** essere in moto; **whose ~ is it?** a chi tocca?; **he's going to do sta per fare**; **to ~ for a walk** andare a fare una passeggiata; **to ~ dancing/shopping** andare a ballare/fare la spesa; **how did it ~?** com'è andato?; **to ~ about** *vi* (*rumour*) correre, circolare // *vt fus*: **how do I ~ about this?** qual'è la prassi per questo?; **to ~ ahead** *vi* andare avanti; ~ **ahead!** faccia pure!; **to ~ along** *vi* andare, avanzare // *vt fus* percorrere; **to ~ away** *vi* partire, andarsene; **to ~ back** *vi* tornare, ritornare; (*go again*) andare di nuovo; **to ~ back on** *vt fus* (*promise*) non mantenere; **to ~ by** *vi* (*years, time*) scorrere // *vt fus* attenersi a, seguire (alla lettera); prestar fede a; **to ~ down** *vi* scendere; (*ship*) affondare; (*sun*) tramontare // *vt fus* scendere; **to ~ for** *vt fus* (*fetch*) andare a prendere; (*like*) andar matto(a) per; (*attack*) attaccare; saltare addosso a; **to ~ in** *vi* entrare; **to ~ in for** *vt fus* (*competition*) iscriversi a; (*like*) interessarsi di; **to ~ into** *vt fus* entrare in; (*investigate*) indagare, esaminare; (*embark on*) lanciarsi in; **to ~ off** *vi* partire, andar

via; (*food*) guastarsi; (*explode*) esplodere, scoppiare; (*event*) passare // *vt fus*: **I've gone off chocolate** la cioccolata non mi piace più; **the gun went off** il fucile si scaricò; **to ~ on** *vi* continuare; (*happen*) succedere; **to ~ on doing** continuare a fare; **to ~ on with** *vt fus* continuare, proseguire; **to ~ out** *vi* uscire; (*fire, light*) spegnersi; **to ~ over** *vi* (*ship*) ribaltarsi // *vt fus* (*check*) esaminare; **to ~ through** *vt fus* (*town etc*) attraversare; **to ~ up** *vi*, *vt fus* salire; **to ~ without** *vt fus* fare a meno di.

goad [gəʊd] *vt* spronare.

go-ahead ['gəʊəhɛd] *a* intraprendente // *n* via *m*.

goal [gəʊl] *n* (*SPORT*) gol *m*, rete *f*; (: *place*) porta; (*fig: aim*) fine *m*, scopo; ~**keeper** *n* portiere *m*; ~**post** *n* palo (della porta).

goat [gəʊt] *n* capra.

gobble ['gɔbl] *vt* (*also*: ~ **down**, ~ **up**) ingoiare.

go-between ['gəʊbɪtwi:n] *n* intermediario/a.

goblet ['gɔblɪt] *n* calice *m*, coppa.

goblin ['gɔblɪn] *n* folletto.

god [gɔd] *n* dio; **G~** *n* Dio; ~**child** *n* figlioccio/a; ~**dess** *n* dea; ~**father** *n* padrino; ~**-forsaken** *a* desolato(a), sperduto(a); ~**mother** *n* madrina; ~**send** *n* dono del cielo; ~**son** *n* figlioccio.

goggles ['gɔglz] *npl* occhiali *mpl* (di protezione).

going ['gəʊɪŋ] *n* (*conditions*) andare *m*, stato del terreno // *a*: **the ~ rate** la tariffa in vigore; **a ~ concern** un'azienda avviata.

gold [gəʊld] *n* oro // *a* d'oro; ~**en** *a* (*made of gold*) d'oro; (*gold in colour*) dorato(a); ~**en rule** regola prima; ~**en age** età d'oro; ~**fish** *n* pesce *m* dorato *or* rosso; ~**mine** *n* miniera d'oro.

golf [gɔlf] *n* golf *m*; ~ **club** *n* circolo di golf; (*stick*) bastone *m or* mazza da golf; ~ **course** *n* campo di golf; ~**er** *n* giocatore/trice di golf.

gondola ['gɔndələ] *n* gondola.

gone [gɔn] *pp of* **go** // *a* partito(a).

gong [gɔŋ] *n* gong *m inv*.

good [gud] *a* buono(a); (*kind*) buono(a), gentile; (*child*) bravo(a) // *n* bene *m*; ~**s** *npl* beni *mpl*; merci *fpl*; **she is ~ with children/her hands** lei sa fare coi bambini/è abile nei lavori manuali; **would you be ~ enough to ...?** avrebbe la gentilezza di ...?; **a ~ deal (of)** molto(a), una buona quantità (di); **a ~ many** molti(e); ~ **morning!** buon giorno!; ~ **afternoon/evening!** buona sera!; ~ **night!** buona notte!; ~**bye!** arrivederci!; **G~ Friday** *n* Venerdì Santo; ~**-looking** *a* bello(a); ~**ness** *n* (*of person*) bontà; **for ~ness sake!** per amor di Dio!; ~**will** *n* amicizia, benevolenza; (*COMM*) avviamento.

goose, *pl* **geese** [gu:s, gi:s] *n* oca.

gooseberry ['guzbərɪ] *n* uva spina.

gooseflesh ['gu:sfleʃ] n pelle f d'oca.
gore [gɔː*] vt incornare // n sangue m (coagulato).
gorge [gɔːdʒ] n gola // vt: to ~ o.s. (on) ingozzarsi (di).
gorgeous ['gɔːdʒəs] a magnifico(a).
gorilla [gə'rilə] n gorilla m inv.
gorse [gɔːs] n ginestrone m.
gory ['gɔːrı] a sanguinoso(a).
go-slow ['gəu'sləu] n rallentamento dei lavori (per agitazione sindacale).
gospel ['gɔspl] n vangelo.
gossamer ['gɔsəmə*] n (cobweb) fili mpl della Madonna or di ragnatela; (light fabric) stoffa sottilissima.
gossip ['gɔsip] n chiacchiere fpl; pettegolezzi mpl; (person) pettegolo/a // vi chiacchierare; (maliciously) pettegolare.
got [gɔt] pt,pp of get; ~ten (US) pp of get.
gout [gaut] n gotta.
govern ['gʌvən] vt governare; (LING) reggere.
governess ['gʌvənıs] n governante f.
government ['gʌvnmənt] n governo; (ministers) ministero // cpd statale; ~al [-'mentl] a governativo(a).
governor ['gʌvənə*] n (of state, bank) governatore m; (of school, hospital) amministratore m.
Govt abbr of government.
gown [gaun] n vestito lungo; (of teacher, judge) toga.
G.P. n abbr see general.
grab [græb] vt afferrare, arraffare; (property, power) impadronirsi di.
grace [greıs] n grazia // vt onorare; 5 Jays' ~ dilazione f di 5 giorni; to say ~ dire il benedicite; ~ful a elegante, aggraziato(a); **gracious** ['greıʃəs] a grazioso(a); misericordioso(a).
gradation [grə'deıʃən] n gradazione f.
grade [greıd] n (COMM) qualità f inv; classe f; categoria; (in hierarchy) grado; (US: SCOL) voto; classe f // vt classificare; ordinare; graduare; ~ crossing n (US) passaggio a livello.
gradient ['greıdıənt] n pendenza, inclinazione f.
gradual ['grædjuəl] a graduale; ~ly ad man mano, a poco a poco.
graduate n ['grædjuıt] laureato/a // vi ['grædjueıt] laurearsi; **graduation** [-'eıʃən] n cerimonia del conferimento della laurea.
graft [grɑːft] n (AGR, MED) innesto // vt innestare; **hard** ~ n (col): by sheer hard ~ lavorando da matti.
grain [greın] n grano; (of sand) granello; (of wood) venatura; **it goes against the** ~ va contro la propria natura.
gram [græm] n grammo.
grammar ['græmə*] n grammatica.
grammatical [grə'mætıkl] a grammaticale.
gramme [græm] n = gram.

gramophone ['græməfəun] n grammofono.
granary ['grænərı] n granaio.
grand [grænd] a grande, magnifico(a); grandioso(a); ~children npl nipoti mpl; ~dad n nonno; ~daughter n nipote f; ~father n nonno; ~iose ['grændıəuz] a grandioso(a); (pej) pomposo(a); ~ma n nonna; ~mother n nonna; ~pa n = ~dad; ~ piano n pianoforte m a coda; ~son n nipote m; ~stand n (SPORT) tribuna.
granite ['grænıt] n granito.
granny ['grænı] n nonna.
grant [grɑːnt] vt accordare; (a request) accogliere; (admit) ammettere, concedere // n (SCOL) borsa; (ADMIN) sussidio, sovvenzione f; to take sth for ~ed dare qc per scontato.
granulated ['grænjuleıtıd] a: ~ sugar n zucchero cristallizzato.
granule ['grænju:l] n granello.
grape [greıp] n chicco d'uva, acino.
grapefruit ['greıpfru:t] n pompelmo.
graph [grɑːf] n grafico; ~ic a grafico(a); (vivid) vivido(a).
grapple ['græpl] vi: to ~ with essere alle prese con.
grasp [grɑːsp] vt afferrare // n (grip) presa; (fig) potere m; comprensione f; ~ing a avido(a).
grass [grɑːs] n erba; ~hopper n cavalletta; ~land n prateria; ~y a erboso(a).
grate [greıt] n graticola (del focolare) // vi cigolare, stridere // vt (CULIN) grattugiare.
grateful ['greıtful] a grato(a), riconoscente; ~ly ad con gratitudine.
grater ['greıtə*] n grattugia.
gratify ['grætıfaı] vt appagare; (whim) soddisfare; ~ing a gradito(a); soddisfacente.
grating ['greıtıŋ] n (iron bars) grata // a (noise) stridente, stridulo(a).
gratitude ['grætıtju:d] n gratitudine f.
gratuity [grə'tju:ıtı] n mancia.
grave [greıv] n tomba // a grave, serio(a).
gravel ['grævl] n ghiaia.
gravestone ['greıvstəun] n pietra tombale.
graveyard ['greıvjɑːd] n cimitero.
gravitate ['grævıteıt] vi gravitare.
gravity ['grævıtı] n (PHYSICS) gravità; pesantezza; (seriousness) gravità, serietà.
gravy ['greıvı] n intingolo della carne; salsa.
gray [greı] a = grey.
graze [greız] vi pascolare, pascere // vt (touch lightly) sfiorare; (scrape) escoriare // n (MED) escoriazione f.
grease [gri:s] n (fat) grasso; (lubricant) lubrificante m // vt ingrassare; lubrificare; ~proof paper n carta oleata; **greasy** a grasso(a), untuoso(a).
great [greıt] a grande; (col) magnifico(a), meraviglioso(a); G~ Britain n Gran

Bretagna; ~-**grandfather** n bisnonno; ~-**grandmother** n bisnonna; ~**ly** ad molto; ~**ness** n grandezza.
Grecian ['gri:ʃən] a greco(a).
Greece [gri:s] n Grecia.
greed [gri:d] n (also: ~**iness**) avarizia; (for food) golosità, ghiottoneria; ~**ily** ad avidamente; golosamente; ~**y** a avido(a); goloso(a), ghiotto(a).
Greek [gri:k] a greco(a) // n greco/a; (LING) greco.
green [gri:n] a verde; (inexperienced) inesperto(a), ingenuo(a) // n verde m; (stretch of grass) prato; (also: **village** ~) ≈ piazza del paese; ~**s** npl verdura; ~**grocer** n fruttivendolo/a, erbivendolo/a; ~**house** n serra.
Greenland ['gri:nlənd] n Groenlandia.
greet [gri:t] vt salutare; ~**ing** n saluto; **Christmas/birthday** ~**ings** auguri mpl di Natale/di compleanno.
gregarious [grə'gɛərɪəs] a gregario(a); socievole.
grenade [grə'neɪd] n granata.
grew [gru:] pt of **grow**.
grey [greɪ] a grigio(a); ~-**haired** a dai capelli grigi; ~**hound** n levriere m.
grid [grɪd] n grata; (ELEC) rete f; ~**iron** n graticola.
grief [gri:f] n dolore m.
grievance ['gri:vəns] n doglianza, lagnanza.
grieve [gri:v] vi addolorarsi; rattristarsi // vt addolorare.
grill [grɪl] n (on cooker) griglia // vt cuocere ai ferri; (question) interrogare senza sosta.
grille [grɪl] n grata; (AUT) griglia.
grill(room) ['grɪl(rum)] n rosticceria.
grim [grɪm] a sinistro(a), brutto(a).
grimace [grɪ'meɪs] n smorfia // vi fare smorfie; fare boccacce.
grime [graɪm] n sudiciume m.
grimy ['graɪmɪ] a sudicio(a).
grin [grɪn] n sorriso smagliante // vi sorridere.
grind [graɪnd] vt (pt, pp ground [graund]) macinare; (make sharp) arrotare // n (work) sgobbata; **to ~ one's teeth** digrignare i denti.
grip [grɪp] n impugnatura; presa; (holdall) borsa da viaggio // vt impugnare; afferrare; **to come to ~s with** affrontare; cercare di risolvere.
gripe(s) [graɪp(s)] n(pl) colica.
gripping ['grɪpɪŋ] a avvincente.
grisly ['grɪzlɪ] a macabro(a), orrido(a).
gristle ['grɪsl] n cartilagine f.
grit [grɪt] n ghiaia; (courage) fegato // vt (road) coprire di sabbia; **to ~ one's teeth** stringere i denti.
groan [grəun] n gemito // vi gemere.
grocer ['grəusə*] n negoziante m di generi alimentari; ~**ies** npl provviste fpl.
groggy ['grɔgɪ] a barcollante.
groin [grɔɪn] n inguine m.
groom [gru:m] n palafreniere m; (also:

bride~) sposo // vt (horse) strigliare; (fig): **to ~ sb for** avviare qd a.
groove [gru:v] n scanalatura, solco.
grope [grəup] vi andar tentoni; **to ~ for** vt fus cercare a tastoni.
gross [grəus] a grossolano(a); (COMM) lordo(a) // n, pl inv (twelve dozen) grossa; ~**ly** ad (greatly) molto.
grotesque [grə'tɛsk] a grottesco(a).
grotto ['grɔtəu] n grotta.
ground [graund] pt, pp of **grind** // n suolo, terra; (land) terreno; (SPORT) campo; (reason: gen pl) ragione f // vt (plane) tenere a terra // vi (ship) arenarsi; ~**s** npl (of coffee etc) fondi mpl; (gardens etc) terreno, giardini mpl; **on/to the ~** per/a terra; ~ **floor** n pianterreno; ~**ing** n (in education) basi fpl; ~**sheet** n pavimento a catino per tenda; ~ **staff** n personale m di terra; ~**work** n preparazione f.
group [gru:p] n gruppo // vt raggruppare // vi raggrupparsi.
grouse [graus] n, pl inv (bird) tetraone m // vi (complain) brontolare.
grove [grəuv] n boschetto.
grovel ['grɔvl] vi (fig): **to ~ (before)** avvilirsi (ai piedi di).
grow [grəu], pt **grew**, pp **grown** [grəu, gru:, grəun] vi crescere; (increase) aumentare; (become): **to ~ rich/weak** arricchirsi/indebolirsi // vt coltivare, far crescere; **to ~ up** vi farsi grande, crescere; ~**er** n coltivatore/trice; ~**ing** a (fear, amount) crescente.
growl [graul] vi ringhiare.
grown [grəun] pp of **grow** // a adulto(a), maturo(a); ~-**up** n adulto/a, grande m/f.
growth [grəuθ] n crescita, sviluppo; (what has grown) crescita; (MED) escrescenza, tumore m.
grub [grʌb] n larva; (col: food) roba (da mangiare).
grubby ['grʌbɪ] a sporco(a).
grudge [grʌdʒ] n rancore m // vt: **to ~ sb sth** dare qc a qd di malavoglia; invidiare qc a qd; **to bear sb a ~ (for)** serbar rancore a qd (per); **grudgingly** ad di malavoglia, di malincuore.
gruelling ['gruəlɪŋ] a strapazzoso(a).
gruesome ['gru:səm] a orribile.
gruff [grʌf] a rozzo(a).
grumble ['grʌmbl] vi brontolare, lagnarsi.
grumpy ['grʌmpɪ] a stizzito(a).
grunt [grʌnt] vi grugnire // n grugnito.
guarantee [gærən'ti:] n garanzia // vt garantire.
guarantor [gærən'tɔ:*] n garante m/f.
guard [gɑ:d] n guardia, custodia; (squad, FENCING) guardia; (BOXING) difesa; (one man) guardia, sentinella; (RAIL) capotreno // vt fare la guardia a; ~-**ed** a (fig) cauto(a), guardingo(a); ~-**ian** n custode m; (of minor) tutore/trice; ~-**'s van** n (RAIL) vagone m di servizio.
guerrilla [gə'rɪlə] n guerrigliero; ~ **warfare** n guerriglia.
guess [gɛs] vi indovinare // vt indovinare; (US) credere, pensare // n congettura; **to**

have a ~ cercare di indovinare.
guest [gɛst] *n* ospite *m/f*; (*in hotel*) cliente *m/f*; **~-house** *n* pensione *f*; **~ room** *n* camera degli ospiti.
guffaw [gʌˈfɔː] *n* risata sonora // *vi* scoppiare di una risata sonora.
guidance ['gaɪdəns] *n* guida, direzione *f*.
guide [gaɪd] *n* (*person, book etc*) guida // *vt* guidare; (**girl**) ~ *n* giovane esploratrice *f*; **~book** *n* guida; **~d missile** *n* missile *m* telecomandato; ~ **dog** *n* cane *m* guida *inv*; **~lines** *npl* (*fig*) indicazioni *fpl*, linee *fpl* direttive.
guild [gɪld] *n* arte *f*, corporazione *f*; associazione *f*; **~hall** *n* (*Brit*) palazzo municipale.
guile [gaɪl] *n* astuzia.
guillotine ['gɪlətiːn] *n* ghigliottina.
guilt [gɪlt] *n* colpevolezza; **~y** *a* colpevole.
guinea ['gɪnɪ] *n* (*Brit*) ghinea (= 21 shillings: valuta ora fuori uso).
guinea pig ['gɪnɪpɪg] *n* cavia.
guise [gaɪz] *n* maschera.
guitar [gɪˈtɑː*] *n* chitarra; **~ist** *n* chitarrista *m/f*.
gulf [gʌlf] *n* golfo; (*abyss*) abisso.
gull [gʌl] *n* gabbiano.
gullet ['gʌlɪt] *n* gola.
gullible ['gʌlɪbl] *a* credulo(a).
gully ['gʌlɪ] *n* burrone *m*; gola; canale *m*.
gulp [gʌlp] *vi* deglutire; (*from emotion*) avere il nodo in gola // *vt* (*also*: ~ **down**) tracannare, inghiottire.
gum [gʌm] *n* (*ANAT*) gengiva; (*glue*) colla; (*sweet*) gelatina di frutta; (*also*: **chewing-~**) chewing-gum *m* // *vt* incollare; **~boots** *npl* stivali *mpl* di gomma.
gumption ['gʌmpʃən] *n* buon senso, senso pratico.
gun [gʌn] *n* fucile *m*; (*small*) pistola, rivoltella; (*rifle*) carabina; (*shotgun*) fucile da caccia; (*cannon*) cannone *m*; **~boat** *n* cannoniera; **~fire** *n* spari *mpl*; **~man** *n* bandito armato; **~ner** *n* artigliere *m*; **at ~point** sotto minaccia di fucile; **~powder** *n* polvere *f* da sparo; **~shot** *n* sparo; **within ~shot** a portata di fucile.
gurgle ['gəːgl] *n* gorgoglio // *vi* gorgogliare.
gush [gʌʃ] *n* fiotto, getto // *vi* sgorgare; (*fig*) abbandonarsi ad effusioni.
gusset ['gʌsɪt] *n* gherone *m*.
gust [gʌst] *n* (*of wind*) raffica; (*of smoke*) buffata.
gusto ['gʌstəu] *n* entusiasmo.
gut [gʌt] *n* intestino, budello; (*MUS etc*) minugia; **~s** *npl* (*courage*) fegato.
gutter ['gʌtə*] *n* (*of roof*) grondaia; (*in street*) cunetta.
guttural ['gʌtərl] *a* gutturale.
guy [gaɪ] *n* (*also*: **~-rope**) cavo or corda di fissaggio; (*col*: *man*) tipo, elemento.
guzzle ['gʌzl] *vi* gozzovigliare // *vt* tranguriare.
gym [dʒɪm] *n* (*also*: **gymnasium**) palestra; (*also*: **gymnastics**) ginnastica; ~ **slip** *n*

grembiule *m* da scuola (*per ragazze*).
gymnast ['dʒɪmnæst] *n* ginnasta *m/f*; **~ics** [-'næstɪks] *n*, *npl* ginnastica.
gynaecology [gaɪnəˈkɔlədʒɪ] *n* ginecologia.
gypsy ['dʒɪpsɪ] *n* = **gipsy**.
gyrate [dʒaɪˈreɪt] *vi* girare.

H

haberdashery ['hæbəˈdæʃərɪ] *n* merceria.
habit ['hæbɪt] *n* abitudine *f*; (*costume*) abito; (*REL*) tonaca.
habitation [hæbɪˈteɪʃən] *n* abitazione *f*.
habitual [həˈbɪtjuəl] *a* abituale; (*drinker, liar*) inveterato(a); **~ly** *ad* abitualmente, di solito.
hack [hæk] *vt* tagliare, fare a pezzi // *n* (*cut*) taglio; (*blow*) colpo; (*pej*: *writer*) negro.
hackney cab ['hæknɪˈkæb] *n* carrozza a nolo.
hackneyed ['hæknɪd] *a* comune, trito(a).
had [hæd] *pt, pp of* **have**.
haddock ['hædək] *n* eglefino.
haemorrhage ['hɛmərɪdʒ] *n* emorragia.
haemorrhoids ['hɛmərɔɪdz] *npl* emorroidi *fpl*.
haggard ['hægəd] *a* smunto(a).
haggle ['hægl] *vi* mercanteggiare.
Hague [heɪg] *n*: **The ~** L'Aia.
hail [heɪl] *n* grandine *f* // *vt* (*call*) chiamare; (*greet*) salutare // *vi* grandinare; **~stone** *n* chicco di grandine.
hair [hɛə*] *n* capelli *mpl*; (*single hair*: *on head*) capello; (: *on body*) pelo; **to do one's ~** pettinarsi; **~brush** *n* spazzola per capelli; **~ cut** *n* taglio di capelli; **I need a ~cut** ho bisogno di farmi i capelli; **~do** ['hɛəduː] *n* acconciatura, pettinatura; **~-dresser** *n* parrucchiere/a; **~-drier** *n* asciugacapelli *m inv*; **~net** *n* retina (per capelli); ~ **oil** *n* brillantina; **~piece** *n* toupet *m inv*; **~pin** *n* forcina; **~pin bend** *n* tornante *m*; **~raising** *a* orripilante; **~style** *n* pettinatura, acconciatura; **~y** *a* irsuto(a); peloso(a); (*fig*) spaventoso(a).
hake [heɪk] *n* nasello.
half [hɑːf] *n* (*pl*: **halves** [hɑːvz]) mezzo, metà *f inv* // *a* mezzo(a) // *ad* a mezzo, a metà; **~-an-hour** mezz'ora; **two and a ~** due e mezzo; **a week and a ~** una settimana e mezza; **~ (of it)** la metà; **~ (of)** la metà di; **~ the amount of** la metà di; **to cut sth in ~** tagliare qc in due; **~-back** *n* (*SPORT*) mediano; **~-breed**, **~-caste** *n* meticcio/a; **~-hearted** *a* tiepido(a); **~-hour** *n* mezz'ora; **~-penny** ['heɪpnɪ] *n* mezzo penny *m inv*; (*at*) **~-price** a metà prezzo; **~-time** *n* intervallo; **~way** *ad* a metà strada.
halibut ['hælɪbət] *n*, *pl inv* ippoglosso.
hall [hɔːl] *n* sala, salone *m*; (*entrance way*) entrata; (*corridor*) corridoio; (*mansion*) grande villa, maniero; ~ **of residence** *n* casa dello studente.
hallmark ['hɔːlmɑːk] *n* marchio di garanzia; (*fig*) caratteristica.

hallo [hə'ləʊ] *excl* = **hello**.
hallucination [həluːsɪ'neɪʃən] *n* allucinazione *f*.
halo ['heɪləʊ] *n* (*of saint etc*) aureola; (*of sun*) alone *m*.
halt [hɔːlt] *n* fermata // *vt* fermare // *vi* fermarsi.
halve [hɑːv] *vt* (*apple etc*) dividere a metà; (*expense*) ridurre di metà.
halves [hɑːvz] *npl of* **half**.
ham [hæm] *n* prosciutto.
hamburger ['hæmbɜːgɜ*] *n* hamburger *m inv*.
hamlet ['hæmlɪt] *n* paesetto.
hammer ['hæmɜ*] *n* martello // *vt* martellare; (*fig*) sconfiggere duramente.
hammock ['hæmɔk] *n* amaca.
hamper ['hæmpɔ*] *vt* impedire // *n* cesta.
hand [hænd] *n* mano *f*; (*of clock*) lancetta; (*handwriting*) scrittura; (*at cards*) carte *fpl* (*: game*) partita; (*worker*) operaio/a // *vt* dare, passare; **to give sb a ~** dare una mano a qd; **at ~** a portata di mano; **in ~** a disposizione; (*work*) in corso; **on the one ~ ...**, **on the other ~** da un lato ..., dall'altro; **to ~ in** *vt* consegnare; **to ~ out** *vt* distribuire; **to ~ over** *vt* passare; cedere; **~bag** *n* borsetta; **~ball** *n* pallamano *f*; **~basin** *n* lavandino; **~book** *n* manuale *m*; **~brake** *n* freno a mano; **~cuffs** *npl* manette *fpl*; **~ful** *n* manata, pugno.
handicap ['hændɪkæp] *n* handicap *m inv* // *vt* andicappare.
handicraft ['hændɪkrɑːft] *n* lavoro d'artigiano.
handkerchief ['hæŋkətʃɪf] *n* fazzoletto.
handle ['hændl] *n* (*of door etc*) maniglia; (*of cup etc*) ansa; (*of knife etc*) impugnatura; (*of saucepan*) manico; (*for winding*) manovella // *vt* toccare, maneggiare; (*deal with*) occuparsi di; (*treat: people*) trattare; **'~ with care'** 'fragile'; **~bar(s)** *n(pl)* manubrio.
hand-luggage ['hændlʌgɪdʒ] *n* bagagli *mpl* a mano.
handmade ['hændmeɪd] *a* fatto(a) a mano.
handsome ['hænsəm] *a* bello(a); generoso(a); considerevole.
handwriting ['hændraɪtɪŋ] *n* scrittura.
handwritten ['hændrɪtn] *a* scritto(a) a mano, manoscritto(a).
handy ['hændɪ] *a* (*person*) destro(a); (*close at hand*) a portata di mano; (*convenient*) comodo(a); **~man** *n* tuttofare *m inv*; **tools for the ~man** arnesi per il fateloda-voi.
hang, *pt, pp* **hung** [hæŋ, hʌŋ] *vt* appendere; (*criminal: pt,pp* **hanged**) impiccare // *vi* pendere; (*hair*) scendere; (*drapery*) cadere; **to ~ about** *vi* bighellonare, ciondolare; **to ~ on** *vi* (*wait*) aspettare; **to ~ up** *vi* (*TEL*) riattaccare // *vt* appendere.
hangar ['hæŋɔ*] *n* hangar *m inv*.
hanger ['hæŋɔ*] *n* gruccia.
hanger-on [hæŋɔr'ɔn] *n* parassita *m*.

hang-gliding ['hæŋglaɪdɪŋ] *n* volo col deltaplano.
hangover ['hæŋəʊvɜ*] *n* (*after drinking*) postumi *mpl* di sbornia.
hang-up ['hæŋʌp] *n* complesso.
hank [hæŋk] *n* matassa.
hanker ['hæŋkɜ*] *vi*: **to ~ after** bramare.
hankie, hanky ['hæŋkɪ] *n abbr of* **handkerchief**.
haphazard [hæp'hæzəd] *a* a casaccio, alla carlona.
happen ['hæpən] *vi* accadere, succedere; **I ~ed to be out** mi capitò di essere fuori; **as it ~s** guarda caso; **~ing** *n* avvenimento.
happily ['hæpɪlɪ] *ad* felicemente; fortunatamente.
happiness ['hæpɪnɪs] *n* felicità, contentezza.
happy ['hæpɪ] *a* felice, contento(a); **~ with** (*arrangements etc*) soddisfatto(a) di; **~-go-lucky** *a* spensierato(a).
harass ['hærəs] *vt* molestare; **~ment** *n* molestia.
harbour ['hɑːbɔ*] *n* porto // *vt* dare rifugio a; **~ master** *n* capitano di porto.
hard [hɑːd] *a* duro(a) // *ad* (*work*) sodo; (*think, try*) bene; **to drink ~** bere forte; **~ luck!** peccato!; **no ~ feelings!** senza rancore!; **to be ~ of hearing** essere duro(a) d'orecchio; **to be ~ done by** essere trattato(a) ingiustamente; **~back** *n* libro rilegato; **~board** *n* legno precompresso; **~-boiled egg** *n* uovo sodo; **~ cash** *n* denaro in contanti; **~en** *vt, vi* indurire; **~ labour** *n* lavori forzati *mpl*.
hardly ['hɑːdlɪ] *ad* (*scarcely*) appena; **it's ~ the case** non è proprio il caso; **~ anyone/ anywhere** quasi nessuno/da nessuna parte.
hardness ['hɑːdnɪs] *n* durezza.
hard sell ['hɑːd'sɛl] *n* (*COMM*) intensa campagna promozionale.
hardship ['hɑːdʃɪp] *n* avversità *f inv*; privazioni *fpl*.
hard-up [hɑːd'ʌp] *a* (*col*) al verde.
hardware ['hɑːdwɛə*] *n* ferramenta *fpl*; (*COMPUTERS*) hardware *m*; **~ shop** *n* (negozio di) ferramenta *fpl*.
hardy ['hɑːdɪ] *a* robusto(a); (*plant*) resistente al gelo.
hare [hɛə*] *n* lepre *f*; **~-brained** *a* folle, scervellato(a); **~lip** *n* (*MED*) labbro leporino.
harem [hɑː'riːm] *n* harem *m inv*.
harm [hɑːm] *n* male *m*; (*wrong*) danno // *vt* (*person*) fare male a; (*thing*) danneggiare; **to mean no ~** non avere l'intenzione d'offendere; **out of ~'s way** al sicuro; **~ful** *a* dannoso(a); **~less** *a* innocuo(a), inoffensivo(a).
harmonica [hɑː'mɔnɪkə] *n* armonica.
harmonics [hɑː'mɔnɪks] *npl* armonia.
harmonious [hɑː'məʊnɪəs] *a* armonioso(a).
harmonium [hɑː'məʊnɪəm] *n* armonium *m inv*.

harmonize ['hɑːmənaɪz] *vt, vi* armonizzare.

harmony ['hɑːmənɪ] *n* armonia.

harness ['hɑːnɪs] *n* bardatura, finimenti *mpl* // *vt* (*horse*) bardare; (*resources*) sfruttare.

harp [hɑːp] *n* arpa // *vi*: to ~ **on about** insistere tediosamente su; ~**ist** *n* arpista *m/f*.

harpoon [hɑːˈpuːn] *n* arpione *m*.

harpsichord ['hɑːpsɪkɔːd] *n* clavicembalo.

harrow ['hærəʊ] *n* (*AGR*) erpice *m*.

harrowing ['hærəʊɪŋ] *a* straziante.

harsh [hɑːʃ] *a* (*hard*) duro(a); (*severe*) severo(a); (*unpleasant: sound*) rauco(a); (: *colour*) chiassoso(a); violento(a); ~**ly** *ad* duramente; severamente; ~**ness** *n* durezza; severità.

harvest ['hɑːvɪst] *n* raccolto, (*of grapes*) vendemmia // *vt* fare il raccolto di, raccogliere; vendemmiare; ~**er** *n* (*machine*) mietitrice *f*.

has [hæz] *see* **have**.

hash [hæʃ] *n* (*CULIN*) specie di spezzatino fatto con carne già cotta; (*fig: mess*) pasticcio; *also abbr of* **hashish**.

hashish ['hæʃɪʃ] *n* hascisc *m*.

haste [heɪst] *n* fretta; precipitazione *f*; ~**n** ['heɪsn] *vt* affrettare // *vi* affrettarsi; **hastily** *ad* in fretta; precipitosamente; **hasty** *a* affrettato(a); precipitoso(a).

hat [hæt] *n* cappello; ~**box** *n* cappelliera.

hatch [hætʃ] *n* (*NAUT: also:* ~**way**) boccaporto; (*also:* **service** ~) portello di servizio // *vi* schiudersi // *vt* covare.

hatchback ['hætʃbæk] *n* (*AUT*) tre (*or* cinque) porte *f inv*.

hatchet ['hætʃɪt] *n* accetta.

hate [heɪt] *vt* odiare, detestare // *n* odio; to ~ **to do** *or* **doing** detestare fare; ~**ful** *a* odioso(a), detestabile.

hatred ['heɪtrɪd] *n* odio.

hat trick ['hættrɪk] *n* (*SPORT, also fig*) tris *m inv* (*3 reti segnate durante una partita etc*).

haughty ['hɔːtɪ] *a* altero(a), arrogante.

haul [hɔːl] *vt* trascinare, tirare // *n* (*of fish*) pescata; (*of stolen goods etc*) bottino; ~**age** *n* trasporto; autotrasporto; ~**ier** *n* trasportatore *m*.

haunch [hɔːntʃ] *n* anca.

haunt [hɔːnt] *vt* (*subj: fear*) pervadere; (: *person*) frequentare // *n* rifugio; **a ghost** ~**s this house** questa casa è abitata da un fantasma.

have *pt,pp* **had** [hæv, hæd] *vt* avere; (*meal, shower*) fare; **to** ~ **sth done** far fare qc; **he had a suit made** si fece fare un abito; **she has to do it** lo deve fare; **I had better leave** è meglio che io vada; **to** ~ **it out with sb** metterlo in chiaro con qd; **I won't** ~ **it** questo non mi va affatto; **he's been had** (*col*) c'è cascato dentro.

haven ['heɪvn] *n* porto; (*fig*) rifugio.

haversack ['hævəsæk] *n* zaino.

havoc ['hævək] *n* caos *m*.

hawk [hɔːk] *n* falco.

hawker ['hɔːkə*] *n* venditore *m* ambulante.

hay [heɪ] *n* fieno; ~ **fever** *n* febbre *f* da fieno; ~**stack** *n* mucchio di fieno.

haywire ['heɪwaɪə*] *a* (*col*): **to go** ~ perdere la testa; impazzire.

hazard ['hæzəd] *n* azzardo, ventura; pericolo, rischio; ~**ous** *a* pericoloso(a), rischioso(a).

haze [heɪz] *n* foschia.

hazelnut ['heɪzlnʌt] *n* nocciola.

hazy ['heɪzɪ] *a* fosco(a); (*idea*) vago(a); (*photograph*) indistinto(a).

he [hiː] *pronoun* lui, egli; **it is** ~ **who ...** è lui che ...; **here** ~ **is** eccolo; ~-**bear** *n* orso maschio.

head [hɛd] *n* testa, capo; (*leader*) capo // *vt* (*list*) essere in testa a; (*group*) essere a capo di; ~**s (or tails)** testa (o croce), pari (o gaffo); **to** ~ **the ball** dare di testa alla palla; **to** ~ **for** *vt fus* dirigersi verso; ~**ache** *n* mal *m* di testa; ~**ing** *n* titolo; intestazione *f*; ~**lamp** *n* fanale *m*; ~**land** *n* promontorio; ~**light** = ~**lamp**; ~**line** *n* titolo; ~**long** *ad* (*fall*) a capofitto; (*rush*) precipitosamente; ~**master** *n* preside *m*; ~**mistress** *n* preside *f*; ~ **office** *n* sede *f* (centrale); ~-**on** *a* (*collision*) frontale; ~**quarters (HQ)** *npl* ufficio centrale; (*MIL*) quartiere *m* generale; ~-**rest** *n* poggiacapo; ~**room** *n* (*in car*) altezza dell'abitacolo; (*under bridge*) altezza limite; ~**scarf** *n* foulard *m inv*; ~**strong** *a* testardo(a); ~ **waiter** *n* capocameriere *m*; ~ **way** *n* progresso, cammino; ~**wind** *n* controvento; ~**y** *a* che dà alla testa; inebriante.

heal [hiːl] *vt,vi* guarire.

health [hɛlθ] *n* salute *f*; **the H**~ **Service** ≈ il Servizio Sanitario Statale; ~**y** *a* (*person*) in buona salute; (*climate*) salubre; (*food*) salutare; (*attitude etc*) sano(a).

heap [hiːp] *n* mucchio // *vt* ammucchiare.

hear, *pt, pp* **heard** [hɪə*, hɜːd] *vt* sentire; (*news*) ascoltare; (*lecture*) assistere a // *vi* sentire; **to** ~ **about** avere notizie di; sentire parlare di; **to** ~ **from sb** ricevere notizie da qd; ~**ing** *n* (*sense*) udito; (*of witnesses*) audizione *f*; (*of a case*) udienza; ~**ing aid** *n* apparecchio acustico; **by** ~**say** *ad* per sentito dire.

hearse [hɜːs] *n* carro funebre.

heart [hɑːt] *n* cuore *m*; ~**s** *npl* (*CARDS*) cuori *mpl*; **at** ~ in fondo; **by** ~ (*learn, know*) a memoria; **to lose** ~ perdere coraggio, scoraggiarsi; ~ **attack** *n* attacco di cuore; ~**beat** *n* battito del cuore; ~**breaking** *a* straziante; **to be** ~**broken** avere il cuore spezzato; ~**burn** *n* bruciore *m* di stomaco; ~**felt** *a* sincero(a).

hearth [hɑːθ] *n* focolare *m*.

heartily ['hɑːtɪlɪ] *ad* (*laugh*) di cuore; (*eat*) di buon appetito.

heartless ['hɑːtlɪs] *a* senza cuore, insensibile; crudele.

heartwarming ['hɑːtwɔːmɪŋ] *a* confortante, che scalda il cuore.

hearty ['hɑːtɪ] a caloroso(a); robusto(a), sano(a); vigoroso(a).

heat [hiːt] n calore m; (fig) ardore m; fuoco; (SPORT: also: **qualifying ~**) prova eliminatoria // vt scaldare; **to ~ up** vi (liquids) scaldarsi; (room) riscaldarsi // vt riscaldare; **~ed** a riscaldato(a); (fig) appassionato(a); acceso(a), eccitato(a); **~er** n stufa; radiatore m.

heath [hiːθ] n (Brit) landa.

heathen ['hiːðn] a, n pagano(a).

heather ['hɛðə*] n erica.

heating ['hiːtɪŋ] n riscaldamento.

heatstroke ['hiːtstrəuk] n colpo di sole.

heatwave ['hiːtweɪv] n ondata di caldo.

heave [hiːv] vt sollevare (con sforzo) // vi sollevarsi // n conato di vomito; (push) grande spinta.

heaven ['hɛvn] n paradiso, cielo; **~ forbid!** Dio ce ne guardi!; **~ly** a divino(a), celeste.

heavily ['hɛvɪlɪ] ad pesantemente; (drink, smoke) molto.

heavy ['hɛvɪ] a pesante; (sea) grosso(a); (rain) forte; (drinker, smoker) gran (before noun); **it's ~ going** è una gran fatica; **~weight** n (SPORT) peso massimo.

Hebrew ['hiːbruː] a ebreo(a) // n (LING) ebraico.

heckle ['hɛkl] vt interpellare e dare noia a (un oratore).

hectic ['hɛktɪk] a movimentato(a).

he'd [hiːd] = **he would, he had**.

hedge [hɛdʒ] n siepe f // vi essere elusivo(a); **to ~ one's bets** (fig) coprirsi dai rischi.

hedgehog ['hɛdʒhɒg] n riccio.

heed [hiːd] vt (also: **take ~ of**) badare a, far conto di; **~less** a sbadato(a).

heel [hiːl] n (ANAT) calcagno; (of shoe) tacco // vt (shoe) rifare i tacchi a.

hefty ['hɛftɪ] a (person) solido(a); (parcel) pesante; (piece, price) grosso(a).

heifer ['hɛfə*] n giovenca.

height [haɪt] n altezza; (high ground) altura; (fig: of glory) apice m; (: of stupidity) colmo; **~en** vt innalzare; (fig) accrescere.

heir [ɛə*] n erede m; **~ess** n erede f; **~loom** n mobile m (or gioiello or quadro) di famiglia.

held [hɛld] pt, pp of **hold**.

helicopter ['hɛlɪkɒptə*] n elicottero.

hell [hɛl] n inferno; **a ~ of a ...** (col) un(a) maledetto(a) ...

he'll [hiːl] = **he will, he shall**.

hellish ['hɛlɪʃ] a infernale.

hello [hə'ləu] excl buon giorno!; ciao! (to sb one addresses as 'tu'); (surprise) ma guarda!

helm [hɛlm] n (NAUT) timone m.

helmet ['hɛlmɪt] n casco.

helmsman ['hɛlmzmən] n timoniere m.

help [hɛlp] n aiuto; (charwoman) donna di servizio; (assistant etc) impiegato // vt aiutare; **~!** aiuto!; **~ yourself (to bread)** si serva (del pane); **I can't ~ saying** non posso evitare di dire; **he can't ~ it** non ci

può far niente; **~er** n aiutante m/f, assistente m/f; **~ful** a di grande aiuto; (useful) utile; **~ing** n porzione f; **~less** a impotente; debole.

hem [hɛm] n orlo // vt fare l'orlo a; **to ~ in** vt cingere.

hemisphere ['hɛmɪsfɪə*] n emisfero.

hemp [hɛmp] n canapa.

hen [hɛn] n gallina.

hence [hɛns] ad (therefore) dunque; **2 years ~** di qui a 2 anni; **~forth** ad d'ora in poi.

henchman ['hɛntʃmən] n (pej) caudatario.

henpecked ['hɛnpɛkt] a dominato dalla moglie.

her [həː*] pronoun (direct) la, l' + vowel; (indirect) le; (stressed, after prep) lei; see note at **she** // a il(la) suo(a), i(le) suoi(sue); **I see ~** la vedo; **give ~ a book** le dia un libro; **after ~** dopo (di) lei.

herald ['hɛrəld] n araldo // vt annunciare.

heraldry ['hɛrəldrɪ] n araldica.

herb [həːb] n erba; **~s** npl (CULIN) erbette fpl.

herd [həːd] n mandria.

here [hɪə*] ad qui, qua // excl ehi!; **~!** presente!; **~'s my sister** ecco mia sorella; **~ she is** eccola; **~ she comes** eccola che viene; **~after** ad in futuro; dopo questo // n: **the ~after** l'al di là m; **~by** ad (in letter) con la presente.

hereditary [hɪ'rɛdɪtrɪ] a ereditario(a).

heredity [hɪ'rɛdɪtɪ] n eredità.

heresy ['hɛrəsɪ] n eresia.

heretic ['hɛrətɪk] n eretico/a; **~al** [hɪ'rɛtɪkl] a eretico(a).

herewith [hɪə'wɪð] ad qui accluso.

heritage ['hɛrɪtɪdʒ] n eredità; (fig) retaggio.

hermetically [həː'mɛtɪklɪ] ad ermeticamente.

hermit ['həːmɪt] n eremita m.

hernia ['həːnɪə] n ernia.

hero, ~es ['hɪərəu] n eroe m; **~ic** [hɪ'rəuɪk] a eroico(a).

heroin ['hɛrəuɪn] n eroina.

heroine ['hɛrəuɪn] n eroina.

heroism ['hɛrəuɪzm] n eroismo.

heron ['hɛrən] n airone m.

herring ['hɛrɪŋ] n aringa.

hers [həːz] pronoun il(la) suo(a), i(le) suoi(sue).

herself [həː'sɛlf] pronoun (reflexive) si; (emphatic) lei stessa; (after prep) se stessa, sé.

he's [hiːz] = **he is, he has**.

hesitant ['hɛzɪtənt] a esitante, indeciso(a).

hesitate ['hɛzɪteɪt] vi: **to ~ (about/to do)** esitare (su/a fare); **hesitation** [-'teɪʃən] n esitazione f.

het up [hɛt'ʌp] a agitato(a).

hew [hjuː] vt tagliare (con l'accetta).

hexagon ['hɛksəgən] n esagono; **~al** [-'sægənl] a esagonale.

heyday ['heɪdeɪ] n: **the ~ of** i bei giorni di, l'età d'oro di.

hi [haɪ] excl ciao!

hibernate ['haɪbəneɪt] vi svernare.

hiccough, hiccup ['hɪkʌp] vi singhiozzare // n singhiozzo; **to have (the) ~s** avere il singhiozzo.

hid [hɪd] pt of **hide**.

hidden ['hɪdn] pp of **hide**.

hide [haɪd] n (skin) pelle f // vb (pt hid, pp **hidden** [hɪd, 'hɪdn]) vt: **to ~ sth (from sb)** nascondere qc (a qd) // vi: **to ~ (from sb)** nascondersi (da qd); **~-and-seek** n rimpiattino; **~away** n nascondiglio.

hideous ['hɪdɪəs] a laido(a); orribile.

hiding ['haɪdɪŋ] n (beating) bastonata; **to be in ~** (concealed) tenersi nascosto(a); **~ place** n nascondiglio.

hierarchy ['haɪərɑːkɪ] n gerarchia.

high [haɪ] a alto(a); (speed, respect, number) grande; (wind) forte // ad alto, in alto; **20m ~** alto(a) 20m; **~brow** a, n intellettuale (m/f); **~chair** n seggiolone m; **~-flying** a (fig) ambizioso(a); **~-handed** a prepotente; **~-heeled** a a tacchi alti; **~jack** = **hijack**; **~ jump** n (SPORT) salto in alto; **~light** n (fig: of event) momento culminante // vt lumeggiare; **~ly** ad molto; **~ly strung** a teso(a) di nervi, eccitabile; **H~ Mass** n messa cantata or solenne; **~ness** n altezza; **Her H~ness** Sua Altezza; **~-pitched** a acuto(a); **~-rise block** n palazzone m.

high school ['haɪskuːl] n scuola secondaria; (US) istituto superiore d'istruzione.

high street ['haɪstriːt] n strada principale.

highway ['haɪweɪ] n strada maestra.

hijack ['haɪdʒæk] vt dirottare; **~er** n dirottatore/trice.

hike [haɪk] vi fare un'escursione a piedi // n escursione f a piedi; **~r** n escursionista m/f.

hilarious [hɪ'lɛərɪəs] a (behaviour, event) che fa schiantare dal ridere.

hilarity [hɪ'lærɪtɪ] n ilarità.

hill [hɪl] n collina, colle m; (fairly high) montagna; (on road) salita; **~side** n fianco della collina; **~y** a collinoso(a); montagnoso(a).

hilt [hɪlt] n (of sword) elsa.

him [hɪm] pronoun (direct) lo, l' + vowel; (indirect) gli; (stressed, after prep) lui; **I see ~** lo vedo; **give ~ a book** gli dia un libro; **after ~** dopo (di) lui; **~self** pronoun (reflexive) si; (emphatic) lui stesso; (after prep) se stesso, sé.

hind [haɪnd] a posteriore // n cerva.

hinder ['hɪndə*] vt ostacolare; (delay) tardare; (prevent): **to ~ sb from doing** impedire a qd di fare; **hindrance** ['hɪndrəns] n ostacolo, impedimento.

Hindu ['hɪnduː] n indù m/f inv.

hinge [hɪndʒ] n cardine m // vi (fig): **to ~ on** dipendere da.

hint [hɪnt] n accenno, allusione f; (advice) consiglio // vt: **to ~ that** lasciar capire che // vi: **to ~ at** accennare a.

hip [hɪp] n anca, fianco.

hippopotamus [hɪpə'pɒtəməs] n ippopotamo.

hire ['haɪə*] vt (car, equipment) noleggiare; (worker) assumere, dare lavoro a // n nolo, noleggio; **for ~** da nolo; (taxi) libero(a); **~ purchase (H.P.)** n acquisto (or vendita) rateale.

his [hɪz] a, pronoun il(la) suo(sua), i(le) suoi(sue).

hiss [hɪs] vi fischiare; (cat, snake) sibilare // n fischio; sibilo.

historian [hɪ'stɔːrɪən] n storico/a.

historic(al) [hɪ'stɒrɪk(l)] a storico(a).

history ['hɪstərɪ] n storia.

hit [hɪt] vt (pt, pp hit) colpire, picchiare; (knock against) battere; (reach: target) raggiungere; (collide with: car) urtare contro; (fig: affect) colpire; (find) incontrare // n colpo; (success, song) successo; **to ~ it off with sb** andare molto d'accordo con qd; **~-and-run driver** n pirata m della strada.

hitch [hɪtʃ] vt (fasten) attaccare; (also: ~ up) tirare su // n (difficulty) intoppo, difficoltà f inv; **to ~ a lift** fare l'autostop.

hitch-hike ['hɪtʃhaɪk] vi fare l'autostop; **~r** n autostoppista m/f.

hive [haɪv] n alveare m.

H.M.S. abbr of His(Her) Majesty's Ship.

hoard [hɔːd] n (of food) provviste fpl; (of money) gruzzolo // vt ammassare.

hoarding ['hɔːdɪŋ] n tabellone m per affissioni.

hoarse [hɔːs] a rauco(a).

hoax [həʊks] n scherzo; falso allarme.

hob [hɒb] n piastra (con fornelli).

hobble ['hɒbl] vi zoppicare.

hobby ['hɒbɪ] n hobby m inv, passatempo.

hobo ['həʊbəʊ] n (US) vagabondo.

hock [hɒk] n vino del Reno.

hockey ['hɒkɪ] n hockey m.

hoe [həʊ] n zappa.

hog [hɒg] n maiale m // vt (fig) arraffare; **to go the whole ~** farlo fino in fondo.

hoist [hɔɪst] n paranco // vt issare.

hold [həʊld] vb (pt, pp held [held]) vt tenere; (contain) contenere; (keep back) trattenere; (believe) mantenere; considerare; (possess) avere, possedere; detenere // vi (withstand pressure) tenere; (be valid) essere valido(a) // n presa; (fig) potere m; (NAUT) stiva; **~ the line!** (TEL) resti in linea!; **to ~ one's own** (fig) difendersi bene; **to catch or get (a) ~ of** afferrare; **to get ~ of** (fig) trovare; **to ~ back** vt trattenere; (secret) tenere celato(a); **to ~ down** vt (person) tenere a terra; (job) tenere; **to ~ off** vt tener lontano; **to ~ on** vi tener fermo; (wait) aspettare; **to ~ on to** vt fus tenersi stretto(a) a; (keep) conservare; **to ~ out** vt offrire // vi (resist) resistere; **to ~ up** vt (raise) alzare; (support) sostenere; (delay) ritardare; **~all** n borsone m; **~er** n (of ticket, title) possessore/posseditrice; (of office etc) incaricato/a; (of record) detentore/trice; **~ing** n (share) azioni fpl, titoli mpl; (farm) podere m, tenuta; **~ing**

company *n* holding *f inv*; ~**up** *n* (*robbery*) rapina a mano armata; (*delay*) ritardo; (*in traffic*) blocco.

hole [həul] *n* buco, buca // *vt* bucare.

holiday ['hɔlədi] *n* vacanza; (*day off*) giorno di vacanza; (*public*) giorno festivo; ~**-maker** *n* villeggiante *m/f;* ~ **resort** *n* luogo di villeggiatura.

holiness ['həulinis] *n* santità.

Holland ['hɔlənd] *n* Olanda.

hollow ['hɔləu] *a* cavo(a), vuoto(a); (*fig*) falso(a); vano(a) // *n* cavità *f inv*; (*in land*) valletta, depressione *f* // *vt:* **to** ~ **out** scavare.

holly ['hɔli] *n* agrifoglio.

holster ['həulstə*] *n* fondina (di pistola).

holy ['həuli] *a* santo(a); (*bread*) benedetto(a), consacrato(a); (*ground*) consacrato(a); **H**~ **Ghost** or **Spirit** *n* Spirito Santo; ~ **orders** *npl* ordini *mpl* (sacri).

homage ['hɔmidʒ] *n* omaggio; **to pay** ~ **to** rendere omaggio a.

home [həum] *n* casa; (*country*) patria; (*institution*) casa, ricovero // *a* familiare; (*cooking etc*) casalingo(a); (ECON, POL) nazionale, interno(a) // *ad* a casa; in patria; (*right in: nail etc*) fino in fondo; **at** ~ a casa; **to go** (*or* **come**) ~ tornare a casa (*or* in patria); **make yourself at** ~ si metta a suo agio; ~ **address** *n* indirizzo di casa; ~**land** *n* patria; ~**less** *a* senza tetto; spatriato(a); ~**ly** *a* semplice, alla buona; accogliente; ~**-made** *a* casalingo(a); ~ **rule** *n* autogoverno; **H**~ **Secretary** *n* (*Brit*) ministro dell'Interno; ~**sick** *a:* **to be** ~**sick** avere la nostalgia; ~ **town** *n* città *f* inv natale; ~**ward** ['həumwəd] *a* (*journey*) di ritorno; ~**work** *n* compiti *mpl* (per casa).

homicide ['hɔmisaid] *n* (*US*) omicidio.

homoeopathy [həumi'ɔpəθi] *n* omeopatia.

homogeneous [hɔməu'dʒi:niəs] *a* omogeneo(a).

homosexual [hɔməu'sɛksjuəl] *a,n* omosessuale (*m/f*).

honest ['ɔnist] *a* onesto(a); sincero(a); ~**ly** *ad* onestamente; sinceramente; ~**y** *n* onestà.

honey ['hʌni] *n* miele *m;* ~**comb** *n* favo; ~**moon** *n* luna di miele; (*trip*) viaggio di nozze.

honk [hɔŋk] *n* (AUT) colpo di clacson // *vi* suonare il clacson.

honorary ['ɔnərəri] *a* onorario(a); (*duty, title*) onorifico(a).

honour ['ɔnə*] *vt* onorare // *n* onore *m;* ~**able** *a* onorevole; ~**s degree** *n* (SCOL) laurea specializzata.

hood [hud] *n* cappuccio; (*Brit: AUT*) capote *f;* (*US: AUT*) cofano; ~**wink** *vt* infinocchiare.

hoof, ~**s** or **hooves** [hu:f, hu:vz] *n* zoccolo.

hook [huk] *n* gancio; (*for fishing*) amo // *vt* uncinare; (*dress*) agganciare.

hooligan ['hu:ligən] *n* giovinastro, teppista *m.*

hoop [hu:p] *n* cerchio.

hoot [hu:t] *vi* (AUT) suonare il clacson // *n* colpo di clacson; (NAUT) sirena; ~**er** *n* (AUT) clacson *m inv;* (NAUT) sirena.

hooves [hu:vz] *npl of* **hoof.**

hop [hɔp] *vi* saltellare, saltare; (*on one foot*) saltare su una gamba // *n* salto.

hope [həup] *vt,vi* sperare // *n* speranza; **I** ~ **so/not** spero di sì/no; ~**ful** *a* (*person*) pieno(a) di speranza; (*situation*) promettente; ~**fully** *ad* con speranza; ~**less** *a* senza speranza, disperato(a); (*useless*) inutile.

hops [hɔps] *npl* luppoli *mpl.*

horde [hɔ:d] *n* orda.

horizon [hə'raizn] *n* orizzonte *m;* ~**tal** [hɔri'zɔntl] *a* orizzontale.

hormone ['hɔ:məun] *n* ormone *m.*

horn [hɔ:n] *n* corno; (AUT) clacson *m inv;* ~**ed** *a* (*animal*) cornuto(a).

hornet ['hɔ:nit] *n* calabrone *m.*

horny ['hɔ:ni] *a* corneo(a); (*hands*) calloso(a).

horoscope ['hɔrəskəup] *n* oroscopo.

horrible ['hɔribl] *a* orribile, tremendo(a).

horrid ['hɔrid] *a* orrido(a); (*person*) antipatico(a).

horrify ['hɔrifai] *vt* scandalizzare.

horror ['hɔrə*] *n* orrore *m;* ~ **film** *n* film *m inv* dell'orrore.

hors d'œuvre [ɔ:'də:vrə] *n* antipasto.

horse [hɔ:s] *n* cavallo; **on** ~**back** a cavallo; ~ **chestnut** *n* ippocastano; ~**-drawn** *a* tirato(a) da cavallo; ~**man** *n* cavaliere *m;* ~**power** (**h.p.**) *n* cavallo (vapore); ~**-racing** *n* ippica; ~**radish** *n* barbaforte *m;* ~**shoe** *n* ferro di cavallo.

horticulture ['hɔ:tikʌltʃə*] *n* orticoltura.

hose [həuz] *n* (*also:* ~**pipe**) tubo; (*also:* **garden** ~) tubo per annaffiare.

hosiery ['həuziəri] *n* (*in shop*) (reparto di) calze *fpl* e calzini *mpl.*

hospitable [hɔs'pitəbl] *a* ospitale.

hospital ['hɔspitl] *n* ospedale *m.*

hospitality [hɔspi'tæliti] *n* ospitalità.

host [həust] *n* ospite *m;* (*large number*): **a** ~ **of** una schiera di; (REL) ostia.

hostage ['hɔstidʒ] *n* ostaggio/a.

hostel ['hɔstl] *n* ostello; (**youth**) ~ *n* ostello della gioventù.

hostess ['həustis] *n* ospite *f.*

hostile ['hɔstail] *a* ostile.

hostility [hɔ'stiliti] *n* ostilità.

hot [hɔt] *a* caldo(a); (*as opposed to only warm*) molto caldo(a); (*spicy*) piccante; (*fig*) accanito(a); ardente; violento(a), focoso(a); ~ **dog** *n* hot dog *m inv.*

hotel [həu'tɛl] *n* albergo; ~**ier** *n* albergatore/trice.

hot: ~**headed** *a* focoso(a), eccitabile; ~**house** *n* serra; ~**ly** *ad* violentemente; ~**plate** *n* fornello; piastra riscaldante; ~**-water bottle** *n* borsa dell'acqua calda.

hound [haund] *vt* perseguitare // *n* segugio.

hour ['auə*] *n* ora; ~**ly** *a* ogni ora.

house *n* [haus] (*pl:* ~**s** ['hauziz]) (*also:*

firm) casa; (POL) camera; (THEATRE) sala; pubblico; spettacolo // vt [hauz] (person) ospitare, alloggiare; **the H~** (of **Commons**) la Camera dei Comuni; **on the ~** (fig) offerto(a) dalla casa; **~ arrest** n confino (a casa); **~boat** n house boat f inv; **~breaking** n furto con scasso; **~hold** n famiglia; casa; **~keeper** n governante f; **~keeping** n (work) governo della casa; **~warming party** n festa per inaugurare la casa nuova; **~wife** n massaia; **~work** n faccende fpl domestiche.

housing ['hauzɪŋ] n alloggio; **~ estate** n zona residenziale con case popolari e/o private.

hovel ['hɔvl] n casupola.

hover ['hɔvə°] vi librarsi a volo; **to ~ round sb** aggirarsi intorno a qd; **~craft** n hovercraft m inv.

how [hau] ad come; **~ are you?** come sta?; **~ long have you been here?** da quanto tempo sta qui?; **~ lovely/how bello!; ~ many?** quanti(e)?; **~ much?** quanto(a)?; **~ many people/much milk?** quante persone/quanto latte?; **~ is it that ...?** com'è che ...? + sub; **~ever** ad in qualsiasi modo or maniera che; (+ adjective) per quanto + sub; (in questions) come // cj comunque, però.

howl [haul] n ululato // vi ululare.

howler ['haulə°] n marronata.

h.p., H.P. see **hire**; **horse**.

HQ abbr of **headquarters**.

hub [hʌb] n (of wheel) mozzo; (fig) fulcro.

hubbub ['hʌbʌb] n baccano.

huddle ['hʌdl] vi: **to ~ together** rannicchiarsi l'uno contro l'altro.

hue [hju:] n tinta; **~ and cry** n clamore m.

huff [hʌf] n: **in a ~** stizzito(a).

hug [hʌg] vt abbracciare; (shore, kerb) stringere // n abbraccio, stretta.

huge [hju:dʒ] a enorme, immenso(a).

hulk [hʌlk] n carcassa; **~ing** a: **~ing (great)** grosso(a) e goffo(a).

hull [hʌl] n (of ship) scafo.

hullo [hə'ləu] excl = **hello**.

hum [hʌm] vt (tune) canticchiare // vi canticchiare; (insect, plane, tool) ronzare.

human ['hju:mən] a umano(a) // n essere m umano.

humane [hju:'meɪn] a umanitario(a).

humanity [hju:'mænɪtɪ] n umanità; **the humanities** gli studi umanistici.

humble ['hʌmbl] a umile, modesto(a) // vt umiliare; **humbly** ad umilmente, modestamente.

humbug ['hʌmbʌg] n inganno; sciocchezze fpl.

humdrum ['hʌmdrʌm] a monotono(a), tedioso(a).

humid ['hju:mɪd] a umido(a); **~ity** [-'mɪdɪtɪ] n umidità.

humiliate [hju:'mɪlɪeɪt] vt umiliare; **humiliation** [-'eɪʃən] n umiliazione f.

humility [hju:'mɪlɪtɪ] n umiltà.

humorist ['hju:mərɪst] n umorista m/f.

humorous ['hju:mərəs] a umoristico(a); (person) buffo(a).

humour ['hju:mə°] n umore m // vt (person) compiacere; (sb's whims) assecondare.

hump [hʌmp] n gobba; **~back** n schiena d'asino.

hunch [hʌntʃ] n gobba; (premonition) intuizione f; **~back** n gobbo/a; **~ed** a incurvato(a).

hundred ['hʌndrəd] num cento; **~weight** n (Brit) = 50.8 kg; 112 lb; (US) = 45.3 kg; 100 lb.

hung [hʌŋ] pt, pp of **hang**.

Hungarian [hʌŋ'geərɪən] a ungherese // n ungherese m/f; (LING) ungherese m.

Hungary ['hʌŋgərɪ] n Ungheria.

hunger ['hʌŋgə°] n fame f // vi: **to ~ for** desiderare ardentemente.

hungrily ['hʌŋgrəlɪ] ad voracemente; (fig) avidamente.

hungry ['hʌŋgrɪ] a affamato(a); **to be ~** aver fame.

hunt [hʌnt] vt (seek) cercare; (SPORT) cacciare // vi andare a caccia // n caccia; **~er** n cacciatore m; **~ing** n caccia.

hurdle ['hə:dl] n (SPORT, fig) ostacolo.

hurl [hə:l] vt lanciare con violenza.

hurrah, hurray [hu'rɑ:, hu'reɪ] excl urrà!, evviva!

hurricane ['hʌrɪkən] n uragano.

hurried ['hʌrɪd] a affrettato(a); (work) fatto(a) in fretta; **~ly** ad in fretta.

hurry ['hʌrɪ] n fretta // vi affrettarsi // vt (person) affrettare; (work) far in fretta; **to be in a ~** aver fretta; **to do sth in a ~** fare qc in fretta; **to ~ in/out** entrare/uscire in fretta.

hurt [hə:t] vb (pt, pp hurt) vt (cause pain to) far male a; (injure, fig) ferire // vi far male // a ferito(a); **~ful** a (remark) che ferisce.

hurtle ['hə:tl] vt scagliare // vi: **to ~ past/down** passare/scendere a razzo.

husband ['hʌzbənd] n marito.

hush [hʌʃ] n silenzio, calma // vt zittire; **~!** zitto(a)!

husk [hʌsk] n (of wheat) cartoccio; (of rice, maize) buccia.

husky ['hʌskɪ] a roco(a) // n cane m esquimese.

hustle ['hʌsl] vt spingere, incalzare // n pigia pigia m inv; **~ and bustle** n trambusto.

hut [hʌt] n rifugio; (shed) ripostiglio.

hutch [hʌtʃ] n gabbia.

hyacinth ['haɪəsɪnθ] n giacinto.

hybrid ['haɪbrɪd] a ibrido(a) // n ibrido.

hydrant ['haɪdrənt] n idrante m.

hydraulic [haɪ'drɔ:lɪk] a idraulico(a).

hydroelectric [haɪdrəu'lektrɪk] a idroelettrico(a).

hydrogen ['haɪdrədʒən] n idrogeno.

hyena [haɪ'i:nə] n iena.

hygiene ['haɪdʒi:n] n igiene f.

hygienic [haɪ'dʒi:nɪk] a igienico(a).

hymn [hɪm] n inno; cantica.

hyphen ['haɪfn] n trattino.
hypnosis [hɪp'nəʊsɪs] n ipnosi f.
hypnotism ['hɪpnətɪzm] n ipnotismo.
hypnotist ['hɪpnətɪst] n ipnotizzatore/trice.
hypnotize ['hɪpnətaɪz] vt ipnotizzare.
hypocrisy [hɪ'pɒkrɪsɪ] n ipocrisia.
hypocrite ['hɪpəkrɪt] n ipocrita m/f; **hypocritical** [-'krɪtɪkl] a ipocrita.
hypothesis, pl **hypotheses** [haɪ'pɒθɪsɪs, -siːz] n ipotesi f inv.
hypothetical [haɪpəʊ'θetɪkl] a ipotetico(a).
hysteria [hɪ'stɪərɪə] n isteria.
hysterical [hɪ'sterɪkl] a isterico(a).
hysterics [hɪ'sterɪks] npl accesso di isteria; (laughter) attacco di riso.

I

I [aɪ] pronoun io.
ice [aɪs] n ghiaccio; (on road) gelo // vt (cake) glassare; (drink) mettere in fresco // vi (also: ~ **over**) ghiacciare; (also: ~ **up**) gelare; ~ **axe** n picozza da ghiaccio; ~**berg** n iceberg m inv; ~**box** n (US) frigorifero; (Brit) reparto ghiaccio; (insulated box) frigo portatile; ~**-cold** a gelato(a); ~ **cream** n gelato; ~ **hockey** n hockey m su ghiaccio.
Iceland ['aɪslənd] n Islanda; ~**er** n islandese m/f; ~**ic** [-'lændɪk] a islandese // n (LING) islandese m.
ice rink ['aɪsrɪŋk] n pista di pattinaggio.
icicle ['aɪsɪkl] n ghiacciolo.
icing ['aɪsɪŋ] n (AVIAT etc) patina di ghiaccio; (CULIN) glassa; ~ **sugar** n zucchero a velo.
icon ['aɪkɔn] n icona.
icy ['aɪsɪ] a ghiacciato(a); (weather, temperature) gelido(a).
I'd [aɪd] = **I would, I had**.
idea [aɪ'dɪə] n idea.
ideal [aɪ'dɪəl] a, n ideale (m); ~**ist** n idealista m/f.
identical [aɪ'dentɪkl] a identico(a).
identification [aɪdentɪfɪ'keɪʃən] n identificazione f; **means of** ~ carta d'identità.
identify [aɪ'dentɪfaɪ] vt identificare.
identity [aɪ'dentɪtɪ] n identità f inv.
ideology [aɪdɪ'ɔlədʒɪ] n ideologia.
idiocy ['ɪdɪəsɪ] n idiozia.
idiom ['ɪdɪəm] n idioma m; (phrase) espressione f idiomatica.
idiosyncrasy [ɪdɪəʊ'sɪŋkrəsɪ] n idiosincrasia.
idiot ['ɪdɪət] n idiota m/f; ~**ic** [-'ɔtɪk] a idiota.
idle ['aɪdl] a inattivo(a); (lazy) pigro(a), ozioso(a); (unemployed) disoccupato(a); (question, pleasures) inutile, ozioso(a); **to lie** ~ stare fermo, non funzionare; ~**ness** n ozio; pigrizia; ~**r** n ozioso/a; fannullone/a.
idol ['aɪdl] n idolo; ~**ize** vt idoleggiare.
idyllic [ɪ'dɪlɪk] a idillico(a).

i.e. ad (abbr of id est) cioè.
if [ɪf] cj se.
igloo ['ɪgluː] n igloo m inv.
ignite [ɪg'naɪt] vt accendere // vi accendersi.
ignition [ɪg'nɪʃən] n (AUT) accensione f; **to switch on/off the** ~ accendere/spegnere il motore; ~ **key** n (AUT) chiave f dell'accensione.
ignorance ['ɪgnərəns] n ignoranza.
ignorant ['ɪgnərənt] a ignorante.
ignore [ɪg'nɔː] vt non tener conto di; (person, fact) ignorare.
I'll [aɪl] = **I will, I shall**.
ill [ɪl] a (sick) malato(a); (bad) cattivo(a) // n male m; **to take** ~ **to be taken** ~ ammalarsi; ~**-advised** a (decision) poco giudizioso(a); (person) mal consigliato(a); ~**-at-ease** a a disagio.
illegal [ɪ'liːgl] a illegale.
illegible [ɪ'ledʒɪbl] a illeggibile.
illegitimate [ɪlɪ'dʒɪtɪmət] a illegittimo(a).
ill-fated [ɪl'feɪtɪd] a nefasto(a).
ill feeling [ɪl'fiːlɪŋ] n rancore m.
illicit [ɪ'lɪsɪt] a illecito(a).
illiterate [ɪ'lɪtərət] a illetterato(a); (letter) scorretto(a).
ill-mannered [ɪl'mænəd] a maleducato(a), sgarbato(a).
illness ['ɪlnɪs] n malattia.
illogical [ɪ'lɒdʒɪkl] a illogico(a).
ill-treat [ɪl'triːt] vt maltrattare.
illuminate [ɪ'luːmɪneɪt] vt illuminare; **illumination** [-'neɪʃən] n illuminazione f.
illusion [ɪ'luːʒən] n illusione f.
illusive, illusory [ɪ'luːsɪv, ɪ'luːsərɪ] a illusorio(a).
illustrate ['ɪləstreɪt] vt illustrare; **illustration** [-'streɪʃən] n illustrazione f.
illustrious [ɪ'lʌstrɪəs] a illustre.
ill will [ɪl'wɪl] n cattiva volontà.
I'm [aɪm] = **I am**.
image ['ɪmɪdʒ] n immagine f; (public face) immagine (pubblica); ~**ry** n immagini fpl.
imaginary [ɪ'mædʒɪnərɪ] a immaginario(a).
imagination [ɪmædʒɪ'neɪʃən] n immaginazione f, fantasia.
imaginative [ɪ'mædʒɪnətɪv] a immaginoso(a).
imagine [ɪ'mædʒɪn] vt immaginare.
imbalance [ɪm'bæləns] n sbilancio.
imbecile ['ɪmbəsiːl] n imbecille m/f.
imitate ['ɪmɪteɪt] vt imitare; **imitation** [-'teɪʃən] n imitazione f; **imitator** n imitatore/trice.
immaculate [ɪ'mækjulət] a immacolato(a); (dress, appearance) impeccabile.
immaterial [ɪmə'tɪərɪəl] a immateriale, indifferente.
immature [ɪmə'tjuə*] a immaturo(a).
immediate [ɪ'miːdɪət] a immediato(a); ~**ly** ad (at once) subito, immediatamente; ~**ly next to** proprio accanto a.
immense [ɪ'mens] a immenso(a); enorme.
immerse [ɪ'mɜːs] vt immergere.

immersion heater [ɪˈmɜːʃnhiːtə*] n riscaldatore m a immersione.

immigrant [ˈɪmɪɡrənt] n immigrante m/f; immigrato/a.

immigration [ɪmɪˈɡreɪʃən] n immigrazione f.

imminent [ˈɪmɪnənt] a imminente.

immobilize [ɪˈməʊbɪlaɪz] vt immobilizzare.

immoral [ɪˈmɔrl] a immorale; ~ity [-ˈrælɪtɪ] n immoralità.

immortal [ɪˈmɔːtl] a, n immortale (m/f); ~ize vt rendere immortale.

immune [ɪˈmjuːn] a: ~ (to) immune (da).

immunize [ˈɪmjunaɪz] vt immunizzare.

impact [ˈɪmpækt] n impatto.

impair [ɪmˈpɛə*] vt danneggiare.

impale [ɪmˈpeɪl] vt impalare.

impartial [ɪmˈpɑːʃl] a imparziale; ~ity [ɪmpɑːʃɪˈælɪtɪ] n imparzialità.

impassable [ɪmˈpɑːsəbl] a insuperabile; (road) impraticabile.

impatience [ɪmˈpeɪʃəns] n impazienza.

impatient [ɪmˈpeɪʃənt] a impaziente.

impeach [ɪmˈpiːtʃ] vt accusare, attaccare; (public official) incriminare.

impeccable [ɪmˈpekəbl] a impeccabile.

impede [ɪmˈpiːd] vt impedire.

impediment [ɪmˈpedɪmənt] n impedimento; (also: **speech** ~) difetto di pronuncia.

impending [ɪmˈpendɪŋ] a imminente.

imperative [ɪmˈperətɪv] a imperativo(a); necessario(a), urgente; (voice) imperioso(a) // n (LING) imperativo.

imperceptible [ɪmpəˈseptɪbl] a impercettibile.

imperfect [ɪmˈpɜːfɪkt] a imperfetto(a); (goods etc) difettoso(a) // n (LING: also: ~ tense) imperfetto; ~ion [-ˈfekʃən] n imperfezione f.

imperial [ɪmˈpɪərɪəl] a imperiale; (measure) legale.

impersonal [ɪmˈpɜːsənl] a impersonale.

impersonate [ɪmˈpɜːsəneɪt] vt impersonare; (THEATRE) fare la mimica di; **impersonation** [-ˈneɪʃən] n (LAW) usurpazione f d'identità; (THEATRE) mimica.

impertinent [ɪmˈpɜːtɪnənt] a insolente, impertinente.

impervious [ɪmˈpɜːvɪəs] a impermeabile; (fig): ~ to insensibile a; impassibile di fronte a.

impetuous [ɪmˈpetjuəs] a impetuoso(a), precipitoso(a).

impetus [ˈɪmpətəs] n impeto.

impinge [ɪmˈpɪndʒ]: to ~ on vt fus (person) colpire; (rights) ledere.

implausible [ɪmˈplɔːzɪbl] a non plausibile.

implement n [ˈɪmplɪmənt] attrezzo; (for cooking) utensile m // vt [ˈɪmplɪment] effettuare.

implicate [ˈɪmplɪkeɪt] vt implicare; **implication** [-ˈkeɪʃən] n implicazione f.

implicit [ɪmˈplɪsɪt] a implicito(a); (complete) completo(a).

implore [ɪmˈplɔː*] vt implorare.

imply [ɪmˈplaɪ] vt insinuare; suggerire.

impolite [ɪmpəˈlaɪt] a scortese.

imponderable [ɪmˈpɔndərəbl] a imponderabile.

import vt [ɪmˈpɔːt] importare // n [ˈɪmpɔːt] (COMM) importazione f; (meaning) significato, senso.

importance [ɪmˈpɔːtns] n importanza.

important [ɪmˈpɔːtnt] a importante.

imported [ɪmˈpɔːtɪd] a importato(a).

importer [ɪmˈpɔːtə*] n importatore/trice.

impose [ɪmˈpəʊz] vt imporre // vi: to ~ on sb sfruttare la bontà di qd.

imposing [ɪmˈpəʊzɪŋ] a imponente.

impossibility [ɪmpɔsəˈbɪlɪtɪ] n impossibilità.

impossible [ɪmˈpɔsɪbl] a impossibile.

impostor [ɪmˈpɔstə*] n impostore/a.

impotence [ˈɪmpətns] n impotenza.

impotent [ˈɪmpətnt] a impotente.

impound [ɪmˈpaʊnd] vt confiscare.

impoverished [ɪmˈpɔvərɪʃt] a impoverito(a).

impracticable [ɪmˈpræktɪkəbl] a impraticabile.

impractical [ɪmˈpræktɪkl] a non pratico(a).

imprecise [ɪmprɪˈsaɪs] a impreciso(a).

impregnable [ɪmˈpregnəbl] a (fortress) inespugnabile; (fig) inoppugnabile; irrefutabile.

impregnate [ˈɪmpregneɪt] vt impregnare; (fertilize) fecondare.

impresario [ɪmprɪˈsɑːrɪəʊ] n impresario/a.

impress [ɪmˈpres] vt impressionare; (mark) imprimere, stampare; to ~ sth on sb far capire qc a qd.

impression [ɪmˈpreʃən] n impressione f; to be under the ~ that avere l'impressione che; ~able a impressionabile; ~ist n impressionista m/f.

impressive [ɪmˈpresɪv] a impressionante.

imprison [ɪmˈprɪzn] vt imprigionare; ~ment n imprigionamento.

improbable [ɪmˈprɔbəbl] a improbabile; (excuse) inverosimile.

impromptu [ɪmˈprɔmptjuː] a improvvisato(a).

improper [ɪmˈprɔpə*] a scorretto(a); (unsuitable) inadatto(a), improprio(a); sconveniente, indecente; **impropriety** [ɪmprəˈpraɪətɪ] n sconvenienza; (of expression) improprietà.

improve [ɪmˈpruːv] vt migliorare // vi migliorare; (pupil etc) fare progressi; ~ment n miglioramento; progresso.

improvisation [ɪmprəvaɪˈzeɪʃən] n improvvisazione f.

improvise [ˈɪmprəvaɪz] vt,vi improvvisare.

impudent [ˈɪmpjudnt] a impudente, sfacciato(a).

impulse [ˈɪmpʌls] n impulso.

impulsive [ɪmˈpʌlsɪv] a impulsivo(a).

impunity [ɪm'pjuːnɪtɪ] *n* impunità.

impure [ɪm'pjuə*] *a* impuro(a).

impurity [ɪm'pjuərɪtɪ] *n* impurità *f inv.*

in [ɪn] *prep* in; (*with time: during, within*): ~ May/2 days in maggio/2 giorni; (: *after*): ~ 2 weeks entro 2 settimane; (*with town*) a; (*with country*): **it's ~ France** è in Francia // *ad* entro, dentro; (*fashionable*) alla moda; **is he ~?** lui c'è?; **~ town/the country** in città/campagna; **~ the sun** al sole; **~ the rain** sotto la pioggia; **~ French** in francese; **a man ~ 10** un uomo su 10; **~ hundreds** a centinaia; **the best pupil ~ the class** il migliore alunno della classe; **~ saying this** nel dire questo; **their party is ~** il loro partito è al potere; **to run/limp** *etc* **~** entrare correndo/zoppicando; **the ~s and outs of** i dettagli di.

in., ins *abbr of* **inch(es)**.

inability [ɪnə'bɪlɪtɪ] *n* inabilità, incapacità.

inaccessible [ɪnæk'sɛsɪbl] *a* inaccessibile.

inaccuracy [ɪn'ækjurəsɪ] *n* inaccuratezza; imprecisione *f.*

inaccurate [ɪn'ækjurət] *a* inesatto(a), impreciso(a).

inactivity [ɪnæk'tɪvɪtɪ] *n* inattività.

inadequacy [ɪn'ædɪkwəsɪ] *n* insufficienza.

inadequate [ɪn'ædɪkwət] *a* insufficiente.

inadvertently [ɪnəd'vəːtntlɪ] *ad* senza volerlo.

inadvisable   [ɪnəd'vaɪzəbl]   *a* sconsigliabile.

inane [ɪ'neɪn] *a* vacuo(a), stupido(a).

inanimate [ɪn'ænɪmət] *a* inanimato(a).

inappropriate   [ɪnə'prəuprɪət]   *a* disadatto(a); (*word, expression*) improprio(a).

inapt [ɪn'æpt] *a* maldestro(a); fuori luogo; **~itude** *n* improprietà.

inarticulate [ɪnɑː'tɪkjulət] *a* (*person*) che si esprime male; (*speech*) inarticolato(a).

inasmuch as [ɪnəz'mʌtʃæz] *ad* in quanto che; (*seeing that*) poiché.

inattention [ɪnə'tɛnʃən] *n* mancanza di attenzione.

inattentive [ɪnə'tɛntɪv] *a* disattento(a), distratto(a); negligente.

inaudible [ɪn'ɔːdɪbl] *a* impercettibile.

inaugural [ɪ'nɔːgjurəl] *a* inaugurale.

inaugurate [ɪ'nɔːgjureɪt] *vt* inaugurare; (*president, official*) insediare; **inauguration** [-'reɪʃən] *n* inaugurazione *f*; insediamento in carica.

in-between [ɪnbɪ'twiːn] *a* fra i (*or* le) due.

inborn [ɪn'bɔːn] *a* (*feeling*) innato(a); (*defect*) congenito(a).

inbred [ɪn'brɛd] *a* innato(a); (*family*) connaturato(a).

inbreeding [ɪn'briːdɪŋ] *n* incrocio ripetuto di animali consanguinei; unioni *fpl* fra consanguinei.

Inc. *abbr see* **incorporated**.

incapability [ɪnkeɪpə'bɪlɪtɪ] *n* incapacità.

incapable [ɪn'keɪpəbl] *a* incapace.

incapacitate [ɪnkə'pæsɪteɪt] *vt*: **to ~ sb from doing** rendere qd incapace di fare.

incarnate [ɪn'kɑːnɪt] *a* incarnato(a); **incarnation** [-'neɪʃən] *n* incarnazione *f.*

incendiary [ɪn'sɛndɪərɪ] *a* incendiario(a).

incense *n* ['ɪnsɛns] incenso // *vt* [ɪn'sɛns] (*anger*) infuriare.

incentive [ɪn'sɛntɪv] *n* incentivo.

incessant [ɪn'sɛsnt] *a* incessante; **~ly** *ad* di continuo, senza sosta.

incest ['ɪnsɛst] *n* incesto.

inch [ɪntʃ] *n* pollice *m* (= *25 mm*; *12 in a foot*); **within an ~ of** a un pelo da.

incidence ['ɪnsɪdns] *n* (*of crime, disease*) incidenza.

incident ['ɪnsɪdnt] *n* incidente *m*; (*in book*) episodio.

incidental [ɪnsɪ'dɛntl] *a* accessorio(a), d'accompagnamento; (*unplanned*) incidentale; **~ to** marginale a; **~ expenses** *npl* spese *fpl* accessorie; **~ly** [-'dɛntəlɪ] *ad* (*by the way*) a proposito.

incinerator [ɪn'sɪnəreɪtə*] *n* inceneritore *m.*

incipient [ɪn'sɪpɪənt] *a* incipiente.

incision [ɪn'sɪʒən] *n* incisione *f.*

incisive [ɪn'saɪsɪv] *a* incisivo(a); tagliante; acuto(a).

incite [ɪn'saɪt] *vt* incitare.

inclination [ɪnklɪ'neɪʃən] *n* inclinazione *f.*

incline *n* ['ɪnklaɪn] pendenza, pendio // *vb* [ɪn'klaɪn] *vt* inclinare // *vi*: **to ~ to** tendere a; **to be ~d to do** tendere a fare; essere propenso(a) a fare; **to be well ~d towards sb** essere ben disposto(a) verso qd.

include [ɪn'kluːd] *vt* includere, comprendere; **including** *prep* compreso(a), incluso(a).

inclusion [ɪn'kluːʒən] *n* inclusione *f.*

inclusive [ɪn'kluːsɪv] *a* incluso(a), compreso(a).

incognito [ɪnkɔg'niːtəu] *ad* in incognito.

incoherent [ɪnkəu'hɪərənt] *a* incoerente.

income ['ɪŋkʌm] *n* reddito; **~ tax** *n* imposta sul reddito; **~ tax return** *n* dichiarazione *f* annuale dei redditi.

incoming ['ɪnkʌmɪŋ] *a*: **~ tide** *n* marea montante.

incompatible [ɪnkəm'pætɪbl] *a* incompatibile.

incompetence [ɪn'kɔmpɪtns] *n* incompetenza, incapacità.

incompetent [ɪn'kɔmpɪtnt] *a* incompetente, incapace.

incomplete [ɪnkəm'pliːt] *a* incompleto(a).

incomprehensible [ɪnkɔmprɪ'hɛnsɪbl] *a* incomprensibile.

inconclusive [ɪnkən'kluːsɪv] *a* improduttivo(a); (*argument*) poco convincente.

incongruous [ɪn'kɔŋgruəs] *a* poco appropriato(a); (*remark, act*) incongruo(a).

inconsequential [ɪnkɔnsɪ'kwɛnʃl] *a* senza importanza.

inconsiderate   [ɪnkən'sɪdərət]   *a* sconsiderato(a).

inconsistent [ɪnkən'sɪstnt] *a* incoerente;

poco logico(a); contraddittorio(a).

inconspicuous [ɪnkən'spɪkjuəs] *a* incospicuo(a); (*colour*) poco appariscente; (*dress*) dimesso(a).

inconstant [ɪn'kɔnstnt] *a* incostante; mutevole.

incontinent [ɪn'kɔntɪnənt] *a* incontinente.

inconvenience [ɪnkən'viːnjəns] *n* inconveniente *m*; (*trouble*) disturbo // *vt* disturbare.

inconvenient [ɪnkən'viːnjənt] *a* scomodo(a).

incorporate [ɪn'kɔːpəreɪt] *vt* incorporare; (*contain*) contenere; ~d *a*: ~d **company** (*US, abbr* **Inc.**) società *f inv* anonima (S.A.).

incorrect [ɪnkə'rɛkt] *a* scorretto(a); (*opinion, statement*) impreciso(a).

incorruptible [ɪnkə'rʌptɪbl] *a* incorruttibile.

increase *n* [ɪn'kriːs] aumento // *vi* [ɪn'kriːs] aumentare.

increasing [ɪn'kriːsɪŋ] *a* (*number*) crescente; ~ly *ad* sempre più.

incredible [ɪn'krɛdɪbl] *a* incredibile.

incredulous [ɪn'krɛdjuləs] *a* incredulo(a).

increment ['ɪnkrɪmənt] *n* aumento, incremento.

incriminate [ɪn'krɪmɪneɪt] *vt* compromettere.

incubation [ɪnkju'beɪʃən] *n* incubazione *f.*

incubator ['ɪnkjubeɪtə*] *n* incubatrice *f.*

incur [ɪn'kɔː*] *vt* (*expenses*) incorrere; (*anger, risk*) esporsi a; (*debt*) contrarre; (*loss*) subire.

incurable [ɪn'kjuərəbl] *a* incurabile.

incursion [ɪn'kɔːʃən] *n* incursione *f.*

indebted [ɪn'dɛtɪd] *a*: **to be ~ to sb** (**for**) essere obbligato(a) verso qd (per).

indecent [ɪn'diːsnt] *a* indecente.

indecision [ɪndɪ'sɪʒən] *n* indecisione *f.*

indecisive [ɪndɪ'saɪsɪv] *a* indeciso(a); (*discussion*) non decisivo(a).

indeed [ɪn'diːd] *ad* infatti; veramente; **yes ~!** certamente!

indefinable [ɪndɪ'faɪnəbl] *a* indefinibile.

indefinite [ɪn'dɛfɪnɪt] *a* indefinito(a); (*answer*) vago(a); (*period, number*) indeterminato(a); ~ly *ad* (*wait*) indefinitamente.

indelible [ɪn'dɛlɪbl] *a* indelebile.

indemnify [ɪn'dɛmnɪfaɪ] *vt* indennizzare.

indentation [ɪndɛn'teɪʃən] *n* intaccatura.

independence [ɪndɪ'pɛndns] *n* indipendenza.

independent [ɪndɪ'pɛndnt] *a* indipendente.

indescribable [ɪndɪ'skraɪbəbl] *a* indescrivibile.

index ['ɪndɛks] *n* (*pl:* ~**es**: *in book*) indice *m*; (: *in library etc*) catalogo; (*pl:* **indices** ['ɪndɪsiːz]: *ratio, sign*) indice *m*; ~ **card** *n* scheda; ~ **finger** *n* (dito) indice *m*; ~-**linked** *a* legato(a) al costo della vita.

India ['ɪndɪə] *n* India; ~**n** *a, n* indiano(a); ~**n ink** *n* inchiostro di china; ~**n Ocean** *n* Oceano Indiano.

indicate ['ɪndɪkeɪt] *vt* indicare;

indication [ɪndɪ'keɪʃən] *n* indicazione *f*, segno.

indicative [ɪn'dɪkətɪv] *a* indicativo(a) // *n* (*LING*) indicativo.

indicator ['ɪndɪkeɪtə*] *n* indicatore *m*.

indices ['ɪndɪsiːz] *npl of* **index**.

indict [ɪn'daɪt] *vt* accusare; ~**able** *a* passibile di pena; ~**ment** *n* accusa.

indifference [ɪn'dɪfrəns] *n* indifferenza.

indifferent [ɪn'dɪfrənt] *a* indifferente; (*poor*) mediocre.

indigenous [ɪn'dɪdʒɪnəs] *a* indigeno(a).

indigestible [ɪndɪ'dʒɛstɪbl] *a* indigeribile.

indigestion [ɪndɪ'dʒɛstʃən] *n* indigestione *f.*

indignant [ɪn'dɪgnənt] *a*: ~ (**at sth/with sb**) indignato(a) (per qc/contro qd).

indignation [ɪndɪg'neɪʃən] *n* indignazione *f.*

indignity [ɪn'dɪgnɪtɪ] *n* affronto.

indirect [ɪndɪ'rɛkt] *a* indiretto(a).

indiscreet [ɪndɪ'skriːt] *a* indiscreto(a); (*rash*) imprudente.

indiscretion [ɪndɪ'skrɛʃən] *n* indiscrezione *f*; imprudenza.

indiscriminate [ɪndɪ'skrɪmɪnət] *a* (*person*) che non sa discernere; (*admiration*) cieco(a); (*killings*) indiscriminato(a).

indispensable [ɪndɪ'spɛnsəbl] *a* indispensabile.

indisposed [ɪndɪ'spəuzd] *a* (*unwell*) indisposto(a).

indisputable [ɪndɪ'spjuːtəbl] *a* incontestabile, indiscutibile.

indistinct [ɪndɪ'stɪŋkt] *a* indistinto(a); (*memory, noise*) vago(a).

individual [ɪndɪ'vɪdjuəl] *n* individuo // *a* individuale; (*characteristic*) particolare, originale; ~**ist** *n* individualista *m/f*; ~**ity** [-'ælɪtɪ] *n* individualità.

indoctrinate [ɪn'dɔktrɪneɪt] *vt* indottrinare; **indoctrination** [-'neɪʃən] *n* indottrinamento.

indolent ['ɪndələnt] *a* indolente.

indoor ['ɪndɔː*] *a* da interno; (*plant*) d'appartamento; (*swimming-pool*) coperto(a); (*sport, games*) fatto(a) al coperto; ~**s** [ɪn'dɔːz] *ad* all'interno; (*at home*) in casa.

indubitable [ɪn'djuːbɪtəbl] *a* indubitabile.

induce [ɪn'djuːs] *vt* persuadere; (*bring about*) provocare; ~**ment** *n* incitamento; (*incentive*) stimolo, incentivo.

induction [ɪn'dʌkʃən] *n* (*MED: of birth*) parto indotto; ~ **course** *n* corso di avviamento.

indulge [ɪn'dʌldʒ] *vt* (*whim*) compiacere, soddisfare; (*child*) viziare // *vi*: **to ~ in sth** concedersi qc; abbandonarsi a qc; ~**nce** *n* lusso (che uno si permette); (*leniency*) indulgenza; ~**nt** *a* indulgente.

industrial [ɪn'dʌstrɪəl] *a* industriale; (*injury*) sul lavoro; (*dispute*) di lavoro; ~ **action** *n* azione *f* rivendicativa; ~ **estate** *n* zona industriale; ~**ist** *n* industriale *m*; ~**ize** *vt* industrializzare.

industrious [ɪn'dʌstrɪəs] a industrioso(a), assiduo(a).

industry ['ɪndəstrɪ] n industria; (diligence) operosità.

inebriated [ɪ'ni:brɪeɪtɪd] a ubriaco(a).

inedible [ɪn'ɛdɪbl] a immangiabile.

ineffective [ɪnɪ'fɛktɪv] a inefficace.

ineffectual [ɪnɪ'fɛktʃuəl] a inefficace; incompetente.

inefficiency [ɪnɪ'fɪʃənsɪ] n inefficienza.

inefficient [ɪnɪ'fɪʃənt] a inefficiente.

ineligible [ɪn'ɛlɪdʒɪbl] a (candidate) ineleggibile; **to be ~ for sth** non avere il diritto a qc.

inept [ɪ'nɛpt] a inetto(a).

inequality [ɪnɪ'kwɒlɪtɪ] n ineguaglianza.

inert [ɪ'nɜːt] a inerte.

inertia [ɪ'nɜːʃə] n inerzia.

inescapable [ɪnɪ'skeɪpəbl] a inevitabile.

inestimable [ɪn'ɛstɪməbl] a inestimabile, incalcolabile.

inevitable [ɪn'ɛvɪtəbl] a inevitabile.

inexact [ɪnɪg'zækt] a inesatto(a).

inexhaustible [ɪnɪg'zɔːstɪbl] a inesauribile; (person) instancabile.

inexorable [ɪn'ɛksərəbl] a inesorabile.

inexpensive [ɪnɪk'spɛnsɪv] a poco costoso(a).

inexperience [ɪnɪk'spɪərɪəns] n inesperienza; **~d** a inesperto(a), senza esperienza.

inexplicable [ɪnɪk'splɪkəbl] a inesplicabile.

inextricable [ɪnɪk'strɪkəbl] a inestricabile.

infallibility [ɪnfælə'bɪlɪtɪ] n infallibilità.

infallible [ɪn'fælɪbl] a infallibile.

infamous ['ɪnfəməs] a infame.

infamy ['ɪnfəmɪ] n infamia.

infancy ['ɪnfənsɪ] n infanzia.

infant ['ɪnfənt] n (baby) infante m/f; (young child) bambino/a; **~ile** a infantile; **~ school** n scuola elementare (per bambini dall'età di 5 a 7 anni).

infantry ['ɪnfəntrɪ] n fanteria; **~man** n fante m.

infatuated [ɪn'fætjueɪtɪd] a: **~ with** infatuato(a) di.

infatuation [ɪnfætju'eɪʃən] n infatuazione f.

infect [ɪn'fɛkt] vt infettare; **~ed with** (illness) affetto(a) da; **~ion** [ɪn'fɛkʃən] n infezione f; contagio; **~ious** [ɪn'fɛkʃəs] a infettivo(a); (also: fig) contagioso(a).

infer [ɪn'fɜː*] vt inferire, dedurre; **~ence** ['ɪnfərəns] n deduzione f, conclusione f.

inferior [ɪn'fɪərɪə*] a inferiore; (goods) di qualità scadente // n inferiore m/f; (in rank) subalterno/a; **~ity** [ɪnfɪərɪ'ɔrətɪ] n inferiorità; **~ity complex** n complesso di inferiorità.

infernal [ɪn'fɜːnl] a infernale.

inferno [ɪn'fɜːnəu] n inferno.

infertile [ɪn'fɜːtaɪl] a sterile; **infertility** [-'tɪlɪtɪ] n sterilità.

infested [ɪn'fɛstɪd] a: **~ (with)** infestato(a) (di).

infidelity [ɪnfɪ'dɛlɪtɪ] n infedeltà.

in-fighting ['ɪnfaɪtɪŋ] n lotte fpl intestine.

infiltrate ['ɪnfɪltreɪt] vt (troops etc) far penetrare; (enemy line etc) infiltrare // vi infiltrarsi.

infinite ['ɪnfɪnɪt] a infinito(a).

infinitive [ɪn'fɪnɪtɪv] n infinito.

infinity [ɪn'fɪnɪtɪ] n infinità; (also MATH) infinito.

infirmary [ɪn'fɜːmərɪ] n ospedale m; (in school, factory) infermeria.

infirmity [ɪn'fɜːmɪtɪ] n infermità f inv.

inflame [ɪn'fleɪm] vt infiammare.

inflammable [ɪn'flæməbl] a infiammabile.

inflammation [ɪnflə'meɪʃən] n infiammazione f.

inflate [ɪn'fleɪt] vt (tyre, balloon) gonfiare; (fig) esagerare; gonfiare; **to ~ the currency** far ricorso all'inflazione; **~d a** (style) gonfio(a); (value) esagerato(a); **inflation** [ɪn'fleɪʃən] n (ECON) inflazione f.

inflexible [ɪn'flɛksɪbl] a inflessibile, rigido(a).

inflict [ɪn'flɪkt] vt: **to ~ on** infliggere a; **~ion** [ɪn'flɪkʃən] n infliggere m; inflizione f; afflizione f.

inflow ['ɪnfləu] n afflusso.

influence ['ɪnfluəns] n influenza // vt influenzare; **under the ~ of** sotto l'influenza di.

influential [ɪnflu'ɛnʃl] a influente.

influenza [ɪnflu'ɛnzə] n (MED) influenza.

influx ['ɪnflʌks] n afflusso.

inform [ɪn'fɔːm] vt: **to ~ sb (of)** informare qd (di); **to ~ sb about** mettere qd al corrente di.

informal [ɪn'fɔːml] a (person, manner) alla buona, semplice; (visit, discussion) informale; (announcement, invitation) non ufficiale; '**dress ~**' 'non è richiesto l'abito scuro'; **~ity** [-'mælɪtɪ] n semplicità, informalità; carattere m non ufficiale.

information [ɪnfə'meɪʃən] n informazioni fpl; notizie fpl; (knowledge) particolari mpl; **a piece of ~** un'informazione.

informative [ɪn'fɔːmətɪv] a istruttivo(a).

informer [ɪn'fɔːmə*] n informatore/trice.

infra-red [ɪnfrə'rɛd] a infrarosso(a).

infrequent [ɪn'friːkwənt] a infrequente, raro(a).

infringe [ɪn'frɪndʒ] vt infrangere // vi: **to ~ on** calpestare; **~ment** n: **~ment (of)** infrazione f (di).

infuriating [ɪn'fjuərɪeɪtɪŋ] a molto irritante.

ingenious [ɪn'dʒiːnjəs] a ingegnoso(a).

ingenuity [ɪndʒɪ'njuːɪtɪ] n ingegnosità.

ingot ['ɪŋgət] n lingotto.

ingrained [ɪn'greɪnd] a radicato(a).

ingratiate [ɪn'greɪʃɪeɪt] vt: **to ~ o.s. with** ingraziarsi.

ingratitude [ɪn'grætɪtjuːd] n ingratitudine f.

ingredient [ɪn'griːdɪənt] n ingrediente m; elemento.

inhabit [ɪn'hæbɪt] vt abitare.

inhabitant [ɪn'hæbɪtnt] n abitante m/f.
inhale [ɪn'heɪl] vt inalare // vi (in smoking) aspirare.
inherent [ɪn'hɪərənt] a: ~ (in or to) inerente (a).
inherit [ɪn'herɪt] vt ereditare; ~ance n eredità.
inhibit [ɪn'hɪbɪt] vt (PSYCH) inibire; to ~ sb from doing impedire a qd di fare; ~ion [-'bɪʃən] n inibizione f.
inhospitable [ɪnhɔs'pɪtəbl] a inospitale.
inhuman [ɪn'hju:mən] a inumano(a).
inimitable [ɪ'nɪmɪtəbl] a inimitabile.
iniquity [ɪ'nɪkwɪtɪ] n iniquità f inv.
initial [ɪ'nɪʃl] a iniziale // n iniziale f // vt siglare; ~s npl iniziali fpl; (as signature) sigla; ~ly ad inizialmente, all'inizio.
initiate [ɪ'nɪʃɪeɪt] vt (start) avviare; intraprendere; iniziare; (person) iniziare; **initiation** [-'eɪʃən] n (into secret etc) iniziazione f.
initiative [ɪ'nɪʃətɪv] n iniziativa.
inject [ɪn'dʒekt] vt (liquid) iniettare; (person) fare una puntura a; ~ion [ɪn-'dʒekʃən] n iniezione f, puntura.
injure [ɪndʒə*] vt ferire; (wrong) fare male or torto a; (damage: reputation etc) nuocere a.
injury [ɪndʒərɪ] n ferita; (wrong) torto; ~ time n (SPORT) tempo di ricupero.
injustice [ɪn'dʒʌstɪs] n ingiustizia.
ink [ɪŋk] n inchiostro.
inkling [ɪŋklɪŋ] n sentore m, vaga idea.
inlaid [ɪnleɪd] a incrostato(a); (table etc) intarsiato(a).
inland a [ɪnlənd] interno(a) // ad [ɪn-'lænd] all'interno; I~ Revenue n (Brit) fisco, entrate fpl fiscali.
in-laws [ɪnlɔ:z] npl suoceri mpl; cognati mpl.
inlet [ɪnlet] n (GEO) insenatura, baia; ~ pipe n (TECH) tubo d'immissione.
inmate [ɪnmeɪt] n (in prison) carcerato/a; (in asylum) ricoverato/a.
inn [ɪn] n locanda.
innate [ɪ'neɪt] a innato(a).
inner [ɪnə*] a interno(a), interiore; ~ tube n camera d'aria.
innocence [ɪnəsns] n innocenza.
innocent [ɪnəsnt] a innocente.
innocuous [ɪ'nɔkjuəs] a innocuo(a).
innovation [ɪnəʊ'veɪʃən] n innovazione f.
innuendo, ~es [ɪnju'endəʊ] n insinuazione f.
innumerable [ɪ'nju:mrəbl] a innumerevole.
inoculation [ɪnɔkju'leɪʃən] n inoculazione f.
inopportune [ɪn'ɔpətju:n] a inopportuno(a).
inordinately [ɪ'nɔːdɪnətlɪ] ad smoderatamente.
inorganic [ɪnɔː'gænɪk] a inorganico(a).
in-patient [ɪnpeɪʃənt] n ricoverato/a.
input [ɪnput] n (ELEC) energia, potenza; (of machine) alimentazione f; (of computer) input m.

inquest [ɪnkwest] n inchiesta.
inquire [ɪn'kwaɪə*] vi informarsi // vt domandare, informarsi di; to ~ about or fus informarsi di; to ~ into vt fus fare indagini su; **inquiring** a (mind) inquisitivo(a); **inquiry** n domanda; (LAW) indagine f, investigazione f.
inquisitive [ɪn'kwɪzɪtɪv] a curioso(a).
inroad [ɪnrəʊd] n incursione f.
insane [ɪn'seɪn] a matto(a), pazzo(a); (MED) alienato(a).
insanitary [ɪn'sænɪtərɪ] a insalubre.
insanity [ɪn'sænɪtɪ] n follia; (MED) alienazione f mentale.
insatiable [ɪn'seɪʃəbl] a insaziabile.
inscribe [ɪn'skraɪb] vt iscrivere.
inscription [ɪn'skrɪpʃən] n iscrizione f, dedica.
inscrutable [ɪn'skru:təbl] a imperscrutabile.
insect [ɪnsekt] n insetto; ~icide [ɪn-'sektɪsaɪd] n insetticida m.
insecure [ɪnsɪ'kjuə*] a malfermo(a); malsicuro(a); (person) ansioso(a); **insecurity** n mancanza di sicurezza.
insensible [ɪn'sensɪbl] a insensibile; (unconscious) privo(a) di sensi.
insensitive [ɪn'sensɪtɪv] a insensibile.
inseparable [ɪn'seprəbl] a inseparabile.
insert vt [ɪn'sɔːt] inserire, introdurre // n [ɪnsɔːt] inserto; ~ion [ɪn'sɔːʃən] n inserzione f.
inshore [ɪn'ʃɔː*] a costiero(a) // ad presso la riva; verso la riva.
inside [ɪn'saɪd] n interno, parte f interiore // a interno(a), interiore // ad dentro, all'interno // prep dentro, all'interno di; (of time): ~ 10 minutes entro 10 minuti; ~s npl (col) ventre m; ~ lane n (AUT) corsia di marcia; ~ out (turn) a rovescio; (know) in fondo.
insidious [ɪn'sɪdɪəs] a insidioso(a).
insight [ɪnsaɪt] n acume m, perspicacia; (glimpse: idea) percezione f.
insignificant [ɪnsɪg'nɪfɪknt] a insignificante.
insincere [ɪnsɪn'sɪə*] a insincero(a).
insinuate [ɪn'sɪnjueɪt] vt insinuare; **insinuation** [-'eɪʃən] n insinuazione f.
insipid [ɪn'sɪpɪd] a insipido(a), insulso(a).
insist [ɪn'sɪst] vi insistere; to ~ on doing insistere per fare; to ~ that insistere perché + sub; (claim) sostenere che; ~ence n insistenza; ~ent a insistente.
insolence [ɪnsələns] n insolenza.
insolent [ɪnsələnt] a insolente.
insoluble [ɪn'sɔljubl] a insolubile.
insolvent [ɪn'sɔlvənt] a insolvente.
insomnia [ɪn'sɔmnɪə] n insonnia.
inspect [ɪn'spekt] vt ispezionare; (ticket) controllare; ~ion [ɪn'spekʃən] n ispezione f; controllo; ~or n ispettore/trice; controllore m.
inspiration [ɪnspə'reɪʃən] n ispirazione f.
inspire [ɪn'spaɪə*] vt ispirare; **inspiring** a stimolante.
instability [ɪnstə'bɪlɪtɪ] n instabilità.

install [ɪn'stɔːl] vt installare; ~ation [ɪnstə'leɪʃən] n installazione f.

instalment [ɪn'stɔːlmənt] n rata; (of TV serial etc) puntata.

instance ['ɪnstəns] n esempio, caso; for ~ per or ad esempio.

instant ['ɪnstənt] n istante m, attimo // a immediato(a); urgente; (coffee, food) in polvere; the 10th — il 10 corrente; ~ly ad immediatamente, subito.

instead [ɪn'stɛd] ad invece; ~ of invece di.

instep ['ɪnstɛp] n collo del piede; (of shoe) collo della scarpa.

instigation [ɪnstɪ'geɪʃən] n istigazione f.

instil [ɪn'stɪl] vt: to ~ (into) inculcare (in).

instinct ['ɪnstɪŋkt] n istinto.

instinctive [ɪn'stɪŋktɪv] a istintivo(a); ~ly ad per istinto.

institute ['ɪnstɪtjuːt] n istituto // vt istituire, stabilire; (inquiry) avviare; (proceedings) iniziare.

institution [ɪnstɪ'tjuːʃən] n istituzione f; istituto (d'istruzione); istituto (psichiatrico).

instruct [ɪn'strʌkt] vt istruire; to ~ sb in sth insegnare qc a qd; to ~ sb to do sth dare ordini a qd di fare; ~ion [ɪn'strʌkʃən] n istruzione f; ~ive a istruttivo(a); ~or n istruttore/trice; (for skiing) maestro/a.

instrument ['ɪnstrumənt] n strumento; ~al [-'mɛntl] a (MUS) strumentale; to be ~al in essere d'aiuto in; ~alist [-'mɛntəlɪst] n strumentista m/f; ~ panel n quadro m portastrumenti inv.

insubordinate [ɪnsə'bɔːdənɪt] a insubordinato(a); **insubordination** [-'neɪʃən] n insubordinazione f.

insufferable [ɪn'sʌfrəbl] a insopportabile.

insufficient [ɪnsə'fɪʃənt] a insufficiente.

insular ['ɪnsjulə*] a insulare; (person) di mente ristretta.

insulate ['ɪnsjuleɪt] vt isolare; **insulating tape** n nastro isolante; **insulation** [-'leɪʃən] n isolamento.

insulin ['ɪnsjulɪn] n insulina.

insult n ['ɪnsʌlt] insulto, affronto // vt [ɪn'sʌlt] insultare; ~ing a offensivo(a), ingiurioso(a).

insuperable [ɪn'sjuːprəbl] a insormontabile, insuperabile.

insurance [ɪn'ʃuərəns] n assicurazione f; fire/life ~ assicurazione contro gli incendi/sulla vita; ~ policy n polizza d'assicurazione.

insure [ɪn'ʃuə*] vt assicurare.

insurrection [ɪnsə'rɛkʃən] n insurrezione f.

intact [ɪn'tækt] a intatto(a).

intake ['ɪnteɪk] n (TECH) immissione f; (of food) consumo; (of pupils etc) afflusso.

intangible [ɪn'tændʒɪbl] a intangibile.

integral ['ɪntɪɡrəl] a integrale; (part) integrante.

integrate ['ɪntɪɡreɪt] vt integrare.

integrity [ɪn'tɛɡrɪtɪ] n integrità.

intellect ['ɪntəlɛkt] n intelletto; ~ual [-'lɛktjuəl] a, n intellettuale (m/f).

intelligence [ɪn'tɛlɪdʒəns] n intelligenza; (MIL etc) informazioni fpl.

intelligent [ɪn'tɛlɪdʒənt] a intelligente.

intelligible [ɪn'tɛlɪdʒɪbl] a intelligibile.

intemperate [ɪn'tɛmpərət] a immoderato(a); (drinking too much) intemperante nel bere.

intend [ɪn'tɛnd] vt (gift etc): to ~ sth for destinare qc a; to ~ to do aver l'intenzione di fare.

intense [ɪn'tɛns] a intenso(a); (person) di forti sentimenti; ~ly ad intensamente; profondamente.

intensify [ɪn'tɛnsɪfaɪ] vt intensificare.

intensity [ɪn'tɛnsɪtɪ] n intensità.

intensive [ɪn'tɛnsɪv] a intensivo(a); ~ care unit n reparto terapia intensiva.

intent [ɪn'tɛnt] n intenzione f // a: ~ (on) intento(a) (a), immerso(a) (in); to all ~s and purposes a tutti gli effetti; to be ~ on doing sth essere deciso a fare qc.

intention [ɪn'tɛnʃən] n intenzione f; ~al a intenzionale, deliberato(a); ~ally ad apposta.

intently [ɪn'tɛntlɪ] ad attentamente.

inter [ɪn'tɜː*] vt sotterrare.

interact [ɪntər'ækt] vi agire reciprocamente; ~ion [-'ækʃən] n azione f reciproca.

intercede [ɪntə'siːd] vi: to ~ (with) intercedere (presso).

intercept [ɪntə'sɛpt] vt intercettare; (person) fermare; ~ion [-'sɛpʃən] n intercettamento.

interchange n ['ɪntətʃeɪndʒ] (exchange) scambio; (on motorway) incrocio pluridirezionale // vt [ɪntə'tʃeɪndʒ] scambiare; sostituire l'uno(a) per l'altro(a); ~able a intercambiabile.

intercom ['ɪntəkɔm] n interfono.

interconnect [ɪntəkə'nɛkt] vi (rooms) essere in comunicazione.

intercourse ['ɪntəkɔːs] n rapporti mpl.

interest ['ɪntrɪst] n interesse m; (COMM: stake, share) interessi mpl // vt interessare; ~ed a interessato(a); to be ~ed in interessarsi di; ~ing a interessante.

interfere [ɪntə'fɪə*] vi: to ~ in (quarrel, other people's business) immischiarsi in; to ~ with (object) toccare; (plans) ostacolare; (duty) interferire con.

interference [ɪntə'fɪərəns] n interferenza.

interim ['ɪntərɪm] a provvisorio(a) // n: in the ~ nel frattempo.

interior [ɪn'tɪərɪə*] n interno; (of country) entroterra // a interiore, interno(a).

interjection [ɪntə'dʒɛkʃən] n interiezione f.

interlock [ɪntə'lɔk] vi ingranarsi // vt ingranare.

interloper ['ɪntələupə*] n intruso/a.

interlude ['ɪntəluːd] n intervallo; (THEATRE) intermezzo.

intermarry [ɪntə'mærɪ] vi imparentarsi

per mezzo di matrimonio; sposarsi tra parenti.

intermediary [ɪntəˈmiːdɪərɪ] *n* intermediario/a.

intermediate [ɪntəˈmiːdɪət] *a* intermedio(a); (*SCOL: course, level*) medio(a).

intermission [ɪntəˈmɪʃən] *n* pausa; (*THEATRE, CINEMA*) intermissione *f*, intervallo.

intermittent [ɪntəˈmɪtnt] *a* intermittente.

intern *vt* [ɪnˈtəːn] internare // *n* [ˈɪntəːn] (*US*) medico interno.

internal [ɪnˈtəːnl] *a* interno(a); ~**ly** *ad* all'interno; I~ **Revenue** *n* (*US*) fisco.

international [ɪntəˈnæʃənl] *a* internazionale // *n* (*SPORT*) partita internazionale.

internment [ɪnˈtəːnmənt] *n* internamento.

interplay [ˈɪntəpleɪ] *n* azione e reazione *f*.

interpret [ɪnˈtəːprɪt] *vt* interpretare // *vi* fare da interprete; ~**ation** [-ˈteɪʃən] *n* interpretazione *f*; ~**er** *n* interprete *m/f*.

interrelated [ɪntərɪˈleɪtɪd] *a* correlato(a).

interrogate [ɪnˈtɛrəʊgeɪt] *vt* interrogare; **interrogation** [-ˈgeɪʃən] *n* interrogazione *f*; (*of suspect etc*) interrogatorio; **interrogative** [ɪntəˈrɔgətɪv] *a* interrogativo(a) // *n* (*LING*) interrogativo; **interrogator** *n* interrogante *m/f*.

interrupt [ɪntəˈrʌpt] *vt* interrompere; ~**ion** [-ˈrʌpʃən] *n* interruzione *f*.

intersect [ɪntəˈsɛkt] *vt* intersecare // *vi* (*roads*) intersecarsi; ~**ion** [-ˈsɛkʃən] *n* intersezione *f*; (*of roads*) incrocio.

intersperse [ɪntəˈspəːs] *vt*: to ~ **with** costellare di.

intertwine [ɪntəˈtwaɪn] *vt* intrecciare // *vi* intrecciarsi.

interval [ˈɪntəvl] *n* intervallo; at ~**s** a intervalli.

intervene [ɪntəˈviːn] *vi* (*time*) intercorrere; (*event, person*) intervenire; **intervention** [-ˈvɛnʃən] *n* intervento.

interview [ˈɪntəvjuː] *n* (*RADIO, TV etc*) intervista; (*for job*) colloquio // *vt* intervistare; avere un colloquio con; ~**er** *n* intervistatore/trice.

intestate [ɪnˈtɛsteɪt] *a* intestato(a).

intestine [ɪnˈtɛstɪn] *n* intestino.

intimacy [ˈɪntɪməsɪ] *n* intimità.

intimate *a* [ˈɪntɪmət] intimo(a); (*knowledge*) profondo(a) // *vt* [ˈɪntɪmeɪt] sottintendere, suggerire; ~**ly** *ad* intimamente.

intimation [ɪntɪˈmeɪʃən] *n* annuncio.

intimidate [ɪnˈtɪmɪdeɪt] *vt* intimidire, intimorire; **intimidation** [-ˈdeɪʃən] *n* intimidazione *f*.

into [ˈɪntu] *prep* dentro, in; **come** ~ **the house** vieni dentro la casa.

intolerable [ɪnˈtɔlərəbl] *a* intollerabile.

intolerance [ɪnˈtɔlərns] *n* intolleranza.

intolerant [ɪnˈtɔlərnt] *a* intollerante.

intonation [ɪntəʊˈneɪʃən] *n* intonazione *f*.

intoxicate [ɪnˈtɔksɪkeɪt] *vt* inebriare; ~**d**

a inebriato(a); **intoxication** [-ˈkeɪʃən] *n* ebbrezza.

intractable [ɪnˈtræktəbl] *a* intrattabile.

intransigent [ɪnˈtrænsɪdʒənt] *a* intransigente.

intransitive [ɪnˈtrænsɪtɪv] *a* intransitivo(a).

intravenous [ɪntrəˈviːnəs] *a* endovenoso(a).

intrepid [ɪnˈtrɛpɪd] *a* intrepido(a).

intricacy [ˈɪntrɪkəsɪ] *n* complessità *f inv*.

intricate [ˈɪntrɪkət] *a* intricato(a), complicato(a).

intrigue [ɪnˈtriːg] *n* intrigo // *vt* affascinare; **intriguing** *a* affascinante.

intrinsic [ɪnˈtrɪnsɪk] *a* intrinseco(a).

introduce [ɪntrəˈdjuːs] *vt* introdurre; to ~ **sb (to sb)** presentare qd (a qd); to ~ **sb to** (*pastime, technique*) iniziare qd a; **introduction** [-ˈdʌkʃən] *n* introduzione *f*; (*of person*) presentazione *f*; **introductory** *a* introduttivo(a).

introspective [ɪntrəʊˈspɛktɪv] *a* introspettivo(a).

introvert [ˈɪntrəʊvəːt] *a* introverso(a) // *n* introverso.

intrude [ɪnˈtruːd] *vi* (*person*) intrudersi; to ~ **on** *or* **into** intrudersi in; **am I intruding?** disturbo?; ~**r** *n* intruso/a; **intrusion** [-ʒən] *n* intrusione *f*.

intuition [ɪntjuːˈɪʃən] *n* intuizione *f*.

intuitive [ɪnˈtjuːɪtɪv] *a* intuitivo(a); dotato(a) di intuito.

inundate [ˈɪnʌndeɪt] *vt*: to ~ **with** inondare di.

invade [ɪnˈveɪd] *vt* invadere; ~**r** *n* invasore *m*.

invalid *n* [ˈɪnvəlɪd] malato/a; (*with disability*) invalido/a // *a* [ɪnˈvælɪd] (*not valid*) invalido(a), non valido(a); ~**ate** [ɪnˈvælɪdeɪt] *vt* invalidare.

invaluable [ɪnˈvæljuəbl] *a* inapprezzabile, inestimabile.

invariable [ɪnˈvɛərɪəbl] *a* invariabile; (*fig*) scontato(a).

invasion [ɪnˈveɪʒən] *n* invasione *f*.

invective [ɪnˈvɛktɪv] *n* invettiva.

invent [ɪnˈvɛnt] *vt* inventare; ~**ion** [ɪnˈvɛnʃən] *n* invenzione *f*; ~**ive** *a* inventivo(a); ~**or** *n* inventore *m*.

inventory [ˈɪnvəntrɪ] *n* inventario.

inverse [ɪnˈvəːs] *a* inverso(a) // *n* inverso, contrario.

invert [ɪnˈvəːt] *vt* invertire; (*cup, object*) rovesciare; ~**ed commas** *npl* virgolette *fpl*.

invertebrate [ɪnˈvəːtɪbrət] *n* invertebrato.

invest [ɪnˈvɛst] *vt* investire // *vi* fare investimenti.

investigate [ɪnˈvɛstɪgeɪt] *vt* investigare, indagare; (*crime*) fare indagini su; **investigation** [-ˈgeɪʃən] *n* investigazione *f*; (*of crime*) indagine *f*; **investigator** *n* investigatore/trice.

investiture [ɪnˈvɛstɪtʃə*] *n* investitura.

investment [ɪnˈvɛstmənt] *n* investimento.

investor [ɪnˈvɛstə°] n investitore/trice; azionista m/f.

inveterate [ɪnˈvɛtərət] a inveterato(a).

invidious [ɪnˈvɪdɪəs] a odioso(a); (task) spiacevole.

invigorating [ɪnˈvɪgəreɪtɪŋ] a stimolante; vivificante.

invincible [ɪnˈvɪnsɪbl] a invincibile.

inviolate [ɪnˈvaɪələt] a inviolato(a).

invisible [ɪnˈvɪzɪbl] a invisibile.

invitation [ɪnvɪˈteɪʃən] n invito.

invite [ɪnˈvaɪt] vt invitare; (opinions etc) sollecitare; (trouble) provocare; **inviting** a invitante, attraente.

invoice [ˈɪnvɔɪs] n fattura // vt fatturare.

invoke [ɪnˈvəuk] vt invocare.

involuntary [ɪnˈvɒləntrɪ] a involontario(a).

involve [ɪnˈvɒlv] vt (entail) richiedere, comportare; (associate): to ~ sb (in) implicare qd (in); coinvolgere qd (in); ~d a involuto(a), complesso(a); to feel ~d sentirsi coinvolto(a); ~ment n implicazione f; coinvolgimento; ~ment (in) impegno m (in); partecipazione f (in).

invulnerable [ɪnˈvʌlnərəbl] a invulnerabile.

inward [ˈɪnwəd] a (movement) verso l'interno; (thought, feeling) interiore, intimo(a); ~ly ad (feel, think etc) nell'intimo, entro di sé; ~(s) ad verso l'interno.

iodine [ˈaɪəudiːn] n iodio.

iota [aɪˈəutə] n (fig) ette m, briciolo.

IOU n (abbr of I owe you) pagherò m inv.

IQ n (abbr of intelligence quotient) quoziente m d'intelligenza.

Iran [ɪˈrɑːn] n Iran m; ~ian [ɪˈreɪnɪən] a iraniano(a) // n iraniano/a; (LING) iranico.

Iraq [ɪˈrɑːk] n Iraq m; ~i a iracheno(a) // n iracheno/a; (LING) iracheno.

irascible [ɪˈræsɪbl] a irascibile.

irate [aɪˈreɪt] a irato(a).

Ireland [ˈaɪlənd] n Irlanda.

iris, ~es [ˈaɪrɪs, -ɪz] n iride f; (BOT) giaggiolo, iride.

Irish [ˈaɪrɪʃ] a irlandese // npl: the ~ gli Irlandesi; ~man n irlandese m; ~ sea n Mar m d'Irlanda; ~woman n irlandese f.

irk [əːk] vt seccare; ~some a seccante.

iron [ˈaɪən] n ferro; (for clothes) ferro da stiro // a di or in ferro // vt (clothes) stirare; ~s npl (chains) catene fpl; to ~ out vt (crease) appianare; (fig) spianare; far sparire; the ~ curtain la cortina di ferro.

ironic(al) [aɪˈrɒnɪk(l)] a ironico(a).

ironing [ˈaɪənɪŋ] n stiratura; ~ board n cavalletto da stiro.

ironmonger [ˈaɪənmʌŋgə°] n negoziante m in ferramenta; ~'s (shop) n (negozio di) ferramenta.

ironworks [ˈaɪənwəːks] n ferriera.

irony [ˈaɪrənɪ] n ironia.

irrational [ɪˈræʃənl] a irrazionale; irragionevole; illogico(a).

irreconcilable [ɪrɛkənˈsaɪləbl] a

irreconciliabile; (opinion): ~ with inconciliabile con.

irredeemable [ɪrɪˈdiːməbl] a (COMM) irredimibile.

irrefutable [ɪrɪˈfjuːtəbl] a irrefutabile.

irregular [ɪˈrɛgjulə°] a irregolare; ~ity [-ˈlærɪtɪ] n irregolarità f inv.

irrelevance [ɪˈrɛləvəns] n inappropriatezza.

irrelevant [ɪˈrɛləvənt] a non appropriato(a).

irreparable [ɪˈrɛprəbl] a irreparabile.

irreplaceable [ɪrɪˈpleɪsəbl] a insostituibile.

irrepressible [ɪrɪˈprɛsbl] a irrefrenabile.

irreproachable [ɪrɪˈprəutʃəbl] a irreprensibile.

irresistible [ɪrɪˈzɪstɪbl] a irresistibile.

irresolute [ɪˈrɛzəluːt] a irresoluto(a), indeciso(a).

irrespective [ɪrɪˈspɛktɪv]: ~ of prep senza riguardo a.

irresponsible [ɪrɪˈspɒnsɪbl] a irresponsabile.

irreverent [ɪˈrɛvərnt] a irriverente.

irrevocable [ɪˈrɛvəkəbl] a irrevocabile.

irrigate [ˈɪrɪgeɪt] vt irrigare; **irrigation** [-ˈgeɪʃən] n irrigazione f.

irritable [ˈɪrɪtəbl] a irritabile.

irritate [ˈɪrɪteɪt] vt irritare; **irritation** [-ˈteɪʃən] n irritazione f.

is [ɪz] vb see be.

Islam [ˈɪzlɑːm] n Islam m.

island [ˈaɪlənd] n isola; (also: traffic ~) salvagente m inv; ~er n isolano/a.

isle [aɪl] n isola.

isn't [ˈɪznt] = is not.

isolate [ˈaɪsəleɪt] vt isolare; ~d a isolato(a); **isolation** [-ˈleɪʃən] n isolamento.

isotope [ˈaɪsəutəup] n isotopo.

Israel [ˈɪzreɪl] n Israele m; ~i [ɪzˈreɪlɪ] a, n israeliano/a.

issue [ˈɪsjuː] n questione f, problema m; (outcome) esito, risultato; (of banknotes etc) emissione f; (of newspaper etc) numero; (offspring) discendenza // vt (rations, equipment) distribuire; (orders) dare; (book) pubblicare; (banknotes, cheques, stamps) emettere; at ~ in gioco, in discussione.

isthmus [ˈɪsməs] n istmo.

it [ɪt] pronoun (subject) esso(a); (direct object) lo(la), l'; (indirect object) gli(le); ~'s raining piove; it's on ~ è il sopra; he's proud of ~ ne è fiero; he agreed to ~ ha acconsentito.

Italian [ɪˈtæljən] a italiano(a) // n italiano/a; (LING) italiano; the ~s gli Italiani.

italic [ɪˈtælɪk] a corsivo(a); ~s npl corsivo.

Italy [ˈɪtəlɪ] n Italia.

itch [ɪtʃ] n prurito // vi (person) avere il prurito; (part of body) prudere; I'm ~ing to do non vedo l'ora di fare; ~y a che prude.

it'd [ˈɪtd] = it would; it had.

item ['aɪtəm] n articolo; (on agenda) punto; (in programme) numero; (also: **news ~**) notizia; **~ize** vt specificare, dettagliare.
itinerant [ɪ'tɪnərənt] a ambulante.
itinerary [aɪ'tɪnərərɪ] n itinerario.
it'll ['ɪtl] = **it will, it shall**.
its [ɪts] a, pronoun il(la) suo(a), i(le) suoi(sue).
it's [ɪts] = **it is; it has**.
itself [ɪt'self] pronoun (emphatic) esso(a) stesso(a); (reflexive) si.
ITV n abbr of Independent Television (canale televisivo in concorrenza con la BBC).
I've [aɪv] = **I have**.
ivory ['aɪvərɪ] n avorio.
ivy ['aɪvɪ] n edera.

J

jab [dʒæb] vt: to ~ sth into affondare or piantare qc dentro // n colpo; (MED: col) puntura.
jabber ['dʒæbə*] vt, vi borbottare.
jack [dʒæk] n (AUT) cricco; (CARDS) fante m; to ~ up vt sollevare sul cricco.
jacket ['dʒækɪt] n giacca; (of book) copertura; **potatoes in their ~s** patate fpl con la buccia.
jack-knife ['dʒæknaɪf] vi: **the lorry ~d** l'autotreno si è piegato su se stesso.
jackpot ['dʒækpɔt] n bottino.
jade [dʒeɪd] n (stone) giada.
jaded ['dʒeɪdɪd] a sfinito(a), spossato(a).
jagged ['dʒægɪd] a sbocconcellato(a); (cliffs etc) frastagliato(a).
jail [dʒeɪl] n prigione f; **~break** n evasione f; **~er** n custode m del carcere.
jam [dʒæm] n marmellata; (of shoppers etc) ressa; (also: **traffic ~**) ingorgo // vt (passage etc) ingombrare, ostacolare; (mechanism, drawer etc) bloccare; (RADIO) disturbare con interferenze // vi (mechanism, sliding part) incepparsi, bloccarsi; (gun) incepparsi; to ~ sth into forzare qc dentro; infilare qc a forza dentro.
Jamaica [dʒə'meɪkə] n Giamaica.
jangle ['dʒæŋgl] vi risuonare; (bracelet) tintinnare.
janitor ['dʒænɪtə*] n (caretaker) portiere m; (: SCOL) bidello.
January ['dʒænjuərɪ] n gennaio.
Japan [dʒə'pæn] n Giappone m; **~ese** [dʒæpə'niːz] a giapponese // n, pl inv giapponese m/f; (LING) giapponese m.
jar [dʒɑ:*] n (glass) barattolo, vasetto // vi (sound) stridere; (colours etc) stonare.
jargon ['dʒɑːgən] n gergo.
jasmin(e) ['dʒæzmɪn] n gelsomino.
jaundice ['dʒɔːndɪs] n itterizia; **~d** a (fig) invidioso(a) e critico(a).
jaunt [dʒɔːnt] n gita; **~y** a vivace, disinvolto(a).
javelin ['dʒævlɪn] n giavellotto.
jaw [dʒɔː] n mascella.
jaywalker ['dʒeɪwɔːkə*] n pedone(a) indisciplinato(a).
jazz [dʒæz] n jazz m; to ~ **up** vt rendere

vivace; **~y** a vistoso(a), chiassoso(a).
jealous ['dʒeləs] a geloso(a); **~y** n gelosia.
jeans [dʒiːnz] npl (blue-)jeans mpl.
jeep [dʒiːp] n jeep m inv.
jeer [dʒɪə*] vi: to ~ (at) fischiare; beffeggiare.
jelly ['dʒelɪ] n gelatina; **~fish** n medusa.
jeopardize ['dʒepədaɪz] vt mettere in pericolo.
jeopardy ['dʒepədɪ] n: **in ~** in pericolo.
jerk [dʒəːk] n scossa; strappo; contrazione f, spasimo // vt dare una scossa a // vi (vehicles) sobbalzare.
jerkin ['dʒəːkɪn] n giubbotto.
jerky ['dʒəːkɪ] a a scatti; a sobbalzi.
jersey ['dʒəːzɪ] n maglia.
jest [dʒest] n scherzo; **in ~** per scherzo.
jet [dʒet] n (of gas, liquid) getto; (AVIAT) aviogetto; **~-black** a nero(a) come l'ebano, corvino(a); **~ engine** n motore m a reazione.
jetsam ['dʒetsəm] n relitti mpl di mare.
jettison ['dʒetɪsn] vt gettare in mare.
jetty ['dʒetɪ] n molo.
Jew [dʒuː] n ebreo.
jewel ['dʒuːəl] n gioiello; **~ler** n orefice m, gioielliere/a; **~ler's (shop)** n oreficeria, gioielleria; **~lery** n gioielli mpl.
Jewess ['dʒuːɪs] n ebrea.
Jewish ['dʒuːɪʃ] a giudeo(a); giudaico(a).
jib [dʒɪb] n (NAUT) fiocco; (of crane) braccio.
jibe [dʒaɪb] n beffa.
jiffy ['dʒɪfɪ] n (col): **in a ~** in un batter d'occhio.
jigsaw ['dʒɪgsɔː] n (also: **~ puzzle**) puzzle m inv.
jilt [dʒɪlt] vt piantare in asso.
jingle ['dʒɪŋgl] n (advert) sigla pubblicitaria // vi tintinnare, scampanellare.
jinx [dʒɪŋks] n (col) iettatura; (person) iettatore/trice.
jitters ['dʒɪtəz] npl (col): **to get the ~** aver fifa.
job [dʒɔb] n lavoro; (employment) impiego, posto; **~less** a senza lavoro, disoccupato(a).
jockey ['dʒɔkɪ] n fantino, jockey m inv // vi: to ~ **for position** manovrare per una posizione di vantaggio.
jocular ['dʒɔkjulə*] a gioviale, scherzoso(a); faceto(a).
jog [dʒɔg] vt scossare // vi (SPORT) fare il footing; to ~ **along** trottare; (fig) andare avanti piano piano; to ~ **sb's memory** stimolare la memoria di qd; **~ging** n footing m.
join [dʒɔɪn] vt unire, congiungere; (become member of) iscriversi a; (meet) raggiungere; riunirsi a // vi (roads, rivers) confluire // n giuntura; to ~ **up** vi arruolarsi.
joiner ['dʒɔɪnə*] n falegname m; **~y** n falegnameria.
joint [dʒɔɪnt] n (TECH) giuntura; giunto; (ANAT) articolazione f, giuntura; (CULIN)

arrosto; (col: place) locale m // a comune;
~ly ad in comune, insieme.

joist [dʒɔɪst] n trave f.

joke [dʒəuk] n scherzo; (funny story)
barzelletta; (also: **practical** ~) beffa // vi
scherzare; ~r n buffone/a, burlone/a;
(CARDS) matta, jolly m inv.

jolly ['dʒɔlɪ] a allegro(a), gioioso(a) // ad
(col) veramente, proprio.

jolt [dʒəult] n scossa, sobbalzo // vt
scossare.

Jordan [dʒɔːdən] n Giordania.

jostle ['dʒɔsl] vt spingere coi gomiti // vi
farsi spazio coi gomiti.

jot [dʒɔt] n: **not one** ~ nemmeno un po';
to ~ **down** vt annotare in fretta, gettare
giù; ~ter n quaderno; blocco.

journal ['dʒəːnl] n giornale m; rivista;
diario; ~ese [-'liːz] n (pej) stile m
giornalistico; ~ism n giornalismo; ~ist
n giornalista m/f.

journey ['dʒəːnɪ] n viaggio; (distance
covered) tragitto.

jowl [dʒaul] n mandibola; guancia.

joy [dʒɔɪ] n gioia; ~ful, ~ous a gioioso(a),
allegro(a); ~ ride n gita in automobile
(specialmente rubata).

J.P. n abbr see **justice**.

Jr, Jun., Junr abbr of **junior**.

jubilant ['dʒuːbɪlnt] a giubilante;
trionfante.

jubilation [dʒuːbɪ'leɪʃən] n giubilo.

jubilee ['dʒuːbɪliː] n giubileo.

judge [dʒʌdʒ] n giudice m/f // vt giudicare;
judg(e)ment n giudizio; (punishment)
punizione f.

judicial [dʒuː'dɪʃl] a giudiziale,
giudiziario(a).

judicious [dʒuː'dɪʃəs] a giudizioso(a).

judo ['dʒuːdəu] n judo m.

jug [dʒʌg] n brocca, bricco.

juggernaut ['dʒʌgənɔːt] n (huge truck)
bestione m.

juggle ['dʒʌgl] vi fare giochi di destrezza;
~r n giocoliere/a.

Jugoslav ['juːgəu'slɑːv] a,n = **Yugoslav**.

juice [dʒuːs] n succo.

juicy ['dʒuːsɪ] a succoso(a).

jukebox ['dʒuːkbɔks] n juke-box m inv.

July [dʒuː'laɪ] n luglio.

jumble ['dʒʌmbl] n miscuglio // vt (also:
~ up) mischiare; ~ **sale** n (Brit) vendita
di oggetti per beneficenza.

jumbo ['dʒʌmbəu] a: ~ **jet** jumbo-jet m
inv.

jump [dʒʌmp] vi saltare, balzare; (start)
sobbalzare; (increase) rincarare // vt
saltare // n salto; balzo; sobbalzo.

jumper ['dʒʌmpə*] n maglia.

jumpy ['dʒʌmpɪ] a nervoso(a), agitato(a).

junction ['dʒʌŋkʃən] n (of roads) incrocio;
(of rails) nodo ferroviario.

juncture ['dʒʌŋktʃə*] n: **at this** ~ in
questa congiuntura.

June [dʒuːn] n giugno.

jungle ['dʒʌŋgl] n giungla.

junior ['dʒuːnɪə*] a, n: **he's** ~ **to me** (by 2

years), **he's my** ~ (**by 2 years**) è più
giovane di me (di 2 anni); **he's** ~ **to me**
(seniority) è al di sotto di me, ho più
anzianità di lui; ~ **school** n scuola
elementare (da 8 a 11 anni).

juniper ['dʒuːnɪpə*] n: ~ **berry** bacca di
ginepro.

junk [dʒʌŋk] n (rubbish) chincaglia; (ship)
giunca; ~**shop** n chincaglieria.

junta ['dʒʌntə] n giunta.

jurisdiction [dʒuərɪs'dɪkʃən] n
giurisdizione f.

jurisprudence [dʒuərɪs'pruːdəns] n
giurisprudenza.

juror ['dʒuərə*] n giurato.

jury ['dʒuərɪ] n giuria.

just [dʒʌst] a giusto(a) // ad: **he's** ~ **done
it/left** lui lo ha appena fatto/è appena
partito; ~ **as I expected** proprio come
me lo aspettavo; ~ **right** proprio giusto;
~ **2 o'clock** le 2 precise; **it was** ~
before/enough/here era poco
prima/appena assai/proprio qui; **it's** ~
me sono solo io; **it's** ~ **a mistake** non è
che uno sbaglio; ~ **missed/caught**
appena perso/preso; ~ **listen to this!**
senta un po' questo!

justice ['dʒʌstɪs] n giustizia; **J**~ **of the
Peace (J.P.)** n giudice m conciliatore.

justification [dʒʌstɪfɪ'keɪʃən] n
giustificazione f.

justify ['dʒʌstɪfaɪ] vt giustificare.

justly ['dʒʌstlɪ] ad giustamente.

justness ['dʒʌstnɪs] n giustezza.

jut [dʒʌt] vi (also: ~ **out**) sporgersi.

juvenile ['dʒuːvənaɪl] a giovane, giovanile;
(court) dei minorenni; (books) per ragazzi
// n giovane m/f, minorenne m/f.

juxtapose ['dʒʌkstəpəuz] vt giustapporre.

K

kaleidoscope [kə'laɪdəskəup] n
caleidoscopio.

kangaroo [kæŋgə'ruː] n canguro.

keel [kiːl] n chiglia; **on an even** ~ (fig) in
uno stato normale.

keen [kiːn] a (interest, desire) vivo(a); (eye,
intelligence) acuto(a); (competition)
serrato(a); (edge) affilato(a); (eager)
entusiastico(a); **to be** ~ **to do** or **on
doing sth** avere una gran voglia di fare
qc; **to be** ~ **on sth** essere
appassionato(a) di qc; **to be** ~ **on sb**
avere un debole per qd; ~**ness** n
(eagerness) entusiasmo.

keep [kiːp] vb (pt,pp kept) [kɛpt] vt tenere;
(hold back) trattenere; (feed: one's family
etc) mantenere, sostentare; (a promise)
mantenere; (chickens, bees, pigs etc)
allevare // vi (food) mantenersi; (remain:
in a certain state or place) restare // n (of
castle) maschio; (food etc): **enough for
his** ~ abbastanza per vitto e alloggio; **to**
~ **doing sth** continuare a fare qc; fare qc
di continuo; **to** ~ **sb from doing/sth
from happening** impedire a qd di
fare/che qc succeda; **to** ~ **sb happy/a**

place tidy tenere qd occupato(a)/un
luogo in ordine; **to ~ sth to o.s.** tenere qc
per sé; **to ~ sth (back) from sb** celare
qc a qd; **to ~ time** (clock) andar bene; **to
~ on** vi continuare; **to ~ on doing**
continuare a fare; **to ~ out** vt tener fuori;
'~ **out**' 'vietato l'accesso'; **to ~ up** vi
mantenersi // vt continuare, mantenere;
to ~ up with tener dietro a, andare di
pari passo con; (work etc) farcela a
seguire; **~er** n custode m/f, guardiano/a;
~ing n (care) custodia; **in ~ing with** in
armonia con; in accordo con; **~sake** n
ricordo.

keg [kɛg] n barilotto.

kennel ['kɛnl] n canile m.

Kenya ['kɛnjə] n Kenia m.

kept [kɛpt] pt,pp of **keep**.

kerb [kɔːb] n orlo del marciapiede.

kernel ['kɔːnl] n nocciolo.

kerosene ['kɛrəsiːn] n cherosene m.

ketchup ['kɛtʃəp] n ketchup m inv.

kettle ['kɛtl] n bollitore m; **~ drum** n
timpano.

key [kiː] n (gen, MUS) chiave f; (of piano,
typewriter) tasto // cpd chiave inv;
~board n tastiera; **~hole** n buco della
serratura; **~note** n (MUS) tonica; (fig)
nota dominante; **~ring** n portachiavi m
inv.

khaki ['kɑːki] a,n cachi (m).

kick [kik] vt calciare, dare calci a // vi
(horse) tirar calci // n calcio; (of rifle)
contraccolpo; (thrill): **he does it for ~s**
lo fa giusto per il piacere di farlo; **to ~
off** vi (SPORT) dare il primo calcio; **~off**
n (SPORT) calcio d'inizio.

kid [kid] n ragazzino/a; (animal, leather)
capretto // vi (col) scherzare // vt (col)
prendere in giro.

kidnap ['kidnæp] vt rapire; **~per** n
rapitore/trice; **~ping** n rapimento.

kidney ['kidni] n (ANAT) rene m; (CULIN)
rognone m.

kill [kil] vt uccidere, ammazzare; (fig)
sopprimere; sopraffare; ammazzare // n
uccisione f; **~er** n uccisore m, killer m
inv; assassino/a; **~ing** n assassinio;
(massacre) strage f.

kiln [kiln] n forno.

kilo ['kiːləu] n chilo; **~gram(me)**
['kiːləugræm] n chilogrammo; **~metre**
['kiləmiːtə°] n chilometro; **~watt**
['kiləwɔt] n chilowatt m inv.

kilt [kilt] n gonnellino scozzese.

kimono [ki'məunəu] n chimono.

kin [kin] n see **next, kith**.

kind [kaind] a gentile, buono(a) // n sorta,
specie f; (species) genere m; **in ~** (COMM)
in natura; (fig): **to repay sb in ~**
ripagare qd della stessa moneta.

kindergarten ['kindəgɑːtn] n giardino
d'infanzia.

kind-hearted [kaind'hɑːtid] a di buon
cuore.

kindle ['kindl] vt accendere, infiammare.

kindly ['kaindli] a pieno(a) di bontà,
benevolo(a) // ad con bontà, gentilmente;

will you ~... vuole... per favore; **he
didn't take it ~** se l'è presa a male.

kindness ['kaindnis] n bontà, gentilezza.

kindred ['kindrid] a imparentato(a); **~
spirit** n spirito affino.

kinetic [ki'nɛtik] a cinetico(a).

king [kiŋ] n re m inv; **~dom** n regno,
reame m; **~fisher** n martin m inv
pescatore; **~-size** a super inv; gigante.

kink [kiŋk] n (of rope) storta.

kinky ['kiŋki] a (fig) eccentrico(a); dai
gusti particolari.

kiosk ['kiːɔsk] n edicola, chiosco; cabina
(telefonica).

kipper ['kipə°] n aringa affumicata.

kiss [kis] n bacio // vt baciare; **to ~ (each
other)** baciarsi.

kit [kit] n equipaggiamento, corredo; (set of
tools etc) attrezzi mpl; (for assembly)
scatola di montaggio; **~bag** n zaino;
sacco militare.

kitchen ['kitʃin] n cucina; **~ sink** n
acquaio.

kite [kait] n (toy) aquilone m; (ZOOL)
nibbio.

kith [kiθ] n: **~ and kin** amici e parenti
mpl.

kitten ['kitn] n gattino/a, micino/a.

kitty ['kiti] n (money) fondo comune.

kleptomaniac [klɛptəu'meiniæk] n
cleptomane m/f.

knack [næk] n: **to have a ~ (for doing)**
avere una pratica (per fare); **to have the
~ of** avere l'abitudine di; **there's a ~** c'è
un modo.

knapsack ['næpsæk] n zaino, sacco da
montagna.

knave [neiv] n (CARDS) fante m.

knead [niːd] vt impastare.

knee [niː] n ginocchio; **~cap** n rotula.

kneel [niːl] vi (pt,pp **knelt** [nɛlt])
inginocchiarsi.

knell [nɛl] n intocco.

knew [njuː] pt of **know**.

knickers ['nikəz] npl mutandine fpl.

knife, knives [naif, naivz] n coltello // vt
accoltellare, dare una coltellata a.

knight [nait] n cavaliere m; (CHESS)
cavallo; **~hood** n cavalleria; (title): **to get
a ~hood** essere fatto cavaliere.

knit [nit] vt fare a maglia; (fig): **to ~
together** unire // vi lavorare a maglia;
(broken bones) saldarsi; **~ting** n lavoro a
maglia; **~ting needle** n ferro; **~wear** n
maglieria.

knives [naivz] npl of **knife**.

knob [nɔb] n bottone m; manopola; (fig): **a
~ of butter** una noce di burro.

knock [nɔk] vt colpire; urtare; (fig: col)
criticare // vi (engine) battere; (at door
etc): **to ~ at/on** bussare a // n bussata;
colpo, botta; **to ~ down** vt abbattere; **to
~ off** vi (col: finish) smettere (di
lavorare); **to ~ out** vt stendere; (BOXING)
mettere K.O.; **~-kneed** a che ha le gambe ad x; **~out** n
(BOXING) knock out m inv.

knot [nɔt] n nodo // vt annodare; ~ty a (fig) spinoso(a).

know [nəʊ] vt (pt **knew**, pp **known** [njuː, nəʊn]) sapere; (person, author, place) conoscere; **to ~ that...** sapere che...; **to ~ how to do** sapere fare; **~how** n tecnica; pratica; **~ing** a (look etc) d'intesa; **~ingly** ad consapevolmente; di complicità.

knowledge ['nɔlɪdʒ] n consapevolezza; (learning) conoscenza, sapere m; **~able** a ben informato(a).

known [nəʊn] pp of **know**.

knuckle ['nʌkl] n nocca.

K.O. n (abbr of knockout) K.O. m // vt mettere K.O.

Koran [kɔˈrɑːn] n Corano.

kw abbr of **kilowatt(s)**.

L

l. abbr of litre.

lab [læb] n (abbr of **laboratory**) laboratorio.

label ['leɪbl] n etichetta, cartellino; (brand: of record) casa // vt etichettare.

laboratory [ləˈbɔrətəri] n laboratorio.

laborious [ləˈbɔːrɪəs] a laborioso(a).

labour ['leɪbəˈ] n (task) lavoro; (workmen) manodopera; (MED) travaglio del parto, doglie fpl // vi: **to ~ (at)** lavorare duro (a); **in ~** (MED) in travaglio; **L~**, **the L~ party** il partito laburista; i laburisti; **~ camp** n campo dei lavori forzati; **~er** n manovale m; (on farm) lavoratore m agricolo; **~ force** n manodopera; **~ pains** npl doglie fpl.

labyrinth ['læbɪrɪnθ] n labirinto.

lace [leɪs] n merletto, pizzo; (of shoe etc) laccio // vt (shoe) allacciare.

lack [læk] n mancanza // vt mancare di; **through or for ~ of** per mancanza di; **to be ~ing** mancare; **to be ~ing in** mancare di.

lackadaisical [lækəˈdeɪzɪkl] a disinteressato(a), noncurante.

laconic [ləˈkɔnɪk] a laconico(a).

lacquer ['lækəˈ] n lacca.

lad [læd] n ragazzo, giovanotto.

ladder ['lædəˈ] n scala; (in tights) smagliatura // vt (tights) smagliare // vi smagliarsi.

laden ['leɪdn] a: **~ (with)** carico(a) or caricato(a) (di).

ladle ['leɪdl] n mestolo.

lady ['leɪdɪ] n signora; dama; **L~ Smith** lady Smith; **the ladies' (toilets)** gabinetti mpl per signore; **~bird**, **~bug** (US) n coccinella; **~-in-waiting** n dama di compagnia; **~like** a da signora, distinto(a).

lag [læg] n = **time ~** // vi (also: **~ behind**) trascinarsi // vt (pipes) rivestire di materiale isolante.

lager ['lɑːgəˈ] n lager m inv.

lagging ['lægɪŋ] n rivestimento di materiale isolante.

lagoon [ləˈguːn] n laguna.

laid [leɪd] pt, pp of **lay**.

lain [leɪn] pp of **lie**.

lair [lɛəˈ] n covo, tana.

laity ['leɪətɪ] n laici mpl.

lake [leɪk] n lago.

lamb [læm] n agnello; **~ chop** n cotoletta d'agnello; **~swool** n lamb's wool m.

lame [leɪm] a zoppo(a).

lament [ləˈmɛnt] n lamento // vt lamentare, piangere; **~able** ['læməntəbl] a doloroso(a); deplorevole.

laminated ['læmɪneɪtɪd] a laminato(a).

lamp [læmp] n lampada.

lampoon [læmˈpuːn] n pasquinata.

lamp: **~post** n lampione m; **~shade** n paralume m.

lance [lɑːns] n lancia // vt (MED) incidere; **~ corporal** n caporale m.

land [lænd] n (as opposed to sea) terra (ferma); (country) paese m; (soil) terreno; suolo; (estate) terreni mpl, terre fpl // vi (from ship) sbarcare; (AVIAT) atterrare; (fig: fall) cadere // vt (obtain) acchiappare; (passengers) sbarcare; (goods) scaricare; **to ~ up** vi andare a finire; **~ing** n sbarco; atterraggio; (of staircase) pianerottolo; **~ing stage** n pontile m da sbarco; **~ing strip** n pista d'atterraggio; **~lady** n padrona or proprietaria di casa; **~locked** a senza sbocco sul mare; **~lord** n padrone m or proprietario di casa; (of pub etc) oste m; **~lubber** n marinaio d'acqua dolce; **~mark** n punto di riferimento; **~owner** n proprietario(a) terriero(a).

landscape ['lænskeɪp] n paesaggio.

landslide ['lændslaɪd] n (GEO) frana; (fig: POL) valanga.

lane [leɪn] n (in country) viottolo; (in town) stradetta; (AUT, in race) corsia.

language ['læŋgwɪdʒ] n lingua; (way one speaks) linguaggio; **bad ~** linguaggio volgare.

languid ['læŋgwɪd] a languente; languido(a).

languish ['læŋgwɪʃ] vi languire.

lank [læŋk] a (hair) liscio(a) e opaco(a).

lanky ['læŋkɪ] a allampanato(a).

lantern ['læntn] n lanterna.

lap [læp] n (of track) giro; (of body): **in or on one's ~** in grembo // vt (also: **~ up**) papparsi, leccare // vi (waves) sciabordare.

lapel [ləˈpɛl] n risvolto.

Lapland ['læplænd] n Lapponia.

Lapp [læp] a lappone // n lappone m/f; (LING) lappone m.

lapse [læps] n lapsus m inv; (longer) caduta // vi (law, act) passare; (ticket, passport) scadere; **to ~ into bad habits** pigliare cattive abitudini; **~ of time** spazio di tempo.

larceny ['lɑːsənɪ] n furto.

lard [lɑːd] n lardo.

larder ['lɑːdəˈ] n dispensa.

large [lɑːdʒ] a grande; (person, animal)

grosso(a); **at ~** (*free*) in libertà; (*generally*) in generale; nell'insieme; **~ly** *ad* in gran parte.

lark [lɑːk] *n* (*bird*) allodola; (*joke*) scherzo, gioco; **to ~ about** *vi* fare lo stupido.

larva, *pl* **larvae** ['lɑːvə, -iː] *n* larva.

laryngitis [lærɪn'dʒaɪtɪs] *n* laringite *f.*

larynx ['lærɪŋks] *n* laringe *f.*

lascivious [lə'sɪvɪəs] *a* lascivo(a).

laser ['leɪzə*] *n* laser *m.*

lash [læʃ] *n* frustata; (*gen: eyelash*) ciglio // *vt* frustare; (*tie*) assicurare con una corda; **to ~ out** *vi*: **to ~ out** (at or against sb/sth) attaccare violentemente (qd/qc); **to ~ out (on sth)** (*col: spend*) spendere un sacco di soldi (per qc).

lass [læs] *n* ragazza.

lasso [læ'suː] *n* laccio // *vt* acchiappare con il laccio.

last [lɑːst] *a* ultimo(a); (*week, month, year*) scorso(a), passato(a) // *ad* per ultimo // *vi* durare; **~ week** la settimana scorsa; **~ night** ieri sera, la notte scorsa; **at ~** finalmente, alla fine; **~ing** *a* durevole; **~-minute** *a* fatto(a) (or preso(a) etc) all'ultimo momento.

latch [lætʃ] *n* serratura a scatto; **~key** *n* chiave *f* di casa.

late [leɪt] *a* (*not on time*) in ritardo; (*far on in day etc*) tardi *inv*; tardo(a); (*recent*) recente, ultimo(a); (*former*) ex; (*dead*) defunto(a) // *ad* tardi; (*behind time, schedule*) in ritardo; **of ~** di recente; **in ~ May** verso la fine di maggio; **~comer** *n* ritardatario/a; **~ly** *ad* recentemente; **~ness** *n* (*of person*) ritardo; (*of event*) tardezza, ora tarda.

latent ['leɪtnt] *a* latente.

later ['leɪtə*] *a* (*date etc*) posteriore; (*version etc*) successivo(a) // *ad* più tardi.

lateral ['lætərl] *a* laterale.

latest ['leɪtɪst] *a* ultimo(a), più recente; **at the ~** al più tardi.

lath, ~s [læθ, læðz] *n* assicella.

lathe [leɪð] *n* tornio.

lather ['lɑːðə*] *n* schiuma di sapone // *vt* insaponare.

Latin ['lætɪn] *n* latino // *a* latino(a); **~ America** *n* America Latina; **~-American** *a* sudamericano(a).

latitude ['lætɪtjuːd] *n* latitudine *f.*

latrine [lə'triːn] *n* latrina.

latter ['lætə*] *a* secondo(a); più recente // *n*: **the ~** quest'ultimo, il secondo; **~ly** *ad* recentemente, negli ultimi tempi.

lattice ['lætɪs] *n* traliccio; graticolato.

laudable ['lɔːdəbl] *a* lodevole.

laugh [lɑːf] *n* risata // *vi* ridere; **to ~ at** *vt fus* (*misfortune etc*) ridere di; **I ~ed at his joke** la sua barzelletta mi fece ridere; **to ~ off** *vt* prendere alla leggera; **~able** *a* ridicolo(a); **~ing** *a* (*face*) ridente; **the ~ing stock of** lo zimbello di; **~ter** *n* riso; risate *fpl.*

launch [lɔːntʃ] *n* (*of rocket etc*) lancio; (*of new ship*) varo; (*boat*) scialuppa; (*also: motor ~*) lancia // *vt* (*rocket*) lanciare; (*ship, plan*) varare; **~ing** *n* lancio; varo;

~(ing) pad *n* rampa di lancio.

launder ['lɔːndə*] *vt* lavare e stirare.

launderette [lɔːn'drɛt] *n* lavanderia (automatica).

laundry ['lɔːndrɪ] *n* lavanderia; (*clothes*) biancheria; **to do the ~** fare il bucato.

laureate ['lɔːrɪət] *a see* poet.

laurel ['lɔrl] *n* lauro.

lava ['lɑːvə] *n* lava.

lavatory ['lævətərɪ] *n* gabinetto.

lavender ['lævəndə*] *n* lavanda.

lavish ['lævɪʃ] *a* copioso(a); abbondante; (*giving freely*): **~ with** prodigo(a) di, largo(a) in // *vt*: **to ~ on sb/sth** (*care*) profondere a qd/qc.

law [lɔː] *n* legge *f*; **~-abiding** *a* ubbidiente alla legge; **~ and order** *n* l'ordine *m* pubblico; **~breaker** *n* violatore/trice della legge; **~ court** *n* tribunale *m*, corte *f* di giustizia; **~ful** *a* legale; lecito(a); **~less** *a* senza legge; illegale.

lawn [lɔːn] *n* tappeto erboso; **~mower** *n* tosaerba *m or f inv*; **~ tennis** ['-tɛnɪs] *n* tennis *m* su prato.

law: ~ school *n* facoltà di legge; **~ student** *n* studente/essa di legge.

lawsuit ['lɔːsuːt] *n* processo, causa.

lawyer ['lɔːjə*] *n* (*consultant, with company*) giurista *m/f*; (*for sales, wills etc*) ≈ notaio; (*partner, in court*) ≈ avvocato/essa.

lax [læks] *a* rilassato(a).

laxative ['læksətɪv] *n* lassativo.

laxity ['læksɪtɪ] *n* rilassamento.

lay [leɪ] *pt of* **lie** // *a* laico(a); secolare // *vt* (*pt, pp* **laid** [leɪd]) posare, mettere; (*eggs*) fare; (*trap*) tendere; (*plans*) fare, elaborare; **to ~ the table** apparecchiare la tavola; **to ~ aside** or **by** *vt* mettere da parte; **to ~ down** *vt* mettere giù; **to ~ off** *vt* (*workers*) licenziare; **to ~ on** *vt* (*water, gas*) installare, mettere; (*provide*) fornire; (*paint*) applicare; **to ~ out** *vt* (*design*) progettare; (*display*) presentare; (*spend*) sborsare; **to ~ up** *vt* (*to store*) accumulare; (*ship*) mettere in disarmo; (*subj: illness*) costringere a letto; **~about** *n* sfaccendato/a, fannullone/a; **~-by** *n* piazzola (di sosta).

layer ['leɪə*] *n* strato.

layman ['leɪmən] *n* laico; profano.

layout ['leɪaut] *n* lay-out *m inv*, disposizione *f*; (*PRESS*) impaginazione *f.*

laze [leɪz] *vi* oziare.

laziness ['leɪzɪnɪs] *n* pigrizia.

lazy ['leɪzɪ] *a* pigro(a).

lb. *abbr of* **pound** (*weight*).

lead [liːd] *see also next headword*; *n* (*front position*) posizione *f* di testa; (*distance, time ahead*) vantaggio; (*clue*) indizio; (*to battery*) filo conduttore; (*ELEC*) conduttore *m* isolato; (*for dog*) guinzaglio; (*THEATRE*) parte *f* principale // *vb* (*pt,pp* **led** [lɛd]) *vt* menare, guidare, condurre; (*induce*) indurre; (*be leader of*) essere a capo di; (*SPORT*) essere in testa a // *vi* condurre, essere in testa; **to ~ to** menare a; condurre a; portare a; **to ~ astray** *vt* sviare; **to ~ away** *vt* condurre via; **to ~ back** to ricondurre a; **to ~ on** *vt* (*tease*) tenere sulla corda; **to ~ on** to *vt* (*induce*) portare a; **to ~ up** to portare a; (*fig*) preparare la strada per.

lead [lɛd] *see also previous headword*; *n* piombo; (*in pencil*) mina; **~en** *a* di piombo.

leader ['liːdə*] *n* capo; direttore/trice, leader *m inv*; (*in newspaper*) articolo di fondo; **~ship** *n* direzione *f*; capacità di comando.

leading ['liːdɪŋ] *a* primo(a); principale; **~ man/lady** *n* (*THEATRE*) primo attore/prima attrice.

leaf, leaves [liːf, liːvz] *n* foglia; (*of table*) ribalta.

leaflet ['liːflɪt] *n* dépliant *m inv*; (*POL, REL*) volantino.

league [liːg] *n* lega; (*FOOTBALL*) campionato; **to be in ~ with** essere in lega con.

leak [liːk] *n* (*out, also fig*) fuga; (*in*) infiltrazione *f* // *vi* (*pipe, liquid etc*) perdere; (*shoes*) lasciar passare l'acqua // *vt* (*liquid*) spandere; (*information*) divulgare; **to ~ out** *vi* perdere; (*information*) trapelare.

lean [liːn] *a* magro(a) // *n* (*of meat*) carne *f* magra // *vb* (*pt,pp* **leaned** *or* **leant** [lɛnt]) *vt*: **to ~ sth on** appoggiare qc su // *vi* (*slope*) pendere; (*rest*): **to ~ against** appoggiarsi contro; essere appoggiato(a) a; **to ~ on** appoggiarsi a; **to ~ back/forward** *vi* sporgersi in avanti/indietro; **to ~ over** *vi* inclinarsi; **~ing** *a*: **~ing (towards)** propensione *f* (per).

leap [liːp] *n* salto, balzo // *vi* (*pt,pp* **leaped** *or* **leapt** [lɛpt]) saltare, balzare; **~frog** *n* gioco di saltamontone; **~ year** *n* anno bisestile.

learn, learned *or* **learnt** [lɜːn, -t] *vt,vi* imparare; **~ed** ['lɜːnɪd] *a* erudito(a), dotto(a); **~er** *n* principiante *m/f*; apprendista *m/f*; **~ing** *n* erudizione *f*, sapienza.

lease [liːs] *n* contratto d'affitto // *vt* affittare.

leash [liːʃ] *n* guinzaglio.

least [liːst] *a*: **the ~ + noun** il(la) più piccolo(a), il(la) minimo(a); (*smallest amount of*) il(la) meno; **the ~ + adjective**: **the ~ beautiful girl** la ragazza meno bella; **the ~ expensive** il(la) meno caro(a); **the ~ money** il meno denaro; **at ~** almeno; **not in the ~** affatto, per nulla.

leather ['lɛðə*] *n* cuoio // *cpd* di cuoio.

leave [liːv] *vb* (*pt,pp* **left** [lɛft]) *vt* lasciare; (*go away from*) partire da // *vi* partire, andarsene // *n* (*time off*) congedo; (*MIL, also: consent*) licenza; **to be left** rimanere; **there's some milk left over** c'è rimasto del latte; **on ~** in congedo; **to take one's ~ of** congedarsi di; **to ~ out** *vt* omettere, tralasciare.

leaves [liːvz] *npl of* **leaf**.

Lebanon ['lɛbənən] *n* Libano.

lecherous ['lɛtʃərəs] *a* lascivo(a), lubrico(a).

lectern ['lɛktɔːn] *n* leggio.

lecture ['lɛktʃə*] *n* conferenza; (*SCOL*) lezione *f* // *vi* fare conferenze; fare lezioni; **to ~ on** fare una conferenza su.

lecturer ['lɛktʃərə*] *n* (*speaker*) conferenziere/a; (*at university*) professore/essa, docente *m/f*.

led [lɛd] *pt,pp of* **lead**.

ledge [lɛdʒ] *n* (*of window*) davanzale *m*; (*on wall etc*) sporgenza; (*of mountain*) cornice *f*, cengia.

ledger ['lɛdʒə*] *n* libro maestro, registro.

lee [liː] *n* lato sottovento.

leech [liːtʃ] *n* sanguisuga.

leek [liːk] *n* porro.

leer [lɪə*] *vi*: **to ~ at sb** gettare uno sguardo voglioso *or* maligno su qd.

leeway ['liːweɪ] *n* (*fig*): **to have some ~** avere una certa libertà di agire.

left [lɛft] *pt,pp of* **leave** // *a* sinistra(a) // *ad* a sinistra // *n* sinistra; **the L~** (*POL*) la sinistra; **~-handed** *a* mancino(a); **~-hand side** *n* lato *or* fianco sinistro; **~-luggage (office)** *n* deposito *m* bagagli *inv*; **~overs** *npl* avanzi *mpl*, resti *mpl*; **~ wing** *n* (*MIL, SPORT*) ala sinistra; (*POL*) sinistra; **~-wing** *a* (*POL*) di sinistra.

leg [lɛg] *n* gamba; (*of animal*) zampa; (*of furniture*) piede *m*; (*CULIN: of chicken*) coscia; (*of journey*) tappa; **1st/2nd ~** (*SPORT*) partita di andata/ritorno.

legacy ['lɛgəsɪ] *n* eredità *f inv*.

legal ['liːgl] *a* legale; **~ize** *vt* legalizzare.

legation [lɪ'geɪʃən] *n* legazione *f*.

legend ['lɛdʒənd] *n* leggenda; **~ary** *a* leggendario(a).

leggings ['lɛgɪŋz] *npl* ghette *fpl*.

legible ['lɛdʒəbl] *a* leggibile.

legion ['liːdʒən] *n* legione *f*.

legislate ['lɛdʒɪsleɪt] *vi* legiferare; **legislation** [-'leɪʃən] *n* legislazione *f*; **legislative** ['lɛdʒɪslətɪv] *a* legislativo(a); **legislator** *n* legislatore/trice; **legislature** ['lɛdʒɪslətʃə*] *n* corpo legislativo.

legitimacy [lɪ'dʒɪtɪməsɪ] *n* legittimità.

legitimate [lɪ'dʒɪtɪmət] *a* legittimo(a).

leg-room ['lɛgruːm] *n* spazio per le gambe.

leisure ['lɛʒə*] *n* agio, tempo libero; ricreazioni *fpl*; **at ~** all'agio; a proprio comodo; **~ centre** *n* centro di ricreazione; **~ly** *a* tranquillo(a); fatto(a) con comodo *or* senza fretta.

lemon ['lɛmən] *n* limone *m*; **~ade** *n* [-'neɪd] limonata.

lend, lent [lɛnd, lɛnt] *vt*: **to ~ sth (to sb)** prestare qc (a qd); **~er** *n* prestatore/trice; **~ing library** *n* biblioteca circolante.

length [lɛŋθ] *n* lunghezza; (*section: of road, pipe etc*) pezzo, tratto; **at ~** (*at last*) finalmente, alla fine; (*lengthily*) a lungo; **~en** *vt* allungare, prolungare // *vi* allungarsi; ~ways ad per il lungo; ~y a molto lungo(a).

leniency ['li:nɪənsɪ] n indulgenza, clemenza.

lenient ['li:nɪənt] a indulgente, clemente.

lens [lɛnz] n lente f; (of camera) obiettivo.

lent [lɛnt] pt,pp of **lend**.

Lent [lɛnt] n Quaresima.

lentil ['lɛntl] n lenticchia.

Leo ['li:əu] n Leone m.

leopard ['lɛpəd] n leopardo.

leotard ['li:əta:d] n calzamaglia.

leper ['lɛpə*] n lebbroso/a.

leprosy ['lɛprəsɪ] n lebbra.

lesbian ['lɛzbɪən] n lesbica.

less [lɛs] det, pronoun, ad meno; ~ than you/ever meno di Lei/che mai; ~ and ~ sempre meno; the ~ he works ... meno lui lavora ...

lessen ['lɛsn] vi diminuire, attenuarsi // vt diminuire, ridurre.

lesson ['lɛsn] n lezione f.

lest [lɛst] cj per paura di + infinitive, per paura che + sub.

let, pt,pp **let** [lɛt] vt lasciare; (lease) dare in affitto; he ~ me go mi ha lasciato andare; ~'s go andiamo; ~ him come lo lasci venire; 'to ~' 'affittasi'; to ~ down vt (lower) abbassare; (dress) allungare; (hair) sciogliere; (disappoint) deludere; to ~ go vi mollare // vt lasciare andare; to ~ in vt lasciare entrare; (visitor etc) far entrare; to ~ off vt lasciare andare; (firework etc) far partire; (smell etc) emettere; to ~ out vt lasciare uscire; (dress) allargare; (scream) emettere; to ~ up vi diminuire.

lethal ['li:θl] a letale, mortale.

lethargic [lɛ'θɑ:dʒɪk] a letargico(a).

lethargy ['lɛθədʒɪ] n letargia.

letter ['lɛtə*] n lettera; ~s npl (LITERATURE) lettere; ~ bomb n lettera esplosiva; ~box n buca delle lettere; ~ing n iscrizione f; caratteri mpl.

lettuce ['lɛtɪs] n lattuga, insalata.

leukaemia [lu:'ki:mɪə] n leucemia.

level ['lɛvl] a piatto(a), piano(a); orizzontale // n livello // vt livellare, spianare; to be ~ with essere alla pari di; 'A' ~s npl ≈ esami mpl di maturità; 'O' ~s npl esami fatti in Inghilterra all'età di 16 anni; on the ~ piatto(a); (fig) onesto(a); to ~ off or out vi (prices etc) stabilizzarsi; ~ crossing n passaggio a livello; ~-headed a equilibrato(a).

lever ['li:və*] n leva // vt: to ~ up/out sollevare/estrarre con una leva; ~age n: ~age (on or with) ascendente m (su).

levity ['lɛvɪtɪ] n leggerezza, frivolità.

levy ['lɛvɪ] n tassa, imposta // vt imporre, percepire.

lewd [lu:d] a osceno(a), lascivo(a).

liability [laɪə'bɪlɪtɪ] n responsabilità f inv; (handicap) peso; **liabilities** npl debiti mpl; (on balance sheet) passivo.

liable ['laɪəbl] a (subject): ~ to soggetto(a) a; passibile di; (responsible):

~ (for) responsabile di; (likely): ~ to do propenso(a) a fare.

liaison [li:'eɪzɔn] n relazione f; (MIL) collegamento.

liar ['laɪə*] n bugiardo/a.

libel ['laɪbl] n libello; diffamazione f // vt diffamare.

liberal ['lɪbərl] a liberale; (generous): to be ~ with distribuire liberalmente.

liberate ['lɪbəreɪt] vt liberare; **liberation** [-'reɪʃən] n liberazione f.

liberty ['lɪbətɪ] n libertà f inv; at ~ to do libero(a) di fare; to take the ~ of prendersi la libertà di, permettersi di.

Libra ['li:brə] n Bilancia.

librarian [laɪ'brɛərɪən] n bibliotecario/a.

library ['laɪbrərɪ] n biblioteca.

libretto [lɪ'brɛtəu] n libretto.

Libya ['lɪbɪə] n Libia; ~n a, n libico(a).

lice [laɪs] npl of **louse**.

licence ['laɪsns] n autorizzazione f, permesso; (COMM) licenza; (RADIO, TV) canone m, abbonamento; (also: **driving** ~) patente f di guida; (excessive freedom) licenza; ~ plate n targa.

license ['laɪsns] n (US) = **licence** // vt dare una licenza a; ~d a (for alcohol) che ha la licenza di vendere bibite alcoliche.

licentious [laɪ'sɛnʃəs] a licenzioso(a).

lichen ['laɪkən] n lichene m.

lick [lɪk] vt leccare // n leccata; a ~ of paint una passata di vernice.

licorice ['lɪkərɪs] n = **liquorice**.

lid [lɪd] n coperchio.

lido ['laɪdəu] n piscina all'aperto.

lie [laɪ] n bugia, menzogna // vi mentire, dire bugie; (pt **lay**, pp **lain** [leɪ, leɪn]) (rest) giacere, star disteso(a); (in grave) giacere, riposare; (of object: be situated) trovarsi, essere; to ~ low (fig) latitare; to have a ~-down sdraiarsi, riposarsi; to have a ~-in rimanere a letto.

lieutenant [lɛf'tɛnənt] n tenente m.

life, **lives** [laɪf, laɪvz] n vita // cpd di vita; della vita; a ~ vita; ~ assurance n assicurazione f sulla vita; ~belt n cintura di salvataggio; ~boat n scialuppa di salvataggio; ~ expectancy n durata media della vita; ~guard n bagnino; ~ jacket n salvagente m, cintura di salvataggio; ~less a senza vita; ~like a verosimile; rassomigliante; ~line n cavo di salvataggio; ~long a per tutta la vita; ~ preserver n (US) salvagente m, cintura di salvataggio; (Brit: col) sfollagente m inv; ~-raft n zattera di salvataggio; ~-saver n bagnino; ~-sized a a grandezza naturale; ~time n: in his ~time durante la sua vita; in a ~time nell'arco della vita; in tutta la vita.

lift [lɪft] vt sollevare, levare; (steal) prendere, rubare // vi (fog) alzarsi // n (elevator) ascensore m; to give sb a ~ dare un passaggio a qd; ~-off n decollo.

ligament ['lɪgəmənt] n legamento.

light [laɪt] n luce f, lume m; (daylight) luce f, giorno; (lamp) lampada; (AUT: rear ~) luce f di posizione; (: headlamp) fanale m;

(for cigarette etc): **have you got a ~?** ha del fuoco?; **~s** *npl* (*AUT*: *traffic* ~s)
semaforo // *vt* (*pt, pp* **lighted** *or* **lit** [lit]) (*candle, cigarette, fire*) accendere; (*room*) illuminare // *a* (*room, colour*) chiaro(a); (*not heavy, also fig*) leggero(a); **to ~ up** *vi* illuminarsi // *vt* (*illuminate*) illuminare; ~ **bulb** *n* lampadina; ~**en** *vi* schiarirsi // *vt* (*give light to*) illuminare; (*make lighter*) schiarire; (*make less heavy*) alleggerire; ~**er** *n* (*also*: **cigarette** ~) accendino; (*boat*) chiatta; ~**-headed** *a* stordito(a); ~**-hearted** *a* gioioso(a), gaio(a); ~**house** *n* faro; ~**ing** *n* illuminazione *f*; ~**ing-up time** *n* orario per l'accensione delle luci; ~**ly** *ad* leggermente; ~ **meter** *n* (*PHOT*) esposimetro; ~**ness** *n* chiarezza; (*in weight*) leggerezza.
lightning ['laɪtnɪŋ] *n* lampo, fulmine *m*; ~ **conductor** *n* parafulmine *m*.
lightweight ['laɪtweɪt] *a* (*suit*) leggero(a); (*boxer*) peso leggero *inv*.
light year ['laɪtjɪə°] *n* anno *m* luce *inv*.
like [laɪk] *vt* (*person*) volere bene a; (*activity, object, food*): **I ~ swimming/that book/chocolate** mi piace nuotare/quel libro/il cioccolato // *prep* come // *a* simile, uguale // *n*: **the ~** un(a) simile; uno(a) uguale; (*pej*) una cosa simile; uno(a) uguale; **his ~s and dislikes** i suoi gusti; **I would ~, I'd ~** mi piacerebbe, vorrei; **to be/look ~ sb/sth** somigliare a qd/qc; **that's just ~ him** è proprio da lui; ~**able** *a* simpatico(a).
likelihood ['laɪklɪhud] *n* probabilità.
likely ['laɪklɪ] *a* probabile; plausibile; **he's ~ to leave** probabilmente partirà, è probabile che parta.
like-minded [laɪk'maɪndɪd] *a* che pensa allo stesso modo.
liken ['laɪkən] *vt*: **to ~ sth to** paragonare qc a.
likewise ['laɪkwaɪz] *ad* similmente, nello stesso modo.
liking ['laɪkɪŋ] *n*: ~ (**for**) simpatia (per); debole *m* (per).
lilac ['laɪlək] *n* lilla *m inv* // *a* lilla *inv*.
lilting ['lɪltɪŋ] *a* melodioso(a).
lily ['lɪlɪ] *n* giglio; ~ **of the valley** *n* mughetto.
limb [lɪm] *n* membro.
limber ['lɪmbə°]: **to ~ up** *vi* riscaldarsi i muscoli.
limbo ['lɪmbəu] *n*: **to be in ~** (*fig*) essere in sospeso.
lime [laɪm] *n* (*tree*) tiglio; (*fruit*) limetta; (*GEO*) calce *f*.
limelight ['laɪmlaɪt] *n*: **in the ~** (*fig*) alla ribalta, in vista.
limerick ['lɪmərɪk] *n* poesiola umoristica di 5 versi.
limestone ['laɪmstəun] *n* pietra calcarea; (*GEO*) calcare *m*.
limit ['lɪmɪt] *n* limite *m* // *vt* limitare; ~**ation** [-'teɪʃən] *n* limitazione *f*, limite *m*; ~**ed** *a* limitato(a), ristretto(a); ~**ed** (**liability**) **company** (**Ltd**) *n* ≈ società *f*

inv a responsabilità limitata (S.r.l.).
limousine ['lɪməziːn] *n* limousine *f inv*.
limp [lɪmp] *vi* zoppicare // *a* floscio(a), flaccido(a).
limpet ['lɪmpɪt] *n* patella.
line [laɪn] *n* linea; (*rope*) corda; (*wire*) filo; (*of poem*) verso; (*row, series*) fila, riga; coda // *vt* (*clothes*): **to ~ (with)** foderare (di); (*box*): **to ~ (with)** rivestire *or* foderare (di); (*subj*: *trees, crowd*) fiancheggiare; **in ~ with** d'accordo con; **to ~ up** *vi* allinearsi, mettersi in fila // *vt* mettere in fila.
linear ['lɪnɪə°] *a* lineare.
linen ['lɪnɪn] *n* biancheria, panni *mpl*; (*cloth*) tela di lino.
liner ['laɪnə°] *n* nave *f* di linea.
linesman ['laɪnzmən] *n* guardalinee *m inv*.
line-up ['laɪnʌp] *n* allineamento, fila; (*SPORT*) formazione *f* di gioco.
linger ['lɪŋgə°] *vi* attardarsi; indugiare; (*smell, tradition*) persistere; ~**ing** *a* lungo(a); persistente; (*death*) lento(a).
lingo, ~**es** ['lɪŋgəu] *n* (*pej*) gergo.
linguist ['lɪŋgwɪst] *n* linguista *m/f*; poliglotta *m/f*; ~**ic** [lɪŋ'gwɪstɪk] *a* linguistico(a); ~**ics** *n* linguistica.
lining ['laɪnɪŋ] *n* fodera.
link [lɪŋk] *n* (*of a chain*) anello; (*connection*) legame *m*, collegamento // *vt* collegare, unire, congiungere; ~**s** *npl* pista *or* terreno da golf; **to ~ up** *vt* collegare, unire // *vi* riunirsi; associarsi.
linoleum [lɪ'nəuliəm] *n* linoleum *m inv*.
lint [lɪnt] *n* garza.
lintel ['lɪntl] *n* architrave *f*.
lion ['laɪən] *n* leone *m*; ~ **cub** leoncino; ~**ess** *n* leonessa.
lip [lɪp] *n* labbro; (*of cup etc*) orlo; (*insolence*) sfacciataggine *f*; ~**read** *vi* leggere sulle labbra; **to pay ~ service to sth** essere favorevole a qc solo a parole; ~**stick** *n* rossetto.
liqueur [lɪ'kjuə°] *n* liquore *m*.
liquid ['lɪkwɪd] *n* liquido *a* liquido(a); ~ **assets** *npl* attività *fpl* liquide, crediti *mpl* liquidi.
liquidate ['lɪkwɪdeɪt] *vt* liquidare; **liquidation** [-'deɪʃən] *n* liquidazione *f*; **liquidator** *n* liquidatore *m*.
liquidize ['lɪkwɪdaɪz] *vt* (*CULIN*) passare al frullatore.
liquor ['lɪkə°] *n* alcool *m*.
liquorice ['lɪkərɪs] *n* liquirizia.
lisp [lɪsp] *n* difetto nel pronunciare le sibilanti.
list [lɪst] *n* lista, elenco; (*of ship*) sbandamento // *vt* (*write down*) mettere in lista; fare una lista di; (*enumerate*) elencare // *vi* (*ship*) sbandare.
listen ['lɪsn] *vi* ascoltare; **to ~ to** ascoltare; ~**er** *n* ascoltatore/trice.
listless ['lɪstlɪs] *a* apatico(a).
lit [lɪt] *pt, pp* of **light**.
litany ['lɪtənɪ] *n* litania.
literacy ['lɪtərəsɪ] *n* fatto di sapere leggere e scrivere; cultura.

literal ['lɪtərl] a letterale; **~ly** ad alla lettera, letteralmente.

literary ['lɪtərərɪ] a letterario(a).

literate ['lɪtərət] a che sa leggere e scrivere, istruito(a).

literature ['lɪtərɪtʃə*] n letteratura; (brochures etc) materiale m.

lithe [laɪð] a agile, snello(a).

litigate ['lɪtɪgeɪt] vt muovere causa a // vi litigare; **litigation** [-'geɪʃən] n causa.

litre ['liːtə*] n litro.

litter ['lɪtə*] n (rubbish) rifiuti mpl; (young animals) figliata // vt sparpagliare; lasciare rifiuti in; ~ **bin** n cestino per rifiuti; **~ed with** coperto(a) di.

little ['lɪtl] a (small) piccolo(a); (not much) poco(a) // ad poco; a ~ un po' (di); a ~ milk un po' di latte; ~ **by** ~ a poco a poco; **to make** ~ **of** dare poca importanza a.

liturgy ['lɪtədʒɪ] n liturgia.

live vi [lɪv] vivere; (reside) vivere, abitare // a [laɪv] (animal) vivo(a); (wire) sotto tensione; (broadcast) diretto(a); **to ~ down** vt far dimenticare (alla gente); **to ~ in** vi essere interno(a); avere vitto e alloggio; **to ~ on** vt fus (food) vivere di // vi sopravvivere, continuare a vivere; **to ~ up to** vt fus tener fede a, non venir meno a.

livelihood ['laɪvlɪhud] n vita, mezzi mpl di sussistenza.

liveliness ['laɪvlɪnəs] n vivacità.

lively ['laɪvlɪ] a vivace, vivo(a).

liver ['lɪvə*] n fegato.

livery ['lɪvərɪ] n livrea.

lives [laɪvz] npl of **life**.

livestock ['laɪvstɔk] n bestiame m.

livid ['lɪvɪd] a livido(a); (furious) livido(a) di rabbia, furibondo(a).

living ['lɪvɪŋ] a vivo(a), vivente // n: **to earn** or **make a** ~ guadagnarsi la vita; ~ **room** n soggiorno; ~ **standards** npl tenore m di vita; ~ **wage** n salario sufficiente per vivere.

lizard ['lɪzəd] n lucertola.

llama ['lɑːmə] n lama m inv.

load [ləud] n (weight) peso; (ELEC, TECH, thing carried) carico // vt: **to ~ (with)** (lorry, ship) caricare (di); (gun, camera) caricare (con); a ~ **of**, **~s of** (fig) un sacco di; **~ed** a (dice) falsato(a); (question, word) capzioso(a).

loaf, loaves [ləuf, ləuvz] n pane m, pagnotta // vi (also: ~ **about**, ~ **around**) bighellonare.

loam [ləum] n terra di marna.

loan [ləun] n prestito // vt dare in prestito; **on** ~ in prestito.

loath [ləuθ] a: **to be** ~ **to do** essere restio(a) a fare.

loathe [ləuð] vt detestare, aborrire; **loathing** n aborrimento, disgusto.

loaves [ləuvz] npl of **loaf**.

lobby ['lɔbɪ] n atrio, vestibolo; (POL: pressure group) gruppo di pressione // vt fare pressione su.

lobe [ləub] n lobo.

lobster ['lɔbstə*] n aragosta.

local ['ləukl] a locale // n (pub) bar m inv or caffè m inv vicino; **the ~s** npl la gente della zona; ~ **call** n telefonata urbana; ~ **government** n amministrazione f locale.

locality [ləu'kælɪtɪ] n località f inv; (position) posto, luogo.

locally ['ləukəlɪ] ad da queste parti; nel vicinato.

locate [ləu'keɪt] vt (find) trovare; (situate) collocare.

location [ləu'keɪʃən] n posizione f; **on** ~ (CINEMA) all'esterno.

loch [lɔx] n lago.

lock [lɔk] n (of door, box) serratura; (of canal) chiusa; (of hair) ciocca, riccio // vt (with key) chiudere a chiave; (immobilize) bloccare // vi (door etc) chiudersi a chiave; (wheels) bloccarsi, incepparsi.

locker ['lɔkə*] n armadietto.

locket ['lɔkɪt] n medaglione m.

lockjaw ['lɔkdʒɔː] n tetano.

locomotive [ləukə'məutɪv] n locomotiva.

locust ['ləukəst] n locusta.

lodge [lɔdʒ] n casetta, portineria // vi (person): **to ~ (with)** essere a pensione (presso or da) // vt (appeal etc) presentare, fare; **to ~ a complaint** presentare un reclamo; **to ~ (itself) in/between** piantarsi dentro/fra; **~r** n affittuario/a; (with room and meals) pensionante m/f.

lodgings ['lɔdʒɪŋz] npl camera d'affitto; camera ammobiliata.

loft [lɔft] n soffitto; (AGR) granaio.

lofty ['lɔftɪ] a alto(a); (haughty) altezzoso(a).

log [lɔg] n (of wood) ceppo; (book) = **logbook**.

logbook ['lɔgbuk] n (NAUT, AVIAT) diario di bordo; (of lorry-driver) registro di viaggio; (of events, movement of goods etc) registro; (of car) libretto di circolazione.

loggerheads ['lɔgəhɛdz] npl: **at ~ (with)** ai ferri corti (con).

logic ['lɔdʒɪk] n logica; ~**al** a logico(a); ~**ally** ad logicamente.

logistics [lɔ'dʒɪstɪks] n logistica.

loin [lɔɪn] n (CULIN) lombata; ~**s** npl reni fpl.

loiter ['lɔɪtə*] vi attardarsi; **to ~ (about)** indugiare, bighellonare.

loll [lɔl] vi (also: ~ **about**) essere stravaccato(a).

lollipop ['lɔlɪpɔp] n lecca lecca m inv; ~ **man/lady** n impiegato/a che aiuta i bambini ad attraversare la strada in vicinanza di scuole.

London ['lʌndən] n Londra; ~**er** n londinese m/f.

lone [ləun] a solitario(a).

loneliness ['ləunlɪnɪs] n solitudine f, isolamento.

lonely ['ləunlɪ] a solo(a); solitario(a), isolato(a); **to feel** ~ sentirsi solo.

loner ['ləunə*] n solitario/a.

long [lɔŋ] a lungo(a) // ad a lungo, per molto tempo // vi: to ~ **for sth/to do** desiderare qc/di fare; non veder l'ora di aver qc/di fare; **he had ~ understood that...** aveva capito da molto tempo che...; **how ~ is this river/course?** quanto è lungo questo fiume/corso?; **6 metres ~** lungo 6 metri; **6 months ~** che dura 6 mesi, di 6 mesi; **all night ~** tutta la notte; **~ before** molto tempo prima; **before ~** (+ *future*) presto, fra poco; (+ *past*) poco tempo dopo; **at ~ last** finalmente; ~**distance** a (*race*) di fondo; (*call*) interurbano(a); ~**hand** n scrittura normale; ~**ing** n desiderio, voglia, brama // a di desiderio; pieno(a) di nostalgia.

longitude ['lɔŋgitjuːd] n longitudine f.

long: ~ **jump** n salto in lungo; ~**lost** a perduto(a) da tempo; ~**playing** a: ~**playing record (L.P.)** n (*disco*) 33 giri m inv; ~**range** a a lunga portata; ~**sighted** a presbite; (*fig*) lungimirante; ~**standing** a di vecchia data; ~**suffering** a estremamente paziente; infinitamente tollerante; ~**term** a a lungo termine; ~ **wave** n onde fpl lunghe; ~**winded** a prolisso(a), interminabile.

loo [luː] n (*col*) W.C. m inv, cesso.

look [luk] vi guardare; (*seem*) sembrare, parere; (*building etc*): to ~ **south/on to** the sea dare a sud/sul mare // n sguardo; (*appearance*) aspetto, aria; ~**s** npl aspetto; bellezza; to ~ **like** assomigliare a; to ~ **after** vt fus occuparsi di, prendere cura di; guardare, badare a; to ~ **at** vt fus guardare; to ~ **down on** vt fus (*fig*) guardare dall'alto, disprezzare; to ~ **for** vt fus cercare; to ~ **forward to** vt fus non veder l'ora di; to ~ **on** vi fare da spettatore; to ~ **out** vi (*beware*): to ~ **out (for)** stare in guardia (per); to ~ **out for** vt fus stare in aspetto per; cercare; to ~ **to** vt fus stare attento(a) a; (*rely on*) contare su; to ~ **up** vi alzare gli occhi; (*improve*) migliorare // vt (*word*) cercare; (*friend*) andare a trovare; to ~ **up to** vt fus avere rispetto per; ~**out** n posto d'osservazione; guardia; **to be on the** ~**out (for)** stare in guardia (per).

loom [luːm] n telaio // vi sorgere; (*fig*) minacciare.

loop [luːp] n cappio; ~**hole** n via d'uscita; scappatoia.

loose [luːs] a (*knot*) sciolto(a); (*screw*) allentato(a); (*stone*) cadente; (*clothes*) ampio(a), largo(a); (*animal*) in libertà, scappato(a); (*life*, *morals*) dissoluto(a); (*discipline*) allentato(a); (*thinking*) poco rigoroso(a), vago(a); **to be at a ~ end** non saper che fare; ~**ly** ad lentamente; approssimativamente; ~**n** vt sciogliere.

loot [luːt] n bottino // vt saccheggiare; ~**ing** n saccheggio.

lop [lɔp]: to ~ **off** vt tagliare via, recidere.

lop-sided ['lɔp'saidid] a non equilibrato(a), assimetrico(a).

lord [lɔːd] n signore m; **L~ Smith** lord Smith; **the L~** il Signore; **the (House of)** L~**s** la Camera dei Lord; ~**ly** a nobile, maestoso(a); (*arrogant*) altero(a); ~**ship** n: **your L~ship** Sua Eccellenza.

lore [lɔːʳ] n tradizioni fpl.

lorry ['lɔri] n camion m inv; ~ **driver** n camionista m.

lose, pt,pp **lost** [luːz, lɔst] vt perdere; (*pursuers*) distanziare // vi perdere; to ~ (*time*) (*clock*) ritardare; ~**r** n perdente m/f.

loss [lɔs] n perdita; **to be at a ~** essere perplesso(a).

lost [lɔst] pt,pp of **lose** // a perduto(a); ~ **property** n oggetti mpl smarriti.

lot [lɔt] n (*at auctions*) lotto; (*destiny*) destino, sorte f; **the ~** tutto(a) quanto(a); tutti(e) quanti(e); **a ~** molto; **a ~ of** una gran quantità di, un sacco di; ~**s of** molto(a); **to draw ~s (for sth)** tirare a sorte (per qc).

lotion ['ləuʃən] n lozione f.

lottery ['lɔtəri] n lotteria.

loud [laud] a forte, alto(a); (*gaudy*) vistoso(a), sgargiante // ad (*speak etc*) forte; ~**hailer** n portavoce m inv; ~**ly** ad fortemente, ad alta voce; ~**speaker** n altoparlante m.

lounge [laundʒ] n salotto, soggiorno // vi oziare; starsene colle mani in mano; ~ **suit** n abito completo; abito da passeggio.

louse, pl **lice** [laus, lais] n pidocchio.

lousy ['lauzi] a (*fig*) orrendo(a), schifoso(a).

lout [laut] n zoticone m.

lovable ['lʌvəbl] a simpatico(a), carino(a); amabile.

love [lʌv] n amore m // vt amare; voler bene a; to ~ **to do:** **I ~ to do** mi piace fare; **to be in ~ with** essere innamorato(a) di; to ~ **to make ~** fare l'amore; **'15 ~'** (*TENNIS*) '15 a zero'; ~ **affair** n intrigo amoroso; ~ **letter** n lettera d'amore.

lovely ['lʌvli] a bello(a); incantevole; gradevole, piacevole.

lover ['lʌvəʳ] n amante m/f; (*amateur*): **a ~ of** un(un')amante di; un(un')appassionato(a) di.

loving ['lʌviŋ] a affettuoso(a), amoroso(a), tenero(a).

low [ləu] a basso(a) // ad in basso // n (*METEOR*) depressione f // vi (*cow*) muggire; **to feel ~** sentirsi giù; **he's very ~** (*ill*) è molto debole; **to turn (down)** vt abbassare; ~**cut** a (*dress*) scollato(a); ~**ly** a umile, modesto(a); ~**lying** a a basso livello; ~**paid** a mal pagato(a).

loyal ['lɔiəl] a fedele, leale; ~**ty** n fedeltà, lealtà.

lozenge ['lɔzindʒ] n (*MED*) pastiglia; (*GEOM*) losanga.

L.P. n abbr see **long-playing**.

Ltd abbr see **limited**.

lubricant ['luːbrikənt] n lubrificante m.

lubricate ['luːbrikeit] vt lubrificare.

lucid ['luːsid] a lucido(a); ~**ity** [-'siditi] n lucidità.

luck [lʌk] n fortuna, sorte f; **bad ~**

sfortuna, mala sorte; **~ily** *ad* fortunatamente, per fortuna; **~y** *a* fortunato(a); *(number etc)* che porta fortuna.

lucrative ['lu:krətıv] *a* lucrativo(a), lucroso(a), profittevole.

ludicrous ['lu:dıkrəs] *a* ridicolo(a), assurdo(a).

lug [lʌg] *vt* trascinare.

luggage ['lʌgıdʒ] *n* bagagli *mpl*; **~ rack** *n* portabagagli *m inv*.

lukewarm ['lu:kwɔ:m] *a* tiepido(a).

lull [lʌl] *n* intervallo di calma // *vt (child)* cullare; *(person, fear)* acquietare, calmare.

lullaby ['lʌləbaı] *n* ninnananna.

lumbago [lʌm'beıgəʊ] *n* lombaggine *f*.

lumber ['lʌmbə*] *n* roba vecchia; **~jack** *n* boscaiolo.

luminous ['lu:mınəs] *a* luminoso(a).

lump [lʌmp] *n* pezzo; *(in sauce)* grumo; *(swelling)* gonfiore *m* // *vt (also: ~ together)* riunire, mettere insieme; **a ~ sum** somma globale; **~y** *a (sauce)* grumoso(a).

lunacy ['lu:nəsı] *n* demenza, follia, pazzia.

lunar ['lu:nə*] *a* lunare.

lunatic ['lu:nətık] *a, n* pazzo(a), matto(a).

lunch [lʌntʃ] *n* pranzo.

luncheon ['lʌntʃən] *n* pranzo; **~ voucher** *n* buono *m* pasto *inv*.

lung [lʌŋ] *n* polmone *m*.

lunge [lʌndʒ] *vi (also: ~ forward)* fare un balzo in avanti.

lurch [lɔ:tʃ] *vi* vacillare, barcollare // *n* scatto improvviso.

lure [luə*] *n* richiamo; lusinga // *vt* allettare.

lurid ['luərıd] *a* sgargiante; *(details etc)* impressionante.

lurk [lɔ:k] *vi* stare in agguato.

luscious ['lʌʃəs] *a* succulento(a), delizioso(a).

lush [lʌʃ] *a* lussureggiante.

lust [lʌst] *n* lussuria; cupidigia; desiderio; *(fig)*: **~ for** sete *f* di; **to ~ after** *vt fus* bramare, desiderare; **~ful** *a* lascivo(a), voglioso(a).

lustre ['lʌstə*] *n* lustro, splendore *m*.

lusty ['lʌstı] *a* vigoroso(a), robusto(a).

lute [lu:t] *n* liuto.

Luxembourg ['lʌksəmbɔ:g] *n* Lussemburgo.

luxuriant [lʌg'zjuərıənt] *a* lussureggiante.

luxurious [lʌg'zjuərıəs] *a* sontuoso(a), di lusso.

luxury ['lʌkʃərı] *n* lusso // *cpd* di lusso.

lying ['laııŋ] *n* mentire *m*.

lynch [lıntʃ] *vt* linciare.

lynx [lıŋks] *n* lince *f*.

lyre ['laıə*] *n* lira.

lyric ['lırık] *a* lirico(a); **~s** *npl (of song)* parole *fpl*; **~al** *a* lirico(a).

M

m. *abbr of* **metre, mile, million**.

M.A. *abbr see* **master**.

mac [mæk] *n* impermeabile *m*.

macaroni [mækə'rəʊnı] *n* maccheroni *mpl*.

mace [meıs] *n* mazza; *(spice)* macis *m or f*.

machine [mə'ʃi:n] *n* macchina // *vt (dress etc)* cucire a macchina; **~ gun** *n* mitragliatrice *f*; **~ry** *n* macchinario, macchine *fpl*; *(fig)* macchina; **machinist** *n* macchinista *m/f*.

mackerel ['mækrl] *n, pl inv* sgombro.

mackintosh ['mækıntɔʃ] *n* impermeabile *m*.

mad [mæd] *a* matto(a), pazzo(a); *(foolish)* sciocco(a); *(angry)* furioso(a).

madam ['mædəm] *n* signora.

madden ['mædn] *vt* fare infuriare.

made [meıd] *pt, pp of* **make**; **~-to-measure** *a* fatto(a) su misura.

madly ['mædlı] *ad* follemente; *(love)* alla follia.

madman ['mædmən] *n* pazzo, alienato.

madness ['mædnıs] *n* pazzia.

magazine [mægə'zi:n] *n (PRESS)* rivista; *(MIL: store)* magazzino, deposito; *(of firearm)* caricatore *m*.

maggot ['mægət] *n* baco, verme *m*.

magic ['mædʒık] *n* magia // *a* magico(a); **~al** *a* magico(a); **~ian** [mə'dʒıʃən] *n* mago/a.

magistrate ['mædʒıstreıt] *n* magistrato; giudice *m/f*.

magnanimous [mæg'nænıməs] *a* magnanimo(a).

magnate ['mægneıt] *n* magnate *m*.

magnet ['mægnıt] *n* magnete *m*, calamita; **~ic** [-'nɛtık] *a* magnetico(a); **~ism** *n* magnetismo.

magnification [mægnıfı'keıʃən] *n* ingrandimento.

magnificence [mæg'nıfısns] *n* magnificenza.

magnificent [mæg'nıfısnt] *a* magnifico(a).

magnify ['mægnıfaı] *vt* ingrandire; **~ing glass** *n* lente *f* d'ingrandimento.

magnitude ['mægnıtju:d] *n* grandezza; importanza.

magnolia [mæg'nəʊlıə] *n* magnolia.

magpie ['mægpaı] *n* gazza.

mahogany [mə'hɔgənı] *n* mogano // *cpd* di *or* in mogano.

maid [meıd] *n* domestica; *(in hotel)* cameriera; **old ~** *(pej)* vecchia zitella.

maiden ['meıdn] *n* fanciulla // *a (aunt etc)* nubile; *(speech, voyage)* inaugurale; **~ name** *n* nome *m* nubile *or* da ragazza.

mail [meıl] *n* posta // *vt* spedire (per posta); **~box** *n (US)* cassetta per la posta; **~ing list** *n* elenco d'indirizzi; **~-order** *n* vendita *(or* acquisto) per corrispondenza.

maim [meım] *vt* mutilare.

main [meın] *a* principale // *n (pipe)*

conduttura principale; **the ~s** (ELEC) la linea principale; **~s operated** a che funziona a elettricità; **in the ~** nel complesso, nell'insieme; **~land** n continente m; **~stay** n (fig) sostegno principale.

maintain [meɪn'teɪn] vt mantenere; (affirm) sostenere; **maintenance** ['meɪntənəns] n manutenzione f; (alimony) alimenti mpl.

maisonette [meɪzə'nɛt] n appartamento a due piani.

maize [meɪz] n granturco, mais m.

majestic [mə'dʒɛstɪk] a maestoso(a).

majesty ['mædʒɪstɪ] n maestà f inv.

major ['meɪdʒə°] n (MIL) maggiore m // a (greater, MUS) maggiore; (in importance) principale, importante.

majority [mə'dʒɔrɪtɪ] n maggioranza.

make [meɪk] vt (pt, pp made [meɪd]) fare; (manufacture) fare, fabbricare; (cause to be): to ~ sb sad etc rendere qd triste etc; (force): to ~ sb do sth costringere qd a fare qc, far fare qc a qd; (equal): 2 and 2 ~ 4 2 più 2 fa 4 // n fabbricazione f; (brand) marca; to ~ do with arrangiarsi con; to ~ for vt fus (place) avviarsi verso; to ~ out vt (write out) scrivere; (understand) capire; (see) distinguere; (: numbers) decifrare; to ~ up vt (invent) inventare; (parcel) fare // vi conciliarsi; (with cosmetics) truccarsi; to ~ up for vt fus compensare; ricuperare; **~-believe** a immaginario(a); **~r** n fabbricante m/f; creatore/trice, autore/trice; **~shift** a improvvisato(a); **~-up** n trucco; (articles) cosmetici mpl.

making ['meɪkɪŋ] n (fig): **in the ~** in formazione.

maladjusted [mælə'dʒʌstɪd] a incapace di adattarsi.

malaise [mæ'leɪz] n malessere m.

malaria [mə'lɛərɪə] n malaria.

Malaysia [mə'leɪzɪə] n Malaysia.

male [meɪl] n (BIOL, ELEC) maschio // a maschile; maschio(a); **~ and female students** studenti e studentesse; **~ sex** sesso maschile.

malevolent [mə'lɛvələnt] a malevolo(a).

malfunction [mæl'fʌŋkʃən] n funzione f difettosa.

malice ['mælɪs] n malevolenza; **malicious** [mə'lɪʃəs] a malevolo(a); (LAW) doloso(a).

malign [mə'laɪn] vt malignare su; calunniare.

malignant [mə'lɪgnənt] a (MED) maligno(a).

malingerer [mə'lɪŋgərə°] n scansafatiche m/f inv.

malleable ['mælɪəbl] a malleabile.

mallet ['mælɪt] n maglio.

malnutrition [mælnju:'trɪʃən] n denutrizione f.

malpractice [mæl'præktɪs] n prevaricazione f; negligenza.

malt [mɔ:lt] n malto.

Malta ['mɔ:ltə] n Malta; **Maltese** [-'ti:z] a, n (pl inv) maltese (m/f).

maltreat [mæl'tri:t] vt maltrattare.

mammal ['mæml] n mammifero.

mammoth ['mæməθ] n mammut m inv // a enorme, gigantesco(a).

man, pl **men** [mæn, mɛn] n uomo; (CHESS) pezzo; (DRAUGHTS) pedina // vt fornire d'uomini; stare a; essere di servizio a.

manage ['mænɪdʒ] vi farcela // vt (be in charge of) occuparsi di; gestire; **~able** a maneggevole; fattibile; **~ment** n amministrazione f, direzione f; **~r** n direttore m; (COMM) gerente m; (of artist) manager m inv; **~ress** [-'rɛs] n direttrice f; gerente f; **~rial** [-ə'dʒɪərɪəl] a dirigenziale; **managing** a: **managing director** amministratore m delegato.

mandarin ['mændərɪn] n mandarino.

mandate ['mændeɪt] n mandato.

mandatory ['mændətərɪ] a obbligatorio(a); (powers etc) mandatorio(a).

mandolin(e) ['mændəlɪn] n mandolino.

mane [meɪn] n criniera.

maneuver [mə'nu:və°] etc (US) = **manoeuvre** etc.

manful ['mænful] a coraggioso(a), valoroso(a).

mangle ['mæŋgl] vt straziare; mutilare // n mangano.

mango, **~es** ['mæŋgəu] n mango.

mangy ['meɪndʒɪ] a rognoso(a).

manhandle ['mænhændl] vt malmenare.

manhole ['mænhəul] n botola stradale.

manhood ['mænhud] n età virile; virilità.

manhunt ['mænhʌnt] n caccia all'uomo.

mania ['meɪnɪə] n mania; **~c** ['meɪnɪæk] n maniaco/a.

manicure ['mænɪkjuə°] n manicure f inv; **~ set** n trousse f inv della manicure.

manifest ['mænɪfɛst] vt manifestare // a manifesto(a), palese; **~ation** [-'teɪʃən] n manifestazione f.

manifesto [mænɪ'fɛstəu] n manifesto.

manipulate [mə'nɪpjuleɪt] vt manipolare.

mankind [mæn'kaɪnd] n umanità, genere m umano.

manly ['mænlɪ] a virile; coraggioso(a).

man-made ['mæn'meɪd] a sintetico(a); artificiale.

manner ['mænə°] n maniera, modo; **~s** npl maniere fpl; **~ism** n vezzo, tic m inv.

manoeuvre [mə'nu:və°] vt manovrare // vi far manovre // n manovra.

manor ['mænə°] n (also: ~ **house**) maniero.

manpower ['mænpauə°] n manodopera.

mansion ['mænʃən] n casa signorile.

manslaughter ['mænslɔːtə°] n omicidio preterintenzionale.

mantelpiece ['mæntlpiːs] n mensola del caminetto.

mantle ['mæntl] n mantello.

manual ['mænjuəl] a manuale // n manuale m.

manufacture [mænju'fæktʃə°] vt fabbricare // n fabbricazione f, manifattura; **~r** n fabbricante m.

manure [mə'njuə*] n concime m.
manuscript ['mænjuskrɪpt] n manoscritto.
many ['menɪ] det molti(e) // pronoun molti(e), un gran numero; **a great ~** moltissimi(e), un gran numero (di); **~ a...** molti(e)..., più di un(a)... .
map [mæp] n carta (geografica) // vt fare una carta di; **to ~ out** vt tracciare un piano di.
maple ['meɪpl] n acero.
mar [mɑ:*] vt sciupare.
marathon ['mærəθən] n maratona.
marauder [mə'rɔːdə*] n saccheggiatore m; predatore m.
marble ['mɑːbl] n marmo; (toy) pallina, bilia; **~s** n (game) palline, bilie.
March [mɑːtʃ] n marzo.
march [mɑːtʃ] vi marciare; sfilare // n marcia; (demonstration) dimostrazione f; **~past** n sfilata.
mare [mɛə*] n giumenta.
margarine [mɑːdʒə'riːn] n margarina.
margin ['mɑːdʒɪn] n margine m; **~al** a marginale.
marigold ['mærɪgəuld] n calendola.
marijuana [mærɪ'wɑːnə] n marijuana.
marina [mə'riːnə] n marina.
marine [mə'riːn] a (animal, plant) marino(a); (forces, engineering) marittimo(a) // n fante m di marina; (US) marine m inv.
marital ['mærɪtl] a maritale, coniugale.
maritime ['mærɪtaɪm] a marittimo(a).
mark [mɑːk] n segno; (stain) macchia; (of skid etc) traccia; (SCOL) voto; (SPORT) bersaglio; (currency) marco // vt segnare; (stain) macchiare; (SCOL) dare un voto a; correggere; **to ~ time** segnare il passo; **to ~ out** vt delimitare; **~ed** a spiccato(a), chiaro(a); **~er** n (sign) segno; (bookmark) segnalibro.
market ['mɑːkɪt] n mercato // vt (COMM) mettere in vendita; **~ day** n giorno di mercato; **~ garden** n (Brit) orto industriale; **~ing** n marketing m; **~ place** n piazza del mercato.
marksman ['mɑːksmən] n tiratore m scelto; **~ship** n abilità nel tiro.
marmalade ['mɑːməleɪd] n marmellata d'arance.
maroon [mə'ruːn] vt (fig): **to be ~ed (in** or **at)** essere abbandonato(a) (in) // a bordeaux inv.
marquee [mɑː'kiː] n padiglione m.
marquess, marquis ['mɑːkwɪs] n marchese m.
marriage ['mærɪdʒ] n matrimonio; **~ bureau** n agenzia matrimoniale.
married ['mærɪd] a sposato(a); (life, love) coniugale, matrimoniale.
marrow ['mærəu] n midollo; (vegetable) zucca.
marry ['mærɪ] vt sposare, sposarsi con; (subj: father, priest etc) dare in matrimonio // vi (also: **get married**) sposarsi.
Mars [mɑːz] n (planet) Marte m.

marsh [mɑːʃ] n palude f.
marshal ['mɑːʃl] n maresciallo; (US: fire) capo; (: police) capitano // vt adunare.
marshy ['mɑːʃɪ] a paludoso(a).
martial ['mɑːʃl] a marziale; **~ law** n legge f marziale.
Martian ['mɑːʃən] n marziano/a.
martyr ['mɑːtə*] n martire m/f // vt martirizzare; **~dom** n martirio.
marvel ['mɑːvl] n meraviglia // vi: **to ~ (at)** meravigliarsi (di); **~lous** a meraviglioso(a).
Marxism ['mɑːksɪzəm] n marxismo; **Marxist** a, n marxista (m/f).
marzipan ['mɑːzɪpæn] n marzapane m.
mascara [mæs'kɑːrə] n mascara m.
mascot ['mæskət] n mascotte f inv.
masculine ['mæskjulɪn] a maschile (: di genere m maschile; **masculinity** [-'lɪnɪtɪ] n mascolinità.
mashed [mæʃt] a: **~ potatoes** purè m di patate.
mask [mɑːsk] n maschera // vt mascherare.
masochist ['mæsəukɪst] n masochista m/f.
mason ['meɪsn] n (also: **stone~**) scalpellino; (also: **free~**) massone m; **~ry** n muratura.
masquerade [mæskə'reɪd] n ballo in maschera; (fig) mascherata // vi: **to ~ as** farsi passare per.
mass [mæs] n moltitudine f, massa; (PHYSICS) massa; (REL) messa // vi ammassarsi; **the ~es** le masse.
massacre ['mæsəkə*] n massacro // vt massacrare.
massage ['mæsɑːʒ] n massaggio // vt massaggiare.
masseur [mæ'sɜː*] n massaggiatore m; **masseuse** [-'sɜːz] n massaggiatrice f.
massive ['mæsɪv] a enorme, massiccio(a).
mass media ['mæs'miːdɪə] npl mass media mpl.
mass-produce ['mæsprə'djuːs] vt produrre in serie.
mast [mɑːst] n albero.
master ['mɑːstə*] n padrone m; (ART etc, teacher: in primary school) maestro; (: in secondary school) professore m; (title for boys): **M~ X** Signorino X // vt domare; (learn) imparare a fondo; (understand) conoscere a fondo; **M~'s degree** n titolo accademico superiore al 'Bachelor'; **~ key** n chiave f maestra; **~ly** a magistrale; **~mind** n mente f superiore // vt essere il cervello di; **~piece** n capolavoro; **~ plan** n piano generale; **~ stroke** n colpo maestro; **~y** n dominio; padronanza.
masturbate ['mæstəbeɪt] vi masturbare; **masturbation** [-'beɪʃən] n masturbazione f.
mat [mæt] n stuoia; (also: **door~**) stoino, zerbino // a = **matt**.
match [mætʃ] n flammifero; (game) partita, incontro; (fig) uguale m/f; matrimonio; partito // vt intonare; (go well with) andare benissimo con; (equal) uguagliare // vi combaciare; **to be a good**

~ andare bene; to ~ up *vt* intonare; ~box *n* scatola di fiammiferi; ~ing *a* ben assortito(a); ~less *a* senza pari.

mate [meɪt] *n* compagno/a di lavoro; (*col*) amico/a; (*animal*) compagno/a; (*in merchant navy*) secondo // *vi* accoppiarsi // *vt* accoppiare.

material [mə'tɪərɪəl] *n* (*substance*) materiale *m*, materia; (*cloth*) stoffa /i *a* materiale; (*important*) essenziale; ~s *npl* materiali *mpl*; ~istic [-ə'lɪstɪk] *a* materialistico(a); ~ize *vi* realizzarsi.

maternal [mə'tɜːnl] *a* materno(a).

maternity [mə'tɜːnɪti] *n* maternità // *cpd* di maternità; (*clothes*) pre-maman *inv*; ~ hospital *n* ≈ clinica ostetrica.

mathematical [mæθə'mætɪkl] *a* matematico(a).

mathematician [mæθəmə'tɪʃən] *n* matematico/a.

mathematics [mæθə'mætɪks] *n* matematica.

maths [mæθs] *n* matematica.

matinée ['mætɪneɪ] *n* matinée *f inv.*

mating ['meɪtɪŋ] *n* accoppiamento; ~ call *n* chiamata all'accoppiamento; ~ season *n* stagione *f* degli amori.

matriarchal [meɪtrɪ'ɑːkl] *a* matriarcale.

matriculation [mətrɪkju'leɪʃən] *n* immatricolazione *f.*

matrimonial [mætrɪ'məʊnɪəl] *a* matrimoniale, coniugale.

matrimony ['mætrɪmənɪ] *n* matrimonio.

matron ['meɪtrən] *n* (*in hospital*) capoinfermiera; (*in school*) infermiera; ~ly *a* matronale; dignitoso(a).

matt [mæt] *a* opaco(a).

matted ['mætɪd] *a* ingarbugliato(a).

matter ['mætə*] *n* questione *f*; (*PHYSICS*) materia, sostanza; (*content*) contenuto; (*MED: pus*) pus *m* // *vi* importare; **it doesn't** ~ non importa; (*I don't mind*) non fa niente; **what's the** ~? che cosa c'è?; **no** ~ **what** qualsiasi cosa accada; **that's another** ~ quello è un altro affare; **as a** ~ **of course** come cosa naturale; **as a** ~ **of fact** in verità; ~-of-fact *a* prosaico(a).

matting ['mætɪŋ] *n* stuoia.

mattress ['mætrɪs] *n* materasso.

mature [mə'tjuə*] *a* maturo(a); (*cheese*) stagionato(a) // *vi* maturare; stagionare; (*COMM*) scadere; **maturity** *n* maturità.

maudlin ['mɔːdlɪn] *a* lacrimoso(a).

maul [mɔːl] *vt* lacerare.

mausoleum [mɔːsə'lɪəm] *n* mausoleo.

mauve [məʊv] *a* malva *inv.*

mawkish ['mɔːkɪʃ] *a* sdolcinato(a); insipido(a).

max. *abbr of* **maximum.**

maxim ['mæksɪm] *n* massima.

maximum ['mæksɪməm] *a* massimo(a) // *n* (*pl* **maxima** ['mæksɪmə]) massimo.

May [meɪ] *n* maggio.

may [meɪ] *vi* (*conditional:* **might**) (*indicating possibility*): **he** ~ **come** può darsi che venga; (*be allowed to*): ~ **I smoke?** posso fumare?; (*wishes*): ~ **God**

bless you! Dio la benedica!; **he might be there** può darsi che ci sia; **I might as well go** potrei anche andarmene; **you might like to try** forse le piacerebbe provare.

maybe ['meɪbiː] *ad* forse, può darsi; ~ **he'll...** può darsi che lui... +sub, forse lui... .

mayday ['meɪdeɪ] *n* S.O.S. *m.*

May Day ['meɪdeɪ] *n* il primo maggio.

mayhem ['meɪhɛm] *n* cagnara.

mayonnaise [meɪə'neɪz] *n* maionese *f.*

mayor [mɛə*] *n* sindaco; ~ess *n* sindaca; moglie *f* del sindaco.

maze [meɪz] *n* labirinto, dedalo.

me [miː] *pronoun* mi, m' + *vowel*; (*stressed, after prep*) me.

meadow ['mɛdəʊ] *n* prato.

meagre ['miːgə*] *a* magro(a).

meal [miːl] *n* pasto; (*flour*) farina; ~time *n* l'ora di mangiare; ~y-mouthed *a* che parla attraverso eufemismi.

mean [miːn] *a* (*with money*) avaro(a), gretto(a); (*unkind*) meschino(a), maligno(a); (*average*) medio(a) // *vt* (*pt, pp* **meant** [mɛnt]) (*signify*) significare, voler dire; (*intend*): **to** ~ **to do** aver l'intenzione di fare // *n* mezzo; (*MATH*) media; ~s *npl* mezzi *mpl*; **by** ~s **of** per mezzo di; (*person*) a mezzo di; **by all** ~s ma certo, prego; **to be meant for** essere destinato(a) a; **what do you** ~? che cosa vuol dire?

meander [mɪ'ændə*] *vi* far meandri; (*fig*) divagare.

meaning ['miːnɪŋ] *n* significato, senso; ~ful *a* significativo(a); ~less *a* senza senso.

meanness ['miːnnɪs] *n* avarizia; meschinità.

meant [mɛnt] *pt, pp of* **mean.**

meantime ['miːntaɪm] *ad*, **meanwhile** ['miːnwaɪl] *ad* (*also:* **in the** ~) nel frattempo.

measles ['miːzlz] *n* morbillo.

measly ['miːzlɪ] *a* (*col*) miserabile.

measure ['mɛʒə*] *vt, vi* misurare // *n* misura; (*ruler*) metro; ~d *a* misurato(a); ~ments *npl* misure *fpl*; **chest/hip** ~ment giro petto/fianchi.

meat [miːt] *n* carne *f*; ~y *a* che sa di carne; (*fig*) sostanzioso(a).

Mecca ['mɛkə] *n* Mecca.

mechanic [mɪ'kænɪk] *n* meccanico; ~s *n* meccanica // *npl* meccanismo; ~al *a* meccanico(a).

mechanism ['mɛkənɪzəm] *n* meccanismo.

mechanization [mɛkənaɪ'zeɪʃən] *n* meccanizzazione *f.*

medal ['mɛdl] *n* medaglia; ~lion [mɪ'dælɪən] *n* medaglione *m*; ~list *n* (*SPORT*) vincitore/trice di medaglia.

meddle ['mɛdl] *vi*: **to** ~ **in** immischiarsi in, mettere le mani in; **to** ~ **with** toccare.

media ['miːdɪə] *npl* media *mpl.*

mediaeval [mɛdɪ'iːvl] *a* = **medievale.**

mediate ['miːdɪeɪt] *vi* interporsi; fare da mediatore/trice; **mediation** [-'eɪʃən] *n* mediazione f; **mediator** n mediatore/trice.

medical ['mɛdɪkl] a medico(a); ~ **student** n studente/essa di medicina.

medicated ['mɛdɪkeɪtɪd] a medicato(a).

medicinal [mɛ'dɪsɪnl] a medicinale.

medicine ['mɛdsɪn] n medicina; ~ **chest** n armadietto farmaceutico.

medieval [mɛdɪ'iːvl] a medievale.

mediocre [miːdɪ'əʊkə°] a mediocre; **mediocrity** [-'ɔkrɪti] a mediocrità.

meditate ['mɛdɪteɪt] vi: to ~ (on) meditare (su); **meditation** [-'teɪʃən] n meditazione f.

Mediterranean [mɛdɪtə'reɪnɪən] a mediterraneo(a); the ~ (Sea) il (mare) Mediterraneo.

medium ['miːdɪəm] a medio(a) // n (pl media: means) mezzo; (pl mediums: person) medium m inv; the happy ~ il giusto medio.

medley ['mɛdlɪ] n selezione f.

meek [miːk] a dolce, umile.

meet, pt, pp **met** [miːt, mɛt] vt incontrare; (for the first time) fare la conoscenza di; (go and fetch): I'll ~ you at the station verrò a prenderla alla stazione; (fig) affrontare; soddisfare; raggiungere // vi incontrarsi; (in session) riunirsi; (join: objects) unirsi; to ~ with vt fus incontrare; ~ing n incontro; (session: of club etc) riunione f; (interview) intervista; she's at a ~ing (comm) è in riunione.

megaphone ['mɛgəfəʊn] n megafono.

melancholy ['mɛlənkəlɪ] n malinconia // a malinconico(a).

mellow ['mɛləʊ] a (wine, sound) ricco(a); (person, light) dolce; (colour) caldo(a); (fruit) maturo(a) // vi (person) addolcirsi.

melodious [mɪ'ləʊdɪəs] a melodioso(a).

melodrama ['mɛləʊdrɑːmə] n melodramma m.

melody ['mɛlədɪ] n melodia.

melon ['mɛlən] n melone m.

melt [mɛlt] vi (gen) sciogliersi, struggersi; (metals) fondersi; (fig) intenerirsi // vt sciogliere, struggere; fondere; (person) commuovere; to ~ away vi sciogliersi completamente; to ~ down vt fondere; ~ing point n punto di fusione.

member ['mɛmbə°] n membro; ~ **country/state** n paese m/stato membro; M~ of Parliament (M.P.) n deputato; ~ship n iscrizione f; (numero d')iscritti mpl, membri mpl.

membrane ['mɛmbreɪn] n membrana.

memento [mə'mɛntəʊ] n ricordo, souvenir m inv.

memo ['mɛməʊ] n appunto; (comm etc) comunicazione f di servizio.

memoir ['mɛmwɑː°] n memoria; ~s npl memorie fpl, ricordi mpl.

memorable ['mɛmərəbl] a memorabile.

memorandum, pl **memoranda** [mɛmə'rændəm, -də] n appunto; (comm etc) comunicazione f di servizio; (diplomacy) memorandum m inv.

memorial [mɪ'mɔːrɪəl] n monumento

commemorativo // a commemorativo(a).

memorize ['mɛmə raɪz] vt imparare a memoria.

memory ['mɛmərɪ] n memoria; (recollection) ricordo; in ~ of in memoria di.

men [mɛn] npl of **man**.

menace ['mɛnəs] n minaccia // minacciare; **menacing** a minaccioso(a).

menagerie [mɪ'nædʒərɪ] n serraglio.

mend [mɛnd] vt aggiustare, riparare; (darn) rammendare // n rammendo; on the ~ in via di guarigione.

menial [mɪ'nɪəl] a da servo, domestico(a); umile.

meningitis [mɛnɪn'dʒaɪtɪs] n meningite f.

menopause ['mɛnəʊpɔːz] n menopausa.

menstruate ['mɛnstrueɪt] vi mestruare; **menstruation** [-'eɪʃən] n mestruazione f.

mental ['mɛntl] a mentale.

mentality [mɛn'tælɪt] n mentalità f inv.

mention ['mɛnʃən] n menzione f // vt menzionare, far menzione di; don't ~ it! non c'è di che!, prego!

menu ['mɛnjuː] n (set ~) menu m inv; (printed) carta.

mercantile ['mɜːkəntaɪl] a mercantile; (law) commerciale.

mercenary ['mɜːsɪnərɪ] a venale // n mercenario.

merchandise ['mɜːtʃəndaɪz] n merci fpl.

merchant ['mɜːtʃənt] n mercante m, commerciante m; ~ timber/wine negoziante m di legno/vino; ~ bank n banca d'affari; ~ navy n marina mercantile.

merciful ['mɜːsɪful] a pietoso(a), clemente.

merciless ['mɜːsɪlɪs] a spietato(a).

mercury ['mɜːkjurɪ] n mercurio.

mercy ['mɜːsɪ] n pietà; (rel) misericordia; to have ~ on sb aver pietà di qd; at the ~ of alla mercé di.

mere [mɪə°] a semplice; by a ~ chance per mero caso; ~ly ad semplicemente, non ... che.

merge [mɜːdʒ] vt unire // vi fondersi, unirsi; (comm) fondersi; ~r n (comm) fusione f.

meridian [mə'rɪdɪən] n meridiano.

meringue [mə'ræŋ] n meringa.

merit ['mɛrɪt] n merito, valore m // vt meritare.

mermaid ['mɜːmeɪd] n sirena.

merriment ['mɛrɪmənt] n gaiezza, allegria.

merry ['mɛrɪ] a gaio(a), allegro(a); ~-go-round n carosello.

mesh [mɛʃ] n maglia; rete f // vi (gears) ingranarsi.

mesmerize ['mɛzmə raɪz] vt ipnotizzare; affascinare.

mess [mɛs] n confusione f, disordine m; (fig) pasticcio; (mil) mensa; to ~ about vi (col) trastullarsi; to ~ about with vt fus (col) gingillarsi con; (: plans) fare un pasticcio di; **to ~ up** *vt* sporcare; fare un pasticcio di; rovinare.

message ['mɛsɪdʒ] *n* messaggio.

messenger ['mɛsɪndʒə*] *n* messaggero/a.

messy ['mɛsɪ] *a* sporco(a); disordinato(a).

met [mɛt] *pt, pp of* **meet**.

metabolism [mɛ'tæbəlɪzəm] *n* metabolismo.

metal ['mɛtl] *n* metallo // *vt* massicciare; **~lic** [-'tælɪk] *a* metallico(a); **~lurgy** [-'tælədʒɪ] *n* metallurgia.

metamorphosis, *pl* **phoses** [mɛtə'mɔːfəsɪs, -iːz] *n* metamorfosi *f inv*.

metaphor ['mɛtəfə*] *n* metafora.

metaphysics [mɛtə'fɪzɪks] *n* metafisica.

mete [miːt]: **to ~ out** *vt* fus infliggere.

meteor ['miːtɪə*] *n* meteora.

meteorology [miːtɪə'rɔlədʒɪ] *n* meteorologia.

meter ['miːtə*] *n* (*instrument*) contatore *m*; (*US*) = **metre**.

method ['mɛθəd] *n* metodo; **~ical** [mɪ'θɔdɪkl] *a* metodico(a).

methylated spirit ['mɛθɪleɪtɪd'spɪrɪt] *n* (*also*: **meths**) alcool *m* denaturato.

meticulous [mɛ'tɪkjuləs] *a* meticoloso(a).

metre ['miːtə*] *n* metro.

metric ['mɛtrɪk] *a* metrico(a); **~al** *a* metrico(a); **~ation** [-'keɪʃən] *n* conversione *f* al sistema metrico.

metronome ['mɛtrənəum] *n* metronomo.

metropolis [mɪ'trɔpəlɪs] *n* metropoli *f inv*.

mettle ['mɛtl] *n* coraggio.

mew [mjuː] *vi* (*cat*) miagolare.

Mexican ['mɛksɪkən] *a, n* messicano(a).

Mexico ['mɛksɪkəu] *n* Messico; **~ City** Città del Messico.

mezzanine ['mɛtsəniːn] *n* mezzanino.

miaow [miː'au] *vi* miagolare.

mice [maɪs] *npl of* **mouse**.

microbe ['maɪkrəub] *n* microbio.

microfilm ['maɪkrəufɪlm] *n* microfilm *m inv* // *vt* microfilmare.

microphone ['maɪkrəfəun] *n* microfono.

microscope ['maɪkrəskəup] *n* microscopio; **microscopic** [-'skɔpɪk] *a* microscopico(a).

mid [mɪd] *a*: **~ May** metà maggio; **~ afternoon** metà pomeriggio; **in ~ air** a mezz'aria; **~day** *n* mezzogiorno.

middle ['mɪdl] *n* mezzo; centro; (*waist*) vita // *a* di mezzo; **~aged** *a* di mezza età; **the M~ Ages** *npl* il Medioevo; **~class** ≈ borghese; **the ~ class(es)** ≈ la borghesia; **M~ East** *n* Medio Oriente *m*; **~man** *n* intermediario; agente *m* rivenditore.

middling ['mɪdlɪŋ] *a* medio(a).

midge [mɪdʒ] *n* moscerino.

midget ['mɪdʒɪt] *n* nano/a.

Midlands ['mɪdləndz] *npl* contee del centro dell'Inghilterra.

midnight ['mɪdnaɪt] *n* mezzanotte *f*.

midriff ['mɪdrɪf] *n* diaframma *m*.

midst [mɪdst] *n*: **in the ~ of** in mezzo a.

midsummer [mɪd'sʌmə*] *n* mezza *or* piena estate *f*.

midway [mɪd'weɪ] *a, ad*: **~ (between)** a mezza strada (fra).

midwife, midwives ['mɪdwaɪf, -vz] *n* levatrice *f*; **~ry** [-wɪfərɪ] *n* ostetrica.

midwinter [mɪd'wɪntə*] *n* pieno inverno.

might [maɪt] *vb see* **may** // *n* potere *m*, forza; **~y** *a* forte, potente // *ad* (*col*) molto.

migraine ['miːgreɪn] *n* emicrania.

migrant ['maɪgrənt] *n* (*bird, animal*) migratore *m*; (*person*) migrante *m/f*; nomade *m/f* // *a* migratore(trice); nomade; (*worker*) emigrato(a).

migrate [maɪ'greɪt] *vi* migrare; **migration** [-'greɪʃən] *n* migrazione *f*.

mike [maɪk] *n* (*abbr of* **microphone**) microfono.

mild [maɪld] *a* mite; (*person, voice*) dolce; (*flavour*) delicato(a); (*illness*) leggero(a) // *n* birra leggera.

mildew ['mɪldjuː] *n* muffa.

mildly ['maɪldlɪ] *ad* mitemente; dolcemente; delicatamente; leggeramente; **to put it ~** a dire poco.

mile [maɪl] *n* miglio; **~age** *n* distanza in miglia, ≈ chilometraggio; **~ometer** *n* = **milometer**; **~stone** *n* pietra miliare.

milieu ['miːljəː] *n* ambiente *m*.

militant ['mɪlɪtnt] *a, n* militante (*m/f*).

military ['mɪlɪtərɪ] *a* militare // *n*: **the ~** i militari, l'esercito.

militate ['mɪlɪteɪt] *vi*: **to ~ against** essere d'ostacolo a.

militia [mɪ'lɪʃə] *n* milizia.

milk [mɪlk] *n* latte *m* // *vt* (*cow*) mungere; (*fig*) sfruttare; **~ chocolate** *n* cioccolato al latte; **~ing** *n* mungitura; **~man** *n* lattaio; **~ shake** *n* frappé *m inv*; **~y** *a* lattiginoso(a); (*colour*) latteo(a); **M~y Way** *n* Via Lattea.

mill [mɪl] *n* mulino; (*small: for coffee, pepper etc*) macinino; (*factory*) fabbrica; (*spinning* ~) filatura // *vt* macinare // *vi* (*also*: ~ **about**) formicolare.

millennium, *pl* **~s** *or* **millennia** [mɪ'lɛnɪəm, -'lɛnɪə] *n* millennio.

miller ['mɪlə*] *n* mugnaio.

millet ['mɪlɪt] *n* miglio.

milli... ['mɪlɪ] *prefix*: **~gram(me)** *n* milligrammo; **~litre** *n* millilitro; **~metre** *n* millimetro.

milliner ['mɪlɪnə*] *n* modista; **~y** *n* modisteria.

million ['mɪljən] *n* milione *m*; **~aire** *n* milionario, ≈ miliardario.

millstone ['mɪlstəun] *n* macina.

milometer [maɪ'lɔmɪtə*] *n* ≈ contachilometri *m inv*.

mime [maɪm] *n* mimo // *vt, vi* mimare.

mimic ['mɪmɪk] *n* imitatore/trice // *vt* fare la mimica di // *vi* fare la mimica; **~ry** *n* mimica; (*ZOOL*) mimetismo.

min. *abbr of* **minute(s), minimum**.

minaret [mɪnə'rɛt] *n* minareto.

mince [mɪns] *vt* tritare, macinare // *vi* (*in walking*) camminare a passettini // *n* (*CULIN*) carne *f* tritata *or* macinata; **he**

does not ~ (his) **words** parla chiaro e tondo; ~**meat** n frutta secca tritata per uso in pasticceria; ~ **pie** n specie di torta con frutta secca; ~**r** n tritacarne m inv.

mind [maind] n mente f // vt (attend to, look after) badare a, occuparsi di; (be careful) fare attenzione a, stare attento(a) a; (object to): **I don't** ~ **the noise** il rumore non mi dà alcun fastidio; **do you** ~ **if ...?** le dispiace se ...?; **I don't** ~ non m'importa; **it is on my** ~ mi preoccupa; **to my** ~ secondo me, a mio parere; **to be out of one's** ~ essere uscito(a) di mente; **never** ~ non importa, non fa niente; **to keep sth in** ~ non dimenticare qc; **to make up one's** ~ decidersi; '~ **the step** 'attenzione allo scalino'; **to have in** ~ to do aver l'intenzione di fare; ~**ful a**: ~**ful of** attento(a) a; memore di; ~**less a** idiota.

mine [main] pronoun il(la) mio(a), pl i(le) miei(mie); **this book is** ~ questo libro è mio // n miniera; (explosive) mina // vt (coal) estrarre; (ship, beach) minare; ~**detector** n rivelatore m di mine; ~**field** n campo minato; ~**r** n minatore m.

mineral ['minərəl] a minerale // n minerale m; ~**s** npl (soft drinks) bevande fpl gasate; ~**ogy** [-'rælədʒi] n mineralogia; ~ **water** n acqua minerale.

minesweeper ['mainswi:pə*] n dragamine m inv.

mingle ['mingl] vt mescolare, mischiare // vi: **to** ~ **with** mescolarsi a, mischiarsi con.

miniature ['minətʃə*] a in miniatura // n miniatura.

minibus ['minibʌs] n minibus m inv.

minim ['minim] n (MUS) minima.

minimal ['miniml] a minimo(a).

minimize ['minimaiz] vt minimizzare.

minimum ['minimom] n (pl: **minima** ['minimə]) minimo // a minimo(a).

mining ['mainiŋ] n industria mineraria // a minerario(a); di minatori.

minion ['minjon] n (pej) caudatario; favorito/a.

miniskirt ['miniskə:t] n minigonna.

minister ['ministə*] n (POL) ministro; (REL) pastore m; ~**ial** [-'tiəriəl] a (POL) ministeriale.

ministry ['ministri] n ministero; (REL): **to go into the** ~ diventare pastore.

mink [miŋk] n visone m; ~ **coat** n pelliccia di visone.

minnow ['minəu] n pesciolino d'acqua dolce.

minor ['mainə*] a minore, di poca importanza; (MUS) minore // n (LAW) minorenne m/f.

minority [mai'nɔriti] n minoranza.

minstrel ['minstrəl] n giullare m, menestrello.

mint [mint] n (plant) menta; (sweet) pasticca di menta // vt (coins) battere; **the (Royal) M~** la Zecca; **in** ~ **condition** come nuovo(a) di zecca; ~ **sauce** n salsa di menta.

minuet [minju'et] n minuetto.

minus ['mainəs] n (also: ~ **sign**) segno meno // prep meno.

minute a [mai'nju:t] minuscolo(a); (detail) minuzioso(a) // n ['minit] minuto; (official record) processo verbale, resoconto sommario; ~**s** npl verbale m, verbali mpl.

miracle ['mirəkl] n miracolo; **miraculous** [mi'rækjuləs] a miracoloso(a).

mirage ['mirɑ:ʒ] n miraggio.

mirror ['mirə*] n specchio // vt rispecchiare, riflettere.

mirth [mɔ:θ] n galezza.

misadventure [misəd'ventʃə*] n disavventura; **death by** ~ morte f accidentale.

misanthropist [mi'zænθrəpist] n misantropo/a.

misapprehension ['misæpri'henʃən] n malinteso.

misappropriate [misə'prəuprieit] vt appropriarsi indebitamente di.

misbehave [misbi'heiv] vi comportarsi male; **misbehaviour** n comportamento scorretto.

miscalculate [mis'kælkjuleit] vt calcolare male; **miscalculation** [-'leiʃən] n errore m di calcolo.

miscarriage ['miskæridʒ] n (MED) aborto spontaneo; ~ **of justice** errore m giudiziario.

miscellaneous [misi'leiniəs] a (items) vario(a); (selection) misto(a).

miscellany [mi'seləni] n raccolta.

mischief ['mistʃif] n (naughtiness) birichineria; (harm) male m, danno; (maliciousness) malizia; **mischievous** a (naughty) birichino(a); (harmful) dannoso(a).

misconception ['miskən'sepʃən] n idea sbagliata.

misconduct [mis'kɔndʌkt] n cattiva condotta; **professional** ~ reato professionale.

misconstrue [miskən'stru:] vt interpretare male.

miscount [mis'kaunt] vt,vi contare male.

misdemeanour [misdi'mi:nə*] n misfatto; infrazione f.

misdirect [misdi'rekt] vt mal indirizzare.

miser ['maizə*] n avaro.

miserable ['mizərəbl] a infelice; (wretched) miserabile.

miserly ['maizəli] a avaro(a).

misery ['mizəri] n (unhappiness) tristezza; (pain) sofferenza; (wretchedness) miseria.

misfire [mis'faiə*] vi far cilecca; (car engine) dare accensione irregolare.

misfit ['misfit] n (person) spostato/a.

misfortune [mis'fɔ:tʃən] n sfortuna.

misgiving(s) [mis'giviŋ(z)] n(pl) dubbi mpl, sospetti mpl.

misguided [mis'gaidid] a sbagliato(a); poco giudizioso(a).

mishandle [mis'hændl] vt (treat roughly) maltrattare; (mismanage) trattare male.

mishap ['mishæp] n disgrazia.

misinform [mɪsɪn'fɔːm] vt informare male.

misinterpret [mɪsɪn'tɜːprɪt] vt interpretare male.

misjudge [mɪs'dʒʌdʒ] vt giudicare male.

mislay [mɪs'leɪ] vt irg smarrire.

mislead [mɪs'liːd] vt irg sviare; ~**ing** a ingannevole.

mismanage [mɪs'mænɪdʒ] vt gestire male; trattare male; ~**ment** n cattiva amministrazione f.

misnomer [mɪs'nəumə*] n termine m sbagliato or improprio.

misplace [mɪs'pleɪs] vt smarrire; collocare fuori posto.

misprint ['mɪsprɪnt] n errore m di stampa.

mispronounce [mɪsprə'nauns] vt pronunziare male.

misread [mɪs'riːd] vt irg leggere male.

misrepresent [mɪsreprɪ'zɛnt] vt travisare.

miss [mɪs] vt (fail to get) perdere; (regret the absence of): **I ~ him/it** sento la sua mancanza, lui/esso mi manca // vi mancare // n (shot) colpo mancato; (fig): **that was a near ~** c'è mancato poco; **to ~ out** vt omettere.

Miss [mɪs] n Signorina.

missal ['mɪsl] n messale m.

misshapen [mɪs'ʃeɪpən] a deforme.

missile ['mɪsaɪl] n (AVIAT) missile m; (object thrown) proiettile m.

missing ['mɪsɪŋ] a perso(a), smarrito(a); (after escape, disaster: person) mancante; **to go ~** sparire.

mission ['mɪʃən] n missione f; ~**ary** n missionario/a.

misspent ['mɪs'spɛnt] a: **his ~ youth** la sua gioventù sciupata.

mist [mɪst] n nebbia, foschia // vi (also: ~ **over**, ~ **up**) annebbiarsi; (windows) appannarsi.

mistake [mɪs'teɪk] n sbaglio, errore m // vt (irg: like take) sbagliarsi di; fraintendere; **to ~ for** prendere per; ~**n** a (idea etc) sbagliato(a); **to be ~n** sbagliarsi; ~**n identity** n errore m di persona.

mister ['mɪstə*] n (col) signore m; see **Mr**.

mistletoe ['mɪsltəu] n vischio.

mistook [mɪs'tuk] pt of **mistake**.

mistranslation [mɪstræns'leɪʃən] n traduzione f errata.

mistreat [mɪs'triːt] vt maltrattare.

mistress ['mɪstrɪs] n padrona; (lover) amante f; (in primary school) maestra; see **Mrs**.

mistrust [mɪs'trʌst] vt diffidare di.

misty ['mɪstɪ] a nebbioso(a), brumoso(a).

misunderstand [mɪsʌndə'stænd] vt, vi irg capire male, fraintendere; ~**ing** n malinteso, equivoco.

misuse n [mɪs'juːs] cattivo uso; (of power) abuso // vt [mɪs'juːz] far cattivo uso di; abusare di.

mitigate ['mɪtɪgeɪt] vt mitigare.

mitre ['maɪtə*] n mitra; (CARPENTRY) ugnatura.

mitt(en) ['mɪt(n)] n mezzo guanto; manopola.

mix [mɪks] vt mescolare // vi mescolarsi // n mescolanza; preparato; **to ~ up** vt mescolare; (confuse) confondere; ~**ed** a misto(a); ~**ed grill** n misto alla griglia; ~**ed-up** a (confused) confuso(a); ~**er** n (for food) sbattitore m; (person): **he is a good ~er** è molto socievole; ~**ture** n mescolanza; (blend: of tobacco etc) miscela; (MED) sciroppo; ~-**up** n confusione f.

moan [məun] n gemito // vi gemere; (col: complain): **to ~ (about)** lamentarsi (di); ~**ing** n gemiti mpl.

moat [məut] n fossato.

mob [mɔb] n folla; (disorderly) calca; (pej): **the ~** la plebaglia // vt accalcarsi intorno a.

mobile ['məubaɪl] a mobile; ~ **home** n grande roulotte f inv (utilizzata come domicilio).

mobility [məu'bɪlɪtɪ] n mobilità.

moccasin ['mɔkəsɪn] n mocassino.

mock [mɔk] vt deridere, burlarsi di // a falso(a); ~**ery** n derisione f; ~**ing** a derisorio(a); ~-**up** n modello dimostrativo; abbozzo.

mod [mɔd] a see **convenience**.

mode [məud] n modo.

model ['mɔdl] n modello; (person: for fashion) indossatore/trice; (: for artist) modello/a // vt modellare // vi fare l'indossatore (or l'indossatrice) // a (railway: toy) modello inv in scala; (child, factory) modello inv; **to ~ clothes** presentare degli abiti.

moderate a, n ['mɔdərət] moderato(a) // vb ['mɔdəreɪt] vi moderarsi, placarsi // vt moderare; **moderation** [-'reɪʃən] n moderazione f, misura.

modern ['mɔdən] a moderno(a); ~**ize** vt modernizzare.

modest ['mɔdɪst] a modesto(a); ~**y** n modestia.

modicum ['mɔdɪkəm] n: **a ~ of** un minimo di.

modification [mɔdɪfɪ'keɪʃən] n modificazione f.

modify ['mɔdɪfaɪ] vt modificare.

module ['mɔdjuːl] n modulo.

mohair ['məuhɛə*] n mohair m.

moist [mɔɪst] a umido(a); ~**en** ['mɔɪsn] vt inumidire; ~**ure** ['mɔɪstʃə*] n umidità; (on glass) goccioline fpl di vapore; ~**urizer** ['mɔɪstʃəraɪzə*] n idratante f.

molar ['məulə*] n molare m.

molasses [məu'læsɪz] n molassa.

mold [məuld] n, vt (US) = **mould**.

mole [məul] n (animal) talpa; (spot) neo.

molecule ['mɔlɪkjuːl] n molecola.

molest [məu'lɛst] vt molestare.

mollusc ['mɔləsk] n mollusco.

mollycoddle ['mɔlɪkɔdl] vt coccolare, vezzeggiare.

molt [məult] vi (US) = moult.

molten ['məultən] a fuso(a).

moment ['məumənt] n momento, istante m; importanza; ~ary a momentaneo(a), passeggero(a); ~ous [-'mentəs] a di grande importanza.

momentum [məu'mentəm] n velocità acquista, slancio; (PHYSICS) momento; to gather ~ aumentare di velocità.

monarch ['mɒnək] n monarca m; ~ist n monarchico/a; ~y n monarchia.

monastery ['mɒnəstəri] n monastero.

monastic [mə'næstik] a monastico(a).

Monday ['mʌndi] n lunedì m inv.

monetary ['mʌnitəri] a monetario(a).

money ['mʌni] n denaro, soldi mpl; ~lender n prestatore m di denaro; ~ order n vaglia m inv.

mongol ['mɒŋgəl] a,n (MED) mongoloide (m/f).

mongrel ['mʌŋgrəl] n (dog) cane m bastardo.

monitor ['mɒnitə*] n (SCOL) capoclasse m/f; (also: television ~) monitor m inv // vt controllare.

monk [mʌŋk] n monaco.

monkey ['mʌŋki] n scimmia; ~ nut n nocciolina americana; ~ wrench n chiave f a rullino.

mono... ['mɒnəu] prefix: ~chrome a monocromo(a).

monocle ['mɒnəkl] n monocolo.

monogram ['mɒnəgræm] n monogramma m.

monologue ['mɒnəlɒg] n monologo.

monopolize [mə'nɒpəlaiz] vt monopolizzare.

monopoly [mə'nɒpəli] n monopolio.

monosyllabic ['mɒnəusi'læbik] a monosillabico(a); (person) che parla a monosillabi.

monotone ['mɒnətəun] n pronunzia (or voce f) monotona.

monotonous [mə'nɒtənəs] a monotono(a).

monotony [mə'nɒtəni] n monotonia.

monsoon [mɒn'su:n] n monsone m.

monster ['mɒnstə*] n mostro.

monstrosity [mɒns'trɒsiti] n mostruosità f inv.

monstrous ['mɒnstrəs] a mostruoso(a).

montage [mɒn'tɑ:ʒ] n montaggio.

month [mʌnθ] n mese m; ~ly a mensile // ad al mese; ogni mese // n (magazine) rivista mensile.

monument ['mɒnjumənt] n monumento; ~al [-'mentl] a monumentale; (fig) colossale.

moo [mu:] vi muggire, mugghiare.

mood [mu:d] n umore m; to be in a good/bad ~ essere di buon/cattivo umore; to be in the ~ for essere disposto(a), a aver voglia di; ~y a (variable) capriccioso(a), lunatico(a); (sullen) imbronciato(a).

moon [mu:n] n luna; ~beam n raggio di luna; ~light n chiaro di luna; ~lit a illuminato(a) dalla luna.

moor [muə*] n brughiera // vt (ship) ormeggiare // vi ormeggiarsi.

moorings ['muəriŋz] npl (chains) ormeggi mpl; (place) ormeggio.

moorland ['muələnd] n brughiera.

moose [mu:s] n, pl inv alce m.

moot [mu:t] vt sollevare // a: ~ point punto discutibile.

mop [mɒp] n lavapavimenti m inv // vt lavare con lo straccio; to ~ one's brow asciugarsi la fronte; to ~ up vt asciugare con uno straccio; ~ of hair n zazzera.

mope [məup] vi fare il broncio.

moped ['məuped] n (Brit) ciclomotore m.

moral ['mɒrl] a morale // n morale f; ~s npl moralità.

morale [mɒ'rɑ:l] n morale m.

morality [mə'ræliti] n moralità.

morass [mə'ræs] n palude f, pantano.

morbid ['mɔ:bid] a morboso(a).

more [mɔ:*] det più // ad più, di più; ~ people più gente; I want ~ ne voglio ancora or di più; ~ dangerous than più pericoloso di (or che); ~ or less più o meno; ~ than ever più che mai.

moreover [mɔ:'rəuvə*] ad inoltre, di più.

morgue [mɔ:g] n obitorio.

morning ['mɔ:niŋ] n mattina, mattino; mattinata; in the ~ la mattina; 7 o'clock in the ~ le 7 di or della mattina.

Morocco [mə'rɒkəu] n Marocco.

moron ['mɔ:rɒn] n deficiente m/f; ~ic [mə'rɒnik] a deficiente.

morose [mə'rəus] a cupo(a), tetro(a).

morphine ['mɔ:fi:n] n morfina.

Morse [mɔ:s] n (also: ~ code) alfabeto Morse.

morsel ['mɔ:sl] n boccone m.

mortal ['mɔ:tl] a, n mortale (m); ~ity [-'tæliti] n mortalità.

mortar ['mɔ:tə*] n (CONSTR) malta; (dish) mortaio.

mortgage ['mɔ:gidʒ] n ipoteca; (loan) prestito ipotecario // vt ipotecare.

mortified ['mɔ:tifaid] a umiliato(a).

mortuary ['mɔ:tjuəri] n camera mortuaria; obitorio.

mosaic [məu'zeiik] n mosaico.

Moscow ['mɒskəu] n Mosca.

Moslem ['mɒzləm] a, n = Muslim.

mosque [mɒsk] n moschea.

mosquito, ~es [mɒs'ki:təu] n zanzara; ~ net n zanzariera.

moss [mɒs] n muschio; ~y a muscoso(a).

most [məust] det la maggior parte di; il più di // pronoun la maggior parte // ad (+ adjective) il(la) più; (work, sleep etc) di più; (very) molto, estremamente; the ~ (also: + adjective) il(la) più; ~ fish la maggior parte dei pesci; ~ of la maggior parte di; at the (very) ~ al massimo; to make the ~ of trarre il massimo vantaggio da; ~ly ad per lo più.

MOT n (abbr of Ministry of Transport): the ~ (test) revisione annuale obbligatoria degli autoveicoli.

motel [məu'tel] n motel m inv.

moth [mɔθ] *n* farfalla notturna; tarma; ~**ball** *n* palla di canfora; ~**eaten** *a* tarmato(a).

mother ['mʌðə*] *n* madre *f* // *vt* (*care for*) fare da madre a; ~**hood** *n* maternità; ~**in-law** *n* suocera; ~**ly** *a* materno(a); ~**of-pearl** *n* madreperla; ~**to-be** *n* futura mamma; ~ **tongue** *n* madrelingua.

mothproof ['mɔθpru:f] *a* antitarmico(a).

motif [məu'ti:f] *n* motivo.

motion ['məuʃən] *n* movimento, moto; (*gesture*) gesto; (*at meeting*) mozione *f* // *vt*, *vi*: to ~ (to) **sb** to do fare cenno a qd di fare; ~**less** *a* immobile; ~ **picture** *n* film *m* inv.

motivated ['məutiveitid] *a* motivato(a).

motivation [məuti'veiʃən] *n* motivazione *f*.

motive ['məutiv] *n* motivo // *a* motore(trice).

motley ['mɔtli] *a* eterogeneo(a), molto vario(a).

motor ['məutə*] *n* motore *m*; (*col*: *vehicle*) macchina *f* // *a* motore(trice); ~**bike** *n* moto *f* inv; ~**boat** *n* motoscafo; ~**car** *n* automobile *f*; ~**cycle** *n* motocicletta; ~**cyclist** *n* motociclista *m/f*; ~**ing** *n* turismo automobilistico // *a*: ~**ing holiday** *n* vacanza in macchina; ~**ist** *n* automobilista *m/f*; ~ **racing** *n* corse *fpl* automobilistiche; ~ **scooter** *n* motorscooter *m* inv; ~ **vehicle** *n* autoveicolo; ~**way** *n* (*Brit*) autostrada.

mottled ['mɔtld] *a* chiazzato(a), marezzato(a).

motto, ~**es** ['mɔtəu] *n* motto.

mould [məuld] *n* forma, stampo; (*mildew*) muffa // *vt* formare; (*fig*) foggiare; ~**er** *vi* (*decay*) ammuffire; ~**y** *a* ammuffito(a).

moult [məult] *vi* far la muta.

mound [maund] *n* rialzo, collinetta.

mount [maunt] *n* monte *m*, montagna; (*horse*) cavalcatura; (*for jewel etc*) montatura // *vt* montare; (*horse*) montare a // *vi* salire, montare; (*also*: ~ **up**) aumentare.

mountain ['mauntin] *n* montagna // *cpd* di montagna; ~**eer** [-'niə*] *n* alpinista *m/f*; ~**eering** [-'niəriŋ] *n* alpinismo; to go ~**eering** fare dell'alpinismo; ~**ous** *a* montagnoso(a); ~**side** *n* fianco della montagna.

mourn [mɔ:n] *vt* piangere, lamentare // *vi*: to ~ (for) piangere, lamentarsi (di); ~**er** *n* parente *m/f* or amico/a del defunto; persona venuta a rendere omaggio al defunto; ~**ful** *a* triste, lugubre; ~**ing** *n* lutto // *cpd* (*dress*) da lutto; **in ~ing** in lutto.

mouse, *pl* **mice** [maus, mais] *n* topo; ~**trap** *n* trappola per i topi.

moustache [məs'ta:ʃ] *n* baffi *mpl*.

mousy ['mausi] *a* (*person*) timido(a); (*hair*) marrone indefinito(a).

mouth, ~**s** [mauθ, -ðz] *n* bocca; (*of river*) bocca, foce *f*; (*of bottle*) orifizio; ~**ful** *n* boccata; ~ **organ** *n* armonica; ~**watering** *a* che fa venire l'acquolina in bocca.

movable ['mu:vəbl] *a* mobile.

move [mu:v] *n* (*movement*) movimento; (*in game*) mossa; (: *turn to play*) turno; (*change of house*) trasloco // *vt* muovere, spostare; (*emotionally*) commuovere; (*POL*: *resolution etc*) proporre // *vi* (*gen*) muoversi, spostarsi; (*traffic*) circolare; (*also*: ~ **house**) cambiar casa, traslocare; to ~ **towards** andare verso; to ~ **sb** to do **sth** indurre or spingere qd a fare qc; to get **a** ~ **on** affrettarsi, sbrigarsi; to ~ **about** *vi* (*fidget*) agitarsi; (*travel*) viaggiare; to ~ **along** *vi* muoversi avanti; to ~ **away** *vi* allontanarsi, andarsene; to ~ **back** *vi* indietreggiare; (*return*) ritornare; to ~ **forward** *vi* avanzare // *vt* avanzare, spostare in avanti; (*people*) far avanzare; to ~ **in** *vi* (*to a house*) entrare (in una nuova casa); to ~ **on** *vi* riprendere la strada // *vt* (*onlookers*) far circolare; to ~ **out** *vi* (*of house*) sgombrare; to ~ **up** *vi* avanzare.

movement ['mu:vmənt] *n* (*gen*) movimento; (*gesture*) gesto; (*of stars*, *water*, *physical*) moto.

movie ['mu:vi] *n* film *m* inv; **the** ~**s** il cinema; ~ **camera** *n* cinepresa.

moving ['mu:viŋ] *a* mobile; commovente.

mow, *pt* **mowed**, *pp* **mowed** or **mown** [məu, -n] *vt* falciare; (*lawn*) mietere; to ~ **down** *vt* falciare; ~**er** *n* falciatore/trice.

M.P. *n abbr see* **member**.

m.p.g. *abbr* = *miles per gallon* (*30 m.p.g.* = *9.5 l. per 100 km*).

m.p.h. *abbr* = *miles per hour* (*60 m.p.h.* = *96 km/h*).

Mr ['mistə*] *n*: ~ X Signor X, Sig. X.

Mrs ['misiz] *n*: ~ X Signora X, Sig.ra X.

Ms [miz] *n* (= *Miss or Mrs*): ~ X ≈ Signora X, Sig.ra X.

much [mʌtʃ] *det* molto(a) // *ad*, *n* or *pronoun* molto; ~ **milk** molto latte; **how** ~ **is it?** quanto costa?

muck [mʌk] *n* (*mud*) fango; (*dirt*) sporcizia; to ~ **about** *vi* (*col*) fare lo stupido; (*waste time*) gingillarsi; ~**y** *a* (*dirty*) sporco(a), lordo(a).

mucus ['mju:kəs] *n* muco.

mud [mʌd] *n* fango.

muddle ['mʌdl] *n* confusione *f*, disordine *m*; pasticcio // *vt* (*also*: ~ **up**) impasticciare; **to be in a** ~ (*person*) non riuscire a raccapezzarsi; **to get in a** ~ (*while explaining etc*) imbrogliarsi; to ~ **through** *vi* cavarsela alla meno peggio.

mud: ~**dy** *a* fangoso(a); ~**guard** *n* parafango; ~**slinging** *n* (*fig*) infangamento.

muff [mʌf] *n* manicotto.

muffin ['mʌfin] *n* specie di pasticcino soffice da tè.

muffle ['mʌfl] *vt* (*sound*) smorzare, attutire; (*against cold*) imbacuccare; ~**d** *a* smorzato(a), attutito(a).

mufti ['mʌfti] *n*: **in** ~ in borghese.

mug [mʌg] *n* (*cup*) tazzone *m*; (: *for beer*) boccale *m*; (*col*: *face*) muso; (: *fool*) scemo/a // vt (assault) assalire; ~ging n assalto.

muggy ['mʌgɪ] a afoso(a).

mule [mju:l] n mulo.

mull [mʌl]: to ~ over vt rimuginare.

mulled [mʌld] a: ~ wine vino caldo.

multi... ['mʌltɪ] prefix multi...; ~coloured a multicolore, variopinto(a).

multiple ['mʌltɪpl] a multiplo(a); molteplice // n multiplo; ~ sclerosis n sclerosi f a placche.

multiplication [ˌmʌltɪplɪ'keɪʃən] n moltiplicazione f.

multiply ['mʌltɪplaɪ] vt moltiplicare // vi moltiplicarsi.

multitude ['mʌltɪtju:d] n moltitudine f.

mum [mʌm] n mamma // a: to keep ~ non aprire bocca; ~'s the word! acqua in bocca!

mumble ['mʌmbl] vt, vi borbottare.

mummy ['mʌmɪ] n (mother) mamma; (embalmed) mummia.

mumps [mʌmps] n orecchioni mpl.

munch [mʌntʃ] vt, vi sgranocchiare.

mundane [mʌn'deɪn] a terra a terra inv.

municipal [mju:'nɪsɪpl] a municipale; ~ity [-'pælɪtɪ] n municipio.

munitions [mju:'nɪʃənz] npl munizioni fpl.

mural ['mjuərɪl] n dipinto murale.

murder ['mɔ:də*] n assassinio, omicidio // vt assassinare; ~er n omicida m, assassino; ~ous a micidiale.

murk [mɔ:k] n oscurità, buio; ~y a tenebroso(a), buio(a).

murmur ['mɔ:mə*] n mormorio // vt, vi mormorare.

muscle ['mʌsl] n muscolo; to ~ in vi immischiarsi.

muscular ['mʌskjulə*] a muscolare; (person, arm) muscoloso(a).

muse [mju:z] vi meditare, sognare // n musa.

museum [mju:'zɪəm] n museo.

mushroom ['mʌʃrum] n fungo // vi (fig) svilupparsi rapidamente.

music ['mju:zɪk] n musica; ~al a musicale // n (show) commedia musicale; ~al box n scatola armonica; ~al instrument n strumento musicale; ~ hall n teatro di varietà; ~ian [-'zɪʃən] n musicista m/f.

musket ['mʌskɪt] n moschetto.

Muslim ['mʌzlɪm] a, n musulmano(a).

muslin ['mʌzlɪn] n mussolina.

mussel ['mʌsl] n cozza.

must [mʌst] auxiliary vb (obligation): I ~ do it devo farlo; (probability): he ~ be there by now dovrebbe essere arrivato ormai; I ~ have made a mistake devo essermi sbagliato // n cosa da non mancare; cosa d'obbligo.

mustard ['mʌstəd] n senape f, mostarda.

muster ['mʌstə*] vt radunare.

mustn't ['mʌsnt] = must not.

musty ['mʌstɪ] a che sa di muffa or di rinchiuso.

mute [mju:t] a, n muto(a).

mutilate ['mju:tɪleɪt] vt mutilare;

mutilation [-'leɪʃən] n mutilazione f.

mutinous ['mju:tɪnəs] a (troops) ammutinato(a); (attitude) ribelle.

mutiny ['mju:tɪnɪ] n ammutinamento // vi ammutinarsi.

mutter ['mʌtə*] vt, vi borbottare, brontolare.

mutton ['mʌtn] n carne f di montone.

mutual ['mju:tʃuəl] a mutuo(a), reciproco(a).

muzzle ['mʌzl] n muso; (protective device) museruola; (of gun) bocca // vt mettere la museruola a.

my [maɪ] a il(la) mio(a), pl i(le) miei(mie).

myself [maɪ'self] pronoun (reflexive) mi; (emphatic) io stesso(a); (after prep) me.

mysterious [mɪs'tɪərɪəs] a misterioso(a).

mystery ['mɪstərɪ] n mistero; ~ story n racconto del mistero.

mystic ['mɪstɪk] n mistico // a (mysterious) esoterico(a); ~al a mistico(a).

mystify ['mɪstɪfaɪ] vt mistificare; (puzzle) confondere.

mystique [mɪs'ti:k] n fascino.

myth [mɪθ] n mito; ~ology [mɪ'θɔlədʒɪ] n mitologia.

N

nab [næb] vt (col) beccare, acchiappare.

nag [næg] n (pej: horse) ronzino; (: person) brontolone/a // vt tormentare // vi brontolare in continuazione; ~ging a (doubt, pain) persistente.

nail [neɪl] n (human) unghia; (metal) chiodo // vt inchiodare; to ~ sb down to a date/price costringere qd a un appuntamento/ad accettare un prezzo; ~brush n spazzolino da or per unghie; ~file n lima da or per unghie; ~ polish n smalto da or per unghie; ~ scissors npl forbici fpl da or per unghie; ~ varnish n = ~ polish.

naïve [naɪ'i:v] a ingenuo(a).

naked ['neɪkɪd] a nudo(a).

name [neɪm] n nome m; (reputation) nome, reputazione f // vt (baby etc) chiamare; (plant, illness) nominare; (person, object) identificare; (price, date) fissare; in the ~ of in nome di; ~ dropping n menzionare qd o qc per fare bella figura; ~less a senza nome; ~ly ad cioè; ~sake n omonimo.

nanny ['nænɪ] n bambinaia.

nap [næp] n (sleep) pisolino; (of cloth) peluria; to have a ~ schiacciare un pisolino; to be caught ~ping essere preso alla sprovvista.

napalm ['neɪpa:m] n napalm m.

nape [neɪp] n: ~ of the neck nuca.

napkin ['næpkɪn] n tovagliolo; (Brit: for baby) pannolino.

nappy ['næpɪ] n pannolino.

narcotic [na:'kɔtɪk] n narcotico.

nark [na:k] vt (col) scocciare.

narrate [nə'reɪt] vt raccontare, narrare.

narrative ['nærǝtɪv] n narrativa // a narrativo(a).

narrow ['nærǝu] a stretto(a); (fig): **to take a ~ view of** avere una visione limitata di // vi restringersi; **to have a ~ escape** farcela per un pelo; **to ~ sth down to** ridurre qc a; **~ly** ad per un pelo; (time) per poco; **~-minded** a meschino(a).

nasal ['neɪzl] a nasale.

nasty ['nɑːstɪ] a (person, remark) cattivo(a); (smell, wound, situation) brutto(a).

nation ['neɪʃǝn] n nazione f.

national ['næʃǝnl] a nazionale // n cittadino/a; **~ dress** n costume m nazionale; **~ism** n nazionalismo; **~ist** a,n nazionalista (m/f); **~ity** [-'nælɪtɪ] n nazionalità f inv; **~ization** [-aɪ'zeɪʃǝn] n nazionalizzazione f; **~ize** vt nazionalizzare; **~ly** ad a livello nazionale.

nation-wide ['neɪʃǝnwaɪd] a diffuso(a) in tutto il paese // ad in tutto il paese.

native ['neɪtɪv] n abitante m/f del paese; (in colonies) indigeno/a // a indigeno(a); (country) natio(a); (ability) innato(a); **a ~ of Russia** un nativo della Russia; **a ~ speaker of French** una persona di madrelingua francese; **~ language** madrelingua.

natter ['nætǝ*] vi chiacchierare.

natural ['nætʃrǝl] a naturale; (ability) innato(a); (manner) semplice; **~ gas** n gas m metano; **~ist** n naturalista m/f; **~ize** vt naturalizzare; **~ly** ad naturalmente; (by nature: gifted) di natura.

nature ['neɪtʃǝ*] n natura; (character) carattere m; **by ~** di natura.

naught [nɔːt] n zero.

naughty ['nɔːtɪ] a (child) birichino(a), cattivello(a); (story, film) spinto(a).

nausea ['nɔːsɪǝ] n (MED) nausea; (fig: disgust) schifo; **~te** ['nɔːsɪeɪt] vt nauseare; far schifo a.

nautical ['nɔːtɪkl] a nautico(a).

naval ['neɪvl] a navale; **~ officer** n ufficiale m di marina.

nave [neɪv] n navata centrale.

navel ['neɪvl] n ombelico.

navigable ['nævɪgǝbl] a navigabile.

navigate ['nævɪgeɪt] vt percorrere navigando // vi navigare; **navigation** [-'geɪʃǝn] n navigazione f; **navigator** n (NAUT, AVIAT) ufficiale m di rotta; (explorer) navigatore m; (AUT) copilota m/f.

navvy ['nævɪ] n manovale m.

navy ['neɪvɪ] n marina; **~(-blue)** a blu scuro inv.

near [nɪǝ*] a vicino(a); (relation) prossimo(a) // ad vicino // prep (also: **~ to**) vicino a, presso; (time) verso // vi avvicinarsi a; **to come ~** vi avvicinarsi; **~by** [nɪǝ'baɪ] a vicino(a) // ad vicino; **N~ East** n Medio Oriente m; **~ly** ad quasi; **~ miss** n: **that was a ~ miss** c'è mancato poco; **~ness** n vicinanza; **~side** n (AUT: right-hand drive) lato sinistro; **~-sighted** a miope.

neat [niːt] a (person, room) ordinato(a); (work) pulito(a); (solution, plan) ben indovinato(a), azzeccato(a); (spirits) liscio(a); **~ly** ad con ordine; (skilfully) abilmente.

nebulous ['nɛbjuləs] a nebuloso(a); (fig) vago(a).

necessarily ['nɛsɪsrɪlɪ] ad necessariamente.

necessary ['nɛsɪsrɪ] a necessario(a).

necessitate [nɪ'sɛsɪteɪt] vt rendere necessario(a).

necessity [nɪ'sɛsɪtɪ] n necessità f inv.

neck [nɛk] n collo; (of garment) colletto; **~ and ~** testa a testa.

necklace ['nɛklɪs] n collana.

neckline ['nɛklaɪn] n scollatura.

née [neɪ] a: **~ Scott** nata Scott.

need [niːd] n bisogno // vt aver bisogno di.

needle ['niːdl] n ago // vt punzecchiare.

needless ['niːdlɪs] a inutile.

needlework ['niːdlwɜːk] n cucito.

needy ['niːdɪ] a bisognoso(a).

negation [nɪ'geɪʃǝn] n negazione f.

negative ['nɛgǝtɪv] n negativo // a negativo(a).

neglect [nɪ'glɛkt] vt trascurare // n (of person, duty) negligenza; (state of) ~ stato di abbandono.

negligee ['nɛglɪʒeɪ] n négligé m inv.

negligence ['nɛglɪdʒǝns] n negligenza.

negligent ['nɛglɪdʒǝnt] a negligente; **~ly** ad con negligenza.

negligible ['nɛglɪdʒɪbl] a insignificante, trascurabile.

negotiable [nɪ'gǝuʃɪǝbl] a negoziabile; (cheque) trasferibile; (road) transitabile.

negotiate [nɪ'gǝuʃɪeɪt] vi negoziare // vt (COMM) negoziare; (obstacle) superare; **negotiation** [-'eɪʃǝn] n negoziato, trattativa; **negotiator** n negoziatore/trice.

Negress ['niːgrɪs] n negra.

Negro ['niːgrǝu] a, n (pl: **~es**) negro(a).

neighbour ['neɪbǝ*] n vicino/a; **~hood** n vicinato; **~ing** a vicino(a); **~ly** a: **he is a ~ly person** è un buon vicino.

neither ['naɪðǝ*] a, pronoun né l'uno(a) né l'altro(a), nessuno(a) dei(delle) due // cj neanche, nemmeno, neppure // ad: **~ good nor bad né** buono né cattivo; **I didn't move and ~ did Claude** io non mi mossi e nemmeno Claude.

neon ['niːɔn] n neon m; **~ light** n luce f al neon; **~ sign** n insegna al neon.

nephew ['nɛvjuː] n nipote m.

nerve [nɜːv] n nervo; (fig) coraggio; (impudence) faccia tosta; **a fit of ~s** una crisi di nervi; **~-racking** a che spezza i nervi.

nervous ['nɜːvǝs] a nervoso(a); **~ breakdown** n esaurimento nervoso; **~ness** n nervosismo.

nest [nɛst] n nido.

nestle ['nɛsl] vi accoccolarsi.

net [nɛt] n rete f // a netto(a); **~ball** n specie di pallacanestro.

Netherlands ['neðələndz] npl: the ~ i Paesi Bassi.

nett [net] a = **net**.

netting ['netɪŋ] n (for fence etc) reticolato.

nettle ['netl] n ortica.

network ['netwə:k] n rete f.

neurosis, pl **neuroses** [njuə'rəusɪs, -siːz] n nevrosi f inv.

neurotic [njuə'rɔtɪk] a, n nevrotico(a).

neuter ['njuːtə*] a neutro(a) // n neutro // vt (cat etc) castrare.

neutral ['njuːtrəl] a neutro(a); (person, nation) neutrale // n (AUT): **in** ~ in folle; ~**ity** [-'trælɪtɪ] n neutralità.

never ['nevə*] ad (non...) mai; ~ **again** mai più; **I'll** ~ **go there again** non ci vado più; ~**-ending** a interminabile; ~**theless** [nevəðə'les] ad tuttavia, ciò nonostante, ciò nondimeno.

new [njuː] a nuovo(a); (brand new) nuovo(a) di zecca; ~**born** a neonato(a); ~**comer** ['njuːkʌmə*] n nuovo(a) venuto(a); ~**ly** ad di recente; ~ **moon** n luna nuova.

news [njuːz] n notizie fpl; (RADIO) giornale m radio; (TV) telegiornale m; **a piece of** ~ una notizia; ~ **agency** n agenzia di stampa; ~**agent** n giornalaio; ~ **flash** n notizia f lampo inv; ~**paper** n giornale m; ~ **stand** n edicola.

New Year ['njuː'jɪə*] n Anno Nuovo; ~**'s Day** n il Capodanno; ~**'s Eve** n la vigilia di Capodanno.

New Zealand [njuː'ziːlənd] n Nuova Zelanda.

next [nekst] a prossimo(a) // ad accanto; (in time) dopo; **when do we meet** ~? quando ci rincontriamo?; ~ **door** ad accanto; ~**-of-kin** n parente m/f prossimo(a); ~ **time** ad la prossima volta; ~ **to** prep accanto a; ~ **to nothing** quasi niente.

N.H.S. n abbr of National Health Service.

nib [nɪb] n (of pen) pennino.

nibble ['nɪbl] vt mordicchiare.

nice [naɪs] a (holiday, trip) piacevole; (flat, picture) bello(a); (person) simpatico(a), gentile; (distinction, point) sottile; ~**-looking** a bello(a); ~**ly** ad bene.

niceties ['naɪsɪtɪz] npl finezze fpl.

nick [nɪk] n tacca // vt (col) rubare; **in the** ~ **of time** appena in tempo.

nickel ['nɪkl] n nichel m; (US) moneta da cinque centesimi di dollaro.

nickname ['nɪkneɪm] n soprannome m // vt soprannominare.

nicotine ['nɪkətiːn] n nicotina.

niece [niːs] n nipote f.

Nigeria [naɪ'dʒɪərɪə] n Nigeria.

niggling ['nɪglɪŋ] a pignolo(a).

night [naɪt] n notte f; (evening) sera; **at** ~ la sera; **by** ~ di notte; ~**cap** n bicchierino prima di andare a letto; ~ **club** n locale m notturno; ~**dress** n camicia da notte; ~**fall** n crepuscolo; ~**ie** ['naɪtɪ] n camicia da notte.

nightingale ['naɪtɪŋgeɪl] n usignolo.

night life ['naɪtlaɪf] n vita notturna.

nightly ['naɪtlɪ] a di ogni notte or sera; (by night) notturno(a) // ad ogni notte or sera.

nightmare ['naɪtmeə*] n incubo.

night school ['naɪtskuːl] n scuola serale.

night-time ['naɪttaɪm] n notte f.

night watchman ['naɪt'wɔtʃmən] n guardiano notturno.

nil [nɪl] n nulla m; (SPORT) zero.

nimble ['nɪmbl] a agile.

nine [naɪn] num nove; ~**teen** num diciannove; ~**ty** num novanta.

ninth [naɪnθ] a nono(a).

nip [nɪp] vt pizzicare.

nipple ['nɪpl] n (ANAT) capezzolo.

nippy ['nɪpɪ] a (weather) pungente; (car, person) svelto(a).

nitrogen ['naɪtrədʒən] n azoto.

no [nəu] det nessuno(a), non; **I have** ~ **money** non ho soldi; **there is** ~ **reason to believe...** non c'è nessuna ragione per credere...; **I have** ~ **books** non ho libri // ad non; **I have** ~ **more wine** non ho più vino // excl n no (m inv); ~ **entry** vietata l'entrata.

nobility [nəu'bɪlɪtɪ] n nobiltà.

noble ['nəubl] a, n nobile (m).

nobody ['nəubədɪ] pronoun nessuno.

nod [nɔd] vi accennare col capo, fare un cenno; (sleep) sonnecchiare // n cenno; **to** ~ **off** vi assopirsi.

noise [nɔɪz] n rumore m; (din, racket) chiasso; **noisy** a (street, car) rumoroso(a); (person) chiassoso(a).

nomad ['nəumæd] n nomade m/f.

no man's land ['nəumænzlænd] n terra di nessuno.

nominal ['nɔmɪnl] a nominale.

nominate ['nɔmɪneɪt] vt (propose) proporre come candidato; (elect) nominare.

nomination [nɔmɪ'neɪʃən] n nomina, candidatura.

nominee [nɔmɪ'niː] n persona nominata; candidato.

non... [nɔn] prefix non...; ~**-alcoholic** a analcolico(a).

nonchalant ['nɔnʃələnt] a incurante, indifferente.

non-committal ['nɔnkə'mɪtl] a evasivo(a).

nondescript ['nɔndɪskrɪpt] a qualunque inv.

none [nʌn] pronoun (not one thing) niente; (not one person) nessuno(a).

nonentity [nɔ'nentɪtɪ] n persona insignificante.

non: ~**-fiction** n saggistica; ~**-flammable** a ininfiammabile.

nonplussed [nɔn'plʌst] a sconcertato(a).

nonsense ['nɔnsəns] n sciocchezze fpl.

non: ~**-smoker** n non fumatore/trice; ~**-stick** a antiaderente, antiadesivo(a); ~**-stop** a continuo(a); (train, bus) direttissimo(a) // ad senza sosta.

noodles ['nuːdlz] npl taglierini mpl.

nook [nuk] n: ~**s and crannies** angoli mpl.

noon [nu:n] n mezzogiorno.

no one ['nəʊwʌn] pronoun = **nobody**.

nor [nɔ:°] cj = neither // ad see **neither**.

norm [nɔ:m] n norma.

normal ['nɔ:ml] a normale; **~ly** ad normalmente.

north [nɔ:θ] n nord m, settentrione m // a nord inv, del nord, settentrionale // ad verso nord; **N~ America** n America del Nord; **~-east** n nord-est m; **~ern** ['nɔ:ðən] a del nord, settentrionale; **N~ern Ireland** n Irlanda del Nord; **N~ Pole** n Polo Nord; **N~ Sea** n Mare m del Nord; **~ward(s)** ['nɔ:θwəd(z)] ad verso nord; **~-west** n nord-ovest m.

Norway ['nɔ:wei] n Norvegia.

Norwegian [nɔ:'wi:dʒən] a norvegese // n norvegese m/f; (LING) norvegese m.

nose [nəuz] n naso; (of animal) muso; **~dive** n picchiata; **~y** a curioso(a).

nostalgia [nɔs'tældʒiə] n nostalgia; **nostalgic** a nostalgico(a).

nostril ['nɔstril] n narice f; (of horse) frogia.

nosy ['nəuzi] a = **nosey**.

not [nɔt] ad non; **~ at all** niente affatto; **you must ~ or mustn't do this** non deve fare questo; **he isn't...** egli non è... .

notable ['nəutəbl] a notevole.

notably ['nəutəbli] ad notevolmente.

notch [nɔtʃ] n tacca.

note [nəut] n nota; (letter, banknote) biglietto // vt prendere nota di; **to take ~s** prendere appunti; **~book** n taccuino; **~d** ['nəutid] a celebre; **~paper** n carta da lettere.

nothing ['nʌθiŋ] n nulla m, niente m; **~ new** niente di nuovo; **for ~** (free) per niente.

notice ['nəutis] n avviso; (of leaving) preavviso // vt notare, accorgersi di; **to take ~ of** fare attenzione a; **to bring sth to sb's ~** far notare qc a qd; **~able** a evidente; **~ board** n (Brit) tabellone m per affissi.

notify ['nəutifai] vt: **to ~ sth to sb** far sapere qc a qd; **to ~ sb of sth** avvisare qd di qc.

notion ['nəuʃən] n idea; (concept) nozione f.

notorious [nəu'tɔ:riəs] a famigerato(a).

notwithstanding [nɔtwiθ'stændiŋ] ad nondimeno // prep nonostante, malgrado.

nougat ['nu:gɑ:] n torrone m.

nought [nɔ:t] n zero.

noun [naun] n nome m, sostantivo.

nourish ['nʌriʃ] vt nutrire; **~ing** a nutriente; **~ment** n nutrimento.

novel ['nɔvl] n romanzo // a nuovo(a); **~ist** n romanziere/a; **~ty** n novità f inv.

November [nəu'vembə°] n novembre m.

novice ['nɔvis] n principiante m/f, (REL) novizio/a.

now [nau] ad ora, adesso; **~ and then, ~ and again** ogni tanto; **from ~ on** da ora in poi; **~adays** ['nauədeiz] ad oggidì.

nowhere ['nəuwɛə°] ad in nessun luogo, da nessuna parte.

nozzle ['nɔzl] n (of hose) boccaglio.

nuance ['nju:ɑ:ns] n sfumatura.

nuclear ['nju:kliə°] a nucleare.

nucleus, pl **nuclei** ['nju:kliəs, 'nju:kliai] n nucleo.

nude [nju:d] a nudo(a) // n (ART) nudo; **in the ~** tutto(a) nudo(a).

nudge [nʌdʒ] vt dare una gomitata a.

nudist ['nju:dist] n nudista m/f.

nudity ['nju:diti] n nudità.

nuisance ['nju:sns] n: **it's a ~** è una seccatura; **he's a ~** lui dà fastidio.

null [nʌl] a: **~ and void** nullo(a); **~ify** ['nʌlifai] vt annullare.

numb [nʌm] a intormentito(a).

number ['nʌmbə°] n numero // vt numerare; (include) contare; **a ~ of** un certo numero di; **the staff ~s 20** gli impiegati sono in 20; **~ plate** n targa.

numeral ['nju:mərəl] n numero, cifra.

numerical [nju:'merikl] a numerico(a).

numerous ['nju:mərəs] a numeroso(a).

nun [nʌn] n suora, monaca.

nurse [nɔ:s] n infermiere/a // vt (patient, cold) curare; (hope) nutrire; **~(maid)** n bambinaia.

nursery ['nɔ:səri] n (room) camera dei bambini; (institution) asilo; (for plants) vivaio; **~ rhyme** n filastrocca; **~ school** n scuola materna; **~ slope** n (SKI) pista per principianti.

nursing ['nɔ:siŋ] n (profession) professione f di infermiere (or di infermiera); **~ home** n casa di cura.

nut [nʌt] n (of metal) dado; (fruit) noce f; **he's ~s** (col) è matto; **~case** n (col) mattarello/a; **~crackers** npl schiaccianoci m inv; **~meg** ['nʌtmeg] n noce f moscata.

nutrition [nju:'triʃən] n nutrizione f.

nutritious [nju:'triʃəs] a nutriente.

nutshell ['nʌtʃel] n guscio di noce; **in a ~** in poche parole.

nylon ['nailən] n nailon m; **~s** npl calze fpl di nailon.

O

oaf [əuf] n zoticone m.

oak [əuk] n quercia.

O.A.P. abbr see **old**.

oar [ɔ:°] n remo.

oasis, pl **oases** [əu'eisis, əu'eisi:z] n oasi f inv.

oath [əuθ] n giuramento; (swear word) bestemmia; **on ~** sotto giuramento; giurato(a).

oatmeal ['əutmi:l] n farina d'avena.

oats [əuts] a avena.

obedience [ə'bi:diəns] n ubbidienza; **in ~ to** conformemente a.

obedient [ə'bi:diənt] a ubbidiente.

obelisk ['ɔbilisk] n obelisco.

obesity [əu'bi:siti] n obesità.

obey [ə'bei] vt ubbidire a; (instructions, regulations) osservare // vi ubbidire.

obituary [ə'bitjuəri] n necrologia.

object *n* ['ɔbdʒɪkt] oggetto; (*purpose*) scopo, intento; (*LING*) complemento oggetto // *vi* [əb'dʒɛkt]: **to ~ to** (*attitude*) disapprovare; (*proposal*) protestare contro, sollevare delle obiezioni contro; **I ~! mi oppongo!; he ~ed that ...** obiettò che ...; **~ion** [əb'dʒɛkʃən] *n* obiezione *f*; (*drawback*) inconveniente *m*; **~ionable** [əb'dʒɛkʃənəbl] *a* antipatico(a); (*smell*) sgradevole; (*language*) scostumato(a); **~ive** *n* obiettivo // *a* obiettivo(a); **~ivity** [ɔbdʒɪk'tɪvɪtɪ] *n* obiettività; **~or** *n* oppositore/trice.

obligation [ɔblɪ'geɪʃən] *n* obbligo, dovere *m*; (*debt*) obbligo (di riconoscenza).

obligatory [ə'blɪgətərɪ] *a* obbligatorio(a).

oblige [ə'blaɪdʒ] *vt* (*force*): **to ~ sb to do** costringere qd a fare; (*do a favour*) fare una cortesia a; **to be ~d to sb for sth** essere grato a qd per qc; **obliging** *a* servizievole, compiacente.

oblique [ə'bliːk] *a* obliquo(a); (*allusion*) indiretto(a).

obliterate [ə'blɪtəreɪt] *vt* cancellare.

oblivion [ə'blɪvɪən] *n* oblio.

oblivious [ə'blɪvɪəs] *a*: **~ of** incurante di; inconscio(a) di.

oblong ['ɔblɔŋ] *a* oblungo(a) // *n* rettangolo.

obnoxious [əb'nɔkʃəs] *a* odioso(a); (*smell*) disgustoso(a), ripugnante.

oboe ['əubəu] *n* oboe *m*.

obscene [əb'siːn] *a* osceno(a).

obscenity [əb'senɪtɪ] *n* oscenità *f inv*.

obscure [əb'skjuə*] *a* oscuro(a) // *vt* oscurare; (*hide: sun*) nascondere; **obscurity** *n* oscurità.

obsequious [əb'siːkwɪəs] *a* ossequioso(a).

observable [əb'zə:vəbl] *a* osservabile; (*appreciable*) notevole.

observance [əb'zə:vns] *n* osservanza.

observant [əb'zə:vnt] *a* attento(a).

observation [ɔbzə'veɪʃən] *n* osservazione *f*; (*by police etc*) sorveglianza.

observatory [əb'zə:vətrɪ] *n* osservatorio.

observe [əb'zə:v] *vt* osservare; (*remark*) fare osservare; **~r** *n* osservatore/trice.

obsess [əb'ses] *vt* ossessionare; **~ion** [əb-'seʃən] *n* ossessione *f*; **~ive** *a* ossessivo(a).

obsolescence [ɔbsə'lesns] *n* obsolescenza.

obsolete ['ɔbsəliːt] *a* obsoleto(a); (*word*) desueto(a).

obstacle ['ɔbstəkl] *n* ostacolo; **~ race** *n* corsa agli ostacoli.

obstetrics [ɔb'stetrɪks] *n* ostetrica.

obstinacy ['ɔbstɪnəsɪ] *n* ostinatezza.

obstinate ['ɔbstɪnɪt] *a* ostinato(a).

obstreperous [əb'strepərəs] *a* turbolento(a).

obstruct [əb'strʌkt] *vt* (*block*) ostruire, ostacolare; (*halt*) fermare; (*hinder*) impedire; **~ion** [əb'strʌkʃən] *n* ostruzione *f*; ostacolo; **~ive** *a* ostruttivo(a).

obtain [əb'teɪn] *vt* ottenere // *vi* essere in uso; **~able** *a* ottenibile.

obtrusive [əb'truːsɪv] *a* (*person*) importuno(a); (*smell*) invadente; (*building etc*) imponente e invadente.

obtuse [əb'tjuːs] *a* ottuso(a).

obviate ['ɔbvɪeɪt] *vt* ovviare a, evitare.

obvious ['ɔbvɪəs] *a* ovvio(a), evidente; **~ly** *ad* ovviamente; certo.

occasion [ə'keɪʒən] *n* occasione *f*; (*event*) avvenimento // *vt* cagionare; **~al** *a* occasionale; **I smoke an ~al cigarette** ogni tanto fumo una sigaretta.

occupation [ɔkju'peɪʃən] *n* occupazione *f*; (*job*) mestiere *m*, professione *f*; **~al hazard** *n* rischio del mestiere.

occupier ['ɔkjupaɪə*] *n* occupante *m/f*.

occupy ['ɔkjupaɪ] *vt* occupare; **to ~ o.s. by doing** occuparsi a fare.

occur [ə'kə:*] *vi* accadere; (*difficulty, opportunity*) capitare; (*phenomenon, error*) trovarsi; **to ~ to sb** venire in mente a qd; **~rence** *n* caso, fatto; presenza.

ocean ['əuʃən] *n* oceano; **~-going** *a* d'alto mare.

ochre ['əukə*] *n* ocra *inv*.

o'clock [ə'klɔk] *ad*: **it is 5 ~** sono le 5.

octagonal [ɔk'tægənl] *a* ottagonale.

octane ['ɔkteɪn] *n* ottano.

octave ['ɔktɪv] *n* ottava.

October [ɔk'təubə*] *n* ottobre *m*.

octopus ['ɔktəpəs] *n* polpo, piovra.

odd [ɔd] *a* (*strange*) strano(a), bizzarro(a); (*number*) dispari *inv*; (*left over*) in più; (*not of a set*) spaiato(a); **60~** 60 e oltre; **at ~ times** di tanto in tanto; **the ~ one out** l'eccezione *f*; **~ity** *n* bizzarria; (*person*) originale *m*; **~-job man** *n* tuttofare *m inv*; **~ jobs** *npl* lavori *mpl* occasionali; **~ly** *ad* stranamente; **~ments** *npl* (*COMM*) rimanenze *fpl*; **~s** *npl* (*in betting*) quota; **the ~s are against his coming** c'è poca probabilità che venga; **it makes no ~s** non importa; **at ~s in** contesa.

ode [əud] *n* ode *f*.

odious ['əudɪəs] *a* odioso(a), ripugnante.

odour ['əudə*] *n* odore *m*; **~less** *a* inodoro(a).

of [ɔv, əv] *prep* di; **a friend ~ ours** un nostro amico; **3 ~ them** went 3 di loro sono andati; **the 5th ~ July** il 5 luglio; **a boy ~ 10** un ragazzo di 10 anni.

off [ɔf] *a,ad* (*engine*) spento(a); (*tap*) chiuso(a); (*food: bad*) andato(a) a male; (*absent*) assente; (*cancelled*) sospeso(a) // *prep* da; a poca distanza da; **to be ~** (*to leave*) partire, andarsene; **to be ~ sick** essere assente per malattia; **a day ~** un giorno di vacanza; **to have an ~ day** non essere in forma; **he had his coat ~** si era tolto il cappotto; **10% ~** (*COMM*) con uno sconto di 10%; **5 km ~** (**the road**) a 5 km (dalla strada); **~ the coast** al largo della costa; **a house ~ the main road** una casa fuori dalla strada maestra; **I'm ~ meat** la carne non mi va più; non mangio più la carne; **on the ~ chance** a caso.

offal ['ɔfl] *n* (*CULIN*) frattaglie *fpl*.

offbeat ['ɔfbiːt] *a* eccentrico(a).

off-colour ['ɔf'kʌlə*] a (ill) malato(a), indisposto(a).

offence, offense (US) [ə'fɛns] n (LAW) contravvenzione f; (: more serious) reato; **to take ~ at** offendersi per.

offend [ə'fɛnd] vt (person) offendere; **~er** n delinquente m/f; (against regulations) contravventore/trice.

offensive [ə'fɛnsɪv] a offensivo(a); (smell etc) sgradevole, ripugnante // n (MIL) offensiva.

offer ['ɔfə*] n offerta, proposta // vt offrire; **'on ~'** (COMM) 'in offerta speciale'; **~ing** n offerta.

offhand [ɔf'hænd] a disinvolto(a), noncurante // ad all'improvviso.

office ['ɔfɪs] n (place) ufficio; (position) carica; **to take ~** entrare in carica; **~ block** n complesso di uffici; **~ boy** n garzone m; **~r** n (MIL etc) ufficiale m; (of organization) funzionario; (also: **police ~r**) agente m di polizia; **~ worker** n impiegato/a d'ufficio.

official [ə'fɪʃl] a (authorized) ufficiale // n ufficiale m; (civil servant) impiegato/a statale; funzionario; **~ly** ad ufficialmente.

officious [ə'fɪʃəs] a invadente.

offing ['ɔfɪŋ] n: **in the ~** (fig) in vista.

off: **~-licence** n (Brit: shop) spaccio di bevande alcoliche; **~-peak** a (ticket etc) a tariffa ridotta; (time) non di punta; **~ season** a, ad fuori stagione.

offset ['ɔfsɛt] vt irg (counteract) controbilanciare, compensare.

offshore [ɔf'ʃɔ:*] a (breeze) di terra; (island) vicino alla costa; (fishing) costiero(a).

offside [ɔf'saɪd] a (SPORT) fuori gioco // a (AUT: with right-hand drive) lato destro.

offspring ['ɔfsprɪŋ] n prole f, discendenza.

off: **~stage** ad dietro le quinte; **~-white** a bianco sporco inv.

often ['ɔfn] ad spesso; **as ~ as not** quasi sempre.

ogle ['əugl] vt occhieggiare.

oil [ɔɪl] n olio; (petroleum) petrolio; (for central heating) nafta // vt (machine) lubrificare; **~can** n oliatore m a mano; (for storing) latta da olio; **~field** n giacimento petrolifero; **~-fired** a a nafta; **~ level** n livello dell'olio; **~ painting** n quadro a olio; **~ refinery** n raffineria di petrolio; **~ rig** n derrick m inv; (at sea) piattaforma per trivellazioni subacquee; **~skins** npl indumenti mpl di tela cerata; **~ slick** n chiazza d'olio; **~ tanker** n petroliera; **~ well** n pozzo petrolifero; **~y** a unto(a), oleoso(a); (food) untuoso(a).

ointment ['ɔɪntmənt] n unguento.

O.K., okay ['əu'keɪ] excl d'accordo! // vt approvare; **is it ~?, are you ~?** tutto bene?

old [əuld] a vecchio(a); (ancient) antico(a), vecchio(a); (person) vecchio(a), anziano(a); **how ~ are you?** quanti anni ha?; **he's 10 years ~** ha 10 anni; **~ age** n vecchiaia; **~-age pensioner (O.A.P.)** n

pensionato/a; **~er brother/sister** fratello/sorella maggiore; **~-fashioned** a antiquato(a), fuori moda; (person) all'antica.

olive ['ɔlɪv] n (fruit) oliva; (tree) olivo // a (also: **~-green**) verde oliva inv; **~ oil** n olio d'oliva.

Olympic [əu'lɪmpɪk] a olimpico(a); **the ~ Games, the ~s** i giochi olimpici, le Olimpiadi.

omelet(te) ['ɔmlɪt] n omelette f inv.

omen ['əumən] n presagio, augurio.

ominous ['ɔmɪnəs] a minaccioso(a); (event) di malaugurio.

omission [əu'mɪʃən] n omissione f.

omit [əu'mɪt] vt omettere.

on [ɔn] prep su; (on top of) sopra // ad (machine) in moto; (light, radio) acceso(a); (tap) aperto(a); **is the meeting still ~?** avrà sempre luogo la riunione?; la riunione è ancora in corso?; **when is this film ~?** quando c'è questo film?; **~ the train** in treno; **~ the wall** sul or al muro; **~ television** alla televisione; **~ learning this** imparando questo; **~ arrival** all'arrivo; **~ the left** sulla or a sinistra; **~ Friday** venerdì; **~ Fridays** di or il venerdì; **a week ~ Friday** venerdì fra otto giorni; **put your coat ~** mettiti il cappotto; **to walk ~** continuare a camminare etc; **it's not ~!** non è possibile!; **~ and off** ogni tanto.

once [wʌns] ad una volta // cj non appena, quando; **at ~** subito; (simultaneously) a un tempo; **all at ~** ad (tutto) ad un tratto; **~ a week** una volta alla settimana; **~ more** ancora una volta; **~ and for all** una volta per sempre.

oncoming ['ɔnkʌmɪŋ] a (traffic) che viene in senso opposto.

one [wʌn] det, num un(uno) m, una(un') f // pronoun uno(a); (impersonal) si; **this ~** questo(a) qui; **that ~** quello(a) là; **the ~ book which...** l'unico libro che...; **~ by ~** a uno(a) a uno(a); **~ never knows** non si sa mai; **to express ~'s opinion** esprimere la propria opinione; **~ another** l'un(a) l'altro(a); **~-man** a (business) diretto(a) etc da un solo uomo; **~-self** pronoun si; (after prep, also emphatic) sé, se stesso(a); **~-way** a (street, traffic) a senso unico.

ongoing ['ɔngəuɪŋ] a in corso; in attuazione.

onion ['ʌnjən] n cipolla.

onlooker ['ɔnlukə*] n spettatore/trice.

only ['əunlɪ] ad solo, soltanto // a solo(a), unico(a) // cj solo che, ma; **an ~ child** un figlio unico; **not ~** non solo; **I ~ took one** ne ho preso soltanto uno, non ne ho preso che uno.

onset ['ɔnsɛt] n inizio; (of winter, old age) approssimarsi m.

onshore ['ɔnʃɔ:*] a (wind) di mare.

onslaught ['ɔnslɔ:t] n attacco, assalto.

onto ['ɔntu] prep = **on to**.

onus ['əunəs] n onere m, peso.

onward(s) ['ɔnwəd(z)] ad (move) in

avanti; **from this time** ~ d'ora in poi.
onyx ['ɔnɪks] n onice f.
ooze [u:z] vi stillare.
opal ['əupl] n opale m or f.
opaque [əu'peɪk] a opaco(a).
open ['əupn] a aperto(a); (road) libero(a); (meeting) pubblico(a); (admiration) evidente, franco(a); (question) insoluto(a); (enemy) dichiarato(a) // vt aprire // vi (eyes, door, debate) aprirsi; (flower) sbocciare; (shop, bank, museum) aprire; (book etc: commence) cominciare; **to ~ on to** vt fus (subj: room, door) dare su; **to ~ out** vt aprire // vi aprirsi; **to ~ up** vt aprire; (blocked road) sgombrare // vi aprirsi; **in the ~ (air)** all'aperto; **~-air** a all'aperto; **~ing** n apertura; (opportunity) occasione f, opportunità f inv; (job) posto vacante; **~ly** ad apertamente; **~-minded** a che ha la mente aperta; **~ sandwich** n canapè m inv; **the ~ sea** il mare aperto, l'alto mare.
opera ['ɔprə] n opera; **~ glasses** npl binocolo da teatro; **~ house** n opera.
operate ['ɔpəreɪt] vt (machine) azionare, far funzionare; (system) usare // vi funzionare; (drug) essere efficace; **to ~ on sb (for)** (MED) operare qd (di).
operatic [ɔpə'rætɪk] a dell'opera, lirico(a).
operating ['ɔpəreɪtɪŋ] a: **~ table** tavolo operatorio; **~ theatre** sala operatoria.
operation [ɔpə'reɪʃən] n operazione f; **to be in ~** (machine) essere in azione or funzionamento; (system) essere in vigore; **~al** a in funzione; d'esercizio.
operative ['ɔprətɪv] a (measure) operativo(a) // n (in factory) operaio/a.
operator ['ɔpəreɪtə*] n (of machine) operatore/trice; (TEL) centralinista m/f.
operetta [ɔpə'rɛtə] n operetta.
opinion [ə'pɪnɪən] n opinione f, parere m; **in my ~** secondo me, a mio avviso; **~ated** a dogmatico(a).
opium ['əupɪəm] n oppio.
opponent [ə'pəunənt] n avversario/a.
opportune ['ɔpətju:n] a opportuno(a); **opportunist** [-'tju:nɪst] n opportunista m/f.
opportunity [ɔpə'tju:nɪtɪ] n opportunità f inv, occasione f.
oppose [ə'pəuz] vt opporsi a; **~d to** a contrario(a) a; **as ~d to** in contrasto con; **opposing** a opposto(a); (team) avversario/a.
opposite ['ɔpəzɪt] a opposto(a); (house etc) di fronte // ad di fronte, dirimpetto // prep di fronte a // n opposto, contrario; (of word) contrario; **his ~ number** il suo corrispondente.
opposition [ɔpə'zɪʃən] n opposizione f.
oppress [ə'prɛs] vt opprimere; **~ion** [ə'prɛʃən] n oppressione f; **~ive** a oppressivo(a).
opt [ɔpt] vi: **to ~ for** optare per; **to ~ to do** scegliere di fare; **to ~ out of** ritirarsi da.
optical ['ɔptɪkl] a ottico(a).
optician [ɔp'tɪʃən] n ottico.
optimism ['ɔptɪmɪzəm] n ottimismo.

optimist ['ɔptɪmɪst] n ottimista m/f; **~ic** [-'mɪstɪk] a ottimistico(a).
optimum ['ɔptɪməm] a ottimale.
option ['ɔpʃən] n scelta; (SCOL) materia facoltativa; (COMM) opzione f; **to keep one's ~s open** (fig) non impegnarsi; **~al** a facoltativo(a); (COMM) a scelta.
opulence ['ɔpjuləns] n opulenza; abbondanza.
or [ɔ:*] cj o, oppure; (with negative): **he hasn't seen ~ heard anything** non ha visto né sentito niente; **~ else** se no, altrimenti; oppure.
oracle ['ɔrəkl] n oracolo.
oral ['ɔ:rəl] a orale // n esame m orale.
orange ['ɔrɪndʒ] n (fruit) arancia // a arancione.
oration [ɔ:'reɪʃən] n orazione f.
orator ['ɔrətə*] n oratore/trice.
oratorio [ɔrə'tɔ:rɪəu] n oratorio.
orb [ɔ:b] n orbe m.
orbit ['ɔ:bɪt] n orbita // vt orbitare intorno a.
orchard ['ɔ:tʃəd] n frutteto.
orchestra ['ɔ:kɪstrə] n orchestra; **~l** [-'kɛstrəl] a orchestrale; (concert) sinfonico(a).
orchid ['ɔ:kɪd] n orchidea.
ordain [ɔ:'deɪn] vt (REL) ordinare; (decide) decretare.
ordeal [ɔ:'di:l] n prova, travaglio.
order ['ɔ:də*] n ordine m; (COMM) ordinazione f // vt ordinare; **in ~** in ordine; (of document) in regola; **in ~ of size** in ordine di grandezza; **in ~ to do** per fare; **in ~ that** affinché +sub; **to ~ sb to do** ordinare a qd di fare; **the lower ~s** (pej) i ceti inferiori; **~ form** n modulo d'ordinazione; **~ly** n (MIL) attendente m // a (room) in ordine; (mind) metodico(a); (person) ordinato(a), metodico(a).
ordinal ['ɔ:dɪnl] a (number) ordinale.
ordinary ['ɔ:dnrɪ] a normale, comune; (pej) mediocre.
ordination [ɔ:dɪ'neɪʃən] n ordinazione f.
ore [ɔ:*] n minerale m grezzo.
organ ['ɔ:gən] n organo; **~ic** [ɔ:'gænɪk] a organico(a).
organism ['ɔ:gənɪzəm] n organismo.
organist ['ɔ:gənɪst] n organista m/f.
organization [ɔ:gənaɪ'zeɪʃən] n organizzazione f.
organize ['ɔ:gənaɪz] vt organizzare; **~r** n organizzatore/trice.
orgasm ['ɔ:gæzəm] n orgasmo.
orgy ['ɔ:dʒɪ] n orgia.
Orient ['ɔ:rɪənt] n: **the ~** l'Oriente m; **oriental** [-'ɛntl] a, n orientale (m/f).
orientate ['ɔ:rɪənteɪt] vt orientare.
orifice ['ɔrɪfɪs] n orifizio.
origin ['ɔrɪdʒɪn] n origine f.
original [ə'rɪdʒɪnl] a originale; (earliest) originario(a) // n originale m; **~ity** [-'nælɪtɪ] n originalità; **~ly** ad (at first) all'inizio.
originate [ə'rɪdʒɪneɪt] vi: **to ~ from**

venire da, essere originario(a) di; (*suggestion*) provenire da.

ornament ['ɔːnəmənt] *n* ornamento; (*trinket*) ninnolo; ~**al** [-'mɛntl] *a* ornamentale.

ornate [ɔː'neit] *a* molto ornato(a).

ornithologist [ɔːni'θɔlədʒist] *n* ornitologo/a.

ornithology [ɔːni'θɔlədʒi] *n* ornitologia.

orphan ['ɔːfn] *n* orfano/a // *vt*: **to be ~ed** diventare orfano; ~**age** *n* orfanotrofio.

orthodox ['ɔːθədɔks] *a* ortodosso(a).

orthopaedic [ɔːθə'piːdik] *a* ortopedico(a).

oscillate ['ɔsileit] *vi* oscillare.

ostensible [ɔs'tɛnsibl] *a* preteso(a); apparente; **ostensibly** *ad* all'apparenza.

ostentation [ɔstɛn'teiʃən] *n* ostentazione *f*.

ostentatious [ɔstɛn'teiʃəs] *a* pretenzioso(a); ostentato(a).

osteopath ['ɔstiəpæθ] *n* specialista *m/f* di osteopatia.

ostracize ['ɔstrəsaiz] *vt* dare l'ostracismo a.

ostrich ['ɔstritʃ] *n* struzzo.

other ['ʌðə*] *a* altro(a); ~ **than** altro che; a parte; ~**wise** *ad,cj* altrimenti.

otter ['ɔtə*] *n* lontra.

ought [ɔːt] *pt* **ought** [ɔːt] *auxiliary vb*: **I ~ to do it** dovrei farlo; **this ~ to have been corrected** questo avrebbe dovuto essere corretto; **he ~ to win** dovrebbe vincere.

ounce [auns] *n* oncia (= *28.35 g; 16 in a pound*).

our ['auə*] *a* il(la) nostro(a), *pl* i(le) nostri(e); ~**s** *pronoun* il(la) nostro(a), *pl* i(le) nostri(e); ~**selves** *pronoun pl* (*reflexive*) ci; (*after preposition*) noi; (*emphatic*) noi stessi(e).

oust [aust] *vt* cacciare, espellere.

out [aut] *ad* fuori; (*published, not at home etc*) uscito(a); (*light, fire*) spento(a); ~ **here** qui fuori; ~ **there** là fuori; **he's ~** è uscito; (*unconscious*) ha perso conoscenza; **to be ~ in one's calculations** essersi sbagliato nei calcoli; **to run/back etc ~** uscire di corsa/a marcia indietro *etc*; ~ **loud** *ad* ad alta voce; ~ **of** (*outside*) fuori di; (*because of: anger etc*) per; (*from among*): ~ **of 10** su 10; (*without*): ~ **of petrol** senza benzina, a corto di benzina; **made ~ of wood** di or in legno; ~ **of order** (*machine etc*) guasto(a).

outboard ['autbɔːd] *n*: ~ (**motor**) (motore *m*) fuoribordo.

outbreak ['autbreik] *n* scoppio; epidemia.

outbuilding ['autbildiŋ] *n* dipendenza.

outburst ['autbɔːst] *n* scoppio.

outcast ['autkɑːst] *n* esule *m/f*, (*socially*) paria *m inv*.

outclass [aut'klɑːs] *vt* surclassare.

outcome ['autkʌm] *n* esito, risultato.

outcry ['autkrai] *n* protesta, clamore *m*.

outdated [aut'deitid] *a* (*custom, clothes*) fuori moda; (*idea*) sorpassato(a).

outdo [aut'duː] *vt irg* sorpassare.

outdoor [aut'dɔː*] *a* all'aperto; ~**s** *ad* fuori; all'aria aperta.

outer ['autə*] *a* esteriore; ~ **space** *n* spazio cosmico.

outfit ['autfit] *n* equipaggiamento; (*clothes*) abito; '~**ter's**' 'confezioni da uomo'.

outgoings ['autgɔuiŋz] *npl* (*expenses*) spese *fpl*.

outgrow [aut'grɔu] *vt irg* (*clothes*) diventare troppo grande for.

outing ['autiŋ] *n* gita; escursione *f*.

outlandish [aut'lændiʃ] *a* strano(a).

outlaw ['autlɔː] *n* fuorilegge *m/f* // *vt* (*person*) mettere fuori della legge; (*practice*) proscrivere.

outlay ['autlei] *n* spese *fpl*; (*investment*) sborsa, spesa.

outlet ['autlɛt] *n* (*for liquid etc*) sbocco, scarico; (*for emotion*) sfogo; (*for goods*) sbocco; (*also*: **retail** ~) punto di vendita.

outline ['autlain] *n* contorno, profilo; (*summary*) abbozzo, grandi linee *fpl*.

outlive [aut'liv] *vt* sopravvivere a.

outlook ['autluk] *n* prospettiva, vista.

outlying ['autlaiiŋ] *a* periferico(a).

outmoded [aut'mɔudid] *a* passato(a) di moda; antiquato(a).

outnumber [aut'nʌmbə*] *vt* superare in numero.

outpatient ['autpeiʃənt] *n* paziente *m/f* ambulatoriale.

outpost ['autpɔust] *n* avamposto.

output ['autput] *n* produzione *f*.

outrage ['autreidʒ] *n* oltraggio; scandalo // *vt* oltraggiare; ~**ous** [-'reidʒəs] *a* oltraggioso(a); scandaloso(a).

outrider ['autraidə*] *n* (*on motorcycle*) battistrada *m inv*.

outright *ad* [aut'rait] completamente; schiettamente; apertamente; sul colpo // *a* ['autrait] completo(a); schietto(a) e netto(a).

outset ['autsɛt] *n* inizio.

outside [aut'said] *n* esterno, esteriore *m* // *a* esterno(a), esteriore // *ad* fuori, all'esterno // *prep* fuori di, all'esterno di; **at the ~** (*fig*) al massimo; ~ **lane** *n* (*AUT*) corsia di sorpasso; ~**r** *n* (*in race etc*) outsider *m inv*; (*stranger*) straniero/a*.

outsize ['autsaiz] *a* enorme; (*clothes*) per taglie forti.

outskirts ['autskɜːts] *npl* sobborghi *mpl*.

outspoken [aut'spoukən] *a* molto franco(a).

outstanding [aut'stændiŋ] *a* eccezionale, di rilievo; (*unfinished*) non completo(a); non evaso(a); non regolato(a).

outstay [aut'stei] *vt*: **to ~ one's welcome** diventare un ospite sgradito.

outstretched [aut'strɛtʃt] *a* (*hand*) teso(a); (*body*) disteso(a).

outward ['autwəd] *a* (*sign, appearances*) esteriore; (*journey*) d'andata; ~**ly** *ad* esteriormente; in apparenza.

outweigh [aut'wei] *vt* avere maggior peso di.

outwit [aut'wit] *vt* superare in astuzia.

oval ['ɔuvl] *a,n* ovale (*m*).

ovary ['əuvəri] *n* ovaia.
ovation [əu'veiʃən] *n* ovazione *f*.
oven ['ʌvn] *n* forno; ~ **proof** *a* da forno.
over ['əuvə*] *ad* al di sopra // *a* (*or* ad) (*finished*) finito(a), terminato(a); (*too*) troppo; (*remaining*) che avanza // *prep* su; sopra; (*above*) al di sopra di; (*on the other side of*) di là di; (*more than*) più di; (*during*) durante; ~ **here** qui; ~ **there** là; **all** ~ (*everywhere*) dappertutto; (*finished*) tutto(a) finito(a); ~ **and** ~ (**again**) più e più volte; ~ **and above** oltre (a); **to ask sb** ~ invitare qd (a passare).
over... ['əuvə*] *prefix*: ~**abundant** sovrabbondante.
overact [əuvər'ækt] *vi* (THEATRE) esagerare *or* strafare la propria parte.
overall *a,n* ['əuvərɔːl] *a* totale // *n* (*Brit*) grembiule *m* // *ad* [əuvər'ɔːl] nell'insieme, complessivamente; ~**s** *npl* tuta (da lavoro).
overawe [əuvər'ɔː] *vt* intimidire.
overbalance [əuvə'bæləns] *vi* perdere l'equilibrio.
overbearing [əuvə'bɛəriŋ] *a* imperioso(a), prepotente.
overboard ['əuvəbɔːd] *ad* (NAUT) fuori bordo, in mare.
overcast ['əuvəkɑːst] *a* coperto(a).
overcharge [əuvə'tʃɑːdʒ] *vt*: **to** ~ **sb for sth** far pagare troppo caro a qd per qc.
overcoat ['əuvəkəut] *n* soprabito, cappotto.
overcome [əuvə'kʌm] *vt irg* superare; sopraffare.
overcrowded [əuvə'kraudid] *a* sovraffollato(a).
overcrowding [əuvə'kraudiŋ] *n* sovraffollamento; (*in bus*) calca.
overdo [əuvə'duː] *vt irg* esagerare; (*overcook*) cuocere troppo.
overdose ['əuvədəus] *n* dose *f* eccessiva.
overdraft ['əuvədrɑːft] *n* scoperto (di conto).
overdrawn [əuvə'drɔːn] *a* (*account*) scoperto(a).
overdue [əuvə'djuː] *a* in ritardo; (*recognition*) tardivo(a).
overestimate [əuvər'ɛstimeit] *vt* sopravvalutare.
overexertion [əuvərig'zɜːʃən] *n* logorio (fisico).
overexpose [əuvərik'spəuz] *vt* (PHOT) sovraesporre.
overflow [əuvə'fləu] *vi* traboccare.
overgrown [əuvə'grəun] *a* (*garden*) ricoperto(a) di vegetazione.
overhaul *vt* [əuvə'hɔːl] revisionare // *n* ['əuvəhɔːl] revisione *f*.
overhead *ad* [əuvə'hɛd] di sopra // *a* ['əuvəhɛd] aereo(a); (*lighting*) verticale; ~**s** *npl* spese *fpl* generali.
overhear [əuvə'hiə*] *vt irg* sentire (per caso).
overjoyed [əuvə'dʒɔid] *a* pazzo(a) di gioia.
overland ['əuvəlænd] *a*, *ad* per via di terra.
overlap [əuvə'læp] *vi* sovrapporsi.

overload [əuvə'ləud] *vt* sovraccaricare.
overlook [əuvə'luk] *vt* (*have view of*) dare su; (*miss*) trascurare; (*forgive*) passare sopra a.
overnight [əuvə'nait] *ad* (*happen*) durante la notte; (*fig*) tutto ad un tratto // *a* di notte; fulmineo(a); **he stayed there** ~ ci ha passato la notte; **if you travel** ~**...** se viaggia di notte... .
overpass ['əuvəpɑːs] *n* cavalcavia *m inv*.
overpower [əuvə'pauə*] *vt* sopraffare; ~**ing** *a* irresistibile; (*heat, stench*) soffocante.
overrate [əuvə'reit] *vt* sopravvalutare.
overreact [əuvəriː'ækt] *vi* reagire in modo esagerato.
override [əuvə'raid] *vt* (*irg: like ride*) (*order, objection*) passar sopra a; (*decision*) annullare; **overriding** *a* preponderante.
overrule [əuvə'ruːl] *vt* (*decision*) annullare; (*claim*) respingere.
overseas [əuvə'siːz] *ad* oltremare; (*abroad*) all'estero // *a* (*trade*) estero(a); (*visitor*) straniero(a).
overseer ['əuvəsiə*] *n* (*in factory*) caposquadra *m*.
overshadow [əuvə'ʃædəu] *vt* (*fig*) eclissare.
overshoot [əuvə'ʃuːt] *vt irg* superare.
oversight ['əuvəsait] *n* omissione *f*, svista.
oversimplify [əuvə'simplifai] *vt* rendere troppo semplice.
oversleep [əuvə'sliːp] *vi irg* dormire troppo a lungo.
overspill ['əuvəspil] *n* eccedenza di popolazione.
overstate [əuvə'steit] *vt* esagerare; ~**ment** *n* esagerazione *f*.
overt [əu'vɔːt] *a* palese.
overtake [əuvə'teik] *vt irg* sorpassare; **overtaking** *n* (AUT) sorpasso.
overthrow [əuvə'θrəu] *vt irg* (*government*) rovesciare.
overtime ['əuvətaim] *n* (*lavoro*) straordinario.
overtone ['əuvətəun] *n* (*also*: ~**s**) sottinteso.
overture ['əuvətʃuə*] *n* (MUS) ouverture *f inv*; (*fig*) approccio.
overturn [əuvə'tɜːn] *vt* rovesciare // *vi* rovesciarsi.
overweight [əuvə'weit] *a* (*person*) troppo grasso(a); (*luggage*) troppo pesante.
overwhelm [əuvə'wɛlm] *vt* sopraffare; sommergere; schiacciare; ~**ing** *a* (*victory, defeat*) schiacciante; (*desire*) irresistibile.
overwork [əuvə'wɜːk] *vt* far lavorare troppo // *vi* lavorare troppo, strapazzarsi.
overwrought [əuvə'rɔːt] *a* molto agitato(a).
owe [əu] *vt* dovere; **to** ~ **sb sth**, **to** ~ **sth to sb** dovere qc a qd.
owing to ['əuiŋtuː] *prep* a causa di, a motivo di.
owl [aul] *n* gufo.
own [əun] *vt* possedere // *a* proprio(a); **a**

room of my ~ la mia propria camera; to get one's ~ back vendicarsi; on one's ~ tutto(a) solo(a); to ~ up vi confessare; ~er n proprietario/a; ~ership n possesso.

ox, pl oxen [ɔks, 'ɔksn] n bue m.

oxide ['ɔksaɪd] n ossido.

oxtail ['ɔksteɪl] n: ~ soup minestra di coda di bue.

oxygen ['ɔksɪdʒən] n ossigeno; ~ mask/tent n maschera/tenda ad ossigeno.

oyster ['ɔɪstə*] n ostrica.

oz. abbr of ounce(s).

ozone ['əuzəun] n ozono.

P

p [pi:] abbr of penny, pence.

p.a. abbr of per annum.

pa [pɑ:] n (col) papà m inv, babbo.

pace [peɪs] n passo; (speed) passo; velocità // vi: to ~ up and down camminare su e giù; to keep ~ with camminare di pari passo a; (events) tenersi al corrente di; ~maker n (MED) segnapasso.

pacific [pə'sɪfɪk] n: the P~ (Ocean) il Pacifico, l'Oceano Pacifico.

pacifist ['pæsɪfɪst] n pacifista m/f.

pacify ['pæsɪfaɪ] vt pacificare; (soothe) calmare.

pack [pæk] n pacco; balla; (of hounds) muta; (of thieves etc) banda; (of cards) mazzo // vt (goods) impaccare, imballare; (in suitcase etc) mettere; (box) riempire; (cram) stipare, pigiare; (press down) tamponare; turare; to ~ (one's bags) fare la valigia.

package ['pækɪdʒ] n pacco; balla; (also: ~ deal) pacchetto; forfait m inv; ~ tour n viaggio organizzato.

packet ['pækɪt] n pacchetto.

pack ice ['pækaɪs] n banchisa.

packing ['pækɪŋ] n imballaggio; ~ case n cassa da imballaggio.

pact [pækt] n patto, accordo; trattato.

pad [pæd] n blocco; (for inking) tampone m; (col: flat) appartamentino // vt imbottire; ~ding n imbottitura; (fig) riempitivo.

paddle ['pædl] n (oar) pagaia // vi sguazzare; ~ steamer n vapore m con ruote a pala; paddling pool n piscina per bambini.

paddock ['pædək] n recinto; paddock m inv.

paddy ['pædɪ] n: ~ field n risaia.

padlock ['pædlɔk] n lucchetto.

padre ['pɑ:drɪ] n cappellano.

paediatrics [pi:dɪ'ætrɪks] n pediatria.

pagan ['peɪgən] a,n pagano(a).

page [peɪdʒ] n pagina; (also: ~ boy) fattorino; (at wedding) paggio // vt (in hotel etc) (far) chiamare.

pageant ['pædʒənt] n spettacolo storico; grande cerimonia; ~ry n pompa.

paid [peɪd] pt, pp of pay // a (work, official)

rimunerato(a); to put ~ to mettere fine a.

pail [peɪl] n secchio.

pain [peɪn] n dolore m; to be in ~ soffrire, aver male; to have a ~ in aver male or un dolore a; to take ~s to do mettercela tutta per fare; ~ed a addolorato(a), afflitto(a); ~ful a doloroso(a), che fa male; difficile, penoso(a); ~killer n antalgico, antidolorifico; ~less a indolore; ~staking ['peɪnzteɪkɪŋ] a sollecito(a).

paint [peɪnt] n vernice f, colore m // vt dipingere; (walls, door etc) verniciare; to ~ the door blue verniciare la porta di azzurro; ~brush n pennello; ~er n pittore m; imbianchino; ~ing n pittura; verniciatura; (picture) dipinto, quadro; ~-stripper n prodotto sverniciante.

pair [pɛə*] n (of shoes, gloves etc) paio; (of people) coppia; duo m inv; a ~ of scissors un paio di forbici.

pajamas [pɪ'dʒɑ:məz] npl (US) pigiama m.

Pakistan [pɑ:kɪ'stɑ:n] n Pakistan m; ~i a, n pakistano(a).

pal [pæl] n (col) amico/a, compagno/a.

palace ['pæləs] n palazzo.

palatable ['pælɪtəbl] a gustoso(a).

palate ['pælɪt] n palato.

palaver [pə'lɑ:və*] n chiacchiere fpl; storie fpl.

pale [peɪl] a pallido(a); ~ blue a azzurro or blu pallido inv; ~ness n pallidezza.

Palestine ['pælɪstaɪn] n Palestina; Palestinian [-'tɪnɪən] a, n palestinese (m/f).

palette ['pælɪt] n tavolozza.

palisade [pælɪ'seɪd] n palizzata.

pall [pɔ:l] n (of smoke) cappa // vi: to ~ (on) diventare noioso(a) (a).

pallid ['pælɪd] a pallido(a), smorto(a).

pally ['pælɪ] a (col) amichevole.

palm [pɑ:m] n (ANAT) palma, palmo; (also: ~ tree) palma // vt: to ~ sth off on sb (col) rifilare qc a qd; ~ist n chiromante m/f; P~ Sunday n la Domenica delle Palme.

palpable ['pælpəbl] a palpabile.

palpitation [pælpɪ'teɪʃən] n palpitazione f.

paltry ['pɔ:ltrɪ] a derisorio(a); insignificante.

pamper ['pæmpə*] vt viziare, accarezzare.

pamphlet ['pæmflət] n dépliant m inv.

pan [pæn] n (also: sauce~) casseruola; (also: frying ~) padella // vi (CINEMA) fare una panoramica.

panacea [pænə'sɪə] n panacea.

Panama ['pænəmɑ:] n Panama; ~ canal n canale m di Panama.

pancake ['pænkeɪk] n frittella.

panda ['pændə] n panda m inv.

pandemonium [pændɪ'məunɪəm] n pandemonio.

pander ['pændə*] vi: to ~ to lusingare; concedere tutto a.

pane [peɪn] n vetro.

panel ['pænl] n (of wood, cloth etc)

pannello; (RADIO, TV) giuria; ~**ling** n
rivestimento a pannelli.

pang [pæŋ] n: ~**s of hunger** spasimi mpl
della fame; ~**s of conscience** morsi mpl
di coscienza.

panic ['pænɪk] n panico // vi perdere il
sangue freddo; ~**ky** a (person)
pauroso(a).

pannier ['pænɪə*] n (on animal) bisaccia;
(on bicycle) borsa.

panorama [pænə'rɑːmə] n panorama m.

pansy ['pænzɪ] n (BOT) viola del pensiero,
pensée f inv; (col) femminuccia.

pant [pænt] vi ansare.

panther ['pænθə*] n pantera.

panties ['pæntɪz] npl slip m, mutandine fpl.

pantomime ['pæntəmaɪm] n pantomima.

pantry ['pæntrɪ] n dispensa.

pants [pænts] npl mutande fpl, slip m; (US:
trousers) pantaloni mpl.

papacy ['peɪpəsɪ] n papato.

papal ['peɪpəl] a papale, pontificio(a).

paper ['peɪpə*] n carta; (also: **wall~**)
carta da parati, tappezzeria; (also:
news~) giornale m; (study, article)
saggio; (exam) prova scritta // a di carta
// vt tappezzare; (identity) ~**s** npl carte
fpl, documenti mpl; ~**back** n tascabile m;
edizione f economica; ~**bag** n sacchetto
di carta; ~ **clip** n graffetta, clip f inv; ~
mill n cartiera; ~**weight** n fermacarte m
inv; ~**work** n lavoro amministrativo.

papier-mâché ['pæpɪeɪ'mæʃeɪ] n
cartapesta.

paprika ['pæprɪkə] n paprica.

par [pɑː*] n parità, pari f; (GOLF) norma; **on
a ~ with** alla pari con.

parable ['pærəbl] n parabola.

parachute ['pærəʃuːt] n paracadute m inv
// vi scendere col paracadute;
parachutist n paracadutista m/f.

parade [pə'reɪd] n parata; (inspection)
rivista, rassegna // vt fare sfoggio di
// vi sfilare in parata.

paradise ['pærədaɪs] n paradiso.

paradox ['pærədɔks] n paradosso; ~**ical**
[-'dɔksɪkl] a paradossale.

paraffin ['pærəfɪn] n: ~ (oil) paraffina.

paragraph ['pærəgrɑːf] n paragrafo.

parallel ['pærəlɛl] a parallelo(a); (fig)
analogo(a) // n (line) parallela; (fig, GEO)
parallelo.

paralysis [pə'rælɪsɪs] n paralisi f inv.

paralyze ['pærəlaɪz] vt paralizzare.

paramount ['pærəmaunt] a: **of ~
importance** di capitale importanza.

paranoia [pærə'nɔɪə] n paranoia.

paraphernalia [pærəfə'neɪlɪə] n attrezzi
mpl, roba.

paraphrase ['pærəfreɪz] vt parafrasare.

paraplegic [pærə'pliːdʒɪk] n
paraplegico(a).

parasite ['pærəsaɪt] n parassita m.

paratrooper ['pærətruːpə*] n
paracadutista m (soldato).

parcel ['pɑːsl] n pacco, pacchetto // vt
(also: ~ **up**) impaccare.

parch [pɑːtʃ] vt riardere; ~**ed** a (person)
assetato(a).

parchment ['pɑːtʃmənt] n pergamena.

pardon ['pɑːdn] n perdono; grazia // vt
perdonare; (LAW) graziare; ~**! scusi!**; ~
me! mi scusi!; **I beg your** ~**! scusi!**; **I beg
your** ~? prego?

parent ['pɛərənt] n genitore m; ~**s** npl
genitori mpl; ~**al** [pə'rɛntl] a dei genitori.

parenthesis, pl **parentheses**
[pə'rɛnθɪsɪs, -siːz] n parentesi f inv.

Paris ['pærɪs] n Parigi.

parish ['pærɪʃ] n parrocchia; (civil) ≈
municipio // a parrocchiale; ~**ioner**
[pə'rɪʃənə*] n parrocchiano/a.

parity ['pærɪtɪ] n parità.

park [pɑːk] n parco // vt, vi parcheggiare;
~**ing** n parcheggio; ~**ing lot** n (US)
posteggio, parcheggio; ~**ing meter** n
parchimetro; ~**ing place** n posto di
parcheggio.

parliament ['pɑːləmənt] n parlamento;
~**ary** [-'mɛntərɪ] a parlamentare.

parlour ['pɑːlə*] n salotto.

parochial [pə'rəukɪəl] a parrocchiale;
(pej) provinciale.

parody ['pærədɪ] n parodia.

parole [pə'rəul] n: **on ~** lasciato(a)
libero(a) sulla parola.

parquet ['pɑːkeɪ] n: ~ **floor(ing)** parquet
m.

parrot ['pærət] n pappagallo; ~ **fashion**
ad in modo pappagallesco.

parry ['pærɪ] vt parare.

parsimonious [pɑːsɪ'məunɪəs] a
parsimonioso(a).

parsley ['pɑːslɪ] n prezzemolo.

parsnip ['pɑːsnɪp] n pastinaca.

parson ['pɑːsn] n prete m; (Church of
England) parroco.

part [pɑːt] n parte f; (of machine) pezzo;
(MUS) voce f; parte f; **in part** in parte // ad =
partly // vt separare // vi (people)
separarsi; (roads) dividersi; **to take ~ in**
prendere parte a; **on his ~** da parte sua,
for my ~ per parte mia; **for the most
part** in generale; nella maggior parte dei
casi; **to ~ with** vt fus separarsi da;
rinunciare a; (take leave) lasciare; **in ~
exchange** in pagamento parziale.

partial ['pɑːʃl] a parziale; **to be ~ to**
avere un debole per.

participate [pɑː'tɪsɪpeɪt] vi: **to ~ (in)**
prendere parte (a), partecipare (a);
participation [-'peɪʃən] n partecipazione
f.

participle ['pɑːtɪsɪpl] n participio.

particle ['pɑːtɪkl] n particella.

particular [pə'tɪkjulə*] a particolare;
speciale; (fussy) difficile; meticoloso(a);
~**s** npl particolari mpl, dettagli mpl;
(information) informazioni fpl; ~**ly** ad
particolarmente; in particolare.

parting ['pɑːtɪŋ] n separazione f; (in hair)
scriminatura // a d'addio.

partisan [pɑːtɪ'zæn] n partigiano/a // a
partigiano(a); di parte.

partition [pɑːˈtɪʃən] n (POL) partizione f; (wall) tramezzo.

partly [ˈpɑːtlɪ] ad parzialmente; in parte.

partner [ˈpɑːtnəʳ] n (COMM) socio/a; (SPORT) compagno/a; (at dance) cavaliere/dama; ~ship n associazione f; (COMM) società f inv.

partridge [ˈpɑːtrɪdʒ] n pernice f.

part-time [ˈpɑːtˈtaɪm] a,ad a orario ridotto.

party [ˈpɑːtɪ] n (POL) partito; (team) squadra; gruppo; (LAW) parte f; (celebration) ricevimento; serata; festa.

pass [pɑːs] vt (gen) passare; (place) passare davanti a; (exam) passare, superare; (candidate) promuovere; (overtake, surpass) sorpassare, superare; (approve) approvare // vi passare // n (permit) lasciapassare m inv; permesso; (in mountains) passo, gola; (SPORT) passaggio; (SCOL: also: ~ mark): to get a ~ prendere la sufficienza; could you ~ the vegetables round? potrebbe far passare i contorni?; to ~ away vi morire; to ~ by vi passare // vt trascurare; to ~ for passare per; to ~ out vi svenire; ~able a (road) praticabile; (work) accettabile.

passage [ˈpæsɪdʒ] n (gen) passaggio; (also: ~way) corridoio; (in book) brano, passo; (by boat) traversata.

passenger [ˈpæsɪndʒəʳ] n passeggero/a.

passer-by [pɑːsəˈbaɪ] n passante m/f.

passing [ˈpɑːsɪŋ] a (fig) fuggevole; a ~ reference un accenno; in ~ incidentalmente.

passion [ˈpæʃən] n passione f; amore m; ~ate a appassionato(a).

passive [ˈpæsɪv] a (also LING) passivo(a).

passport [ˈpɑːspɔːt] n passaporto.

password [ˈpɑːswɜːd] n parola d'ordine.

past [pɑːst] prep (further than) oltre, di là di; dopo; (later than) dopo // a passato(a); (president etc) ex inv // n passato; he's ~ forty ha più di quarant'anni; for the ~ few days da qualche giorno; in questi ultimi giorni; to run ~ passare di corsa.

pasta [ˈpæstə] n pasta.

paste [peɪst] n (glue) colla; (CULIN) pâté m inv; pasta // vt collare.

pastel [ˈpæstl] a pastello(a).

pasteurized [ˈpæstəraɪzd] a pastorizzato(a).

pastille [ˈpæstl] n pastiglia.

pastime [ˈpɑːstaɪm] n passatempo.

pastoral [ˈpɑːstərl] a pastorale.

pastry [ˈpeɪstrɪ] n pasta.

pasture [ˈpɑːstʃəʳ] n pascolo.

pasty n [ˈpæstɪ] pasticcio di carne // a [ˈpeɪstɪ] pastoso(a); (complexion) pallido(a).

pat [pæt] vt accarezzare, dare un colpetto (affettuoso) a // n: a ~ of butter un panetto di burro.

patch [pætʃ] n (of material) toppa; (spot) macchia; (of land) pezzo // vt (clothes) rattoppare; a bad ~ un brutto periodo; to ~ up vt rappezzare; ~work n patchwork m; ~y a irregolare.

pâté [ˈpæteɪ] n pâté m inv.

patent [ˈpeɪtnt] n brevetto // vt brevettare // a patente, manifesto(a); ~ leather n cuoio verniciato.

paternal [pəˈtɜːnl] a paterno(a).

paternity [pəˈtɜːnɪtɪ] n paternità.

path [pɑːθ] n sentiero, viottolo; viale m; (fig) via, strada; (of planet, missile) traiettoria.

pathetic [pəˈθetɪk] a (pitiful) patetico(a); (very bad) penoso(a).

pathologist [pəˈθɔlədʒɪst] n patologo/a.

pathology [pəˈθɔlədʒɪ] n patologia.

pathos [ˈpeɪθɔs] n pathos m.

pathway [ˈpɑːθweɪ] n sentiero, viottolo.

patience [ˈpeɪʃns] n pazienza; (CARDS) solitario.

patient [ˈpeɪʃnt] n paziente m/f; malato/a // a paziente.

patio [ˈpætɪəʊ] n terrazza.

patriot [ˈpeɪtrɪət] n patriota m/f; ~ic [pætrɪˈɔtɪk] a patriottico(a).

patrol [pəˈtrəʊl] n pattuglia // vt pattugliare; ~ car n autoradio f inv (della polizia); ~man n (US) poliziotto.

patron [ˈpeɪtrən] n (in shop) cliente m/f; (of charity) benefattore/trice; ~age [ˈpætrənɪdʒ] n patronato; ~ize [ˈpætrənaɪz] vt essere cliente abituale di; (fig) trattare con condiscendenza; ~ saint n patrono.

patter [ˈpætəʳ] n picchiettio; (sales talk) propaganda di vendita // vi picchiettare.

pattern [ˈpætən] n modello; (design) disegno, motivo; (sample) campione m.

paunch [pɔːntʃ] n pancione m.

pauper [ˈpɔːpəʳ] n indigente m/f.

pause [pɔːz] n pausa // vi fare una pausa, arrestarsi.

pave [peɪv] vt pavimentare; to ~ the way for aprire la via a.

pavement [ˈpeɪvmənt] n (Brit) marciapiede m.

pavilion [pəˈvɪlɪən] n padiglione m; tendone m.

paving [ˈpeɪvɪŋ] n pavimentazione f; ~ stone n lastra di pietra.

paw [pɔː] n zampa // vt dare una zampata a; (subj: person: pej) palpare.

pawn [pɔːn] n pegno; (CHESS) pedone m; (fig) pedina // vt dare in pegno; ~broker n prestatore m su pegno; ~shop n monte m di pietà.

pay [peɪ] n stipendio; paga // vb (pt,pp paid [peɪd]) vt pagare // vi pagare; (be profitable) rendere; to ~ attention (to) fare attenzione (a); to ~ back vt rimborsare; to ~ for vt fus pagare; to ~ in vt versare; to ~ up vt saldare; ~able a pagabile; ~ day n giorno di paga; ~ee n beneficiario/a; ~ment n pagamento; versamento; saldamento; ~ packet n busta f paga inv; ~roll n ruolo (organico).

p.c. abbr of per cent.

pea [piː] n pisello.

peace [pi:s] n pace f; (calm) calma, tranquillità; ~able a pacifico(a); ~ful a pacifico(a), calmo(a); ~keeping n mantenimento della pace.

peach [pi:tʃ] n pesca.

peacock ['pi:kɔk] n pavone m.

peak [pi:k] n (of mountain) cima, vetta; (mountain itself) picco; (fig) massimo; (: of career) acme f; ~ period n periodo di punta.

peal [pi:l] n (of bells) scampanio, carillon m inv; ~s of laughter scoppi mpl di risa.

peanut ['pi:nʌt] n arachide f, nocciolina americana; ~ butter n burro di arachidi.

pear [pɛə°] n pera.

pearl [pə:l] n perla.

peasant ['pɛznt] n contadino/a.

peat [pi:t] n torba.

pebble ['pebl] n ciottolo.

peck [pɛk] vi (also: ~ at) beccare; (food) mangiucchiare // n colpo di becco; (kiss) bacetto; ~ish a (col): I feel ~ish ho un languorino.

peculiar [pi'kju:liə°] a strano(a), bizzarro(a); peculiare; ~ to peculiare di; ~ity [pikjuli'ɛriti] n peculiarità f inv; (oddity) bizzarria.

pecuniary [pi'kju:niəri] a pecuniario(a).

pedal ['pɛdl] n pedale m // vi pedalare.

pedantic [pi'dæntik] a pedantesco(a).

pedestal ['pɛdəstl] n piedestallo.

pedestrian [pi'dɛstriən] n pedone/a // a pedonale; (fig) prosaico(a), pedestre.

pediatrics [pi:di'ætriks] n (US) = paediatrics.

pedigree ['pɛdigri:] n stirpe f; (of animal) pedigree m inv // cpd (animal) di razza.

pedlar ['pɛdlə°] n venditore m ambulante.

peek [pi:k] vi guardare furtivamente.

peel [pi:l] n buccia; (of orange, lemon) scorza // vt sbucciare // vi (paint etc) staccarsi.

peep [pi:p] n (look) sguardo furtivo, sbirciata; (sound) pigolio // vi guardare furtivamente; to ~ out n mostrarsi furtivamente; ~hole n spioncino.

peer [piə°] vi: to ~ at scrutare // n (noble) pari m inv; (equal) pari m/f inv, uguale m/f; ~age n dignità di pari; pari mpl.

peeved [pi:vd] a stizzito(a).

peevish ['pi:viʃ] a stizzoso(a).

peg [pɛg] n caviglia; (for coat etc) attaccapanni m inv; (also: clothes ~) molletta; off the ~ ad confezionato(a).

pejorative [pi'dʒɔrətiv] a peggiorativo(a).

pekingese [pi:ki'ni:z] n pechinese m.

pelican ['pɛlikən] n pellicano.

pellet ['pɛlit] n pallottola, pallina.

pelmet ['pɛlmit] n mantovana; cassonetto.

pelt [pɛlt] vt: to ~ sb (with) bombardare qd (con) // vi (rain) piovere a dirotto // n pelle f.

pelvis ['pɛlvis] n pelvi f inv, bacino.

pen [pɛn] n penna; (for sheep) recinto.

penal ['pi:nl] a penale; ~ize vt punire; (SPORT) penalizzare; (fig) svantaggiare.

penalty ['pɛnlti] n penalità f inv; sanzione f penale; (fine) ammenda; (SPORT) penalizzazione f; ~ (kick) n (FOOTBALL) calcio di rigore.

penance ['pɛnəns] n penitenza.

pence [pɛns] npl of penny.

pencil ['pɛnsl] n matita; ~ sharpener n temperamatite m inv.

pendant ['pɛndnt] n pendaglio.

pending ['pɛndiŋ] prep in attesa di // a in sospeso.

pendulum ['pɛndjuləm] n pendolo.

penetrate ['pɛnitreit] vt penetrare; penetrating a penetrante; penetration [-'treiʃən] n penetrazione f.

penfriend ['pɛnfrɛnd] n corrispondente m/f.

penguin ['pɛŋgwin] n pinguino.

penicillin [pɛni'silin] n penicillina.

peninsula [pə'ninsjulə] n penisola.

penis ['pi:nis] n pene m.

penitence ['pɛnitns] n penitenza.

penitent ['pɛnitnt] a penitente.

penitentiary [pɛni'tɛnʃəri] n (US) carcere m.

penknife ['pɛnnaif] n temperino.

pennant ['pɛnənt] n banderuola.

penniless ['pɛnilis] a senza un soldo.

penny ['pɛni], pl pennies or pence ['pɛni, pɛns] n penny m (pl pence).

pension ['pɛnʃən] n pensione f; ~able a che ha diritto a una pensione; ~er n pensionato/a.

pensive ['pɛnsiv] a pensoso(a).

pentagon ['pɛntəgən] n pentagono.

Pentecost ['pɛntikɔst] n Pentecoste f.

penthouse ['pɛnthaus] n appartamento (di lusso) nell'attico.

pent-up ['pɛntʌp] a (feelings) represso(a).

penultimate [pɛ'nʌltimət] a penultimo(a).

people ['pi:pl] npl gente f; persone fpl; (citizens) popolo // n (nation, race) popolo // vt popolare; 4/several ~ came 4/parecchie persone sono venute; the room was full of ~ la stanza era piena di gente; ~ say that... si dice or la gente dice che... .

pep [pɛp] n (col) dinamismo; to ~ up vt vivacizzare; (food) rendere più gustoso(a).

pepper ['pɛpə°] n pepe m; (vegetable) peperone m // vt pepare; ~mint n (plant) menta peperita; (sweet) pasticca di menta.

peptalk ['pɛptɔk] n (col) discorso di incoraggiamento.

per [pə:°] prep per; a; ~ hour all'ora; ~ kilo etc il chilo etc; ~ day al giorno; ~ cent per cento; ~ annum all'anno.

perceive [pə'si:v] vt percepire; (notice) accorgersi di.

percentage [pə'sɛntidʒ] n percentuale f.

perceptible [pə'sɛptibl] a percettibile.

perception [pə'sɛpʃən] n percezione f; sensibilità; perspicacia.

perceptive [pə'sɛptiv] a percettivo(a); perspicace.

perch [pə:tʃ] n (fish) pesce m persico; (for

bird) sostegno, ramo // *vi* appollaiarsi.
percolator ['pɔːkəleɪtə*] *n* **caffettiera a pressione; caffettiera elettrica.**
percussion [pə'kʌʃən] *n* percussione *f.*
peremptory [pə'remptərɪ] *a* perentorio(a).
perennial [pə'renɪəl] *a* perenne // *n* pianta perenne.
perfect *a,n* ['pɔːfɪkt] *a* perfetto(a) // *n* (*also*: ~ **tense**) perfetto, passato prossimo // *vt* [pə'fɛkt] perfezionare; **mettere a punto; ~ion** [-'fɛkʃən] *n* perfezione *f;* ~**ionist** *n* perfezionista *m/f.*
perforate ['pɔːfəreɪt] *vt* perforare; **perforation** [-'reɪʃən] *n* perforazione *f;* (*line of holes*) dentellatura.
perform [pə'fɔːm] *vt* (*carry out*) eseguire, fare; (*symphony etc*) suonare; (*play, ballet*) dare; (*opera*) fare // *vi* suonare; recitare; ~**ance** *n* esecuzione *f;* (*at theatre etc*) rappresentazione *f,* spettacolo; (*of an artist*) interpretazione *f;* (*of player etc*) performance *f;* (*of car, engine*) prestazione *f;* ~**er** *n* artista *m/f;* ~**ing** *a* (*animal*) ammaestrato(a).
perfume ['pɔːfjuːm] *n* profumo.
perfunctory [pə'fʌŋktərɪ] *a* superficiale, per la forma.
perhaps [pə'hæps] *ad* forse.
peril ['perɪl] *n* pericolo; ~**ous** *a* pericoloso(a).
perimeter [pə'rɪmɪtə*] *n* perimetro; ~ **wall** *n* muro di cinta.
period ['pɪərɪəd] *n* periodo; (*HISTORY*) epoca; (*SCOL*) lezione *f;* (*full stop*) punto; (*MED*) mestruazioni *fpl* // *a* (*costume, furniture*) d'epoca; ~**ic** [-'ɔdɪk] *a* periodico(a); ~**ical** [-'ɔdɪkl] *a* periodico(a) // *n* periodico.
peripheral [pə'rɪfərəl] *a* periferico(a).
periphery [pə'rɪfərɪ] *n* periferia.
periscope ['perɪskəup] *n* periscopio.
perish ['perɪʃ] *vi* perire, morire; (*decay*) deteriorarsi; ~**able** *a* deperibile; ~**ing** *a* (*col. cold*) da morire.
perjure ['pɔːdʒə*] *vt*: **to ~ o.s.** spergiurare; **perjury** *n* spergiuro.
perk [pɔːk] *n* vantaggio; **to ~ up** *vi* (*cheer up*) rianimarsi; ~**y** *a* (*cheerful*) vivace, allegro(a).
perm [pɔːm] *n* (*for hair*) permanente *f.*
permanence ['pɔːmənəns] *n* permanenza.
permanent ['pɔːmənənt] *a* permanente.
permeate ['pɔːmɪeɪt] *vi* penetrare // *vt* permeare.
permissible [pə'mɪsɪbl] *a* permissibile, ammissibile.
permission [pə'mɪʃən] *n* permesso.
permissive [pə'mɪsɪv] *a* tollerante; **the ~ society** la società permissiva.
permit *n* [pə'mɪt] permesso // *vt* [pə'mɪt] permettere; **to ~ sb to do** permettere a qd di fare, dare il permesso a qd di fare.
permutation [pɔːmju'teɪʃən] *n* permutazione *f.*
pernicious [pɔː'nɪʃəs] *a* pernicioso(a), nocivo(a).

perpendicular [pɔːpən'dɪkjulə*] *a,n* perpendicolare (*f*).
perpetrate ['pɔːpɪtreɪt] *vt* perpetrare, commettere.
perpetual [pə'petjuəl] *a* perpetuo(a).
perpetuity [pɔːpɪ'tjuːɪtɪ] *n*: **in ~** in perpetuo.
perplex [pə'pleks] *vt* rendere perplesso(a); (*complicate*) imbrogliare.
persecute ['pɔːsɪkjuːt] *vt* perseguitare; **persecution** [-'kjuːʃən] *n* persecuzione *f.*
persevere [pɔːsɪ'vɪə*] *vi* perseverare.
Persian ['pɔːʃən] *a* persiano(a) // *n* (*LING*) persiano; **the (~) Gulf** *n* il Golfo Persico.
persist [pə'sɪst] *vi*: **to ~ (in doing)** persistere (nel fare); ostinarsi (a fare); ~**ence** *n* persistenza, ostinazione *f;* ~**ent** *a* persistente; ostinato(a).
person ['pɔːsn] *n* persona; ~**able** *a* di bell'aspetto; ~**al** *a* personale; individuale; ~**ality** [-'nælɪtɪ] *n* personalità *f inv;* ~**ally** *ad* personalmente; ~**ify** [-'sɔnɪfaɪ] *vt* personificare.
personnel [pɔːsə'nel] *n* personale *m;* ~ **manager** *n* direttore/trice del personale.
perspective [pə'spektɪv] *n* prospettiva.
perspicacity [pɔːspɪ'kæsɪtɪ] *n* perspicacia.
perspiration [pɔːspɪ'reɪʃən] *n* traspirazione *f,* sudore *m.*
perspire [pə'spaɪə*] *vi* traspirare.
persuade [pə'sweɪd] *vt* persuadere.
persuasion [pə'sweɪʒən] *n* persuasione *f.*
persuasive [pə'sweɪsɪv] *a* persuasivo(a).
pert [pɔːt] *a* (*bold*) sfacciato(a), impertinente.
pertaining [pɔː'teɪnɪŋ]: ~ **to** *prep* che riguarda.
pertinent ['pɔːtɪnənt] *a* pertinente.
perturb [pə'tɔːb] *vt* turbare.
Peru [pə'ruː] *n* Perù *m.*
perusal [pə'ruːzl] *n* attenta lettura.
Peruvian [pə'ruːvjən] *a, n* peruviano(a).
pervade [pə'veɪd] *vt* pervadere.
perverse [pə'vɔːs] *a* perverso(a).
perversion [pə'vɔːʃn] *n* pervertimento, perversione *f.*
perversity [pə'vɔːsɪtɪ] *n* perversità.
pervert *n* ['pɔːvɔːt] pervertito/a // *vt* [pə'vɔːt] pervertire.
pessimism ['pesɪmɪzəm] *n* pessimismo.
pessimist ['pesɪmɪst] *n* pessimista *m/f;* ~**ic** [-'mɪstɪk] *a* pessimistico(a).
pest [pest] *n* animale *m* (*or* insetto) pestifero; (*fig*) peste *f.*
pester ['pestə*] *vt* tormentare, molestare.
pesticide ['pestɪsaɪd] *n* pesticida *m.*
pestle ['pesl] *n* pestello.
pet [pet] *n* animale *m* domestico; (*favourite*) favorito/a // *vt* accarezzare // *vi* (*col*) fare il petting; ~ **lion** *n* leone *m* ammaestrato.
petal ['petl] *n* petalo.
peter ['piːtə*]: **to ~ out** *vi* esaurirsi; estinguersi.
petite [pə'tiːt] *a* piccolo(a) e aggraziato(a).
petition [pə'tɪʃən] *n* petizione *f.*

petrified ['petrıfaıd] a (fig) morto(a) di paura.

petrol ['petrəl] n (Brit) benzina.

petroleum [pə'trəulıəm] n petrolio.

petrol: ~ **pump** n (in car, at garage) pompa di benzina; ~ **station** n stazione f di rifornimento; ~ **tank** n serbatoio della benzina.

petticoat ['petıkəut] n sottana.

pettiness ['petınıs] n meschinità.

petty ['petı] a (mean) meschino(a); (unimportant) insignificante; ~ **cash** n piccola cassa; ~ **officer** n sottufficiale m di marina.

petulant ['petjulənt] a irritabile.

pew [pju:] n panca (di chiesa).

pewter ['pju:tə*] n peltro.

phallic ['fælık] a fallico(a).

phantom ['fæntəm] n fantasma m.

Pharaoh ['fɛərəu] n faraone m.

pharmacist ['fɑːməsıst] n farmacista m/f.

pharmacy ['fɑːməsı] n farmacia.

phase [feız] n fase f, periodo // vt: to ~ sth in/out introdurre/eliminare qc progressivamente.

Ph.D. (abbr = Doctor of Philosophy) n (degree) dottorato di ricerca.

pheasant ['feznt] n fagiano.

phenomenon, pl **phenomena** [fə'nəmınən, -nə] n fenomeno.

phew [fju:] excl uff!

phial ['faıəl] n fiala.

philanthropic [fılən'θrɔpık] a filantropico(a).

philanthropist [fı'lænθrəpıst] n filantropo.

philately [fı'lætəlı] n filatelia.

Philippines ['fılıpi:nz] npl (also: Philippine Islands) Filippine fpl.

philosopher [fı'lɔsəfə*] n filosofo/a.

philosophical [fılə'sɔfıkl] a filosofico(a).

philosophy [fı'lɔsəfı] n filosofia.

phlegm [flɛm] n flemma; ~**atic** [flɛg'mætık] a flemmatico(a).

phobia ['fəubjə] n fobia.

phone [fəun] n telefono // vt telefonare; to ~ **back** vt, vi richiamare.

phonetics [fə'nɛtıks] n fonetica.

phon(e)y ['fəunı] a falso(a), fasullo(a) // n (person) ciarlatano.

phonograph ['fəunəgrɑːf] n (US) giradischi m.

phosphate ['fɔsfeıt] n fosfato.

phosphorus ['fɔsfərəs] n fosforo.

photo ['fəutəu] n foto f inv.

photo... ['fəutəu] prefix: ~**copier** n fotocopiatrice f; ~**copy** n fotocopia // vt fotocopiare; ~**genic** [-'dʒɛnık] a fotogenico(a); ~**graph** n fotografia // vt fotografare; ~**grapher** [fə'tɔgrəfə*] n fotografo; ~**graphic** [-'græfık] a fotografico(a); ~**graphy** [fə'tɔgrəfı] n fotografia.

phrase [freız] n espressione f; (LING) locuzione f; (MUS) frase f // vt esprimere; ~ **book** n vocabolarietto.

physical ['fızıkl] a fisico(a); ~**ly** ad fisicamente.

physician [fı'zıʃən] n medico.

physicist ['fızısıst] n fisico.

physics ['fızıks] n fisica.

physiology [fızı'ɔlədʒı] n fisiologia.

physiotherapist [fızıəu'θerəpıst] n fisioterapista m/f.

physiotherapy [fızıəu'θerəpı] n fisioterapia.

physique [fı'zi:k] n fisico; costituzione f.

pianist ['pi:ənıst] n pianista m/f.

piano [pı'ænəu] n pianoforte m.

piccolo ['pıkələu] n ottavino.

pick [pık] n (tool: also: ~-axe) piccone m // vt scegliere; (gather) cogliere; take your ~ scelga; the ~ of il fior fiore di; to ~ one's teeth stuzzicarsi i denti; to ~ pockets borseggiare; to ~ on vt fus (person) avercela con; to ~ out vt scegliere; (distinguish) distinguere; to ~ up vi (improve) migliorarsi // vt raccogliere; (collect) passare a prendere; (AUT: give lift to) far salire; (learn) imparare; to ~ up speed acquistare velocità; to ~ o.s. up rialzarsi.

picket ['pıkıt] n (in strike) scioperante m/f che fa parte di un picchetto; picchetto // vt picchettare; ~ **line** n controllo del picchetto.

pickle ['pıkl] n (also: ~s: as condiment) sottaceti mpl // vt mettere sottaceto; mettere in salamoia.

pick-me-up ['pıkmiːʌp] n tiramisù m inv.

pickpocket ['pıkpɔkıt] n borsaiolo.

pickup ['pıkʌp] n (on record player) pick-up m inv; (small truck) camioncino.

picnic ['pıknık] n picnic m inv // vi fare un picnic.

pictorial [pık'tɔːrıəl] a illustrato(a).

picture ['pıktʃə*] n quadro; (painting) pittura; (photograph) foto(grafia); (drawing) disegno; (film) film m inv // vt raffigurarsi; the ~s il cinema; ~ **book** n libro illustrato.

picturesque [pıktʃə'rɛsk] a pittoresco(a).

piddling ['pıdlıŋ] a (col) insignificante.

pidgin ['pıdʒın] a: ~ **English** n inglese semplificato misto ad elementi indigeni.

pie [paı] n torta; (of meat) pasticcio.

piebald ['paıbɔːld] a pezzato(a).

piece [pi:s] n pezzo; (of land) appezzamento; (item): a ~ of furniture/advice un mobile/consiglio // vt: to ~ together mettere insieme; in ~s (broken) in pezzi; (not yet assembled) smontato(a); to take to ~s smontare; ~**meal** ad pezzo a pezzo, a spizzico; ~**work** n (lavoro a) cottimo.

pier [pıə*] n molo; (of bridge etc) pila.

pierce [pıəs] vt forare; (with arrow etc) trafiggere.

piercing ['pıəsıŋ] a (cry) acuto(a).

piety ['paıətı] n pietà, devozione f.

pig [pıg] n maiale m, porco.

pigeon ['pıdʒən] n piccione m; ~**hole** n

casella; ~-toed a che cammina con i piedi in dentro.

piggy bank ['pɪgɪbæŋk] n salvadanaro.

pigheaded ['pɪg'hɛdɪd] a caparbio(a), cocciuto(a).

piglet ['pɪglɪt] n porcellino.

pigment ['pɪgmənt] n pigmento.

pigmy ['pɪgmɪ] n = **pygmy**.

pigsty ['pɪgstaɪ] n porcile m.

pigtail ['pɪgteɪl] n treccina.

pike [paɪk] n (spear) picca; (fish) luccio.

pilchard ['pɪltʃəd] n specie di sardina.

pile [paɪl] n (pillar, of books) pila; (heap) mucchio; (of carpet) pelo // vb (also: ~ up) vt ammucchiare // vi ammucchiarsi.

piles [paɪlz] npl emorroidi fpl.

pileup ['paɪlʌp] n (AUT) tamponamento a catena.

pilfering ['pɪlfərɪŋ] n rubacchiare m.

pilgrim ['pɪlgrɪm] n pellegrino/a; ~age n pellegrinaggio.

pill [pɪl] n pillola; **the** ~ la pillola.

pillage ['pɪlɪdʒ] vt saccheggiare.

pillar ['pɪlə*] n colonna; ~ **box** n (Brit) cassetta postale.

pillion ['pɪljən] n (of motor cycle) sellino posteriore.

pillory ['pɪlərɪ] n berlina // vt mettere alla berlina.

pillow ['pɪləu] n guanciale m; ~**case** n federa.

pilot ['paɪlət] n pilota m/f // cpd (scheme etc) pilota inv // vt pilotare; ~ **boat** n battello pilota; ~ **light** n fiamma pilota.

pimp [pɪmp] n mezzano.

pimple ['pɪmpl] n foruncolo.

pin [pɪn] n spillo; (TECH) perno // vt attaccare con uno spillo; ~**s and needles** formicolio; **to** ~ **sb down** (fig) obbligare qd a pronunziarsi.

pinafore ['pɪnəfɔ:*] n grembiule m (senza maniche); ~ **dress** n scamiciato.

pincers ['pɪnsəz] npl pinzette fpl.

pinch [pɪntʃ] n pizzicotto, pizzico // vt pizzicare; (col: steal) grattare // vi (shoe) stringere; **at a** ~ in caso di bisogno.

pincushion ['pɪnkuʃən] n puntaspilli m inv.

pine [paɪn] n (also: ~ **tree**) pino // vi: ~ **for** struggersi dal desiderio di; **to** ~ **away** vi languire.

pineapple ['paɪnæpl] n ananas m inv.

ping [pɪŋ] n (noise) tintinnio; ~-**pong** n * ping-pong m *.

pink [pɪŋk] a rosa inv // n (colour) rosa m inv; (BOT) garofano.

pinnacle ['pɪnəkl] n pinnacolo.

pinpoint ['pɪnpɔɪnt] vt indicare con precisione.

pinstripe ['pɪnstraɪp] n stoffa gessata.

pint [paɪnt] n pinta (= 0.56 l).

pinup ['pɪnʌp] n pin-up girl f inv.

pioneer [paɪə'nɪə*] n pioniere/a.

pious ['paɪəs] a pio(a).

pip [pɪp] n (seed) seme m; (time signal on radio) segnale m orario.

pipe [paɪp] n tubo; (for smoking) pipa; (MUS) piffero // vt portare per mezzo di

tubazione; ~**s** npl (also: **bag**~**s**) cornamusa (scozzese); **to** ~ **down** vi (col) calmarsi; ~ **dream** n vana speranza; ~**line** n conduttura; (for oil) oleodotto; ~**r** n piffero; suonatore/trice di cornamusa.

piping ['paɪpɪŋ] ad: ~ **hot** caldo bollente.

pique [pi:k] n picca.

piracy ['paɪərəsɪ] n pirateria.

pirate ['paɪərət] n pirata m; ~ **radio** n radio pirata f inv.

pirouette [pɪru'ɛt] n piroetta // vi piroettare.

Pisces ['paɪsi:z] n Pesci mpl.

pistol ['pɪstl] n pistola.

piston ['pɪstən] n pistone m.

pit [pɪt] n buca, fossa; (also: **coal** ~) miniera; (also: **orchestra** ~) orchestra // vt: **to** ~ **sb against sb** opporre qd a qd; ~**s** npl (AUT) box m; **to** ~ **o.s. against** opporsi a.

pitch [pɪtʃ] n (throw) lancia; (MUS) tono; (of voice) altezza; (SPORT) campo; (NAUT) beccheggio; (tar) pece f // vt (throw) lanciare // vi (fall) cascare; (NAUT) beccheggiare; **to** ~ **a tent** piantare una tenda; ~-**black** a nero(a) come la pece; ~**ed battle** n battaglia campale.

pitcher ['pɪtʃə*] n brocca.

pitchfork ['pɪtʃfɔ:k] n forcone m.

piteous ['pɪtɪəs] a pietoso(a).

pitfall ['pɪtfɔ:l] n trappola.

pith [pɪθ] n (of plant) midollo; (of orange) parte f interna della scorza; (fig) essenza, succo; vigore m.

pithy ['pɪθɪ] a conciso(a); vigoroso(a).

pitiable ['pɪtɪəbl] a pietoso(a).

pitiful ['pɪtɪful] a (touching) pietoso(a); (contemptible) miserabile.

pitiless ['pɪtɪlɪs] a spietato(a).

pittance ['pɪtns] n miseria, magro salario.

pity ['pɪtɪ] n pietà // vt aver pietà di; **what a** ~! che peccato!; ~**ing** a compassionevole.

pivot ['pɪvət] n perno // vi imperniarsi.

pixie ['pɪksɪ] n folletto.

placard ['plækɑ:d] n affisso.

placate [plə'keɪt] vt placare, calmare.

place [pleɪs] n posto, luogo; (proper position, rank, seat) posto; (house) casa, alloggio; (home) **at/to his** ~ a casa sua // vt (object) posare, mettere; (identify) riconoscere; individuare; **to take** ~ aver luogo; succedere; **to** ~ **an order** dare un'ordinazione; **out of** ~ (not suitable) inopportuno(a); **in the first** ~ in primo luogo; ~ **mat** n sottopiatto.

placid ['plæsɪd] a placido(a), calmo(a).

plagiarism ['pleɪdʒjərɪzm] n plagio.

plagiarize ['pleɪdʒjəraɪz] vt plagiare.

plague [pleɪg] n piaga; (MED) peste f.

plaice [pleɪs] n, pl inv pianuzza. -

plaid [plæd] n plaid m inv.

plain [pleɪn] a (clear) chiaro(a), palese; (simple) semplice; (frank) franco(a), aperto(a); (not handsome) bruttino(a); (without seasoning etc) scondito(a);

naturale; (in one colour) tinta unita inv //
ad francamente, chiaramente // n
pianura; **in ~ clothes** (police) in
borghese; **~ly** ad chiaramente; (frankly)
francamente; **~ness** n semplicità.
plaintiff ['pleintif] n attore/trice.
plait [plæt] n treccia.
plan [plæn] n pianta; (scheme) progetto,
piano // vt (think in advance) progettare;
(prepare) organizzare // vi far piani or
progetti; **to ~ to** do progettare di fare.
plane [plein] n (AVIAT) aereo; (tree)
platano; (tool) pialla; (ART, MATH etc) piano
// a piano(a), piatto(a) // vt (with tool)
piallare.
planet ['plænit] n pianeta m.
planetarium [plæni'tɛəriəm] n planetario.
plank [plæŋk] n tavola, asse f.
plankton ['plæŋktən] n plancton m.
planner ['plænə°] n pianificatore/trice.
planning ['plæniŋ] n progettazione f;
family ~ pianificazione f delle nascite.
plant [plɑ:nt] n pianta; (machinery)
impianto; (factory) fabbrica // vt piantare;
(bomb) mettere.
plantation [plæn'teiʃən] n piantagione f.
plaque [plæk] n placca.
plasma ['plæzmə] n plasma m.
plaster ['plɑ:stə°] n intonaco; (also: ~ of
Paris) gesso; (also: sticking ~) cerotto
// vt intonacare; ingessare; (cover): **to ~
with** coprire di; **in ~** (leg etc)
ingessato(a); **~ed** a (col) ubriaco(a)
fradicio(a); **~er** n intonacatore m.
plastic ['plæstik] n plastica // a (made of
plastic) di or in plastica; (flexible)
plastico(a), malleabile; (art) plastico(a).
plasticine ['plæstisi:n] a ⓇC plastilina Ⓡ.
plastic surgery ['plæstik'sə:dʒəri] a
chirurgia plastica.
plate [pleit] n (dish) piatto; (sheet of metal)
lamiera; (PHOT) lastra; (in book) tavola;
gold ~ (dishes) vasellame m d'oro; **silver
~** (dishes) argenteria.
plateau, **~s** or **~x** ['plætou, -z] n
altipiano.
plateful ['pleitful] n piatto.
plate glass [pleit'glɑ:s] n vetro piano.
platform ['plætfɔ:m] n (at meeting)
piattaforma; (stage) palco; (RAIL)
marciapiede m; **~ ticket** n biglietto
d'ingresso ai binari.
platinum ['plætinəm] n platino.
platitude ['plætitju:d] n luogo comune.
platoon [plə'tu:n] n plotone m.
platter ['plætə°] n piatto.
plausible ['plɔ:zibl] a plausibile, credibile;
(person) convincente.
play [plei] n gioco; (THEATRE) commedia //
vt (game) giocare a; (team, opponent)
giocare contro; (instrument, piece of music)
suonare; (play, part) interpretare // vi
giocare; suonare; recitare; **to ~ down** vt
minimizzare; **to ~ up** vi (cause trouble)
fare i capricci; **to ~act** vi fare la
commedia; **~ed-out** a spossato(a); **~er**
n giocatore/trice; (THEATRE) attore/trice;
(MUS) musicista m/f; **~ful** a giocoso(a);

~ground n campo di ricreazioni;
~group n giardino d'infanzia; **~ing
card** n carta da gioco; **~ing field** n
campo sportivo; **~ mate** n compagno/a di
gioco; **~-off** n (SPORT) bella; **~ on words**
n gioco di parole; **~pen** n box m inv;
~thing n giocattolo; **~wright** n dram-
maturgo/a.
plea [pli:] n (request) preghiera, domanda;
(excuse) scusa; (LAW) (argomento di)
difesa.
plead [pli:d] vt patrocinare; (give as
excuse) addurre a pretesto // vi (LAW)
perorare la causa; (beg): **to ~ with sb**
implorare qd.
pleasant ['pleznt] a piacevole, gradevole;
~ly ad piacevolmente; **~ness** n (of
person) amabilità; (of place) amenità;
~ry n (joke) scherzo.
please [pli:z] vt piacere a // vi (think fit):
do as you ~ faccia come le pare; **~!** per
piacere!; **my bill, ~** il conto, per piacere;
~ yourself! come ti or le pare!; **~d** a:
~d (with) contento(a) di; **pleasing** a
piacevole, che fa piacere.
pleasurable ['pleʒərəbl] a molto
piacevole, molto gradevole.
pleasure ['pleʒə°] n piacere m; **'it's a ~'**
'prego'; **~ steamer** n vapore m da
diporto.
pleat [pli:t] n piega.
plebiscite ['plebisit] n plebiscito.
plectrum ['plektrəm] n plettro.
pledge [pledʒ] n pegno; (promise)
promessa // vt impegnare; promettere.
plentiful ['plentiful] a abbondante,
copioso(a).
plenty ['plenti] n abbondanza; **~ of**
tanto(a), molto(a); un'abbondanza di.
pleurisy ['pluərisi] n pleurite f.
pliable ['plaiəbl] a flessibile; (person)
malleabile.
pliers ['plaiəz] npl pinza.
plight [plait] n situazione f critica.
plimsolls ['plimsəlz] npl scarpe fpl da
tennis.
plinth [plinθ] n plinto; piedistallo.
plod [plod] vi camminare a stento; (fig)
sgobbare; **~der** n sgobbone m.
plonk [plɔŋk] (col) n (wine) vino da poco
// vt: **to ~ sth down** buttare giù qc
bruscamente.
plot [plot] n congiura, cospirazione f; (of
story, play) trama; (of land) lotto // vt
(mark out) fare la pianta di; rilevare; (:
diagram etc) tracciare; (conspire)
congiurare, cospirare // vi congiurare;
~ter n cospiratore/trice.
plough, plow (US) [plau] n aratro // vt
(earth) arare; **to ~ back** vt (COMM)
reinvestire; **to ~ through** vt fus (snow
etc) procedere a fatica in.
ploy [plɔi] n stratagemma m.
pluck [plʌk] vt (fruit) cogliere; (musical
instrument) pizzicare; (bird) spennare // n
coraggio, fegato; **to ~ up courage** farsi
coraggio; **~y** a coraggioso(a).
plug [plʌg] n tappo; (ELEC) spina; (AUT)

candela // vt (hole) tappare; (col: advertise) spingere.

plum [plʌm] n (fruit) susina // a: ~ **job** n (col) impiego ottimo or favoloso.

plumb [plʌm] a verticale // n piombo // ad (exactly) esattamente // vt sondare.

plumber ['plʌmə°] n idraulico.

plumbing ['plʌmɪŋ] n (trade) lavoro di idraulico; (piping) tubature fpl.

plumbline ['plʌmlaɪn] n filo a piombo.

plume [pluːm] n piuma, penna; (decorative) pennacchio.

plummet ['plʌmɪt] vi cadere a piombo.

plump [plʌmp] a grassoccio(a); **to ~ for** vt fus (col: choose) decidersi per.

plunder ['plʌndə°] n saccheggio // vt saccheggiare.

plunge [plʌndʒ] n tuffo // vt immergere // vi (fall) cadere, precipitare; **to take the ~** saltare il fosso; **plunging** a (neckline) profondo(a).

pluperfect [pluː'pəːfɪkt] n piucchepperfetto.

plural ['pluərl] a, n plurale (m).

plus [plʌs] n (also: ~ **sign**) segno più // prep più; **ten/twenty ~** più di dieci/venti; ~ **fours** npl calzoni mpl alla zuava.

plush [plʌʃ] a lussuoso(a).

ply [plaɪ] n (of wool) capo; (of wood) strato // vt (tool) maneggiare; (a trade) esercitare // vi (ship) fare il servizio; **to ~ sb with drink** dare di bere continuamente a qd; ~**wood** n legno compensato.

P.M. abbr see **prime**.

p.m. ad (abbr of post meridiem) del pomeriggio.

pneumatic [njuː'mætɪk] a pneumatico(a).

pneumonia [njuː'məunɪə] n polmonite f.

P.O. abbr see **post office**.

poach [pəutʃ] vt (cook) affogare; (steal) cacciare (or pescare) di frodo // vi fare il bracconiere; ~**ed** a (egg) affogato(a); ~**er** n bracconiere m; ~**ing** n caccia (or pesca) di frodo.

pocket ['pɔkɪt] n tasca // vt intascare; **to be out of ~** rimetterci; ~**book** n (wallet) portafoglio; (notebook) taccuino; ~ **knife** n temperino; ~ **money** n paghetta, settimana.

pockmarked ['pɔkmɑːkt] a (face) butterato(a).

pod [pɔd] n guscio // vt sgusciare.

podgy ['pɔdʒɪ] a grassoccio(a).

poem ['pəuɪm] n poesia.

poet ['pəuɪt] n poeta/essa; ~**ic** [-'etɪk] a poetico(a); ~ **laureate** n poeta m laureato (nominato dalla Corte Reale); ~**ry** n poesia.

poignant ['pɔɪnjənt] a struggente; (sharp) pungente.

point [pɔɪnt] n (gen) punto; (tip: of needle etc) punta; (in time) punto, momento; (SCOL) voto; (main idea, important part) nocciolo; (also: **decimal ~**): **2 ~ 3 (2.3)** 2 virgola 3 (2,3) // vt (show) indicare; (gun etc): **to ~ sth at** puntare qc contro // vi

mostrare a dito; ~**s** npl (AUT) puntine fpl; (RAIL) scambio; **to make a ~** fare un'osservazione; **to get the ~** capire; **to come to the ~** venire al fatto; **there's no ~ (in doing)** è inutile (fare); **good ~s** vantaggi mpl; (of person) qualità fpl; **to ~ out** vt far notare; **to ~ to** indicare; (fig) dimostrare; ~**-blank** ad (also: at ~**-blank range**) a bruciapelo; (fig) categoricamente; ~**ed** a (shape) aguzzo(a), appuntito(a); (remark) specifico(a); ~**edly** ad in maniera inequivocabile; ~**er** n (stick) bacchetta; (needle) lancetta; (dog) pointer m, cane m da punta; ~**less** a inutile, vano(a); ~ **of view** n punto di vista.

poise [pɔɪz] n (balance) equilibrio; (of head, body) portamento; (calmness) calma // vt tenere in equilibrio; **to be ~d for** (fig) essere pronto(a) a.

poison ['pɔɪzn] n veleno // vt avvelenare; ~**ing** n avvelenamento; ~**ous** a velenoso(a).

poke [pəuk] vt (fire) attizzare; (jab with finger, stick etc) punzecchiare; (put): **to ~ sth in(to)** spingere qc dentro; **to ~ about** vi frugare.

poker ['pəukə°] n attizzatoio; (CARDS) poker m; ~**-faced** a dal viso impassibile.

poky ['pəukɪ] a piccolo(a) e stretto(a).

Poland ['pəulənd] n Polonia.

polar ['pəulə°] a polare; ~ **bear** n orso bianco.

polarize ['pəuləraɪz] vt polarizzare.

pole [pəul] n (of wood) palo; (ELEC, GEO) polo.

Pole [pəul] n polacco/a.

polecat ['pəulkæt] n (US) puzzola.

polemic [pɔ'lemɪk] n polemica.

pole star ['pəulstɑː°] n stella polare.

pole vault ['pəulvɔːlt] n salto con l'asta.

police [pɔ'liːs] n polizia // vt mantenere l'ordine in; ~ **car** n macchina della polizia; ~**man** n poliziotto, agente m di polizia; ~ **station** n posto di polizia; ~**woman** n donna f poliziotto inv.

policy ['pɔlɪsɪ] n politica; (also: **insurance ~**) polizza (d'assicurazione).

polio ['pəulɪəu] n polio f.

Polish ['pəulɪʃ] a polacco(a) // n (LING) polacco.

polish ['pɔlɪʃ] n (for shoes) lucido; (for floor) cera; (for nails) smalto; (shine) lucentezza, lustro; (fig: refinement) raffinatezza // vt lucidare; (fig: improve) raffinare; **to ~ off** vt (work) sbrigare; (food) mangiarsi; ~**ed** a (fig) raffinato(a).

polite [pɔ'laɪt] a cortese; ~**ly** ad cortesemente; ~**ness** n cortesia.

politic ['pɔlɪtɪk] a diplomatico(a); ~**al** [pɔ'lɪtɪkl] a politico(a); ~**ian** [-'tɪʃən] n politico; ~**s** npl politica.

polka ['pɔlkə] n polca; ~ **dot** n pois m inv.

poll [pəul] n scrutinio; (votes cast) voti mpl; (also: **opinion ~**) sondaggio (d'opinioni) // vt ottenere.

pollen ['pɔlən] n polline m.

pollination [pɒlɪ'neɪʃən] n impollinazione f.

polling ['pəʊlɪŋ]: ~ **booth** n cabina elettorale; ~ **day** n giorno delle elezioni; ~ **station** n sezione f elettorale.

pollute [pə'luːt] vt inquinare.

pollution [pə'luːʃən] n inquinamento.

polo ['pəʊləʊ] n polo; ~-**neck** a a collo alto risvoltato.

polyester [pɒlɪ'estə°] n poliestere m.

polygamy ['pɒlɪgəmɪ] n poligamia.

Polynesia [pɒlɪ'niːzɪə] n Polinesia.

polytechnic [pɒlɪ'teknɪk] n (college) istituto superiore ad indirizzo tecnologico.

polythene ['pɒlɪθiːn] n politene m; ~ **bag** n sacco di plastica.

pomegranate ['pɒmɪgrænɪt] n melagrana.

pommel ['pɒml] n pomo.

pomp [pɒmp] n pompa, fasto.

pompous ['pɒmpəs] a pomposo(a).

pond [pɒnd] n pozza; stagno.

ponder ['pɒndə°] vt ponderare, riflettere su; ~-**ous** a ponderoso(a), pesante.

pontiff ['pɒntɪf] n pontefice m.

pontificate [pɒn'tɪfɪkeɪt] vi (fig): to ~ (about) pontificare (su).

pontoon [pɒn'tuːn] n pontone m.

pony ['pəʊnɪ] n pony m inv; ~-**tail** n coda di cavallo.

poodle ['puːdl] n barboncino, barbone m.

pooh-pooh ['puː'puː] vt deridere.

pool [puːl] n (of rain) pozza; (pond) stagno; (artificial) vasca; (also: **swimming** ~) piscina; (sth shared) fondo comune; (billiards) specie di biliardo a buca // vt mettere in comune.

poor [pʊə°] a povero(a); (mediocre) mediocre, cattivo(a) // npl: **the** ~ i poveri; ~**ly** ad poveramente; male // a indisposto(a), malato(a).

pop [pɒp] n (noise) schiocco; (MUS) musica pop; (US: col: father) babbo // vt (put) mettere (in fretta) // vi scoppiare; (cork) schioccare; to ~ **in** vi passare; to ~ **out** vi fare un salto fuori; to ~ **up** vi apparire, sorgere; ~ **concert** n concerto m pop inv; ~-**corn** n pop-corn m.

pope [pəʊp] n papa m.

poplar ['pɒplə°] n pioppo.

poplin ['pɒplɪn] n popeline f.

poppy ['pɒpɪ] n papavero.

populace ['pɒpjʊləs] n popolo.

popular ['pɒpjʊlə°] a popolare; (fashionable) in voga; ~**ity** [-'lærɪtɪ] n popolarità; ~**ize** vt divulgare; (science) volgarizzare.

population [pɒpjʊ'leɪʃən] n popolazione f.

populous ['pɒpjʊləs] a popolato(a).

porcelain ['pɔːslɪn] n porcellana.

porch [pɔːtʃ] n veranda.

porcupine ['pɔːkjʊpaɪn] n porcospino.

pore [pɔː°] n poro // vi: to ~ **over** essere immerso(a) in.

pork [pɔːk] n carne f di maiale.

pornographic [pɔːnə'græfɪk] a pornografico(a).

pornography [pɔː'nɒgrəfɪ] n pornografia.

porous ['pɔːrəs] a poroso(a).

porpoise ['pɔːpəs] n focena.

porridge ['pɒrɪdʒ] n porridge m.

port [pɔːt] n porto; (opening in ship) portello; (NAUT: left side) babordo; (wine) porto.

portable ['pɔːtəbl] a portatile.

portal ['pɔːtl] n portale m.

portcullis [pɔːt'kʌlɪs] n saracinesca.

portend ['pɔːtend] n presagio.

porter ['pɔːtə°] n (for luggage) facchino, portabagagli m inv; (doorkeeper) portiere m, portinaio.

porthole ['pɔːthəʊl] n oblò m inv.

portico ['pɔːtɪkəʊ] n portico.

portion ['pɔːʃən] n porzione f.

portly ['pɔːtlɪ] a corpulento(a).

portrait ['pɔːtreɪt] n ritratto.

portray [pɔː'treɪ] vt fare il ritratto di; (character on stage) rappresentare; (in writing) ritrarre; ~-**al** n ritratto; rappresentazione f.

Portugal ['pɔːtjʊgl] n Portogallo.

Portuguese [pɔːtjʊ'giːz] a portoghese // n, pl inv portoghese m/f; (LING) portoghese m.

pose [pəʊz] n posa // vi posare; (pretend): to ~ **as** atteggiarsi a, posare a // vt porre.

posh [pɒʃ] a (col) elegante; (family) per bene.

position [pə'zɪʃən] n posizione f; (job) posto // vt mettere in posizione, collocare.

positive ['pɒzɪtɪv] a positivo(a); (certain) sicuro(a), certo(a); (definite) preciso(a), definitivo(a).

posse ['pɒsɪ] n (US) drappello.

possess [pə'zes] vt possedere; ~-**ion** [pə'zeʃən] n possesso; (object) bene m; ~-**ive** a possessivo(a); ~-**or** n possessore/posseditrice.

possibility [pɒsɪ'bɪlɪtɪ] n possibilità f inv.

possible ['pɒsɪbl] a possibile; **if** ~ se possibile; **as big as** ~ il più grande possibile.

possibly ['pɒsɪblɪ] ad (perhaps) forse; **if you** ~ **can** se le è possibile; **I cannot** ~ **come** proprio non posso venire.

post [pəʊst] n posta; (collection) levata; (job, situation) posto; (pole) palo // vt (send by post) impostare; (MIL) appostare; (appoint): to ~ **to** assegnare a; (notice) affiggere; ~-**age** n affrancatura; ~-**al** a postale; ~-**al order** n vaglia m inv postale; ~-**box** n cassetta postale; ~-**card** n cartolina.

postdate ['pəʊst'deɪt] vt (cheque) postdatare.

poster ['pəʊstə°] n manifesto, affisso.

poste restante [pəʊst'rɛstɑ̃ːnt] n fermo posta m.

posterity [pɒs'terɪtɪ] n posterità.

postgraduate ['pəʊst'grædjʊət] n ≈ laureato/a che continua gli studi.

posthumous ['pɒstjuməs] a postumo(a); ~**ly** ad dopo la mia (or sua etc) morte.

postman ['pəustmən] n postino.
postmark ['pəustmɑːk] n bollo or timbro postale.
postmaster ['pəustmɑːstə°] n direttore m d'un ufficio postale.
post-mortem [pəust'mɔːtəm] n autopsia.
post office ['pəustɔfis] n (building) ufficio postale; (organization) poste fpl; ~ **box** (P.O. box) n casella postale (C.P.).
postpone [pəs'pəun] vt rinviare; ~**ment** n rinvio.
postscript ['pəustskript] n poscritto.
postulate ['pɔstjuleit] vt postulare.
posture ['pɔstʃə°] n portamento; (pose) posa, atteggiamento // vi posare.
postwar ['pəust'wɔː°] a del dopoguerra.
posy ['pəuzi] n mazzetto di fiori.
pot [pɔt] n (for cooking) pentola; casseruola; (for plants, jam) vaso; (col: marijuana) erba // vt (plant) piantare in vaso; **to go to** ~ andare in malora.
potash ['pɔtæʃ] n potassa.
potato, ~**es** [pə'teitəu] n patata.
potency ['pəutnsi] n potenza; (of drink) forza.
potent ['pəutnt] a potente, forte.
potentate ['pəutnteit] n potentato.
potential [pə'tenʃl] a potenziale // n possibilità fpl; ~**ly** ad potenzialmente.
pothole ['pɔthəul] n (in road) buca; (underground) marmitta; ~**r** n speleologo/a; **potholing** n: **to go potholing** fare la speleologia.
potion ['pəuʃən] n pozione f.
potluck [pɔt'lʌk] n: **to take** ~ tentare la sorte.
potshot ['pɔtʃɔt] n: **to take** ~**s at** tirare a vanvera contro.
potted ['pɔtid] a (food) in conserva; (plant) in vaso.
potter ['pɔtə°] n vasaio // vi: **to** ~ **around**, ~ **about** lavoracchiare; ~**y** n ceramiche fpl.
potty ['pɔti] a (col: mad) tocco(a) // n (child's) vasino.
pouch [pautʃ] n borsa; (zool.) marsupio.
pouf(fe) [puːf] n (stool) pouf m inv.
poultice ['pəultis] n impiastro, cataplasma.
poultry ['pəultri] n pollame m.
pounce [pauns] vi: **to** ~ **(on)** balzare addosso a, piombare su // n balzo.
pound [paund] n (weight) libbra; (money) (lira) sterlina; (for dogs) canile m municipale // vt (beat) battere; (crush) pestare, polverizzare // vi (beat) battere, martellare.
pour [pɔː°] vt versare // vi riversarsi; (rain) piovere a dirotto; **to** ~ **in** vi (people) entrare a flotti; **to** ~ **out** vi vuotare; versare; (serve: a drink) mescere; ~**ing** a: ~**ing rain** pioggia torrenziale.
pout [paut] vi sporgere le labbra; fare il broncio.
poverty ['pɔvəti] n povertà, miseria;

~**-stricken** a molto povero(a), misero(a).
powder ['paudə°] n polvere f // vt spolverizzare; (face) incipriare; ~ **room** n toilette f inv (per signore); ~**y** a polveroso(a).
power ['pauə°] n (strength) potenza, forza; (ability, POL: of party, leader) potere m; (MATH) potenza; (ELEC) corrente f // vt fornire di energia; **mental** ~**s** capacità fpl mentali; ~ **cut** n interruzione f or mancanza di corrente; ~**ed** a: ~**ed by** azionato(a) da; ~**ful** a potente, forte; ~**less** a impotente, senza potere; ~ **point** n presa di corrente; ~ **station** n centrale f elettrica.
powwow ['pauwau] n riunione f.
pox [pɔks] n see **chicken**.
p.p. abbr: ~ **J. Smith** per il Signor J. Smith.
P.R. abbr of **public relations**.
practicability [præktikə'biliti] n praticabilità.
practicable ['præktikəbl] a (scheme) praticabile.
practical ['præktikl] a pratico(a); ~ **joke** n beffa; ~**ly** ad (almost) quasi.
practice ['præktis] n pratica; (of profession) esercizio; (at football etc) allenamento; (business) gabinetto; clientela // vt,vi (US) = **practise**; **in** ~ (in reality) in pratica; **out of** ~ fuori esercizio; **2 hours' piano** ~ 2 ore di esercizio al pianoforte.
practise, (US) **practice** ['præktis] vt (work at: piano, one's backhand etc) esercitarsi a; (train for: skiing, running etc) allenarsi a; (a sport, religion) praticare; (method) usare; (profession) esercitare // vi esercitarsi; (train) allenarsi; **practising** a (Christian etc) praticante; (lawyer) che esercita la professione.
practitioner [præk'tiʃənə°] n professionista m/f.
pragmatic [præg'mætik] a prammatico(a).
prairie ['preəri] n prateria.
praise [preiz] n elogio, lode f // vt elogiare, lodare; ~**worthy** a lodevole.
pram [præm] n carrozzina.
prance [prɑːns] vi (horse) impennarsi.
prank [præŋk] n burla.
prattle ['prætl] vi cinguettare.
prawn [prɔːn] n gamberetto.
pray [prei] vi pregare.
prayer [preə°] n preghiera; ~ **book** n libro di preghiere.
preach [priːtʃ] vi,vi predicare; ~**er** n predicatore/trice.
preamble [pri'æmbl] n preambolo.
precarious [pri'keəriəs] a precario(a).
precaution [pri'kɔːʃən] n precauzione f; ~**ary** a (measure) precauzionale.
precede [pri'siːd] vt,vi precedere.
precedence ['presidəns] n precedenza; **to take** ~ **over** avere la precedenza su.
precedent ['presidənt] n precedente m.
preceding [pri'siːdiŋ] a precedente.

precept ['pri:sept] n precetto.
precinct ['pri:sıŋkt] n (round cathedral) recinto; ~s npl (neighbourhood) dintorni mpl, vicinanze fpl; **pedestrian** ~ n zona pedonale.
precious ['preʃəs] a prezioso(a).
precipice ['presıpıs] n precipizio.
precipitate [prı'sıpıtıt] a (hasty) precipitoso(a); **precipitation** [-'teıʃən] n precipitazione f.
precipitous [prı'sıpıtəs] a (steep) erto(a), ripido(a).
précis, pl **précis** ['preısı:, -z] n riassunto.
precise [prı'saıs] a preciso(a); ~ly ad precisamente; ~ly! appunto!
preclude [prı'klu:d] vt precludere, impedire; to ~ sb from doing impedire a qd di fare.
precocious [prı'kəuʃəs] a precoce.
preconceived [pri:kən'si:vd] a (idea) preconcetto(a).
precondition [pri:kən'dıʃən] n condizione f necessaria.
precursor [pri:'kə:sə*] n precursore m.
predator ['predətə*] n predatore m; ~y a predatore(trice).
predecessor ['pri:dısesə*] n predecessore/a.
predestination [pri:destı'neıʃən] n predestinazione f.
predetermine [pri:dı'tə:mın] vt predeterminare.
predicament [prı'dıkəmənt] n situazione f difficile.
predicate ['predıkıt] n (LING) predicativo.
predict [prı'dıkt] vt predire; ~ion [-'dıkʃən] n predizione f.
predominant [prı'dɔmınənt] a predominante; ~ly ad in maggior parte, soprattutto.
predominate [prı'dɔmıneıt] vi predominare.
pre-eminent [pri:'emınənt] a preminente.
pre-empt [pri:'emt] vt acquistare per diritto di prelazione.
preen [pri:n] vt: to ~ itself (bird) lisciarsi le penne.
prefab ['pri:fæb] n casa prefabbricata.
prefabricated [pri:'fæbrıkeıtıd] a prefabbricato(a).
preface ['prefəs] n prefazione f.
prefect ['pri:fekt] n (Brit: in school) studente/essa con funzioni disciplinari; (in Italy) prefetto.
prefer [prı'fə:*] vt preferire; ~able ['prefrəbl] a preferibile; ~ably ['prefrəblı] ad preferibilmente; ~ence ['prefrəns] n preferenza; ~ential [prefə'renʃəl] a preferenziale.
prefix ['pri:fıks] n prefisso.
pregnancy ['pregnənsı] n gravidanza.
pregnant ['pregnənt] a incinta af.
prehistoric ['pri:hıs'tɔrık] a preistorico(a).
prejudge [pri:'dʒʌdʒ] vt pregiudicare.
prejudice ['predʒudıs] n pregiudizio; (harm) torto, danno // vt pregiudicare,

ledere; ~d a (person) pieno(a) di pregiudizi; (view) prevenuto(a).
prelate ['prelət] n prelato.
preliminary [prı'lımınərı] a preliminare; **preliminaries** npl preliminari mpl.
prelude ['prelju:d] n preludio.
premarital ['pri:'mærıtl] a prematrimoniale.
premature ['premətʃuə*] a prematuro(a).
premeditated [pri:'medıteıtıd] a premeditato(a).
premier ['premıə*] a primo(a) // n (POL) primo ministro.
première ['premıeə*] n première f inv.
premise ['premıs] n premessa; ~s npl locale m; on the ~s sul posto.
premium ['pri:mıəm] n premio.
premonition [premə'nıʃən] n premonizione f.
preoccupation [pri:ɔkju'peıʃən] n preoccupazione f.
preoccupied [pri:'ɔkjupaıd] a preoccupato(a).
prep [prep] n (SCOL: study) studio; ~ **school** n = **preparatory school.**
prepaid [pri:'peıd] a pagato(a) in anticipo.
preparation [prepə'reıʃən] n preparazione f; ~s npl (for trip, war) preparativi mpl.
preparatory [prı'pærətərı] a preparatorio(a); ~ **school** n scuola elementare privata.
prepare [prı'peə*] vt preparare // vi: to ~ **for** prepararsi a; ~d **for** preparato(a) a; ~d **to** pronto(a) a.
preponderance [prı'pɔndərns] n preponderanza.
preposition [prepə'zıʃən] n preposizione f.
preposterous [prı'pɔstərəs] a assurdo(a).
prerequisite [pri:'rekwızıt] n requisito indispensabile.
prerogative [prı'rɔgətıv] n prerogativa.
presbytery ['prezbıtərı] n presbiterio.
prescribe [prı'skraıb] vt prescrivere; (MED) ordinare.
prescription [prı'skrıpʃən] n prescrizione f; (MED) ricetta.
presence ['prezns] n presenza; ~ **of mind** n presenza di spirito.
present ['preznt] a presente; (wife, residence, job) attuale // n regalo; (also: ~ **tense**) tempo presente // vt [prı'zent] presentare; (give): to ~ sb with sth offrire qc a qd; at ~ al momento; ~able [prı'zentəbl] a presentabile; ~ation [-'teıʃən] n presentazione f; (gift) regalo, dono; (ceremony) cerimonia per il conferimento di un regalo; ~day a attuale, d'oggigiorno; ~ly ad (soon) fra poco, presto; (at present) al momento.
preservation [prezə'veıʃən] n preservazione f, conservazione f.
preservative [prı'zə:vətıv] n conservante m.
preserve [prı'zə:v] vt (keep safe) preservare, proteggere; (maintain) conservare; (food) mettere in conserva //

n (for game, fish) riserva; *(often pl: jam)* marmellata; *(: fruit)* frutta sciroppata.

preside [prɪ'zaɪd] *vi* presiedere.

presidency ['prezɪdənsɪ] *n* presidenza.

president ['prezɪdənt] *n* presidente *m*; **~ial** [-'denʃl] *a* presidenziale.

press [pres] *n (tool, machine)* pressa; *(for wine)* torchio; *(newspapers)* stampa; *(crowd)* folla // *vt (push)* premere, pigiare; *(squeeze)* spremere; *(: hand)* stringere; *(clothes: iron)* stirare; *(pursue)* incalzare; *(insist)*: to ~ sth on sb far accettare qc da qd // *vi* premere; accalcare; **we are ~ed for time** ci manca il tempo; **to ~ for sth** insistere per avere qc; **to ~ on** *vi* continuare; **~ agency** *n* agenzia di stampa; **~ conference** *n* conferenza stampa; **~ cutting** *n* ritaglio di giornale; **~ing** *a* urgente // *n* stiratura; **~ stud** *n* bottone *m* a pressione.

pressure ['preʃə*] *n* pressione *f*; **~ cooker** *n* pentola a pressione; **~ gauge** *n* manometro; **~ group** *n* gruppo di pressione; **pressurized** *a* pressurizzato(a).

prestige [pres'tiːʒ] *n* prestigio.

prestigious [pres'tɪdʒəs] *a* prestigioso(a).

presumably [prɪ'zjuːməblɪ] *ad* presumibilmente.

presume [prɪ'zjuːm] *vt* supporre; **to ~ to do** *(dare)* permettersi di fare.

presumption [prɪ'zʌmpʃən] *n* presunzione *f*; *(boldness)* audacia.

presumptuous [prɪ'zʌmpʃəs] *a* presuntuoso(a).

presuppose [prɪsə'pəuz] *vt* presupporre.

pretence, pretense *(US)* [prɪ'tens] *n (claim)* pretesa; **to make a ~ of doing** far finta di fare.

pretend [prɪ'tend] *vt (feign)* fingere // *vi (feign)* far finta; *(claim)*: **to ~ to sth** pretendere a qc; **to ~ to do** far finta di fare.

pretentious [prɪ'tenʃəs] *a* pretenzioso(a).

preterite ['pretərɪt] *n* preterito.

pretext ['priːtekst] *n* pretesto.

pretty ['prɪtɪ] *a* grazioso(a), carino(a) // *ad* abbastanza, assai.

prevail [prɪ'veɪl] *vi (win, be usual)* prevalere; *(persuade)*: **to ~ (up)on sb to do** persuadere qd a fare; **~ing** *a* dominante.

prevalent ['prevələnt] *a (belief)* predominante; *(customs)* diffuso(a); *(fashion)* corrente; *(disease)* comune.

prevarication [prɪværɪ'keɪʃən] *n* tergiversazione *f*.

prevent [prɪ'vent] *vt* prevenire; **to ~ sb from doing** impedire a qd di fare; **~able** *a* evitabile; **~ative** *a* preventivo(a); **~ion** [-'venʃən] *n* prevenzione *f*; **~ive** *a* preventivo(a).

preview ['priːvjuː] *n (of film)* anteprima.

previous ['priːvɪəs] *a* precedente; anteriore; **~ly** *ad* prima.

prewar ['priː'wɔː*] *a* anteguerra *inv*.

prey [preɪ] *n* preda // *vi*: **to ~ on** far

preda di; **it was ~ing on his mind** gli rodeva la mente.

price [praɪs] *n* prezzo // *vt (goods)* fissare il prezzo di; valutare; **~less** *a* inapprezzabile.

prick [prɪk] *n* puntura // *vt* pungere; **to ~ up one's ears** drizzare gli orecchi.

prickle ['prɪkl] *n (of plant)* spina; *(sensation)* pizzicore *m*.

prickly ['prɪklɪ] *a* spinoso(a); *(fig: person)* permaloso(a); **~ heat** *n* sudamina.

pride [praɪd] *n* orgoglio; superbia // *vt*: **to ~ o.s. on** essere orgoglioso(a) di; vantarsi di.

priest [priːst] *n* prete *m*, sacerdote *m*; **~ess** *n* sacerdotessa; **~hood** *n* sacerdozio.

prig [prɪg] *n*: **he's a ~** è compiaciuto di se stesso.

prim [prɪm] *a* pudico(a); contegnoso(a).

primarily ['praɪmərɪlɪ] *ad* principalmente, essenzialmente.

primary ['praɪmərɪ] *a* primario(a); *(first in importance)* primo(a); **~ school** *n* scuola elementare.

primate *n* (REL: ['praɪmɪt], ZOOL: ['praɪmeɪt]) primate *m*.

prime [praɪm] *a* primario(a), fondamentale; *(excellent)* di prima qualità // *vt (gun)* innescare; *(pump)* adescare; *(fig)* mettere al corrente; **in the ~ of life** nel fiore della vita; **~ minister (P.M.)** *n* primo ministro; **~r** *n (book)* testo elementare.

primeval [praɪ'miːvl] *a* primitivo(a).

primitive ['prɪmɪtɪv] *a* primitivo(a).

primrose ['prɪmrəuz] *n* primavera.

primus (stove) ['praɪməs(stəuv)] *n* (®) fornello a petrolio.

prince [prɪns] *n* principe *m*.

princess [prɪn'ses] *n* principessa.

principal ['prɪnsɪpl] *a* principale // *n (headmaster)* preside *m*.

principality [prɪnsɪ'pælɪtɪ] *n* principato.

principle ['prɪnsɪpl] *n* principio.

print [prɪnt] *n (mark)* impronta; *(letters)* caratteri *mpl*; *(fabric)* tessuto stampato; (ART, PHOT) stampa // *vt* imprimere; *(publish)* stampare, pubblicare; *(write in capitals)* scrivere in stampatello; **out of ~** esaurito(a); **~ed matter** *n* stampe *fpl*; **~er** *n* tipografo; **~ing** *n* stampa; **~ing press** *n* macchina tipografica; **~-out** *n* tabulato.

prior ['praɪə*] *a* precedente // *n* priore *m*; **~ to doing** prima di fare.

priority [praɪ'ɔrɪtɪ] *n* priorità *f inv*; precedenza.

priory ['praɪərɪ] *n* monastero.

prise [praɪz] *vt*: **to ~ open** forzare.

prism ['prɪzəm] *n* prisma *m*.

prison ['prɪzn] *n* prigione *f*; **~er** *n* prigioniero/a.

pristine ['prɪstiːn] *a* originario(a); intatto(a); puro(a).

privacy ['prɪvəsɪ] *n* solitudine *f*, intimità.

private ['praɪvɪt] *a* privato(a); personale

// *n* soldato semplice; '~' (*on envelope*) 'riservata'; **in ~** in privato; **~ eye** *n* investigatore *m* privato; **~ly** *ad* in privato; (*within oneself*) dentro di sé.

privet ['privit] *n* ligustro.

privilege ['priviidʒ] *n* privilegio; **~d** *a* privilegiato(a).

privy ['privi] *a*: **to be ~ to** essere al corrente di; **P~ Council** *n* Consiglio della Corona.

prize [praiz] *n* premio // *a* (*example, idiot*) perfetto(a); (*bull, novel*) premiato(a) // *vt* apprezzare, pregiare; **~ fight** *n* incontro di pugilato tra professionisti; **~ giving** *n* premiazione *f*; **~winner** *n* premiato/a.

pro [prəu] *n* (*SPORT*) professionista *m/f*; **the ~s and cons** il pro e il contro.

probability [prɔbə'biliti] *n* probabilità *f* inv.

probable ['prɔbəbl] *a* probabile; **probably** *ad* probabilmente.

probation [prə'beiʃən] *n* (*in employment*) periodo di prova; (*LAW*) libertà vigilata; **on ~** (*employee*) in prova; (*LAW*) in libertà vigilata.

probe [prəub] *n* (*MED, SPACE*) sonda; (*enquiry*) indagine *f*, investigazione *f* // *vt* sondare, esplorare; indagare.

probity ['prəubiti] *n* probità.

problem ['prɔbləm] *n* problema *m*; **~atic** [-'mætik] *a* problematico(a).

procedure [prə'si:dʒə*] *n* (*ADMIN, LAW*) procedura; (*method*) metodo, procedimento.

proceed [prə'si:d] *vi* (*go forward*) avanzare, andare avanti; (*go about it*) procedere; (*continue*): **to ~ (with)** continuare; **to ~ to** andare a; passare a; **to ~ to do** mettersi a fare; **~ing** *n* procedimento, modo d'agire; **~ings** *npl* misure *fpl*; (*LAW*) procedimento; (*meeting*) riunione *f*; (*records*) rendiconti *mpl*; atti *mpl*; **~s** ['prəusi:dz] *npl* profitto, incasso.

process ['prəuses] *n* processo; (*method*) metodo, sistema *m* // *vt* trattare; (*information*) elaborare; **~ing** *n* trattamento; elaborazione *f*.

procession [prə'seʃən] *n* processione *f*, corteo.

proclaim [prə'kleim] *vt* proclamare, dichiarare.

proclamation [prɔklə'meiʃən] *n* proclamazione *f*.

procrastination [prəukræsti'neiʃən] *n* procrastinazione *f*.

procreation [prəukri'eiʃən] *n* procreazione *f*.

procure [prə'kjuə*] *vt* (*for o.s.*) procurarsi; (*for sb*) procurare.

prod [prɔd] *vt* pungolare // *n* (*push, jab*) pungolo.

prodigal ['prɔdigl] *a* prodigo(a).

prodigious [prə'didʒəs] *a* prodigioso(a).

prodigy ['prɔdidʒi] *n* prodigio.

produce *n* ['prɔdju:s] (*AGR*) prodotto, prodotti *mpl* // *vt* [prə'dju:s] produrre; (*to show*) esibire, mostrare; (*cause*) cagionare, causare; (*THEATRE*) mettere in

scena; **~r** *n* (*THEATRE*) direttore/trice; (*AGR, CINEMA*) produttore *m*.

product ['prɔdʌkt] *n* prodotto.

production [prə'dʌkʃən] *n* produzione *f*; (*THEATRE*) messa in scena; **~ line** *n* catena di lavorazione.

productive [prə'dʌktiv] *a* produttivo(a).

productivity [prɔdʌk'tiviti] *n* produttività.

profane [prə'fein] *a* profano(a); (*language*) empio(a).

profess [prə'fes] *vt* professare.

profession [prə'feʃən] *n* professione *f*; **~al** *n* (*SPORT*) professionista *m/f* // *a* professionale; (*work*) da professionista; **~alism** *n* professionismo.

professor [prə'fesə*] *n* professore *m* (*titolare di una cattedra*).

proficiency [prə'fiʃənsi] *n* competenza, abilità.

proficient [prə'fiʃənt] *a* competente, abile.

profile ['prəufail] *n* profilo.

profit ['prɔfit] *n* profitto; beneficio // *vi*: **to ~ (by** *or* **from)** approfittare (di); **~ability** [-'biliti] *n* redditività; **~able** *a* redditizio(a).

profiteering [prɔfi'tiəriŋ] *n* (*pej*) affarismo.

profound [prə'faund] *a* profondo(a).

profuse [prə'fju:s] *a* infinito(a), abbondante; **~ly** *ad* con grande effusione; **profusion** [-'fju:ʒən] *n* profusione *f*, abbondanza.

progeny ['prɔdʒini] *n* progenie *f*; discendenti *mpl*.

programme, **program** (*US*) ['prəugræm] *n* programma *m* // *vt* programmare; **programming**, **programing** (*US*) *n* programmazione *f*.

progress *n* ['prəugres] progresso // *vi* [prə'gres] avanzare, procedere; **in ~** in corso; **to make ~** far progressi; **~ion** [-'greʃən] *n* progressione *f*; **~ive** [-'gresiv] *a* progressivo(a); (*person*) progressista *m/f*; **~ively** [-'gresivli] *ad* progressivamente.

prohibit [prə'hibit] *vt* proibire, vietare; **~ion** [prəui'biʃən] *n* (*US*) proibizionismo; **~ive** *a* (*price etc*) proibitivo(a).

project *n* ['prɔdʒekt] (*plan*) piano; (*venture*) progetto; (*SCOL*) studio // *vb* [prə'dʒekt] *vt* proiettare // *vi* (*stick out*) sporgere.

projectile [prə'dʒektail] *n* proiettile *m*.

projection [prə'dʒekʃən] *n* proiezione *f*; sporgenza.

projector [prə'dʒektə*] *n* proiettore *m*.

proletarian [prəuli'teəriən] *a*, *n* proletario(a).

proletariat [prəuli'teəriət] *n* proletariato.

proliferate [prə'lifəreit] *vi* proliferare; **proliferation** [-'reiʃən] *n* proliferazione *f*.

prolific [prə'lifik] *a* prolifico(a).

prologue ['prəulɔg] *n* prologo.

prolong [prə'lɔŋ] *vt* prolungare.

prom [prɔm] *n abbr of* **promenade**; (*US*: *ball*) ballo studentesco.

promenade [prɔmə'nɑ:d] *n* (*by sea*)

lungomare *m*; ~ **concert** *n* concerto di musica classica.

prominence ['prɔmɪnəns] *n* prominenza; importanza.

prominent ['prɔmɪnənt] *a* (*standing out*) prominente; (*important*) importante.

promiscuity [prɔmɪs'kjuːɪti] *n* (*sexual*) rapporti *mpl* multipli.

promiscuous [prə'mɪskjuəs] *a* (*sexually*) di facili costumi.

promise ['prɔmɪs] *n* promessa // *vt,vi* promettere; **promising** *a* promettente.

promontory ['prɔmontri] *n* promontorio.

promote [prə'məut] *vt* promuovere; (*venture, event*) organizzare; ~**r** *n* (*of sporting event*) organizzatore/trice; **promotion** [-'məuʃən] *n* promozione *f*; (*of new product*) promotion *m*.

prompt [prɔmpt] *a* rapido(a), svelto(a); puntuale; (*reply*) sollecito(a) // *ad* (*punctually*) in punto // *vt* incitare; provocare; (*THEATRE*) suggerire a; **to ~ sb to do** spingere qd a fare; ~**er** *n* (*THEATRE*) suggeritore *m*; ~**ly** *ad* prontamente; puntualmente; ~**ness** *n* prontezza; puntualità.

prone [prəun] *a* (*lying*) prono(a); ~ **to** propenso(a) a, incline a.

prong [prɔŋ] *n* rebbio, punta.

pronoun ['prəunaun] *n* pronome *m*.

pronounce [prə'nauns] *vt* pronunziare // *vi*: **to ~ (up)on** pronunziare su; ~**d** *a* (*marked*) spiccato(a); ~**ment** *n* dichiarazione *f*.

pronunciation [prənʌnsɪ'eɪʃən] *n* pronunzia.

proof [pruːf] *n* prova; (*of book*) bozza; (*PHOT*) provino; (*of alcohol*) grado // *a*: ~ **against** a prova di.

prop [prɔp] *n* sostegno, appoggio // *vt* (*also*: ~ **up**) sostenere, appoggiare; (*lean*): **to ~ sth against** appoggiare qc contro *or* a.

propaganda [prɔpə'gændə] *n* propaganda.

propagation [prɔpə'geɪʃən] *n* propagazione *f*.

propel [prə'pɛl] *vt* spingere (in avanti), muovere; ~**ler** *n* elica; ~**ling pencil** *n* matita a mina.

propensity [prə'pɛnsɪti] *n* tendenza.

proper ['prɔpə*] *a* (*suited, right*) adatto(a), appropriato(a); (*seemly*) decente; (*authentic*) vero(a); (*col*: *real*) noun + vero(a) e proprio(a); ~**ly** *ad* decentemente; proprio, del tutto; ~ **noun** *n* nome *m* proprio.

property ['prɔpəti] *n* (*things owned*) beni *mpl*; proprietà *fpl*; bene *m* immobile; tenuta, terra; (*CHEM etc*: *quality*) proprietà *f inv*; ~ **owner** *n* proprietario/a.

prophecy ['prɔfɪsi] *n* profezia.

prophesy ['prɔfɪsaɪ] *vt* predire.

prophet ['prɔfɪt] *n* profeta *m*; ~**ic** [prə'fɛtɪk] *a* profetico(a).

proportion [prə'pɔːʃən] *n* proporzione *f*; (*share*) parte *f* // *vt* proporzionare, commisurare; ~**al** *a* proporzionale; ~**ate** *a* proporzionato(a).

proposal [prə'pəuzl] *n* proposta; (*plan*) progetto; (*of marriage*) proposta di matrimonio.

propose [prə'pəuz] *vt* proporre, suggerire // *vi* fare una proposta di matrimonio; **to ~ to do** proporsi di fare, aver l'intenzione di fare.

proposition [prɔpə'zɪʃən] *n* proposizione *f*.

propound [prə'paund] *vt* proporre, presentare.

proprietor [prə'praɪətə*] *n* proprietario/a.

propulsion [prə'pʌlʃən] *n* propulsione *f*.

prosaic [prəu'zeɪɪk] *a* prosaico(a).

prose [prəuz] *n* prosa; (*SCOL*: *translation*) traduzione *f* dalla madrelingua.

prosecute ['prɔsɪkjuːt] *vt* processare; **prosecution** [-'kjuːʃən] *n* processo; (*accusing side*) accusa; **prosecutor** *n* accusatore/trice; (*also*: **public ~**) pubblico ministero.

prospect *n* ['prɔspɛkt] prospettiva; (*hope*) speranza // *vb* [prə'spɛkt] *vt* fare assaggi in // *vi* fare assaggi; ~**s** *npl* (*for work etc*) prospettive *fpl*; **prospecting** *n* prospezione *f*; **prospective** *a* possibile; futuro(a); **prospector** *n* prospettore *m*.

prospectus [prə'spɛktəs] *n* prospetto, programma *m*.

prosper ['prɔspə*] *vi* prosperare; ~**ity** [-'spɛrɪti] *n* prosperità; ~**ous** *a* prospero(a).

prostitute ['prɔstɪtjuːt] *n* prostituta.

prostrate ['prɔstreɪt] *a* prostrato(a).

protagonist [prə'tægənist] *n* protagonista *m/f*.

protect [prə'tɛkt] *vt* proteggere, salvaguardare; ~**ion** *n* protezione *f*; ~**ive** *a* protettivo(a); ~**or** *n* protettore/trice.

protégé ['prəutɛʒeɪ] *n* protetto; ~**e** *n* protetta.

protein [prəutiːn] *n* proteina.

protest *n* ['prəutɛst] protesta // *vi* [prə'tɛst] protestare.

Protestant ['prɔtɪstənt] *a,n* protestante (*m/f*).

protocol ['prəutəkɔl] *n* protocollo.

prototype ['prəutətaɪp] *n* prototipo.

protracted [prə'træktɪd] *a* tirato(a) per le lunghe.

protrude [prə'truːd] *vi* sporgere.

protuberance [prə'tjuːbərəns] *n* sporgenza.

proud [praud] *a* fiero(a), orgoglioso(a); (*pej*) superbo(a).

prove [pruːv] *vt* provare, dimostrare // *vi*: **to ~ correct** *etc* risultare vero(a) *etc*; **to ~ o.s.** mostrare le proprie capacità; **to o.s./itself (to be) useful** *etc* mostrarsi *or* rivelarsi utile *etc*.

proverb ['prɔvəːb] *n* proverbio; ~**ial** [prə'vəːbɪəl] *a* proverbiale.

provide [prə'vaɪd] *vt* fornire, provvedere; **to ~ sb with sth** fornire *or* provvedere qd di qc; **to ~ for** *vt* provvedere a; ~**d** (**that**) *cj* purché + *sub*, a condizione che + *sub*.

Providence ['prɔvidəns] n Provvidenza.
providing [prə'vaidiŋ] cj purché + sub, a
condizione che + sub.
province ['prɔvins] n provincia;
provincial [prə'vinʃəl] a provinciale.
provision [prə'viʒən] n (supply) riserva;
(supplying) provvista; rifornimento; (stipu-
lation) condizione f; ~s npl (food) provviste fpl; ~al a provvisorio(a).
proviso [prə'vaizəu] n condizione f.
provocation [prɔvə'keiʃən] n
provocazione f.
provocative [prə'vɔkətiv] a (aggressive)
provocatorio(a); (thought-provoking)
stimolante; (seductive) provocante.
provoke [prə'vəuk] vt provocare; incitare.
prow [prau] n prua.
prowess ['prauis] n prodezza.
prowl [praul] vi (also: ~ about, ~
around) aggirarsi furtivamente; ~er n
tipo sospetto (che s'aggira con l'intenzione di
rubare, aggredire etc).
proximity [prɔk'simiti] n prossimità.
proxy ['prɔksi] n procura; by ~ per
procura.
prudence [pru:dns] n prudenza.
prudent ['pru:dnt] a prudente.
prudish ['pru:diʃ] a puritano(a).
prune [pru:n] n prugna secca // vt potare.
pry [prai] vi: to ~ into ficcare il naso in.
psalm [sɑ:m] n salmo.
pseudo- ['sju:dəu] prefix pseudo...; ~nym n
pseudonimo.
psyche ['saiki] n psiche f.
psychiatric [saiki'ætrik] a
psichiatrico(a).
psychiatrist [sai'kaiətrist] n psichiatra
m/f.
psychiatry [sai'kaiətri] n psichiatria.
psychic ['saikik] a (also: ~al)
psichico(a); (person) dotato(a) di qualità
telepatiche.
psychoanalyse [saikəu'ænəlaiz] vt
psicanalizzare.
psychoanalysis, pl lyses [saikəu-
'nælisis, -siːz] n psicanalisi f inv.
psychoanalyst [saikəu'ænəlist] n
psicanalista m/f.
psychological [saikə'lɔdʒikl] a
psicologico(a).
psychologist [sai'kɔlədʒist] n psicologo/a.
psychology [sai'kɔlədʒi] n psicologia.
psychopath ['saikəupæθ] n psicopatico/a.
psychotic [sai'kɔtik] a,n psicotico(a).
P.T.O. abbr (= please turn over) v.r. (vedi
retro).
pub [pʌb] n (abbr of public house) pub m
inv.
puberty ['pju:bəti] n pubertà.
public ['pʌblik] a pubblico(a) // n
pubblico; the general ~ il pubblico.
publican ['pʌblikən] n proprietario di un
pub.
publication [pʌbli'keiʃən] n pubblicazione
f.
public: ~ **company** n società f inv per
azioni (costituita tramite pubblica

sottoscrizione); ~ **convenience** n
gabinetti mpl; ~ **house** n pub m inv.
publicity [pʌb'lisiti] n pubblicità.
publicly ['pʌblikli] ad pubblicamente.
public: ~ **opinion** n opinione f pubblica;
~ **relations** n pubbliche relazioni fpl; ~
school n (Brit) scuola privata;
~**-spirited** a che ha senso civico.
publish ['pʌbliʃ] vt pubblicare; ~**er** n
editore m; ~**ing** n (industry) editoria; (of a
book) pubblicazione f.
puce [pju:s] a color pulce inv.
puck [pʌk] n (ICE HOCKEY) disco.
pucker ['pʌkə*] vt corrugare.
pudding ['pudiŋ] n budino; (dessert) dolce
m.
puddle ['pʌdl] n pozza, pozzanghera.
puerile ['pjuərail] a puerile.
puff [pʌf] n sbuffo; (also: **powder** ~)
piumino // vt: to ~ one's pipe tirare
sboccate di fumo // vi uscire a sbuffi;
(pant) ansare; to ~ out smoke mandar
fuori sbuffi di fumo; ~**ed** a (col: out of
breath) senza fiato.
puffin ['pʌfin] n puffino.
puff pastry ['pʌf'peistri] n pasta sfoglia.
puffy ['pʌfi] a gonfio(a).
pugnacious [pʌg'neiʃəs] a combattivo(a).
pull [pul] n (tug): to give sth a ~ tirare
su qc; (fig) influenza // vt tirare; (muscle)
strappare // vi tirare; to ~ to pieces
fare a pezzi; to ~ one's punches
(BOXING) risparmiare l'avversario; not to
~ one's punches (fig) non avere peli
sulla lingua; to ~ one's weight dare il
proprio contributo; to ~ o.s. together
ricomporsi, riprendersi; to ~ sb's leg
prendere in giro qd; to ~ apart vt
(break) fare a pezzi; to ~ down vt
(house) demolire; (tree) abbattere; to ~
in vi (AUT: at the kerb) accostarsi; (RAIL)
entrare in stazione; to ~ off vt (deal etc)
portare a compimento; to ~ out vi
partire; (AUT: come out of line) spostarsi
sulla mezzeria // vt staccare; far uscire;
(withdraw) ritirare; to ~ through vi
farcela; to ~ up vi (stop) fermarsi // vt
(uproot) sradicare; (stop) fermare.
pulley ['puli] n puleggia, carrucola.
pullover ['puləuvə*] n pullover m inv.
pulp [pʌlp] n (of fruit) polpa; (for paper)
pasta per carta.
pulpit ['pulpit] n pulpito.
pulsate [pʌl'seit] vi battere, palpitare.
pulse [pʌls] n polso.
pulverize ['pʌlvəraiz] vt polverizzare.
puma ['pju:mə] n puma m inv.
pummel ['pʌml] vt dare pugni a.
pump [pʌmp] n pompa; (shoe) scarpetta //
vt pompare; (fig: col) far parlare; to ~ up
vt gonfiare.
pumpkin ['pʌmpkin] n zucca.
pun [pʌn] n gioco di parole.
punch [pʌntʃ] n (blow) pugno; (fig: force)
forza; (tool) punzone m; (drink) ponce m
// vt (hit): to ~ sb/sth dare un pugno a
qd/qc; to ~ a hole (in) fare un buco (in);
~**-up** n (col) rissa.

punctual ['pʌŋktjuəl] a puntuale; ~ity [-'ælɪtɪ] n puntualità.

punctuate ['pʌŋktjueɪt] vt punteggiare; **punctuation** [-'eɪʃən] n interpunzione f, punteggiatura.

puncture ['pʌŋktʃə°] n foratura // vt forare.

pundit ['pʌndɪt] n sapientone/a.

pungent ['pʌndʒənt] a piccante; (fig) mordace, caustico(a).

punish ['pʌnɪʃ] vt punire; ~able a punibile; ~ment n punizione f.

punt [pʌnt] n (boat) barchino; (FOOTBALL) colpo a volo.

puny ['pju:nɪ] a gracile.

pup [pʌp] n cucciolo/a.

pupil ['pju:pl] n allievo/a; alunno/a.

puppet ['pʌpɪt] n burattino.

puppy ['pʌpɪ] n cucciolo/a, cagnolino/a.

purchase ['pɜ:tʃɪs] n acquisto, compera // vt comprare; ~r n compratore/trice.

pure [pjuə°] a puro(a).

purge [pɜ:dʒ] n (MED) purga; (POL) epurazione f // vt purgare; (fig) epurare.

purification [pjuərɪfɪ'keɪʃən] n purificazione f.

purify ['pjuərɪfaɪ] vt purificare.

purist ['pjuərɪst] n purista m/f.

puritan ['pjuərɪtən] n puritano/a; ~ical [-'tænɪkl] a puritano(a).

purity ['pjuərɪtɪ] n purità.

purl [pɜ:l] n punto rovescio.

purple ['pɜ:pl] a di porpora; viola inv.

purport [pɜ:'pɔ:t] vi: to ~ to be/do pretendere di essere/fare.

purpose ['pɜ:pəs] n intenzione f, scopo; on ~ apposta; ~ful a deciso(a), risoluto(a); ~ly ad apposta.

purr [pɜ:°] vi fare le fusa.

purse [pɜ:s] n borsellino // vt contrarre.

purser ['pɜ:sə°] n (NAUT) commissario di bordo.

pursue [pə'sju:] vt inseguire; ~r n inseguitore/trice.

pursuit [pə'sju:t] n inseguimento; (occupation) occupazione f, attività f inv; **scientific** ~s ricerche fpl scientifiche.

purveyor [pə'veɪə°] n fornitore/trice.

pus [pʌs] n pus m.

push [puʃ] n spinta; (effort) grande sforzo; (drive) energia // vt spingere; (button) premere; (thrust): to ~ sth (into) ficcare qc (in); (fig) fare pubblicità a // vi spingere; premere; to ~ aside vt scostare; to ~ off vi (col) filare; to ~ on vi (continue) continuare; to ~ through vt (measure) far approvare; to ~ up vt (total, prices) far salire; ~chair n passeggino; ~over n (col): it's a ~over è un lavoro da bambini; ~y a (pej) opportunista.

puss, pussy(-cat) [pus, 'pusɪ(kæt)] n micio.

put, pt, pp put [put] vt mettere, porre; (say) dire, esprimere; (a question) fare; (estimate) stimare; to ~ about vi (NAUT) virare di bordo // vt (rumour) diffondere;

to ~ across vt (ideas etc) comunicare; far capire; to ~ away vt (return) mettere a posto; to ~ back vt (replace) rimettere (a posto); (postpone) rinviare; (delay) ritardare; to ~ by vt (money) mettere da parte; to ~ down vt (parcel etc) posare, mettere giù; (pay) versare; (in writing) mettere per iscritto; (suppress: revolt etc) reprimere, sopprimere; (attribute) attribuire; to ~ forward vt (ideas) avanzare, proporre; (date) anticipare; to ~ in vt (application, complaint) presentare; to ~ off vt (postpone) rimandare, rinviare; (discourage) dissuadere; to ~ on vt (clothes, lipstick etc) mettere; (light etc) accendere; (play etc) mettere in scena; (food, meal) servire; (brake) mettere; to ~ on weight ingrassare; to ~ on airs darsi delle arie; to ~ out vt mettere fuori; (one's hand) porgere; (light etc) spegnere; (person: inconvenience) scomodare; to ~ up vt (raise) sollevare, alzare; (pin up) affiggere; (hang) appendere; (build) costruire, erigere; (increase) aumentare; (accommodate) alloggiare; to ~ up with vt fus sopportare.

putrid ['pju:trɪd] a putrido(a).

putt [pʌt] vt (ball) colpire leggermente // n colpo leggero; ~er n (GOLF) putter m inv; ~ing green n green m inv; campo da putting.

putty ['pʌtɪ] n stucco.

put-up ['putʌp] a: ~ job n montatura.

puzzle ['pʌzl] n enigma m, mistero; (jigsaw) puzzle m // vt confondere, rendere perplesso(a) // vi scervellarsi; **puzzling** a sconcertante, inspiegabile.

pygmy ['pɪgmɪ] n pigmeo/a.

pyjamas [pɪ'dʒɑ:məz] npl pigiama m.

pylon ['paɪlən] n pilone m.

pyramid ['pɪrəmɪd] n piramide f.

python ['paɪθən] n pitone m.

Q

quack [kwæk] n (of duck) qua qua m inv; (pej: doctor) dottoruccio/a.

quad [kwɔd] abbr of **quadrangle, quadruplet**.

quadrangle ['kwɔdræŋgl] n (MATH) quadrilatero; (courtyard) cortile m.

quadruped ['kwɔdruped] n quadrupede m.

quadruple [kwɔ'drupl] a quadruplo(a) // n quadruplo // vt quadruplicare // vi quadruplicarsi; ~t [-'dru:plɪt] n uno/a di quattro gemelli.

quagmire ['kwægmaɪə°] n pantano.

quail [kweɪl] n (ZOOL) quaglia.

quaint [kweɪnt] a bizzarro(a); (old-fashioned) antiquato(a); grazioso(a), pittoresco(a).

quake [kweɪk] vi tremare // n abbr of **earthquake.**

Quaker ['kweɪkə°] n quacchero/a.

qualification [kwɔlɪfɪ'keɪʃən] n (degree etc) qualifica, titolo; (ability) competenza,

qualificazione *f*; (*limitation*) riserva, restrizione *f*.
qualified ['kwɔlɪfaɪd] *a* qualificato(a); (*able*) competente, qualificato(a); (*limited*) condizionato(a).
qualify ['kwɔlɪfaɪ] *vt* abilitare; (*limit: statement*) modificare, precisare // *vi*: **to ~ (as)** qualificarsi (come); **to ~ (for)** acquistare i requisiti necessari (per); (*SPORT*) qualificarsi (per or a).
qualitative ['kwɔlɪtɪtɪv] *a* qualitativo(a).
quality ['kwɔlɪtɪ] *n* qualità *f inv*.
qualm [kwɑːm] *n* dubbio; scrupolo.
quandary ['kwɔndrɪ] *n*: **in a ~** in un dilemma.
quantitative ['kwɔntɪtətɪv] *a* quantitativo(a).
quantity ['kwɔntɪtɪ] *n* quantità *f inv*; **~ surveyor** *n* geometra *m* (*specializzato nel calcolare la quantità e il costo del materiale da costruzione*).
quarantine ['kwɔrntiːn] *n* quarantena.
quarrel ['kwɔrl] *n* lite *f*, disputa // *vi* litigare; **~some** *a* litigioso(a).
quarry ['kwɔrɪ] *n* (*for stone*) cava; (*animal*) preda // *vt* (*marble etc*) estrarre.
quart [kwɔːt] *n* ≈ litro (= 2 *pints*).
quarter ['kwɔːtə*] *n* quarto; (*of year*) trimestre *m*; (*district*) quartiere *m* // *vt* dividere in quattro; (*MIL*) alloggiare; **~s** *npl* alloggi *mpl*, quadrato; **a ~ of an hour** un quarto d'ora; **~ final** *n* quarto di finale; **~ly** *a* trimestrale // *ad* trimestralmente; **~master** *n* (*MIL*) furiere *m*.
quartet(te) [kwɔː'tɛt] *n* quartetto.
quartz [kwɔːts] *n* quarzo; **~ watch** *n* orologio al quarzo.
quash [kwɔʃ] *vt* (*verdict*) annullare.
quasi- ['kweɪzaɪ] *prefix* quasi + *noun*; quasi, pressoché + *adjective*.
quaver ['kweɪvə*] *n* (*MUS*) croma // *vi* tremolare.
quay [kiː] *n* (*also*: **~side**) banchina.
queasy ['kwiːzɪ] *a* (*stomach*) delicato(a); **to feel ~** aver la nausea.
queen [kwiːn] *n* (*gen*) regina; (*CARDS etc*) regina, donna; **~ mother** *n* regina madre.
queer [kwɪə*] *a* strano(a), curioso(a); (*suspicious*) dubbio(a), sospetto(a); (*sick*): **I feel ~** mi sento poco bene // *n* (*col*) finocchio.
quell [kwɛl] *vt* domare.
quench [kwɛntʃ] *vt* (*flames*) spegnere; **to ~ one's thirst** dissetarsi.
query ['kwɪərɪ] *n* domanda, questione *f*; (*doubt*) dubbio // *vt* mettere in questione.
quest [kwɛst] *n* cerca, ricerca.
question ['kwɛstʃən] *n* domanda, questione *f* // *vt* (*person*) interrogare; (*plan, idea*) mettere in questione or in dubbio; **it's a ~ of doing** si tratta di fare; **beyond ~** fuori di dubbio; **out of the ~** fuori discussione, impossibile; **~able** *a* discutibile; **~ing** *a* interrogativo(a) // *n* interrogatorio; **~ mark** *n* punto interrogativo.

questionnaire [kwɛstʃə'nɛə*] *n* questionario.
queue [kjuː] *n* coda, fila // *vi* fare la coda.
quibble ['kwɪbl] *vi* cavillare.
quick [kwɪk] *a* rapido(a), veloce; (*reply*) pronto(a); (*mind*) pronto(a), acuto(a) // *ad* rapidamente, presto // *n*: **cut to the ~** (*fig*) toccato(a) sul vivo; **be ~!** fa presto!; **~en** *vt* accelerare, affrettare; (*rouse*) animare, stimolare // *vi* accelerare, affrettarsi; **~ly** *ad* rapidamente, velocemente; **~ness** *n* rapidità; prontezza; acutezza; **~sand** *n* sabbie *fpl* mobili; **~step** *n* (*dance*) fox-trot *m inv*; **~-witted** *a* pronto(a) d'ingegno.
quid [kwɪd] *n, pl inv* (*Brit: col*) sterlina.
quiet ['kwaɪət] *a* tranquillo(a), quieto(a); (*ceremony*) semplice; (*colour*) discreto(a) // *n* tranquillità, calma; **keep ~! sta zitto!**; **on the ~** di nascosto; **~en** (*also*: **~en down**) *vi* calmarsi, chetarsi // *vt* calmare, chetare; **~ly** *ad* tranquillamente, calmamente, sommessamente; discretamente; **~ness** *n* tranquillità, calma; silenzio.
quill [kwɪl] *n* penna d'oca.
quilt [kwɪlt] *n* piumino; (*continental*) **~** *n* sofficone *m* imbottito.
quin [kwɪn] *n* abbr of **quintuplet**.
quinine [kwɪ'niːn] *n* chinino.
quintet(te) [kwɪn'tɛt] *n* quintetto.
quintuplet [kwɪn'tjuːplɪt] *n* uno/a di cinque gemelli.
quip [kwɪp] *n* frizzo.
quirk [kwɔːk] *n* ghiribizzo.
quit [kwɪt], *pt, pp* **quit** *or* **quitted** [kwɪt] *vt* lasciare, partire da // *vi* (*give up*) mollare; (*resign*) dimettersi; **notice to ~** preavviso (*dato all'inquilino*).
quite [kwaɪt] *ad* (*rather*) assai; (*entirely*) completamente, del tutto; **I ~ understand** capisco perfettamente; **~ a few of them** non pochi di loro; **~ (so)!** esatto!
quits [kwɪts] *a*: **~ (with)** pari (con).
quiver ['kwɪvə*] *vi* tremare, fremere // *n* (*for arrows*) faretra.
quiz [kwɪz] *n* (*game*) quiz *m inv*; indovinello // *vt* interrogare; **~zical** *a* enigmatico(a).
quoits [kwɔɪts] *npl* gioco degli anelli.
quorum ['kwɔːrəm] *n* quorum *m*.
quota ['kwəʊtə] *n* quota.
quotation [kwəʊ'teɪʃən] *n* citazione *f*; (*of shares etc*) quotazione *f*; (*estimate*) preventivo; **~ marks** *npl* virgolette *fpl*.
quote [kwəʊt] *n* citazione *f* // *vt* (*sentence*) citare; (*price*) dare, fissare; (*shares*) quotare // *vi*: **to ~ from** citare; **to ~ for a job** dare un preventivo per un lavoro.

R

rabbi ['ræbaɪ] *n* rabbino.
rabbit ['ræbɪt] *n* coniglio; **~ hutch** *n* conigliera.
rabble ['ræbl] *n* (*pej*) canaglia, plebaglia.

rabid ['ræbɪd] *a* rabbioso(a);   (*fig*) fanatico(a).

rabies ['reɪbiːz] *n* rabbia.

RAC *n abbr of Royal Automobile Club*.

raccoon [rə'kuːn] *n* procione *m*.

race [reɪs] *n* corsa; (*competition*) gara, corsa // *vt* (*person*) gareggiare (in corsa) con; (*horse*) far correre; (*engine*) imballare // *vi* correre; **~course** *n* campo di corse, ippodromo; **~horse** *n* cavallo da corsa; **~ relations** *npl* rapporto fra le razze.

racial ['reɪʃl] *a* razziale; **~ discrimination** *n* discriminazione *f* razziale; **~ism** *n* razzismo; **~ist** *a, n* razzista (*m/f*).

racing ['reɪsɪŋ] *n* corsa; **~ car** *n* macchina da corsa; **~ driver** *n* corridore *m* automobilista.

racist ['reɪsɪst] *a,n* (*pej*) razzista (*m/f*).

rack [ræk] *n* rastrelliera; (*also*: **luggage ~**) rete *f*, portabagagli *m inv*; (*also*: **roof ~**) portabagagli // *vt* torturare, tormentare; **toast ~** *n* portatoast *m inv*.

racket ['rækɪt] *n* (*for tennis*) racchetta; (*noise*) fracasso, baccano; (*swindle*) imbroglio, truffa; (*organized crime*) racket *m inv*.

racoon [rə'kuːn] *n* = **raccoon**.

racquet ['rækɪt] *n* racchetta.

racy ['reɪsɪ] *a* brioso(a); piccante.

radar ['reɪdɑː°] *n* radar *m* // *cpd* radar *inv*.

radiance ['reɪdɪəns] *n* splendore *m*, radiosità.

radiant ['reɪdɪənt] *a* raggiante; (*PHYSICS*) radiante.

radiate ['reɪdɪeɪt] *vt* (*heat*) irraggiare, irradiare // *vi* (*lines*) irradiarsi.

radiation [reɪdɪ'eɪʃən] *n* irradiamento; (*radioactive*) radiazione *f*.

radiator ['reɪdɪeɪtə°] *n* radiatore *m*; **~ cap** *n* tappo del radiatore.

radical ['rædɪkl] *a* radicale.

radii ['reɪdɪaɪ] *npl of* **radius**.

radio ['reɪdɪəu] *n* radio *f inv*; **on the ~** alla radio; **~ station** *n* stazione *f* radio *inv*.

radio... ['reɪdɪəu] *prefix*: **~active** *a* radioattivo(a); **~activity** *n* radioattività; **~grapher** [-'ɒgrəfə°] *n* radiologo/a; **~graphy** [-'ɒgrəfɪ] *n* radiografia; **~logy** [-'ɒlədʒɪ] *n* radiologia.

radish ['rædɪʃ] *n* ravanello.

radium ['reɪdɪəm] *n* radio.

radius, *pl* **radii** ['reɪdɪəs, -ɪaɪ] *n* raggio; (*ANAT*) radio.

raffia ['ræfɪə] *n* rafia.

raffle ['ræfl] *n* lotteria.

raft [rɑːft] *n* zattera.

rafter ['rɑːftə°] *n* trave *f*.

rag [ræg] *n* straccio, cencio; (*pej*: *newspaper*) giornalaccio, bandiera; (*for charity*) iniziativa studentesca a scopo caritativo // *vt* prendere in giro; **~s** *npl* stracci *mpl*, brandelli *mpl*; **~-and-bone man** *n* straccivendolo; **~bag** *n* (*fig*) guazzabuglio.

rage [reɪdʒ] *n* (*fury*) collera, furia // *vi* (*person*) andare su tutte le furie; (*storm*) infuriare; **it's all the ~** fa furore.

ragged ['rægɪd] *a* (*edge*) irregolare; (*cuff*) logoro(a); (*appearance*) pezzente.

raid [reɪd] *n* (*MIL*) incursione *f*; (*criminal*) rapina; (*by police*) irruzione *f* // *vt* fare un'incursione in; rapinare; fare irruzione in; **~er** *n* rapinatore/trice; (*plane*) aeroplano da incursione.

rail [reɪl] *n* (*on stair*) ringhiera; (*on bridge, balcony*) parapetto; (*of ship*) battagliola; (*for train*) rotaia; **~s** *npl* binario, rotaie *fpl*; **by ~** per ferrovia; **~ing(s)** *n(pl)* ringhiere *fpl*; **~road** *n* (*US*), **~way** *n* ferrovia; **~wayman** *n* ferroviere *m*; **~way station** *n* stazione *f* ferroviaria.

rain [reɪn] *n* pioggia // *vi* piovere; **in the ~** sotto la pioggia; **~bow** *n* arcobaleno; **~coat** *n* impermeabile *m*; **~drop** *n* goccia di pioggia; **~fall** *n* pioggia; (*measurement*) piovosità; **~proof** *a* impermeabile; **~y** *a* piovoso(a).

raise [reɪz] *n* aumento // *vt* (*lift*) alzare; sollevare; (*build*) erigere; (*increase*) aumentare; (*a protest, doubt, question*) sollevare; (*cattle, family*) allevare; (*crop*) coltivare; (*army, funds*) raccogliere; (*loan*) ottenere; **to ~ one's voice** alzare la voce.

raisin ['reɪzn] *n* uva secca.

rajah ['rɑːdʒə] *n* ragià *m inv*.

rake [reɪk] *n* (*tool*) rastrello; (*person*) libertino // *vt* (*garden*) rastrellare; (*with machine gun*) spazzare.

rakish ['reɪkɪʃ] *a* dissoluto(a); disinvolto(a).

rally ['rælɪ] *n* (*POL etc*) riunione *f*; (*AUT*) rally *m inv*; (*TENNIS*) scambio // *vt* riunire, radunare // *vi* raccogliersi, radunarsi; (*sick person, Stock Exchange*) riprendersi; **to ~ round** *vt fus* raggrupparsi intorno a; venire in aiuto di.

ram [ræm] *n* montone *m*; (*also: device*) ariete *m* // *vt* conficcare; (*crash into*) cozzare, sbattere contro; percuotere; speronare.

ramble ['ræmbl] *n* escursione *f* // *vi* (*pej: also: ~ on*) divagare; **~r** *n* escursionista *m/f*; (*BOT*) rosa rampicante; **rambling** *a* (*speech*) sconnesso(a); (*BOT*) rampicante.

ramification [ræmɪfɪ'keɪʃən] *n* ramificazione *f*.

ramp [ræmp] *n* rampa.

rampage [ræm'peɪdʒ] *n*: **to be on the ~** scatenarsi in modo violento // *vi* **they went rampaging through the town** si sono scatenati in modo violento per la città.

rampant ['ræmpənt] *a* (*disease etc*) che infierisce.

rampart ['ræmpɑːt] *n* bastione *m*.

ramshackle ['ræmʃækl] *a* (*house*) cadente; (*car etc*) sgangherato(a).

ran [ræn] *pt of* **run**.

ranch [rɑːntʃ] *n* ranch *m inv*; **~er** *n* proprietario di un ranch; cowboy *m inv*.

rancid ['rænsɪd] *a* rancido(a).

rancour ['ræŋkə*] n rancore m.

random ['rændəm] a fatto(a) or detto(a) per caso // n: at ~ a casaccio.

randy ['rændı] a (col) arrapato(a); lascivo(a).

rang [ræŋ] pt of ring.

range [reındʒ] n (of mountains) catena; (of missile, voice) portata; (of products) gamma; (MIL: also: shooting ~) campo di tiro; (also: kitchen ~) fornello, cucina economica // vi: to ~ over coprire; to ~ from ... to andare da ... a; ~r n guardia forestale.

rank [ræŋk] n fila; (MIL) grado; (also: taxi ~) posteggio di taxi // vi: to ~ among essere nel numero di // a puzzolente; vero(a) e proprio(a); the ~s (MIL) la truppa; the ~ and file (fig) la gran massa.

rankle ['ræŋkl] vi bruciare.

ransack ['rænsæk] vt rovistare; (plunder) saccheggiare.

ransom ['rænsəm] n riscatto; to hold sb to ~ (fig) esercitare pressione su qd.

rant [rænt] vi vociare; ~ing n vociare m.

rap [ræp] n colpo secco e lievo; picchio // vt bussare a; picchiare su.

rape [reıp] n violenza carnale, stupro // vt violentare.

rapid ['ræpıd] a rapido(a); ~s npl (GEO) rapida.

rapist ['reıpıst] n violentatore m.

rapport [ræ'pɔ:*] n rapporto.

rapture ['ræptʃə*] n estasi f inv; to go into ~s over andare in solluchero per; rapturous a estatico(a).

rare [rεə*] a raro(a); (CULIN: steak) al sangue.

rarefied ['rεərıfaıd] a (air, atmosphere) rarefatto(a).

rarely ['rεəlı] ad raramente.

rarity ['rεərıtı] n rarità f inv.

rascal ['rɑːskl] n mascalzone m.

rash [ræʃ] a imprudente, sconsiderato(a) // n (MED) eruzione f.

rasher ['ræʃə*] n fetta sottile (di lardo or prosciutto).

rasp [rɑːsp] n (tool) lima.

raspberry ['rɑːzbərı] n lampone m.

rasping ['rɑːspıŋ] a stridulo(a).

rat [ræt] n ratto.

ratchet ['rætʃıt] n (TECH) dente m d'arresto.

rate [reıt] n (proportion) tasso, percentuale f; (speed) velocità f inv; (price) tariffa // vt giudicare; stimare; to ~ sb/sth as valutare qd/qc come; to ~ sb/sth among annoverare qd/qc tra; ~s npl (Brit) imposte fpl comunali; (fees) tariffe fpl; ~able value n valore m imponibile or locativo (di una proprietà); ~ of exchange n corso dei cambi; ~payer n contribuente m/f (che paga le imposte comunali).

rather ['rɑːðə*] ad piuttosto; it's ~ expensive è piuttosto caro; (too much) è un po' caro; I would or I'd ~ go preferirei andare.

ratification [rætıfı'keıʃən] n ratificazione f.

ratify ['rætıfaı] vt ratificare.

rating ['reıtıŋ] n classificazione f; punteggio di merito; (NAUT: sailor) marinaio semplice.

ratio ['reıʃıəu] n proporzione f.

ration ['ræʃən] n (gen pl) razioni fpl // vt razionare.

rational ['ræʃənl] a razionale, ragionevole; (solution, reasoning) logico(a); ~e [-'nɑːl] n fondamento logico; giustificazione f; ~ize vt razionalizzare; ~ly ad razionalmente; logicamente.

rat race ['rætreıs] n mondo cane.

rattle ['rætl] n tintinnio; (louder) strepito; (object: of baby) sonaglino; (: of sports fan) raganella // vi risuonare, tintinnare; fare un rumore di ferraglia // vt scuotere (con strepito); ~snake n serpente m a sonagli.

raucous ['rɔːkəs] a rauco(a).

ravage ['rævıdʒ] vt devastare; ~s danni mpl.

rave [reıv] vi (in anger) infuriarsi; (with enthusiasm) andare in estasi; (MED) delirare.

raven ['reıvən] n corvo.

ravenous ['rævənəs] a affamato(a).

ravine [rə'viːn] n burrone m.

raving ['reıvıŋ] a: ~ lunatic n pazzo(a) furioso(a).

ravioli [rævı'əulı] n ravioli mpl.

ravish ['rævıʃ] vt (delight) estasiare; ~ing a incantevole.

raw [rɔː] a (uncooked) crudo(a); (not processed) greggio(a); (sore) vivo(a); (inexperienced) inesperto(a); ~ material n materia prima.

ray [reı] n raggio.

rayon ['reıən] n raion m.

raze [reız] vt radere, distruggere.

razor ['reızə*] n rasoio; ~ blade n lama di rasoio.

Rd abbr of road.

re [riː] prep con riferimento a.

reach [riːtʃ] n portata; (of river etc) tratto // vt raggiungere; arrivare a // vi stendersi; out of/within ~ (object) fuori a portata di mano; within easy ~ (of) (place) a breve distanza (di), vicino (a); to ~ out vt: to ~ out for stendere la mano per prendere.

react [riː'ækt] vi reagire; ~ion [-'ækʃən] n reazione f; ~ionary [-'ækʃənrı] a,n reazionario(a).

reactor [riː'æktə*] n reattore m.

read, pt,pp read [riːd, rεd] vi leggere // vt leggere; (understand) intendere, interpretare; (study) studiare; to ~ out vt leggere ad alta voce; ~er n lettore/trice; (book) libro di lettura; (at university) professore con funzioni preminenti di ricerca; ~ership n (of paper etc) numero di lettori.

readily ['rεdılı] ad volentieri; (easily) facilmente.

readiness ['rεdınıs] n prontezza; in ~ (prepared) pronto(a).

reading ['ri:dɪŋ] n lettura; (understanding) interpretazione f; (on instrument) indicazione f; ~ **lamp** n lampada da studio; ~ **room** n sala di lettura.

readjust [ri:ə'dʒʌst] vt raggiustare // vi (person): **to** ~ **(to)** riadattarsi (a).

ready ['rɛdɪ] a pronto(a); (willing) pronto(a), disposto(a); (quick) rapido(a); (available) disponibile // ad: ~-**cooked** già cotto(a) // n: **at the** ~ (MIL) pronto a sparare; (fig) tutto(a) pronto(a); ~ **cash** n denaro in contanti; ~-**made** a prefabbricato(a); (clothes) confezionato(a).

real [rɪəl] a reale; vero(a); **in** ~ **terms** in realtà; ~ **estate** n beni mpl immobili; ~**ism** n (also ART) realismo; ~**ist** n realista m/f; ~**istic** [-'lɪstɪk] a realistico(a).

reality [ri:'ælɪtɪ] n realtà f inv; **in** ~ in realtà, in effetti.

realization [rɪəlaɪ'zeɪʃən] n presa di coscienza; realizzazione f.

realize ['rɪəlaɪz] vt (understand) rendersi conto di; (a project, COMM: asset) realizzare.

really ['rɪəlɪ] ad veramente, davvero.

realm [rɛlm] n reame m, regno.

ream [ri:m] n risma.

reap [ri:p] vt mietere; (fig) raccogliere.

reappear [ri:ə'pɪə*] vi ricomparire, riapparire; ~**ance** n riapparizione f.

rear [rɪə*] a di dietro; (AUT: wheel etc) posteriore // n didietro, parte f posteriore // vt (cattle, family) allevare // vi (also: ~ **up**) (animal) impennarsi; ~**guard** n retroguardia.

rearm [ri:'ɑ.m] vt, vi riarmare; ~**ament** n riarmo.

rearrange [ri:ə'reɪndʒ] vt riordinare.

rear-view ['rɪəvju:] a: ~ **mirror** n (AUT) specchio retrovisivo.

reason ['ri:zn] n ragione f; (cause, motive) ragione, motivo // vi: **to** ~ **with sb** far ragionare qd; **to have** ~ **to think** avere motivi per pensare; **it stands to** ~ **that** è ovvio che; ~**able** a ragionevole; (not bad) accettabile; ~**ably** ad ragionevolmente; ~**ed** a (argument) ponderato(a); ~**ing** n ragionamento.

reassert [ri:ə'sə:t] vt riaffermare.

reassure [ri:ə'ʃuə*] vt rassicurare; **to** ~ **sb of** rassicurare qd di or su; **reassuring** a rassicurante.

rebate ['ri:beɪt] n (on product) ribasso; (on tax etc) sgravio; (repayment) rimborso.

rebel n ['rɛbl] ribelle m/f // vi [rɪ'bɛl] ribellarsi; ~**lion** n ribellione f; ~**llous** a ribelle.

rebirth [ri:'bə:θ] n rinascita.

rebound vi [rɪ'baund] (ball) rimbalzare // n ['ri:baund] rimbalzo.

rebuff [rɪ'bʌf] n secco rifiuto // vt respingere.

rebuild [ri:'bɪld] vt irg ricostruire.

rebuke [rɪ'bju:k] n rimprovero // vt rimproverare.

rebut [rɪ'bʌt] vt rifiutare; ~**tal** n rifiuto.

recall [rɪ'kɔ:l] vt richiamare; (remember) ricordare, richiamare alla mente // n richiamo; **beyond** ~ a irrevocabile.

recant [rɪ'kænt] vi ritrattarsi; (REL) fare abiura.

recap ['ri:kæp] n ricapitolazione f // vt ricapitolare // vi riassumere.

recapture [ri:'kæptʃə*] vt riprendere; (atmosphere) ricreare.

recede [rɪ'si:d] vi allontanarsi; ritirarsi; calare; **receding** a (forehead, chin) sfuggente; **he's got a receding hairline** sta stempiando.

receipt [rɪ'si:t] n (document) ricevuta; (act of receiving) ricevimento; ~**s** npl (COMM) introiti mpl.

receive [rɪ'si:v] vt ricevere; (guest) ricevere, accogliere.

receiver [rɪ'si:və*] n (TEL) ricevitore m; (of stolen goods) ricettatore/trice; (LAW) curatore m fallimentare.

recent ['ri:snt] a recente; ~**ly** ad recentemente.

receptacle [rɪ'sɛptɪkl] n recipiente m.

reception [rɪ'sɛpʃən] n ricevimento; (welcome) accoglienza; (TV etc) ricezione f; ~ **desk** n ricevimento; ~**ist** n receptionist m/f inv.

receptive [rɪ'sɛptɪv] a ricettivo(a).

recess [rɪ'sɛs] n (in room) alcova; (POL etc: holiday) vacanze fpl.

recharge [ri:'tʃɑ:dʒ] vt (battery) ricaricare.

recipe ['rɛsɪpɪ] n ricetta.

recipient [rɪ'sɪpɪənt] n beneficiario/a; (of letter) destinatario.

reciprocal [rɪ'sɪprəkl] a reciproco(a).

reciprocate [rɪ'sɪprəkeɪt] vt ricambiare, contraccambiare.

recital [rɪ'saɪtl] n recital m inv.

recite [rɪ'saɪt] vt (poem) recitare.

reckless ['rɛkləs] a (driver etc) spericolato(a).

reckon ['rɛkən] vt (count) calcolare; (consider) considerare, stimare; (think): **I** ~ **that ...** penso che ...; **to** ~ **on** vt fus contare su; ~**ing** n conto; stima; **the day of** ~**ing** il giorno del giudizio.

reclaim [rɪ'kleɪm] vt (land) bonificare; (demand back) richiedere, reclamare; **reclamation** [rɛklə'meɪʃən] n bonifica.

recline [rɪ'klaɪn] vi stare sdraiato(a); **reclining** a (seat) ribaltabile.

recluse [rɪ'klu:s] n eremita m, appartato/a.

recognition [rɛkəg'nɪʃən] n riconoscimento; **to gain** ~ essere riconosciuto(a); **transformed beyond** ~ irriconoscibile.

recognizable ['rɛkəgnaɪzəbl] a riconoscibile.

recognize ['rɛkəgnaɪz] vt: **to** ~ **(by/as)** riconoscere (a or da/come).

recoil [rɪ'kɔɪl] vi (gun) rinculare; (spring) balzare indietro; (person): **to** ~ **(from)** indietreggiare (davanti a) // n rinculo; contraccolpo.

recollect [rɛkə'lɛkt] vt ricordare; ~**ion** [-'lɛkʃən] n ricordo.

recommend [rekə'mend] vt raccomandare; (advise) consigliare; ~ation [-'deɪʃən] n raccomandazione f; consiglio.

recompense ['rekəmpens] vt ricompensare; (compensate) risarcire.

reconcile ['rekənsaɪl] vt (two people) riconciliare; (two facts) conciliare, quadrare; to ~ o.s. to rassegnarsi a; **reconciliation** [-sɪlɪ'eɪʃən] n riconciliazione f; conciliazione f.

recondition [ri:kən'dɪʃən] vt rimettere a nuovo; rifare.

reconnaissance [rɪ'kɔnɪsns] n (MIL) ricognizione f.

reconnoitre [rekə'nɔɪtə°] (MIL) vt fare una ricognizione di // vi fare una ricognizione.

reconsider [ri:kən'sɪdə°] vt riconsiderare.

reconstruct [ri:kən'strʌkt] vt ricostruire; ~ion [-kʃən] n ricostruzione f.

record n ['rekɔ:d] ricordo, documento; (of meeting etc) nota, verbale m; (register) registro; (file) pratica, dossier m inv; (also: police ~) fedina penale sporca; (MUS: disc) disco; (SPORT) record m inv, primato // vt [rɪ'kɔ:d] (set down) prendere nota di, registrare; (relate) raccontare; (MUS: song etc) registrare; **in ~ time** a tempo di record; **to keep a ~ of** tener nota di; **off the ~** a ufficioso(a); ~ **card** n (in file) scheda; ~er n avvocato che funge da giudice; (MUS) flauto diritto; ~ **holder** n (SPORT) primatista m/f; ~ing n (MUS) registrazione f; ~ **library** n discoteca; ~ **player** n giradischi m inv.

recount [rɪ'kaunt] vt raccontare, narrare.

re-count ['ri:kaunt] n (POL: of votes) nuovo computo.

recoup [rɪ'ku:p] vt ricuperare.

recourse [rɪ'kɔ:s] n ricorso; rimedio; **to have ~ to** ricorrere a.

recover [rɪ'kʌvə°] vt ricuperare // vi (from illness) rimettersi (in salute), ristabilirsi; (country, person: from shock) riprendersi.

re-cover [ri:'kʌvə°] vt (chair etc) ricoprire.

recovery [rɪ'kʌvərɪ] n ricupero; ristabilimento; ripresa.

recreate [ri:krɪ'eɪt] vt ricreare.

recreation [rekrɪ'eɪʃən] n ricreazione f; svago; ~al a ricreativo(a).

recrimination [rɪkrɪmɪ'neɪʃən] n recriminazione f.

recruit [rɪ'kru:t] n recluta // vt reclutare; ~ment n reclutamento.

rectangle ['rektæŋgl] n rettangolo; **rectangular** [-'tæŋgjulə°] a rettangolare.

rectify ['rektɪfaɪ] vt (error) rettificare; (omission) riparare.

rector ['rektə°] n (REL) parroco (anglicano); **rectory** n presbiterio.

recuperate [rɪ'kju:pəreɪt] vi ristabilirsi.

recur [rɪ'kə:°] vi riaccadere; (idea, opportunity) riapparire; (symptoms) ripresentarsi; ~**rence** n recrudescenza; riapparizione f; rinnovo; ~**rent** a

ricorrente, periodico(a); ~**ring** a (MATH) periodico(a).

red [red] n rosso; (POL: pej) rosso/a // a rosso(a); **in the ~** (account) scoperto; (business) in deficit; ~ **carpet treatment** n cerimonia col gran pavese; **R~ Cross** n Croce f Rossa; ~**currant** n ribes m inv; ~**den** vt arrossare // vi arrossire; ~**dish** a rossiccio(a).

redeem [rɪ'di:m] vt (debt) riscattare; (sth in pawn) ritirare; (fig, also REL) redimere; ~**ing** a (feature) che salva.

redeploy [ri:dɪ'plɔɪ] vt (resources) riorganizzare.

red-haired [red'heəd] a dai capelli rossi.

red-handed [red'hændɪd] a: **to be caught ~** essere preso(a) in flagrante or con le mani nel sacco.

redhead ['redhed] n rosso/a.

red herring ['red'herɪŋ] n (fig) falsa pista.

red-hot [red'hɔt] a arroventato(a).

redirect [ri:daɪ'rekt] vt (mail) far seguire.

redistribute [ri:dɪ'strɪbju:t] vt ridistribuire.

red light ['red'laɪt] n: **to go through a ~** (AUT) passare col rosso; **red-light district** n quartiere m luce rossa inv.

redness ['rednɪs] n rossore m; (of hair) rosso.

redo [ri:'du:] vt irg rifare.

redolent ['redəulnt] a: ~ **of** che sa di; (fig) che ricorda.

redouble [ri:'dʌbl] vt: **to ~ one's efforts** raddoppiare gli sforzi.

redress [rɪ'dres] n riparazione f.

red tape ['red'teɪp] n (fig) burocrazia.

reduce [rɪ'dju:s] vt ridurre; (lower) ridurre, abbassare; **reduction** [rɪ'dʌkʃən] n riduzione f; (of price) ribasso; (discount) sconto.

redundancy [rɪ'dʌndənsɪ] n licenziamento.

redundant [rɪ'dʌndnt] a (worker) licenziato(a); (detail, object) superfluo(a); **to make ~** licenziare.

reed [ri:d] n (BOT) canna; (MUS: of clarinet etc) ancia.

reef [ri:f] n (at sea) scogliera.

reek [ri:k] vi: **to ~ (of)** puzzare (di).

reel [ri:l] n bobina, rocchetto; (TECH) aspo; (FISHING) mulinello; (CINEMA) rotolo // vt (TECH) annaspare; (also: ~ **up**) avvolgere // vi (sway) barcollare.

re-election [ri:'lekʃən] n rielezione f.

ref [ref] n (col: abbr of referee) arbitro.

refectory [rɪ'fektərɪ] n refettorio.

refer [rɪ'fə:°] vt: **to ~ sb (or sth) to** (dispute, decision) deferire qc a; (inquirer: for information) indirizzare qd a; (reader: to text) rimandare qd a; **to ~ to vt fus** (allude to) accennare a; (apply to) riferire a; (consult) rivolgersi a; ~**ring to your letter** (COMM) in riferimento alla Vostra lettera.

referee [refə'ri:] n arbitro; (for job application) referenza // vt arbitrare.

reference ['refrəns] n riferimento;

(*mention*) menzione f, allusione f; (*for job application: letter*) referenza; lettera di raccomandazione; (: *person*) referenza; **with ~ to** a riguardo a; (*COMM: in letter*) in or con riferimento a; **~ book** n libro di consultazione.

referendum, pl **referenda** [rɛfə'rɛndəm, -də] n referendum m inv.

refill vt [ri:'fɪl] riempire di nuovo; (*pen, lighter etc*) ricaricare // n ['ri:fɪl] (*for pen etc*) ricambio.

refine [rɪ'faɪn] vt raffinare; **~d** a (*person, taste*) raffinato(a); **~ment** n (*of person*) raffinatezza; **~ry** n raffineria.

reflect [rɪ'flɛkt] vt (*light, image*) riflettere; (*fig*) rispecchiare // vi (*think*) riflettere, considerare; **to ~ on** vt fus (*discredit*) rispecchiarsi su; **~ion** [-'flɛkʃən] n riflessione f; (*image*) riflesso; (*criticism*): **~ion on** giudizio su; attacco a; **on ~ion** pensandoci sopra; **~or** n (*also AUT*) catarifrangente m.

reflex ['ri:flɛks] a riflesso(a) // n riflesso; **~ive** [rɪ'flɛksɪv] a (*LING*) riflessivo(a).

reform [rɪ'fɔ:m] n riforma // vt riformare; **the R~ation** [rɛfə'meɪʃən] n la Riforma; **~ed** a cambiato(a) (per il meglio); **~er** n riformatore/trice.

refrain [rɪ'freɪn] vi: **to ~ from doing** trattenersi dal fare // n ritornello.

refresh [rɪ'frɛʃ] vt rinfrescare; (*subj: food, sleep*) ristorare; **~er course** n corso di aggiornamento; **~ment room** n posto di ristoro; **~ments** npl rinfreschi mpl.

refrigeration [rɪfrɪdʒə'reɪʃən] n refrigerazione f.

refrigerator [rɪ'frɪdʒəreɪtə*] n frigorifero.

refuel [ri:'fjuəl] vt rifornire (di carburante) // vi far rifornimento (di carburante).

refuge ['rɛfju:dʒ] n rifugio; **to take ~ in** rifugiarsi in.

refugee [rɛfju'dʒi:] n rifugiato/a, profugo/a.

refund n ['ri:fʌnd] rimborso // vt [rɪ'fʌnd] rimborsare.

refurbish [ri:'fɔ:bɪʃ] vt rimettere a nuovo.

refusal [rɪ'fju:zəl] n rifiuto.

refuse n ['rɛfju:s] rifiuti mpl // vt, vi [rɪ'fju:z] rifiutare; **~ collector** n netturbino.

refute [rɪ'fju:t] vt confutare.

regain [rɪ'geɪn] vt riguadagnare; riacquistare, ricuperare.

regal ['ri:gl] a regio(a); **~ia** [rɪ'geɪlɪə] n insegne fpl regie.

regard [rɪ'gɑ:d] n riguardo, stima // vt considerare, stimare; **to give one's ~s to** porgere i suoi saluti a; **~ing, as ~s, with ~ to** riguardo a; **~less** ad lo stesso; **~less of** a dispetto di, nonostante.

regatta [rɪ'gætə] n regata.

regency ['ri:dʒənsɪ] n reggenza.

regent ['ri:dʒənt] n reggente m.

régime [reɪ'ʒi:m] n regime m.

regiment ['rɛdʒɪmənt] n reggimento; **~al**

[-'mɛntl] a reggimentale; **~ation** [-'teɪʃən] n irreggimentazione f.

region ['ri:dʒən] n regione f; **in the ~ of** (*fig*) all'incirca di; **~al** a regionale.

register ['rɛdʒɪstə*] n registro; (*also: electoral ~*) lista elettorale // vt registrare; (*vehicle*) immatricolare; (*luggage*) spedire assicurato(a); (*letter*) raccomandare; (*subj: instrument*) segnare // vi iscriversi; (*at hotel*) firmare il registro; (*make impression*) entrare in testa; **~ed** a (*design*) deposito(a); (*letter*) raccomandato(a).

registrar ['rɛdʒɪstrɑ:*] n ufficiale m di stato civile; segretario.

registration [rɛdʒɪs'treɪʃən] n (*act*) registrazione f, iscrizione f; (*AUT: also: ~ number*) numero di targa.

registry ['rɛdʒɪstrɪ] n ufficio del registro; **~ office** n anagrafe f.

regret [rɪ'grɛt] n rimpianto, rincrescimento // vt rimpiangere; **I ~ that** I/he cannot help mi rincresce di non poter aiutare/che lui non possa aiutare; **~fully** ad con rincrescimento; **~table** a deplorevole.

regroup [ri:'gru:p] vt raggruppare // vi raggrupparsi.

regular ['rɛgjulə*] a regolare; (*usual*) abituale, normale; (*soldier*) dell'esercito regolare; (*COMM: size*) normale // n (*client etc*) cliente m/f abituale; **~ity** [-'lærɪtɪ] n regolarità f inv; **~ly** ad regolarmente.

regulate ['rɛgjuleɪt] vt regolare; **regulation** [-'leɪʃən] n (*rule*) regola, regolamento; (*adjustment*) regolazione f.

rehabilitation ['ri:həbɪlɪ'teɪʃən] n (*of offender*) riabilitazione f; (*of disabled*) riadattamento.

rehash [ri:'hæʃ] vt (*col*) rimaneggiare.

rehearsal [rɪ'hə:səl] n prova.

rehearse [rɪ'hə:s] vt provare.

reign [reɪn] n regno // vi regnare; **~ing** a (*monarch*) regnante; (*champion*) attuale.

reimburse [ri:ɪm'bə:s] vt rimborsare.

rein [reɪn] n (*for horse*) briglia.

reincarnation [ri:ɪnkɑ:'neɪʃən] n reincarnazione f.

reindeer ['reɪndɪə*] n, pl inv renna.

reinforce [ri:ɪn'fɔ:s] vt rinforzare; **~d concrete** n cemento armato; **~ment** n (*action*) rinforzamento; **~ments** npl (*MIL*) rinforzi mpl.

reinstate [ri:ɪn'steɪt] vt reintegrare.

reissue [ri:'ɪʃju:] vt (*book*) ristampare, ripubblicare; (*film*) distribuire di nuovo.

reiterate [ri:'ɪtəreɪt] vt reiterare, ripetere.

reject n ['ri:dʒɛkt] (*COMM*) scarto // vt [rɪ'dʒɛkt] rifiutare, respingere; (*COMM: goods*) scartare; **~ion** [rɪ'dʒɛkʃən] n rifiuto.

rejoice [rɪ'dʒɔɪs] vi: **to ~ (at or over)** provare diletto in.

rejuvenate [rɪ'dʒu:vəneɪt] vt ringiovanire.

rekindle [ri:'kɪndl] vt riaccendere.

relapse [rɪ'læps] n (*MED*) ricaduta.

relate [rɪ'leɪt] vt (*tell*) raccontare; (*connect*) collegare; **~d** a imparentato(a);

collegato(a), connesso(a); ~d to imparentato(a) con; collegato(a) or connesso(a) con; **relating**: **relating to** prep che riguarda, rispetto a.

relation [rɪ'leɪʃən] n (person) parente m/f; (link) rapporto, relazione f; ~ship n rapporto; (personal ties) rapporti mpl, relazioni fpl.

relative ['relətɪv] n parente m/f // a relativo(a); (respective) rispettivo(a); ~ly ad relativamente.

relax [rɪ'læks] vi rilasciarsi; (person: unwind) rilassarsi // vt rilasciare; (mind, person) rilassare; ~ation [riːlæk'seɪʃən] n rilasciamento; rilassamento; (entertainment) ricreazione f, svago; ~ed a rilasciato(a); rilassato(a); ~ing a rilassante.

relay ['riːleɪ] n (SPORT) corsa a staffetta // vt (message) trasmettere.

release [rɪ'liːs] n (from prison) rilascio; (from obligation) liberazione f; (of gas etc) emissione f; (of film etc) distribuzione f; (record) disco; (device) disinnesto // vt (prisoner) rilasciare; (from obligation, wreckage etc) liberare; (book, film) fare uscire; (news) rendere pubblico(a); (gas etc) emettere; (TECH: catch, spring etc) disinnestare; (let go) rilasciare; lasciar andare; sciogliere; to ~ one's grip mollare la presa; to ~ the clutch (AUT) staccare la frizione.

relegate ['relɪgeɪt] vt relegare.

relent [rɪ'lent] vi cedere; ~less a implacabile.

relevance ['relɪvəns] n pertinenza; ~ of sth to sth rapporto tra qc e qc.

relevant ['relɪvənt] a pertinente; (chapter) in questione; ~ to pertinente a.

reliability [rɪlaɪə'bɪlɪti] n fidabilità; affidabilità.

reliable [rɪ'laɪəbl] a (person, firm) fidato(a), che dà affidamento; (method) sicuro(a); (machine) affidabile; **reliably** ad: to be **reliably informed** sapere da fonti sicure.

reliance [rɪ'laɪəns] n: ~ (on) fiducia (in); bisogno (di).

relic ['relɪk] n (REL) reliquia; (of the past) resto.

relief [rɪ'liːf] n (from pain, anxiety) sollievo; (help, supplies) soccorsi mpl; (of guard) cambio; (ART, GEO) rilievo.

relieve [rɪ'liːv] vt (pain, patient) sollevare; (bring help) soccorrere; (take over from: gen) sostituire; (: guard) rilevare; to ~ sb of sth alleggerire qd di qc.

religion [rɪ'lɪdʒən] n religione f; **religious** a religioso(a).

relinquish [rɪ'lɪŋkwɪʃ] vt abbandonare; (plan, habit) rinunziare a.

relish ['relɪʃ] n (CULIN) condimento; (enjoyment) gran piacere m // vt (food etc) godere; to ~ **doing** adorare fare.

relive [riː'lɪv] vt rivivere.

reload [riː'ləʊd] vt ricaricare.

reluctance [rɪ'lʌktəns] n riluttanza.

reluctant [rɪ'lʌktənt] a riluttante, mal

disposto(a); ~ly ad di mala voglia, a malincuore.

rely [rɪ'laɪ]: to ~ on vt fus contare su; (be dependent) dipendere da.

remain [rɪ'meɪn] vi restare, rimanere; ~der n resto; (COMM) rimanenza; ~ing a che rimane; ~s npl resti mpl.

remand [rɪ'mɑːnd] n: on ~ in detenzione preventiva // vt: to ~ **in custody** rinviare in carcere; trattenere a disposizione della legge.

remark [rɪ'mɑːk] n osservazione f // vt osservare, dire; (notice) notare; ~able a notevole; eccezionale.

remedial [rɪ'miːdɪəl] a (tuition, classes) di riparazione.

remedy ['remədɪ] n: ~ (for) rimedio (per) // vt rimediare a.

remember [rɪ'membə*] vt ricordare, ricordarsi di; ~ **me to** (in letter) ricordami a; **remembrance** n memoria; ricordo.

remind [rɪ'maɪnd] vt: to ~ **sb of sth** ricordare qc a qd; to ~ **sb to do** ricordare a qd di fare; ~er n richiamo; (note etc) promemoria m inv.

reminisce [remɪ'nɪs] vi: to ~ (about) abbandonarsi ai ricordi (di).

reminiscences [remɪ'nɪsnsɪz] npl reminiscenze fpl, memorie fpl.

reminiscent [remɪ'nɪsnt] a: ~ of che fa pensare a, che richiama.

remission [rɪ'mɪʃən] n remissione f; (of fee) esonero.

remit [rɪ'mɪt] vt (send: money) rimettere; ~tance n rimessa.

remnant ['remnənt] n resto, avanzo; ~s npl (COMM) scampoli mpl; fine f serie.

remorse [rɪ'mɔːs] n rimorso; ~ful a pieno(a) di rimorsi; ~less a (fig) spietato(a).

remote [rɪ'məʊt] a remoto(a), lontano(a); (person) distaccato(a); ~ **control** n telecomando; ~ly ad remotamente; (slightly) vagamente; ~ness n lontananza.

remould ['riːməʊld] n (tyre) gomma rivestita.

removable [rɪ'muːvəbl] a (detachable) staccabile.

removal [rɪ'muːvəl] n (taking away) rimozione f; soppressione f; (from house) trasloco; (from office: sacking) destituzione f; (MED) ablazione f; ~ **van** n furgone m per traslochi.

remove [rɪ'muːv] vt togliere, rimuovere; (employee) destituire; (stain) far sparire; (doubt, abuse) sopprimere, eliminare.

remuneration [rɪmjuːnə'reɪʃən] n rimunerazione f.

rend, pt, pp **rent** [rend, rent] vt lacerare.

render ['rendə*] vt rendere; (CULIN: fat) struggere; ~ing n (MUS etc) interpretazione f.

rendez-vous ['rɒndɪvuː] n appuntamento; (place) luogo d'incontro; (meeting) incontro.

renegade ['renɪgeɪd] n rinnegato/a.

renew [rɪ'njuː] vt rinnovare; (negotiations) riprendere; ~**al** n rinnovamento; ripresa.

renounce [rɪ'naʊns] vt rinunziare a; (disown) ripudiare.

renovate ['renəveɪt] vt rinnovare; (art work) restaurare; **renovation** [-'veɪʃən] n rinnovamento; restauro.

renown [rɪ'naʊn] n rinomanza; ~**ed** a rinomato(a).

rent [rent] pt, pp of rend // n affitto // vt (take for rent) prendere in affitto; (also: ~ out) dare in affitto; ~**al** n (for television, car) fitto.

renunciation [rɪnʌnsɪ'eɪʃən] n rinnegamento; (self-denial) rinunzia.

reopen [riː'əʊpən] vt riaprire; ~**ing** n riapertura.

reorder [riː'ɔːdə*] vt ordinare di nuovo; (rearrange) riorganizzare.

reorganize [riː'ɔːgənaɪz] vt riorganizzare.

rep [rep] n (COMM: abbr of representative) rappresentante m/f; (THEATRE: abbr of repertory) teatro di repertorio.

repair [rɪ'peə*] n riparazione f // vt riparare; **in good/bad** ~ in buona/cattiva condizione; ~ **kit** n corredo per riparazioni; ~ **shop** n (AUT etc) officina.

repartee [repɑː'tiː] n risposta pronta.

repay [riː'peɪ] vt irg (money, creditor) rimborsare, ripagare; (sb's efforts) ricompensare; ~**ment** n rimborsamento; ricompensa.

repeal [rɪ'piːl] n (of law) abrogazione f; (of sentence) annullamento // vt abrogare; annullare.

repeat [rɪ'piːt] n (RADIO, TV) replica // vt ripetere; (pattern) riprodurre; (promise, attack, also COMM: order) rinnovare; ~**edly** ad ripetutamente, spesso.

repel [rɪ'pel] vt respingere; ~**lent** a repellente // n: **insect** ~**lent** prodotto m anti-insetti inv.

repent [rɪ'pent] vi: **to** ~ (**of**) pentirsi (di); ~**ance** n pentimento.

repercussion [riːpə'kʌʃən] n (consequence) ripercussione f.

repertoire ['repətwɑː*] n repertorio.

repertory ['repətərɪ] n (also: ~ **theatre**) teatro di repertorio.

repetition [repɪ'tɪʃən] n ripetizione f; (COMM: order etc) rinnovo.

repetitive [rɪ'petɪtɪv] a (movement) che si ripete; (work) monotono(a); (speech) pieno(a) di ripetizioni.

replace [rɪ'pleɪs] vt (put back) rimettere a posto; (take the place of) sostituire (TEL): '~ **the receiver'** 'riattaccare'; ~**ment** n rimessa; sostituzione f; (person) sostituto/a; ~**ment part** n pezzo di ricambio.

replenish [rɪ'plenɪʃ] vt (glass) riempire; (stock etc) rifornire.

replete [rɪ'pliːt] a ripieno(a); (well-fed) sazio(a).

replica ['replɪkə] n replica, copia.

reply [rɪ'plaɪ] n risposta // vi rispondere.

report [rɪ'pɔːt] n rapporto; (PRESS etc) cronaca; (also: **school** ~) pagella // vt riportare; (PRESS etc) fare una cronaca su; (bring to notice: occurrence) segnalare; (: person) denunciare // vi (make a report) fare un rapporto (or una cronaca); (present o.s.): **to** ~ (**to sb**) presentarsi (a qd); **it is** ~**ed that** si dice che; ~**ed speech** n (LING) discorso indiretto; ~**er** n reporter m inv.

reprehensible [reprɪ'hensɪbl] a riprensibile.

represent [reprɪ'zent] vt rappresentare; ~**ation** [-'teɪʃən] n rappresentazione f; ~**ations** npl (protest) protesta; ~**ative** n rappresentativo/a; (US: POL) deputato/a // a rappresentativo(a), caratteristico(a).

repress [rɪ'pres] vt reprimere; ~**ion** [-'preʃən] repressione f; ~**ive** a repressivo(a).

reprieve [rɪ'priːv] n (LAW) sospensione f dell'esecuzione della condanna; (fig) dilazione f // vt sospendere l'esecuzione della condanna a; accordare una dilazione a.

reprimand ['reprɪmɑːnd] n rampogna // vt rampognare.

reprisal [rɪ'praɪzl] n rappresaglia.

reproach [rɪ'prəʊtʃ] n rimprovero // vt: **to** ~ **sb with sth** rimproverare qd di qc; **beyond** ~ irreprensibile; ~**ful** a di rimprovero.

reproduce [riːprə'djuːs] vt riprodurre // vi riprodursi; **reproduction** [-'dʌkʃən] n riproduzione f; **reproductive** [-'dʌktɪv] a riproduttore(trice); riproduttivo(a).

reprove [rɪ'pruːv] vt (action) disapprovare; (person): **to** ~ (**for**) biasimare (per); **reproving** a di disapprovazione.

reptile ['reptaɪl] n rettile m.

republic [rɪ'pʌblɪk] n repubblica; ~**an** a,n repubblicano(a).

repudiate [rɪ'pjuːdɪeɪt] vt ripudiare.

repugnant [rɪ'pʌgnənt] a ripugnante.

repulse [rɪ'pʌls] vt respingere.

repulsion [rɪ'pʌlʃən] n ripulsione f.

repulsive [rɪ'pʌlsɪv] a ripugnante, ripulsivo(a).

reputable ['repjutəbl] a di buona reputazione; (occupation) rispettabile.

reputation [repju'teɪʃən] n reputazione f.

repute [rɪ'pjuːt] n reputazione f; ~**d** a reputato(a); ~**dly** ad secondo quanto si dice.

request [rɪ'kwest] n domanda; (formal) richiesta // vt: **to** ~ (**of** or **from sb**) chiedere (a qd).

requiem ['rekwɪəm] n requiem m or f inv.

require [rɪ'kwaɪə*] vt (need: subj: person) aver bisogno di; (: thing, situation) richiedere; (want) volere; esigere; (order) obbligare; ~**d** a richiesto(a); **if** ~**d** in caso di bisogno; ~**ment** n esigenza; bisogno; requisito.

requisite ['rekwɪzɪt] n cosa necessaria // a necessario(a); **toilet** ~**s** articoli mpl da toletta.

requisition [rekwɪ'zɪʃən] n: ~ (**for**) richiesta (di) // vt (MIL) requisire.

rescind [rɪ'sɪnd] vt annullare; (law) abrogare; (judgment) rescindere.

rescue ['reskju:] n salvataggio; (help) soccorso // vt salvare; ~ **party** n squadra di salvataggio; ~**r** n salvatore/trice.

research [rɪ'sɜ:tʃ] n ricerca, ricerche fpl // vt fare ricerche su; ~**er** n ricercatore/trice; ~ **work** n ricerche fpl.

resemblance [rɪ'zɛmbləns] n somiglianza.

resemble [rɪ'zɛmbl] vt assomigliare a.

resent [rɪ'zɛnt] vt risentirsi di; ~**ful** a pieno(a) di risentimento; ~**ment** n risentimento.

reservation [rɛzə'veɪʃən] n (booking) prenotazione f; (doubt) dubbio; (protected area) riserva; (on road: also: **central** ~) spartitraffico m inv; **to make a** ~ (**in an hotel/a restaurant/on a plane**) prenotare una camera/una tavola/un posto.

reserve [rɪ'zɜ:v] n riserva // vt (seats etc) prenotare; ~**s** npl (MIL) riserve fpl; **in** ~ in serbo; ~**d** a (shy) riservato(a); (seat) prenotato(a).

reservoir ['rɛzəvwa:*] n serbatoio.

reshape [ri:'ʃeɪp] vt (policy) ristrutturare.

reshuffle [ri:'ʃʌfl] n: **Cabinet** ~ (POL) rimpasto governativo.

reside [rɪ'zaɪd] vi risiedere.

residence ['rɛzɪdəns] n residenza; ~ **permit** n permesso di soggiorno.

resident ['rɛzɪdənt] n residente m/f; (in hotel) cliente m/f fisso(a) // a residente.

residential [rɛzɪ'dɛnʃl] a di residenza; (area) residenziale.

residue ['rɛzɪdju:] n resto; (CHEM, PHYSICS) residuo.

resign [rɪ'zaɪn] vt (one's post) dimettersi da // vi dimettersi; **to** ~ **o.s. to** rassegnarsi a; ~**ation** [rɛzɪg'neɪʃən] n dimissioni fpl; rassegnazione f; ~**ed** a rassegnato(a).

resilience [rɪ'zɪlɪəns] n (of material) elasticità, resilienza; (of person) capacità di recupero.

resilient [rɪ'zɪlɪənt] a (person) che si riprende facilmente.

resin ['rɛzɪn] n resina.

resist [rɪ'zɪst] vt resistere a; ~**ance** n resistenza.

resolute ['rɛzəlu:t] a risoluto(a).

resolution [rɛzə'lu:ʃən] n risoluzione f.

resolve [rɪ'zɔlv] n risoluzione f // vt (decide): **to** ~ **to do** decidere di fare; ~**d** a risoluto(a).

resonant ['rɛzənənt] a risonante.

resort [rɪ'zɔ:t] n (town) stazione f; (recourse) ricorso // vi: **to** ~ **to** aver ricorso a; **as a last** ~ come ultimo ricorso.

resound [rɪ'zaund] vi: **to** ~ (**with**) risonare (di); ~**ing** a risonante.

resource [rɪ'sɔ:s] n risorsa; ~**s** npl risorse fpl; ~**ful** a pieno(a) di risorse, intraprendente.

respect [rɪs'pɛkt] n rispetto // vt rispettare; **with** ~ **to** rispetto a, riguardo a; **in this** ~ per questo riguardo;

~**ability** [-ə'bɪlɪtɪ] n rispettabilità; ~**able** a rispettabile; ~**ful** a rispettoso(a).

respective [rɪs'pɛktɪv] a rispettivo(a); ~**ly** ad rispettivamente.

respiration [rɛspɪ'reɪʃən] n respirazione f.

respite ['rɛspaɪt] n respiro, tregua.

resplendent [rɪs'plɛndənt] a risplendente.

respond [rɪs'pɔnd] vi rispondere.

response [rɪs'pɔns] n risposta.

responsibility [rɪspɔnsɪ'bɪlɪtɪ] n responsabilità f inv.

responsible [rɪs'pɔnsɪbl] a (liable): ~ (**for**) responsabile (di); (trustworthy) fidato(a); (job) di (grande) responsabilità; **responsibly** ad responsabilmente.

responsive [rɪs'pɔnsɪv] a che reagisce.

rest [rɛst] n riposo; (stop) sosta, pausa; (MUS) pausa; (support) appoggio, sostegno; (remainder) resto, avanzi mpl // vi riposarsi; (be supported): **to** ~ **on** appoggiarsi su; (remain) rimanere, restare // vt (lean): **to** ~ **sth on/against** appoggiare qc su/contro; **the** ~ **of them** gli altri; **it** ~**s with him to decide** sta a lui decidere.

restart [ri:'sta:t] vt (engine) rimettere in marcia; (work) ricominciare.

restaurant ['rɛstərɔŋ] n ristorante m; ~ **car** n vagone m ristorante.

restful ['rɛstful] a riposante.

rest home ['rɛsthəum] n casa di riposo.

restitution [rɛstɪ'tju:ʃən] n (act) restituzione f; (reparation) riparazione f.

restive ['rɛstɪv] a agitato(a), impaziente; (horse) restio(a).

restless ['rɛstlɪs] a agitato(a), irrequieto(a).

restock [ri:'stɔk] vt rifornire.

restoration [rɛstə'reɪʃən] n restauro; restituzione f.

restore [rɪ'stɔ:*] vt (building) restaurare; (sth stolen) restituire; (peace, health) ristorare.

restrain [rɪs'treɪn] vt (feeling) contenere, frenare; (person): **to** ~ (**from doing**) trattenere (dal fare); ~**ed** a (style) contenuto(a), sobrio(a); (manner) riservato(a); ~**t** n (restriction) limitazione f; (moderation) ritegno.

restrict [rɪs'trɪkt] vt restringere, limitare; ~**ed area** n (AUT) zona a velocità limitata; ~**ion** [-kʃən] n restrizione f, limitazione f; ~**ive** a restrittivo(a).

rest room n (US) toletta.

result [rɪ'zʌlt] n risultato // vi: **to** ~ **in** avere per risultato.

resume [rɪ'zju:m] vt, vi (work, journey) riprendere.

resumption [rɪ'zʌmpʃən] n ripresa.

resurgence [rɪ'sɜ:dʒəns] n rinascita.

resurrection [rɛzə'rɛkʃən] n risurrezione f.

resuscitate [rɪ'sʌsɪteɪt] vt (MED) risuscitare; **resuscitation** [-'teɪʃən] n rianimazione f.

retail ['ri:teɪl] n (vendita al) minuto // cpd al minuto // vt vendere al minuto; ~**er** n commerciante m/f al minuto, dettagliante

m; ~ **price** n prezzo al minuto.
retain [rɪ'teɪn] vt (keep) tenere, serbare;
~**er** n (servant) servitore m; (fee)
onorario.
retaliate [rɪ'tælɪeɪt] vi: **to** ~ **(against)**
vendicarsi (di); **retaliation** [-'eɪʃən] n
vendetta, rappresaglie fpl.
retarded [rɪ'tɑːdɪd] a ritardato(a); (also:
mentally ~) tardo(a) (di mente).
retch [retʃ] vi aver conati di vomito.
rethink [ˈriː'θɪŋk] vt ripensare.
reticence ['retɪsns] n reticenza.
reticent ['retɪsnt] a reticente.
retina ['retɪnə] n retina.
retinue ['retɪnjuː] n seguito, scorta.
retire [rɪ'taɪə*] vi (give up work) andare in
pensione; (withdraw) ritirarsi, andarsene;
(go to bed) andare a letto, ritirarsi; ~**d** a
(person) pensionato(a); ~**ment** n
pensione f; **retiring** a (person)
riservato(a).
retort [rɪ'tɔːt] n (reply) rimbecco; (container) storta // vi rimbeccare.
retrace [riː'treɪs] vt ricostruire; **to** ~
one's steps tornare sui passi.
retract [rɪ'trækt] vt (statement) ritrattare;
(claws, undercarriage, aerial) ritrarre,
ritirare // vi ritrarsi; ~**able** a retrattile.
retrain [riː'treɪn] vt (worker) riaddestrare;
~**ing** n riaddestramento.
retreat [rɪ'triːt] n ritirata; (place) rifugio
// vi battere in ritirata; (flood) ritirarsi.
retrial [riː'traɪəl] n nuovo processo.
retribution [retrɪ'bjuːʃən] n castigo.
retrieval [rɪ'triːvəl] n ricupero;
riparazione f.
retrieve [rɪ'triːv] vt (sth lost) ricuperare,
ritrovare; (situation, honour) salvare;
(error, loss) riparare; (COMPUTERS)
ricuperare; ~**r** n cane m da riporto.
retrospect ['retrəspekt] n: **in** ~
guardando indietro; ~**ive** [-'spektɪv] a
retrospettivo(a); (law) retroattivo(a).
return [rɪ'tɜːn] n (going or coming back)
ritorno; (of sth stolen etc) restituzione f; (recompense) ricompensa; (FINANCE: from
land, shares) profitto, reddito; (report)
rapporto // cpd (journey, match) di ritorno;
(ticket) di andata e ritorno // vi tornare,
ritornare // vt rendere, restituire; (bring
back) riportare; (send back) mandare
indietro; (put back) rimettere; (POL: candidate) eleggere; ~**s** npl (COMM) incassi
mpl; profitti mpl; **many happy ~s (of
the day)!** auguri!, buon compleanno!
reunion [riː'juːnɪən] n riunione f.
reunite [riːjuː'naɪt] vt riunire.
rev [rev] n (abbr of revolution: AUT) giro
// vb (also: ~ **up**) vt imballare // vi
imballarsi.
revamp ['riː'væmp] vt rinnovare;
riorganizzare.
reveal [rɪ'viːl] vt (make known) rivelare,
svelare; (display) rivelare, mostrare;
~**ing** a rivelatore(trice); (dress)
scollato(a).
reveille [rɪ'vælɪ] n (MIL) sveglia.

revel ['revl] vi: **to** ~ **in sth/in doing**
dilettarsi di qc/a fare.
revelation [revə'leɪʃən] n rivelazione f.
reveller ['revlə*] n crapulone/a,
festaiolo/a.
revelry ['revlrɪ] n crapula, baldoria.
revenge [rɪ'vendʒ] n vendetta; (in game
etc) rivincita // vt vendicare; **to take** ~
vendicarsi; ~**ful** a vendicatore(trice);
vendicativo(a).
revenue ['revənjuː] n reddito.
reverberate [rɪ'vɜːbəreɪt] vi (sound)
rimbombare; (light) riverberarsi; **reverberation** [-'reɪʃən] n (of light, sound)
riverberazione f.
reverence ['revərəns] n venerazione f,
riverenza.
reverent ['revərənt] a riverente.
reverie ['revərɪ] n fantasticheria.
reversal [rɪ'vɜːsl] n capovolgimento.
reverse [rɪ'vɜːs] n contrario, opposto;
(back) rovescio; (AUT: also: ~ **gear**)
marcia indietro // a (order, direction)
contrario(a), opposto(a) // vt (turn)
invertire, rivoltare; (change) capovolgere,
rovesciare; (LAW: judgment) cassare // vi
(AUT) fare marcia indietro; ~**d charge
call** n (TEL) telefonata con addebito al
ricevente.
reversion [rɪ'vɜːʃən] n ritorno.
revert [rɪ'vɜːt] vi: **to** ~ **to** tornare a.
review [rɪ'vjuː] n rivista; (of book, film)
recensione f // vt passare in rivista; fare
la recensione di; ~**er** n recensore/a.
revise [rɪ'vaɪz] vt (manuscript) rivedere,
correggere; (opinion) emendare,
modificare; (study: subject, notes)
ripassare; **revision** [rɪ'vɪʒən] n revisione
f; ripasso.
revitalize [riː'vaɪtəlaɪz] vt ravvivare.
revival [rɪ'vaɪvl] n ripresa;
ristabilimento; (of faith) risveglio.
revive [rɪ'vaɪv] vt (person) rianimare;
(custom) far rivivere; (hope, courage)
ravvivare; (play, fashion) riesumare // vi
(person) rianimarsi; (hope) ravvivarsi; (activity) riprendersi.
revoke [rɪ'vəuk] vt revocare; (promise, decision) rinvenire su.
revolt [rɪ'vəult] n rivolta, ribellione f // vi
rivoltarsi, ribellarsi; ~**ing** a ripugnante.
revolution [revə'luːʃən] n rivoluzione f; (of
wheel etc) rivoluzione, giro; ~**ary** a, n
rivoluzionario(a); ~**ize** vt rivoluzionare.
revolve [rɪ'vɒlv] vi girare.
revolver [rɪ'vɒlvə*] n rivoltella.
revolving [rɪ'vɒlvɪŋ] a girevole.
revue [rɪ'vjuː] n (THEATRE) rivista.
revulsion [rɪ'vʌlʃən] n ripugnanza.
reward [rɪ'wɔːd] n ricompensa, premio //
vt: **to** ~ **(for)** ricompensare (per); ~**ing**
a (fig) soddisfacente.
rewind [riː'waɪnd] vt irg (watch)
ricaricare; (ribbon etc) riavvolgere.
rewire [riː'waɪə*] vt (house) rifare
l'impianto elettrico di.

reword [riː'wəːd] vt formulare or esprimere con altre parole.

rewrite [riː'raɪt] vt irg riscrivere.

rhapsody ['ræpsədɪ] n (MUS) rapsodia; (fig) elogio stravagante.

rhetoric ['retərɪk] n retorica; ~al [rɪ'tɔrɪk] a retorico(a).

rheumatic [ruː'mætɪk] a reumatico(a).

rheumatism ['ruːmətɪzəm] n reumatismo.

Rhine [raɪn] n: the ~ il Reno.

rhinoceros [raɪ'nɔsərəs] n rinoceronte m.

rhododendron [rəudə'dendrn] n rododendro.

Rhone [rəun] n: the ~ il Rodano.

rhubarb ['ruːbɑːb] n rabarbaro.

rhyme [raɪm] n rima; (verse) poesia.

rhythm ['rɪðm] n ritmo; ~ic(al) a ritmico(a); ~ically ad con ritmo.

rib [rɪb] n (ANAT) costola // vt (tease) punzecchiare.

ribald ['rɪbəld] a licenzioso(a), volgare.

ribbed [rɪbd] a (knitting) a coste.

ribbon ['rɪbən] n nastro; in ~s (torn) a brandelli.

rice [raɪs] n riso; ~field n risaia; ~ pudding n budino di riso.

rich [rɪtʃ] a ricco(a); (clothes) sontuoso(a); the ~ i ricchi; ~es npl ricchezze fpl; ~ness n ricchezza.

rickets ['rɪkɪts] n rachitismo.

rickety ['rɪkɪtɪ] a zoppicante.

rickshaw ['rɪkʃɔ] n risciò m inv.

ricochet ['rɪkəʃeɪ] n rimbalzo // vi rimbalzare.

rid, pt, pp **rid** [rɪd] vt: to ~ sb of sbarazzare or liberare qd di; to get ~ of sbarazzarsi di; **good riddance!** che liberazione!

ridden ['rɪdn] pp of ride.

riddle ['rɪdl] n (puzzle) indovinello // vt: to be ~d with essere crivellato(a) di.

ride [raɪd] n (on horse) cavalcata; (outing) passeggiata; (distance covered) cavalcata; corsa // vb (pt **rode**, pp **ridden** [rəud, 'rɪdn]) vi (as sport) cavalcare; (go somewhere: on horse, bicycle) andare a cavallo or in bicicletta etc); (journey: on bicycle, motor cycle, bus) andare, viaggiare // vt (a horse) montare, cavalcare; **we rode all day** abbiamo cavalcato tutto il giorno; to ~ a horse/bicycle/camel montare a cavallo/in bicicletta/in groppa a un cammello; to ~ at anchor (NAUT) essere alla fonda; **horse** ~ cavalcata; **car** ~ passeggiata in macchina; to take sb for a ~ (fig) prendere in giro qd (fig); ~r n cavalcatore/trice; (in race) fantino; (on bicycle) ciclista m/f; (on motorcycle) motociclista m/f; (in document) clausola addizionale, aggiunta.

ridge [rɪdʒ] n (of hill) cresta; (of roof) colmo; (of mountain) giogo; (on object) riga (in rilievo).

ridicule ['rɪdɪkjuːl] n ridicolo; scherno // vt mettere in ridicolo.

ridiculous [rɪ'dɪkjuləs] a ridicolo(a).

riding ['raɪdɪŋ] n equitazione f; ~ school n scuola d'equitazione.

rife [raɪf] a diffuso(a); to be ~ with abbondare di.

riffraff ['rɪfræf] n canaglia.

rifle ['raɪfl] n carabina // vt vuotare; ~ range n campo di tiro; (indoor) tiro al bersaglio.

rift [rɪft] n fessura, crepatura; (fig: disagreement) incrinatura, disaccordo.

rig [rɪg] n (also: **oil** ~: on land) derrick m inv; (: at sea) piattaforma per trivellazioni subacquee // vt (election etc) truccare; to ~ out vt attrezzare; (pej) abbigliare, agghindare; to ~ up vt allestire; ~ging n (NAUT) attrezzatura.

right [raɪt] a giusto(a); (suitable) appropriato(a); (not left) destro(a) // n (title, claim) diritto; (not left) destra // ad (answer) correttamente; (not on the left) a destra // vt raddrizzare; (fig) riparare // excl bene!; to be ~ (person) aver ragione; (answer) essere giusto(a) or corretto(a); ~ now proprio adesso; subito; ~ against the wall proprio contro il muro; ~ ahead sempre diritto; proprio davanti; ~ in the middle proprio nel mezzo; ~ away subito; by ~s di diritto; on the ~ a destra; ~ angle n angolo retto; ~eous ['raɪtʃəs] a retto(a), virtuoso(a); (anger) giusto(a), giustificato(a); ~eousness ['raɪtʃəsnɪs] n rettitudine f, virtù f; ~ful (heir) legittimo(a); ~-handed a (person) che adopera la mano destra; ~-hand man n braccio destro; the ~-hand side il lato destro; ~ly ad bene, correttamente; (with reason) a ragione; ~-minded a sensato(a); ~ of way n diritto di passaggio; (AUT) precedenza; ~ wing n (MIL, SPORT) ala destra; (POL) destra; ~-wing a (POL) di destra.

rigid ['rɪdʒɪd] a rigido(a); (principle) rigoroso(a); ~ity [rɪ'dʒɪdɪtɪ] n rigidità; ~ly ad rigidamente.

rigmarole ['rɪgmərəul] n tiritera; commedia.

rigorous ['rɪgərəs] a rigoroso(a).

rigour ['rɪgəʳ] n rigore m.

rim [rɪm] n orlo; (of spectacles) montatura; (of wheel) cerchione m; ~less a (spectacles) senza montatura; ~med a bordato(a); cerchiato(a).

rind [raɪnd] n (of bacon) cotenna; (of lemon etc) scorza.

ring [rɪŋ] n anello; (also: **wedding** ~) fede f; (of people, objects) cerchio; (of spies) giro; (of smoke etc) spirale m; (arena) pista, arena; (for boxing) ring m inv; (sound of bell) scampanio; (telephone call) colpo di telefono // vb (pt **rang**, pp **rung** [ræŋ, rʌŋ]) vi (person, bell, telephone) suonare; (also: ~ **out**: voice, words) risuonare; (TEL) telefonare // vt (TEL: also: ~ **up**) telefonare a; to ~ the bell suonare; to ~ **back** vt, vi (TEL) richiamare; to ~ **off** vi (TEL) mettere giù, riattaccare; ~leader n (of gang) capobanda m.

ringlets ['rɪŋlɪts] npl boccoli mpl.

ring road ['rɪŋrəud] n raccordo anulare.
rink [rɪŋk] n (also: **ice** ~) pista di pattinaggio.
rinse [rɪns] n risciacquatura; (hair tint) colorito // vt sciacquare; darsi il colorito a.
riot ['raɪət] n sommossa, tumulto // vi tumultuare; **a** ~ **of colours** un'orgia di colori; **to run** ~ creare disordine; ~**ous** a tumultuoso(a); che fa crepare dal ridere; ~**ously funny** che fa crepare dal ridere.
rip [rɪp] n strappo // vt strappare // vi strapparsi; ~**cord** n cavo di sfilamento.
ripe [raɪp] a (fruit) maturo(a); (cheese) stagionato(a); ~**n** vt maturare // vi maturarsi; stagionarsi; ~**ness** n maturità.
ripple ['rɪpl] n increspamento, ondulazione f; mormorio // vi incresparsi.
rise [raɪz] n (slope) salita, pendio; (hill) altura; (increase: in wages) aumento; (: in prices, temperature) rialzo, aumento; (fig: to power etc) ascesa // vi (pt **rose**, pp **risen** [rəuz, 'rɪzn]) alzarsi, levarsi; (prices) aumentarsi; (waters, river) crescere; (sun, wind, person: from chair, bed) levarsi; (also: ~ **up**: rebel) insorgere; ribellarsi; **to give** ~ **to** provocare, dare origine a; **to** ~ **to the occasion** essere all'altezza.
risk [rɪsk] n rischio; pericolo // vt rischiare; **to take** or **run the** ~ **of doing** correre il rischio di fare; **at** ~ in pericolo; ~**y** a rischioso(a).
risqué ['riːskeɪ] a (joke) spinto(a).
rissole ['rɪsəul] n crocchetta.
rite [raɪt] n rito.
ritual ['rɪtjuəl] a, n rituale (m).
rival ['raɪvl] n rivale m/f; (in business) concorrente m/f // a rivale; che fa concorrenza // vt essere in concorrenza con; **to** ~ **sb/sth in** competere con qd/qc in; ~**ry** n rivalità; concorrenza.
river ['rɪvə*] n fiume m // cpd (port, traffic) fluviale; ~**bank** n argine m; ~**bed** n alveo (fluviale); ~**side** n sponda del fiume.
rivet ['rɪvɪt] n ribattino, rivetto // vt ribadire; (fig) concentrare, fissare.
Riviera [rɪvɪ'ɛərə] n: **the (French)** ~ la Costa Azzurra.
RN abbr of Royal Navy.
road [rəud] n strada; (small) cammino; (in town) via; ~**block** n blocco stradale; ~**hog** n guidatore m egoista e spericolato; ~ **map** n carta stradale; ~**side** n margine m della strada; ~**sign** n cartello stradale; ~**way** n carreggiata; ~**worthy** a in buono stato di marcia.
roam [rəum] vi errare, vagabondare // vt vagare per.
roar [rɔː*] n ruggito; (of crowd) tumulto; (of thunder, storm) muggito // vi ruggire; tumultuare; muggire; **to** ~ **with laugh**-ter scoppiare dalle risa; **a** ~**ing fire** un bel fuoco; **to do a** ~**ing trade** fare affari d'oro.
roast [rəust] n arrosto // vt (meat) arrostire.
rob [rɔb] vt (person) rubare; (bank)

svaligiare; **to** ~ **sb of sth** derubare qd di qc; (fig: deprive) privare qd di qc; ~**ber** n ladro; (armed) rapinatore m; ~**bery** n furto; rapina.
robe [rəub] n (for ceremony etc) abito; (also: **bath** ~) accappatoio // vt vestire.
robin ['rɔbɪn] n pettirosso.
robot ['rəubɔt] n robot m inv.
robust [rəu'bʌst] a robusto(a); (material) solido(a).
rock [rɔk] n (substance) roccia; (boulder) masso; roccia; (in sea) scoglio; (sweet) zucchero candito // vt (swing gently: cradle) dondolare; (: child) cullare; (shake) scrollare, far tremare // vi dondolarsi; scrollarsi, tremare; **on the** ~**s** (drink) col ghiaccio; (ship) sugli scogli; (marriage etc) in crisi; ~-**bottom** n (fig) stremo; ~**ery** n giardino roccioso.
rocket ['rɔkɪt] n razzo; (MIL) razzo, missile m.
rock face ['rɔkfeɪs] n parete f della roccia.
rock fall ['rɔkfɔːl] n caduta di massa.
rocking chair ['rɔkɪŋtʃeə*] n sedia a dondolo.
rocking horse ['rɔkɪŋhɔːs] n cavallo a dondolo.
rocky ['rɔkɪ] a (hill) roccioso(a); (path) sassoso(a); (unsteady: table) traballante.
rod [rɔd] n (metallic, TECH) asta; (wooden) bacchetta; (also: **fishing** ~) canna da pesca.
rode [rəud] pt of **ride**.
rodent ['rəudnt] n roditore m.
rodeo ['rəudɪəu] n rodeo.
roe [rəu] n (species: also: ~ **deer**) capriolo; (of fish) uova fpl di pesce; **soft** ~ latte m di pesce.
rogue [rəug] n mascalzone m; **roguish** a birbantesco(a).
role [rəul] n ruolo.
roll [rəul] n rotolo; (of banknotes) mazzo; (also: **bread** ~) panino; (register) lista; (sound: of drums etc) rullio; (movement: of ship) rullio // vt rotolare; (also: ~ **up**: string) aggomitolare; (also: ~ **out**: pastry) stendere // vi rotolare; (wheel) girare; **to** ~ **in** vi (mail, cash) arrivare a bizzeffe; **to** ~ **over** vi rivoltarsi; **to** ~ **up** vi (col: arrive) arrivare // vt (carpet) arrotolare; ~ **call** n appello; ~**ed gold** a d'oro laminato; ~**er** n rullo; (wheel) rotella; ~**er skates** npl pattini mpl a rotelle.
rolling ['rəulɪŋ] a (landscape) ondulato(a); ~ **pin** n matterello; ~ **stock** n (RAIL) materiale m rotabile.
Roman ['rəumən] a, n romano(a); ~ **Catholic** a, n cattolico(a).
romance [rə'mæns] n storia (or avventura or film m inv) romantico(a); (charm) poesia; (love affair) idillio.
Romanesque [rəumə'nɛsk] a romanico(a).
Romania [rəu'meɪnɪə] n Romania; ~**n** a, n romeno(a).
romantic [rə'mæntɪk] a romantico(a); sentimentale.

romanticism [rə'mæntɪsɪzəm] n romanticismo.

Rome [rəum] n Roma.

romp [rɔmp] n gioco rumoroso // vi (also: ~ **about**) far chiasso, giocare in un modo rumoroso.

rompers ['rɔmpəz] npl pagliaccetto.

roof [ru:f] n tetto; (of tunnel, cave) volta // vt coprire (con un tetto); ~ **garden** n giardino pensile; ~**ing** n materiale m per copertura; ~ **rack** n (AUT) portabagagli m inv.

rook [ruk] n (bird) corvo nero; (CHESS) torre f // vt (cheat) truffare, spennare.

room [ru:m] n (in house) stanza, camera; (in school etc) sala; (space) posto, spazio; ~**s** npl (lodging) alloggio; ~**ing house** n (US) casa in cui si affittano camere o appartamentini ammobiliati; ~**mate** n compagno/a di stanza; ~ **service** n servizio da camera; ~**y** a spazioso(a); (garment) ampio(a).

roost [ru:st] n appollaiato // vi appollaiarsi.

rooster ['ru:stə°] n gallo.

root [ru:t] n radice f // vt (plant, belief) far radicare; **to** ~ **about** vi (fig) frugare; **to** ~ **for** vt fus fare il tifo per; **to** ~ **out** vt estirpare.

rope [rəup] n corda, fune f; (NAUT) cavo // vt (box) legare; (climbers) legare in cordata; **to** ~ **sb in** (fig) coinvolgere qd; **to know the** ~**s** (fig) conoscere i trucchi del mestiere; ~ **ladder** n scala di corda.

rosary ['rəuzərɪ] n rosario; roseto.

rose [rəuz] pt of **rise** // n rosa; (on watering can) rosetta // a rosa inv.

rosé ['rəuzeɪ] n vino rosato.

rose: ~**bed** n roseto; ~**bud** n bocciolo di rosa; ~**bush** n rosaio.

rosemary ['rəuzmərɪ] n rosmarino.

rosette [rəu'zɛt] n rosetta; (larger) coccarda.

roster ['rɔstə°] n: **duty** ~ ruolino di servizio.

rostrum ['rɔstrəm] n tribuna.

rosy ['rəuzɪ] a roseo(a).

rot [rɔt] n (decay) putrefazione f; (fig: pej) stupidaggini fpl // vt, vi imputridire, marcire.

rota ['rəutə] n ruolino di servizio.

rotary ['rəutərɪ] a rotante.

rotate [rəu'teɪt] vt (revolve) far girare; (change round: crops) avvicendare; (: jobs) fare a turno // vi (revolve) girare; **rotating** a (movement) rotante; **rotation** [-'teɪʃən] n rotazione f.

rotor ['rəutə°] n rotore m.

rotten ['rɔtn] a (decayed) putrido(a), marcio(a); (dishonest) corrotto(a); (col: bad) brutto(a); (: action) vigliacco(a); **to feel** ~ (ill) sentirsi proprio male.

rotund [rəu'tʌnd] a grassoccio(a); tondo(a).

rouble ['ru:bl] n rublo.

rouge [ru:ʒ] n rossetto.

rough [rʌf] a aspro(a); (person, manner: coarse) rozzo(a), aspro(a); (: violent) brutale; (district) malfamato(a); (weather) cattivo(a); (plan) abbozzato(a); (guess) approssimativo(a) // n (GOLF) macchia; (person) duro; **to** ~ **it** far vita dura; **to play** ~ far il gioco pesante; **to sleep** ~ dormire all'addiaccio; **to feel** ~ sentirsi male; **to** ~ **out** vt (draft) abbozzare; ~**en** vt (a surface) rendere ruvido(a); ~**ly** ad (handle) rudemente, brutalmente; (make) grossolanamente; (approximately) approssimativamente; ~**ness** n asprezza; rozzezza; brutalità; ~ **work** n (at school etc) brutta copia.

roulette [ru:'lɛt] n roulette f.

Roumania [ru:'meɪnɪə] n = **Romania**.

round [raund] a rotondo(a) // n tondo, cerchio; (of toast) fetta; (duty: of policeman, milkman etc) giro; (: of doctor) visite fpl; (game: of cards, in competition) partita; (BOXING) round m inv; (of talks) serie f inv // vt (corner) girare; (cape) doppiare // prep intorno a // ad: **right** ~, **all** ~ tutt'attorno; **all the year** ~ tutto l'anno; **it's just** ~ **the corner** (also fig) è dietro l'angolo; **to go** ~ fare il giro; **to go** ~ **an obstacle** aggirare un ostacolo; **to go** ~ **a house** visitare una casa; **to** ~ **off** vt (speech etc) finire; **to** ~ **up** vt radunare; (criminals) fare una retata di; (prices) arrotondare; ~**about** n (AUT) rotatoria; (at fair) giostra // a (route, means) indiretto(a); ~ **of ammunition** n cartuccia; ~ **of applause** n applausi mpl; ~ **of drinks** n giro di bibite; ~ **of sandwiches** n sandwich m inv; ~**ed** a arrotondato(a); (style) armonioso(a); ~**ly** ad (fig) chiaro e tondo; ~**-shouldered** a dalle spalle tonde; ~ **trip** n (viaggio di) andata e ritorno; ~**up** n raduno; (of criminals) retata.

rouse [rauz] vt (wake up) svegliare; (stir up) destare; provocare; risvegliare; **rousing** a (speech, applause) entusiastico(a).

rout [raut] n (MIL) rotta // vt mettere in rotta.

route [ru:t] n itinerario; (of bus) percorso; (of trade, shipping) rotta.

routine [ru:'ti:n] a (work) corrente, abituale; (procedure) solito(a) // n (pej) routine f, tran tran m; (THEATRE) numero; **daily** ~ orario quotidiano.

roving ['rəuvɪŋ] a (life) itinerante.

row [rəu] n (line) riga, fila; (KNITTING) ferro; (behind one another: of cars, people) fila // vi (in boat) remare; (as sport) vogare // vt (boat) manovrare a remi; **in a** ~ (fig) di fila.

row [rau] n (noise) baccano, chiasso; (dispute) lite f // vi litigare.

rowdiness ['raudɪnɪs] n baccano; (fighting) zuffa.

rowdy ['raudɪ] a chiassoso(a); turbolento(a) // n teppista m/f.

rowing ['rəuɪŋ] n canottaggio; ~ **boat** n barca a remi.

rowlock ['rɔlək] n scalmo.

royal ['rɔɪəl] a reale; ~**ist** a, n realista (m/f).

royalty ['rɔɪəltɪ] n (royal persons) (membri mpl della) famiglia reale; (payment: to author) diritti mpl d'autore; (: to inventor) diritti di brevetto.

r.p.m. abbr (= revs per minute) giri/min. (giri/minuto).

R.S.V.P. abbr (= répondez s'il vous plaît) R.S.V.P.

Rt Hon. abbr (= Right Honourable) ≈ Onorevole.

rub [rʌb] n (with cloth) fregata, strofinata; (on person) frizione f, massaggio // vt fregare, strofinare; frizionare; **to ~ sb up the wrong way** lisciare qd contro pelo; **to ~ off** vi andare via; **to ~ off on** lasciare una traccia su.

rubber ['rʌbə*] n gomma; ~ **band** n elastico; ~ **plant** n ficus elastica m inv; ~ **stamp** n timbro di gomma; ~**y** a gommoso(a).

rubbish ['rʌbɪʃ] n (from household) immondizie fpl, rifiuti mpl; (fig: pej) cose fpl senza valore; robaccia; sciocchezze fpl; ~ **bin** n pattumiera; ~ **dump** n (in town) immondezzaio.

rubble ['rʌbl] n macerie fpl; (smaller) pietrisco.

ruble ['ru:bl] n (US) = **rouble**.

ruby ['ru:bɪ] n rubino.

rucksack ['rʌksæk] n zaino.

rudder ['rʌdə*] n timone m.

ruddy ['rʌdɪ] a (face) fresco(a); (col: damned) maledetto(a).

rude [ru:d] a (impolite: person) scortese, rozzo(a); (: word, manners) grossolano(a), rozzo(a); (shocking) indecente; ~**ly** ad scortesemente; grossolanamente; ~**ness** n scortesia; grossolanità.

rudiment ['ru:dɪmənt] n rudimento; ~**ary** [-'mɛntərɪ] a rudimentale.

rueful ['ru:ful] a mesto(a), triste.

ruff [rʌf] n gorgiera.

ruffian ['rʌfɪən] n briccone m, furfante m.

ruffle ['rʌfl] vt (hair) scompigliare; (clothes, water) increspare; (fig: person) turbare.

rug [rʌg] n tappeto; (for knees) coperta.

rugby ['rʌgbɪ] n (also: ~ **football**) rugby m.

rugged ['rʌgɪd] a (landscape) aspro(a); (features, determination) duro(a); (character) brusco(a).

rugger ['rʌgə*] n (col) rugby m.

ruin ['ru:ɪn] n rovina // vt rovinare; (spoil: clothes) sciupare; ~**s** npl rovine fpl, ruderi mpl; ~**ation** [-'neɪʃən] n rovina; ~**ous** a rovinoso(a); (expenditure) inverosimile.

rule [ru:l] n regola; (regulation) regolamento, regola; (government) governo // vt (country) governare; (person) dominare; (decide) decidere // vi regnare; decidere; (LAW) dichiarare; **as a ~** normalmente; ~**d** a (paper) vergato(a); ~**r** n (sovereign) sovrano/a; (leader) capo (dello Stato); (for measuring) regolo, riga; **ruling** a (party) al potere;

(class) dirigente // n (LAW) decisione f.

rum [rʌm] n rum m // a (col) strano(a).

Rumania [ru:'meɪnɪə] n = **Romania**.

rumble ['rʌmbl] n rimbombo; brontolio // vi rimbombare; (stomach, pipe) brontolare.

rummage ['rʌmɪdʒ] vi frugare.

rumour ['ru:mə*] n voce f // vt: **it is ~ed** that corre voce che.

rump [rʌmp] n (of animal) groppa; ~ **steak** n bistecca di girello.

rumpus ['rʌmpəs] n (col) baccano; (: quarrel) rissa.

run [rʌn] n corsa; (outing) gita (in macchina); (distance travelled) percorso, tragitto; (series) serie f; (THEATRE) periodo di rappresentazione; (SKI) pista // vb (pt ran, pp run [ræn, rʌn]) vt (operate: business) gestire, dirigere; (: competition, course) organizzare; (: hotel) gestire; (: house) governare; (force through: rope, pipe): **to ~ sth through** far passare qc attraverso; (to pass: hand, finger): **to ~ sth over** passare qc su; (water, bath) far scorrere // vi correre; (pass: road etc) passare; (work: machine, factory) funzionare, andare; (bus, train: operate) far servizio; (: travel) circolare; (continue: play, contract) durare; (slide: drawer; flow: river, bath) scorrere; (colours, washing) stemperarsi; (in election) presentarsi candidato; **there was a ~ on ...** c'era una corsa a ...; **in the long ~** alla lunga; in fin dei conti; **on the ~** in fuga; **I'll ~ you to the station** la porto alla stazione; **to ~ a risk** correre un rischio; **to ~ about** vi (children) correre qua e là; **to ~ across** vt fus (find) trovare per caso; **to ~ away** vi fuggire; **to ~ down** vi (clock) scaricarsi // vt (AUT) investire; (criticize) criticare; **to be ~ down** essere esausto(a) or a zero; **to ~ off** vi fuggire; **to ~ out** vi (person) uscire di corsa; (liquid) colare; (lease) scadere; (money) esaurirsi; **to ~ out of** vt fus rimanere a corto di; **to ~ over** vt sep (AUT) investire, arrotare // vt fus (revise) rivedere; **to ~ through** vt fus (instructions) dare una scorsa a; **to ~ up** vt (debt) lasciar accumulare; **to ~ up against** (difficulties) incontrare; ~**away** a (person) fuggiasco(a); (horse) in libertà; (truck) fuori controllo; (inflation) galoppante.

rung [rʌŋ] pp of **ring** // n (of ladder) piolo.

runner ['rʌnə*] n (in race) corridore m; (on sledge) pattino; (for drawer etc, carpet: in hall etc) guida; ~ **bean** n (BOT) fagiolo rampicante; ~**-up** n secondo(a) arrivato(a).

running ['rʌnɪŋ] n corsa; direzione f; organizzazione f; funzionamento // a (water) corrente; (commentary) simultaneo(a); **6 days ~** 6 giorni di seguito.

runny ['rʌnɪ] a che cola.

run-of-the-mill ['rʌnəvðə'mɪl] a solito(a), banale.

runt [rʌnt] n (also: pej) omuncolo; (ZOOL)

animale *m* più piccolo del normale.

run-through ['rʌnθru:] *n* prova.

runway ['rʌnweɪ] *n* (*AVIAT*) pista (di decollo).

rupture ['rʌptʃə*] *n* (*MED*) ernia // *vt*: to ~ o.s. farsi venire un'ernia.

rural ['ruərl] *a* rurale.

ruse [ru:z] *n* trucco.

rush [rʌʃ] *n* corsa precipitosa; (*of crowd*) afflusso; (*hurry*) furia, fretta; (*current*) flusso // *vt* mandare or spedire velocemente; (*attack: town etc*) prendere d'assalto // *vi* precipitarsi; **don't ~ me!** non farmi fretta!; ~**es** *npl* (*BOT*) giunchi *mpl*; ~ **hour** *n* ora di punta.

rusk [rʌsk] *n* biscotto.

Russia ['rʌʃə] *n* Russia; ~**n** *a* russo(a) // *n* russo/a; (*LING*) russo.

rust [rʌst] *n* ruggine *f* // *vi* arrugginirsi.

rustic ['rʌstɪk] *a* rustico(a) // *n* (*pej*) cafone/a.

rustle ['rʌsl] *vi* frusciare // *vt* (*paper*) far frusciare; (*US: cattle*) rubare.

rustproof ['rʌstpru:f] *a* inossidabile.

rusty ['rʌstɪ] *a* arrugginito(a).

rut [rʌt] *n* solco; (*ZOOL*) fregola.

ruthless ['ru:θlɪs] *a* spietato(a).

rye ['raɪ] *n* segale *f*.

S

Sabbath ['sæbəθ] *n* (*Jewish*) sabato; (*Christian*) domenica.

sabbatical [sə'bætɪkl] *a*: ~ **year** *n* anno sabbatico.

sabotage ['sæbətɑ:ʒ] *n* sabotaggio // *vt* sabotare.

saccharin(e) ['sækərɪn] *n* saccarina.

sack [sæk] *n* (*bag*) sacco // *vt* (*dismiss*) licenziare, mandare a spasso; (*plunder*) saccheggiare; **to get the ~** essere mandato a spasso; **a ~ful of** un sacco di; ~**ing** *n* tela di sacco; (*dismissal*) licenziamento.

sacrament ['sækrəmənt] *n* sacramento.

sacred ['seɪkrɪd] *a* sacro(a).

sacrifice ['sækrɪfaɪs] *n* sacrificio // *vt* sacrificare.

sacrilege ['sækrɪlɪdʒ] *n* sacrilegio.

sacrosanct ['sækrousæŋkt] *a* sacrosanto(a).

sad [sæd] *a* triste; ~**den** *vt* rattristare.

saddle ['sædl] *n* sella // *vt* (*horse*) sellare; **to be ~d with sth** (*col*) avere qc sulle spalle; ~**bag** *n* bisaccia; (*on bicycle*) borsa.

sadism ['seɪdɪzm] *n* sadismo; **sadist** *n* sadico/a; **sadistic** [sə'dɪstɪk] *a* sadico(a).

sadness ['sædnɪs] *n* tristezza.

safari [sə'fɑ:rɪ] *n* safari *m inv*.

safe [seɪf] *a* sicuro(a); (*out of danger*) salvo(a), al sicuro; (*cautious*) prudente // *n* cassaforte *f*; ~ **from** al sicuro da; ~ **and sound** sano(a) e salvo(a); **(just) to be on the ~ side** per non correre rischi; ~**guard** *n* salvaguardia // *vt* salvaguardare; ~**keeping** *n* custodia;

~**ly** *ad* sicuramente; sano(a) e salvo(a); prudentemente.

safety ['seɪftɪ] *n* sicurezza; ~ **belt** *n* cintura di sicurezza; ~ **pin** *n* spilla di sicurezza.

saffron ['sæfrən] *n* zafferano.

sag [sæg] *vi* incurvarsi; afflosciarsi.

sage [seɪdʒ] *n* (*herb*) salvia; (*man*) saggio.

Sagittarius [sædʒɪ'tɛərɪəs] *n* Sagittario.

sago ['seɪɡəʊ] *n* sagù *m*.

said [sɛd] *pt*, *pp* *of* **say**.

sail [seɪl] *n* (*on boat*) vela; (*trip*): **to go for a ~** fare un giro in barca a vela // *vt* (*boat*) condurre, governare // *vi* (*travel: ship*) navigare; (: *passenger*) viaggiare per mare; (*set off*) salpare; (*SPORT*) fare della vela; **they ~ed into Genoa** entrarono nel porto di Genova; **to ~ through** (*fig*) *vt fus* superare senza difficoltà // *vi* farcela senza difficoltà; ~**boat** *n* (*US*) barca a vela; ~**ing** *n* (*SPORT*) vela; **to go ~ing** fare della vela; ~**ing boat** *n* barca a vela; ~**ing ship** *n* veliero; ~**or** *n* marinaio.

saint [seɪnt] *n* santo/a.

sake [seɪk] *n*: **for the ~ of** per, per amore di, per il bene di; **for pity's ~** per pietà.

salad ['sæləd] *n* insalata; ~ **bowl** *n* insalatiera; ~ **cream** *n* (*tipo di*) maionese *f*; ~ **dressing** *n* condimento per insalata; ~ **oil** *n* olio da tavola.

salary ['sælərɪ] *n* stipendio.

sale [seɪl] *n* vendita; (*at reduced prices*) svendita, liquidazione *f*; **'for ~'** 'in vendita'; **on ~ or return** da vendere o rimandare; ~**room** *n* sala delle aste; ~**sman** *n* commesso; (*representative*) rappresentante *m*; ~**swoman** *n* commessa.

salient ['seɪlɪənt] *a* saliente.

saliva [sə'laɪvə] *n* saliva.

sallow ['sæləʊ] *a* giallastro(a).

salmon ['sæmən] *n*, *pl inv* salmone *m*.

saloon [sə'lu:n] *n* (*US*) saloon *m inv*, bar *m inv*; (*AUT*) berlina; (*ship's lounge*) salone *m*.

salt [sɔlt] *n* sale *m* // *vt* salare // *cpd* di sale; (*CULIN*) salato(a); ~ **cellar** *n* saliera; ~**y** *a* salato(a).

salutary ['sæljutərɪ] *a* salutare.

salute [sə'lu:t] *n* saluto // *vt* salutare.

salvage ['sælvɪdʒ] *n* (*saving*) salvataggio; (*things saved*) beni *mpl* salvati or recuperati // *vt* salvare, mettere in salvo.

salvation [sæl'veɪʃən] *n* salvezza; **S~ Army** *n* Esercito della Salvezza.

salvo ['sælvəʊ] *n* salva.

same [seɪm] *a* stesso(a), medesimo(a) // *pronoun*: **the ~** lo(la) stesso(a), gli(le) stessi(e); **the ~ book as** lo stesso libro di (*or che*); **all or just the ~** tuttavia; **to do the ~** fare la stessa cosa; **to do the ~ as sb** fare come qd.

sample ['sɑ:mpl] *n* campione *m* // *vt* (*food*) assaggiare; (*wine*) degustare.

sanatorium, *pl* **sanatoria** [sænə'tɔ:rɪəm, -rɪə] *n* sanatorio.

sanctimonious [sæŋktɪ'məʊnɪəs] *a* bigotto(a), bacchettone(a).

sanction ['sæŋkʃən] n sanzione f // vt sancire, sanzionare.

sanctity ['sæŋktɪtɪ] n santità.

sanctuary ['sæŋktjuərɪ] n (holy place) santuario; (refuge) rifugio; (for wildlife) riserva.

sand [sænd] n sabbia // vt cospargere di sabbia; ~s npl spiaggia.

sandal ['sændl] n sandalo.

sandcastle ['sændkɑːsl] n castello di sabbia.

sand dune ['sænddjuːn] n duna di sabbia.

sandpaper ['sændpeɪpə*] n carta vetrata.

sandpit ['sændpɪt] n (for children) buca di sabbia per i giochi dei bambini.

sandstone ['sændstəun] n arenaria.

sandwich ['sændwɪtʃ] n tramezzino, panino, sandwich m inv // vt (also: ~ in) intramezzare, interporre; **cheese/ham ~ sandwich** al formaggio/prosciutto; ~ **course** n corso di formazione professionale.

sandy ['sændɪ] a sabbioso(a); (colour) color sabbia inv, biondo(a) o rossiccio(a).

sane [seɪn] a (person) sano(a) di mente; (outlook) sensato(a).

sang [sæŋ] pt of **sing**.

sanguine ['sæŋgwɪn] a ottimista.

sanitary ['sænɪtərɪ] a (system, arrangements) sanitario(a); (clean) igienico(a); ~ **towel**, ~ **napkin** (US) n assorbente m (igienico).

sanitation [sænɪ'teɪʃən] n (in house) impianti mpl sanitari; (in town) fognature fpl.

sanity ['sænɪtɪ] n sanità mentale; (common sense) buon senso.

sank [sæŋk] pt of **sink**.

Santa Claus [sæntə'klɔːz] n Babbo Natale.

sap [sæp] n (of plants) linfa // vt (strength) fiaccare.

sapling ['sæplɪŋ] n alberello.

sapphire ['sæfaɪə*] n zaffiro.

sarcasm ['sɑːkæzm] n sarcasmo.

sarcastic [sɑː'kæstɪk] a sarcastico(a).

sardine [sɑː'diːn] n sardina.

Sardinia [sɑː'dɪnɪə] n Sardegna.

sash [sæʃ] n fascia; ~ **window** n finestra a ghigliottina.

sat [sæt] pt,pp of **sit**.

Satan ['seɪtən] n Satana m.

satchel ['sætʃl] n cartella.

satellite ['sætəlaɪt] a, n satellite (m).

satin ['sætɪn] n raso, satin m // a di or in satin.

satire ['sætaɪə*] n satira; **satirical** [sə'tɪrɪkl] a satirico(a).

satisfaction [sætɪs'fækʃən] n soddisfazione f.

satisfactory [sætɪs'fæktərɪ] a soddisfacente.

satisfy ['sætɪsfaɪ] vt soddisfare; (convince) convincere; ~ing a soddisfacente.

saturate ['sætʃəreɪt] vt: to ~ (with) saturare (di).

Saturday ['sætədɪ] n sabato.

sauce [sɔːs] n salsa; (containing meat, fish) sugo; ~ **pan** n casseruola.

saucer ['sɔːsə*] n sottocoppa m, piattino.

saucy ['sɔːsɪ] a impertinente.

saunter ['sɔːntə*] vi andare a zonzo, bighellonare.

sausage ['sɔsɪdʒ] n salsiccia;· ~ **roll** n rotolo di pasta sfoglia ripiena di salsiccia.

savage ['sævɪdʒ] a (cruel, fierce) selvaggio(a), feroce; (primitive) primitivo(a) // n selvaggio/a // vt attaccare selvaggiamente; ~ry n crudeltà, ferocia.

save [seɪv] vt (person, belongings) salvare; (money) risparmiare, mettere da parte; (time) risparmiare; (food) conservare; (avoid: trouble) evitare // vi (also: ~ up) economizzare // n (SPORT) parata // prep salvo, a eccezione di.

saving ['seɪvɪŋ] n risparmio // a: the ~ **grace of** l'unica cosa buona di; ~s npl risparmi mpl; ~s **bank** n cassa di risparmio.

saviour ['seɪvjə*] n salvatore m.

savour ['seɪvə*] n sapore m, gusto // vt gustare; ~y a saporito(a); (dish: not sweet) salato(a).

saw [sɔː] pt of **see** // n (tool) sega // vt (pt sawed, pp sawed or sawn [sɔːn]) segare; ~**dust** n segatura; ~**mill** n segheria.

saxophone ['sæksəfəun] n sassofono.

say [seɪ] n: to have one's ~ fare sentire il proprio parere; to have a ~ avere voce in capitolo // vt (pt, pp said [sed]) dire; **could you ~ that again?** potrebbe ripeterlo?; **that is to ~** cioè, vale a dire; **to ~ nothing of** per non parlare di; ~ **that ...** mettiamo or diciamo che ...; **that goes without** ~ing va da sé; ~ing n proverbio, detto.

scab [skæb] n crosta; (pej) crumiro/a; ~**by** a crostoso(a).

scaffold ['skæfəuld] n impalcatura; (gallows) patibolo; ~**ing** n impalcatura.

scald [skɔːld] n scottatura // vt scottare.

scale [skeɪl] n scala; (of fish) squama // vt (mountain) scalare; ~s npl bilancia; on a **large ~** su vasta scala; ~ **model** n modello in scala; **small-~ model** n modello in scala ridotta.

scallop ['skɔləp] n pettine m.

scalp [skælp] n cuoio capelluto // vt scotennare.

scalpel ['skælpl] n bisturi m inv.

scamper ['skæmpə*] vi: to ~ **away**, ~ **off** darsela a gambe.

scan [skæn] vt scrutare; (glance at quickly) scorrere, dare un'occhiata a; (poetry) scandire; (TV) analizzare; (RADAR) esplorare.

scandal ['skændl] n scandalo; (gossip) pettegolezzi mpl; ~**ize** vt scandalizzare; ~**ous** a scandaloso(a).

Scandinavia [skændɪ'neɪvɪə] n Scandinavia; ~**n** a, n scandinavo(a).

scant [skænt] a scarso(a); ~y a insufficiente; (swimsuit) ridotto(a).

scapegoat ['skeɪpgəut] n capro espiatorio.

scar [skɑː] n cicatrice f // vt sfregiare.

scarce [skɛəs] a scarso(a); (copy, edition) raro(a); **~ly** ad appena; **scarcity** n scarsità, mancanza.

scare [skɛə°] n spavento; panico // vt spaventare, atterrire; **to ~ sb stiff** spaventare a morte qd; **~crow** n spaventapasseri m inv; **~d** a: **to be ~d** aver paura; **~monger** n allarmista m/f.

scarf, scarves [skɑːf, skɑːvz] n (long) sciarpa; (square) fazzoletto da testa, foulard m inv.

scarlet ['skɑːlit] a scarlatto(a); **~ fever** n scarlattina.

scarves [skɑːvz] npl of **scarf**.

scathing ['skeiðiŋ] a aspro(a).

scatter ['skætə°] vt spargere; (crowd) disperdere // vi disperdere; **~brained** a scervellato(a), sbadato(a); **~ed** a sparso(a), sparpagliato(a).

scatty ['skæti] a (col) scervellato(a), sbadato(a).

scavenger ['skævəndʒə°] n spazzino.

scene [siːn] n (THEATRE, fig etc) scena; (of crime, accident) scena, luogo; (sight, view) vista, veduta; **~ry** n (THEATRE) scenario; (landscape) panorama m; **scenic** a scenico(a); panoramico(a).

scent [sɛnt] n odore m, profumo; (fig: track) pista; (sense of smell) olfatto, odorato.

sceptic ['skɛptik] n scettico/a; **~al** a scettico(a); **~ism** ['skɛptisizm] n scetticismo.

sceptre ['sɛptə°] n scettro.

schedule ['ʃɛdjuːl] n programma m, piano; (of trains) orario; (of prices etc) lista, tabella // vt stabilire; **as ~d** come stabilito; **on ~** in orario; in regola con la tabella di marcia; **to be ahead of/behind ~** essere in anticipo/ritardo sul previsto.

scheme [skiːm] n piano, progetto; (method) sistema m; (dishonest plan, plot) intrigo, trama; (arrangement) disposizione f, sistemazione f // vt progettare; (plot) ordire // vi fare progetti; (intrigue) complottare; **scheming** a intrigante // n intrighi mpl, macchinazioni fpl.

schism ['skizəm] n scisma m.

schizophrenic [skitsə'frɛnik] a schizofrenico(a).

scholar ['skɔlə°] n erudito/a; **~ly** a dotto(a), erudito(a); **~ship** n erudizione f; (grant) borsa di studio.

school [skuːl] n scuola; (in university) scuola, facoltà f inv // cpd scolare, scolastico(a) // vt (animal) addestrare; **~book** n libro scolastico; **~boy** n scolaro; **~days** npl giorni mpl di scuola; **~girl** n scolara; **~ing** n istruzione f; **~-leaving age** n età dell'adempimento dell'obbligo scolastico; **~master** n (primary) maestro; (secondary) insegnante m; **~mistress** n maestra; insegnante f; **~teacher** n insegnante m/f, docente m/f; (primary) maestro/a.

schooner ['skuːnə°] n (ship) goletta,

schooner m inv; (glass) bicchiere m alto da sherry.

sciatica [saɪ'ætɪkə] n sciatica.

science ['saiəns] n scienza; **~ fiction** n fantascienza; **scientific** [-'tifik] a scientifico(a); **scientist** n scienziato/a.

scintillating ['sintileitiŋ] a scintillante.

scissors ['sizəz] npl forbici fpl; **a pair of ~** un paio di forbici.

scoff [skɔf] vt (col: eat) tranguiare, ingozzare // vi: **to ~ (at)** (mock) farsi beffe (di).

scold [skəuld] vt rimproverare.

scone [skɔn] n focaccina da tè.

scoop [skuːp] n mestolo; (for ice cream) cucchiaio dosatore; (PRESS) colpo giornalistico, notizia (in) esclusiva; **to ~ out** vt scavare; **to ~ up** vt tirare su, sollevare.

scooter ['skuːtə°] n (motor cycle) motoretta, scooter m inv; (toy) monopattino.

scope [skəup] n (capacity: of plan, undertaking) portata; (: of person) competenza; (opportunity) opportunità; **within the ~ of** entro la competenza di.

scorch [skɔːtʃ] vt (clothes) strinare, bruciacchiare; (earth, grass) seccare, bruciare; **~er** n (col: hot day) giornata torrida; **~ing** a cocente, scottante.

score [skɔː°] n punti mpl, punteggio; (MUS) partitura, spartito; (twenty) venti // vt (goal, point) segnare, fare; (success) ottenere // vi segnare; (FOOTBALL) fare un gol; (keep score) segnare i punti; **on that ~** a questo riguardo; **~board** n tabellone m segnapunti; **~card** n (SPORT) cartoncino segnapunti; **~r** n marcatore/trice; (keeping score) segnapunti m inv.

scorn [skɔːn] n disprezzo // vt disprezzare.

Scorpio ['skɔːpiəu] n Scorpione m.

scorpion ['skɔːpiən] n scorpione m.

Scot [skɔt] n scozzese m/f.

scotch [skɔtʃ] vt (rumour etc) soffocare; **S~** n whisky m scozzese, scotch m.

scot-free ['skɔt'friː] a impunito(a).

Scotland ['skɔtlənd] n Scozia.

Scots [skɔts] a scozzese; **~man/woman** n scozzese m/f.

Scottish ['skɔtiʃ] a scozzese.

scoundrel ['skaundrl] n farabutto/a; (child) furfantello/a.

scour ['skauə°] vt (clean) pulire strofinando; raschiare via; ripulire; (search) battere, perlustrare.

scourge [skəːdʒ] n flagello.

scout [skaut] n (MIL) esploratore m; (also: boy ~) giovane esploratore, scout m inv; **to ~ around** vi cercare in giro.

scowl [skaul] vi accigliarsi, aggrottare le sopracciglia; **to ~ at** guardare torvo.

scraggy ['skrægi] a scarno(a), molto magro(a).

scram [skræm] vi (col) filare via.

scramble ['skræmbl] n arrampicata // vi inerpicarsi; **to ~ for** azzuffarsi per; **~d eggs** npl uova fpl strapazzate.

scrap [skræp] *n* pezzo, pezzetto; (*fight*) zuffa; (*also*: ~ **iron**) rottami *mpl* di ferro, ferraglia // *vt* demolire; (*fig*) scartare; ~**s** *npl* (*waste*) scarti *mpl*; ~**book** *n* album *m inv* di ritagli.

scrape [skreip] *vt,vi* raschiare, grattare // *n*: **to get into a** ~ cacciarsi in un guaio; ~**r** *n* raschietto.

scrap: ~ **heap** *n* mucchio di rottami; ~ **merchant** *n* commerciante *m* di ferraglia; ~ **paper** *n* cartaccia; ~**py** *a* frammentario(a), sconnesso(a).

scratch [skrætʃ] *n* graffio // *a*: ~ **team** *n* squadra raccogliticcia // *vt* graffiare, rigare // *vi* grattare, graffiare; **to start from** ~ cominciare *or* partire da zero; **to be up to** ~ essere all'altezza.

scrawl [skrɔːl] *n* scarabocchio // *vi* scarabocchiare.

scrawny [ˈskrɔːnɪ] *a* scarno(a), pelle e ossa *inv*.

scream [skriːm] *n* grido, urlo // *vi* urlare, gridare.

scree [skriː] *n* ghiaione *m*.

screech [skriːtʃ] *n* strido; (*of tyres, brakes*) stridore *m* // *vi* stridere.

screen [skriːn] *n* schermo; (*fig*) muro, cortina, velo // *vt* schermare, fare schermo a; (*from the wind etc*) riparare; (*film*) proiettare; (*book*) adattare per lo schermo; (*candidates etc*) selezionare; ~**ing** *n* (*MED*) dépistage *m inv*.

screw [skruː] *n* vite *f*; (*propeller*) elica // *vt* avvitare; ~**driver** *n* cacciavite *m*; ~**y** *a* (*col*) svitato(a).

scribble [ˈskrɪbl] *n* scarabocchio // *vt* scribacchiare in fretta // *vi* scarabocchiare.

script [skrɪpt] *n* (*CINEMA etc*) copione *m*; (*in exam*) elaborato *or* compito d'esame.

Scripture [ˈskrɪptʃə*] *n* sacre Scritture *fpl*.

scriptwriter [ˈskrɪptraɪtə*] *n* soggettista *m/f*.

scroll [skrəul] *n* rotolo di carta.

scrounge [skraundʒ] *vt* (*col*): **to** ~ **sth** (**off** *or* **from sb**) scroccare (qc a qd) // *vi*: **to** ~ **on sb** vivere alle spalle di qd; ~**r** *n* scroccone/a.

scrub [skrʌb] *n* (*clean*) strofinata; (*land*) boscaglia // *vt* pulire strofinando; (*reject*) annullare.

scruff [skrʌf] *n*: **by the** ~ **of the neck** per la collottola.

scruffy [ˈskrʌfɪ] *a* sciatto(a).

scrum(mage) [ˈskrʌm(ɪdʒ)] *n* mischia.

scruple [ˈskruːpl] *n* scrupolo.

scrupulous [ˈskruːpjuləs] *a* scrupoloso(a).

scrutinize [ˈskruːtɪnaɪz] *vt* scrutare, esaminare attentamente.

scrutiny [ˈskruːtɪnɪ] *n* esame *m* accurato.

scuff [skʌf] *vt* (*shoes*) consumare strascicando.

scuffle [ˈskʌfl] *n* baruffa, tafferuglio.

scullery [ˈskʌlərɪ] *n* retrocucina *m or f*.

sculptor [ˈskʌlptə*] *n* scultore *m*.

sculpture [ˈskʌlptʃə*] *n* scultura.

scum [skʌm] *n* schiuma; (*pej: people*) feccia.

scurrilous [ˈskʌrɪləs] *a* scurrile, volgare.

scurry [ˈskʌrɪ] *vi* sgambare, affrettarsi.

scurvy [ˈskɜːvɪ] *n* scorbuto.

scuttle [ˈskʌtl] *n* (*NAUT*) portellino; (*also*: **coal** ~) secchio del carbone // *vt* (*ship*) autoaffondare // *vi* (*scamper*): **to** ~ **away**, ~ **off** darsela a gambe, scappare.

scythe [saɪð] *n* falce *f*.

sea [siː] *n* mare *m* // *cpd* marino(a), del mare; (*ship, sailor, port*) marittimo(a), di mare; **on the** ~ (*boat*) in mare; (*town*) di mare; **to be all at** ~ (*fig*) non sapere che pesci pigliare; ~ **bird** *n* uccello di mare; ~**board** *n* costa; ~ **breeze** *n* brezza di mare; ~**farer** *n* navigante *m*; ~**food** *n* frutti *mpl* di mare; ~ **front** *n* lungomare *m*; ~**going** *a* (*ship*) d'alto mare; ~**gull** *n* gabbiano.

seal [siːl] *n* (*animal*) foca; (*stamp*) sigillo; (*impression*) impronta del sigillo // *vt* sigillare.

sea level [ˈsiːlɛvl] *n* livello del mare.

sea lion [ˈsiːlaɪən] *n* leone *m* marino.

seam [siːm] *n* cucitura; (*of coal*) filone *m*.

seaman [ˈsiːmən] *n* marinaio.

seamy [ˈsiːmɪ] *a* orribile.

seance [ˈseɪɔns] *n* seduta spiritica.

seaplane [ˈsiːpleɪn] *n* idrovolante *m*.

seaport [ˈsiːpɔːt] *n* porto di mare.

search [sɜːtʃ] *n* (*for person, thing*) ricerca; (*of drawer, pockets*) esame *m* accurato; (*LAW: at sb's home*) perquisizione *f* // *vt* perlustrare, frugare; (*examine*) esaminare minuziosamente // *vi*: **to** ~ **for** ricercare; **to** ~ **through** *vt fus* frugare; **in** ~ **of** alla ricerca di; ~**ing** *a* minuzioso(a); penetrante; ~**light** *n* proiettore *m*; ~ **party** *n* squadra di soccorso; ~ **warrant** *n* mandato di perquisizione.

seashore [ˈsiːʃɔː*] *n* spiaggia.

seasick [ˈsiːsɪk] *a* che soffre il mal di mare.

seaside [ˈsiːsaɪd] *n* spiaggia; ~ **resort** *n* stazione *f* balneare.

season [ˈsiːzn] *n* stagione *f* // *vt* condire, insaporire; ~**al** *a* stagionale; ~**ing** *n* condimento; ~ **ticket** *n* abbonamento.

seat [siːt] *n* sedile *m*; (*in bus, train: place*) posto; (*PARLIAMENT*) seggio; (*buttocks*) didietro; (*of trousers*) fondo // *vt* far sedere; (*have room for*) avere *or* essere fornito(a) di posti a sedere per; ~ **belt** *n* cintura di sicurezza.

sea water [ˈsiːwɔːtə*] *n* acqua di mare.

seaweed [ˈsiːwiːd] *n* alga.

seaworthy [ˈsiːwɜːðɪ] *a* atto(a) alla navigazione.

sec. *abbr of* **second(s).**

secluded [sɪˈkluːdɪd] *a* isolato(a), appartato(a).

seclusion [sɪˈkluːʒən] *n* isolamento.

second [ˈsɛkənd] *num* secondo(a) // *ad* (*in race etc*) al secondo posto; (*RAIL-*) in seconda // *n* (*unit of time*) secondo; (*in series, position*) secondo/a; (*AUT: also*: ~ **gear**) seconda; (*COMM: imperfect*) scarto

// vt (motion) appoggiare; ~ary a secondario(a); ~ary school n scuola secondaria; ~-class a di seconda classe; ~er n sostenitore/trice; ~hand a di seconda mano, usato(a); ~ hand n (on clock) lancetta dei secondi; ~ly ad in secondo luogo; ~-rate a scadente; ~ thoughts npl ripensamenti mpl; on ~ thoughts ripensandoci bene.

secrecy ['si:krəsɪ] n segretezza.

secret ['si:krɪt] a segreto(a) // n segreto.

secretariat [sɛkrɪ'tɛərɪət] n segretariato.

secretary ['sɛkrətərɪ] n segretario/a; S~ of State (for) (Brit: POL) ministro (di).

secretive ['si:krətɪv] a riservato(a).

sect [sɛkt] n setta; ~arian [-'tɛərɪən] a settario(a).

section ['sɛkʃən] n sezione f // vt sezionare, dividere in sezioni.

sector ['sɛktəᵊ] n settore m.

secular ['sɛkjuləᵊ] a secolare.

secure [sɪ'kjuəᵊ] a (free from anxiety) sicuro(a); (firmly fixed) assicurato(a), ben fermato(a); (in safe place) al sicuro // vt (fix) fissare, assicurare; (get) ottenere, assicurarsi.

security [sɪ'kjuərɪtɪ] n sicurezza; (for loan) garanzia.

sedate [sɪ'deɪt] a posato(a); calmo(a) // vt calmare.

sedation [sɪ'deɪʃən] n (MED) l'effetto dei sedativi.

sedative ['sɛdɪtɪv] n sedativo, calmante m.

sediment ['sɛdɪmənt] n sedimento.

seduce [sɪ'dju:s] vt sedurre; **seduction** [-'dʌkʃən] n seduzione f; **seductive** [-'dʌktɪv] a seducente.

see [si:] vb (pt saw, pp seen [sɔ:, si:n]) vt vedere; (accompany): to ~ sb to the door accompagnare qd alla porta // vi vedere; (understand) capire // n sede f vescovile; to ~ that (ensure) badare che + sub, fare in modo che + sub; to ~ off vt salutare alla partenza; to ~ through vt portare a termine // vt fus non lasciarsi ingannare da; to ~ to vt fus occuparsi di.

seed [si:d] n seme m; (fig) germe m; (TENNIS) testa di serie; to go to ~ fare seme; (fig) scadere; ~ling n piantina di semenzaio; ~y a (shabby: person) sciatto(a); (: place) cadente.

seeing ['si:ɪŋ] cj: ~ (that) visto che.

seek, pt,pp **sought** [si:k, sɔ:t] vt cercare.

seem [si:m] vi sembrare, parere; **there seems to be** ... sembra che ci sia ...; ~ingly ad apparentemente.

seen [si:n] pp of **see**.

seep [si:p] vi filtrare, trapelare.

seer [sɪəᵊ] n profeta/essa, veggente m/f.

seesaw ['si:sɔ:] n altalena a bilico.

seethe [si:ð] vi ribollire; to ~ **with anger** fremere di rabbia.

see-through ['si:θru:] a trasparente.

segment ['sɛgmənt] n segmento.

segregate ['sɛgrɪgeɪt] vt segregare, isolare.

seismic ['saɪzmɪk] a sismico(a).

seize [si:z] vt (grasp) afferrare; (take possession of) impadronirsi di; (LAW) sequestrare; to ~ **up** on vt fus ricorrere a; to ~ **up** vi (TECH) grippare.

seizure ['si:ʒəᵊ] n (MED) attacco; (LAW) confisca, sequestro.

seldom ['sɛldəm] ad raramente.

select [sɪ'lɛkt] a scelto(a) // vt scegliere, selezionare; ~**ion** [-'lɛkʃən] n selezione f, scelta; ~**ive** a selettivo(a).

self [sɛlf] n (pl **selves** [sɛlvz]): **the** ~ l'io m // prefix auto...; ~-**assured** a sicuro(a) di sé; ~-**catering** a in cui ci si cucina da sé; ~-**centred** a egocentrico(a); ~-**coloured** a monocolore; ~-**confidence** n sicurezza di sé; ~-**conscious** a timido(a); ~-**contained** a (flat) indipendente; ~-**control** n autocontrollo; ~-**defence** n autodifesa; (LAW) legittima difesa; ~-**discipline** n autodisciplina; ~-**employed** a che lavora in proprio; ~-**evident** a evidente; ~-**explanatory** a ovvio(a); ~-**indulgent** a indulgente verso se stesso(a); ~-**interest** n interesse m personale; ~-**ish** a egoista; ~-**ishness** n egoismo; ~-**lessly** ad altruisticamente; ~-**pity** n autocommiserazione f; ~-**portrait** n autoritratto; ~-**possessed** a controllato(a); ~-**preservation** n istinto di conservazione; ~-**respect** n rispetto di sé, amor proprio; ~-**respecting** a che ha rispetto di sé; ~-**righteous** a soddisfatto(a) di sé; ~-**sacrifice** n abnegazione f; ~-**satisfied** a compiaciuto(a) di sé; ~-**seal** a autosigillante; ~-**service** n autoservizio, self-service m; ~-**sufficient** a autosufficiente; ~-**supporting** a economicamente indipendente.

sell, pt,pp **sold** [sɛl, səuld] vt vendere // vi vendersi; to ~ **at** or **for 1000 lire** essere in vendita a 1000 lire; to ~ **off** vt svendere, liquidare; ~**er** n venditore/trice; ~**ing price** n prezzo di vendita.

sellotape ['sɛləuteɪp] n ⊛ nastro adesivo, scotch m ⊛.

sellout ['sɛlaut] n tradimento; (of tickets): **it was a** ~ registrò un tutto esaurito.

selves [sɛlvz] npl of **self**.

semantic [sɪ'mæntɪk] a semantico(a); ~**s** n semantica.

semaphore ['sɛməfɔ:ᵊ] n segnali mpl con bandiere; (RAIL) semaforo.

semen ['si:mən] n sperma m.

semi ['sɛmɪ] prefix semi...; ~-**breve** n semibreve f; ~-**circle** n semicerchio; ~-**colon** n punto e virgola; ~-**conscious** a parzialmente cosciente; ~-**detached** (house) n casa gemella; ~-**final** n semifinale f.

seminar ['sɛmɪnɑ:ᵊ] n seminario.

semiquaver ['sɛmɪkweɪvəᵊ] n semicroma.

semiskilled ['sɛmɪ'skɪld] a: ~ **worker** n operaio(a) non specializzato(a).

semitone ['sɛmɪtəun] n (MUS) semitono.

semolina [sɛmə'liːnə] n semolino.
senate ['sɛnɪt] n senato; **senator** n senatore/trice.
send, pt,pp **sent** [sɛnd, sɛnt] vt mandare; **to ~ sb to Coventry** dare l'ostracismo a qd; **to ~ away** vt (letter, goods) spedire; (person) mandare via; **to ~ away for** vt fus richiedere per posta, farsi spedire; **to ~ back** vt rimandare; **to ~ for** vt fus mandare a chiamare, far venire; **to ~ off** vt (goods) spedire; (SPORT: player) espellere; **to ~ out** vt (invitation) diramare; **to ~ up** vt (person, price) far salire; (parody) mettere in ridicolo; **~er** n mittente m/f.
senile ['siːnaɪl] a senile.
senior ['siːnɪə*] a (older) più vecchio(a); (of higher rank) di grado più elevato // n persona più anziana; (in service) persona con maggiore anzianità; **~ity** [-'ɔrɪti] n anzianità.
sensation [sɛn'seɪʃən] n sensazione f; **to create a ~** fare scalpore; **~al** a sensazionale; (marvellous) eccezionale.
sense [sɛns] n senso; (feeling) sensazione f, senso; (meaning) significato; (wisdom) buonsenso // vt sentire, percepire; **it makes ~** ha senso; **~s** npl ragione f; **~less** a sciocco(a); (unconscious) privo(a) di sensi.
sensibility [sɛnsɪ'bɪlɪti] n sensibilità; **sensibilities** npl sensibilità sg.
sensible ['sɛnsɪbl] a sensato(a), ragionevole.
sensitive ['sɛnsɪtɪv] a: **~ (to)** sensibile (a); **sensitivity** [-'tɪvɪti] n sensibilità.
sensual ['sɛnsjuəl] a sensuale.
sensuous ['sɛnsjuəs] a sensuale.
sent [sɛnt] pt,pp of **send**.
sentence ['sɛntns] n (LING) frase f; (LAW: judgment) sentenza; (: punishment) condanna // vt: **to ~ sb to death/to 5 years** condannare qd a morte/a 5 anni.
sentiment ['sɛntɪmənt] n sentimento; (opinion) opinione f; **~al** [-'mɛntl] a sentimentale.
sentry ['sɛntrɪ] n sentinella.
separate a ['sɛprɪt] separato(a) // vb ['sɛpəreɪt] vt separare // vi separarsi; **~ly** ad separatamente; **~s** npl (clothes) coordinati mpl; **separation** [-'reɪʃən] n separazione f.
September [sɛp'tɛmbə*] n settembre m.
septic ['sɛptɪk] a settico(a); (wound) infettato(a).
sequel ['siːkwl] n conseguenza; (of story) seguito.
sequence ['siːkwəns] n (series) serie f; (order) ordine m.
sequin ['siːkwɪn] n lustrino, paillette f inv.
serenade [sɛrə'neɪd] n serenata.
serene [sɪ'riːn] a sereno(a), calmo(a); **serenity** [sə'rɛnɪti] n serenità, tranquillità.
sergeant ['sɑːdʒənt] n sergente m; (POLICE) brigadiere m.
serial ['sɪərɪəl] n (PRESS) romanzo a puntate; (RADIO, TV) trasmissione f a

puntate // a (number) di serie; **~ize** vt pubblicare a puntate; trasmettere a puntate.
series ['sɪəriːs] n serie f inv; (PUBLISHING) collana.
serious ['sɪərɪəs] a serio(a), grave; **~ly** ad seriamente; **~ness** n serietà, gravità.
sermon ['sɜːmən] n sermone m.
serrated [sɪ'reɪtɪd] a seghettato(a).
serum ['sɪərəm] n siero.
servant ['sɜːvənt] n domestico/a.
serve [sɜːv] vt (employer etc) servire, essere a servizio di; (purpose) servire a; (customer, food, meal) servire; (apprenticeship) fare; (prison term) scontare // vi (also TENNIS) servire; (be useful): **to ~ as/for/to do** servire da/per/per fare // n (TENNIS) servizio; **it ~s him right** ben gli sta, se l'èmeritata; **to ~ out, ~ up** vt (food) servire.
service ['sɜːvɪs] n servizio; (AUT: maintenance) assistenza, revisione f // vt (car, washing machine) revisionare; **the S~s** le forze armate; **to be of ~ to sb, to do sb a ~** essere d'aiuto a qd; **to put one's car in for (a) ~** portare la macchina in officina per una revisione; **dinner ~** n servizio da tavola; **~able** a pratico(a), utile; **~ area** n (on motorway) area di servizio; **~man** n militare m; **~ station** n stazione f di servizio.
serviette [sɜːvɪ'ɛt] n tovagliolo.
servile ['sɜːvaɪl] a servile.
session ['sɛʃən] n (sitting) seduta, sessione f; (SCOL) anno scolastico (or accademico); **to be in ~** essere in seduta.
set [sɛt] n serie f inv; (RADIO, TV) apparecchio; (TENNIS) set m inv; (group of people) mondo, ambiente m; (CINEMA) scenario; (THEATRE: stage) scene fpl; (: scenery) scenario; (MATH) insieme m; (HAIRDRESSING) messa in piega // a (fixed) stabilito(a), determinato(a); (ready) pronto(a) // vb (pt, pp set) (place) posare, mettere; (fix) fissare; (adjust) regolare; (decide: rules etc) stabilire, fissare; (TYP) comporre // vi (sun) tramontare; (jam, jelly) rapprendersi; (concrete) fare presa; **to be ~ on doing** essere deciso a fare; **to be (dead) ~ against** essere completamente contrario a; **to ~ (to music)** mettere in musica; **to ~ on fire** dare fuoco a; **to ~ free** liberare; **to ~ sail** prendere il mare; **to ~ about** vt fus (task) intraprendere, mettersi a; **to ~ aside** vt mettere da parte; **to ~ back** (in time): **to ~ back (by)** mettere indietro (di); **to ~ off** vi partire // vt (bomb) far scoppiare; (cause to start) mettere in moto; (show up well) dare risalto a; **to ~ out** vi: **to ~ out to do** proporsi di fare // vt (arrange) disporre; (state) esporre, presentare; **to ~ up** vt (organization) fondare, costituire; (record) stabilire; (monument) innalzare; **~back** n (hitch) contrattempo, inconveniente m.
settee [sɛ'tiː] n divano, sofà m inv.

setting ['sɛtɪŋ] n ambiente m; (of jewel) montatura.

settle ['sɛtl] vt (argument, matter) appianare; (problem) risolvere; (MED: calm) calmare // vi (bird, dust etc) posarsi; (sediment) depositarsi; (also: ~ **down**) sistemarsi, stabilirsi; calmarsi; **to** ~ **to sth** applicarsi a qc; **to** ~ **for sth** accontentarsi di qc; **to** ~ **in** vi sistemarsi; **to** ~ **on sth** decidersi per qc; **to** ~ **up with sb** regolare i conti con qd; ~**ment** n (payment) pagamento, saldo; (agreement) accordo; (colony) colonia; (village etc) villaggio, comunità f inv; ~**r** n colonizzatore/trice.

setup ['sɛtʌp] n (arrangement) situazione f; sistemazione f; (situation) situazione.

seven ['sɛvn] num sette; ~**teen** num diciassette; ~**th** num settimo(a); ~**ty** num settanta.

sever ['sɛvə*] vt recidere, tagliare; (relations) troncare.

several ['sɛvərl] a, pronoun alcuni(e), diversi(e); ~ **of us** alcuni di noi.

severe [sɪ'vɪə*] a severo(a); (serious) serio(a), grave; (hard) duro(a); (plain) semplice, sobrio(a); **severity** [sɪ'vɛrɪtɪ] n severità; gravità; (of weather) rigore m.

sew, pt **sewed**, pp **sewn** [sɔu, sɔud, sɔun] vt, vi cucire; **to** ~ **up** vt ricucire.

sewage ['su:ɪdʒ] n acque fpl di scolo.

sewer ['su:ə*] n fogna.

sewing ['sɔuɪŋ] n cucitura; cucito; ~ **machine** n macchina da cucire.

sewn [sɔun] pp of **sew**.

sex [sɛks] n sesso; **to have** ~ **with** avere rapporti sessuali con; ~ **act** n atto sessuale.

sexual ['sɛksjuəl] a sessuale.

sexy ['sɛksɪ] a provocante, sexy inv.

shabby ['ʃæbɪ] a malandato(a); (behaviour) vergognoso(a).

shack [ʃæk] n baracca, capanna.

shackles ['ʃæklz] npl ferri mpl, catene fpl.

shade [ʃeɪd] n ombra; (for lamp) paralume m; (of colour) tonalità f inv; (small quantity): **a** ~ **of** un po' or un'ombra di // vt ombreggiare, fare ombra a; **in the** ~ all'ombra; **a** ~ **smaller** un tantino più piccolo.

shadow ['ʃædəu] n ombra // vt (follow) pedinare; ~ **cabinet** n (POL) governo m ombra inv; ~**y** a ombreggiato(a), ombroso(a); (dim) vago(a), indistinto(a).

shady ['ʃeɪdɪ] a ombroso(a); (fig: dishonest) losco(a), equivoco(a).

shaft [ʃɑːft] n (of arrow, spear) asta; (AUT, TECH) albero; (of mine) pozzo; (of lift) tromba; (of light) raggio.

shaggy ['ʃægɪ] a ispido(a).

shake [ʃeɪk] vb (pt **shook**, pp **shaken** [ʃuk, 'ʃeɪkn]) vt scuotere; (bottle, cocktail) agitare // vi tremare // n scossa; **to** ~ **hands with sb** stringere or dare la mano a qd; **to** ~ **off** vt scrollare (via); (fig) sbarazzarsi di; **to** ~ **up** vt scuotere; ~**-up** n riorganizzazione f drastica; **shaky** a

(hand, voice) tremante; (building) traballante.

shale [ʃeɪl] n roccia scistosa.

shall [ʃæl] auxiliary vb: **I** ~ **go** andrò.

shallow ['ʃæləu] a poco profondo(a); (fig) superficiale.

sham [ʃæm] n finzione f, messinscena; (jewellery, furniture) imitazione f // a finto(a) // vt fingere, simulare.

shambles ['ʃæmblz] n confusione f, baraonda, scompiglio.

shame [ʃeɪm] n vergogna // vt far vergognare; **it is a** ~ **(that/to do)** è un peccato (che + sub/fare); **what a** ~! che peccato!; ~**faced** a vergognoso(a); ~**ful** a vergognoso(a); ~**less** a sfrontato(a); (immodest) spudorato(a).

shampoo [ʃæm'puː] n shampoo m inv // vt fare lo shampoo a.

shamrock ['ʃæmrɔk] n trifoglio (simbolo nazionale dell'Irlanda).

shandy ['ʃændɪ] n birra con gassosa.

shanty ['ʃæntɪ] n baracca, capanna; ~ **town** n bidonville f inv.

shape [ʃeɪp] n forma // vt formare; (statement) formulare; (sb's ideas) condizionare // vi (also: ~ **up**) (events) andare, mettersi; (person) cavarsela; **to take** ~ prendere forma; **-shaped** suffix: **heart-shaped** a a forma di cuore; ~**less** a senza forma, informe; ~**ly** a ben proporzionato(a).

share [ʃɛə*] n (thing received, contribution) parte f; (COMM) azione f // vt dividere; (have in common) condividere, avere in comune; **to** ~ **out** (among or between) dividere (tra); ~**holder** n azionista m/f.

shark [ʃɑːk] n squalo, pescecane m.

sharp [ʃɑːp] a (razor, knife) affilato(a); (point) acuto(a), acuminato(a); (nose, chin) aguzzo(a); (outline) netto(a); (cold, pain) pungente; (MUS) diesis; (voice) stridulo(a); (person: quick-witted) sveglio(a); (: unscrupulous) disonesto(a) // n (MUS) diesis m inv // ad: **at 2 o'clock** ~ alle due in punto; ~**en** vt affilare; (pencil) fare la punta a; (fig) aguzzare; ~**ener** n (also: **pencil** ~**ener**) temperamatite m inv; (also: **knife** ~**ener**) affilacoltelli m inv; ~**eyed** a dalla vista acuta.

shatter ['ʃætə*] vt mandare in frantumi, frantumare; (fig: upset) distruggere; (: ruin) rovinare // vi frantumarsi, andare in pezzi.

shave [ʃeɪv] vt radere, rasare // vi radersi, farsi la barba // n: **to have a** ~ farsi la barba; ~**n** a (head) rasato(a), tonsurato(a); ~**r** n (also: **electric** ~) rasoio elettrico.

shaving ['ʃeɪvɪŋ] n (action) rasatura; ~**s** npl (of wood etc) trucioli mpl; ~ **brush** n pennello da barba; ~ **cream** n crema da barba; ~ **soap** n sapone m da barba.

shawl [ʃɔːl] n scialle m.

she [ʃiː] pronoun ella, lei, essa; ~**-cat** n gatta; ~**-elephant** n elefantessa; NB: for ships, countries follow the gender of your translation.

sheaf, sheaves [ʃi:f, ʃi:vz] n covone m.

shear [ʃiə°] vt (pt ~ed, pp ~ed or **shorn** [ʃɔ:n]) (sheep) tosare; **to ~ off** vt tosare; (branch) tagliare; **~s** npl (for hedge) cesoie fpl.

sheath [ʃi:θ] n fodero, guaina; (contraceptive) preservativo.

sheaves [ʃi:vz] npl of **sheaf**.

shed [ʃed] n capannone m // vt (pt,pp **shed**) (leaves, fur etc) perdere; (tears) versare.

sheep [ʃi:p] n, pl inv pecora; **~dog** n cane m da pastore; **~ish** a vergognoso(a), timido(a); **~skin** n pelle f di pecora.

sheer [ʃiə°] a (utter) vero(a) (e proprio(a)); (steep) a picco, perpendicolare; (almost transparent) sottile // ad a picco.

sheet [ʃi:t] n (on bed) lenzuolo; (of paper) foglio; (of glass) lastra; (of metal) foglio, lamina; **~ lightning** n lampo diffuso.

sheik(h) [ʃeik] n sceicco.

shelf, shelves [ʃelf, ʃelvz] n scaffale m, mensola.

shell [ʃel] n (on beach) conchiglia; (of egg, nut etc) guscio; (explosive) granata; (of building) scheletro // vt (peas) sgranare; (MIL) bombardare, cannoneggiare.

shellfish ['ʃelfiʃ] n, pl inv (crab etc) crostaceo; (scallop etc) mollusco; (pl: as food) crostacei; molluschi.

shelter ['ʃeltə°] n riparo, rifugio // vt riparare, proteggere; (give lodging to) dare rifugio or asilo a // vi ripararsi, mettersi al riparo; **~ed** a (life) ritirato(a); (spot) riparato(a), protetto(a).

shelve [ʃelv] vt (fig) accantonare, rimandare; **~s** npl of **shelf**.

shepherd ['ʃepəd] n pastore m // vt (guide) guidare.

sheriff ['ʃerif] n sceriffo.

sherry ['ʃeri] n sherry m.

shield [ʃi:ld] n scudo // vt: **to ~ (from)** riparare (da), proteggere (da or contro).

shift [ʃift] n (change) cambiamento; (of workers) turno // vt spostare, muovere; (remove) rimuovere // vi spostarsi, muoversi; **~ work** n lavoro a squadre; **~y** a ambiguo(a); (eyes) sfuggente.

shilling ['ʃiliŋ] n scellino (= 12 old pence; 20 in a pound).

shilly-shally ['ʃiliʃæli] vi tentennare, esitare.

shimmer ['ʃimə°] vi brillare, luccicare.

shin [ʃin] n tibia.

shine [ʃain] n splendore m, lucentezza // vb (pt, pp **shone** [ʃɔn]) vi (ri)splendere, brillare // vt far brillare, far risplendere; (torch): **to ~ sth on** puntare qc verso.

shingle ['ʃiŋgl] n (on beach) ciottoli mpl; (on roof) assicella di copertura; **~s** n (MED) erpete m.

shiny ['ʃaini] a lucente, lucido(a).

ship [ʃip] n nave f // vt trasportare (via mare); (send) spedire (via mare); (load) imbarcare, caricare; **~building** n costruzione f navale; **~ment** n carico; **~ping** n (ships) naviglio; (traffic)

navigazione f; **~shape** a in perfetto ordine; **~wreck** n relitto; (event) naufragio; **~yard** n cantiere m navale.

shire ['ʃaiə°] n contea.

shirk [ʃə:k] vt sottrarsi a, evitare.

shirt [ʃə:t] n (man's) camicia; **in ~ sleeves** in maniche di camicia; **~y** a (col) incavolato(a).

shiver ['ʃivə°] n brivido // vi rabbrividire, tremare.

shoal [ʃəul] n (of fish) banco.

shock [ʃɔk] n (impact) urto, colpo; (ELEC) scossa; (emotional) colpo, shock m inv; (MED) shock // vt colpire, scioccare; scandalizzare; **~ absorber** n ammortizzatore m; **~ing** a scioccante, traumatizzante; scandaloso(a), oltraggioso(a); **~proof** a antiurto inv.

shod [ʃɔd] pt, pp of **shoe**.

shoddy ['ʃɔdi] a scadente.

shoe [ʃu:] n scarpa; (also: **horse~**) ferro di cavallo // vt (pt,pp **shod** [ʃɔd]) (horse) ferrare; **~brush** n spazzola per le scarpe; **~horn** n calzante m; **~lace** n stringa; **~polish** n lucido per scarpe; **~shop** n calzoleria; **~tree** n forma per scarpe.

shone [ʃɔn] pt,pp of **shine**.

shook [ʃuk] pt of **shake**.

shoot [ʃu:t] n (on branch, seedling) germoglio // vb (pt,pp **shot** [ʃɔt]) vt (game) cacciare, andare a caccia di; (person) sparare a; (execute) fucilare; (film) girare // vi (with gun): **to ~ (at)** sparare (a), fare fuoco (su); (with bow): **to ~ (at)** tirare (su); (FOOTBALL) sparare, tirare (forte); **to ~ down** vt (plane) abbattere; **to ~ in/out** vi entrare/uscire come una freccia; **to ~ up** vi (fig) salire alle stelle; **~ing** n (shots) sparatoria; (HUNTING) caccia; **~ing range** n poligono (di tiro), tirassegno; **~ing star** n stella cadente.

shop [ʃɔp] n negozio; (workshop) officina // vi (also: **go ~ping**) fare spese; **~ assistant** n commesso/a; **~ floor** n officina; (fig) operai mpl, maestranze fpl; **~keeper** n negoziante m/f, bottegaio/a; **~lifting** n taccheggio; **~per** n compratore/trice; **~ping** n (goods) spesa, acquisti mpl; **~ping bag** n borsa per la spesa; **~ping centre** n centro commerciale; **~soiled** a sciupato(a) a forza di stare in vetrina; **~ steward** n (INDUSTRY) rappresentante m sindacale; **~ window** n vetrina.

shore [ʃɔ:°] n (of sea) riva, spiaggia; (of lake) riva // vt: **to ~ (up)** puntellare.

shorn [ʃɔ:n] pp of **shear**.

short [ʃɔ:t] a (not long) corto(a); (soon finished) breve; (person) basso(a); (curt) brusco(a), secco(a); (insufficient) insufficiente // n (also: **~ film**) cortometraggio; (a pair of) **~s** (i) calzoncini; **to be ~ of sth** essere a corto di or mancare di qc; **I'm 3 ~** me ne mancano 3; **in ~** in breve; **~ of doing** a meno che non si faccia; **everything ~ of** tutto fuorché; **it is ~ for** è l'abbreviazione or il diminutivo di; to cut ~ (speech, visit) accorciare, abbreviare; (person) interrompere; **to fail** ~ **of** non essere all'altezza di; to stop ~ fermarsi di colpo; to stop ~ of non arrivare fino a; ~**age** n scarsezza, carenza; ~**bread** n biscotto di pasta frolla; ~**circuit** n cortocircuito // vt cortocircuitare // vi fare cortocircuito; ~**coming** n difetto; ~(**crust**) **pastry** n pasta frolla; ~**cut** n scorciatoia; ~**en** vt accorciare, ridurre; ~**hand** n stenografia; ~**hand typist** n stenodattilografo/a; ~**list** n (for job) rosa dei candidati; ~**lived** a effimero(a), di breve durata; ~**ly** ad fra poco; ~**sighted** a miope; ~**story** n racconto, novella; ~**tempered** a irascibile; ~**term** a (effect) di or a breve durata; ~**wave** n (RADIO) onde fpl corte.

shot [ʃɔt] pt,pp of **shoot** // n sparo, colpo; (person) tiratore m; (try) prova; (injection) iniezione f; (PHOT) foto f inv; **like a** ~ come un razzo; (very readily) immediatamente; ~**gun** n fucile m da caccia.

should [ʃud] auxiliary vb: **I** ~ **go now** dovrei andare ora; **he** ~ **be there now** dovrebbe essere arrivato ora; **I** ~ **go if I were you** se fossi in te andrei; **I** ~ **like to** mi piacerebbe.

shoulder ['ʃəuldə⁰] n spalla; (of road): **hard** ~ banchina // vt (fig) addossarsi, prendere sulle proprie spalle; ~ **bag** n borsa a tracolla; ~ **blade** n scapola; ~ **strap** n bretella, spallina.

shout [ʃaut] n urlo, grido // vt gridare // vi urlare, gridare; **to give sb a** ~ chiamare qd gridando; **to** ~ **down** vt zittire gridando; ~**ing** n urli mpl.

shove [ʃʌv] vt spingere; (col: put): **to** ~ **sth in** ficcare qc in; **to** ~ **off** vi (NAUT) scostarsi.

shovel ['ʃʌvl] n pala // vt spalare.

show [ʃəu] n (of emotion) dimostrazione f, manifestazione f; (semblance) apparenza f; (exhibition) mostra, esposizione f; (THEATRE, CINEMA) spettacolo // vb (pt ~**ed**, pp **shown** [ʃəun]) vt far vedere, mostrare; (courage etc) dimostrare, dar prova di; (exhibit) esporre // vi vedersi, essere visibile; **to** ~ **sb in** far entrare qd; **to** ~ **off** vi (pej) esibirsi, mettersi in mostra // vt (display) mettere in risalto; (pej) mettere in mostra; **to** ~ **sb out** accompagnare qd alla porta; **to** ~ **up** vi (stand out) essere ben visibile; (col: turn up) farsi vedere // vt mettere in risalto; (unmask) smascherare; ~ **business** n industria dello spettacolo; ~**down** n prova di forza.

shower ['ʃauə⁰] n (rain) acquazzone m; (of stones etc) pioggia; (also: ~**bath**) doccia // vi fare la doccia // vt: **to** ~ **sb with** (gifts, abuse etc) coprire qd di; (missiles) lanciare contro qd una pioggia di.

showground ['ʃəugraund] n terreno d'esposizione.

showing ['ʃəuiŋ] n (of film) proiezione f.

show jumping ['ʃəudʒʌmpiŋ] n concorso ippico (di salto ad ostacoli).

showmanship ['ʃəumənʃip] n abilità d'impresario.

shown [ʃəun] pp of **show**.

show-off ['ʃəuɔf] n (col: person) esibizionista m/f.

showroom ['ʃəurum] n sala d'esposizione.

shrank [ʃræŋk] pt of **shrink**.

shrapnel ['ʃræpnl] n shrapnel m.

shred [ʃred] n (gen pl) brandello // vt fare a brandelli; (CULIN) sminuzzare, tagliuzzare.

shrewd [ʃru:d] a astuto(a), scaltro(a).

shriek [ʃri:k] n strillo // vt, vi strillare.

shrift [ʃrift] n: **to give sb short** ~ sbrigare qd.

shrill [ʃril] a acuto(a), stridulo(a), stridente.

shrimp [ʃrimp] n gamberetto.

shrine [ʃrain] n reliquario; (place) santuario.

shrink [ʃriŋk] vb (pt **shrank**, pp **shrunk** [ʃræŋk, ʃrʌŋk]) vi restringersi; (fig) ridursi // vt (wool) far restringere // n (col: pej) psicanalista m/f; ~**age** n restringimento.

shrivel ['ʃrivl] (also: ~ **up**) vt raggrinzare, avvizzire // vi raggrinzirsi, avvizzire.

shroud [ʃraud] n sudario // vt: ~**ed in mystery** avvolto(a) nel mistero.

Shrove Tuesday ['ʃrəuv'tju:zdi] n martedì m grasso.

shrub [ʃrʌb] n arbusto; ~**bery** n arbusti mpl.

shrug [ʃrʌg] n scrollata di spalle // vt,vi: **to** ~ **(one's shoulders)** alzare le spalle, fare spallucce; **to** ~ **off** vt passare sopra a.

shrunk [ʃrʌŋk] pp of **shrink**; ~**en** a rattrappito(a).

shudder ['ʃʌdə⁰] n brivido // vi rabbrividire.

shuffle ['ʃʌfl] vt (cards) mescolare; **to** ~ **(one's feet)** strascicare i piedi.

shun [ʃʌn] vt sfuggire, evitare.

shunt [ʃʌnt] vt (RAIL: direct) smistare; (: divert) deviare // vi: **to** ~ **(to and fro)** fare la spola.

shut, pt, pp **shut** [ʃʌt] vt chiudere // vi chiudersi, chiudere; **to** ~ **down** vt, vi chiudere definitivamente; **to** ~ **off** vt fermare, bloccare; **to** ~ **up** vi (col: keep quiet) stare zitto(a), fare silenzio // vt (close) chiudere; (silence) far tacere; ~**ter** n imposta; (PHOT) otturatore m.

shuttle ['ʃʌtl] n spola, navetta; (also: ~ **service**) servizio m navetta inv.

shuttlecock ['ʃʌtlkɔk] n volano.

shy [ʃai] a timido(a).

Siamese [saiə'mi:z] a: ~ **cat** gatto siamese.

Sicily ['sisili] n Sicilia.

sick [sik] a (ill) malato(a); (vomiting): **to be** ~ vomitare; (humour) macabro(a); **to feel** ~ avere la nausea; **to be** ~ **of** (fig) averne abbastanza di; ~ **bay** n infermeria; ~**en** vt nauseare; ~**ening** a (fig) disgustoso(a), rivoltante.

sickle ['sıkl] n falcetto.

sick: ~ **leave** n congedo per malattia; ~**ly** a malaticcio(a); (causing nausea) nauseante; ~**ness** n malattia; (vomiting) vomito; ~ **pay** n sussidio per malattia.

side [saɪd] n lato; (of lake) riva // cpd (door, entrance) laterale // vi: **to ~ with sb** parteggiare per qd, prendere le parti di qd; **by the ~ of** a fianco di; (road) sul ciglio di; ~ **by** ~ fianco a fianco; **to take ~s (with)** schierarsi (con); ~**board** n credenza; ~**boards**, ~**burns** npl (whiskers) basette fpl; ~ **effect** n (MED) effetto collaterale; ~**light** n (AUT) luce di posizione; ~**line** n (SPORT) linea laterale; (fig) attività secondaria; ~**long** a obliquo(a); ~ **road** n strada secondaria; ~**saddle** ad all'amazzone; ~ **show** n attrazione f; ~**track** vt (fig) distrarre; ~**walk** n (US) marciapiede m; ~**ways** ad di traverso.

siding ['saɪdıŋ] n (RAIL) binario di raccordo.

sidle ['saɪdl] vi: **to ~ up (to)** avvicinarsi furtivamente (a).

siege [si:dʒ] n assedio.

sieve [sɪv] n setaccio // vt setacciare.

sift [sıft] vt passare al crivello; (fig) vagliare.

sigh [saɪ] n sospiro // vi sospirare.

sight [saɪt] n (faculty) vista; (spectacle) spettacolo; (on gun) mira // vt avvistare; **in ~** in vista; **out of ~** non visibile; ~**seeing** n giro turistico; **to go ~seeing** visitare una località; ~**seer** n turista m/f.

sign [saɪn] n segno; (with hand etc) segno, gesto; (notice) insegna, cartello // vt firmare; **to ~ in/out** vi firmare il registro (all'arrivo/alla partenza); **to ~ up** (MIL) vt arruolare // vi arruolarsi.

signal ['sıgnl] n segnale m // vt (person) fare segno a; (message) segnalare.

signature ['sıgnətʃə*] n firma; ~ **tune** n sigla musicale.

signet ring ['sıgnətrıŋ] n anello con sigillo.

significance [sıg'nıfıkəns] n significato; importanza.

significant [sıg'nıfıkənt] a significante.

signify ['sıgnıfaı] vt significare.

signpost ['saınpəust] n cartello indicatore.

silence ['saıləns] n silenzio // vt far tacere, ridurre al silenzio; ~**r** n (on gun, AUT) silenziatore m.

silent ['saılnt] a silenzioso(a); (film) muto(a).

silhouette [sılu:'ɛt] n silhouette f inv.

silicon chip ['sılıkən'tʃıp] n plastrina di silicio.

silk [sılk] n seta // cpd di seta; ~**y** a di seta.

silly ['sılı] a stupido(a), sciocco(a).

silt [sılt] n limo.

silver ['sılvə*] n argento; (money) monete da 5, 10 o 50 pence; (also: ~**ware**) argenteria // cpd d'argento; ~ **paper** n carta argentata, (carta) stagnola; ~-**plated** a argentato(a); ~**smith** n argentiere m; ~**y** a (colour) argenteo(a); (sound) argentino(a).

similar ['sımılə*] a: ~ **(to)** simile (a); ~**ity** [-'lærıtı] n somiglianza, rassomiglianza.

simile ['sımılı] n similitudine f.

simmer ['sımə*] vi cuocere a fuoco lento.

simple ['sımpl] a semplice; **simplicity** [-'plısıtı] n semplicità; **simplify** ['sımplıfaı] vt semplificare; **simply** ad semplicemente.

simulate ['sımjuleıt] vt fingere, simulare.

simultaneous [sıməl'teınıəs] a simultaneo(a).

sin [sın] n peccato // vi peccare.

since [sıns] ad da allora // prep da // cj (time) da quando; (because) poiché, dato che; ~ **then** da allora.

sincere [sın'sıə*] a sincero(a); **sincerity** [-'serıtı] n sincerità.

sine [saın] n (MATH) seno.

sinew ['sınju:] n tendine m; ~**s** npl muscoli mpl.

sinful ['sınful] a peccaminoso(a).

sing, pt **sang**, pp **sung** [sıŋ, sæŋ, sʌŋ] vt, vi cantare.

singe [sındʒ] vt bruciacchiare.

singer ['sıŋə*] n cantante m/f.

single ['sıŋgl] a solo(a), unico(a); (unmarried: man) celibe; (: woman) nubile; (not double) semplice // n (also: ~ **ticket**) biglietto di (sola) andata; (record) 45 giri m; ~**s** npl (TENNIS) singolo; **to ~ out** vt scegliere; (distinguish) distinguere; ~-**breasted** a a un petto; **in ~ file** in fila indiana; ~-**handed** ad senza aiuto, da solo(a); ~-**minded** a tenace, risoluto(a); ~ **room** n camera singola.

singlet ['sıŋglıt] n canottiera.

singly ['sıŋglı] ad separatamente.

singular ['sıŋgjulə*] a (exceptional, LING) singolare; (unusual) strano(a) // n (LING) singolare m.

sinister ['sınıstə*] a sinistro(a).

sink [sıŋk] n lavandino, acquaio // vb (pt **sank**, pp **sunk** [sæŋk, sʌŋk]) vt (ship) (fare) affondare, colare a picco; (foundations) scavare; (piles etc): **to ~ sth into** conficcare qc in // vi (ship) andare a fondo; (ground etc) cedere, avvallarsi; **to ~ in** vi conficcarsi, penetrare.

sinner ['sınə*] n peccatore/trice.

sinuous ['sınjuəs] a sinuoso(a).

sinus ['saınəs] n (ANAT) seno.

sip [sıp] n sorso // vt sorseggiare.

siphon ['saıfən] n sifone m; **to ~ off** vt travasare (con un sifone).

sir [sə*] n signore m; S~ **John Smith** Sir John Smith; **yes** ~ sì, signore.

siren ['saıərn] n sirena.

sirloin ['sə:lɔın] n lombata di manzo.

sirocco [sı'rɔkəu] n scirocco.

sissy ['sısı] n (col) femminuccia.

sister ['sıstə*] n sorella; (nun) suora;

(*nurse*) infermiera *f* caposala *inv*; ~-**in-law** *n* cognata.

sit, *pt,pp* **sat** [sɪt, sæt] *vi* sedere, sedersi; (*assembly*) essere in seduta // *vt* (*exam*) sostenere, dare; **to ~ down** *vi* sedersi; **to ~ up** *vi* tirarsi su a sedere; (*not go to bed*) stare alzato(a) fino a tardi.

site [saɪt] *n* posto; (*also:* **building ~**) cantiere *m* // *vt* situare.

sit-in ['sɪtɪn] *n* (*demonstration*) sit-in *m inv*, manifestazione *f* di protesta con occupazione.

sitting ['sɪtɪŋ] *n* (*of assembly etc*) seduta; (*in canteen*) turno; **~ room** *n* soggiorno.

situated ['sɪtjueɪtɪd] *a* situato(a).

situation [sɪtju'eɪʃən] *n* situazione *f*.

six [sɪks] *num* sei; **~teen** *num* sedici; **~th** *a* sesto(a); **~ty** *num* sessanta.

size [saɪz] *n* dimensioni *fpl*; (*of clothing*) taglia, misura; (*of shoes*) numero; (*glue*) colla; **to ~ up** *vt* giudicare, farsi un'idea di; **~able** *a* considerevole.

sizzle ['sɪzl] *vi* sfrigolare.

skate [skeɪt] *n* pattino; (*fish: pl inv*) razza // *vi* pattinare; **~board** *n* skateboard *m inv*; **~r** *n* pattinatore/trice; **skating** *n* pattinaggio; **skating rink** *n* pista di pattinaggio.

skeleton ['skɛlɪtn] *n* scheletro; **~ staff** *n* personale *m* ridotto.

sketch [skɛtʃ] *n* (*drawing*) schizzo, abbozzo; (*THEATRE*) scenetta comica, sketch *m inv* // *vt* abbozzare, schizzare; **~ book** *n* album *m inv* per schizzi; **~ pad** *n* blocco per schizzi; **~y** *a* incompleto(a), lacunoso(a).

skewer ['skjuːə*] *n* spiedo.

ski [skiː] *n* sci *m inv* // *vi* sciare; **~ boot** *n* scarpone *m* da sci.

skid [skɪd] *n* slittamento // *vi* slittare.

skier ['skiːə*] *n* sciatore/trice.

skiing ['skiːɪŋ] *n* sci *m*.

skiful ['skɪlful] *a* abile.

ski lift ['skiːlɪft] *n* sciovia.

skill [skɪl] *n* abilità *f inv*, capacità *f inv*; **~ed** *a* esperto(a); (*worker*) qualificato(a), specializzato(a).

skim [skɪm] *vt* (*milk*) scremare; (*soup*) schiumare; (*glide over*) sfiorare // *vi*: **to ~ through** (*fig*) scorrere, dare una scorsa a.

skimp [skɪmp] *vt* (*work*) fare alla carlona; (*cloth etc*) lesinare; **~y** *a* misero(a); striminzito(a); frugale.

skin [skɪn] *n* pelle *f* // *vt* (*fruit etc*) sbucciare; (*animal*) scuoiare, spellare; **~-deep** *a* superficiale; **~ diving** *n* nuoto subacqueo; **~ graft** *n* innesto epidermico; **~ny** *a* molto magro(a), pelle e ossa *inv*; **~ test** *n* prova di reazione cutanea.

skip [skɪp] *n* saltello, balzo; (*container*) benna // *vi* saltare; (*with rope*) saltare la corda // *vt* (*pass over*) saltare.

skipper ['skɪpə*] *n* (*NAUT, SPORT*) capitano.

skipping rope ['skɪpɪŋrəup] *n* corda per saltare.

skirmish ['skəːmɪʃ] *n* scaramuccia.

skirt [skəːt] *n* gonna, sottana // *vt*

fiancheggiare, costeggiare; **~ing board** *n* zoccolo.

skit [skɪt] *n* parodia; scenetta satirica.

ski tow ['skiːtəu] *n* = **ski lift**.

skittle ['skɪtl] *n* birillo; **~s** *n* (*game*) (gioco dei) birilli *mpl*.

skive [skaɪv] *vi* (*Brit: col*) fare il lavativo.

skulk [skʌlk] *vi* muoversi furtivamente.

skull [skʌl] *n* cranio, teschio.

skunk [skʌŋk] *n* moffetta.

sky [skaɪ] *n* cielo; **~light** *n* lucernario; **~scraper** *n* grattacielo.

slab [slæb] *n* lastra.

slack [slæk] *a* (*loose*) allentato(a); (*slow*) lento(a); (*careless*) negligente // *n* (*in rope etc*) parte *f* non tesa; **~s** *npl* pantaloni *mpl*; **~en** (*also:* **~en off**) *vi* rallentare, diminuire // *vt* allentare.

slag [slæg] *n* scorie *fpl*; **~ heap** *n* ammasso di scorie.

slam [slæm] *vt* (*door*) sbattere; (*throw*) scaraventare; (*criticize*) stroncare // *vi* sbattere.

slander ['slɑːndə*] *n* calunnia; diffamazione *f* // *vt* calunniare; diffamare.

slang [slæŋ] *n* gergo; slang *m*.

slant [slɑːnt] *n* pendenza, inclinazione *f*; (*fig*) angolazione *f*, punto di vista; **~ed** *a* tendenzioso(a); **~ing** *a* in pendenza, inclinato(a).

slap [slæp] *n* manata, pacca; (*on face*) schiaffo // *vt* dare una manata a; schiaffeggiare // *ad* (*directly*) in pieno; **~dash** *a* abborracciato(a); **~stick** *n* (*comedy*) farsa grossolana; **a ~-up meal** un pranzo (*or* una cena) coi fiocchi.

slash [slæʃ] *vt* squarciare; (*face*) sfregiare; (*fig: prices*) ridurre drasticamente, tagliare.

slate [sleɪt] *n* ardesia // *vt* (*fig: criticize*) stroncare, distruggere.

slaughter ['slɔːtə*] *n* strage *f*, massacro // *vt* (*animal*) macellare; (*people*) trucidare, massacrare; **~house** *n* macello, mattatoio.

Slav [slɑːv] *a* slavo(a).

slave [sleɪv] *n* schiavo/a // *vi* (*also:* **~ away**) lavorare come uno schiavo; **~ry** *n* schiavitù *f*.

sleazy ['sliːzɪ] *a* trasandato(a).

sledge [slɛdʒ] *n* slitta; **~hammer** *n* mazza, martello da fabbro.

sleek [sliːk] *a* (*hair, fur*) lucido(a), lucente; (*car, boat*) slanciato(a), affusolato(a).

sleep [sliːp] *n* sonno // *vi* (*pt, pp* **slept** [slɛpt]) dormire; **to go to ~** addormentarsi; **to ~ in** *vi* (*lie late*) alzarsi tardi; (*oversleep*) dormire fino a tardi; **~er** *n* (*person*) dormiente *m/f*; (*RAIL: on track*) traversina; (: *train*) treno di vagoni letto; **~ing bag** *n* sacco a pelo; **~ing car** *n* vagone *m* letto *inv*, carrozza *f* letto *inv*; **~ing pill** *n* sonnifero; **~lessness** *n* insonnia; **a ~less night** una notte in bianco; **~walker** *n* sonnambulo/a; **~y** *a* assonnato(a), sonnolento(a); (*fig*) addormentato(a).

sleet [sli:t] n nevischio.

sleeve [sli:v] n manica; ~**less** a (garment) senza maniche.

sleigh [sleɪ] n slitta.

sleight [slaɪt] n: ~ **of hand** gioco di destrezza.

slender ['slendə*] a snello(a), sottile; (not enough) scarso(a), esiguo(a).

slept [slɛpt] pt,pp of **sleep**.

slice [slaɪs] n fetta // vt affettare, tagliare a fette.

slick [slɪk] a (clever) brillante; (insincere) untuoso(a), falso(a) // n (also: oil ~) chiazza di petrolio.

slid [slɪd] pt,pp of **slide**.

slide [slaɪd] n (in playground) scivolo; (PHOT) diapositiva; (also: **hair** ~) fermaglio (per capelli); (in prices) caduta // vb (pt,pp **slid** [slɪd]) vt far scivolare // vi scivolare; ~ **rule** n regolo calcolatore; **sliding** a (door) scorrevole; **sliding scale** n scala mobile.

slight [slaɪt] a (slim) snello(a), sottile; (frail) delicato(a), fragile; (trivial) insignificante; (small) piccolo(a) // n offesa, affronto // vt (offend) offendere, fare un affronto a; **the** ~**est** il minimo (or la minima); **not in the** ~**est** affatto, neppure per sogno; ~**ly** ad lievemente, un po'.

slim [slɪm] a magro(a), snello(a) // vi dimagrire; fare (or seguire) una dieta dimagrante.

slime [slaɪm] n limo, melma; viscidume m.

sling [slɪŋ] n (MED) benda al collo // vt (pt,pp **slung** [slʌŋ]) lanciare, tirare.

slip [slɪp] n scivolata, scivolone m; (mistake) errore m, sbaglio; (underskirt) sottoveste f; (of paper) striscia di carta; tagliando, scontrino // vt (slide) far scivolare // vi (slide) scivolare; (move smoothly): **to** ~ **into/out of** scivolare in/via da; (decline) declinare; **to give sb the** ~ sfuggire qd; **a** ~ **of the tongue** un lapsus linguae; **to** ~ **away** vi svignarsela; **to** ~ **in** vt introdurre casualmente; **to** ~ **out** vi uscire furtivamente; ~**ped disc** n spostamento della vertebre.

slipper ['slɪpə*] n pantofola.

slippery ['slɪpərɪ] a scivoloso(a).

slip road ['slɪprəud] n (to motorway) rampa di accesso.

slipshod ['slɪpʃɔd] a sciatto(a), trasandato(a).

slip-up ['slɪpʌp] n granchio.

slipway ['slɪpweɪ] n scalo di costruzione.

slit [slɪt] n fessura, fenditura; (cut) taglio; (tear) squarcio; strappo // vt (pt,pp **slit**) tagliare; (make a **slit**) squarciare; strappare.

slither ['slɪðə*] vi scivolare, sdrucciolare.

slog [slɔg] n faticata // vi lavorare con accanimento, sgobbare.

slogan ['sləugən] n motto, slogan m inv.

slop [slɔp] vi (also: ~ **over**) traboccare; versarsi // vt spandere; versare; ~**s** npl acqua sporca; sbobba.

slope [sləup] n pendio; (side of mountain) versante m; (of roof) pendenza; (of floor) inclinazione f // vi: **to** ~ **down** declinare; **to** ~ **up** essere in salita.

sloppy ['slɔpɪ] a (work) tirato(a) via; (appearance) sciatto(a); (film etc) sdolcinato(a).

slot [slɔt] n fessura // vt: **to** ~ **into** introdurre in una fessura; ~ **machine** n distributore m automatico.

slouch [slautʃ] vi ciondolare.

slovenly ['slʌvənlɪ] a sciatto(a), trasandato(a).

slow [sləu] a lento(a); (watch): **to be** ~ essere indietro // ad lentamente // vt,vi (also: ~ **down**, ~ **up**) rallentare; ' ~ ' (road sign) 'rallentare'; ~**ly** ad lentamente; **in** ~ **motion** al rallentatore.

sludge [slʌdʒ] n fanghiglia.

slug [slʌg] n lumaca; (bullet) pallottola; ~**gish** a lento(a).

sluice [slu:s] n chiusa.

slum [slʌm] n catapecchia.

slumber ['slʌmbə*] n sonno.

slump [slʌmp] n crollo, caduta; depressione f, crisi f inv // vi crollare.

slung [slʌŋ] pt,pp of **sling**.

slur [slə:*] n pronuncia indistinta; (stigma) diffamazione f, calunnia; (smear): ~ **(on)** macchia (su); (MUS) legatura // vt pronunciare in modo indistinto.

slush [slʌʃ] n neve mista a fango.

slut [slʌt] n donna trasandata, sciattona.

sly [slaɪ] a furbo(a), scaltro(a); **on the** ~ di soppiatto.

smack [smæk] n (slap) pacca; (on face) schiaffo // vt schiaffeggiare; (child) picchiare // vi: **to** ~ **of** puzzare di; **to** ~ **one's lips** fare uno schiocco con le labbra.

small [smɔ:l] a piccolo(a); ~ **ads** npl piccola pubblicità; **in the** ~ **hours** alle ore piccole; ~**pox** n vaiolo; ~ **talk** n chiacchiere fpl.

smarmy ['smɑ:mɪ] a (col) untuoso(a), strisciante.

smart [smɑ:t] a elegante; (clever) intelligente; (quick) sveglio(a) // vi bruciare; **to** ~**en up** vi farsi bello(a) // vt (people) fare bello(a); (things) abbellire.

smash [smæʃ] n (also: ~**up**) scontro, collisione f // vt frantumare, fracassare; (opponent) annientare, schiacciare; (hopes) distruggere; (SPORT: record) battere // vi frantumarsi, andare in pezzi; ~**ing** a (col) favoloso(a), formidabile.

smattering ['smætərɪŋ] n: **a** ~ **of** un'infarinatura di.

smear [smɪə*] n macchia; (MED) striscio // vt ungere; (fig) denigrare, diffamare.

smell [smɛl] n odore m; (sense) olfatto, odorato // vb (pt,pp **smelt** or **smelled** [smɛlt, smɛld]) vt sentire (l')odore di // vi (food etc): **to** ~ **(of)** avere odore (di); (pej) puzzare, avere un cattivo odore; ~**y** a puzzolente.

smile [smaɪl] n sorriso // vi sorridere.

smirk [smə:k] n sorriso furbo; sorriso compiaciuto.

smith [smiθ] *n* fabbro; **~y** *n* fucina.

smitten ['smɪtn] *a*: **~ with** colpito(a) da.

smock [smɔk] *n* grembiule *m*, camice *m*.

smog [smɔg] *n* smog *m*.

smoke [sməuk] *n* fumo // *vt, vi* fumare; **to have a ~** fumarsi una sigaretta; **~d** *a* (*bacon, glass*) affumicato(a); **~r** *n* (*person*) fumatore/trice; (*RAIL*) carrozza per fumatori; **smoking** *n*: **'no smoking'** (*sign*) 'vietato fumare'; **smoky** *a* fumoso(a); (*surface*) affumicato(a).

smooth [smuːð] *a* liscio(a); (*sauce*) omogeneo(a); (*flavour, whisky*) amabile; (*movement*) regolare; (*person*) mellifluo(a) // *vt* lisciare, spianare; (*also:* **~ out**: *difficulties*) appianare.

smother ['smʌðə*] *vt* soffocare.

smoulder ['sməuldə*] *vi* covare sotto la cenere.

smudge [smʌdʒ] *n* macchia; sbavatura // *vt* imbrattare, sporcare.

smug [smʌg] *a* soddisfatto(a), compiaciuto(a).

smuggle ['smʌgl] *vt* contrabbandare **~r** *n* contrabbandiere/a; **smuggling** *n* contrabbando.

smutty ['smʌtɪ] *a* (*fig*) osceno(a), indecente.

snack [snæk] *n* spuntino; **~ bar** *n* tavola calda, snack bar *m inv*.

snag [snæg] *n* intoppo, ostacolo imprevisto.

snail [sneɪl] *n* chiocciola.

snake [sneɪk] *n* serpente *m*.

snap [snæp] *n* (*sound*) schianto, colpo secco; (*photograph*) istantanea; (*game*) rubamazzo // *a* improvviso(a) // *vt* (far) schioccare; (*break*) spezzare di netto; (*photograph*) scattare un'istantanea di // *vi* spezzarsi con un rumore secco; **to ~ open/shut** aprirsi/chiudersi di scatto; **to ~ at** *vt fus* (*subj: dog*) cercare di mordere; **to ~ off** *vt* (*break*) schiantare; **to ~ up** *vt* afferrare; **~py** *a* rapido(a); **~shot** *n* istantanea.

snare [snɛə*] *n* trappola.

snarl [snɑːl] *vi* ringhiare.

snatch [snætʃ] *n* (*fig*) furto con strappo, scippo; (*small amount*): **~es** *of* frammenti *mpl* di // *vt* strappare (con violenza); (*steal*) rubare.

sneak [sniːk] *vi*: **to ~ in/out** entrare/uscire di nascosto; **~y** *a* falso(a), disonesto(a).

sneer [snɪə*] *n* ghigno, sogghigno // *vi* ghignare, sogghignare.

sneeze [sniːz] *n* starnuto // *vi* starnutire.

snide [snaɪd] *a* maligno(a).

sniff [snɪf] *n* fiutata, annusata // *vi* fiutare, annusare; tirare su col naso; (*in contempt*) arricciare il naso // *vt* fiutare, annusare.

snigger ['snɪgə*] *n* riso represso // *vi* ridacchiare, ridere sotto i baffi.

snip [snɪp] *n* pezzetto; (*bargain*) (buon) affare *m*, occasione *f* // *vt* tagliare.

sniper ['snaɪpə*] *n* (*marksman*) franco tiratore *m*, cecchino.

snippet ['snɪpɪt] *n* frammento.

snivelling ['snɪvlɪŋ] *a* (*whimpering*) piagnucoloso(a).

snob [snɔb] *n* snob *m/f inv*; **~bery** *n* snobismo; **~bish** *a* snob *inv*.

snooker ['snuːkə*] *n* tipo di gioco del biliardo.

snoop ['snuːp] *vi*: **to ~ on sb** spiare qd.

snooty ['snuːtɪ] *a* borioso(a), snob *inv*.

snooze [snuːz] *n* sonnellino, pisolino // *vi* fare un sonnellino.

snore [snɔː*] *vi* russare.

snorkel ['snɔːkl] *n* (*of swimmer*) respiratore *m* a tubo.

snort [snɔːt] *n* sbuffo // *vi* sbuffare.

snout [snaut] *n* muso.

snow [snəu] *n* neve *f* // *vi* nevicare; **~ball** *n* palla di neve; **~bound** *a* bloccato(a) dalla neve; **~drift** *n* cumulo di neve (ammucchiato dal vento); **~drop** *n* bucaneve *m inv*; **~fall** *n* nevicata; **~flake** *n* fiocco di neve; **~man** *n* pupazzo di neve; **~plough** *n* spazzaneve *m inv*; **~storm** *n* tormenta.

snub [snʌb] *vt* snobbare // *n* offesa, affronto; **~-nosed** *a* dal naso camuso.

snuff [snʌf] *n* tabacco da fiuto.

snug [snʌg] *a* comodo(a); (*room, house*) accogliente, comodo(a).

so [səu] *ad* (*degree*) così, tanto; (*manner: thus*) così, in questo modo // *cj* perciò; **~ as to do** in modo da *or* così da fare; **~ that** (*purpose*) affinché + *sub*; (*result*) così che; **~ do I, ~ am I** *etc* anch'io *etc*; **if ~** se è così; **I hope ~** spero di sì; **10 or ~** circa 10; **~ far** fin qui, finora; (*in past*) fino ad allora; **~ long!** arrivederci!; **~ many** tanti(e); **~ much** ad tanto // *det* tanto(a); **~ and ~** *n* tale *m/f* dei tali.

soak [səuk] *vt* inzuppare; (*clothes*) mettere a mollo // *vi* inzupparsi; (*clothes*) essere a mollo; **to be ~ed through** essere fradicio; **to ~ in** *vi* penetrare; **to ~ up** *vt* assorbire.

soap [səup] *n* sapone *m*; **~ powder** *n* detersivo; **~y** *a* insaponato(a).

soar [sɔː*] *vi* volare in alto.

sob [sɔb] *n* singhiozzo // *vi* singhiozzare.

sober ['səubə*] *a* non ubriaco(a); (*sedate*) serio(a); (*moderate*) moderato(a); (*colour, style*) sobrio(a); **to ~ up** *vt* far passare la sbornia a // *vi* farsi passare la sbornia.

Soc. *abbr of* **society**.

so-called ['səu'kɔːld] *a* cosiddetto(a).

soccer ['sɔkə*] *n* calcio.

sociable ['səuʃəbl] *a* socievole.

social ['səuʃl] *a* sociale // *n* festa, serata; **~ club** *n* club *m inv* sociale; **~ism** *n* socialismo; **~ist** *a,n* socialista (*m/f*); **~ science** *n* scienze *fpl* sociali; **~ security** *n* previdenza sociale; **~ welfare** *n* assistenza sociale; **~ work** *n* servizio sociale; **~ worker** *n* assistente *m/f* sociale.

society [sə'saɪətɪ] *n* società *f inv*; (*club*) società, associazione *f*; (*also:* **high ~**) alta società.

sociology [səusɪ'ɔlədʒɪ] *n* sociologia.

sock [sɔk] n calzino // vt (hit) dare un pugno a.

socket ['sɔkɪt] n cavità f inv; (of eye) orbita; (ELEC: also: **wall** ~) presa di corrente; (: for light bulb) portalampada m inv.

sod [sɔd] n (of earth) zolla erbosa; (col!) bastardo/a (!).

soda ['səudə] n (CHEM) soda; (also: ~ **water**) acqua di seltz.

sodden ['sɔdn] a fradicio(a).

sodium ['səudiəm] n sodio.

sofa ['səufə] n sofà m inv.

soft [sɔft] a (not rough) morbido(a); (not hard) soffice; (not loud) sommesso(a); (kind) gentile; (weak) debole; (stupid) stupido(a); ~ **drink** n analcolico; **~en** ['sɔfn] vt ammorbidire; addolcire; attenuare // vi ammorbidirsi; addolcirsi; attenuarsi; ~**-hearted** a sensibile; ~**ly** ad dolcemente; morbidamente; ~**ness** n dolcezza; morbidezza; ~**ware** n software m.

soggy ['sɔgi] a inzuppato(a).

soil [sɔɪl] n (earth) terreno, suolo // vt sporcare; (fig) macchiare.

solar ['səulə*] a solare.

sold [səuld] pt,pp of **sell**; ~ **out** a (COMM) esaurito(a).

solder ['səuldə*] vt saldare // n saldatura.

soldier ['səuldʒə*] n soldato, militare m.

sole [səul] n (of foot) pianta (del piede); (of shoe) suola; (fish: pl inv) sogliola // a solo(a), unico(a).

solemn ['sɔləm] a solenne; grave; serio(a).

solicitor [sə'lɪsɪtə*] n (for wills etc) ≈ notaio; (in court) ≈ avvocato.

solid ['sɔlɪd] a (not hollow) pieno(a); (strong, sound, reliable, not loud) solido(a); (meal) sostanzioso(a) // n solido.

solidarity [sɔlɪ'dærɪti] n solidarietà.

solidify [sə'lɪdɪfaɪ] vi solidificarsi // vt solidificare.

solitaire [sɔlɪ'tɛə*] n (game, gem) solitario.

solitary ['sɔlɪtəri] a solitario(a).

solitude ['sɔlɪtjuːd] n solitudine f.

solo ['səuləu] n assolo; ~**ist** n solista m/f.

solstice ['sɔlstɪs] n solstizio.

soluble ['sɔljubl] a solubile.

solution [sə'luːʃən] n soluzione f.

solve [sɔlv] vt risolvere.

solvent ['sɔlvənt] a (COMM) solvibile // n (CHEM) solvente m.

sombre, (US) **somber** ['sɔmbə*] a scuro(a); (mood, person) triste.

some [sʌm] det (a few) alcuni(e), qualche; (certain) certi(e); (a certain number or amount) see phrases below; (unspecified) un(a)... qualunque // pronoun alcuni(e); un po' // ad: ~ **10 people** circa 10 persone; **I have ~ books** ho qualche libro o alcuni libri; **have ~ tea/ice-cream/water** prendi un po' di tè/gelato/acqua; **there's ~ milk in the fridge** c'è un po' di latte nel frigo; ~ (**of it**) **was left** ne è rimasto un po'; **I've got ~** (i.e. books etc) ne ho

alcuni; (i.e. milk, money etc) ne ho un po'; ~**body** pronoun qualcuno; ~ **day** ad uno di questi giorni, un giorno o l'altro; ~**how** ad in un modo o nell'altro, in qualche modo; (for some reason) per qualche ragione; ~**one** pronoun = **somebody**; ~**place** ad (US) = **somewhere**.

somersault ['sʌməsɔːlt] n capriola; salto mortale // vi fare una capriola (or un salto mortale); (car) cappottare.

something ['sʌmθɪŋ] pronoun qualcosa; ~ **interesting** qualcosa di interessante.

sometime ['sʌmtaɪm] ad (in future) una volta o l'altra; (in past): ~ **last month** durante il mese scorso.

sometimes ['sʌmtaɪmz] ad qualche volta.

somewhat ['sʌmwɔt] ad piuttosto.

somewhere ['sʌmwɛə*] ad in or da qualche parte.

son [sʌn] n figlio.

song [sɔŋ] n canzone f; ~**book** n canzoniere m.

sonic ['sɔnɪk] a (boom) sonico(a).

son-in-law ['sʌnɪnlɔː] n genero.

sonnet ['sɔnɪt] n sonetto.

sonny ['sʌnɪ] n (col) ragazzo mio.

soon [suːn] ad presto, fra poco; (early) presto; ~ **afterwards** subito dopo; see also **as**; ~**er** ad (time) prima; (preference): **I would** ~**er do** preferirei fare; ~**er or later** prima o poi.

soot [sut] n fuliggine f.

soothe [suːð] vt calmare.

sop [sɔp] n: **that's only a** ~ è soltanto un'offa.

sophisticated [sə'fɪstɪkeɪtɪd] a sofisticato(a); raffinato(a); altamente perfezionato(a); complesso(a).

sopping ['sɔpɪŋ] a (also: ~ **wet**) bagnato(a) fradicio(a).

soppy ['sɔpɪ] a (pej) sentimentale.

soprano [sə'prɑːnəu] n (voice) soprano m; (singer) soprano m.

sorcerer ['sɔːsərə*] n stregone m, mago.

sordid ['sɔːdɪd] a sordido(a).

sore [sɔː*] a (painful) dolorante; (col: offended) offeso(a) // n piaga; ~**ly** ad (tempted) fortemente.

sorrow ['sɔrəu] n dolore m; ~**ful** a triste.

sorry ['sɔri] a spiacente; (condition, excuse) misero(a); ~**!** scusa! (or scusi! or scusate!); **to feel** ~ **for sb** rincrescersi per qd.

sort [sɔːt] n specie f, genere m // vt (also: ~ **out**: papers) classificare; ordinare; (: letters etc) smistare; (: problems) risolvere; ~**ing office** n ufficio m smistamento inv.

SOS n (abbr of save our souls) S.O.S. m inv.

so-so ['səusəu] ad così così.

soufflé ['suːfleɪ] n soufflé m inv.

sought [sɔːt] pt,pp of **seek**.

soul [səul] n anima; ~**-destroying** a demoralizzante; ~**ful** a pieno(a) di sentimento.

sound [saund] a (healthy) sano(a); (safe, not damaged) solido(a), in buono stato; (reliable, not superficial) solido(a); (sensible) giudizioso(a), di buon senso //

ad: ~ **asleep** profondamente addormentato // n (*noise*) suono; rumore m; (GEO) stretto // vt (*alarm*) suonare; (*also*: ~ **out**: *opinions*) sondare // vi suonare; (*fig*: *seem*) sembrare; **to ~ like** rassomigliare a; ~ **barrier** n muro del suono; **~ing** n (NAUT *etc*) scandagliamento; **~ly** ad (*sleep*) profondamente; (*beat*) duramente; **~proof** vt insonorizzare, isolare acusticamente // a insonorizzato(a), isolato(a) acusticamente; **~track** n (*of film*) colonna sonora.

soup [su:p] n minestra; brodo; zuppa; **in the ~** (*fig*) nei guai; **~spoon** n cucchiaio da minestra.

sour ['sauə°] a aspro(a); (*fruit*) acerbo(a); (*milk*) acido(a), fermentato(a); (*fig*) arcigno(a); acido(a); **it's ~ grapes** è soltanto invidia.

source [sɔːs] n fonte f, sorgente f; (*fig*) fonte.

south [sauθ] n sud m, meridione m, mezzogiorno // a del sud, sud *inv*, meridionale // ad verso sud; **S~ Africa** n Sudafrica m; **S~ African** a, n sudafricano(a); **S~ America** n Sudamerica, America del sud; **S~ American** a, n sudamericano(a); **~east** n sud-est m; **~erly** ['sʌðəlı] a dal sud, meridionale; **~ern** ['sʌðən] a del sud, meridionale; esposto(a) a sud; **S~ Pole** Polo Sud; **~ward(s)** ad verso sud; **~west** n sud-ovest m.

souvenir [su:və'nıə°] n ricordo, souvenir m *inv*.

sovereign ['sɔvrın] a,n sovrano(a); **~ty** n sovranità.

soviet ['sauvıət] a sovietico(a); **the S~ Union** l'Unione f Sovietica.

sow n (sau) scrofa f // vt (səu) (pt ~**ed**, pp **sown** [səun]) seminare.

soya bean ['sɔıəbi:n] n seme m di soia.

spa [spa:] n (*resort*) stazione f termale.

space [speıs] n spazio; (*room*) posto; spazio; (*length of time*) intervallo // cpd spaziale // vt (*also*: ~ **out**) distanziare; **~craft** n veicolo spaziale; **~man/woman** n astronauta m/f, cosmonauta m/f; **spacing** n spaziatura.

spacious ['speıʃəs] a spazioso(a), ampio(a).

spade [speıd] n (*tool*) vanga; pala; (*child's*) paletta; **~s** npl (CARDS) picche fpl; **~work** n (*fig*) duro lavoro preparatorio.

Spain [speın] n Spagna.

span [spæn] pt of **spin** // n (*of bird, plane*) apertura alare; (*of arch*) campata; (*in time*) periodo; durata // vt attraversare; (*fig*) abbracciare.

Spaniard ['spænjəd] n spagnolo/a.

spaniel ['spænjəl] n spaniel m *inv*.

Spanish ['spænıʃ] a spagnolo(a) // n (LING) spagnolo.

spank [spæŋk] vt sculacciare.

spanner ['spænə°] n chiave f inglese.

spare [spɛə°] a di riserva, di scorta; (*surplus*) in più, d'avanzo // n (*part*) pezzo

di ricambio // vt (*do without*) fare a meno di; (*afford to give*) concedere; (*refrain from hurting, using*) risparmiare; **to ~** (*surplus*) d'avanzo; **~ part** n pezzo di ricambio; **~ time** n tempo libero.

sparing ['spɛərıŋ] a (*amount*) scarso(a); (*use*) parsimonioso(a); **~ of words** che risparmia le proprie parole; **~ly** ad moderatamente.

spark [spɑ:k] n scintilla; **~(ing) plug** n candela.

sparkle ['spɑ:kl] n scintillio, sfavillio // vi scintillare, sfavillare; (*bubble*) spumeggiare, frizzare; **sparkling** a scintillante, sfavillante; (*wine*) spumante.

sparrow ['spærəu] n passero.

sparse [spɑ:s] a sparso(a), rado(a).

spasm ['spæzəm] n (MED) spasmo; (*fig*) accesso, attacco; **~odic** [spæz'mɔdık] a spasmodico(a); (*fig*) intermittente.

spastic ['spæstık] n spastico/a.

spat [spæt] pt,pp of **spit**.

spate [speıt] n (*fig*): ~ **of** diluvio or fiume m di; **in ~** (*river*) in piena.

spatter ['spætə°] vt, vi schizzare.

spatula ['spætjulə] n spatola.

spawn [spɔ:n] vt deporre // vi deporre le uova // n uova fpl.

speak, pt **spoke**, pp **spoken** [spi:k, spəuk, 'spəukn] vt (*language*) parlare; (*truth*) dire // vi parlare; **to ~ to sb/of or about sth** parlare a qd/di qc; **~ up!** parla più forte!; **~er** n (*in public*) oratore/trice; (*also*: **loud~er**) altoparlante m; (POL): **the S~er** il presidente della Camera dei Comuni; **to be on ~ing terms** parlarsi.

spear [spıə°] n lancia.

spec [spɛk] n (*col*): **on ~** sperando bene.

special ['spɛʃl] a speciale; **take ~ care** siate particolarmente prudenti; **~ist** n specialista m/f; **~ity** [spɛʃı'ælıtı] n specialità f *inv*; **~ize** vi: **to ~ize (in)** specializzarsi (in); **~ly** ad specialmente, particolarmente.

species ['spi:ʃi:z] n, pl *inv* specie f *inv*.

specific [spə'sıfık] a specifico(a); preciso(a); **~ation** [spɛsıfı'keıʃən] n specificazione f.

specify ['spɛsıfaı] vt specificare, precisare.

specimen ['spɛsımən] n esemplare m, modello; (MED) campione m.

speck [spɛk] n puntino, macchiolina; (*particle*) granello.

speckled ['spɛkld] a macchiettato(a).

specs [spɛks] npl (*col*) occhiali mpl.

spectacle ['spɛktəkl] n spettacolo; **~s** npl occhiali mpl; **spectacular** [-'tækjulə°] a spettacolare // n (CINEMA *etc*) film m *inv* etc spettacolare.

spectator [spɛk'teıtə°] n spettatore m.

spectre ['spɛktə°] n spettro.

spectrum, pl **spectra** ['spɛktrəm, -rə] n spettro; (*fig*) gamma.

speculate ['spɛkjuleıt] vi speculare; (*try to guess*): **to ~ about** fare ipotesi su; **speculation** [-'leıʃən] n speculazione f;

congettura; **speculative** [-lətɪv] a speculativo(a).

speech [spi:tʃ] n (faculty) parola; (talk) discorso; (manner of speaking) parlata; (enunciation) elocuzione f, ~less a ammutolito(a), muto(a); ~ therapy n cura dei disturbi del linguaggio.

speed [spi:d] n velocità f inv; (promptness) prontezza; at full or top ~ a tutta velocità; to ~ up vi, vt accelerare; ~boat n motoscafo; fuoribordo m inv; ~ily ad velocemente; prontamente; ~ing n (AUT) eccesso di velocità; ~ limit n limite m di velocità; ~ometer [spɪˈdɔmɪtə°] n tachimetro; ~way n (SPORT) pista per motociclismo; ~y a veloce, rapido(a); pronto(a).

spell [spɛl] n (also: magic ~) incantesimo; (period of time) (breve) periodo // vt (pt,pp spelt or ~ed [spɛlt, spɛld]) (in writing) scrivere (lettera per lettera); (aloud) dire il nome delle lettere di; (fig) significare; to cast a ~ on sb fare un incantesimo a qd; he can't ~ lui fa errori di ortografia; ~bound a incantato(a); affascinato(a); ~ing n ortografia.

spelt [spɛlt] pt,pp of spell.

spend, pt,pp spent [spɛnd, spɛnt] vt (money) spendere; (time, life) passare; ~ing money n denaro per le piccole spese; ~thrift n spendaccione/a.

spent [spɛnt] pt,pp of spend // a (patience) esaurito(a).

sperm [spə:m] n spermatozoo; (semen) sperma m; ~ whale n capodoglio.

spew [spju:] vt vomitare.

sphere [sfɪə°] n sfera.

spice [spaɪs] n spezia // vt aromatizzare.

spick-and-span [ˈspɪkənˈspæn] a impeccabile.

spicy [ˈspaɪsɪ] a piccante.

spider [ˈspaɪdə°] n ragno.

spike [spaɪk] n punta.

spill, pt,pp spilt or ~ed [spɪl, -t, -d] vt versare, rovesciare // vi versarsi, rovesciarsi.

spin [spɪn] n (revolution of wheel) rotazione f; (AVIAT) avvitamento; (trip in car) giretto // vb (pt spun, span, pp spun [spʌn, spæn]) vt (wool etc) filare; (wheel) far girare // vi girare; to ~ a yarn raccontare una storia; to ~ out vt far durare.

spinach [ˈspɪnɪtʃ] n spinacio; (as food) spinaci mpl.

spinal [ˈspaɪnl] a spinale; ~ cord n midollo spinale.

spindly [ˈspɪndlɪ] a lungo(a) e sottile, filiforme.

spin-drier [spɪnˈdraɪə°] n centrifuga.

spine [spaɪn] n spina dorsale; (thorn) spina; ~less a invertebrato(a), senza spina dorsale; (fig) smidollato(a).

spinning [ˈspɪnɪŋ] n filatura; ~ top n trottola; ~ wheel n filatoio.

spinster [ˈspɪnstə°] n nubile f; zitella.

spiral [ˈspaɪərl] n spirale f // a a spirale //

vi (fig) salire a spirale; ~ staircase n scala a chiocciola.

spire [spaɪə°] n guglia.

spirit [ˈspɪrɪt] n (soul) spirito, anima; (ghost) spirito, fantasma m; (mood) stato d'animo, umore m; (courage) coraggio; ~s npl (drink) alcolici mpl; in good ~s di buon umore; in low ~s triste, abbattuto(a); ~ed a vivace, vigoroso(a); (horse) focoso(a); ~ level n livella a bolla (d'aria).

spiritual [ˈspɪrɪtjuəl] a spirituale // n (also: Negro ~) spiritual m inv; ~ism n spiritismo.

spit [spɪt] n (for roasting) spiedo // vi (pt, pp spat [spæt]) sputare; (fire, fat) scoppiettare.

spite [spaɪt] n dispetto // vt contrariare, far dispetto a; in ~ of nonostante, malgrado; ~ful a dispettoso(a).

spittle [ˈspɪtl] n saliva; sputo.

splash [splæʃ] n spruzzo; (sound) ciac m inv; (of colour) schizzo // vt spruzzare // vi (also: ~ about) sguazzare.

spleen [spli:n] n (ANAT) milza.

splendid [ˈsplɛndɪd] a splendido(a), magnifico(a).

splendour [ˈsplɛndə°] n splendore m.

splice [splaɪs] vt (rope) impiombare; (wood) calettare.

splint [splɪnt] n (MED) stecca.

splinter [ˈsplɪntə°] n scheggia // vi scheggiarsi.

split [splɪt] n spaccatura; (fig: POL) scissione f // vb (pt, pp split) vt spaccare; (party) dividere; (work, profits) spartire, ripartire // vi (divide) dividersi; to ~ up vi (couple) separarsi, rompere; (meeting) sciogliersi; ~ting headache n mal m di testa da impazzire.

splutter [ˈsplʌtə°] vi farfugliare; sputacchiare.

spoil, pt,pp spoilt or ~ed [spɔɪl, -t, -d] vt (damage) rovinare, guastare; (mar) sciupare; (child) viziare; ~s npl bottino; ~sport n guastafeste m/f inv.

spoke [spəuk] pt of speak // n raggio.

spoken [ˈspəukn] pp of speak.

spokesman [ˈspəuksmən] n portavoce m inv.

sponge [spʌndʒ] n spugna // vt spugnare, pulire con una spugna // vi: to ~ on scroccare a; ~ cake n pan m di Spagna; ~r n (pej) parassita m/f, scroccone/a; spongy a spugnoso(a).

sponsor [ˈspɔnsə°] n (RADIO, TV) finanziatore/trice (a scopo pubblicitario) // vt sostenere; patrocinare; ~ship n finanziamento (a scopo pubblicitario); patrocinio.

spontaneous [spɔnˈteɪnɪəs] a spontaneo(a).

spooky [ˈspu:kɪ] a che fa accapponare la pelle.

spool [spu:l] n bobina.

spoon [spu:n] n cucchiaio; ~-feed vt nutrire con il cucchiaio; (fig) imboccare; ~ful n cucchiaiata.

sporadic [spɔ'rædɪk] a sporadico(a).

sport [spɔːt] n sport m inv; (person) sportivo/a // vt sfoggiare; ~**ing** a sportivo(a); **to give sb a** ~**ing chance** dare a qd una possibilità (di vincere); ~**s car** n automobile f sportiva; ~**s jacket** n giacca sportiva; ~**sman** n sportivo; ~**smanship** n spirito sportivo; ~**s page** n pagina sportiva; ~**swear** n abiti mpl sportivi; ~**swoman** n sportiva; ~**y** a sportivo(a).

spot [spɔt] n punto; (mark) macchia; (dot: on pattern) pallino; (pimple) foruncolo; (place) posto; (small amount): **a** ~ **of** un po' di // vt (notice) individuare, distinguere; **on the** ~ sul posto; su due piedi; ~ **check** n controllo senza preavviso; ~**less** a immacolato(a); ~**light** n proiettore m; (AUT) faro ausiliario; ~**ted** a macchiato(a); a puntini, a pallini; ~**ted with** punteggiato(a) di; ~**ty** a (face) foruncoloso(a).

spouse [spauz] n sposo/a.

spout [spaut] n (of jug) beccuccio; (of liquid) zampillo, getto // vi zampillare.

sprain [spreɪn] n storta, distorsione f // vt: **to** ~ **one's ankle** storcersi una caviglia.

sprang [spræŋ] pt of **spring**.

sprawl [sprɔːl] vi sdraiarsi (in modo scomposto).

spray [spreɪ] n spruzzo; (container) nebulizzatore m, spray m inv; (of flowers) mazzetto // vt spruzzare; (crops) irrorare.

spread [sprɛd] n diffusione f; (distribution) distribuzione f; (CULIN) pasta (da spalmare) // vb (pt,pp **spread**) vt (cloth) stendere, distendere; (butter etc) spalmare; (disease, knowledge) propagare, diffondere // vi stendersi, distendersi; spalmarsi; propagarsi, diffondersi.

spree [spriː] n: **to go on a** ~ fare baldoria.

sprig [sprɪg] n ramoscello.

sprightly ['spraɪtlɪ] a vivace.

spring [sprɪŋ] n (leap) salto, balzo; (coiled metal) molla; (season) primavera; (of water) sorgente f // vi (pt **sprang**, pp **sprung** [spræŋ, sprʌŋ]) saltare, balzare; **to** ~ **from** provenire da; **to** ~ **up** vi (problem) presentarsi; ~**board** n trampolino; ~**-clean** n (also: ~**-cleaning**) grandi pulizie fpl di primavera; ~**time** n primavera; ~**y** a elastico(a).

sprinkle ['sprɪŋkl] vt spruzzare; spargere; **to** ~ **water** etc **on**, ~ **with water** etc spruzzare dell'acqua etc su; **to** ~ **sugar** etc **on**, ~ **with sugar** etc spolverizzare di zucchero etc; ~**d with** (fig) cosparso(a) di.

sprint [sprɪnt] n volata, scatto // vi correre di volata, scattare; ~**er** n velocista m/f.

sprite [spraɪt] n elfo, folletto.

sprout [spraut] vi germogliare; (Brussels) ~**s** npl cavolini mpl di Bruxelles.

spruce [spruːs] n abete m rosso // a lindo(a); azzimato(a).

sprung [sprʌŋ] pp of **spring**.

spry [spraɪ] a arzillo(a), sveglio(a).

spun [spʌn] pt, pp of **spin**.

spur [spəː°] n sperone m; (fig) sprone m, incentivo // vt (also: ~ **on**) spronare; **on the** ~ **of the moment** lì per lì.

spurious ['spjuərɪəs] a falso(a).

spurn [spəːn] vt rifiutare con disprezzo, sdegnare.

spurt [spəːt] n getto; (of energy) esplosione f // vi sgorgare; zampillare.

spy [spaɪ] n spia // vi: **to** ~ **on** spiare // vt (see) scorgere; ~**ing** n spionaggio.

sq. (MATH), **Sq.** (in address) abbr of **square**.

squabble ['skwɔbl] vi bisticciarsi.

squad [skwɔd] n (MIL) plotone m; (POLICE) squadra.

squadron ['skwɔdrn] n (MIL) squadrone m; (AVIAT, NAUT) squadriglia.

squalid ['skwɔlɪd] a sordido(a).

squall [skwɔːl] n raffica; burrasca.

squalor ['skwɔlə°] n squallore m.

squander ['skwɔndə°] vt dissipare.

square [skwɛə°] n quadrato; (in town) piazza; (instrument) squadra // a quadrato(a); (honest) onesto(a); (col: ideas, tastes) di vecchio stampo // vt (arrange) regolare; (MATH) elevare al quadrato // vi (agree) accordarsi; **all** ~ pari; **a** ~ **meal** un pasto abbondante; **2 metres** ~ di 2 metri per 2; **1** ~ **metre** 1 metro quadrato; ~**ly** ad diritto; fermamente.

squash [skwɔʃ] n (drink): **lemon/orange** ~ sciroppo di limone/arancia; (SPORT) squash m // vt schiacciare.

squat [skwɔt] a tarchiato(a), tozzo(a) // vi accovacciarsi; ~**ter** n occupante m/f abusivo(a).

squawk [skwɔːk] vi emettere strida rauche.

squeak [skwiːk] vi squittire.

squeal [skwiːl] vi strillare.

squeamish ['skwiːmɪʃ] a schizzinoso(a); disgustato(a).

squeeze [skwiːz] n pressione f; (also ECON) stretta // vt premere; (hand, arm) stringere; **to** ~ **out** vt spremere.

squelch [skwɛltʃ] vi fare ciac; sguazzare.

squib [skwɪb] n petardo.

squid [skwɪd] n calamaro.

squint [skwɪnt] vi essere strabico(a) // n: **he has a** ~ è strabico.

squire ['skwaɪə°] n proprietario terriero.

squirm [skwəːm] vi contorcersi.

squirrel ['skwɪrəl] n scoiattolo.

squirt [skwəːt] n schizzo // vi schizzare; zampillare.

Sr abbr of **senior**.

St abbr of **saint**, **street**.

stab [stæb] n (with knife etc) pugnalata; (col: try): **to have a** ~ **at (doing) sth** provare a fare qc // vt pugnalare.

stability [stə'bɪlɪtɪ] n stabilità.

stabilize ['steɪbəlaɪz] vt stabilizzare.

stable ['steɪbl] n (for horses) scuderia; (for cattle) stalla // a stabile.

stack [stæk] n catasta, pila // vt accatastare, ammucchiare.

stadium ['steɪdɪəm] n stadio.

staff [stɑːf] n (work force) personale m; (: scol) personale insegnante; (: servants) personale di servizio; (mil) stato maggiore; (stick) bastone m // vt fornire di personale.

stag [stæg] n cervo.

stage [steɪdʒ] n palcoscenico; (profession): the ~ il teatro, la scena; (point) punto; (platform) palco // vt (play) allestire, mettere in scena; (demonstration) organizzare; (fig: perform: recovery etc) effettuare; in ~s per gradi; a tappe; ~coach n diligenza; ~ door n ingresso degli artisti; ~ fright n paura del pubblico; ~ manager n direttore m di scena.

stagger ['stægə°] vi barcollare // vt (person) sbalordire; (hours, holidays) scaglionare; ~ing a (amazing) incredibile, sbalorditivo(a).

stagnant ['stægnənt] a stagnante.

stagnate [stæg'neɪt] vi stagnare.

stag party ['stægpɑːtɪ] n festa di addio al celibato.

staid [steɪd] a posato(a), serio(a).

stain [steɪn] n macchia; (colouring) colorante m // vt macchiare; (wood) tingere; ~ed glass window n vetrata; ~less a (steel) inossidabile; ~ remover n smacchiatore m.

stair [stɛə°] n (step) gradino; ~s npl scale fpl, scala; on the ~s sulle scale; ~case, ~way n scale fpl, scala.

stake [steɪk] n palo, piolo; (betting) puntata, scommessa // vt (bet) scommettere; (risk) rischiare; to be at ~ essere in gioco.

stalactite ['stæləktaɪt] n stalattite f.

stalagmite ['stæləgmaɪt] n stalagmite f.

stale [steɪl] a (bread) raffermo(a), stantio(a); (beer) svaporato(a); (smell) di chiuso.

stalemate ['steɪlmeɪt] n stallo; (fig) punto morto.

stalk [stɔːk] n gambo, stelo // vt inseguire // vi camminare con sussiego.

stall [stɔːl] n bancarella; (in stable) box m inv di stalla // vt (aut) far spegnere // vi (aut) spegnersi, fermarsi; (fig) temporeggiare; ~s npl (in cinema, theatre) platea.

stalwart ['stɔːlwət] n membro fidato.

stamina ['stæmɪnə] n vigore m, resistenza.

stammer ['stæmə°] n balbuzie f // vi balbettare.

stamp [stæmp] n (postage =) francobollo; (implement) timbro; (mark, also fig) marchio, impronta; (on document) bollo; timbro // vi battere il piede // vt battere; (letter) affrancare; (mark with a ~) timbrare; ~ album n album m inv per francobolli; ~ collecting n filatelia.

stampede [stæm'piːd] n fuggi fuggi m inv.

stance [stæns] n posizione f.

stand [stænd] n (position) posizione f; (mil) resistenza; (structure) supporto, sostegno; (at exhibition) stand m inv; (in shop) banco; (at market) bancarella; (booth) chiosco; (sport) tribuna // vb (pt,pp stood [stud]) vi stare in piedi; (rise) alzarsi in piedi; (be placed) trovarsi // vt (place) mettere, porre; (tolerate, withstand) resistere, sopportare; to make a ~ prendere posizione; to ~ for parliament presentarsi come candidato (per il parlamento); it ~s to reason è logico; to ~ by vi (be ready) tenersi pronto // vt fus (opinion) sostenere; to ~ for vt fus (signify) rappresentare, significare; (tolerate) sopportare, tollerare; to ~ in for vt fus sostituire; to ~ out vi (be prominent) spiccare; to ~ up vi (rise) alzarsi in piedi; to ~ up for vt fus difendere; to ~ up to vt fus tener testa a, resistere a.

standard ['stændəd] n modello, standard m inv; (level) livello; (flag) stendardo // a (size etc) normale, standard inv; ~s npl (morals) principi mpl, valori mpl; ~ize vt normalizzare, standardizzare; ~ lamp n lampada a stelo; ~ of living n livello di vita.

stand-by ['stændbaɪ] n riserva, sostituto; ~ ticket n (aviat) biglietto senza garanzia.

stand-in ['stændɪn] n sostituto/a; (cinema) controfigura.

standing ['stændɪŋ] a diritto(a), in piedi // n rango, condizione f, posizione f; of many years' ~ che esiste da molti anni; ~ committee n commissione f permanente; ~ order n (at bank) ordine m permanente (di pagamento periodico); ~ orders npl (mil) regolamento; ~ room n posto all'impiedi.

stand-offish [stænd'ɔfɪʃ] a scostante, freddo(a).

standpoint ['stændpɔɪnt] n punto di vista.

standstill ['stændstɪl] n: at a ~ alla fermata; (fig) a un punto morto; to come to a ~ fermarsi; giungere a un punto morto.

stank [stæŋk] pt of **stink**.

staple ['steɪpl] n (for papers) graffetta // a (food etc) di base // vt cucire; ~r n cucitrice f.

star [stɑː°] n stella; (celebrity) divo/a; (principal actor) vedette f inv // vi: to ~ (in) essere il (or la) protagonista (di) // vt (cinema) essere interpretato(a) da.

starboard ['stɑːbəd] n dritta; to ~ a dritta.

starch [stɑːtʃ] n amido; ~ed a (collar) inamidato(a).

stardom ['stɑːdəm] n celebrità.

stare [stɛə°] n sguardo fisso // vi: to ~ at fissare.

starfish ['stɑːfɪʃ] n stella di mare.

stark [stɑːk] a (bleak) desolato(a) // ad: ~ naked completamente nudo(a).

starling ['stɑːlɪŋ] n storno.

start [stɑːt] *n* inizio; (*of race*) partenza; (*sudden movement*) sobbalzo // *vt* cominciare, iniziare // *vi* partire, mettersi in viaggio; (*jump*) sobbalzare; **to ~ doing** sth (in)cominciare a fare qc; **to ~ off** *vi* cominciare; (*leave*) partire; **to ~ up** *vi* cominciare; (*car*) avviarsi // *vt* iniziare; (*car*) avviare; **~er** *n* (AUT) motorino d'avviamento; (SPORT: *official*) starter *m inv*; (: *runner, horse*) partente *m/f*; (CULIN) primo piatto; **~ing point** *n* punto di partenza.

startle [stɑːtl] *vt* far trasalire; **startling** *a* sorprendente, sbalorditivo(a).

starvation [stɑːˈveɪʃən] *n* fame *f*, inedia.

starve [stɑːv] *vi* morire di fame; soffrire la fame // *vt* far morire di fame, affamare; **I'm starving** muoio di fame.

state [steɪt] *n* stato // *vt* dichiarare, affermare; annunciare; **the S~s** gli Stati Uniti; **to be in a ~** essere agitato(a); **~d** *a* fissato(a), stabilito(a); **~ly** *a* maestoso(a), imponente; **~ment** *n* dichiarazione *f*; (LAW) deposizione *f*; **~sman** *n* statista *m*.

static [stætɪk] *n* (RADIO) scariche *fpl* // *a* statico(a); **~ electricity** *n* elettricità statica.

station [steɪʃən] *n* stazione *f*; (*rank*) rango, condizione *f* // *vt* collocare, disporre.

stationary [steɪʃənərɪ] *a* fermo(a), immobile.

stationer [steɪʃənə*] *n* cartolaio/a; **~'s** (*shop*) *n* cartoleria; **~y** *n* articoli *mpl* di cancelleria.

station master [steɪʃənmɑːstə*] *n* (RAIL) capostazione *m*.

station wagon [steɪʃənwægən] *n* (US) giardinetta.

statistic [stəˈtɪstɪk] *n* statistica; **~s** *npl* (*science*) statistica; **~al** *a* statistico(a).

statue [stætjuː] *n* statua.

stature [stætʃə*] *n* statura.

status [steɪtəs] *n* posizione *f*, condizione *f* sociale; prestigio; stato; **the ~ quo** lo statu quo; **~ symbol** *n* simbolo di prestigio.

statute [stætjuːt] *n* legge *f*; **~s** *npl* (*of club etc*) statuto; **statutory** *a* stabilito(a) dalla legge, statutario(a).

staunch [stɔːntʃ] *a* fidato(a), leale.

stave [steɪv] *n* (MUS) rigo // *vt*: **to ~ off** (*attack*) respingere; (*threat*) evitare.

stay [steɪ] *n* (*period of time*) soggiorno, permanenza // *vi* rimanere; (*reside*) alloggiare, stare; (*spend some time*) trattenersi, soggiornare; **to ~ put** non muoversi; **to ~ with friends** stare presso amici; **to ~ the night** passare la notte; **to ~ behind** *vi* restare indietro; **to ~ in** *vi* (*at home*) stare in casa; **to ~ on** *vi* restare, rimanere; **to ~ out** *vi* (*of house*) rimanere fuori (di casa); **to ~ up** *vi* (*at night*) rimanere alzato(a).

STD *n* (*abbr of Subscriber Trunk Dialling*) teleselezione *f*.

steadfast [stɛdfɑːst] *a* fermo(a), risoluto(a).

steadily [stɛdɪlɪ] *ad* continuamente; (*walk*) con passo sicuro.

steady [stɛdɪ] *a* stabile, solido(a), fermo(a); (*regular*) costante; (*person*) calmo(a), tranquillo(a) // *vt* stabilizzare; calmare; **to ~ oneself** ritrovare l'equilibrio.

steak [steɪk] *n* (*meat*) bistecca; (*fish*) trancia.

steal, *pt* **stole**, *pp* **stolen** [stiːl, stəul, stəuln] rubare.

stealth [stɛlθ] *n*: **by ~** furtivamente; **~y** *a* furtivo(a).

steam [stiːm] *n* vapore *m* // *vt* trattare con vapore; (CULIN) cuocere a vapore // *vi* fumare; (*ship*): **to ~ along** filare; **~ engine** *n* macchina a vapore; (RAIL) locomotiva a vapore; **~er** *n* piroscafo, vapore *m*; **~roller** *n* rullo compressore.

steel [stiːl] *n* acciaio // *cpd* di acciaio; **~works** *n* acciaieria.

steep [stiːp] *a* ripido(a), scosceso(a); (*price*) eccessivo(a) // *vt* inzuppare; (*washing*) mettere a mollo.

steeple [stiːpl] *n* campanile *m*; **~chase** *n* corsa a ostacoli, steeplechase *m inv*.

steer [stɪə*] *n* manzo // *vt* (*ship*) governare; (*car*) guidare // *vi* (NAUT: *person*) governare; (: *ship*) rispondere al timone; (*car*) guidarsi; **~ing** *n* (AUT) sterzo; **~ing column** *n* piantone *m* dello sterzo; **~ing wheel** *n* volante *m*.

stem [stɛm] *n* (*of flower, plant*) stelo; (*of tree*) fusto; (*of glass*) gambo; (*of fruit, leaf*) picciolo; (NAUT) prua, prora // *vt* contenere, arginare; **to ~ from** *vt fus* provenire da, derivare da.

stench [stɛntʃ] *n* puzzo, fetore *m*.

stencil [stɛnsl] *n* (*of metal, cardboard*) stampino, mascherina; (*in typing*) matrice *f*.

step [stɛp] *n* passo; (*stair*) gradino, scalino; (*action*) mossa, azione *f* // *vi*: **to ~ forward** fare un passo avanti; **~s** *npl* = **stepladder**; **to ~ down** *vi* (*fig*) ritirarsi; **to ~ off** *vt fus* scendere da; **to ~ up** *vt* aumentare; intensificare; **~brother** *n* fratellastro; **~child** *n* figliastro/a; **~father** *n* patrigno; **~ladder** *n* scala a libretto; **~mother** *n* matrigna; **stepping stone** *n* pietra di un guado; (*fig*) trampolino; **~sister** *n* sorellastra.

stereo [stɛrɪəu] *n* (*system*) sistema *m* stereofonico; (*record player*) stereo *m inv* // *a* (*also*: **~phonic**) stereofonico(a).

stereotype [stɪərɪətaɪp] *n* stereotipo.

sterile [stɛraɪl] *a* sterile; **sterilize** [stɛrɪlaɪz] *vt* sterilizzare.

sterling [stɛːlɪŋ] *a* (*gold, silver*) di buona lega; (*fig*) autentico(a), genuino(a) // *n* (ECON) (*lira*) sterlina; **a pound ~** una lira sterlina.

stern [stɛːn] *a* severo(a) // *n* (NAUT) poppa.

stethoscope [stɛθəskəup] *n* stetoscopio.

stew [stjuː] *n* stufato // *vt*, *vi* cuocere in umido.

steward [stjuːəd] *n* (AVIAT, NAUT, RAIL)

steward *m inv*; (*in club etc*) dispensiere *m*; ~**ess** *n* assistente *f* di volo, hostess *f inv*.

stick [stɪk] *n* stecco; bastone *m* // *vb* (*pt, pp* stuck [stʌk]) *vt* (*glue*) attaccare; (*thrust*): to ~ sth into conficcare or piantare or infiggere qc in; (*col: put*) ficcare; (*col: tolerate*) sopportare // *vi* conficcarsi; tenere; (*remain*) restare, rimanere; to ~ out, to ~ up *vi* sporgere, spuntare; to ~ up for *vt fus* difendere; ~er *n* cartellino adesivo.

stickler ['stɪklə°] *n*: to be a ~ for essere pignolo(a) su, tenere molto a.

sticky ['stɪkɪ] *a* attaccaticcio(a), vischioso(a); (*label*) adesivo(a).

stiff [stɪf] *a* rigido(a), duro(a); (*muscle*) legato(a), indolenzito(a); (*difficult*) difficile, arduo(a); (*cold*) freddo(a), formale; (*strong*) forte; (*high: price*) molto alto(a); ~en *vt* irrigidire; rinforzare // *vi* irrigidirsi; indurirsi; ~neck *n* torcicollo.

stifle ['staɪfl] *vt* soffocare; stifling *a* (*heat*) soffocante.

stigma ['stɪgmə] *n* (*BOT, fig*) stigma *m*; ~ta [stig'mɑːtə] *npl* (*REL*) stigmate *fpl*.

stile [staɪl] *n* cavalcasiepe *m*; cavalcasteccato.

stiletto [stɪ'lɛtəu] *n* (*also:* ~ heel) tacco a spillo.

still [stɪl] *a* fermo(a); silenzioso(a) // *ad* (*up to this time, even*) ancora; (*nonetheless*) tuttavia, ciò nonostante; ~born *a* nato(a) morto(a); ~ life *n* natura morta.

stilt [stɪlt] *n* trampolo; (*pile*) palo.

stilted ['stɪltɪd] *a* freddo(a), formale; artificiale.

stimulate ['stɪmjuleɪt] *vt* stimolare; stimulating *a* stimolante.

stimulus, *pl* stimuli ['stɪmjuləs, 'stɪmjulaɪ] *n* stimolo.

sting [stɪŋ] *n* puntura; (*organ*) pungiglione *m* // *vt* (*pt, pp* stung [stʌŋ]) pungere.

stingy ['stɪndʒɪ] *a* spilorcio(a), tirchio(a).

stink [stɪŋk] *n* fetore *m*, puzzo // *vi* (*pt* stank, *pp* stunk [stæŋk, stʌŋk]) puzzare; ~er *n* (*col*) porcheria; fetente *m/f*; ~ing *a* (*col*): a ~ing... uno schifo di..., un(a) maledetto(a)...

stint [stɪnt] *n* lavoro, compito // *vi*: to ~ on lesinare su.

stipulate ['stɪpjuleɪt] *vt* stipulare.

stir [stə:°] *n* agitazione *f*, clamore *m* // *vt* rimescolare; (*move*) smuovere, agitare // *vi* muoversi; to ~ up *vt* provocare, suscitare; ~ring *a* eccitante; commovente.

stirrup ['stɪrəp] *n* staffa.

stitch [stɪtʃ] *n* (*SEWING*) punto; (*KNITTING*) maglia; (*MED*) punto (di sutura); (*pain*) fitta // *vt* cucire, attaccare; suturare.

stoat [stəut] *n* ermellino.

stock [stɔk] *n* riserva, provvista; (*COMM*) giacenza, stock *m inv*; (*AGR*) bestiame *m*; (*CULIN*) brodo; (*FINANCE*) titoli *mpl*, azioni *fpl* // *a* (*fig: reply etc*) consueto(a); classico(a) // *vt* (*have in stock*) avere, vendere; well-~ed ben fornito(a); to

take ~ (*fig*) fare il punto; to ~ up with *vt fus* fare provvista di.

stockade [stɔ'keɪd] *n* palizzata.

stockbroker ['stɔkbrəukə°] *n* agente *m* di cambio.

stock exchange ['stɔkɪkstʃeɪndʒ] *n* Borsa (Valori).

stocking ['stɔkɪŋ] *n* calza.

stockist ['stɔkɪst] *n* fornitore *m*.

stock market ['stɔkmɑːkɪt] *n* Borsa, mercato finanziario.

stock phrase ['stɔk'freɪz] *n* cliché *m inv*.

stockpile ['stɔkpaɪl] *n* riserva // *vt* accumulare riserve.

stocktaking ['stɔkteɪkɪŋ] *n* (*COMM*) inventario.

stocky ['stɔkɪ] *a* tarchiato(a), tozzo(a).

stodgy ['stɔdʒɪ] *a* pesante, indigesto(a).

stoical ['stəuɪkəl] *a* stoico(a).

stoke [stəuk] *vt* alimentare; ~r *n* fochista *m*.

stole [stəul] *pt of* steal // *n* stola.

stolen ['stəuln] *pp of* steal.

stolid ['stɔlɪd] *a* impassibile.

stomach ['stʌmək] *n* stomaco; (*abdomen*) ventre *m* // *vt* sopportare, digerire; ~ache *n* mal *m* di stomaco.

stone [stəun] *n* pietra; (*pebble*) sasso, ciottolo; (*in fruit*) nocciolo; (*MED*) calcolo; (*weight*) misura di peso = 6.348 kg.; 14 libbre // *cpd* di pietra // *vt* lapidare; ~-cold *a* gelido(a); ~-deaf *a* sordo(a) come una campana; ~work *n* muratura; stony *a* pietroso(a), sassoso(a).

stood [stud] *pt,pp of* stand.

stool [stuːl] *n* sgabello.

stoop [stuːp] *vi* (*also:* have a ~) avere una curvatura; (*bend*) chinarsi, curvarsi.

stop [stɔp] *n* arresto, (*stopping place*) fermata; (*in punctuation*) punto // *vt* arrestare, fermare; (*break off*) interrompere; (*also:* put a ~ to) porre fine a // *vi* fermarsi; (*rain, noise etc*) cessare, finire; to ~ doing sth cessare or finire di fare qc; to ~ dead fermarsi di colpo; to ~ off *vi* sostare brevemente; to ~ up *vt* (*hole*) chiudere, turare; ~lights *npl* (*AUT*) stop *mpl*; ~over *n* breve sosta; (*AVIAT*) scalo.

stoppage ['stɔpɪdʒ] *n* arresto, fermata; (*of pay*) trattenuta; (*strike*) interruzione *f* del lavoro.

stopper ['stɔpə°] *n* tappo.

stop-press ['stɔp'pres] *n* ultimissime *fpl*.

stopwatch ['stɔpwɔtʃ] *n* cronometro.

storage ['stɔːrɪdʒ] *n* immagazzinamento; (*COMPUTERS*) memoria.

store [stɔ:°] *n* provvista, riserva; (*depot*) deposito; (*large shop*) grande magazzino // *vt* immagazzinare; to ~ up *vt* mettere in serbo, conservare; ~room *n* dispensa.

storey ['stɔːrɪ] *n* piano.

stork [stɔːk] *n* cicogna.

storm [stɔːm] *n* tempesta, temporale *m*, burrasca; uragano // *vi* (*fig*) infuriarsi // *vt* prendere d'assalto; ~y *a* tempestoso(a), burrascoso(a).

story ['stɔːrɪ] n storia; favola; racconto; (US) = **storey**; ~**book** n libro di racconti.

stout [staut] a solido(a), robusto(a); (brave) coraggioso(a); (fat) corpulento(a), grasso(a) // n birra scura.

stove [stəuv] n (for cooking) fornello; (: small) fornelletto; (for heating) stufa.

stow [stəu] vt mettere via; ~**away** n passeggero(a) clandestino(a).

straddle ['strædl] vt stare a cavalcioni di.

strafe [strɑːf] vt mitragliare.

straggle ['strægl] vi crescere (or estendersi) disordinatamente; trascinarsi; rimanere indietro; ~**d along the coast** disseminati(e) lungo la costa; ~**r** n sbandato(a); **straggling, straggly** a (hair) in disordine.

straight [streɪt] a dritto(a); (frank) onesto(a), franco(a) // ad diritto; (drink) liscio // n: the ~ la linea retta; (RAIL) il rettilineo; (SPORT) la dirittura d'arrivo; **to put** or **get** ~ mettere in ordine, mettere ordine in; ~ **away**, ~**off** (at once) immediatamente; ~ **off**, ~ **out** senza esitare; ~**en** vt (also: ~**en out**) raddrizzare; ~**forward** a semplice; onesto(a), franco(a).

strain [streɪn] n (TECH) sollecitazione f; (physical) sforzo; (mental) tensione f; (MED) strappo; distorsione f; (streak, trace) tendenza; elemento // vt tendere; (muscle) sforzare; (ankle) storcere; (friendship, marriage) mettere a dura prova; (filter) colare, filtrare // vi sforzarsi; ~**s** npl (MUS) motivo; ~**ed** a (laugh etc) forzato(a); (relations) teso(a); ~**er** n passino, colino.

strait [streɪt] n (GEO) stretto; ~ **jacket** n camicia di forza; ~-**laced** a bacchettone(a).

strand [strænd] n (of thread) filo; ~**ed** a nei guai; senza mezzi di trasporto.

strange [streɪndʒ] a (not known) sconosciuto(a); (odd) strano(a), bizzarro(a); ~**r** n sconosciuto/a; estraneo/a.

strangle ['stræŋgl] vt strangolare; ~**hold** n (fig) stretta (mortale).

strap [stræp] n cinghia; (of slip, dress) spallina, bretella // vt legare con una cinghia; (child etc) punire (con una cinghia).

strapping ['stræpɪŋ] a ben piantato(a).

strata ['strɑːtə] npl of **stratum**.

strategic [strə'tiːdʒɪk] a strategico(a).

strategy ['strætɪdʒɪ] n strategia.

stratum, pl **strata** ['strɑːtəm, 'strɑːtə] n strato.

straw [strɔː] n paglia.

strawberry ['strɔːbərɪ] n fragola.

stray [streɪ] a (animal) randagio(a) // vi perdersi; ~ **bullet** n proiettile m vagante.

streak [striːk] n striscia; (fig: of madness etc): a ~ of una vena di // vt striare, screziare // vi: to ~ **past** passare vicino(a) come un fulmine; ~**y** a

screziato(a), striato(a); ~**y bacon** n ≈ pancetta.

stream [striːm] n ruscello; corrente f; (of people) fiume m // vt (SCOL) dividere in livelli di rendimento // vi scorrere; to ~ **in/out** entrare/uscire a fiotti.

streamer ['striːmə°] n (flag) fiamma; (of paper) stella filante.

streamlined ['striːmlaɪnd] a aerodinamico(a); affusolato(a); (fig) razionalizzato(a).

street [striːt] n strada, via; ~**car** n (US) tram m inv; ~ **lamp** n lampione m.

strength [strɛŋθ] n forza; (of girder, knot etc) resistenza, solidità; ~**en** vt rinforzare; fortificare; consolidare.

strenuous ['strɛnjuəs] a vigoroso(a), energico(a); (tiring) duro(a), pesante.

stress [strɛs] n (force, pressure) pressione f; (mental strain) tensione f; (accent) accento // vt insistere su, sottolineare.

stretch [strɛtʃ] n (of sand etc) distesa // vi stirarsi; (extend): to ~ **to/as far as** estendersi fino a // vt tendere, allungare; (spread) distendere; (fig) spingere (al massimo); at a ~ ininterrottamente; to ~ **out** vi allungarsi, estendersi // vt (arm etc) allungare, tendere; (to spread) distendere; to ~ **out for sth** allungare la mano per prendere qc.

stretcher ['strɛtʃə°] n barella, lettiga.

strewn [struːn] a: ~ **with** cosparso(a) di.

stricken ['strɪkən] a provato(a); affranto(a); ~ **with** colpito(a) da.

strict [strɪkt] a (severe) rigido(a), severo(a); (precise) preciso(a), stretto(a); ~**ly** ad severamente; strettamente, assolutamente.

stride [straɪd] n passo lungo // vi (pt **strode**, pp **stridden** [strəud, 'strɪdn]) camminare a grandi passi.

strident ['straɪdnt] a stridente.

strife [straɪf] n conflitto; litigi mpl.

strike [straɪk] n sciopero; (of oil etc) scoperta; (attack) attacco // vb (pt,pp **struck** [strʌk]) vt colpire; (oil etc) scoprire, trovare // vi far sciopero, scioperare; (attack) attaccare; (clock) suonare; to ~ **a match** accendere un fiammifero; to ~ **down** vt (fig) atterrare; to ~ **out** vt depennare; to ~ **up** vt (MUS) attaccare; to ~ **up a friendship with** fare amicizia con; ~**breaker** n crumiro/a; ~**r** n scioperante m/f; (SPORT) attaccante m; **striking** a impressionante.

string [strɪŋ] n spago; (row) fila; sequenza; catena; (MUS) corda // vt (pt,pp **strung** [strʌŋ]): to ~ **out** disporre di fianco; the ~**s** npl (MUS) gli archi; ~ **bean** n fagiolino; ~(-**ed**) **instrument** n (MUS) strumento a corda; ~ **of pearls** filo di perle.

stringent ['strɪndʒənt] a rigoroso(a); (need) stringente, impellente.

strip [strɪp] n striscia // vt spogliare; (also: ~ **down**: machine) smontare // vi spogliarsi; ~ **cartoon** n fumetto.

stripe [straɪp] *n* striscia, riga; ~**d** *a* a strisce *or* righe.

strip light ['strɪplaɪt] *n* tubo al neon.

stripper ['strɪpə*] *n* spogliarellista.

striptease ['strɪptiːz] *n* spogliarello.

strive, *pt* **strove**, *pp* **striven** [straɪv, strəʊv, 'strɪvn] *vi*: **to ~ to do** sforzarsi di fare.

strode [strəʊd] *pt of* **stride**.

stroke [strəʊk] *n* colpo; (*MED*) colpo apoplettico; (*caress*) carezza // *vt* accarezzare; **at a ~** in un attimo; **on the ~ of 5** alle 5 in punto, allo scoccare delle 5.

stroll [strəʊl] *n* giretto, passeggiatina // *vi* andare a spasso.

strong [strɔŋ] *a* forte; vigoroso(a); solido(a); vivo(a); **they are 50 ~** sono in 50; ~**hold** *n* fortezza, roccaforte *f*; ~**ly** *ad* fortemente, con forza; energicamente; vivamente; ~**room** *n* camera di sicurezza.

strove [strəʊv] *pt of* **strive**.

struck [strʌk] *pt,pp of* **strike**.

structural ['strʌktʃərəl] *a* strutturale; (*CONSTR*) di costruzione; di struttura.

structure ['strʌktʃə*] *n* struttura; (*building*) costruzione *f*, fabbricato.

struggle ['strʌgl] *n* lotta // *vi* lottare.

strum [strʌm] *vt* (*guitar*) strimpellare.

strung [strʌŋ] *pt,pp of* **string**.

strut [strʌt] *n* sostegno, supporto // *vi* pavoneggiarsi.

stub [stʌb] *n* mozzicone *m*; (*of ticket etc*) matrice *f*, talloncino; **to ~ out** *vt* schiacciare.

stubble ['stʌbl] *n* stoppia; (*on chin*) barba ispida.

stubborn ['stʌbən] *a* testardo(a), ostinato(a).

stuck [stʌk] *pt,pp of* **stick** // *a* (*jammed*) bloccato(a); ~**-up** *a* presuntuoso(a).

stud [stʌd] *n* bottoncino; borchia; (*of horses*) scuderia, allevamento di cavalli; (*also*: ~ **horse**) stallone *m* // *vt* (*fig*): ~**ded with** tempestato(a) di.

student ['stjuːdənt] *n* studente/essa // *cpd* studentesco(a); universitario(a); degli studenti.

studied ['stʌdɪd] *a* studiato(a), calcolato(a).

studio ['stjuːdɪəʊ] *n* studio.

studious ['stjuːdɪəs] *a* studioso(a); (*studied*) studiato(a), voluto(a); ~**ly** *ad* (*carefully*) deliberatamente, di proposito.

study ['stʌdɪ] *n* studio // *vt* studiare; esaminare // *vi* studiare.

stuff [stʌf] *n* cosa, roba; (*belongings*) cose *fpl*, roba; (*substance*) sostanza, materiale *m* // *vt* imbottire; (*CULIN*) farcire; ~**ing** *n* imbottitura, (*CULIN*) ripieno; ~**y** *a* (*room*) mal ventilato(a), senz'aria; (*ideas*) antiquato(a).

stumble ['stʌmbl] *vi* inciampare; **to ~ across** (*fig*) imbattersi in; **stumbling block** *n* ostacolo, scoglio.

stump [stʌmp] *n* ceppo; (*of limb*) moncone *m*.

stun [stʌn] *vt* stordire; sbalordire.

stung [stʌŋ] *pt, pp of* **sting**.

stunk [stʌŋk] *pp of* **stink**.

stunning ['stʌnɪŋ] *a* (*piece of news etc*) sbalorditivo(a); (*girl, dress*) favoloso(a), stupendo(a).

stunt [stʌnt] *n* bravata; trucco pubblicitario; (*AVIAT*) acrobazia // *vt* arrestare; ~**ed** *a* stentato(a), rachitico(a); ~**man** *n* cascatore *m*.

stupefy ['stjuːpɪfaɪ] *vt* stordire; intontire; (*fig*) stupire.

stupendous [stjuː'pɛndəs] *a* stupendo(a), meraviglioso(a).

stupid ['stjuːpɪd] *a* stupido(a); ~**ity** [-'pɪdɪtɪ] *n* stupidità *f inv*, stupidaggine *f*.

stupor ['stjuːpə*] *n* torpore *m*.

sturdy ['stɜːdɪ] *a* robusto(a), vigoroso(a); solido(a).

sturgeon ['stɜːdʒən] *n* storione *m*.

stutter ['stʌtə*] *n* balbuzie *f* // *vi* balbettare.

sty [staɪ] *n* (*of pigs*) porcile *m*.

stye [staɪ] *n* (*MED*) orzaiolo.

style [staɪl] *n* stile *m*; (*distinction*) eleganza, classe *f*; **stylish** *a* elegante.

stylized ['staɪlaɪzd] *a* stilizzato(a).

stylus ['staɪləs] *n* (*of record player*) puntina.

suave [swɑːv] *a* untuoso(a).

sub... [sʌb] *prefix* sub..., sotto...; **subconscious** *a*, *n* subcosciente (*m*); **subdivide** *vt* suddividere.

subdue [səb'djuː] *vt* sottomettere, soggiogare; ~**d** *a* pacato(a), (*light*) attenuato(a); (*person*) poco esuberante.

subject *n* ['sʌbdʒɪkt] soggetto; (*citizen etc*) cittadino/a; (*SCOL*) materia // *vt* [səb'dʒɛkt]: **to ~** to sottomettere a; esporre a; **to be ~** to (*law*) essere sottomesso(a) a; (*disease*) essere soggetto(a) a; ~**ive** *a* soggettivo(a); ~ **matter** *n* argomento; contenuto.

subjunctive [səb'dʒʌŋktɪv] *a* congiuntivo(a) // *n* congiuntivo.

sublime [sə'blaɪm] *a* sublime.

submachine gun ['sʌbmə'ʃiːngʌn] *n* mitra *m inv*.

submarine [sʌbmə'riːn] *n* sommergibile *m*.

submerge [səb'mɜːdʒ] *vt* sommergere; immergere // *vi* immergersi.

submission [səb'mɪʃən] *n* sottomissione *f*.

submissive [səb'mɪsɪv] *a* remissivo(a).

submit [səb'mɪt] *vt* sottomettere // *vi* sottomettersi.

subordinate [sə'bɔːdɪnət] *a,n* subordinato(a).

subscribe [səb'skraɪb] *vi* contribuire; **to ~ to** (*opinion*) approvare, condividere; (*fund*) sottoscrivere; (*newspaper*) abbonarsi a; essere abbonato(a) a; ~**r** *n* (*to periodical, telephone*) abbonato/a.

subscription [səb'skrɪpʃən] *n* sottoscrizione *f*; abbonamento.

subsequent ['sʌbsɪkwənt] *a* successivo(a),

seguente; conseguente; ~ly *ad* in seguito, successivamente.

subside [səb'saɪd] *vi* cedere, abbassarsi; (*flood*) decrescere; (*wind*) calmarsi; ~nce [-'saɪdns] *n* cedimento, abbassamento.

subsidiary [səb'sɪdɪərɪ] *a* sussidiario(a); accessorio(a) // *n* filiale *f*.

subsidize ['sʌbsɪdaɪz] *vt* sovvenzionare.

subsidy ['sʌbsɪdɪ] *n* sovvenzione *f*.

subsistence [səb'sɪstəns] *n* esistenza; mezzi *mpl* di sostentamento.

substance ['sʌbstəns] *n* sostanza; (*fig*) essenza.

substantial [səb'stænʃl] *a* solido(a); (*amount, progress etc*) notevole; (*meal*) sostanzioso(a).

substantiate [səb'stænʃɪeɪt] *vt* comprovare.

substitute ['sʌbstɪtjuːt] *n* (*person*) sostituto/a; (*thing*) succedaneo, surrogato // *vt*: to ~ sth/sb for sostituire qc/qd con; **substitution** [-'tjuːʃən] *n* sostituzione *f*.

subtitle ['sʌbtaɪtl] *n* (*CINEMA*) sottotitolo.

subtle ['sʌtl] *a* sottile; ~ty *n* sottigliezza.

subtract [səb'trækt] *vt* sottrarre; ~ion [-'trækʃən] *n* sottrazione *f*.

suburb ['sʌbəːb] *n* sobborgo; the ~s la periferia; ~an [sə'bəːbən] *a* suburbano(a).

subversive [səb'vəːsɪv] *a* sovversivo(a).

subway ['sʌbweɪ] *n* (*US*) metropolitana; (*Brit*) sottopassaggio.

succeed [sək'siːd] *vi* riuscire; avere successo // *vt* succedere a; to ~ in doing riuscire a fare; ~ing *a* (*following*) successivo(a).

success [sək'sɛs] *n* successo; ~ful *a* (*venture*) coronato(a) da successo, riuscito(a); to be ~ful (in doing) riuscire (a fare).

succession [sək'sɛʃən] *n* successione *f*.

successive [sək'sɛsɪv] *a* successivo(a); consecutivo(a).

successor [sək'sɛsə*] *n* successore *m*.

succinct [sək'sɪŋkt] *a* succinto(a), breve.

succulent ['sʌkjulənt] *a* succulento(a).

succumb [sə'kʌm] *vi* soccombere.

such [sʌtʃ] *a, det* tale; (*of that kind*): ~ a book un tale libro, un libro del genere; ~ books tali libri, libri del genere; (*so much*): ~ courage tanto coraggio; ~ a long trip un viaggio così lungo; ~ good books libri così buoni; ~ a lot of talmente or così tanto(a); making ~ a noise that facendo un rumore tale che; ~ as (*like*) come; a noise ~ as to un rumore tale da; as ~ *ad* come or in quanto tale; ~-and-~ *det* tale (*after noun*).

suck [sʌk] *vt* succhiare; (*breast, bottle*) poppare; ~er *n* (*ZOOL, TECH*) ventosa; (*BOT*) pollone *m*; (*col*) gonzo/a, babbeo/a.

suckle ['sʌkl] *vt* allattare.

suction ['sʌkʃən] *n* succhiamento; (*TECH*) aspirazione *f*.

sudden ['sʌdn] *a* improvviso(a); all of a ~ improvvisamente, all'improvviso; ~ly

ad bruscamente, improvvisamente, di colpo.

suds [sʌdz] *npl* schiuma (di sapone).

sue [suː] *vt* citare in giudizio.

suede [sweɪd] *n* pelle *f* scamosciata // *cpd* scamosciato(a).

suet ['suɪt] *n* grasso di rognone.

suffer ['sʌfə*] *vt* soffrire, patire; (*bear*) sopportare, tollerare // *vi* soffrire; ~ing *n* sofferenza.

suffice [sə'faɪs] *vi* essere sufficiente, bastare.

sufficient [sə'fɪʃənt] *a* sufficiente; ~ money abbastanza soldi; ~ly *ad* sufficientemente, abbastanza.

suffix ['sʌfɪks] *n* suffisso.

suffocate ['sʌfəkeɪt] *vi* (*have difficulty breathing*) soffocare; (*die through lack of air*) asfissiare; **suffocation** [-'keɪʃən] *n* soffocamento; (*MED*) asfissia.

sugar ['ʃugə*] *n* zucchero // *vt* zuccherare; ~ beet *n* barbabietola da zucchero; ~ cane *n* canna da zucchero; ~y *a* zuccherino(a), dolce; (*fig*) sdolcinato(a).

suggest [sə'dʒɛst] *vt* proporre, suggerire; indicare; ~ion [-'dʒɛstʃən] *n* suggerimento, proposta; ~ive *a* suggestivo(a).

suicide ['suɪsaɪd] *n* (*person*) suicida *m/f*; (*act*) suicidio.

suit [suːt] *n* (*man's*) vestito; (*woman's*) completo, tailleur *m inv*; (*CARDS*) seme *m*, colore *m* // *vt* andar bene a or per; essere adatto(a) a or per; (*adapt*): to ~ sth to adattare qc a; ~able *a* adatto(a); appropriato(a).

suitcase ['suːtkeɪs] *n* valigia.

suite [swiːt] *n* (*of rooms*) appartamento; (*MUS*) suite *f inv*; (*furniture*): bedroom/dining room ~ arredo or mobilia per la camera da letto/sala da pranzo.

sulk [sʌlk] *vi* fare il broncio; ~y *a* imbronciato(a).

sullen ['sʌlən] *a* scontroso(a); cupo(a).

sulphur ['sʌlfə*] *n* zolfo; ~ic [-'fjuərɪk] *a*: ~ic acid acido solforico.

sultana [sʌl'tɑːnə] *n* (*fruit*) uva (secca) sultanina.

sultry ['sʌltrɪ] *a* afoso(a).

sum [sʌm] *n* somma; (*SCOL etc*) addizione *f*; to ~ up *vt,vi* ricapitolare.

summarize ['sʌmaraɪz] *vt* riassumere, riepilogare.

summary ['sʌmərɪ] *n* riassunto // *a* (*justice*) sommario(a).

summer ['sʌmə*] *n* estate *f* // *cpd* d'estate, estivo(a); ~house *n* (*in garden*) padiglione *m*; ~time *n* (*season*) estate *f*; ~ time *n* (*by clock*) ora legale (estiva).

summit ['sʌmɪt] *n* cima, sommità; vertice *m*; ~ (conference) *n* (conferenza al) vertice.

summon ['sʌmən] *vt* chiamare, convocare; to ~ up *vt* raccogliere, fare appello a; ~s *n* ordine *m* di comparizione // *vt* citare.

sump [sʌmp] *n* (*AUT*) coppa dell'olio.

sumptuous ['sʌmptjuəs] a sontuoso(a).
sun [sʌn] n sole m; **in the ~** al sole; **~bathe** vi prendere un bagno di sole; **~burnt** a abbronzato(a); (painfully) scottato(a) dal sole; **~ cream** n crema solare.
Sunday ['sʌndaɪ] n domenica.
sundial ['sʌndaɪəl] n meridiana.
sundry ['sʌndrɪ] a vari(e), diversi(e); **all and ~** tutti quanti; **sundries** npl articoli diversi, cose diverse.
sunflower ['sʌnflauə°] n girasole m.
sung [sʌŋ] pp of **sing**.
sunglasses ['sʌnglɑːsɪz] npl occhiali mpl da sole.
sunk [sʌŋk] pp of **sink**; **~en** a sommerso(a); infossato(a).
sun: ~light n (luce f del) sole m; **~lit** a assolato(a), soleggiato(a); **~ny** a assolato(a), soleggiato(a); (fig) allegro(a), felice; **~rise** n levata del sole, alba; **~set** n tramonto; **~shade** n parasole m; **~shine** n (luce f del) sole m; **~stroke** n insolazione f, colpo di sole; **~tan** n abbronzatura; **~tan oil** n olio solare; **~trap** n luogo molto assolato, angolo pieno di sole.
super ['suːpə°] a (col) fantastico(a).
superannuation [suːpərænju'eɪʃən] n contributi mpl pensionistici; pensione f.
superb [suː'pɜːb] a magnifico(a).
supercilious [suːpə'sɪlɪəs] a sprezzante, sdegnoso(a).
superficial [suːpə'fɪʃəl] a superficiale.
superfluous [suː'pɜːfluəs] a superfluo(a).
superhuman [suːpə'hjuːmən] a sovrumano(a).
superimpose ['suːpərɪm'pəuz] vt sovrapporre.
superintendent [suːpərɪn'tɛndənt] n direttore/trice; (POLICE) ≈ commissario (capo).
superior [suː'pɪərɪə°] a,n superiore (m/f); **~ity** [-'ɔrɪtɪ] n superiorità.
superlative [suː'pɜːlətɪv] a superlativo(a), supremo(a) // n (LING) superlativo.
superman ['suːpəmæn] n superuomo.
supermarket ['suːpəmɑːkɪt] n supermercato.
supernatural [suːpə'nætʃərəl] a soprannaturale.
superpower ['suːpəpauə°] n (POL) superpotenza.
supersede [suːpə'siːd] vt sostituire, soppiantare.
supersonic ['suːpə'sɔnɪk] a supersonico(a).
superstition [suːpə'stɪʃən] n superstizione f.
superstitious [suːpə'stɪʃəs] a superstizioso(a).
supervise ['suːpəvaɪz] vt (person etc) sorvegliare; (organization) soprintendere a; **supervision** [-'vɪʒən] n sorveglianza; supervisione f; **supervisor** n sorvegliante m/f; soprintendente m/f; (in shop) capocommesso/a.
supper ['sʌpə°] n cena.

supple ['sʌpl] a flessibile; agile.
supplement n ['sʌplɪmənt] supplemento // vt [sʌplɪ'mɛnt] completare, integrare; **~ary** [-'mɛntərɪ] a supplementare.
supplier [sə'plaɪə°] n fornitore m.
supply [sə'plaɪ] vt (provide) fornire; (equip): to **~ (with)** approvvigionare (di); attrezzare (con) // n riserva, provvista; (supplying) approvvigionamento; (TECH) alimentazione f // cpd (teacher etc) supplente; **supplies** npl (food) viveri mpl; (MIL) sussistenza; **~ and demand** la domanda e l'offerta.
support [sə'pɔːt] n (moral, financial etc) sostegno, appoggio; (TECH) supporto // vt sostenere; (financially) mantenere; (uphold) sostenere, difendere; **~er** n (POL etc) sostenitore/trice, fautore/ trice; (SPORT) tifoso/a.
suppose [sə'pəuz] vt, vi supporre; immaginare; to be **~d** to do essere tenuto(a) a fare; **~dly** [sə'pəuzɪdlɪ] ad presumibilmente; (seemingly) apparentemente; **supposing** cj se, ammesso che + sub; **supposition** [sʌpə'zɪʃən] n supposizione f, ipotesi f inv.
suppress [sə'prɛs] vt reprimere; sopprimere; tenere segreto(a); **~ion** [sə'prɛʃən] n repressione f, soppressione f; **~or** n (ELEC etc) soppressore m.
supremacy [suː'prɛməsɪ] n supremazia.
supreme [suː'priːm] a supremo(a).
surcharge ['sɜːtʃɑːdʒ] n supplemento; (extra tax) soprattassa.
sure [ʃuə°] a sicuro(a); (definite, convinced) sicuro(a), certo(a); **~!** (of course) senz'altro!, certo!; **~ enough** infatti; to make **~** of assicurarsi di; **~-footed** a dal passo sicuro; **~ly** ad sicuramente, certamente.
surety ['ʃuərətɪ] n garanzia.
surf [sɜːf] n risacca; cresta dell'onda; frangenti mpl.
surface ['sɜːfɪs] n superficie f // vt (road) asfaltare // vi risalire alla superficie; (fig: person) venire a galla, farsi vivo(a); **~ mail** n posta ordinaria.
surfboard ['sɜːfbɔːd] n tavola per surfing.
surfeit ['sɜːfɪt] n: a **~ of** un eccesso di; un'indigestione di.
surfing ['sɜːfɪŋ] n surfing m.
surge [sɜːdʒ] n (strong movement) ondata; (of feeling) impeto // vi (waves) gonfiarsi; (ELEC: power) aumentare improvvisamente; (fig) sollevarsi.
surgeon ['sɜːdʒən] n chirurgo.
surgery ['sɜːdʒərɪ] n chirurgia; (room) studio or gabinetto medico, ambulatorio; **~ hours** npl orario delle visite or di consultazione.
surgical ['sɜːdʒɪkl] a chirurgico(a); **~ spirit** n alcool denaturato.
surly ['sɜːlɪ] a scontroso(a), burbero(a).
surmise [sɜː'maɪz] vt supporre, congetturare.
surmount [sɜː'maunt] vt sormontare.
surname ['sɜːneɪm] n cognome m.
surpass [sɜː'pɑːs] vt superare.

surplus ['sɔ:pləs] n eccedenza; (ECON) surplus m inv // a eccedente, d'avanzo.

surprise [sə'praɪz] n sorpresa; (astonishment) stupore m // vt sorprendere; stupire; **surprising** a sorprendente, stupefacente.

surrender [sə'rɛndə*] n resa, capitolazione f // vi arrendersi.

surreptitious [sʌrəp'tɪʃəs] a furtivo(a).

surround [sə'raund] vt circondare; (MIL etc) accerchiare; **~ing** a circostante; **~ings** npl dintorni mpl; (fig) ambiente m.

surveillance [sɔ:'veɪləns] n sorveglianza, controllo.

survey n ['sɔ:veɪ] vista; (study) esame m; (in housebuying etc) perizia; (of land) rilevamento, rilievo topografico // vt [sɔ:'veɪ] osservare; esaminare; valutare; rilevare; **~ing** n (of land) agrimensura; **~or** n perito; geometra m; (of land) agrimensore m.

survival [sə'vaɪvl] n sopravvivenza; (relic) reliquia, vestigio.

survive [sə'vaɪv] vi sopravvivere // vt sopravvivere a; **survivor** n superstite m/f, sopravvissuto/a.

susceptible [sə'sɛptəbl] a: **~ (to)** sensibile (a); (disease) predisposto(a) (a).

suspect a, n ['sʌspɛkt] a sospetto(a) // n persona sospetta // vt [səs'pɛkt] sospettare; (think likely) supporre; (doubt) dubitare.

suspend [səs'pɛnd] vt sospendere; **~ed sentence** n condanna con la condizionale; **~er belt** n reggicalze m inv; **~ers** npl giarrettiere fpl; (US) bretelle fpl.

suspense [səs'pɛns] n apprensione f; (in film etc) suspense m.

suspension [səs'pɛnʃən] n (gen AUT) sospensione f; (of driving licence) ritiro temporaneo; **~ bridge** n ponte m sospeso.

suspicion [səs'pɪʃən] n sospetto.

suspicious [səs'pɪʃəs] a (suspecting) sospettoso(a); (causing suspicion) sospetto(a).

sustain [səs'teɪn] vt sostenere; sopportare; (LAW: charge) confermare; (suffer) subire; **~ed** a (effort) prolungato(a).

sustenance ['sʌstɪnəns] n nutrimento; mezzi mpl di sostentamento.

swab [swɔb] n (MED) tampone m.

swagger ['swægə*] vi pavoneggiarsi.

swallow ['swɔləu] n (bird) rondine f // vt inghiottire; (fig: story) bere; **to ~ up** vt inghiottire.

swam [swæm] pt of swim.

swamp [swɔmp] n palude f // vt sommergere.

swan [swɔn] n cigno.

swap [swɔp] n scambio // vt: **to ~ (for)** scambiare (con).

swarm [swɔ:m] n sciame m // vi formicolare; (bees) sciamare.

swarthy ['swɔ:ðɪ] a di carnagione scura.

swastika ['swɔstɪkə] n croce f uncinata, svastica.

swat [swɔt] vt schiacciare.

sway [sweɪ] vi (building) oscillare; (tree) ondeggiare; (person) barcollare // vt (influence) influenzare, dominare.

swear, pt **swore**, pp **sworn** [swɛə*, swɔ:*, swɔ:n] vi (witness etc) giurare; (curse) bestemmiare, imprecare; **to ~ to sth** giurare qc; **~word** n parolaccia.

sweat [swɛt] n sudore m, traspirazione f // vi sudare; **in a ~** in un bagno di sudore.

sweater ['swɛtə*] n maglione m.

sweaty ['swɛtɪ] a sudato(a); bagnato(a) di sudore.

swede [swi:d] n rapa svedese.

Swede [swi:d] n svedese m/f.

Sweden ['swi:dn] n Svezia.

Swedish ['swi:dɪʃ] a svedese // n (LING) svedese m.

sweep [swi:p] n spazzata; (curve) curva; (expanse) distesa; (range) portata; (also: **chimney ~**) spazzacamino // vb (pt, pp **swept**) vt spazzare, scopare // vi camminare maestosamente; precipitarsi, lanciarsi; (e)stendersi; **to ~ away** vt spazzare via; trascinare via; **to ~ past** vi sfrecciare accanto; passare accanto maestosamente; **to ~ up** vt, vi spazzare; **~ing** a (gesture) largo(a); circolare; a **~ing statement** una affermazione generica.

sweet [swi:t] n dolce m; (candy) caramella // a dolce; (fresh) fresco(a); (fig) piacevole; delicato(a), grazioso(a); gentile; **~bread** n animella; **~corn** n granturco dolce; **~en** vt addolcire; zuccherare; **~heart** n innamorato/a; **~ness** n sapore m dolce; dolcezza; **~ pea** n pisello odoroso; **to have a ~ tooth** avere un debole per i dolci.

swell [swɛl] n (of sea) mare m lungo // a (col: excellent) favoloso(a) // vb (pt **~ed**, pp **swollen**, **~ed** ['swəulən]) vt gonfiare, ingrossare; aumentare // vi gonfiarsi, ingrossarsi; (sound) crescere; (MED) gonfiarsi; **~ing** n (MED) tumefazione f, gonfiore m.

sweltering ['swɛltərɪŋ] a soffocante.

swept [swɛpt] pt,pp of sweep.

swerve [swə:v] vi deviare; (driver) sterzare; (boxer) scartare.

swift [swɪft] n (bird) rondone m // a rapido(a), veloce.

swig [swɪg] n (col: drink) sorsata.

swill [swɪl] n broda // vt (also: **~ out**, **~ down**) risciacquare.

swim [swɪm] n: **to go for a ~** andare a fare una nuotata // vb (pt **swam**, pp **swum** [swæm, swʌm]) vi nuotare; (SPORT) fare del nuoto; (head, room) girare // vt (river, channel) attraversare or percorrere a nuoto; (length) nuotare; **~mer** n nuotatore/trice; **~ming** n nuoto; **~ming baths** npl piscina; **~ming cap** n cuffia; **~ming costume** n costume m da bagno; **~ming pool** n piscina; **~suit** n costume m da bagno.

swindle ['swɪndl] n truffa // vt truffare; **~r** n truffatore/trice.

swine [swaɪn] *n, pl inv* maiale *m*, porco; (*col!*) porco.

swing [swɪŋ] *n* altalena; (*movement*) oscillazione *f*; (*MUS*) ritmo; swing *m* // *vb* (*pt, pp* **swung** [swʌŋ]) *vt* dondolare, far oscillare; (*also*: ~ **round**) far girare // *vi* oscillare, dondolare; (*also*: ~ **round**) (*object*) roteare; (*person*) girarsi, voltarsi; **to be in full** ~ (*activity*) essere in piena attività; (*party etc*) essere nel pieno; ~ **bridge** *n* ponte *m* girevole; ~ **door** *n* porta battente.

swingeing ['swɪndʒɪŋ] *a* (*defeat*) violento(a); (*price increase*) enorme.

swinging ['swɪŋɪŋ] *a* (*step*) cadenzato(a), ritmico(a); (*rhythm, music*) trascinante.

swipe [swaɪp] *n* forte colpo; schiaffo // *vt* (*hit*) colpire con forza; dare uno schiaffo a; (*col: steal*) sgraffignare.

swirl [swəːl] *n* turbine *m*, mulinello // *vi* turbinare, far mulinello.

swish [swɪʃ] *a* (*col: smart*) all'ultimo grido, alla moda // *vi* sibilare.

Swiss [swɪs] *a, n, pl inv* svizzero(a); ~ **German** *a* svizzero(a) tedesco(a).

switch [swɪtʃ] *n* (*for light, radio etc*) interruttore *m*; (*change*) cambiamento // *vt* (*change*) cambiare; scambiare; **to** ~ **off** *vt* spegnere; **to** ~ **on** *vt* accendere; (*engine, machine*) mettere in moto, avviare; ~**back** *n* montagne *fpl* russe; ~**board** *n* (*TEL*) centralino; ~**board operator** centralinista *m/f*.

Switzerland ['swɪtsələnd] *n* Svizzera.

swivel ['swɪvl] *vi* (*also*: ~ **round**) girare.

swollen ['swəʊlən] *pp* of **swell** // *a* (*ankle etc*) gonfio(a).

swoon [swuːn] *vi* svenire.

swoop [swuːp] *n* (*by police etc*) incursione *f* // *vi* (*also*: ~ **down**) scendere in picchiata, piombare.

swop [swɒp] *n, vt* = **swap**.

sword [sɔːd] *n* spada; ~**fish** *n* pesce *m* spada *inv*.

swore [swɔː*] *pt* of **swear**.

sworn [swɔːn] *pp* of **swear**.

swot [swɒt] *vt* sgobbare su // *vi* sgobbare.

swum [swʌm] *pp* of **swim**.

swung [swʌŋ] *pt, pp* of **swing**.

sycamore ['sɪkəmɔː*] *n* sicomoro.

syllable ['sɪləbl] *n* sillaba.

syllabus ['sɪləbəs] *n* programma *m*.

symbol ['sɪmbl] *n* simbolo; ~**ic(al)** [-'bɒlɪk(l)] *a* simbolico(a); ~**ism** *n* simbolismo; ~**ize** *vt* simbolizzare.

symmetrical [sɪ'mɛtrɪkl] *a* simmetrico(a).

symmetry ['sɪmɪtrɪ] *n* simmetria.

sympathetic [sɪmpə'θɛtɪk] *a* (*showing pity*) compassionevole; (*kind*) comprensivo(a); ~ **towards** ben disposto(a) verso.

sympathize ['sɪmpəθaɪz] *vi*: **to** ~ **with** *sb* compatire qd; partecipare al dolore di qd; ~**r** *n* (*POL*) simpatizzante *m/f*.

sympathy ['sɪmpəθɪ] *n* compassione *f*; **in** ~ **with** d'accordo con; (*strike*) per solidarietà con; **with our deepest** ~ con

le nostre più sincere condoglianze.

symphony ['sɪmfənɪ] *n* sinfonia.

symposium [sɪm'pəʊzɪəm] *n* simposio.

symptom ['sɪmptəm] *n* sintomo; indizio.

synagogue ['sɪnəgɒg] *n* sinagoga.

synchronize ['sɪŋkrənaɪz] *vt* sincronizzare // *vi*: **to** ~ **with** essere contemporaneo(a) a.

syncopated ['sɪŋkəpeɪtɪd] *a* sincopato(a).

syndicate ['sɪndɪkɪt] *n* sindacato.

syndrome ['sɪndrəʊm] *n* sindrome *f*.

synonym ['sɪnənɪm] *n* sinonimo; ~**ous** [sɪ'nɒnɪməs] *a*: ~**ous (with)** sinonimo(a) (di).

synopsis, *pl* **synopses** [sɪ'nɒpsɪs, -siːz] *n* sommario, sinossi *f inv*.

syntax ['sɪntæks] *n* sintassi *f inv*.

synthesis, *pl* **syntheses** [sɪn'θəsɪs, -siːz] *n* sintesi *f inv*.

synthetic [sɪn'θɛtɪk] *a* sintetico(a).

syphilis ['sɪfɪlɪs] *n* sifilide *f*.

syphon ['saɪfən] *n, vb* = **siphon**.

Syria ['sɪrɪə] *n* Siria; ~**n** *a, n* siriano(a).

syringe [sɪ'rɪndʒ] *n* siringa.

syrup ['sɪrəp] *n* sciroppo; (*also*: **golden** ~) melassa raffinata.

system ['sɪstəm] *n* sistema *m*; (*order*) metodo; (*ANAT*) organismo; ~**atic** [-'mætɪk] *a* sistematico(a); metodico(a); ~**s analyst** *n* analista programmatore *m*.

T

ta [tɑː] *excl* (*Brit: col*) grazie!

tab [tæb] *n* (*loop on coat etc*) laccetto; (*label*) etichetta; **to keep** ~**s on** (*fig*) tenere d'occhio.

tabby ['tæbɪ] *n* (*also*: ~ **cat**) (*gatto*) soriano, gatto tigrato.

table ['teɪbl] *n* tavolo, tavola // *vt* (*motion etc*) presentare; **to lay** *or* **set the** ~ apparecchiare *or* preparare la tavola; ~ **of contents** *n* indice *m*; ~**cloth** *n* tovaglia; ~ **d'hôte** [tɑːbl'dəʊt] *a* (*meal*) a prezzo fisso; ~ **lamp** *n* lampada da tavolo; ~**mat** *n* sottopiatto; ~ **salt** *n* sale *m* fino *or* da tavola; ~**spoon** *n* cucchiaio da tavola; (*also*: ~**spoonful**: *as measurement*) cucchiaiata.

tablet ['tæblɪt] *n* (*MED*) compressa; (: *for sucking*) pastiglia; (*for writing*) blocco; (*of stone*) targa.

table: ~ **tennis** *n* tennis *m* da tavolo, ping-pong *m* ®; ~ **wine** *n* vino da tavola.

taboo [tə'buː] *a, n* tabù (*m inv*).

tabulate ['tæbjʊleɪt] *vt* (*data, figures*) tabulare, disporre in tabelle.

tacit ['tæsɪt] *a* tacito(a).

taciturn ['tæsɪtəːn] *a* taciturno(a).

tack [tæk] *n* (*nail*) bulletta; (*stitch*) punto d'imbastitura; (*NAUT*) bordo, bordata // *vt* imbullettare; imbastire // *vi* bordeggiare; **to change** ~ virare di bordo; **on the wrong** ~ (*fig*) sulla strada sbagliata.

tackle ['tækl] *n* attrezzatura, equipaggiamento; (*for lifting*) paranco; (*RUGBY*) placcaggio // *vt* (*difficulty*)

affrontare; (RUGBY) placcare.
tacky ['tækɪ] a colloso(a), appiccicaticcio(a); ancora bagnato(a).
tact [tækt] n tatto; **~ful** a delicato(a), discreto(a).
tactical ['tæktɪkl] a tattico(a).
tactics ['tæktɪks] n,npl tattica.
tactless ['tæktlɪs] a che manca di tatto.
tadpole ['tædpəul] n girino.
tag [tæg] n etichetta; to ~ along vi seguire.
tail [teɪl] n coda; (of shirt) falda // vt (follow) seguire, pedinare; to ~ away, ~ off vi (in size, quality etc) diminuire gradatamente; **~back** n ingorgo; ~ **coat** n marsina; ~ **end** n (of train, procession etc) coda; (of meeting etc) fine f.
tailor ['teɪlə*] n sarto; **~ing** n (cut) stile m; **~-made** a (also fig) fatto(a) su misura.
tailwind ['teɪlwɪnd] n vento di coda.
tainted ['teɪntɪd] a (food) guasto(a); (water, air) infetto(a); (fig) corrotto(a).
take, pt **took**, pp **taken** [teɪk, tuk, 'teɪkn] vt prendere; (gain: prize) ottenere, vincere; (require: effort, courage) occorrere, volerci; (tolerate) accettare, sopportare; (hold: passengers etc) contenere; (accompany) accompagnare; (bring, carry) portare; (exam) sostenere, presentarsi a; **it ~s a lot of time/courage** occorre or ci vuole molto tempo/coraggio; **I ~ it that** suppongo che; to ~ **for a walk** (child, dog) portare a fare una passeggiata; to ~ **after** vt fus assomigliare a; to ~ **apart** vt smontare; to ~ **away** vt portare via; togliere; to ~ **back** vt (return) restituire; riportare; (one's words) ritirare; to ~ **down** vt (building) demolire; (letter etc) scrivere; to ~ **in** vt (deceive) imbrogliare, abbindolare; (understand) capire; (include) prendere, ospitare; to ~ **off** vi (AVIAT) decollare // vt (remove) togliere; (imitate) imitare; to ~ **on** vt (work) accettare, intraprendere; (employee) assumere; (opponent) sfidare, affrontare; to ~ **out** vt portare fuori; (remove) togliere; (licence) prendere, ottenere; to ~ **sth out of** tirare qc fuori da; estrarre qc da; to ~ **over** vt (business) rilevare // vi: to ~ **over from** sb prendere le consegne or il controllo da qd; to ~ **to** vt fus (person) prendere in simpatia; (activity) prendere gusto a; to ~ **up** vt (one's story) riprendere; (dress) accorciare; (occupy: time, space) occupare; (engage in: hobby etc) mettersi a; **~away** a (food) da portar via; **~-home pay** n stipendio netto; **~off** n (AVIAT) decollo; **~over** n (COMM) rilevamento.
takings ['teɪkɪŋz] npl (COMM) incasso.
talc [tælk] n (also: **~um powder**) talco.
tale [teɪl] n racconto, storia; (pej) fandonia.
talent ['tælnt] n talento.
talk [tɔːk] n discorso; (gossip) chiacchiere fpl; (conversation) conversazione f; (interview) discussione f // vi (chatter)

chiacchierare; to ~ **about** parlare di; (converse) discorrere or conversare su; to ~ **sb out of/into doing** dissuadere qd da/convincere qd a fare; to ~ **shop** parlare del lavoro or degli affari; to ~ **over** vt discutere; **~ative** a loquace, ciarliero(a).
tall [tɔːl] a alto(a); **to be 6 feet ~** ≈ essere alto 1 metro e 80; **~boy** n cassettone m alto; ~ **story** n panzana, frottola.
tally ['tælɪ] n conto, conteggio // vi: to ~ (with) corrispondere (con).
tambourine [tæmbə'riːn] n tamburello.
tame [teɪm] a addomesticato(a); (fig: story, style) insipido(a), scialbo(a).
tamper ['tæmpə*] vi: to ~ **with** manomettere.
tampon ['tæmpɒn] n assorbente m interno.
tan [tæn] n (also: **sun~**) abbronzatura // vt abbronzare // vi abbronzarsi // a (colour) marrone rossiccio inv.
tandem ['tændəm] n tandem m inv.
tang [tæŋ] n odore m penetrante; sapore m piccante.
tangent ['tændʒənt] n (MATH) tangente f.
tangerine [tændʒə'riːn] n mandarino.
tangible ['tændʒəbl] a tangibile.
tangle ['tæŋgl] n groviglio // vt aggrovigliare; **to get in(to) a ~** finire in un groviglio.
tango ['tæŋgəu] n tango.
tank [tæŋk] n serbatoio; (for processing) vasca; (for fish) acquario; (MIL) carro armato.
tankard ['tæŋkəd] n boccale m.
tanker ['tæŋkə*] n (ship) nave f cisterna inv; (truck) autobotte f, autocisterna.
tantalizing ['tæntəlaɪzɪŋ] a allettante.
tantamount ['tæntəmaunt] a: ~ **to** equivalente a.
tantrum ['tæntrəm] n accesso di collera.
tap [tæp] n (on sink etc) rubinetto; (gentle blow) colpetto // vt dare un colpetto a; (resources) sfruttare, utilizzare; **~-dancing** n tip tap m.
tape [teɪp] n nastro; (also: **magnetic ~**) nastro (magnetico) // vt (record) registrare (su nastro); ~ **measure** n metro a nastro.
taper ['teɪpə*] n candelina // vi assottigliarsi.
tape recorder ['teɪprɪkɔːdə*] n registratore m (a nastro).
tapestry ['tæpɪstrɪ] n arazzo; tappezzeria.
tapioca [tæpɪ'əukə] n tapioca.
tar [tɑː] n catrame m.
tarantula [tə'ræntjulə] n tarantola.
tardy ['tɑːdɪ] a tardo(a); tardivo(a).
target ['tɑːgɪt] n bersaglio; (fig: objective) obiettivo; ~ **practice** n tiro al bersaglio.
tariff ['tærɪf] n (COMM) tariffa; (taxes) tariffe fpl doganali.
tarmac ['tɑːmæk] n macadam m al catrame; (AVIAT) pista di decollo.
tarnish ['tɑːnɪʃ] vt offuscare, annerire; (fig) macchiare.

tarpaulin [tɑːˈpɔːlɪn] *n* tela incatramata.
tart [tɑːt] *n* (*CULIN*) crostata; (*col: pej: woman*) sgualdrina // *a* (*flavour*) aspro(a), agro(a).
tartan [ˈtɑːtn] *n* tartan *m inv*.
tartar [ˈtɑːtəˈ] *n* (*on teeth*) tartaro; ~ **sauce** *n* salsa tartara.
task [tɑːsk] *n* compito; **to take to** ~ rimproverare; ~ **force** *n* (*MIL, POLICE*) unità operativa.
Tasmania [tæzˈmeɪnɪə] *n* Tasmania.
tassel [ˈtæsl] *n* fiocco.
taste [teɪst] *n* gusto; (*flavour*) sapore *m*, gusto; (*fig: glimpse, idea*) idea // *vt* gustare; (*sample*) assaggiare // *vi*: **to ~ of** (*fish etc*) sapere *o* avere sapore di; **it ~s like fish** sa di pesce; **can I have a ~ of this wine?** posso assaggiare un po' di questo vino?; **to have a ~ of sth** assaggiare qc; **to have a ~ for sth** avere un'inclinazione per qc; ~**ful** *a* di buon gusto; ~**less** *a* (*food*) insipido(a); (*remark*) di cattivo gusto; **tasty** *a* saporito(a), gustoso(a).
tatters [ˈtætəz] *npl*: **in ~** (*also:* **tattered**) a brandelli, sbrindellato(a).
tattoo [təˈtuː] *n* tatuaggio; (*spectacle*) parata militare // *vt* tatuare.
tatty [ˈtætɪ] *a* (*col*) malandato(a).
taught [tɔːt] *pt,pp* of **teach**.
taunt [tɔːnt] *n* scherno // *vt* schernire.
Taurus [ˈtɔːrəs] *n* Toro.
taut [tɔːt] *a* teso(a).
tavern [ˈtævən] *n* taverna.
tawdry [ˈtɔːdrɪ] *a* pacchiano(a).
tawny [ˈtɔːnɪ] *a* fulvo(a).
tax [tæks] *n* (*on goods*) imposta; (*on services*) tassa; (*on income*) imposte *fpl*, tasse *fpl* // *vt* tassare; (*fig: strain: patience etc*) mettere alla prova; ~**ation** [-ˈseɪʃən] *n* tassazione *f*; tasse *fpl*, imposte *fpl*; ~ **avoidance** *n* l'evitare legalmente il pagamento di imposte; ~ **collector** *n* esattore *m* delle imposte; ~ **evasion** *n* evasione *f* fiscale; ~ **exile** *n* chi ripara all'estero per evadere le imposte; ~**-free** *a* esente da imposte.
taxi [ˈtæksɪ] *n* taxi *m inv* // *vi* (*AVIAT*) rullare; ~ **driver** *n* tassista *m/f*; ~ **rank**, ~ **stand** *n* posteggio dei taxi.
tax: ~ **payer** *n* contribuente *m/f*; ~ **return** *n* dichiarazione *f* dei redditi.
TB *abbr of* **tuberculosis**.
tea [tiː] *n* tè *m inv*; (*snack: for children*) merenda; **high** ~ cena leggera (*presa nel tardo pomeriggio*); ~ **bag** *n* bustina di tè; ~ **break** *n* intervallo per il tè.
teach, *pt, pp* **taught** [tiːtʃ, tɔːt] *vt*: **to ~ sb sth,** ~ **sth to sb** insegnare qc a qd // *vi* insegnare; ~**er** *n* insegnante *m/f*; (*in secondary school*) professore/essa; (*in primary school*) maestro/a; ~**ing** *n* insegnamento; ~**ing staff** *n* insegnanti *mpl*, personale *m* insegnante.
tea cosy [ˈtiːkəuzɪ] *n* copriteiera *m inv*.
teacup [ˈtiːkʌp] *n* tazza da tè.
teak [tiːk] *n* teak *m*.
tea leaves [ˈtiːliːvz] *npl* foglie *fpl* di tè.

team [tiːm] *n* squadra; (*of animals*) tiro; ~ **games/work** giochi *mpl*/lavoro di squadra.
tea party [ˈtiːpɑːtɪ] *n* tè *m inv* (*ricevimento*).
teapot [ˈtiːpɔt] *n* teiera.
tear *n* [tɛəˈ] strappo; [tɪəˈ] lacrima // *vb* [tɛəˈ] (*pt* **tore**, *pp* **torn** [tɔːˈ, tɔːn]) *vt* strappare // *vi* strapparsi; **in ~s** in lacrime; **to burst into ~s** scoppiare in lacrime; **to ~ along** *vi* (*rush*) correre all'impazzata; ~**ful** *a* piangente, lacrimoso(a); ~ **gas** *n* gas *m* lacrimogeno.
tearoom [ˈtiːruːm] *n* sala da tè.
tease [tiːz] *vt* canzonare; (*unkindly*) tormentare.
tea set [ˈtiːsɛt] *n* servizio da tè.
teaspoon [ˈtiːspuːn] *n* cucchiaino da tè; (*also:* ~**ful:** *as measurement*) cucchiaino.
tea strainer [ˈtiːstreɪnəˈ] *n* colino da tè.
teat [tiːt] *n* capezzolo.
teatime [ˈtiːtaɪm] *n* l'ora del tè.
tea towel [ˈtiːtauəl] *n* strofinaccio (per i piatti).
technical [ˈtɛknɪkl] *a* tecnico(a); ~**ity** [-ˈkælɪtɪ] *n* tecnicità; (*detail*) dettaglio tecnico.
technician [tɛkˈnɪʃən] *n* tecnico/a.
technique [tɛkˈniːk] *n* tecnica.
technological [tɛknəˈlɔdʒɪkl] *a* tecnologico(a).
technology [tɛkˈnɔlədʒɪ] *n* tecnologia.
teddy (bear) [ˈtɛdɪ(bɛəˈ)] *n* orsacchiotto.
tedious [ˈtiːdɪəs] *a* noioso(a), tedioso(a).
tedium [ˈtiːdɪəm] *n* noia, tedio.
tee [tiː] *n* (*GOLF*) tee *m inv*.
teem [tiːm] *vi* abbondare, brulicare; **to ~ with** brulicare di; **it is ~ing (with rain)** piove a dirotto.
teenage [ˈtiːneɪdʒ] *a* (*fashions etc*) per giovani, per adolescenti; ~**r** *n* adolescente *m/f*.
teens [tiːnz] *npl*: **to be in one's ~** essere adolescente.
tee-shirt [ˈtiːʃɔːt] *n* = **T-shirt**.
teeter [ˈtiːtəˈ] *vi* barcollare, vacillare.
teeth [tiːθ] *npl* of **tooth**.
teethe [tiːð] *vi* mettere i denti.
teething [ˈtiːðɪŋ] *a*: ~ **ring** *n* dentaruolo; ~ **troubles** *npl* (*fig*) difficoltà *fpl* iniziali.
teetotal [ˈtiːˈtəutl] *a* astemio(a).
telecommunications [ˈtɛlɪkəmjuːnɪˈkeɪʃənz] *n* telecomunicazioni *fpl*.
telegram [ˈtɛlɪgræm] *n* telegramma *m*.
telegraph [ˈtɛlɪgrɑːf] *n* telegrafo; ~**ic** [-ˈgræfɪk] *a* telegrafico(a); ~ **pole** *n* palo del telegrafo.
telepathy [təˈlɛpəθɪ] *n* telepatia.
telephone [ˈtɛlɪfəun] *n* telefono // *vt* (*person*) telefonare a; (*message*) telefonare; ~ **booth**, ~ **box** *n* cabina telefonica; ~ **call** *n* telefonata; ~ **directory** *n* elenco telefonico; ~ **exchange** *n* centralino telefonico; ~ **number** *n* numero di telefono;

telephonist [tə'lefənist] n telefonista m/f.
telephoto ['tɛlı'fəutəu] a: ~ **lens** n teleobiettivo.
teleprinter ['tɛlıprıntə*] n telescrivente f.
telescope ['tɛlıskəup] n telescopio // vt incastrare a cannocchiale.
televise ['tɛlıvaız] vt teletrasmettere.
television ['tɛlıvıʒən] n televisione f; ~ **programme** n programma m televisivo; ~ **set** n televisore m.
tell, pt, pp **told** [tɛl, təuld] vt dire; (relate: story) raccontare; (distinguish): to ~ **sth from** distinguere qc da // vi (have effect) farsi sentire, avere effetto; to ~ **sb to do** dire a qd di fare; to ~ **on** vt fus (inform against) denunciare; to ~ **off** vt rimproverare, sgridare; ~**er** n (in bank) cassiere/a; ~**ing** a (remark, detail) rivelatore(trice); ~**tale** a (sign) significativo(a) // n malalingua, pettegolo/a.
telly ['tɛlı] n (col: abbr of **television**) tivù f inv.
temerity [tə'mɛrıtı] n temerarietà.
temp [tɛmp] n (abbr of **temporary**) segretaria temporanea.
temper ['tɛmpə*] n (nature) carattere m; (mood) umore m; (fit of anger) collera // vt (moderate) temperare, moderare; **to be in a** ~ essere in collera; **to lose one's** ~ andare in collera.
temperament ['tɛmprəmənt] n (nature) temperamento; ~**al** [-'mɛntl] a capriccioso(a).
temperance ['tɛmpərns] n moderazione f; (in drinking) temperanza nel bere.
temperate ['tɛmprət] a moderato(a); (climate) temperato(a).
temperature ['tɛmprətʃə*] n temperatura; **to have** or **run a** ~ avere la febbre.
tempered ['tɛmpəd] a (steel) temprato(a).
tempest ['tɛmpıst] n tempesta.
tempi ['tɛmpi:] npl of **tempo**.
template ['tɛmplıt] n sagoma.
temple ['tɛmpl] n (building) tempio; (ANAT) tempia.
tempo, ~**s** or **tempi** ['tɛmpəu, 'tɛmpi:] n tempo; (fig: of life etc) ritmo.
temporal ['tɛmpərl] a temporale.
temporary ['tɛmpərərı] a temporaneo(a); (job, worker) avventizio(a), temporaneo(a); ~ **secretary** n segretaria temporanea.
tempt [tɛmpt] vt tentare; **to** ~ **sb into doing** indurre qd a fare; ~**ation** [-'teıʃən] n tentazione f; ~**ing** a allettante, seducente.
ten [tɛn] num dieci.
tenacious [tə'neıʃəs] a tenace.
tenacity [tə'næsıtı] n tenacia.
tenancy ['tɛnənsı] n affitto; condizione f di inquilino.
tenant ['tɛnənt] n inquilino/a.
tend [tɛnd] vt badare a, occuparsi di // vi: **to** ~ **to do** tendere a fare; (colour): **to** ~ **to** tendere a.
tendency ['tɛndənsı] n tendenza.

tender ['tɛndə*] a tenero(a); (delicate) fragile; (sore) dolorante; (affectionate) affettuoso(a) // n (COMM: offer) offerta; (money): **legal** ~ valuta (a corso legale) // vt offrire; ~**ize** vt (CULIN) far intenerire.
tendon ['tɛndən] n tendine m.
tenement ['tɛnəmənt] n casamento.
tenet ['tɛnət] n principio.
tennis ['tɛnıs] n tennis m; ~ **ball** n palla da tennis; ~ **court** n campo da tennis; ~ **racket** n racchetta da tennis.
tenor ['tɛnə*] n (MUS, of speech etc) tenore m.
tense [tɛns] a teso(a) // n (LING) tempo.
tension ['tɛnʃən] n tensione f.
tent [tɛnt] n tenda.
tentacle ['tɛntəkl] n tentacolo.
tentative ['tɛntətıv] a esitante, incerto(a); (conclusion) provvisorio(a).
tenterhooks ['tɛntəhuks] npl: **on** ~ sulle spine.
tenth [tɛnθ] num decimo(a).
tent: ~ **peg** n picchetto da tenda; ~ **pole** n palo da tenda, montante m.
tenuous ['tɛnjuəs] a tenue.
tenure ['tɛnjuə*] n (of property) possesso; (of job) permanenza; titolarità.
tepid ['tɛpıd] a tiepido(a).
term [tə:m] n (limit) termine m; (word) vocabolo, termine; (SCOL) trimestre m; (LAW) sessione f // vt chiamare, definire; ~**s** npl (conditions) condizioni fpl; (COMM) prezzi mpl, tariffe fpl; ~ **of imprisonment** periodo di prigionia; **in the short/long** ~ a breve/lunga scadenza; **to be on good** ~**s with** essere in buoni rapporti con; **to come to** ~**s with** (person) arrivare a un accordo con; (problem) affrontare.
terminal ['tə:mınl] a finale, terminale; (disease) nella fase terminale // n (ELEC) morsetto; (for oil, ore etc) terminal m inv; (also: **air** ~) aerostazione f; (also: **coach** ~) capolinea m.
terminate ['tə:mıneıt] vt mettere fine a // vi: **to** ~ **in** finire in or con.
terminology [tə:mı'nɔlədʒı] n terminologia.
terminus, pl **termini** ['tə:mınəs, 'tə:mınaı] n (for buses) capolinea m; (for trains) stazione f terminale.
termite ['tə:maıt] n termite f.
terrace ['tɛrəs] n terrazza; (row of houses) fila di case (unite); **the** ~**s** (SPORT) le gradinate; ~**d** a (garden) a terrazze.
terrain [tɛ'reın] n terreno.
terrible ['tɛrıbl] a terribile; (weather) bruttissimo(a); (work) orribile; **terribly** ad terribilmente; (very badly) spaventosamente male.
terrier ['tɛrıə*] n terrier m inv.
terrific [tə'rıfık] a incredibile, fantastico(a); (wonderful) formidabile, eccezionale.
terrify ['tɛrıfaı] vt terrorizzare.
territory ['tɛrıtərı] n territorio.

terror ['tɛrə°] n terrore m; ~**ism** n terrorismo; ~**ist** n terrorista m/f; ~**ize** vt terrorizzare.

terse [tɜːs] a (style) conciso(a); (reply) laconico(a).

test [tɛst] n (trial, check, of courage etc) prova; (: of goods in factory) controllo, collaudo; (MED) esame m; (CHEM) analisi f inv; (exam: of intelligence etc) test m inv; (: in school) saggio; (also: **driving** ~) esame m di guida // vt provare; controllare, collaudare; esaminare; analizzare; saggiare; sottoporre ad esame.

testament ['tɛstəmənt] n testamento; **the Old/New T~** il Vecchio/Nuovo testamento.

test: ~ **case** n (LAW, fig) caso da annali or che farà testo; ~ **flight** n volo di prova.

testicle ['tɛstɪkl] n testicolo.

testify ['tɛstɪfaɪ] vi (LAW) testimoniare, deporre.

testimonial [tɛstɪ'məunɪəl] n (reference) benservito; (gift) testimonianza di stima.

testimony ['tɛstɪmənɪ] n (LAW) testimonianza, deposizione f.

test: ~ **match** n (CRICKET, RUGBY) partita internazionale; ~ **paper** n (SCOL) interrogazione f scritta; ~ **pilot** n pilota m collaudatore; ~ **tube** n provetta.

testy ['tɛstɪ] a irritabile.

tetanus ['tɛtənəs] n tetano.

tether ['tɛðə°] vt legare, impastoiare // n: **at the end of one's** ~ al limite (della pazienza).

text [tɛkst] n testo; ~**book** n libro di testo.

textile ['tɛkstaɪl] n tessile m.

texture ['tɛkstʃə°] n tessitura; (of skin, paper etc) struttura.

Thai [taɪ] a tailandese // n tailandese m/f; (LING) tailandese m; ~**land** n Tailandia.

Thames [tɛmz] n: **the** ~ il Tamigi.

than [ðæn, ðən] cj che; (with numerals, pronouns, proper names): **more** ~ 10/me/Maria più di 10/me/Maria; **you know her better** ~ **I do** la conosce meglio di me or di quanto non la conosca io; **she has more apples** ~ **pears** ha più mele che pere.

thank [θæŋk] vt ringraziare; ~ **you (very much)** grazie (tante); ~**s** npl ringraziamenti mpl, grazie fpl // excl grazie!; ~**s to** prep grazie a; ~**ful** a: ~**ful (for)** riconoscente (per); ~**less** a ingrato(a); **T~sgiving (Day)** n giorno del ringraziamento.

that [ðæt, ðət] cj che // det quel (quell', quello) m; quella(quell') f // pronoun ciò; (the one, not 'this one') quello(a); (relative) che; prep + il(la) quale; (with time): **on the day** ~ **he came** il giorno in cui or quando venne // ad: ~ **high** così alto; alto così; ~ **one** quello(a) (là); **what's** ~? cos'è?; **who's** ~? chi è?; **is** ~ **you?** sei tu?; ~**'s what he said** questo è or ecco quello che ha detto; ~ **is...** cioè è..., vale a dire...; **I can't work** ~ **much** non posso lavorare così tanto.

thatched [θætʃt] a (roof) di paglia; ~

cottage n cottage m inv col tetto di paglia.

thaw [θɔː] n disgelo // vi (ice) sciogliersi; (food) scongelarsi // vt (food) (fare) scongelare; **it's** ~**ing** (weather) sta sgelando.

the [ðiː, ðə] det il(lo, l') m; la(l') f; i(gli) mpl; le fpl.

theatre ['θɪətə°] n teatro; ~-**goer** n frequentatore/trice di teatri.

theatrical [θɪ'ætrɪkl] a teatrale.

theft [θɛft] n furto.

their [ðɛə°] a il(la) loro, pl i(le) loro; ~**s** pronoun il(la) loro, pl i(le) loro; **it is** ~**s** è loro; **a friend of** ~**s** un loro amico.

them [ðɛm, ðəm] pronoun (direct) li(le); (indirect) gli, loro (after vb); (stressed, after prep: people) loro; (: people, things) essi(e); **I see** ~ li vedo; **give** ~ **the book** dà loro or dagli il libro.

theme [θiːm] n tema m; ~ **song/tune** n tema musicale.

themselves [ðəm'sɛlvz] pl pronoun (reflexive) si; (emphatic) loro stessi(e); (after prep) se stessi(e); **between** ~ tra (di) loro.

then [ðɛn] ad (at that time) allora; (next) poi, dopo; (and also) e poi // cj (therefore) perciò, dunque, quindi // a: **the** ~ **president** il presidente di allora; **from** ~ **on** da allora in poi.

theologian [θɪə'ləudʒən] n teologo/a.

theology [θɪ'ɔlədʒɪ] n teologia.

theorem ['θɪərəm] n teorema m.

theoretical [θɪə'rɛtɪkl] a teorico(a).

theorize ['θɪəraɪz] vi teorizzare.

theory ['θɪərɪ] n teoria.

therapeutic(al) [θɛrə'pjuːtɪk(l)] a terapeutico(a).

therapy ['θɛrəpɪ] n terapia.

there [ðɛə°] ad là, lì; ~, ~! su, su!; **it's** ~ è lì; **he went** ~ ci è andato; ~ **is** c'è; ~ **are** ci sono; ~ **he is** eccolo; ~ **has been** c'è stato; **on/in** ~ lassù/lì dentro; **to go** ~ **and back** andarci e ritornare; ~**abouts** ad (place) nei pressi, da quelle parti; (amount) giù di lì, all'incirca; ~**after** ad da allora in poi; ~**fore** ad perciò, quindi.

thermal ['θɜːml] a termico(a).

thermometer [θə'mɔmɪtə°] n termometro.

thermonuclear ['θɜːməu'njuːklɪə°] a termonucleare.

Thermos ['θɜːməs] n ® (also: ~ **flask**) thermos m inv ®.

thermostat ['θɜːməstæt] n termostato.

thesaurus [θɪ'sɔːrəs] n dizionario dei sinonimi.

these [ðiːz] pl pronoun, det questi(e).

thesis, pl theses ['θiːsɪs, 'θiːsiːz] n tesi f inv.

they [ðeɪ] pl pronoun essi(esse); (people only) loro; ~ **say that...** (it is said that) si dice che...

thick [θɪk] a spesso(a); (crowd) compatto(a); (stupid) ottuso(a), lento(a) // n: **in the** ~ **of** nel folto di; **it's 20 cm** ~ ha uno spessore di 20 cm; ~**en** vi spessire // vt (sauce etc) ispessire, rendere più denso(a); ~ness n spessore m; ~set a tarchiato(a), tozzo(a); ~skinned a (fig) insensibile.

thief, thieves [θi:f, θi:vz] n ladro/a.

thigh [θaɪ] n coscia; ~bone n femore m.

thimble ['θɪmbl] n ditale m.

thin [θɪn] a sottile; (person) magro(a); (soup) brodoso(a); (hair, crowd) rado(a); (fog) leggero(a) // vt (hair) sfoltire; to ~ (down) (sauce, paint) diluire.

thing [θɪŋ] n cosa; (object) oggetto; (contraption) aggeggio; ~s npl (belongings) cose fpl; for one ~ tanto per cominciare; the best ~ would be to la cosa migliore sarebbe di; how are ~s? come va?

think, pt, pp thought [θɪŋk, θɔ:t] vi pensare, riflettere // vt pensare, credere; (imagine) immaginare; to ~ of pensare a; what did you ~ of them? cosa ne hai pensato?; to ~ about sth/sb pensare a qc/qd; I'll ~ about it ci penserò; to ~ of doing something pensare di fare; I ~ so penso di sì; to ~ well of avere una buona opinione di; to ~ over vt riflettere su; to ~ up vt ideare.

third [θə:d] num terzo(a) // n terzo/a; (fraction) terzo, terza parte f; (SCOL: degree) ≈ laurea col minimo dei voti; ~ly ad in terzo luogo; ~ party insurance n assicurazione f contro terzi; ~rate a di qualità scadente; the T~ World n il Terzo Mondo.

thirst [θə:st] n sete f; ~y a (person) assetato(a), che ha sete.

thirteen ['θə:'ti:n] num tredici.

thirty ['θə:tɪ] num trenta.

this [ðɪs] det, pronoun questo(a); ~ one questo(a) (qui); ~ is what he said questo è quello or ciò che ha detto.

thistle ['θɪsl] n cardo.

thong [θɒŋ] n cinghia.

thorn [θɔ:n] n spina; ~y a spinoso(a).

thorough ['θʌrə] a (search) minuzioso(a); (knowledge, research) approfondito(a), profondo(a); (cleaning) a fondo; ~bred a (horse) purosangue m/f inv; ~fare n strada transitabile; 'no ~fare' 'divieto di transito'; ~ly ad minuziosamente; in profondità; a fondo; he ~ly agreed fu completamente d'accordo.

those [ðəuz] pl pronoun quelli(e) // pl det quei(quegli) mpl; quelle fpl.

though [ðəu] cj benché, sebbene // ad comunque.

thought [θɔ:t] pt, pp of think // n pensiero; (opinion) opinione f; (intention) intenzione f; ~ful a pensieroso(a), pensoso(a); ponderato(a); (considerate) premuroso(a); ~less a irriguardoso(a).

thousand ['θauzənd] num mille; ~th num millesimo(a); one ~ mille; ~s of migliaia di.

thrash [θræʃ] vt picchiare; bastonare; (defeat) battere; to ~ about vi dibattersi; to ~ out vt dibattere, sviscerare.

thread [θrɛd] n filo; (of screw) filetto // vt

(needle) infilare; to ~ one's way between infilarsi tra; ~bare a consumato(a), logoro(a).

threat [θrɛt] n minaccia; ~en vi (storm) minacciare // vt: to ~en sb with sth/to do minacciare qd con qc/di fare.

three [θri:] num tre; ~-dimensional a tridimensionale; (film) stereoscopico(a); ~-piece suit n completo (con gilè); ~-piece suite n salotto comprendente un divano e due poltrone; ~-ply a (wool) a tre strati; (wool) a tre fili; ~-wheeler n (car) veicolo a tre ruote.

thresh [θrɛʃ] vt (AGR) trebbiare; ~ing machine n trebbiatrice f.

threshold ['θrɛʃhəuld] n soglia.

threw [θru:] pt of throw.

thrifty ['θrɪftɪ] a economico(a).

thrill [θrɪl] n brivido // vi eccitarsi, tremare // vt (audience) elettrizzare; to be ~ed (with gift etc) essere commosso(a); ~er n film m inv (or dramma m or libro) del brivido.

thrive, pt thrived, throve pp thrived, thriven [θraɪv, θrəuv, 'θrɪvn] vi crescere or svilupparsi bene; (business) prosperare; he ~s on it gli fa bene, ne gode.

throat [θrəut] n gola; to have a sore ~ avere (un or il) mal di gola.

throb [θrɒb] n (of heart) battito; (of engine) vibrazione f; (of pain) fitta // vi (heart) palpitare; (engine) vibrare; (with pain) pulsare.

throes [θrəuz] npl: in the ~ of alle prese con; in preda a; in the ~ of death in agonia.

thrombosis [θrɒm'bəusɪs] n trombosi f.

throne [θrəun] n trono.

throttle ['θrɒtl] n (AUT) valvola a farfalla // vt strangolare.

through [θru:] prep attraverso; (time) per, durante; (by means of) per mezzo di; (owing to) a causa di // a (ticket, train, passage) diretto(a) // ad attraverso; to put sb ~ to sb (TEL) passare qd a qd; to be ~ (TEL) ottenere la comunicazione; (have finished) avere finito; 'no ~ way' 'strada senza sbocco'; ~out prep (place) dappertutto in; (time) per or durante tutto(a) // ad dappertutto; sempre.

throve [θrəuv] pt of thrive.

throw [θrəu] n tiro, getto; (SPORT) lancio // vt (pt threw, pp thrown [θru:, θrəun]) tirare, gettare; (SPORT) lanciare; (rider) disarcionare; (fig) confondere; (pottery) formare al tornio; to ~ a party dare una festa; to ~ away vt gettare or buttare via; to ~ off vt sbarazzarsi di; to ~ out vt buttare fuori; (reject) respingere; to ~ up vi vomitare; ~away a da buttare; ~-in n (SPORT) rimessa in gioco.

thru [θru:] prep, a, ad (US) = through.

thrush [θrʌʃ] n tordo.

thrust [θrʌst] n (TECH) spinta // vt (pt, pp thrust) spingere con forza; (push in) conficcare.

thud [θʌd] n tonfo.

thug [θʌg] n delinquente m.

thumb [θʌm] n (ANAT) pollice m // vt (book) sfogliare; **to ~ a lift** fare l'autostop; **~ index** n indice m a rubrica; **~tack** n (US) puntina da disegno.

thump [θʌmp] n colpo forte; (sound) tonfo // vt battere su // vi picchiare, battere.

thunder ['θʌndə*] n tuono // vi tuonare; (train etc): **to ~ past** passare con un rombo; **~clap** n rombo di tuono; **~ous** a fragoroso(a); **~storm** n temporale m; **~y** a temporalesco(a).

Thursday ['θə:zdɪ] n giovedì m inv.

thus [ðʌs] ad così.

thwart [θwɔ:t] vt contrastare.

thyme [taɪm] n timo.

thyroid ['θaɪrɔɪd] n tiroide f.

tiara [tɪ'ɑ:rə] n (woman's) diadema m.

Tiber ['taɪbə*] n: **the ~** il Tevere.

tic [tɪk] a tic m inv.

tick [tɪk] n (sound: of clock) tic tac m inv; (mark) segno; spunta; (ZOOL) zecca; (col): **in a ~** in un attimo // vi fare tic tac // vt spuntare; **to ~ off** vt spuntare; (person) sgridare.

ticket ['tɪkɪt] n biglietto; (in shop: on goods) etichetta; (: from cash register) scontrino; (for library) scheda; **~ collector** n bigliettaio; **~ holder** n persona munita di biglietto; **~ office** n biglietteria.

tickle ['tɪkl] n solletico // vt fare il solletico a, solleticare; (fig) stuzzicare; piacere a; far ridere; **ticklish** a che soffre il solletico.

tidal ['taɪdl] a di marea.

tiddlywinks ['tɪdlɪwɪŋks] n gioco della pulce.

tide [taɪd] n marea; (fig: of events) corso.

tidy ['taɪdɪ] a (room) ordinato(a), lindo(a); (dress, work) curato(a), in ordine; (person) ordinato(a) // vt (also: ~ up) riordinare, mettere in ordine; **to ~ o.s. up** rassettarsi.

tie [taɪ] n (string etc) legaccio; (also: **neck~**) cravatta; (fig: link) legame m; (SPORT: draw) pareggio // vt (parcel) legare; (ribbon) annodare // vi (SPORT) pareggiare; **'black/white ~'** 'smoking/abito di rigore'; **to ~ sth in a bow** annodare qc; **to ~ a knot in sth** fare un nodo a qc; **to ~ down** vt fissare con una corda; (fig): **to ~ sb down to** costringere qd a accettare; **to ~ up** vt (parcel, dog) legare; (boat) ormeggiare; (arrangements) concludere; **to be ~d up** (busy) essere occupato or preso.

tier [tɪə*] n fila; (of cake) piano, strato.

tiff [tɪf] n battibecco.

tiger ['taɪgə*] n tigre f.

tight [taɪt] a (rope) teso(a), tirato(a); (clothes) stretto(a); (budget, programme, bend) stretto(a); (control) severo(a), fermo(a); (col: drunk) sbronzo(a) // ad (squeeze) fortemente; (shut) ermeticamente; **~s** npl collant m inv; **~en** vt (rope) tendere; (screw) stringere; (control) rinforzare // vi tenderi; stringersi; **~-fisted** a avaro(a); **~ly** ad

(grasp) bene, saldamente; **~-rope** n corda (da acrobata).

tile [taɪl] n (on roof) tegola; (on wall or floor) piastrella, mattonella.

till [tɪl] n registratore m di cassa // vt (land) coltivare // prep, cj = **until**.

tiller ['tɪlə*] n (NAUT) barra del timone.

tilt [tɪlt] vt inclinare, far pendere // vi inclinarsi, pendere.

timber ['tɪmbə*] n (material) legname m; (trees) alberi mpl da legname.

time [taɪm] n tempo; (epoch: often pl) epoca, tempo; (by clock) ora; (moment) momento; (occasion, also MATH) volta; (MUS) tempo // vt (race) cronometrare; (programme) calcolare la durata di; (remark etc) dire (or fare) al momento giusto; **a long ~** molto tempo; **for the ~ being** per il momento; **from ~ to ~** ogni tanto; **in ~** (soon enough) in tempo; (after some time) col tempo; (MUS) a tempo; **in a week's ~** fra una settimana; **on ~** puntualmente; **5 ~s 5** 5 volte or per 5; **what ~ is it?** che ora è?, che ore sono?; **to have a good ~** divertirsi; **~'s up!** è (l')ora!; **~ bomb** n bomba a orologeria; **~keeper** n (SPORT) cronometrista m/f; **~ lag** n intervallo, ritardo; (in travel) differenza di fuso orario; **~less** a eterno(a); **~ limit** n limite m di tempo; **~ly** a opportuno(a); **~ off** n tempo libero; **~r** n (in kitchen) contaminuti m inv; **~-saving** a che fa risparmiare tempo; **~ switch** n interruttore m a tempo; **~table** n orario; **~ zone** n fuso orario.

timid ['tɪmɪd] a timido(a); (easily scared) pauroso(a).

timing ['taɪmɪŋ] n sincronizzazione f; (fig) scelta del momento opportuno, tempismo; (SPORT) cronometraggio.

timpani ['tɪmpənɪ] npl timpani mpl.

tin [tɪn] n stagno; (also: ~ **plate**) latta; (can) barattolo (di latta), lattina, scatola; (for baking) teglia; **~ foil** n stagnola.

tinge [tɪndʒ] n sfumatura // vt: **~d with** tinto/a di.

tingle ['tɪŋgl] vi pizzicare.

tinker ['tɪŋkə*] n calderaio ambulante; (gipsy) zingaro/a; **to ~ with** vt fus armeggiare intorno a; cercare di riparare.

tinkle ['tɪŋkl] vi tintinnare.

tinned [tɪnd] a (food) in scatola.

tinny ['tɪnɪ] a metallico(a).

tin opener ['tɪnəupnə*] n apriscatole m inv.

tinsel ['tɪnsl] n decorazioni fpl natalizie (argentate).

tint [tɪnt] n tinta.

tiny ['taɪnɪ] a minuscolo(a).

tip [tɪp] n (end) punta; (protective: on umbrella etc) puntale m; (gratuity) mancia; (for coal) discarica; (for rubbish) immondezzaio; (advice) suggerimento // vt (waiter) dare la mancia a; (tilt) inclinare; (overturn: also: ~ **over**) capovolgere; (empty: also: ~ **out**) scaricare; **~-off** n (hint) soffiata; **~ped** a (cigarette) col

filtro; **steel-~ped** con la punta d'acciaio.
tipple ['tɪpl] *vi* sbevazzare // *n*: **to have a ~** prendere un bicchierino.
tipsy ['tɪpsɪ] *a* brillo(a).
tiptoe ['tɪptəʊ] *n*: **on ~** in punta di piedi.
tiptop ['tɪp'tɒp] *a*: **in ~ condition** in ottime condizioni.
tire ['taɪə*] *vt* stancare // *vi* stancarsi; **~d** *a* stanco(a); **to be ~d of** essere stanco or stufo di; **~less** *a* instancabile; **~some** *a* noioso(a); **tiring** *a* faticoso(a).
tissue ['tɪʃuː] *n* tessuto; (*paper handkerchief*) fazzoletto di carta; **~ paper** *n* carta velina.
tit [tɪt] *n* (*bird*) cinciallegra; **to give ~ for tat** rendere pan per focaccia.
titbit ['tɪtbɪt] *n* (*food*) leccornia; (*news*) notizia ghiotta.
titillate ['tɪtɪleɪt] *vt* titillare.
titivate ['tɪtɪveɪt] *vt* agghindare.
title ['taɪtl] *n* titolo; **~ deed** *n* (*LAW*) titolo di proprietà; **~ role** *n* ruolo or parte *f* principale.
titter ['tɪtə*] *vi* ridere scioccamente.
tittle-tattle ['tɪtltætl] *n* chiacchiere *fpl*, pettegolezzi *mpl*.
tizzy ['tɪzɪ] *n*: **to be in a ~** essere in agitazione.
to [tuː, tə] *prep* a; (*towards*) verso; **give it ~ me** dammelo; **the key ~ the front door** la chiave della porta d'ingresso; **the main thing is ~ ...** l'importante è di...; **to go ~ France/Portugal** andare in Francia/Portogallo; **I went ~ Claudia's** sono andato da Claudia; **to go ~ town/school** andare in città/a scuola; **to pull/push the door ~** tirare/spingere la porta; **to go ~ and fro** andare e tornare.
toad [təʊd] *n* rospo; **~stool** *n* fungo (velenoso); **~y** *vi* adulare.
toast [təʊst] *n* (*CULIN*) toast *m*, pane *m* abbrustolito; (*drink, speech*) brindisi *m inv* // *vt* (*CULIN*) abbrustolire; (*drink to*) brindare a; **a piece or slice of ~** una fetta di pane abbrustolito; **~er** *n* tostapane *m inv*; **~master** *n* direttore *m* dei brindisi.
tobacco [tə'bækəʊ] *n* tabacco; **~nist** *n* tabaccaio/a; **~nist's (shop)** *n* tabaccheria.
toboggan [tə'bɒgən] *n* toboga *m inv*; (*child's*) slitta.
today [tə'deɪ] *ad,n* (*also fig*) oggi (*m*).
toddler ['tɒdlə*] *n* bambino/a che impara a camminare.
toddy ['tɒdɪ] *n* grog *m inv*.
to-do [tə'duː] *n* (*fuss*) storie *fpl*.
toe [təʊ] *n* dito del piede; (*of shoe*) punta; **to ~ the line** (*fig*) stare in riga, conformarsi; **~nail** *n* unghia del piede.
toffee ['tɒfɪ] *n* caramella.
toga ['təʊgə] *n* toga.
together [tə'geðə*] *ad* insieme; (*at same time*) allo stesso tempo; **~ with** *prep* insieme a; **~ness** *n* solidarietà; intimità.
toil [tɔɪl] *n* travaglio, fatica // *vi* affannarsi; sgobbare.
toilet ['tɔɪlət] *n* (*lavatory*) gabinetto // *cpd*

(*bag, soap etc*) da toletta; **~ bowl** *n* vaso or tazza del gabinetto; **~ paper** *n* carta igienica; **~ries** *npl* articoli *mpl* da toletta; **~ roll** *n* rotolo di carta igienica; **~ water** *n* colonia.
token ['təʊkən] *n* (*sign*) segno; (*voucher*) buono; **book/record ~** *n* buono-libro/disco.
told [təʊld] *pt, pp of* **tell**.
tolerable ['tɒlərəbl] *a* (*bearable*) tollerabile; (*fairly good*) passabile.
tolerance ['tɒlərns] *n* (*also: TECH*) tolleranza.
tolerant ['tɒlərnt] *a*: **~ (of)** tollerante (nei confronti di).
tolerate ['tɒləreɪt] *vt* sopportare; (*MED, TECH*) tollerare; **toleration** [-'reɪʃən] *n* tolleranza.
toll [təʊl] *n* (*tax, charge*) pedaggio // *vi* (*bell*) suonare; **the accident ~ on the roads** il numero delle vittime della strada; **~bridge** *n* ponte *m* a pedaggio.
tomato, **~es** [tə'mɑːtəʊ] *n* pomodoro.
tomb [tuːm] *n* tomba.
tombola [tɒm'bəʊlə] *n* tombola.
tomboy ['tɒmbɔɪ] *n* maschiaccio.
tombstone ['tuːmstəʊn] *n* pietra tombale.
tomcat ['tɒmkæt] *n* gatto.
tomorrow [tə'mɒrəʊ] *ad,n* (*also fig*) domani (*m inv*); **the day after ~** dopodomani; **~ morning** domani mattina.
ton [tʌn] *n* tonnellata (*=1016 kg; 20 cwt*); (*NAUT: also: register ~*) tonnellata di stazza (*=2.83 cu.m; 100 cu. ft*); **~s of** (*col*) un mucchio or sacco di.
tone [təʊn] *n* tono // *vi* intonarsi; **to ~ down** *vt* (*colour, criticism, sound*) attenuare; **to ~ up** *vt* (*muscles*) tonificare; **~-deaf** *a* che non ha orecchio (musicale).
tongs [tɒŋz] *npl* tenaglie *fpl*; (*for coal*) molle *fpl*; (*for hair*) arricciacapelli *m inv*.
tongue [tʌŋ] *n* lingua; **~ in cheek** *ad* ironicamente; **~-tied** *a* (*fig*) muto(a); **~-twister** *n* scioglilingua *m inv*.
tonic ['tɒnɪk] *n* (*MED*) tonico; (*MUS*) nota tonica; (*also: ~ water*) acqua tonica.
tonight [tə'naɪt] *ad* stanotte; (*this evening*) stasera // *n* questa notte; questa sera.
tonnage ['tʌnɪdʒ] *n* (*NAUT*) tonnellaggio, stazza.
tonne [tʌn] *n* (*metric ton*) tonnellata.
tonsil ['tɒnsl] *n* tonsilla; **~litis** [-'laɪtɪs] *n* tonsillite *f*.
too [tuː] *ad* (*excessively*) troppo; (*also*) anche; **~ much** *ad* troppo // *det* troppo(a); **~ many** *det* troppi(e); **~ bad!** tanto peggio!, peggio così!
took [tʊk] *pt of* **take**.
tool [tuːl] *n* utensile *m*, attrezzo // *vt* lavorare con un attrezzo; **~ box/kit** *n* cassetta *f* portautensili/attrezzi *inv*.
toot [tuːt] *vi* suonare; (*with car-horn*) suonare il clacson.
tooth, *pl* **teeth** [tuːθ, tiːθ] *n* (*ANAT, TECH*) dente *m*; **~ache** *n* mal *m* di denti; **~brush** *n* spazzolino da denti; **~paste** *n*

dentifricio (in pasta); ~**pick** *n* stuzzicadenti *m inv.*

top [tɔp] *n* (*of mountain, page, ladder*) cima; (*of box, cupboard, table*) sopra *m inv*, parte *f* superiore; (*lid: of box, jar*) coperchio; (: *of bottle*) tappo; (*toy*) trottola // *a* più alto(a); (*in rank*) primo(a); (*best*) migliore // *vt* (*exceed*) superare; (*be first in*) essere in testa a; **on** ~ **of** sopra, in cima a; (*in addition to*) oltre a; **from** ~ **to toe** dalla testa ai piedi; **to** ~ **up** *vt* riempire; ~ **floor** *n* ultimo piano; ~ **hat** *n* cilindro; ~**heavy** *a* (*object*) con la parte superiore troppo pesante.

topic ['tɔpɪk] *n* argomento; ~**al** *a* d'attualità.

top: ~**less** *a* (*bather etc*) col seno scoperto; ~**less swimsuit** *n* topless *m inv*; ~**level** *a* (*talks*) ad alto livello; ~**most** *a* il(la) più alto(a).

topple ['tɔpl] *vt* rovesciare, far cadere // *vi* cadere; traballare.

topsy-turvy ['tɔpsɪ'tə:vɪ] *a,ad* sottosopra.

torch [tɔ:tʃ] *n* torcia; (*electric*) lampadina tascabile.

tore [tɔ:*] *pt of* tear.

torment *n* ['tɔ:mɛnt] tormento // *vt* [tɔ:'mɛnt] tormentare; (*fig: annoy*) infastidire.

torn [tɔ:n] *pp of* tear // *a*: ~ **between** (*fig*) combattuto(a) tra.

tornado, ~**es** [tɔ:'neɪdəu] *n* tornado.

torpedo, ~**es** [tɔ:'pi:dəu] *n* siluro.

torpor ['tɔ:pə*] *n* torpore *m.*

torque [tɔ:k] *n* coppia di torsione.

torrent ['tɔrnt] *n* torrente *m*; ~**ial** [-'rɛnʃl] *a* torrenziale.

torso ['tɔ:səu] *n* torso.

tortoise ['tɔ:təs] *n* tartaruga; ~**shell** ['tɔ:təʃɛl] *a* di tartaruga.

tortuous ['tɔ:tjuəs] *a* tortuoso(a).

torture ['tɔ:tʃə*] *n* tortura // *vt* torturare.

Tory ['tɔ:rɪ] *a* dei tories, conservatore(trice) // *n* tory *m inv*, conservatore/trice.

toss [tɔs] *vt* gettare, lanciare; (*pancake*) far saltare; (*head*) scuotere; **to** ~ **a coin** fare a testa o croce; **to** ~ **up for sth** fare a testa o croce per qc; **to** ~ **and turn** (*in bed*) girarsi e rigirarsi.

tot [tɔt] *n* (*drink*) bicchierino; (*child*) bimbo/a.

total ['təutl] *a* totale // *n* totale *m* // *vt* (*add up*) sommare; (*amount to*) ammontare a.

totalitarian [təutælɪ'tɛərɪən] *a* totalitario(a).

totem pole ['təutəmpəul] *n* totem *m inv.*

totter ['tɔtə*] *vi* barcollare.

touch [tʌtʃ] *n* tocco; (*sense*) tatto; (*contact*) contatto; (*FOOTBALL*) fuori gioco *m* // *vt* toccare; **a** ~ **of** (*fig*) un tocco di; un pizzico di; **in** ~ **with** in contatto con; **to get in** ~ **with** mettersi in contatto con; **to lose** ~ (*friends*) perdersi di vista; **to** ~ **on** *vt fus* (*topic*) sfiorare, accennare a; **to** ~ **up** *vt* (*paint*) ritoccare; ~**and-go** *a* incerto(a); **it was** ~**and-go whether**

we did it c'è mancato poco che non lo facessimo; ~**down** *n* atterraggio; (*on sea*) ammaraggio; ~**ed** *a* commosso(a); (*col*) tocco(a), toccato(a); ~**ing** *a* commovente; ~**line** *n* (*SPORT*) linea laterale; ~**y** *a* (*person*) suscettibile.

tough [tʌf] *a* duro(a); (*resistant*) resistente; (*meat*) duro(a), tiglioso(a); ~ **luck!** che disdetta!; peggio per me (*or te etc*)!; ~**en** *vt* indurire, rendere più resistente.

toupee ['tu:peɪ] *n* parrucchino.

tour ['tuə*] *n* viaggio; (*also:* **package** ~) viaggio organizzato *or* tutto compreso; (*of town, museum*) visita; (*by artist*) tournée *f inv* // *vt* visitare; ~**ing** *n* turismo.

tourism ['tuərɪzəm] *n* turismo.

tourist ['tuərɪst] *n* turista *m/f* // *ad* (*travel*) in classe turistica // *cpd* turistico(a); ~ **office** *n* pro loco *f inv.*

tournament ['tuənəmənt] *n* torneo.

tousled ['tauzld] *a* (*hair*) arruffato(a).

tout [taut] *vi*: **to** ~ **for** procacciare, raccogliere; cercare clienti per; **to** ~ **sth (around)** cercare di (ri)vendere qc.

tow [təu] *vt* rimorchiare; **'on** ~**'** (*AUT*) 'veicolo rimorchiato'.

toward(s) [tə'wɔ:d(z)] *prep* verso; (*of attitude*) nei confronti di; (*of purpose*) per.

towel ['tauəl] *n* asciugamano; (*also:* **tea** ~) strofinaccio; ~**ling** *n* (*fabric*) spugna; ~ **rail** *n* portasciugamano.

tower ['tauə*] *n* torre *f*; ~ **block** *n* palazzone *m*; ~**ing** *a* altissimo(a), imponente.

town [taun] *n* città *f inv*; **to go to** ~ andare in città; (*fig*) mettercela tutta; ~ **clerk** *n* segretario comunale; ~ **council** *n* consiglio comunale; ~ **hall** *n* ≈ municipio; ~ **planner** *n* urbanista *m/f*; ~ **planning** *n* urbanistica.

towpath ['təupɑ:θ] *n* alzaia.

towrope ['təurəup] *n* (cavo da) rimorchio.

toxic ['tɔksɪk] *a* tossico(a).

toy [tɔɪ] *n* giocattolo; **to** ~ **with** *vt fus* giocare con; (*idea*) accarezzare, trastullarsi con; ~**shop** *n* negozio di giocattoli.

trace [treɪs] *n* traccia // *vt* (*draw*) tracciare; (*follow*) seguire; (*locate*) rintracciare.

track [træk] *n* (*mark*) traccia; (*on tape, SPORT, path: gen*) pista; (: *of bullet etc*) traiettoria; (: *of suspect, animal*) pista, tracce *fpl*; (*RAIL*) binario, rotaie *fpl* // *vt* seguire le tracce di; **to keep** ~ **of** seguire; **to** ~ **down** *vt* (*prey*) scovare; snidare; (*sth lost*) rintracciare; ~**er dog** *n* cane *m* poliziotto *inv*; ~ **suit** *n* tuta sportiva.

tract [trækt] *n* (*GEO*) tratto, estensione *f*; (*pamphlet*) opuscolo, libretto; **respiratory** ~ (*ANAT*) apparato respiratorio.

tractor ['træktə*] *n* trattore *m.*

trade [treɪd] *n* commercio; (*skill, job*) mestiere *m* // *vi* commerciare; **to** ~ **with/in** commerciare con/in; **to** ~ **in** *vt* (*old car etc*) dare come pagamento parziale; ~**mark** *n* marchio di fabbrica;

~**name** n marca, nome m deposito; ~**r** n commerciante m/f; ~**sman** n (shopkeeper) negoziante m; ~ **union** n sindacato; ~ **unionist** sindacalista m/f; **trading** n commercio; **trading estate** n zona industriale.

tradition [trə'dɪʃən] n tradizione f; ~**s** npl tradizioni, usanze fpl; ~**al** a tradizionale.

traffic ['træfɪk] n traffico // vi: **to** ~ **in** (pej: liquor, drugs) trafficare in; ~ **circle** n (US) isola rotatoria; ~ **jam** n ingorgo (del traffico); ~ **lights** npl semaforo; ~ **warden** n addetto/a al controllo del traffico e del parcheggio.

tragedy ['trædʒədɪ] n tragedia.

tragic ['trædʒɪk] a tragico(a).

trail [treɪl] n (tracks) tracce fpl, pista; (path) sentiero; (of smoke etc) scia // vt trascinare, strascicare; (follow) seguire // vi essere al traino; (dress etc) strusciare; (plant) arrampicarsi; strisciare; **to** ~ **behind** vi essere al traino; ~**er** n (AUT) rimorchio; (US) roulotte f inv; (CINEMA) prossimamente m inv.

train [treɪn] n treno; (of dress) coda, strascico // vt (apprentice, doctor etc) formare; (sportsman) allenare; (dog) addestrare; (memory) esercitare; (point: gun etc): **to** ~ **sth on** puntare qc contro // vi formarsi; allenarsi; **one's** ~ **of thought** il filo dei propri pensieri; ~**ed** a qualificato(a); allenato(a); addestrato(a); ~**ee** [treɪ'niː] n allievo/a; (in trade) apprendista m/f; ~**er** n (SPORT) allenatore/trice; (of dogs etc) addestratore/trice; ~**ing** n formazione f; allenamento; addestramento; **in** ~**ing** (SPORT) in allenamento; (fit) in forma; ~**ing college** n istituto professionale; (for teachers) ≈ istituto magistrale.

traipse [treɪps] vi girovagare, andare a zonzo.

trait [treɪt] n tratto.

traitor ['treɪtə*] n traditore m.

tram [træm] n (also: ~**car**) tram m inv; ~**line** n linea tranviaria.

tramp [træmp] n (person) vagabondo/a // vi camminare con passo pesante // vt (walk through: town, streets) percorrere a piedi.

trample ['træmpl] vt: **to** ~ (**underfoot**) calpestare.

trampoline ['træmpəliːn] n trampolino.

trance [trɑːns] n trance f inv; (MED) catalessi f inv.

tranquil ['træŋkwɪl] a tranquillo(a); ~**lity** n tranquillità; ~**lizer** n (MED) tranquillante m.

transact [træn'zækt] vt (business) trattare; ~**ion** [-'zækʃən] n transazione f; ~**ions** npl (minutes) atti mpl.

transatlantic ['trænzət'læntɪk] a transatlantico(a).

transcend [træn'send] vt trascendere; (excel over) superare.

transcript ['trænskrɪpt] n trascrizione f; ~**ion** [-'skrɪpʃən] n trascrizione f.

transept ['trænsept] n transetto.

transfer n ['trænsfə*] (gen, also SPORT) trasferimento; (POL: of power) passaggio; (picture, design) decalcomania; (: stick-on) autoadesivo // vt [træns'fə:*] trasferire; passare; decalcare; **to** ~ **the charges** (TEL) telefonare con addebito al ricevente; ~**able** [-'fɜːrəbl] a trasferibile.

transform [træns'fɔːm] vt trasformare; ~**ation** [-'meɪʃən] n trasformazione f; ~**er** n (ELEC) trasformatore m.

transfusion [træns'fjuːʒən] n trasfusione f.

transient ['trænzɪənt] a transitorio(a), fugace.

transistor [træn'zɪstə*] n (ELEC) transistor m inv; (also: ~ **radio**) radio f inv a transistor.

transit ['trænzɪt] n: **in** ~ in transito; ~ **lounge** n sala di transito.

transition [træn'zɪʃən] n passaggio, transizione f; ~**al** a di transizione.

transitive ['trænzɪtɪv] a (LING) transitivo(a).

transitory ['trænzɪtərɪ] a transitorio(a).

translate [trænz'leɪt] vt tradurre; **translation** [-'leɪʃən] n traduzione f; (SCOL: as opposed to prose) versione f; **translator** n traduttore/trice.

transmission [trænz'mɪʃən] n trasmissione f.

transmit [trænz'mɪt] vt trasmettere; ~**ter** n trasmettitore m.

transparency [træns'pɛərnsɪ] n (PHOT) diapositiva.

transparent [træns'pærnt] a trasparente.

transplant vt [træns'plɑːnt] trapiantare // n ['trænsplɑːnt] (MED) trapianto.

transport n ['trænspɔːt] trasporto // vt [træns'pɔːt] trasportare; ~**ation** [-'teɪʃən] n (mezzo di) trasporto; (of prisoners) deportazione f; ~ **café** n trattoria per camionisti.

transvestite [trænz'vɛstaɪt] n travestito/a.

trap [træp] n (snare, trick) trappola; (carriage) calesse m // vt prendere in trappola, intrappolare; (immobilize) bloccare; (jam) chiudere, schiacciare; ~ **door** n botola.

trapeze [trə'piːz] n trapezio.

trapper ['træpə*] n cacciatore m di animali da pelliccia.

trappings ['træpɪŋz] npl ornamenti mpl; indoratura, sfarzo.

trash [træʃ] n (pej: goods) ciarpame m; (: nonsense) sciocchezze fpl; ~ **can** n (US) secchio della spazzatura.

trauma ['trɔːmə] n trauma m; ~**tic** [-'mætɪk] a traumatico(a).

travel ['trævl] n viaggio; viaggi mpl; // vi viaggiare; (move) andare, spostarsi // vt (distance) percorrere; ~**ler** n viaggiatore/trice; ~**ler's cheque** n assegno turistico; ~**ling** n viaggi mpl // cpd (bag, clock) da viaggio; (expenses) di viaggio; ~ **sickness** n mal m d'auto (or di mare or d'aria).

travesty ['trævəstɪ] n parodia.

trawler ['trɔ:lə*] n peschereccio (a strascico).

tray [treɪ] n (for carrying) vassoio; (on desk) vaschetta.

treacherous ['trɛtʃərəs] a traditore(trice).

treachery ['trɛtʃərɪ] n tradimento.

treacle ['tri:kl] n melassa.

tread [trɛd] n passo; (sound) rumore m di passi; (of tyre) battistrada m inv // vi (pt **trod**, pp **trodden** [trɔd, 'trɔdn]) camminare; to ~ on vt fus calpestare.

treason ['tri:zn] n tradimento.

treasure ['trɛʒə*] n tesoro // vt (value) tenere in gran conto, apprezzare molto; (store) custodire gelosamente.

treasurer ['trɛʒərə*] n tesoriere/a.

treasury ['trɛʒərɪ] n tesoreria; the T~ (POL) il ministero del tesoro.

treat [tri:t] n regalo // vt trattare; (MED) curare; **it was a** ~ **mi** (or ci etc) ha fatto veramente piacere; **to** ~ **sb to sth** offrire qc a qd.

treatise ['tri:tɪz] n trattato.

treatment ['tri:tmənt] n trattamento.

treaty ['tri:tɪ] n patto, trattato.

treble ['trɛbl] a triplo(a), triplice // n (MUS) soprano m/f // vt triplicare // vi triplicarsi; ~ **clef** n chiave f di violino.

tree [tri:] n albero; ~ **trunk** n tronco d'albero.

trek [trɛk] n viaggio; camminata; (tiring walk) tirata a piedi // vi (as holiday) fare dell'escursionismo.

trellis ['trɛlɪs] n graticcio, pergola.

tremble ['trɛmbl] vi tremare; (machine) vibrare.

tremendous [trɪ'mɛndəs] a (enormous) enorme; (excellent) meraviglioso(a), formidabile.

tremor ['trɛmə*] n tremore m, tremito; (also: **earth** ~) scossa sismica.

trench [trɛntʃ] n trincea.

trend [trɛnd] n (tendency) tendenza; (of events) corso; (fashion) moda; ~y a (idea) di moda; (clothes) all'ultima moda.

trepidation [trɛpɪ'deɪʃən] n trepidazione f, agitazione f.

trespass ['trɛspəs] vi: **to** ~ **on** entrare abusivamente in; (fig) abusare di; **'no** ~ **ing'** 'proprietà privata', 'vietato l'accesso'.

trestle ['trɛsl] n cavalletto; ~ **table** n tavolo su cavalletti.

trial ['traɪəl] n (LAW) processo; (test: of machine etc) collaudo; (hardship) prova, difficoltà f inv; (worry) cruccio; **to be on** ~ essere sotto processo; **by** ~ **and error** a tentoni.

triangle ['traɪæŋgl] n (MATH, MUS) triangolo.

tribe [traɪb] n tribù f inv; ~**sman** n membro della tribù.

tribulation [trɪbju'leɪʃən] n tribolazione f.

tribunal [traɪ'bju:nl] n tribunale m.

tributary ['trɪbjutərɪ] n (river) tributario, affluente m.

tribute ['trɪbju:t] n tributo, omaggio; **to**

pay ~ **to** rendere omaggio a.

trice [traɪs] n: **in a** ~ in un attimo.

trick [trɪk] n trucco; (clever act) stratagemma m; (joke) tiro; (CARDS) presa // vt imbrogliare, ingannare; **to play a** ~ **on sb** giocare un tiro a qd; ~**ery** n inganno.

trickle ['trɪkl] n (of water etc) rivolo; gocciolio // vi gocciolare; **to** ~ **in/out** (people) entrare/uscire alla spicciolata.

tricky ['trɪkɪ] a difficile, delicato(a).

tricycle ['traɪsɪkl] n triciclo.

trifle ['traɪfl] n sciocchezza; (CULIN) ≈ zuppa inglese // ad: **a** ~ **long** un po' lungo; **trifling** a insignificante.

trigger ['trɪgə*] n (of gun) grilletto; **to** ~ **off** vt dare l'avvio a.

trigonometry [trɪgə'nɔmətrɪ] n trigonometria.

trim [trɪm] a ordinato(a); (house, garden) ben tenuto(a); (figure) snello(a) // n (haircut etc) spuntata, regolata; (embellishment) finiture fpl; (on car) guarnizioni fpl // vt spuntare; (decorate): **to** ~ **(with)** decorare (con); (NAUT: a sail) orientare; ~**mings** npl decorazioni fpl; (extras: gen CULIN) guarnizione f.

Trinity ['trɪnɪtɪ] n: **the** ~ la Trinità.

trinket ['trɪŋkɪt] n gingillo; (piece of jewellery) ciondolo.

trio ['tri:əu] n trio.

trip [trɪp] n viaggio; (excursion) gita, escursione f; (stumble) passo falso // vi inciampare; (go lightly) camminare con passo leggero; **on a** ~ in viaggio; **to** ~ **up** vi inciampare // vt fare lo sgambetto a.

tripe [traɪp] n (CULIN) trippa; (pej: rubbish) sciocchezze fpl, fesserie fpl.

triple ['trɪpl] a triplo(a).

triplets ['trɪplɪts] npl bambini(e) trigemini(e).

triplicate ['trɪplɪkət] n: **in** ~ in triplice copia.

tripod ['traɪpɔd] n treppiede m.

trite [traɪt] a banale, trito(a).

triumph ['traɪʌmf] n trionfo // vi: **to** ~ **(over)** trionfare (su); ~**al** ['ʌmfl] a trionfale; ~**ant** ['ʌmfənt] a trionfante.

trivia ['trɪvɪə] npl banalità fpl.

trivial ['trɪvɪəl] a insignificante; (commonplace) banale.

trod [trɔd] pt of **tread**; ~**den** pp of **tread**.

trolley ['trɔlɪ] n carrello; ~ **bus** n filobus m inv.

trollop ['trɔləp] n prostituta.

trombone [trɔm'bəun] n trombone m.

troop [tru:p] n gruppo, truppa; ~**s** npl (MIL) truppe fpl; **to** ~ **in/out** vi entrare/uscire a frotte; ~**er** n (MIL) soldato di cavalleria; ~**ing the colour** (ceremony) sfilata della bandiera.

trophy ['trəufɪ] n trofeo.

tropic ['trɔpɪk] n tropico; **in the** ~**s** ai tropici; **T**~ **of Cancer/Capricorn** n tropico del Cancro/Capricorno; ~**al** a tropicale.

trot [trɔt] n trotto // vi trottare; **on the** ~

(fig: col) di fila, uno(a) dopo l'altro(a).

trouble ['trʌbl] n difficoltà f inv, problema m; difficoltà fpl, problemi; (worry) preoccupazione f; (bother, effort) sforzo; (POL) conflitti mpl, disordine m; (MED): **stomach** etc ~ disturbi mpl gastrici etc // vt disturbare; (worry) preoccupare // vi: **to** ~ **to do** disturbarsi a fare; ~**s** npl (POL etc) disordini mpl; **to be in** ~ avere dei problemi; **to go to the** ~ **of doing** darsi la pena di fare; **it's no** ~! di niente!; **what's the** ~? cosa c'è che non va?; ~**d** a (person) preoccupato(a), inquieto(a); (epoch, life) agitato(a), difficile; ~**-free** a senza problemi; ~**maker** n elemento disturbatore, agitatore/trice; ~**shooter** n (in conflict) conciliatore m; ~**some** a fastidioso(a), seccante.

trough [trɔf] n (also: **drinking** ~) abbeveratoio; (also: **feeding** ~) trogolo, mangiatoia; (channel) canale m; (of low pressure) n (GEO) depressione f.

trounce [trauns] vt (defeat) sgominare.

troupe [tru:p] n troupe f inv.

trousers ['trauzəz] npl pantaloni mpl, calzoni mpl; **short** ~ npl calzoncini mpl.

trousseau, pl ~**x** or ~**s** ['tru:səu, -z] n corredo da sposa.

trout [traut] n, pl inv trota.

trowel ['trauəl] n cazzuola.

truant ['truənt] n: **to play** ~ marinare la scuola.

truce [tru:s] n tregua.

truck [trʌk] n autocarro, camion m inv; (RAIL) carro merci aperto; (for luggage) carrello m portabagagli inv; ~ **driver** n camionista m/f.

trudge [trʌdʒ] vi arrancare.

true [tru:] a vero(a); (accurate) accurato(a), esatto(a); (genuine) reale; (faithful) fedele.

truffle ['trʌfl] n tartufo.

truly ['tru:lɪ] ad veramente; (truthfully) sinceramente; (faithfully) fedelmente.

trump [trʌmp] n briscola; ~**ed-up** a inventato(a).

trumpet ['trʌmpɪt] n tromba.

truncated [trʌŋ'keɪtɪd] a tronco(a).

truncheon ['trʌntʃən] n sfollagente m inv.

trundle ['trʌndl] vt, vi: **to** ~ **along** rotolare rumorosamente.

trunk [trʌŋk] n (of tree, person) tronco; (of elephant) proboscide f; (case) baule m; ~**s** npl (also: **swimming** ~**s**) calzoncini mpl da bagno; ~ **call** n (TEL) (telefonata) interurbana.

truss [trʌs] n (MED) cinto erniario; **to** ~ (**up**) vt (CULIN) legare.

trust [trʌst] n fiducia; (LAW) amministrazione f fiduciaria; (COMM) trust m inv // vt (rely on) contare su; (entrust): **to** ~ **sth to sb** affidare qc a qd; ~**ed** a fidato(a); ~**ee** [trʌs'ti:] n (LAW) amministratore(trice) fiduciario(a); (of school etc) amministratore/trice; ~**ful**, ~**ing** a fiducioso(a); ~**worthy** a fidato(a), degno(a) di fiducia; ~**y** a fidato(a).

truth, ~**s** [tru:θ, tru:ðz] n verità f inv; ~**ful** a (person) sincero(a); (description) veritiero(a), esatto(a).

try [traɪ] n prova, tentativo; (RUGBY) meta // vt (LAW) giudicare; (test: sth new) provare; (strain) mettere alla prova // vi provare; **to** ~ **to do** provare a fare; (seek) cercare di fare; **to** ~ **on** vt (clothes) provare; **to** ~ **it on** (with sb) (fig) cercare di farla a qd; **to** ~ **out** vt provare, mettere alla prova; ~**ing** a (day, experience) logorante, pesante; (child) difficile, insopportabile.

tsar [zɑ:*] n zar m inv.

T-shirt ['ti:ʃə:t] n maglietta.

T-square ['ti:skwɛə*] n riga a T.

tub [tʌb] n tinozza; mastello; (bath) bagno.

tuba ['tju:bə] n tuba.

tubby ['tʌbɪ] a grassoccio(a).

tube [tju:b] n tubo; (underground) metropolitana; (for tyre) camera d'aria.

tuberculosis [tjubə:kju'ləusɪs] n tubercolosi f.

tubing ['tju:bɪŋ] n tubazione f; **a piece of** ~ un tubo.

tubular ['tju:bjulə*] a tubolare.

TUC n (abbr of Trades Union Congress) confederazione f dei sindacati britannici.

tuck [tʌk] n (SEWING) piega // vt (put) mettere; **to** ~ **away** vt riporre; **to** ~ **in** vt mettere dentro; (child) rimboccare // vi (eat) mangiare di buon appetito; abbuffarsi; **to** ~ **up** vt (child) rimboccare; ~ **shop** n negozio di pasticceria (in una scuola).

Tuesday ['tju:zdɪ] n martedì m inv.

tuft [tʌft] n ciuffo.

tug [tʌg] n (ship) rimorchiatore m // vt tirare con forza; ~**-of-war** n tiro alla fune.

tuition [tju:'ɪʃən] n lezioni fpl.

tulip ['tju:lɪp] n tulipano.

tumble ['tʌmbl] n (fall) capitombolo // vi capitombolare, ruzzolare; (somersault) fare capriole // vt far cadere; ~**-down** a cadente, diroccato(a); ~ **dryer** n asciugatrice f.

tumbler ['tʌmblə*] n bicchiere m (senza piede); acrobata m/f.

tummy ['tʌmɪ] n (col) pancia.

tumour ['tju:mə*] n tumore m.

tumult ['tju:mʌlt] n tumulto; ~**uous** [-'mʌltjuəs] a tumultuoso(a).

tuna ['tju:nə] n, pl inv (also: ~ **fish**) tonno.

tune [tju:n] n (melody) melodia, aria // vt (MUS) accordare; (RADIO, TV, AUT) regolare, mettere a punto; **to be in/out of** ~ (instrument) essere accordato(a)/scordato(a); (singer) essere intonato(a)/stonato(a); **to** ~ **in** (to) (RADIO, TV) sintonizzarsi (su); **to** ~ **up** vi (musician) accordare lo strumento; ~**ful** a melodioso(a); ~**r** n (radio set) sintonizzatore m; **piano** ~**r** accordatore/trice di pianoforte.

tungsten ['tʌŋstn] n tungsteno.

tunic ['tju:nɪk] n tunica.

tuning ['tju:nɪŋ] n messa a punto; ~ **fork** n diapason m inv.

Tunisia [tju:'nɪzɪə] n Tunisia.

tunnel ['tʌnl] n galleria // vi scavare una galleria.

tunny ['tʌnɪ] n tonno.

turban ['tɔːbən] n turbante m.

turbine ['tɔːbaɪn] n turbina.

turbojet ['tɔːbəʊ'dʒɛt] n turboreattore m.

turbot ['tɔːbət] n, pl inv rombo gigante.

turbulence ['tɔːbjʊləns] n (AVIAT) turbolenza.

turbulent ['tɔːbjʊlənt] a turbolento(a); (sea) agitato(a).

tureen [tə'riːn] n zuppiera.

turf [tɔːf] n terreno erboso; (clod) zolla // vt coprire di zolle erbose; **the T~** n l'ippodromo; **to ~ out** vt (col) buttar fuori.

turgid ['tɔːdʒɪd] a (speech) ampolloso(a), pomposo(a).

Turk [tɔːk] n turco/a.

turkey ['tɔːkɪ] n tacchino.

Turkey ['tɔːkɪ] n Turchia.

Turkish ['tɔːkɪʃ] a turco(a) // n (LING) turco; ~ **bath** n bagno turco.

turmoil ['tɔːmɔɪl] n confusione f, tumulto.

turn [tɔːn] n giro; (in road) curva; (tendency: of mind, events) tendenza; (performance) numero; (MED) crisi f inv, attacco // vt girare, voltare; (milk) far andare a male; (change): **to ~ sth into** trasformare qc in // vi girare; (person: look back) girarsi, voltarsi; (reverse direction) girarsi indietro; (change) cambiare; (become) diventare; **to ~ into** trasformarsi in; **a good ~** un buon servizio; **a bad ~** un brutto tiro; **it gave me quite a ~** mi ha fatto prendere un bello spavento; **'no left ~'** (AUT) 'divieto di svolta a sinistra'; **it's your ~** tocca a lei; **in ~** a sua volta; a turno; **to take ~s (at sth)** fare (qc) a turno; **to ~ about** vi girarsi indietro; **to ~ away** vi girarsi (dall'altra parte); **to ~ back** vi ritornare, tornare indietro; **to ~ down** vt (refuse) rifiutare; (reduce) abbassare; (fold) ripiegare; **to ~ in** vi (col: go to bed) andare a letto // vt (fold) voltare in dentro; **to ~ off** vi (from road) girare, voltare // vt (light, radio, engine etc) spegnere; **to ~ on** vt (light, radio etc) accendere; (engine) avviare; **to ~ out** vt (light, gas) chiudere, spegnere // vi: **to ~ out to be...** rivelarsi ..., risultare ...; **to ~ up** vi (person) arrivare, presentarsi; (lost object) saltar fuori // vt (collar, sound) alzare; **~ed-up** a (nose) all'insù; **~ing** n (in road) curva; **~ing point** n (fig) svolta decisiva.

turnip ['tɔːnɪp] n rapa.

turnout ['tɔːnaʊt] n presenza, affluenza.

turnover ['tɔːnəʊvə*] n (COMM) giro di affari.

turnpike ['tɔːnpaɪk] n (US) autostrada a pedaggio.

turnstile ['tɔːnstaɪl] n tornella.

turntable ['tɔːnteɪbl] n (on record player) piatto.

turn-up ['tɔːnʌp] n (on trousers) risvolto.

turpentine ['tɔːpəntaɪn] n (also: **turps**) acqua ragia.

turquoise ['tɔːkwɔɪz] n (stone) turchese m // a color turchese; di turchese.

turret ['tʌrɪt] n torretta.

turtle ['tɔːtl] n testuggine f; **~neck (sweater)** n maglione m con il collo alto.

tusk [tʌsk] n zanna.

tussle ['tʌsl] n baruffa, mischia.

tutor ['tjuːtə*] n (in college) docente m/f (responsabile di un gruppo di studenti); (private teacher) precettore m; **~ial** [-'tɔːrɪəl] n (SCOL) lezione f con discussione (a un gruppo limitato).

tuxedo [tʌk'siːdəʊ] n (US) smoking m inv.

T.V. [tiː'viː] n (abbr of television) tivù f inv.

twang [twæŋ] n (of instrument) suono vibrante; (of voice) accento nasale.

tweed [twiːd] n tweed m inv.

tweezers ['twiːzəz] npl pinzette fpl.

twelfth [twɛlfθ] num dodicesimo(a).

twelve [twɛlv] num dodici; **at ~** alle dodici, a mezzogiorno; (midnight) a mezzanotte.

twentieth ['twɛntɪɪθ] num ventesimo(a).

twenty ['twɛntɪ] num venti.

twice [twaɪs] ad due volte; **~ as much** due volte tanto.

twig [twɪg] n ramoscello // vt, vi (col) capire.

twilight ['twaɪlaɪt] n crepuscolo.

twill [twɪl] n spigato.

twin [twɪn] a,n gemello(a).

twine [twaɪn] n spago, cordicella // vi (plant) attorcigliarsi; (road) serpeggiare.

twinge [twɪndʒ] n (of pain) fitta; **a ~ of conscience/regret** un rimorso/rimpianto.

twinkle ['twɪŋkl] n scintillio; guizzo // vi scintillare; (eyes) brillare.

twirl [twɔːl] n mulinello; piroetta // vt mulinare // vi roteare.

twist [twɪst] n torsione f; (in wire, flex) storta; (in story) colpo di scena // vt attorcigliare; (weave) intrecciare; (roll around) arrotolare; (fig) deformare // vi attorcigliarsi; arrotolarsi; (road) serpeggiare.

twit [twɪt] n (col) minchione/a.

twitch [twɪtʃ] n strattone m; (nervous) tic m inv // vi contrarsi; avere un tic.

two [tuː] num due; **to put ~ and ~ together** (fig) trarre le conclusioni; **~-door** a (AUT) a due porte; **~-faced** a (pej: person) falso(a); **~-piece (suit)** n due pezzi m inv; **~-piece (swimsuit)** n (costume m da bagno a) due pezzi m inv; **~-seater** n (plane) biposto; (car) macchina a due posti; **~some** n (people) coppia; **~-way** a (traffic) a due sensi.

tycoon [taɪ'kuːn] n: **(business) ~** magnate m.

type [taɪp] n (category) genere m; (model) modello; (example) tipo; (TYP) tipo, carattere *m* // *vt* (*letter etc*) battere (a macchina), dattilografare; ~**cast** *a* (*actor*) a ruolo fisso; ~**script** *n* dattiloscritto; ~**writer** *n* macchina da scrivere.

typhoid ['taɪfɔɪd] *n* tifoidea.

typhoon [taɪ'fuːn] *n* tifone *m*.

typhus ['taɪfəs] *n* tifo.

typical ['tɪpɪkl] *a* tipico(a).

typify ['tɪpɪfaɪ] *vt* essere tipico(a) di.

typing ['taɪpɪŋ] *n* dattilografia.

typist ['taɪpɪst] *n* dattilografo/a.

tyranny ['tɪrənɪ] *n* tirannia.

tyrant ['taɪərnt] *n* tiranno.

tyre ['taɪə*] *n* pneumatico, gomma; ~ **pressure** *n* pressione *f* (delle gomme).

tzar [zaː°] *n* = **tsar**.

U

ubiquitous [ju:'bɪkwɪtəs] *a* onnipresente.

udder ['ʌdə°] *n* mammella.

UFO ['juːfəu] *n* (*abbr of unidentified flying object*) UFO *m inv*.

ugh [ɔːh] *excl* puah!

ugliness ['ʌglɪnɪs] *n* bruttezza.

ugly ['ʌglɪ] *a* brutto(a).

UHF *abbr of ultra-high frequency*.

U.K. *n abbr see* **united**.

ulcer ['ʌlsə°] *n* ulcera.

Ulster ['ʌlstə°] *n* Ulster *m*.

ulterior [ʌl'tɪərɪə°] *a* ulteriore; ~ **motive** *n* secondo fine *m*.

ultimate ['ʌltɪmət] *a* ultimo(a), finale; (*authority*) massimo(a), supremo(a); ~**ly** *ad* alla fine; in definitiva, in fin dei conti.

ultimatum [ʌltɪ'meɪtəm] *n* ultimatum *m inv*.

ultraviolet   ['ʌltrə'vaɪəlɪt]   *a* ultravioletto(a).

umbilical [ʌm'bɪlɪkl] *a*: ~ **cord** cordone *m* ombelicale.

umbrage ['ʌmbrɪdʒ] *n*: **to take** ~ offendersi, impermalirsi.

umbrella [ʌm'brɛlə] *n* ombrello.

umpire ['ʌmpaɪə°] *n* arbitro.

umpteen [ʌmp'tiːn] *a* non so quanti(e); **for the** ~**th time** per l'ennesima volta.

UN, UNO *abbr see* **united**.

unabashed [ʌnə'bæʃt] *a* imperturbato(a).

unabated [ʌnə'beɪtɪd] *a* non diminuito(a).

unable [ʌn'eɪbl] *a*: **to be** ~ **to** non potere, essere nell'impossibilità di; essere incapace di.

unaccompanied [ʌnə'kʌmpənɪd] *a* (*child, lady*) non accompagnato(a).

unaccountably [ʌnə'kauntəblɪ] *ad* inesplicabilmente.

unaccustomed   [ʌnə'kʌstəmd]   *a* insolito(a); **to be** ~ **to sth** non essere abituato a qc.

unanimity [juːnə'nɪmɪtɪ] *n* unanimità.

unanimous [juː'nænɪməs] *a* unanime; ~**ly** *ad* all'unanimità.

unashamed [ʌnə'ʃeɪmd] *a* sfacciato(a); senza vergogna.

unassuming [ʌnə'sjuːmɪŋ] *a* modesto(a), senza pretese.

unattached [ʌnə'tætʃt] *a* senza legami, libero(a).

unattended [ʌnə'tɛndɪd] *a* (*car, child, luggage*) incustodito(a).

unattractive [ʌnə'træktɪv] *a* privo(a) di attrattiva, poco attraente.

unauthorized [ʌn'ɔ:θəraɪzd] *a* non autorizzato(a).

unavoidable [ʌnə'vɔɪdəbl] *a* inevitabile.

unaware [ʌnə'wɛə°] *a*: **to be** ~ **of** non sapere, ignorare; ~**s** *ad* di sorpresa, alla sprovvista.

unbalanced [ʌn'bælənst] *a* squilibrato(a).

unbearable [ʌn'bɛərəbl] *a* insopportabile.

unbeatable [ʌn'biːtəbl] *a* imbattibile.

unbeknown(st) [ʌnbɪ'nəun(st)] *ad*: ~ **to** all'insaputa di.

unbelievable [ʌnbɪ'liːvəbl] *a* incredibile.

unbend [ʌn'bɛnd] *vb* (*irg*) *vi* distendersi // *vt* (*wire*) raddrizzare.

unbreakable [ʌn'breɪkəbl] *a* infrangibile.

unbridled [ʌn'braɪdld] *a* sbrigliato(a).

unbroken [ʌn'brəukən] *a* intero(a); continuo(a).

unburden [ʌn'bəːdn] *vt*: **to** ~ **o.s.** sfogarsi.

unbutton [ʌn'bʌtn] *vt* sbottonare.

uncalled-for [ʌn'kɔːldfɔː°] *a* (*remark*) fuori luogo *inv*; (*action*) ingiustificato(a).

uncanny [ʌn'kænɪ] *a* misterioso(a), strano(a).

unceasing [ʌn'siːsɪŋ] *a* incessante.

uncertain [ʌn'səːtn] *a* incerto(a); dubbio(a); ~**ty** *n* incertezza.

unchanged [ʌn'tʃeɪndʒd] *a* immutato(a).

uncharitable [ʌn'tʃærɪtəbl] *a* duro(a), severo(a).

uncharted [ʌn'tʃɑːtɪd] *a* inesplorato(a).

unchecked [ʌn'tʃɛkt] *a* incontrollato(a).

uncle ['ʌŋkl] *n* zio.

uncomfortable [ʌn'kʌmfətəbl] *a* scomodo(a); (*uneasy*) a disagio, agitato(a); fastidioso(a).

uncommon [ʌn'kɔmən] *a* raro(a), insolito(a), non comune.

uncompromising [ʌn'kɔmprəmaɪzɪŋ] *a* intransigente, inflessibile.

unconditional [ʌnkən'dɪʃənl] *a* incondizionato(a), senza condizioni.

unconscious [ʌn'kɔnʃəs] *a* privo(a) di sensi, svenuto(a); (*unaware*) inconsapevole, inconscio(a) // *n*: **the** ~ l'inconscio; ~**ly** *ad* inconsciamente.

uncontrollable [ʌnkən'trəuləbl] *a* incontrollabile; indisciplinato(a).

uncouth [ʌn'kuːθ] *a* maleducato(a), grossolano(a).

uncover [ʌn'kʌvə°] *vt* scoprire.

unctuous ['ʌŋktjuəs] *a* untuoso(a).

undaunted [ʌn'dɔːntɪd] *a* intrepido(a).

undecided [ʌndɪ'saɪdɪd] *a* indeciso(a).

undeniable [ʌndɪ'naɪəbl] *a* innegabile, indiscutibile.

under ['ʌndə°] *prep* sotto; (*less than*) meno di; al disotto di; (*according to*) secondo, in conformità a // ad (al) disotto; from ~ sth da sotto a or dal disotto di qc; ~ there là sotto; ~ repair in riparazione.

under... ['ʌndə*] prefix sotto..., sub...; ~-age a minorenne; ~carriage n carrello (d'atterraggio); ~clothes npl biancheria (intima); ~coat n (paint) mano f di fondo; ~cover a segreto(a), clandestino(a); ~current n corrente f sottomarina; ~cut vt irg vendere a prezzo minore di; ~developed a sottosviluppato(a); ~dog n oppresso/a; ~done a (CULIN) al sangue; (pej) poco cotto(a); ~estimate vt sottovalutare; ~exposed a (PHOT) sottoesposto(a); ~fed a denutrito(a); ~foot ad sotto i piedi; ~go vt irg subire; (treatment) sottoporsi a; ~graduate n studente(essa) universitario(a); ~ground n metropolitana; (POL) movimento clandestino // ad sottoterra; clandestinamente; ~growth n sottobosco; ~hand(ed) a (fig) furtivo(a), subdolo(a); ~lie vt irg essere alla base di; ~line vt sottolineare; ~ling ['ʌndəlɪŋ] n (pej) subalterno/a, tirapiedi m/f inv; ~mine vt minare; ~neath [ʌndə'ni:θ] ad sotto, disotto // prep sotto, al di sotto di; ~paid a mal pagato(a); ~pants npl (Brit) mutande fpl, slip m inv; ~pass n sottopassaggio; ~play vt minimizzare; ~privileged a non abbiente; meno favorito(a); ~rate vt sottovalutare; ~shirt n (US) maglietta; ~shorts npl (US) mutande fpl, slip m inv; ~side n disotto; ~skirt n sottoveste f.

understand [ʌndə'stænd] vb (irg: like stand) vt, vi capire, comprendere; I ~ that... sento che...; credo di capire che...; ~able a comprensibile; ~ing a comprensivo(a) // n comprensione f; (agreement) accordo.

understatement [ʌndə'steɪtmənt] n: that's an ~! a dire poco!

understood [ʌndə'stud] pt, pp of understand // a inteso(a); (implied) sottinteso(a); to make o.s. ~ farsi capire.

understudy ['ʌndəstʌdɪ] n sostituto/a, attore/trice supplente.

undertake [ʌndə'teɪk] vt irg intraprendere; impegnarsi a.

undertaker ['ʌndəteɪkə*] n impresario di pompe funebri.

undertaking [ʌndə'teɪkɪŋ] n impresa; (promise) promessa.

underwater [ʌndə'wɔːtə*] ad sott'acqua // a subacqueo(a).

underwear ['ʌndəwɛə*] n biancheria (intima).

underworld ['ʌndəwɜːld] n (of crime) malavita.

underwriter ['ʌndəraɪtə*] n (INSURANCE) sottoscrittore/trice.

undesirable [ʌndɪ'zaɪərəbl] a indesiderabile; sgradito(a).

undies ['ʌndɪz] npl (col) robina, biancheria intima da donna.

undisputed [ʌndɪs'pjuːtɪd] a indiscusso(a).

undistinguished [ʌndɪs'tɪŋgwɪʃt] a mediocre, qualunque.

undo [ʌn'duː] vt irg disfare; ~ing n rovina, perdita.

undoubted [ʌn'dautɪd] a sicuro(a), certo(a); ~ly ad senza alcun dubbio.

undress [ʌn'drɛs] vi spogliarsi.

undue [ʌn'djuː] a eccessivo(a).

undulating ['ʌndjuleɪtɪŋ] a ondeggiante; ondulato(a).

unduly [ʌn'djuːlɪ] ad eccessivamente.

unearth [ʌn'ɜːθ] vt dissotterrare; (fig) scoprire.

unearthly [ʌn'ɜːθlɪ] a soprannaturale; (hour) impossibile.

uneasy [ʌn'iːzɪ] a a disagio; (worried) preoccupato(a).

uneconomic(al) [ʌniːkə'nɔmɪk(l)] a non economico(a); antieconomico(a).

unemployed [ʌnɪm'plɔɪd] a disoccupato(a) // n: the ~ i disoccupati.

unemployment [ʌnɪm'plɔɪmənt] n disoccupazione f.

unending [ʌn'ɛndɪŋ] a senza fine.

unerring [ʌn'ɜːrɪŋ] a infallibile.

uneven [ʌn'iːvn] a ineguale; irregolare.

unexpected [ʌnɪk'spɛktɪd] a inatteso(a), imprevisto(a).

unfailing [ʌn'feɪlɪŋ] a inesauribile; infallibile.

unfair [ʌn'fɛə*] a: ~ (to) ingiusto(a) (nei confronti di).

unfaithful [ʌn'feɪθful] a infedele.

unfamiliar [ʌnfə'mɪlɪə*] a sconosciuto(a), strano(a).

unfasten [ʌn'fɑːsn] vt slacciare; sciogliere.

unfavourable [ʌn'feɪvərəbl] a sfavorevole.

unfeeling [ʌn'fiːlɪŋ] a insensibile, duro(a).

unfinished [ʌn'fɪnɪʃt] a incompiuto(a).

unfit [ʌn'fɪt] a inadatto(a); (ill) malato(a), in cattiva salute; (incompetent): ~ (for) incompetente (in); (: work, service) inabile (a); ~ for habitation inabitabile.

unflagging [ʌn'flægɪŋ] a instancabile.

unflappable [ʌn'flæpəbl] a calmo(a), composto(a).

unflinching [ʌn'flɪntʃɪŋ] a che non indietreggia, risoluto(a).

unfold [ʌn'fəuld] vt spiegare; (fig) rivelare // vi (view, countryside) distendersi; (story, plot) svelarsi.

unforeseen ['ʌnfɔː'siːn] a imprevisto(a).

unforgivable [ʌnfə'gɪvəbl] a imperdonabile.

unfortunate [ʌn'fɔːtʃnət] a sfortunato(a); (event, remark) infelice; ~ly ad sfortunatamente, purtroppo.

unfounded [ʌn'faundɪd] a infondato(a).

unfriendly [ʌn'frɛndlɪ] a poco amichevole, freddo(a).

ungainly [ʌn'geɪnlɪ] a goffo(a), impacciato(a).

ungodly [ʌn'gɔdlɪ] a empio(a); at an ~ hour a un'ora impossibile.

unguarded [ʌn'gɑːdɪd] a: ~ moment n

momento di distrazione or di disattenzione.

unhappiness [ʌn'hæpɪnɪs] *n* infelicità.

unhappy [ʌn'hæpɪ] *a* infelice; ~ **with** (*arrangements etc*) insoddisfatto(a) di.

unharmed [ʌn'hɑːmd] *a* incolume, sano(a) e salvo(a).

unhealthy [ʌn'helθɪ] *a* (*gen*) malsano(a); (*person*) malaticcio(a).

unheard-of [ʌn'hɜːdɔv] *a* inaudito(a), senza precedenti.

unhook [ʌn'huk] *vt* sganciare; sfibbiare.

unhurt [ʌn'hɜːt] *a* incolume, sano(a) e salvo(a).

unicorn ['juːnɪkɔːn] *n* unicorno.

unidentified [ʌnaɪ'dentɪfaɪd] *a* non identificato(a).

uniform ['juːnɪfɔːm] *n* uniforme f, divisa // *a* uniforme; ~**ity** [-'fɔːmɪtɪ] *n* uniformità.

unify ['juːnɪfaɪ] *vt* unificare.

unilateral [juːnɪ'lætərəl] *a* unilaterale.

unimaginable [ʌnɪ'mædʒɪnəbl] *a* inimmaginabile, inconcepibile.

uninhibited [ʌnɪn'hɪbɪtɪd] *a* senza inibizioni; senza ritegno.

unintentional [ʌnɪn'tenʃənəl] *a* involontario(a).

union ['juːnjən] *n* unione f; (*also*: trade ~) sindacato // *cpd* sindacale, dei sindacati; U~ **Jack** *n bandiera nazionale britannica*.

unique [juː'niːk] *a* unico(a).

unison ['juːnɪsn] *n*: **in** ~ all'unisono.

unit ['juːnɪt] *n* unità f inv; (*section: of furniture etc*) elemento; (*team, squad*) reparto, squadra.

unite [juː'naɪt] *vt* unire // *vi* unirsi; ~**d** *a* unito(a); unificato(a); (*efforts*) congiunto(a); U~**d Kingdom (U.K.)** *n* Regno Unito; U~**d Nations (Organization) (UN, UNO)** *n* (Organizzazione f delle) Nazioni Unite (O.N.U.); U~**d States (of America) (US, USA)** *n* Stati *mpl* Uniti (d'America) (USA).

unit trust ['juːnɪttrʌst] *n* (*Brit*) fondo d'investimento.

unity ['juːnɪtɪ] *n* unità f.

universal [juːnɪ'vɜːsl] *a* universale.

universe ['juːnɪvɜːs] *n* universo.

university [juːnɪ'vɜːsɪtɪ] *n* università f inv.

unjust [ʌn'dʒʌst] *a* ingiusto(a).

unkempt [ʌn'kempt] *a* trasandato(a); spettinato(a).

unkind [ʌn'kaɪnd] *a* scortese; crudele.

unknown [ʌn'nəun] *a* sconosciuto(a).

unladen [ʌn'leɪdn] *a* (*ship, weight*) a vuoto.

unlawful [ʌn'lɔːful] *a* illecito(a), illegale.

unleash [ʌn'liːʃ] *vt* sguinzagliare; (*fig*) scatenare.

unleavened [ʌn'levnd] *a* non lievitato(a), azzimo(a).

unless [ʌn'les] *cj* a meno che (non) + *sub*; ~ **otherwise stated** salvo indicazione contraria.

unlicensed [ʌn'laɪsənst] *a* senza licenza per la vendita di alcolici.

unlike [ʌn'laɪk] *a* diverso(a) // *prep* a differenza di, contrariamente a.

unlikely [ʌn'laɪklɪ] *a* improbabile; inverosimile.

unlimited [ʌn'lɪmɪtɪd] *a* illimitato(a).

unload [ʌn'ləud] *vt* scaricare.

unlock [ʌn'lɔk] *vt* aprire.

unlucky [ʌn'lʌkɪ] *a* sfortunato(a); (*object, number*) che porta sfortuna, di malaugurio.

unmarried [ʌn'mærɪd] *a* non sposato(a); (*man only*) scapolo, celibe; (*woman only*) nubile; ~ **mother** *n ragazza f madre inv*.

unmask [ʌn'mɑːsk] *vt* smascherare.

unmistakable [ʌnmɪs'teɪkəbl] *a* indubbio(a); facilmente riconoscibile.

unmitigated [ʌn'mɪtɪɡeɪtɪd] *a* non mitigato(a), assoluto(a), vero(a) e proprio(a).

unnatural [ʌn'nætʃrəl] *a* innaturale; contro natura.

unnecessary [ʌn'nesəsərɪ] *a* inutile, superfluo(a).

unobtainable [ʌnəb'teɪnəbl] *a* (*TEL*) non ottenibile.

unofficial [ʌnə'fɪʃl] *a* non ufficiale; (*strike*) non dichiarato(a) dal sindacato.

unorthodox [ʌn'ɔːθədɔks] *a* non ortodosso(a).

unpack [ʌn'pæk] *vi* disfare la valigia (or le valigie).

unpalatable [ʌn'pælətəbl] *a* (*truth*) sgradevole.

unparalleled [ʌn'pærəleld] *a* incomparabile, impareggiabile.

unpleasant [ʌn'pleznt] *a* spiacevole.

unplug [ʌn'plʌɡ] *vt* staccare.

unpopular [ʌn'pɔpjulə*] *a* impopolare.

unprecedented [ʌn'presɪdəntɪd] *a* senza precedenti.

unpredictable [ʌnprɪ'dɪktəbl] *a* imprevedibile.

unpretentious [ʌnprɪ'tenʃəs] *a* senza pretese.

unqualified [ʌn'kwɔlɪfaɪd] *a* (*teacher*) non abilitato(a); (*success*) assoluto(a), senza riserve.

unravel [ʌn'rævl] *vt* dipanare, districare.

unreal [ʌn'rɪəl] *a* irreale.

unreasonable [ʌn'riːznəbl] *a* irragionevole.

unrelated [ʌnrɪ'leɪtɪd] *a*: ~ **(to)** senza rapporto (con); non imparentato(a) (con).

unrelenting [ʌnrɪ'lentɪŋ] *a* implacabile; accanito(a).

unreliable [ʌnrɪ'laɪəbl] *a* (*person, machine*) che non dà affidamento; (*news, source of information*) inattendibile.

unrelieved [ʌnrɪ'liːvd] *a* (*monotony*) uniforme.

unremitting [ʌnrɪ'mɪtɪŋ] *a* incessante, infaticabile.

unrepentant [ʌnrɪ'pentənt] *a* impenitente.

unrest [ʌn'rest] *n* agitazione f.

unroll [ʌn'rəul] *vt* srotolare.

unruly [ʌn'ruːlɪ] *a* indisciplinato(a).

unsafe [ʌn'seɪf] *a* pericoloso(a), rischioso(a).

unsaid [ʌn'sɛd] *a*: **to leave sth ~** passare qc sotto silenzio.

unsatisfactory ['ʌnsætɪs'fæktərɪ] *a* che lascia a desiderare, insufficiente.

unsavoury [ʌn'seɪvərɪ] *a* (*fig*: *person*) losco(a); (: *reputation*, *subject*) disgustoso(a), ripugnante.

unscathed [ʌn'skeɪðd] *a* incolume.

unscrew [ʌn'skru:] *vt* svitare.

unscrupulous [ʌn'skru:pjuləs] *a* senza scrupoli.

unseemly [ʌn'si:mlɪ] *a* sconveniente.

unsettled [ʌn'sɛtld] *a* turbato(a); instabile; indeciso(a).

unsightly [ʌn'saɪtlɪ] *a* brutto(a), sgradevole a vedersi.

unskilled [ʌn'skɪld] *a*: **~ worker** *n* manovale *m*.

unsophisticated [ʌnsə'fɪstɪkeɪtɪd] *a* semplice, naturale.

unspeakable [ʌn'spi:kəbl] *a* (*bad*) abominevole.

unsteady [ʌn'stɛdɪ] *a* instabile, malsicuro(a).

unstuck [ʌn'stʌk] *a*: **to come ~** scollarsi; (*fig*) fare fiasco.

unsuccessful [ʌnsək'sɛsful] *a* (*writer*, *proposal*) che non ha successo; (*marriage*, *attempt*) mal riuscito(a), fallito(a); **to be ~** (*in attempting sth*) non riuscire; non avere successo; (*application*) non essere considerato(a); **~ly** *ad* senza successo.

unsuitable [ʌn'su:təbl] *a* inadatto(a); inopportuno(a); sconveniente.

unsuspecting [ʌnsə'spɛktɪŋ] *a* che non sospetta niente.

unswerving [ʌn'swə:vɪŋ] *a* fermo(a).

untangle [ʌn'tæŋgl] *vt* sbrogliare.

untapped [ʌn'tæpt] *a* (*resources*) non sfruttato(a).

unthinkable [ʌn'θɪŋkəbl] *a* impensabile, inconcepibile.

untidy [ʌn'taɪdɪ] *a* (*room*) in disordine; (*appearance*, *work*) trascurato(a); (*person*, *writing*) disordinato(a).

untie [ʌn'taɪ] *vt* (*knot*, *parcel*) disfare; (*prisoner*, *dog*) slegare.

until [ən'tɪl] *prep* fino a; (*after negative*) prima di // *cj* finché, fino a quando; (*in past*, *after negative*) prima che + *sub*, prima di + *infinitive*.

untimely [ʌn'taɪmlɪ] *a* intempestivo(a), inopportuno(a); (*death*) prematuro(a).

untold [ʌn'təʊld] *a* incalcolabile; indescrivibile.

untoward [ʌntə'wɔ:d] *a* sfortunato(a), sconveniente.

unused [ʌn'ju:zd] *a* nuovo(a).

unusual [ʌn'ju:ʒuəl] *a* insolito(a), eccezionale, raro(a).

unveil [ʌn'veɪl] *vt* scoprire; svelare.

unwavering [ʌn'weɪvərɪŋ] *a* fermo(a), incrollabile.

unwell [ʌn'wɛl] *a* indisposto(a).

unwieldy [ʌn'wi:ldɪ] *a* poco maneggevole.

unwilling [ʌn'wɪlɪŋ] *a*: **to be ~ to do** non voler fare; **~ly** *ad* malvolentieri.

unwind [ʌn'waɪnd] *vb* (*irg*) *vt* svolgere, srotolare // *vi* (*relax*) rilassarsi.

unwitting [ʌn'wɪtɪŋ] *a* involontario(a).

unworthy [ʌn'wə:ðɪ] *a* indegno(a).

unwrap [ʌn'ræp] *vt* disfare; aprire.

unwritten [ʌn'rɪtn] *a* (*agreement*) tacito(a).

up [ʌp] *prep*: **to go/be ~ sth** salire/essere su qc // *ad* su, (di) sopra; in alto; **~ there** lassù; **~ above** al di sopra; **~ to** fino a; **to be ~** (*out of bed*) essere alzato(a) or in piedi; **it is ~ to you** tocca a lei decidere; **what is he ~ to?** cosa sta tramando?; **he is not ~ to it** non ne è capace; **~-and-coming** *a* pieno(a) di promesse, promettente; **~s and downs** *npl* (*fig*) alti e bassi *mpl*.

upbringing ['ʌpbrɪŋɪŋ] *n* educazione *f*.

update [ʌp'deɪt] *vt* aggiornare.

upgrade [ʌp'greɪd] *vt* promuovere; (*job*) rivalutare.

upheaval [ʌp'hi:vl] *n* sconvolgimento; tumulto.

uphill [ʌp'hɪl] *a* in salita; (*fig*: *task*) difficile // *ad*: **to gd ~** andare in salita, salire.

uphold [ʌp'həʊld] *vt irg* approvare; sostenere.

upholstery [ʌp'həʊlstərɪ] *n* tappezzeria.

upkeep ['ʌpki:p] *n* manutenzione *f*.

upon [ə'pɔn] *prep* su.

upper ['ʌpə*] *a* superiore // *n* (*of shoe*) tomaia; **the ~ class** ≈ l'alta borghesia; **~-class** *a* dell'alta borghesia; **~most** *a* il(la) più alto(a); predominante.

upright ['ʌpraɪt] *a* diritto(a); verticale; (*fig*) diritto(a), onesto(a) // *n* montante *m*.

uprising ['ʌpraɪzɪŋ] *n* insurrezione *f*, rivolta.

uproar ['ʌprɔ:*] *n* tumulto, clamore *m*.

uproot [ʌp'ru:t] *vt* sradicare.

upset *n* ['ʌpsɛt] turbamento // *vt* [ʌp'sɛt] (*irg*: *like* **set**) (*glass etc*) rovesciare; (*plan*, *stomach*) scombussolare; (*person*: *offend*) contrariare; (: *grieve*) addolorare; sconvolgere // *a* [ʌp'sɛt] contrariato(a); addolorato(a); (*stomach*) scombussolato(a), disturbato(a).

upshot ['ʌpʃɔt] *n* risultato.

upside ['ʌpsaɪd]: **~-down** *ad* sottosopra; **to turn ~-down** capovolgere; (*fig*) mettere sottosopra.

upstairs [ʌp'stɛəz] *ad*, *a* di sopra, al piano superiore.

upstart ['ʌpstɑ:t] *n* nuovo(a) ricco(a).

upstream [ʌp'stri:m] *ad* a monte.

uptake ['ʌpteɪk] *n*: **he is quick/slow on the ~** è pronto/lento di comprendonio.

up-to-date ['ʌptə'deɪt] *a* moderno(a); aggiornato(a).

upturn ['ʌptə:n] *n* (*in luck*) svolta favorevole.

upward ['ʌpwəd] *a* ascendente; verso l'alto; **~(s)** *ad* in su, verso l'alto.

uranium [juə'reɪnɪəm] *n* uranio.

urban ['ə:bən] *a* urbano(a).

urbane [ə:'beɪn] *a* civile, urbano(a), educato(a).

urchin ['əːtʃɪn] n monello; sea ~ n riccio di mare.

urge [əːdʒ] n impulso; stimolo; forte desiderio // vt: to ~ sb to do esortare qd a fare, spingere qd a fare; raccomandare a qd di fare; to ~ on vt spronare.

urgency ['əːdʒənsɪ] n urgenza; (of tone) insistenza.

urgent ['əːdʒənt] a urgente.

urinate ['juərɪneɪt] vi orinare.

urn [əːn] n urna; (also: tea ~) bollitore m per il tè.

us [ʌs] pronoun ci; (stressed, after prep) noi.

US, USA n abbr see **united**.

usage ['juːzɪdʒ] n uso.

use n [juːs] uso; impiego, utilizzazione f // vt [juːz] usare, utilizzare, servirsi di; **she ~d to do it** lo faceva (una volta), era solita farlo; **in** ~ in uso; **out of** ~ fuori uso; **it's no** ~ non serve, è inutile; **to be ~d to** avere l'abitudine di; **to** ~ **up** vt consumare; esaurire; ~**d** a (car) d'occasione; ~**ful** a utile; ~**fulness** n utilità; ~**less** a inutile; ~**r** n utente m/f.

usher ['ʌʃə*] n usciere m; (in cinema) maschera; ~**ette** [-'rɛt] n (in cinema) maschera.

USSR n: **the** ~ l'URSS f.

usual ['juːʒuəl] a solito(a); ~**ly** ad di solito.

usurer ['juːʒərə*] n usuraio/a.

usurp [juːˈzəːp] vt usurpare.

utensil [juːˈtɛnsl] n utensile m.

uterus ['juːtərəs] n utero.

utilitarian [juːtɪlɪˈtɛərɪən] a utilitario(a).

utility [juːˈtɪlɪtɪ] n utilità; (also: **public** ~) servizio pubblico.

utilization [juːtɪlaɪˈzeɪʃən] n utilizzazione f.

utilize ['juːtɪlaɪz] vt utilizzare; sfruttare.

utmost ['ʌtməust] a estremo(a) // n: **to do one's** ~ fare il possibile or di tutto.

utter ['ʌtə*] a assoluto(a), totale // vt pronunciare, proferire; emettere; ~**ance** n espressione f; parole fpl.

U-turn ['juːˈtəːn] n inversione f a U.

V

v. abbr of **verse, versus, volt**; (abbr of **vide**) vedi, vedere.

vacancy ['veɪkənsɪ] n (job) posto libero; (room) stanza libera; '**no vacancies**' 'completo'.

vacant ['veɪkənt] a (job, seat etc) libero(a); (expression) assente.

vacate [vəˈkeɪt] vt lasciare libero(a).

vacation [vəˈkeɪʃən] n vacanze fpl; ~ **course** n corso estivo.

vaccinate ['væksɪneɪt] vt vaccinare; **vaccination** [-ˈneɪʃən] n vaccinazione f.

vaccine ['væksiːn] n vaccino.

vacuum ['vækjum] n vuoto; ~ **cleaner** n aspirapolvere m inv; ~ **flask** n thermos m inv (®).

vagina [vəˈdʒaɪnə] n vagina.

vagrant ['veɪgrnt] n vagabondo/a.

vague [veɪg] a vago(a); (blurred: photo, memory) sfocato(a); ~**ly** ad vagamente.

vain [veɪn] a (useless) inutile, vano(a); (conceited) vanitoso(a); **in** ~ inutilmente, invano.

valentine ['væləntaɪn] n (also: ~ **card**) cartolina or biglietto di San Valentino.

valiant ['vælɪənt] a valoroso(a), coraggioso(a).

valid ['vælɪd] a valido(a), valevole; (excuse) valido(a); ~**ity** [-'lɪdɪtɪ] n validità.

valley ['vælɪ] n valle f.

valuable ['væljuəbl] a (jewel) di (grande) valore; (time) prezioso(a); ~**s** npl oggetti mpl di valore.

valuation [væljuˈeɪʃən] n valutazione f, stima.

value ['væljuː] n valore m // vt (fix price) valutare, dare un prezzo a; (cherish) apprezzare, tenere a; ~ **added tax** (VAT) n imposta sul valore aggiunto (I.V.A.); ~**d** a (appreciated) stimato(a), apprezzato(a).

valve [vælv] n valvola.

van [væn] n (AUT) furgone m; (RAIL) vagone m.

vandal ['vændl] n vandalo/a; ~**ism** n vandalismo.

vanguard ['vængɑːd] n avanguardia.

vanilla [vəˈnɪlə] n vaniglia // cpd (ice cream) alla vaniglia.

vanish ['vænɪʃ] vi svanire, scomparire.

vanity ['vænɪtɪ] n vanità; ~ **case** n valigetta per cosmetici.

vantage ['vɑːntɪdʒ] n: ~ **point** n posizione f or punto di osservazione; (fig) posizione vantaggiosa.

vapour ['veɪpə*] n vapore m.

variable ['vɛərɪəbl] a variabile; (mood) mutevole.

variance ['vɛərɪəns] n: **to be at** ~ (**with**) essere in disaccordo (con); (facts) essere in contraddizione (con).

variant ['vɛərɪənt] n variante f.

variation [vɛərɪˈeɪʃən] n variazione f; (in opinion) cambiamento.

varicose ['værɪkəus] a: ~ **veins** npl varici fpl.

varied ['vɛərɪd] a vario(a), diverso(a).

variety [vəˈraɪətɪ] n varietà f inv; (quantity) quantità, numero; ~ **show** n varietà m inv.

various ['vɛərɪəs] a vario(a), diverso(a); (several) parecchi(e), molti(e).

varnish ['vɑːnɪʃ] n vernice f // vt verniciare.

vary ['vɛərɪ] vt, vi variare, mutare; ~**ing** a variabile.

vase [vɑːz] n vaso.

vast [vɑːst] a vasto(a); (amount, success) enorme; ~**ly** ad enormemente.

vat [væt] n tino.

VAT [væt] n abbr see **value**.

Vatican ['vætɪkən] n: **the** ~ il Vaticano.

vault [vɔːlt] n (of roof) volta; (tomb) tomba; (in bank) camera blindata; (jump) salto // vt (also: ~ **over**) saltare (d'un balzo).

vaunted ['vɔːntɪd] *a*: **much-~** tanto celebrato(a).

VD *n abbr see* **venereal**.

veal [viːl] *n* vitello.

veer [vɪə*] *vi* girare; virare.

vegetable ['vedʒtəbl] *n* verdura, ortaggio // *a* vegetale.

vegetarian [vedʒɪ'tɛərɪən] *a*, *n* vegetariano(a).

vegetate ['vedʒɪteɪt] *vi* vegetare.

vegetation [vedʒɪ'teɪʃən] *n* vegetazione *f*.

vehemence ['viːɪməns] *n* veemenza, violenza.

vehicle ['viːɪkl] *n* veicolo.

veil [veɪl] *n* velo // *vt* velare.

vein [veɪn] *n* vena; (*on leaf*) nervatura; (*fig: mood*) vena, umore *m*.

velocity [vɪ'lɒsɪtɪ] *n* velocità.

velvet ['velvɪt] *n* velluto.

vending machine ['vendɪŋməʃiːn] *n* distributore *m* automatico.

vendor ['vendə*] *n* venditore/trice.

veneer [və'nɪə*] *n* impiallacciatura; (*fig*) vernice *f*.

venerable ['venərəbl] *a* venerabile.

venereal [vɪ'nɪərɪəl] *a*: **~ disease (VD)** *n* malattia venerea.

Venetian [vɪ'niːʃən] *a* veneziano(a); **~ blind** *n* (tenda alla) veneziana.

Venezuela [venɪ'zweɪlə] *n* Venezuela *m*; **~ n** *a*, *n* venezuelano(a).

vengeance ['vendʒəns] *n* vendetta; **with a ~** (*fig*) davvero; furiosamente.

Venice ['venɪs] *n* Venezia.

venison ['venɪsn] *n* carne *f* di cervo.

venom ['venəm] *n* veleno; **~ous** *a* velenoso(a).

vent [vent] *n* foro, apertura; (*in dress, jacket*) spacco // *vt* (*fig: one's feelings*) sfogare, dare sfogo a.

ventilate ['ventɪleɪt] *vt* (*room*) dare aria a, arieggiare; **ventilation** [-'leɪʃən] *n* ventilazione *f*; **ventilator** *n* ventilatore *m*.

ventriloquist [ven'trɪləkwɪst] *n* ventriloquo/a.

venture ['ventʃə*] *n* impresa (rischiosa) // *vt* rischiare, azzardare // *vi* arrischiarsi, azzardarsi.

venue ['venjuː] *n* luogo di incontro; (*SPORT*) luogo (designato) per l'incontro.

veranda(h) [və'rændə] *n* veranda.

verb [vɜːb] *n* verbo; **~al** *a* verbale; (*translation*) letterale.

verbose [vɜː'bəus] *a* verboso(a).

verdict ['vɜːdɪkt] *n* verdetto.

verge [vɜːdʒ] *n* bordo, orlo; **on the ~ of doing** sul punto di fare; **to ~ on** *vt fus* rasentare.

verger ['vɜːdʒə*] *n* (*REL*) sagrestano.

verification [verɪfɪ'keɪʃən] *n* verifica.

verify ['verɪfaɪ] *vt* verificare.

vermin ['vɜːmɪn] *npl* animali *mpl* nocivi; (*insects*) insetti *mpl* parassiti.

vermouth ['vɜːməθ] *n* vermut *m inv*.

vernacular [və'nækjulə*] *n* vernacolo.

versatile ['vɜːsətaɪl] *a* (*person*) versatile;

(*machine, tool etc*) (che si presta) a molti usi.

verse [vɜːs] *n* versi *mpl*; (*stanza*) stanza, strofa; (*in bible*) versetto.

versed [vɜːst] *a*: **(well-)~ in** versato(a) in.

version ['vɜːʃən] *n* versione *f*.

versus ['vɜːsəs] *prep* contro.

vertebra, *pl* **~e** ['vɜːtɪbrə, -briː] *n* vertebra.

vertebrate ['vɜːtɪbrɪt] *n* vertebrato.

vertical ['vɜːtɪkl] *a*, *n* verticale (*m*); **~ly** *ad* verticalmente.

vertigo ['vɜːtɪgəu] *n* vertigine *f*.

verve [vɜːv] *n* brio; entusiasmo.

very ['verɪ] *ad* molto // *a*: **the ~ book which** proprio il libro che; **at the ~ end** proprio alla fine; **the ~ last** proprio l'ultimo; **at the ~ least** almeno; **~ much** moltissimo.

vespers ['vespəz] *npl* vespro.

vessel ['vesl] *n* (*ANAT*) vaso; (*NAUT*) nave *f*; (*container*) recipiente *m*.

vest [vest] *n* maglia; (*sleeveless*) canottiera; (*US: waistcoat*) gilè *m inv* // *vt*: **to ~ sb with sth**, **to ~ sth in sb** conferire qc a qd; **~ed interests** *npl* (*COMM*) diritti *mpl* acquisiti.

vestibule ['vestɪbjuːl] *n* vestibolo.

vestige ['vestɪdʒ] *n* vestigio.

vestment ['vestmənt] *n* (*REL*) paramento liturgico.

vestry ['vestrɪ] *n* sagrestia.

vet [vet] *n* (*abbr of* **veterinary surgeon**) veterinario // *vt* esaminare minuziosamente; (*text*) rivedere.

veteran ['vetərn] *n* veterano; (*also: war ~*) reduce *m*; **~ car** *n* auto *f inv* d'epoca.

veterinary ['vetrɪnərɪ] *a* veterinario(a); **~ surgeon** *n* veterinario.

veto ['viːtəu] *n*, *pl* **~es** veto // *vt* opporre il veto a.

vex [veks] *vt* irritare, contrariare; **~ed** *a* (*question*) controverso(a), dibattuto(a).

VHF *abbr of* very high frequency.

via ['vaɪə] *prep* (*by way of*) via; (*by means of*) tramite.

viable ['vaɪəbl] *a* attuabile; vitale.

viaduct ['vaɪədʌkt] *n* viadotto.

vibrate [vaɪ'breɪt] *vi*: **to ~ (with)** vibrare (di); (*resound*) risonare (di); **vibration** [-'breɪʃən] *n* vibrazione *f*.

vicar ['vɪkə*] *n* pastore *m*; **~age** *n* presbiterio.

vice [vaɪs] *n* (*evil*) vizio; (*TECH*) morsa.

vice- [vaɪs] *prefix* vice...; **~chairman** *n* vicepresidente *m*.

vice squad ['vaɪsskwɔd] *n* (squadra del) buon costume *f*.

vice versa ['vaɪsɪ'vɜːsə] *ad* viceversa.

vicinity [vɪ'sɪnɪtɪ] *n* vicinanze *fpl*.

vicious ['vɪʃəs] *a* (*remark*) maligno(a), cattivo(a); (*blow*) violento(a); **~ness** *n* malignità, cattiveria; ferocia.

vicissitudes [vɪ'sɪsɪtjuːdz] *npl* vicissitudini *fpl*.

victim ['vɪktɪm] *n* vittima; **~ization**

[-aɪʃən] *n* persecuzione *f*; rappresaglie *fpl*; ~**ize** *vt* perseguitare; compiere delle rappresaglie contro.

victor ['vɪktə*] *n* vincitore *m*.

Victorian [vɪk'tɔ:rɪən] *a* vittoriano(a).

victorious [vɪk'tɔ:rɪəs] *a* vittorioso(a).

victory ['vɪktərɪ] *n* vittoria.

video ['vɪdɪəʊ] *cpd* video...; ~(-**tape**) **recorder** *n* videoregistratore *m*.

vie [vaɪ] *vi*: to ~ **with** competere con, rivaleggiare con.

Vienna [vɪ'enə] *n* Vienna.

view [vju:] *n* vista, veduta; (*opinion*) opinione *f* // *vt* (*situation*) considerare; (*house*) visitare; **on** ~ (*in museum etc*) esposto(a); **in my** ~ a mio avviso, secondo me; **in** ~ **of the fact that** considerato che; ~**er** *n* (*viewfinder*) mirino; (*small projector*) visore *m*; (*TV*) telespettatore/trice; ~**finder** *n* mirino; ~**point** *n* punto di vista.

vigil ['vɪdʒɪl] *n* veglia; ~**ance** *n* vigilanza; ~**ant** *a* vigile.

vigorous ['vɪgərəs] *a* vigoroso(a).

vigour ['vɪgə*] *n* vigore *m*.

vile [vaɪl] *a* (*action*) vile; (*smell*) disgustoso(a), nauseante; (*temper*) pessimo(a).

villa ['vɪlə] *n* villa.

village ['vɪlɪdʒ] *n* villaggio; ~**r** *n* abitante *m/f* di villaggio.

villain ['vɪlən] *n* (*scoundrel*) canaglia; (*criminal*) criminale *m*; (*in novel etc*) cattivo.

vindicate ['vɪndɪkeɪt] *vt* comprovare; giustificare.

vindictive [vɪn'dɪktɪv] *a* vendicativo(a).

vine [vaɪn] *n* vite *f*; (*climbing plant*) rampicante *m*.

vinegar ['vɪnɪgə*] *n* aceto.

vineyard ['vɪnjɑːd] *n* vigna, vigneto.

vintage ['vɪntɪdʒ] *n* (*year*) annata, produzione *f*; ~ **wine** *n* vino d'annata.

vinyl ['vaɪnl] *n* vinile *m*.

viola [vɪ'əʊlə] *n* viola.

violate ['vaɪəleɪt] *vt* violare; **violation** [-'leɪʃən] *n* violazione *f*.

violence ['vaɪələns] *n* violenza; (*POL etc*) incidenti *mpl* violenti.

violent ['vaɪələnt] *a* violento(a); ~**ly** *ad* violentemente; estremamente.

violet ['vaɪələt] *a* (*colour*) viola *inv*, violetto(a) // *n* (*plant*) violetta.

violin [vaɪə'lɪn] *n* violino; ~**ist** *n* violinista *m/f*.

VIP *n* (*abbr of very important person*) V.I.P. *m/f inv*.

viper ['vaɪpə*] *n* vipera.

virgin ['vɜːdʒɪn] *n* vergine *f* // *a* vergine; **the Blessed V~** la Beatissima Vergine; ~**ity** [-'dʒɪnɪtɪ] *n* verginità.

Virgo ['vɜːgəʊ] *n* (*sign*) Vergine *f*.

virile ['vɪraɪl] *a* virile.

virility [vɪ'rɪlɪtɪ] *n* virilità.

virtually ['vɜːtjʊəlɪ] *ad* (*almost*) praticamente.

virtue ['vɜːtjuː] *n* virtù *f inv*; (*advantage*) pregio, vantaggio; **by** ~ **of** grazie a.

virtuoso [vɜːtjuˈəʊzəʊ] *n* virtuoso.

virtuous ['vɜːtjʊəs] *a* virtuoso(a).

virus ['vaɪərəs] *n* virus *m inv*.

visa ['viːzə] *n* visto.

vis-à-vis [viːzə'viː] *prep* rispetto a, nei riguardi di.

viscount ['vaɪkaʊnt] *n* visconte *m*.

visibility [vɪzɪ'bɪlɪtɪ] *n* visibilità.

visible ['vɪzəbl] *a* visibile.

vision ['vɪʒən] *n* (*sight*) vista; (*foresight, in dream*) visione *f*; ~**ary** *n* visionario/a.

visit ['vɪzɪt] *n* visita; (*stay*) soggiorno // *vt* (*person*) andare a trovare; (*place*) visitare; ~**ing card** *n* biglietto da visita; ~**or** *n* visitatore/trice; (*guest*) ospite *m/f*; (*in hotel*) cliente *m/f*; ~**ors' book** *n* libro d'oro; (*in hotel*) registro.

visor ['vaɪzə*] *n* visiera.

vista ['vɪstə] *n* vista, prospettiva.

visual ['vɪzjʊəl] *a* visivo(a); visuale; ottico(a); ~ **aid** *n* sussidio visivo.

visualize ['vɪzjʊəlaɪz] *vt* immaginare, figurarsi; (*foresee*) prevedere.

vital ['vaɪtl] *a* vitale; ~**ity** [-'tælɪtɪ] *n* vitalità; ~**ly** *ad* estremamente; ~ **statistics** *npl* (*fig*) misure *fpl*.

vitamin ['vɪtəmɪn] *n* vitamina.

vivacious [vɪ'veɪʃəs] *a* vivace.

vivacity [vɪ'væsɪtɪ] *n* vivacità.

vivid ['vɪvɪd] *a* vivido(a); ~**ly** *ad* (*describe*) vividamente; (*remember*) con precisione.

vivisection [vɪvɪ'sekʃən] *n* vivisezione *f*.

vocabulary [vəʊ'kæbjʊlərɪ] *n* vocabolario.

vocal ['vəʊkl] *a* (*MUS*) vocale; (*communication*) verbale; (*noisy*) rumoroso(a); ~**ist** *n* cantante *m/f* di musica vocale, vocalist *m/f inv*.

vocation [vəʊ'keɪʃən] *n* vocazione *f*; ~**al** *a* professionale.

vociferous [və'sɪfərəs] *a* rumoroso(a).

vodka ['vɒdkə] *n* vodka *f inv*.

vogue [vəʊg] *n* moda; (*popularity*) popolarità, voga.

voice [vɔɪs] *n* voce *f* // *vt* (*opinion*) esprimere.

void [vɔɪd] *n* vuoto // *a*: ~ **of** privo(a) di.

volatile ['vɒlətaɪl] *a* volatile; (*fig*) volubile.

volcanic [vɒl'kænɪk] *a* vulcanico(a).

volcano [vɒl'keɪnəʊ] *n*, ~**es** [vɒl'keɪnəʊz] *n* vulcano.

volition [və'lɪʃən] *n*: **of one's own** ~ di sua volontà.

volley ['vɒlɪ] *n* (*of gunfire*) salva; (*of stones etc*) raffica, gragnola; (*TENNIS etc*) volata; ~**ball** *n* pallavolo *f*.

volt [vəʊlt] *n* volt *m inv*; ~**age** *n* tensione *f*, voltaggio.

voluble ['vɒljʊbl] *a* loquace, ciarliero(a).

volume ['vɒljuːm] *n* volume *m*; ~ **control** *n* (*RADIO, TV*) regolatore *m or* manopola del volume.

voluntarily ['vɒləntrɪlɪ] *ad* volontariamente; gratuitamente.

voluntary ['vɒləntərɪ] *a* volontario(a); (*unpaid*) gratuito(a), non retribuito(a).

volunteer [vɒlən'tɪə*] *n* volontario/a // *vi*

(MIL) arruolarsi volontario; **to ~ to do** offrire (volontariamente) di fare.

voluptuous [və'lʌptjuəs] *a* voluttuoso(a).

vomit ['vɔmɪt] *n* vomito // *vt, vi* vomitare.

vote [vəut] *n* voto, suffragio; *(cast)* voto; *(franchise)* diritto di voto // *vi* votare; **~ of thanks** *n* discorso di ringraziamento; **~r** *n* elettore/trice; **voting** *n* scrutinio.

vouch [vautʃ]: **to ~ for** *vt* farsi garante di.

voucher ['vautʃə*] *n (for meal, petrol)* buono; *(receipt)* ricevuta.

vow [vau] *n* voto, promessa solenne // *vi* giurare.

vowel ['vauəl] *n* vocale *f*.

voyage ['vɔɪdʒ] *n* viaggio per mare, traversata.

vulgar ['vʌlgə*] *a* volgare; **~ity** [-'gærɪtɪ] *n* volgarità.

vulnerable ['vʌlnərəbl] *a* vulnerabile.

vulture ['vʌltʃə*] *n* avvoltoio.

W

wad [wɔd] *n (of cotton wool, paper)* tampone *m; (of banknotes etc)* fascio.

wade [weɪd] *vi*: **to ~ through** camminare a stento in // *vt* guadare.

wafer ['weɪfə*] *n (CULIN)* cialda; *(REL)* ostia.

waffle ['wɔfl] *n (CULIN)* cialda; *(col)* ciance *fpl*; riempitivo // *vi* cianciare; parlare a vuoto.

waft [wɔft] *vt* portare // *vi* diffondersi.

wag [wæg] *vt* agitare, muovere // *vi* agitarsi.

wage [weɪdʒ] *n* salario, paga // *vt*: **to ~ war** fare la guerra; **~s** *npl* salario, paga.

wager ['weɪdʒə*] *n* scommessa.

waggle ['wægl] *vt* dimenare, agitare // *vi* dimenarsi, agitarsi.

wag(g)on ['wægən] *n (horse-drawn)* carro; *(truck)* furgone *m; (RAIL)* vagone *m* (merci).

wail [weɪl] *n* gemito; *(of siren)* urlo // *vi* gemere; urlare.

waist [weɪst] *n* vita, cintola; **~coat** *n* panciotto, gilè *m inv;* **~line** *n* (giro di) vita.

wait [weɪt] *n* attesa // *vi* aspettare, attendere; **to lie in ~ for** stare in agguato a; **I can't ~ to** *(fig)* non vedo l'ora di; **to ~ behind** *vi* rimanere (ad aspettare); **to ~ for** aspettare; **to ~ on** *vt fus* servire; **~er** *n* cameriere *m;* **'no ~ing'** *(AUT)* 'divieto di sosta'; **~ing list** *n* lista di attesa; **~ing room** *n* sala d'aspetto or d'attesa; **~ress** *n* cameriera.

waive [weɪv] *vt* rinunciare a, abbandonare.

wake [weɪk] *vb (pt* **woke,** **~d,** *pp* **woken,** **~d** [wəuk, 'wəukn]) *vt (also:* **~ up)** svegliare // *vi (also:* **~ up)** svegliarsi // *n (for dead person)* veglia funebre; *(NAUT)* scia; **~n** *vt, vi* = **wake.**

Wales [weɪlz] *n* Galles *m.*

walk [wɔːk] *n* passeggiata; *(short)* giretto; *(gait)* passo, andatura; *(path)* sentiero; *(in*

park etc) sentiero, vialetto // *vi* camminare; *(for pleasure, exercise)* passeggiare // *vt (distance)* fare or percorrere a piedi; *(dog)* accompagnare, portare a passeggiare; **10 minutes' ~ from** 10 minuti di cammino *or* a piedi da; **from all ~s of life** di tutte le condizioni sociali; **~er** *n (person)* camminatore/trice; **~ie-talkie** ['wɔːkɪ'tɔːkɪ] *n* radiotelefono portatile; **~ing** *n* camminare *m;* **~ing stick** *n* bastone *m* da passeggio; **~out** *n (of workers)* sciopero senza preavviso *or* a sorpresa; **~over** *n (col)* vittoria facile, gioco da ragazzi.

wall [wɔːl] *n* muro; *(internal, of tunnel, cave)* parete *f;* **~ed** *a (city)* fortificato(a).

wallet ['wɔlɪt] *n* portafoglio.

wallflower ['wɔːlflauə*] *n* violacciocca; **to be a ~** *(fig)* fare da tappezzeria.

wallop ['wɔləp] *vt (col)* pestare.

wallow ['wɔləu] *vi* sguazzare, voltolarsi.

wallpaper ['wɔːlpeɪpə*] *n* carta da parati.

walnut ['wɔːlnʌt] *n* noce *f; (tree)* noce *m.*

walrus, *pl* **~** *or* **~es** ['wɔːlrəs] *n* tricheco.

waltz [wɔːlts] *n* valzer *m inv* // *vi* ballare il valzer.

wan [wɔn] *a* pallido(a), smorto(a); triste.

wand [wɔnd] *n (also:* **magic ~)** bacchetta (magica).

wander ['wɔndə*] *vi (person)* girare senza meta, girovagare; *(thoughts)* vagare; *(river)* serpeggiare; **~er** *n* vagabondo/a.

wane [weɪn] *vi (moon)* calare; *(reputation)* declinare.

want [wɔnt] *vt* volere; *(need)* aver bisogno di; *(lack)* mancare di // *n:* **for ~ of** per mancanza di; **~s** *npl (needs)* bisogni *mpl;* **to ~ to do** volere fare; **to ~ sb to do** volere che qd faccia; **to be found ~ing** non risultare all'altezza.

wanton ['wɔntn] *a* sfrenato(a); senza motivo.

war [wɔː*] *n* guerra; **to go to ~** entrare in guerra.

ward [wɔːd] *n (in hospital: room)* corsia; (: *section)* reparto; *(POL)* circoscrizione *f;* *(LAW: child)* pupillo/a; **to ~ off** *vt* parare, schivare.

warden ['wɔːdn] *n (of institution)* direttore/trice; *(of park, game reserve)* guardiano/a; *(also:* **traffic ~)** addetto/a al controllo del traffico e del parcheggio.

warder ['wɔːdə*] *n* guardia carceraria.

wardrobe ['wɔːdrəub] *n (cupboard)* guardaroba *m inv,* armadio; *(clothes)* guardaroba; *(THEATRE)* costumi *mpl.*

warehouse ['wɛəhaus] *n* magazzino.

wares [wɛəz] *npl* merci *fpl.*

warfare ['wɔːfɛə*] *n* guerra.

warhead ['wɔːhɛd] *n (MIL)* testata, ogiva.

warily ['wɛərɪlɪ] *ad* cautamente, con prudenza.

warlike ['wɔːlaɪk] *a* guerriero(a).

warm [wɔːm] *a* caldo(a); *(thanks, welcome, applause)* caloroso(a); **it's ~** fa caldo; **I'm ~** ho caldo; **to ~ up** *vi* scaldarsi, riscaldarsi; *(athlete, discussion)* riscaldarsi

// vt scaldare, riscaldare; (*engine*) far scaldare; ~-hearted a affettuoso(a); ~ly ad caldamente; calorosamente; vivamente; ~th n calore m.

warn [wɔːn] vt avvertire, avvisare; ~ing n avvertimento; (*notice*) avviso; ~ing light n spia luminosa.

warp [wɔːp] vi deformarsi // vt deformare; (*fig*) corrompere.

warrant ['wɔrnt] n (*LAW*: *to arrest*) mandato di cattura; (: *to search*) mandato di perquisizione.

warranty ['wɔrənti] n garanzia.

warrior ['wɔriə°] n guerriero/a.

warship ['wɔːʃip] n nave f da guerra.

wart [wɔːt] n verruca.

wartime ['wɔːtaim] n: **in** ~ in tempo di guerra.

wary ['wɛəri] a prudente.

was [wɔz] pt of be.

wash [wɔʃ] vt lavare // vi lavarsi // n: to give sth a ~ lavare qc, dare una lavata a qc; **to have a** ~ lavarsi; **to** ~ **away** vt (*stain*) togliere lavando; (*subj*: *river etc*) trascinare via; **to** ~ **down** vt lavare; **to** ~ **off** vi andare via con il lavaggio; **to** ~ **up** vi lavare i piatti; ~basin n lavabo; ~er n (*TECH*) rondella; ~ing n (*linen etc*) bucato; ~ing machine n lavatrice f; ~ing powder n detersivo (in polvere); ~ing-up n rigovernatura, lavatura dei piatti; ~-out n (*col*) disastro; ~room n gabinetto.

wasn't ['wɔznt] = was not.

wasp [wɔsp] n vespa.

wastage ['weistidʒ] n spreco; (*in manufacturing*) scarti mpl.

waste [weist] n spreco; (*of time*) perdita; (*rubbish*) rifiuti mpl // a (*material*) di scarto; (*food*) avanzato(a) // vt sprecare; (*time, opportunity*) perdere; ~s npl distesa desolata; **to** ~ **away** vi deperire; ~bin n bidone m or secchio della spazzatura; ~disposal unit n eliminatore m di rifiuti; ~ful a sprecone(a); (*process*) dispendioso(a); ~ ground n terreno incolto or abbandonato; ~paper basket n cestino per la carta straccia.

watch [wɔtʃ] n orologio; (*act of watching*) sorveglianza; (*guard*: MIL, NAUT) guardia; (NAUT: *spell of duty*) quarto // vt (*look at*) osservare; (: *match, programme*) guardare; (*spy on, guard*) sorvegliare, tenere d'occhio; (*be careful of*) fare attenzione a // vi osservare, guardare; (*keep guard*) fare or montare la guardia; **to** ~ **out** vi fare attenzione; ~dog n cane m da guardia; ~ful a attento(a), vigile; ~maker n orologiaio/a; ~man n guardiano; (*also*: night ~man) guardiano notturno; ~ strap n cinturino da orologio.

water ['wɔːtə°] n acqua // vt (*plant*) annaffiare; **in British** ~s nelle acque territoriali britanniche; **to** ~ **down** vt (*milk*) diluire; (*fig*: *story*) edulcorare; ~closet n W.C. m inv, gabinetto; ~colours npl colori mpl per acquarello; ~cress n crescione m; ~fall n cascata; ~ing can

n annaffiatoio; ~ level n livello dell'acqua; (*of flood*) livello delle acque; ~ lily n ninfea; ~line n (NAUT) linea di galleggiamento; ~logged a saturo(a) d'acqua; imbevuto(a) d'acqua; (*football pitch etc*) allagato(a); ~ main n conduttura dell'acqua; ~mark n (*on paper*) filigrana; ~melon n anguria, cocomero; ~ polo n pallanuoto f; ~proof a impermeabile; ~shed n (GEO, fig) spartiacque m; ~skiing n sci m acquatico; ~tight a stagno(a); ~works npl impianto idrico; ~y a (*colour*) slavato(a); (*coffee*) acquoso(a).

watt [wɔt] n watt m inv.

wave [weiv] n onda; (*of hand*) gesto, segno; (*in hair*) ondulazione f // vi fare un cenno con la mano; (*flag*) sventolare // vt (*handkerchief*) sventolare; (*stick*) brandire; (*hair*) ondulare; ~length n lunghezza d'onda.

waver ['weivə°] vi vacillare; (*voice*) tremolare.

wavy ['weivi] a ondulato(a); ondeggiante.

wax [wæks] n cera // vt dare la cera a; (*car*) lucidare // vi (*moon*) crescere; ~works npl cere fpl; museo delle cere.

way [wei] n via, strada; (*path, access*) passaggio; (*distance*) distanza; (*direction*) parte f, direzione f; (*manner*) modo, stile m; (*habit*) abitudine f; (*condition*) condizione f; **which** ~? – **this** ~ da che parte or in quale direzione? – da questa parte, per di qua; **to be on one's** ~ essere in cammino or sulla strada; **to be in the** ~ bloccare il passaggio; (*fig*) essere tra i piedi or d'impiccio; **to go out of one's** ~ **to do** (*fig*) mettercela tutta or fare di tutto per fare; **in a** ~ in un certo senso; **in some** ~s sotto certi aspetti; '~ in' 'entrata', 'ingresso'; '~ out' 'uscita'; **the** ~ **back** la via del ritorno.

waylay [wei'lei] vt irg tendere un agguato a; attendere al passaggio.

wayward ['weiwəd] a capriccioso(a); testardo(a).

W.C. ['dʌbljuː'siː] n W.C. m inv, gabinetto.

we [wiː] pl pronoun noi.

weak [wiːk] a debole; (*health*) precario(a); (*beam etc*) fragile; ~en vi indebolirsi // vt indebolire; ~ling n ['wiːkliŋ] n smidollato(a); debole m/f; ~ness n debolezza; (*fault*) punto debole, difetto.

wealth [welθ] n (*money, resources*) ricchezza, ricchezze fpl; (*of details*) abbondanza, profusione f; ~y a ricco(a).

wean [wiːn] vt svezzare.

weapon ['wepən] n arma.

wear [wɛə°] n (*use*) uso; (*deterioration through use*) logorio, usura; (*clothing*): sports/baby~ abbigliamento sportivo/per neonati // vb (*pt* wore, *pp* worn [wɔː°, wɔːn]) vt (*clothes*) portare; mettersi; (*damage*: *through use*) consumare // vi (*last*) durare; (*rub etc through*) consumarsi; town/evening ~ n abiti mpl or tenuta da città/sera; ~ and tear n usura, consumo; **to** ~ **away** vt

consumare; erodere // vi consumarsi;
essere eroso(a); to ~ down vt
consumare; (strength) esaurire; to ~ off
vi sparire lentamente; to ~ on vi passare;
to ~ out vt consumare; (person, strength)
esaurire.

weariness ['wɪərɪnɪs] n stanchezza.

weary ['wɪərɪ] a stanco(a); (tiring)
faticoso(a) // vi: to ~ of stancarsi di.

weasel ['wiːzl] n (ZOOL) donnola.

weather ['wɛðə°] n tempo // vt (wood)
stagionare; (storm, crisis) superare;
~-beaten a (person) segnato(a) dalle
intemperie; (building) logorato(a) dalle
intemperie; ~ cock n banderuola; ~
forecast n previsioni fpl del tempo,
bollettino meteorologico.

weave, pt wove, pp woven [wiːv, wəuv,
'wəuvn] vt (cloth) tessere; (basket)
intrecciare; ~r n tessitore/trice;
weaving n tessitura.

web [wɛb] n (of spider) ragnatela; (on foot)
palma; (fabric, also fig) tessuto; ~bed a
(foot) palmato(a).

wed [wɛd] vt (pt, pp wedded) sposare // n:
the newly-~s gli sposi novelli.

we'd [wiːd] = we had, we would.

wedding ['wɛdɪŋ] n matrimonio;
silver/golden ~ n nozze fpl
d'argento/d'oro; ~ day n giorno delle
nozze or del matrimonio; ~ dress n abito
nuziale; ~ present n regalo di nozze; ~
ring n fede f.

wedge [wɛdʒ] n (of wood etc) cuneo; (under
door etc) zeppa; (of cake) spicchio, fetta //
vt (fix) fissare con zeppe; (push)
incuneare.

wedlock ['wɛdlɔk] n vincolo
matrimoniale.

Wednesday ['wɛdnzdɪ] n mercole-dì m
inv.

wee [wiː] a (Scottish) piccolo(a);
piccolissimo(a).

weed [wiːd] n erbaccia // vt diserbare;
~-killer n diserbante m.

week [wiːk] n settimana; ~day n giorno
feriale; (COMM) giornata lavorativa; ~end
n fine settimana m or f inv, weekend m inv;
~ly ad ogni settimana, settimanalmente
// a,n settimanale (m).

weep, pt, pp wept [wiːp, wɛpt] vi (person)
piangere; ~ing willow n salice m
piangente.

weigh [weɪ] vt,vi pesare; to ~ anchor
salpare or levare l'ancora; to ~ down vt
(branch) piegare; (fig: with worry)
opprimere, caricare; to ~ up vt valutare.

weight [weɪt] n peso; sold by ~
venduto(a) a peso; ~lessness n
mancanza di peso; ~ lifter n pesista m;
~y a pesante; (fig) importante, grave.

weir [wɪə°] n diga.

weird [wɪəd] a strano(a), bizzarro(a);
(eerie) soprannaturale.

welcome ['wɛlkəm] a benvenuto(a) // n
accoglienza, benvenuto // vt accogliere
cordialmente; (also: bid ~) dare il
benvenuto a; (be glad of) rallegrarsi di; to

be ~ essere il(la) benvenuto(a);
welcoming a accogliente.

weld [wɛld] n saldatura // vt saldare; ~er
n (person) saldatore m; ~ing n saldatura
(autogena).

welfare ['wɛlfɛə°] n benessere m; ~
state n stato assistenziale; ~ work n
assistenza sociale.

well [wɛl] n pozzo // ad bene // a: to be ~
andare bene; (person) stare bene // excl
allora!; mai; ebbene!; ~ done! bravo(a)!;
get ~ soon! guarisci presto!; to do ~ in
sth riuscire in qc.

we'll [wiːl] = we will, we shall.

well: ~-behaved a ubbidiente; ~-being
n benessere m; ~-built a (person) ben
fatto(a); ~-developed a (girl) sviluppata;
~-earned a (rest) meritato(a);
~-groomed a curato(a), azzimato(a);
~-heeled a (col: wealthy) agiato(a),
facoltoso(a).

wellingtons ['wɛlɪŋtənz] npl (also:
wellington boots) stivali mpl di gomma.

well: ~-known a (person) ben noto(a); (:
famous) famoso(a); ~-meaning a ben
intenzionato(a); ~-off a benestante,
danaroso(a); ~-read a colto(a); ~-to-do
a abbiente, benestante.

Welsh [wɛlʃ] a gallese // n (LING) gallese
m; ~man/woman n gallese m/f; ~
rarebit n crostino al formaggio.

went [wɛnt] pt of go.

wept [wɛpt] pt, pp of weep.

were [wəː°] pt of be.

we're [wɪə°] = we are.

weren't [wəːnt] = were not.

west [wɛst] n ovest m, occidente m,
ponente m // a (a) ovest inv, occidentale
// ad verso ovest; the W~ n l'Occidente
m; the W~ Country n il sud-ovest
dell'Inghilterra; ~erly a (wind)
occidentale, da ovest; ~ern a
occidentale, dell'ovest // n (CINEMA)
western m inv; W~ Germany n
Germania occidentale or ovest; W~
Indies npl Indie fpl occidentali;
~ward(s) ad verso ovest.

wet [wɛt] a umido(a), bagnato(a); (soaked)
fradicio(a); (rainy) piovoso(a); to get ~
bagnarsi; ~ blanket n (fig) guastafeste
m/f; '~ paint' 'vernice fresca'; ~ suit n
tuta da sub.

we've [wiːv] = we have.

whack [wæk] vt picchiare, battere; ~ed a
(col: tired) sfinito(a), a pezzi.

whale [weɪl] n (ZOOL) balena.

wharf, wharves [wɔːf, wɔːvz] n banchina.

what [wɔt] excl cosa!, come! // det quale //
pronoun (interrogative) che cosa, cosa,
che; (relative) quello che, ciò che; ~ a
mess! che disordine!; ~ is it called?
come si chiama?; ~ about doing ...?
cosa ne diresti di fare ...?; ~ about me? e
io?; ~ever det: ~ever book qualunque
or qualsiasi libro + sub // pronoun: do
~ever is necessary/you want faccia
qualunque or qualsiasi cosa sia
necessaria/lei voglia; ~ever happens

qualunque cosa accada; **no reason** ~**ever** or ~**soever** nessuna ragione affatto or al mondo.

wheat [wi:t] n grano, frumento.

wheel [wi:l] n ruota; (AUT: also: **steering** ~) volante m; (NAUT) (ruota del) timone m // vt spingere // vi (also: ~ **round**) girare; ~**barrow** n carriola; ~**chair** n sedia a rotelle.

wheeze [wi:z] n respiro affannoso // vi ansimare.

when [wɛn] ad quando // cj quando, nel momento in cui; (whereas) mentre; ~**ever** ad quando mai // cj quando; (every time that) ogni volta che.

where [wɛə*] ad,cj dove; **this is** ~ è qui che; ~**abouts** ad dove qd si trova; ~**as** cj mentre; ~**by** ad da cui // cj dovunque + sub.

whet [wɛt] vt (tool) affilare; (appetite etc) stimolare.

whether ['wɛðə*] cj se; **I don't know** ~ **to accept or not** non so se accettare o no; **it's doubtful** ~ è poco probabile che; ~ **you go or not** che tei vada o no.

which [wɪtʃ] det (interrogative) che, quale; ~ **one of you?** chi di voi?; **tell me** ~ **one you want** mi dica quale vuole // pronoun (interrogative, indirect) quale; (relative: subject) che; (: object) che, prep + cui, il(la) quale; **I don't mind** ~ non mi importa quale; **the apple** ~ **you ate/**~ **is on the table** la mela che ha mangiato/che è sul tavolo; **the chair on** ~ **la sedia sulla quale** or su cui; **the book of** ~ il libro del quale or di cui; **he said he knew,** ~ **is true/I feared** disse che lo sapeva, il che è vero/ciò che temevo; **after** ~ dopo di che; **in** ~ **case** nel qual caso; ~**ever** det: **take** ~**ever book you prefer** prenda qualsiasi libro che preferisce; ~**ever book you take** qualsiasi libro prenda.

whiff [wɪf] n soffio; sbuffo; odore m.

while [waɪl] n momento // cj mentre; (as long as) finché; (although) sebbene + sub; per quanto + sub; **for a** ~ per un po'.

whim [wɪm] n capriccio.

whimper ['wɪmpə*] n piagnucolìo // vi piagnucolare.

whimsical ['wɪmzɪkl] a (person) capriccioso(a); (look) strano(a).

whine [waɪn] n gemito // vi gemere; uggiolare; piagnucolare.

whip [wɪp] n frusta; (for riding) frustino; (Brit: POL: person) capogruppo (che sovrintende alla disciplina dei colleghi di partito) // vt frustare; (snatch) sollevare (or estrarre) bruscamente; ~**ped cream** n panna montata; ~-**round** n colletta.

whirl [wə:l] n turbine m // vt (far) girare rapidamente; (far) turbinare // vi turbinare; ~**pool** n mulinello; ~**wind** n turbine m.

whirr [wə:*] vi ronzare; rombare; frullare.

whisk [wɪsk] n (CULIN) frusta; frullino // vt sbattere, frullare; **to** ~ **sb away** or **off**

portar via qd a tutta velocità.

whisker ['wɪskə*] n: ~**s** npl (of animal) baffi mpl; (of man) favoriti mpl.

whisk(e)y ['wɪskɪ] n whisky m inv.

whisper ['wɪspə*] n sussurro; (rumour) voce f // vt,vi sussurrare.

whist [wɪst] n whist m.

whistle ['wɪsl] n (sound) fischio; (object) fischietto // vi fischiare.

white [waɪt] a bianco(a); (with fear) pallido(a) // n bianco; (person) bianco/a; ~-**collar worker** n impiegato; ~ **lie** n bugia pietosa; ~**ness** n bianchezza; ~**wash** n (paint) bianco di calce // vt imbiancare; (fig) coprire.

Whitsun ['wɪtsn] n la Pentecoste.

whittle ['wɪtl] vt: **to** ~ **away,** ~ **down** ridurre, tagliare.

whizz [wɪz] vi sfrecciare; ~ **kid** n (col) ragazzo/a prodigio.

WHO n (abbr of World Health Organization) O.M.S. f (Organizzazione mondiale della sanità).

who [hu:] pronoun (interrogative) chi; (relative) che; ~**dunit** [hu:'dʌnɪt] n (col) giallo; ~**ever** pronoun: ~**ever finds it** chiunque lo trovi; **ask** ~**ever you like** lo chieda a chiunque vuole; ~**ever told you that?** chi mai gliel'ha detto?

whole [həul] a (complete) tutto(a), completo(a); (not broken) intero(a), intatto(a) // n (total) totale m; (sth not broken) tutto; **the** ~ **of the time** tutto il tempo; **on the** ~, **as a** ~ nel complesso, nell'insieme; ~**hearted** a sincero(a); ~**sale** n commercio or vendita all'ingrosso // a all'ingrosso; (destruction) totale; ~**saler** n grossista m/f; ~**some** a sano(a); salutare; **wholly** ad completamente, del tutto.

whom [hu:m] pronoun che, prep + il(la) quale; (interrogative) chi.

whooping cough ['hu:pɪŋkɔf] n pertosse f.

whopping ['wɔpɪŋ] a (col: big) enorme.

whore [hɔ:*] n (pej) puttana.

whose [hu:z] det: ~ **book is this?** di chi è questo libro?; ~ **pencil have you taken?** di chi è la matita che ha preso?; **the man** ~ **son you rescued** l'uomo di cui or del quale ha salvato il figlio; **the girl** ~ **sister you were speaking to** la ragazza alla sorella di cui or della quale stava parlando // pronoun: ~ **is this?** di chi è questo?; **I know** ~ **it is** so di chi è.

why [waɪ] ad perché // excl oh!; ma come!; **the reason** ~ **la ragione perché** or **per la quale;** ~**ever** ad perché mai.

wick [wɪk] n lucignolo, stoppino.

wicked ['wɪkɪd] a cattivo(a), malvagio(a); maligno(a); perfido(a); (mischievous) malizioso(a).

wicker ['wɪkə*] n vimine m; (also: ~**work**) articoli mpl di vimini.

wicket ['wɪkɪt] n (CRICKET) porta; area tra le due porte.

wide [waɪd] a largo(a); (region, knowledge) vasto(a); (choice) ampio(a) // ad: **to open** ~ spalancare; **to shoot** ~ tirare a vuoto

or fuori bersaglio; **~-angle lens** *n*
grandangolare *m*; **~-awake** *a*
completamente sveglio(a); **~ly** *ad*
(*different*) molto, completamente;
(*believed*) generalmente; **~ly spaced**
molto distanziati(e); **~n** *vt* allargare,
ampliare; **~ open** *a* spalancato(a);
~spread *a* (*belief etc*) molto *or* assai
diffuso(a).

widow ['wɪdəu] *n* vedova; **~ed** *a* (che è
rimasto(a)) vedovo(a); **~er** *n* vedovo.

width [wɪdθ] *n* larghezza.

wield [wi:ld] *vt* (*sword*) maneggiare;
(*power*) esercitare.

wife, wives [waɪf, waɪvz] *n* moglie *f*.

wig [wɪg] *n* parrucca.

wiggle ['wɪgl] *vt* dimenare, agitare // *vi*
(*loose screw etc*) traballare; (*worm*)
torcersi.

wild [waɪld] *a* selvatico(a); selvaggio(a);
(*sea*) tempestoso(a); (*idea, life*) folle;
stravagante; **~s** *npl* regione *f* selvaggia;
~erness ['wɪldənɪs] *n* deserto; **~goose
chase** *n* (*fig*) pista falsa; **~life** *n* natura;
~ly *ad* (*applaud*) freneticamente; (*hit,
guess*) a casaccio; (*happy*) follemente.

wilful ['wɪlful] *a* (*person*) testardo(a),
ostinato(a); (*action*) intenzionale; (*crime*)
premeditato(a).

will [wɪl] *auxiliary vb*: he **~ come** verrà //
vt (*pt, pp* **~ed**): to **~ sb to do** volere che
qd faccia; he **~ed himself to go on**
continuò grazie a un grande sforzo di
volontà // *n* volontà; testamento; **~ing** *a*
volonteroso(a); **~ing to do** disposto(a) a
fare; **~ingly** *ad* volentieri; **~ingness** *n*
buona volontà.

willow ['wɪləu] *n* salice *m*.

will power ['wɪlpauə*] *n* forza di volontà.

wilt [wɪlt] *vi* appassire.

wily ['waɪlɪ] *a* furbo(a).

win [wɪn] *n* (*in sports etc*) vittoria // *vb* (*pt,
pp* **won** [wʌn]) *vt* (*battle, prize*) vincere;
(*money*) guadagnare; (*popularity*) conquistare // *vi* vincere; to **~ over**, **~
round** *vt* convincere.

wince [wɪns] *n* trasalimento, sussulto // *vi*
trasalire.

winch [wɪntʃ] *n* verricello, argano.

wind *n* [wɪnd] vento; (*MED*) flatulenza,
ventosità // *vb* (*pt, pp* **wound**
[waund]) *vt* attorcigliare; (*wrap*)
avvolgere; (*clock, toy*) caricare; (*take
breath away*: [wɪnd]) far restare senza
fiato // *vi* (*road, river*) serpeggiare; to **~
up** *vt* (*clock*) caricare; (*debate*)
concludere; **~break** *n* frangivento; **~fall**
n colpo di fortuna; **~ing** ['waɪndɪŋ] *a*
(*road*) serpeggiante; (*staircase*) a
chiocciola; **~ instrument** *n* (*MUS*)
strumento a fiato; **~mill** *n* mulino a
vento.

window ['wɪndəu] *n* finestra; (*in car, train*)
finestrino; (*in shop etc*) vetrina; (*also*: **~
pane**) vetro; **~ box** *n* cassetta da fiori; **~
cleaner** *n* (*person*) pulitore *m* di finestre;
~ ledge *n* davanzale *m*; **~ pane** *n* vetro;
~ sill *n* davanzale *m*.

windpipe ['wɪndpaɪp] *n* trachea.

windscreen, windshield (*US*)
['wɪndskri:n, 'wɪndʃi:ld] *n* parabrezza *m*
inv; **~ washer** *n* lavacristallo; **~ wiper**
n tergicristallo.

windswept ['wɪndswɛpt] *a* spazzato(a) dal
vento.

windy ['wɪndɪ] *a* ventoso(a); **it's ~** c'è
vento.

wine [waɪn] *n* vino; **~ cellar** *n* cantina; **~
glass** *n* bicchiere *m* da vino; **~ list** *n* lista
dei vini; **~ tasting** *n* degustazione *f* dei
vini; **~ waiter** *n* sommelier *m inv*.

wing [wɪŋ] *n* ala; **~s** *npl* (*THEATRE*) quinte
fpl; **~er** *n* (*SPORT*) ala.

wink [wɪŋk] *n* ammiccamento // *vi*
ammiccare, fare l'occhiolino.

winner ['wɪnə*] *n* vincitore/trice.

winning ['wɪnɪŋ] *a* (*team*) vincente; (*goal*)
decisivo(a); **~s** *npl* vincite *fpl*; **~ post** *n*
traguardo.

winter ['wɪntə*] *n* inverno; **~ sports** *npl*
sport *mpl* invernali.

wintry ['wɪntrɪ] *a* invernale.

wipe [waɪp] *n* pulita, passata // *vt* pulire
(strofinando); (*dishes*) asciugare; to **~ off**
vt cancellare; (*stains*) togliere strofinando;
to **~ out** *vt* (*debt*) pagare, liquidare;
(*memory*) cancellare; (*destroy*)
annientare; to **~ up** *vt* asciugare.

wire ['waɪə*] *n* filo; (*ELEC*) filo elettrico;
(*TEL*) telegramma *m*.

wireless ['waɪəlɪs] *n* telegrafia senza fili;
(*set*) (apparecchio *m*) radio *f inv*.

wiry ['waɪərɪ] *a* magro(a) e nerboruto(a).

wisdom ['wɪzdəm] *n* saggezza; (*of action*)
prudenza; **~ tooth** *n* dente *m* del giudizio.

wise [waɪz] *a* saggio(a); prudente;
giudizioso(a).

...wise [waɪz] *suffix*: **time~** per quanto
riguarda il tempo, in termini di tempo.

wisecrack ['waɪzkræk] *n* battuta
spiritosa.

wish [wɪʃ] *n* (*desire*) desiderio; (*specific
desire*) richiesta // *vt* desiderare, volere;
best ~es (*on birthday etc*) i migliori
auguri; **with best ~es** (*in letter*) cordiali
saluti, con i migliori saluti; to **~ sb
goodbye** dire arrivederci a qd; **he ~ed**
me well mi augurò di riuscire; to **~ to
do/sb to do** desiderare *or* volere fare/che
qd faccia; to **~ for** desiderare; **it's ~ful**
thinking è prendere i desideri per realtà.

wisp [wɪsp] *n* ciuffo, ciocca; (*of smoke,
straw*) filo.

wistful ['wɪstful] *a* malinconico(a).

wit [wɪt] *n* (*gen pl*) intelligenza; presenza di
spirito; (*wittiness*) spirito, arguzia; (*person*)
bello spirito; to be at one's **~s' end** (*fig*)
non sapere più cosa fare; to **~ ad** cioè.

witch [wɪtʃ] *n* strega; **~craft** *n*
stregoneria.

with [wɪð, wɪθ] *prep* con; **red ~ anger**
rosso dalla *or* per la rabbia; **covered ~**
snow coperto di neve; **the man ~ the**
grey hat l'uomo dal *or* col cappello grigio; **to be**
~ it (*fig*) essere al corrente; essere

sveglio(a); **I am ~ you** (*I understand*) la
seguo.

withdraw [wɪð'drɔ:] *vb* (*irg*) *vt* ritirare;
(*money from bank*) ritirare; prelevare // *vi*
ritirarsi; (*go back on promise*) ritrattarsi;
~al *n* ritiro; prelievo; (*of army*) ritirata;
(*MED*) stato di privazione.

wither ['wɪðə*] *vi* appassire; **~ed a**
appassito(a); (*limb*) atrofizzato(a).

withhold [wɪð'hauld] *vt irg* (*money*)
trattenere; (*decision*) rimettere,
rimandare; (*permission*): **to ~ (from)**
rifiutare (a); (*information*): **to ~ (from)**
nascondere (a).

within [wɪð'ɪn] *prep* all'interno; (*in time,
distances*) entro // *ad* all'interno, dentro;
~ sight of in vista di; **~ a mile of** entro
un miglio da; **~ the week** prima della
fine della settimana.

without [wɪð'aut] *prep* senza.

withstand [wɪð'stænd] *vt irg* resistere a.

witness ['wɪtnɪs] *n* (*person*) testimone *m/f*
// *vi* (*event*) essere testimone di;
(*document*) attestare l'autenticità di; **to
bear ~ to sth** testimoniare qc; **~ box,
~ stand** (*US*) *n* banco dei testimoni.

witticism ['wɪtɪsɪzm] *n* spiritosaggine *f.*

witty ['wɪtɪ] *a* spiritoso(a).

wives [waɪvz] *npl of* **wife.**

wizard ['wɪzəd] *n* mago.

wk *abbr of* **week.**

wobble ['wɔbl] *vi* tremare; (*chair*)
traballare.

woe [wəu] *n* dolore *m*; disgrazia.

woke [wəuk] *pt of* **wake; ~n** *pp of* **wake.**

wolf, wolves [wulf, wulvz] *n* lupo.

woman, *pl* **women** ['wumən, 'wɪmɪn] *n*
donna; **~ doctor** *n* dottoressa; **~ly** *a*
femminile.

womb [wu:m] *n* (*ANAT*) utero.

women ['wɪmɪn] *npl of* **woman.**

won [wʌn] *pt,pp of* **win.**

wonder ['wʌndə*] *n* meraviglia // *vi*: **to
~ whether** domandarsi se; **to ~ at**
essere sorpreso(a) di; meravigliarsi di; **to
~ about** domandarsi di; pensare a; **it's
no ~ that** c'è poco *or* non c'è da
meravigliarsi **che +** *sub*; **~ful a**
meraviglioso(a); **~fully** *ad* (+ *adjective*)
meravigliosamente; (+ *vb*) a meraviglia.

wonky ['wɔŋkɪ] *a* (*col*) traballante.

won't [wəunt] = **will not.**

woo [wu:] *vt* (*woman*) fare la corte a.

wood [wud] *n* legno; (*timber*) legname *m*;
(*forest*) bosco; **~ carving** *n* scultura in
legno, intaglio; **~ed a** boschivo(a);
boscoso(a); **~en a** di legno; (*fig*)
rigido(a); inespressivo(a); **~pecker** *n*
picchio; **~wind** *n* (*MUS*) strumento a fiato
in legno; **the ~wind** (*MUS*) i legni;
~work *n* parti *fpl* in legno; (*craft, subject*)
falegnameria; **~worm** *n* tarlo del legno.

wool [wul] *n* lana; **to pull the ~ over sb's
eyes** (*fig*) imbrogliare qd; **~len** *a* di lana;
~lens *npl* indumenti *mpl* di lana; **~ly** *a*
lanoso(a); (*fig*: *ideas*) confuso(a).

word [wɜːd] *n* parola; (*news*) notizie *fpl* //
vt esprimere, formulare; **in other ~s** in

altre parole; **to break/keep one's ~** non
mantenere/mantenere la propria parola;
I'll take your ~ for it la crederò sulla
parola; **~ing** *n* formulazione *f*; **~y** *a*
verboso(a).

wore [wɔ:*] *pt of* **wear.**

work [wɜːk] *n* lavoro; (*ART, LITERATURE*)
opera // *vi* lavorare; (*mechanism, plan etc*)
funzionare; (*medicine*) essere efficace //
vt (*clay, wood etc*) lavorare; (*mine etc*)
sfruttare; (*machine*) far funzionare; **to be
out of ~** essere disoccupato(a); **~s** *n*
(*factory*) fabbrica // *npl* (*of clock,
machine*) meccanismo; **to ~ loose** *vi*
allentarsi; **to ~ on** *vt fus* lavorare a;
(*principle*) basarsi su; **to ~ out** *vi* (*plans
etc*) riuscire, andare bene // *vt* (*problem*)
risolvere; (*plan*) elaborare; **it ~s out at
£100** fa 100 sterline; **to get ~ed up**
andare su tutte le furie; eccitarsi; **~able a**
(*solution*) realizzabile; **~er** *n*
lavoratore/trice, operaio/a; **~ing class** *n*
classe *f* operaia *or* lavoratrice; **~ing-
class a** operaio(a); **~ing man** *n*
lavoratore *m*; **in ~ing order**
funzionante; **~man** *n* operaio;
~manship *n* abilità; lavoro; fattura;
~shop *n* officina; **~-to-rule** *n* sciopero
bianco.

world [wɜːld] *n* mondo // *cpd* (*champion*)
del mondo; (*power, war*) mondiale; **to
think the ~ of sb** (*fig*) pensare un gran
bene di qd; **out of this ~** a formidabile;
~ly *a* di questo mondo; **~-wide a**
universale.

worm [wɜːm] *n* verme *m.*

worn [wɔ:n] *pp of* **wear** // *a* usato(a);
~-out a (*object*) consumato(a), logoro(a);
(*person*) sfinito(a).

worried ['wʌrɪd] *a* preoccupato(a).

worrier ['wʌrɪə*] *n* ansioso/a.

worry ['wʌrɪ] *n* preoccupazione *f* // *vt*
preoccupare // *vi* preoccuparsi; **~ing a**
preoccupante.

worse [wɜːs] *a* peggiore // *ad, n* peggio; **a
change for the ~** un peggioramento;
~n *vt, vi* peggiorare; **~ off a** in
condizioni (economiche) peggiori.

worship ['wɜːʃɪp] *n* culto // *vt* (*God*)
adorare, venerare; (*person*) adorare;
Your W~ (*to mayor*) signor sindaco; (*to
judge*) signor giudice; **~per** *n*
adoratore/trice; (*in church*) fedele *m/f,*
devoto/a.

worst [wɜːst] *a* il(la) peggiore // *ad, n*
peggio; **at ~** al peggio, per male che
vada.

worsted ['wustɪd] *n*: (**wool**) **~ lana**
pettinata.

worth [wɜːθ] *n* valore *m* // *a*: **to be ~**
valere; **it's ~** it ne vale la pena; **50
pence ~ of apples** 50 pence di mele;
~less a di nessun valore; **~while a**
(*activity*) utile; (*cause*) lodevole; **a
~while book** un libro che vale la pena
leggere.

worthy ['wɜːðɪ] *a* (*person*) degno(a);
(*motive*) lodevole; **~ of** degno di.

would [wud] *auxiliary vb*: **she ~ come** verrebbe; **he ~ have come** sarebbe venuto; **~ you like a biscuit?** vuole *or* vorrebbe un biscotto?; **he ~ go there on Mondays** ci andava il lunedì; **~-be** *a* (*pej*) sedicente.

wound *vb* [waund] *pt, pp of* **wind** // *n*,*vt* [wu:nd] *n* ferita // *vt* ferire; **~ed in the leg** ferito(a) alla gamba.

wove [wəuv] *pt of* **weave;** **~n** *pp of* **weave.**

wrangle ['ræŋgl] *n* litigio // *vi* litigare.

wrap [ræp] *n* (*stole*) scialle *m*; (*cape*) mantellina // *vt* (*also*: **~ up**) avvolgere; (*parcel*) incartare; **~per** *n* (*of book*) copertina; **~ping paper** *n* carta da pacchi; (*for gift*) carta da regali.

wrath [rɔθ] *n* collera, ira.

wreath, **~s** [ri:θ, ri:ðz] *n* corona.

wreck [rek] *n* (*sea disaster*) naufragio; (*ship*) relitto; (*pej: person*) rottame *m* // *vt* demolire; (*ship*) far naufragare; (*fig*) rovinare; **~age** *n* rottami *mpl*; (*of building*) macerie *fpl*; (*of ship*) relitti *mpl*.

wren [ren] *n* (*ZOOL*) scricciolo.

wrench [rentʃ] *n* (*TECH*) chiave *f*; (*tug*) torsione *f* brusca; (*fig*) strazio // *vt* strappare; storcere; **to ~ sth from** strappare qc a *or* da.

wrestle ['resl] *vi*: **to ~ (with sb)** lottare (con qd); **to ~ with** (*fig*) combattere *or* lottare contro; **~r** *n* lottatore/trice; **wrestling** *n* lotta; (*also*: **all-in wrestling**) catch *m*, lotta libera.

wretched ['retʃid] *a* disgraziato(a); (*col: weather, holiday*) orrendo(a), orribile; (: *child, dog*) pestifero(a).

wriggle ['rɪgl] *n* contorsione *f* // *vi* dimenarsi; (*snake, worm*) serpeggiare, muoversi serpeggiando.

wring, *pt, pp* **wrung** [rɪŋ, rʌŋ] *vt* torcere; (*wet clothes*) strizzare; (*fig*): **to ~ sth out of** strappare qc a.

wrinkle ['rɪŋkl] *n* (*on skin*) ruga; (*on paper etc*) grinza // *vt* corrugare; raggrinzire // *vi* corrugarsi; raggrinzirsi.

wrist [rist] *n* polso; **~ watch** *n* orologio da polso.

writ [rit] *n* ordine *m*; mandato.

write, *pt* **wrote,** *pp* **written** [rait, rəut, 'ritn] *vt, vi* scrivere; **to ~ down** *vt* annotare; (*put in writing*) mettere per iscritto; **to ~ off** *vt* (*debt*) cancellare; (*depreciate*) deprezzare; **to ~ out** *vt* scrivere; (*copy*) ricopiare; **to ~ up** *vt* redigere; **~-off** *n* perdita completa; **the car is a ~-off** la macchina va bene per il demolitore; **~r** *n* autore/trice, scrittore/trice.

writhe [raið] *vi* contorcersi.

writing ['raitiŋ] *n* scrittura; (*of author*) scritto, opera; **in ~** per iscritto; **~ paper** *n* carta da scrivere.

written ['ritn] *pp of* **write.**

wrong [rɔŋ] *a* sbagliato(a); (*not suitable*) inadatto(a); (*wicked*) cattivo(a); (*unfair*) ingiusto(a) // *ad* in modo sbagliato, erroneamente // *n* (*evil*) male *m*;

(*injustice*) torto // *vt* fare torto a; **you are ~ to do it** hai torto a farlo; **you are ~ about that** ti sbagli; **to be in the ~** avere torto; **what's ~?** cosa c'è che non va?; **to go ~** (*person*) sbagliarsi; (*plan*) fallire, non riuscire; (*machine*) guastarsi; **~ful** *a* illegittimo(a); ingiusto(a); **~ly** *ad* a torto.

wrote [rəut] *pt of* **write.**

wrought [rɔ:t] *a*: **~ iron** ferro battuto.

wrung [rʌŋ] *pt, pp of* **wring.**

wry [rai] *a* storto(a).

wt. *abbr of* **weight.**

X Y Z

Xmas ['eksməs] *n abbr of* **Christmas.**

X-ray ['eks'rei] *n* raggio X; (*photograph*) radiografia // *vt* radiografare.

xylophone ['zailəfəun] *n* xilofono.

yacht [jɔt] *n* panfilo, yacht *m inv*; **~ing** *n* yachting *m*, sport *m* della vela; **~sman** *n* yachtsman *m inv*.

Yank [jæŋk] *n* (*pej*) yankee *m/f inv*.

yap [jæp] *vi* (*dog*) guaire, abbaiare.

yard [jɑ:d] *n* (*of house etc*) cortile *m*; (*measure*) iarda (= 914 mm; 3 feet); **~stick** *n* (*fig*) misura, criterio.

yarn [jɑ:n] *n* filato; (*tale*) lunga storia.

yawn [jɔ:n] *n* sbadiglio // *vi* sbadigliare; **~ing** *a* (*gap*) spalancato(a).

yd. *abbr of* **yard(s).**

year [jiə*] *n* anno; (*referring to harvest, wine etc*) annata; **~ly** *a* annuale // *ad* annualmente.

yearn [jɔ:n] *vi*: **to ~ for sth/to do** desiderare ardentemente qc/di fare; **~ing** *n* desiderio intenso.

yeast [ji:st] *n* lievito.

yell [jel] *n* urlo // *vi* urlare.

yellow ['jeləu] *a* giallo(a).

yelp [jelp] *n* guaito, uggiolio // *vi* guaire, uggiolare.

yes [jes] *ad, n* sì (*m inv*).

yesterday ['jestədi] *ad,n* ieri (*m inv*).

yet [jet] *ad* ancora; già // *cj* ma, tuttavia; **it is not finished ~** non è ancora finito; **the best ~** finora il migliore; **as ~** finora.

yew [ju:] *n* tasso.

Yiddish ['jidiʃ] *n* yiddish *m*.

yield [ji:ld] *n* produzione *f*, resa; reddito // *vt* produrre, rendere; (*surrender*) cedere // *vi* cedere.

yodel ['jəudl] *vi* cantare lo jodel *or* alla tirolese.

yoga ['jəugə] *n* yoga *m*.

yog(h)ourt, yog(h)urt ['jəugət] *n* iogurt *m inv*.

yoke [jəuk] *n* giogo.

yolk [jəuk] *n* tuorlo, rosso d'uovo.

yonder ['jɔndə*] *ad* là.

you [ju:] *pronoun* tu; (*polite form*) lei; (*pl*) voi; (: *very formal*) loro; (*complement: direct*) ti; la; vi; li; (: *indirect*) ti; le; vi; gli; (*stressed*) te; lei; voi; loro; (*one*): **fresh air**

does ~ **good** l'aria fresca fa bene; ~ **never know** non si sa mai.

you'd [ju:d] = **you had; you would.**

you'll [ju:l] = **you will; you shall.**

young [jʌŋ] a giovane // npl (of animal) piccoli mpl; (people): **the** ~ i giovani, la gioventù; ~**ster** n giovanotto, ragazzo; (child) bambino/a.

your [jɔː°] a il(la) tuo(a), pl i(le) tuoi(tue); il(la) suo(a), pl i(le) suoi(sue); il(la) vostro(a), pl i(le) vostri(e); il(la) loro, pl i(le) loro.

you're [juə°] = **you are.**

yours [jɔːz] pronoun il(la) tuo(a), pl i(le) tuoi(tue); (polite form) il(la) suo(a), pl i(le) suoi(sue); (pl) il(la) vostro(a), pl i(le) vostri(e); (: very formal) il(la) loro, pl i(le) loro; ~ **sincerely/faithfully** cordiali/distinti saluti.

yourself [jɔː'sɛlf] pronoun (reflexive) ti; si; (after prep) te; sé; (emphatic) tu stesso(a); lei stesso(a); **yourselves** pl pronoun (reflexive) vi; si; (after prep) voi; loro; (emphatic) voi stessi(e); loro stessi(e).

youth [ju:θ] n gioventù f; (young man: pl ~**s** [ju:ðz]) giovane m, ragazzo; ~**ful** a giovane; da giovane; giovanile; ~ **hostel** n ostello della gioventù.

you've [ju:v] = **you have.**

Yugoslav ['ju:gəʊ'slɑ:v] a, n jugoslavo(a).

Yugoslavia ['ju:gəʊ'slɑ:vɪə] n Jugoslavia.

zany ['zeɪnɪ] a un po' pazzo(a).

zeal [zi:l] n zelo; entusiasmo; ~**ous** ['zɛləs] a zelante; premuroso(a).

zebra ['zi:brə] n zebra; ~ **crossing** n (passaggio pedonale a) strisce fpl, zebre fpl.

zero ['zɪərəʊ] n zero; ~ **hour** n l'ora zero.

zest [zɛst] n gusto; (CULIN) buccia.

zigzag ['zɪgzæg] n zigzag m inv // vi zigzagare.

zinc [zɪŋk] n zinco.

zip [zɪp] n (also: ~ **fastener,** ~**per**) chiusura f or cerniera f lampo inv // vt (also: ~ **up**) chiudere con una cerniera lampo.

zither ['zɪðə°] n cetra.

zodiac ['zəʊdɪæk] n zodiaco.

zombie ['zɒmbɪ] n (fig): **like a** ~ come un morto che cammina.

zone [zəʊn] n zona; (subdivision of town) quartiere m.

zoo [zu:] n zoo m inv.

zoologist [zu:'ɒlədʒɪst] n zoologo/a.

zoology [zu:'ɒlədʒɪ] n zoologia.

zoom [zu:m] vi: **to** ~ **past** sfrecciare; ~ **lens** n zoom m inv, obiettivo a focale variabile.

ITALIAN VERBS

1 Gerundio *2* Participio passato *3* Presente *4* Imperfetto *5* Passato remoto *6* Futuro *7* Condizionale *8* Congiuntivo presente *9* Congiuntivo passato *10* Imperativo

andare *3* vado, vai, va, andiamo, andate, vanno *6* andrò *etc 8* vada *10* va'!, vada!, andate!, vadano!

apparire *2* apparso *3* appaio, appari *o* apparisci, appare *o* apparisce, appaiono *o* appariscono *5* apparvi *o* apparsi, apparisti, apparve *o* appari *o* apparse, apparvero *o* apparirono *o* apparsero *8* appaia *o* apparisca

aprire *2* aperto *3* apro *5* aprii *o* apersi, apristi *8* apra

AVERE *3* ho, hai, ha, abbiamo, avete, hanno *5* ebbi, avesti, ebbe, avemmo, aveste, ebbero *6* avrò *etc 8* abbia *etc 10* abbi!, abbia!, abbiate!, abbiano!

bere *1* bevendo *2* bevuto *3* bevo *etc 4* bevevo *etc 5* bevvi *o* bevetti, bevesti *6* berrò *etc 8* beva *etc 9* bevessi *etc*

cadere *5* caddi, cadesti *6* cadrò *etc*

cogliere *2* colto *3* colgo, colgono *5* colsi, cogliesti *8* colga

correre *2* corso *5* corsi, corresti

cuocere *2* cotto *3* cuocio, cociamo, cuociono *5* cossi, cocesti

dare *3* do, dai, da, diamo, date, danno *5* diedi *o* detti, desti *6* darò *etc 8* dia *etc 9* dessi *etc 10* da'!, dia!, date!, diano!

dire *1* dicendo *2* detto *3* dico, dici, dice, diciamo, dite, dicono *4* dicevo *etc 5* dissi, dicesti *6* dirò *etc 8* dica, diciamo, diciate, dicano *9* dicessi *etc 10* di'!, dica!, dite!, dicano!

dolere *3* dolgo, duoli, duole, dolgono *5* dolsi, dolesti *6* dorrò *etc 8* dolga

dovere *3* devo *o* debbo, devi, deve, dobbiamo, dovete, devono *o* debbono *6* dovrò *etc 8* debba, dobbiamo, dobbiate, devano *o* debbano

ESSERE *2* stato *3* sono, sei, è, siamo, siete, sono *4* ero, eri, era, eravamo, eravate, erano *5* fui, fosti, fu, fummo, foste, furono *6* sarò *etc 8* sia *etc 9* fossi, fossi, fosse, fossimo, foste, fossero *10* sii!, sia!, siate!, siano!

fare *1* facendo *2* fatto *3* faccio, fai, fa, facciamo, fate, fanno *4* facevo *etc 5* feci, facesti *6* farò *etc 8* faccia *etc 9* facessi *etc 10* fa'!, faccia!, fate!, facciano!

FINIRE *1* finendo *2* finito *3* finisco, finisci, finisce, finiamo, finite, finiscono *4* finivo, finivi, finiva, finivamo, finivate, finivano *5* finii, finisti, finì, finimmo, finiste, finirono *6* finirò, finirai, finirà, finiremo, finirete, finiranno *7* finirei, finiresti, finirebbe, finiremmo, finireste, finirebbero *8* finisca, finisca, finisca, finiamo, finiate, finiscano *9* finissi, finissi, finisse, finissimo, finiste, finissero *10* finisci!, finisca!, finite!, finiscano!

giungere *2* giunto *5* giunsi, giungesti

leggere *2* letto *5* lessi, leggesti

mettere *2* messo *5* misi, mettesti

morire *2* morto *3* muoio, muori, muore, moriamo, morite, muoiono *6* morirò *o* morrò *etc 8* muoia

muovere *2* mosso *5* mossi, movesti

nascere *2* nato *5* nacqui, nascesti

nuocere *2* nuociuto *3* nuoccio, nuoci, nuoce, nociamo *o* nuociamo, nuocete, nuocciono *4* nuocevo *etc 5* nocqui, nuocesti *6* nuocerò *etc 7* nuoccia

offrire *2* offerto *3* offro *5* offersi *o* offrii, offristi *8* offra

parere *2* parso *3* paio, paiamo, paiono *5* parvi *o* parsi, paresti *6* parrò *etc 8* paia, paiamo, pariate, paiano

PARLARE *1* parlando *2* parlato *3* parlo, parli, parla, parliamo, parlate, parlano *4* parlavo, parlavi, parlava, parlavamo, parlavate, parlavano *5* parlai, parlasti, parlò, parlammo, parlaste, parlarono *6* parlerò, parlerai, parlerà, parleremo, parlerete, parleranno *7* parlerei, parleresti, parlerebbe, parleremmo, parlereste, parlerebbero *8* parli, parli, parli, parliamo, parliate, parlino *9* parlassi, parlassi, parlasse, parlassimo, parlaste, parlassero *10* parla!, parli!, parlate!, parlino!

piacere *2* piaciuto *3* piaccio, piacciamo, piacciono *5* piacqui, piacesti *8* piaccia *etc*

porre *1* ponendo *2* posto *3* pongo, poni, pone, poniamo, ponete, pongono *4* ponevo *etc* *5* posi, ponesti *6* porrò *etc* *8* ponga, poniamo, poniate, pongano *9* ponessi *etc*

potere *3* posso, puoi, può, possiamo, potete, possono *6* potrò *etc* *8* possa, possiamo, possiate, possano

prendere *2* preso *5* presi, prendesti

ridurre *1* riducendo *2* ridotto *3* riduco *etc* *4* riducevo *etc* *5* ridussi, riducesti *6* ridurrò *etc* *8* riduca *etc* *9* riducessi *etc*

riempire *1* riempiendo *3* riempio, riempi, riempie, riempiono

rimanere *2* rimasto *3* rimango, rimangono *5* rimasi, rimanesti *6* rimarrò *etc* *8* rimanga

rispondere *2* risposto *5* risposi, rispondesti

salire *3* salgo, sali, salgono *8* salga

sapere *3* so, sai, sa, sappiamo, sapete, sanno *5* seppi, sapesti *6* saprò *etc* *8* sappia *etc* *10* sappi!, sappia!, sappiate!, sappiano!

scrivere *2* scritto *5* scrissi, scrivesti

sedere *3* siedo, siedi, siede, siedono *8* sieda

spegnere *2* spento *3* spengo, spengono *5* spensi, spegnesti *8* spenga

stare *2* stato *3* sto, stai, sta, stiamo, state, stanno *5* stetti, stesti *6* starò *etc* *8* stia *etc* *9* stessi *etc* *10* sta'!, stia!, state!, stiano!

tacere *2* taciuto *3* taccio, tacciono *5* tacqui, tacesti *8* taccia

tenere *3* tengo, tieni, tiene, tengono *5* tenni, tenesti *6* terrò *etc* *8* tenga

trarre *1* traendo *2* tratto *3* traggo, trai, trae, traiamo, traete, traggono *4* traevo *etc* *5* trassi, traesti *6* trarrò *etc* *8* tragga *9* traessi *etc*

udire *3* odo, odi, ode, odono *8* oda

uscire *3* esco, esci, esce, escono *8* esca

valere *2* valso *3* valgo, valgono *5* valsi, valesti *6* varrò *etc* *8* valga

vedere *2* visto *o* veduto *5* vidi, vedesti *6* vedrò *etc*

VENDERE *1* vendendo *2* venduto *3* vendo, vendi, vende, vendiamo, vendete, vendono *4* vendevo, vendevi, vendeva, vendevamo, vendevate, vendevano *5* vendei *o* vendetti, vendesti, vendé *o* vendette, vendemmo, vendeste, venderono *o* vendettero *6* venderò, venderai, venderà, venderemo, venderete, venderanno *7* venderei, venderesti, venderebbe, venderemmo, vendereste, venderebbero *8* venda, venda, venda, vendiamo, vendiate, vendano *9* vendessi, vendessi, vendesse, vendessimo, vendeste, vendessero *10* vendi!, venda!, vendete!, vendano!

venire *2* venuto *3* vengo, vieni, viene, vengono *5* venni, venisti *6* verrò *etc* *8* venga

vivere *2* vissuto *5* vissi, vivesti

volere *3* voglio, vuoi, vuole, vogliamo, volete, vogliono *5* volli, volesti *6* vorrò *etc* *8* voglia *etc* *10* vogli!, voglia!, vogliate!, vogliano!

VERBI INGLESI

present	pt	pp	present	pt	pp
arise	arose	arisen	eat	ate	eaten
awake	awoke	awaked	fall	fell	fallen
be (am,	was,	been	feed	fed	fed
is, are;	were		feel	felt	felt
being)			fight	fought	fought
bear	bore	born(e)	find	found	found
beat	beat	beaten	flee	fled	fled
become	became	become	fling	flung	flung
befall	befell	befallen	fly	flew	flown
begin	began	begun	forbid	forbade	forbidden
behold	beheld	beheld	forecast	forecast	forecast
bend	bent	bent	forget	forgot	forgotten
beset	beset	beset	forgive	forgave	forgiven
bet	bet,	bet,	forsake	forsook	forsaken
	betted	betted	freeze	froze	frozen
bid	bid	bid	get	got	got, (US)
bind	bound	bound			gotten
bite	bit	bitten	give	gave	given
bleed	bled	bled	go	went	gone
blow	blew	blown	(goes)		
break	broke	broken	grind	ground	ground
breed	bred	bred	grow	grew	grown
bring	brought	brought	hang	hung,	hung,
build	built	built		hanged	hanged
burn	burnt,	burnt,	have	had	had
	burned	burned	hear	heard	heard
burst	burst	burst	hide	hid	hidden
buy	bought	bought	hit	hit	hit
can	could	(been able)	hold	held	held
cast	cast	cast	hurt	hurt	hurt
catch	caught	caught	keep	kept	kept
choose	chose	chosen	kneel	knelt,	knelt,
cling	clung	clung		kneeled	kneeled
come	came	come	know	knew	known
cost	cost	cost	lay	laid	laid
creep	crept	crept	lead	led	led
cut	cut	cut	lean	leant,	leant,
deal	dealt	dealt		leaned	leaned
dig	dug	dug	leap	leapt,	leapt,
do (3rd	did	done		leaped	leaped
person;			learn	learnt,	learnt,
he/she/				learned	learned
it/does)			leave	left	left
draw	drew	drawn	lend	lent	lent
dream	dreamed,	dreamed,	let	let	let
	dreamt	dreamt	lie	lay	lain
drink	drank	drunk	(lying)		
drive	drove	driven	light	lit,	lit,
dwell	dwelt	dwelt		lighted	lighted

present	pt	pp	present	pt	pp
lose	lost	lost	speed	sped,	sped,
make	made	made		speeded	speeded
may	might	—	spell	spelt,	spelt,
mean	meant	meant		spelled	spelled
meet	met	met	spend	spent	spent
mistake	mistook	mistaken	spill	spilt,	spilt,
mow	mowed	mown,		spilled	spilled
		mowed	spin	spun	spun
must	(had to)	(had to)	spit	spat	spat
pay	paid	paid	split	split	split
put	put	put	spoil	spoiled,	spoiled,
quit	quit,	quit,		spoilt	spoilt
	quitted	quitted	spread	spread	spread
read	read	read	spring	sprang	sprung
rend	rent	rent	stand	stood	stood
rid	rid	rid	steal	stole	stolen
ride	rode	ridden	stick	stuck	stuck
ring	rang	rung	sting	stung	stung
rise	rose	risen	stink	stank	stunk
run	ran	run	stride	strode	strode
saw	sawed	sawn	strike	struck	struck,
say	said	said			stricken
see	saw	seen	strive	strove	striven
seek	sought	sought	swear	swore	sworn
sell	sold	sold	sweep	swept	swept
send	sent	sent	swell	swelled	swollen,
set	set	set			swelled
shake	shook	shaken	swim	swam	swum
shall	should	—	swing	swung	swung
shear	sheared	shorn,	take	took	taken
		sheared	teach	taught	taught
shed	shed	shed			
shine	shone	shone	tear	tore	torn
shoot	shot	shot	tell	told	told
show	showed	shown	think	thought	thought
shrink	shrank	shrunk	throw	threw	thrown
shut	shut	shut	thrust	thrust	thrust
sing	sang	sung	tread	trod	trodden
sink	sank	sunk	wake	woke,	woken,
sit	sat	sat		waked	waked
slay	slew	slain	wear	wore	worn
sleep	slept	slept	weave	wove,	woven,
slide	slid	slid		weaved	weaved
sling	slung	slung	wed	wedded,	wedded,
slit	slit	slit		wed	wed
smell	smelt,	smelt,	weep	wept	wept
	smelled	smelled	win	won	won
sow	sowed	sown,	wind	wound	wound
		sowed	wring	wrung	wrung
speak	spoke	spoken	write	wrote	written

NOTES TO THE USER OF THIS DICTIONARY

I. Using the dictionary

In using this book, you will either want to check the meaning of an Italian word you don't know, or find the Italian for an English word. These two operations are quite different, and so are the problems you may face when using one side of the dictionary or the other. In order to help you, we have tried to explain below the main features of this book.

The 'wordlist' is the alphabetical list of all the items in large bold type, i.e. all the 'headwords'. Each 'entry', or article, is introduced by a headword, and may contain additional 'references' in smaller bold type, such as phrases, derivatives, and compound words. Section 1. below deals with the way references are listed.

The typography distinguishes between three broad categories of text within the dictionary. All items in bold type, large or smaller, are 'source language' references, for which an equivalent in the other language is provided. All items in standard type are translations. Items in italics are information about the words being translated, i.e. either labels, or 'signposts' pinpointing the appropriate translation, or explanations.

1. *Where to look for a word*

1.1 Derivatives

In order to save space, a number of derivatives have been listed within entries, provided this does not break alphabetical order. Thus, **borsellino** and **borsista** are listed under the entry for **borsa**, and **caller** and **calling** under **call**. You must remember this when looking for a word you don't find listed as a headword. These derivatives are always listed last within an entry (see also I.2 on entry layout).

1.2 Homographs

Homographs are words which are spelt in exactly the same way, like Italian **fine** (thin, fine) and **fine** (end), or English **fine** (nice etc.) and **fine** (penalty). As a rule, in order to save space, such words have been treated as one headword only.

1.3 Phrases

Because of the constraints of space, there can be only a limited number of idiomatic phrases in a pocket dictionary like this one. Particular emphasis is given to verbal phrases like **mettersi al lavoro, mettere via, prendere fuoco, andare via, farsi avanti,** etc., and also to basic constructions (see for instance the entries for **apply, agree**). Verbal phrases with the ten or so basic verbs (like *fare, mettere, prendere,* or English *set, do, get,* etc.) are listed under the noun. Other phrases and idioms are listed under the first key word (i.e. not a preposition), for instance **filare diritto** under **filare**.

1.4 Abbreviations and proper names

For easier reference, abbreviations, acronyms and proper names have been listed alphabetically in the wordlist, as opposed to being relegated to the appendices. **M.O.T.** is used in every way like **certificate** or **permit, I.V.A.** like **imposta,** and these words are treated like other nouns.

1.5 Compounds

Housewife, smoke screen, terremoto and **doposcuola** are all compounds. One-word compounds like 'housewife' are not a problem when consulting the dictionary, since they can appear only in one place and in strict alphabetical order. When it comes to other compounds, however – hyphenated compounds and compounds made up of separate words – each language presents its own peculiar problems.

1.5.1 Italian compounds

Most compounds in Italian are of the solid variety, e.g.: 'doposcuola', 'portacenere'. There are also compounds made up of two juxtaposed words in Italian. Some are not hyphenated but are two separate words, e.g.: 'vagone ristorante', 'verde bottiglia'. Others, chiefly political and technical compounds, are hyphenated, e.g.: 'radico-socialista', 'vegeto-minerale'. Compounds made up of two separate words are listed under the first word, i.e. 'vagone ristorante' under 'vagone'.

1.5.2 Italian pronominal verbs

Verbs like 'svegliarsi', 'sbagliarsi', 'ricordarsi' are called 'pronominal' because they are used with a personal pronoun: 'mi sono svegliato alle otto' etc. They must be distinguished from truly reflexive or reciprocal uses like 'egli si guarda nello specchio' (he is looking at himself in the mirror) and 'si parlano ogni giorno' (they talk to each other every day). They are intransitive or transitive verbs in their own right.

There are no such verbs in English (which has another type of 'compound verb', the phrasal verb, see 1.5.4), where a verb used with 'oneself' is, as a rule, truly reflexive. Compare for instance the translations for 'annegarsi' (accidentalmente) and 'annegarsi' (deliberatamente). These verbs have been listed as phrases under the entry for the key word. See for instance the entries for 'svegliare', 'sbagliare', 'ricordare'.

1.5.3 English compounds

Here there is a problem of where to find a compound because of less predictable spelling than is the case with Italian: is it **airgun, air-gun** or **air gun**? This is why we choose to list them according to strict alphabetical order. Thus **coal face** and **coalman** are separated by **coalition.** The entries between **tax** and **technical** will provide a good illustration of the system of listing. It has drawbacks, for instance in that **tax-free** and **taxpayer** are separated by **taxi**, and three 'taxi' compounds. However, in a short dictionary used by beginners, it has the merit of simplicity and consistency.

1.5.4 English 'phrasal verbs'

'Phrasal verbs' are verbs like **go off, blow up, cut down** etc. Here you have the advantage of knowing that these words belong together, whereas it will take the foreign user some time before he can identify these verbs immediately. They have been listed under the entry for the basic verb (e.g. **go, blow, cut**), grouped alphabetically before any other derivative or compound. Thus, **pull up** comes before **pulley.** See also **to back out, to look up** (a word), **to look out.**

1.6 Irregular forms

When looking up an Italian word, you may not immediately find the form you are looking for, although the word in question has been duly entered in the dictionary. This is possibly because you are looking up an irregular noun or verb form, and these are not always given as entries in their own right.

We have assumed that you know basic Italian grammar. Thus you will be expected to know that 'cantano' is a form of the verb **cantare** and so on. However, in order to help you, we have included some of the main irregular forms as entries in their own right, with a cross-reference to the basic form. Thus, if you come across the word 'esce' and attempt to look up a verb 'escere', you won't find it, but what you will find under 'esce', between 'escandescenza' and 'esclamare', is the entry **'esce, esci** *forme del vb* **uscire'**. Similarly, **faccio** etc.

With past participles, it sometimes happens that in addition to the purely verbal form there is an adjectival or noun use, for instance **conosciuto**. These usages are translated as autonomous words, but they are also cross-referred to the verb whenever appropriate (see for instance entry for **coperto**).

2. Entry layout

All entries, however long or complex, are arranged in a systematic way. But it may be a little difficult at first to find one's way through an entry like Italian **passare**, or English **back, round** or **run** because the text is run on without any breakdown into paragraphs, in order to save space. Ease of reference comes with practice, but the guidelines below will make it easier for you.

2.1 'Signposting'

If you look up an Italian word and find a string of quite different English translations, you are unlikely to have much trouble finding out which is the relevant one for your context, because you know what the English words mean, and the context will almost automatically rule out unsuitable translations. It is quite a different matter when you want to find the Italian for, say, **lock**, in the context 'we got to the lock around lunchtime', and are faced with an entry that reads 'lock: serratura; chiusa; ciocca, riccio'. You can of course go to the other side and check what each translation means. But this is time-consuming, and it doesn't always work. This is why we have provided the user with signposts which pinpoint the relevant translation. For instance with **lock**, the entry reads: '... (*of door, box*) serratura; (*of canal*) chiusa; (*of hair*) ciocca, riccio ...'. For the context suggested above, it is now clear that 'chiusa' is the right word.

2.2 Grammatical categories and meaning categories

Complex entries are first broken down into grammatical categories, e.g.: **lock** *n* // *vt* // *vi*. Be prepared to go through entries like **run** or **back** carefully and you will find how useful all these 'signposts' are. Each grammatical category is then split where appropriate into the various meanings, e.g.:

> **lock** *n* (*of door, box*) serratura; (*of canal*) chiusa; (*of hair*) ciocca, riccio // *vt* (*with key*) chiudere a chiave;

      (*immobilize*) bloccare // *vi* (*door etc*) chiudersi a
      chiave; (*wheels*) bloccarsi, incepparsi.

3. *Using the translations*

3.1   Gender

All feminine endings for Italian adjectives have been given on the
English-Italian side of the dictionary. This may appear to duplicate
information given on the other side, but we feel it is a useful reminder
where and when it matters. The feminine version is given as a translation
of words like **driver, teacher, researcher** etc., where appropriate.
Remember that the Italian equivalents of **his, her, its** or **the** do not
behave like their English counterparts: see section II for more
information.

3.2   Plurals

We have assumed knowledge on the part of the user of plural formation
in Italian (see section II), including the plural of compounds. Irregular
plural forms are shown only on the Italian-English side of the dictionary.

3.3   Verb forms

Irregular Italian verbs appearing as translations have not been marked as
such, and the user should refer to the Italian verb tables when in doubt
(pp. 402–403).

3.4   Colloquial language

You should as a rule proceed with great caution when handling foreign
language which has a degree of informality. When an English word or
phrase has been labelled (*col*), i.e. colloquial, you must assume that the
translation belongs to a similar level of informality. If the translation is
followed by (!) you should use it with extreme care, or better still avoid it
unless you are with close friends!

3.5   'Grammatical words'

It is exceedingly difficult to give adequate treatment to words like **for,
away, whose, off,** or Italian **quale** etc. in a short dictionary such as
this one. We have tried to go some way towards providing as much
relevant information as possible about the most frequent uses of these
words. However, for further information use a good monolingual
dictionary of Italian and a good modern Italian grammar.

3.6 'Approximate' translations and cultural equivalents

It is not always possible to give a genuine translation, when for instance an English word denotes a thing or institution which either doesn't exist in Italy, or is quite different. Therefore, only an approximate equivalent can be given, or else an explanation. See for instance **whip**, **comprehensive school**, and on the Italian-English side **A.C.I.**

3.7 Alternative translations

As a rule, translations separated by commas can be regarded as broadly interchangeable for the meaning indicated. Translations separated by a semi-colon are not interchangeable and when in doubt you should consult either a larger bilingual dictionary or a good monolingual Italian dictionary. You will find however that there are very few cases of translations separated by a semi-colon without an intervening 'signpost'.

II. Notes on Italian grammar

When you are first confronted with Italian at school, or if you happen to be at a business meeting where you are the only one speaking little or no Italian, it may seem to you that Italian is very different from English. On the other hand, if you stand back and consider a wider range of related and unrelated languages, Italian can come to look very close to English.

We have tried here to show some of the main differences, especially with the beginner and the dictionary user in mind, without dwelling on subtleties or aspects of Italian that are broadly similar to English. Among the greatest obstacles for the beginner are gender, verb forms and tenses, the position of adjectives, the use of prepositions and of course the sounds of Italian.

1. *Nouns and 'satellite' words (articles, adjectives)*

1.1   Gender

One basic difference: 'the knife and the fork' but '*il* coltello e *la* forchetta'. Gender must be learned as a feature to be remembered with each new word. However, words ending in -o are almost always masculine and words ending in -a are almost always feminine, whereas words ending in -e can be either. It is most important to get the article right, and of course the agreement of adjectives and past participles: '**la** vecchia casa ed **il** vecchio palazzo'.

See also 1.4 (possessive adjectives)

1.2   Articles: *il, lo, la, un, del, dei* etc.

Apart from the problem of gender, there is the question of whether the article is used or not, and the Italian does not always follow the English pattern. For instance you say 'I like wine' but the Italians say 'mi piace il vino'. Conversely, 'my father is a teacher' but 'mio padre è professore'.

1.2.1   *il, l', lo, la, i, gli, le*

(a)   The definite article is used more often in Italian than in English.

For instance:

apples are good for you   **le** mele fanno bene
meat is expensive   **la** carne è cara
love is not enough   **l'**amore non basta
he likes ice-cream   gli piace **il** gelato
France is beautiful   **la** Francia è bella

Note that no article is used with the names of towns or small islands.

(b)   Use of *il/la* with parts of the body

Where the possessive is used in English, 'il/la' tends to be used in Italian, (sometimes together with an additional pronoun):

I broke **my** leg   **mi** sono rotto **la** gamba
put up **your** hand   alza **la** mano
he trod on **my** foot   **mi** ha calpestato **il** piede

(c)   'il' and 'i' are used before all masculine nouns beginning with a consonant
   'lo' and 'gli' are used before 'z', 'gn', 'ps', 'x', 's' impure (i.e. 's' plus a consonant, as in 'sbagliare') and the semi-vowel 'i'
   'l'' and 'gli' are used with all masculine nouns beginning with a vowel
   'la' and 'le' are used with feminine nouns beginning with a consonant
   'la' becomes 'l'' before feminine nouns beginning with a vowel, whereas 'le' is used in the plural for all feminine nouns

	singular	plural
masculine	il libro	i libri
	lo sportello	gli sportelli
	lo gnomo	gli gnomi
	lo psicologo	gli psicologi
	l'uomo	gli uomini
feminine	la scuola	le scuole
	l'entrata	le entrate

(d)   *a + il, di + il, da + il, in + il, su + il*

Remember the articulated forms with prepositions (shown under the appropriate entries). For instance: 'vado al cinema', 'la porta della casa' etc.

1.2.2 *Un(o), una*

(a)   In structures of the type 'with incredible strength', the article 'un(o), una' is used in Italian:

he has incredible courage   lui ha **un** coraggio incredibile
a building of frightening size   un palazzo di **una** grandezza paurosa

(b)   On the other hand this article is not used in Italian in structures equivalent to:

my father is **a** teacher   mio padre è professore
my sister is **a** nurse   mia sorella è infermiera

But this only applies with names of professions and crafts:

his brother is an idiot!   suo fratello è un idiota!
my sister is a very liberated young lady   mia sorella è una ragazza molto emancipata

(c)   without a pen, without bread: no article in Italian

Where the English uses the article with a so-called 'countable noun' (like 'hat' as opposed to 'milk' or 'water' or 'bread'), the Italian doesn't: 'senza penna, non si può scrivere'.

1.2.3   *di, del, dello, della, dei, degli, delle* = some, any

Remember not to confuse 'del' as in 'il titolo del libro' and 'del' as in 'mi piacerebbe del pane' (see entry **di**). Where there is 'some' or 'any' or sometimes nothing in English, the Italian uses 'del' etc., as shown below:

voglio del pane   I want some bread
vuoi del pane/della minestra/delle sigarette?   would you like any bread/soup/cigarettes?

BUT: non voglio pane   I don't want (any) bread

1.3   Adjectives

Apart from the question of gender agreement, the main difficulty is the position of adjectives. As a general rule, the adjectives follow the noun they qualify when they have a distinguishing function e.g.: 'egli portava una sciarpa vecchia' he was wearing an old scarf (a particular old scarf compared to one that wasn't old).

Adjectives precede the noun when they have a purely descriptive function e.g. 'egli portava una vecchia sciarpa' he was wearing an old scarf (any scarf which was old).

Among adjectives usually found before the noun are cardinal numbers, ordinal numbers, possessives, indefinites, 'ultimo', 'unico'. Among adjectives usually following the noun are adjectives of nationality, past participles used as adjectives, and restrictive adjectives.

1.4 Possessives

1.4.1 *il suo, la sua/i suoi, le sue, il mio, la mia/i miei, le mie, il tuo, la tua/i tuoi, le tue* etc. *vs* his/her/its, my, your.

Unlike English, the possessive varies in Italian according to the gender and number of the noun it qualifies. Whether the owner is male or female it is:

la sua valigia ed il suo ombrello   his(her) suitcase and his(her) umbrella
le sue valigie ed i suoi ombrelli   his(her) suitcases and his(her) umbrellas

1.4.2 *il mio, la mia, i miei, le mie* etc. *vs* mine etc.

Here again, watch the variation depending on gender and number of the qualified noun.

1.5 Demonstratives: *questo, questa, questi, queste/quel, quello, quella, quei, quegli, quelle*

For the purpose of this book the 'questo' form corresponds broadly to 'this', the 'quello' form corresponds broadly to 'that'.

1.6 Comparative and superlative: *più … che* etc.

There is no form in Italian similar to '-er' or '-est' as in 'bigger/ biggest'. Always use 'più' + *adjective* or 'il più' + *adjective*.

2. *Verbs*

This is one of the main areas of difficulty for English-speaking learners.

There are three major problems. First the variety of endings (io vedo, noi vediamo etc.) and the number of irregular or semi-irregular forms. Second the difference in the formation of negative or interrogative phrases (no equivalent of 'do' as in 'I didn't go, did you?'). Third the use of 'avere' and 'essere' in compound tenses.

2.1 Verb forms

The verb tables on pp. 424 and 425 will give you ending patterns for the main verb groups; irregular verbs are shown on page 402. There is no substitute for practice in this, but try not to look on these forms as a great number of separate and very different forms: there are two basic combining patterns, one relating to the person (a 'noi' form *vs* a 'voi' form etc.), one relating to the tense ('ved-' or 'vedr-' etc. + *ending*). Also don't learn and practise too many different tenses at once, parrot-fashion. The present tense, the imperfect, the future and conditional, the 'passato prossimo' will cater for most of your needs as a beginner when it comes to expressing yourself in Italian.

2.2 Negatives and questions

(*Personal pronoun* +) 'non' + *verb form* (+ *past participle*) is the basic pattern of negative verb phrases. 'Io non credo (veramente) che', 'egli non è andato (subito)', 'egli non ha risposto (subito)'. In sentences of this type the adverb cannot fit between the noun and the verb form.

Interrogatives in Italian are conveyed by the use of intonation (voice raised on the last syllable), or by verb-subject inversion:

e.g.: è partito   he has gone
       è partito? has he gone?
       Luisa è partita   Luisa has gone
       è partita Luisa? *or* Luisa è partita?   has Luisa gone?

except where there is an interrogative word:
e.g.: chi viene?   who is coming?

2.3 Tenses

2.3.1   When the English has the sense of 'to be in the process of doing ...' there is an equivalent in Italian of the 'progressive' '-ing' form e.g.: 'sto leggendo un libro'   I am reading a book. In other cases the present tense or the 'imperfetto' will do:

lavoravo per il governo   I was working for the Government
lo vediamo domani   we are seeing him tomorrow

2.3.2   The two tenses of the past in English (I went there, he has taken it) do not correspond closely to the Italian. Of the 'imperfetto' (abitavo), the 'passato prossimo' (ho risposto) and the 'passato remoto' (io partii), the last is used in the south of Italy and is the literary tense. The 'passato prossimo' is used much more widely than its counterpart in English and tends to be a substitute for the 'passato remoto' in spoken Italian except in the South. It can be used in many cases when the English would use the preterite (I went, he gave etc.).

2.3.3 The 'passato prossimo'

The use of 'avere' as an auxiliary verb is by far the most common, hence it is convenient to concentrate on the few verbs which use 'essere'. They are all intransitive and are verbs expressing movement or becoming, like 'andare', 'venire', 'partire', 'arrivare', '(ri)tornare', 'entrare', 'uscire', 'nascere', 'morire', 'diventare'.

The second thing to remember is that the past participle will occasionally take the marks of gender or plural. Two basic rules should enable you to cope with most problems. The past participle remains in the form of the masculine singular (io ho risposto, egli è andato) unless:

(a) with a verb used transitively a direct object pronoun precedes the verb:

l'ho comprata (where 'l'' stands for la casa, la sciarpa etc.)

(b) The auxiliary 'essere' is used:

lei è partita ieri   she left yesterday

There are exceptions, but these rules should suffice on most occasions.

2.3.4 The 'imperfetto'

This is used for an action or state without definite limits in time. Compare for instance:

He lived in London during the war   egli abitava a Londra durante la guerra
He stood near the window   stava vicino alla finestra

with:

they lived here from '64 to '68   sono vissuti qui dal '64 al '68.

2.3.5 The 'congiuntivo'

It is not possible to give here a single rule showing when the subjunctive ('congiuntivo') should be used. The dictionary will occasionally show you when a particular construction requires the use of the subjunctive (see for instance under **may**). It generally follows a *verb* + 'che' construction where the sentence expresses doubt, a hypothesis rather than a fact, a question, an interdiction. It is always used after certain conjunctions e.g.: 'affinché', 'benché', 'prima che', and certain impersonal expressions e.g.: 'è meglio che', 'bisogna che', 'è inutile che'.

III. Italian verb conjugations

1. The table of irregular verbs on p. 402 is self-explanatory. Unless stated otherwise, if one form only is given, it is that of the first person singular; if two forms are given, they are the first and second person singular; if four forms are shown, they are the first, second and third person singular and third person plural. If not shown, the first and second person plural are regularly formed on the stem of the infinitive.

2. Note that verbs in '-ire' fall into two distinct categories:

   (a) those which add '-isc-' to the stem and follow the pattern of 'finire', shown in the tables;

   (b) those which follow the pattern of 'dormire' (see model conjugation table B).

3. Verbs in '-durre' follow the pattern of 'ridurre', shown in the tables.

4. Verbs in '-scere' follow the pattern of 'conoscere', shown in the tables.

5. Do not forget to use the appropriate pronoun with pronominal verbs: *mi* lavo, *si* lava, *vi* siete sbagliati.

6. 'Semi-irregular' verbs

   Some verbs are only irregular in a few predictable ways:

   6.1 A 'c' will change to a 'ch' before 'e' or 'i' (the corresponding sound remaining [k]): **cercare** – tu cerchi, noi cerchiamo, io cercherò.

   6.2 A 'g' will change to a 'gh' before 'e' or 'i' (the corresponding sound remaining [g]): **pagare** – tu paghi, noi paghiamo, io pagherò.

6.3   Verbs of the first conjugation ending in '-ciare' drop the 'i' whenever it precedes 'e' or 'i': **cominciare** – tu cominci, io comincerò, noi cominceremmo; **baciare** – tu baci, io bacerò, noi baceremmo.

6.4   Verbs of the first conjugation ending in '-giare' drop the 'i' whenever it precedes 'i' or 'e': **mangiare** – tu mangi, io mangerò, noi mangeremmo; **assegiare** – tu assaggi, io assaggerò, noi assaggeremmo.

7. Compound tenses ('tempi composti') are formed as follows:

7.1   Perfect ('passato prossimo'): with 'essere' – sono partito, sei partito etc. (see *essere*); with 'avere' – ho finito, hai finito etc. (see *avere*).

7.2   Pluperfect ('piuccheperfetto'): ero partito etc.; avevo finito etc.

7.3   Future anterior ('future anteriore'): sarò partito etc.; avrò finito etc.

7.4   Past conditional ('condizionale passato'): sarei partito etc.; avrei finito etc.

7.5   Past anterior ('trapassato remoto'): ebbi finito etc. This tense is rarely used.

A. A regular '-are' verb: 'parl*are*'

PRESENT: Indicative		Subjunctive	
	o		i
	i		i
parl	a	parl	i
	iamo		iamo
	ate		iate
	ano		ino

IMPERFECT: Indicative		Subjunctive	
	avo		assi
	avi		assi
parl	ava	parl	asse
	avamo		assimo
	avate		aste
	avano		assero

PRETERITE	
	ai
	asti
parl	ò
	ammo
	aste
	arono

FUTURE		CONDITIONAL	
	ò		ei
	ai		esti
parler	à	parler	ebbe
	emo		emmo
	ete		este
	anno		ebbero

IMPERATIVE: parla, parli, parlate

PAST PARTICIPLE: parlato

GERUND: parlando

B. A regular '-ire' verb: 'dormire'

PRESENT:	Indicative	Subjunctive
	o	a
	i	a
	e	a
dorm	iamo	dorm iamo
	ite	iate
	ono	ano

IMPERFECT:	Indicative	Subjunctive
	ivo	issi
	ivi	issi
	iva	isse
dorm	ivamo	dorm issimo
	ivate	iste
	ivano	issero

PRETERITE		
	ii	
	isti	
	ì	
dorm	immo	
	iste	
	irono	

FUTURE		CONDITIONAL
	ò	ei
	ai	esti
	à	ebbe
dormir	emo	dormir emmo
	ete	este
	anno	ebbero

IMPERATIVE: dormi, dorma, dormite

PAST PARTICIPLE: dormito

GERUND: dormendo

IV. The sounds of Italian

1. *General remarks*. Unlike English, Italian is to all intents and purposes a phonetic language. In other words there is a direct and regular connection between written and spoken Italian. This means, in practical terms, that once you have learned the pronunciation of a letter or combination of letters in Italian, you can apply that pronunciation confidently to any word – even one you are unfamiliar with. For instance, having learned that the Italian group of letters 'azione' is pronounced [ats'jone], we can be sure of the pronunciation of 'conversazione' (conversation) and 'relazione' (report). English provides no such certainty: the group '-ough' has, for example, at least five distinct pronunciations, as in 'rough', 'though', 'through', 'trough', 'plough'. Learning and applying the sounds of Italian is therefore a relatively straightforward matter.

In the following account, the phonetic symbols employed are those of the International Phonetic Association.

2. *Stress*. In Italian, as in English, one syllable of any given word is always pronounced with greater force than the others. We say that the stress falls on that particular syllable. Both Italian and English are called free-stress languages since it is not possible to predict with certainty which syllable of a word will be stressed. In English, the word politics, for example, is stressed on the first syllable, whereas police has the stress on the second syllable. Similarly in the equivalent Italian words, the stress falls on the second syllable of politica and the third syllable of polizia.

Knowing where stress falls in a word is vital in Italian as well as in English. In 'escort bureau' the noun is stressed on the first syllable; in 'may I escort you', stress on the second syllable has turned 'escort' into a verb. The meaning of a word can be altered entirely by a change in stress: 'ancora' in Italian means anchor, but 'ancora' means again.

Although we cannot predict with certainty where the stress will fall on an Italian word, there are some useful guidelines:

1. Most Italian words are stressed on the last but one syllable, for example 'amico' (friend), 'cioccolata' (chocolate), 'cucina' (kitchen), 'arrivare' (to arrive).

2. The next most common pattern is for the stress to fall on the final syllable, for example 'verità' (truth), 'città' (city), 'gioventù' (youth), 'caffè' (coffee). Only in words stressed on the final syllable, will you find the stress indicated by a written accent. As stress alone (not pronunciation) is indicated by the written accent, the type of written accent employed is not important (as it is in French). In Italian the grave accent (ˋ) is most generally used.

3. Less commonly, stress may fall on the third-last syllable, for example 'popolo' (people) or even more rarely on the fourth-last syllable, for example 'continuano' (they continue).

4. The stress is as follows on these common word-endings: -astro ('verdastro' greenish); -one ('portone' main door); -accio ('tempaccio' bad weather); -ino ('gattino' kitten); -ello ('coltello' knife); -oso ('famoso' famous); -etto ('berretto' beret); -azione ('conversazione' conversation).

3. *Quality of pronunciation.* Each syllable in an Italian word — irrespective of whether it is stressed or not — is pronounced clearly and distinctly; each vowel, especially, must be given its full value. All vowels in words such as cioccolata (chocolate) and lattuga (lettuce) are enunciated vigorously to give [tʃokkoˈlata] and [latˈtuga]. The lip-tension and energetic delivery characteristic of Italian are much less important in English; thus in 'chocolate' and 'lettuce' only the initial, stressed vowels receive their full value, while all others are slurred — giving the typical pronunciations [ˈtʃɔklɪt], [ˈlɛtɪs]. Italians tend to give themselves away when speaking English by the clarity they try to restore to such slurred vowels.

4. The pronunciation of Italian letters

(a) *Vowels*. Particular attention should be paid to the pronunciation of Italian vowels. They differ considerably from their English counterparts.

A   This letter always represents the sound [a] in Italian, whether in a stressed or unstressed syllable. It resembles the a in 'cat' but is shorter and purer, with the lips not drawn so far back – rather like the Northern English a. Its pronunciation is never modified, for example in combination with any other letter e.g. 'camera' (bedroom); 'caro' (dear); 'aiuto' (help); 'aereo' (aeroplane).

E   This letter is always pronounced in Italian. There is no 'silent' e as in English 'mate'. The Italian vowel has two sounds: either [ɛ] similar to the sound in 'end', or [e] like the French é (e.g. rosé). If the vowel is unstressed it always has the [e] sound. If stressed, there is no way of predicting which sound applies. (Italians themselves vary in which sound they use, according to their region of origin). However, comprehension is rarely affected. The following are usually pronounced [ɛ]: 'bello' (beautiful); 'c'è' (there is); 'era' (he/she/it was); 'finestra' (window). The [e] is generally used in 'mentre' (while), 'nero' (black), 'mela' (apple).

I   This vowel is pronounced [i] – rather like the vowel sound in English 'meal, wheel, feel'. The Italian sound is purer, however, with no glide; the lips are tenser in Italian and the sound is produced more energetically e.g. 'vino' (wine), 'dormire' (to sleep), 'Fellini'.

O   Basically, the letter O represents two sounds in English: open and pure as in 'chop', closed and diphthongized as in 'hope'. Italian makes a similar distinction. On the one hand there is the open sound [ɔ] similar to 'chop', but pronounced with greater lip-tension and energy e.g. 'oggi' (today), 'ogni' (every), 'ho' (I have). On the other hand there is the closed sound [o] like the vowel sound in the Scots English pronunciation of 'home', French 'hôte' or German 'Brot', e.g. 'sole' (sun), 'come' (how), 'amore' (love). This closed sound is always employed if the vowel is unstressed. If stressed, the observations made about the two sounds of E also apply to O.

U   This letter has only one pronunciation in Italian: [u]. The vowel sound of 'moon' is close to it, but the Italian vowel is pronounced with lips more rounded and pushed forward (cf. French, 'vous' or German, 'Ruhr') e.g. 'uno' (one), 'luna' (moon), 'nessuno' (nobody).

(b) *Diphthongs.* When two vowels come together in a syllable, we have what is called a diphthong, i.e. a sound like most English vowels, as opposed to the 'purer' Italian single vowels. There are two basic combinations between so-called hard vowels (A, E, O) and soft vowels (U, I):

1.1 'i' not accented and followed by a vowel, where 'i' becomes the semi-vowel [j]:
p*i*ano (slowly) ['pjano]; p*i*eno (full) ['pjɛno]; f*i*ore (flower) ['fjore]

1.2 'u' not accented and followed by a vowel, where 'u' becomes the semi-vowel [w]:
g*u*ardare (to look) [gwar'dare]; g*u*erra (war) ['gwɛrra]; *u*omo (man) ['wɔmo]

AND:

2.1 an accented vowel followed by 'i' or 'u' produces the following diphthongs:
m*ai* (never) [maj]; s*ei* (six) [sej]; p*oi* (then) [poj]; *au*tostrada (motorway) [autos'trada]; *Eu*ropa (Europe) [eu'ropa]

NOTE:

3. 'i' accented followed by a vowel gives two separate vowels and two syllables:
mio (mine) ['mio]

(c) *Consonants.* Italian consonants and consonantal groups are pronounced like their English equivalents except in the following instances:

C and G   Normally C and G have the sound of English 'cat' and 'gone'. If they are followed by the vowels I or E, however, they are softer ('palatalized') and become the sounds [tʃ] and [dʒ] respectively – as in the English 'cheese' and 'jeer', e.g. Botti*c*elli, da Vin*c*i, violon*c*ello, con*c*erto, *g*enerale (general), *g*elato (ice-cream), *g*iro (turn).

In order to make C or G soft when they occur in front of the vowels A, O, U, the vowel I is placed after them: thus '*ci*ao' (hello) pronounced ['tʃao] and 'ada*gio*' (softly) pronounced [a'dadʒo]. Notice that in these cases, the I itself is *not* pronounced.

On the other hand, if the hard [k] sound or [g] sound is required for C or G when they occur before I or E, the hardening is achieved by adding H, e.g. Ma*ch*iavelli, Mi*ch*elangelo, spa*gh*etti, *gh*etto.

GL   Normally the group GL is followed by the vowels I or E. It is pronounced [ʎ], rather like the L sound in the English 'million', e.g. famiglia (family), figlia (daughter).

GN   This group is pronounced [ɲ] – the sound of French 'montagne', e.g. montagna (mountain), lasagne, gnocchi.

H   This consonant is not pronounced in Italian. Its usual function is to 'harden' C and G (cf. above).

R   The Italian R is strongly trilled, rather like the Scottish R, e.g. Roma, raro (rare). It is always pronounced, even in combination with a vowel, e.g. mercato (market), pronounced [mer'kato].

SC   This group usually has the sound of English 'scan'. If followed by I or E, it is pronounced [ʃ] as in English 'ship', e.g. Fascismo (Fascism), scendere (to go down).

Z or ZZ   Single or double Z never has the characteristic English Z sound. It is pronounced either [dz] as in English 'be*ds*', e.g. zero or mezzo (half) or [ts] as in English 'hi*ts*', e.g. forza (strength) or pezzo (piece). There is no rule about which of the two sounds to employ; the pronunciation of each word has to be learned individually.

(d) *Double Consonants*. Most Italian consonants can be doubled, greatly affecting pronunciation and also meaning. In English, double consonants do not differ in pronunciation from single ones, e.g. there is no difference in the quality of the single p in 'paper' and the double p in 'pepper'. In Italian there is a marked difference between 'nono' (ninth) and 'nonno' (grandfather) or between 'pala' (shovel) and 'palla' (ball). To gain some idea of this difference try pronouncing 'I gave i*t*/I gave i*t* *t*o him' or 'go u*p*/go u*p* *p*lease'.

The following points should be noted. Doubling does not affect Z which has the same pronunciation whether it is single or double. The group QU is doubled by placing C before it, e.g. the sound is single in 'liquore' (liqueur) but double in 'acqua' (water); likewise CH is doubled by placing C in front of it, e.g. 'dichiarare' (to declare) *vs* 'acchiappare' (to grab), while GH is doubled by placing G in front of it, e.g. 'aghi' (needles) *vs* 'mugghiare' (to bellow).

V. The time

what time is it?	che ora è?, che ore sono?
it is ...	è ..., sono ...
at what time?	a che ora?
at ...	a ...
at midnight	a mezzanotte
at one p.m.	alle tredici, all'una, al tocco

00.00	mezzanotte
00.10	mezzanotte e dieci
00.15	mezzanotte e un quarto, mezzanotte e quindici
00.30	mezzanotte e mezzo
00.45	l'una meno un quarto, un quarto all'una
01.00	l'una (della mattina)
01.10	l'una e dieci
01.15	l'una e un quarto, l'una e quindici
01.30	l'una e mezzo
01.45	l'una e quarantacinque, un quarto alle due, le due meno un quarto
01.50	l'una e cinquanta, le due meno dieci
12.00	mezzogiorno
12.30	mezzogiorno e mezzo
13.00	le tredici, l'una, il tocco
01.30	l'una e mezzo
19.00	le diciannove, le sette (di sera)
19.30	le diciannove e mezzo, le sette e mezzo
23.00	le ventitré
23.45	le ventitré e quarantacinque, mezzanotte meno un quarto

in 20 minutes	fra venti minuti
20 minutes ago	venti minuti fa
wake me up at 7	svegliami alle sette
20 kmph	venti chilometri all'ora, 20 km/o

Dates and numbers

1. The date

what's the date today?	quanti ne abbiamo oggi?, che giorno è oggi?
it's the ...	è il ...

1st of February	primo febbraio
2nd of February	due febbraio
28th of February	ventotto febbraio

he's coming on the 7th of May viene il sette (di) maggio

NB: use cardinal numbers except for the first day of the month

I was born in 1945
io sono nato nel millenovecentoquarantacinque

I was born on the 15th of July 19...
io sono nato il quindici luglio millenovecento...

during the sixties	negli anni sessanta
in the twentieth century	nel ventesimo secolo, nel Novecento
in May	in maggio
on Monday (the 15th)	lunedì (il quindici)
on Mondays	il lunedì
next/last Monday	lunedì prossimo/scorso
in 10 days' time	fra dieci giorni

2. Telephone numbers

I would like Florence 24 35 56
mi dia Firenze ventiquattro / trentacinque / cinquantasei

could you get me Rome 22 00 79, extension 2233
mi chiami Roma ventidue / zero zero / settanta nove interno ventidue / trentatré

the Milan prefix is 02
il prefisso per Milano è zero due

3. Using numbers

he lives at number 10	abita al numero dieci
it's in chapter 7, on page 7	si trova nel capitolo sette, a pagina sette
he lives on the 3rd floor	abita al terzo piano
he came in 4th	arrivò quarto
a share of one seventh	una parte di un settimo
scale 1:25,000	scala uno a venticinquemila

Numbers

1	uno(una)	21	ventuno
2	due	22	ventidue
3	tre	23	ventitré
4	quattro	30	trenta
5	cinque	31	trentuno
6	sei	32	trentadue
7	sette		
8	otto	40	quaranta
9	nove	50	cinquanta
10	dieci	60	sessanta
		70	settanta
11	undici	80	ottanta
12	dodici	90	novanta
13	tredici		
14	quattordici	100	cento
15	quindici	101	cento uno
16	sedici	300	trecento
17	diciasette	1,000	mille
18	diciotto	1,001	mille uno
19	diciannove	1,202	milleduecentodue
20	venti	5,000	cinquemila

1,000,000 un milione

$2 + 2 =$	due più due sono	$2 - 2$	due meno due
2×2	due per due	$2 \div 2$	due diviso per due

6^2 sei quadrato 6^3 sei al cubo, sei alla terza potenza
20 m^2 venti metri quadrati 20 m^3 venti metri cubi

0	zero
0.5	zero virgola cinque (0,5)
5.2	cinque virgola due (5,2)

Numbers (*cont.*)

1st	primo(a)
2nd	secondo(a)
3rd	terzo(a)
4th	quarto(a)
5th	quinto(a)
6th	sesto(a)
7th	settimo(a)
8th	ottavo(a)
9th	nono(a)
10th	decimo(a)

11th	undicesimo(a)
12th	dodicesimo(a)
13th	tredicesimo(a)
14th	quattordicesimo(a)
15th	quindicesimo(a)
16th	sedicesimo(a)
17th	diciasettesimo(a)
18th	diciottesimo(a)
19th	diciannovesimo(a)
20th	ventesimo(a)

21st	ventunesimo(a)
22nd	ventiduesimo(a)
23rd	ventitreesimo(a)
30th	trentesimo(a)
31st	trentunesimo(a)
32nd	trentaduesimo(a)

100th	centesimo(a)

1/2	mezzo		1/5	quinto
1/3	terzo		2 1/3	due e un terzo
1/4	quarto		5 1/2	cinque e mezzo
10%	dieci per cento		100%	cento per cento